Encyclopedia
of the
American Constitution

Original 1986 Editorial Board

Encyclopedia
of the
American Constitution

SECOND EDITION

Edited by
LEONARD W. LEVY
and
KENNETH L. KARST

ADAM WINKLER, Associate Editor for the Second Edition

DENNIS J. MAHONEY, Assistant Editor for the First Edition
JOHN G. WEST, JR., Assistant Editor for Supplement I

MACMILLAN REFERENCE USA
An imprint of the Gale Group
New York

Macmillan Library Reference USA
1633 Broadway
New York, NY 10019

Printed in the United States of America

Printing Number
10 9 8 7 6 5 4 3 2 1

Library of Congress Cataloging-in-Publication Data
Encyclopedia of the American Constitution / edited by Leonard W. Levy and Kenneth L. Karst.—2nd ed. / Adam Winkler, associate editor for the second edition.
    p. cm.
   Includes bibliographical references and indexes.
   ISBN 0-02-864880-3 (hard cover : alk. paper)
     1. Constitutional law—United States—Encyclopedias.   I. Levy, Leonard Williams, 1923– II. Karst, Kenneth L. III. Winkler, Adam.
  KF4548 .E53 2000
  342.73—dc21

                            00-029203

This paper meets the requirements of ANSI-NISO Z39.48-1992 (Permanence of Paper).

KAHRIGER, UNITED STATES v.

See: *Marchetti v. United States*

KALVEN, HARRY, JR.
(1914–1974)

Commencing the lectures that became his book, *The Negro and the First Amendment* (1965), Harry Kalven remarked that constitutional law was his hobby. He considered himself a torts teacher who had become interested in some constitutional subjects, and certainly his writings on the constitutional law of DEFAMATION and invasions of PRIVACY show deep understanding of the underlying private law. But Kalven was no constitutional amateur; his work on the jury system and on the FIRST AMENDMENT placed him in the first rank of scholars in both fields.

A long collaboration with Hans Zeisel culminated in the publication of *The American Jury* (1966), a work still hailed for its pathbreaking combination of traditional legal analysis and imaginative empirical study. His essays on defamation and OBSCENITY set patterns of thought that can be seen in scores of later scholarly works, and his article on "the PUBLIC FORUM" probably influenced the course of Supreme Court decisions more than any other single work of its era. (See also: TWO-LEVEL THEORY.)

An effervescent man, Kalven was much beloved by a generation of his students at the University of Chicago Law School, some of whom are numbered today among our leading constitutional scholars. His legacy to them, and to all of us through his scholarship, was a passion for applying careful, particularized analysis—in short, the lawyer's craft—to the ends of justice.

KENNETH L. KARST
(1986)

Bibliography

In Memoriam: Harry Kalven, Jr. 1975 *The University of Chicago Law Review* 43:1–149. (Includes a complete bibliography of Kalven's writings.)

KANSAS-NEBRASKA ACT
10 Stat 277 (1854)

The Kansas-Nebraska Act declared the MISSOURI COMPROMISE of 1820 void and in its place enacted the policy of "POPULAR SOVEREIGNTY," thereby potentially opening all American territories to SLAVERY.

Democrats had extolled the finality of the COMPROMISE OF 1850 as a permanent resolution of the slavery controversy. Its constitutional elements included the stringent Fugitive Slave Act of 1850; the organization of New Mexico and Utah Territories without a prohibition of slavery; abolition of the slave trade in the DISTRICT OF COLUMBIA; and the "Clayton Compromise," which made all questions arising in the TERRITORIAL COURTS involving blacks' personal freedom or title to slaves directly appealable to the Supreme Court of the United States. The Illinois Democrat STEPHEN A. DOUGLAS, chairman of the Senate Committee on the Territories, disrupted this settlement in 1854, however, by introducing a bill to organize the remainder of the LOUISANA PURCHASE territory in order to facilitate construction of a transcontinental railroad that would have Chicago as its midcontinent terminus.

Douglas's original bill contained minor concessions to slavery, including reenactment of the Clayton Compromise provisions for Kansas Territory. But dissatisfied pro-slavery senators wrested further concessions. These included the declaration that the Missori Compromise of 1820 (which prohibited slavery in the Louisiana Purchase territory north of latitude 36° 30′, except in Missouri) had been superseded by the Compromise of 1850 and was void. The Kansas-Nebraska Bill enacted the principle of popular sovereignty, declaring that "all questions pertaining to SLAVERY IN THE TERRITORIES . . . are to be left to the decision of the people residing therein." It included a vague suggestion that the federal Constitution might in some unspecified way inhibit the power of a territorial legislature to exclude slaves. The bill explicitly endorsed "nonintervention," a code word for an indefinite congeries of proslavery constitutional principles that hinted at an absence of power in any government to inhibit the intrusion of slavery into the territories prior to statehood.

The Kansas-Nebraska Act, together with the Compromise of 1850, surrounded the free states and the free territory of Minnesota with a cordon of territories open to slavery, thus threatening to make the Great Plains a vast proslavery chasm between the free states of the northeast and the free states and territories of the Pacific coast. The Whig party distintegrated, and its place in the North was taken by the new Republican party, which combined Whig economic objectives (free homesteads, federal aid to INTERNAL IMPROVEMENTS) with elements of the Free Soil platform of 1848. These Free Soil principles included the idea that Congress could not establish or permit slavery in a territory and that it could not constitutionally support slavery anywhere outside the extant slave states. Thus the proslavery concessions of 1854 paradoxically resulted in no immediate practical gain for slavery but rather in a widespread dissemination of antislavery constitutional beliefs.

Kansas Territory, organized by the Act, became a theater of struggle for sectional advantage between proslavery Missourians and free-state settlers. The ensuing violence disrupted the Democratic party, especially after President JAMES BUCHANAN tried to force the proslavery LECOMPTON CONSTITUTION on the free-soil majority of Kansas settlers. The Kansas-Nebraska Act thus contributed substantially to the disruption of the Union.

WILLIAM M. WIECEK
(1986)

Bibliography

RUSSEL, ROBERT R.   1963   The Issues in the Congressional Struggle over the Kansas-Nebraska Bill, 1854. *Journal of Southern History* 29:187–210.

KASSEL v. CONSOLIDATED FREIGHTWAYS CORPORATION

See: *Raymond Motor Transportation Company v. Rice*

KASTIGAR v. UNITED STATES
406 U.S. 441 (1972)

Until this case the rule was that the Fifth Amendment requires a grant of transactional immunity to displace a claim of the RIGHT AGAINST SELF-INCRIMINATION. Title II of the ORGANIZED CRIME CONTROL ACT of 1970 fixed a single comprehensive standard applicable to grants of immunity in all federal judicial, GRAND JURY, administrative, and legislative proceedings. The new law provided that when a witness is required to testify over his claim of the Fifth Amendment right, "no testimony or other information compelled under the order (or any information directly or indirectly derived from such testimony or other information) may be used against the witness in any criminal cases," except in a prosecution for perjury or failure to comply. The statute thus provided for use immunity, permitting a prosecution based on EVIDENCE not derived from the testimony forced by a grant of immunity. (See IMMUNITY GRANT.)

Kastigar was cited for contempt after he persisted in his refusal to testify concerning unnecessary dental services affecting the draft status of persons seeking to evade the draft. His refusal to testify raised the question whether the grant of use immunity was sufficient to displace the Fifth Amendment right.

A seven-member Supreme Court, voting 5–2, sustained the constitutionality of use immunity. Justice LEWIS F. POWELL declared: "We hold that such immunity from use and derivative use is coextensive with the scope of the privilege against self-incrimination, and therefore is sufficient to compel testimony over a claim of the privilege. . . . Transactional immunity, which accords full immunity from prosecution for the offense to which the compelled testimony relates, affords the witness considerably broader protection than does the Fifth Amendment privilege. The privilege has never been construed to mean that one who invokes it cannot subsequently be prosecuted." Powell dismissed COUNSELMAN V. HITCHCOCK (1892) and its progeny, which established the transactional immunity standard, as OBITER DICTA and therefore not binding. Powell reasoned that a witness who had use immunity against his compelled testimony is in substantially the same position as if he had invoked the Fifth Amendment in the absence of a grant of immunity.

But one who relies on his constitutional right to silence

gives the state no possible way to use his testimony, however indirectly, against him, and he has not remotely, from the standpoint of the law, criminally implicated himself. Use immunity permits compulsion without removing the implication of criminality. On the other hand, the values of the Fifth Amendment are not infringed if the state prosecutes on evidence not related to the compelled testimony, and the state has the burden of proving that the prosecution relies on evidence from sources independent of the compelled testimony. The trouble is, as Justice THURGOOD MARSHALL pointed out in dissent, that only the prosecuting authorities know, if even they can know, the chains of information by which evidence was gathered. In any case, use immunity compels a person to be a witness against himself criminally.

LEONARD W. LEVY
(1986)

Bibliography

LEVY, LEONARD W. 1974 *Against the Law: The Nixon Court and Criminal Justice.* Pages 173–187. New York: Harper & Row.

KATZ v. UNITED STATES
389 U.S. 347 (1967)

Katz ended one era of constitutional protection for FOURTH AMENDMENT rights and began another. In OLMSTEAD V. UNITED STATES (1928) the Supreme Court had virtually exempted from the Fourth Amendment's ban on UNREASONABLE SEARCHES and seizures any search that did not involve a physical intrusion on property and a seizure of tangible things. Although eroded by subsequent decisions, and superseded by a federal statute where wiretapping was required, *Olmstead's* physical intrusion requirement inhibited constitutional control of aural and visual surveillance for forty years, until *Katz* was decided.

Federal agents, believing that Katz was using a pay telephone to transmit gambling information, attached a listening and recording device to the outside of the phone booth without trying to meet Fourth Amendment requirements. With the information obtained from the device, the police were able to convict Katz, but the Supreme Court overturned the conviction. The Court ruled that Katz was entitled to Fourth Amendment protection for his conversations and that a physical intrusion into an area occupied by Katz was not necessary to bring the amendment into play. "The Fourth Amendment protects people, not places," wrote Justice POTTER STEWART for a virtually unanimous Court (only Justice HUGO L. BLACK dissented). Justice JOHN MARSHALL HARLAN, concurring, developed a test for

determining what interests are protected, which has come to be the accepted standard: "first that a person have exhibited an actual (subjective) expectation of privacy and second, that the expectation be one that society is prepared to recognize as "reasonable."

The Court also set out some of the requirements for lawful ELECTRONIC EAVESDROPPING, supplementing those in BERGER V. NEW YORK (1967), many of which were incorporated in Title III of the OMNIBUS CRIME CONTROL AND SAFE STREETS ACT of 1968.

HERMAN SCHWARTZ
(1986)

KATZENBACH v. MCCLUNG

See: *Heart of Atlanta Motel v. United States*

KATZENBACH v. MORGAN
384 U.S. 641 (1966)

This decision upheld the constitutionality of section 4(e) of the VOTING RIGHTS ACT of 1965. Section 4(e) provided that no person who had successfully completed sixth grade in a school in which the language of instruction was other than English should be denied the right to vote in any election because of his inability to read or write English. In *Lassiter v. Northampton County Board of Elections* (1959) a unanimous Supreme Court had rejected a black citizen's attack on North Carolina's LITERACY TEST for voting. In *Morgan* the Court, in an opinion by Justice WILLIAM J. BRENNAN and over the dissents of Justices JOHN MARSHALL HARLAN and POTTER STEWART, rejected New York State's argument that in enforcing section 5 of the FOURTEENTH AMENDMENT Congress may prohibit enforcement of state law only if courts determine that the state law violates the FOURTEENTH AMENDMENT. In light of *Lassiter,* it seemed unlikely that New York's literacy requirement would be judicially found to violate the Constitution. Instead, the Court found Section 4(e) appropriate legislation to enforce the Fourteenth Amendment by assuring the franchise to those who migrated to New York from PUERTO RICO after completing sixth grade, whether or not that right to vote had been unconstitutionally infringed. The *Morgan* view that the Fourteenth Amendment confers discretion upon Congress to act both remedially and prophylactically to protect Fourteenth Amendment rights makes the case a centerpeice for analysis of how far Congress may go to protect or restrict Fourteenth Amendment rights.

THEODORE EISENBERG
(1986)

KEATING-OWEN CHILD LABOR ACT
39 Stat. 675 (1916)

This law marked the federal government's first attempt to regulate the use of child labor, culminating a decade-long effort by organized labor, social reformers and workers, publicists, and progressive politicians. The act prohibited the shipment in interstate or foreign commerce of any commodity produced in a mine or factory that employed children under the ages of sixteen and fourteen respectively.

Congressional debates over child labor legislation centered on the scope of national power. Opponents of the measure insisted that it involved a regulation of PRODUCTION, not commerce, and hence violated the TENTH AMENDMENT and the controlling precedent of UNITED STATES V. E. C. KNIGHT (1895). Although that decision had been distinguished in other cases involving NATIONAL POLICE POWER uses of the COMMERCE CLAUSE, such as the regulation of adulterated foods, STATES RIGHTS' oriented southern congressmen insisted that the national government could only prohibit harmful items from INTERSTATE COMMERCE. Goods made by children, they insisted, were not harmful in and of themselves. Supporters of a child labor law countered that congressional power over interstate commerce was plenary except for Fifth Amendment limitations. They also maintained that congressional action was imperative because state regulations had proven ineffective.

Supporters of the bill mobilized a broad array of interested groups, coordinated by the highly effective National Child Labor Committee. In addition, some traditionally conservative northern manufacturers lobbied for national action to counter the competitive advantage of new southern industries that operated under ineffectual state laws against child labor. A House committee report reflected this concern, noting that only national power could maintain a national marketplace and prevent unfair competition among the states. Finally, in the summer of 1916, independent progressives convinced a hitherto reluctant President WOODROW WILSON that his support was necessary to insure progressive backing in the forthcoming presidential election. Wilson decisively intervened with southern senators who had prevented passage for nearly six months, and the bill became law on September 1, 1916.

The Keating-Owen Act proved short-lived, for in less than two years the Supreme Court invalidated it in HAMMER V. DAGENHART (1918). A 5–4 majority held that the act regulated production, not interstate commerce, and violated the Tenth Amendment. The *Knight* precedent was reconfirmed, and the Court distinguished its approval of police power regulations of the flow of lottery tickets, adulterated foods, prostitutes, and liquor on the grounds that child labor products were not injurious.

Congress followed the Court's action with a new law based on the taxing power, but it, too, was voided. An effort to secure a child labor amendment to the Constitution languished in the 1920s and 1930s, but finally, in 1938, the FAIR LABOR STANDARDS ACT revived the essential elements of Keating-Owen. The Court sustained the new law in UNITED STATES V. DARBY (1941), expressly overruling *Hammer v. Dagenhart*.

STANLEY I. KUTLER
(1986)

Bibliography

WOOD, STEPHEN 1968 *Constitutional Politics in the Progressive Era: Child Labor and the Law.* Chicago: University of Chicago Press.

KELLY, ALFRED H.
(1907–1976)

Alfred Hinsey Kelly taught constitutional history for many years at Wayne State University. With his colleague Winfred A. Harbison he wrote *The American Constitution: Its Origins and Development* (1948; 6th ed., with Herman Belz, 1982), now widely regarded as the best single-volume constitutional history ever written. In 1953 Kelly researched the background of the FOURTEENTH AMENDMENT for the NAACP LEGAL DEFENSE FUND's brief in BROWN V. BOARD OF EDUCATION (1954), concentrating on establishing the views of the framers of the amendment. He and Fund attorneys THURGOOD MARSHALL and William R. Ming prepared the final version of the historical sections of the brief submitted to the Court; in this brief and in later articles on the Amendment, Kelly distinguished "between the narrow scope of the CIVIL RIGHTS ACT OF 1866 and the much broader purposes of the Fourteenth Amendment itself" and emphasized the "broad equalitarian objectives" advocated by Representatives JOHN A. BINGHAM, THADDEUS STEVENS, and other members of Congress in the debates on the amendment. Kelly also provided inside accounts of the *Brown* litigation in his essay in *Quarrels That Shaped the Constitution* (John Garraty, ed., 1962) and in interviews with Richard Kluger for the latter's *Simple Justice* (1976).

RICHARD B. BERNSTEIN
(1986)

KEMMLER, IN RE
136 U.S. 436 (1890)

MCELVAINE v. BRUSH
142 U.S. 155 (1891)

O'NEIL v. VERMONT
144 U.S. 155 (1892)

These cases dealt with the meaning of the ban on CRUEL AND UNUSUAL PUNISHMENT and with the INCORPORATION DOCTRINE of the FOURTEENTH AMENDMENT. Kemmler was sentenced to die in the electric chair, then recently invented. He argued that infliction of death by that device would violate the Fourteenth Amendment, because its PRIVILEGES AND IMMUNITIES clause or its DUE PROCESS clause meant that no state could inflict a cruel execution. The Court unanimously ruled that a cruel execution would be one involving torture or lingering death, "something inhuman and barbarous," but that the electric chair was a "humane" form of execution. The Court also held that no clause of the Fourteenth Amendment banned punishments not deemed cruel by state courts. Unlike Kemmler, McElvaine explicitly argued that the Fourteenth Amendment incorporated the Eighth Amendment's ban on cruel punishments; he also argued that solitary confinement of a convict sentenced to death was cruel. Unanimously the Court met and rejected both contentions. In O'Neil's case, however, Justices STEPHEN J. FIELD, DAVID J. BREWER, and JOHN MARSHALL HARLAN in DISSENTING OPINIONS declared that the Fourteenth Amendment applied Eighth Amendment rights and all "fundamental" rights to the states.

LEONARD W. LEVY
(1986)

KENNEDY, ANTHONY M.
(1936–)

Anthony M. Kennedy has fulfilled the objectives of President RONALD REAGAN in choosing him to fill the vacancy on the Supreme Court created by the retirement of Justice LEWIS F. POWELL.

First, President Reagan expected that Kennedy's noncontroversial background would ensure him swift confirmation by the Senate. After graduating from Harvard Law School in 1961, Kennedy had worked as a lawyer and lobbyist in California until President GERALD R. FORD appointed him to the Ninth Circuit Court of Appeals in 1975. While on the bench, Kennedy, who also taught constitutional law at McGeorge School of Law, evolved as a relatively colorless, nonideological conservative, but gained notoriety for writing the lower court opinion striking down the LEGISLATIVE VETO—a result subsequently affirmed by the Supreme Court in IMMIGRATION AND NATURALIZATION SERVICE V. CHADHA (1983). In February 1988 the Senate unanimously confirmed Kennedy.

President Reagan also hoped that Kennedy would join Chief Justice WILLIAM H. REHNQUIST and Justices BYRON R. WHITE, SANDRA DAY O'CONNOR, and ANTONIN SCALIA to form a conservative majority that would curtail the initiatives of both the WARREN COURT and the BURGER COURT. During his first two terms on the Court, Kennedy did in fact cast the crucial fifth vote with these Justices in several 5–4 decisions expanding state control in the fields of ABORTION, CAPITAL PUNISHMENT, CRIMINAL PROCEDURE, and CIVIL RIGHTS.

However, Kennedy has demonstrated little potential as a leader of the current conservative Justices, others of whom have striven to apply complex interpretative theories to constitutional issues. Instead, Kennedy has emerged as a classically conservative Justice: he has thus far avoided articulating any overarching philosophy of CONSTITUTIONAL INTERPRETATION and has been reluctant to challenge PRECEDENT.

Kennedy's votes support a view of FEDERALISM under which the states check federal power and are responsible for matters on which the Constitution provides no clear prohibitions. For example, Kennedy joined Justice Scalia's separate opinion in *Pennsylvania v. Union Gas Co.* (1989), which would have denied Congress the power to lift the states' ELEVENTH AMENDMENT immunity in exercising its legislative powers under Article I. Kennedy also joined *Will v. Michigan* (1989) and DESHANEY V. WINNEBAGO COUNTY DEPARTMENT OF SOCIAL SERVICES (1989), which effectively held that neither the FOURTEENTH AMENDMENT nor SECTION 1983, TITLE 42, U.S. CODE significantly altered state sovereignty. Similarly, Kennedy maintained in dissent in MISSOURI V. JENKINS (1990) that by upholding a federal court order commanding a school district to impose a tax, the majority impermissibly expanded federal court power at the expense of "fundamental precepts for the democratic control of public institutions."

Kennedy's opinions reflect his belief in a living constitution that recognizes, even against claims of individual liberties, the need for government to adapt to changes in technology and its responsibilities. For example, in SKINNER V. RAILWAY LABOR EXECUTIVES ASSOCIATION (1989) and TREASURY EMPLOYEES UNION V. VON RAAB (1989) Kennedy explained that the FOURTH AMENDMENT did not preclude DRUG TESTING of railway workers after railroad accidents and of customs workers when there was no individualized suspicion and no evidence of drug abuse in the customs service. Similarly, Kennedy rejected FIRST AMENDMENT challenges to a municipal regulation in *Ward v. Rock Against Racism* (1989) that required performers at an outdoor theater to use the city's sound system and technician, even though the requirement restricted certain speakers and messages.

Kennedy's hesitancy to reverse or to expand precedent reflects his preference for deciding cases on the narrowest available grounds and to affect settled doctrine as little as possible. Accordingly, in *Saffle v. Parks* (1990) Kennedy read precedents narrowly in order to deny federal HABEAS CORPUS relief because the respondent had raised a new legal claim that could not be applied retroactively on collateral review. Kennedy also hewed closely to precedent in *Barnard v. Thorstenn* (1989) in holding that residency requirements for admission to the Virgin Islands bar violated the PRIVILEGES AND IMMUNITIES clause of Article IV.

In WEBSTER V. REPRODUCTIVE HEALTH SERVICES (1989), Kennedy refused to join Justice Scalia's concurrence urging overruling of ROE V. WADE (1973), but joined Chief Justice Rehnquist's PLURALITY OPINION that rejected the trimester analysis used by the *Roe* Court for measuring the importance of the state's interest. Similarly, in CITY OF RICHMOND V. J. A. CROSON CO. (1989) Kennedy refused to join Justice Scalia's concurrence challenging a city's set-aside of public funds for minority contractors, as well as the congressional program on which it was modeled, which had been upheld in FULLILOVE V. KLUTZNICK (1980). Kennedy's concurrence emphasized that *Fullilove* posed a difficult but separate issue concerning the scope of congressional power under section 5 of the FOURTEENTH AMENDMENT.

In PATTERSON V. MCLEAN CREDIT UNION (1989), Kennedy narrowly reaffirmed RUNYON V. MCCRARY (1976). Although the *Runyon* Court had applied 42 U.S.C. section 1981 to restrict racial discrimination in private school admissions, Kennedy refused to apply the statute's prohibitions of discrimination in the "formation" or "making" of contracts to racial harassment in the conditions of employment.

Dissenting in *James v. Illinois* (1990), Kennedy reluctantly accepted precedents imposing the EXCLUSIONARY RULE on the states, but suggested the rule should not have been applied to prevent the prosecution from using illegally obtained evidence to impeach the defendant and other defense witnesses in a criminal trial. Similarly, in *Jones v. Thomas* (1989), Kennedy acknowledged, but refused to extend, the traditional DOUBLE JEOPARDY prohibition (against multiple sentences for the same offense) to preclude the petitioner's continued confinement under a longer sentence after he had completed a commuted sentence imposed for the same offense. He also explained in WASHINGTON V. HARPER (1990) that the involuntary administration of antipsychotic drugs to a violent prisoner

comported with both SUBSTANTIVE DUE PROCESS and PROCEDURAL DUE PROCESS.

However, in his dissent in COUNTY OF ALLEGHENY V. ACLU (1989), Kennedy urged abandoning the Court's traditional test in ESTABLISHMENT CLAUSE cases. He argued that the Court's test separated church and state more than the Framers intended.

The major exception to Kennedy's narrow construction of individual rights is his concurrence in TEXAS V. JOHNSON (1989), in which the Court held 5–4 that the First Amendment protected flag burning as political speech. Kennedy explained that "the flag protects even those who would hold it in contempt."

Kennedy's steadfast refusal to offer a sophisticated alternative to the grander constitutional visions of his fellow conservatives may foretell a modest role for him. Ironically, such a role would reflect Kennedy's vision of the Court's modest role in a system governed by traditional notions of federalism.

MICHAEL J. GERHARDT
(1992)

(SEE ALSO: *Flag Desecration; Fourteenth Amendment, Section 5 (Framing); Fourteenth Amendment, Section 5 (Judicial Construction).*)

Bibliography

CHEMERINSKY, ERWIN 1989 Foreword: The Vanishing Constitution. *Harvard Law Review* 103:43–104.

MALTZ, EARL M. 1990 The Prospects for a Revival of Conservative Activism in Constitutional Jurisprudence. *Georgia Law Review* 24:629–668.

KENNEDY, ANTHONY M.
(1936–   )
(Update)

After spending his first few terms on the Supreme Court as a reliable if nonideological conservative Justice, Anthony M. Kennedy has emerged as a "swing vote" on the REHNQUIST COURT. His predecessor, Justice LEWIS F. POWELL, JR., played a similar role on the BURGER COURT, but unlike Powell, Kennedy does not tend to stake out intermediate positions on controversial issues. Instead, Kennedy has strong views that happen to place him at the Court's center. In some areas he joins the conservative bloc, consisting of Chief Justice WILLIAM H. REHNQUIST, and Justices ANTONIN SCALIA, CLARENCE THOMAS, and (on many issues) SANDRA DAY O'CONNOR. In other areas, Kennedy joins the moderate-to-liberal bloc, consisting of Justices JOHN PAUL STEVENS, DAVID H. SOUTER, RUTH BADER GINSBURG, and STE-

PHEN G. BREYER. The one near-constant is that Kennedy's position commands at least four other votes.

Kennedy's views about the relation between the states and the federal government are illustrative. He has joined the conservative bloc in a string of decisions invalidating federal laws as infringing upon state SOVEREIGNTY. These cases alternatively invoke the TENTH AMENDMENT, *Printz v. United States* (1997); the ELEVENTH AMENDMENT, *Seminole Tribe of Florida v. Florida* (1996); or Congress's limited enumerated powers, UNITED STATES V. LÓPEZ (1995), *City of Boerne v. Flores* (1997); but they consistently display a skepticism toward federal power. Kennedy does not, however, romanticize the states in the way that the other conservatives appear to do. He was the only member of the Court who voted to invalidate both the federal Gun-Free School Zones Act and a state's efforts to impose TERM LIMITS on members of its congressional delegation, *Thornton v. U.S. Term Limits* (1995). As he wrote in a concurrence in the latter case: "That the States may not invade the sphere of federal sovereignty is as incontestable, in my view, as the corollary proposition that the Federal Government must be held within the boundaries of its own power when it intrudes upon matters reserved to the States." The driving force behind Kennedy's FEDERALISM jurisprudence is neither nationalism nor STATES' RIGHTS, but an abiding belief in limited government at all levels.

Kennedy's libertarian streak also informs his individual rights jurisprudence. He generally takes an expansive view of FREEDOM OF SPEECH rights under the FIRST AMENDMENT, although he recognizes a legitimate role for government regulation in cases involving a risk of private monopolization of speech, TURNER BROADCASTING SYSTEM V. FCC (1997), and government-funded speech, RUST V. SULLIVAN (1991), *NEA v. Finley* (1998). The funding "exception" has its limits, though, as Kennedy argued in a (partially) DISSENTING OPINION sympathetic to speakers claiming a right to access to public spaces, even nontraditional spaces such as public airports, INTERNATIONAL SOCIETY FOR KRISHNA CONSCIOUSNESS V. LEE (1992).

Kennedy's sharpest disagreement with the conservative bloc concerns the role of the Court in enforcing constitutional rights beyond those expressly enumerated in the text, under the doctrine of SUBSTANTIVE DUE PROCESS. In PLANNED PARENTHOOD V. CASEY (1992), Kennedy, O'Connor, and Souter jointly authored an opinion reaffirming the "central holding" of ROE V. WADE (1973). Although the *Casey* opinion relied in part on the doctrine of STARE DECISIS, it also contained a ringing endorsement of the practice of judicial protection for unenumerated rights. In other contexts as well, Kennedy has disagreed with the claim that the Constitution protects only those rights spelled out in the text or widely accepted at the time of its adoption.

If Kennedy's endorsement of a right to ABORTION and other unenumerated rights has disappointed conservatives' hopes, they have found his jurisprudence on questions of race more to their liking. He interprets the constitutional requirement of EQUAL PROTECTION OF THE LAWS to mandate "color-blindness" in nearly all circumstances, and has thus voted to strike down AFFIRMATIVE ACTION programs and ELECTORAL DISTRICTING in which race was the predominant factor in the drawing of district lines.

The principal themes of Kennedy's equal protection jurisprudence—and much of his rights jurisprudence more generally—are inclusion and fairness. Outside the context of affirmative action, this has often led Kennedy to cast liberal votes. For example, in *Edmonson v. Leesville Concrete Co.* (1991), he found that the Constitution bars race-based PEREMPTORY JURY CHALLENGES, even in civil cases. Kennedy's opinion in that case reflects an extremely expansive view of the doctrine of what constitutes STATE ACTION, because he saw this approach as necessary to ensure that persons not be denied the opportunity to carry out their duty as jurors simply on the basis of their race. The theme of inclusion also explains his opinion for a 5–4 Court in LEE V. WEISMAN (1992). Although Kennedy usually votes to permit significant state ACCOMMODATION OF RELIGION, his opinion in *Lee* invalidated an official prayer at a public high school graduation. The opinion roundly condemns the suggestion that no violation occurred simply because the students were not required to participate in the graduation ceremony in order to receive their degrees: "to say a teenage student has a real choice not to attend her high school graduation is formalistic in the extreme," Kennedy wrote.

ROMER V. EVANS (1996) may be the apotheosis of Kennedy's individual rights jurisprudence. In that case, the Court addressed a challenge to an amendment to the Colorado constitution prohibiting the state or any of its subdivisions from enacting or enforcing laws protecting homosexuals from discrimination. Without deciding whether governmental discrimination on the basis of SEXUAL ORIENTATION is inherently suspect, and without even citing BOWERS V. HARDWICK (1986), which upheld the criminalization of homosexual sodomy, Kennedy's opinion in *Romer* invalidates the Colorado amendment as born of an irrational antipathy towards an unpopular group. Although Kennedy nominally uses the least demanding test for constitutionality under the equal protection clause— the RATIONAL BASIS test—the opinion's great strength (or from the perspective of those who disagree, its glaring weakness), is its extremely sparse use of formal legal categories.

In *Romer*, Kennedy appears to be speaking to the nation at large, explaining why the Colorado amendment offends basic principles of fairness and inclusion, and thus offends the Constitution as well. These principles lie at the center of Kennedy's constitutional vision, and thus at the center of the Rehnquist Court's constitutional vision as well.

MICHAEL C. DORF
(2000)

Bibliography

AMAR, AKHIL R. 1997 Justice Kennedy and the Ideal of Equality. *Pacific Law Journal* 28:515–532.

EDELMAN, PAUL H. and CHEN, JIM 1996 The Most Dangerous Justice: The Supreme Court at the Bar of Mathematics. *Southern California Law Review* 70:63–105.

FRIEDMAN, LAWRENCE 1993 The Limitations of Labeling: Justice Anthony M. Kennedy and the First Amendment. *Ohio Northern University Law Review* 20:225–262.

SULLIVAN, KATHLEEN M. 1992 The Supreme Court 1991 Term—Foreword: The Justices of Rules and Standards. *Harvard Law Review* 106:22–123.

KENNEDY, JOHN F.
(1917–1963)

John Fitzgerald Kennedy entered the White House in 1961 as the heir to the liberal, Democratic party tradition of WOODROW WILSON, FRANKLIN D. ROOSEVELT, and HARRY S. TRUMAN. Youthful, vigorous, and blessed with extraordinary rhetorical powers, Kennedy saw himself as an activist chief executive and pledged to "get the country moving again," especially with respect to economic growth and international competition with the Soviet Union. But during his one thousand days in office, Kennedy's performance often lagged behind his promises.

His appointments to the Supreme Court were unexceptional. To the first vacancy, created by the retirement of CHARLES WHITTAKER, he named deputy attorney general BYRON R. WHITE, a former All American football player, Rhodes Scholar, and campaign adviser. White's intellect and productivity exceeded those of his predecessor; he often aligned himself with the conservative faction on the WARREN COURT. To replace Justice FELIX FRANKFURTER and to fill the chair once occupied by OLIVER WENDELL HOLMES and BENJAMIN N. CARDOZO, Kennedy named ARTHUR GOLDBERG, a hard-working, conscientious labor lawyer, who usually voted with the liberals on the Warren Court but was blessed with neither intellectual brilliance nor a dashing prose style.

Kennedy's appointments to the lower federal courts were often dreadful, especially in the southern circuits, where "senatorial courtesy" gave great influence to segregationist Democratic senators. The result was Kennedy's appointment of a number of federal district judges who were openly segregationist and, in some instances, openly racist. On the other hand, Kennedy did place THURGOOD MARSHALL on the circuit court in New York; the Department of Justice, under the prodding of Attorney General ROBERT F. KENNEDY, began to intervene to protect CIVIL RIGHTS workers in the South; and Solicitor General Archibald Cox became a forceful and articulate spokesman for racial justice.

The struggle of black Americans to batter down the walls of segregation and win access to the voting booths of the deep South was the great domestic constitutional issue of the Kennedy years. The administration's response to this crisis blended pragmatism and expediency with idealism and occasional moral outrage. While forcing the South to accept the token integration of higher education, the administration did not push hard for similar results in the primary and secondary grades. The official violence inflicted upon civil rights activists during the Birmingham, Alabama, demonstrations led Kennedy to propose to Congress legislation which became, after his death, the landmark CIVIL RIGHTS ACT OF 1964. Many students of the Kennedy presidency regard his televised address in support of this legislation as his finest hour. On the other hand, the Kennedy brothers were not enthusiastic supporters of the 1963 March on Washington, and under pressure from FBI Director J. EDGAR HOOVER they endorsed the electronic surveillance of civil rights leader MARTIN LUTHER KING, JR.

If civil rights received growing constitutional protection from the Kennedy administration, CIVIL LIBERTIES often suffered at the hands of a regime that espoused vigorous presidential leadership and believed that the ends usually justified the means. Outraged that the nation's leading steel producers had raised prices in defiance of an informal agreement with labor and the White House, Kennedy threatened the offending corporations with tax audits, securities law investigations, and cancellation of defense contracts. Robert Kennedy's unremitting war against organized crime figures skirted the boundary of assorted illegalities, including WARRANTLESS SEARCHES and ELECTRONIC EAVESDROPPING. By waging a clandestine war against Fidel Castro's communist regime in Cuba, the Kennedy brothers also displayed a cavalier attitude about the RULE OF LAW. Operation Mongoose, directed by the attorney general, involved acts of sabotage and terrorism against the Cuban regime, most of them in violation of the neutrality laws.

Although their motives were sometimes the highest, John Kennedy and his closest advisers often fostered a disrespect for legal norms and an inflated conception of executive power that would haunt the nation during the decade after his assassination in 1963.

MICHAEL E. PARRISH
(1986)

Bibliography

NAVASKY, VICTOR 1977 *Kennedy Justice.* New York: Atheneum.
PARMET, HERBERT S. 1983 *JFK: The Presidency of John F. Kennedy.* New York: Dial Press.

KENNEDY, ROBERT F.
(1925–1968)

After brief service in the Department of Justice, Robert F. Kennedy joined the Permanent Subcommittee on Investigations of the United States Senate (then headed by JOSEPH MCCARTHY) in 1953 as assistant counsel. When John McClellan became chairman in 1955 he appointed Kennedy chief counsel. In 1957 Kennedy became chief counsel of McClellan's Senate Rackets Committee and achieved national fame during the committee's investigations of teamsters' union leaders David Beck and James Hoffa.

Kennedy was appointed attorney general in 1961 by his brother, President JOHN F. KENNEDY. In this post he distinguished himself by vigorous enforcement of CIVIL RIGHTS—desegregating schools and interstate transportation facilities—and by finally securing the conviction of Hoffa on jury-tampering charges. (See HOFFA V. UNITED STATES.) As the President's closest adviser he exerted more influence on FOREIGN AFFAIRS than most attorneys general, heading the "executive committee" of the National Security Council during the Cuban missile crisis of 1962.

As a United States senator from New York (1965–1968), Kennedy voted for the GULF OF TONKIN RESOLUTION but later opposed President LYNDON B. JOHNSON's conduct of the VIETNAM WAR. He was assassinated by a Palestinian nationalist while campaigning for the Democratic presidential nomination in 1968.

DENNIS J. MAHONEY
(1986)

Bibliography

LASKY, VICTOR 1968 *Robert F. Kennedy: The Man and the Myth.* New York: Trident.

KENNEDY, ROBERT F.
(1925–1968)
(Update)

Robert Kennedy was named ATTORNEY GENERAL of the United States in 1961 by his brother President JOHN F. KENNEDY. A graduate of Harvard College and the University of Virginia Law School, he had served as counsel for Senate committees in the 1950s and acquired a reputation as an able and relentless prosecutor. His appointment was ascribed to nepotism and provoked widespread criticism.

Kennedy surrounded himself with an exceptionally able group of lawyers, headed by Archibald Cox of the Harvard Law School as SOLICITOR GENERAL and by BYRON R. WHITE, later of the Supreme Court, as deputy attorney general. In time, he won general respect for capable, humane, and nonpolitical administration of the Department of Justice.

The major challenge was the enforcement of CIVIL RIGHTS statutes and decisions. Robert Kennedy brought about the end of SEGREGATION in interstate transportation and used government intervention, including federal marshals, to support black students seeking entry to the University of Mississippi (1962) and the University of Alabama (1963).

Civil rights activists criticized the Justice Department for segregationist appointments to the southern bench and for unwillingness to assume local POLICE POWER in protection of civil rights workers. The problem of FEDERALISM and civil rights caused Kennedy anguish, but he believed that LOCAL GOVERNMENTS had primary responsibility for law enforcement and feared the implications of a national police force.

The key to racial justice in his view was voting: "From participation in the elections," he said, "flow all other rights." Department of Justice lawyers fanned out across the South to fight VOTING RIGHTS cases. In 1963, after outrages in Birmingham and elsewhere in the South, the Kennedys submitted a comprehensive civil rights bill to Congress. The CIVIL RIGHTS ACT OF 1964, passed after President Kennedy's assassination, was the most far-reaching civil rights statute since RECONSTRUCTION.

Like all attorneys general from 1920 to 1970, Kennedy had the problem of J. EDGAR HOOVER, the autocratic and increasingly tendentious chief of the FEDERAL BUREAU OF INVESTIGATION (FBI). Kennedy required the FBI to hire black agents, to reduce its obsession with communism, and to move into such neglected fields as civil rights and organized crime.

Kennedy personally argued the case of GRAY V. SANDERS (1963), in which the Supreme Court struck down the Georgia county-unit system and affirmed the principle of ONE PERSON, ONE VOTE. He secured provision of counsel and reform of the BAIL system in the interests of INDIGENT defendants, and his Committee on Juvenile Delinquency laid the foundation for the War on Poverty in the later 1960s.

He also played a role in FOREIGN AFFAIRS but as the President's troubleshooter, not as his legal adviser. The Central Intelligence Agency covert action that the younger

Kennedy promoted against Fidel Castro's Cuba, like all covert action, violated international law. During the Cuban missile crisis, however, he opposed a surprise air strike on Cuba, observing that "a sneak attack was not in our traditions." After serving nine prickly months as LYNDON B. JOHNSON's attorney general, Kennedy resigned and ran successfully for the Senate from New York. He was assassinated in 1968.

As attorney general, Robert Kennedy, though not a legal technician himself, had a high appreciation of technical legal ability in others, sought impartial enforcement of domestic law, gave new impetus to the movement for racial justice, and organized one of the strongest Departments of Justice in recent times.

ARTHUR M. SCHLESINGER, JR.
(1992)

Bibliography

NAVASKY, VICTOR 1971 *Kennedy Justice.* New York: Atheneum.
SCHLESINGER, ARTHUR M., JR. 1978 *Robert F. Kennedy and His Times.* Boston: Houghton Mifflin.

KENT, JAMES
(1763–1847)

James Kent, a New York jurist, influenced American constitutional jurisprudence through both his writings and his judicial opinions. Largely because of his *Commentaries on American Law*, Kent was as important a legal figure as any in nineteenth-century America. The *Commentaries* went through fourteen editions by 1900 and innumerable popular abridgments. After publication of the fifth edition, editors came and went, but they wrought their changes mostly in the notes, leaving Kent's work intact. For approximately three-quarters of a century Kent was for many lawyers, throughout the country, their primary legal authority.

Originally a two-volume set when it appeared in 1826, the *Commentaries* were quickly expanded to four. Ostensibly the book was commenced after Kent's mandatory retirement from the bench on reaching age sixty in 1823. Yet, it is possible to see the work in process through Kent's carefully crafted opinions beginning with his appointment to the New York Supreme Court in 1798, and continuing while he was the state's chancellor, 1814–1823. And it is scarcely stretching matters to consider the writing of the *Commentaries* a lifelong process.

Kent's twenty-five years of judicial opinions were imbued with the federalism of the late eighteenth century. At the heart of Kent's jurisprudence was an independent judiciary whose role was to maintain society's moral order. Because of a quirk in New York's 1777 constitution, Kent participated in the veto process as a member of the Council of Revision, which considered all bills passed by the legislature. This process meant that New York judges would have little reason to exercise JUDICIAL REVIEW when a statute's constitutionality was questioned in a case. Having approved the steamboat monopoly bill on several occasions while sitting on the council, for example, New York judges would be unlikely to declare the law contrary to the federal constitution when such a challenge was made in *Livingston v. Van Ingen* (1812) and GIBBONS V. OGDEN (1819, 1820).

The moral order that Kent and his brethren sought to maintain covered many facets of life, including freedom of expression. There was no room in Kent's order of things for BLASPHEMY—"it tends to corrupt the morals of the people, and to destroy good order," he wrote in *People v. Ruggles* (1811)—but a Federalist printer was afforded the defense of truth to the COMMON LAW charge of criminal libel against THOMAS JEFFERSON in PEOPLE V. CROSWELL (1804). The New York Supreme Court was evenly divided in *Croswell*, so that Kent's opinion, based on ALEXANDER HAMILTON's argument, did not become law in itself. A year later the legislature made truth a defense in libel suits, provided the alleged libelous matter "was published with good motives and for justifiable ends." Kent and his colleagues were careful, moreover, in their interpretation of the law, subsequently inserted in the state constitution of 1821, to protect officeholders, setting the groundwork for *Root v. King* (1829), which kept a bridle on attacks on New York public officials until NEW YORK TIMES V. SULLIVAN (1964).

Kent made another major contribution to constitutional law in *Livingston v. Van Ingen* (1812), by elaborately enunciating the doctrine of concurrent commerce powers. The Livingston-Fulton steamboat monopoly symbolized New York's encouragement of commercial enterprise. Under the statute creating the monopoly, any competitor was required to get a license in order to run a steamboat on New York waters. In his opinion for the state's court of last resort, Kent legitimized the monopoly in a decision that reversed Chancellor JOHN LANSING's refusal to grant the monopoly an INJUNCTION against unlicensed competition. Of particular constitutional moment was the argument that the monopoly violated the federal Constitution's COMMERCE CLAUSE. In rejecting this argument, Kent asserted that in the absence of actual conflict between state and national laws, states retained the powers to regulate commerce. Seven years later in *Ogden v. Gibbons* (1819), Kent found no such conflict between the monopoly and the federal coasting act of 1793. In the United States Supreme Court, however, that served as the basis for JOHN MARSHALL's invalidation of the monopoly in GIBBONS V. OGDEN (1824). Kent's doctrine of concurrent commerce powers persisted, though, largely through the efforts of his former law clerk and judicial colleague, SMITH THOMPSON, and for a time it won the support of the TANEY COURT.

Kent was also responsible for first enunciating what would become the Cherokee doctrine. Speaking for the New York court in *Goodell v. Jackson* (1823), Kent fully developed the paternalistic notion that American Indian peoples, though subject, were sovereign nations, a theme adopted by Thompson in his *Cherokee Nation v. Georgia* dissent (1831), which in turn was adopted by Marshall for the Supreme Court in *Worcester v. Georgia* (1832). (See CHEROKEE INDIAN CASES.)

Important as Kent's occasional constitutional opinions may have been, his major contribution to constitutional development remains the *Commentaries*. There is apparent irony in this accomplishment because Kent did not emphasize constitutional law; instead, he salted that subject into the great body of American law between the law of nations and the construction of wills. Kent succeeded in putting constitutional law in its proper perspective compared to other important aspects of the law. In addition, Kent admirably digested the great Marshall opinions so as, in the opinion of THOMAS REED POWELL, to make them decidedly more palatable than they were in the original. Needless to say, the *Commentaries* continued to vote Federalist.

DONALD ROPER
(1986)

Bibliography

BAUER, ELIZABETH KELLEY 1952 *Commentaries on the Constitution 1790–1860.* New York: Columbia University Press.
HORTON, JOHN T. 1939 *James Kent: A Study in Conservatism 1763–1847.* New York: Appleton-Century Co.

KENT v. DULLES
357 U.S. 116 (1958)

This decision severely limited the State Department's discretionary passport policies. During the Cold War era, the department routinely denied passports to those who refused to sign a noncommunist affidavit. The Supreme Court held that the department lacked statutory authority for this policy and went on to remark in OBITER DICTUM that the RIGHT TO TRAVEL, which it traced back to MAGNA CARTA, was protected by the DUE PROCESS clause of the FIFTH AMENDMENT.

STANLEY I. KUTLER
(1986)

KENTUCKY RESOLUTIONS

See: Virginia and Kentucky Resolutions

KER v. CALIFORNIA
374 U.S. 23 (1963)

In *Ker* the Supreme Court clarified the constitutional standards governing the states in SEARCH AND SEIZURE cases. MAPP V. OHIO (1961), in applying the federal EXCLUSIONARY RULE against the states, had left undetermined whether they would retain some latitude to fashion their own search rules. The Court answered this question in *Ker,* holding that the protection against state searches granted by the FOURTEENTH AMENDMENT is coextensive with that of the FOURTH AMENDMENT against federal searches. Only Justice JOHN MARSHALL HARLAN disagreed. The Court's single-standard position, he feared, might lead to dilution of federal search safeguards because the Court would be reluctant to fetter the states with standards beyond their reach.

JACOB W. LANDYNSKI
(1986)

KEYES v. SCHOOL DISTRICT NO. 1
413 U.S. 189 (1973)

Keyes, the Denver school DESEGREGATION case, was the first such case to reach the Supreme Court from a district outside the South. The case gave the Court an opportunity to decide whether the fact of separation of the races in a city's schools was sufficient to justify desegregation remedies, even in the absence of any history of state law commanding SEGREGATION or any deliberate segregative action by the school board. The Court found it unnecessary to decide this question. Deliberate segregative actions of the board in one substantial part of the city, the Court said, raised a presumption of de jure segregation affecting the whole district; absent a showing that the district's parts were truly unrelated, a districtwide remedy would be approved on the basis of SWANN V. CHARLOTTE-MECKLENBURG BOARD OF EDUCATION (1971). The Court thus affirmed a busing order affecting twelve percent of the district's pupils. Justice WILLIAM J. BRENNAN wrote for a Court that was no longer unanimous.

Justice LEWIS F. POWELL, in a separate opinion that was more dissent than concurrence, argued that the time had come to scrap the DE FACTO/DE JURE distinction. In his view, *Swann* effectively required a school board to provide a remedy not only for segregation deliberately brought about by its own action or by state law but also for residential segregation—a fact of urban life throughout the country. "Segregative intent" was an illusory concept, he said. Once the fact of racial separation is shown, a board should have the duty to take appropriate steps to minimize school segregation. Massive busing, however, was not an appropriate remedy in his opinion, chiefly because of its costs to the values of the neighborhood school. Justice WILLIAM O. DOUGLAS, concurring, also thought that the de facto-de jure distinction made no sense but thought busing an appropriate remedy. Chief Justice WARREN E. BURGER concurred in the result, Justice WILLIAM H. REHNQUIST dissented, and Justice BYRON R. WHITE did not participate.

KENNETH L. KARST
(1986)

(SEE ALSO: *Columbus Board of Education v. Penick; School Busing.*)

KEYISHIAN v. BOARD OF REGENTS
385 U.S. 589 (1967)

ADLER V. BOARD OF EDUCATION (1952) was one of the cases in which the Supreme Court upheld a wide range of regulations barring "subversives" from government employment. *Keyishian* overruled *Adler* and was the culmination of a series of later decisions restricting LOYALTY-SECURITY PROGRAMS, typically by invoking the VAGUENESS and OVERBREADTH doctrines. *Keyishian* struck down some parts of a complex New York law limiting employment in public teaching; the law's use of the term "seditious" was unconstitutionally vague. Other parts of the law were invalid because they prohibited *mere* knowing membership in the Communist party without the specific intent required by ELFBRANDT V. RUSSELL (1966). *Keyishian* confirmed the Court's previous decisions rejecting the doctrine that public employment is a privilege to which government may attach whatever conditions it pleases.

MARTIN SHAPIRO
(1986)

KIDD v. PEARSON
128 U.S. 1 (1888)

A unanimous Court distinguished manufacturing and all forms of PRODUCTION from INTERSTATE COMMERCE, holding that a state act prohibiting the manufacture of intoxicants did not conflict with the national power to regulate interstate commerce and that the manufacture of a product for export to other states did not make it an article of interstate commerce.

LEONARD W. LEVY
(1986)

KILBOURN v. THOMPSON
103 U.S. 168 (1881)

Until this case Congress believed that its power of conducting investigations was unlimited and that its judicial authority to punish contumacious witnesses for contempt was unquestionable. After this case both the investigatory and CONTEMPT POWERS of Congress were distinctly limited and subject to JUDICIAL REVIEW. Not until MCGRAIN V. DAUGHERTY (1927) did the Court firmly establish the constitutional basis for oversight and investigatory powers. The decision in *Kilbourn* was so negative in character that the legitimate area of LEGISLATIVE INVESTIGATIONS seemed murky.

Kilbourn developed out of the House's investigation, by a select committee, into the activities of a bankrupt banking firm that owed money to the United States. The committee subpoenaed Kilbourn's records, which he refused to produce, and interrogated him, but he refused to answer on the ground that the questions concerned private matters. The House cited him for contempt and jailed him. He in turn sued for false arrest, and on a writ of HABEAS CORPUS he obtained a review of his case before the Supreme Court.

Unanimously, in an opinion by Justice SAMUEL F. MILLER, the Court held that neither house of Congress can punish a witness for contumacy unless his testimony is required on a matter concerning which "the House has jurisdiction to inquire," and, Miller added, neither house has "the general power of making inquiry into the private affairs of the citizen." The subject of this inquiry, Miller said, was judicial in nature, not legislative, and a case was pending in a lower federal court. The investigation was fruitless also because "it could result in no valid legislation" on the subject of the inquiry. Thus, the courts hold final power to decide what constitutes a contempt of Congress, and Congress cannot compel a witness to testify in an investigation that cannot assist remedial legislation.

LEONARD W. LEVY
(1986)

KING, MARTIN LUTHER, JR.
(1929–1968)

Martin Luther King, Jr., preeminent leader of the black freedom movement of the 1950s and 1960s, repeatedly challenged America to live up to the egalitarian principles set forth in the three RECONSTRUCTION era amendments. "If we are wrong, the Constitution of the United States is wrong," King told his Alabama colleagues in an unpublished speech on December 5, 1955, the day that Montgomery's black citizens began a year-long campaign against discriminatory seating practices on city buses. Victory in that struggle catapulted King to national prominence as an exponent of nonviolent protest against racial oppression, and throughout the twelve remaining years of his life King pursued and expanded his challenge to injustice and exploitation internationally as well as domestically.

Pointing out in his 1964 book, *Why We Can't Wait,* that the United States was "a society where the supreme law of the land, the Constitution, is rendered inoperative in vast areas of the nation" because of explicit RACIAL DISCRIMINATION, King described the CIVIL RIGHTS struggle as a resumption "of that noble journey toward the goals reflected in the PREAMBLE to the Constitution, the Constitution itself, the BILL OF RIGHTS and the Thirteenth, Fourteenth, and FIFTEENTH AMENDMENTS." Protest campaigns in segregationist strongholds such as Birmingham and Selma, Alabama, stimulated national support for landmark legislative achievements such as the CIVIL RIGHTS ACT OF 1964 and the VOTING RIGHTS ACT OF 1965, and produced an all-but-complete victory over de jure segregation by the middle of that decade.

Recognizing that other evils more subtle than segregation also tangibly afflicted the daily lives of millions of black people, King broadened his attack to include all forms of poverty and economic injustice, saying that the movement had to go beyond civil rights to human rights. That progression, coupled with King's outspoken condemnations of America's militaristic foreign policy, particularly its participation in the VIETNAM WAR, led King to advocate basic changes in American society reaching far beyond his previous attacks on racial discrimination.

Identified as a prominent advocate of CIVIL DISOBEDIENCE against immoral segregation statutes even before his influential 1963 "Letter from Birmingham Jail," King defended his position by reference to the long tradition of NATURAL RIGHTS thinking. In his early years of civil rights activism King said that peaceful, willing violation of such statutes forced courts to void unconstitutional provisions, but toward the end of his life King expanded his argument, contending that the weightier moral demands of social justice sometimes required that nondiscriminatory laws also be violated. If any laws blocked the oppressed from confronting the nation with moral issues of human rights and economic justice, then such laws rightfully could be breached. Although King until 1966 had believed that depicting the brutalities of racism best attracted national support for civil rights, in his final years King repeatedly suggested that protesters might have to coerce concessions from unwilling federal officials by obstructing the orderly functioning of society until the desired policy changes were made.

King's challenge to American racism helped to close the gap between constitutional principles and discriminatory practices; his broader struggle against other forms of human injustice left a legacy that will stimulate future generations for years to come.

DAVID J. GARROW
(1986)

Bibliography

GARROW, DAVID J. 1986 *Bearing the Cross: Martin Luther King, Jr., and the Southern Christian Leadership Conference, 1955–1968.* New York: William Morrow.

KING, MARTIN LUTHER, JR. 1964 *Why We Can't Wait.* New York: New American Library.

KING, RUFUS
(1755–1827)

Rufus King, a Harvard-educated lawyer who had been an officer in the Revolutionary War, represented Massachusetts in the Congress of the Confederation from 1784 to 1787. He was a principal author of the NORTHWEST ORDINANCE, and wrote its provisions prohibiting SLAVERY and protecting the OBLIGATION OF CONTRACTS against legislative impairment.

Although he originally opposed either calling a convention or radically altering the ARTICLES OF CONFEDERATION, he represented Massachusetts at the CONSTITUTIONAL CONVENTION OF 1787. King soon became a spokesman for those who favored a strong national government and for the interests of the large northern states. Very early in the debates he advocated consolidation rather than confederation; although he recognized that it was impossible to annihilate the states, he thought they should be stripped of much of their power. He argued against equal representation of the states in the SENATE, and he favored popular election of the President. King proposed the CONTRACT CLAUSE, and, although it was voted down in the Committee of the Whole, he saw that it was inserted into the Constitution by the Committee on Style, of which he was a member. In opposition to GOUVERNEUR MORRIS, he supported the admission of new states on terms of equality with the old. King was also one of the first to recognize publicly that the politically important division of the country was not between large and small states, but between North and South.

Almost immediately after attending the Massachusetts ratifying convention, he moved to New York and was elected one of its original United States senators. King served in the Senate from 1789 to 1796, and was a leading spokesman for ALEXANDER HAMILTON (his political patron) and the Federalist administration.

King returned to the Senate in 1813. Although an opponent of the War of 1812, he refused to attend the HART-FORD CONVENTION, denounced New England's threat of SECESSION, and supported the government financially. Serving in the Senate until 1825, King participated in the debates over the MISSOURI COMPROMISE. Although not an abolitionist, King opposed the extension of slavery, and he contended that it was within the power of Congress to make permanent abolition of slavery a condition of Missouri's admission as a state. He insisted upon constitutional guarantees of the rights of black Missourians.

In his public career, King was the Federalist candidate for vice-president (1804, 1808) and President (1816), and was twice minister to Great Britain (1796–1803, 1825–1826).

DENNIS J. MAHONEY
(1986)

KINGSLEY BOOKS, INC. v. BROWN
354 U.S. 436 (1957)

Kingsley authorized broad civil remedies to control the merchandising of OBSCENITY. The Supreme Court upheld a New York statute permitting state officials to obtain IN-JUNCTIONS against the sale of allegedly obscene materials before a judicial determination that the materials were obscene and, after trial, to seize and destroy any material found to be obscene. Rejecting assertions that the statutory scheme was an unconstitutional PRIOR RESTRAINT, the majority concluded that the scheme in actual application did not differ from the criminal remedies sanctioned in *Alberts v. California* (1957), decided the same day. (See ROTH V. UNITED STATES.)

The dissenters argued that numerous procedural defects rendered the statute unconstitutional. The seizure and destruction of the obscene books were tantamount to "book burning," according to Chief Justice EARL WARREN, for books were judged outside the context of their use. Justices WILLIAM O. DOUGLAS and HUGO L. BLACK, jointly dissenting, argued that an injunction before trial was censorship. They also would have required a finding of obscenity for each publication of the condemned work rather than regulating speech like "diseased cattle and impure butter." Justice WILLIAM J. BRENNAN contended that the statute was vastly defective for permitting a judge, rather than a jury, to determine a work's obscenity.

KIM MCLANE WARDLAW
(1986)

KINGSLEY INTERNATIONAL PICTURES CORP. v. REGENTS
360 U.S. 684 (1959)

In *Kingsley International Pictures Corp. v. Regents* the state of New York had refused to issue a license for the motion picture *Lady Chatterley's Lover* because it "alluringly portrays adultery as proper behavior." There was no claim that the film constituted an INCITEMENT TO UNLAWFUL CONDUCT. Without deciding whether all licensing schemes for motion pictures were unconstitutional the Supreme Court held that the refusal to grant this license violated the FIRST AMENDMENT. The Court reaffirmed that motion pictures were within the scope of the First Amendment and proclaimed that the amendment's "basic guarantee" is "the freedom to advocate ideas," including the idea that adultery may in some cases be justified.

STEVEN SHIFFRIN
(1986)

KINSELLA v. KRUEGER

See: *Reid v. Covert*

KIRBY v. ILLINOIS
406 U.S. 682 (1972)

In an effort to eviscerate UNITED STATES V. WADE (1967) without overruling it, a plurality of the Supreme Court held that the RIGHT TO COUNSEL does not apply to pretrial identification procedures that occur before INDICTMENT or other indicia of formal criminal charges. The case involved the most suggestive confrontation imaginable: a one-to-one presentation of the person upon whom police had found a robbery victim's credit cards. Yet the Court held that because this confrontation occurred before Kirby had been formally charged, it was not a "critical stage" of the proceedings requiring counsel to preserve a future right to a FAIR TRIAL.

The distinction between pre- and postindictment identification procedures is dubious for two reasons. First, the vast majority of LINEUPS occur while cases are under investigation, and thus before indictment. Second, all the dangers of irreparable mistaken identification and the inability of counsel to reconstruct the pretrial confrontation—which had been the foundation of *Wade*—apply whether the identification occurs before or after formal charging. The plurality's startling misreading of precedent was highlighted when Justice BYRON R. WHITE, who dissented in *Wade*, dissented in *Kirby* also, saying that *Wade* compelled the opposite result.

Kirby leaves untouched the possible DUE PROCESS objections to an unfair pretrial confrontation. Proof of unfairness would require suppression of testimony about the pretrial procedure as well as the in-court identification by a witness whose perceptions were possibly tainted. A due process objection may be made whether the pretrial confrontation has occurred before or after formal charging.

Of course, it is much more difficult for the accused to show that a confrontation was fundamentally unfair than to prove that it was done without counsel.

BARBARA ALLEN BABCOCK
(1986)

KIRSCHBAUM v. WALLING
316 U.S. 517 (1942)

After UNITED STATES V. DARBY (1941) the Court decided many cases on the coverage of the FAIR LABOR STANDARDS ACT, which benefited employees "engaged in commerce or in the PRODUCTION of goods for commerce." Congress by no means had made the statute coextensive with the limits of its power over INTERSTATE COMMERCE, but every time the Court ruled that the statute covered certain employees, it brought their activities within the scope of the COMMERCE CLAUSE. The leading case is *Kirschbaum*, which extended statutory coverage—and thus the commerce power—to employees who were at least one step away from production. On the theory that service and maintenance employees kept a building safe and habitable, the Court held that a landlord who rented space to a firm that manufactured goods destined for interstate commerce had to pay his janitors and elevator operators the minima fixed by the statute. In *Borden Milk Co. v. Barella* (1945), the Court upheld application of the statute to service employees in a building occupied by the executive offices of a company that carried on its interstate manufacturing elsewhere. In *Martino v. Michigan Window Cleaning Co.* (1946), the employees who benefited from the statute— window cleaners employed by a company to service an industrial building—were two steps removed from production for commerce. Similarly, in *D. A. Schulte v. Gangi* (1946), the Court extended the statute and the commerce power to the maintenance people employed by a building owner who rented space to a firm that worked on intrastate goods and returned them to a contractor who subsequently shipped some of them across state lines. Employees sometimes did lose, but the Court's interpretations in these cases showed that the commerce power virtually authorized Congress to regulate any business, however remote its economic connection with interstate commerce.

LEONARD W. LEVY
(1986)

KLOPFER v. NORTH CAROLINA
386 U.S. 213 (1967)

Prior to the Supreme Court's decision in *Klopfer*, only defendants in federal courts enjoyed the Sixth Amendment right to a SPEEDY TRIAL. Consequently, legislation in many states permitted prosecutors to postpone bringing pending cases to trial indefinitely. Declaring such state laws unconstitutional, the Court, in an opinion by Chief Justice EARL WARREN, held that the right to a speedy trial is a FUNDAMENTAL RIGHT incorporated by the DUE PROCESS CLAUSE of the FOURTEENTH AMENDMENT and thus fully applicable in state trials.

WENDY E. LEVY
(1986)

(SEE ALSO: *Incorporation Doctrine*.)

KNIGHT COMPANY, E. C., UNITED STATES v.
156 U.S. 1 (1895)

The issue in the Supreme Court's first interpretation of the SHERMAN ANTITRUST ACT hung on the lawfulness of the Sugar Trust's acquisition of its competitors, and the decision nearly eviscerated the act. An 8–1 Court used the doctrine of DUAL FEDERALISM in dismissing a government suit to dissolve the trust.

When the American Sugar Refining Company (the Sugar Trust) acquired four Philadelphia refineries in 1892 it controlled ninety-eight percent of domestic sugar manufacturing. Attorney General RICHARD OLNEY, who inherited the case from his predecessor, believed that the Sherman Act was founded on a false economic theory; he believed that free competition had been "thoroughly discredited" and that the act should have regulated trusts as a natural development, not prohibited them. There is, however, little evidence of deliberate carelessness in Olney's preparation of the case. Although the MAJORITY OPINION commented upon a lack of EVIDENCE to demonstrate a restraint of trade, the government never believed that such a showing was necessary. Prior decisions had clearly held sales to be a part of commerce; the majority would admit as much here, and a lower court conceded that the trust had sought control of both refining and sales. Clever defense strategy successfully shifted the Court's attention from restraint of INTERSTATE COMMERCE to a consideration whether the commerce power extended to manufacturing.

Chief Justice MELVILLE W. FULLER's opinion for the Court endorsed the defendants' argument. By repeating that manufacturing was separable from commerce, the Court made a formally plausible distinction based solely on precedent. (See KIDD V. PEARSON.) Although the Sugar Trust had monopolized manufacturing, the Court found no Sherman Act violation because the acquisition of the Philadelphia refineries involved INTRASTATE COMMERCE. Although manufacturing "involves in a certain sense the control of its disposition . . . this is a secondary and not the primary sense." The trust did not lead to control of interstate commerce and so "affects it only incidentally and indirectly." This direct-indirect effects test of the reach of federal regulation had been mentioned in earlier cases (see EFFECTS ON COMMERCE) and was here employed to reach unrealistic ends: "Contracts, combinations, or conspiracies to control domestic enterprise in manufacture, agriculture, mining, PRODUCTION in all its forms, or to raise or lower prices or wages, might unquestionably tend to restrain external as well as domestic trade, but the restraint would be an indirect result, however inevitable and whatever its extent, and such result would not necessarily determine the object of the contract, combination or conspiracy."

Justice JOHN MARSHALL HARLAN, dissenting, posed the basic question: "What, in a legal sense, is a restraint of trade?" The trust was in business to sell as well as manufacture sugar, and most of its sales obviously constituted interstate commerce. Relying on GIBBONS V. OGDEN (1824), Harlan posited a broad view of the commerce power. Any obstruction of commerce among the states was an impairment of that commerce and must be treated as such. The majority's construction of the Sherman Act left the public "at the mercy of combinations." The Sugar Trust's inevitable purpose of preventing free competition doomed it as a restraint of trade. "The general government is not placed by the Constitution in such a condition of helplessness that it must fold its arms and remain inactive while capital combines . . . to destroy competition." Harlan correctly believed that the issue should not have been the contracts of acquisition but rather the trust's control over commerce in sugar.

By excluding manufacturing monopolies from the scope of the antitrust act, the decision in *Knight* cleared the way for the greatest merger and consolidation movement in American history. Chief among the industries taking advantage of the opportunities given them by the Supreme Court were manufacturing and the railroads. Such massive combines as United States Steel Corporation, American Can Company, International Harvester, and Standard Oil of New Jersey can trace their origins to this period. From 1879 to 1897 fewer than a dozen important combinations had been formed, with a total capital of around one billion dollars. Before the century ended, nearly two hundred more combinations formed, with a total capital exceeding three billion dollars. Of some 318 CORPORATIONS in business in 1904, nearly seventy-five percent had been formed after 1897.

The Court's opinion also seriously injured the concept of national supremacy; Fuller's distinction between production and commerce lasted until 1937. In the meantime, the Court had created what EDWARD S. CORWIN called a "twilight zone" in which national regulation of corporations was uncertain and haphazard. Although the Court

would apply the Sherman Act to railroads within two years (see UNITED STATES V. TRANS-MISSOURI FREIGHT ASSOCIATION), not until the reinterpretation in NORTHERN SECURITIES CO. V. UNITED STATES (1904) would the Sherman Act become an effective tool against big business.

DAVID GORDON
(1986)

Bibliography
EICHNER, ALFRED S. 1969 *Emergence of Oligopoly: Sugar Refining as a Case Study.* Westport, Conn.: Greenwood Press.

KNOX, PHILANDER C.
(1853–1921)

Although Philander Chase Knox, a Pittsburgh corporation lawyer, had helped create the United States Steel Corporation, he became an active antitrust prosecutor as THEODORE ROOSEVELT'S ATTORNEY GENERAL (1901–1904). Knox initiated the efficient and meticulous prosecution in NORTHERN SECURITIES CO. V. UNITED STATES (1904) and successfully argued that case before the Supreme Court. He also began victorious cases against the Salt Trust, the Coal Trust, and the Beef Trust, the latter culminating in the STREAM OF COMMERCE doctrine in SWIFT & COMPANY V. UNITED STATES (1905). Knox's actions helped revive the SHERMAN ANTITRUST ACT and insured a prominent political career after his resignation in 1904. He served as WILLIAM HOWARD TAFT'S secretary of state (1909–1913) and later, in the Senate, played a major role in railroad rate legislation. An "irreconcilable" over the League of Nations, Knox believed it imposed unconstitutional obligations under the TREATY POWER.

DAVID GORDON
(1986)

KNOX v. LEE

See: Legal Tender Cases

KOLENDER v. LAWSON
461 U.S. 352 (1983)

The facts of this case, not revealed by the official report, enhanced its interest. Lawson was a law-abiding black man of unorthodox attire and grooming who suffered frequent police harassment when he walked in white neighborhoods. A 7–2 Supreme Court held VOID FOR VAGUENESS a California statute obligating persons who "wander" the streets to provide credible and reliable identification and to explain their business to the police. The majority reasoned that the statute vested excessive discretion in the police to decide whether to stop and interrogate a suspect or leave him alone in the absence of PROBABLE CAUSE to arrest him. The Court also suggested that the statute compromised the constitutional right to freedom of movement.

LEONARD W. LEVY
(1986)

KONIGSBERG v. STATE BAR
353 U.S. 252 (1957)
366 U.S. 36 (1961)

In *Konigsberg* I the Supreme Court held that refusal to answer questions about political associations was constitutionally insufficient to justify a state bar association finding of failure to demonstrate good moral character, and consequent denial of bar admission. In *Konigsberg* II the Court upheld a second denial of admission based on the ground that refusal to answer obstructed full investigation of the applicant's qualifications.

MARTIN SHAPIRO
(1986)

KOREAN WAR

In June 1950 North Korea attacked South Korea; within a week President HARRY S. TRUMAN committed American air, sea, and ground forces to South Korea's defense. The resulting three-year involvement lasted into the administration of DWIGHT D. EISENHOWER and became the largest undeclared war in American history prior to the Vietnam involvement.

The initial rush of events created enduring confusion about the constitutional basis for the American intervention. On June 25, the day following the attack, the United States obtained a United Nations Security Council resolution ordering North Korean withdrawal. Two days later, with fighting continuing, the Security Council requested U.N. members to assist in repelling the aggression. That day, without congressional approval, President Truman publicly ordered American air and naval support for the South Koreans, and throughout his remaining tenure in office he persistently called the conflict a United Nations POLICE ACTION. The key American decisions had actually preceded the U.N. request, however, and critics, led by Senator Robert A. Taft, convincingly demonstrated that pertinent provisions of the UNITED NATIONS CHARTER (having status as treaty law in the United States) and the United Nations Participation Act gave no constitutional authority to the American President. The necessary agreements for United States peacekeeping forces had never been concluded with the Security Council.

Careful defenders of Truman's actions, especially Secretary of State Dean Acheson, argued that Truman's authority derived from his duty as COMMANDER-IN-CHIEF to protect American interests. One such interest was the preservation of the United Nations as an instrument for peace; another was the security of American forces in the Pacific area. The defenders relied, too, on presidential control of FOREIGN AFFAIRS and on the alleged precedent of eighty-five prior instances of presidential use of military forces without a DECLARATION OF WAR. Not surprisingly, critics also found these sources insufficient, strongly disagreeing about the meaning of Congress's power "to declare war" and about the legal relevance of past episodes of unilateral presidential action. Truman nonetheless followed Acheson's advice and explicitly refused to request formal authorization from Congress.

The war had other constitutional dimensions, as well. In April 1951, after serious policy disagreements, Truman dismissed his outspoken Korean and Far Eastern commander, General of the Army Douglas MacArthur, thereby reaffirming the principle of civilian control over the military. (See CIVIL-MILITARY RELATIONS). Later, in April 1952, when a strike threatened military production for Korea, the President seized American steel mills, an action subsequently held unconstitutional in YOUNGSTOWN SHEET AND TUBE CO. V. SAWYER (1952), a decision that arguably narrowed future presidential prerogatives. The Korean engagement also intensified clashes over the FIRST AMENDMENT by contributing to the anticommunist sentiment tapped by Senator Joseph R. McCarthy. Similarly, the war provided context and impulse for the partially successful congressional effort, in the "Great Debate" of 1951, to restrict additional presidential commitment of troops to Europe. Finally, the war figured rhetorically in calls for limiting the TREATY POWER and EXECUTIVE AGREEMENTS through the BRICKER AMENDMENT.

By the time of the Korean armistice on July 27, 1953, American casualties numbered 142,000, including 33,600 deaths. The war thus stands squarely as de facto precedent for presidential war-making of substantial magnitude, and more so because American courts, in typical fashion, refrained from ruling on its constitutional base. Ironically, memories of the domestic debates over Korea helped generate later efforts, such as the GULF OF TONKIN RESOLUTION (1964), to obtain prior congressional endorsement of foreign military ventures.

CHARLES A. LOFGREN
(1986)

Bibliography
LOFGREN, CHARLES A. 1969 Mr. Truman's War: A Debate and Its Aftermath. *Review of Politics* 31:223–241.

MURPHY, PAUL L. 1972 *The Constitution in Crisis Times, 1918–1969.* New York: Harper & Row.

KOREMATSU v. UNITED STATES

See: Japanese American Cases

KOVACS v. COOPER
336 U.S. 77 (1949)

After earlier suggesting that a ban on SOUND TRUCKS would be invalid, the Supreme Court held that "loud and raucous" loudspeakers could be prohibited as a reasonable regulation of time, place, and manner of speech. The opinion by Justice STANLEY REED noted interests in residential tranquillity, and it is cited as a PRIVACY decision. Justice FELIX FRANKFURTER, concurring, delivered a major attack on the PREFERRED FREEDOM doctrine.

MARTIN SHAPIRO
(1986)

KRAMER v. UNION FREE SCHOOL DISTRICT NO. 15
395 U.S. 621 (1969)

New York limited school district VOTING RIGHTS to residents who owned (or leased) real property or were parents (or guardians) of public school children. Following HARPER V. VIRGINIA BOARD OF ELECTIONS (1966), the Supreme Court held, 6–3, that this restriction denied the EQUAL PROTECTION OF THE LAWS to an adult resident living in his parents' home.

Chief Justice EARL WARREN wrote for the Court. A RATIONAL BASIS for the voting limitation was not enough; it must be justified as necessary to promote a COMPELLING STATE INTEREST. Assuming that New York could limit voting to persons especially interested in school affairs, this law's classification was insufficiently tailored to that purpose; an uninterested, non-taxpaying renter could vote, but Kramer, a taxpayer interested in school matters, could not.

The *Harper* dissenters also dissented here, speaking through Justice POTTER STEWART. The Constitution conferred no right to vote, and no racial classification was involved. Thus there was no reason to heighten judicial scrutiny, and there was a rational basis for limiting the vote to probably-interested persons.

On the same day, in *Cipriano v. Houma*, the Court unanimously invalidated a Louisiana law allowing only property taxpayers to vote on a revenue bond issue.

KENNETH L. KARST
(1986)

KU KLUX KLAN ACT

See: Force Acts

KUNZ v. NEW YORK
340 U.S. 290 (1951)

In a case involving a street-corner preacher whose sermons vigorously denounced other religions, the Supreme Court struck down an ordinance requiring a permit to hold religious meetings in public places. Chief Justice FRED M. VINSON, for an 8–1 majority, wrote that "New York cannot vest restraining control over the right to speak on religious subjects in an administrative official where there are no appropriate standards to guide his action." The ordinance was "clearly invalid as a PRIOR RESTRAINT on the exercise of FIRST AMENDMENT rights."

DENNIS J. MAHONEY
(1986)

KURLAND, PHILIP B.
(1921–1996)

Philip B. Kurland was, with ALEXANDER M. BICKEL, one of the principal scholarly critics of the WARREN COURT. Beginning with a sharply pointed and controversial foreword in 1964 to the *Harvard Law Review*'s annual survey of the Supreme Court's work, Kurland condemned what he saw as the Court's penchant to undertake social reform at the expense of PRECEDENT, history, and practical consequences. His Cooley Lectures at the University of Michigan, published as *Politics, the Constitution, and the Warren Court* (1970), were a lawyer's meticulous, and often sarcastic, critique of almost every aspect of the Court's work. He also edited collections of extrajudicial essays (*Felix Frankfurter and the Supreme Court*, 1970) and judicial opinions by Justice FELIX FRANKFURTER (*Mr. Justice Frankfurter and the Constitution*, 1971), for whom he had clerked after a clerkship with JEROME N. FRANK following his graduation from Harvard Law School and the University of Pennsylvania. Kurland readily identified himself with Frankfurter's view of the judicial role. The emphasis of both was on "judicial restraint," although not to the point of ignoring what both viewed as bright lines established either by the text of the Constitution or by settled precedent.

Although often mentioned in speculative short lists for an appointment to the Court in the 1970s, he never sought judicial office and spent all but three years of his forty-three-year career teaching at the University of Chicago, in both the College and the Law School. He served as an adviser to numerous federal and state governmental bodies, including the SENATE JUDICIARY COMMITTEE on several occasions. Senator SAMUEL J. ERVIN consulted him during the WATERGATE affair. Near the end of his career, Kurland played a prominent role in op-ed pages and as an adviser to the chairman of the Senate Judiciary Committee, opposing the nomination of Robert H. Bork to the Court in 1987.

Kurland's scholarly legacy rests less on his theoretical work—although *Religion and the Law* (1960) remains influential—than on his trenchant critiques of particular cases or issues, such as school DESEGREGATION and SEPA-RATION OF POWERS (*Watergate and the Constitution*, 1978); and on his editorial work, which included founding *The Supreme Court Review* in 1960 and co-editing the multi-volume collection of commentaries on the Constitution, *The Founders' Constitution* (1986, with Ralph Lerner). At his death, he left two unfinished projects, an edition of Frankfurter's letters and the authorized biography of ROBERT H. JACKSON.

DENNIS J. HUTCHINSON
(2000)

(SEE ALSO: *Judicial Activism and Judicial Restraint.*)

LABOR AND THE ANTITRUST LAWS

Problems relating to the application of antitrust law to labor result from a basic incompatibility between two public policies: the first, embodied in the SHERMAN ACT of 1890, prohibits efforts by anyone to monopolize or restrain competition in the product market; the second, embodied in the NORRIS-LAGUARDIA ACT of 1932 and the WAGNER ACT of 1935, permits workers to combine into unions in order to bargain collectively with employers. COLLECTIVE BARGAINING necessarily assumes, however, the elimination of competition between employees in dealings with their employers; hence the unions' need to achieve a monopoly of the labor market. The ultimate goal of every union is to remove wages, hours, and working conditions as factors in the competition between employers.

The hotly debated question whether Congress intended to include unions within the coverage of the Sherman Act was resolved by the Supreme Court in LOEWE V. LAWLOR (1908), which held a union liable for violation of the Act. Efforts to reverse this result in the CLAYTON ACT of 1914, which declared that the "labor of a human being is not a commodity or article of commerce," and which forbade federal courts from granting INJUNCTIONS against specified kinds of peaceful conduct in labor disputes, were frustrated by extremely narrow constructions of the statutory language by the Supreme Court.

United States v. Hutcheson (1941), which held that the Sherman Act does not reach acts by a union in its own self-interest that do not involve combination with nonlabor groups, marked the beginning of a new period of virtual immunity for unions under the antitrust laws. And in *Allen Bradley v. Local 3, International Brotherhood of Electrical Workers* (1945) the Court, while holding that a conspiracy between the union and electrical parts manufacturers and contractors to monopolize the industry in New York City violated the Sherman Act, declared that if the union had achieved the same result through parallel but separate agreements with each employer, the arrangement would not have been illegal. Thus, Norris-LaGuardia's comprehensive prohibition against the issuance by federal courts of injunctions in labor disputes, the Wagner Act's authorization of the granting by the National Labor Relations Board of "official patents of monopoly" through its certification procedures, and the rise of industry-wide bargaining combined to create a doctrine of "licit monopoly" of the labor market by unions, while the Sherman Act continued to prevent similar domination of the product market by business enterprises.

By the mid-1960s, however, the pendulum had begun to swing back. In *United Mine Workers v. Pennington* (1965) a badly divided Supreme Court held that a union's conspiracy with large mine operators to drive small operators out of the market by establishing wage scales that the latter could not afford to pay violated the antitrust laws. Ten years later, in *Connell Construction Company v. Plumbers & Steamfitters Local 100* (1975), the Supreme Court distinguished union activity that eliminates competition over wages and working conditions—immune under the antitrust laws, even though it affects price competition among employers, because such restriction is the inevitable consequence of collective bargaining—from union activity restricting competition in the product market—unprotected because (in this case) its effect was to drive all nonunion employers, including the more efficient ones, out of the market, whether or not they met union standards for wages and working conditions. The Court's 5–4 decision also held that even though the union's conduct violated the secondary boycott and "hot cargo" provisions of the TAFT-HARTLEY ACT of 1947, for which express penalties are prescribed in that statute, the union was not shielded from additional liability under the Sherman Act.

The critics of the Court's decisions in *Pennington* and *Connell* point out that in both cases the issues involved were mandatory subjects of bargaining under the labor laws. They contend that the legislative history of those laws makes clear that Congress intended to provide specific and exclusive remedies for violations of their substantive provisions (e.g., illegal "secondary boycotts" and "hot cargo" clauses) and rejected the proposed revival of remedies such as injunctions at the request of private parties, as well as punitive damages, which are available under the antitrust laws.

Unquestionably, judicial application of the antitrust laws to labor not only has seriously hampered union efforts to impose uniform wages, hours, and working conditions in the labor market but also has created considerable confusion in the administration of laws governing labor-management relations. It is also true, however, that unrestricted union efforts to monopolize labor markets adversely affect product markets in respect of the cost and availability of products. The question is whether antitrust laws are the proper mechanism for striking a proper balance between the right of workers to organize and to bargain collectively and the right of employers and the general public to be free of union coercive practices that raise prices, restrict output, or otherwise control the product to the detriment of consumers.

Inasmuch as unions derive their coercive powers from industry-wide and market-wide organizations, it is often proposed that they should be precluded from organizing more than one employer in an industry, and that collusion between separate unions should be proscribed. This proposal for "fragmented bargaining" probably is not politically feasible; moreover, it would have its least effect in oligopolistic industries, where, presumably, it is needed the most, and would have its greatest impact in atomized industries, where it is needed the least. Finally, fragmented bargaining would so weaken union organizations as to undermine completely the national labor policy favoring collective bargaining.

It appears that no satisfactory way has been found to reconcile free-market competitive policies with those permitting workers to combine and to engage in peaceful concerted activities for their mutual aid and protection. The preferable way to establish the necessarily shifting equilibrium between them would seem to be through legisla-tion dealing with specific problems rather than through the application by the judiciary of antitrust laws designed primarily for other purposes.

BENJAMIN AARON
(1986)

Bibliography

HILDEBRAND, GEORGE H. 1962 *Public Policy and Collective Bargaining.* Pages 152–187. New York: Harper & Row.

MELTZER, BERNARD D. 1965 Labor Unions, Collective Bargaining, and the Antitrust Laws. *University of Chicago Law Review* 32:659–734.

ST. ANTOINE, THEODORE J. 1976 *Connell:* Antitrust Law at the Expense of Labor Law. *Virginia Law Review* 62:603–631.

LABOR AND THE CONSTITUTION

An important aspect of constitutional law has been the connection between individual rights and state or national power to regulate economic affairs. The constitutional treatment of employment is a paradigmatic example: what is the status of the relationship between employer and employee? What power does government have to change it? Of course, the answers to these questions depend on whether they are asked about the pre- or post-NEW DEAL era.

Before the mid-1930s, labor legislation was subjected to searching JUDICIAL REVIEW by a Supreme Court committed to a laissez-faire treatment of economic issues under the DUE PROCESS clauses and a limited conception of federal authority under the COMMERCE CLAUSE. Since the New Deal, constitutional questions involving labor have been dominated by issues of expression and association, and the classification of labor activity as "economic" or "political."

The constitutional treatment of employment prior to the New Deal is best understood against the background of the COMMON LAW, a law dominated by concepts of FREEDOM OF CONTRACT and employment at will. The employer had the right to discharge an employee at any time, and the employee had supposedly equivalent right to quit at any time.

At an early stage, concerted actions by workers to affect contractual relations sometimes were treated as criminal conspiracies. Thus, in the *Philadelphia Cordwainers' Case* (1806), a strike for higher wages by a group of shoemakers was held to be illegal. "A combination of workmen to raise their wages may be considered in a twofold view: one is to benefit themselves, the other is to injure those who do not join their society. The rule of law condemns both."

Later in the nineteenth century, the courts recognized the right of workers to join together. *Commonwealth v.*

Hunt (1842) is the landmark. Chief Justice LEMUEL SHAW, for the Supreme Judicial Court of Massachusetts, held that, for a combination of workers to constitute a CRIMINAL CONSPIRACY, the state must prove that the workers had specific criminal objectives or used specific criminal methods. Thereafter, the common law treatment of labor focused on the limits of legitimate labor activity—whether combinations of workers had illegal purposes or used illegal methods.

But many courts at common law continued to take a restrictive view of legal labor activity. In *Vegelahn v. Gunter* (1869), for example, the Massachusetts Court found that strikers had used "intimidation" to interfere with the contractual relationship of the employer and strikebreakers. The "coercive" methods ranged from threats of personal injury to simple "persuasion and social pressure." Similarly, in *Plant v. Woods* (1900), the same court found that a threat by strikers that the employer could "expect trouble in his business" indicated that the strike was "only the preliminary skirmish" in violent industrial warfare; the workers had given "the signal, and in doing so must be held to avail themselves of the degree of fear and dread which the knowledge of such consequences will cause in the minds of those ... against whom the strike is directed." Thus, in measuring "illegal" objectives and methods, common law courts often assumed that even a low level of labor activity constituted a "signal" that was inherently coercive.

This common law view of the permissible limits of labor activity was read into the Constitution by the Supreme Court in the late nineteenth century, as it interpreted SUBSTANTIVE DUE PROCESS and elaborated a restrictive conception of the federal commerce power.

The Supreme Court constitutionalized the common law of employment by placing "freedom of contract" within the liberty protected by the FIFTH and FOURTEENTH AMENDMENTS, Many important cases concerned legislation designed to regulate the labor market as to hours, wages, and working conditions. This type of legislation—such as the wages and hours law in the leading case of LOCHNER V. NEW YORK (1905)—was invalidated if, in the Court's view, it unreasonably interfered with the contractual freedom of employer and employee. Even when such legislation was upheld, as in MULLER V. OREGON (1908), the Court made a detailed inquiry into the substantive reasonableness of the law.

Notions of freedom of contract were also applied to the activities of labor unions. In 1898, in the aftermath of a violent Pullman strike, Congress passed the ERDMAN ACT, outlawing YELLOW DOG CONTRACTS—contracts by which employees agreed not to join labor unions. In *Adair v. United States* (1908) the Supreme Court held that the act violated the due process clause of the Fifth Amendment:

"the employer and the employee have equality of right, and any legislation that disturbs that equality is an arbitrary interference with the liberty of contract which no government can legally justify in a free land. ..." The Court struck down a similar state statute in COPPAGE V. KANSAS (1915), and, in the 1917 case of HITCHMAN COAL V. MITCHELL, relied on the constitutional protection of yellow dog contracts in holding that federal courts could prevent unions from organizing at plants they knew to be covered by such contracts. And in TRUAX V. CORRIGAN (1921) the Court held that an Arizona statute forbidding INJUNCTIONS against PICKETING was unconstitutional, since it protected an activity (picketing) that wrongfully interfered with employers' property rights, in violation of due process.

The Supreme Court narrowly interpreted the commerce power at the beginning of the New Deal, striking down measures such as "Hot Oil" Codes, the AGRICULTURAL ADJUSTMENT ACT, and the NATIONAL INDUSTRIAL RECOVERY ACT. This development was nothing new. Although there had been swings in doctrine, the Court had generally viewed congressional power under the commerce clause with suspicion in the area of employment relations. In HAMMER V. DAGENHART (1918), for example, the Court struck down an act banning commerce in goods produced by child labor, and twenty years later, in CARTER V. CARTER COAL CO. (1936), it struck down an act regulating hours and wages in the coal industry.

The constitutional treatment of employment was changed radically by the watershed events of the New Deal. This period saw the Supreme Court reject its earlier laissez-faire interpretations of due process and its narrow vision of federal commerce power.

During the New Deal the Court abandoned its view of freedom of contract in employment relations. In WEST COAST HOTEL V. PARRISH (1937) the Court sustained a state minimum wage law for women, holding that contractual freedom could be limited by a reasonable exercise of STATE POLICE POWERS: "Even if the wisdom of the policy be regarded as debatable and its effect uncertain, still the legislature is entitled to its judgment."

National Labor Relations Board v. Jones & Laughlin Steel Corp. (1937) upheld the WAGNER NATIONAL LABOR RELATIONS ACT (NLRA), which entitled workers to organize and required employers to bargain with their employees' chosen representatives. The Court found that the act did not invade freedom of contract: an employer was not compelled to make any agreement, but only to bargain with the employees' representatives in recognition of the "fundamental right" of workers to organize. The Court distinguished the "yellow dog" contract cases on the grounds that the NLRA did not interfere with an employer's right to discharge employees, but only prohibited coercion of employees in the guise of discharge. Despite this disclaimer, it is clear that the Court was departing radically from the rule of its prior cases: the employer was prohibited from discharging employees for union activities, and was required to bargain in good faith with its employees' unions. (See WAGNER ACT CASES.) This new treatment of labor activity was reinforced the same year in *Senn v. Tile Layers Union,* in which the Court upheld a state law permitting peaceful picketing in conjunction with a labor dispute; although the Court distinguished cases such as *Truax,* the picketing involved was neither more peaceful nor less coercive than in prior cases.

The new approach to due process was exemplified by Justice FELIX FRANKFURTER, writing for the Court in *Osborn v. Ozlin* (1940), in an opinion reminiscent of Justice OLIVER WENDELL HOLMES's classic dissent in *Lochner:* "It is immaterial that state action may run counter to the economic wisdom either of Adam Smith or of J. Maynard Keynes, or may be ultimately mischievous even from the point of view of avowed state policy. Our inquiry must be much narrower. It is whether [the state] has taken hold of a matter within her power, or has reached beyond her borders to regulate a subject which was none of her concern. . . ."

In the 1937 *Jones & Laughlin* case, the Court upheld the NLRA under the commerce clause. The act regulated industrial strife, which had a "close and substantial relation" to commerce, and which was therefore within Congress's "plenary" power to regulate commerce.

The Court also upheld the NATIONAL POLICE POWER in the field of employment relations. UNITED STATES V. DARBY (1941) sustained the constitutionality of the FAIR LABOR STANDARDS ACT, which prohibited the interstate shipment of goods not meeting wage and hour requirements. Overruling the *Hammer* and *Carter Coal* cases, the Court confined its inquiry to the question whether the activity regulated had substantial EFFECTS ON COMMERCE. "The motive and purpose of a regulation of interstate commerce are matters for the legislative judgment upon which the Constitution places no restriction and over which the courts are given no control. . . ."

In sum, the New Deal saw the Supreme Court abandon its protection of the common law of employment in the name of the Constitution. The Court dropped its laissez-faire reading of due process and its restrictive interpretation of the commerce power. Employers are no longer apt to be successful if they claim that their constitutional rights to liberty or property are invaded by ECONOMIC REGULATION, or by state protection of union activity. They have little chance should they claim that congressional regulation of employment exceeds the commerce power.

While the Court has never explicitly revived the due process protection for freedom of contrast or similar economic rights in the context of labor relations, it has continued to see a residuum of inherent employer economic freedom that has a quasi-constitutional dimension manifested in statutory interpretation. This residuum has emerged around the issues of the right of an employer to subcontract work formerly done by its employees, or to close down all or part of its operations. Two questions have presented themselves: whether the employer may be required to bargain with its employees' union about such a decision, and whether such a decision would constitute discriminatory discharge of employees if motivated by antiunion animus.

The NLRA requires an employer to bargain over wages, hours, and working conditions; as to subjects not affecting these areas, an employer may act unilaterally. In *Fibreboard Paper Products v. NLRB* (1964) the Supreme Court held that an employer is required to bargain over a decision to subcontract work, where such subcontracting would simply replace employees with nonemployees doing the same work, and where the employer's motive is to cut costs by reducing the work force. Justice POTTER STEWART, in a concurring opinion, argued that an employer could not be compelled to bargain over managerial decisions "which lie at the core of entrepreneurial control," "those management decisions which are fundamental to the basic direction of a corporate enterprise. . . ."

The Court adopted Justice Stewart's position in *First National Maintenance v. NLRB* (1981), holding that the employer may unilaterally "shut down part of its business purely for economic reasons. . . ." The Court, as if this were a constitutional holding, read Congress's intent narrowly to avoid interference with entrepreneurial freedom: "Congress had no expectation that the elected union representative would become an equal partner in the running of the business enterprise. . . . Management must be free from the restraints of the bargaining process to the extent essential for the running of a profitable business."

The NLRA also prohibits an employer from discharging employees in retaliation for union activities. In *Textile Workers Union v. Darlington Manufacturing Co.* (1965) the Court held that it was not a discriminatory discharge for an employer to close his entire operation and discharge his entire work force, even if motivated by antiunion animus, because the employer would derive no "future benefit" from such a decision. As for a partial shutdown, this would constitute a discriminatory discharge only if it served to discourage union activity in the remainder of the employer's enterprise. Again, the Court construed congressional intent narrowly, as if it were avoiding a constitutional issue: the proposition that a single businessman cannot choose to go out of business if he wants to would represent such a startling innovation that it should not be entertained without the clearest manifestation of legislative intent or unequivocal judicial precedent so construing the Labor Relations Act. These cases were decided on statutory grounds, but they have clear constitutional emanations. The decisions are couched in terms of an inherent, absolute economic liberty untouched by regulatory statutes that look in a contrary direction.

For four decades after the New Deal, no congressional enactment was declared to have exceeded the limits of the commerce power. Congress was allowed virtually unlimited discretion. The consensus was that, as the Supreme Court stated in WICKARD V. FILBURN (1942), "effective restraints on its exercise must proceed from political rather than judicial processes"—anything Congress passed was within the commerce power.

In 1976, in NATIONAL LEAGUE OF CITIES V. USERY, however, the Court invalidated the application of the Fair Labor Standards Act to public employees, holding that the TENTH AMENDMENT prevents Congress from exercising its commerce power with respect to "functions essential to [the] separate and independent existence" of states and their subdivisions. Nevertheless, it does not seem likely in the labor field that Congress will lose much power to regulate by further restriction of the commerce power or the rebirth of economic due process. Indeed, early in 1985 in GARCIA V. SAN ANTONIO METROPOLITAN TRANSIT AUTHORITY, the Court explicitly overruled *National League of Cities*.

With the proposition established during the New Deal that government support of organized labor does not threaten the constitutional freedom of employers, the fundamental issues shifted to problems of association and expression. These problems arise in the framework of a constitutional jurisprudence which generally distinguishes sharply, for purposes of legislative authority and judicial review, between issues of economic regulation (narrow judicial review) and of the regulation of political activity (substantial review).

In this jurisprudence a key question becomes the classification of activity as "economic" or "political." With a few early exceptions, labor activity generally has been viewed, by both Congress and the Supreme Court, as economic. The "proper" role of unions has been confined to "economic" issues surrounding the collective bargaining process, with the consequence that labor's rights of expression are narrower than those attaching to organizations classified as political, and that Congress has a broader power to regulate association and expression in the labor context.

Prior to the New Deal, the right to organize a union was constitutionally unprotected. Since the New Deal, however, it has become well established (for example, in NAACP V. ALABAMA, 1958) that the protection of the FIRST AMENDMENT encompasses a right of association. But in the labor context it has not been necessary for the Supreme Court explicitly to find that the right to join a union is protected by FREEDOM OF ASSEMBLY AND ASSOCIATION. The right is protected by statute, most prominently Section 7 of the National Labor Relations Act: "Employees shall have the right to self-organization, to form, join, or assist labor organizations, to bargain collectively through representatives of their own choosing, and to engage in other concerted activities for the purpose of collective bargaining or other mutual aid or protection. . . ."

What the Supreme Court has held is that peaceful organizing activities are constitutionally protected. In HAGUE V. CONGRESS OF INDUSTRIAL ORGANIZATIONS (1939) the Court held that FREEDOM OF SPEECH and assembly attached to the dissemination of information regarding the NLRA, as well as peaceful assembly "for the discussion of the Act, and of the opportunities and advantages offered by it. . . ." And in *Thomas v. Collins* (1945) the Court held that freedom of speech and assembly were violated by a statute requiring union organizers to register prior to engaging in any organizing activities, including giving speeches to groups of workers. Although the Court characterized the union activity as economic, it rejected the proposition that "the First Amendment's safeguards are wholly inapplicable to business or economic activity." The case was therefore treated under the First Amendment's requirement that a restriction on speech or assembly be justified by clear public interest, threatened not doubtfully or remotely but by CLEAR AND PRESENT DANGER.

Most lower courts have interpreted the *Hague* and *Thomas* cases to establish a constitutional right to join a labor union. Thus, despite being clearly classified as economic activity, joining a union is protected by the First Amendment. However, the classification of labor activity as economic has consequences for the constitutional treatment of strikes and picketing.

The THIRTEENTH AMENDMENT, prohibiting involuntary servitude, probably protects the right of an individual employee to withhold his or her services. The constitutional status of strikes, however, is unclear. One reason for this is that strikes are "concerted activity" protected by the NLRA; it is therefore usually possible to decide strike questions without facing the constitutional question. However, extensive regulation and limitation of the right to strike has been permitted ever since the New Deal; it thus seems that, at most, the right has a low level of constitutional protection.

Legal limitations on strikes have been based on both their objectives and their methods. Prior to the NLRA, strikes were treated under the "illegal objectives" test of the common law; work stoppages with purposes held by courts to be illegal were prohibited. And today, strikes with certain objectives are unprotected under Section 7 of the NLRA. Thus, for example, a strike loses its protection if its purpose is to compel the employer to commit an unfair labor practice or violate other laws.

Section 7 also withholds protection from strikes that use illegal methods. For example, in *NLRB v. Fansteel Metallurgical Corp.* (1939) the Supreme Court declared unprotected a sitdown strike involving TRESPASS, destruction of property, and violation of state court injunctions. In *Mastro Plastics v. NLRB* (1956) the strike violated the NLRA's requirement of NOTICE to the employer; in *Local 174 v. Lucas Flour* (1962) the strike violated a "no-strike" clause in the union's contract with the employer.

Prior to the New Deal, labor picketing was readily enjoined, either because the ends sought were disapproved or because it was assumed to be intrinsically coercive. The Supreme Court turned this law around in the leading case of THORNHILL V. ALABAMA (1940). That case held unconstitutional a state statute banning all picketing near a business where the purpose of the picketing was to hinder the business. The Court adopted the "clear and present danger" test, treating labor activity as political activity: "The freedom of speech and of the press guaranteed by the constitution embraces at least the liberty to discuss publicly and truthfully all matters of public concern without previous restraint or fear of subsequent punishment. . . . In the circumstances of our times the dissemination of information concerning the facts of a labor dispute must be regarded as within that area of free discussion that is guaranteed by the Constitution." The Court explicitly rejected the assumption that all labor picketing is inherently coercive; it also stated that some "coercion" is permitted by the First Amendment: "Every expression of opinion on matters that are important has the potentiality of inducing action in the interests of one rather than another group in society. But the Group in power at any moment may not impose penal sanctions on peaceful and truthful discussions of matters of public interest merely on showing that others might thereby be persuaded to take action inconsistent with their interests." The Court thus treated labor picketing as full-fledged political activity.

But the Court quickly retreated from this position. Since *Thornhill*, it has become well accepted that labor picketing may be regulated, without violating freedom of speech and assembly, if the picketing is found to be illegal in method or objective.

While violence is an easy case, the Court has—to some extent—returned implicitly to the old assumption that labor picketing is an inherently coercive "signal." This means that picketing can be extensively regulated. Justice WILLIAM O. DOUGLAS, concurring in *Bakery Drivers v. Wohl* (1942), put it this way: "Picketing by an organized group is more than free speech, since it involves patrol of a particular locality and since the very presence of a picket line may induce action of one kind or another, quite irrespective of the nature of the ideas which are being disseminated."

The Court has also, as with other types of labor activity, maintained an "illegal objectives" limitation on picketing. The limitation has been most visible in two areas. The first is picketing with an objective to compel violation of state law or policy. This limitation was first articulated in *Carpenters' & Joiners Union v. Ritter's Cafe* (1942), where the Court held that the First Amendment did not protect picketing that urged an employer to act contrary to a state antitrust statute. By 1950, in *Hughes v. Superior Court*, the Court found a sufficient basis for prohibition in a purpose to violate a state "policy" announced by its courts.

The second visible category of picketing for an improper purpose is picketing for an object outlawed by the NLRA as "union unfair labor practices." For instance, the act explicitly prohibits some types of picketing designed to persuade an employer to recognize and bargain with the picketing union. But it is the secondary boycott that is the union unfair labor practice that is constitutionally most troublesome.

The act forbids a union to "threaten, coerce, or restrain" any person—usually a business—with the object of "forcing or requiring" that person to stop dealing with an employer with whom the union has a labor dispute.

The Supreme Court has recognized the potential conflict between such a prohibition and the First Amendment. In the *Tree Fruits* case, *NLRB v. Fruit & Vegetable Packers* (1964), the Court announced that it would construe the statute narrowly to avoid this constitutional difficulty: "Congress has consistently refused to prohibit peaceful picketing except where used as a means to achieve specific ends which experience has shown are undesirable." The Court therefore distinguished between picketing that attempted to persuade persons not to deal with the secondary employer (which was prohibited), and picketing attempting to persuade people not to buy products made by the primary employer (which was outside the act's prohibition). The Court thus permitted secondary picketing that was narrowly confined to the labor dispute with the primary employer. Subsequently, it limited even this narrow protection. In *Safeco NLRB v. Retail Store Employees Union* (1980), the Court held that the NLRA prohibits picketing confined to the primary employer's products, if those products constitute most of the secondary employer's business. In such a situation, boycotting the struck product is the same as boycotting the secondary employer.

Comparisons of the constitutional treatment of picketing with the treatment of other uses of the PUBLIC FORUM show that labor picketing is treated under standards different from other, similar activities. Consider two cases decided in 1982 by the Supreme Court, both decided without dissent. The cases had one thing in common: each involved a BOYCOTT and picketing by a group. The first, *Longshoremen's Association v. Allied International, Inc.*, was a suit for damages arising out of the refusal of the Longshoremen's Union to unload cargo shipped from the Soviet Union, in protest against the Russian invasion of Afghanistan. The boycott was entirely peaceful, it was totally effective, and it was unanimously held to be illegal. The boycott violated the labor statute, and that statute, as applied to this situation, did not infringe anyone's First Amendment rights.

Two months later the Court handed down its opinion in *NAACP v. Claiborne Hardware*. That case involved a suit for damages brought by white merchants in Claiborne County, Mississippi. Their businesses had been disrupted by a boycott, organized by the NAACP in protest against the failure of public officials in the county to desegregate public schools and facilities, hire black policemen, select blacks for jury duty, and end verbal abuse of blacks by law enforcement officers. The boycott, which was held by the Mississippi courts to violate state law, was executed in a less than peaceful, if considerably effective fashion. And it was—in most respects—found by the Supreme Court to be protected by the First Amendment.

Although there are a number of nice legal distinctions that might be noted between these cases and although it may be that the NAACP could not have survived if the Mississippi courts had been affirmed, one is forced to conclude that the two decisions are deeply inconsistent with one another. Of course, there is considerable inconsistency in our decisional law. The trouble here is that the inconsistency grows out of stereotypical thinking. Although labor unions ordinarily are organizations dedicated to economic activity and although economic activity is subject to substantial governmental regulation, sometimes unions engage in political action. The NAACP is often, but perhaps not always, a political action organization and political activity is rightly subject to substantial government protection.

The distinction between economic and political activity is difficult to maintain. At the margin it is difficult to designate conduct as economic and not political, or as political and not economic. But maintenance of the distinction is necessary unless we are prepared either to reduce substantially our political freedom or to reestablish substantive judicial review of economic regulation. (See COMMERCIAL SPEECH.)

Nor is the difficulty of sustaining the distinction in these cases really the problem. All legal distinctions, after all, give actors and decision makers trouble at the margin.

The real problem is that even as it is wrong to stereotype individuals, so too is it wrong to stereotype the organizations through which individuals seek to achieve their economic and political goals. In deciding what is protected and what may be regulated, legislatures and courts should look at the organizations' specific conduct, not their general characteristics.

Employer speech—communications by employers with their employees during union organization campaigns—is given significantly lower protection than is the political speech often said to be at the core of the First Amendment. During the early post-New Deal period, the National Labor Relations Board viewed any antiunion speeches or literature from the employer as "interference, restraint or coercion," in violation of the NLRA. This position was rejected in *NLRB v. Virginia Electric & Power Co.* (1941). The Supreme Court held that the act could not, within the First Amendment, prohibit employer speech unless it could be demonstrated, from a total course of conduct, that the speech was coercive. This view was codified in 1947, when the NLRA was amended to provide that speech may be used as evidence of an unfair labor practice only if it contains a "threat of reprisal or force or promise of benefit." In *NLRB v. Gissel Packing* (1969), the Supreme Court made clear that employer speech is entitled to some First Amendment protection, and that the 1947 amendment to the NLRA simply "implements the First Amendment. . . ."

But the actual treatment of employer speech in union organization campaigns makes clear the low level of First Amendment protection that speech enjoys. The NLRB announced as long ago as 1948 that it would regulate union certification elections under a "laboratory conditions" standard: "it is the Board's function to provide a laboratory in which an experiment may be conducted, under conditions as nearly ideal as possible, to determine the uninhibited desires of the employees." This approach has entailed extensive restriction and regulation of employer speech, on several grounds. For example, implied threats of harm to employees for unionization have been held to be illegal except where the consequences are beyond the employer's control and are based on demonstrable probabilities. And under NLRB rulings racial appeals are prohibited unless the party making the appeal proves "that it was truthful and germane. . . ."

As with employee speech and association, this framework differs significantly from mainstream First Amendment doctrine. First, this framework suffers from a vagueness problem; the NLRB and the courts regulate, on an ad hoc basis, speech that in the political arena could be regulated, if at all, only under narrow and precise statutes. Second, with respect to employer threats, labor law turns the First Amendment on its head: an employer may

vised in 1947 and 1959, forbids both employers and unions in INTERSTATE COMMERCE from coercing employees in their right to join, or not join, a labor organization. In addition, the 1947 Taft-Hartley Act amendments made the contracts of such employers and unions enforceable in the courts under federal law. Previously, state law generally applied to all these matters. In *San Diego Building Trades v. Garmon* (1959), the Supreme Court held that if activity in the labor field is "arguably subject" to federal protection or prohibition, the states must ordinarily yield jurisdiction. The Court added in *Machinists Lodge 76 v. Wisconsin Employment Relations Commission* (1976) that the states also cannot regulate conduct that Congress intended to leave unregulated.

There are several exceptions to this doctrine of federal PREEMPTION. Compelling local interests in the maintenance of domestic peace or minimum labor standards enable the states to deal with violence, malicious LIBEL, or TRESPASS to private property, and to prescribe requirements for job safety and insured health care plans. Even if conduct is arguably protected by federal law such as union access to employer premises during an organizing campaign—thus implicating federal supremacy most acutely—preemption does not follow invariably. In *Sears, Roebuck and Co. v. San Diego Carpenters* (1978), the Court concluded that a state court could determine whether a union's trespassory picketing was actually protected by federal law when the union had declined to seek a federal ruling on the issue, the employer had no way of obtaining one, and the trespass was "far more likely to be unprotected than protected." Finally, although federal substantive law is now applicable to union-employer contracts, the Supreme Court held in *Dowd Box Co. v. Courtney* (1962) that state courts retain concurrent jurisdiction over suits for their violation.

Federal and state labor legislation enacted during the twentieth century has often abrogated COMMON LAW claims, created new statutory rights and obligations, and substituted administrative proceedings for TRIAL BY JURY. These laws have posed due process and other constitutional questions. After some initial opposition, the courts have tended to sustain these innovations. The Supreme Court upheld the constitutionality of a state WORKERS' COMPENSATION law in NEW YORK CENTRAL RAILROAD COMPANY V. WHITE (1917), of the federal unemployment tax in STEWARD MACHINE COMPANY V. DAVIS (1937), and of the National Labor Relations Act in *NLRB v. Jones and Laughlin Steel Corp.* (1937). But to avoid constitutional problems, the Court declared in *Steele v. Louisville & Nashville Railroad Co.* (1944) that the federal labor laws, in granting majority unions the power of exclusive representation, also implied a duty to represent all the members of a bargaining unit fairly and nondiscriminatorily. A new round of battles over

due process may have opened when the Montana Supreme Court ruled 4–3 in *Meech v. Hillhaven West, Inc.* (1989) that the state's pioneering "wrongful discharge" statute, which displaced common law claims for dismissal, did not violate the Montana Constitution's guarantee of "full legal redress."

THEODORE J. ST.ANTOINE
(1992)

(SEE ALSO: *Freedom of Assembly and Association; Freedom of Speech.*)

Bibliography

GORMAN, ROBERT A.   1976   *Basic Text on Labor Law: Unionization and Collective Bargaining.* Pages 209–215, 257–262, 655–661, 695–728. St. Paul, Minn.: West Publishing Co.
WELLINGTON, HARRY H.   1968   *Labor and the Legal Process.* Pages 145–184, 223–266. New Haven, Conn.: Yale University Press.

LABOR BOARD CASES

See: Wagner Act Cases

LABOR MOVEMENT

The American labor movement has had a passionate, paradoxical, and often bitter relationship with the Constitution. During the era of LOCHNER V. NEW YORK (1905), from the 1880s to the 1920s, most judges agreed that labor was a commodity like any other; the Constitution guaranteed workers the right freely to sell their labor "just as the employer may sell his iron or coal." During these decades, state and federal courts protected employers' and individual workers' rights to contract and compete in the marketplace free from what judges deemed unwarranted governmental interferences. Courts voided many hours and safety laws as unconstitutional interferences with liberty of contract. Courts enjoined strikes and BOYCOTTS as tortious interferences with employers' freedom of enterprise. Even in "legal" strikes, many state and federal courts held that there was no such thing as peaceful PICKETING.

The burdens of repression and semi-outlawry drove trade unionists to develop an alternative constitutional outlook. They assailed the COMMON LAW view that labor was a mere commodity and that employers could acquire a property right in their workers' labor or "human capacities." The INJUNCTIONS that forbade strikers' "interference" with this right were, in labor's view, "judicial re-enactments of slavery." The THIRTEENTH AMENDMENT— even some of the Supreme Court's own Thirteenth

Amendment decisions—seemed to support these claims. According to the unions, the Thirteenth Amendment, which abolished slavery, was a "glorious labor amendment" that stood not only for self-owernship but also for labor's dignity and independence. These ideas drew upon the Lincolnian "Free Labor" philosophy of the Thirteenth Amendment's framers who vowed that the amendment would always stand as a shield against the oppression of "free labor both black and white."

Labor's constitutional critique of the injunction also invoked the FIRST AMENDMENT. However slight a feature of official constitutional doctrine, the First Amendment, in the eyes of nineteenth-century trade unionists, always stood for the sanctity of association by citizens and "uniting peaceably to redress wrongs." Injunctions against peaceful persuasion, meetings, publications, parades, and picketing "trampled on" this vision of the First Amendment.

During the *Lochner* era, only a few dissenting jurists embraced aspects of labor's constitutional vision. But labor's constitutional views were seconded by many NEW DEAL congressmen who championed the NORRIS-LAGUARDIA ACT and WAGNER ACT. These statutes supplanted the old common law regime and ushered in the modern labor-law era. Then, with the demise of *Lochner*-era SUBSTANTIVE DUE PROCESS and the emergence of a New Deal majority on the Supreme Court, the Court began to extend First Amendment protection to labor protest.

In THORNHILL V. ALABAMA (1940) the Court struck down a state antipicketing statute, declaring that "the dissemination of information concerning the facts of a labor dispute must be regarded as within that area of free discussion that is guaranteed by the Constitution." Picketing was a means of communicating with the public about matters of public concern. Although decided on the narrow ground of OVERBREADTH, *Thornhill* established that restrictions on picketing were subject to the constraints of the First Amendment.

In *Thornhill*, the Court did not adopt organized labor's—and New Deal reformers'—view that liberty of labor protest was bound up with an alternative conception of labor and of industrial democracy. Instead, the *Thornhill* Court classified picketing as political speech, perhaps because it had just abandoned the economic due-process doctrines of the *Lochner* era and did not want to appear to be meddling anew in economic affairs. But the marketplace dimension of picketing was inescapable. Picketing is inextricable from strikes and boycotts: a form of moral and political expression at the same time it aims to produce marketplace pressure and advantage. The Court could not recognize and define a constitutional right to picket without confronting the question of constitutional protection for strikes and boycotts. After *Thornhill*, sev-

eral lower federal courts began to forge substantial First and Thirteenth Amendment limits on the states' power to bar peaceful strikes and boycotts.

But the Supreme Court soon dissappointed those who expected it to recognize these nascent rights. Instead, the Court returned the issue to the common-law terrain, reaffirming the law's traditional role of restricting the scope of allowable protest and mutaul aid. In *Carpenters & Joiners Union, Locale 213 v. Ritter's Cafe* (1942) the Court upheld a state court injunction against peaceful picketing. "[R]ecognition of peaceful picketing as an exercise of free speech," the Court reasoned, "does not imply that the states must be without power" to confine the bounds of industrial disputes—in this case, to forbid any pickets urging the public to boycott a cafe whose owner "had awarded a building contract to a man who was unfair to organized labor." The state court had found that the boycott violated the state's ANTITRUST LAWS; the Supreme Court held that state courts and legislatures remained free to "draw the line" in this fashion, balancing "the effort of the employer to carry on his business free from the interference of others against the effort of labor to further its economic self-interest."

But the Supreme Court soon disappointed those who expected it to recognize these nascent rights. Instead, the Court returned the issue to the common-law terrain, reaffirming the law's tradtional role of restricting the scope of allowable protest and mutual aid. In *Carpenter and Joiners Union, Local No. 213 v. Ritter's Cafe* (1942) the Court upheld a state court injunction against peaceful picketing. "[R]ecognition of peaceful picketing as an excercise of free speach," the Court reasoned, "does not imply that the state must be without power" to confine the bounds of industrial disputes—in this case, to forbid any pickets urging the public to boycott a cafe whose owner "had awarded a building contract to a man who was unfair to organized labor." The state courts had found that the boycott violated the state's ANTITRUST LAWS; the Supreme Court held that state courts and legislatures remained free to "draw the line" in this fashion, balancing "the effort of the employer to carry on his business free from the interference of others against the effort of labor to further its economic self-interest.

In the new regime of judicial deference toward state regulation of business and commerce, this characterization of labor conflicts—as clashes of private economic interests—was a gloomy sign from labor's perspective. Beginning with *Ritter's Cafe*, the Court ceased characterizing industrial disputes and labor picketing as involving matters of public concern. By the 1950s, labor protest was held to involve "purely commercial activities which may be regulated by the state upon any reasonable basis." Organized workers once again were sellers of a commodity like any other, and judicial restraint was therefore the appropriate posture. Since the New Deal, primary strikes over wages and working conditions have enjoyed considerable statutory protection; but strikes or boycotts that fall outside the narrow circle of statutory or state court approval have found almost no shelter in the Constitution. Today, even peaceful picketing urging consumers not to buy the products of "unfair" employers continues to be routinely enjoined, and First Amendment challenges are routinely rebuffed.

Meanwhile, First Amendment doctrine has undergone transformations that render its treatment of labor protest anomalous. Nonlabor picketing now enjoys full First Amendment protection from content-based restrictions. Moreover, in *NAACP v. Claiborne Hardware Co.* (1982), the Court held that peaceful picketing by CIVIL RIGHTS groups in support of a boycott of white merchants was fully shielded by the First Amendment. The Court rejected the argument that the picketing was unprotected because the pickets frequently had no direct dispute with the merchants. The pickets' main goal was DESEGREGATION of local public facilities; thus, the boycott was largely a "secondary" one, in labor-law jargon. The *Claiborne* Court noted that no similar First Amendment protection shields picketing in support of labor boycotts, but the Court found the difference in constitutional status justified by the difference it perceived between the two kinds of boycotts. The black citizens' boycott involved "expression on public issues, which has always rested on the highest rung of the hierarchy of first amendment values." Labor boycotts, by contrast, involve mere clashes of economic interests. Forgetting what it once had recognized—that labor protest also involves "public issues"—the Court relegated labor picketing to a second-class status.

Many commentators have assailed the Court's "public issue" versus "labor" picketing distinction, particularly in light of the elevation of commercial advertising to the status of constitutionally protected speech. At the time of *Thornhill*, the Court regarded government regulation of COMMERCIAL SPEECH as falling within that domain of social and economic policy that it behooved the Court to leave alone. More recently, however, the Court in CENTRAL HUDSON GAS AND ELECTRIC CORP. V. PUBLIC SERVICE COMMISSION (1980) extended substantial First Amendment protection to commercial advertising so that it now enjoys more constitutional protection than peaceful labor picketing.

It may be that the Court continues to relegate labor protest to a second-class constitutional status because it does not view industrial conflict as a matter of much public concern. Other factors may also figure. Many current decisions rest on the hoary nineteenth-century assumption that picketing is inherently coercive. Today's courts still frequently seem unable to distinguish physical coercion on the part of pickets from the economic force exerted on an employer if uncoerced listeners are simply persuaded by the pickets' message.

Courts may also tolerate severe governmental restraints on labor protest in part because they see unions as powerful political and economic players, more or less evenly matched with their employer-adversaries. In fact, this parity has rarely existed; today, the labor movement is extremely weak—as weak, in some respects, as it was before the New Deal reforms. But it is unlikely that the courts will change the Constitution's treatment of labor protest unless workers and unions themselves again create on a massive scale a protest movement that appeals beyond existing law to an alternative constitutional tradition and the moral imagination of the public.

WILLIAM E. FORBATH
(1992)

Bibliography

FORBATH, WILLIAM 1989 The Shaping of the American Labor Movement. *Harvard Law Review* 102:1109–1256.
NOTE (Cynthia Estlund) 1982 Labor Picketing and Commercial Speech: Free Enterprise Values in the Doctrine of Free Speech. *Yale Law Journal* 91:938–960.
POPE, JAMES 1987 Labor and the Constitution: From Abolition to Deindustrialization. *Texas Law Review* 65:1071–1136.

LADUE (CITY OF) v. GILLEO
512 U.S. 43 (1994)

For communities seeking order and stability, political speech is often disruptive and disquieting. In recent years, private homeowners associations and public municipalities have sought to preserve order and aesthetic values by prohibiting political signs and placards from public display on lawns and from windows of homes. The Supreme Court held one such effort, by the City of Ladue in Missouri, to be an unconstitutional infringement of the FREEDOM OF SPEECH.

Ladue banned homeowners from posting on their property signs other than "for sale" and identification signs. Margaret Gilleo, who wished to post a small sign advocating a peaceful resolution to the GULF WAR, challenged the municipal ordinance as violative of the FIRST AMENDMENT. Justice JOHN PAUL STEVENS, writing for a unanimous Court, invalidated the law, reasoning that political signs on residential property were a "venerable means of communication" important for political campaigns and for "animat[ing] change in the life of a community."

The Court rejected the city's argument that the ban was essential to avoid "visual blight and clutter" and was justifiable as a "time, place or manner" restriction. Commercial signs also created visual clutter, and even if content neutral the ban foreclosed a vehicle of political speech for which persons of "modest means" had "no practical substitute." Residential signs, the Court explained, were too important a feature of American political culture to be prohibited absent truly compelling reasons.

ADAM WINKLER
(2000)

LA FOLLETTE, ROBERT M.
(1855–1925)

Robert Marion La Follette was one of the few giants in the history of the United States SENATE, ranking with HENRY CLAY and DANIEL WEBSTER. Born in a Wisconsin log cabin, he was graduated from his state's university in Madison, began his legal practice there, and spent three undistinguished terms (1885–1891) in Congress. During the farmer-labor unrest of the 1890s, La Follette grew considerably more liberal, and in 1901 he entered the governor's mansion with a reform program later called the "Wisconsin idea." It became the basis of the Progressive movement. La Follette, always a Republican, advocated the direct PRIMARY ELECTION as a method of nominating candidates, MINIMUM WAGE AND MAXIMUM HOURS laws, trade unionism, the popular REFERENDUM, strict regulation of the rates and services of railroads and public utilities by government commissions of experts, and radical tax reforms. His success as governor led to his election in 1905 as a United States senator.

During his twenty-year career as a senator he rivaled THEODORE ROOSEVELT and WOODROW WILSON as an influence for political liberalism. The leader of the Senate's Republican insurgents, he exerted special efforts on behalf of increasing the powers of the Interstate Commerce Commission, energetic enforcement of ANTITRUST LAW, a federal income tax law, direct election of senators, and women's suffrage. After the Supreme Court decided STANDARD OIL COMPANY V. UNITED STATES (1911), La Follette denounced the RULE OF REASON and judicial usurpation of the legislative function. Unlike most Republicans he supported the appointment to the Supreme Court of LOUIS D. BRANDEIS; the two men were close friends, thought alike on most matters of political economy, and had collaborated in framing many reform measures. They differed on foreign policy. La Follette opposed American entry into WORLD WAR I and the League of Nations. Although unpopular for a while during the war, because of pro-German and pacifist sympathies, La Follette emerged from the war as the undisputed leader of American liberalism.

He excoriated illiberal decisions of the Supreme Court. When the Court held unconstitutional congressional measures against child labor and construed antitrust laws to cover trade union activities, La Follette began a national campaign to curb the Court. Because he opposed JUDICIAL REVIEW over Congress, he proposed a constitutional amendment that would have authorized Congress to overcome a judicial veto in the same way as it did a presidential veto, by reenacting the statute by a two-thirds majority.

In 1924, at the peak of his career, La Follette refused to support CALVIN COOLIDGE and formed the Independent Progressive party, which nominated him and BURTON K. WHEELER, a Democrat. The party had only a presidential ticket, no local, state, or other federal candidates. It supported La Follette's Court-curbing amendment and would have restricted judicial invalidation of congressional acts to the Supreme Court only; in addition, it would have fixed a ten-year tenure for federal judges. The Progressives also denounced the Ku Klux Klan, then at the height of its popularity, and the Communist party. They also favored collective bargaining by labor through union representatives of their choice, antimonopoly measures, the restoration of competition, and extensive government ECONOMIC REGULATION. La Follette drew one vote out of every six, compared to the one in twelve received by the Populists in 1892, but carried only his own state.

When "Fighting Bob" died in 1925, his casket was placed in the rotunda of the Capitol, a rare honor, and the nation remembered him, in the words of his own epitaph, as one who "stood to the end for the ideals of American democracy."

LEONARD W. LEVY
(1986)

Bibliography

LA FOLLETTE, BELLE CASE and LA FOLLETTE, FOLA 1953 *Robert M. La Follette.* 2 Vols. New York: Macmillan.

LAIRD v. TATUM
408 U.S. 1 (1972)

Protesters against American involvement in the VIETNAM WAR sued to stop Army intelligence surveillance which they claimed had a CHILLING EFFECT on the exercise of their FIRST AMENDMENT rights. Chief Justice WARREN E. BURGER's opinion for the Court, in a 5–4 decision, held that the case lacked RIPENESS because the protesters had presented no "claim of specific present objective . . . or . . . future harm" but only the fear that "the army may at some future date misuse the information in some way" that would harm them.

MARTIN SHAPIRO
(1986)

LAKE COUNTRY ESTATES, INC. v. TAHOE REGIONAL PLANNING AGENCY
440 U.S. 391 (1979)

Landowners claimed that an appointed bi-state agency regulating development had, through overregulation, unconstitutionally destroyed the economic value of their property. The Supreme Court, over Justice THURGOOD MARSHALL's dissent, extended TENNEY V. BRANDHOVE (1951) to acts of unelected officials and found members of the planning agency to be absolutely immune from suit under SECTION 1983, TITLE 42, UNITED STATES CODE for their legislation-like acts. The Court also found the agency not to be protected by the ELEVENTH AMENDMENT immunity available to states.

THEODORE EISENBERG
(1986)

LALLI v. LALLI
439 U.S. 259 (1978)

In *Lalli* a fragmented Supreme Court brought further confusion to the body of EQUAL PROTECTION doctrine governing classifications based on ILLEGITIMACY. A 5–4 majority upheld a New York law that allowed an illegitimate child to inherit from his or her father only if a court, during the father's lifetime and no later than two years after the child's birth, had declared the father's paternity. Justice LEWIS F. POWELL, who had written the MAJORITY OPINION in TRIMBLE V. GORDON (1977), wrote for a plurality of three Justices. Powell distinguished *Trimble* as a case in which even a judicial order declaring paternity would not have allowed inheritance; only the marriage of the child's parents would suffice. In *Lalli* the state could properly insist on the "evidentiary" requirement of a judicial order to establish paternity. The other six Justices all thought *Lalli* and *Trimble* indistinguishable: the four *Lalli* dissenters, plus two who joined the majority in upholding the law. The latter two Justices voted in accordance with their *Trimble* dissents.

The precedential force of *Trimble* may be uncertain, but at least seven Justices (the *Lalli* plurality and dissenters) all agreed that the STANDARD OF REVIEW for testing classifications based on illegitimacy was more rigorous than the RATIONAL BASIS test. Such classifications, said the plurality, would be invalid unless they were "substantially related to permissible state interests."

The state's interest in *Lalli* was the achievement of finality in the settlement of decedents' estates. The court order requirement provided sure proof of paternity. The artificiality of the requirement, however, was illustrated dramatically by the facts of *Lalli* itself, as Justice BYRON R. WHITE, for the dissenters, made clear. The decedent had often acknowledged his children openly; he had even executed a notarized document referring to one of them as "my son" and consenting to his marriage. Paternity had been proved clearly; what was missing was the formality of a court order. Such a judicial proceeding, of course, is least likely in the case in which the father and his illegitimate child are closest, and the father's acknowledgment of paternity has been most clearly established by nonjudicial means. The New York estate planners who wrote the law contrived its inertia to lean against the children of informal unions. *Lalli* is thus reminiscent of an earlier legal order designed to assure a man that his wealth and status would attach to a woman only when he chose to formalize their union and would pass only to the children of such a union.

KENNETH L. KARST
(1986)

(SEE ALSO: *Freedom of Intimate Association.*)

LAMAR, JOSEPH R.
(1857–1916)

Joseph Rucker Lamar, "an old-fashioned southern gentleman," served on the Supreme Court from 1911 until his death in 1916. As a Justice, Lamar approved the received doctrines of the time such as FREEDOM OF CONTRACT and AFFECTATION WITH A PUBLIC INTEREST. Lamar had been a leading Georgia attorney and had served as a state legislator and member of the Georgia Supreme Court (1903–1905) before his appointment to the Court. He was the fourth of President WILLIAM HOWARD TAFT's appointees and replaced EDWARD D. WHITE, whom Taft had promoted from Associate to Chief Justice.

Lamar joined a Court that included Justices OLIVER WENDELL HOLMES and JOHN MARSHALL HARLAN, leaning to the progressive side. Lamar usually voted with the majority of the Court; he wrote only eight dissents in four years, and one writer counted agreement in 150 of 154 cases sustaining exercise of STATE POLICE POWER and in 71 of 74 cases striking down such legislation. Lamar's apparent conciliation should not be taken to indicate disinterested acquiescence. In UNITED STATES V. GRIMAUD (1911) Lamar substantially strengthened the force of administrative rulings. *Grimaud* placed the law squarely behind such rulings; Lamar denied that administrative decisions constituted legislative DELEGATIONS OF POWER, and he upheld Congress's right to punish violations as criminal acts if it chose. Although he sometimes supported CIVIL RIGHTS, his most famous opinion came in a labor case: GOMPERS V. BUCK'S STOVE AND RANGE COMPANY (1911). Writing for a unanimous Court, Lamar declared that a secondary boycott constituted an illegal conspiracy in restraint of trade which could be forbidden by INJUNCTION. He rejected the union's claim of FREEDOM OF SPEECH.

Lamar served on the WHITE COURT, a Court that increasingly favored propertied interests. His lack of imagination and creativity were likely seen as virtues by his contemporaries, characteristics of a man well-fitted for the Court.

DAVID GORDON
(1986)

Bibliography

DINNERSTEIN, LEONARD   1969   Joseph R. Lamar. Pages 1973–1997 in Leon Friedman and Fred L. Israel, eds., *The Justices of the United States Supreme Court, 1789–1969.* New York: Chelsea House.

LAMAR, L. Q. C.
(1825–1893)

Lucius Quintus Cincinnatus Lamar, draftsman of the Mississippi Ordinance of Secession, celebrated eulogist of CHARLES SUMNER, and "Great Pacificator" during the electoral crisis of 1877, was appointed to the Supreme Court by GROVER CLEVELAND in 1888. He was the first Democrat to be appointed in a quarter-century and the first ex-Confederate to serve on the Court. Lamar was sixty-two years old when he received his commission, the second oldest new Justice in the Court's history. But he had been the South's most prominent apostle of sectional reconciliation for more than a decade and the President was primarily interested in the nomination's symbolic dimensions.

Judging exhilarated Lamar, and he was among the Court's most productive members until debilitated by ill health in the spring of 1892. Construction of the public land laws was his specialty, reflecting his experience as Cleveland's reform-minded secretary of the interior. He was also valuable at the conference table. "His was the most suggestive mind that I ever knew," Chief Justice MELVILLE W. FULLER reported, "and not one of us but has drawn from his inexhaustible store." Lamar was equally impressed by his brethren, calling them "the smartest old fellows I ever saw." In 1893, when reminiscing about a long career of public service as Confederate diplomat, congressman, senator, and cabinet official, he described his judicial experience as "the most impressive incident in my entire intellectual and moral life."

STRICT CONSTRUCTION and traditional canons of interpretation characterized his work in constitutional law. Lamar had no sympathy for the newly fashioned concept of SUBSTANTIVE DUE PROCESS, and he concurred with Justice JOSEPH P. BRADLEY's strident dissent in *Chicago, Milwaukee & St. Paul Ry. Co. v. Minnesota* (1890), maintaining that the REASONABLENESS of price regulations was a legislative, not a judicial, question. He also resisted extension of the SWIFT V. TYSON (1842) "general jurisprudence" doctrine to industrial accident cases. Only in the well-trodden COMMERCE CLAUSE field did Lamar consistently vote to restrict the autonomy of the states. And though he was quick to strike down tax laws and police regulations that burdened interstate transactions, Lamar remained obsessed with the necessity of setting limits to Congress's commerce power. In KIDD V. PEARSON (1888), his most influential opinion, Lamar not only formulated the mischievous distinction between commerce and manufacturing but also stated its rationale. "If it be held that the term [commerce] includes the regulation of all such manufactures as are intended to be the subject of commercial transactions in the future," he explained, "it is impossible to deny that it would also include all productive industries that contemplate the same thing. The result would be that Congress would be invested, to the exclusion of the States, with the power to regulate, not only manufacture, but also agriculture, horticulture, stock raising, domestic fisheries, mining—in short, every branch of human industry." For a former Confederate whose cherished doctrine of state SOVEREIGNTY already had been extinguished, such a state of affairs was at once imaginable and unthinkable.

CHARLES W. MCCURDY
(1986)

Bibliography

MAYES, EDWARD   1896   *Lucius Q. C. Lamar; His Life, Times, and Speeches.* Nashville, Tenn.: Publishing House of the Methodist Episcopal Church South.
MURPHY, JAMS B.   1973   *L. Q. C. Lamar, Pragmatic Patriot.* Baton Rouge: Louisiana State University Press.

LAMB'S CHAPEL v. CENTER MORICHES UNION FREE SCHOOL DISTRICT
508 U.S. 384 (1993)

In *Lamb's Chapel v. Center Moriches Union Free School District*, the Supreme Court first established the important proposition that religion is a "viewpoint" that is entitled to protection from the unequal allocation of government benefits. Prior to this decision, it was often argued that religion is merely a subject matter, and that the government could exclude "religious" speakers from government benefits so long as it remained neutral among religions, and between religion and atheism or agnosticism. In a wide range of cases involving access to government PROPERTY or public benefits, the state may discriminate on the basis of subject matter but not viewpoint.

The case arose when a church, named Lamb's Chapel, sought to use an auditorium in a public school during nonschool hours to show a religious film on the subject of child rearing. Under rules set by the school district, school facilities could be used during nonschool hours for social, civic, or recreational meetings or entertainment. Pursuant to state law, however, the district adopted a rule prohibiting the use of this property "by any group for religious purposes."

The church sued, arguing that the school property was a designated PUBLIC FORUM and that it is unconstitutional to exclude a group from such a forum on the basis of the religious viewpoint of its speech. Although the DISTRICT COURT and the Court of Appeals for the Second Circuit rejected this argument, the Supreme Court unanimously reversed and adopted the plaintiffs' position.

The decision was an extension of WIDMAR V. VINCENT (1981), which had permitted university students to use university facilities for religious speech. *Lamb's Chapel* further opened the door to expanded FREEDOM OF SPEECH rights by religious groups on government property and in other government-subsidized forums. If religion is a "viewpoint" then it cannot be used as a basis for exclusion, no matter what type of forum may be involved, in the absence of a COMPELLING STATE INTEREST to justify it. The only such justification that appears plausible is compliance with the ESTABLISHMENT CLAUSE. The Court held that the establishment clause does not bar a religious group from using government property on a neutral basis.

That analysis sparked a colorful CONCURRING OPINION by Justice ANTONIN SCALIA, who objected to the Court's reliance on the three-part test of LEMON V. KURTZMAN (1971), which he described as similar to "some ghoul in a late-night horror movie that repeatedly sits up in its grave and shuffles abroad, after being repeatedly killed and buried."

MICHAEL W. MCCONNELL
(2000)

(SEE ALSO: *Accommodation of Religion; Government Aid to Religious Institutions; Lemon Test; Religion and Free Speech; Religious Liberty.*)

LAMONT v. POSTMASTER GENERAL OF THE UNITED STATES
381 U.S. 301 (1965)

A 1962 act of Congress required the postmaster general to detain all unsealed mail of foreign origin determined to be "communist political propaganda," and to notify the addressee that the mail would be delivered only if he requested it by returning an official reply card. The Supreme Court, 8–0, held the act unconstitutional as an abridgment of the addressee's FIRST AMENDMENT rights. Justice WILLIAM O. DOUGLAS, for the Court, declared that the act sought to control the flow of ideas and was at war with the wide-open discussion of ideas protected by the amendment.

LEONARD W. LEVY
(1986)

(SEE ALSO: *Listeners' Rights.*)

LANDIS, JAMES M.
(1899–1964)

James McCauley Landis was a gifted lawyer, professor and dean at Harvard Law School, and writer, whose outstanding contribution to American law was his theoretical analysis and practical championing of REGULATORY COMMISSIONS. He was a student of FELIX FRANKFURTER and co-authored *The Business of the Supreme Court* (1928) with him. Landis chaired both the Securities and Exchange Commission (1934–1937) and the Civil Aeronautics Board (1946–1947), served on the Federal Trade Commission (1933–1934), and wrote *The Administrative Process* (1938), a sympathetic analysis of regulatory commissions. The book discussed the limits on agencies imposed by Congress and the checks on them afforded by JUDICIAL REVIEW, and Landis downplayed the likelihood of administrative abuses of power, arguing that the true danger lay in lethargic enforcement of congressional policy. The efficiency with which these commissions could focus on economic problems by merging executive, legislative, and judicial powers impressed Landis, who saw administrative action as a practical means to achieve realistic ends.

DAVID GORDON
(1986)

Bibliography

RITCHIE, DONALD A. 1980 *James M. Landis, Dean of the Regulators.* Cambridge, Mass.: Harvard University Press.

LAND ORDINANCE OF 1784

See: Ordinance of 1784

LANDRUM-GRIFFIN ACT
73 Stat. 519 (1959)

Known as the Labor Management Reporting and Disclosure Act, Landrum-Griffin brought internal administration of labor unions within the realm of federal regulation and guaranteed union members certain basic rights. Its goal was union self-regulation and voluntary democratization.

Passage of the measure resulted from a growing national concern influenced by a Senate committee's findings of union leaders' corruption and autocratic behavior. Relying on Congress's constitutional authority to insure the free flow of INTERSTATE COMMERCE, the act restricted secondary BOYCOTTS; strictly controlled union elections; required strict reporting of the unions' financial transactions; outlawed extortion PICKETING; authorized state JURISDICTION over labor disputes not handled by the National Labor Relations Board; and modified union security provisions for certain national unions. In setting forth a Bill of Rights of Members of Labor Organizations, the act reversed the courts' tendency to allow union governance by self-established rules.

The act also made it a criminal offense for a Communist party member to serve as an officer or employee of a labor union until five years after termination of party membership. In UNITED STATES V. BROWN (1965) the Supreme Court ruled this section unconstitutional as a BILL OF ATTAINDER.

PAUL L. MURPHY
(1986)

Bibliography

MCLAUGHLIN, DORIS and SCHOOMAKER, ANITA 1979 *The Landrum-Griffin Act and Union Democracy.* Ann Arbor: University of Michigan Press.

LAND USE

See: Eminent Domain; Zoning

LANE v. WILSON

See: Literacy Test

LANGDON, JOHN
(1741–1819)

John Langdon, a financier and businessman who risked his large personal fortune in support of the Revolution, had, by 1787, already served in the Continental Congress and as a colonel in the Revolutionary War; he had also supervised shipbuilding for the navy and had been president of New Hampshire.

As chairman of New Hampshire's delegation to the CONSTITUTIONAL CONVENTION OF 1787, Langdon personally paid the delegation's expenses. He spoke often at the Convention and served on three committees. He favored such nationalist measures as a congressional veto over state legislation and a prohibition of state taxes on exports. He advocated prohibiting Congress, as well as the states, from emitting BILLS OF CREDIT.

After signing the Constitution, Langdon returned home to become leader of the proratification forces in the state convention. He was elected to the United States Senate and became its first president *pro tempore;* and he served seven more years as governor of New Hampshire.

DENNIS J. MAHONEY
(1986)

Bibliography

ROSSITER, CLINTON 1966 *1787: The Grand Convention.* New York: Macmillan.

LANSING, JOHN, JR.
(1754–1829?)

Mayor John Lansing of Albany was one of three delegates from New York to the CONSTITUTIONAL CONVENTION OF 1787. A former member of Congress and an ally of Governor George Clinton, Lansing was chosen to represent the antinationalist sentiment of the state's political leadership. Lansing was a coauthor of the PATERSON PLAN and a spokesman for the faction that opposed creating a strong national government. He and fellow New York delegate ROBERT YATES withdrew on July 10 charging that the convention was exceeding its congressional mandate to propose amendments to the ARTICLES OF CONFEDERATION.

In the New York debate over RATIFICATION OF THE CONSTITUTION Lansing was one of the anti-Federalist leaders. He was a delegate to the state ratifying convention where he urged defeat of the new Constitution and summoning of a new federal convention. After a proratification majority was assured, Lansing urged conditional ratification and then ratification reserving the right to secede. The long series of proposed amendments—including a BILL OF RIGHTS—that accompanied New York's instrument of ratification was largely Lansing's work.

After 1788 Lansing held state judicial office—serving as Chief Justice and Chancellor—but he never held any federal office except presidential elector.

DENNIS J. MAHONEY
(1986)

Bibliography
ROSSITER, CLINTON   1966   *1787: The Grand Convention.* New York: Macmillan.

LANZA, UNITED STATES v.
260 U.S. 377 (1922)

There is no DOUBLE JEOPARDY when both state and federal governments outlaw an offense and each prosecutes an individual for the same act. The United States indicted Lanza for violating the VOLSTEAD ACT after the state of Washington had already prosecuted him under a state statute enforcing PROHIBITION. A unanimous Supreme Court, dismissing Lanza's double jeopardy claim, declared that the double jeopardy forbidden by the Fifth Amendment was a second trial for the same offense in the same JURISDICTION. The Court concluded: "It follows that an act denounced as a crime by both national and state sovereignties is an offense against the peace and dignity of both, and may be punished by each." *Lanza* is still good law.

DAVID GORDON
(1986)

LARKIN v. GRENDEL'S DEN, INCORPORATED
459 U.S. 116 (1982)

Dissenting alone, Justice WILLIAM H. REHNQUIST observed that "silly cases" like this one, as well as great or hard cases, make bad law. Chief Justice WARREN E. BURGER for the Court aimed its "heavy FIRST AMENDMENT artillery," in Rehnquist's phrase, at a statute that banned the sale of alcoholic beverages within 500 feet of a school or church, should either object to the presence of a neighboring tavern. Originally, Massachusetts had absolutely banned such taverns but found that the objective of the STATE POLICE POWER, promoting neighborhood peace, could be fulfilled by the less drastic method of allowing schools and churches to take the initiative of registering objections. In this case a church objected to a tavern located ten feet away. Burger held that vesting the church with the state's veto power breached the prohibition against an ESTABLISHMENT OF RELIGION, on the grounds that the church's involvement vitiated the secular purposes of the statute, advanced the cause of religion, and excessively entangled state and church. Rehnquist argued that a sensible statute had not breached the wall of SEPARATION OF CHURCH AND STATE.

LEONARD W. LEVY
(1986)

LARSON v. DOMESTIC AND FOREIGN COMMERCE CORPORATION
337 U.S. 682 (1949)

This is a leading decision concerning the SOVEREIGN IMMUNITY of the United States. Plaintiff sued the head of the War Assets Administration (WAA), alleging that the Administrator had sold certain surplus coal to plaintiff, had refused to deliver the coal, and had entered into a contract to sell the coal to others. Because plaintiff sought injunctive relief against WAA officials, ordering them not to sell the coal or to deliver it to anyone other than plaintiff, and because the suit concerned property of the United States, the Supreme Court found the suit to be one against the United States and, therefore, to be barred by sovereign immunity. The Court distinguished *Larson* from suits against officers for acts beyond their statutory powers and from suits seeking to enjoin allegedly unconstitutional behavior, both of which the Court stated would not constitute suits against the sovereign, even if the plaintiff alleges the officer acted unconstitutionally or beyond his statutory powers, "if the relief requested cannot be granted merely by ordering the cessation of the conduct complained of but will require affirmative action by the sovereign or the disposition of unquestionably sovereign property." In cases involving suits against state officials, part of this passage apparently was contradicted by EDELMAN V. JORDAN (1974) and MILLIKEN V. BRADLEY (1977). In each of these cases the Court found that litigation to require a state to pay the costs of future compliance with the Constitution did not constitute a suit against the sovereign. The precise holding in *Larson* became an important and debated issue in PENNHURST STATE SCHOOL AND HOSPITAL V. HALDERMAN (1984), where the Court relied in part on *Larson* to hold that actions in federal court against state officials, alleging violations of state law, are prohibited by the ELEVENTH AMENDMENT.

THEODORE EISENBERG
(1986)

LARSON v. VALENTE
456 U.S. 228 (1982)

Minnesota required charitable organizations to register and make disclosure when they solicited contributions. Religious organizations were exempted if more than half their contributions came from members. Members of the Unification Church sued in federal court to challenge the law's constitutionality. The Supreme Court, 5–4, held the law invalid.

Justice WILLIAM J. BRENNAN, for the Court, said that the law effectively granted denominational preferences, favoring well-established churches and disfavoring newer churches or churches that preferred public solicitation. This discrimination took the case out of the purpose-effects-entanglement test of LEMON V. KURTZMAN (1971) for ESTABLISHMENT OF RELIGION. Instead, Brennan invoked a searching form of STRICT SCRUTINY, which the state here failed to pass. The state's purported interests in preventing abuse in solicitation were not supported in the record. In any case, Brennan said, the Minnesota law failed *Lemon's* "entanglement" test by risking the politicizing of religion; one Minnesota legislator had remarked, "I'm not sure why we're so hot to regulate the Moonies [Unification Church] anyway."

The four dissenters thought the plaintiffs lacked STANDING to challenge the law. Two of them also dissented on the merits of the case, arguing that the law did not constitute an intentional discrimination among religions.

KENNETH L. KARST
(1986)

LASKI, HAROLD J.
(1893–1950)

British political scientist and Socialist party leader Harold Joseph Laski influenced American constitutional thought both through his public writings and through his friendship with leading American jurists and political leaders. Laski studied political science at Oxford University under Ernest Barker, and from 1916 to 1920 was an instructor in government at Harvard University. While teaching at Harvard he met, and began a twenty-year correspondence with, Justice OLIVER WENDELL HOLMES, and he established an even longer-lasting friendship with Professor (later Justice) FELIX FRANKFURTER. He also numbered among his friends and correspondents President FRANKLIN D. ROOSEVELT and Justice BENJAMIN N. CARDOZO.

From 1920 until his death in 1950 Laski taught at the London School of Economics and Political Science. He continued to correspond with his American friends and frequently visited the United States. He affected American jurisprudence mainly by influencing those whose general approach to legal and constitutional problems is called LEGAL REALISM.

Although in his early books, written in America, he had embraced a pluralist doctrine of politics, Laski had by 1931 adopted the Marxist theory of history as class struggle, and thereafter he attempted to formulate a non-Soviet Marxist political theory. He never lost interest in American

politics, and his last book was *The American Democracy*, a Marxist account of American history and institutions.

DENNIS J. MAHONEY
(1986)

Bibliography

DEANE, HERBERT A.   1954   *The Political Ideas of Harold Laski.* Ph.D. dissertation, Columbia University.
HOWE, MARK DEWOLFE   1953   *The Holmes-Laski Correspondence.* 2 Vols. Cambridge, Mass.: Harvard University Press.

LASSITER v. DEPARTMENT OF SOCIAL SERVICES

See: Right to Counsel

LAU v. NICHOLS
414 U.S. 563 (1974)

San Francisco failed to provide non-English-speaking students of Chinese ancestry with an adequate education. The Supreme Court, without dissent, found such an effect to violate Title VI of the CIVIL RIGHTS ACT OF 1964 even absent any intent to discriminate against the students. *Lau's* employment of an "effects" test under Title VI may not have survived REGENTS OF THE UNIVERSITY OF CALIFORNIA V. BAKKE (1978), a question that divided the Court in *Guardians Association v. Civil Service Commission* (1983). Congress later expressed approval of *Lau* in enacting legislation to assist non-English-speaking students.

THEODORE EISENBERG
(1986)

LAW AND ECONOMICS THEORY

The "positive" economic theory of law argues that one can discern an economic logic implicit in law, constitutional as well as any other. Economic analysis can also play a normative role, providing a benchmark for assessing the soundness of any particular constitutional clause or interpretation. (As economics itself does not establish indisputable criteria of judgment, the benchmark itself may be blurry.) For some constitutional provisions or doctrines, the relevance of economics is obvious; the Fifth Amendment's takings clause is an example.

A market economy requires private property. One can imagine an economy of government firms relating to each other, to workers, and to consumers primarily through market operations. But if capital were allocated by government, this would be an odd parody of a market economy, and if capital were allocated by markets in the sense that individuals were free to place their capital where they chose, the firms would not be government firms. The Fifth Amendment's requirement of JUST COMPENSATION for the TAKING OF PROPERTY thus supplies a qualified protection for the market economy. The economist naturally asks how alternative constructions of the clause will affect incentives—the feature of a market economy that accounts in large measure for its productivity.

One might view the clause as aimed at assuring owners correct incentives to invest and improve property. The Supreme Court's focus on "investment-backed expectations" in PENN CENTRAL TRANSPORTATION CO. V. NEW YORK CITY (1978) suggests such a concern. But insurance against such risks could be provided by private insurers, and so the question arises why the duty to pay should fall on government. At least one answer—again look ing at incentives—is that such a duty will improve incentives for government decision makers, deterring the pursuit of programs that sacrifice a greater value than they produce.

Does such a view lead to a rule that compensation is required for government acts that fail some sort of cost-benefit test, and not for ones that pass? Clearly not. To resolve claims on such a basis would require the courts to assess the wisdom of virtually every government decision, a costly repetition of other branches' work. Because many of the benefits and costs of a program are political, this inquiry would take courts into areas where other institutions might have a comparative advantage. Finally, the Constitution establishes rights. Whether created for instrumental or for ethical reasons (e.g., a sense of the moral fitness of people's owning themselves and what they receive in free exchanges with others), a right would hardly be worthy of the name if it succumbed whenever a cost-benefit test ran against it. Thus, the economist, along with everyone else, would not define the protections of the taking clause by reference to "case utilitarianism" (assessing particular acts in terms of their direct effect on aggregate utility).

But the criterion of maximizing utility may help define the rules that embody constitutional rights—"rule utilitarianism." Reading the takings clause to require compensation for all government acts, for instance, would provide a strong incentive against wasteful government acts. But such a rule would entail enormous administrative and information costs—though never the costs of evaluating the program's benefits, as the rejected case-utilitarian view would. The concern for administrative costs suggests a reading of the takings clause that requires compensation for any act (or class of acts), except where its costs are relatively widespread—in the extreme case, for example, those of a change in monetary policy—so that the administrative costs of awarding compensation are high. (The compensation itself is not a social cost, but a transfer from taxpayers or users to whoever's property is taken. Effecting the transfer through raising taxes will usually impose secondary costs, however, by reducing economic incentives to engage in the taxed activity.)

In fact, many features of taking law seem to fit such a notion comfortably: the refusal to view all regulatory losses as automatically compensable, coupled with compensability for at least some extreme cases; consideration of "average reciprocity of advantage," offsetting benefits that a property owner may gain from a scheme as a whole, such as a historic district, and that would complicate any effort to compute compensation; and award of compensation for even a very small loss where it takes the form of a complete taking of all rights in a diminutive piece of property.

On the other hand, the courts' relative indifference to regulations sweeping away much of the value of undeveloped land raises a question about the judicial vision of the clause. Focus on incentives for property owners might support such relative indifference; the existence of land, as opposed to buildings, typically requires no investor effort. (In *Kaiser Aetna v. United States*, 1979, where human effort had created a waterway, the Supreme Court extended protections to private interests beyond what it would have afforded similar interests in a natural waterway.) Focus on incentives for government and recognition of the opportunity costs of undeveloped resources preempted by government might tilt the balance toward protection in some of these cases.

The takings clause may seem easy territory for demonstrating a constitutional concern for economic incentives, but broadly defined, such a concern pervades the document. The Framers' fear of excessive governmental power led them to rely on institutional incentives as a check. The SEPARATION OF POWERS rests on an assumption about human behavior familiar to economists: even in government, people will pursue personal advantage to a large degree. Thus, as in the private marketplace, the Constitution used private incentives to achieve a public end, ambition being made to counteract ambition, as JAMES MADISON put it in THE FEDERALIST #51.

The system of checks exposes a complex relation between efficiency at different levels. While Judge Richard Posner has argued that seperation of powers is at least in part an effort to increase government efficiency by tailoring the institutional structure to particular government tasks, the structure also impedes government action, making it less efficient as an institution, But if some sort of overall efficiency by forstalling inefficient ECONOMIC REGULATION. On the other hand, once inefficient regulations exist, seperation of powers may decrease efficiency by delaying deregulation long after a consensus has developed that government intervention is unwise.

Another example of a per se inefficient activity may be

the FIRST AMENDMENT ban on an ESTABLISHMENT OF RELI-
GION, which would seem to negate even government subsidies to religion that offset market failure and would thus
presumably be efficient. But reading the clause as a requirement of government neutrality in religion, one can
readily find a justification in economics, broadly conceived. The Framers could easily have thought that the
costs of any government nonneutrality, in social and political divisiveness, would generally outweigh benefits.

If the Constitution does prefer a set of social "goods,"
such as minimal government and government neutrality
toward religion and speech, there remains the problem of
defining the degree of preference. Few good things come
without costs, and one would naturally expect courts to be
wary of constitutional interpretations that extend constitutional goods to a point of extravagant cost. The Constitution is not a "suicide pact," as Justice ROBERT H. JACKSON
cautioned in TERMINIELLO V. CHICAGO (1949). Similarly, if
"cost-benefit" sounds like an economist's approach, "balancing" the costs of alternative rules is surely no more
than recognition that at some point one set of rights must
yield to another. Justice OLIVER WENDELL HOLMES, JR.,
wrote in *Hudson County Water Co. v. McCarter* (1908),
"All rights tend to declare themselves absolute to their
logical extreme. Yet all in fact are limited by the neighborhood of principles of policy which are other than those
on which the particular right is founded, and which become strong enough to hold their own when a certain
point is reached."

Still, the economist's concern for cost may be special.
The subject of economics is the problem of maximizing
something (e.g., utility, wealth), subject to the constraint
of scarcity. Whether the relevant scarcity is of conventional commodities or of constitutional goods, such as opportunities to communicate, the economist should have
something useful to say. Indeed, an important insight of
economics is that costs are simply benefits (goods) given
up in pursuit of other goods. An economist should be
quicker than most to spot opportunity costs and to dispel
the fallacy that costs could ever be purely pecuniary. The
costs of a policy, including a constitutional rule, are the
goods, services, and benefits that it destroys or sacrifices.
To the extent economic analysis of law flourishes, one may
expect to find cost arguments more common, explicit, and
sophisticated. Thus, although in CLEVELAND BOARD OF EDU-
CATION V. LAFLEUR (1974) the Court declared that "administrative convenience alone is insufficient to make valid
what is otherwise a violation of due process of law," MA-
THEWS V. ELDRIDGE (1976) made such costs integral to its
analysis of procedural due process.

What, then, is distinctive about the economic approach? Neither the interest in costs nor the balancing of
the costs of various approaches seems unique to analysts

of economic bent, even if economists typically press them
furthest. There are, however, analytic tools employed by
economists as a matter of course, but by others rarely, if
at all.

One specialty of economics is the search for the true
incidence of the costs of taxes, subsidies, and regulations.
Inelastic suppliers and demanders bear these costs. A supply is inelastic if suppliers have few alternative uses of the
relevant resources. A tax on coal production is likely to fall
largely on the owners of coal in place, as there are few
activities to which they can divert their coal-mining property. This is still more true if users of coal have many alternatives—that is, if demand is quite elastic. This is
clearest where the coal tax of a single state is at issue, and
demanders' substitutes include the supply of all coal producers outside the taxing state.

Use of the analysis is obvious for issues of the constitutionality of state taxes or regulations that are challenged
as offending the DORMANT COMMERCE CLAUSE, that is, the
courts' implied authority to strike down state rules that
unduly intrude on INTERSTATE COMMERCE, even where
Congress has been silent. Indeed, in assessing a coal sev-
erance tax against a COMMERCE CLAUSE attack, the Court
alluded in *Commonwealth Edison Co. v. Montana* (1981)
to the elasticity of demand as an important consideration,
but declined to pursue the matter. The decision not to
pursue it appears correct, for the "export" of the tax seems
unlikely unless the taxing state has market power in the
good. This will not be true unless the state accounts for a
high proportion of supply or colludes with other supplying
states. In either case, the state is likely to be so drastically
outnumbered by importing states as to make a congressional remedy easy.

The search for incidence is useful in other, less obvious
areas. The Supreme Court's PUBLIC FORUM jurisprudence,
for example, rests on the notion that for a special class of
speakers the burden of restrictions on the communicative
use of public property is relatively severe because of their
lack of alternative means of reaching an audience. Thus,
Justice HUGO L. BLACK argued in *Martin v. City of Struthers*
(1943) that "door to door distribution of circulars is essential to the poorly financed causes of little people." The
question raised is a good one, but the asserted answer may
be an oversimplification. Though doubtless the poor buy
a lower per capita share of the food supply than the nonpoor, the nonpoor obviously do not "buy up" all the food.
Similarly, it is far from clear that messages relating to
causes involving the poor are underrepresented in market
channels of communication. (To the extent that the poor
are a demoralized underclass, they likely would not initiate
many communications of any kind, including circulars and
street demonstrations.)

The economist's training generally leads to a search for

effects on ultimate consumers and providers. Where would-be speakers challenge a private property owner's speech restrictions, as at the shopping center in *Lloyd Corp. v. Tanner* (1972), or where a shopping center owner challenges a state's limits on his ability to restrain speech, as in PRUNEYARD SHOPPING CENTER V. ROBINS (1980), the Court has framed the dispute as one between the property rights of the owner and the free speech rights of speakers. But to the economist a more relevant formulation is the conflict between one set of property users' interest in communication and another set's interest in being free from the communications. A profit-seeking owner of a shopping center is a middleman, presumably seeking an economically optimal tradeoff: to allow speech up to the point where the benefit (captured by him in rents) exceeds the costs (suffered by him as diminished rentals as result of user resistance). The point suggests yet another perspective on the idea that the cost of communication on sidewalks, streets, or other government property is low. The speaker's out-of-pocket cost is low, to be sure, but in part because some of the burden is borne by those whose convenience or tranquillity is reduced. Of course, if government officials cannot charge fees to capture some of the benefits of free communication, yet do bear some of its costs (in the form of less personal tranquillity themselves), the public forum doctrine may be a justifiable subsidy to offset their skewed incentives in other branches.

If there is an economic logic implicit in constitutional law, is the reason that the Framers and the courts hace used the tools of ecconomic analysis intuitively rather than explicitly or that some process (e.g., the selectionof cases for litigation as a opposed to settlement) tends to screen out economically unsound precedents? To the extent that the first explaination is sound, there may appear some tension between the positive economic theory—with incentives, with maximizing values subject to constraints, with tradeoffs at the margin, with identifying the true nature and incidence of costs—seem basic to any coherent approach to social nomic analysis thus seems inextricably linked to CONSTITUTIONAL INTERPRETATION, with perhaps no more at stake than degrees of sophistication.

STEPHEN F. WILLIAMS
(1992)

(SEE ALSO: *Economic Analysis and the Constitution; Economic Equal Protection; Economic Liberties and the Constitution.*)

Bibliography

COASE, R. H. 1977 Advertising and Free Speech. *Journal of Legal Studies* 6:1–34.
CONFERENCE 1975 Economic Analysis of Political Behavior. *Journal of Law and Economics* 18:587–918.
EASTERBROOK, FRANK H. 1984 Foreword: The Court and the Economic System. *Harvard Law Review* 98:1–60.
EPSTEIN, RICHARD A. 1985 *Takings.* Cambridge, Mass.: Harvard University Press.
McCONNELL, MICHAEL W. and POSNER, RICHARD A. 1989 An Economic Approach to Issues of Religious Freedom. *University of Chicago Law Review* 56:1–60.
POSNER, RICHARD A. 1986 *Economic Analysis of Law,* 3rd ed. Boston: Little, Brown.
SOWELL, THOMAS 1980 *Knowledge and Decisions.* New York: Basic Books.
SYMPOSIUM 1987 The Constitution as an Economic Document. *George Washington Law Review* 56:1–186.

LAW ENFORCEMENT AND FEDERAL–STATE RELATIONS

This country has long been committed to the notion that primary responsibility for law enforcement should reside in state and local governments. Over the past century, however, changes in the federal criminal system have affected the traditional balance among federal, state, and local responsibilities for law enforcement. We may be slowly moving in the direction of a national police force.

The Supreme Court has affirmed the constitutionality of an expanded federal legislative authority in the realm of criminal enforcement. Congress has enacted numerous statutes under this expanded federal authority. As a result, the federal criminal code has begun to look more and more like a state criminal code in its substantive content and even in its jurisdictional reach and form.

Over the long term, the balance among the several law enforcement JURISDICTIONS will be determined not only by the breadth of the law on the books but also by its implementation in practice. The type and magnitude of police resources available to the federal government and the attitudes of the electorate and decision makers in key governmental institutions are likely to determine whether a broad federal criminal authority will supplant state and local responsibilities. Here, too, some changes have begun.

The traditional allocation of law enforcement responsibilities assigns to local governments the basic policing of crimes such as homicide, theft, robbery, rape, burglary, muggings, and the like. Local police have responsibility for patrol, for immediate response to reports of crime, and for investigations. A huge number of local officers presently performs those functions nationwide, particularly in metropolitan areas. The idea of a "national police force" directed from Washington, D.C. taking over these functions seems far-reaching. But one can imagine substantial shifts in the traditional division between federal and local responsibilities that would be accompanied by growth of a significantly larger corps of federal police that might fairly be called a national police force.

The jurisdictional reach of the federal criminal code has expanded in many ways over the past century. Most federal criminal legislation not aimed at protecting direct federal interests, such as federal funds or property, has been constitutionally based in Congress's enumerated powers—for example, the POSTAL POWER, the TAXING AND SPENDING POWER, and the power to regulate commerce among the states. (See NATIONAL POLICE POWER.)

Use of the postal and taxing powers as a basis for federal criminal jurisdiction has not changed much over the years. The use of the mails was relied upon early in the mail fraud statute enacted in 1872. A comprehensive registration-tax scheme was utilized in the original major antinarcotics legislation, the HARRISON ACT of 1914. The COMMERCE CLAUSE which began its criminal law history as a fairly narrow jurisdictional base—requiring transportation or travel across a state line—in modern times has been expanded. In a number of statutes, federal jurisdiction is now based on the use of the facilities of commerce such as interstate telephone calls, telegrams, and any kind of interstate movement of persons or goods.

The EFFECT ON COMMERCE formula, originally developed in the economic regulation sphere, has also broadened the bases for federal criminal jurisdiction. The nexus with commerce required under that formula is not very substantial. And the "effect on commerce" formula itself has been extended to situations where the criminal activity merely takes place on the premises of a business whose operations affect commerce. Furthermore, in PEREZ V. UNITED STATES (1971) the Court accepted congressional findings that a type of criminal conduct was part of a class of activities affecting commerce, and held that that type of conduct could be made a federal crime without any showing of an effect upon commerce in the individual case. Although in most cases similar to *Perez* proof of an effect upon commerce probably can be shown, *Perez* represents the furthest expansion of the reach of federal criminal jurisdiction under the commerce power.

The necessity to rely upon enumerated powers led Congress to enact crimes in forms differing markedly from the usual state penal code. Often, otherwise innocuous conduct that provided the basis for federal jurisdiction became the central element of the offense. Congress made criminal the transportation in commerce of lottery tickets, or obscene literature, or women for immoral purposes; depositing a letter in the mails to execute a fraudulent scheme; or affecting commerce by robbery or extortion.

The odd form of these crimes has produced concerns peculiar to federal criminal law. The prosecution of federal crimes often overemphasizes the jurisdiction element. The Supreme Court in four decades has, in five mail fraud cases, faced the question whether mailing was done for purposes of the fraudulent scheme; during the same pe-

riod, the Court has not once considered the sometimes perplexing question of what constitutes fraudulant conduct under the statute.

The jurisdictional reach of federal criminal statutes has also developed in an odd checkerboard pattern. For example, originally, federal law made it a crime to use the mails to defraud but not the telegraph or telephone. Many such inconsistencies have been eliminated, but some still remain.

The *Perez* decision may also have far-reaching effects on the form of federal crimes. The case is usually cited for its effect in expanding the jurisdictional reach of federal criminal laws. However, the more important impact of the case may be that Congress can now, if it is so minded, draft a criminal code in a form substantially identical to a state penal code. Under such a code, the federal prosecutor would not have to prove the jurisdictional element in a crime belonging to a commerce-related class of activity; the proof would resemble the evidence offered in comparable state prosecutions.

Congress has not yet fully taken up the *Perez* invitation. In addition to the consumer credit statute enacted in 1964, the most significant statutes using this drafting approach are the illegal gambling business statute and the Comprehensive Drug Abuse Prevention and Control Act, both enacted in 1970. Federal drug crimes, which were historically based on the taxing power, are now based on the commerce power and defined in traditional criminal law terms.

Many traditional crimes have long been subject to punishment under the federal criminal code where a direct federal interest is involved, when the offense occurs on federal property or in a location for which the federal government has a special responsibility, or when federal funds are involved or persons are injured. Thus murder, manslaughter, and rape are federal crimes when committed "within the special maritime and territorial jurisdiction of the United States." And where criminal conduct on federal lands is not punishable by any specific federal enactment but would be a crime under state law, federal law incorporates state law and makes the conduct punishable.

However, traditional crimes have also been made federal offenses where no direct federal interest is involved. Legislation of this type is usually justified on the ground that the crimes involved are often committed by criminal groups organized and operating in more than one state, thus calling for nationwide investigation and prosecution. Such offenses are broadly defined, however, and do not limit federal prosecution to instances where the conduct involved can conveniently only be investigated and prosecuted by federal authorities.

There is today hardly a major crime category treated in state penal codes that is not also a federal crime, even in the absence of a direct federal interest. Ignoring for the moment the jurisdictional limits, examples of such crimes include: prostitution (MANN ACT, 1910); various forms of theft involving stolen motor vehicles, other stolen property, and theft from interstate shipments (Dyer Act, 1919); bank robbery (1934); robbery (Anti-Racketeering Act, 1934); extortion (Anti-Racketeering Act, 1934); kidnaping (1932); threats (1934); arson (Travel Act, 1961); bribery (Travel Act, 1961); rioting (1968); sexual exploitation of children (1978); and murder (RACKETEER INFLUENCED AND CORRUPT ORGANIZATIONS ACT, RICO, 1970).

In several instances, state crimes have played a more direct role in the federal criminal code. In three important pieces of complex criminal legislation—the Travel Act of 1961, the gambling business statute of 1970, and the RICO statute of 1970—Congress adopted the legislative technique of making the commission of certain crimes in violation of state law a federal crime under specified circumstances. In these instances, federal law did not simply cover the same ground as the state crime; it became identical to it.

The effect of these changes in jurisdictional reach, form, and substantive coverage has been to move the federal criminal code closer to the form and content of the fifty state penal codes with which it overlaps. Certain benefits have resulted from these changes. Many anomalies and inconsistencies in federal crime coverage have been eliminated. It is now also easier for the federal government, in a limited fashion, directly to supplement state and local efforts to combat ordinary crime.

These changes also have their costs. The old emphasis on jurisdiction and the checkerboard pattern of coverage have served as a constant reminder of the limited role of the federal government in protecting local communities against ordinary crime. As these elements in the code are eliminated, it becomes easier to think in terms of an expanded federal role.

The balance of responsibility necessarily will continue to remain with the states as long as federal law enforcement resources remain small in comparison to state and local forces, and federal prosecutions remain a small percentage of the total prosecutorial caseload of the country. Overall, there are about fifty major federal criminal enforcement agencies with approximately 50,000 field personnel. Most of these have specialized duties and limited jurisdiction. Approximately 35,000 federal felony prosecutions are initiated annually by about 2,000 federal prosecutors. This federal picture should be contrasted with that at the state and local levels where approximately 19,000 police agencies employ about 500,000 sworn officers, and in excess of 700,000 prosecutions are begun each year by more than 20,000 state and local prosecutors.

A dramatic increase in the number of federal law enforcement personnel or their combination in a single agency would have to occur in order to create the conditions for a major shift of law enforcement responsibilities to the federal realm. However, such a shift could also conceivably occur through a shift of military personnel into domestic law enforcement, or by the development of federal control over state and local agencies.

The growth of existing federal law enforcement agencies has been significant although not dramatic. In the past thirty years, the FEDERAL BUREAU OF INVESTIGATION (FBI), the largest federal law enforcement agency and the one with the most general criminal enforcement authority, has grown from 3,000 to 8,000 agents; the Secret Service has expanded from 300 to 1,500; and the Customs Service, from 150 to 600 agents. The Drug Enforcement Administration (DEA) has grown tenfold from 200 to 2,000 agents.

The 1970s and 1980s have seen moves toward consolidation of separate agencies. The Bureau of Narcotics, originally located in the Treasury Department, was shifted to the Department of Justice, and later became the DEA. Recently the FBI, which had never before had any significant investigative responsibility for drug matters, moved strongly into that field and began working closely with DEA. DEA personnel may eventually be absorbed into the FBI, a move that would increase the personnel of that agency by more than one-fifth.

Even if agencies continue to grow and merge, a dramatic shift of law enforcement responsibility from state and local governments to the federal government seems unlikely in the foreseeable future. The creation of a single, really large corps of federal enforcement personnel would require considerable expansion of either the rate of growth or the practice of combining agencies.

Resources for a national police operation might also conceivably become available through increased use of the military to enforce domestic law. There is a strong tradition, founded in part in the same concerns as the commitment to local responsibility for law enforcement, against the involvement of the military in law enforcement. In the context of military surveillance activities directed against civilians, Justice WILLIAM O. DOUGLAS once suggested that "turning the military loose on civilians even if sanctioned by act of Congress . . . would raise serious and profound constitutional questions." A statutory prohibition against the use of the military to enforce domestic law, the POSSE COMITATUS ACT, was enacted in 1878. The act makes it a crime to use the military forces "to execute the laws" except as expressly authorized by Congress or the Constitution.

The Supreme Court has not yet authoritatively interpretated the Posse Comitatus Act. Existing lower court interpretations permit some limited involvement of the military in domestic law enforcement. Several different constructions of the act were advanced in a series of decisions growing out of the occupation of Wounded Knee, South Dakota, by American Indian Movement members, for example, that the act is violated only by direct active use of federal troops in domestic law enforcement. Specific statutory exceptions also allow the domestic use of the military to enforce the laws, in cases of civil disorder, threats to federal property, and protection of federal parks, foreign dignitaries, and certain federal officials.

Increased federal efforts to combat drug smuggling have strained the Posse Comitatus Act. The desire to use navy ships and air force planes against smugglers led to enactment in 1982 of a statute that made further inroads on the act. Though limited, the new law is important because it is the first statutory modification of the Posse Comitatus Act for ordinary law enforcement purposes in the more than 100 years since its enactment. This is an area where special care should be taken; by a single stroke, Congress can effect a major change in the traditional law enforcement balance.

In the decades of the 1970s and 1980s there has been increasing federal involvement with state and local law enforcement. The Law Enforcement Assistance Administration, established in 1968 and terminated in the late 1970s, involved a massive FEDERAL GRANT-IN-AID program to state and local governments for law enforcement purposes. The potential of this technique for giving the federal government control over local law enforcement policy decisions has not been fully realized.

Formal arrangements of cooperation between federal and state and local agencies are also increasing. Fourteen federal organized crime strike forces and twelve special drug task forces involving cooperating teams of federal, state, and local law enforcement agents have been established in major cities throughout the country. Policymaking committees composed of federal, state, and local law enforcement officials also meet.

The picture presented is one of increasingly close cooperation and interdependence of law enforcement agencies at the federal, state, and local levels. The existing programs do not yet, however, add up to the establishment of a basis for federal control.

As long as there is a national consensus that the primary responsibility for law enforcement should remain at the local level there is no serious likelihood that Congress would authorize the resources to create a national police force to enforce what is becoming a true national criminal code. Any assessment of trends in the national consensus on an issue of this nature is, of course, difficult to make. One can only point to certain factors which serve as general indicators.

The focus and rhetoric of national discourse on the role of federal criminal law enforcement have changed somewhat in recent years. Crime has increasingly become a source of public concern and a standard topic of national political discussion. Correspondingly, the federal government's public pronouncements have assumed increasingly larger responsibilities for federal law enforcement. The federal emphasis in the 1950s and 1960s focused on organized crime and political corruption. In the 1970s the emphasis shifted to white-collar crime. In the 1980s the federal government has added to its emphasized responsibilities a massive attack on drugs and violence.

In the 1960s, the ATTORNEY GENERAL of the United States never spoke of the federal government's role in law enforcement without at least paying lip service to the principle that primary responsibility rests at the local level. In the 1980s the attorney general in his major addresses generally speaks of working closely with state and local law enforcement officials and the development of a national strategy.

Any serious moves toward substantial enlargement of federal law enforcement responsibilities might be opposed by state and local governments. As matters stand, these authorities typically welcome increasing federal assistance and involvement, because the crime problem is too big for local officials to handle alone. Of course, this condition augurs continued growth of the federal arm. One wonders when that growth will begin to be seen as a threat.

Congress itself continues to recite the local responsibility credo even while it expands the scope of the federal code. Although the Supreme Court has not imposed significant constitutional restraints on the reach of federal penal legislation, it has adopted a restrictive maxim of interpretation: unless Congress expresses itself unambiguously it will be presumed not to have intended to change the traditional state-federal balance in law enforcement. If the prospect of a national police force loomed on the horizon, would the Court resurrect significant constitutional limits?

Perceiving the prospect of a national police force simply in the continued expansion of the federal criminal code would be foolish. That growth, however, creates one of the conditions that would enable a national police force to function. And the very existence of an enlarged code may generate some pressure to enforce it actively. Nothing can happen, of course, unless the national consensus breaks down. There, too, some signals could mean that the "impossible" is at least possible. The development of a national police force is not imminent, but there are enough portents to suggest that we should keep in mind words uttered by Justice FELIX FRANKFURTER in YOUNGSTOWN SHEET & TUBE CO. V. SAWYER (1952), a case involving assertion of national executive power: "The accretion of dangerous power does not come in a day. It does come, however slowly, from the generative force of unchecked disregard of the restrictions that fence in even the most disinterested assertion of authority."

NORMAN ABRAMS
(1986)

Bibliography

ABRAMS, NORMAN 1970 Report on Jurisdiction. Pages 33–66 in *National Commission on Reform of Federal Criminal Laws: Working Papers*, vol. 1. Washington, D.C.: The Commission.
——— 1986 Federal Criminal Law and Its Enforcement. St. Paul, Minn.: West Publishing Co.
SCHWARTZ, LOUIS B. 1948 Federal Criminal Jurisdiction and Prosecutors' Discretion. *Law and Contemporary Problems* 13:64–87.
STERN, ROBERT L. 1973 The Commerce Clause Revisited: The Federalization of Intrastate Crime. *Arizona Law Review* 15: 271–285.

LAW ENFORCEMENT AND FEDERAL–STATE RELATIONS
(Update)

In 1995, the Supreme Court handed down an opinion that had the potential to rewrite federal–state relations in criminal enforcement. The ruling in UNITED STATES V. LÓPEZ, a decision on the power of Congress to regulate INTERSTATE COMMERCE, involved a criminal prosecution of a twelfth-grade student for a violation of the Gun-Free School Zones Act of 1990, which made it a federal offense "for any individual knowingly to possess a firearm at a place that the individual knows, or has reasonable cause to believe, is a school zone."

In *López*, the Court held that this statute was "invalid as beyond the power of Congress under the Commerce Clause." For the first time since the 1930s, the Court declared a federal statute unconstitutional on such a ground and thereby raised doubts about the COMMERCE CLAUSE underpinnings of much of the Federal Criminal Code.

Chief Justice WILLIAM H. REHNQUIST reviewed the traditional commerce power bases that have been upheld by the Court and found none of them present in *López*. Initially the Court's decision seems sound; upon reflection, however, doubts arise. After all, what is the guiding principle in the decision? Simply the absence of express connection to interstate commerce? If so, could Congress cure the constitutional defect by including findings in the statute regarding the impact on commerce of the possession of guns on school grounds; or using another approach, by requiring that the gun, or some of its parts, or the possessor of the gun, have traveled recently in interstate commerce? If so, the decision loses its significance and becomes formalistic in the extreme.

In the wake of the decision, numerous symposia were organized discussing the impact of *López*. Nor was there a stirring only in academia. Within the next few years, in reliance on the decision, frequent challenges to the constitutionality of other commerce-based federal criminal LEGISLATION were raised in the lower federal courts. A key question addressed in the academic consideration of the implications of the decision was whether this was an opening salvo in an attack by the Court on the practically unlimited scope of the exercise of commerce power authority by the Congress. Or was it simply "an isolated deviation from the strong current of precedents"?

If the lower court decisions are any index, *López* does not signal a revolution in commerce power DOCTRINE. Although there have been some decisions holding federal statutes unconstitutional, most of the case law has upheld the challenged statutes. Yet, the issue has not returned to the Court, and until that body rules again, the significance of *López* remains uncertain.

If *López* is not the harbinger of a revolution, one wonders why the Court chose this particular case to draw a constitutional line in the sand. Examining the case in light of how its facts bear on the federal–state relationship in criminal enforcement may shed some light on this issue. While such an examination may not produce a doctrinal principle underlying the decision, it does steer us toward pragmatic policy concerns relating to the enforcement of federal criminal statutes that may be quite relevant to the constitutional issues in such cases.

Articulated concerns about the federal–state relationship in criminal enforcement have surfaced in a set of Supreme Court cases involving issues of STATUTORY INTERPRETATION. One such early case is *Rewis v. United States* (1971), which involved the interpretation of the Travel Act that, among other things, makes it a federal crime to travel across a state line in aid of gambling. In *Rewis*, the Court construed the act as not covering the interstate travel of mere customers of a gambling establishment, stating, "an expansive Travel Act [i.e., one that would include the interstate travel of gambling customers within its coverage] would alter sensitive federal–state relationships, could overextend limited federal police resources, and . . . would transform relatively minor state offenses into federal felonies."

One can examine *López* through the same prism as *Rewis* and make strikingly similar observations. As in *Rewis*, the likely number of persons who would violate the federal statute, countrywide, might be substantial. Extensive enforcement of the *López* statute would disproportionately use up limited federal police resources, while limited enforcement inevitably would involve prosecutors in selecting a very few cases from a large number of possible prosecutions, making the selection, inevitably, rather arbitrary and capricious. Either way, serious stresses would be put on the sensitive federal–state relationship.

Further, although the nature of the crime and the criminal in *López* is undoubtedly different from that in *Rewis*, there nevertheless are similarities. However concerned we are about not having guns present where children are regularly found, the nature of the conduct involved in *López* is not, in and of itself, directly a form of serious criminality. The perpetrator is likely to be "a local student at a local school," and most of the persons likely to be prosecuted under the statute would not be typical criminals. While the underlying concern about potential violence in *López* is quite different from *Rewis*, federal prosecution of school children may be viewed, arguably, as not significantly different from prosecuting gambling customers. In *Rewis*, the Court had the luxury of being able to construe the statute narrowly to avoid federal–state concerns. Where that option is not available, the same type of concerns may have some impact on the constitutional decision that is rendered.

López probably is not the forerunner of a major upheaval in federal–state relations in criminal enforcement. Such a change may one day come, but it is more likely to come from the actions of legislators and officials in the U.S. Department of Justice and the work of scholars in the field, than from a sea change in commerce clause doctrine handed down by the Supreme Court.

NORMAN ABRAMS
(2000)

(SEE ALSO: *Federal Criminal Law.*)

Bibliography

SYMPOSIUM 1995 Federalization of Crime: The Roles of the Federal and State Governments in the Criminal Justice System. *Hastings Law Journal* 46:965–1338.
——— 1995 Reflections on *United States v. López. Michigan Law Review* 94:533–831.
——— 1996 The Federal Role in Criminal Law. *The Annals* 543:9–166.

LAW OF THE LAND

The phrase "law of the land" has two connotations of constitutional dimension. In general usage it refers to a HIGHER LAW than that of COMMON LAW declaration or legislative enactment. As a result of the SUPREMACY CLAUSE, the Constitution is such a higher law; it is the "supreme law of the land." In the exercise of JUDICIAL REVIEW, the SUPREME COURT claims the office of ultimate interpreter of

the Constitution. It has thus become commonplace to think of decisions of the Court as the law of the land.

A second connotation has a specialized meaning that reaches far back into English history and leaves its indelible mark on American constitutional law. In 1215, the barons of England forced King John to sign MAGNA CARTA, pledging his observance of obligations owed to them in return for their fealty to him. Among the provisions was one that declared (in translation from the Latin): "No freeman shall be taken or imprisoned or dispossessed or outlawed or banished, or in any way destroyed, nor will we go upon him, nor send upon him, except by the judgment of his peers, or by the law of the land." Magna Carta was necessarily a feudal document, but this provision was so worded that it retained meaning long after feudalism gave way to the modern constitutional state.

The term "law of the land" consequently continued in English usage, representing that body of FUNDAMENTAL LAW to which appeal was made against any oppression by the sovereign, whether procedural or substantive. By 1354 there had appeared an alternate formulation, "due process of law." In his *Second Institute of the Laws of England* (1642), Sir EDWARD COKE asserted that "law of the land" and "due process of law" possessed interchangeable meanings; nevertheless, the older version was not thereby supplanted. The PETITION OF RIGHT (1628) played no favorites with the two terms, demanding "that freemen be imprisoned or detained only by the law of the land, or by due process of law and not by the king's special command, without any charge."

In the politically creative period after Independence, American statesmen preferred "law of the land" to "due process," apparently because of its historic association with Magna Carta. All eight of the early state CONSTITUTIONS incorporating the guarantee in full or partial form employed the term "law of the land"; and the same was true of the NORTHWEST ORDINANCE (1787). The first appearance of "due process of law" in American organic law occurred in the Fifth Amendment to the United States Constitution (1791). But that switch of usage did not displace "law of the land." Throughout the nineteenth century state constitutions and state courts spoke in one voice or the other, or even both. As of 1903 a listing by THOMAS M. COOLEY of state constitutions incorporating the legacy from Magna Carta showed "law of the land" outrunning "due process of law." The trend subsequently has been to the latter phrase; yet a 1980 count found eleven states still expressing the guarantee as "law of the land."

The Glorious Revolution of 1688, embodying the political theory that parliamentary enactment was the practical equivalent of the "law of the land," presented a dilemma in interpretation when the versions of the guarantee were introduced into American thought and incorporated into most American constitutions. Legislative supremacy was unacceptable in the New World; the American view was that when sovereignty changed hands the English concept of limitations upon the crown now applied to the legislative as well as the executive branch. It followed that to construe the guarantee as forbidding deprivation of life, liberty, or property except by legislative enactment would be to render its protection meaningless. The puzzlement of American judges is understandable; only in the latter part of the nineteenth century had the concept been fully disentangled from the related concepts of regularized legislative process and SEPARATION OF POWERS.

The guarantee inherited from Magna Carta is unusual among constitutional limitations. On its face it is not absolute but conditional. The government may not act against persons except by the law of the land or by due process. The thrust is arguably procedural, suggesting original intent may have been to guarantee the protection of a trial. But it can carry substantive meanings as well; those meanings emerged early and had fully developed in England by the late seventeenth century.

Although the wording and position of the state constitutional guarantees varied—some using "law of the land," others "due process of law"; some appending the guarantee to a list of procedural rights, others making it a separate provision—the variation made little difference in judicial response at the procedural level. Not so, however, with respect to substantive content. Where, as in the constitutions of the Carolinas, Illinois, Maryland, and Tennessee, the wording was close to a literal translation of Magna Carta, the guarantee was extended to VESTED RIGHTS, independently of the criminal provisions of the procedural connotation. On the other hand, Connecticut and Rhode Island courts sustained PROHIBITION laws in the 1850s, holding that the phrase "due process of law" in their state constitutions was so enmeshed with entitlements of the criminally accused as to preclude inclusion of substantive right. A third series of cases, from Massachusetts, New Hampshire, New York, and Pennsylvania, read substantive content into the guarantee despite close interrelation with procedural protections. WYNEHAMER V. NEW YORK (1856) requires special consideration. In that case the state's highest court invalidated a prohibition law, insofar as it destroyed property rights in existing liquor stocks, resting its decision on separate constitutional guarantees of both "due process" and "law of the land." Contrary to the opinion of some scholars, *Wynehamer* was not overruled by *Metropolitan Board v. Barrie* (1866); the former case applied to a law with retroactive application, the latter to one that was purely prospective.

The Fifth Amendment associates "due process" with other constitutional guarantees clearly procedural in char-

acter, and separates the guarantee of due process from the RIGHT AGAINST SELF-INCRIMINATION only by a comma. Yet in major decisions, DRED SCOTT V. SANDFORD (1857), *Hepburn v. Griswold* (1870), and *Adair v. United States* (1908), the Supreme Court found substantive content in the clause.

In the FOURTEENTH AMENDMENT, due process is not linked to criminal procedure protections, but resembles those state constitutional provisions that had been held in state courts to have substantive content. However, the Supreme Court has disregarded the distinction between the two due process clauses in the federal Constitution. The Court has been abetted by numerous COMMENTATORS ON THE CONSTITUTION who, intent on denying the substantive element in due process, have ignored or misinterpreted the history of state constitutional guarantees of "due process" and "law of the land." The freedom from procedural connotation of Fourteenth Amendment due process made easier the path of substantive content from dissent in the SLAUGHTERHOUSE CASES (1873), to reception in *Chicago, Milwaukee & St. Paul Railway Company v. Minnesota,* (1890), to full embrace in LOCHNER V. NEW YORK (1905). The Court's acceptance of the INCORPORATION DOCTRINE, with consequent reading into the Fourteenth Amendment of the various procedural protections enumerated in the BILL OF RIGHTS, largely equates the content of the two due process clauses. This development has written the final chapter in the reinterpretation of "law of the land."

FRANK R. STRONG
(1986)

Bibliography

HOWARD, A. E. DICK 1968 *The Road from Runnymede: Magna Carta and Constitutionalism in America.* Charlottesville: University Press of Virginia.

REMBAR, CHARLES 1980 *The Law of the Land: The Evolution of Our Legal System.* New York: Simon and Schuster.

LEARY v. UNITED STATES
395 U.S. 6 (1969)

Timothy Leary, a celebrated 1960s connoisseur of mind-altering substances, was found in possession of marijuana and convicted of (1) failure to pay the federal marijuana tax; and (2) transportation and concealment of marijuana, knowing it had been illegally imported into the country. A unanimous Supreme Court held both convictions unconstitutional. Paying the tax would have incriminated Leary under state law; his omission to pay was justified by his RIGHT AGAINST SELF-INCRIMINATION. His other conviction had rested on a statutory presumption that a person in possession of marijuana knew it had been illegally imported. This presumption was irrational; much marijuana was grown in the United States. The presumption thus violated PROCEDURAL DUE PROCESS.

KENNETH L. KARST
(1986)

LEAST RESTRICTIVE MEANS TEST

When the Supreme Court, in reviewing the constitutionality of legislation, uses the permissive RATIONAL BASIS standard, it demands only that a law be a rational means for achieving a legitimate governmental purpose. When the STANDARD OF REVIEW is more exacting, however, the Court looks more closely at the legislative choice of means, insisting on more than some minimal showing of rationality. In a SEX DISCRIMINATION case, for example, the legislation must be "substantially related" to achieving some important governmental purpose; when STRICT SCRUTINY is the appropriate standard of review, the law must be "necessary" to achieving a COMPELLING STATE INTEREST. However such a heightened standard of review may be phrased, it aims at providing as much protection for constitutional values and interests as may be consistent with the accomplishment of legislative goals. One commonly used formulation of this aim is the Court's insistence that legislation be the "least restrictive means" for attaining the ends the legislature seeks—that is, least restrictive on such constitutionally protected interests as the FREEDOM OF SPEECH, or equality, or the free flow of INTERSTATE COMMERCE.

Some commentators have urged the Supreme Court to use a similar analysis in testing the reasonableness of legislative means even under the "rational basis" standard of review, as in cases involving challenges to ECONOMIC REGULATION. Thus far, however, the Court has employed "least restrictive means" reasoning only when it has consciously used a more demanding standard of review. Thus, in DEAN MILK COMPANY V. MADISON (1951), the Court struck down an ordinance specifying that milk sold in the city as "pasteurized" be pasteurized at an approved plant within five miles of the city center. The Court emphasized that "reasonable nondiscriminatory alternatives" were available to serve the city's health interests. (See STATE REGULATION OF COMMERCE.) And in *Shelton v. Tucker* (1960) the Court invalidated a law requiring every Arkansas teacher to file an annual affidavit listing every organization to which he or she had belonged or made contributions within five years. The Court agreed that Arkansas had a strong interest in teacher fitness, but said the legislature's sweeping intrusion into associational privacy "must be viewed in the light of less drastic means for achieving the same basic purpose." A narrower inquiry, presumably, would serve that purpose.

Both decisions illustrate how the "least restrictive means" formula can help a court avoid casting aspersions on legislative motive. (See Legislation; Legislative Intent.) Madison's ordinance might have been designed to capture the pasteurization business; Arkansas undoubtedly was seeking to expose and dismiss teachers who were members of the NAACP. In neither case did the Supreme Court openly question the legitimacy of the legislative purpose; taking the government's statement of objective at face value, it said, in effect, "There are ways you could have accomplished that without intruding on constitutionally protected ground." One excellent reason for heightening the standard of review—and thus for insisting on "least restrictive means"—is the suspicion that legislators have acted for questionable purposes. (See SUSPECT CLASSIFICATION.)

KENNETH L. KARST
(1986)

Bibliography

NOTE 1969 Less Drastic Means and the First Amendment. *Yale Law Journal* 78:464–474.

LEBRON v. NATIONAL RAILROAD PASSENGER CORP.
513 U.S. 374 (1995)

In *Lebron v. National Railroad Passenger Corp.*, the Supreme Court held that the National Railroad Passenger Corporation (Amtrak) must comply with the Constitution. Amtrak is a CORPORATION created by federal law, with a governing board appointed by the President and it receives substantial federal funding. However, the statute creating Amtrak declares that it "will not be an agency or establishment of the United States government."

Michael Lebron signed a contract to display an advertisement on a huge billboard—about 103 feet long and 10 feet high—at Amtrak's Penn Station in New York City. Lebron's advertisement was a photomontage criticizing the Coors beer company's conservative political activities and especially its involvement in Central America. When Amtrak refused to allow display of the advertisement, Lebron sued, claiming infringement on his FIRST AMENDMENT right of FREEDOM OF SPEECH.

The Supreme Court ruled that Amtrak is the government for STATE ACTION purposes. Justice ANTONIN SCALIA, writing for the majority, declared: "We hold that where, as here, the Government creates a corporation by special law, for the furtherance of governmental objectives, and retains for itself permanent authority to appoint a majority of the directors of that corporation, the corporation is part of the Government for purposes of the First Amendment."

The Court emphasized that Amtrak was created by a federal statute to serve the national interest of providing railroad passenger service.

Lebron is important in that it makes it clear that government-created corporations such as the Overseas Private Investment Corporation, the Communications Satellite Corporation (COMSAT), the Corporation for Public Broadcasting, and the Legal Services Corporation, are part of the government and thus the Constitution applies to their activities.

ERWIN CHEMERINSKY
(2000)

LECOMPTON CONSTITUTION

In June 1857 less than thirty percent of registered voters in Kansas Territory elected a CONSTITUTIONAL CONVENTION dominated by proslavery delegates. Meeting in Lecompton, the convention drew up a constitution preparatory for statehood that guaranteed the rights of owners of slaves in the territory, excluded free blacks, and submitted to a REFERENDUM the question whether the constitution should be accepted with or without a clause prohibiting the importation of slaves into Kansas (rather than a referendum on the constitution as a whole). Viewing this as a travesty of his principle of territorial SOVEREIGNTY, Illinois Senator STEPHEN A. DOUGLAS broke with the administration of JAMES BUCHANAN, which was pressuring Congress to accept the Lecompton constitution, and led the struggle against it. In three referenda on the constitution, Kansas voted first to accept the constitution with slavery (6,226 to 569, with free-state voters abstaining), then to reject the constitution entirely (10,226 to 166 with proslavery voters abstaining), then finally to reject it entirely again (11,300 to 1,788).

The struggle over the Lecompton constitution left Kansas a territory until 1861, dissipated the influence of the Buchanan administration, drove Douglas into opposition, and destroyed the capacity of the Democratic party to serve as a unifying transsectional force.

WILLIAM M. WIECEK
(1986)

Bibliography

JOHANSES, ROBERT W.   1973   *Stephen A. Douglas.* New York: Oxford University Press.

LEE, REX EDWIN
(1935–1996)

United States SOLICITOR GENERAL, educator, and one of the nation's foremost Supreme Court advocates, Rex E. Lee was born in Los Angeles on February 27, 1935. He was undergraduate student body president at Brigham Young University and first in his class at the University of Chicago Law School. After law school, he served as a law clerk to Supreme Court Justice BYRON R. WHITE.

As a public servant, Lee held the positions of Assistant U.S. Attorney General in the administration of President GERALD R. FORD and Solicitor General in the administration of President RONALD REAGAN. During his four years as Solicitor General, he Served as the chief appellate advocate for the federal government and argued a number of cases of constitutional significance, with a particular emphasis on RELIGIOUS LIBERTY, SEPARATION OF POWERS, and FEDERALISM. In total, Lee presented oral argument before the U.S. Supreme Court on fifty-nine occasions.

In 1972, at the age of thirty-seven, Lee became the founding dean of the J. Reuben Clark Law School at Brigham Young University. After serving in the federal government and practicing law in the firm of Sidley & Austin, Lee returned to Brigham Young University where he became its tenth president.

A man of faith, Lee served his church, The Church of Jesus Christ of Latter-Day Saints, in a number of capacities throughout his life. At the young age of nineteen, he worked as a missionary in Mexico. Later in life, he served as a lay leader of congregations in the Washington, D.C. area and in Utah. Probably his most significant church service occurred while he served as law school dean and university president for Brigham Young University, the nation's largest church-owned university.

During his life, Lee wrote a number of books and essays on subjects ranging from law to religion. Two of his books, *A Lawyer Looks at the Constitution* (1981) and *A Lawyer Looks at the Equal Rights Amendment* (1980) provide insight into his moderate conservative philosophy of government. Lee also published a number of essays on religion and a book entitled *What Do Mormons Believe* (1992).

Lee had a family of seven children with his wife, Janet. He often depended on his family for support as he suffered the effects of cancer during the final eight years of his life. On March 11, 1996, Lee died after a ten-month battle with pneumonia. It was reported that from his hospital bed before his death he was preparing to give his sixtieth oral argument before the Supreme Court.

MICHAEL W. MCCONNELL
(2000)

Bibliography

FRIED, CHARLES   1991   *Order and Law: Arguing the Reagan Revolution.* New York: Simon & Schuster.
LEE, REX E.   1980   *A Lawyer Looks at the Equal Rights Amendment.* Provo, Utah: Brigham Young University Press.

—— 1981 *A Lawyer Looks at the Constitution.* Provo, Utah: Brigham Young University Press.

LEE, RICHARD HENRY
(1732–1794)

Educated in England, Richard Henry Lee practiced law in his native Virginia and became a justice of the peace in 1757. The next year he was elected to the House of Burgesses where his first speech was in favor of a measure to check the spread of SLAVERY. Lee was a leader of opposition to parliamentary taxation of the colonies and wrote the protest of the House of Burgesses against the Sugar Act (1764). When the royal governor dissolved the House of Burgesses in 1774, Lee introduced a resolution, adopted by the rump of the house, calling for a continental congress. As a delegate to the FIRST CONTINENTAL CONGRESS Lee proposed formation of committees of correspondence (a plan he originated with PATRICK HENRY and THOMAS JEFFERSON) and adoption of the continental ASSOCIATION. In June 1776 Lee made the original motions in the Continental Congress for a DECLARATION OF INDEPENDENCE, confederation, and seeking of foreign alliances. He later advocated Virginia's cession of western territorial claims in order to facilitate ratification of the ARTICLES OF CONFEDERATION; and, in 1784, he was elected President of the United States in Congress Assembled.

Lee was chosen as a delegate to the CONSTITUTIONAL CONVENTION OF 1787 but declined appointment, citing conflict with his responsibilities as a member of Congress. When the new Constitution was submitted to Congress, Lee opposed it on the ground that the convention had exceeded its mandate. Seeing that he could not block the proposal, he attempted, but failed, to have Congress add a BILL OF RIGHTS (drafted by GEORGE MASON).

Lee was a leading opponent of RATIFICATION OF THE CONSTITUTION. His seventeen "Letters from the Federal Farmer," widely printed in newspapers, were among the most influential of the various ANTI-FEDERALIST writings. In the letters Lee presented a wide-ranging critique of the new Constitution: it was consolidationist, not federal, and would rob the states of their SOVEREIGNTY; it was aristocratic, or even monarchical, in tendency, not republican; the coexistence of state and federal courts would lead inevitably to conflict; the JUDICIAL POWER OF THE UNITED STATES was so broadly drawn as to permit foreigners and citizens of other states to sue a state in federal court; and, most important, there was no bill of rights. Lee argued and voted against ratification in the Virginia convention of 1788.

Lee was one of Virginia's original United States senators (1789–1792). He was chairman of the committee that drafted the JUDICIARY ACT OF 1789 and floor leader in the Senate for the Bill of Rights. Later in his senatorial career he became a supporter of the Federalist party and the economic program of ALEXANDER HAMILTON. A fervent opponent of slavery, Lee himself held about three dozen slaves.

DENNIS J. MAHONEY
(1986)

LEE, UNITED STATES v.
455 U.S. 252 (1982)

Members of the Amish religion object, on religious grounds, to paying taxes or receiving benefits under the SOCIAL SECURITY ACT. An Amish employer of Amish workers claimed a constitutional right to refuse to pay Social Security taxes. The Supreme Court unanimously rejected that claim. Chief Justice WARREN E. BURGER, for the Court, accepted STRICT SCRUTINY as the appropriate STANDARD OF REVIEW in cases involving RELIGIOUS LIBERTY, but concluded that the government had established that mandatory participation was necessary to achieving the "overriding governmental interest" in maintaining the Social Security system. In a concurring opinion, Justice JOHN PAUL STEVENS argued against the strict scrutiny standard, saying that claimants of special religious exemptions from laws of general applicability must demonstrate "unique" reasons for being exempted—a standard that would be nearly impossible to meet.

KENNETH L. KARST
(1986)

LEE v. WEISMAN
505 U.S. 577 (1992)

The principal of a public junior high school in Providence, Rhode Island, invited a clergyman, a rabbi, to give opening and closing prayers as part of the school's graduation ceremony. Although the rabbi composed the prayers himself, the officials gave him guidelines and advised that the prayers should be "nonsectarian." When a student challenged the constitutionality of this practice, the Supreme Court held, 5–4, that the school violated the ESTABLISHMENT CLAUSE of the FIRST AMENDMENT by informally pressuring students to participate in a state-sponsored and state-controlled religious exercise.

Before *Weisman*, it was widely thought that the appointment of several "conservative" Justices might lead the REHNQUIST COURT to overrule WARREN COURT decisions and permit school-sponsored prayers or other religious exercises as long as the school did not directly coerce anyone to participate. *Weisman* did not decide the broad question of whether noncoercive exercises would ever be an unconstitutional ESTABLISHMENT OF RELIGION. Instead, the opinion (authored by Justice ANTHONY M. KENNEDY, an appointee of President RONALD REAGAN) held that the school placed "subtle" coercive pressure on students to participate in prayer. The graduation ceremony, though formally voluntary, was important enough to students that they should not have to miss it in order to avoid exposure to prayer. And although the audience was only required to stand silently during the prayers, the Court said that a "reasonable dissenter" might feel this forced her to signify her approval of them.

Weisman showed that even those who limit the establishment clause's prohibitions to government "coercion" can disagree on the meaning of that term. Justice ANTONIN SCALIA, dissenting, argued that only coercion "by threat of penalty" should be unconstitutional; the majority's broader notion of "psychological" coercion, he argued, would require forbidding the Pledge of Allegiance in schools as well (since the state cannot compel citizens to endorse political ideas either).

The broad coercion analysis suggested that most official religious exercises by public schools would be forbidden. The majority also looked beyond issues of coercion, stating that with religious ideas, unlike political or social ideas, "government is not a prime participant" in debate and should remain uninvolved. However, *Weisman* did leave open the possible permissibility of religious acts sponsored by government in settings that arguably are less important or pressure-laden than a high school graduation, such as a courthouse open to all citizens, or even a high school football game.

THOMAS C. BERG
(2000)

Bibliography

CONKLE, DANIEL O. 1993 Lemon Lives. *Case Western Reserve Law Review* 43:865–882.
GREENE, ABNER S. 1995 The Pledge of Allegiance Problem. *Fordham Law Review* 64:451–490.
PAULSEN, MICHAEL STOKES 1993 Lemon is Dead. *Case Western Reserve Law Review* 43:795–863.

LEGAL CULTURE

The expression "legal culture" refers to opinions, attitudes, values, and expectations with regard to law and legal institutions. Every man and woman in society has at least some opinions on this subject—about judges, courts, the Supreme Court, or lawyers—but the expression, as the word "culture" implies, refers not so much to individuals as to generalizations about the opinions and values of members of some distinct group, class, category, or jurisdiction. One can speak about the legal culture of men as opposed to women, blacks as opposed to whites, or of salespeople, teachers, drug addicts, or people who live on farms. It may also be possible to make statistical generalizations about particular countries, so that it may make sense to talk about American legal culture as opposed to Portuguese or Korean legal culture.

One can distinguish between an "external" and an "internal" legal culture. The internal legal culture is the legal culture of those members of society "inside" the legal system, so to speak—that is, those who perform specialized legal tasks, for example, lawyers and judges. The legal culture of everybody else is external legal culture.

Concepts of legal culture are, or ought to be, significant for the understanding of constitutional history and in explaining how constitutional doctrine gets made. Political and social movements always provide the motor force for constitution making and for constitutional change; the decisions of high courts, which create the fabric of constitutional law, are always the product of concrete lawsuits, in which real parties with real social and economic interests are contending. In both cases, purposes, goals, and ideals of litigators and other actors (and of lawyers and judges) are the immediate cause of both stasis or change. Hence, legal culture, it can be argued, is what creates constitutional law and gives meaning and life to the constitutional system.

It is obvious that the texture of constitutional law has changed radically in the course of American history; yet the text of the Constitution itself has been extremely durable, not to say sluggish. The leading cases of modern constitutional law are or pretend to be "interpretations" or glosses on the post-CIVIL WAR amendments, which have not been altered in over a century; the BILL OF RIGHTS; or the text of the original Constitution, which is now some two centuries old. A scholar of 1870 or 1880 who woke from a century's sleep would simply not recognize today's body of constitutional doctrine; current EQUAL PROTECTION doctrine, for example, would be totally beyond his or her comprehension. Yet much of the standard work on both CONSTITUTIONAL THEORY and constitutional history has a strongly normative flavor, and it fails to come to grips with the powerful forces that have turned old doctrines topsy-turvy and pulled new doctrines into existence like rabbits from a magician's hat.

The radical changes in constitutional doctrine imply radical changes in internal legal culture; but these in turn are reflexes of radical changes in external legal culture, the culture of the educated community, of business and political leaders, and indeed, of the public at large. The Constitution, in fact, is always interpreted (and necessarily so) in the light of ruling ideas of the times. The Justices may make use of general social norms either consciously or unconsciously; because of the standardized and formalistic style in which Supreme Court decisions are written, it is not easy to know the level of awareness of the Justices or the way in which they conceive of their judicial role.

In the broadest sense, studies of constitutional doctrine and constitutional history that are sensitive to social context are studies of legal culture, although they do not necessarily use this term. Other studies deal with American culture and the Constitution more explicitly: Michael Kammen, for example, has written a history of the meaning and imagery of the Constitution in American culture—an exploration, among other things, of the symbolic importance of the Constitution in American politics and the cult of the Constitution as a "sacred" document.

Constitutional doctrine itself is a reflection of legal culture, but it would be naive to assume that the general public or any particular segment of it share the same views as the justices who enunciate legal doctrine. There has been some research on public attitudes toward CIVIL LIBERTIES and the Bill of Rights; such studies are necessarily studies of the congruence (or lack of congruence) of external and internal legal culture. The most important recent study (by Herbert McClosky and Alida Brill, in 1983) found that the general public tends to agree strongly with the general ideas behind the Bill of Rights, but on many specific issues, public opinion differs from the current state of doctrine—and from the views of legal and political elites. These differences tilt in a particular direction. The general public is less "liberal" than the Court and less "liberal" than legal and political elites on such issues as whether PORNOGRAPHY can be banned, whether atheists should be allowed to teach or hold public office, or how far to carry the SEPARATION OF CHURCH AND STATE.

So-called impact studies are also relevant to the study of legal culture. These are studies of the ways in which decisions of the Supreme Court, or other courts, are received, used, followed, evaded, or flouted by the public, or some particular part of the public. Legal culture is not only the source of doctrine; it monitors the reaction to doctrine and to specific decisions of the courts. There is a sizeable literature, for example, on reactions to the Supreme Court's decisions barring prayers from public schools. In the broadest sense, much of the vast literature on the controversy over ABORTION or on school DESEGREGATION is impact literature and, hence, relevant to the role of legal culture in the constitutional system. But there has not been much success as yet in framing general theories about impact or about the role of legal culture in producing compliant or noncompliant behavior.

The neglect of legal culture by constitutional scholars has undoubtedly impoverished the understanding of constitutional law. Normative arguments are tossed back and forth on many crucial issues: for example, what ways of "interpreting" the Constitution are legitimate and what ways are illegitimate. "Originalists" claim that the duty of judges is to seek out the ORIGINAL INTENT of the Framers; judges have no legitimate right to read their own values into the Constitution. Such arguments, rhetorically speaking, put the issue very starkly as a kind of either-or position. Apparently, the only alternative to STRICT CONSTRUCTION is a situation in which judges act arbitrarily, according to whim, and simply spin constitutional doctrines out of their heads. In a system of CHECKS AND BALANCES, where are the checks and balances on the power of the Supreme Court Justices to create law out of thin air?

One answer (there are many others) is that the Justices are constrained by internal and external legal cultures. The internal legal culture is inescapably inside the heads of the Justices. The Justices are lawyers, trained in a particular tradition. The internal legal culture has its own powerful symbols, its own language and etiquette; and the Justices operate in this context. Of course, each Justice is an individual man or woman; each has his or her own take on the internal legal culture. But this culture sets boundaries and limits within which the Court, of necessity, does its work.

The external legal culture is an even more powerful curb, in fact, if not in theory. The concept of legal culture assumes that judges never "invent" doctrine; that in any given period, the general legal culture sets limits, defines boundaries, and establishes a range of opinions no less than does the internal legal culture (the legal tradition). It is out of the question for a Supreme Court Justice today, no matter how "conservative," to be as retrograde on racial issues as the most "liberal" judge of the 1880s. The whole spectrum of opinion has shifted in the direction of racial equality, and the corresponding interpretation of the meaning of equal protection has shifted accordingly. The social context is the source of the norms that mold general opinion on matters of race. The norms change over time as context changes. The Justices today live in a world of computers, gene-splicing, and communication satellites, and their views are profoundly affected by the world all about them. They also live in a society dedicated more deeply to individual rights and to race and gender equality than the world of their predecessors. The study of legal culture is a study of this world, and those who stress this factor believe it is one of the best ways to understand where the Court has been, where it is, and where it is going.

LAWRENCE M. FRIEDMAN
(1992)

Bibliography
FRIEDMAN, LAWRENCE M. 1975 *The Legal System: A Social Science Perspective.* New York: Russell Sage Foundation.

—— 1990 *The Republic of Choice: Law, Authority, and Culture*. Cambridge, Mass.: Harvard University Press.

KAMMEN, MICHAEL   1986   *A Machine that Would Go of Itself: The Constitution in American Culture*. New York: Alfred A. Knopf.

McCLOSKY, HERBERT and BRILL, ALIDA   1983   *Dimensions of Tolerance: What Americans Believe About Civil Liberties*. New York: Russell Sage Foundation.

MUIR, WILLIAM K., JR.   1967   *Prayer in the Public Schools: Law and Attitude Change*. Chicago: University of Chicago Press.

UROFSKY, MELVIN I.   1988   *A March of Liberty: A Constitutional History of the United States*. New York: Alfred A. Knopf.

LEGAL POSITIVISM

See: Philosophy and the Constitution

LEGAL PROCESS

The legal process school of legal theory was a movement among legal scholars beginning in the 1950s and continuing through the end of the 1960s, a movement that represented an effort to craft a comprehensive theory of legal decisionmaking, especially in the public law area, to combat LEGAL REALISM and the doctrinal shifts reflected in the jurisprudence of the WARREN COURT. The foundation of this work was laid in a series of influential books and articles, most notably HENRY M. HART, JR., and Albert Sacks's magnum opus *The Legal Process: Basic Problems in the Making and Application of Law* (1958).

Although the sources of the legal process school are complex, the basic principles grew out of public law scholars' critiques of modern legal thought in both its theoretical and doctrinal aspects. Out of the post-war period came a skepticism about legal positivism, that is, the view that law represents nothing more nor less than the executable commands of the sovereign, and a skepticism about NATURAL LAW theory. Scholars working within the legal process tradition were determined to substitute both for positivism and natural law theory a theory of legal decisionmaking which would help students, scholars, and judges focus not on the outcomes of legal decisions but on the *processes* of legal institutions, especially courts. Moreover, in the period of the late 1950s and 1960s, these same scholars grew ever more concerned with the direction of the Warren Court's decisions. Critics of the era described the Warren Court as substituting a "jurisprudence of values" for the previously more restrained and moderate patterns of decisions in the NEW DEAL era. The problem, as these critics viewed it, was that the Court was writing particular ideological values and preferences into DOCTRINE, thus leaving the Court vulnerable to the essential legal realist charge that judicial decisionmaking was unprincipled, subjective, and chaotic.

In response both to the post-war angst about positivistic and natural law jurisprudence and to the perceived subjectivity of Warren Court jurisprudence, there emerged a cadre of legal academics who set out to rescue judicial decisionmaking from these threats. The result was the legal process movement of this era. While the legal process school describes a large and diverse collection of academic agendas, the school can be described as a project following four basic tenets: (1) a focus on neutral principles as guides to judicial decisionmaking, (2) a focus on reasoned elaboration as a method of adjudication, (3) a focus on comparative institutional competence in considering which institutions and processes ought to be employed in legal decisionmaking, and (4) a focus on restrained innovation in the implementation and development of law and legal reasoning.

The focus on neutral principles grew out of the legal realists' critique of judicial decisionmaking. In its strong form, legal realists decried the courts' tendencies toward inconsistent, unprincipled decisionmaking. Legal reasoning was, critics argued, at least unpredictable and at most nihilistic and driven by judges' personal ideologies. Scholars working in the legal process tradition, most notably Herbert Wechsler in his influential article "Toward Neutral Principles of Constitutional Law," reacted decisively to legal realists' somewhat fatalistic view by offering the insight that there are durable legal principles worth following. These principles are drawn from various sources including legal texts, earlier decisions applied through STARE DECISIS, and general legal principles. Moreover, the task of the judge in adjudication is to recover these principles and to apply them in a neutral, principled way.

Neil Duxbury argues that this strain in legal process theory echoes classical legal thought in its rigid adherence to principled decisionmaking; therefore, he suggests, there is a fundamental connection between Langdellian formalism and process theory. Upon closer reflection, however, the differences outweigh the similarities. Whereas Langdellian classical legal thought emphasized logically coherent decisionmaking and syllogistic reasoning, the emphasis in legal process theory is on reason and neutral principles and not on the uncritical application of logical reasoning to legal disputes. Process theorists were dissatisfied with Langdell and his disciples on the one hand and with Karl Llewelyn and his fellow legal realists on the other.

Related to this emphasis on neutral principles is a focus on reasoned elaboration in adjudication. Process theorists maintained a scrupulous faith in reason. They favored a system of law in which legal institutions would make and apply law in a deeply analytical, transparent, and purposive way. Here the key intellectual figure was Lon Fuller.

In analyzing the "forms and limits of adjudication" and in tracing through the judicial reasoning process with the use of his famous hypothetical, the "Case of the Spelunchean Explorers," Fuller brought to life his conclusion that courts were well situated to resolve cases and further the sound development of law through fidelity to reason. This system of reasoned elaboration was juxtaposed against what process theorists regarded as the excesses of the jurisprudence of the era, especially the "incoherent" decisions of the Warren Court. For the most part, these theorists demurred on questions concerning the desirability of the results reached in cases such as BROWN V. BOARD OF EDUCATION (1954), BAKER V. CARR (1962), and MIRANDA V. ARIZONA (1966), decisions that obviously touched ideological nerves in the body politic. Rather, process theorists criticized these and other decisions for failing to accord with either neutral, principled decisionmaking or the recommended process of reasoned elaboration.

A third tenet of process theory is a focus on comparative institutional competence. In their legal process materials, Hart and Sacks offered through various extended examples and commentary an approach to legal reasoning and decisionmaking in the context of adjudication, LEGISLATION, and administration. Hart and Sacks began with the premise that law is made and applied in many different institutional contexts; they developed an analysis not only for the use of courts, legislatures, and ADMINISTRATIVE AGENCIES in carrying out their functions, but also for decisionmakers in assessing and evaluating the strengths and weaknesses of different institutions. A key assumption in this normative enterprise is that the legislature—the key lawmaker in a democratic polity—is made up of "reasonable persons pursuing reasonable aims reasonably." From this assumption, process theorists derived a structure of circumspect institutional power in matters concerning, for example, STATUTORY INTERPRETATION and the development of the law through COMMON LAW reasoning. They insisted on attention to the question of which institution is best suited to decide a particular dispute. Beyond offering rich comparative institutional analysis, perhaps the main contribution of Hart and Sacks's legal process enterprise is the intellectual spotlight it shines on the multiple sources and functions of law in modern society. In this respect, it provides a bridge to the law and society movement that emerged somewhat later as a significant enterprise emphasizing, among other things, the role of law in action and the complementary and competing institutions of legal decisionmaking in the modern era.

A fourth and final tenet of legal process theory is restrained innovation in the making and application of law. Process scholars emphasized the limits of adjudication and also the limited capacities of all legal institutions to move forward with legal change. In his influential Holmes lectures, *The Bill of Rights* (1958), Judge LEARNED HAND built upon the foundations of process theory in counseling caution on the part of judges in deciding constitutional cases. Hand's message was that courts ought to be extremely circumspect in the face of social and political change. Restrained innovation is counseled not merely by a particularly narrow conception of the judge's proper role but also by the anticipation of adverse effects of unnecessarily ambitious judicial creativity. In offering faith in reason and attentiveness to process values, scholars working in the legal process tradition hoped to elide some of the more serious consequences that, in their view, plagued more dynamic, expansive approaches to legal interpretation.

The legal process movement came under substantial criticism in the 1970s and 1980s. Scholars noted that there was an inadequate positive or empirical basis for process theory. In particular, the assumption of reasonable persons pursuing reasonable aims reasonably was regarded as quaint and unrealistic. Moreover, process theorists were criticized as having a too-crabbed picture of law as an instrument of social engineering. Finally, prominent critics of process theory, such as Ronald Dworkin on the right and the CRITICAL LEGAL STUDIES movement on the left, maintained that process theory ultimately masks substantive outcomes. The test for the utility of the theory, therefore, was whether it produced favorable substantive ends.

Perhaps the principal impact of the legal process movement was on the judges and Justices who came to the bench having been influenced by their legal process–inspired teachers in the 1960s and 1970s. The emphasis on restrained innovation and on reasoned elaboration is especially notable in the Supreme Court's contemporary constitutional and statutory interpretation jurisprudence. At the same time, these proceduralist patterns of restraint are in tension with strains of both liberal and conservative activism in modern judicial decisionmaking.

DANIEL B. RODRIGUEZ
(2000)

Bibliography

DUXBURY, NEIL 1995 *Patterns of American Jurisprudence*. Oxford, England: Clarendon Press.

FULLER, LON L. 1949 The Case of the Spelunchean Explorers. *Harvard Law Review* 62:616–645.

——— 1978 The Forms and Limits of Adjudication. *Harvard Law Review* 92:353–409.

HAND, LEARNED 1958 *The Bill of Rights*. Cambridge, Mass.: Harvard University Press.

HART, HENRY M., JR. and SACKS, ALBERT M. 1994 *The Legal Process: Basic Problems in the Making and Application of Law*, William Eskridge, Jr. and Philip Frickey, eds. St. Paul, Minn.: Foundation Press.

PELLER, GARY   1988   Neutral Principles in the 1950's. *University of Michigan Journal of Law Reform* 21:561–622.

VETTER, JAN   1983   Postwar Legal Scholarship on Judicial Decision Making. *Journal of Legal Education* 33:412–423.

WECHSLER, HERBERT   1959   Toward Neutral Principles of Constitutional Law. *Harvard Law Review* 73:1–35.

WHITE, G. EDWARD   1973   The Evolution of Reasoned Elaboration: Jurisprudential Criticism and Social Change. *Virginia Law Review* 59:279–302.

LEGAL REALISM

Legal realism was the most significant movement that emerged within American jurisprudence during the 1920s and 1930s. Numerous factors conditioned this development, including pragmatism, SOCIOLOGICAL JURISPRUDENCE, and certain ideas of Justice OLIVER WENDELL HOLMES. The legal realists were not, however, an organized or highly unified group of thinkers. Their concepts had diverse sources, their work branched out in many directions, and their responses to particular issues often varied. The substantial differences between Judge JEROME N. FRANK and Karl N. Llewellyn illustrate these tendencies. Even so, these men and the other realists shared a number of distinctive attitudes and ideas.

The term "legal realism" signifies the basic thrust of the movement, which was to uncover and to explain legal realities. This effort reflects the allegation that some of the most cherished beliefs of lawyers are myths or fictions. The major purpose of the realists' provocative criticisms of these beliefs was not, however, to undermine the American legal system. Rather, it was to facilitate development of an accurate understanding of the nature, interpretation, operation, and effects of law. The realists insisted that achievement of this goal was essential for intelligent reform of legal rules, doctrines, and practices.

This outlook contributed to the realists' intense dissatisfaction with prevailing modes of legal education and scholarship. Both were under the spell of the case method pioneered by Christopher Columbus Langdell, the influential dean of the Harvard Law School from 1870 to 1895. He conceived of legal science as a small number of fundamental principles derived from study of relatively few cases. This conception was anathema to the realists, most of whom taught at leading American law schools. Their objective was to reform and to supplement, however, rather than to discard, the case method. The changes they advocated included focus on the *behavior* of judges and other officials, on their actual *decisions* rather than broad precepts. This emphasis was essential for the understanding of "real" instead of mere "paper" rules. The realists also urged the broadening of legal education to embrace not only the law on the books but also its administration and social impact. The development of this approach required a much closer integration of law and the social sciences than was traditional.

Some of these ideas were an outgrowth of major themes of ROSCOE POUND's sociological jurisprudence. Still, the realists tended to develop criticisms of legal orthodoxies more radical than Pound's. This tendency is apparent from both the fact-skepticism of Judge Frank and the rule-skepticism of virtually all of the realists. The first of these doctrines stresses the difficulty of predicting findings of fact by judges or jurors, while the second emphasizes the limitations of legal rules. Rule-skepticism takes various forms, one of which is the conception of law as the past or future decisions of judges or other officials. Legal rules are descriptive or predictive rather than prescriptive generalizations about their behavior. This idea stems from Justice Holmes's predictive conception of law, which is one reason for the large shadow he cast over the realist movement.

Rule-skepticism also signifies distrust of the assumption that traditional legal rules or principles are the most influential determinant of judicial decisions. Numerous considerations explain this distrust, the degree of which varied among the realists. The most important factors were: a conviction of the possibility of widely different interpretations of established legal rules and principles; a belief in the existence of competing precedents, each of which could justify conflicting decisions in most cases; an awareness of the ambiguity inherent in legal language; a perception of the rapidity of socioeconomic change; and a study of the teachings of modern psychology. This last factor also influenced the realists' critique of judicial opinions. They attacked the syllogistic reasoning of judges on the ground that it failed to explain their choice of premises, which was all-important. This failure meant that opinions were often misleading rationalizations of decisions, the real reasons for which were unstated.

Rule-skepticism is the basis of some of the most important ideas of the legal realists. Their rejection of the conventional belief that judges do or should interpret rather than make law is a significant example. That belief is untenable because judicial legislation is unavoidable. Judges frequently must choose between competing decisions or interpretations, each of which is consistent with at least some precedents, rules, or principles. Although these generalizations limit judicial freedom, judges retain a substantial amount of room to maneuver.

This analysis underlies the realists' pragmatic approach to the evaluation of law, which emphasizes its practical results or effects. Rule-skepticism also influenced their de-emphasis of legal doctrine for the purpose of explaining and predicting judicial decisions. Instead, the realists stressed the importance of such factors as the personality, attitudes, or policies of judges. A similar emphasis characterized the behavioral jurisprudence developed largely by political scientists after WORLD WAR II.

Although most of the realists did not specialize in constitutional law, their ideas facilitate understanding of the decisions of the Supreme Court. The Justices frequently must choose between conflicting interpretations of the Constitution, each of which has some legal basis. Their choices depend most basically upon their values, which may vary among Justices and may change over time. These variations help to explain disagreements among the Justices as well as changes in constitutional doctrine. Realism was also a formative influence on the legal philosophy of Justice WILLIAM O. DOUGLAS.

Despite the influence of the realists on American legal thought, the reaction to their ideas has not been uniform. In fact, large numbers of lawyers expressed varying degrees of dissatisfaction with the realist movement from its inception. If some of the concepts of the realists are unsatisfactory, others are enduring contributions to the study of law and the judicial process. Legal realism therefore warrants close scrutiny by students of constitutional law and judicial behavior.

WILFRID E. RUMBLE
(1986)

Bibliography

FRANK, JEROME 1949 Law and the Modern Mind. New York: Coward-McCann.
LLEWELLYN, KARL N. 1962 Jurisprudence: Realism in Theory and Practice. Chicago: University of Chicago Press.
RUMBLE, WILFRID E. 1968 American Legal Realism: Skepticism, Reform, and the Judicial Process. Ithaca, N.Y.: Cornell University Press.
TWINING, WILLIAM 1973 Karl Llewellyn and the Realist Movement. London: Weidenfeld & Nicolson.

LEGAL TENDER CASES

The Legal Tender Cases include the decisions in *Hepburn v. Griswold* (1870), invalidating CIVIL WAR legislation authorizing paper money, and *Knox v. Lee* (1871) and *Parker v. Davis* (1871), sustaining postwar legal tender legislation. The various decisions reflect important developments in the nation's economic history, as well as in the Supreme Court's history, concerning the judicial role in questions of political economy, the nature and scope of judicial power, and the relation of politics to judicial opinions.

The greenback legislation of 1862 was designed to facilitate the financing of the Civil War, authorizing payments in demand notes, redeemable not in gold or silver but in interest-bearing twenty-year bonds. The notes were made "lawful money and a legal tender in payment of all debts, public and private, within the United States." The Treasury issued over $400 million in paper money during the war. After 1865, as inflation grew and greenbacks depreciated, creditors demanded payment in specie or at least in paper money equivalent to the rising premium on specie.

Secretary of the Treasury SALMON P. CHASE presided over the government's wartime greenback program. His outward support for paper money only masked his deepseated hostility. In March 1864, he composed an epigram reflecting his true feelings: "When public exigencies require, Coin must become paper. When public exigencies allow, Paper must become coin." Six years later, as Chief Justice, he invalidated his previous policy.

Chase's role in the first legal tender case provoked intense partisan wrangling, both on and off the bench, and raised questions of the Chief Justice's behavior as the Court's administrative leader. The legal tender controversy had become entangled in partisan politics, as Republicans defended their greenback policy and the opposition Democrats attacked it as unconstitutional and improper. The Justices lined up on the same political grounds. (Chase and the Republicans by then were mutually alienated and the Chief Justice already was courting the Democrats in hopes of winning their presidential nomination.) In numerous state cases, judges similarly voted along party lines.

Chase apparently was determined to project the Court into the political maelstrom of monetary policy. But he did so with a precarious majority. Following the arguments in *Hepburn v. Griswold* in 1869, Republican Justices DAVID DAVIS, SAMUEL F. MILLER, and NOAH SWAYNE unhesitatingly endorsed the greenback policy. Chase, joined by Democrats NATHAN CLIFFORD, STEPHEN J. FIELD, ROBERT C. GRIER, and SAMUEL NELSON voted to invalidate the 1862 law. Grier by then was so senile that his colleagues persuaded him to resign. Chase, however, included his vote in the majority.

Meanwhile, Congress had authorized increasing the number of Justices to nine, giving President ULYSSES S. GRANT two new appointments, including Grier's replacement. On February 7, 1870, he nominated WILLIAM STRONG, who as a member of the Pennsylvania Supreme Court had supported the legal tender legislation, and JOSEPH P. BRADLEY, a railroad lawyer whose clients clearly favored the paper money scheme. On that same day, Chase defiantly announced the decision holding the law unconstitutional. The resulting charge of "court packing" against Grant and the Republicans misses the point: Presidents always seek judges who will support their political goals. In this case, Chase and his allies must bear the responsibility for the Court's embarrassment when it reversed itself a year later.

Chase's opinion invoked some of JOHN MARSHALL's best aphorisms. The Court, he insisted, must declare what the law is and not enforce any law inconsistent with the Constitution. To a point, Chase followed Marshall's MCCULLOCH V. MARYLAND (1819) discussions of IMPLIED POWERS, the NECESSARY AND PROPER clause, and the validity of laws consistent with the "letter and spirit of the Constitution." But where Marshall had appealed to the "spirit" of the Constitution to justify a BROAD CONSTRUCTION of congressional powers, Chase turned the notion on its head, construed those powers narrowly, and used the spirit to discover a limitation nowhere mentioned in the Constitution.

The Constitution, Chase maintained, was designed to establish justice, and a fundamental principle of justice was that preexisting private contracts should not be impaired by governmental action. The CONTRACT CLAUSE of the Constitution, however, applied to STATE ACTION; it said nothing regarding the federal government. But, Chase argued that the Constitution's Framers "intended that the spirit" of the contract clause would apply against all legislative bodies. His reliance on the Fifth Amendment was similarly strained. He found that the prohibition of contracts requiring specie payment in effect deprived people of their property without DUE PROCESS OF LAW; indeed, he maintained that the property was "taken" for a PUBLIC USE without the required JUST COMPENSATION.

Justice Miller's dissent pleaded for judicial restraint. He rebuked Chase's "abstract and intangible" arguments about the "spirit" of the Constitution. Following Marshall's broad reading of the necessary and proper clause, Miller suggested that "the degree of that necessity is for the legislature and not for the court to determine."

Partisan reactions to the decision were predictable. But the focused concerns for the result obscured the majority's far-reaching notions of judicial authority. Chase's bold assertions of judicial superintendence provoked virtually no negative reaction. The political and public acceptance of that doctrine gave a new legitimacy to judicial power. The nation had come a great distance from the protests against judicial excesses following DRED SCOTT V. SANDFORD (1857); indeed, Chase's opinion signaled a new chapter in judicial activism.

Significantly, the newly appointed Justice Strong, and not Miller, spoke for the majority in *Knox v. Lee* (1871) when the Court reversed itself. Strong largely followed Miller's interpretation of Congress's power and the necessity of congressional control over currency policy. But he responded only indirectly to Chase's presumptions of judicial power, contending that judges must assume the constitutionality of congressional acts and rely on congressional determination of what was "necessary and proper." He failed to rebuke Chase's reliance on the

"spirit" of the Constitution. Finally, anticipating criticism for the dramatic reversal, Strong chided Chase for having forced the earlier decision when the Court was so divided and on the verge of receiving new appointees. The Chief Justice, joined by Nelson, Clifford, and Field dissented, with the latter two offering additional, separate opinions. The dissenting remarks largely reiterated the majority views of *Hepburn v. Griswold.*

Thirteen years later, in *Juilliard v. Greenman,* the Court, with only Field dissenting, sustained the peacetime use of greenbacks. Justice HORACE GRAY not only used the occasion to reaffirm the constitutionality of greenbacks but flatly declared that the policy involved "a POLITICAL QUESTION, to be determined by Congress when the question of exigency arises, and not a judicial question, to be afterwards passed upon by the Court." A half century later, Chief Justice CHARLES EVANS HUGHES invoked *Juilliard* as the Court, in the GOLD CLAUSE CASES (1935), narrowly acquiesced in President FRANKLIN D. ROOSEVELT's decision to abandon the gold standard. What had begun as one of the most politically conscious and aggrandizing decisions by the Supreme Court ended in self-abnegation and deference to the political branches of the government.

STANLEY I. KUTLER
(1986)

Bibliography

DAM, KENNETH W.   1982   The Legal Tender Cases. *The Supreme Court Review* 1982:367–412.

FAIRMAN, CHARLES   1971   *Reconstruction and Reunion, 1864–1888,* Vol. XVI of the Oliver Wendell Holmes Devise *History of the Supreme Court of the United States.* New York: Macmillan.

KUTLER, STANLEY I.   1968   *Judicial Power and Reconstruction Politics.* Chicago: University of Chicago Press.

LEGISLATION

In addition to the separation of powers, there are at least two intersections of the Constitution and the legislative process. One concerns the obligation and capacity of legislatures to assess the constitutionality of their proposed enactments. The other concerns the federal judiciary's role in inducing legislatures to meet their constitutional obligations. Within this context there are issues common to state and congressional lawmaking.

The American constitutional scheme obligates legislatures to assess the constitutionality of proposed enactments and to enact only legislation they deem constitutionally permissible. Although this proposition may seem obvious, it has often been contradicted by respectable lawmakers, who assert that legislatures should engage in policymaking without regard to the Constitution and leave constitutional questions exclusively to the courts. Therefore the reasons that legislatures are obligated, no less than courts, to determine the constitutionality of proposed enactments deserve explanation.

If, as Chief Justice JOHN MARSHALL asserted in MARBURY V. MADISON (1803), the Constitution is a law paramount to ordinary legislation, then to assert that legislatures need not consult the Constitution is the equivalent of asserting that individuals need not consult the law before acting. To be sure, people sometimes act in disregard of the law, subject only to the risk of sanctions if they are caught and a court holds their actions to be unlawful. But it would be perverse to conclude from this observation that we are not obligated to obey the law.

The structure and text of the Constitution certainly imply that legislatures must initially determine the legality of their enactments. For example, how would Congress know whether it had the authority to enact a bill without consulting Article I and the other provisions that delegate limited powers to the national government? Indeed, some provisions of the Constitution are explicitly addressed to legislators. Article I, section 9, provides, "No bill of attainder or ex post facto law shall be passed." The FIRST AMENDMENT says, "Congress shall make no law," and the FOURTEENTH AMENDMENT's prohibitions begin with the words, "No state shall make or enforce any law. . . ." Article VI binds legislators and officials "by Oath or Affirmation to support this Constitution. . . ." Although this command does not entail that all constitutional questions are open to all institutions at all times, it does imply that a legislator must vote only for legislation that he or she believes is authorized by the Constitution. If history matters, the obligation of legislatures to interpret the Constitution was affirmed and acted on by various of the Framers and by early legislators and Presidents—some of whom, indeed, expressed this duty or prerogative even in the face of contrary judicial interpretations.

The existence of JUDICIAL REVIEW is sometimes thought to relieve legislatures of the obligations to determine the constitutionality of their enactments. But Chief Justice Marshall's classic justifications for judicial review in *Marbury* do not necessarily imply a privileged judicial function. As Herbert Wechsler wrote: "Federal courts, including the Supreme Court, do not pass on constitutional questions because there is a special function vested in them to enforce the Constitution or police the other agencies of government. They do so rather for the reason that they must decide a litigated issue that is otherwise within their jurisdiction and in doing so they must give effect to the supreme law of the land. That is, at least, what *Marbury v. Madison* was all about." (Wechsler, 1965, p. 1006.) Other arguments for judicial review have accorded the judiciary a special role, and in COOPER V. AARON

(1958) the modern Court claimed that it was "supreme in the exposition of the law of the Constitution." But the Court has never implied that JUDICIAL SUPREMACY implies judicial exclusively, or that its privileged position relieves other institutions of the responsibility for making constitutional judgments.

Indeed, some constitutional issues—so-called POLITICAL QUESTIONS—may be committed to the legislative and executive branches to the exclusion of the judiciary. For example, it is widely assumed that the Senate's judgment in an IMPEACHMENT proceeding is not reviewable by the courts even though the decision may involve controverted constitutional questions, and even though the Senate's role in cases of impeachment is more judicial than legislative. In such cases, at least, if the legislature does not consider the constitutional questions, no one will.

If legislatures are obligated to consider constitutional questions, what deference, if any, should they accord prior judicial interpretations of the Constitution? In what might be called the judicial supremacy view, a legislature is in essentially the same position as a state or lower federal court: it must treat the Supreme Court's rulings as authoritative and binding. This was the view expressed by the Court in *Cooper v. Aaron.* Quoting Marshall's assertion in *Marbury* that "[i]t is emphatically the province and the duty of the judicial department to say what the law is," the Justices continued: "This decision declared the basic principle that the federal judiciary is supreme in the exposition of the law of the Constitution, and that principle has ever since been respected by this Court and the Country as a permanent and indispensable feature of our constitutional system."

The polar view is that legislators and other officials may, or must, apply the Constitution according to their best lights. This position was asserted by Thomas Jefferson, ANDREW JACKSON, and ABRAHAM LINCOLN, among others. In vetoing the bill to recharter the Bank of the United States in 1832, Jackson wrote:

It is maintained by advocates of the bank that its constitutionality in all its features ought to be considered settled by the decision of the Supreme Court [in MCCULLOCH V. MARYLAND (1819)]. To this conclusion I can not assent. . . . The Congress, the Executive, and the Court must each for itself be guided by its own opinion of the Constitution. Each public officer who takes an oath to support the Constitution swears that he will support it as he understands it, and not as it is understood by others. It is as much the duty of the House of Representatives, of the Senate, and of the President to decide upon the constitutionality of any bill or resolution which may be presented to them for passage or approval as it is of the supreme judges when it may be brought before them for judicial decision. The opinion of the judges has no more authority over Congress

"there is an element of futility in a judicial attempt to invalidate a law because of the bad motives of its supporters. If a law is struck down for this reason, rather than because of its facial contents or effect, it would presumably be valid as soon as the legislature . . . repassed it for different reasons."

More recently, the Court has repudiated the broadest implications of *O'Brien* and *Palmer.* In ARLINGTON HEIGHTS V. METROPOLITAN HOUSING DEVELOPMENT CORPORATION (1977) Justice LEWIS F. POWELL noted the importance of "[p]roof of racially discriminatory intent or purpose" to claims under the EQUAL PROTECTION clause. The Court held that the complainant was entitled—indeed, required—to prove that the town's refusal to rezone an area to permit multiple-family housing was discriminatorily motivated. The relevent standard was not whether the decision was solely or even dominantly motivated by racial considerations. Rather, proof that racial motivation played any part in the decision shifts to the decision maker "the burden of establishing that the same decision would have resulted even had the impermissible purpose not been considered." In *Mt. Healthy City Board of Education v. Doyle* (1977) the Court applied a similar standard in reviewing an employee's claim that he had been discharged for exercising First Amendment rights.

The current doctrine is correct. Legislative motives are not always obscure; nor does judicial review usually require inquiring into and aggregating the motives of individual legislators. As Justice Powell noted in *Arlington Heights*, the bizarrely shaped boundaries of Tuskeegee in *Gomillion* revealed "a clear pattern, unexplainable on grounds other than race." Sometimes, as in the school- and pool-closing cases, the historical background and sequence of actions leading up to the contested event may reveal invidious purposes. Placing a substantial burden on the complainant and permitting the respondent to show that the decision was in fact overdetermined by legitimate purposes amply protect against judicial invalidation of legislative policies that were based on legitimate considerations.

Indeed, this objective might be better achieved simply by invalidating a law where unconstitutional motives played any substantial role and permitting the legislature to consider the measure anew. Justice Black's concern to the contrary, such a course is not inevitably futile. Although a legislature may disguise its motivation and reenact the law for illicit reasons, it may also choose to reenact the law for entirely legitimate reasons—or the legislature may have lost whatever interest motivated it to act in the first instance. The Alabama legislature did not attempt to gerrymander Tuskeegee again, nor did Prince Edward County try to close its schools again for a "better" reason.

Judicial inquiry into unconstitutional motivation is sometimes said to be especially intrusive because it requires the judiciary to concern itself directly with the legislative process. In an important sense, however, any form of procedural review is less intrusive than substantive review. The Court leaves to the legislature its assigned task of weighing the costs and benefits of proposed legislation, and requires only that the legislature not count a constitutionally illicit objective as a benefit.

When a law is challenged on the ground that it does not further any valid interests, or does not further them sufficiently, the Supreme Court typically does not ask what ends the legislature actually sought to achieve, but hypothesizes possible objectives and asks whether the law can be upheld in terms of them. For example, in *United States v. O'Brien*, lacking any information about what legitimate objectives Congress actually sought to achieve through the draft card destruction law, the Court upheld the law on the basis of several administrative objectives that the Justices thought the law might serve.

In a widely cited 1972 article Gerald Gunther urged that the Court should be "less willing to supply justifying rationale by exercising its imagination. . . . [It] should assess the means in terms of legislative purposes that have substantial basis in actuality, not mere conjecture." Gunther asserted that a court need not delve into "actual legislative motivation" but can rely on legislative materials such as debates and reports or on a "state court's or attorney general office's description of purpose."

The Court has sometimes taken this approach. For example, in GRISWOLD V. CONNECTICUT (1965) the Court held that the state's anticontraceptive law was not justified as a means of deterring illicit sexual intercourse—the only purpose urged by the state attorney general. The Court did not consider whether the law might be upheld on the more plausible (though constitutionally problematic) ground that the Connecticut legislature believed that contraception was immoral. Whatever the justification for this judicial strategy, it is not likely to identify the legislature's actual purposes: state courts and attorneys general have no privileged access to actual legislative purposes but must rely on the same public materials available to the Supreme Court.

In recent years some Justices, and occasionally a majority of the Court, have limited the objectives that can be considered in support of a challenged regulation to the decision maker's (supposed) actual objectives. This course is easiest for a court to follow when statutory limitations on an agency's mandate foreclose it from pursuing a broad range of objectives. For example, HAMPTON V. MOW SUN WONG (1976) invalidated a United States Civil Service regulation barring resident ALIENS from federal civil service jobs. Writing for the Court, Justice JOHN PAUL STEVENS assumed that Congress or the President might constitutionally have adopted such a requirement for reasons of foreign policy, but held that the commission's jurisdiction was limited to adopting regulations to "promote the efficiency of the federal service." Similarly, in REGENTS OF THE UNIVERSITY OF CALIFORNIA V. BAKKE (1978), Justice Powell refused to consider whether the university's preferential admissions policy was justified as a remedy for past discrimination, holding that the regents were empowered only to pursue educational objectives.

The Supreme Court has sometimes relied on legislative history to refuse to uphold legislation on the basis of objectives that were not intended. For example, in *Weinberger v. Wiesenfeld* (1975), in assessing the constitutionality of the "mother's insurance benefit" provision of the SOCIAL SECURITY ACT, Justice WILLIAM J. BRENNAN wrote for the Court that "the mere recitation of a benign, compensatory purpose is not an automatic shield which protects against an inquiry into the actual purposes underlying a statutory scheme." Although the provision might have been designed to compensate for past economic discrimination against women, the legislative history belied this purpose and the Court refused to uphold the law on a false basis.

Legislative history is often sparse or nonexistent, however. A complex legislative scheme may make a myriad of classifications; the chances are slight that legislative materials will illuminate the classification challenged in any particular case; and the absence of legislative history does not mean that the legislators did not intend to pursue a particular objective. Partly because of these complexities, judicial efforts to limit the purposes on the basis of which laws can be justified have not followed a consistent pattern. The current state of the law is captured in *Kassell v. Consolidated Freightways Corporation* (1981), which struck down a state's highway regulation prohibiting double trailers as an undue burden on INTERSTATE COMMERCE. In a concurring opinion, Justice Brennan wrote that he would give no deference to the state's arguments based on safety because the law was not actually designed to promote safety but to protect local industries. Justice WILLIAM H. REHNQUIST, dissenting, asserted that there was "no authority for the proposition that possible legislative purposes suggested by a state's lawyers should not be considered in COMMERCE CLAUSE cases." The plurality avoided the issue by rejecting the state's safety claims on the merits.

In *McCulloch* Marshall implied that the BANK OF THE UNITED STATES ACT was entitled to special deference because of the attention paid to the constitutional issues within the executive and legislative branches. Because of the difficulty of such an inquiry, however, and perhaps because of its perceived impropriety, the court has seldom conditioned deference on the extent to which the legislature actually considered the factual and legal issues

bearing on the constitutional questions at stake. In *Textile Workers Union v. Lincoln Mills* (1957) the Court gave a strained interpretation to a federal statute in order to avoid a difficult constitutional question of federal jurisdiction, to which Congress had apparently paid no attention. In a separate opinion, Justice FELIX FRANKFURTER noted that "this Court cannot do what a President sometimes does in returning a bill to Congress. We cannot return this provision to Congress and respectfully request that body to assume the responsibility placed upon it by the Constitution."

In an article on the *Lincoln Mills* case, ALEXANDER M. BICKEL and Harry Wellington responded that the Court could properly perform such a "remanding function" and that it had sometimes done so, albeit surreptitiously. KENT V. DULLES (1958) is often cited as an example. Rather than decide whether the secretary of state could constitutionally refuse to issue passports to members of the Communist party, the Court held that Congress had not delegated the secretary this authority, thus in effect returning the matter to Congress. More recently, Justice Stevens, dissenting in FULLILOVE V. KLUTZNICK (1980), explicitly urged such a "remand." *Fullilove* upheld a congressional provision requiring that ten percent of the federal funds allocated to public work projects be used to procure services from minority contractors. Justice Stevens's dissent started from the premise that the Constitution disfavors all racial classifications. Noting that the challenged provision was scarcely discussed in committee or on the floor of the Congress, he wrote:

Although it is traditional for judges to accord the same presumption of regularity to the legislative process no matter how obvious it may be that a busy Congress has acted precipitately, I see no reason why the character of their procedures may not be considered relevant to the decision whether the legislative product has [violated the Constitution]. A holding that the classification was not adequately preceded by a consideration of less drastic alternatives or adequately explained by a statement of legislative purpose would be far less intrusive than a final decision [of unconstitutionality]. ... [T]here can be no separation-of-powers objection to a more tentative holding of unconstitutionality based on a failure to follow procedures that guarantee the kind of deliberation that a fundamental constitutional decision of this kind obviously merits.

"Procedural" judicial review, which takes account of the legislature's consideration of relevant constitutional issues, has two objectives. First, it may foster legislative attention to the Constitution in the first instance. Second, it prevents constitutional concerns from falling between two stools—which happens when a court blindly defers to a judgment that the legislature did not in fact make.

Procedural review seems appropriate where a legislature evidently has ignored issues of law or fact that bear on the constitutionality of an enactment. It is questionable whether a general practice of procedural review would prove workable, however. Among other things, a court will have difficulty in assessing the adequacy of constitutional deliberation from external indicia. Justice Powell, concurring in *Fullilove*, thus responded to the argument that the legislation was not adequately supported by factual findings or debate:

> The creation of national rules for the governance of our society simply does not entail the same concept of record-making that is appropriate to a judicial or administrative proceeding. Congress has no responsibility to confine its vision to the facts and evidence adduced by particular parties. One appropriate source [of facts] is the information and expertise that Congress acquires in the consideration and enactment of earlier legislation. After Congress has legislated repeatedly in an area of national concern, its Members gain experience that may reduce the need for fresh hearings or prolonged debate when Congress again considers action in that area.

In addition to the specific powers and limitations found in the Constitution, the Court has interpreted the DUE PROCESS and equal protection clauses to impose general requirements of "rationality" on the outcome of the legislative process. As stated in *F. S. Royster Guano Company v. Virginia* (1920), the equal protection STANDARD OF REVIEW requires that "the classification must be reasonable, not arbitrary, and must rest upon some ground of difference having a fair and substantial relation to the object of the legislation. . . ." The modern Court has usually articulated an even less demanding RATIONAL BASIS requirement: the law, and any classifications it makes, must plausibly promote some permissible ends to some extent.

The rationality standards may provide a minimal judicial safeguard against laws whose only purpose is constitutionally illicit, without requiring a direct inquiry into legislative motivation. But they may also impose a broader requirement on the legislative process. They may imply what Frank Michelman has described as a "public interest" rather than a "public choice" model of the legislative process.

The public interest model is premised on the possibility of shared public values or ends. "[T]he legislature is regarded as the forum for identifying or defining, and acting towards those ends. The process is one of mutual search through joint deliberation, relying on the use of reason supposed to have persuasive force" (Michelman, 1977, p. 149). The public choice model regards "all substantive values and ends . . . as strictly private. . . . There is no public or general social interest, there are only concatenations of particular interests or private preferences. There is no

reason, only strategy. . . . There are no good legislators, only shrewd ones; no statesmen; only messengers" (ibid., p. 148).

The constitutional implications of the two models can be illustrated by the city ordinance challenged in RAILWAY EXPRESS AGENCY V. NEW YORK (1949). The ordinance prohibited advertisements on the side of vehicles but exempted business delivery vehicles advertising their own business. The most obvious beneficiaries of the exemption were the city's newspapers.

If the Court had adopted a "public choice" model, it would have been pointless to subject the New York ordinance to a rationality requirement: the exemption would be permissible even if its only rationale were to "buy off" the newspapers to get the ordinance enacted or, indeed, to favor the newspapers over other advertisers. Under a "public interest" model, however, the Court would at least ask whether the exemption was related to some extrinsic purpose—and this it did. Justice WILLIAM O. DOUGLAS wrote for the Court that the "local authorities may well have concluded that those who advertise their own wares on their trucks do not present the same traffic problem in view of the nature or extent of the advertising which they use." In a concurring opinion, Justice ROBERT H. JACKSON pointed to "a real difference between doing in self-interest and doing for hire."

Thus, the Court seems nominally to adhere to a public interest model. But the weakness of the rationality standards, and the Court's generosity in imagining possible rationales for classifications (exemplified by *Railway Express Agency* itself), suggest some judicial ambivalence about the extent to which this model should be treated as a constitutional norm. There is some academic controversy about both the norm itself and its judicial enforceability.

JAMES BRADLEY THAYER asserted in his 1901 biography of John Marshall that judicial review implies a distrust of legislatures and that the legislatures "are growing accustomed to this distrust, and more and more readily incline to justify it, and to shed the consideration of constitutional restraints, . . . turning that subject over to the courts; and what is worse, they insensibly fall into a habit of assuming that whatever they can constitutionally do they may do. . . . The tendency of a common and easy resort to this great function is to dwarf the political capacity of the people, and to deaden its sense of moral responsibility." Assessing Thayer's argument is practically impossible, but it seems at least as plausible that the practice of judicial review is a necessary reminder to legislators that their actions are constrained by fundamental public law and not only by their constituents' interests or even their own moral principles.

Thayer's argument nonetheless underscores the point

that the Constitution speaks directly to legislatures. In a properly functioning constitutional system, judicial review should be just that—the review of the legislature's considered judgment that the challenged act is constitutionally permissible. Whether this position is "realistic" is another matter. Surely, however, one cannot expect legislators to take their constitutional responsibilities seriously if they and the citizenry at large assume that they have none.

PAUL BREST
(1986)

Bibliography

BENNETT, ROBERT 1979 "Mere" Rationality in Constitutional Law: Judicial Review and Democratic Theory. *California Law Review* 67:1049–1103.

BICKEL, ALEXANDER and WELLINGTON, HARRY 1957 Legislative Purpose and the Judicial Function: The Lincoln Mills Case. *Harvard Law Review* 71:1–39.

BREST, PAUL 1971 An Approach to the Problem of Unconstitutional Legislative Motive. *Supreme Court Review* 1971:95–146.

ELY, JOHN H. 1970 Legislative and Administrative Motivation in Constitutional Law. *Yale Law Journal* 79:1205–1341.

GUNTHER, GERALD 1982 In Search of Evolving Doctrine on a Changing Court: A Model for a Newer Equal Protection. *Harvard Law Review* 86:1–48.

LINDE, HANS 1976 Due Process of Lawmaking. *Nebraska Law Review* 55:197–255.

MICHELMAN, FRANK 1977 Political Markets and Community Self-Determination: Competing Judicial Models of Local Government Legitimacy. *Indiana Law Journal* 53:145–206.

MORGAN, DONALD G. 1966 *Congress and the Constitution: A Study in Responsibility.* Cambridge, Mass.: Belknap Press.

THAYER, JAMES BRADLEY 1901 *John Marshall.* Boston: Houghton Mifflin.

WECHSLER, HERBERT 1965 The Courts and the Constitution. *Columbia Law Review* 65:1001–1014.

LEGISLATIVE CONTEMPT POWER

Anglo-American legislative bodies have exercised the power to punish nonmembers for contempt of their dignity and proceedings since the time when the High Court of Parliament exercised undifferentiated legislative and judicial power. There is no explicit constitutional warrant for the exercise of the power by Congress, but Congress has exercised it, nonetheless, at least since 1795. There were several instances in the nineteenth century of summary judgments being rendered against nonmembers for such acts of contempt as publishing abusive language about Congress or attempting to bribe its members. In *Anderson v. Dunn* (1821) the Supreme Court held that the power to punish contempts—at least of the latter sort—was inherent in "a deliberate assembly, clothed with the majesty of the people." In KILBOURNE V. THOMPSON (1881), however, the Supreme Court held that Congress did not possess COMMON LAW power to punish as contempt Kilbourne's failure to produce documents subpoenaed by an investigatory committee for a nonlegislative purpose.

Congress defined the statutory offense of contempt of Congress in 1857; this offense was triable before the house against which the contempt was committed, and a contemnor, once convicted, might be confined in the Capitol for the duration of the congressional session. Contempt of Congress remains a statutory offense, but it is no longer prosecuted at the bar of the house. Because bribery of members of Congress is now punishable as a separate offense, the most common contemporary form of contempt of Congress is refusal to testify at or to provide evidence for LEGISLATIVE INVESTIGATIONS. The presiding officer of the offended house (ordinarily only if directed by a vote of the full house) certifies the circumstances of the contempt to the United States attorney in the district where the contempt was committed; the federal attorney may then prosecute the contemnor in federal court.

DENNIS J. MAHONEY
(1986)

Bibliography

GOLDFARB, RONALD L. 1963 *The Contempt Power.* New York: Columbia University Press.

LEGISLATIVE COURT

The term "legislative court" was coined by Chief Justice JOHN MARSHALL to describe the status of courts created by Congress to serve United States TERRITORIES lying outside the boundaries of any state. Congress had not given the judges of the territorial courts the life tenure and salary guarantees that Article III of the Constitution required for judges of CONSTITUTIONAL COURTS, and Marshall needed to explain the anomaly of federal courts outside the contemplation of Article III. In AMERICAN INSURANCE CO. V. CANTER (1828) he concluded that Congress, in exercising its power to govern the territories, could establish courts that did not fit Article III's specifications. Today this concept of legislative courts embraces all courts created by Congress and staffed by judges who do not enjoy constitutional protection of their tenure and salaries. Examples include territorial courts, consular courts, the Tax Court of the United States, the Bankruptcy Court, the Court of Military Appeals, and the courts of local jurisdiction operating in the DISTRICT OF COLUMBIA and the Commonwealth of PUERTO RICO.

Just as a legislative court's judges fall outside Article III's guarantees of independence, so it is capable of handling business outside that Article's definition of "the JUDICIAL POWER OF THE UNITED STATES"—something a constitutional court cannot constitutionally do. A legislative court, for example, can be assigned JURISDICTION to give ADVISORY OPINIONS to the President or Congress. Yet, despite Marshall's OBITER DICTUM in the *Canter* opinion that a legislative court is "incapable of receiving" jurisdiction lying within the judicial power, it is clear today that such courts, like administrative agencies, can constitutionally be assigned the initial decision of a great many cases within Article III's definition of that power. (See NORTHERN PIPELINE CONSTRUCTION CO. V. MARATHON PIPE LINE CO.) Their decisions on such Article III matters are reviewable by constitutional courts, including the Supreme Court, when Congress so provides.

With some difficulty, the Supreme Court has resolved controversies over the status of several courts. The federal courts formerly serving the District of Columbia were held protected by Article III's guarantees of life tenure and salary protection. In this sense, they were constitutional courts. However, the Court also held that the same courts could constitutionally be given work falling outside Article III's specification of CASES AND CONTROVERSIES within the judicial power. In 1970, Congress replaced these "hybrid" courts with a dual court system: the constitutional courts operate under Article III's strictures and the legislative courts handle the local judicial business of the District. In *Palmore v. United States* (1973) the Supreme Court upheld the local courts' power to try local crimes (established by congressional statute), despite their judges' lack of life tenure and salary guarantees.

Similarly, in *Glidden Co. v. Zdanok* (1962), the Court staggered to the ruling—based on two inconsistent opinions, pieced together to make a majority for the result—that the old Court of Claims (see CLAIMS COURT; UNITED STATES COURT OF APPEALS FOR THE FEDERAL CIRCUIT) and the COURT OF CUSTOMS AND PATENT APPEALS were constitutional courts, not legislative courts.

In essence a legislative court is merely an administrative agency with an elegant name. While Congress surely has the power to transfer portions of the business of the federal judiciary to legislative courts, a wholesale transfer of that business would work a fundamental change in the status of our independent judiciary and would seem vulnerable to constitutional attack.

KENNETH L. KARST
(1986)

Bibliography

NOTE 1962 Legislative and Constitutional Courts: What Lurks Ahead for Bifurcation. *Yale Law Journal* 71:979–1012.

LEGISLATIVE FACTS

The growth of American constitutional doctrine has been influenced, from the beginning, by the traditions of the Anglo-American COMMON LAW. Judges make constitutional law, as they make other kinds of law, partly on the basis of factual premises. Sometimes these premises are merely assumed, but sometimes they are developed with the aid of counsel. However they may be determined, the facts on which a court's lawmaking is premised are called "legislative facts." In modern usage they are sometimes contrasted with "adjudicative facts," the facts of the particular case before the court.

Not all constitutional questions concern the validity of legislation. In the 1970s and 1980s, for example, the Supreme Court went through a period of reappraisal of the EXCLUSIONARY RULE, which excludes from a criminal case some types of EVIDENCE obtained in violation of the Constitution. One factual issue repeatedly raised during this reconsideration was whether the rule actually served to deter police misconduct. In considering that question, the Court was not second-guessing the judgment of a legislature. Yet the question was properly regarded as one of legislative fact; its resolution would provide one of the premises for the Court's constitutional lawmaking.

More frequently, however, the courts consider issues of legislative fact in reviewing the constitutionality of legislation. In many cases, particularly when the laws under review are acts of Congress, the legislature itself has already given consideration to the same fact questions. Congress sometimes writes its own factual findings into the text of a law, explicitly declaring the actual basis for the legislation. In such cases the courts typically defer to the congressional versions of reality. Similar legislative findings are only infrequently written into the enactments of state and local legislative bodies, but even there the practice has recently increased. It seems unlikely, however, that judges, especially federal judges, will pay the same degree of deference to those legislative findings.

The courts' treatment of issues of legislative fact is thus seen as a function of the STANDARD OF REVIEW used to test a law's validity. When a court uses the most permissive form of the RATIONAL BASIS standard, it asks only whether the legislature could rationally conclude that the law under review was an appropriate means for achieving a legitimate legislative objective. The BRANDEIS BRIEF was invented for use in just such cases, presenting evidence to show that a legislature's factual premises were not irrational. When the standard of review is heightened—for example, when the courts invoke the rhetoric of STRICT SCRUTINY—arguments addressed to questions of legislative fact can be expected to come from both the challengers and the defenders of legislation. A court's fact-finding task in such a case is apt to be more complicated; the complication is implicit in any standard of review more demanding than the "rational basis" standard, any real interest-balancing by the courts. Arguments about the proper judicial approach to the factual premises for legislation are, in fact, arguments about the proper role of the judiciary in the governmental system. (See JUDICIAL REVIEW; JUDICIAL ACTIVISM AND JUDICIAL RESTRAINT.)

The technique of the Brandeis brief was invented for the occasion of the Supreme Court's consideration of MULLER V. OREGON (1908), upholding a law regulating women's working hours, and has been in fairly frequent use ever since. Increasingly, however, counsel have sought to present evidence on issues of legislative fact to trial courts. An early example was SOUTHERN PACIFIC CO. V. ARIZONA (1945), in which the Supreme Court struck down a law limiting the length of railroad trains. For five and a half months the trial judge heard evidence filling some 3,000 pages in the record; he made findings of legislative fact covering 148 printed pages. Justice HUGO L. BLACK, dissenting, complained that this procedure made the judiciary into a "super-legislature," but courts cannot escape from this kind of factual inquiry unless they adopt Justice Black's permissive views and abandon most constitutional limits on STATE REGULATION OF COMMERCE.

Nor are such trials of legislative fact limited to issues lying within the competence of people like safety engineers. When the California school finance case, SERRANO V. PRIEST (1972), was remanded for trial, the court took six months of expert testimony centered on a single question: Does differential spending on education produce differences in educational quality? (The court's unsurprising answer: Yes.)

As the *Serrano* and *Southern Pacific* cases show, proving legislative facts at trial is considerably more costly than filing a Brandeis brief. It permits cross-examination, however, and sharpens the focus for evidentiary offerings. Even when appellate review seems certain, the trial court's sorting and evaluation of a complex record can aid the appellate court greatly. Expert testimony, the staple of such a trial, typically rests on the sort of opinion and hearsay about which nonexperts ordinarily would not be permitted to testify. Legislative facts, of course, are tried to the judge and not to a jury; furthermore, questions of legislative fact, by definition, touch a great many "cases" not in court that will be "decided" by the precedent made in the court's constitutional ruling. Just as a constitutional case is an especially appropriate occasion for hearing the views of an AMICUS CURIAE, the widest latitude should be allowed to the parties (and to an amicus) to present evidence broadly relevant to the lawmaking issues before the court.

Ultimately there is no assurance that counsel's efforts to educate a court about the factual setting for constitutional lawmaking will improve the lawmaking itself. Yet our courts, with the Supreme Court's encouragement, continue to invite counsel to make these efforts. One of America's traditional faiths, which judges share with the rest of us, is a belief in the value of education.

KENNETH L. KARST
(1986)

Bibliography

FREUND, PAUL A. 1951 *On Understanding the Supreme Court.* Boston: Little, Brown.
KARST, KENNETH L. 1960 Legislative Facts in Constitutional Litigation. *Supreme Court Review* 1960:75–112.

LEGISLATIVE IMMUNITY

The SPEECH OR DEBATE CLAUSE immunizes federal legislators from civil or criminal actions based on legislative acts. In TENNEY V. BRANDHOVE (1951) the Supreme Court, relying on the COMMON LAW immunity of legislators and the speech or debate clause, held legislators to be immune from federal civil suits based on legislative acts. This legislative immunity, however, does not preclude evidence of legislative acts in criminal prosecutions for corruption.

In what may be an expansion of common law legislative immunity, LAKE COUNTRY ESTATES, INC. V. TAHOE REGIONAL PLANNING AGENCY (1979) held that the appointed members of a bistate agency enjoyed legislative immunity from suits for constitutional violations. The Court also suggested that state legislative immunity does not depend on the existence of the speech or debate clause. *Lake Country Estates'* extension of absolute legislative immunity to un-elected officials may enable many public bodies or officials that promulgate rules of general application to rely on legislative immunity. For example, in *Supreme Court of Virginia v. Consumers Union of the United States* (1980) the Court concluded that state supreme court justices enjoyed legislative immunity from damages actions based on their promulgation of unconstitutional rules of conduct for the state bar.

THEODORE EISENBERG
(1986)

Bibliography

EISENBERG, THEODORE 1982 Section 1983: Doctrinal Foundations and an Empirical Study. *Cornell Law Review* 67:492–505.

LEGISLATIVE INTENT

Legislative intent is a construct that courts use to discern the meaning of legislative action, usually in the form of

LEGISLATION. The concept is employed in many fields of law—including constitutional law—in the interpretation and application of statutes. In constitutional law, courts also use the concept in determining the purposes or goals of a legislature when they are relevant to deciding the constitutionality of the legislation.

In searching for legislative intent, courts appear to assume that legislation is aimed, in an instrumentally rational fashion, at achieving certain objectives or goals. Sometimes these objectives or goals are stated in rather discrete terms. In HINES V. DAVIDOWITZ (1941), for example, the Supreme Court decided that in passing a law requiring ALIENS to register with federal authorities, Congress had the objective of barring enforcement of state laws that required aliens to register with state officials. At other times, legislative intent is cast in more general terms. Thus in RAILWAY EXPRESS AGENCY V. NEW YORK (1949), the Supreme Court decided that the legislative goal in banning advertisements from some motor vehicles was the promotion of traffic safety.

There has been controversy about reference to legislative intent as a method of giving meaning to legislation, much as there has been controversy about reference to the Framers' intent as a means of giving meaning to the provisions of the Constitution itself. Two lines of criticism have developed, one rooted in doubt about the intelligibility of the concept of legislative intent, the other grounded in skepticism about the legitimacy of the political theory that an appeal to legislative intent presupposes.

Those who question the intelligibility of attempting to ascertain the intent of a legislature argue that it is impossible to ascribe an intent to a multi-member body. First, they point out the difficulty of ascertaining the individual intents of all the legislators and, second, they argue that even if the individual intents could be ascertained, there is no theoretically sound way to combine them to produce a coherent intent of the group.

Those who question the legitimacy of an appeal to legislative intent argue that as a matter of political theory, courts should not be bound by beliefs or wishes of legislators that were not written into the text of the statute but rather only the printed words of the legislation. OLIVER WENDELL HOLMES, for example, urged that courts should ask not what the legislature intended but rather only what the statute means. Instead of looking for evidence of legislative intent, courts should, according to Holmes, consult dictionaries and evidence of contemporary usage to construct the most acceptable interpretation of the statute's meaning.

More recent scholarly criticism has also questioned the validity of the assumption about legislative behavior that legislative intent presupposes. According to these critics, legislatures are merely market arenas in which private interests trade with each other through their legislators to further their own particular advantages. A search for a legislative intent beyond the immediate effects that the statute accomplishes is, according to his view, nonsensical and perhaps politically illegitimate as well.

Legislative intent has remained an important concept in constitutional law in spite of these criticisms. First, courts have developed various methods of dealing with the practical difficulties of constructing a legislative intent. Thus the difficulties associated with discovering the intent of each legislator and of aggregating these individual intents into a group intent have been addressed through the use of presumptions and, in some cases, outright fictions. Often, particularly in the case of state legislation, there is no evidence of legislative intent beyond the words of the statute, but the courts nevertheless generally say they are seeking legislative intention when they are deciding what the legislation means.

The courts indulge in similar assumptions when additional evidence does exist. For example, courts generally credit statements in committee reports as evidence of legislative purpose, even though there may be little reason to believe that many legislators read the report or agreed with it. Similarly, the speeches of proponents during floor debates (or even in public discourse outside the legislative arena) are also treated as evidence of legislative intent, even though few legislators may have been present during the floor debate (or heard the nonlegislative remarks). Some have argued that the legislative draftsmen or proponents are the "agents" of the legislature and therefore that their intent is the relevant legislative intent. Others urge that silent legislators who vote for the enactment share the intent of those who do speak in favor of the legislation. Another view is that legislatures in effect delegate to identifiable subgroups, such as committees, the task of setting legislative goals in the areas of the subgroups' specialties. Thus the intent of the legislature with respect to a transportation law would be assumed to be the same as the intent of the legislative committee on transportation. Whatever the rationale, courts have created a concept of legislative intent that does not purport to be a true measurement of the intents of the individual legislators. In effect, courts have personified legislatures and sought to ascribe to them an intent as if the legislature were a single person, one who sometimes speaks with several, often conflicting voices about what he wants to accomplish.

The more fundamental questions of political theory which challenge the legitimacy of looking to legislative intent have not been systematically addressed, at least by the courts. Courts have, by and large, assumed that if legislative intent can be constructed, it is relevant and even controlling in the interpretation of legislative action, at least where the terms of the statute are perceived to provide leeway for interpretation.

Legislative intent may have remained important for several reasons. First, the concept is used widely outside of constitutional law for statutory interpretation. Legislatures have learned what courts will consider in searching for legislative intent, and they have adjusted their processes in some measure to provide the appropriate signals to the courts—thus encouraging continued judicial reliance on legislative intent.

Second, adherence to legislative intent may be grounded in judicial support of what the judges believe to be a political ideal. Although courts may recognize that trading among private interests does occur, they may believe that our society nevertheless aspires to a model of legislation that is an instrumentally rational pursuit of objectives that further the public interest.

Finally, courts have evolved several STANDARDS OF REVIEW in constitutional law that make the legislature's goals or objectives relevant to the constitutionality of the legislation. These standards, such as the RATIONAL BASIS test, LEAST RESTRICTIVE MEANS analysis, and the tests for federal PREEMPTION of state regulatory authority, have no doubt helped insure that the search for legislative intent remains a significant part of constitutional adjudication.

Legislative intent is thus important in several areas of constitutional adjudication. Three examples are illustrative. First, courts look to legislative intent to determine whether a legislature gave an administrative official power to take the challenged action. In KENT V. DULLES (1958), for example, the secretary of state denied a passport because the applicant failed to state whether or not he was or had been a communist. The Supreme Court held that Congress had not intended to give the secretary of state the power to deny passports on those grounds. Similarly, courts have ruled on numerous occasions—Hines is an example—that a state statute cannot be enforced because Congress, by enacting legislation on the same subject matter, "intended" to preempt the field from state regulation.

Second, courts often look to legislative intent because the constitutionality of the challenged legislative action depends on the legislature's purpose. Thus legislation mandating that only single-family residences may be built in a certain zone is constitutional if the purposes of the law are to reduce traffic, limit demand on municipal resources, and provide a suburban atmosphere. It will be unconstitutional, however, if the legislative purpose is to exclude minorities from the municipality, as the Supreme Court suggested in ARLINGTON HEIGHTS V. METROPOLITAN HOUSING DEVELOPMENT CORPORATION (1977).

Third, legislative intent is relevant in those areas of constitutional decision making in which courts purportedly scrutinize the "fit" between legislative means and ends. In EQUAL PROTECTION law, for example, legislative classification that disadvantages one person vis-à-vis another is said to be constitutional only if the classification is rationally related to a legitimate legislative goal. While courts tend to hypothesize rather freely about what the legislature could have intended to achieve with the classification, evidence of legislative intent is clearly relevant. More important, when circumstances call for more rigorous scrutiny—as when the classification is based on sex or race—the courts are less willing to speculate about the legislature's possible purposes, and they search for concrete evidence of legislative intent.

The meaning of legislation—what the legislature sought to accomplish—is often important in constitutional law. Even though theoretical and practical problems are attendant on the concept of legislative intent, courts use the concept in ascribing meaning to legislation in the numerous doctrinal areas in which the courts themselves have made that meaning relevant.

SCOTT H. BICE
(1986)

Bibliography

DICKERSON, REED 1975 Statutory Interpretation: A Peek into the Mind and Will of a Legislature. *Indiana Law Journal* 50: 206–237.
MacCALLUM, GERALD C., JR. 1966 Legislative Intent. *Yale Law Journal* 75:754–787.
RADIN, MAX 1930 Statutory Interpretation. *Harvard Law Review* 43:863–885.

LEGISLATIVE INVESTIGATION

Although congressional power to conduct investigations and punish recalcitrant witnesses is nowhere mentioned in the United States Constitution, the inherent investigative power of legislatures was well established, both in the British Parliament and in the American colonial legislatures, more than a century before the Constitution was adopted. Mention of such power in the early state constitutions was generally regarded as unnecessary, but the Massachusetts and Maryland constitutions both gave explicit authorization; the latter, adopted in 1776, empowered the House of Delegates to ". . . inquire on the oath of witnesses, into all complaints, grievances, and offenses, as the grand inquest of this state," and to ". . . call for all public or official papers and records, and send for persons, whom they may judge necessary in the course of inquiries concerning affairs relating to the public interest."

The basic theory of the power was and is that a legislative house needs it in order to obtain information, so that its law-making and other functions may be discharged on an enlightened rather than a benighted basis. Under the Constitution, the power was first exercised by the HOUSE OF REPRESENTATIVES in 1792, when it appointed a select committee to inquire into the defeat by the Indians suffered the previous year by federal forces commanded by General Arthur St. Clair. The House empowered the committee "to call for such persons, papers and records as may be necessary to assist in their inquiries." After examining the British precedents, President GEORGE WASHINGTON and his cabinet agreed that the House "was an inquest and therefore might institute inquiries" and "call for papers generally," and that although the executive ought to refuse to release documents "the disclosure of which would endanger the public," in the matter at hand "there was not a paper which might not be properly produced," and therefore the committee's requests should be granted.

For nearly a century thereafter, investigations were conducted frequently and without encountering serious challenge, in Congress and the state legislatures alike. They covered a wide range of subjects, and their history is in large part the history of American politics. Among the most interesting state investigations were those conducted in 1855 by the Massachusetts legislature and the New York City Council, under the leadership of the "Know-Nothing" party, in which Irish Roman Catholicism was the target. Inquiries by the New York City Council into alleged Irish domination of the police force were challenged in the New York Court of Common Pleas, and Judge Charles Patrick Daly's opinion in *Briggs v. McKellar* (1855) was the first to hold that, unlike in Britain, in the United States the legislative investigative power is limited by the Constitution.

Fifteen years later, a congressional investigation was for the first time successfully challenged on constitutional grounds, in KILBOURN V. THOMPSON (1881). The House of Representatives had authorized a select committee to investigate the bankruptcy of the Jay Cooke banking firm (which was a depository of federal funds), and when the witness Kilbourn refused to answer questions, the House cited him for contempt and imprisoned him. After his release on HABEAS CORPUS, Kilbourn sued the House sergeant-at-arms for damages from false imprisonment. In an opinion by Justice SAMUEL F. MILLER, the Supreme Court sustained his claim on the grounds of constitutional SEPARATION OF POWERS, declaring that the Jay Cooke bankruptcy presented no legislative grounds for inquiry and that "the investigation . . . could only be properly and successfully made by a court of justice." The Court has never since invalidated a legislative inquiry on that particular basis, and it is probable that today, under comparable circumstances, a sufficient legislative purpose would be found. But the Court's ruling, that Congress's investigative and contempt powers are subject to JUDICIAL REVIEW and

must conform to constitutional limitations, has not since been seriously questioned.

Exclusively until 1857, and commonly until 1935, Congress enforced its investigative power against recalcitrant witnesses by its own contempt proceedings: a congressional citation for contempt, and its execution through arrest and confinement of the witness by the sergeant-at-arms. (See LEGISLATIVE CONTEMPT POWER.) Judicial review of the contempt was usually obtained by habeas corpus. But the system was cumbersome, and effective only when Congress was in session. To remedy these shortcomings, Congress in 1857 enacted a statute making it a federal offense to refuse to produce documents demanded, or to answer questions put, by a duly authorized congressional investigatory committee. For some years both the contempt and the statutory criminal procedures were used, but since 1935 the contempt procedure has fallen into disuse. Challenges to congressional investigative authority are currently dealt with by INDICTMENT and trial under the criminal statute, now found in section 192, Title 2, United States Code, the constitutionality of which was upheld by the Supreme Court in *In re Chapman* (1897).

The tone of Justice Miller's opinion in the *Kilbourn* case raised doubts about the scope and even the existence of the congressional contempt power, which were repeatedly voiced during the early years of the twentieth century, when Congress conducted investigations damaging to powerful business and financial institutions. In 1912 the House Committee on Banking and Currency launched what became known as the "Money Trust Investigation," in which practically all the leading financiers of the time— J. P. Morgan the elder, George F. Baker, James J. Hill, and others—were called to answer charges of undue concentration of control of railroads and heavy industries in the hands of a few New York bankers. In 1924, SENATE committees probed allegations of corruption and maladministration in the Justice, Interior, and Navy departments.

The legality and propriety of these inquiries aroused vigorous public debate. The famous jurist JOHN HENRY WIGMORE wrote of a "debauch of investigations" which raised a "stench" and caused the Senate to fall "in popular esteem to the level of professional searchers of the municipal dunghills," while then Professor FELIX FRANKFURTER accused the critics of seeking to "divert attention and shackle the future," and argued that the investigative power should be left "untrammeled." The doubters and critics were encouraged when a federal district judge, relying on the *Kilbourn* case, quashed a Senate contempt citation against Attorney General Harry M. Daugherty's brother, but the investigative and contempt powers were vindicated when the Supreme Court reversed that decision and ruled in MCGRAIN V. DAUGHERTY (1927) that the investigation was proper as an aid to legislation, and that

Mally Daugherty could be required to testify on pain of imprisonment. Consequently, there were no serious or successful legal challenges to the many congressional investigations born of the Great Depression and the "NEW DEAL" period of President FRANKLIN D. ROOSEVELT's administration. (See CONSTITUTIONAL HISTORY, 1933–1945.)

Until this time the main subjects of legislative investigations had been the civil and military operations of the executive branch, industrial and financial problems, and the operation of social forces such as the labor movement. Except for state investigations in the middle years of the nineteenth century directed at Masons and Roman Catholics, ideological matters had not been much involved.

The Russian Revolution of 1917, the spread of communist doctrine, and the Nazi seizure of dictatorial power in Germany soon emerged as major subjects of congressional concern. There were short-lived congressional investigations of communist propaganda in 1919 and 1930, and of Nazi propaganda in 1934. With the establishment of the HOUSE COMMITTEE OF UN-AMERICAN ACTIVITIES in May 1938, SUBVERSIVE ACTIVITIES emerged as the most publicized subject of congressional investigation.

During WORLD WAR II, in which the United States and the Soviet Union were allies, there was a lull in these inquiries, but the "Iron Curtain" and "Cold War" revived them, and by 1947 they were again front-page news. Soon, names of prosecutors and witnesses—for example, MARTIN DIES, RICHARD M. NIXON, Alger Hiss, Whittaker Chambers, JOSEPH R. MCCARTHY, and Patrick McCarran—became household words. The Senate authorized two bodies to join in the hunt for subversion: the Judiciary Committee's Subcommittee on Internal Security headed by Senator McCarran, and the Government Operations Committee's Subcommittee on Investigations under Senator McCarthy, respectively established in 1946 and 1950.

The principal activity of these agencies was summoning individuals to testify about the communist connections of themselves or others, and their proceedings contributed mightily to a period of public recrimination and bitter controversy that lasted for more than a decade. It was also a period of frequent criminal litigation involving congressional investigative power, as numerous witnesses were indicted for refusing to answer such questions. Some witnesses invoked the Fifth Amendment RIGHT AGAINST SELF-INCRIMINATION, and the Supreme Court, in three cases decided in 1955, was unanimously of the opinion that the right is available to witnesses before legislative committees, though three of the Justices thought that the witnesses had not clearly invoked it. Writing for the majority, Chief Justice EARL WARREN confirmed the congressional investigative power and stated further (*Quinn v. United States*):

But the power to investigate, broad as it may be, is also subject to recognized limitations. It cannot be used to inquire into private affairs unrelated to a valid legislative purpose. Nor does it extend to an area in which Congress is forbidden to legislate. Similarly, the power to investigate must not be confused with any of the powers of law enforcement; these powers are assigned under our Constitution to the Executive and Judiciary. Still further limitations on the power to investigate are found in the specific individual guarantees of the BILL OF RIGHTS, such as the Fifth Amendment's privilege against self-incrimination which is in issue here.

Other witnesses, however, invoked the FIRST AMENDMENT's guarantee of FREEDOM OF SPEECH as justification for their refusal to answer, and in 1956 and 1957 two such cases, SWEEZY V. NEW HAMPSHIRE and WATKINS V. UNITED STATES, the first involving a congressional and the second a state investigation, reached the Court. With only Justice TOM C. CLARK dissenting, the Court held that, as a general proposition, First Amendment rights are enjoyed by witnesses in legislative investigations.

But did the First Amendment protect these witnesses from the obligation to answer questions about individual connections with communism? The Court did not meet that issue and based its reversal of both convictions on nonconstitutional grounds. Watkins had not been told that the questions put to him were (as the federal statute requires) "pertinent to the question under inquiry," while in Sweezy's case it was not shown that the state legislature had authorized the investigative agency to ask the questions he declined to answer.

Three years later, however, by a 5–4 vote, the Court held that the First Amendment did not bar requiring a witness to answer questions regarding his own or others' communist connections. (See BARENBLATT V. UNITED STATES; UPHAUS V. WYMAN.) In his opinion for the Court in the former case, Justice JOHN MARSHALL HARLAN undertook a "balancing . . . of the private and public interests at stake," and concluded that since the Communist party was not "an ordinary political party" and sought overthrow of the government "by force and violence," Congress had "the right to identify a witness as a member of the Communist Party." (See BALANCING TESTS.)

The authority of these two cases was somewhat tarnished in 1963 after Justice ARTHUR J. GOLDBERG had replaced Justice Frankfurter, who had been in the five-member majority. A Florida court authorized a state investigatory committee to require a local branch of the NAACP to produce its membership lists so that the committee could determine whether certain individuals suspected of communist connections were members of the NAACP. Once again the Court divided 5–4, and Justice Goldberg, writing for the majority in GIBSON V. FLORIDA

LEGISLATIVE COMMITTEE, ruled that, in the absence of any prior showing of connection between the NAACP and communist activities, such required disclosure was barred by the First Amendment. Three years later, in another New Hampshire investigations case, *DeGregory v. New Hampshire Attorney General*, the Court ruled, 6–3, that the state's interest was "too remote and conjectural" to justify compelling a witness in 1964 to testify about communist activities in 1957.

Since then there have been no Supreme Court and no important state or lower federal court decisions on the constitutional aspects of legislative investigative power. The *Barenblatt* case has not been overruled, and it is perhaps noteworthy that both the *Gibson* and *DeGregory* cases involved state rather than congressional investigations. The attitudes of the Justices who have joined the Court since 1966 remain untested.

It may be surmised, for the future, that if a plausible relation between a legislative inquiry and a valid legislative purpose can be shown, and there are no procedural flaws or manifestations of gross abuse, the Court will be reluctant to deny, on constitutional grounds, the power of a legislative investigating committee to require witnesses to answer questions or produce records.

A different situation might well obtain if a congressional investigating committee should seek to enforce the production of government documents involving NATIONAL SECURITY or for some other reason inappropriate for public disclosure. Presidents have on numerous occasions exercised the right first asserted by George Washington in 1792, to withhold documents "the disclosure of which would endanger the public" or otherwise contravene the public interest. (See EXECUTIVE PRIVILEGE.) Congressional committee efforts to force the production of records of judicial conferences, or other confidential court papers, might likewise encounter constitutional objections based on the separation of powers. Up to the present time, these issues have not confronted the Supreme Court, and the political wisdom of avoiding such confrontations is manifest.

TELFORD TAYLOR
(1986)

Bibliography

CARR, ROBERT K.   1952   *The House Committee on Un-American Activities.* Ithaca, N.Y.: Cornell University Press.
GOODMAN, WALTER   1968   *The Committee.* New York: Farrar, Straus & Giroux.
LANDIS, JAMES M.   1926   Constitutional Limits on the Congressional Power of Investigation. *Harvard Law Review* 40:153–226.
OGDEN, AUGUST RAYMOND   1945   *The Dies Committee.* Washington, D.C.: Catholic University of America Press.
POTTS, CHARLES S.   1926   Power of Legislative Bodies to Punish for Contempt. *University of Pennsylvania Law Review* 74:691–780.
TAYLOR, TELFORD   1955   *Grand Inquest: The Story of Congressional Investigations.* New York: Simon & Schuster.

LEGISLATIVE JURISDICTION

See: Jurisdiction

LEGISLATIVE POWER

"Legislative power" is a distinctly modern conception which presupposes a modern understanding of "law." In medieval Europe the authority of laws was variously attributed to God, nature, or custom; human authorities "found" or "declared" or enforced the law but were not thought to create it. Consequently, medieval jurists did not distinguish "legislative" from "judicial" powers. Through the end of the sixteenth century, the English Parliament (like its continental counterparts) was primarily regarded as a court, an ultimate court of APPEAL for individuals as well as communities. It was at most an incidental consideration whether Parliament was "representative" because law was not a matter of will but of knowledge.

The modern conception traces the authority of law precisely to the will of the lawmakers. It is this assumption of a pure power to make or unmake the laws that allows for our artificially clear distinction between "legislative" (that is lawmaking) and "judicial" or "executive" (law-applying) powers. In acknowledging law as the creation of particular human wills, the modern view liberates government from encrusted tradition, from folklore and superstition, above all from manipulation by legalistic conjurings. At the same time, however, this view of law opens the chilling prospect of an unlimited coercive power, since the power to create the laws seems, by its very nature, superior to the constraints of law. This sort of reasoning, powerfully advanced by theorists of SOVEREIGNTY in the seventeenth century, was treated by WILLIAM BLACKSTONE in the next century as virtually self-evident: for any court to declare invalid an act of Parliament, he observed, "were to set the judicial power above that of the legislature, which would be subversive of all government."

The Framers of the American Constitution were nonetheless intent on curbing legislative power. Historians have noted that by the standards of their European contemporaries the constitutional perspective of the American Framers was somewhat archaic, most notably in the Framers' acceptance of a HIGHER LAW limitation on legislative power and in their indifference to questions about sovereignty or ultimate authority. But in the decisive respect, the concerns and accomplishments of the Framers reflected their quite modern recognition that no laws are simply given, that the scope of legislative assertion is vast and, as THE FEDERALIST conceded, "the legislative authority necessarily predominates." Thus they set out the legislative powers in the first and longest article of the Constitution, suggesting the primacy of these powers in the governmental scheme and implicitly identifying the reach of the federal government with the reach of its legislative powers. At the same time, the language of Article I emphasizes the open-endedness of legislative power precisely by its focus on the powers rather than the duties, objectives, or obligations of the legislative branch.

Perhaps the most important checks on legislative power in the Constitution are those that seem merely procedural or institutional. In the first place, the Constitution sets up a formidable institutional gauntlet for legislative proposals, requiring that they obtain majorities in each house of Congress and then secure approval from the President (or extraordinary majorities in Congress). The Constitution also seeks to assure some independent authority for the executive branch and the judiciary by removing the selection and tenure of these officers from immediate congressional control. Ultimately, almost all executive and judicial action depends on prior statutory authority and funding from Congress. And it is impossible to say with confidence when a legislative enactment (apart from an actual BILL OF ATTAINDER—imposing criminal sanctions on particular individuals) would be so specific and peremptory as to infringe the essential law-applying authority of the executive or the judiciary. But in practice the institutional reality of the SEPARATION OF POWERS usually does preserve a protective screen of independent judgment between the legislative will and the force of law as applied.

Direct limitations on legislative power in the Constitution are perhaps the most dramatic legacy of the Framers' distrust of legislative power, but they are probably not the most efficacious or important. From the outset, Congress has been emboldened to exercise powers beyond those specifically enumerated in Article I, either by construing implied powers or appealing to the requisites of national SOVEREIGNTY. The Supreme Court sought to give some force to these limitations in the early decades of this century in order to prevent Congress from preempting the legislative authority of the states. But these efforts were repudiated by the Court after the 1930s and the repudiation of judicially enforceable limits has been explicitly reconfirmed in the current era. Even the limitations imposed by the BILL OF RIGHTS on behalf of individual liberty have very rarely been construed by the Supreme Court in ways that threatened federal legislation.

As it has expanded, however, federal legislative power has also been dispersed in striking ways. In recent decades, the federal courts, invoking vague or general constitutional clauses, have assumed the power to impose elaborate requirements on states and localities in a more or less openly legislative (law-creating) manner. Meanwhile, since the 1930s, Congress has delegated more and more legislative power to federal administrative agencies. Though Congress retains the ultimate power to block what courts and agencies do, its passivity may or may not be properly construed as acquiescence. Thus the dispersal of legislative powers seems to threaten the central promise in the modern conception of law—that there is always an identifiable human authority to hold responsible for the law.

JEREMY RABKIN
(1986)

Bibliography

CORWIN, EDWARD S. 1955 *The "Higher Law" Background of American Constitutional Law.* Ithaca, N.Y.: Cornell University Press.

FISHER, LOUIS 1985 *Constitutional Conflicts between Congress and the President.* Princeton, N.J.: Princeton University Press.

LEGISLATIVE PURPOSES AND MOTIVES

Article I of the Constitution vests all legislative powers in the Congress of the United States. Congress is thus ordained to be the policymaking arm of the government. Since Congress exercises this authority through the separate flexing of 435 members of the HOUSE OF REPRESENTATIVES and the 100 members of the SENATE, the statutes passed by Congress are always collective works—written, amended, and propounded by many. As a result, discerning a single purpose or motive for most statutes is not easy.

An individual member of Congress proposes legislation to solve a problem. As that proposal winds its way through the legislative process, many forces affect the proposal and its meaning. Witnesses favoring and opposing the proposal testify before committees, and their testimony may present an interpretation altogether different from that intended by the proposal's sponsor. While the bill remains in committee, amendments may be offered and voted upon, further changing the purposes or effects of the proposal. Constituents, hearing about the proposal, will express their views to their representatives, voicing still other potentially competing concerns and perceptions about the proposal. After the proposal comes out of the committee, frequently in amended form, it is further refined and amended in floor debate. Again, the purposes and perceptions of the legislators are vast and varied.

Once the proposal is approved in one chamber, the whole process is replicated in the other chamber. If further amendments are adopted in the second chamber, the differences between the two chambers' versions are ironed out in a "conference committee," consisting of legislators from both chambers. Only when the House and Senate approve an identical bill does the proposal go to the President for his approval.

With such a tortuous journey to complete, a piece of legislation rarely survives its odyssey with a clear purpose intact. As a result, judges and lawyers must devote much of their time and attention to the process of interpreting statutes. Although the judges, lawyers, and lawmakers have developed many rules and strictures for performing this task, there is much disagreement on what rules or strictures apply in a particular case.

Sometimes a legislative body will seek to ease the task of interpretation by putting a "preamble" or "statement of purposes" into the statute. Unfortunately, such efforts frequently end up as broad platitudes that do not help readers to discern more subtle nuances, such as the LEGISLATIVE INTENT or purpose of a statute. On occasion, the preamble is used to reassure dubious legislators that the statute does not have the effect that its plain words imply. Because these preambles are usually included as window dressing, most courts have rejected efforts to use the preamble to "trump" the plain meaning of the words of the statute. The title of a statute can also be misleading as to the law's real purposes. An infamous example from one of the state legislatures involved a statute entitled An Act Relative to Sheep and Swine that also imposed a residence requirement for candidates for public office.

The rules that the courts use in interpreting statutes are usually called the "canons of construction." There are perhaps a dozen well-known canons that are most frequently employed. The most commonly accepted canon is the "plain-meaning rule," which requires that a court first look at the words of the statute without regard to the floor debate or committee reports. On this view, if the plain meaning of the statute can be discerned from such a review of the wording, the court should look no further; the statute should be construed in accord with such plain meaning. Few statutes lend themselves easily to the plain-meaning approach. When the meaning is not clear, both judges and lawyers differ as to where to look next. Some look to the floor debate, and others look to the committee reports that accompany such a legislative proposal when it goes to the floor for debate. Some judges and scholars apply other canons of construction, on the theory that the legislators knew and used such canons in deciding what words to use. Still others delve into the testimony of committee witnesses for clues about congressional intent. All of the congressional activities that took place before the statute was passed are called collectively the "legislative history" of the statute. Because the activities are so multifarious, use of legislative history by the courts is sometimes disparaged as being comparable to a performer looking out at an audience and waving to his friends.

There is not much to indicate that the legislators in fact do their work with the canons of construction in mind. One of the canons states that expression of one thing excludes another, similar thing. Legislators frequently will insert specific amendments to emphasize a particular concern without considering this canon. Another canon (ejusdem generis) states that when an enumeration of examples is followed by a general catchall phrase, the catchall phrase can apply only to persons or things of the same general kind or class that were specifically mentioned. Notwithstanding this canon, the statutes and court decisions are full of examples where the catchall phrase was not so limited. In any event, the canons frequently contradict each other, and even when they are consistent, they are not always consistently applied.

All agree that the individual expressions of purposes by individual members of Congress ought not be controlling—not even when such an expression comes from the sponsor of the legislation. Statements of purpose voiced after the statute is passed are almost never given any weight; the theory of legislative interpretation turns on deciphering the purposes of the legislative body *before* the statute was voted upon.

Even the record of congressional debate may be suspect. Members of Congress frequently engage in artificial floor debate in an effort to influence the way in which a statute will be interpreted in the future. A dialogue will be written out between two or more members in which questions of interpretation of particular parts of the statute will be asked and answered. Because these dialogues usually involve only a few members and are not voted upon by the entire membership, the weight to be accorded such "debate" should be light. However, many judges are beguiled by such artificial legislative maneuvers.

Congress sometimes avoids elaborating the minute details of its intent by delegating the effectuation and elaboration of its purpose to an ADMINISTRATIVE AGENCY. A large number of statutes establish agencies to administer programs created by Congress. Two examples are the Environmental Protection Agency, which is mandated to administer and enforce the environmental laws passed by Congress, and the Securities and Exchange Commission, which is mandated to administer and enforce the securities laws passed by Congress. The laws usually provide that an appeal may be taken from the final decision of the administrative agency to the federal courts. In such an appeal, the interpretation placed on the statute by the agency charged with its administration is to be given great weight by the reviewing courts. Unless the agency has violated the plain meaning of the statute, the courts are supposed to defer to whatever interpretation the agency places upon the statute. The theory behind this doctrine, derived from *Chevron USA, Inc. v. Natural Resources Defense Council* (1984), is that the agency has been charged by Congress to be the main actor in that particular field, and the courts should not interfere with the discretion exercised by the agency.

Many STATE CONSTITUTIONS require the state legislatures to enact statutes limited to a single subject. This limitation makes it easier for the legislators and the citizenry to know what is in a statute and assists courts in interpreting the meaning of a statute. The United States Constitution has never contained such a limitation, and Congress routinely includes a variety of provisions and subjects in a single bill. A single continuing appropriation bill passed by the Congress can contain substantive law provisions covering a wide range of topics. Because some of these provisions are inserted during floor debate and do not have much legislative history, it is frequently difficult to decipher a provision intention or purpose except from the brief explanation that may be made by the sponsor.

Finding the legislative purpose or motive of a particular statute is one of the difficult tasks given over to administrative agencies and the courts.

ABNER J. MIKVA
(1992)

(SEE ALSO: *Environmental Regulation and the Constitution; Securities Law and the Constitution*.)

Bibliography

FRANKFURTER, FELIX 1947 Some Reflections on the Reading of Statutes. *Columbia Law Review* 47:527–546.

LLEWELLYN, KARL N. 1950 Remarks on the Theory of Appellate Decision and the Rules or Canons About How Statutes Are to Be Construed. *Vanderbilt Law Review* 3:395–406.

MIKVA, ABNER J. 1987 Reading and Writing Statutes. *University of Pittsburgh Law Review* 48:627–637.

LEGISLATIVE VETO

The legislative veto emerged in the 1930s as an effort to reconcile two conflicting needs. Executive officials sought greater discretionary authority, while Congress wanted to retain control over delegated authority without having to adopt new legislation for that purpose. The resulting accommodation permitted administrators to submit proposals that would become law unless Congress acted to disapprove by simple resolution (a one-house veto) or concurrent resolution (a two-house veto). Evolving forms of the legislative veto came to include requirements of congressional approval as well as opportunities for disapproval; Congress even vested some of the controls in its committees.

Although the legislative veto acquired a reputation as a congressional usurpation of executive power, initially the device favored the President. In 1932 Congress authorized President HERBERT C. HOOVER to reorganize the executive branch. His plans would become law within sixty days unless either house disapproved. The President did not have to secure the support of both houses, as would have been necessary through the regular legislative process. Instead, the burden was placed on Congress to veto his initiatives. Furthermore, to prevent presidential proposals from being buried in committee, filibustered, or changed by Congress, the law limited each opportunity for legislative veto by rules for discharging committees, restricting congressional debate, and prohibiting committee or floor amendments.

The executive branch began to view the legislative veto apprehensively when Congress attached it to statutes governing such important subjects as lend lease, IMMIGRATION, public works, energy, IMPOUNDMENT, federal salaries, foreign trade, and the WAR POWERS. As part of the congressional reassertion after the VIETNAM WAR and WATERGATE, legislative vetoes proliferated in the 1970s. By the late 1970s, Congress seemed on the verge of subjecting every federal regulation to some form of legislative veto.

The lower federal courts upheld some legislative vetoes and invalidated others, but carefully restricted their opinions to the particular statutes challenged. In 1982, however, the UNITED STATES COURT OF APPEALS for the District of Columbia Circuit struck down three laws on such broad grounds as to cast a shadow of illegality over every type of legislative veto. The Supreme Court adopted this comprehensive approach in IMMIGRATION AND NATURALIZATION SERVICE V. CHADHA (1983), invalidating the Immigration and Nationality Act's authorization for either house of Congress to set aside the attorney general's decision to suspend the DEPORTATION of an alien.

Chief Justice WARREN E. BURGER, joined by five Justices, wrote the OPINION OF THE COURT. The one-house legislative veto in *Chadha* was unconstitutional because it violated both the principle of BICAMERALISM and the presentment clause of the Constitution, which requires every bill, resolution, or vote to which the concurrence of the SENATE and the HOUSE OF REPRESENTATIVES is necessary (except a vote of adjournment) to be presented to the President. Whenever congressional action has the "purpose and effect of altering the legal rights, duties and relations of persons" outside the legislative branch, the Court said, Congress must act through both houses in a bill presented to the President.

Justice LEWIS F. POWELL concurred in the judgment on

a narrower ground. Justice BYRON R. WHITE delivered a lengthy dissent, generally supporting the constitutionality of the legislative veto. Justice WILLIAM H. REHNQUIST also dissented, but only on the question of SEVERABILITY. He said that if the Court declared the legislative veto invalid, it should also strike down the attorney general's authority to suspend deportations.

The majority's opinion raises numerous questions. First, in holding the legislative veto severable from the attorney general's authority, the Court ignored clear evidence of a quid pro quo between Congress and the President. If severability could be discerned in this legislative history, presumably it can be found in nearly every statute establishing a legislative veto. This reasoning gives the executive branch a temporary one-sided advantage from an accommodation meant to balance executive and legislative interests.

Second, the Court asserted that the legislative veto's efficiency or convenience would not save it "if it is contrary to the Constitution. Convenience and efficiency are not the primary objectives—or the hallmarks—of democratic government. . . ." Although the legislative veto might be a "convenient shortcut" and an "appealing compromise," the Court said, it is "crystal clear from the records of the Convention, contemporaneous writings and debates, that the Framers ranked other values higher than efficiency." Here the Court played loose with history, for efficiency was indeed an important consideration for the Framers. The decade prior to the CONSTITUTIONAL CONVENTION saw an anxious and persistent search for a form of government that would perform more efficiently than the ARTICLES OF CONFEDERATION.

Third, the Court characterized the presentment clause as a means of giving the President the power of self-defense against an encroaching Congress. The President's veto would check "oppressive, improvident, or ill-considered measures." This argument is misleading in suggesting that the legislative veto, by evading the President's veto, threatened the independence of the executive branch. In fact, the legislative veto was directed only against measures submitted by the President. Congress could not amend his proposals, but must vote yes or no. A legislative veto, if exercised, simply reestablished the status quo. For example, if either house defeated a reorganization plan the structure of government would remain as before. The President did not need his veto for purposes of "self-defense."

Fourth, the Court said that the Framers had unmistakably expressed their "determination that legislation by the national Congress be a step-by-step, deliberate and deliberative process." But both houses of Congress regularly use "shortcut" methods that pose no problems under *Chadha:* suspending the rules, asking for unanimous consent, placing legislative riders on appropriations bills, and even passing bills that have never been sent to committee.

The Court's theory of government contradicts practices developed over a period of decades by the political branches. Neither administrators nor members of Congress want the static model proffered by the Court. The conditions that spawned the legislative veto over a half-century ago have not disappeared. Executive officials still want substantial latitude in administering delegated authority; legislators still want to maintain control without having to pass new legislation. Surely the executive and legislative branches will develop substitutes to serve as the functional equivalent of the legislative veto. Forms will change; the substance will not.

Instead of a one-house veto over executive reorganization, Congress is likely to require a joint resolution of approval. This device, which satisfies the tests of bicameralism and presentment, requires the President to obtain the support of both Houses within a specified number of days. If one house withholds its support, the effect is a one-house veto.

Internal House and Senate rules offer another option. Congress can require that funds be appropriated only after an authorizing committee has passed a resolution of approval. Although this procedure amounts to a committee veto, the Justice Department may acquiesce, accepting Congress's distinction between authorization and appropriation and reasoning that Congress can control its own internal processes.

Congress can also attach a rider to an appropriations bill to prevent an agency from implementing a proposed action. Because a President will rarely veto an appropriations bill (and probably will never do so because of an objectionable rider), the practical effect of this device is that of a two-house veto. Indeed, House-Senate comity will often produce the effect of a one-house veto.

Statutes can require that selected committees be notified before agency implementation of certain programs. Notification raises no constitutional issue, for it falls within the report-and-wait category already sanctioned by court rulings. But "notification" can become a code word for prior committee approval. Only in unusual circumstances would an agency defy the wishes of its oversight committees.

After *Chadha,* Congress will continue to use informal and nonstatutory methods to control the executive branch. Congress allows agencies to shift funds within an appropriation account provided they obtain committee approval for major changes. Agencies comply because they want to retain this administrative flexibility. Because these "gentlemen's agreements" are not placed in statutes, they are unaffected by *Chadha.* They are not legal in effect. They are, however, in effect legal.

Last, Congress has continued to authorize legislative vetoes in statutes adopted after *Chadha.* Although these provisions are unconstitutional under the Court's decision, agencies are likely to abide by them rather than alienate powerful support committees on Capitol Hill. When the practical needs of executive officials and legislators coincide, they nearly always prevail over formalistic notions of SEPARATION OF POWERS.

LOUIS FISHER
(1986)

Bibliography

BOLTON, JOHN R. and ABRAMS, KEVIN G. 1984 The Judicial and Congressional Response to the Invalidation of the Legislative Veto. *Journal of Law and Politics* 1:299–355.
STRAUSS, PETER L. 1983 Was There a Baby in the Bathwater? A Comment on the Supreme Court's Legislative Veto Decision. *Duke Law Journal* 1983:789–819.
SYLVESTER, KATHLEEN 1984 After Chadha, A Legal Void. *National Law Journal*, April 23, 1984, pp. 1, 8, 10.

LEHMAN v. SHAKER HEIGHTS

See: Captive Audience

LEISY v. HARDIN
135 U.S. 100 (1890)

Chief Justice MELVILLE W. FULLER, speaking for a six-member majority, ruled that because Congress possesses an EXCLUSIVE POWER under the COMMERCE CLAUSE to regulate interstate transportation, no state may enact a liquor PROHIBITION statute that bars the sale in that state of liquors imported from other states and sold in their original packages. That Congress had not exercised its commerce power was equivalent to a declaration that commerce shall be free. Any DOCTRINE to the contrary, deriving from the LICENSE CASES (1847), said Fuller, was "overthrown." Congress might, however, specifically authorize a state to ban interstate liquors; the Court sustained such an act of Congress in *In re Rahrer* (1891).

LEONARD W. LEVY
(1986)

LELAND, JOHN
(1754–1841)

A native of Massachusetts and a Baptist minister, John Leland preached in Virginia from 1776 to 1791, becoming a leader in the Baptists' struggle against the Anglican church establishment there and helping to bring about its dismantlement. At first he opposed the federal Constitution on the grounds that it lacked a BILL OF RIGHTS and safeguards against taxsupported clergy; but he later switched his stand—possibly converted by JAMES MADISON personally—and swung Virginia's Baptists behind ratification.

Leland held that state attempts to foster religion only corrupted religion. A defender of both civil and RELIGIOUS LIBERTY, he supported religious rights for all, repudiating the notion of a Christian commonwealth. He opposed attempts to halt Sunday mail delivery, and by denying that government had power to pass sabbath laws, proclaim public days of prayer, or pay chaplains, he assumed a more radical stance on church and state than did most contemporary evangelicals.

THOMAS CURRY
(1986)

Bibliography

BUTTERFIELD, L. H. 1952 Elder John Leland, Jeffersonian Itinerant. *American Antiquarian Society Proceedings* 62:155–242.

LEMON v. KURTZMAN
403 U.S. 602 (1971) (I)
411 U.S. 192 1973) (II)

This case involved one of the school aid statutes produced by state legislatures in the wake of BOARD OF EDUCATION V. ALLEN (1968). *Lemon* I stands for three cases joined for decision by the Court. Lemon challenged the constitutionality of a Pennsylvania statute that authorized the Superintendent of Public Instruction to reimburse nonpublic schools for teachers' salaries, textbooks, and instructional materials in secular subjects. *Erley v. DiCenso* and *Robinson v. DiCenso* (1971) challenged a Rhode Island statute that made available direct payments to teachers in nonpublic schools in amounts of up to fifteen percent of their regular salaries.

Both statutes were unconstitutional, Chief Justice WARREN BURGER concluded, and he set forth a threefold test which continues to be invoked in ESTABLISHMENT OF RELIGION cases: any program aiding a church-related institution must have an adequate secular purpose; it must have a primary effect that neither advances nor inhibits religion; and government must not be excessively entangled with religious institutions in the administration of the program. The Pennsylvania and Rhode Island schemes provided GOVERNMENT AID TO RELIGIOUS INSTITUTIONS. Burger argued that in order to see that these dollars were not used for religious instruction, the states would have to monitor compliance in ways involving excessive entanglement.

Lemon v. Kurtzman returned to the Court (*Lemon* II) two years later on the question of whether the Pennsylvania schools could retain the monies that had been paid out in the period between the implementation of law and the decision of the Supreme Court invalidating it in *Lemon* I. In a PLURALITY OPINION for himself and Justices HARRY BLACKMUN, LEWIS F. POWELL, and WILLIAM H. REHNQUIST, Chief Justice Burger held that they could. An unconstitutional statute, he suggested, is not absolutely void but is a practical reality upon which people are entitled to rely until authoritatively informed otherwise. Justice BYRON R. WHITE concurred. Justice WILLIAM O. DOUGLAS, joined by Justices WILLIAM J. BRENNAN and POTTER STEWART, dissented. Douglas argued that there was "clear warning to those who proposed such subsidies" that they were treading on unconstitutional ground. "No consideration of EQUITY," Douglas suggested, should allow them "to profit from their unconstitutional venture."

RICHARD E. MORGAN
(1986)

LEMON TEST

The *Lemon* test is the three-part formula used by the Supreme Court to decide whether or not a government action violates the ESTABLISHMENT CLAUSE. The first part requires that the government action have a secular purpose; the second part demands that the action neither advance nor inhibit religion as its primary effect; and the final part dictates that the act not cause an excessive entanglement between church and state. The test was first announced in LEMON V. KURTZMAN (1971), though its major components date back, at least, to the majority opinion in ABINGTON TOWNSHIP SCHOOL DISTRICT V. SCHEMPP (1963).

The test's first prong remained noncontroversial throughout most of the 1970s, with the Court invariably finding a secular purpose for statutes under review. Then came the Court's decision in *Stone v. Graham* (1979), which struck down a Kentucky law requiring the posting of the Ten Commandments in public classrooms. Kentucky claimed that the purpose of the posting was to inform students of the influence of the Ten Commandments on secular history—and, in fact, the Commandments were to be accompanied by a message pointing out their influence on the development of Western law. But the Court found this "avowed" secular purpose insufficient and claimed that the state's actual purpose was to promote religion. This distinction between "actual" and "avowed" secular purposes was adopted by Justice SANDRA DAY O'CONNOR in her restatement of the *Lemon* test in LYNCH V. DONNELLY (1984), and the distinction became increasingly important thereafter. In WALLACE V. JAFFREE (1984) the Court struck down a law providing for a schoolroom moment of silence because the legislators' actual motive was to promote religion; and in *Edwards v. Aguillard* (1987) the Court invalidated for the same reason Louisiana's Balanced Treatment Act, which claimed to promote ACADEMIC FREEDOM in the discussion of CREATIONISM.

The actual-purpose approach has drawn serious criticism; the most sustained critique of the approach was delivered by Justice ANTONIN SCALIA in his dissent in *Aguillard.* If religious motivation by itself invalidates a piece of legislation, wrote Scalia, then a great deal of legislation indeed may have to be invalidated: "Today's religious activism may give us the Balanced Treatment Act, but yesterday's resulted in the abolition of slavery, and tomorrow's may bring relief for famine victims." Moreover, if the Court really wants to strike down legislation on the basis of motivations, it had better go about it in a more thorough manner. Scalia suggested that to ascertain the dominant motivation behind a bill reliably, one would need to tally the views of every legislator. Scalia's criticism may have had an effect, for Justice O'Connor took a step back from the actual-purpose standard in her majority opinion in WESTSIDE COMMUNITY SCHOOLS V. MERGENS (1990).

But the first prong of *Lemon* is not the only part of the test to spark debate in recent years; controversy has also erupted over its second prong—spurred in part by the Court's maze of contradictory decisions involving GOVERNMENT AID TO RELIGIOUS INSTITUTIONS. Seeking greater clarity in the application of the second prong, Justice O'Connor has convinced a majority of her colleagues to reformulate it. The inquiry under the second prong has shifted from determining the primary effect of a government act to ascertaining whether the government action has "in fact conveyed a message of endorsement or disapproval" of religion. Under this new inquiry, an act may (or may not) violate the establishment clause, regardless of whether it advances or inhibits religion as a primary effect; the crucial factor is the public message conveyed by the act.

Justice ANTHONY M. KENNEDY has been the Court's most vocal critic of O'Connor's endorsement inquiry, and in COUNTY OF ALLEGHENY V. AMERICAN CIVIL LIBERTIES UNION (1989) he offered his own reformulation of *Lemon's* second prong in response. Kennedy's reformulation prohibits two types of government action: direct government benefits that tend to establish a state religion, and government coercion to engage in religious activity. Kennedy's opinion was joined by Chief Justice WILLIAM H. REHNQUIST and Justices Antonin Scalia and BYRON R. WHITE. All four Justices have indicated a dislike for the *Lemon* test, and

Kennedy may be laying the groundwork to replace it altogether.

JOHN G. WEST, JR.
(1992)

(SEE ALSO: *Religious Fundamentalism; Separation of Church and State.*)

Bibliography

LEVY, LEONARD W. 1986 *The Establishment Clause: Religion and the First Amendment.* Chapter 6. New York: Macmillan.
THEUER, JEFFREY S. 1988 The Lemon Test and Subjective Intent in Establishment Clause Analysis: The Case for Abandoning the Purpose Prong. *Kentucky Law Journal* 76:1061–1075.

LEMON TEST
(Update)

In LEMON V. KURTZMAN (1971), the Supreme Court announced a three-part ESTABLISHMENT CLAUSE test, under which a challenged government action, to be valid, must satisfy each of the following criteria: (1) it must have a secular purpose, (2) its "primary effect" must neither advance nor inhibit religion, and (3) it must not create an "excessive government entanglement with religion." The Court applied this test regularly for about fifteen years. Since the mid-1980s, however, the test increasingly has been criticized as excessively hostile to religion, historically misguided, and incoherent. Although the three *Lemon* factors remain relevant to judicial decisions, their strength has been modified substantially, and the future of even this modified *Lemon* test remains uncertain.

Only rarely has the Court invalidated a statute under the first part of the *Lemon* test. In *Stone v. Graham* (1979), the Court held that a statute requiring posting of the Ten Commandments in public classrooms was unconstitutional for want of a secular purpose. Similarly, in WALLACE V. JAFFREE (1984) and *Edwards v. Aguillard* (1987), the Court invalidated statutes that required, respectively, a moment of silence in public classrooms and the teaching of creationism in public schools. In other cases, the Court readily has found a secular purpose and proceeded to *Lemon*'s effects and entanglement inquiries.

The Court has developed and modified its criteria for unconstitutional effects and entanglement primarily in cases reviewing GOVERNMENT AID TO RELIGIOUS INSTITUTIONS. Through the 1970s and 1980s, the premise of the Court's effects analysis was that religious schools are "pervasively sectarian" institutions in which religious and secular education are inextricably intertwined; accordingly, any "direct and substantial aid" to religious schools' "edu-

cational function" unconstitutionally advances religion. On this approach, modified substantially in recent years, the Court was most concerned that government-paid teachers or guidance counselors, sent into religious schools to perform even secular tasks, might conform to the sectarian environment and engage in religious indoctrination. The Court invariably invalidated such programs. Government must be certain that its employees do not engage in religious indoctrination, the Court said, and the sectarian environment made such certainty unattainable. Furthermore, even when government tried to avoid these unconstitutional effects—by monitoring its aid programs to ensure that they neither provided nor subsidized religious indoctrination—the Court held that these monitoring efforts unconstitutionally entangled government and religion.

The high-water mark of this approach came in the 1985 companion cases, *School District of Grand Rapids v. Ball* and AGUILAR V. FELTON. Even by that time, however, sharp criticism had begun to develop, both off the Court and among the Justices. The year before, in her LYNCH V. DONNELLY (1984) concurrence, Justice SANDRA DAY O'CONNOR had proposed what she called a "clarification" of the *Lemon* test, under which courts should inquire whether government has acted with the purpose or effect of conveying its endorsement or disapproval of religion. Alongside this endorsement test, O'Connor presented a weakened version of the *Lemon* entanglement inquiry. O'Connor's approach was less aggressively separationist than the conventional *Lemon* analysis, but more demanding than the other theories that began to proliferate on the Court.

One of those other theories was the "nonpreferentialist" approach that then-Justice WILLIAM H. REHNQUIST, announced in his 1985 *Wallace v. Jaffree* dissent. According to Rehnquist, the establishment clause's meaning is defined by its drafters' intention to bar only governmental preference for one sect over another. Four years later, Justice ANTHONY M. KENNEDY proposed yet another alternative test, under which the clause prohibits government from coercing participation in religious activity or delegating government power to religious groups. While Kennedy obtained a bare majority for his opinion in LEE V. WEISMAN (1992), holding that a clergy-led SCHOOL PRAYER at a public-school graduation was unconstitutionally coercive, he was unable to persuade his majority that coercion is the appropriate test.

Many commentators in the late 1980s and early 1990s believed that the *Lemon* test was either dead or in its death throes. But the Court was unable to establish majority support for any of the alternative tests. Still, by 1994 it became clear that five Justices agreed on a more limited modification of the *Lemon* framework. In three separate opinions filed in BOARD OF EDUCATION OF KIRYAS JOEL VILLAGE SCHOOL DISTRICT V. GRUMET (1994), Chief Justice Rehnquist, and Justices O'Connor, ANTONIN SCALIA, Kennedy, and CLARENCE THOMAS, suggested OVERRULING the *Ball* and *Aguilar* PRECEDENTS at the next opportunity.

Those five Justices seized that opportunity in AGOSTINI V. FELTON (1997). *Agostini*'s procedural context was unusual: the City of New York, still enjoined from providing the program of remedial instruction invalidated in *Aguilar*, moved for relief from the *Aguilar* judgment. This context had an important effect: under the Court's earlier interpretation of the relevant procedural rule, the Court could not change the law in its *Agostini* decision. Instead, the Court could only recognize post-*Aguilar* changes already in place. *Agostini*'s five-Justice majority, with O'Connor writing, found those changes in WITTERS V. WASHINGTON DEPARTMENT OF SERVICES FOR THE BLIND (1986), and *Zobrest v. Catalina Foothills School District* (1993). Both decisions had held that if government aid is available generally and neutrally, without regard to the nature of the institution at which it is expended, then the program is not readily subject to establishment clause challenge. Both decisions, further, held that because the challenged aid reached religious schools only through recipients' private choices, the state had not unconstitutionally subsidized religious indoctrination.

In *Agostini*'s revised establishment clause test, *Lemon*'s purpose inquiry remains unchanged, and the clause still bars the effect of advancing or inhibiting religion. But entanglement now is but one of three factors in the effects test, not a separate inquiry. The other two criteria of unconstitutional effect are whether the government action results in government indoctrination—either by government employees' own actions, or by state subsidization of religious education—and whether the action operates by reference to religion.

Some aspects of this revision are clear. *Agostini* decisively repudiates the presumption that publicly employed teachers and guidance counselors are likely to engage in religious indoctrination when charged with purely secular tasks. *Agostini* is clear, also, that government monitoring for indoctrination is not by itself unconstitutional entanglement. But other aspects are unclear, particularly when one considers the issue of school vouchers, or SCHOOL CHOICE, that seems destined for Court review. On one hand, a program making vouchers available to all needy students, regardless of whether they attend sectarian or nonsectarian schools, would have the generality and neutrality that now point toward constitutionality. Further, whether vouchers actually benefit religious schools would depend on recipients' private choices—a second factor *Agostini* identified as favoring constitutionality. On the other hand, however, the Court could invalidate such a program as an unconstitutional subsidy to religious indoctrination. A comprehensive voucher program would have the two consequences *Agostini* considers relevant to unconstitutional subsidy: government money would flow into religious schools' coffers, and the program likely would relieve religious schools of costs they otherwise would have borne. A program making vouchers generally available for specifically religious education, not just for secular instruction, would go well beyond the programs so far approved.

No doubt one reason for *Agostini*'s ambiguity is continuing disagreement as to the proper establishment clause test. Another reason concerns the case's procedural context, which prevented the Court from reformulating—or admitting it was reformulating—establishment clause DOCTRINE. The Court would have done better to reconsider *Aguilar* and *Ball* in a context that would have allowed *Lemon*'s systematic reexamination. The Court's claim not to have innovated in *Agostini* is unpersuasive, and the apparent agreement on a constitutional test could dissolve in the next case, in which the Court would be more free to revise its doctrinal position.

That next case will be before the Court in its 1999–2000 term. The issue in *Mitchell v. Helms* (CERTIORARI granted on June 14, 1999) is whether the government may provide secular instructional materials, such as computers, to sectarian as well as non-sectarian schools. The lower court applied *Lemon* precedents from the 1970s to invalidate the challenged aid. Those precedents are at least in tension with *Agostini*'s rendition of the *Lemon* test, and the Court may well overrule them. Because the Court will be free in *Mitchell* from the procedural complications that affected *Agostini*, it could use the case as a vehicle for altering the constitutional test more systematically—perhaps adopting one of the alternative tests that various Justices have urged in separate opinions, or perhaps adopting a compromise version that presses the neutrality theme less ambiguously than did *Agostini*. But the Court need not do so to uphold the aid challenged in *Mitchell*, and nothing indicates that the Court is less divided as to the ideal establishment clause inquiry than it has been in the past. The long-term durability of *Agostini*'s modified *Lemon* test likely will remain uncertain until the Court considers the voucher issue.

HUGH BAXTER
(2000)

Bibliography

BAXTER, HUGH 1998 Managing Legal Change: The Transformation of Establishment Clause Law. *UCLA Law Review* 46: 343–457.

LAYCOCK, DOUGLAS 1997 The Underlying Unity of Separation and Neutrality. *Emory Law Review* 46:43–74.

LEVINSON, SANFORD 1997 Religious Language and the Public Square. *Harvard Law Review* 105:2061–2079.

LEVY, LEONARD W. 1986 *The Establishment Clause: Religion and the First Amendment.* New York: Macmillan.

McCONNELL, MICHAEL 1992 Religious Freedom at a Crossroads. *University of Chicago Law Review* 59:115–194.

LEON, UNITED STATES v.

See: Good Faith Exception

LESBIANISM

See: *Bowers v. Hardwick*; Same-Sex Marriage; Sexual Discrimination; Sexual Orientation; Sexual Preference and the Constitution

LETTERS OF MARQUE AND REPRISAL

Letters of marque and reprisal are commissions that governments of belligerent powers grant to private shipowners (called "privateers") authorizing them to seize the vessels and property of enemy subjects on the high seas. During the Revolutionary War both the STATES and the CONTINENTAL CONGRESS issued letters of marque; but the Constitution grants Congress the power to issue them and denies it to the states. Although not a signatory to the Declaration of Paris (1856), which condemned privateering as contrary to the law of nations, the United States has issued no letters of marque since that time.

DENNIS J. MAHONEY
(1986)

LEVER FOOD AND DRUG CONTROL ACT
40 Stat. 276 (1917)

The administration proposed this legislation to Congress, arguing that "the existence of a STATE OF WAR" made it "essential to the national security and defense" for the federal government to control the supply and pricing of food and fuel. By subjecting those industries AFFECTED WITH A PUBLIC INTEREST to federal regulation, Congress effectively delegated control of significant sectors of the economy to the President. Section 4, the heart of the act, outlawed the destruction, waste, hoarding, or price-fixing of commodities. Further sections, in an exceptionally broad DELEGATION OF POWER, authorized the President to regulate the food industry and to seize and operate "any factory, packing house, oil pipe line, mine, or other plant" engaged in commodity production.

In *United States v. L. Cohen Grocery Company* (1921), a unanimous Supreme Court struck down section 4 for failing to set adequate standards for prices. The criminal provisions unconstitutionally delegated "legislative power to courts and juries" and deprived "the citizen of the right to be informed of the nature and cause of the accusation against him," violating the Fifth and Sixth Amendments. Although the Court struck down particular provisions for VAGUENESS, it did not reach the issue of the government's authority to regulate prices under the WAR POWERS, and the Lever Act would later serve as a model for other regulatory legislation

DAVID GORDON
(1986)

LEVY v. LOUISIANA
391 U.S. 68 (1968)
GLONA v. AMERICAN GUARANTEE & LIABILITY INSURANCE CO.
391 U.S. 73 (1968)

In these decisions the Supreme Court began to subject legislative classifications based on ILLEGITIMACY of parentage to heightened judicial scrutiny. Both cases arose out of Louisiana's statute allowing an action for damages on behalf of the survivors of a decedent against a person who wrongfully caused the decedent's death. *Levy* invalidated, 6–3, a provision denying an illegitimate child the right to recover damages for the death of a parent, and *Glona* invalidated, 6–3, a corresponding provision disallowing a parent's recovery of damages for the death of an illegitimate child.

The two opinions for the Court, by Justice WILLIAM O. DOUGLAS, were very brief. Douglas purported to accept the RATIONAL BASIS STANDARD OF REVIEW. The rights asserted, however, involved "the intimate, familial relationship between a child and his own mother." And illegitimacy bore no relation to the nature of the harm inflicted in either case. The accident of a child's illegitimate birth did not justify denying his rights, and if the state sought to punish the mother of an illegitimate child for her "sin," denying her wrongful death damages was an irrational means for doing so.

It is plain that in these cases the Court was employing a standard of review considerably more demanding than its "rational basis" language suggested. Justice JOHN MARSHALL HARLAN, for the dissenters, took note of this heightened scrutiny, and opposed it. Any definition of the plaintiff class in a wrongful death statute must be artificial; a biological definition would attune the law neither to degrees of love nor to degrees of economic dependence between decedents and survivors. It was not irrational for Louisiana to "simplify" its wrongful death proceedings by using formal marriage as the key to defining the plaintiff class.

Left unspoken by both Douglas and Harlan was the time-dishonored use of the law of illegitimacy in many southern states as a covert form of RACIAL DISCRIMINATION in controlling the transmission of wealth from white fathers to their racially diverse offspring.

KENNETH L. KARST
(1986)

LIBEL AND THE FIRST AMENDMENT

A central historical question about the FIRST AMENDMENT is to what extent it embodied the received eighteenth-century legal traditions of English law and governmental practice as they were reshaped and renewed in the colonial, revolutionary, and formative periods in America. Or was the amendment a break from these traditions? This issue can be stated either as a question of the intent of the Framers and ratifiers or as a matter of the normative impact of an authoritative text, elaborated in our century within an institutional matrix of JUDICIAL REVIEW radically different from that of the eighteenth century on either side of the Atlantic. However the question be stated, the historical problem is in essence whether the First Amendment is to be regarded as expressing a principle of continuity with the received legal tradition or as constituting a declaration of independence from English law, thereby projecting the American law of freedom of expression on a path of autonomous development.

The general view emphasizes continuity, both as a matter of the original understanding of the Framers of the First Amendment and as a matter of the amendment's later—much later—doctrinal elaborations. Indeed, we conventionally measure continuity or discontinuity by reference to the basic conceptual dichotomy of the English legal tradition, as formulated by WILLIAM BLACKSTONE, the oracle of the COMMON LAW for the framing generation:

> where blasphemous, immoral, treasonable, schismatical, seditious, or scandalous libels are punished by the English law . . . the liberty of the press, properly understood, is by no means infringed or violated. The *liberty of the press* is indeed essential to the nature of a free state, but this consists in laying no previous restraints upon publications, and not in freedom from censure for criminal matter when published. Every freeman has an undoubted right to lay what sentiments he pleases before the public: to forbid this is to destroy the freedom of the press: but if he publishes what is improper, mischievous, or illegal, he must take the consequences of his own temerity [*Commentaries on the Laws of England*, 1765, Bk. 4, chap. II, pp. 151–52].

The issue whether the First Amendment embraced or departed from the English legal tradition with respect to subsequent punishment tends to be fixed on the treatment of SEDITIOUS LIBEL. The historical argument for the law of seditious libel has been that government ought to have power to punish its most abusive or subversive critics because criticism of government contains the seeds of a variety of evils—disobedience to government, public disorder, even violence—and that no government can subsist if people have the right to criticize it or to call its agents corrupt or incompetent. This is seen in the work of Leonard W. Levy, ZECHARIAH CHAFEE, and others who have lately examined the First Amendment's historical foundations by looking at seditious libel as the exclusive focus for probing the question of continuity and discontinuity with respect to subsequent punishments. Having narrowed the issue to seditious libel, the scholarly tradition put the question of continuity and discontinuity in all-or-nothing terms: Does the First Amendment as a matter of original understanding, or as a matter of latter doctrinal connotation, repudiate or embrace the concept of seditious libel?

When a question about the relationship of a controversial legal tradition to a broadly phrased constitutional text is put in such terms, the answers are likely to fall out along dialectical lines. So it has been with the rejection-or-reception issue concerning seditious libel. The heated debate on the question by the Federalists and Republicans in connection with the passage of the ALIEN AND SEDITION ACTS of 1798 has been echoed through our history. In modern scholarship, the dialectic begins in 1919 when Zechariah Chafee, troubled deeply by the World War I ESPIONAGE ACT prosecutions, wrote in the *Harvard Law Review* that the Framers of the First Amendment "intended to wipe out the common law of SEDITION, and to make further prosecutions for criticism of the government, without any incitement to law-breaking, forever impossible in the United States of America." Six months later, and plainly in emulation, Justice OLIVER WENDELL HOLMES added the weight of his and LOUIS D. BRANDEIS's authority to the Chafee thesis, when he declared in his great dissent in the *Abrams* case: "I wholly disagree with the argument . . . that the first Amendment left the common law as to seditious libel in force. History seems to me against the notion." But the Chafee position never won the broad adherence that most modern scholars seem to think it had. In the World War I free speech cases before the Supreme court, John Lord O'Brien, who briefed the cases for the Justice Department, stated as the official view of the government that seditious libel prosecutions were not rendered invalid by the First Amendment, either as a matter of original intent or as correctly understood in 1919. And others, including EDWARD S. CORWIN, dissented from the Chafee position. Indeed, Chafee himself seems to have changed his tune by 1949, at least on the issue of the Framers' original intent: "The truth is, I think, that the framers had no very clear idea as to what they meant by 'the freedom of speech or the press.'" The dialectic about seditious libel and the First Amendment entered a new phase with the publication of Leonard W. Levy's seminal work, *Legacy of Suppression,* in 1960. This book argued that with respect to the general conceptions of FREEDOM OF THE PRESS prevalent at the time of the framing and ratification of the First Amendment, there was no solid evidence of a consensus to move away from a purely Blackstonian conception of freedom, that is, a conception limited to protecting only against previous restraints. In particular, Levy found considerable evidence that supported the continuing validity of seditious libel prosecutions, and no clear evidence that any lawyer, pamphleteer, philosopher, or statesman repudiated the concept of seditious libel. There was, Levy recognized, a growing sense of the necessity of the defense of truth, although far from a clear consensus even on that. And there was also a growing insistence on the independent power of the jury in a seditious libel prosecution to determine the issue of truth and the question of the seditious quality of any publication, as well as the other factual issues in the case.

Levy's account of the relationship of the First Amendment as a formal constitutional limitation on the power of Congress and his overall conception of intellectual and legal history respecting freedom of expression has from the beginning been confused by the problem of FEDERALISM. At the same time that he has insisted that the conception of freedom of the press guarded against abridgment by the First Amendment does not invalidate seditious libel, he has described the amendment as denying any power whatever by Congress to legislate with respect to the press, except to protect COPYRIGHT. Thus, he concluded that Congress had no power to pass the Sedition Act of 1798, but on federalism grounds, not because the Sedition Act violated any understandings about press freedom embodied in the First Amendment. The states and the federal courts remained empowered to try seditious libel prosecutions.

But Levy's interpretation of the "Congress shall make no law" language in the First Amendment has taken a distant backseat, in his own writing and in that of others, to his overriding emphasis that "the freedom of speech or of the press" was not understood to repudiate the concept of seditious libel. In other words, the First Amendment was understood to embody a Blackstonian conception of freedom of expression as a matter of original intent.

In NEW YORK TIMES CO. V. SULLIVAN (1964) the Supreme Court gave an authoritative modern answer to the question whether prosecution of seditious libel would survive the First Amendment. An advertisement in March 1960, placed by supporters of MARTIN LUTHER KING, JR., in the *New York Times;* recited the repressive activities of Alabama police with several minor inaccuracies and exaggerations. An Alabama jury awarded a local official $500,000 damages against the *New York Times.* The Supreme Court reacted with sweeping changes in the constitutional status of defamation law. Libel would no longer be viewed as a category of expression beneath First Amendment protection. Instead, the Court found that the political repudiation of the Sedition Act of 1798 had revealed the "central meaning" of the First Amendment: a right to criticize government and public officials. As the Court put it, "[A] rule compelling the critic of official conduct to guarantee the truth of all his factual assertions . . . leads to . . . 'self-censorship.'" The Alabama act, "because of the restraint it imposed upon criticism of government and public officials," was inconsistent with the First Amendment.

In place of actual falsity as a basis for liability, the Court imposed a new standard to govern defamation actions brought by public officials. Now, a public official could recover damages for a defamatory falsehood relating to his official conduct only upon a showing "that the statement was made with 'actual malice'—that is, with knowledge that it was false or with reckless disregard of whether it was false or not."

Sullivan effected important changes in constitutional law and practice. Defamation law previously had been left to the states, subject to gradual common law evolution in state courts not often exposed to First Amendment issues. *Sullivan* federalized this diversity of local rules into a single national body of doctrine overseen by a Court peculiarly sensitive to First Amendment problems. Furthermore, the intangibility of defamation law had left wide discretion in trial court juries; *Sullivan* imposed independent appellate court review of the facts in defamation actions as a First Amendment guarantee. And, in place of the complexity of overlapping liabilities, offsetting privileges, and jurisdictional diversity, *Sullivan* instituted a simple national rule that put a stringent burden of proof on plaintiffs.

Decisions following *Sullivan* extended the "actual malice" limitation on the law of defamation beyond the case of criticism of high public officials. The rule was expanded to apply to PUBLIC FIGURES in *Curtis Publishing Co. v. Butts* and *Associated Press v. Walker* (1967). A plurality of the Court even stretched the rule to cover private figures, if the matter was "a subject of public or general interest," in *Rosenbloom v. Metromedia, Inc.* (1971). But the Court retreated from *Rosenbloom* three years later in GERTZ V. ROBERT WELCH, INC. (1974). *Gertz* held that a private person may recover without meeting the actual malice standard. Because private figures have only limited access to the media to correct misstatements of others, and because they have not assumed the risk of injury due to defamatory falsehoods against them, the Court found the interests of private figures to weigh more heavily than those of public figures. The states were left free to establish an appropriate standard of liability, provided they do not impose liability without fault. Moreover, the states were forbidden from awarding presumed or punitive DAMAGES absent a showing of actual malice. More recently, in DUN & BRADSTREET, INC. V. GREENMOSS BUILDERS, INC. (1985), the Court retreated still further, permitting recovery of presumed and punitive damages by a private plaintiff without a showing of actual malice, because the defamatory statements did not involve a matter of public concern.

The defamation decisions beginning with *New York Times Co. v. Sullivan* have had the twofold effect of highlighting the core purpose of the First Amendment and constitutionalizing the law of defamation. By invalidating the law of seditious libel, the Court recognized that criticism of government is the type of speech most deserving of First Amendment protection. By establishing minimum standards of liability and limitations on damages for public figures and some private plaintiffs, the Court federalized the law of defamation.

BENNO C. SCHMIDT, JR.
(1986)

Bibliography

KALVEN, HARRY, JR. 1964 The New York Times Case: A Note on "The Central Meaning of the First Amendment." *Supreme Court Review* 1964:191.

LEVY, LEONARD W. 1960 *Legacy of Suppression: Freedom of Speech and Press in Early American History.* Cambridge, Mass.: Harvard University Press.

——— 1984 *Emergence of a Free Press.* New York: Oxford University Press.

LIBEL AND THE
FIRST AMENDMENT
(Update)

The structure of the Supreme Court's libel DOCTRINE has changed very little since the mid-1980s—remarkably so given the breadth and depth of dissatisfaction that this doctrine has engendered. While NEW YORK TIMES V. SULLIVAN (1964) deservedly remains an icon of modern FIRST AMENDMENT law, *Sullivan*'s progeny—an extensive and highly complex body of cases constitutionalizing almost every aspect of the law of defamation—has come under attack for failing to protect the legitimate interests of either defamed individuals or the press and other speakers. Yet the Court's libel law doctrine by now has acquired, seemingly despite itself, the virtue of stability—an achievement itself likely to prevent any ambitious reform proposals from making headway.

Sullivan derives its importance from two essentially independent features. First, the decision stands as the Court's strongest statement of general First Amendment principle—that the "central meaning" of the First Amendment, revealed in the controversy over the ALIEN AND SEDITION ACTS of 1798, is to protect against all infringements the right of a sovereign people to criticize government policy and public officials. Second, the decision began the process by which the Court brought the federal Constitution to bear on the state COMMON LAW of defamation. In the course of this doctrinal development, the Court provided some level of constitutional protection to libelous speech extending far beyond attacks on official conduct.

The Court put in place the main building blocks of its libel law doctrine in the two decades following *Sullivan*. First, in *Curtis Publishing Company v. Butts* (1967), the Court held that the "actual malice" standard adopted in *Sullivan* for libel cases brought by public officials also applied in cases brought by PUBLIC FIGURES. The latter, just like the former, would have to show that the speaker had acted with knowledge of a statement's falsity or reckless disregard as to its truth. Although the Court tried on several occasions to put some limits on the "public figure" category, lower courts have interpreted it expansively, to apply both to celebrities of all kinds and to any individual involved, voluntarily or not, in any sort of public controversy. Next, in GERTZ V. ROBERT WELCH, INC. (1974), the Court held that private figures must prove negligence (itself a heightened standard compared to the common law rule of strict liability) to recover compensatory damages and actual malice to obtain presumed or PUNITIVE DAMAGES. Because of the difficulty of proving actual injury to reputation, as well as the expense of bringing libel litigation, many private figures subject to *Gertz* discover that their suits are tenable only with evidence of actual malice. Finally, the Court held in DUN & BRADSTREET V. GREENMOSS BUILDERS, INC. (1985) that in the small category of cases in which a private figure is defamed on "a matter of purely private concern" (like the faulty credit rating in the case), the actual malice standard does not apply to any part of the litigation. The upshot of the system is that the actual malice standard today governs most libel cases, although the occasional plaintiff manages to escape its strict proof requirements.

Since *Dun & Bradstreet*, the Court has tinkered with the actual malice standard, while also elaborating on the lesser included requirement of proving a defamatory statement's falsity. In *Anderson v. Liberty Lobby* (1986), the Court held that a public figure can defeat summary judgment only by showing with "convincing clarity" sufficient evidence of actual malice to create a genuine issue of material fact. And in *Harte-Hanks Communications v. Connaughton* (1989), the Court made clear that the actual malice standard requires proof of a libel defendant's actual state of mind, so that purposeful avoidance of truth, but not a gross failure to comply with professional standards, can establish the requisite liability. Further increasing the difficulty of bringing a libel suit, the Court held in *Philadelphia Newspapers, Inc. v. Hepps* (1986) that not only public but also private figures bear the burden of proving a defamatory statement's falsity, at least if the speech is of public concern and the defendant is a member of the media. With respect to the nature of this proof, MASSON V. NEW YORKER MAGAZINE, INC. (1991) adopted as a constitutional requirement the common law rule that the falsity at issue must be material.

One problem with this body of law is sheer complexity. The Court now categorizes libel suits along multiple dimensions. The primary distinction, established in *Gertz*, relates to the status (public or private) of the plaintiff. A secondary but still important distinction relates to the nature (public or private) of the speech. This inquiry functions in two ways: by entering into the initial determination whether a plaintiff is a public or private figure (because one way to become a public figure is to participate in a "public controversy") and then, as held in *Dun & Bradstreet*, by dividing the private figure category into two. Finally, a possible distinction lurks between media and nonmedia defendants; in *Hepps* and several other cases, the Court explicitly reserved the question whether this distinction too should have constitutional relevance. The intricate, even convoluted nature of this categorical scheme, governing as it does every important aspect of libel litigation, ill comports with the Court's usual concern for certainty and predictability in matters affecting FREEDOM OF SPEECH.

A related though more comprehensive problem is that the Court's libel doctrine often manages to frustrate the interests of both sides in libel cases—and in doing so, to frustrate as well the interests of the public. Application of the *Sullivan* rule usually deprives falsely defamed individuals of the ability to obtain monetary damages or any other effective remedy for reputational injury, however grievous. By the same token, application of the rule may prevent the public from ever learning of the falsity of widely disseminated libelous statements. The justification for accepting these consequences is that the actual malice standard promotes what the *Sullivan* Court called "uninhibited, robust, and wide-open" debate by removing the press's fear of liability for inevitable errors. Whether this trade-off makes sense may depend on whether the speech at issue lies at the core of First Amendment protection, as was true in *Sullivan*, or nearer to its periphery, as in the many libel cases involving celebrity gossip. But even if this issue is set to one side, the question remains whether the trade-off is in fact a trade-off—whether, that is, the public gets the uninhibited debate promised for the price paid. With regard to this question, the press routinely claims, and probably with good reason, that although the actual malice regime reduces the number of libel judgments, it greatly increases the size of judgments and, even more important, the costs of defense. Current libel law thus may thwart the correction and remedy of false defamatory statements without in any way lessening the self-censorship that the *Sullivan* Court acted to prevent.

This arguably miserable accommodation of competing interests spawned in the 1980s a kind of cottage industry in proposals for reforming libel law. Most of these proposals relied on reduced damage awards rather than heightened standards of liability to strike the appropriate balance in the area. One proposal would have relieved the libel plaintiff of any burden of proving fault, but offered as a remedy only a declaratory judgment of the defamatory statement's falsity. Other variants would have allowed the plaintiff to recover modest actual damages or given the plaintiff a choice between bringing a no-money, no-fault suit and trying to recover unlimited damages under the actual malice standard. The essential idea of this reform movement was to create a low-cost mechanism for correcting defamatory error, which would protect better than the *Sullivan* regime both reputational and free speech interests.

Even as these proposals multiplied, however, the Court's libel law doctrine began to acquire a surprising air of permanence. The Court took fewer and fewer libel cases in the 1990s, and the few decisions it did issue had little significance. Perhaps the Court believed that its accommodation of interests was superior to any of the alternatives. Or perhaps the Court thought that the need for stability counseled against further changes, even if a different approach might have been better in the first instance. Regardless of the cause, libel doctrine at the turn of the century seems settled in a way that few commentators would have predicted in the mid-1980s. And this very rootedness, with its attendant virtues, makes the prospects for the significant reforms urged at that time ever more unlikely.

ELENA KAGAN
(2000)

Bibliography

ANDERSON, DAVID 1991 Is Libel Law Worth Reforming? *University of Pennsylvania Law Review* 140:487–554.

EPSTEIN, RICHARD 1986 Was *New York Times v. Sullivan* Wrong? *University of Chicago Law Review* 53:782–818.

FRANKLIN, MARC A. 1986 A Declaratory Judgment Alternative to Current Libel Law. *California Law Review* 74:809–845.

KAGAN, ELENA 1993 A Libel Story: *Sullivan* Then and Now. *Law and Social Inquiry* 18:197–217.

LEVAL, PIERRE N. 1988 The No-Money, No-Fault Libel Suit: Keeping *Sullivan* in its Proper Place. *Harvard Law Review* 101:1287–1302.

LEWIS, ANTHONY 1991 *Make No Law: The Sullivan Case and the First Amendment.* New York: Random House.

POST, ROBERT C. 1986 The Social Foundations of Defamation Law: Reputation and the Constitution. *California Law Review* 74:691–742.

SCHAUER, FREDERICK 1984 Public Figures. *William and Mary Law Review* 25:905–935.

——— 1992 Uncoupling Free Speech. *Columbia Law Review* 92:1321–1357.

SMOLLA, RODNEY A. 1986 *Suing the Press: Libel, the Media, and Power.* New York: Oxford University Press.

SUNSTEIN, CASS R. 1984 Hard Defamation Cases. *William and Mary Law Review* 25:891–904.

LIBERAL CONSTITUTIONAL CONSTRUCTION

The liberal attitude toward the Constitution—admitting a range of internal differences—centers on the proposition that the Framers, as talented a group of democratic politicians as ever lived, expected their descendants to be at least as experimental as they were. When the Framers gathered in Philadelphia, they were improvising a *novus ordo seclorum* without a blueprint. JOHN ADAMS, working feverishly in London compiling the history of attempts at republican government, tried to summarize the lessons of history. JAMES MADISON had prepared himself by reading every relevant work that he and his mentor THOMAS JEFFERSON, then in Paris, could lay their hands on. ALEXANDER HAMILTON was satisfied that Thomas Hobbes had provided the essentials.

But delegates to the CONSTITUTIONAL CONVENTION OF 1787 mainly brought with them their experience in running provincial, state, and Confederation government. Collectively they had well over a thousand years of experience in office, from governor and Chief Justice down to mayor and justice of the peace. Of the fifty-five chosen, forty-four were, or had been, members of the CONTINENTAL CONGRESS; at a time when being a lawyer was very different from emerging from a law school assembly line and vanishing into a vacuum-packed corporate enviroment, thirty-five had done their apprenticeships, and JAMES WILSON and GEORGE WYTHE were eminent professors and legists. The only outstanding absentees from the political class were JOHN JAY a secretary of foreign affairs under the Confederation; John Adams in London; Thomas Jefferson in Paris; and PATRICK HENRY who was elected but refused to attend as he "smelt a rat," that is, he thought Jefferson was masterminding the convention through Madison, as had been the case in the Virginia legislature with the VIRGINIA STATUE OF RELIGIOUS LIBERTY.

Although with the exception of Madison and perhaps Hamilton they had not arrived with specific plans, they clearly shared a sense of mission: The United States government under the ARTICLES OF CONFEDERATION had to be strengthened to prevent the infant nation from being eaten by the sharks that infested the international environment. Here the presence of GEORGE WASHINGTON was of immense symbolic value because of his known dedication to the principles of a free republic and the respect he had from the people. Washington was unanimously elected president of the Convention.

The Framers were well aware that they were not free-floating Platonic "guardians" who could impose their concept of a "republic" upon an unresisting populace. Hence, when the final document was signed on September 17, its principal architects considered it the best they could get rather than the fulfillment of an ideal. George Washington put it well in a letter: "You will readily conceive . . . the difficulties which the Convention had to struggle against. The various and opposit [*sic*] interests which were to be subdued, the diversity of opinions and sentiments which were to be reconciled; and in fine, the sacrifices which were necessary to be made on all sides for the General Welfare, combined to make it work of so intricate and difficult a nature that I think it is much to be wondered at that any thing could have been produced with such unanimity."

Hamilton and Madison, disappointed by the convention's rebuff to their centralizing initiative, agreed that the Constitution was an improvement over the Articles and set to work to get it ratified. South Carolina's PIERCE BUTLER probably spoke for most of his fellow Framers when he wrote, "View the system then as resulting from a spirit of Accommodation to different Interests, and not the most perfect one that the Deputies cou'd devise for a Country better adapted for the reception of it than America is at this day, or perhaps ever will be."

In the course of RATIFICATION OF THE CONSTITUTION by the state conventions, questions inevitably arose on the meaning of various articles. When one reads the replies that were given—in a universe wholly lacking in modern communications techniques—it rapidly becomes clear that a number of the delegates often were not quite sure what they had approved. They knew that in general terms they had established a republic with strong legislative and executive branches—the judicial article received little attention either in the Convention or in ratification debates—and hoped that the new government would provide the United States with the authority and the funds that were so sorely lacking under the Articles.

To head off a potentially dangerous demagogic anticonstitutionalist attack—claiming in essence that Hobbes's Leviathan was being covertly imposed on unsuspecting citizens—the Framers promised a BILL OF RIGHTS. The Constitution was ratified, the states organized presidential and congressional elections for that fall, and the Founding Fathers set to work finding appropriate positions for themselves and their friends in the new administration. Now they had to make this experiment in republican government work.

To summarize, the Framers had not descended from Mount Sinai with the Law carved in stone; they had contrived a mechanism designed to establish law and, if necessary, change it. The FIRST CONGRESS, for example, set up the Treasury Department as a dependency of Congress with the secretary reporting in person or in writing to the House and Senate. Alexander Hamilton's masterful recommendations on the public credit, the BANK OF THE UNITED STATES, and the encouragement of manufactures were in the form of reports to Congress. In practice, however, the secretary was responsible to the President, and the law was later changed to reflect this. The Constitution requires the President to get the ADVICE AND CONSENT of the Senate to treaties; the advice provision vanished after Washington's one attempt to discuss pending Indian treaties with the Senate ended on such a chilly note that no President since has made the pilgrimage.

Indeed, there is a substantial body of evidence to suggest that the widely discussed "intent of the Framers" is a will-o'-the-wisp. We know their intention on structural matters—the division of powers between the executive, legislative, and judicial branches—but beyond that, things get murky. Once again the First Congress gives us a sense of the extent to which the Framers were not sure of their own objectives, for an intense debate arose over the question of the Senate's role in the President's dismissal power. In other words, if Senate approval is necessary for the appointment of, say, an ambassador, is Senate approval required to fire him? The consensus seemed to be that it was not, but the matter was not settled until MYERS V. UNITED STATES in 1926, and even today there is some ambiguity on the status of members of so-called independent regulatory commissions.

Without going into further detail, it is obvious that early generations of politicians and jurists were more concerned with how a problem could be solved than with how the Framers would have dealt with it. ABRAHAM BALDWIN, one of the most intelligent men who was both a politician and jurist, put it thus to his House colleagues in March 1796:

It was not to disparage [the Constitution] to say that it had not definitely, and with precision, absolutely settled everything on which it had spoke. He had sufficient evidence to satisfy his own mind that it was not supposed by the makers of it at the time but that some subjects were left a little ambiguous and uncertain. It was a great thing to get so many difficult subjects definitely settled at once. . . . The few that were left a little unsettled might without any great risk be settled by practice or by amendments. . . . When he reflected on the immense difficulties and dangers of that trying occasion—the old Government prostrated and a chance whether a new one could be agreed on—the recollection recalled to him nothing but the most joyful sensations that so many things had been so well settled, and that experience had shown there was very little difficulty or danger in settling the rest.

This liberal spirit of experimentation was brilliantly exemplified by the Supreme Court under the leadership of Chief Justice JOHN MARSHALL. Marshall's enmity toward his cousin Thomas Jefferson was surely fortified by the latter's penchant (at least before and after he served as President) for STRICT CONSTRUCTION of the Constitution. In the famous 1819 case MCCULLOCH V. MARYLAND, the Chief Justice, in the course of echoing Hamilton's 1791 defense of the constitutionality of the Bank of the United States, took some time out to condemn this unimaginative perception of the nature of the Constitution. Wrote Marshall:

A constitution to contain an accurate detail of all the subdivisions of which its great powers will admit, and of all the means by which they may be carried into execution, would partake of the prolixity of a legal code, and could scarcely be embraced by the human mind. It would probably never be understood by the public. Its nature therefore requires that only its great outlines should be marked, its important objects designated, and the minor ingredients which compose these objects be deducted from the nature of the objects themselves. . . . To have prescribed the means by which government should in all future time execute its powers . . . would have been an unwise attempt to provide by immutable rules for exigencies which, if foreseen at all, must have been seen dimly, and which can best be provided for as they occur.

Five years later in the steamboat case of GIBBONS V. OGDEN (1824) the Chief Justice really dispatched the narrow-minded critics of federal power: "Powerful and ingenious minds taking as postulates that the powers expressly granted to the government of the Union are to be contracted by construction into the narrowest possible compass, and that the original powers of the states be retained if any possible construction will retain them, may by a course of well-digested but refined and metaphysical reasoning, founded on these premises, explain away the constitution of our country and leave it a magnificent structure indeed to look at, but totally unfit for use." So much for metaphysicians and political philosophers.

In concrete terms Marshall's talent for improvisation to cope with pressing problems was spectacular. He invented the doctrine of POLITICAL QUESTIONS to provide the Court with a safe exit from risky enfilades in *Foster v. Nielson* (1829); in AMERICAN INSURANCE COMPANY V. CANTER (1828) he belatedly provided the constitutional rationale for acquiring new territories and, while he was at it, invented LEGISLATIVE COURTS, created under Article I and distinct from the CONSTITUTIONAL COURTS of Article III; and, to mention only two more, he developed the ORIGINAL PACKAGE DOCTRINE in BROWN V. MARYLAND (1827) and the status of Indian tribes as "dependent domestic nations" in *Worcester v. Georgia* (1831). One could argue that John Marshall, following in the footsteps of the Framers (and he had been a delegate to the Virginia ratifying convention), set the pattern of creative experimentation for liberal CONSTITUTIONALISM.

Rather than compiling a catalog of constitutional improvisations, many of which have been initiated by the executive (ABRAHAM LINCOLN moved the power to suspend the writ of HABEAS CORPUS into Article II, where it has since remained) and the legislature (Congress in 1871 conferred citizenship on corporations for federal jurisdictional purposes), it would be wise to narrow the inquiry to a few specific areas. For example, what do steamships and television waves have in common? The answer is that they are subject to regulation by the federal government under the COMMERCE CLAUSE. The first stages in this triumph of fungibility were easy, for interstate water shipping, interstate railways, interstate trucking, and interstate telegraphs were tangible. The big jump took place in 1933 when the Supreme Court, in *Federal Radio Commission v. Nelson Bros.*, held radio waves to be analogous to telegraph signals and subsequently widened this to include television. The principle applied was Marshall's, namely, that it did not make any difference whether a boat was propelled by sail or engine; the vital aspect was that something was going from one state to another.

The liberal approach to constitutionalism has infuriated a lot of individuals and groups of all political persuasions. The focus here is not on whether the experiments were successful but on the modus operandi. At some points the improvisations were considered politically "reactionary" (for example, when the Court in the YELLOW DOG CONTRACT Case assumed that individual workers and industrial giants were bargaining-table equals and when it negated state minimum-wage laws). In other cases a howl went up that the Justices were "radical" (for example, when the Court protected criminal rights and when it legitimized ABOR-

TION). Whatever the outcome, the result was founded on the experimental attitude. To put it differently, it would be extremely difficult to find a decision in which the majority view was buttressed by better probative evidence of the intention of the Framers than was the view of the dissenting minority.

To say that experimentation has been the only game in town since 1787 is a statement of historical fact, a fundament of the liberal tradition. Indeed, one could argue that the one area where stasis set in and experimentation became increasingly difficult and finally impossible was the mesh of SLAVERY and STATES' RIGHTS, leading to a ferocious Civil War in which roughly a million males out of a population of sixteen million ages fifteen to thirty-nine were killed or wounded. The Constitution of 1787 was a sanguinary failure.

If this is the liberal attitude toward the Constitution, what are the critical differences between it and the conservative view? In candor, it is hard to find substantial differences at the level of principle, for America's so-called conservatives have always found themselves carrying the intellectual baggage of that magnificent cadre of improvisers who founded the Republic. In Ireland in the 1690s many a big house had a portrait of the king over the mantelpiece mounted on pivots top and bottom. When the Jacobites came to town one pushed the picture around to display King James II; when the forces of William and Mary appeared, a similar push put their visages front and center. The problem with such a portrait in the context of the founding era is that the same portraits would appear on both sides: conservative constitutionalists have always endorsed experimentation *sub silentio*, but then denied that this in fact was their methodology. Presumably they have learned the technique at the feet of John Marshall.

For example, JOHN C. CALHOUN has been described as a man of rigid conservative principles, the hero of the states' rights cause. Yet in 1817 Calhoun casually observed that the Constitution "was not intended as a thesis for the logician to exercise his ingenuity on it. It ought to be construed with plain good sense."

Similarly, Robert H. Bork has become an icon of contemporary conservative jurisprudence, but in his book *The Tempting of America: The Political Seduction of the Law* (1990) he provides us with an example of the liberal, experimental mode worthy of John Marshall himself. In discussing BAKER V. CARR (1962)—which required states to establish election districts based on the formula ONE PERSON, ONE VOTE—Bork excoriated the WARREN COURT not for the result ("There is no doubt in my mind . . . that plaintiffs [demanding the end of rigged districting] deserved to win") but because the Court based its decision on the EQUAL PROTECTION clause of the FOURTEENTH AMENDMENT.

As it happens, the authors of the Fourteenth Amendment, like the Framers, had a talent for ambiguity, so it is an exercise in soothsaying to attempt a reconstruction of the precise meaning of equal protection. Let us simply say that the jury is still out, and will doubtless remain out indefinitely, on the legal consequences the drafting Committee of Fifteen had in mind in 1866. What is interesting is Bork's solution to the inequities created by malapportionment and how he explicates the constitutional rationale that would enable those who "deserved to win" to win. Let no one deny his imaginative creativity: he indicates that the Court could have avoided the equal protection quagmire quite simply by using the provision in Article IV, section 4, that "the United States shall guarantee to every State in this Union a REPUBLICAN FORM OF GOVERNMENT."

This provision, launched by Madison in the VIRGINIA PLAN, was discussed on two occasions during the Convention. The weight of the evidence suggests it was designed to prevent any state from setting up, or having imposed upon it from without, a monarchical form of government. When it was invoked by the Dorrite rebels against the obsolete Rhode Island Charter in 1849, the Court said in LUTHER V. BORDEN that the legitimacy of Rhode Island's government was a "political question"; and when the clause was subsequently invoked in a desultory fashion in several other cases, the Justices echoed Chief Justice ROGER BROOKE TANEY's decision in *Luther* and held that the determination of republican governance was nonjusticiable.

Bork states that "for no very good reason" the Court held the proviso to be judicially unenforceable and suggests it should be overruled after 113 years as STARE DECISIS. Actually, some supporters of the liberal, experimental approach who thought of this at the time of COLEGROVE V. GREEN (1946) (the first major assault on malapportionment) and hit a brick wall would cheer Bork on. However, the historical evidence for the use of the "guarantee clause" is tenuous, at least as flimsy as that underpinning the equal protection clause of the Fourteenth Amendment, for at the time of the ratification of the Constitution malapportionment was a major concern in a number of states. ELBRIDGE GERRY, a Framer, refused to sign the document, but not because it forbade the GERRYMANDER. It would seem that even Bork cannot resist temptation. As David Hume pointed out, creating a useful past is a delightful form of political entertainment. It is also a persistent highlight of American judicial behavior.

JOHN P. ROCHE
(1992)

(SEE ALSO: *Bork Nomination; Cherokee Indian Cases; Conservatism; Justiciability; Original Intent; Political Philosophy of the Constitution; Pragmatism; Progressive Constitutional Thought; Progressivism.*)

Bibliography

BORK, ROBERT H.   1990   *The Tempting of America: The Political Seduction of the Law.* New York: Free Press.
JACKSON, ROBERT H.   1941   *The Struggle for Judicial Supremacy.* New York: Knopf.
LEVY, LEONARD W.   1988   *Original Intent and the Framers' Constitution.* New York: Macmillan.
MCDONALD, FORREST   1985   *Novus Ordo Seclorum.* Lawrence: University Press of Kansas.
PETERSON, MERRILL   1987   *The Great Triumvirate.* New York: Oxford University Press.
ROCHE JOHN P.   1961   *Courts and Rights.* New York: Random House.
———   1974   *Shadow and Substance.* New York: Macmillan.
WARREN, CHARLES   1922   *The Supreme Court in United States History,* 2 vols. Boston: Little, Brown.

LIBERALISM

In today's America the term "liberalism" is circulated mainly by those who pronounce it with scorn—by the political right and by academic theorists who have little else in common with the right. Yet the American nation was conceived in liberalism. The DECLARATION OF INDEPENDENCE proclaimed the liberal ideals of individual liberty, legal equality, and the rule of law. It also embraced the liberal doctrine that located the legitimacy of governmental power not in divine right but in the consent of the governed.

The Constitution, too, was mainly seen by its Framers through liberal lenses. What they saw was a SOCIAL COMPACT deriving its authority from "the people of the United States" and designed in major part to serve liberal purposes: "to establish justice," "to secure the blessings of liberty," and by dampening the causes of civil strife, "to insure domestic tranquility." What they did not see—or would not see—was the fundamental inconsistency of SLAVERY with all these purposes. Putting this enormity out of their minds, the Framers of the Constitution and the BILL OF RIGHTS saw the chief source of oppression in the power of the state and placed much of their hope for achieving liberal ends in a system of LIMITED GOVERNMENT.

The limits were both structural and substantive. Liberty was to be achieved both by the dispersal of the powers of government (see FEDERALISM; SEPARATION OF POWERS) and by broadly worded prohibitions on various kinds of governmental interference with the rights of individuals. Although the liberalism of the Framers was strongly influenced by the Enlightenment's notions of rationality, these substantive limitations were not the product of abstract reason. Rather, they were designed to serve intensely practical purposes for the new nation. The liberal doctrines of FREEDOM OF SPEECH and FREEDOM OF THE PRESS, for example, seemed essential to the citizen participation on which the continued legitimacy of government would depend. Similarly, the liberal doctrine rejecting divine authority as the basis for governmental legitimacy served the cause of domestic peace. The Framers, well versed in recent British history, need not stretch their imaginations to see how the interactions of religion and government might plunge a nation into civil strife. A major purpose of both the SEPARATION OF CHURCH AND STATE and the guarantee of RELIGIOUS LIBERTY was to promote tolerance and thereby to moderate religion's capacity for political divisiveness.

Today's Constitution, the product of two centuries' worth of interpretation, differs dramatically from the Constitution of the Framers. Yet, what Louis Hartz called "the liberal tradition" has remained central in American constitutional law, surviving political and social upheavals and even a civil war of our own. Like all paradoxes, this contradiction of continuity and change is more apparent than real. Over the years liberalism, like the Constitution, has taken on a series of new meanings in response to changes in America's economic, social, and political conditions. Jacksonian democracy, the CIVIL WAR and RECONSTRUCTION, the late-nineteenth-century industrial expansion, the NEW DEAL, and the CIVIL RIGHTS MOVEMENT each brought a new version of liberalism that made its mark on the Constitution. The constitutional law of our time—like the term liberalism itself—evidences overlays of all these eras of social change, from the days of Adam Smith to the days of MARTIN LUTHER KING, JR. The decisions of the Supreme Court, the nation's leading expositor of the Constitution, have both reflected the transformations of liberalism and contributed to them.

In the nation's early years the individualist liberalism of JOHN LOCKE was tempered by a vision of REPUBLICANISM that imposed on the people's governors a moral responsibility to attune their public decisions to the general good, not merely their own self-interest or the interests of their constituents. This republican ideal was not wholly unrealistic so long as government was largely in the hands of the gentry. By around 1820, however, gentry rule had crumbled under the dual pressures of democratization and geographical expansion. In the era of ANDREW JACKSON the consent of the governed implied an electorate that was expanded to include most adult white men, and the body of citizens who could make effective use of individual freedom—especially economic freedom—was similarly expanded by a doctrine of equal liberties. The widening of the franchise was almost entirely the work of legislatures. The protection of economic freedom, however, became

the business of the courts, acting in the name of the Constitution. The JUDICIAL ACTIVISM of the MARSHALL COURT (1803–1835) led the way in promoting a nationwide free-trade unit by striking down a number of state regulatory laws (see STATE REGULATION OF COMMERCE; CONTRACT CLAUSE).

During the period before the Civil War, another doctrine of liberalism came to the fore, with major assists from the adherents of ABOLITIONIST CONSTITUTIONAL THEORY and from those who opposed SLAVERY IN THE TERRITORIES. "Free labor" became a slogan of the new REPUBLICAN PARTY and of ABRAHAM LINCOLN in particular (see LABOR MOVEMENT AND CONSTITUTIONAL DOCTRINE). The doctrine of free labor, infused with the liberal goals of democracy and individualism, received a strong impetus when the EMANCIPATION PROCLAMATION converted a war to save the Union into a war to free the slaves—a process that culminated in the THIRTEENTH AMENDMENT, ratified in 1865.

Generously interpreted, the Thirteenth Amendment might have served as a foundation for a sweeping constitutional guarantee of racial equality and for congressional legislation serving this end. The politics of Reconstruction impeded such an expansive interpretation, but did produce the FOURTEENTH AMENDMENT, with its broad guarantees of EQUAL PROTECTION and DUE PROCESS, and the FIFTEENTH AMENDMENT, prohibiting racial discrimination in VOTING RIGHTS. The three Civil War amendments, along with a series of civil rights acts, were seen by their proponents as establishing a principle of equal citizenship that would carry out some of the unfulfilled liberal promises of the Declaration of Independence.

These hopes were soon dashed. By the end of the century, politics—North and South—had turned away from a concern for racial equality. The Supreme Court had followed suit in a series of decisions that converted the Civil War amendments and the Reconstruction CIVIL RIGHTS laws into guarantees of formal equality that offered little real protection for the substantive values of equal citizenship: respect, responsibility, and participation (see CIVIL RIGHTS CASES; PLESSY V. FERGUSON).

As politics increasingly turned to the business of industrial expansion, the dominant version of liberal individualism now focused on the freedom of industry and enterprise from ECONOMIC REGULATION. Beginning in the 1880s, for half a century the Supreme Court policed the boundaries of economic liberty, striking down a great many regulatory laws in the name of ECONOMIC DUE PROCESS and holding a number of federal statutes invalid as exceeding the power of Congress under the COMMERCE CLAUSE. During this period, and especially during WORLD WAR I and the Red Scare of 1919–1920, the Court gave little comfort to those who were urging a similarly expansive reading of other constitutional legacies of the Framers' liberal individualism—such as FIRST AMENDMENT freedoms.

It took the Great Depression and WORLD WAR II to effect a realignment that would give the center of the political stage to the liberalism of the New Deal. This rendering of liberalism, like the liberalism of Reconstruction, emphasized the necessity of substantive underpinnings for individual liberty. The New Deal's legislative program centered on economic democracy and social welfare, and to achieve these ends its leaders sought to guide the national economy with governmental regulation on an unprecedented scale. During the first term of President FRANKLIN D. ROOSEVELT, an activist majority of the Supreme Court fought a rear-guard action against the new liberalism in the name of the old. In 1937, however, before Roosevelt had made a single appointment to the Court, the majority shifted. From that day to the present, the Court has routinely upheld economic regulation both by Congress and by the states and has also upheld the legislative framework of the modern welfare state (see TAXING AND SPENDING POWERS; SPENDING POWER). During the 1930s and 1940s, the Court also took its first steps toward reinvigorating the First Amendment.

All these developments in constitutional doctrine supported a liberalism in which equality meant not just formally equal laws but the substance of equal citizenship. The Court cooperated with the political branches in an effort to bring freedom and security to people who had been seen as outsiders and so to achieve a more inclusive definition of the national community. For a time, the Cold War, like the Red Scare before it, laid a restraining hand on political freedom and also marked a group of dissidents as outsiders. But just as the Cold War reached the peak of its influence on domestic politics, the new liberalism, with its impulse to extend the blessings of liberty to all Americans, took a giant step forward. The WARREN COURT opened the modern civil rights era with the decision in BROWN V. BOARD OF EDUCATION (1954).

The *Brown* decision began a "second Reconstruction," not only by expanding the meaning of constitutional doctrines of racial equality, but also by providing a catalyst for a vigorous political movement, Congress responded with two momentous laws aimed at extending the substance of equal citizenship to the members of racial and ethnic minorities: the CIVIL RIGHTS ACT OF 1964 and the VOTING RIGHTS ACT OF 1965. In its active liberal reshaping of constitutional doctrine, the Warren Court began in the civil rights field, but did not end there. Particularly during the last six years of the tenure of EARL WARREN as Chief Justice, the court not only extended judicial remedies for racial DESEGREGATION but also promoted political equality by or-

dering REAPPORTIONMENT of legislatures on the principle of "one person, one vote." The court also greatly expanded the substantive protections of the First Amendment and recognized a constitutional RIGHT OF PRIVACY. In the field of criminal justice the Court accomplished the INCORPORATION of nearly all the guarentees of the Bill of Rights into the Fourteenth Ammendment, thus applying them to the states as well as the national government. Furthermore, the court tightened the requirements of many of those guarantees, making th Constitution a significant limitation on police practices and the proceedures of state criminal courts.

Even after Chief Justice Warren retired in 1969, the constitutional momentum of the Warren Court carried the Court to further liberal activism. Most notably, the BURGER COURT in the 1970s expanded the reach of the equal protection clause to the field of SEX DISCRIMINATION and held in ROE V. WADE (1973) that the right of privacy largely forbade a state to criminalize a woman's choice to have an ABORTION. These two developments were closely related; women's right to control their own sexuality and maternity is critical to their ability to participate in society as equal citizens.

Political liberals generally have applauded all these constitutional developments. Yet each of them has produced its own "backlash" in the political arena. When President LYNDON B. JOHNSON signed the 1964 act into law, he predicted that the South would thus be handed to the Republican party. In Presidential politics, this prediction has been validated, starting with the successful "southern strategy" of RICHARD M. NIXON in 1968. Nixon explicitly criticized the Warren Court's decisions in the criminal justice area, and the four Justices that he appointed to the Court began the process that would eventually dismantle a considerable part of that doctrinal structure. As for civil rights, critics of the REHNQUIST COURT have said that the second Reconstruction lasted only a little longer than the first one did. In the 1980s a firm majority of the Court has embraced a doctrinal model centered on formal racial equality, sharply limiting the uses of AFFIRMATIVE ACTION and other group-based remedies for the group harm of racial discrimination. The right of privacy has not yet fulfilled its promise as a generalized protection of individual freedom in matters of intimate personal relations, but rather has been narrowed even in the area of abortion rights. Recent First Amendment developments are typified by the PUBLIC FORUM doctrine, which began as a means to expand expressive freedom and now serves mainly as a threshold barrier to turn away would-be speakers' claims. In the world of constitutional doctrine, as in the larger political world, modern liberalism has been obliged to assume a posture of defense.

The constitutional liberalism that animates political liberals today—and serves as the political right's *bête noire*—is a far cry from the liberalism of nineteenth-century economics that dominated constitutional doctrine for five decades. Its primary modern sources are the New Deal's social welfare concerns and the Warren Court's concerns for CIVIL LIBERTIES and for the inclusion of subordinated groups in the promise of America. Even so, today's liberalism continues to draw on the liberalism that infused the framing of the Constitution and the Fourteenth Amendment: the rule of law, tolerance as a means to civil peace, individual rights to freedom from excessive governmental intrusion, and equal citizenship.

Although the political resistance to the New Deal had its main base in the business sector, today business has largely made its peace with the newer liberalism—not exactly embracing regulation, but accepting it. The most vehement opposition to affirmative action programs, for example, comes not from business groups, but from "social issues" conservatives who equally oppose the recognition of abortion rights or claims to sexual freedom. These citizens, who are presently the dominant voices on the political right, do not reject the liberal constitutional ideals of equality, individual rights, or tolerance, but argue that in recent decades liberals on the bench have abused their power to write a perverted version of those ideals into constitutional law.

For the "social issues" conservatives, these constitutional ideals are unchangeable; they took permanent shape when they were written into the Constitution. In this view constitutional equality means formally equal laws and no more; individual constitutional rights are limited to the specific rights of life, liberty, and property that the Framers had in mind; and the reach of constitutionally required tolerance is permanently confined by the morality of the Framers (see CONSERVATISM AND THE CONSTITUTION). They emphatically reject, for example, any claim to equality or rights of tolerance in the context of governmental discrimination on the basis of SEXUAL ORIENTATION, insisting that such matters be left to majoritarian community morality.

Constitutional liberalism is also under attack from quite another political direction, notably by theorists in the CRITICAL LEGAL STUDIES movement. These writers seek to "deconstruct" the very idea of rights by showing that all legal doctrine is indeterminate and therefore subject to manipulation in the interest of the powerful. Here, a countercurrent has developed among racial and ethnic minority writers who argue the practical utility of claims of rights in overcoming group subordination and point to the civil rights movement as an example of the liberating possibilities of rights—an argument the Framers of the Constitution surely would understand.

Another attack on liberalism by critical theorists, now joined by a number of feminist writers, centers on the potential of liberal-individualist attitudes for impoverishing the sense of self and submerging the sense of community responsibility—especially responsibility toward the down-and-out. Related to these concerns is the criticism that classical liberalism, locating the threat to individual freedom in the power of the state, neglects the oppressive capacity of nongovernmental actors, compounding the wrong by insisting on a strong public-private distinction. (See STATE ACTION—BEYOND RACE.)

From both sides, then, liberalism is challenged for undercutting the claims of community. A liberal tolerance may result in constitutional protections not only for consensual homosexual behavior but for racist speech or PORNOGRAPHY. (The antipornography cause in particular has produced an alliance between the political right and one branch of feminists.) Similarly, liberalism's long-standing devotion to Enlightenment-style rationality is under attack from both sides. The dominance of secular rationality is attacked by those who would promote SCHOOL PRAYERS or the teaching of CREATIONISM in public schools; and feminists and others argue that the instrumental rationality of the liberal welfare state's BUREAUCRACY is alienating and dehumanizing.

The critical theorists' critique of liberalism has yet to make a significant impact on constitutional law. The critique from the right, however, has been warmly received by the federal judiciary, which in large measure was reconstituted during the 1980s. Now it is liberal judges who are fighting a rear-guard action. Yet some important elements of the liberal constitutional inheritance from the New Deal and the Warren Court seem secure. Citizens at all points on the political spectrum continue to hold the federal government responsible for maintaining the health of the national economy, including high levels of employment. Although social welfare programs perceived as aiding the minority poor are anything but robust, SOCIAL SECURITY is the nearest thing we have to a political sacred cow, and some form of national health insurance seems likely to emerge soon. Explicit governmental discrimination against the members of subordinated racial or ethnic groups, we can assume, will be unconstitutional as long as we have the Constitution.

These examples are modest when they are measured against the modern liberal agenda; saying that the constitutional clock will not be turned back to 1950 or 1930 is not saying very much. For the moment, surely, liberals must seek their goals primarily in political arenas. In these arenas, however, we have already seen some important effects of racial equality in voting rights—for example, in the process of confirmation of Supreme Court Justices.

Undoubtedly, "the liberal tradition" will remain central

in American constitutional jurisprudence because our constitutional culture is indelibly imprinted with the rhetoric of liberalism: equality, tolerance, individual rights. Another certainty, however, is that the meanings of these large abstractions will change in response to changes in American society. Today's political liberals will applaud some of those changes and regret others. But the process is one that no true liberal can lament.

KENNETH L. KARST
(1992)

Bibliography

ALTMAN, ANDREW 1990 *Critical Legal Studies: A Liberal Critique.* Princeton, N.J.: Princeton University Press.

CRENSHAW, KIMBERLÉ 1988 Race, Reform and Retrenchment: Transformation and Legitimation in Antidiscrimination Law. *Harvard Law Review* 101:1331–1387.

DIGGINS, JOHN P. 1984 *The Lost Soul of American Politics: Virtue, Self-Interest, and the Foundations of Liberalism.* New York: Basic Books.

FERGUSON, KATHY E. 1984 *The Feminist Case Against Bureaucracy.* Philadelphia: Temple University Press.

HARTZ, LOUIS 1955 *The Liberal Tradition in America: An Interpretation of American Political Thought Since the Revolution.* New York: Harcourt Brace Jovanovich.

KARST, KENNETH L. 1989 *Belonging to America: Equal Citizenship and the Constitution.* New Haven, Conn.: Yale University Press.

SHIFFRIN, STEVEN 1983 Liberalism, Radicalism, and Legal Scholarship. *UCLA Law Review* 30:1103–1217.

SMITH, ROGERS M. 1985 *Liberalism and American Constitutional Law.* Cambridge, Mass.: Harvard University Press.

UNGER, ROBERTO MANGABEIRA 1975 *Knowledge and Politics.* New York: Free Press.

WOLFF, ROBERT PAUL 1968 *The Poverty of Liberalism.* Boston: Beacon Press.

LIBERTY OF CONTRACT

See: Freedom of Contract

LICENSE CASES
5 Howard 504 (1847)

In three related cases decided the same day, the Court sustained the constitutionality of temperance statutes of states that had restricted the sale of liquor and required all dealers to be licensed. Although the Justices unanimously concurred in the disposition of the cases, six men wrote nine opinions, and there was no opinion for the Court because a majority could not agree on the reasoning. At one extreme Justice JOHN MCLEAN took the position that the DORMANT POWERS of Congress under the COM-

MERCE CLAUSE utterly excluded the exercise of CONCURRENT POWERS by the states; but McLean found that the statutes were not regulations of commerce but reasonable exercises of the POLICE POWER. At the other extreme Justice PETER DANIEL supported an exaggerated view of concurrent state commerce powers.

Chief Justice ROGER B. TANEY's view was the least doctrinaire. He observed that two of the three *License Cases* dealt with the retail sale of liquor that was no longer in the original package and therefore raised no INTERSTATE COMMERCE issue. (See ORIGINAL PACKAGE DOCTRINE.) The third case, however, involved liquor imported in the original package from another state and sold in that unbroken package. Thus the business affected by the state's license law was in interstate commerce. Taney therefore confronted the question "whether the grant of power to Congress is of itself a prohibition to the States, and renders all State laws on the subject null and void." His answer to the question, unlike Chief Justice JOHN MARSHALL's, was that unless a state act came into conflict with a law of Congress, the state could constitutionally exercise a concurrent commerce power. On the other hand, he muddled his position by arguing that such a power was no more than the police power of the state, which he defined, promiscuously, as "nothing more or less than the powers of government inherent in every sovereignty to the extent of its dominions." His refusal to distinguish the police power from the commerce power and other powers left his opinion doctrinally murky, and like the opinions by the other Justices it failed to provide a usable test. At least two state judges, JAMES KENT and LEMUEL SHAW, avoided the Supreme Court's quest for a system of definitional categories by suggesting that if Congress did not brush away state legislation, it should be sustained in the absence of an actual or operational conflict with national legislation.

LEONARD W. LEVY
(1986)

LIEBER, FRANCIS

See: Commentators on the Constitution

LILBURNE, JOHN
(1614–1657)

John Lilburne, whose entire career was a precedent for freedom, was the catalytic agent in the history of the RIGHT AGAINST SELF-INCRIMINATION. Primarily because of him, that right became a respected, established rule of the COMMON LAW. An agitator with an incurably inflamed sense of injustice, Lilburne was called Freeborn John, because of his incessant demands on behalf of the rights of every free-born Englishman. No one in England could silence or out-talk him, no one was a greater pamphleteer, and no one was more principled in his devotion to political liberty, the rights of the criminally accused, and the freedoms of conscience and press. Making CIVIL DISOBEDIENCE a way of life, Lilburne successively defied king, parliament, and protectorate.

He first focused the attention of England on the injustice of forcing anyone to answer incriminating questions during his 1637 trial. After his release from prison in 1641, he joined the parliamentary cause, rose to a high military position, and became close to Oliver Cromwell; but he resigned his commission to be free to oppose the government. Four times he stood trial for his life, and he spent much of his last twenty years in jail, from which he smuggled out a torrent of tracts. He advocated a special CONSTITUTIONAL CONVENTION to write a constitution for England embodying the reforms proposed by the Levellers, the faction of constitutional democrats that he led.

When Parliament itself arrested and interrogated him, Lilburne became the first hostile witness in a LEGISLATIVE INVESTIGATION to claim a right not to answer questions against or concerning himself. He successfully made the same claim, under his view of MAGNA CARTA and the PETITION OF RIGHT, before a common law court in 1649, when tried for TREASON. He appealed to the jury above the heads of the judges and convinced the jury to decide on the injustice of the laws used to persecute political prisoners. Twice he persuaded juries to acquit him. In his trials and writings he educated England on the relation of liberty to fair play and DUE PROCESS OF LAW. At his last trial he won the unprecedented right to secure a copy of the INDICTMENT against him and to be represented by counsel in a capital case. Cromwell finally imprisoned him without trial, and Lilburne died in jail.

LEONARD W. LEVY
(1986)

Bibliography

LEVY, LEONARD W. 1968 *Origins of the Fifth Amendment.* Pages 271–312. New York: Oxford University Press.

LIMITED GOVERNMENT

The idea of limited government is closely associated with political thinkers, mostly of medieval and modern periods, who placed special emphasis on preventing abuses of government. Some spoke of limitations connected with divine law and natural law; others spoke of a SOCIAL COMPACT establishing government for the sake of protecting property and other individual rights. Limited government was also a corollary of the more affirmative approach of ancient philosophers, who taught that ruling bodies could best maintain themselves by respecting social customs, moderating their policies, honoring the contributions of each social class in distributing governmental offices, and fostering self-restraint, patriotism, and other attitudes conducive to the general welfare.

In American constitutional thought limited government is often synonymous with CONSTITUTIONALISM itself. It has three more specific connotations resulting from the three principal ways in which the government can be said to be constitutionally limited: in a jurisdictional sense, limited in the objectives it may pursue; in a procedural sense, limited in the ways it may decide policy questions and adjudicate disputes involving individuals; and limited by the requirement that its policies be compatible with individual rights.

The first sense of limited government refers to the ENUMERATION OF POWERS through which the Constitution outlines the jurisdictional concerns of the national government. This method of limitation has failed. The enumeration of powers is now a dead letter as a result of the nationalizing tendencies of American economic and social life, which the Supreme Court has accommodated through its interpretations of the TENTH AMENDMENT, the COMMERCE CLAUSE, the NECESSARY AND PROPER CLAUSE, the GENERAL WELFARE CLAUSE, and the CIVIL WAR amendments.

As for the second, or procedural, mode of limitation (structural limitations on policy formation and due process limitations on adjudication), some contemporary constitutionalists regard it as the only philosophically acceptable variety. These theorists tend to follow a value-neutral conception of constitutional democracy which is both at odds with citizen presuppositions about the goals of politics and supported by no compelling historical or philosophic argument. Respect for procedural ideas like SEPARATION OF POWERS, representative government, and DUE PROCESS is indeed central to American constitutionalism, but not because that tradition is indifferent to different ways of life and the ends of government. A traditional respect for procedure is rather an aspect of the Enlightenment commitment to liberal toleration or reasoning in human affairs, as opposed especially to precipitous decision and government in the name of divine authority. The value-neutral variety of proceduralism is inconsistent with this tradition because it denies the possibility of rationally defending the practices, conditions, and attitudes conducive to reasoning itself.

Americans typically associate limited government first and foremost with constitutional rights and JUDICIAL REVIEW. "By a limited constitution," wrote ALEXANDER HAMILTON in THE FEDERALIST #78, "I understand one which contains certain specified exceptions to the legislative authority; such, for instance, as that it shall pass no BILLS OF ATTAINDER, no EX POST FACTO laws, and the like. Limitations of this kind can be preserved in practice no other way than through the medium of courts of justice, whose duty it must be to declare all acts contrary to the manifest tenor of the Constitution void."

Yet courts are also agencies of government, and groups throughout American history have opposed judicial protection of some rights as the least majoritarian and therefore least legitimate subordination of other rights. Some theorists believe society has a way of arriving at pragmatic adjustments of conflicting views (lax enforcement of laws against CONTRACEPTION and ABORTION, for example) that cannot be reconciled at the level of moral principle. They regard judicial intervention in behalf of those persons who brook no compromise as divisive to the point of undermining everyone's right to live in a peaceful society. Many citizens seem profoundly bitter over their loss of freedom to live and raise their children in communities that exclude sexually suggestive entertainment, political deviants, and others, including members of other races and religions. Their criticism of the judiciary's protection of rights suggests a community oriented understanding of rights, for they themselves want the right to be members of communities that use official power to exclude some kinds of people as equals or to exclude them altogether. This community-oriented conception is highly visible in the demands of some religious groups for organized prayer in public schools despite offense to others.

But a community orientation of sorts is also implicit in demands for public recognition of the RIGHTS OF PRIVACY like those involving property, sexual freedom, and conscience. In effect, persons who demand these rights seek the right to live in communities that honor the rights demanded. Rights to property, for example, are hardly secure if the general public is unwilling to exercise the restraint and undertake the sacrifices that honoring such rights entails. It is therefore not surprising that defenders of property should treat "free enterprise" as an article of the community's gospel and special identity. For if any rights are genuine exemptions from LEGISLATIVE POWER, their enjoyment must not be left to prudential calculation. And if the government has no authority to invade them, those rights must at once be grounded in higher authority and be essential to the nation's identity in a way that it would make no sense to violate them for the sake of saving the nation. The religious right wing of American politics has a point in contending that "secular humanism" is itself something of a religious imposition on fundamentalists, who are thereby forced to live among what they regard as evil practices. Maxims of liberal toleration are no answer to these people because liberals themselves cannot tolerate being governed by thoroughly dedicated fundamen-

talists—those who would live every aspect of their lives as they think they should, even if that should mean employing coercive government against those who would stop them. Religiously committed folk can be excused for believing that liberalism tolerates illiberalism only by degrading it to a form of play-acting to be confined to churches, the home, or wherever one goes for respite from the serious world of education, work, and government. Defending liberalism thus requires an argument (eventually a persuasive one) that liberalism is a better way of life—that, wherever feasible, it is better for human beings to have a liberal outlook and live in secular communities that tolerate illiberal speech only, not action.

Deepening ideological divisions in American life indicate that constitutional rights can place real limits on government only where public morality favors honoring rights. Hamilton said as much in *The Federalist* #84 where he criticized naïve reliance on BILLS OF RIGHTS to protect the rights themselves. "[W]hatever fine declarations may be inserted in any constitution," he said, the security of rights "must altogether depend on public opinion, and on the general spirit of the people and of the government." It follows that governments that would honor rights effectively should work for the social and economic conditions and attitudes that are favorable to honoring rights. If rights are to remain effective limits on government, the ends of government will have to include the virtue of its citizens. Limited government in a modern sense will have to converge toward limited government in an ancient sense.

SOTIRIOS A. BARBER
(1986)

(SEE ALSO: *Checks and Balances; Unwritten Constitution.*)

Bibliography

BARBER, SOTIRIOS A. 1984 *On What the Constitution Means.* Baltimore: Johns Hopkins University Press.

BERNS, WALTER 1982 Judicial Review and the Rights and Laws of Nature. *Supreme Court Review* 1982:49–83.

CORWIN, EDWARD S. 1928 The "Higher Law" Background of American Constitutional Law. *Harvard Law Review* 42:149–365.

DWORKIN, RONALD 1981 The Forum of Principle. *New York University Law Review* 56:469–518.

PURCELL, EDWARD A., JR. 1973 *The Crisis of Democratic Theory.* Lexington: University Press of Kentucky.

LINCOLN, ABRAHAM
(1809–1865)

Abraham Lincoln of Illinois served as President of the United States during the nation's greatest crisis, the CIVIL WAR. He had previously represented Illinois in the HOUSE

OF REPRESENTATIVES for a single term (1847–1849), during which he introduced the SPOT RESOLUTIONS, implicitly critical of President JAMES K. POLK's administration of the Mexican War, and supported the WILMOT PROVISO, which would have banned slavery from the territory acquired in that war. Lincoln rose to national prominence opposing the policies of Senator STEPHEN A. DOUGLAS, especially Douglas's KANSAS-NEBRASKA ACT, which extended SLAVERY IN THE TERRITORIES on a local-option basis. In 1856 he joined the fledgling Republican party. Lincoln opposed Douglas's re-election to the Senate in 1858, and the two candidates toured the state together, publicly debating the issues of slavery, POPULAR SOVEREIGNTY, and CONSTITUTIONALISM. During the LINCOLN-DOUGLAS DEBATES, Lincoln severely criticized Chief Justice ROGER B. TANEY's decision in DRED SCOTT V. SANDFORD (1857) as a betrayal of the principles embodied in the DECLARATION OF INDEPENDENCE.

Lincoln's election to the presidency in 1860 triggered the long-impending SECESSION of several slaveholding southern states. Lincoln's presidency was devoted to saving the Union, which meant, in his mind, the rededication of the nation to the principles of the Declaration of Independence, and especially to the proposition that all men are created equal. This work of saving the Union, tragically cut short by an assassin's bullet, was Lincoln's great contribution to American constitutionalism.

In the Lincoln Memorial, directly behind the statue of the Great Emancipator, these words are inscribed:

> In this temple
> as in the hearts of the people
> for whom he saved the Union
> the memory of Abraham Lincoln
> is enshrined forever.

Lincoln did indeed save the Union. But the Union Lincoln saved was older than the Constitution; the Constitution was intended to form a "more perfect Union." When Lincoln began the Gettysburg Address with the magisterial "Fourscore and seven years ago . . ." he intended his listeners to understand that the birth date of the nation was 1776, not 1787, and that the principles of "government of the people, by the people, for the people" were those of the Declaration of Independence. The Constitution was intended to implement those principles more perfectly than had been done by the ARTICLES OF CONFEDERATION. Lincoln at Gettysburg also intended his listeners—and the world—to know that there would be "a new birth of freedom" that would be accomplished by the EMANCIPATION PROCLAMATION, followed, as he intended that it would be, by the THIRTEENTH AMENDMENT. (We may be confident that, had he lived, Lincoln would also have given his support to the FOURTEENTH and FIFTEENTH AMENDMENTS, as part of that same "new birth.")

To understand the Constitution as Abraham Lincoln did must mean, primarily and essentially, to understand the Constitution as an expression of the principles of the Declaration. To do this is to separate the interpretation of the Constitution from all forms of legal positivism, historicism, and moral relativism, that is to say, from all those forms of interpretation that are dominant today in the law schools, universities, and courts of the nation. For, contrary to Lincoln's expectations, his words at Gettysburg have been greatly noted and long remembered: it is their meaning that has been forgotten.

Lincoln did indeed save the Union. At the time of his inauguration, March 4, 1861, seven states had already seceded and joined together to form an independent government called the Confederate States of America. JAMES BUCHANAN, the outgoing President, had been confronted with the SOUTH CAROLINA ORDINANCE OF SECESSION on December 20, 1860, six weeks after Lincoln's election, and more than ten weeks before his inauguration. Buchanan declared secession to be unconstitutional, but coupled his denunciation of secession with a much harsher denunciation of abolitionism. He denied, moreover, that he as President could take any lawful action against secession. Whatever action the federal government ought to take, he lamely concluded, must originate in laws enacted by Congress. But Buchanan had nothing to suggest to Congress, and Congress, at this juncture—the representatives of eight slave states remaining on March 4, 1861—was as divided as the nation itself. No congressional majority could have been formed then for decisive action against the rebellion. Lincoln waited until Congress had gone home, and cannily maneuvered the South Carolinians into firing those shots against Fort Sumter that electrified the North and consolidated public opinion behind his leadership. He then issued his call for 75,000 troops, and set on foot those measures that eventually resulted in the forcible subjugation of the rebellion.

Lincoln insisted that the Constitution ought not to be construed in such a way as to deny to the government any power necessary for carrying out the Constitution's commands. The Constitution required the President to take an oath "to preserve, protect, and defend the Constitution," and made it the duty of the President to "take care that the laws be faithfully executed." Lincoln held it to be absurd to suppose that it was unlawful for him to do those things that were indispensably necessary to preserve the Constitution by enforcing the execution of the laws. Even an action that might otherwise be unlawful, he said, might become lawful, by becoming thus indispensable. Lincoln never conceded that any of his wartime actions were unconstitutional. But supposing that one of them had been so, he asked, ". . . are all the laws but one to go unexecuted, and the Government itself go to pieces, lest that one be violated?"

Lincoln saved the Union. He prevented the United States from being divided into two or more separate confederacies. It was entirely likely that the North American continent would have been "Balkanized" had the initial secession succeeded. Like the Balkan states, the petty American powers would have formed alliances with greater powers, and North America would have become a cockpit of world conflict. All the evils that the more perfect Union was designed to prevent, those particularly described in the first ten numbers of THE FEDERALIST—large standing armies, heavy taxation, the restriction of individual liberties characteristic of an armed camp—would have come to pass. Civil and religious liberty, the supreme ends of republican government, would, with the failure of the American experiment, "perish from the earth." The "central idea of secession," Lincoln held, "is the essence of anarchy." A constitutional majority, checked and limited, and able to change easily with deliberate changes in public opinion and sentiment, "is the only true sovereign of a free people." To reject majority rule is to turn necessarily either to anarchy or to despotism.

The Lincoln Memorial says that Lincoln saved the Union for "the people." At the outset of the war Lincoln said, "This is essentially a people's contest." Today, when the foulest despotisms call themselves "people's republics," it requires a conscious effort to restore to our minds the intrinsic connection in Lincoln's mind between the cause of the people and fidelity to individual liberty under the rule of law in a constitutional regime. "Our adversaries," Lincoln said, at the outset of the war, "have adopted some declarations of independence, in which, unlike the good old one, penned by THOMAS JEFFERSON, they omit the words 'all men are created equal.' Why? They have adopted a temporary national constitution, in the preamble of which they omit, 'We the People,' and substitute 'We, the deputies of the sovereign and independent States.' Why? Why this deliberate pressing out of view the rights of men and the authority of the people?" Here is the core constitutional question of the Civil War. Lincoln was elected on a platform that called for the recognition of STATES' RIGHTS, "and especially the right of each State to order and control its own domestic institutions according to its own judgment exclusively." Such rights, the Republican platform asserted, and Lincoln repeated in his inaugural, were "essential to that balance of power on which the perfection and endurance of our political fabric depend." For Lincoln, however, the rights of the states were themselves the political expression of the rights of the people, which in turn were the political expression of the rights of men. The proposition that embodied the rights of men was that to which—as he said at Gettysburg—the nation was dedicated at its conception. The Civil War was a result of the fact that the idea of states' rights, and of popular sovereignty, had become divorced, in the public mind of the Confederacy, from the original doctrine of equality in the Declaration of Independence.

The question posed by the Civil War, Lincoln said, was addressed to "the whole family of man." That Lincoln conceived of mankind as in some sense a "family" was of course but another expression of his belief in human equality. Lincoln's question was essentially the same as that addressed by ALEXANDER HAMILTON in *The Federalist* #1: "whether societies of men are really capable or not of establishing good government from reflection and choice, or whether they are forever destined to depend for their political constitutions upon accident and force." The election of Abraham Lincoln was a deliberate decision of the American people, in accordance with the canons of reflection and choice embodied in the Constitution. It remained to be seen therefore whether, in Lincoln's words, "discontented individuals, too few in numbers to control administration according to organic law [can arbitrarily] break up their government, and thus practically put an end to free government upon the earth." But because the leaders of the rebellion "knew their people possessed as much of moral sense, as much devotion to law and order . . . as any other civilized and patriotic people," it was necessary for them to invent "an ingenious sophism which, if conceded, was followed by perfectly logical steps . . . to the complete destruction of the Union. The sophism itself is, that any State of the Union may, consistently with the national Constitution . . . withdraw from the Union without the consent of the Union or of any other State."

The secessionists claimed that membership in the Union resulted from the acts by which the states had ratified the Constitution and that they might therefore withdraw by the same procedure. The Constitution itself, according to this theory, had no higher authority than the will of the people of the several states, acting in their constituent capacity.

In contradiction of this position, Lincoln presented a historical argument, that the Union was older than the states, that the rights of the states were only rights within the Union, and never rights outside of it or independent of it. Although the Declaration of Independence speaks, in its next to last sentence, of all those "Acts and Things which Independent States may of right do," none of them were ever done by any of the United States independently of each other. This argument, however, is not as conclusive as that other argument, independent of history, which follows from that "abstract truth applicable to all men and all times," to which, at Gettysburg, Lincoln said the nation had been dedicated. This argument Lincoln had been developing throughout his mature life, and is the ground of his constitutionalism, as indeed it is of all his moral and political thought. According to Lincoln, the Civil War was a "people's contest" because the rights of the states, and of the United States, were the rights of the people, either severally or generally. But what are the rights of the people? They are the rights with which the Creator has equally endowed all men—all human beings. These are the unalienable rights, among which are the rights to life, to liberty, and to the pursuit of happiness. Since all men have these rights equally, no man can rule another rightfully except with that other man's consent. Nothing better illuminates the division within the American mind that brought about the Civil War than this passage from a speech in reply to Douglas in 1854: "Judge Douglas," said Lincoln, "frequently, with bitter irony and sarcasm, paraphrases our argument by saying: 'The white people of Nebraska are good enough to govern themselves, *but they are not good enough to govern a few miserable negroes!*' Well, I doubt not that the people of Nebraska are, and will continue to be as good as the average of people elsewhere. I do not say the contrary. What I do say is, that no man is good enough to govern another man, *without that other's consent.* I say this is the leading principle—the sheet anchor of American republicanism." Slavery, Lincoln observed, is a violation of this principle, not only because "the Master . . . governs the slave without his consent; but he governs him by a set of rules altogether different from those which he prescribes for himself." Republicanism, for Lincoln, meant that those who live under the law share equally in the making of the law they live under, and that those who make the law live equally under the law that they make. Here in essence is the necessary relationship between equality, consent, majority rule, and the rule of law in Lincoln's thought. Here in essence is what unites the principles of the Declaration with the forms of the Constitution. Here is what enables us to distinguish the principles of the Constitution from the compromises of the Constitution (in particular, the compromises with slavery). Here is the essence of Lincoln's understanding of why the argument against slavery and the argument for free government are distinguishable but inseparable aspects of one and the same argument.

The people are collectively sovereign because the people individually, by their consent, have transferred the exercise of certain of their unalienable rights—but not the rights themselves—to civil society. They have done so, the better "to secure these rights." A just government will act by the majority, under a constitution devised to assure with a reasonable likelihood that the action of the majority will fulfill its purpose, which is the equal protection of the indefeasible and equal rights of all. The majority is the surrogate of the community, which is to say, of each individual. Majority rule is not merely obliged to respect minority rights; in the final analysis it has no higher purpose than to secure the rights of that indefeasible minority, the individual. The sovereignty of the people—or of the states—cannot be exerted morally or lawfully for any purpose inconsistent with the security of those original and unalienable rights. Although Lincoln denied any constitutional right to secede, he did not deny a revolutionary right, which might be exercised justly if "by the mere force of numbers, a majority should deprive a minority of any clearly written constitutional right."

In his inaugural address Lincoln repeated his oft-repeated declaration that he had no purpose, "directly or indirectly, to interfere with slavery where it exists." He had, he said, "no lawful right to do so" and he had "no inclination to do so." This, he held, was implied constitutional law, but he was willing to make it express, by an amendment to the Constitution. Lincoln would not, however, agree to any measures that might have as their consequence the extension of slavery to new lands where it did not already exist. As he wrote to his old friend ALEXANDER H. STEPHENS in 1861, "You think slavery is *right,* and ought to be extended; while we think it is *wrong* and ought to be restricted. That I suppose is the rub. It certainly is the only substantial difference between us." Many complex and elaborate explanations have been made of the causes of the Civil War. Lincoln's is at once the shortest and the most profound.

The South claimed the right to extend slavery on the ground that it was a violation of the fundamental equality of the states to allow the citizens of one state or section to emigrate into a federal TERRITORY with their property, while prohibiting the citizens of any other state or section from emigrating into that same federal territory with their property. Lincoln dealt with this argument in 1854—in his first great antislavery speech—as follows: "Equal justice to the South, it is said, requires us to consent to the extending of slavery to new countries. That is to say, inasmuch as you do not object to my taking my hog to Nebraska, therefore I must not object to you taking your slave. Now, I admit this is perfectly logical, if there is no difference between hogs and negroes."

Southerners had come to deny the essential difference between hogs and Negroes, in part because of the enormous economic stake that they had come to have in slave labor, because of the enormous burgeoning of the cotton economy. This was one cause of the change in their opinion of slavery, from a necessary evil to a positive good. Another may be seen in the following from one of Lincoln's 1859 speeches. Douglas, Lincoln said, had "declared that while in all contests between the negro and the white man, he was for the white man . . . that in all questions between the negro and the crocodile he was for the negro." Lincoln interpreted Douglas's statements as "a sort of proposition in proportion, which may be stated thus: As the negro is to the white man, so is the crocodile to the negro; and as the negro may rightfully treat the crocodile as a beast or reptile, so the white man may rightfully treat the negro as a beast or reptile." Douglas's references to "contests" between negroes and crocodiles, and between negroes and whites, reflected popular ideas of "the survival of the fittest" in the evolutionary process. Lincoln, in commenting on these remarks of Douglas, also went out of his way to deny the necessity of any such "contests." Alexander Stephens, who was inaugurated vice-president of the Confederacy in February 1861, conceded that the United States had been founded upon the proposition "that all men are created equal," and that that proposition had indeed (contrary to what Chief Justice Roger B. Taney had said in *Dred Scott v. Sandford*) included black men as well as white. But, Stephens went on, the Confederacy was "founded [and] its corner stone rests upon . . . the great truth that the negro is not the equal of the white man. That slavery—the subordination to the superior race, is his natural and normal condition." "This our new Government," Stephens added, "is the first in the history of the world, based upon this great physical and moral truth." The doctrine of racial superiority became a vital element in the conviction that slavery was a positive good. Without the conviction and the doctrine there could not have been a belief in the South of a constitutional right to extend slavery. That science, in one or another version of evolution, had established the inequality of the races, became the ground for the rejection of the doctrine that all men are created equal.

In fact, the doctrine of racial inequality involves the denial that there is any natural right, or that there are any "laws of nature and of nature's God." And this is to deny that constitutionalism and the RULE OF LAW rest upon anything besides blind preference. Justice would then be nothing but the interest of the stronger. Abraham Lincoln's speeches, before and during the Civil War, are the supreme repository for that wisdom that teaches us that we as moral beings ought to live under the rule of law. According to this wisdom, it is also in our interest to do so, because upon our recognition of the humanity of other men depends the recognition of our own humanity. And upon the recognition of our own humanity—by ourselves and by others—depends the possibility of our own happiness as human beings. Surely Lincoln was right in saying that the source of all moral principle—no less than of all political and constitutional right—was the proposition "that all men are created equal."

It is doubtful that the history of the world records another life displaying an integrity of speech and deed equal to that of Abraham Lincoln. With an almost perfect understanding of the theoretical ground of free, constitutional government was united an unflinching courage, and a practical wisdom, in doing what had to be done, lest popular government "perish from the earth." Whether, in the third century of the Constitution, Lincoln's legacy will survive in deed depends upon whether we can recover anything of his character and intelligence. But whether or not this republic lasts, as long as the world lasts Lincoln's speeches and deeds will remain as an emblem and a beacon of humanity to all men everywhere who may be struggling out of the dark valley of despotism and aspiring to the broad, sunlit uplands of freedom.

HARRY V. JAFFA
(1986)

Bibliography

BELZ, HERMAN 1969 *Reconstructing the Union.* Ithaca, N.Y.: Cornell University Press.

FEHRENBACHER, DON E. 1978 *The Dred Scott Case: Its Significance in American Law and Politics.* New York: Oxford University Press.

—— 1979 Lincoln and the Constitution. Pages 121–166 in Cullom Davis, ed., *The Public and Private Lincoln: Contemporary Perspectives.* Carbondale: Southern Illinois University Press.

JAFFA, HARRY V. (1952) 1983 *Crisis of the House Divided: An Interpretation of the Lincoln-Douglas Debates.* Chicago: University of Chicago Press.

NEVINS, ALAN 1950 *The Emergence of Lincoln.* 2 Vols. New York: Scribner's.

RANDALL, JAMES G. 1951 *Constitutional Problems under Lincoln,* rev. ed. Urbana: University of Illinois Press.

LINCOLN, LEVI
(1749–1820)

Graduated from Harvard University and trained in law, Levi Lincoln fought as a Minuteman in the AMERICAN REVOLUTION and subsequently held several offices in the revolutionary government of Massachusetts. In 1780 he was a delegate to the convention that drafted the state constitution. After the Revolution he became a leader of the Massachusetts bar as well as a member of the legislature.

In 1781, Lincoln successfully argued in *Quock Walker's Case (Caldwell v. Jennison)* that the passage in the MASSACHUSETTS CONSTITUTION declaring that "all men are born free and equal" prohibited any legal recognition of slavery in the state. The decision effectively abolished slavery in Massachusetts.

Having early become a leader of the Republican party,

Lincoln served from 1801 to 1805 as attorney general of the United States in the first administration of THOMAS JEFFERSON. In 1811 he declined, on the ground of failing eyesight, President JAMES MADISON's offer of appointment as an associate Justice of the Supreme Court.

DENNIS J. MAHONEY
(1986)

LINCOLN AND CONSTITUTIONAL THEORY

Throughout his political career, most notably in the performance of his duties as chief executive during the CIVIL WAR, ABRAHAM LINCOLN was required to construe the Constitution. Three of Lincoln's constitutional constructions have assumed fundamental significance in American CONSTITUTIONAL THEORY. Basic to the decision to resist disruption of the Union, these constructions were presented in Lincoln's first inaugural address, on March 4, 1861.

The first of Lincoln's constitutional constructions denied a monopoly of CONSTITUTIONAL INTERPRETATION to the judicial branch and asserted the authority of the political branches of the government to determine the meaning of the Constitution. Discussing the nature of a liberal REPUBLICAN FORM OF GOVERNMENT, Lincoln considered the proposition that constitutional questions are to be decided by the Supreme Court. He said that constitutional decisions of the Court were binding on the parties to a suit as to the object of that suit, and were entitled to very high respect and consideration by the other departments of government in parallel cases. Nevertheless, "if the policy of the government, upon vital questions, affecting the whole people, is to be irrevocably fixed by the decisions of the Supreme Court, the instant they are made, in ordinary litigation between parties, in personal actions, the people will have ceased to be their own rulers, having to that extent, practically resigned their government, into the hands of that eminent tribunal." Reiterating his criticism of the DRED SCOTT V. SANDFORD (1857) decision, Lincoln affirmed the SEPARATION OF POWERS and the POLITICAL QUESTION DOCTRINE as essential elements in constitutional interpretation.

Lincoln's second constitutional construction asserted the necessity of majority rule as a fundamental principle in liberal republican government. Rejecting the Southern view that the right of SECESSION was the basic principle in the American political tradition, Lincoln said: "A majority, held in restraint by constitutional checks, and limitations, and always changing easily, with deliberate changes of popular opinions and sentiments, is the only true sovereign of a free people." Stating that unanimity was impossible and that the rule of a minority was not legitimate as a permanent arrangement, Lincoln declared the majority principle to be the only alternative to anarchy or despotism. In deciding constitutional controversies, he reasoned: "If the minority will not acquiesce, the majority must, or the government must cease." And if "a minority, in such case, will secede rather than acquiesce, they make a precedent which, in turn, will divide and ruin them; for a minority of their own will secede from them, whenever a majority refuses to be controlled by such minority."

The third theoretically significant constitutional construction, providing further reason for rejecting secession as an American constitutional principle, concerned the nature of the Union and the Constitution. Claiming authority to prevent the disruption of the Union, Lincoln said: "I hold, that in contemplation of universal law, and of the Constitution, the Union of these States is perpetual. Perpetuity is implied, if not expressed, in the fundamental law of all national governments. It is safe to assert that no government proper, ever had a provision in its organic law for its own termination." Lincoln meant that the federal government, in essence, was the sovereign government of a nation and national people, not the coordinating authority or agent of "an association of States in the nature of a contract merely." Like all national governments, the government of the Union-nation was intended to last indefinitely. By the principles of political science and the law of nations, it possessed rightful authority to maintain its own existence against disintegration, as a means to the end of maintaining the purposes of the nation and of the Constitution by which the establishment of the government was ordained.

Lincoln's constitutional constructions crystallized earlier constitutional arguments and had a formative effect on constitutional law and theory for the indefinite future. Politically controversial, they were integral to practical decisions aimed at upholding the ends of the Constitution. Lincoln did not conceive of constitutional theory as an activity aimed at developing abstract normative propositions based on principles of moral philosophy external to the existing constitutional order.

HERMAN BELZ
(2000)

(SEE ALSO: Nonjudicial Interpretation of the Constitution.)

Bibliography

ABBOT, PHILIP 1996 The Lincoln Propositions and the Spirit of Secession. Studies in American Political Development 10: 103–129.

BELZ, HERMAN 1998 Abraham Lincoln, Constitutionalism, and Equal Rights in the Civil War Era. New York: Fordham University Press.

DIETZE, GOTTFRIED 1968 America's Political Dilemma: From

Limited to Unlimited Democracy. Baltimore, Maryland: Johns Hopkins Press.

LINCOLN-DOUGLAS DEBATES
(1858)

STEPHEN A. DOUGLAS, running for reelection to the United States Senate, agreed to debate his Republican challenger, ABRAHAM LINCOLN, at seven joint appearances in rural Illinois during the summer of 1858. The resulting discourse, promptly reprinted in full in newspapers, produced a classic survey of alternatives for the future of SLAVERY and black people in the American constitutional system.

Douglas defended the concept of territorial SOVEREIGNTY: let the people of the territories, rather than Congress, decide the future of slavery there. He stated that he "cared not whether slavery be voted up or voted down" and accused Lincoln of advocating racial equality. Lincoln emphasized the incompatibility of Douglas's position with the decision in DRED SCOTT V. SANDFORD (1857), in which Chief Justice ROGER B. TANEY had stated that a territorial legislature lacked power to exclude slavery. Douglas responded with the "FREEPORT DOCTRINE": a territorial legislature could exclude slavery simply by not enacting legislation supporting it. Lincoln hinted at a conspiracy involving Taney, Douglas, and the Pierce and BUCHANAN administrations to force slavery into the free states, an allegation Douglas indignantly denied by reasserting the power of each state to fully control its domestic policy.

WILLIAM M. WIECEK
(1986)

Bibliography

JAFFA, HARRY V. 1959 *Crisis of the House Divided: An Interpretation of the Lincoln-Douglas Debates.* Garden City, N.Y.: Doubleday.

LINCOLN'S PLAN OF RECONSTRUCTION
(1863)

By 1863, President ABRAHAM LINCOLN adopted policies that affected RECONSTRUCTION in some of the seceded states. He appointed military governors in Louisiana, Tennessee, and North Carolina and recognized the provisional government of Virginia. The EMANCIPATION PROCLAMATION took effect on January 1, 1863.

Lincoln issued his Proclamation of Amnesty and Reconstruction on December 8, 1863. In it, he offered AMNESTY to all participants in the rebellion, except high-ranking military and civilian officers. He announced his intention to appoint a military governor in each occupied state and to require each occupied state to accept all extant and future policy concerning SLAVERY and emancipation. But otherwise Lincoln's policy was conservative. It assumed preservation of the states' boundaries, constitutions, and laws (except those relating to slavery) and required neither black suffrage nor confiscation. Lincoln proposed to recreate an enfranchised citizenry in each state by requiring all persons to take an oath of future loyalty and support of the laws. When ten percent of a state's 1860 voters had taken the oath, they could reorganize the state's government.

The President's authority to recreate loyal state governments derived from several provisions of Article II, including his powers as COMMANDER-IN-CHIEF, his PARDONING POWER, and his duty to see to the faithful execution of the laws. But, as with his earlier actions in calling for volunteers and suspending HABEAS CORPUS, Lincoln had to make the most of a document that had not contemplated SECESSION, CIVIL WAR, or Reconstruction.

Though Arkansas and Louisiana complied with Lincoln's terms, Congress refused to seat their representatives. Lincoln and Congress clashed over the more stringent congressional plan of Reconstruction embodied in the WADE-DAVIS BILL of 1864. President ANDREW JOHNSON later pursued Reconstruction policies similar to Lincoln's.

WILLIAM M. WIECEK
(1986)

Bibliography

BELZ, HERMAN 1969 *Reconstructing the Union: Theory and Policy During the Civil War.* Ithaca, N.Y.: Cornell University Press.

LINE-ITEM VETO

The Constitution permits the President to sign or veto a bill as a whole. He may not pick and choose among the parts of a bill, signing some portions while vetoing others. Although most governors have VETO POWER over individual items, constitutional amendments to grant similar authority to the President have thus far been unsuccessful.

The Framers were familiar with the powers exerted by the British Board of Trade, which routinely reviewed thousands of acts submitted by the mainland of American colonies and disallowed some "in whole or in part." These disapprovals were more similar to JUDICIAL REVIEW than to an item veto, in the sense that vetoes prevent proposals from taking effect, while the board's actions came after the colonial measures were law. In any event, the Framers did not find the British precedent appealing for the Constitution being drafted.

The item veto did not materialize until the CONFEDER- ATE CONSTITUTION of 1861. Since that time, forty-three states have adopted some variation of the item veto for their governors. In 1873 President ULYSSES S. GRANT re- quested an item veto for the national executive, and at least a dozen Presidents have made similar appeals.

The fact that so many governors have the item veto is not a sufficient justification for giving the same power to the President. The federal-state analogy suffers from a number of deficiencies. The item veto exercised by gov- ernors is inseparable from a constitutional design that differs dramatically from the design of the federal Con- stitution, especially in the distribution of executive and legislative powers. A much greater bias against LEGISLA- TIVE POWER operates at the state level. State budget pro- cedures also differ substantially from federal procedures. Appropriation bills in the state are structured to facilitate item vetoes by governors, but appropriation bills passed by Congress contain few items. Money is provided in large, lump-sum accounts.

Presidents regularly claim that with item-veto power they could carve out the "boondoggles and pork" that Congress supposedly includes in bills. However, Congress does not specify "pork barrel" projects in the bills pre- sented to the President. Particular projects are identified in the conference report that accompanies a bill. These reports, which are not submitted to the President for his signature or veto, explain to executive departments and agencies how lump-sum funds are to be spent. The Pres- ident cannot veto items, because there are no items to veto.

Congress could pattern itself after the states, taking the details from conference reports and inserting them into public laws. The results would not be attractive for agency officials, who like the latitude and flexibility of lump-sum funding. They do not want details, or items, locked into public law.

During the administration of RONALD REAGAN, the edi- torial page of the *Wall Street Journal* argued that the Pres- ident already had item-veto authority. The theory is that the Framers anticipated that each discrete subject would be placed in a separate bill and presented to the President, giving him maximum discretion in using the veto power. Because Congress currently passes omnibus bills—in- cluding continuing funding and authorization for various programs—it is argued that an effective veto requires a power in the President to exercise item veto within these massive bills.

The historical record does not support this theory's view of the Framers' expectations. The first appropriations bill passed in 1789 was an omnibus measure, containing all funds for civilian and military programs. The same kinds of bills were enacted in 1790 and 1791. Evidently the members of the First Congres, which included many of the Framers who had participated in the CONSTITU- TIONAL CONVENTION OF 1787, did not believe that Congress should pass seperate appropriations bills for every discrete program or activity.

A presidential item veto would have little effect on re- ducing federal deficits. Most of the federal budget is "un- controllable" because of fixed costs to pay interest on the federal deficit, provide ENTITLEMENTS (such as SOCIAL SE- CURITY) for individuals, and reimburse contractors for work already done. Those appropriations could not be ve- toed. However, an item veto could greatly increase EXEC- UTIVE POWER. Presidents and their assistants could use the threat of an item veto to coerce legislators into supporting presidential nominees, treaties, legislative goals, and spending priorities.

LOUIS FISHER
(1992)

(SEE ALSO: *Budget Process.*)

Bibliography

FEIN, BRUCE and REYNOLDS, WILLIAM BRADFORD 1989 Wishful Thinking on a Line-Item Veto. *Legal Times*, November 13, pp. 20, 24.
FISHER, LOUIS and DEVINS, NEAL 1986 How Successfully Can the States' Item Veto Be Transferred to the President? *Georgetown Law Journal* 75:159–197.

LINE-ITEM VETO
(Update)

The Line Item Veto Act of 1996 authorized the President to cancel in whole any dollar amount of discretionary bud- get authority (appropriations), any item of new direct spending (entitlements), and any limited tax benefit. Un- like the item veto available to forty-three governors, this measure did not allow the President to cancel items in bills presented to him. Only after signing a bill into law could the President exercise the cancellation authority, and he had to do that within five days. Congress could pass a bill disapproving the cancellations, but the President could veto that bill. Congress would then need a two-thirds ma- jority in each chamber to override the veto.

President WILLIAM J. CLINTON canceled eighty-two items, all of them appearing in appropriations bills except for one item of direct spending and two items of limited tax benefits. The seventy-nine appropriation items totaled $477 million, a tiny percentage of the $526 billion appro- priated in those bills. After Congress successfully reversed the cancellation of thirty-eight military construction proj- ects ($287 million), the net reduction in appropriations was only $190 million. The three nonappropriation items amounted to $225 million, but the administration conceded that Clinton lacked authority to cancel one involving the federal retirement system.

Senator Robert C. Byrd and several colleagues challenged the constitutionality of the Line Item Veto Act. In *Raines v. Byrd* (1997), the Supreme Court ruled that the legislators lacked STANDING to bring the suit. A year later, the Court accepted a case from private parties who had been denied federal assistance because of Clinton's cancellations. In *Clinton v. City of New York* (1998), the Court held that the act violated the lawmaking procedures established by the Constitution, especially the PRESENTMENT clause that requires that all bills and resolutions be presented to the President for his signature or veto. Congress, said the Court, could not authorize the President to repeal parts of a statute.

Writing for a 6–3 majority, Justice JOHN PAUL STEVENS acknowledged that Congress in previous years had authorized the President to suspend certain statutory provisions in the field of international trade. He argued that those statutes "all relate to foreign trade," suggesting that the issue was not merely procedural (presentment clause) but possibly substantive as well (foreign versus domestic affairs).

Stevens said that if Congress wanted to give the President item-veto authority, it would have to act by constitutional amendment, not by statute. However, several of the dissenters identified line-item options that would have no problems under the presentment clause. Justice ANTONIN SCALIA pointed out that Congress could direct the President to spend "not in excess" of certain amounts, allowing the President not to spend anything. In a separate dissent, Justice STEPHEN G. BREYER said that Congress could direct the President to carry out certain programs unless he issued a certification that the program not take effect. In 1995, the U.S. SENATE passed a version of line-item authority that would not raise presentment problems either. Under a procedure called "separate enrollment," Congress could break the large appropriations bills into individual items and present each one to the President. Thus, despite the Court's opinion, the item-veto issue might return under a different name.

LOUIS FISHER
(2000)

(SEE ALSO: *Veto Power.*)

Bibliography

DEVINS, NEAL E. 1997 In Search of the Lost Chord: Reflections on the 1996 Item Veto Act. *Case Western Reserve Law Review* 47:1605–1642.

FISHER, LOUIS 1997 Line Item Veto Act of 1996: Heads-up from the States. *Public Budgeting & Finance* 17:3–17.
JOST, KENNETH 1997 Line-Item Veto: Can It Control Wasteful Federal Spending? *CQ Researcher* 7:529–552.
JOYCE, PHILIP G. and REISCHAUER, ROBERT D. 1997 The Federal Line-Item Veto: What Is It and What Will It Do? *Public Administration Review* 57:95–104.

LINEUP

In opinions whose subtext is unease about eyewitness identification procedures and testimony, the Supreme Court ruled in 1967 that a suspect is entitled to the presence of counsel at a lineup in order to preserve a FAIR TRIAL at which the witnesses can be meaningfully cross-examined. The opinions were delivered in the cases of UNITED STATES V. WADE and *Gilbert v. California.*

If a lineup is conducted without counsel, testimony about the lineup identification is automatically excluded. The question then becomes whether the witness who attended the illegally conducted lineup should be allowed to identify the witness at trial. This question centers on whether the witness could have made the in-court identification without having attended the lineup at which counsel was not present: whether, in other words, the witness had an independent source for the identification.

The lineup cases have generated much litigation and writing, both of a practical and a scholarly sort, about the role of counsel. The Court seemed to envision the attorney as a passive observer who would use what he saw to reconstruct for the fact-finder any unfairness in the lineup procedure. But a lawyer's skills are not necessary for observing, and reconstruction on cross-examination creates the risk that through the knowledge he displays in asking questions a lawyer may become a witness in his own case. Perhaps recognizing that having counsel at lineups was an interim measure and perceiving the analytical difficulties, the Court suggested that other techniques, such as photographing or videotaping lineups, could obviate the need for counsel.

The RIGHT TO COUNSEL at lineups was greatly undercut in *Kirby v. Illinois* (1972), in which the Court held that the right begins only "at or after the initiation of adversary criminal proceedings—whether by way of formal charge, preliminary hearing, INDICTMENT, INFORMATION, or arraignment." Because most lineups are part of the investigative stage of a case and occur before any of the indices of a formal charge, *Kirby* necessarily implied that a lawyer or some other observer was not, in fact, generally required.

Untouched by *Kirby,* however, is the argument, made in *Stovall v. Denno* (1967), that identification procedures may be so "unnecessarily suggestive and conducive to irreparable mistaken identification" as to violate DUE PROCESS OF LAW. An example of a due process violation would be showing a crime victim only the suspect dressed in clothes like those of the perpetrator when there was time to arrange a proper lineup. Once such a due process violation is proven, the issue shifts to whether it tainted the in-court identification: whether there was "a very substantial likelihood of irreparable mistaken identification." This decision mirrors that of a court in deciding whether a victim can make an in-court identification after attending a lineup where counsel was not present.

The effect of the lineup decisions has been to focus attention on all of the procedures used in pretrial CONFRONTATION of witnesses and suspects and thus to improve the fairness of these previously unobserved, but critically important, occasions.

BARBARA ALLEN BABCOCK
(1986)

Bibliography

LEVY, LEONARD W.   1974   *Against the Law.* Pages 242–258. New York: Harper & Row.

LINMARK ASSOCIATES v. WILLINGBORO
431 U.S. 85 (1977)

Without dissent, the BURGER COURT invalidated a local ordinance prohibiting real estate "For Sale" and "Sold" signs. The ordinance sought to reduce the flight by white homeowners from racially integrated neighborhoods. Although a ban upon all signs for aesthetic purposes might survive a constitutional test, wrote Justice THURGOOD MARSHALL, this ordinance violated the FIRST AMENDMENT because the township had selected a particular message for prohibitions.

MICHAEL E. PARRISH
(1986)

LISTENERS' RIGHTS

The constitutional commitment to FREEDOM OF SPEECH is in part based on the simple idea that people have a right to say what they want to say without government interference. That is, freedom of speech protects the speaker. Yet the FIRST AMENDMENT themes of self-expression and speaker liberty have been recognized only sporadically in Supreme Court opinions. The more prevalent themes in First Amendment jurisprudence have been audience-oriented, albeit implicitly.

One classic justification of freedom of speech has been based on optimistic assessments about the capacity of the marketplace of ideas to distinguish between the false and the true. The emphasis of this justification is not that speakers have a right to say what they want to say, but that speakers must be free to speak so that the society can find truth, that is, so that listeners can hear and evaluate what is said. Listeners' rights are also strongly implicated by the notion that freedom of speech reflects a commitment to democratic self-government. If citizens are to decide how to respond to public issues, they must hear what others have to say. The listeners' rights emphasis of the self-government perspective is best illustrated by ALEXANDER MEIKLEJOHN's observation, approvingly cited by the Supreme Court in COLUMBIA BROADCASTING SYSTEM V. DEMOCRATIC NATIONAL COMMITTEE (1981): "What is essential is not that everyone shall speak, but that everything worth saying shall be said."

For many years, listeners' rights were protected with nary a listener before the Court. In routine cases, the aggrieved speaker invoked the rights of the listeners. In *Thomas v. Collins* (1945), for example, the Court invalidated an attempted prior restraint at the behest of the speaker, in part because of the rights of others "to hear what he had to say."

Ultimately, listeners were permitted to invoke their own rights without any speakers before the Court. In VIRGINIA STATE BOARD OF PHARMACY V. VIRGINIA CITIZENS CONSUMER COUNCIL (1976), for example, consumers challenged a statute that prohibited pharmacists from advertising the prices of prescription drugs. No pharmacist was before the Court, only potential members of the audience for drug price advertising. The Court recognized the rights of "listener" plaintiffs to sue on their own behalf, observing that the First Amendment gives protection "to the communication, to its source and its recipients both."

LAMONT V. POSTMASTER GENERAL (1965) stands for an even broader principle. There the Court struck down a statute directing the postmaster general not to deliver certain "communist political propaganda" unless the addressee, upon notification, requested its delivery. The Court found this to be "an unconstitutional abridgment of the addressee's rights." Many of the potential senders of this "propaganda" were aliens outside the country who had no First Amendment rights of their own. The Court made this distinction explicit in *Kleindeist v. Mandel* (1972). Thus recipients of messages have a First Amendment right to hear that does not depend upon corresponding rights in the speaker. Such rights may extend to situations where the speaker is unwilling to speak; they are then usually referred to as the RIGHT TO KNOW. On the other hand, an unwilling recipient of a message may have a right not to hear, deriving from notions such as a right of privacy.

STEVEN SHIFFRIN
(1986)

Bibliography

BEVIER, LILLIAN 1980 An Informed Public, an Informing Press: The Search for a Constitutional Principle. *Stanford Law Review* 68:482–517.

EMERSON, THOMAS I. 1976 Legal Foundations of the Right to Know. *Washington University Law Quarterly* 1976:1–24.

LITERACY TEST

Many states used to require voters to be literate in English. The main constitutional problems raised by this practice arose from the use of literacy tests in southern and border states as a form of RACIAL DISCRIMINATION aimed at denying black citizens their VOTING RIGHTS in violation of the FIFTEENTH AMENDMENT. A typical law conditioned voter registration on the ability to read and write a provision of the state constitution selected by the registrar, to the registrar's "satisfaction." (An Alabama registrar once wrote this explanation for rejecting a black applicant: "Error in spilling.") Some laws also required the applicant to "interpret" or "explain" the constitutional provision, offering even greater opportunities for discriminatory application.

In *Davis v. Schnell* (1949) the Supreme Court summarily affirmed a lower court decision invalidating a requirement that a voter "understand and explain" an article of the United States Constitution; the registrar's discretion was so great that the test was an obvious "device to make racial discrimination easy." However, in *Lassiter v. Northampton County Board of Elections* (1959) the Court unanimously upheld a bare literacy requirement, in the absence of any showing of discriminatory application. This distinction had been suggested by the Court as early as WILLIAMS V. MISSISSIPPI (1898).

Meanwhile, the Court had fought two minor voting rights skirmishes with Oklahoma. That state had required voters to pass a literacy test, but excepted any voter whose ancestors had been registered to vote in 1866. Because of this GRANDFATHER CLAUSE, only black registrants were required to take literacy tests; the Court readily invalidated this law in GUINN V. UNITED STATES (1915). After the decision, Oklahoma adopted a law requiring all new voters to register within a twelve-day period; because virtually all the new voters were black, this onerous procedure fell before the Fifteenth Amendment, which "nullifies sophisticated as well as simple-minded modes of discrimination," in *Lane v. Wilson* (1939).

The death blow to voter literacy tests was delivered not by the Court but by Congress, which approached the question gingerly. The VOTING RIGHTS ACT OF 1965 required certain states and counties to suspend their use of literacy tests for five years. This feature of the law was upheld in SOUTH CAROLINA V. KATZENBACH (1966). In the same year, KATZENBACH V. MORGAN (1966) upheld another feature of the 1965 act requiring states to confer the vote on some citizens who, having been educated in Puerto Rico, were literate in Spanish. In 1970, Congress suspended literacy tests for voting throughout the nation, a provision which the Court upheld in OREGON V. MITCHELL (1970) as a valid exercise of the power to enforce the Fifteenth Amendment. Finally, in 1975, Congress made the ban on literacy tests permanent. In practical terms, literacy tests for voters are a thing of the past, and the Supreme Court is unlikely to confront the *Lassiter* issue again.

KENNETH L. KARST
(1986)

Bibliography

LEIBOWITZ, ARNOLD H. 1969 English Literacy: Legal Sanction for Discrimination. *Notre Dame Lawyer* 45:7–67.

LITIGATION

See: Public Law Litigation

LITIGATION STRATEGY

Litigation strategy in constitutional cases is shaped by a single animating principle—a desire to increase the likelihood that a black-robed bureaucrat called a judge will act on behalf of a politically vulnerable applicant to alter or set aside the act of a popularly accountable official. Although the degree of tension that exists between democratic political theory and constitutional litigation varies widely depending on the nature of the case and the attributes of the forum—a police brutality case litigated before an elected state judge poses no threat to democratic decision making; an EQUAL PROTECTION challenge to an act of Congress argued before an appointed, life-tenured, federal judge poses a more direct conflict—constitutional cases generally involve persons who are unable to secure redress through more conventional appeals to the political process. Litigation strategy in constitutional cases is designed to increase the potential that a judicial forum will rule in favor of such politically disfavored plaintiffs.

Sustained constitutional litigation in the United States has involved many sets of litigants, including abolitionists versus slaveholders in the period prior to the CIVIL WAR; radical reconstructionists versus southern revisionists in the period immediately following the Civil War; business CORPORATIONS versus populist reformers during the first third of the twentieth century; and civil libertarians versus majoritarians during the modern era. Although the political goals of the participants have varied widely, the strategic choices of the contestants have remained remarkably stable, involving five areas: choice of forum; selection of parties; articulation of theories of recovery; choice of tactics; and articulation of antidemocratic apologia.

Choice of forum is the most important strategic decision for a constitutional litigator. In choosing a forum, a constitutional litigator must choose between state and federal court; between a judge and jury; and sometimes between one judge and another. The outcome of many, if not most, constitutional cases turns as much on the wisdom of those strategic choices as on the intrinsic merits of the cases.

Because a constitutional plaintiff is generally seeking to trump a decision that enjoys the imprimatur of democratic decision making, the institutional capacity of the forum to render sustained anti- (or, at least, counter-) majoritarian doctrine is critical to the success of any constitutional litigation campaign. Judges who are themselves elected by the political majority or who are otherwise closely tied to the political process are least likely to enunciate sustained countermajoritarian doctrine. Judges who enjoy maximum political insulation are, on the other hand, in a position to ignore the short-term political consequences of their unpopular decisions. It would, for example, have been impossible for elected judges to have effectively enforced the fugitive slave clause in the pre-Civil War North on behalf of southern slaveholders, or the equal protection clause in the post-World War II South on behalf of black schoolchildren seeking an integrated education.

The search for an insulated judge in constitutional cases has generally led politically vulnerable plaintiffs— whether slaveholders, business corporations, or CIVIL RIGHTS activists—to seek a federal judicial forum, for federal judges are appointed and enjoy life tenure. Much of the procedural infighting that characterizes constitutional litigation revolves around attempts by plaintiffs to force claims into insulated federal forums and by defendants to deflect them to more politically accountable state courts.

The search for an insulated forum has led many constitutional litigators to view juries with suspicion. Not surprisingly, a principal litigation strategy of the abolitionist bar was to choreograph disputes about alleged fugitive slaves before free state juries in the hope that juries would decline to enforce the Fugitive Slave Act. (See FUGITIVE SLAVERY.) Modern civil rights lawyers have experienced analogous difficulty in persuading juries to return verdicts in favor of unpalatable plaintiffs whose rights may have been violated by a popularly responsible official.

Finally, the choice of forum involves a decision about the identity of the judge or, in less polite terms, judge-shopping. The identity of the judge in a constitutional case is extremely important for two reasons, one obvious and one less well understood. The obvious reason for judge-shopping involves the judge's politics. Because constitutional cases often turn on a clash of values and because the urgency with which a judge views a constitutional case may well depend on his or her view of the relative importance of the conflicting values, the same case may be decided differently by equally competent judges with differing value systems.

The less obvious reason why judge-shopping is important in constitutional cases involves the judge's technical competence. Victory for the plaintiff in constitutional cases depends upon persuading a judge that constitutional doctrine requires the overturning of a presumptively valid decision by another government official. Unless a judge is equipped to understand and evaluate complex argumentation about the meaning of ambiguous textual provisions and judicial PRECEDENT, it will be impossible to persuade the judge that doctrinal factors compel a decision for the plaintiff. Because the inertial advantage in constitutional cases almost always favors government defendants—failure to persuade the judge to act results in perpetuation of the challenged status quo—the inability of a judge to grapple with complex argumentation generally works to the disadvantage of a constitutional plaintiff.

In addition to care in selecting a forum, constitutional litigators expend a good deal of energy on the choice of a plaintiff, seeking to project the most sympathetic and appealing fact pattern. Because the judge's view of the equities may play a substantial role in the outcome of a constitutional case, the capacity of a constitutional plaintiff to evoke sympathy can be crucial. Constitutional lawyers have learned, moreover, that courts respond most favorably to fact patterns that emerge naturally from the interrelationship between a constitutional plaintiff and the government, but balk at being asked to decide artificially constructed TEST CASES.

A difficult decision constitutional litigators face in selecting a plaintiff is whether to bring the case as an individual action involving only named individuals or as a CLASS ACTION on behalf of all similarly situated persons. Militating in favor of class action status is its increased impact. A single class action can provide relief to thousands of people. Class actions, however, have drawbacks. Against the prospect of increased impact must be weighed the risk of loss, for members of a losing class are generally bound by the loss. Moreover, class actions can act as red flags to judges who would be sensitive to the claims of an individual plaintiff but who are reluctant to become involved in litigation seeking institutional change.

The selection of a defendant in a constitutional case also requires careful thought. Most important, the defendant must be capable of providing adequate relief. If injunctive relief is sought, the defendant must be sufficiently senior in the bureaucratic hierarchy to be able to promulgate and implement the changes sought by the action. At the same time, of course, the defendant must be sufficiently involved in the factual dispute giving rise to the lawsuit to justify naming him as an adverse party. If DAMAGES are sought, the defendant must have a sufficiently "deep pocket" to pay the judgment. A damage award against a judgment-proof defendant is hardly worth the effort.

One method of dealing with both the need for a high-ranking defendant and the quest for financial solvency is the naming of an entity-defendant such as the City of New York or the United States in addition to the individual defendants. The extremely complicated interplay between rules limiting the extent to which government entities can be sued in constitutional cases and plaintiffs' interest in suing government entities poses one of the serious tactical dilemmas in constitutional litigation.

A final—and less empirically verifiable—concern in selecting a defendant flows from what may be called the "Redneck-Mandarin dichotomy," which seeks to match a defendant and a judge from different educational and social backgrounds in the hope that the judge will be less constrained in exercising vigorous review powers. Although such an assumption is highly speculative, many constitutional litigators believe, for example, that they perceive a difference between many judges' willingness to exercise vigorous review of the actions of low-ranking police officers and the same judges' willingness to review the decisions of police commissioners.

Given the difficulty of overcoming the inertial advantage enjoyed by the government in constitutional cases, strategic considerations often play a role in the articulation of plaintiff's theory of recovery. It is often advisable to proceed by incremental stages and to develop alternatives to the primary constitutional theory. Thus, for example, litigation aimed at the OVERRULING of the SEPARATE BUT EQUAL DOCTRINE enunciated by PLESSY V. FERGUSON (1896) proceeded by carefully calibrated constitutional steps designed to develop sufficient momentum to make the final decision in BROWN V. BOARD OF EDUCATION (1954) possible. It is, however, extremely difficult to execute a sustained litigation campaign over time, for the factors of chance and changing tides of legal analysis are difficult to predict. On the other hand, asking for too much too soon in the absence of a carefully laid doctrinal foundation places an intolerable degree of pressure on even a sympathetic judge.

In an effort to lessen the tension between constitutional litigation and democratic political theory, litigators often seek to articulate a process-based alternative to their principal substantive theory. Thus, litigators attacking FIRST AMENDMENT violations often invite the court to seize upon a narrower, process-based claim such as VAGUENESS or OVERBREADTH as the basis for invalidating a statute, rather than confront the substantive question of the legislature's power to enact it at all. Similarly, constitutional litigators often seek to link their constitutional theories with non-constitutional claims, such as a claim based on a statute or a COMMON LAW tort. Posing alternative theories of recovery provides a judge with a less dramatic means of protecting a constitutional value while providing effective relief to the plaintiff. Of course, many such alternative theories of recovery are subject to modification by the legislature, but the short-term result is often indistinguishable from success of the constitutional claim.

Although much litigation strategy depends on a perception of the degree to which constitutional law is shaped by value judgments, constitutional lawyers also recognize the extent to which constitutional litigation shapes community values. The process of bringing a constitutional lawsuit is educational as well as remedial. It seeks to expose the judge to a set of facts and a legal reality that would ordinarily be far from his or her consciousness. It seeks to inform the public of the existence of a social problem that, even if not ultimately amenable to constitutional resolution, requires increased public attention. Viewed as a part of the process by which the interests of the politically powerless can be protected in a democracy, constitutional litigation provides a mechanism not only for classic remedial action but for a sharpening of the underlying social issues for ultimate political resolution. Thus, for example, although under current legal standards it is difficult to establish a violation of the constitutional right of a minority community to receive equal municipal services (discriminatory purpose, not merely disparate effect, must be proven), constitutional litigation provides a forum for the dramatization of unequal treatment as a first step to a political resolution. Similarly, although only the most optimistic believed that courts would actually stop the VIETNAM WAR because it was supposedly carried on in violation of Article 1, section 8, of the Constitution, the repeated presentation of the issue both shaped public perception of the war and helped pave the way for the passage of the War Powers Resolution which attempted to deal with the legal issue of undeclared war.

Two major constraints limit the use of constitutional litigation as an educational vehicle. First is the ethical obligation to refrain from presenting frivolous or inappropriate claims to a court. Judicial attention is a scarce national resource which must be rationed, and lawyers must be prudent in presenting claims that cannot win. In the absence of a good faith belief in the legal—as opposed to the moral—soundness of a claim, it should not be presented to a court. Moreover, even if a claim is sufficiently substantial to satisfy ethical considerations, tactical considerations often argue against presenting a weak claim for adjudication. Losing a constitutional case risks the enunciation of dangerous precedent and acts to legitimate the challenged activity. Thus, although constitutional litigation plays an educational as well as a remedial role, its educational role should be a by-product of a bona fide attempt to secure a legal remedy.

A significant dilemma in planning and executing litigation strategy in constitutional cases is posed by the potential for conflict between the best interest of a plaintiff and the furtherance of the cause that precipitated the case into court. For example, a plaintiff who has gone to court to vindicate a principle and who poses a powerful TEST CASE may be confronted with a settlement offer which, while advantageous to the plaintiff, leaves the legal issue unresolved. Constitutional lawyers, while recognizing this conflict, generally resolve it in favor of the plaintiff and recommend acceptance to their clients, who then make the final decision. Despite the recognition that the interest of the client in a constitutional case should predominate over the advancement of the cause, a disturbing tendency exists on the part of both bench and bar to use a constitutional plaintiff as a convenient vehicle to trigger the enunciation of norms that may benefit society as a whole but which do little for the parties before the Court. William Marbury never did get his commission. (See MARBURY V. MADISON.)

Once a constitutional case is underway, three recurring tactical issues arise. Should immediate relief be sought, usually in the form of a preliminary INJUNCTION? Should the case be pursued as an abstract issue of law or should substantial resources be expended in developing the facts? And how broad a remedy should be sought? It is impossible to formulate even a general rule governing these three issues, except that attorneys with weak cases rarely seek preliminary injunctions and that issues of law should not be presented to a potentially hostile court in the absence of clearly established fact, given that a judge's freedom of action is greatest in determining the facts on an ambiguous record.

A parallel tactical issue defendants in a constitutional case face is whether to move to dismiss—and, thus, to assume the truth of the facts alleged in the complaint for the purposes of the motion—or to force plaintiffs to prove their facts by going to trial. Surprisingly, most defendants, in an effort to save time and resources, attempt dismissal motions, which require courts to rule on the theoretical validity of plaintiff's case without requiring plaintiff to establish the facts. Much constitutional law has been made in denying motions to dismiss and thus creating important legal precedents in cases where plaintiffs might have experienced difficulty in proving their allegations.

Finally, in presenting a constitutional case to a judge, a constitutional litigator will often seek to place it within one of three categories posing the least tension with democratic political theory in order to free the judge to exercise vigorous review. If the case involves a member of a DISCRETE AND INSULAR MINORITY, constitutional litigators will stress the inability of unpopular or disadvantaged minority groups to protect themselves within the traditional political process, thus invoking the special responsibility of courts to act as a bulwark against majoritarian overreaching. If the case involves significant political values, constitutional litigators will stress the responsibility of courts to guarantee the proper functioning of the democratic process. It is not antidemocratic, they argue, for a court to prevent the majority from refusing to permit the democratic process to function properly. If the case involves a "fundamental" value, like marriage or REPRODUCTIVE AUTONOMY, constitutional litigators will argue that the importance of such values warrants increased judicial protection. This third category involves the most controversial exercises of judicial power, because the selection of "fundamental" values appears subjective.

Ultimately, litigation strategy in constitutional cases, even at its most sophisticated, can exert only a relatively weak influence on the outcome. The adjudication of issues that impinge on deeply held values and in many other systems would be relegated solely to the political process is an inherently unpredictable phenomenon. No other area of law fits Tolstoy's vision of history so well as the claim of constitutional lawyers to be able to influence the ocean on which they most often bob like corks.

BURT NEUBORNE
(1986)

Bibliography

COVER, ROBERT M. 1975 *Justice Accused: Anti-Slavery and the Judicial Process.* New Haven, Conn.: Yale University Press.

GREENBURG, JACK 1977 *Judicial Process and Social Change: Constitutional Litigation.* St. Paul, Minn.: West Publishing Co.

KLUGER, RICHARD 1975 *Simple Justice.* New York: Knopf.

NEUBORNE, BURT 1977 The Myth of Parity. *Harvard Law Review* 90:1105.

LIVING CONSTITUTION

The phrase "the living Constitution" emerged from two developments at the end of the nineteenth century. The first was the influence of Darwinism and PRAGMATISM on traditional CONSTITUTIONAL THEORY, and in particular their challenge to a more traditional, and conservative emphasis on remaining faithful to ORIGINAL INTENT and designs. The second development was the rising constituency for political reform in the early twentieth century after industrialization began putting pressure on eighteenth-century institutional arrangements.

The idea of the living Constitution should be seen in light of a relatively straightforward feature of our constitutional system: the document was intended to be the basis of American government for an indefinite period of time. The Framers believed that the Constitution embodied principles of a REPUBLICAN FORM OF GOVERNMENT that had withstood the test of time. Thus, despite warnings from THOMAS JEFFERSON against imposing on future generations the "dead hand of the past," the supporters of the Constitution felt it was acceptable to entrench these arrangements in a constitutional system that was perpetual and marked by a difficult, formal AMENDING PROCESS.

It is sometimes claimed that the idea of the living Constitution received its first clear expression in MCCULLOCH V. MARYLAND (1819) when Chief Justice JOHN MARSHALL wrote that "we must never forget that it is a *constitution* we are expounding," one that was "intended to endure for ages to come, and consequently, to be adapted to the various *crises* of human affairs." But it should be remembered that Marshall's intent was to offer an explanation for why the doctrine of IMPLIED POWERS, supplemented by the NECESSARY AND PROPER clause, should be interpreted to give the government flexibility in selecting "the necessary means for the execution of the powers conferred on the government." Marshall did not mean to imply that the actual powers of government might be reinterpreted whenever old understandings proved inconvenient or anachronistic. As Justice JOSEPH STORY explained in his *Commentaries on the Constitution of the United States* (1833), while the "means" by which the government pursues its ENUMERATED POWERS "must be subject to perpetual modification" it is equally important "not to enlarge the construction of a given power beyond the fair scope of its terms, merely because the restriction is inconvenient, impolitic, or even mischievous. If it be mischievous, the power of redressing the evil lies with the people by an exercise of the power of amendment. . . . [The Constitution] is to have a fixed, uniform, permanent construction. It should be, so far at least as human infirmity will allow, not dependent upon the passions or parties of particular times, but the same yesterday, to-day, and for ever."

By the end of the nineteenth century Charles Darwin's image of change had begun to replace Sir Isaac Newton's rule-bound universe as the exemplar of natural science, and philosophical pragmatism had begun to challenge older protestant commitments to the ongoing authority of inherited texts or principles. WOODROW WILSON would later explain in his *Constitutional Government in the United States* (1908) that although the Framers believed that politics "was a variety of mechanics" and the Constitution a "display [of] the laws of nature," we have since come to realize that "[s]ociety is a living organism and must obey the laws of life, not of mechanics" and "all that progressives ask or desire is permission—in an era when 'development,' 'evolution,' is the scientific word—to interpret the Constitution according to the Darwinian principle; all they ask is recognition of the fact that a nation is a living thing and not a machine."

Wilson and other reformers were obviously not asking for an opportunity to use the amendment process to establish new structures. Rather, they were challenging the inherited principle that the Constitution is to have a "permanent construction," arguing instead that judges should update their interpretations to make them more consistent with current assumptions and more serviceable to current problems. On the Supreme Court the theory of the living Constitution found expression in two related but distinct judicial traditions. The first is associated with Justice OLIVER WENDELL HOLMES, JR., whose famous aphorism "the life of the law has not been logic: it has been experience" was initially intended as a description of COMMON LAW reasoning but would later inform much of his constitutional decisionmaking. As he put it in MISSOURI V. HOLLAND (1920), the words of the Constitution "have called into life a being the development of which could not have been foreseen completely by the most gifted of its begetters," and to be faithful to this "organism" the "case before us must be considered in the light of our whole experience and not merely in that of what was said a hundred years ago." Importantly, Holmes believed that if the political system was to be capable of addressing the new challenges of a rapidly changing world, it was important for judges to get out of the habit of impeding legislative experimentation with reference to inherited, anachronistic constitutional principles. As he put it in his DISSENTING OPINION in LOCHNER V. NEW YORK (1905), judges should not use the Constitution to prevent the "natural outcome of dominant opinion" from prevailing in LEGISLATION, except in extraordinary circumstances.

The second tradition associated with the new theory of the living Constitution can be traced to Justice LOUIS D. BRANDEIS. Brandies often agreed with Holmes about the advantages of deferring to experimental legislation, but unlike Holmes he also believed that a commitment to a living Constitution meant that judges had an obligation to update constitutional protections to enable them to address contemporary threats to liberty. When the Court ruled in OLMSTEAD V. UNITED STATES (1928) that there was nothing in the language or origin of the FOURTH AMENDMENT that would apply to the practice of WIRETAPPING, Brandeis objected, saying that the Constitution "must have a . . . capacity of adaptation to a changing world"— not just the clauses that empower the government to address innovative problems, but also those clauses "guaranteeing to the individual protection against specific abuses of power. . . . Time works changes, brings into existence new conditions and purposes. Therefore a principle to be vital must be capable of wider application than the mischief which gave it birth."

The years leading up to the NEW DEAL saw a pitched battle between an older tradition of interpretive stability against the emergent reformist tradition of the living Constitution. As increasing numbers of reform-minded lawyers and judges followed the example of Holmes and Brandeis, conservatives on and off the Court kept insisting, like Justice GEORGE SUTHERLAND in his dissent in HOME BUILDING & LOAN ASSOCIATION V. BLAISDELL (1934), that "[c]onstitutional grants of power and restrictions upon the exercise of power are not flexible as the doctrines of the common law are flexible," and that legitimate constitutional change had to take the form of amendment and not interpretive updates. This battle intensified after President FRANKLIN D. ROOSEVELT aligned himself firmly behind those who argued that the meaning of the Constitution had to change with the times. This political development led increasing numbers of scholars sympathetic to the New Deal to speak out more strongly in favor of the living Constitution. Of this group none was more vocal or prolific than EDWARD S. CORWIN, who led the charge in favor of the view "that the Constitution must mean different things at different times if it is to mean what is sensible, applicable, feasible" and that its words must be "construed from a point of view which is sympathetic with the aspirations of the existing generation of American people, rather than that which is furnished by concern for theories as to what was intended by a generation long since dissolved into its native dust."

With the "switch in time" in 1937—when the Court abandoned its *Lochner*-era commitment to limited national government—the theory of the living Constitution became the dominant position on the Court, but it did not congeal into a unified new theory of interpretation. The original Holmes/Brandeis split continued to shape post–New Deal constitutional theory and practice. The Holmes version of constitutional adaptation through judicial deference was given voice by the former progressive, Justice FELIX FRANKFURTER. It is a fairly straight line from this position to the attempts of ALEXANDER M. BICKEL to convince the Court to embrace "the passive virtues" of judicial restraint, and then to the claim of Chief Justice WILLIAM H. REHNQUIST that the key feature of the living Constitution is "to enable the popularly elected branches of government, not the judicial branch, to keep the country abreast of the times."

Alongside this commitment to judicial deference is the modern liberal version of the tradition, articulated by Justices such as WILLIAM J. BRENNAN, JR., who wrote that "the genius of the Constitution rests not in any static meaning it might have had in a world that is dead and gone, but in the adaptability of its great principles to cope with current problems and current needs." Within constitutional theory this Brandeisian version of the living Constitution is most notable in the work of legal philosopher Ronald Dworkin, particularly when he suggests that the specific provisions of the Constitution should be viewed as carriers of more general concepts of political morality that should be abstracted away from the specific understandings (or conceptions) of their drafters and applied in ways that more accurately reflect contemporary convictions and challenges.

Whether either version of the living Constitution can be reconciled with the original understanding of our constitutional system has been a central locus for debate among post–New Deal constitutional theorists. Still, if it be true that the alternative to this move is the kind of activist ORIGINALISM practiced by pre–New Deal conservatives, then we may come to see the theory of the living Constitution as an understandable—but still controversial—response to the pressures for political change within a difficult-to-amend constitutional system.

HOWARD GILLMAN
(2000)

(SEE ALSO: *Amendment Process (Outside Article V); Judicial Activism and Restraint; Nonjudicial Interpretation of the Constitution; Transformation of Constitutional Law.*)

Bibliography

CORWIN, EDWARD S.   1987   *Corwin on the Constitution, Volume Two: The Judiciary,* edited with an introduction by Richard Loss. Ithaca, N.Y. and London, England: Cornell University Press.

GILLMAN, HOWARD   1997   The Collapse of Constitutional Originalism and the Rise of the Notion of the "Living Constitution" in the Course of American State-Building. *Studies in American Political Development* 11:191–247.

HAMBURGER, PHILIP A.   1989   The Constitution's Accommodation of Social Change. *Michigan Law Review* 88:239–327.

HORWITZ, MORTON J.   1993   Foreword: The Constitution of Change: Legal Fundamentality Without Fundamentalism. *Harvard Law Review* 107:30–117.

KAMMEN, MICHAEL   1994   *A Machine That Would Go of Itself.* New York: St. Martin's Press.

KYVIG, DAVID E.   1996   *Explicit and Authentic Acts: Amending the U.S. Constitution, 1776–1995.* Lawrence: University Press of Kansas.

RAKOVE, JACK N., ed.   1990   *Interpreting the Constitution: The Debate Over Original Intent.* Boston, Mass.: Northeastern University Press.

REHNQUIST, WILLIAM H.   1976   The Notion of a Living Constitution. *Texas Law Review* 54:693.

SIEGEL, STEPHEN A.   1990   Historicism in Late Nineteenth-

Century Constitutional Thought. *Wisconsin Law Review* 1990: 1431–1547.

VARIOUS AUTHORS 1936 The Constitution in the Twentieth Century. *The Annals of the American Academy of Political and Social Science* 185:1–200.

WHITE, G. EDWARD 1997 The "Constitutional Revolution" as a Crisis in Adaptivity. *Hastings Law Journal* 48:867–912.

LIVINGSTON, HENRY BROCKHOLST
(1757–1823)

There is a modest puzzle regarding Henry Brockholst Livingston's more than sixteen years on the Supreme Court (1806–1823): why was he comparatively silent? Livingston, a New York Jeffersonian, was among the best qualified appointees ever named to the Court. Before his appointment to the New York Supreme Court in 1802, he was at the top of the legal profession, ranked as an equal of his frequent sparring mate, ALEXANDER HAMILTON. Livingston's opinions during his five years on the New York court demonstrated legal erudition, style, and wit. Some of his opinions are still required reading for law students. The New York reports indicate that Livingston had a constant urge to express his thoughts, and he was not only an extremely active dissenter but also constantly rendered SERIATIM OPINIONS. In his four years of New York judicial tenure, Livingston dissented twenty times, concurred on fourteen occasions, and delivered twenty-four seriatim opinions. Those statistics only begin to indicate the battle on the New York court, largely between Livingston and JAMES KENT, both of whom were first-rate jurists. The business of the New York court involved many significant matters but few constitutional questions. Livingston's dissent in *Hitchcock v. Aicken* (1803) argued that the FULL FAITH AND CREDIT clause should be interpreted broadly; ultimately, the MARSHALL COURT, including Livingston, agreed with this reasoning in *Mills v. Duryee* (1813).

In contrast to his active role on the New York court, Livingston was scarcely noticeable on the Marshall Court. In fifteen TERMS he dissented but three times and delivered only five CONCURRING OPINIONS. The fact that he had not shrunk from confronting some of the ablest judges in the country when on the New York court precludes any notion that he was overwhelmed by JOHN MARSHALL and associates. The difference in Livingston's roles on the state court and the Supreme Court is important largely for what it explains about the Marshall Court's constitutional jurisprudence. By the time of Livingston's appointment, Marshall's practice of having one Justice deliver a single opinion for the Court was settled. The Justices, moreover, willingly stifled their differences, save on questions of great moment, usually constitutional. Within this practice, the Justices' common values, regardless of party affiliation, normally made compromise possible. There are indications that Livingston initially had difficulty in adjusting to the ways of the Marshall Court. In the first few cases he heard, Livingston seemed particularly active in questioning counsel, as if he might have wished to dissent, but did not. Apparently, Livingston's policy preferences blended well with the Marshall Court's general mercantile orientation. While on the New York bench Livingston had served as a precursor for nineteenth-century instrumentalist judges who shaped the law to promote commercial development. In this respect, Livingston resembled a fellow Jeffersonian on the Court, WILLIAM JOHNSON. Because of the commercial atmosphere of his home community of Charleston, South Carolina, Johnson, like Livingston, had good reason for thinking as his brethren did on commercial questions. Johnson was even more nationalistic than Marshall. Unlike Johnson, however, THOMAS JEFFERSON apparently did not attempt to goad Livingston into expressing his differences as he had done while a state judge. Another reason that Livingston did not join Johnson and make plural the "first dissenter" may have been that Livingston got along with the rest of the Court much better than Johnson did. When Livingston died, JOSEPH STORY's rich eulogy to him indicated how fondly he was remembered. Finally, Livingston was a ready adherent to precedent, as he had demonstrated on the New York bench. When a question was settled, Livingston was unlikely to challenge its resolutions, even obliquely. In short, Livingston was a good team player, and our constitutional jurisprudence may be poorer for it. A clear example of the consequences of Livingston's proclivity for compromise is seen in STURGES V. CROWNINSHIELD (1819), in which the Court invalidated a New York insolvent law of 1811 because it had been applied retroactively. On circuit, Livingston had emphatically sustained the same law in *Adams v. Storey* (1817); yet he proceeded to compromise in *Sturges*. It seems likely that Marshall did not wish to say in his opinion that the states had CONCURRENT POWER to pass bankruptcy or insolvency laws, but he did—probably in response to Livingston's urging. Livingston's main role on the Marshall Court and in the development of constitutional jurisprudence was that of a compromiser. His opinions, with few exceptions, are forgettable.

DONLAD ROPER
(1986)

Bibliography

DUNNE, GERALD T. 1969 Brockholst Livingston. In Leon Friedman and Fred L. Israel, eds., *The Justices of the United States Supreme Court.* New York: Chelsea House.

HASKINS, GEORGE LEE, and JOHNSON, HERBERT A. 1981 *Foun-*

dations of Power: John Marshall, 1801–1815, volume II of Freund, Paul A., general editor, *The Oliver Wendell Holmes Devise History of the Supreme Court of the United States.* New York: Macmillan.

LIVINGSTON, ROBERT R., JR.
(1746–1813)

The son of a New York judge, Robert R. Livingston, Jr., was a member of the committees that drafted the DECLARATION OF INDEPENDENCE (which he regarded as premature and did not sign) and the ARTICLES OF CONFEDERATION. With JOHN JAY and GOUVERNEUR MORRIS he drafted the New York constitution of 1777. From 1777 to 1801 he was chancellor of New York. In 1788 he was chairman of the New York state convention where he vigorously supported RATIFICATION OF THE CONSTITUTION. He was later minister to France (1801–1804) and, with JAMES MONROE, negotiated the LOUISIANA PURCHASE TREATY. Livingston became a partner of inventor Robert Fulton and secured a New York steamboat monopoly not broken until GIBBONS V. OGDEN (1824).

DENNIS J. MAHONEY
(1986)

LIVINGSTON, WILLIAM
(1723–1790)

Governor William Livingston, poet, lawyer, and Revolutionary general, signed the Constitution as a New Jersey delegate to the CONSTITUTIONAL CONVENTION OF 1787. Unable to attend regularly, Livingston was not active in the debates; but he was influential in securing New Jersey's early and unanimous ratification. He was the father of Justice BROCKHOLST LIVINGSTON and the guardian of young ALEXANDER HAMILTON.

DENNIS J. MAHONEY
(1986)

LOAN ASSOCIATION v. TOPEKA
20 Wall. (87 U.S.) 655 (1875)

The Supreme Court has frequently resorted to HIGHER LAW doctrine to buttress an opinion, but only twice in its history, in TERRETT V. TAYLOR (1815) and in this case, has it relied exclusively on the higher law as the ground for decision. An 8–1 Court, in an opinion by Justice SAMUEL F. MILLER, held unconstitutional a Kansas statute that authorized the city of Topeka to issue public bonds, payable by taxes, for the benefit of a private company that built iron bridges. In the absence of some usable clause of the Constitution, Miller relied on judicially implied limitations on government power "which grow out of the essential nature of all free governments" and protect individual rights "without which the SOCIAL COMPACT could not exist." Topeka and the state legislature had believed that attracting a bridge company promoted public prosperity as did a railroad or a public utility, but because the Court saw only an improper exercise of the tax power "to aid private enterprise and build up private fortunes," it called the statute "a robbery" of the public. Taxation, the Could held, can be exercised only for a public use or public purpose. Justice NATHAN CLIFFORD, the sole dissenter, believed that JUDICIAL REVIEW should be exercised only when the Constitution imposed a prohibition either express or necessarily implied, but not when the Court believed that a legislature had violated "natural justice" or "a general latent spirit" supposedly underlying the Constitution.

LEONARD W. LEVY
(1986)

LOBBYING DISCLOSURE ACT
109 Stat. 691 (1995)

The first full-scale lobbying reform LEGISLATION passed into law since 1946, the Lobbying Disclosure Act of 1995 requires paid lobbyists to register with a national Office of Lobbying Registration and Public Disclosure and prohibits such lobbyists from providing gifts to legislators.

In previous decisions, the Supreme Court has recognized the protection of lobbyists by the FIRST AMENDMENT guarantee of the RIGHT TO PETITION. The 1946 Federal Regulation of Lobbying Act, the only other omnibus lobbying regulation measure, was severely limited in its scope by the Court in *U.S. v. Harriss* (1954). *Harriss* established a very narrow definition of the term "lobbyist"; only those who have "direct communication with Members of Congress" were so defined for the purpose of the act, effectively excluding nearly all individuals from its regulatory mechanism.

The Lobbying Disclosure Act substantially broadens the definition of "lobbyist" established in *Harriss*. The act also significantly limits the actions of those defined as lobbyists, banning gifts to members of Congress and prohibiting lobbyists from receiving federal grants. The act thus clearly restricts the broad freedoms presently claimed by lobbyists under the First Amendment. Whether the Court will accept or reject this departure from *Harriss* will have a significant effect on its interpretation of First Amendment petitioning guarantees.

DAVID K. RYDEN
(2000)

LOCAL GOVERNMENT

The Constitution does not mention local governments, but because of their ubiquity and importance questions have inevitably arisen about how they are to be fitted into the conceptual world it creates. Differences in the structures and functions of local governments might have led the Supreme Court to develop a complex set of responses to those questions. Both history and state law, for example, furnish materials that would have permitted the Court to conclude that some activities of some local governments should be characterized as "private," thereby freeing those local governments from the limitations the Constitution imposes on the exercise of governmental power and permitting them to claim the protections it confers upon private interests.

Instead, the Court has, with minor exceptions, treated all local governments alike. In all their activities, all are "political subdivisions of the State created as convenient agencies for exercising such of the powers of the State as may be entrusted to them," as the Court wrote of municipal corporations in *Hunter v. City of Pittsburgh* (1907). Several important conclusions flow from this conception of local government.

First, in exercising whatever authority the state may have conferred on them, local governments are subject to the same limitations the Constitution imposes on the exercise of state power. Second, local governments have no constitutional rights against the state that created them. A state may, for example, dispose of a local government's property as though it were the state's own, with no obligation to compensate the local government from which the property is "taken." Third, states have plenary control over the distribution of governmental authority within their borders. Individuals do not have a constitutional right to be governed by local institutions rather than by the state directly, nor do they have a right to be governed by one rather than another local government.

The states' plenary authority over governmental organization is, of course, subject to the limitations the Constitution imposes on the exercise of all state authority. Thus, in GOMILLION V. LIGHTFOOT (1961), a state statute redrawing the boundaries of a municipality so as to exclude virtually all its black, and none of its white, residents was invalidated as racially discriminatory. And in *Washington v. Seattle School District No. 1* (1982), the Court sustained a challenge to a statewide initiative that denied local school boards authority to bus students for the purpose of eliminating DE FACTO school SEGREGATION. Relying on HUNTER V. ERICKSON (1969), the Court held that a state could not structure its decision-making process "in such a way as to place special burdens on the ability of minority groups to achieve beneficial legislation." But in so holding, the Court was careful to reaffirm the state's power to assume control of the schools or, presumably, of all decisions concerning student placement. The invalidated initiative differed from such measures, in the Court's view, because it did not operate "in a race-neutral manner."

The states' plenary authority over their local governments may also be circumscribed by federal legislation. Thus, in *Lawrence County v. Lead-Deadwood School District* (1985) a federal statute authorizing local governments that receive federal payments in lieu of property taxes to spend funds "for any governmental purpose" was held to preempt a state statute which required that the funds be spent in the same way as general tax revenues. Just how far Congress may intrude on the states' power to control their local governments is uncertain, but in principle the question appears to be no different from that which arises whenever Congress regulates internal affairs of the states. In *FERC v. Mississippi* (1982) the Court sustained Congress's power to impose certain duties on state utility commissions, and in GARCIA V. SAN ANTONIO METROPOLITAN TRANSIT AUTHORITY (1985) the Court sustained Congress's power to subject states to the wage and hour provisions of the FAIR LABOR STANDARDS ACT. These decisions establish that the power of Congress is very broad, perhaps extending to the limits of Congress's authority under its ENUMERATED POWERS. Neither decision, however, quite forecloses the possibility that the Court may yet find in the TENTH AMENDMENT a principle of state autonomy that imposes some limits on Congress's power to interfere with state control of the agencies of state government.

The doctrine that local governments are merely state agencies, if taken to a logical extreme, might be understood to undermine the devolution of state authority to them. To the extent that a state relies on local governments for the performance of various governmental functions, differences in the circumstances and policies of the local governments inevitably lead to disparate treatment of the state's citizens. If local governments are merely state agencies, it can be argued, the state should be held responsible for the disparities to the same extent it would if it had directly ordered them. Although territorial discrimination by the state often can be justified and has in particular circumstances been upheld by the Court, it seems plain that the acceptance of that argument would seriously threaten the institution of local self-government. Thus far, however, the Supreme Court has refused to apply the *Hunter* doctrine in so drily logical a fashion.

In SAN ANTONIO INDEPENDENT SCHOOL DISTRICT V. RODRIGUEZ (1973), the Court held that a state policy of relying on local school districts to finance a substantial percentage of the cost of operating local schools did not violate the EQUAL PROTECTION clause of the FOURTEENTH AMENDMENT, even though there were marked differences among the school districts in both taxable resources and expenditures per pupil. Among the considerations that influenced the Court were the deeply embedded national tradition of local financing and control of schools and the more general threat that a contrary decision would have posed to traditional reliance on local governments to support and provide a broad range of other services.

MILLIKEN V. BRADLEY (1974) reflects similar deference to the tradition of local self-government. In that case, the Court reversed a decree ordering interdistrict SCHOOL BUSING as a remedy for unlawful segregation of the Detroit schools. In doing so, it rejected the district court's argument that "school district lines are no more than arbitrary lines on a map drawn "for political conve nience" that may be ignored whenever interdistrict relief is necessary to achieve an effective remedy. Said the Court, "No single tradition in public education is more deeply rooted than local control over the operation of schools." Due respect for that tradition, the Court held, precluded an interdistrict remedy unless other districts participated in bringing about the unlawful segregation or the state drew district lines to foster segregation.

A number of commentators have argued that *Rodriguez, Milliken,* and several other recent Supreme Court decisions that accord weight to the nation's traditions of local self-government are, if not inconsistent with the *Hunter* doctrine, at least in tension with it. But the Court has gone no further than to recognize those traditions when they are expressed in state law. For that reason, its recent decisions seem more an affirmation of the state's plenary authority over governmental organization than a retreat from it.

For reasons that have never been adequately explained, however, the Court has not followed the logic of *Hunter* in determining the reach of federal JUDICIAL POWER. A local government is treated as a "citizen of a state" for purposes of DIVERSITY JURISDICTION, though the same is not true of either the state or those of its political subdivisions of statewide authority that are regarded as merely its alter ego. Nor do local governments share the state's ELEVENTH AMENDMENT immunity from federal court suit.

TERRANCE SANDALOW
(1992)

(SEE ALSO: *Racial Discrimination; State Action.*)

Bibliography

BRIFFAULT, RICHARD 1989 Our Localism. *Columbia Law Review* 89:85–111.

LEE, CAROL F. 1982 The Federal Courts and the Status of Municipalities: A Conceptual Challenge. *Boston University Law Review* 62:1–73.

LOCHNER v. NEW YORK
198 U.S. 45 (1905)

Lochner v. New York, a landmark decision of 1905, has been discredited by the evolution of constitutional law. Justice RUFUS W. PECKHAM, writing for a 5–4 majority of the Supreme Court, invalidated a New York state statute forbidding employment in bakeries for more than sixty hours a week or ten hours a day. The rationale for the Court's opinion was that the statute interfered with the FREEDOM OF CONTRACT and thus the FOURTEENTH AMENDMENT's right to liberty afforded both the employer and the employee. The Court stated that under the statute, viewed as a labor law, the state had no reasonable ground for interfering with liberty by determining the hours of labor. Seen as a health law, the statute affected only the bakers and not the public. Accordingly, the Court concluded that the law was neither necessary nor appropriate to accomplish its health objective. Moreover, the Court was of the view that if the law were upheld for the bakers, laws designed to protect other workers would also have to be upheld. In either case, said the Court, the statute was an illegal interference with the right to contract.

Justice OLIVER WENDELL HOLMES, in an important and historic dissent, concluded that the legislature had the power to enact a law that interfered with full freedom to contract and that the personal biases of judges could not justify declaring a statute unconstitutional. Said Justice Holmes: "The constitution is not intended to embody a particular economic theory," an obvious reference to the laissez-faire view then widely accepted. Holmes's view was that a law interfered with the Fourteenth Amendment's guarantee of liberty only if "a rational and fair man necessarily would admit that the statute proposed would infringe fundamental principles of our people and our law." The dissent's view was that the statute, viewed either as a health or a labor law, did not violate these principles.

Justice JOHN MARSHALL HARLAN also dissented, arguing with Justice Holmes that the wisdom of the statute or of a particular economic theory is judicially irrelevant. Citing studies that showed the hazards of bakery work, Harlan noted that legislatures in many states had enacted legislation dealing with the number of hours in a work day. Said Justice Harlan: "[I]t is enough for the determination of this case, and it is enough for this Court, to know that the question is one about which there is room for debate and for at least honest difference of opinion." If there are "weighty substantial" reasons for enacting a law it ought "to be the end of [the] case, for the State is not amenable to the judiciary, in respect of its legislative enactments, unless such enactments are plainly, palpably, beyond all question, inconsistent with the Constitution of the United States."

The Court implicitly overruled the *Lochner* result in BUNTING V. OREGON (1917), but for three decades the decision influenced the Court as it scrutinized carefully and often struck down economic regulations as violations of SUBSTANTIVE DUE PROCESS. It was not until the mid-1930s, in the wake of the Court-packing furor and especially the Court's approval of the constitutionality of the National Labor Relations Act in *National Labor Relations Board v. Jones & Laughlin Steel Corporation* (1937), that judicial intervention in economic legislation declined. Although *Lochner* is now discredited, its focus upon substantive due process and FUNDAMENTAL RIGHTS has emerged in cases dealing with both contraception and abortion, namely GRISWOLD V. CONNECTICUT (1965) and ROE V. WADE (1973).

WILLIAM B. GOULD

(1986)

LOCKE, JOHN
(1631–1704)

John Locke, the English philosopher of enlightenment, formulated the basic doctrines that influenced the American Framers of 1787. While his famous *Second Treatise*, "Of Civil Government" (1688), alludes to various traditional ways to limit governments, it sets forth an effectual new way, later called liberal CONSTITUTIONALISM. That comprised a sphere of individual liberty, fenced by a right to property, and fixed government, constituted by a majority's consent. Constitutional or civil government is to be representative, responsible, and limited, with powers separated as well as effective, and it is to be kept to its FUNDAMENTAL LAW by a perpetual threat of popular rebellion.

The first of Locke's *Two Treatises of Government* rebutted Robert Filmer's contention that monarchy exists by divine right, derived from the fatherly authority of Adam and of God. Locke thrust at paternalism, which he regarded as the natural foundation of uncivil government and of inhumane civilization in general. Mankind has inclined unthinkingly to obey fathers, who grew to be patriarchs of families and chiefs of tribes, and finally to be oppressive kings and nobles upheld by wealth, power, and the servile flatteries of traditional faiths. The *Letter concerning Toleration* (1689) espoused freedom of conscience and SEPARATION OF CHURCH AND STATE. Locke tried to remove religion from the magistrate's armory and to remake churches into voluntary associations keeping watch on government and on one another. The *Letter* counsels public toleration of religion, but as a thing merely private, and only of civil religions willing to tolerate other faiths and to obey the civil powers. In other writings Locke advocated a reasonable Christianity and a worldly and private edu-

cation, and he explained human understanding prosaically, as reliably derived from sense impressions rather than from intuitions or divinations.

The first chapters of the *Second Treatise* set forth the famous doctrine of individualism: human beings are naturally free, equal, and occupied with securing themselves, not naturally subordinate to a superior or oriented to something noble or true above themselves. They are not subject to fathers or mothers so soon as they can "shift for themselves," or to husbands or wives if they no longer consent to be spouses, or to some gentleman or lord in his vineyard or estate. On the contrary, they have a natural right to acquire the means of life, to obtain the fruits of their own labor. Locke devised a private right of unlimited acquisition which implicitly indicts any leisured class, authorizes opportunity for the "industrious and rational," and provides powerful incentives for work, invention, and production. Locke was the philosophic father of capitalism, his plan whereby freedom of enterprise produces economic growth and the means of collective security. The profits of entrepreneurs, which Locke defended as incentives, occasioned the later attacks on capitalism as unjust and LIMITED GOVERNMENT as callously narrow.

The central chapters of the *Second Treatise* are Locke's prescription for public powers that will serve the people instead of exploiting them. He insisted upon powerful institutions, what THE FEDERALIST was to call effective or energetic government. A condition without government, Locke eventually maintained, is "very unsafe, very insecure," and people are "driven" to establish a LEGISLATIVE POWER to define laws, judges to apply them, and an executive to enforce them. Despite this agreement with the authoritarian Thomas Hobbes, Locke insisted that raising a state is easy compared to domesticating it. For domesticated or civil government the key is constitutionalism—government according to a man-made fundamental law agreeable to a majority. In particular, the supreme power, which Locke defines as a lawmaking power, is to be set up with a majority's consent (immediate or eventual, express or tacit). This supreme legislative power, however, is also and primarily to be shaped by Locke's enlightened prescriptions for a legislative limited, conditional, and rather democratic. Every actual legislature has by right only this legislative power, the natural CONSTITUTION behind any written constitution, and a consenting majority is to be supposed an enlightened majority. The legislature must aim to preserve individual rights, to govern by declared laws, not to impose TAXATION WITHOUT REPRESENTATION, and not to delegate its powers. Also, a legislature must be broadly representative of "populous" places filled with "wealth and inhabitants." Locke required an assembly of "deputies" of the people, while cautiously but pervasively impugning an aristocratic senate or house.

Locke provided for an executive power that is (unlike a monarch) subordinate to law and yet (like a monarch) able to act beyond law when public necessities require. The executive enforces law, unites the nation's forces for FOREIGN AFFAIRS (Locke's "federative" power), includes the judiciary, and remains, unlike the legislature, permanently on duty. For purposes of lawmaking Locke subordinated the executive to the legislature and attacked executives (such as the British king) who shared in lawmaking. Locke's argument led discreetly toward government by a responsible ministry, a dependence on a popular legislature that was rejected when the American Founders devised the Presidency, and a constitutional monarchy, which is only a "head of the republic," "a badge or emblem" representing the people. Still, executive power is extended by political necessity. In extraordinary situations, such as civil war, executive "prerogative" may extend to actions without authorization of law or even in violation of fundamental law, as when ABRAHAM LINCOLN in 1861 raised troops and monies before Congress had assembled. *Salus populi suprema lex est* is the Two Treatises' motto: the people's benefit is the supreme law. Locke repeated this maxim, which shows the limits of constitutional law, as he urged a king to reapportion an oligarchic house into a representative legislature.

The *Second Treatise* ends by insisting on an extraconstitutional RIGHT OF REVOLUTION, to secure a constitutional order against tyranny and also to help bring about popular constitutionalism. While executive prerogative may extend to reform, it is not to include a "godlike" prince with "a distinct and separate interest," a despot who violates the fiduciary "trust" of office, a conqueror, a usurper, a tyrannical king, or a clique of the rich. Such excesses make power revert to the people, who may set up anew their legislature. Locke repeatedly called this doctrine new. Each of the last six chapters ends by holding up to governors and peoples the new right of popular rebellion. In effect, Locke justified rebellion against every regime not a constitutional republic, and justified "revolution" of traditional beliefs inimical to individualism and popular government, that is, of almost all traditional beliefs.

The American Framers accepted Locke's broad framework of NATURAL RIGHTS and civil government, while varying details of the Constitution in accord with the cautious versions of MONTESQUIEU and his followers, David Hume and Sir WILLIAM BLACKSTONE. Fearing a political zealotry that might rival the old religious wars, Montesquieu, in his *Spirit of the Laws* (1748), abstained from Locke's fiery language of natural and popular liberty. His modified Lockeanism would allow forms and structures to vary with circumstance, make the judiciary a third separate power, and allow a senate of the successful and wealthy. Montes-

quieu also sought to introduce humane civilization less by rebellion and more by the spread of commerce and by changes in the private law of contract and inheritance.

ROBERT K. FAULKNER
(1986)

Bibliography

HARTZ, LOUIS 1955 *The Liberal Tradition in America.* New York: Harcourt, Brace.

STRAUSS, LEO 1953 *Natural Right and History.* Chicago: University of Chicago Press.

VILE, M. J. C. 1967 *Constitutionalism and the Separation of Powers.* Oxford: Clarendon Press.

LOCKHART, WILLIAM B.
(1906–1995)

William B. Lockhart was a major constitutional law figure for more than a half century. Closely identified with the University of Minnesota Law School, where he taught for twenty-eight years and was dean from 1956 to 1972, Lockhart also served on the law faculties at Stanford (1938–1946) and the University of California, Hastings (1975–1994). Although he occupied several prestigious administrative positions—president of the Association of American Law Schools, a longtime member of the Council of the American Law Institute, and chairman of President LYNDON B. JOHNSON's controversial National Commission on Obscenity and Pornography—he was most prominently recognized for his seminal contributions to constitutional law scholarship. His series of articles on STATE TAXATION OF COMMERCE and OBSCENITY significantly influenced the Supreme Court and were often cited in its opinions, beginning in 1940 and continuing to the present time. On state taxation, he contended that the Court should abandon the so-called Formal Rule—that states may not tax any activity viewed by the Court as a part of INTERSTATE COMMERCE, even though the tax threatens no discriminatory burden on commerce—which had been used for a century to invalidate many state taxes. His view was finally accepted by the Court in 1977. His position on obscenity—that normal FIRST AMENDMENT protection should be afforded to all sex-related expression except for material treated as hard-core PORNOGRAPHY by its primary audience and the manner in which it is sold—has been less successful as a matter of constitutional DOCTRINE, although essentially followed in actual practice. Finally, Lockhart co-authored eight editions of a widely used casebook on constitutional law— the first edition published in 1964 and the most recent published in 1996—the hallmark of which was the inclusion of many selections from the literature woven into notes and questions that were contained throughout the materials.

JESSE H. CHOPER
(2000)

Bibliography
LOCKHART, WILLIAM B. 1975 Escape from the Chill of Uncertainty: Explicit Sex and the First Amendment. *Georgia Law Review* 9:533–587.
——— 1981 A Revolution in State Taxation of Commerce? *Minnesota Law Review* 65:1025–1061.
LOCKHART, WILLIAM B. and MCCLURE, ROBERT C. 1960 Censorship of Obscenity: The Developing Constitutional Standards. *Minnesota Law Review* 45:5–121.

LODGE, HENRY CABOT
(1850–1924)

A Harvard-trained lawyer who also earned the Ph.D. degree in history, Henry Cabot Lodge was elected three times to the HOUSE OF REPRESENTATIVES and six times to the United States SENATE from Massachusetts. He was a close friend of President THEODORE ROOSEVELT and a national leader of the Republican party.

During his second term in Congress Lodge introduced a bill that would have provided for federal supervision of elections in order to protect the VOTING RIGHTS of black citizens in southern states. But he was wary of such Progressive innovations as women's suffrage and the DIRECT ELECTION of senators. He advocated the constant expansion of the United States through the annexation of Hawaii and other island TERRITORIES, and he supported the Spanish American War because it promised to lead to annexation of the Philippine Islands. During Roosevelt's administration Lodge was a leading congressional supporter of the Panama Canal project.

In 1918, Lodge used his position as chairman of the Senate Foreign Relations Committee to lead the fight against the Treaty of Versailles. He based his opposition to the League of Nations, a key element of the treaty, on the unconstitutionality of commiting American military forces to combat without the express consent of Congress.

Lodge was known during his lifetime as "the scholar in politics." His vision of an American constitutionalism that was both conservative and nationalistic was presented, in part, in his biographies of GEORGE WASHINGTON, ALEXANDER HAMILTON, and DANIEL WEBSTER.

DENNIS J. MAHONEY
(1986)

Bibliography
GARRATY, JOHN A. 1965 *Henry Cabot Lodge: A Biography.* New York: Knopf.

LOEWE v. LAWLOR
208 U.S. 274 (1908)

This case fits a pattern of antilabor decisions that supported INJUNCTIONS against trade unions and struck down maximum hours acts, minimum wage acts, and acts prohibiting YELLOW DOG CONTRACTS. In *Loewe*, the Court, while crippling secondary boycotts, held that unions were subject to the antitrust laws and therefore were civilly liable for triple damages to compensate for injuries inflicted by their restraints on INTERSTATE COMMERCE.

Loewe originated in an attempt by the United Hatters Union, AFL, to organize a manufacturer of hats in Danbury, Connecticut. Most hat firms in the country were unionized. The few nonunion firms sweated their workers and were able to undersell unionized competitors, threatening their survival as well as the jobs of their unionized labor. Loewe's firm refused to negotiate a union contract and defeated a strike. The union retaliated with a secondary boycott, a refusal by the national membership of the AFL to buy Loewe's hats or patronize retailers who sold them. Loewe sued the union under the SHERMAN ANTITRUST ACT after the boycott resulted in a substantial loss of orders. The union demurred to the charges, admitting that it had engaged in the boycott but alleging that it had not violated the antitrust law, because that law did not cover the activities of trade unions and because the boycott in this case was not a conspiracy in restraint of commerce among the states. Invoking the DOCTRINE of the Sugar Trust Case (UNITED STATES V. E. C. KNIGHT CO., 1895) that manufacturing is a purely local activity, the union claimed that neither it nor the manufacturer engaged in interstate commerce. Although Loewe's hats, once manufactured, were shipped to purchasing retailers in twenty-one states, the union argued that it did not interfere with the actual transportation across state lines and that any restraint on interstate commerce resulting from the boycott was, according to the Sugar Trust Case, remote and indirect.

Overruling a lower federal court decision in favor of the union, the Supreme Court, in a unanimous opinion by Chief Justice MELVILLE W. FULLER, for the first time held that the Sherman Act applied to union activities; that a secondary boycott conducted across state lines is a conspiracy in restraint of interstate commerce; and that even if the restraint were remote and indirect, the Sherman Act applied because it covered "every" combination in the form of a trust "or otherwise" in restraint of interstate commerce. In 1911, however, the Court embraced the RULE OF REASON, enabling it subsequently to find that corporations, not unions, might engage in reasonable restraints; that is, the act did not prohibit all restraints except by unions. In *Loewe*, however, the Court construed the act broadly, even to the point of using the STREAM OF COMMERCE DOCTRINE to show the scope of the commerce power. There is no evidence, however, that Congress, when adopting the Sherman Act, intended to cover union activities.

The case presents the phenomenon of a labor union being held within the terms of an antitrust act and contrasting opinions of the Court. In the Sugar Trust Case the Court held a ninety-eight percent monopoly not to violate the act because manufacturing is local and any effect upon or relationship with interstate commerce is necessarily indirect; here, though, a small hatmakers' union came within the act because its boycott was interstate, despite its having done nothing to control the price or transportation of the product of a manufacturer. Moreover, the decision in this case came one week after the decision in *Adair v. United States* (1908), where the Court declared that there is "no connection between interstate commerce and membership in a labor organization," as it struck down an act of Congress prohibiting the use of yellow-dog contracts by railroads against railroad workers engaged in interstate commerce. If *Adair* correctly invalidated the attempt by Congress to protect railroad workers under the commerce power, then a week later the Court should have decided that Congress under the same commerce power cannot, via the Sherman Act, reach an admittedly indirect relationship between a hatters' union and interstate commerce. Both the legislative history of the antitrust law and the Sugar Trust and *Adair* precedents opposed the decision in the Danbury Hatters' Case. Following the Court's decision, a triple-damages suit against the union in the lower federal court resulted in a fine of $252,000. The Danbury Hatters went unorganized, hatmakers everywhere suffered, and unionization everywhere was thwarted to an inestimable extent by the threat of Sherman Act suits. *Loewe* is one of the major cases on the subject of LABOR AND THE CONSTITUTION.

LEONARD W. LEVY
(1986)

Bibliography

LIEBERMAN, ELIAS 1960 *Unions Before the Bar.* Pages 56–70. New York: Harper & Row.

LONG HAUL-SHORT HAUL RATE DISCRIMINATION

Long haul-short haul discrimination was one of the most notorious abuses practiced by railroads in the late nineteenth and early twentieth centuries. The practice involved charging a higher rate for a short haul that was included within a longer haul over the same line. Although Congress outlawed this discriminatory practice in Section 4 of the INTERSTATE COMMERCE ACT (1887), the Supreme Court effectively nullified that section in *ICC v. Alabama Midland Railway Company* (1897). The Court rested its decision on the commission's power to grant exemptions if the long and short hauls did not occur "under substantially similar circumstances and conditions." Sufficient differences existed between hauls to justify departures from Section 4's prohibition. In 1910 Congress revived the prohibition by reenacting the long haul-short haul clause minus the "similar circumstances" clause. Carriers were now forbidden to charge higher rates for shorter (included) hauls *regardless* of different conditions, although the commission was still authorized to make exceptions. A unanimous Supreme Court sustained this provision to *United States v. Atchison, Topeka, & Santa Fe Railway Co.* (1914).

DAVID GORDON
(1986)

Bibliography

SHARFMAN, ISAIAH L. 1931–1937 *The Interstate Commerce Commission.* 4 Vols. New York: Commonwealth Fund.

LONGSHOREMEN'S ASSOCIATION v. ALLIED INTERNATIONAL

See: Labor and the Constitution

LOOSE CONSTRUCTION

See: Broad Construction

LÓPEZ, UNITED STATES v.
514 U.S. 549 (1995)

In *United States v. López,* a 5–4 Supreme Court struck down the Gun-Free School Zones Act, a federal statute that made it unlawful to carry a gun in a school zone. The law was supposedly passed under Congress's power to regulate INTERSTATE COMMERCE, but the statute did not require any specific "commercial" act. That is, the mere possession of a gun in a school zone, no matter how acquired or what its intended use, was made unlawful. In a cautiously stated but revolutionary opinion, Chief Justice WILLIAM H. REHNQUIST objected to the law principally on the ground that the mere possession of a gun had nothing to do with "commerce" or any kind of economic enterprise. The Chief Justice was particularly critical of the statute's failure to require that a particular act of gun possession be shown to have some kind of impact on interstate commerce, in the sense of commercial enterprise. While striking down the statute, the Court also emphasized that Congress had not made "findings regarding the effects of firearm possession in and around schools upon interstate and foreign commerce." To summarize, under the majority's opinion (1) federal power to regulate interstate commerce must have some limits; and (2) those limits are exceeded when the government shows no relationship between interstate commerce and a specific act of gun possession; but (3) Congress probably could save the statute either by requiring that in each particular case an impact on interstate commerce be shown, or by making specific background findings that gun possession generally has such an effect.

Three DISSENTING OPINIONS representing the views of four Justices criticized the majority for (1) underestimating the impact of guns on interstate commerce, which seemed obvious and could well be presumed; and (2) rolling back congressional power to regulate under the COMMERCE CLAUSE—an area where the Court had given Congress virtually unlimited discretion since the NEW DEAL, after several decades of close scrutiny during the late nineteenth and early twentieth centuries.

The most controversial opinion in *López* is a concurrence by Justice CLARENCE THOMAS, arguing that the Court should reconsider the meaning of the commerce clause in light of the way that the constitutional words "commerce among the several states" were used in the late eighteenth century when the Constitution was written. Under his reading those words conveyed to Congress much less power than Congress had actually assumed, and in fact reached only commercial transactions ("commerce") where the goods or services in question actually crossed a state line ("interstate").

The original meaning of "commerce among the several states" has been subject to a great deal of historical scholarship, much of which is inconsistent with Thomas's position. For example, late-eighteenth-century writers were much more careful than most people today about the different usage of "between" and the commerce clause word "among." Thomas's requirement of an activity that moves from one state to another is more consistent with the term "between." Something that happened "among" the states in the eighteenth century could easily have included interstate and purely intrastate activities. For example, "there is a great deal of activity among the bees this morning" would not necessarily mean that the bees were engaging in transactions with one another; each could be busily doing its own work. In his very famous 1953 book, *Politics and the Constitution in the History of the United States,* the late WILLIAM W. CROSSKEY also pointed out that the late-eighteenth-century meaning of "commerce" was significantly less technical than it is today, and could refer to a variety of commercial and noncommercial activities, including such things as conversation or household management. Nevertheless, Thomas's opinion invites constitutional historians to return to these issues.

HERBERT HOVENKAMP
(2000)

(SEE ALSO: *Federalism.*)

Bibliography

GRAGLIA, LINO 1996 *United States v. López:* Judicial Review under the Commerce Clause. *Texas Law Review* 74:719–771.
HOVENKAMP, HERBERT 1996 Judicial Restraint and Constitutional Federalism: the Supreme Court's *López* and *Seminole Tribe* Decisions. *Columbia Law Review* 96:2213–2247.
SYMPOSIUM 1995 Reflections on *United States v. López. Michigan Law Review* 94:533–830.

LOPEZ v. UNITED STATES
373 U.S. 427 (1963)

The Supreme Court held that a government agent may surreptitiously record a conversation with a criminal suspect and use the recording to corroborate his testimony. Lopez, a tavern keeper, offered a bribe to a federal tax agent who thereupon recorded the conversation. The Court refused to exclude the recording. Because the agent was on the premises with Lopez's consent, there was no TRESPASS and therefore no violation of the FOURTH AMENDMENT. Because the agent could testify to the conversation, he could use the recording to corroborate his testimony.

HERMAN SCHWARTZ
(1986)

LORETTO v. TELEPROMPTER MANHATTAN CATV CORP.
458 U.S. 419 (1982)

The Supreme Court in the modern era has used an interest balancing analysis to determine whether government regulation amounts to a TAKING OF PROPERTY for which JUST COMPENSATION must be paid. Here a New York law required landlords to allow cable television companies to install equipment on the landlords' property in order to serve tenants. The Supreme Court, 6–3, held that this governmental authorization of a "permanent physical occupation" of property was, of itself, a "taking"; in such a case no interest balancing need be done.

KENNETH L. KARST
(1986)

LOTTERY CASE

See: *Champion v. Ames*

LOUISIANA PURCHASE TREATY
(1803)

The Louisiana Purchase Treaty (April 30, 1803) provided for the cession of the French province of Louisiana to the United States for approximately $11,250,000. France had reacquired Louisiana from Spain as part of Napoleon's plan to reestablish a French empire in the New World. The United States had tolerated weak Spanish control at the mouth of the Mississippi, especially since the Pinckney Treaty of 1795 gave Americans the right to navigate the river and use the port of New Orleans; but Louisiana in the hands of Napoleonic France threatened the security, commerce, and growth of the country. President THOMAS JEFFERSON sought a diplomatic resolution, hoping to obtain from France at least the continuation of Spanish guarantees and, at best, the cession of New Orleans together with the Floridas, if France possessed them. In a surprising about-face, however, Napoleon renounced the whole of Louisiana.

The acquisition of Louisiana—some 828,000 square miles, virtually doubling the land area of the United States—challenged the government in several ways. First, the boundaries were obscure. Was Texas included? Or West Florida? Jefferson made pretensions to both. Article III of the treaty said that the inhabitants should be incorporated in the Union and enjoy all the rights of citizens of the United States. Unfortunately, the Constitution Jefferson and his party were pledged to construe strictly made no provision for acquiring foreign territory, much less admitting that territory and its people into the Union. The treaty, Jefferson declared, was "an act beyond the Constitution" and ought to be sanctioned retroactively by amendment. He drafted a 375-word amendment. When congressmen objected that Louisiana might be lost because of constitutional scruples, Jefferson acquiesced in

silent expansion of the TREATY POWER even as he reiterated his belief that it made the Constitution "a blank paper by construction." (The Supreme Court, in AMERICAN INSURANCE COMPANY V. CANTER, 1828, later upheld the authority to acquire and govern territory under the treaty and WAR POWERS.) The Senate ratified the treaty on October 20, 1803. Two months later the American flag was raised at New Orleans.

Government of the territory also raised constitutional difficulties. The Enabling Act, in October, vested the President and his agents with full powers, civil and military. Querulous Federalists said it made Jefferson "as despotic as the Grand Turk." The Louisiana Government Act six months later created the Orleans Territory in populous lower Louisiana, extended to it many federal laws, and vested authority in a strong governor and weak legislative council, both appointed by the President. In the view of the President and Congress the rights of self-government, for which Creole Louisianans were unprepared, should be introduced gradually as the territory became "Americanized" in its population, habits, and institutions. The Louisianans demanded immediate statehood. Although this was denied, Congress in March 1805 introduced the second stage of territorial government, including a representative assembly, more or less on the plan of the NORTHWEST ORDINANCE. Five years later the statehood commitment of the treaty was met. The American theory of an expanding union of equal self-governing states thus survived its severest test.

MERRILL D. PERTERSON
(1986)

(SEE ALSO: *Theories of the Union*.)

Bibliography

BROWN, EVERETT S. 1920 *The Constitutional History of the Louisiana Purchase, 1803–1812*. Berkeley: University of California Press.

LOUISVILLE JOINT STOCK LAND BANK v. RADFORD
295 U.S. 555 (1935)

During the Great Depression of the 1930s foreclosure or default on payments threatened to extinguish the small, independent farmer who owned his own property. Congress, exercising its BANKRUPTCY POWER, came to his rescue by passing the FRAZIER-LEMKE (Farm Mortgage) ACT of 1934. The act provided that bankrupt farmers might require a federal bankruptcy court to stay farm mortgage payments for a period of five years, during which time the debtor retained possession of his property and paid his creditor a reasonable rental sum fixed by the court, and at the end of the five years the debtor could buy the property at its appraised value. Because the act operated retroactively it took away rights of the mortgagee, but the CONTRACT CLAUSE limits only the states, not Congress. In the face of that clause the Court had sustained a similar state act in HOME BUILDING & LOAN ASS'N V. BLAISDELL (1934). Nevertheless Justice LOUIS D. BRANDEIS, for a unanimous Court, ruled the act of Congress void. He distinguished *Blaisdell* as less drastic: the statute there had stayed proceedings for two, not five, years. In effect Brandeis read the contract clause into the Fifth Amendment's DUE PROCESS clause, holding that the bankruptcy power of Congress must be exercised subject to SUBSTANTIVE DUE PROCESS. The statute deprived persons of property without due process by not allowing the mortgagee to retain a lien on mortgaged property. The oddest feature of this strained opinion is that it did not mention due process; Brandeis referred only to the clause that prohibited the taking of private property for a public purpose without just compensation, though the government took nothing and sought by the statute to preserve private property. The Court retreated from its position in WRIGHT V. VINTON BRANCH BANK (1937).

LEONARD W. LEVY
(1986)

LOUISVILLE, NEW ORLEANS & TEXAS PACIFIC RAILWAY v. MISSISSIPPI
133 U.S. 587 (1890)

A 7–2 Supreme Court held here that a state might lawfully require railroads to provide "equal but separate accommodations" without burdening INTERSTATE COMMERCE. The majority distinguished HALL V. DECUIR (1878) because the Louisiana Supreme Court had held in that case that the state act prohibiting SEGREGATION unlawfully regulated interstate commerce. Here, the Mississippi Supreme Court had said that the Mississippi statute applied solely to INTRASTATE COMMERCE. Moreover, this case did not involve a refusal of accommodations (as in *DeCuir*), so no question of "personal rights" arose. Justice JOHN MARSHALL HARLAN, dissenting, relied on *DeCuir*.

DAVID GORDON
(1986)

LOVELL v. CITY OF GRIFFIN
303 U.S. 444 (1938)

A municipal ordinance prohibited the distribution of circulars or any other literature within Griffin without a per-

mit from the city manager. Chief Justice CHARLES EVANS HUGHES, for a unanimous Court, held the Griffin ordinance unconstitutional. The ordinance provided no standards to guide the city manager's decision. To vest an official with absolute discretion to issue or deny a permit was an unconstitutional prior restraint that violated the FIRST AMENDMENT. Because the ordinance was INVALID ON ITS FACE, Lovell was entitled to distribute her literature without seeking a permit, and to challenge the ordinance's validity when she was charged with its violation.

RICHARD E. MORGAN
(1986)

LOVETT, UNITED STATES v.
328 U.S. 303 (1946)

In an opinion by Justice HUGO L. BLACK the Court declared unconstitutional a rider to an appropriation act of 1943 which provided that no salary or other compensation could be paid after November 1943 to three specified employees of the executive branch who had been branded as "subversives" by the HOUSE COMMITTEE ON UN-AMERICAN ACTIVITIES. Congress, Black wrote, had passed a BILL OF ATTAINDER, prohibited by Article I, section 9.

Justices FELIX FRANKFURTER and STANLEY F. REED rejected Black's bill of attainder analysis; but both agreed that the employees were entitled to recover money for the value of services rendered to the government, even after Congress had refused to disburse money to pay their salaries.

MICHAEL E. PARRISH
(1086)

LOVING v. VIRGINIA
388 U.S. 1 (1967)

For more than a decade following its decision in BROWN V. BOARD OF EDUCATION (1954) the Supreme Court avoided direct confrontation with the constitutionality of MISCEGENATION laws. In *Loving*, the Court faced the issue squarely and held invalid a Virginia law forbidding any interracial marriage including a white partner. The decision is a major precedent in the area of RACIAL DISCRIMINATION as well as the foundation of the modern "freedom to marry." (See MARRIAGE AND THE CONSTITUTION.)

A black woman and a white man, Virginia residents, went to the DISTRICT OF COLUMBIA to be married, and returned to live in Virginia. They were convicted of violating the Racial Integrity Act and given one-year prison sentences, suspended on condition that they leave Virginia. The Virginia appellate courts modified the sentences but upheld the constitutionality of the law. The Supreme Court unanimously reversed; Chief Justice EARL WARREN wrote for the Court.

Citing the SUSPECT CLASSIFICATION language of *Korematsu v. United States* (1944) (see JAPANESE AMERICAN CASES), Warren said that a "heavy burden of justification" must be carried by a state seeking to sustain any racial classification. The fact that the law punished both the white and black partners to a marriage did not relieve the state of that burden. The law's announced goal of "racial integrity" was promoted only selectively. A white was prohibited from marrying any nonwhite except the descendants of Pocahantas; a black and an Asian, for example, could lawfully marry. The law's obvious goal was the maintenance of white supremacy; it had no legitimate purpose independent of racial discrimination and thus violated the EQUAL PROTECTION clause. PACE V. ALABAMA (1883) was assumed to be overruled.

The Court's opinion also rested on an alternative ground: the statute violated SUBSTANTIVE DUE PROCESS, by interfering with "the freedom to marry." Quoting from the STERILIZATION case, SKINNER V. OKLAHOMA (1942), Chief Justice Warren called marriage "one of the 'basic civil rights of man,' fundamental to our very existence and survival." (See ZABLOCKI V. REDHAIL; FREEDOM OF INTIMATE ASSOCIATION.)

Justice POTTER STEWART, concurring, merely repeated his earlier statement in *McLaughlin v. Florida* (1964) that a state could never make an act's criminality depend on the race of the actor.

KENNETH L. KARST
(1986)

LOW-VALUE SPEECH

The role that assessments of the value of particular speech or categories of speech should play in FIRST AMENDMENT theory is much contested. Everyone agrees, however, that at some point judges should be barred from making assessments about the value of particular speech in deciding whether it may be regulated or prohibited. Moreover, the image of a content-neutral government, at least as a regulative ideal, is a powerful force in First Amendment law.

Commentators ordinarily describe judicial judgments about the value of speech as "exceptions." The norm is said to be that speech is protected and that judgments about the value of speech are foreign to the judiciary. Exceptions are often explained in terms of "low value" theory. Speech does not get protection or it gets less protection than other speech because it has low value.

Geoffrey R, Stone, the theory's principal exponent, argues that low-value theory justifiably plays a major role in

the JURISPRUDENCE of the First Amendment. It is neccesary, he argues, because otherwise we should have to apply the same standards to private blackmail as to public debate. If we do not treat harmful, but relatively unimportant speech differently, we will dilute the expression "at the very heart of the guarentee." As Stone charecterizes the law, "the Court, applying [the low-value] approach, has held that several classes of speech have only low first amendment value, including express incitement, false statements of fact, obscenity, commercial speech, fighting words and child pornography." Once the Court has decided that speech has low value, according to Stone, it engages in "categorical balancing, through which it defines the precise circumstances in which the speech may be restricted." By contrast, in assesing high-value speech, "the court employees, not a balancing approach akin to its content-neutral balancing, but a far more speech-protective analysis." Thus low-value theory functions to preserve the autonomy of high-value speech from government regulation.

No doubt, many categories of unprotected speech are explainable in part because they are thought to be of low value. Moreover, some forms of otherwise protected speech are afforded less generous protection than is given to other forms of protected speech almost exclusively because they are seen to have less value. But no sharp line divides low-value from high-value speech, and low value theory cannot account for all of its important exceptions.

Consider the First Amendment's standard testing ground: advocacy of illegal action. Such advocacy is protected unless it is directed to inciting imminent lawless action and is likely to incite or produce imminent lawless action. Is unprotected advocacy really a form of low-value speech? One approach might be to say that any speech that can be prohibited is low-value by definition. This approach, however, substitutes tautology for analysis, and it does nothing to provide an *ex ante* divide between high-value and low-value speech.

In what sense, then, is INCITEMENT or unprotected advocacy a form of low-value speech? Notice that advocacy of illegal action is not in itself a form of low-value speech. Indeed, noninciting advocacy of illegal action in itself is fully protected by the First Amendment. This conclusion has been reached in light of powerful opinions by Justices OLIVER WENDELL HOLMES, JR., and LOUIS D. BRANDEIS about the value of such speech. Thus, advocacy of illegal action appears to be high-value speech. The reason why some types of advocacy of illegal action can be prohibited seems to have less to do with their value as speech than with their potential for harm.

Alternatively, even if the Court had silently repudiated Holmes and Brandeis, the label "low-value speech" would obscure the decision-making process. The Court did not start, and need not have started, its analysis of illegal action by asking wheter the category of speech was valuable or not. Indeed, in dealing with the issues, the Court has ordinarily begun with an assesssment of state interests. What ultimately is at stake in this context is an accommodation of the values of order and FREEDOM OF SPEECH. If the rules in the context of advocacy of illegal action are good ones, the reason is that those rules have protected order without unneccessary sacrifice of the First Amendment values. But First Amendment values have surely been sacrificed. If the rules governing advocacy of illegal action have the effect of muffling the voices of those who are most agitated against the system, we have suffered a substancial First Amendment loss. It demeans the speech and underestimates that loss to think about this as a part of low-value theory.

The same can be said for the rules attempting to regulate false statements of fact in LIBEL law. Certainly, from one perspective, high-value speech is at risk. Many think criticism of public officials and other PUBLIC FIGURES is "at the very heart of the guarantee." To fashion a set of rules in which plaintiffs succeed in allowing juries to scrutinize that criticism risks a major chilling effect. Moreover, the fact-finding process may simply mask the unleashing of juror prejudices about what speech should be free.

Presumably the protection of reputation requires findings of truth and falsity by juries, but that protection must be accompanied by a sense of First Amendment loss. To characterize any such process as a part of low-value theory would deemphasize the major risk to high-value speech, however the latter might be defined. The conflict between reputation and free speech necessitates a difficult choice. Something important must be abandoned, and that choice deserves emphasis.

Low-value theory avoids that emphasis. It offers the soothing prospect of characterizing free-speech doctrine as generally unthreatening to speech of general importance, but low-value theory cannot deliver. Like it or not, so-called high-value speech is subject to government regulation if a strong enough showing can be made.

STEVEN SHIFFRIN
(1992)

(SEE ALSO: *Balancing Test; Child Pornography; Commercial Speech; Fighting Words; Obscenity; Pornography; Pornography and Feminism.*)

Bibliography

SHIFFRIN, STEVEN H. 1990 *The First Amendment, Democracy, and Romance.* Cambridge, Mass.: Harvard University Press.
STONE, GEOFFREY R. 1983 Content Regulation and the First Amendment. *William and Mary Law Review* 25:189–252.

LOYALTY OATH

A mild form of loyalty oath is embedded in the Constitution itself. The President must swear (or affirm): "that I will faithfully execute the office of President of the United States, and will to the best of my ability, preserve, protect and defend the constitution of the United States." And Article VI, in conjunction with the supremacy clause, requires that members of Congress, state legislators, and "all executive and judicial officers, both of the United States and of the several states, shall be bound by oath or affirmation, to support this constitution." These are usually called affirmative oaths, in contrast to negative oaths in which oath-takers are required to abjure certain beliefs, words, or acts. In their most searching form, negative oaths probe the past as well as the future.

In Article VI, the constitutional oath of support is immediately followed by the proscription of any religious test for holding office. Loyalty oaths, called test oaths, were rife in an age of warring faiths defended by princes. They tested orthodoxy of belief and thus loyalty to the sovereign. Henry VIII launched Anglo-American constitutional practice on a sea of oaths, whose chief purpose was to root out followers of the pope of Rome. The Stuart kings exacted oaths from the first settlers, and the settlers in turn invoked them against each other. When George Calvert, the Roman Catholic first Lord Baltimore, attempted to settle in Virginia, he was confronted with an oath that he could not take. He perforce made the hard voyage back to England; his successors got their own grant to what became Maryland and promptly imposed an oath pledging fidelity to themselves.

Wary though they became of oaths with a religious content, those who made our Revolution, as well as those who resisted it, routinely exacted political loyalty oaths from military and civilians under their control. When one occupying force displaced the other, it could become a matter of life and liberty to have one's name on the wrong roster. At the same time, there was room for claims of duress and duplicity. BENJAMIN FRANKLIN expressed with his usual pithiness what was doubtless a shared cynicism when he wrote in 1776: "I have never regarded oaths otherwise than as the last recourse of liars."

One might have thought that the Framers, with revolutionary excesses fresh in their memories, meant the constitutional oaths to be exclusive of any others; but when the CIVIL WAR came, loyalty oaths again became ubiquitous. In the Confederacy, oaths were linked to the passes routinely required for any travel. Of more gravity, taking an oath was often for captives and hostile civilians the only alternative to rotting in prison or starving. The multiplicity of oaths and the pressure to yield to them resulted in their becoming unreliable indicia of loyalty. Union authorities were impelled to create a bureaucracy to interrogate oath-takers, thus anticipating modern LOYALTY-SECURITY PROGRAMS.

President ABRAHAM LINCOLN favored relatively mild oaths pledging only future loyalty. The sterner Congress fashioned the "ironclad" test oath that required denials of past conduct that secessionists could not possibly make. Those oaths barred even repentant rebels from government and the professions. The Supreme Court plausibly characterized such oaths as legislative punishment, and declared them BILLS OF ATTAINDER, in the TEST OATH CASES (1867).

Little was heard of loyalty oaths in WORLD WAR I. After that war, many states singled out teachers for loyalty oaths; but they were only affirmative oaths on the constitutional model, repugnant chiefly because of the mistrust implicit in demanding them.

The waves of anticommunist sentiment that subsided only during the WORLD WAR II alliance with Russia led to a new proliferation of oaths that penalized membership in subversive organizations (sometimes specifying the Communist party) and advocacy or support of violent overthrow of governments.

All this came to a boil in the tormented Cold War–McCarthy era, when oaths old and new, state and federal, were combined with loyalty-security programs to purge communist influences from public employment and licensed occupations.

When oath cases came before the Court in the 1950s, it first sustained the constitutionality of elaborate oaths, requiring only that communist affiliations must be with knowledge of illegal ends (WIEMAN V. UPDEGRAFF, 1952), and suggesting that an employee must have an opportunity for an explanatory hearing (*Nostrand v. Little*, 1960). But in the 1960s, when the tide of public opinion turned against the excesses of the 1950s, the Court turned too. In half a dozen cases, of which the climactic one was KEYISHIAN V. BOARD OF REGENTS (1967), the Court found oaths that were barely distinguishable from those it had upheld in the 1950s to be void for vagueness or overbreadth. The majority opinions paraded an alarming catalog of possible dilemmas that teachers in particular could not escape and overwhelmed the expostulations of dissenters that the Court had created a "whimsical straw man" who was "not only grim but Grimm." For good measure, the Court, in UNITED STATES V. BROWN (1965), unsheathed the bill of attainder weapon of 1867 to strike down an oath that would exclude a former communist from any office in a labor union.

Such successes against negative oaths emboldened teachers and other public servants who resented having essentially affirmative oaths directed at them. But variants of the Article VI oath to support the Constitution were uniformly upheld. The capstone case was *Cole v. Richardson* (1972). There the Court, while reaffirming in generous FIRST AMENDMENT terms the 1960s cases, found no fault in an obligation first to support and defend the constitutions of the United States and the Commonwealth of Massachusetts and, second, to oppose their violent overthrow. The second clause, Chief Justice WARREN E. BURGER wrote, "does not expand the obligation of the first; it simply makes clear the application of the first clause to a particular issue. Such repetition, whether for emphasis or cadence, seems to be the wont of authors of oaths." He added in a footnote that "The time may come when the value of oaths in routine public employment will be thought not 'worth the candle' for all the division of opinion they engender." Justice THURGOOD MARSHALL, arguing in partial dissent that the second clause should be repudiated, reflected the persisting division between willing and unwilling oath-takers when he wrote, understatedly, that "Loyalty oaths do not have a very pleasant history in this country."

The fear that hellfire would follow a false oath must have faded since the seventeenth century. Nowadays public exposure, and a perjury prosecution, are the serious sanctions. Compulsory oath-taking is welcome to some, a matter of indifference to others, an offense to conscience for a few. A notable instance of a loyalty oath that hit the wrong targets occurred at the University of California in 1949–1952. When the university regents, after prolonged and wounding controversy, insisted on their power to impose a noncommunist oath, twenty-six members of the faculty refused to take it and were ejected. They won a pyrrhic victory in the California Supreme Court, which held that the regents' oath had been supplanted by an oath required of all state employees, but that the statewide oath somehow did not contravene a state constitutional prohibition of any test oath beyond the constitutional oath of support. Some of the nonsigners in time returned; one became president of the university and so did the historian of the episode, who called it "a futile interlude."

RALPH S. BROWN
(1986)

Bibliography

GARDNER, DAVID P. 1967 *The California Oath Controversy.* Berkeley and Los Angeles: University of California Press.

HYMAN, HAROLD M. 1959 *To Try Men's Souls: Loyalty Tests in American History.* Berkeley and Los Angeles: University of California Press.

SAGER, ALAN M. 1972 The Impact of Supreme Court Loyalty Oath Decisions. *American University Law Review* 22:39–78.

LOYALTY-SECURITY PROGRAMS

This hyphenated phrase refers chiefly to the measures that were taken under Presidents HARRY S. TRUMAN and DWIGHT D. EISENHOWER to exclude from public employment, and from defense industries, persons who were believed to pose risks to national security. Because the gravest threat to security was believed to flow from world communism, loyalty and security programs were designed almost entirely to counter communist influence and penetration.

In earlier periods of tension attendant upon wars, LOYALTY OATHS were the preferred device for separating the loyal from the disloyal. If oaths were taken seriously, they were self-enforcing. But when necessity or duplicity led to bales of unreliable oaths, the authorities responded by empowering officials to go behind the oaths with investigations and to make their own judgments. Such procedures, usually under military control and untrammeled by judicial control, were widespread during the CIVIL WAR and RECONSTRUCTION.

WORLD WAR I was distinguished by the overzealous prying of the American Protective League and other amateurs who were given extraordinary aid and comfort by the Department of Justice. In WORLD WAR II the military departments, both determined to avoid the excesses of the crusade against the Kaiser, effectively centralized loyalty screening. They emerged with a minimum of criticism. After the war, the Soviet Union abruptly came to be viewed as enemy rather than ally. The insecurities of the postwar world aroused mistrust and anxiety. President Truman, aiming to forestall harsher congressional action, launched a new kind of program with his EXECUTIVE ORDER 9835 of March 21, 1947.

The Truman loyalty program covered all civilian employees. The Department of Defense had its own program for the armed services. Defense and the Atomic Energy Commission had programs for employees of defense contractors. The Coast Guard screened maritime workers. A few states developed systematic programs of their own. Many millions thus became subject to proceedings that sought to establish whether, in the language of E.O. 9835, there were "reasonable grounds" for a belief that they were disloyal (softened in 1951 to require only a finding of "reasonable doubt" as to loyalty). In 1953 President Eisenhower's Executive Order 10450 replaced the Truman program. It required employment to be "clearly consistent with the interests of the national security." That standard remains in effect.

All of these programs worked from personal histories supplied by the employee (or applicant) backed up by investigative reports. If "derogatory information" led to a tentative adverse judgment, that was usually the end for an applicant's chances of employment. But an incumbent could have the benefit of formal charges, a hearing, and review. The trouble was that the investigations ranged widely into associations, opinions, and flimsy appraisals. The sources of none of these were accessible to the employee. He could only guess who his detractors were.

These programs were only one array in the frantic mobilization against subversion. They were flanked by oaths and affidavits and questionnaires. To falsify any of these was a criminal offense. In order to establish what associations were forbidden, the 1947 executive order systematized the secret preparation and open use of the Attorney General's List of Subversive Organizations. Long before and for some years after the heyday of Senator Joseph R. McCarthy (1950–1954), congressional investigating committees took as their specialty the exposure of groups and individuals with communist ties. Their disclosures encouraged blacklists in private employment, notoriously in films and broadcasting. Senator McCarthy took the lead in stigmatizing the "Fifth-Amendment Communist"—a witness who invoked the RIGHT AGAINST SELF-INCRIMINATION. Senator Patrick A. McCarran initiated the idea that naming names was the only true badge of repentance for those who said they were no longer communists. A mass of legislation sought to expose and condemn the Communist party and its affiliates, while the Department of Justice jailed its leaders for sedition.

All of these measures raised intertwining constitutional problems, so those of loyalty-security programs are not easily isolated. However, two strands can be picked out. First, there were demands for fair process, notably to confront the source of accusations. Second, there were claims for First Amendment rights, set against the supposed necessities of national security. However, the courts often trimmed the reach of the programs without deciding such issues. They would invoke their usual preference for avoiding constitutional collisions, and simply find that executive or legislative authority was lacking.

The position that DUE PROCESS OF LAW was wanting in the rules and administration of employment tests first had to surmount the proposition that employment was not a right but only a privilege that could be summarily withheld. First Amendment claims also encountered this barrier, curtly expressed in Justice OLIVER WENDELL HOLMES's now battered epigram: "The petitioner may have a constitutional right to talk politics, but he has no constitutional right to be a policeman." After some early hesitation, this dismissive argument was itself dismissed, notably by Justice TOM C. CLARK, who was usually a steadfast supporter of security measures. In an oath case, WIEMAN V. UPDEGRAFF (1952), he wrote for the Court: "We need not pause to consider whether an abstract right to public employment exists. It is sufficient to say that constitutional protection does extend to the public servant whose exclusion . . . is patently arbitrary or discriminatory."

What process is then due? The government perennially opposes the right of confrontation by invoking the need to protect confidential informants. The court came close to requiring a trial-type hearing, with confrontation and cross-examination, in the industrial security case of *Greene v. McElroy* (1959). But it used the avoidance technique. It said that there would have to be, at the threshold, explicit authorization from the President or Congress to conceal sources, and that it could not find such authorization. The decision had little effect. The statute authorizing security removals of government employees still requires only that charges "be stated as specifically as security considerations permit." It is doubtful that, in a time of perceived crisis, and in sensitive employment, the Constitution would be read to compel confrontation.

The Court worked its way to a firmer position on narrowing grounds for removal. It found that First Amendment rights to freedom of association were impaired by a flat proscription of employing communists in a "defense facility." In UNITED STATES V. ROBEL (1967) the employee, a shipyard worker, was an avowed Communist party member. A majority of the Court, declaring that "the statute quite literally establishes guilt by association alone," held that some less restrictive means would have to be employed to guard against disruption or sabotage. If *Robel* and like cases are followed where charges of disloyalty are brought, and where the accusation stems from political associations, the government may be unable to remove an employee except for conduct that would support a criminal prosecution.

This does not mean an end to the reliance on prying and gossiping that made loyalty-security programs disreputable. In satisfying itself of the reliability of applicants for employment, the government (or a private employer) can still probe for flaws of character, so long as standards for expulsion do not invade areas protected by the First Amendment or by ANTIDISCRIMINATION LEGISLATION. Investigators may even demand answers to questions, for example, on communist connections, that come close to protected zones, as long as the ultimate standards are correct, and the questions are helpful in seeing that the standards are satisfied. This seems to be the upshot of a tortuous line of cases involving admission to the practice of law.

From these unavoidable clashes between individual rights and security claims, a remarkable course of events has followed. Once the fevers of the 1950s had subsided, loyalty-security programs simply shrank to very modest levels. It is noteworthy that the VIETNAM WAR did not check

the decline. Yet the KOREAN WAR, which broke out in 1950, undoubtedly deepened the fears of that era.

The contraction has been helped along by the courts. Congress and the executive have perhaps done more to limit the scale at which the federal programs have been operating (the last dismissal on loyalty grounds was in 1968). The PRIVACY ACT of 1974 and similar statutes greatly restricted the flow of official information about misbehavior. President RICHARD M. NIXON abolished the Attorney General's List in the same year. Nudged by lower court decisions, the Civil Service Commission first stopped asking applicants for nonsensitive positions about subversive associations, and then in 1977 scrapped the questions for sensitive jobs too. Appropriations for investigative staff both in the Federal Bureau of Investigation and in the Defense Department have declined.

Do recent developments represent a slackening of our defenses? A revulsion against the excesses of McCarthyism? Because the prime mover in all the loyalty-security programs was hostility to communism, the programs may revive if our relations with the Soviet Union worsen. If the programs do revive, it seems unlikely that the courts will check recurrence of past excesses.

RALPH S. BROWN
(1986)

Bibliography

BROWN, RALPH S. 1958 *Loyalty and Security: Employment Tests in the United States.* New Haven, Conn.: Yale University Press.

CAUTE, DAVID 1978 *The Great Fear: The Anti-Communist Purge under Truman and Eisenhower.* New York: Simon & Schuster.

DEVELOPMENTS IN THE LAW 1972 The National Security Interest and Civil Liberties. *Harvard Law Review* 85:1130–1326.

LEWY, GUENTER 1983 *The Federal Loyalty-Security Program: The Need for Reform.* Washington and London: American Enterprise Institute.

LUCAS v. 44TH GENERAL ASSEMBLY OF COLORADO

See: *Reynolds v. Sims*

LUCAS v. SOUTH CAROLINA COASTAL COUNCIL
505 U.S. 1003 (1992)

If the government takes land—say, to build a road—it has to pay the owner JUST COMPENSATION. But one of the most contested issues of constitutional law arises when the government, rather than physically appropriating land, affects its value through legislative or administrative action.

Lucas bought two oceanfront lots before South Carolina adopted the Beachfront Zone Management Act. Although houses had previously been built on neighboring parcels, the Coastal Council prevented Lucas from erecting new structures. Lucas challenged the act as an unconstitutional TAKING OF PROPERTY without just compensation. The Supreme Court, 6–2, agreed.

Writing for five Justices, Justice ANTONIN SCALIA held that where a regulation "denies all economically beneficial or productive use" of private PROPERTY, it requires compensation. This formalizes a per se rule for "total" REGULATORY TAKINGS. The Court remanded the case to determine whether Lucas's construction was already forbidden by COMMON LAW principles of nuisance or property. Of broader significance than the narrow facts of the case is the Court's attempt to clarify and strengthen a line of analysis begun by Justice OLIVER WENDELL HOLMES, JR., in *Pennsylvania Coal Co. v. Mahon* (1922). Justice ANTHONY M. KENNEDY concurred in the judgment.

Justice HARRY A. BLACKMUN, in dissent, accused the Court of "launching a missile to kill a mouse." Justice JOHN PAUL STEVENS questioned the new rule's arbitrariness: "A landowner whose property is diminished in value 95 percent recovers nothing, while an owner whose property is diminished 100 percent recovers the land's full value." Justice DAVID H. SOUTER would have dismissed the WRIT OF CERTIORARI as not ripe for review.

EDWARD J. MCCAFFERY
(2000)

LUJAN v. DEFENDERS OF WILDLIFE
504 U.S. 555 (1992)

The Supreme Court, in an opinion by Justice ANTONIN SCALIA, held that an environmental organization had no STANDING because its members lacked "injury in fact" as required under Article III of the Constitution. Defenders of Wildlife sued under the federal Endangered Species Act (ESA), which provides that "any person" may sue to enjoin a federal agency from violating the ESA. Plaintiff sought expansion of a U.S. Interior Department rule requiring federal agencies to consult with the Secretary of the Interior to ensure that development projects within the United States do not threaten endangered species. Plaintiff contended that the ESA also required such consultation for projects in foreign countries. Two projects that would have been included under the broader rule were located in Egypt and Sri Lanka. Two members of Defenders of Wildlife had previously visited those coun-

tries. Neither had current travel plans, but both intended to return and hoped to see endangered species on their return visits.

The "any person" standing provision of the ESA is based on a "private attorney general" concept under which private individuals are authorized to enforce statutes for the benefit of the general public. Private attorney general statutes have repeatedly been upheld by the Court.

As a practical matter, *Lujan* may not be very important. For example, Scalia's opinion distinguishes *Lujan* from a qui tam standing case in which a plaintiff acting as a private attorney general gets a cash bounty. Further, Justices ANTHONY M. KENNEDY and DAVID H. SOUTER indicated that standing would have been proper if Defenders of Wildlife members had purchased airplane tickets or announced specific dates for future trips. As a theoretical matter, however, *Lujan* is a significant watershed. For the first time, the Court has held unconstitutional a grant of standing to a private person to enforce a federal statutory duty because that person does not satisfy the Court's understanding of injury in fact under Article III.

WILLIAM A. FLETCHER
(2000)

Bibliography

NICHOL, GENE R. 1993 Justice Scalia, Standing, and Public Law Litigation. *Duke Law Journal* 42:1141–1169.

SCALIA, ANTONIN 1983 The Doctrine of Standing as an Essential Element of the Separation of Powers. *Suffolk Law Review* 17:881–899.

SUNSTEIN, CASS R. 1992 What's Standing After Lujan? Of Citizen Suits, "Injuries," and Article III. *Michigan Law Review* 91:163–236.

LURTON, HORACE H.
(1844–1914)

President WILLIAM HOWARD TAFT's nomination of his close friend and former colleague, Horace Lurton, to replace Justice RUFUS PECKHAM in December 1909 engendered some skepticism. A Confederate veteran of the CIVIL WAR, Lurton was sixty-six and a pronounced conservative. He was, however, known as a patient and gentle man who sought compromise, and his experience clearly fitted him for the office. Lurton had sat on the Tennessee Supreme Court and the Sixth Circuit Court of Appeals (with Taft and WILLIAM R. DAY) and had also taught constitutional law and served as dean of the Law School at Vanderbilt University.

Lurton did not write many majority opinions during his tenure on the Supreme Court. He was usually among a silent majority voting in favor of government authority to sustain, for example, the NATIONAL POLICE POWER (e.g., HOKE V. UNITED STATES, 1913) and the SHERMAN ANTITRUST ACT (STANDARD OIL COMPANY V. UNITED STATES, 1911); he dissented without opinion in HOUSTON, EAST & WEST TEXAS RAILWAY CO. V. UNITED STATES (1914). Most of his opinions dealt with procedural technicalities or the intricacies of employer liability laws.

One of the more frequent, though hardly regular, dissenters, Lurton was often in a minority with Justice OLIVER WENDELL HOLMES. Lurton's particular regard for precedent prompted extensive research to uncover those cases that would justify apparently inconsistent stances.

Shortly after his fourth term of court, in June 1914, Lurton died. His belief in law as the cement of society had led him to oppose JUDICIAL ACTIVISM, particularly when "a valid law, under the Constitution, is to be interpreted or modified so as to accomplish . . . [what a court] shall deem to the public advantage." Despite Lurton's prior experience, his career as a Justice provided little evidence of distinguished achievement.

DAVID GORDON
(1986)

Bibliography

WATTS, JAMES F., JR. 1969 Horace H. Lurton. In Leon Friedman and Fred L. Israel, eds., *The Justices of the United States Supreme Court, 1789–1969*. New York: Chelsea House.

LUTHER v. BORDEN
7 Howard (48 U.S.) 1 (1849)

In *Luther v. Borden,* a case arising from the aftermath of the Dorr Rebellion (1842), Chief Justice ROGER B. TANEY enunciated the DOCTRINE of POLITICAL QUESTIONS and provided the first judicial exposition of the clause of the Constitution guaranteeing REPUBLICAN FORMS OF GOVERNMENT (Article IV, section 4).

Though Rhode Island was in the forefront of the Industrial Revolution, its constitutional system, derived from the royal charter of 1663 (which was retained with slight modifications as the state's organic act after the Revolution), was an archaic and peculiar blend of democratic and regressive features. Malapportionment and disfranchisement grew intolerably severe as the industrial cities and mill villages filled with propertyless native and immigrant workers. (Perhaps as many as ninety percent of the adult males of Providence were voteless in 1840.) Reform efforts through the 1820s and 1830s were unsuccessful. In 1841–1842, suffragist reformers adopted more radical tactics derived from the theory of the DECLARATION OF INDE-

PENDENCE, asserting that the people had a right to reform or replace their government, outside the forms of law if need be. They therefore drafted a new state constitution (the "People's Constitution") and submitted it to ratification by a vote open to all adult white male citizens of the state. The regular government, meanwhile, also submitted a revised constitution (the "Freeholders' Constitution") to ratification, but only by those entitled to vote under the Charter. The people's Constitution was ratified, the Freeholders' rejected. Reform leaders then organized elections for a new state government, in which Thomas Wilson Dorr was elected governor. The two governments organized, each claiming exclusive legitimacy. The Freeholders' government declared martial law and, with the tacit support of President John Tyler, used state militia to suppress the Dorrites in an almost bloodless confrontation. It then submitted another revised constitution, ratified in late 1842, that alleviated the problems arising under the Charter.

Dorrites dissatisfied with this outcome created a TEST CASE from an incident of militia harassment and requested the Supreme Court to determine that the Freeholders' government and the subsequent 1842 constitution were illegitimate, on the grounds that the Freeholders' government was not republican and that the people of the state had a right to replace it, without legal sanction if necessary. Taney, for a unanimous Court (Justice LEVI WOODBURY dissenting in part on a martial law point), declined to issue any such ruling. After noting the insuperable practical difficulties of declaring the previous seven years of Rhode Island's government illegitimate, Taney stated that "the courts uniformly held that the inquiry proposed to be made belonged to the political power and not to the judicial." He went on to explain that Dorrite contentions "turned upon political rights and political questions, upon which the court has been urged to express an opinion. We decline doing so." Taney thus amplified a distinction, earlier suggested by Chief Justice JOHN MARSHALL, between judicial questions (which a court can resolve), and political ones, which can be resolved only by the political branches of government (executive and legislative).

Taney further held that the GUARANTEE CLAUSE committed the question of the legitimacy of a state government to Congress for resolution, and that Congress's decision was binding on the courts, a point later reiterated by Chief Justice SALMON P. CHASE in cases involving the legitimacy of congressional Reconstruction policies. Taney concluded his opinion with an empty concession to the political theory of the Dorrites: "No one, we believe, has ever doubted the proposition that, according to the institutions of this country, the SOVEREIGNTY in every State resides in the people of the State, and that they may alter and change their form of government at their pleasure. But whether they have changed it or not," Taney repeated, "is a question to be settled by the political power," not the courts.

Though the political question doctrine thereby created has never been explained by a definitive rationale, it has proved useful in enabling the courts to avoid involvement in controversies that are not justiciable, that is, not suitable for resolution by judges. (See BAKER V. CARR.)

WILLIAM W. WIECEK
(1986)

LYNCH v. DONNELLY
465 U.S. 668 (1984)

The Supreme Court significantly lowered the wall of SEPARATION OF CHURCH AND STATE by sanctioning an official display of a sacred Christian symbol. Pawtucket, Rhode Island, included a crèche, or nativity scene, in its annual Christmas exhibit in the center of the city's shopping district. The case raised the question whether Pawtucket's crèche violated the Constitution's prohibition of ESTABLISHMENT OF RELIGION.

Chief Justice WARREN BURGER for a 5–4 Court ruled that despite the religious nature of the crèche, Pawtucket had a secular purpose in displaying it, as evinced by the fact that it was part of a Christmas exhibit that proclaimed "Season's Greetings" and included Santa Claus, his reindeer, a Christmas tree, and figures of carolers, a clown, an elephant, and a teddy bear. That the FIRST AMENDMENT, Burger argued, did not mandate complete separation is shown by our national motto, paid chaplains, presidential proclamations invoking God, the pledge of allegiance, and religious art in publicly supported museums.

Justice WILLIAM BRENNAN, dissenting, construed Burger's majority opinion narrowly, observing that the question was still open on the constitutionality of a public display on public property of a crèche alone or of the display of some other sacred symbol, such as a crucifixion scene. Brennan repudiated the supposed secular character of the crèche; he argued that "[f]or Christians the essential message of the nativity is that God became incarnate in the person of Christ." The majority's insensitivity toward the feelings of non-Christians disturbed Brennan.

A spokesman for the National Council of Churches complained that the Court had put Christ "on the same level as Santa Claus and Rudolph the Red-Nosed Rein-

deer." Clearly, the Court had a topsy-turvy understanding of what constitutes an establishment of religion, because in LARKIN V. GRENDEL'S DEN (1982) it saw a forbidden establishment in a STATE POLICE POWER measure aimed at keeping boisterous patrons of a tavern from disturbing a church, yet here saw no establishment in a state-sponsored crèche.

LEONARD W. LEVY
(1986)

LYNG v. NORTHWEST INDIAN CEMETERY
485 U.S. 439 (1988)

The U.S. Forest Service planned to build a paved road and allow timber harvesting in an area held sacred by certain AMERICAN INDIANS. The Indians used the area, now part of a national forest, to perform religious rituals. The Supreme Court held 5–3 that the Forest Service action would not violate the free exercise clause of the FIRST AMENDMENT.

Writing for the majority, Justice SANDRA DAY O'CONNOR maintained that the free exercise clause was not implicated here because the Indians would not be coerced by the government's action into violating their religious beliefs. Hence, the government did not have to supply a COMPELLING STATE INTEREST to justify its action. The fact that the government activity would interfere with the Indians' religion was irrelevant because "the Free Exercise Clause is written in terms of what the government cannot do to the individual, not in terms of what the individual can extract from the government." Moreover, even if the Forest Service actions should 'virtually destroy the Indians' ability to practice their religion,' . . . the Constitution simply does not provide a principle that could justify upholding" their claims.

Writing for the dissenters, Justice WILLIAM J. BRENNAN rejected the majority's narrow reading of the free exercise clause and argued that because the beliefs and activities implicated by the government action were "central" to the religion of the American Indians, the government must supply a compelling state interest to justify its action.

JOHN G. WEST, JR.
(1992)

(SEE ALSO: *Religious Liberty.*)

MACDONALD, UNITED STATES v.
456 U.S. 1 (1982)

Chief Justice WARREN E. BURGER for a 6–3 Supreme Court reaffirmed that the protection of the SPEEDY TRIAL provision of the Sixth Amendment does not extend to the period before a defendant is officially accused of the crime and ceases once charges are dismissed. Thus, the period between dismissal of military charges and indictment later in a civil court could not be considered in determining whether delay violated the right to a speedy trial. Dissenters disagreed with the majority's reasoning that the interests served by the right to a speedy trial stood in no jeopardy before accusation or after dismissal of charges.

LEONARD W. LEVY
(1986)

MACON, NATHANIEL
(1757–1837)

Nathaniel Macon, a North Carolina planter, opposed RATIFICATION OF THE CONSTITUTION because he thought the new government too powerful. Joining THOMAS JEFFERSON'S Republican party, Macon was elected to Congress in 1791; with his party he opposed ALEXANDER HAMILTON'S economic policies and the ALIEN AND SEDITION ACTS. As speaker (1801–1807), Macon, with his deputy, JOHN RANDOLPH, firmly guided the HOUSE OF REPRESENTATIVES along administration lines. Although he briefly broke with Jefferson (1807–1809), he supported the unpopular EMBARGO ACTS. In the House (1791–1815) and later in the SENATE (1815–1826), Macon was a spokesman for STRICT CONSTRUCTION, and individual liberty.

DENNIS J. MAHONEY
(1986)

MADDEN v. KENTUCKY
309 U.S. 83 (1940)

A Kentucky statute taxing bank deposits outside the state at a rate five times higher than the tax on intrastate deposits was assailed as breaching several clauses of section one of the FOURTEENTH AMENDMENT. By a 7–2 vote the Supreme Court, speaking through Justice STANLEY F. REED, declared that the states have broad discretion in their tax policies. Reed dismissed the arguments against the statute based on the EQUAL PROTECTION and DUE PROCESS clauses as insubstantial, but the decision in COLGATE V. HARVEY (1935) supported the argument based on the PRIVILEGES AND IMMUNITIES clause. On reconsideration the Court found that lending or depositing money is not a privilege of national CITIZENSHIP and therefore overruled Colgate.

LEONARD W. LEVY
(1986)

MADISON, JAMES
(1751–1836)

James Madison, "the father of the Constitution," matured with the AMERICAN REVOLUTION. Educated at a boarding school and at patriotic Princeton, he returned to the family plantation in Virginia at age twenty-one, two years before the infamous Coercive Acts. As Orange County mobilized behind the recommendations of the CONTINENTAL CONGRESS, he joined his father on the committee of safety, practiced with a rifle, and drilled with the local militia company. As he wrote much later, in a sketch of an autobiography, "he was under very early and strong impressions in favor of liberty both civil and religious."

Civil and religious liberty were intimately linked in Madison's career and thinking. His early revolutionary ardor is the necessary starting point for understanding his distinctive role among the Founders. The young man first involved himself in local politics, in 1774, to raise his voice against the persecution of dissenters in neighboring Virginia counties. When feeble health compelled him to abandon thoughts of active military service, the gratitude of Baptist neighbors may have helped him win election to the state convention of 1776, which framed one of the earliest, most widely imitated revolutionary constitutions. (See VIRGINIA CONSTITUTION AND DECLARATION OF RIGHTS.) It seems appropriate that Madison's first major office should have been in this convention, his first important act to prepare amendatory language that significantly broadened the definition of freedom of conscience in the Virginia Declaration of Rights. The American Revolution, as he understood it, was a grand experiment, of world-historical significance, in the creation and vindication of governments that would combine majority control with individual freedom, popular self-government with security for the private rights of all. Through more than forty years of active public service, he was at the center of the country's search for a structure and practice of government that would secure both sorts of freedom. His conviction that democracy and individual liberty are mutually dependent—and, increasingly, that neither would survive disintegration of the continental Union—guided his distinctive contributions to the writing and interpretation of the Constitution.

Defeated in his bid for reelection to the state assembly—he refused to offer the customary treats to voters—the promising young Madison was soon selected by the legislature as a member of the Council of State. Two years later, in December 1779, the legislature chose him as a delegate to Congress. Here he gradually acquired a national reputation. He was instrumental in the management of Virginia's western cession, which prepared the way for ratification of the ARTICLES OF CONFEDERATION and creation of a national domain. He introduced the compromise that resulted in the congressional recommendations of April 18, 1783, calling on the states to approve an amendment to the Articles granting Congress power to impose a five percent duty on foreign imports, to complete their western cessions, and to levy other taxes sufficient to provide for the continental debt. He learned that the confedera-

tion government's dependence on the states for revenues and for enforcement of its acts and treaties rendered it unable to perform its duties and endangered its very existence.

Reentering Virginia's legislature when his term in Congress ended, Madison became increasingly convinced that liberty in individual states depended on the Union that protected them from foreign intervention and from the wars and rivalries that had fractured Europe and condemned its peoples to oppressive taxes, swollen military forces, and the rule of executive tyrants. In 1786, as he prepared for the Annapolis Convention, Northerners and Southerners clashed bitterly in Congress over the negotiation of a commercial treaty with Spain. When Madison and other delegates decided to propose the meeting of a general convention to revise the Articles of Confederation, they acted in a context of profound, immediate concern for the survival of the Union.

By 1786, however, Madison no longer hoped that a revision of the Articles might reinvigorate the general government, nor was he worried solely by the peril of disunion. In all the states popular assemblies struggled to protect their citizens from economic troubles. Although Virginia managed to avoid the worst abuses, Madison thought continentally. Correspondents warned him of a growing disillusionment with popular misgovernment, particularly in New England, where SHAYS' REBELLION erupted in the winter of 1786. Virginia's own immunity from popular commotions or majority misrule appeared to him in doubt. He had not been able to achieve revision of the revolutionary constitution and had often suffered agonizing losses when he urged support for federal measures or important state reforms. In 1785, in his opinion, only the presence of a multitude of disagreeing sects had blocked the passage of a bill providing tax support for teachers of the Christian religion, which would have been a major blow to freedom of conscience and an egregious violation of the constitution. Personally disgusted by the changeability, injustices, and lack of foresight of even Virginia's laws, Madison feared that the revulsion with democracy, confined thus far to only a tiny (though an influential) few, could spread in time through growing numbers of the people. The crisis of confederation government, as he conceived it, was compounded by a crisis of republican convictions. Either could reverse the Revolution. Neither could be overcome by minor alterations of the Articles of Confederation. To save the Revolution, he wrote to EDMUND PENDLETON, constitutional reform must both "perpetuate the union and redeem the honor of the republican name."

No one played a more important part than Madison in bringing on the CONSTITUTIONAL CONVENTION OF 1787, turning its attention to a sweeping transformation of the federal system, or achieving national approval of its work. Returning from Annapolis, he won Virginia's quick consent to a general convention, wrote the resolutions signaling the Old Dominion's serious commitment to the project, and helped persuade GEORGE WASHINGTON to lead a delegation whose distinguished quality encouraged other states to call upon their best. Reeligible at last, he rushed from Richmond to New York, reentered the Confederation Congress, and worked successfully for measures that significantly improved the prospects for a full, successful meeting. He researched the histories and structures of other ancient and modern confederations and somehow found the time to write a formal memorandum on the "Vices of the Political System of the United States," in which he argued that the mortal ills of the confederation government and the concurrent crisis in the states alike demanded the abandonment of the Articles of Confederation and the creation of a carefully constructed national republic. In Madison's vision, the republic would rise directly from the people; would possess effective, full, and independent powers over matters of general concern; and would incorporate so many different economic interests and religious sects that majorities would seldom form "on any other principles than those of justice and the general good." Urging other members of Virginia's delegation to arrive in Philadelphia in time to frame some general propositions with which the meeting might begin, he reached the city himself the best prepared of all who gathered for the Constitutional Convention.

Madison made several distinctive contributions to the writing of the Constitution. He was primarily responsible for the VIRGINIA PLAN: the resolutions that initiated the Convention's thorough reconstruction of the federal system and served throughout the summer as the outline for reform. In the early weeks of the deliberations, he persuasively explained why no reform could prove effective if it left the general government dependent on the states. Together with JAMES WILSON, he led the delegates who insisted on proportional representation, popular ratification of the fundamental charter, and a careful balance of authority between a democratic House of Representatives and branches more resistant to ill-considered popular demands. He also urged his fellows not to limit their attention to the weaknesses of the confederation, but to come to terms as well with the vices of democratic government in the states. Constitutional reform, he argued, must also overcome the crisis of republican convictions, both by placing limitations on the states and by creating a greater republic free from the structural errors of the local constitutions. With the latter plea particularly, he opened members' minds to a complete rethinking of the problems of democracy and to the possibility that liberty and popular control might both be safest in a large republic. Al-

though the finished Constitution differed in a number of significant respects from his original proposals, Madison was, by general agreement of historians and his colleagues, the most important of the Framers.

All of which was only part of his enormous contribution to the Constitution's great success. Before departing for Virginia, where he led the Federalists to victory in a close and capably contested state convention, Madison reassumed his seat in the Confederation Congress, helped provide some central guidance for the ratification struggle, and joined with ALEXANDER HAMILTON to write the most important explanation and defense of the completed Constitution. His numbers of THE FEDERALIST, perhaps the greatest classic in the history of American political writing, rationalized the compromises made in the Convention, rendered the document intelligible in terms of democratic theory, and thus contributed as surely to the shaping of the Constitution as the work of the preceding summer. Since early in the nineteenth century, these essays have been recognized as an essential source for understanding the intentions of the Framers, and Madison's essential theme—that the Convention's work was perfectly consistent with the principles of the Revolution, a genuinely democratic remedy for the diseases most destructive to democracy—was still but the beginning of his effort to interpret and insure the triumph of the finished plan.

The reconstructed federal government initiated operations in April 1789. Madison immediately assumed the leading role in the first Congress, which was responsible for filling in the outline of the Constitution as well as for the national legislation it had been created to permit. He drafted parts of Washington's inaugural address, prepared the House of Representatives' reply, and helped defeat proposals to address the President as "highness"—important contributions to the early effort to define the protocol between the branches and to set a democratic tone for the infant regime. He initiated the deliberations that resulted in the first federal tariff and assured a steady source of independent federal revenues. He seized the lead again in the creation of executive departments, successfully insisting that the concept of responsibility required a presidential power to remove executive officials without the consent of Congress. Finally, he took upon himself the principal responsibility for preparing the constitutional amendments that became the BILL OF RIGHTS.

Early in the contest over RATIFICATION OF THE CONSTITUTION, Madison had denied the need for such amendments. He argued that the federal government had not been granted any powers that might threaten the liberties protected in the declarations of the states, and he warned that any effort to prepare a federal bill might actually endanger rights it was intended to preserve: an inadvertent error or omission could become the basis for a claim of positive authority to act. This very train of reasoning, however, suggests why he was open to a change of mind and offers some important clues to understanding his political and constitutional position in the years after 1789.

Throughout the course of constitutional reform, Madison had insisted no less strongly on the need for an effective central government than on a governmental structure that would guarantee the continuing responsibility of rulers to the ruled, along with a considerable residual autonomy for the people in their several states. Even as he worried over the excesses of majorities, he reminded correspondents of the perils posed by rulers who escaped a due dependence on the people; and even as he warned the Constitutional Convention not to leave the general government dependent on the states, he recognized the danger of excessive concentration of authority in federal hands. His contributions to *The Federalist* describe the new regime as neither wholly national nor purely federal in nature, but as a novel, complicated mixture under which concurrent state and central governments, each possessed of only limited authority, would each perform the duties for which they were best equipped and would both resist disturbance of a federal equilibrium that offered new protection for the people. During the ratification contest, Madison was forced to promise that amendments would be added once the Constitution was approved. He realized how useful this could be in reconciling skeptics to the system. But he was also predisposed to be receptive when THOMAS JEFFERSON insisted that a bill of rights would be a valuable, additional security for the liberties and powers that the states and people had intended to reserve.

Among the most consistent themes of Madison's career was his profound respect for FUNDAMENTAL LAW. Written constitutions, in his view, were solemn compacts which created governments and granted them the only powers they legitimately possessed. Rulers guilty of transcending them, he had written in his 1785 Memorial and Remonstrance against religious assessments, were "Tyrants," those who submitted "slaves." And usurpations of this sort, he added, ought to be resisted on their first appearance, as they had been early in the Revolution, before they could be strengthened by repeated exercise and "entangle the question in precedents." This scrupulous regard for fundamental charters encouraged Madison to change his mind about a bill of rights and shaped his conduct throughout the rest of his career.

Early in Washington's administration, Madison became alarmed about the sectional inequities and other consequences of Hamilton's political economy. He broke with Hamilton entirely when the secretary of the treasury proposed the creation of a national bank, protesting that the Constitution granted Congress no explicit power to charter such a corporation and that a doctrine of IMPLIED POW-ERS, justifying federal measures by a BROAD CONSTRUCTION of the general clauses, could completely change the character and spirit of a limited, federal system. During the 1790s, as Madison and Jefferson concluded that Hamilton and his supporters were deliberately attempting to subvert the Revolution—to concentrate all power in the general government and most of that in its executive departments—their insistence on a strict construction of the Constitution and a compact theory of its origins became an organizing theme of the Democratic-Republican opposition. Madison's Virginia Resolutions of 1798, part of a larger effort to arouse the states against the ALIEN AND SEDITION ACTS, which the Republicans regarded as a flagrant violation of the FIRST AMENDMENT, identified a Hamiltonian construction of the Constitution as a central feature of a Federalist conspiracy to sweep away all limitations on the exercise of federal power. Madison's great Report of 1800, explaining and defending the resolutions of 1798 against objections from other states, still stands as a striking landmark in the evolution of a modern, literalist interpretation of the First Amendment. In opposition to prevailing understandings that FREEDOM OF THE PRESS afforded guarantees against PRIOR RESTRAINT AND CENSORSHIP, but did not protect a publisher or author from criminal responsibility for statements tending to bring the government or its officers into disrepute, Madison insisted that the federal government was "destitute" of all authority whatever to interfere with the free development and circulation of opinion. In passages with major implications for the future, he denied that a FEDERAL COMMON LAW OF CRIMES had ever operated and suggested that the essence of elective governments was inconsistent with even STATE ACTION to restrain "that right of freely examining public characters and measures and of free communication of the people thereon, which has ever been justly deemed the only effectual guardian of every other right."

In its constitutional dimensions, the Jeffersonian "Revolution of 1800" was intended by its leaders to restore the threatened federal balance and return the general government to the role and limits originally intended by the people. As Jefferson's secretary of state, principal lieutenant, and eventual successor, Madison continued to believe that governmental actions should "conform to the constitution as understood by the Convention that produced and recommended it, and particularly by the state conventions that *adopted* it." He conceded that there were occasions that might justify or even command departures from the letter of the Constitution. He defended the LOUISIANA PURCHASE on these grounds, suggesting that a power to acquire new TERRITORIES was inherent in the concept of a sovereign nation. As President, he acted on the basis of implied executive authority in ordering the occupation of West Florida. He even came to recommend rechartering a national bank, maintaining that repeated acts of every part of government, repeatedly approved of by the nation, had overruled his earlier opinion of the institution's unconstitutionality. In his final days in office, nevertheless, he vetoed a bill providing federal support for INTERNAL IMPROVEMENTS. Although he favored federal action, he insisted on a constitutional amendment in advance. He still believed, as he had written in his "Letters of Helvidius" in 1793, that "a people who are so happy as to possess the inestimable blessing of a free and defined constitution cannot be too watchful against the introduction nor too critical in tracing the consequences of new principles and new constructions that may remove the landmarks of power."

Madison's regard for fundamental law is not to be confused with a minimalist conception of the constitutional scope of federal powers. He recommended the creation of a national university, although the Constitution delegated no explicit power to erect one. He believed that the Constitution granted Congress plenary authority over commerce, not merely ample power to impose a protective tariff but power even to require a temporary end to foreign trade as in the complete embargo or the various non-intercourse experiments preceding the War of 1812. He was as willing to defend the powers plainly granted to the federal government—over state militias, for example—as he was to guard the liberties protected by the Bill of Rights. Nevertheless, his leadership as President was characterized by deep respect for both the letter and the spirit of the federal compact. If he was diffident in leading Congress into proper preparations for a war, his serious regard for legislative independence was as much at fault as personality or circumstances. If he forbore perhaps too much in the face of flagrantly seditious opposition to the war, this forbearance was not for want of an imaginable alternative. ABRAHAM LINCOLN claimed the powers needed for a greater crisis. Madison deliberately attempted to conduct the War of 1812 at minimal expense to the republican and federal nature of the country. It was at once his weakness and his glory.

The father of the Constitution outlived all the other signers, becoming in his final years a rather troubled, though revered, authority on the creation and construction of the federal charter. The source of his discomfort was his own insistence that the Constitution was a compact among the sovereign peoples of the several states, who remained the only power competent to alter it or to deliver a definitive decision on its meaning. The great Virginian repeatedly denied that this interpretation justified the developing southern doctrine of state INTERPOSITION and NULLIFICATION. He had, in fact, warned Jefferson in 1798 against confusing the constituent authority of the peoples of the states with the powers of an individual state government. Yet neither was he willing to permit the federal courts a power of interpretation that would make the general government the final or exclusive judge in its own cause (or even to concede the courts the power to override the constitutional opinions of the executive and legislative branches). Trapped between his love of Union and his fear of grasping power, he was never able, never willing, to identify an agency or a procedure that, in case of a collision of conflicting understandings of the Constitution, could prevent a revolutionary recourse to the sovereign people. But, then, James Madison was Revolution's child. Admitting that the best constructed government could not secure a nation's liberty if it were not supported by a proper public spirit, he trusted to the end that mutual conciliation and restraint would prove sufficient to preserve the Union he had done so much to shape.

LANCE BANNING
(1986)

Bibliography

BANNING, LANCE 1984 "The Hamiltonian Madison: A Reconsideration." *Virginia Magazine of History and Biography* 92: 3–28.

BRANT, IRVING 1941–1961 *James Madison.* 6 Vols. Indianapolis: Bobbs-Merrill.

KETCHAM, RALPH 1971 *James Madison: A Biography.* New York: Macmillan.

McCOY, DREW R. 1980 *The Elusive Republic: Political Economy in Jeffersonian America.* Chapel Hill: University of North Carolina Press.

WOOD, GORDON S. 1969 *The Creation of the American Republic, 1776–1789.* Chapel Hill: University of North Carolina Press.

MADISONIAN CONSTITUTION

Constitutional scholars often describe the original Constitution of 1787 and its first ten amendments as Madisonian, and they have two good reasons to do so. First, JAMES MADISON was arguably the central historical actor in every phase of the political movement that led to the adoption of the Constitution, from the calling of the federal CONSTITUTIONAL CONVENTION OF 1787 to the ratification of the BILL OF RIGHTS in 1791. His preparations for the federal convention shaped its basic agenda and its politics. Even though several of the proposals he most favored were rejected, the completed Constitution still carried the marks of his substantial influence. Second, scholars typically rely on Madison's political writings— especially his most celebrated contributions to THE FEDERALIST—as the most authoritative statements of the underlying theory of politics and government that the Constitution embodied.

If Madison did play the critical role that historians ascribe to him, the reason was not only that experience and intellect suited him to do so, but also that he consciously made the task of promoting the project of constitutional reform his own cause. During his service in the CONTINENTAL CONGRESS (1780–1783), Madison was deeply involved in the effort to ratify and then amend the ARTICLES OF CONFEDERATION, and he pursued the same ends as a member of the Virginia assembly from 1784 to 1786. Though Madison initially worried that the assembly's decision to invite other states to a conference to consider national problems of commerce might backfire, he went to the Annapolis Convention in September 1786 convinced that a radical step was necessary to break the impasse over reforming the Confederation. When it became evident that the meeting was too poorly attended to propose anything of substance, Madison joined the other commissioners in issuing a call for a general convention to meet in Philadelphia in May 1787. He then returned to Virginia to make sure that the assembly took the lead in inviting the other states to appoint delegates for the new convention.

Madison prepared for the convention by reflecting on both the history of other confederations and his own political experiences. These reflections supported one critical conclusion: Any federal union that relied, as did the Confederation, on the voluntary compliance of its member states with national decisions must always prove defective. Instead, the national government needed to be empowered to act directly upon the people, by enacting, executing, and adjudicating its own laws. This conclusion led to two others. First, the convention would need to think seriously about the proper composition of the three essential departments of government—legislative, executive, and judicial. Second, because a well-constructed legislature was bicameral, the rules of apportioning REPRESENTATION in both houses of a future Congress would become a source of controversy. Here Madison was intent on establishing that seats in both houses should be apportioned on the basis of population and perhaps wealth.

The deeper impetus for the solutions Madison wished the convention to adopt reflected his diagnosis of the problems of legislative misrule and popular politics in the individual states. Madison believed that the great source of instability in American government lay in the tendency of the state legislatures to act impulsively and unwisely, especially by enacting laws that violated the due rights of minorities and individuals. The legislature, and especially its lower house, was the branch of government most likely to encroach upon the legitimate powers of the other departments. The great challenge of designing the institutions of republican government was thus to protect the two weaker departments, the executive and judiciary, against legislative domination. But the problem was not merely an institutional one. For when legislatures over-

stepped their bounds or acted unjustly, Madison reasoned, they were likely to be acting in response to the improper desires of their constituents, or more to the point, the popular majorities whom they represented. To bring stability to republican government, Madison believed, required finding ways to insulate elected representatives from the passions and interests that swayed the electorate.

In drafting the VIRGINIA PLAN just before the Constitutional Convention assembled in May 1787, Madison converted this general diagnosis into a program of reform. Over the next four months, however, he met defeat on most of the crucial proposals that he supported most strongly. The rule of representation adopted for the U.S. SENATE, giving each state an equal vote, Madison thought fundamentally unjust. The Senate would also be elected by the state legislatures, which Madison regarded as nests of political demagoguery. To protect the executive and judiciary against legislative domination, Madison had proposed uniting these two weaker branches into a council of revision armed with a limited VETO POWER over Congress; instead the Constitution gave the veto to the President alone. To correct the vices of state LEGISLATION, Madison proposed giving Congress a veto over all state laws; instead, the Constitution envisioned limited JUDICIAL REVIEW of state legislation by a federal judiciary that Madison feared would be too weak to carry out this task.

The completed Constitution was thus far less Madisonian than Madison would have wished. Yet it is equally true that both the debates at Philadelphia and the document they produced were deeply influenced by Madison's diagnosis of what he called the "vices of the political system of the United States." No other delegate played a more important role in framing the convention's agenda, steering its deliberations, or elevating the tenor of its debates. And even if the Constitution disappointed his expectations, Madison's criticisms of the defects of the Confederation were the foundation on which the new plan of government rested.

After the Constitution was published, Madison agreed to contribute to the series of essays that ALEXANDER HAMILTON planned to publish to support its ratification. Madison's first essay, the tenth *Federalist*, appeared on November 22, 1787. Its importance was largely neglected by nineteenth-century commentators. But in his influential work, *An Economic Interpretation of the Constitution* (1913), CHARLES A. BEARD treated *Federalist* No. 10 as the paradigmatic statement of the political theory of the Constitution, and a host of later commentators who rejected most of Beard's reading of this text have nevertheless echoed the same judgment. Several of Madison's other essays for *The Federalist*—notably his discussion of FEDERALISM in Nos. 39, 45, and 46, and of the SEPARATION OF POWERS in Nos. 47–51—have attained nearly the same status.

Federalist No. 10 is a critical document because it disputes the conventional wisdom which then held that stable republican governments could safely exist only in compact, relatively homogeneous societies. This posed a formidable objection to the Constitution, because Americans could never approve a national government that did not take a suitably REPUBLICAN FORM. *Federalist* No. 10 turned this conventional wisdom on its head. The greatest danger to liberty arose when self-interested factions seized control of government, Madison argued, and this was far more likely to happen in small, homogeneous societies than in extended, diverse polities. Creating an extended national republic of diverse interests would reduce this danger, Madison concluded, and it might have the further benefit of enabling a superior class of lawmakers to gain election to Congress, where they could legislate more wisely than their counterparts in the states.

Federalist No. 10 explained why a national republican government was possible, but it did not describe how its institutions would be constructed or how they would operate. These were the subjects to which Madison turned in later essays. In *Federalist* No. 39, he patiently explained why the new government could only be described as a complicated amalgam of national, federal, and republican features—neither a confederation of fully sovereign states nor a consolidated unitary nation-state. The succeeding essays then provided a case-by-case defense of the particular powers that the proposed Constitution delegated to Congress. In *Federalist* Nos. 45–46, Madison further suggested that the states would retain significant political advantages over the national government. All of these essays sought to demonstrate that creating an effective national government would still leave the states in possession of their essential powers and even their political influence.

It was in *Federalist* Nos. 47–51, however, that the second fundamental element of the Madisonian theory of the Constitution became apparent. Here Madison set out to counter two other axioms of contemporary constitutional theory. One held that the best way to protect each of the three branches of government from encroachments by the others was to keep them rigidly separated in their powers and personnel; the other held that the greatest danger to this institutional separation of powers arose from the executive.

Madison countered these positions in several ways. He argued, first, that the theory of rigid separation was rarely followed in either British or American practice, and that indeed some mixture of powers across the branches might prove a better way of preserving the essential separation than an adherence to their rigid separation. Second, in republican governments the real danger to separation came from the "impetuous vortex" of the legislature, which could deploy its rulemaking authority and its superior political influence to overwhelm the other branches. From this it followed, third, that the people could not be expected to rally to the support of the threatened departments; it was far more likely that their passions and interests would inspire the legislature to overstep its bounds. The only security for protecting each branch within its proper sphere, Madison concluded in *Federalist* No. 51, was to give each branch of government some means of defense (the veto for the President, JUDICIAL REVIEW of legislation for the judiciary, the power of the purse for Congress), but also to encourage alliances between the weaker institutions against the stronger. Read carefully, *Federalist* No. 51 is really a defense of the potential alliance between the President and Senate against the danger from the U.S. HOUSE OF REPRESENTATIVES. But its general principle extends further. Rather than rely on a rigid theory of separation, a truly Madisonian constitution would strive to fashion pragmatic mechanisms for preventing any one branch of government from gaining lasting supremacy over the others.

Madison ended *Federalist* No. 51 with a restatement of the argument of *Federalist* No. 10, and this provides a revealing clue to his own understanding of the Constitution. If the extended republic worked as the latter essay had earlier predicted, Madison concluded, the actual danger that Congress would dominate the other branches might be mitigated, for the diversity of interests in the larger society should work to discourage the wrong kinds of majorities from forming to pursue their vicious ends. This restatement confirms that Madison himself believed that the benefits of the extended republic would lay the essential foundation of a truly Madisonian constitution.

JACK N. RAKOVE
(2000)

Bibliography

ADAIR, DOUGLASS 1951 The Tenth Federalist Revisited. William and Mary Quarterly 8:48–67.
——— 1957 "That Politics May Be Reduced to a Science": David Hume, James Madison, and the Tenth Federalist. *Huntington Library Quarterly* 20:343–360.
BANNING, LANCE 1995 *The Sacred Fire of Liberty: James Madison and the Founding of the American Republic.* Ithaca, N.Y.: Cornell University Press.
BEARD, CHARLES A. 1913 *An Economic Interpretation of the Constitution.* New York: Macmillan.
BOURKE, PAUL 1975 The Pluralist Reading of James Madison's Tenth Federalist. *Perspectives in American History* 9:271–295.
DAHL, ROBERT 1956 *A Preface to Democratic Theory.* Chicago: University of Chicago Press.
DIAMOND, MARTIN 1959 Democracy and The Federalist: A Reconsideration of the Framers' Intent. *American Political Science Review* 53:52–68.

EPSTEIN, DAVID F. 1984 *The Political Theory of* The Federalist. Chicago: University of Chicago Press.

KETCHAM, RALPH 1971 *James Madison: A Biography.* New York: Macmillan.

NEDELSKY, JENNIFER 1990 *Private Property and the Limits of American Constitutionalism: The Madisonian Framework and Its Legacy.* Chicago: University of Chicago Press.

RAKOVE, JACK N. 1996 *Original Meanings: Politics and Ideas in the Making of the Constitution.* New York: Alfred Knopf.

ZVESPER, JOHN 1984 The Madisonian Systems. *Western Political Quarterly* 37:236–256.

MADISON'S "MEMORIAL AND REMONSTRANCE"
(1785)

This remonstrance is the best evidence of what JAMES MADISON, the framer of the FIRST AMENDMENT, meant by an ESTABLISHMENT OF RELIGION. In 1784 the Virginia legislature had proposed a bill that benefited "Teachers of the Christian Religion" by assessing a small tax on property owners. Each taxpayer could designate the Christian church of his choice as the recipient of his tax money; the bill allowed non-church members to earmark their taxes for the support of local schools, and it upheld the "liberal principle" that all Christian sects and denominations were equal under the law, none preferred over others. The bill did not speak of the "established religion" of the state as had an aborted bill of 1779, and it purported to be based on only secular considerations, the promotion of the public peace and morality rather than Christ's kingdom on earth. Madison denounced the bill as an establishment of religion, no less dangerous to RELIGIOUS LIBERTY than the proposal of 1779 and differing "only in degree" from the Inquisition.

In an elaborate argument of fifteen parts, Madison advocated a complete SEPARATION OF CHURCH AND STATE as the only guarantee of the equal right of every citizen to the free exercise of religion, including the freedom of those "whose minds have not yet yielded to the evidence which has convinced us." He regarded the right to support religion as an "unalienable" individual right to be exercised only on a voluntary basis. Religion, he contended, must be exempt from the power of society, the legislature, and the magistrate. In his trenchant assault on establishments including the one proposed by this mild bill—"it is proper to take alarm at the first experiment on our liberties"—and in his eloquent defense of separation, Madison stressed the point that separation benefited not only personal freedom but also the free state and even religion itself. His remonstrance, which circulated throughout Virginia in the summer of 1785, actually redirected public opinion, resulting in the election of legislators who opposed the bill, which had previously passed a second reading. Madison then introduced THOMAS JEFFERSON's proposal which was enacted into law as the VIRGINIA STATUTE OF RELIGIOUS FREEDOM.

LEONARD W. LEVY
(1986)

Bibliography

BRANT, IRVING 1948 *James Madison, Nationalist 1780–1787.* Pages 343–355. Indianapolis: Bobbs-Merrill.

MADISON'S *NOTES OF THE DEBATES*

In the oral arguments in OGDEN V. SAUNDERS (1824), a lawyer wondered what the intentions were of those who framed the Constitution when they included the CONTRACT CLAUSE. "Unhappily for this country and for the general interest of political science," he added, "the history of the Convention of 1787 which framed the Constitution of the United States is lost to the world." It was not lost, but no one who was not an intimate of JAMES MADISON knew that. Incredibly, JOHN MARSHALL wrote his great opinions on constitutional law and JOSEPH STORY wrote his *Commentaries on the Constitution* (1833) without knowing that Madison had in his possession his elaborate manuscript record of the CONSTITUTIONAL CONVENTION.

The Father of the Constitution not only wielded the greatest influence on its formation at the Convention, where he delivered over 200 speeches, but he also kept a record of the debates for nearly four months, a task that he later said "almost killed" him. He sat front and center in a "favorable position for hearing all that passed," and daily he composed a transcript from detailed notes kept of each session. Yet the memory that he had performed the task faded from the minds of participants.

In Madison's will of 1835, leaving his papers to his wife, he wrote that given the interest the Constitution "has inspired among friends of free Government, it was not an unreasonable inference that a report of the proceedings and discussions . . . will be particularly gratifying to the people of the United States, and to all who take an interest in the progress of political science and the course of true liberty." Why he failed to publish those records during his lifetime, indeed, why he kept them a secret, is inexplicable.

Madison worked on his manuscript intermittently for many years, revising and expanding as additional information became available. For example, he incorporated material from the official *Journal, Acts and Proceedings of the Convention* (1819) and even from ROBERT YATES's *Secret Proceedings and Debates* (1821), an Anti-Federalist work that contained useful details through July 5, 1787, including versions of Madison's own speeches. Madison's revisions of his original manuscript revealed his objective of making the record as full and accurate as possible.

After his death in 1836, Dolley Madison offered his papers to the United States. In 1837 Congress agreed on a price of $30,000, and in 1840, fifty-three years after the Convention, Madison's *Notes of the Debates* was published for the first of many times. It remains our most important source by far of what happened at the Constitutional Convention.

LEONARD W. LEVY
(1986)

Bibliography

MADISON, JAMES 1977 *The Papers of James Madison*, Robert A. Rutland, ed., vol. 10. Chicago: University of Chicago Press.
WARREN, CHARLES 1928 *The Making of the Constitution*. Boston: Little, Brown.

MAGNA CARTA
(1215)

Magna Carta (Latin, great charter), one of the enduring symbols of LIMITED GOVERNMENT and of the RULE OF LAW, was forced upon an unwilling King John by rebellious barons in June of 1215. Since his accession in 1199, John had made enemies at every quarter. The barons resisted heavy taxation exacted to support the king's expensive and unsuccessful wars with the French. Lesser folk complained that royal officials requisitioned, often without payment, food, timber, horses, and carts. Justice in the courts became more sporadic. Quarreling with Pope Innocent III over the election of a new archbishop of Canterbury, John seized church properties, yielding only when the pope threatened to release the English people from their allegiance to the Crown.

By spring of 1215, the barons' discontent had ripened to the point that they formally renounced their allegiance after the king refused their demands that he confirm their liberties by a charter. Under severe pressure, John agreed to meet the barons at Runnymede. There the barons presented a list of demands, the Articles of the Barons, which were then reduced to the form of a charter—the document that later generations came to call Magna Carta.

The charter to which John agreed is an intensely practical document. Rather than being a philosophical tract redolent with lofty generalities, the charter was drafted to provide concrete remedies for specific abuses. Moreover, although the barons were rebelling against the abuse of royal power, they were not seeking to remake the fabric of feudal society. They sought instead to restore customary

limits on the power of the Crown, distinguishing between rule according to law and rule by the imposition of arbitrary will.

The barons' interests were essentially selfish. They did not see themselves as disinterested advocates for the common good of the realm. Nevertheless, because the abuses of John's reign touched so many elements of English society, his opponents' demands had implications far beyond the barons' own interests. For example, the charter begins with the declaration that the liberties therein guaranteed run to "all the free men of our kingdom."

Many of Magna Carta's provisions concern feudal relationships having no counterpart in modern times. Certain of the charter's decrees, however, raise issues as vital now as then. Indeed, some of its provisions anticipate rights now embedded in American constitutional law. Among the more relevant are the following:

Chapter 39 declares, "No freed man shall be taken, imprisoned, disseised, outlawed, banished, or in any way destroyed, nor will We proceed against or prosecute him, except by the lawful judgment of his peers and by the LAW OF THE LAND." One should not read this language too broadly; for instance, "judgment of his peers" did not mean, as many have supposed, TRIAL BY JURY. But the requirement of proceedings according to the "law of the land" was significant in the development generally of the rule of law and more specifically of the concept of DUE PROCESS OF LAW. Indeed, "due process of law" and "law of the land" became interchangeable.

Chapter 40 states, "To no one will We sell, to none will We deny or delay, right or justice." Like chapter 39, this provision aimed at curbing abuses in the administration of justice. Several chapters (28, 29, 30, 31) relate to abuses in royal officials' requisitioning of private property and thus are the remote ancestor of the requirement of JUST COMPENSATION in the Fifth Amendment to the United States Constitution. Other chapters (20, 21, 22) require that fines be "according to the measure" of the offense and that fines not be so heavy as to jeopardize one's ability to make a living—reflecting the principle that the criminal law ought not to be administered in a vindictive or unduly oppressive way. Still other provisions deal with the liberties and free customs of cities and towns, with the free flow of commerce, and with church and state—all of these subjects being continuing concerns of American constitutional law.

Beginning with Henry III (who at age nine succeeded John in 1216), king after king reaffirmed Magna Carta. By the end of the fourteenth century, Magna Carta (which had been placed on the statute books in 1297) had established itself as more than a venerable statute; by then it was a FUNDAMENTAL LAW. In 1368, for example—over 400 years before MARBURY V. MADISON (1803)—a statute of Edward III commanded that Magna Carta "be holden and kept in all Points; and if there be any Statute made to the contrary, it shall be holden for none." Here one sees an early germ of the principle contained in the SUPREMACY CLAUSE of the United States Constitution.

The political turmoil of seventeenth-century England saw such parliamentarians as Sir EDWARD COKE and such pamphleteers as JOHN LILBURNE ("Free-born John") invoking Magna Carta against the pretensions of the Stuart kings. By the end of that century, climaxed by the Glorious Revolution, three new "liberty documents" had been brought into being to stand alongside Magna Carta as assuring the liberties of the subject—the PETITION OF RIGHT (1628), the HABEAS CORPUS ACT (1679), and the BILL OF RIGHTS (1689).

Magna Carta was early carried to the New World. In 1646, some discontented freemen in the Massachusetts colony complained that the laws and liberties they were entitled to as Englishmen were not being enforced. The colony's magistrates responded by drawing up the famous "parallels" of Massachusetts—one column entitled "Magna Charta," the other "fundamentalls of the Massachusetts," the purpose being to argue that the rights assured by Magna Carta and the common law were indeed not denied to the people of Massachusetts. When WILLIAM PENN founded Pennsylvania, he drew upon Magna Carta in drafting the new colony's Frame of Government and, in 1687, was responsible for the first publication in America of Magna Carta.

In the decade between the STAMP ACT (1765) and the outbreak of hostilities with the mother country, Magna Carta became part of the fabric of colonial arguments against British policies. In the petition by the Stamp Act Congress to the king, the Congress declared that both the colonists' right to tax themselves and the right of trial by jury (a right the Crown had circumvented by giving ADMIRALTY courts JURISDICTION to try cases under the Stamp Act) were "confirmed by the Great Charter of English Liberty."

During the period leading up to revolution, the colonists' arguments, in tracts and resolutions, were essentially eclectic. Appeals to the British Constitution, including Magna Carta, were intertwined with arguments that the colonists' entitlement to such rights as taxation only with their consent were based also on the colonial charters and on natural law. As SAMUEL ADAMS put it, Magna Carta itself was a declaration of Britons' "original, inherent, indefeasible NATURAL RIGHTS."

Independence accomplished, the Americans turned to the work of building their own constitutional governments, both state and ultimately federal. The new constitutions reveal both the legacy of British institutions, including Magna Carta, and their perceived limitations.

By and large, the contributions of Magna Carta and the other British "liberty" documents are most evident in American bills of rights. Virtually every state constitution has a due process clause, some using the phrase "due process," others using Magna Carta's formulation of "law of the land." For example, the debt owed Magna Carta's chapter 39 is obvious in North Carolina's Declaration of Rights, framed in 1776, "That no freeman ought to be taken, imprisoned, or disseized of his freehold, liberties, or privileges, or outlawed, or exiled, or in any manner destroyed, or deprived of his life, liberty, or property, but by the law of the land."

From the outset, however, American constitutional draftsmen understood their handiwork to go beyond Magna Carta. In North Carolina's ratifying convention (1789), JAMES IREDELL (later to serve on the Supreme Court) called Magna Carta "no constitution" but simply a legislative act, "every article of which the legislature may at any time alter." What Britain lacked, he concluded, the new American constitution supplied.

Throughout the nineteenth century, American courts, both state and federal, commonly invoked Magna Carta in shaping constitutional rights. Thus Magna Carta was relied on in cases involving (to give but a few examples) excessive court costs, open courts and certain remedies, notice and hearing, general application of the laws, and BILLS OF ATTAINDER. Gradually, as a corpus of indigenous American law developed, reliance upon Magna Carta became more and more attenuated, indeed largely rhetorical. By the twentieth century, Magna Carta had long since been irrevocably embedded into the fabric of American CONSTITUTIONALISM, both by contributing specific concepts such as due process of law and by being the ultimate symbol of constitutional government under a rule of law.

A. E. DICK HOWARD
(1986)

Bibliography

HOWARD, A. E. DICK   1968   *The Road from Runnymede: Magna Carta and Constitutionalism in America.* Charlottesville: University Press of Virginia.

MAHAN v. HOWELL
410 U.S. 315 (1973)

The ideal REAPPORTIONMENT, following REYNOLDS V. SIMS (1964), would establish state legislative districts of equal populations. The question remained: How much deviation from pure mathematical equality would be tolerated? In *Mahan*, the Supreme Court approved, 6–3, a deviation of sixteen percent in the districting of Virginia's lower house, justified by the state's "policy of maintaining the integrity of district lines."

In congressional districting, no such deviation from equality is tolerated (*White v. Weiser*, 1973). However, state legislative districting may include DE MINIMIS departures from equality (up to around ten percent) without any justification (*White v. Regester*, 1973).

KENNETH L. KARST
(1986)

MAHER v. ROE
432 U.S. 464 (1977)

The Supreme Court here sustained, 6–3, a Connecticut law limiting state medicaid assistance for abortions in the first trimester of pregnancy to "medically necessary" abortions (including "psychiatric necessity"), but providing such aid for childbirth. Justice LEWIS F. POWELL, for the Court, rejected both the claim that the law violated the right of PRIVACY recognized in ROE V. WADE (1973) and the claim that the state's WEALTH DISCRIMINATION violated the EQUAL PROTECTION clause.

There was to be "no retreat from *Roe*," but Connecticut had placed "no obstacles . . . in the pregnant woman's path to an abortion." An indigent woman suffered no disadvantage from the state's funding of childbirth; she might still have an abortion if she could find the wherewithal; Connecticut had not created her indigency. Nor did the scheme deny equal protection. There was no SUSPECT CLASSIFICATION requiring STRICT SCRUTINY of the law; neither had the state invaded any FUNDAMENTAL INTEREST by discriminating against the exercise of a constitutional right. The law satisfied the RATIONAL BASIS standard, for it was rationally related to promoting the state's interest in protecting potential life—an interest recognized in *Roe* itself.

Two companion decisions, *Poelker v. Doe* and *Beal v. Doe*, upheld a city's refusal to provide hospital services for an indigent woman's nontherapeutic abortion, and read the SOCIAL SECURITY ACT not to require a state to aid nontherapeutic abortions in order to receive federal medicaid grants.

Justices WILLIAM J. BRENNAN, THURGOOD MARSHALL, and HARRY BLACKMUN all filed opinions dissenting in the three cases. They emphasized the "coercive" effect on poor women of the state's financial preference for childbirth, and the particularly harsh effect of adding unwanted children to poor households.

Even before *Roe*, wealthy women could have abortions by traveling to other states or abroad. *Roe* brought abortion within the means of middleclass women. The *Maher* majority Justices declined to extend the effective right to

have an abortion beyond the boundaries of their own socioeconomic environment.

KENNETH L. KARST
(1986)

(SEE ALSO: *Abortion and the Constitution; Harris v. McRae; Reproductive Autonomy.*)

MAJORITY OPINION

See: Opinion of the Court

MALLORY v. UNITED STATES

See: McNabb-Mallory Rule

MALLOY v. HOGAN
378 U.S. 1 (1964)

This is one of a series of cases in which the WARREN COURT nationalized the rights of the criminally accused by incorporating provisions of the Fourth through the Eighth Amendments into the FOURTEENTH AMENDMENT. (See INCORPORATION DOCTRINE.) In *Malloy* it was the RIGHT AGAINST SELF-INCRIMINATION. Malloy, a convicted felon on probation, was ordered to testify in a judicial inquiry into gambling activities. He refused to answer any questions concerning the crime for which he had been convicted, and he was held in contempt. Connecticut's highest court, relying on TWINING V. NEW JERSEY (1908) and *Adamson v. California* (1947), ruled that Malloy's invocation of the Fifth Amendment right had no constitutional basis in the state and that the Fourteenth Amendment did not extend the right to a state proceeding.

The Supreme Court reversed on the ground that the "same standards must determine whether an accused's silence in either a federal or a state proceeding is justified." Had the inquiry been a federal one, said Justice WILLIAM J. BRENNAN for a 5–4 majority, Malloy would have been entitled to refuse to answer because his disclosures might have furnished a link in a chain of evidence to connect him to a new crime for which he might be prosecuted. The Court held that "the Fifth Amendment exception from compulsory self-incrimination is also protected by the Fourteenth against abridgment by the States." *Twining* and *Adamson*, which had held to the contrary, were overruled, although the specific holding in *Adamson* relating to comments on the accused's failure to testify was not overruled until GRIFFIN V. CALIFORNIA (1965). Thus, *Malloy* stands for the DOCTRINE that the Fourteenth Amendment protects against state abridgment the same right that the Fifth protects against federal abridgment. Justices BYRON R. WHITE and POTTER STEWART did not expressly dissent from this doctrine; they contended, rather, that Malloy's reliance on his right to silence was groundless on the basis of the facts. Justices JOHN MARSHALL HARLAN and TOM C. CLARK opposed the incorporation of the Fifth Amendment right into the Fourteenth.

LEONARD W. LEVY
(1986)

MANDAMUS, WRIT OF

(Latin: "We command.") A writ of mandamus is a judicial order to a lower court or to any agency or officer of any department of government, commanding the performance of a nondiscretionary act as a duty of office for the purpose of enforcing or recognizing an individual right or privilege. (See MARBURY V. MADISON.)

LEONARD W. LEVY
(1986)

MANN ACT
36 Stat. 825 (1910)

Congress sought to suppress prostitution in the so-called White Slave Act under the commerce power. Anyone transporting or aiding the transportation of a woman in INTERSTATE or FOREIGN COMMERCE "for the purpose of prostitution or debauchery, or for any other immoral purpose, or with the intent and purpose to induce, entice, or compel such woman or girl" to such immoral acts was guilty of a FELONY. Persuasion to cross state lines for these purposes "whether with or without her consent" was likewise a felony. Another section doubled the already stiff penalties (five years imprisonment or $5,000) in cases involving women under eighteen years of age. The act also authorized the Commissioner-General of Immigration to "receive and centralize information concerning the procuration of alien women and girls" for such purposes and required brothel-keepers to file statements regarding alien employees, exempting the keepers from prosecution for "truthful statements."

In HOKE V. UNITED STATES (1913) the Supreme Court sustained congressional power to enact the law under the COMMERCE CLAUSE, relying squarely on CHAMPION V. AMES (1903): "Congress, as an incident to [the commerce power] may adopt not only means necessary but convenient to its exercise, and the means may have the quality of police regulations."

DAVID GORDON
(1986)

MANN-ELKINS ACT
36 Stat. 539 (1910)

The ELKINS ACT of 1903 and the HEPBURN ACT of 1906, as well as the decisions they prompted, had reinvigorated the Interstate Commerce Commission (ICC) after disastrous Supreme Court decisions such as INTERSTATE COMMERCE COMMISSION V. CINCINNATI, NEW ORLEANS & TEXAS PACIFIC RAILWAY CO. (1897). The Mann-Elkins Act granted the ICC, for the first time, the power to set original rates; it also authorized the commission to suspend applications for proposed rate increases until it had ascertained their reasonableness. Despite the statute's vesting the commission with such powers, determinations of reasonableness would still be subject to the extraordinarily flexible guidelines of the FAIR RETURN rule laid down in SMYTH V. AMES (1898). The act placed the ICC firmly in control by shifting the BURDEN OF PROOF on the question of reasonableness from the commission to the carriers. In addition, the act revived a prohibition against LONG HAUL-SHORT HAUL DISCRIMINATION, except where specifically allowed by the commission. The act also brought telephone, telegraph, and cable lines under ICC JURISDICTION. A unanimous Supreme Court sustained many of the act's provisions in *United States v. Atchinson, Topeka & Santa Fe Railroad* (1914).

DAVID GORDON
(1986)

MANSFIELD, LORD

See: Murray, William

MAPP v. OHIO
367 U.S. 643 (1961)

Mapp v. Ohio brought to a close an abrasive constitutional debate within the Supreme Court on the question whether the EXCLUSIONARY RULE, constitutionally required in federal trials since 1914, was also required in state criminal cases. *Mapp* imposed the rule on the states.

WOLF V. COLORADO (1949) had applied to the states the FOURTH AMENDMENT's prohibition against UNREASONABLE SEARCHES, but it had not required state courts to exclude from trial evidence so obtained. *Mapp*'s extension of *Wolf* was based on two considerations. First, in *Wolf* the Court had been persuaded by the rejection of the exclusionary rule by most state courts; by 1961, however, a narrow majority of the states had independently adopted the rule. Second, the *Wolf* majority was convinced that other remedies, such as suits in tort against offending officers, could serve equally in deterring unlawful searches; time, however, had shown that such remedies were useless. "Nothing can destroy a government more quickly than its failure to observe its own laws," wrote Justice TOM C. CLARK for the Court, "or worse, its disregard of the charter of its own existence."

In *Mapp v. Ohio* the Court asserted emphatically that the exclusionary rule was "an essential part" of the Fourth Amendment and hence a fit subject for imposition on the states despite "passing references" in earlier cases to its being a nonconstitutional rule of evidence. Yet, in some hazy phrasing, the opinion also suggested that the Fifth Amendment's RIGHT AGAINST SELF-INCRIMINATION was the exclusionary rule's constitutional backbone. Equally confusing was the Court's characterization of the rule as "the most important constitutional privilege" (that is, personal right) guaranteed by the Fourth Amendment while at the same time pointing to the rule's deterrent effect as justification for its imposition. More recently, the Court has settled on deterrence as the crucial consideration, and thus has refused to apply the rule in situations, such as GRAND JURY proceedings in CALANDRA V. UNITED STATES (1974), where in the Court's view the deterrent effect is minimal.

Three dissenters, in an opinion by Justice JOHN MARSHALL HARLAN, expressed "considerable doubt" that the federal exclusionary rule of WEEKS V. UNITED STATES (1914) was constitutionally based and argued that, in any event, considerations of FEDERALISM should allow the states to devise their own remedies for unlawful searches.

(Unlike the well-entrenched federal exclusionary rule, which has gone well-nigh unchallenged on the Court from the beginning, controversy concerning the rule for the states has continued unabated, both on and off the Court, since *Mapp* was decided.)

JACOB W. LANDYNSKI
(1986)

MARBURY v. MADISON
1 Cranch 137 (1803)

Marbury has transcended its origins in the party battles between Federalists and Republicans, achieving mythic status as the foremost precedent for JUDICIAL REVIEW. For the first time the Court held unconstitutional an act of Congress, establishing, if only for posterity, the doctrine that the Supreme Court has the final word among the co-ordinate branches of the national government in determining what is law under the Constitution. By 1803 no one doubted that an unconstitutional act of government was null and void, but who was to judge? What *Marbury* settled, doctrinally if not in reality, was the Court's ulti-mate authority over Congress and the President. Actually, the historic reputation of the case is all out of proportion to the merits of Chief Justice JOHN MARSHALLS unanimous opinion for the Court. On the issue of judicial review, which made the case live, he said nothing new, and his claim for the power of the Court occasioned little contemporary comment. The significance of the case in its time derived from its political context and from the fact that the Court appeared successfully to interfere with the executive branch. Marshall's most remarkable accomplishment, in retrospect, was his massing of the Court behind a poorly reasoned opinion that section 13 of the JUDICIARY ACT OF 1789 was unconstitutional. Though the Court's legal craftsmanship was not evident, its judicial politics—egregious partisanship and calculated expediency—was exceptionally adroit, leaving no target for Republican retaliation beyond frustrated rhetoric.

Republican hostility to the United States courts, which were Federalist to the last man as well as Federalist in doctrine and interests, had mounted increasingly and passed the threshold of tolerance when the Justices on circuit enforced the Sedition Act. (See ALIEN AND SEDITION ACTS.) Then the lame-duck Federalist administration passed the JUDICIARY ACT OF 1801 and, a week before THOMAS JEFFERSON's inauguration, passed the companion act for the appointment of forty-two justices of the peace for the DISTRICT OF COLUMBIA, prompting the new President to believe that "the Federalists have retired into the Judiciary as a stronghold . . . and from that battery all the works of republicanism are to be beaten down and erased." The new Circuit Court for the District of Columbia sought in vain to obtain the conviction of the editor of the administration's organ in the capital for the common law crime of SEDITIOUS LIBEL. The temperate response of the new administration was remarkable. Instead of increasing the size of the courts, especially the Supreme Court, and packing them with Republican appointees, the administration simply repealed the Judiciary Act of 1801. (See JUDICIARY ACTS OF 1802.) On taking office Jefferson also ordered that the commissions for the forty-two justices of the peace for the district be withheld, though he reappointed twenty-five, all political enemies originally appointed by President JOHN ADAMS.

Marbury v. Madison arose from the refusal of the administration to deliver the commissions of four of these appointees, including one William Marbury. The Senate had confirmed the appointments and Adams had signed their commissions, which Marshall, the outgoing secretary of state, had affixed with the great seal of the United States. But in the rush of the "midnight appointments" on the evening of March 3, the last day of the outgoing administration, Marshall had neglected to deliver the commissions. Marbury and three others sought from the

Supreme Court, in a case of ORIGINAL JURISDICTION, a WRIT OF MANDAMUS compelling JAMES MADISON, the new secretary of state, to issue their commissions. In December 1801 the Court issued an order commanding Madison to show cause why the writ should not be issued.

A congressman reflected the Republican viewpoint when saying that the show-cause order was "a bold stroke against the Executive," and JOHN BRECKINRIDGE, the majority leader of the Senate, thought the order "the most daring attack which the annals of Federalism have yet exhibited." When the debate began on the repeal bill, Federalists defended the show-cause order, the independence of the judiciary, and the duty of the Supreme Court to hold void any unconstitutional acts of Congress. A Republican paper declared that the "mandamus business" had first appeared to be only a contest between the judiciary and the executive but now seemed a political act by the Court to deter repeal of the 1801 legislation. In retaliation the Republicans passed the repealer and altered the terms of the Court so that it would lose its June 1802 session and not again meet until February 1803, fourteen months after the show-cause order. The Republicans hoped, as proved to be the case, that the Justices would comply with the repealer and return to circuit duty, thereby averting a showdown and a constitutional crisis, which the administration preferred to avoid.

By the time the Court met in February 1803 to hear arguments in *Marbury*, which had become a political sensation, talk of IMPEACHMENT was in the air. A few days before the Court's term, Federalists in Congress moved that the Senate should produce for Marbury's benefit records of his confirmation, provoking Senator James Jackson to declare that the Senate would not interfere in the case and become "a party to an accusation which may end in an impeachment, of which the Senate were the constitutional Judges." By no coincidence, a week before the Court met, Jefferson instructed the House to impeach a U.S. District Court judge in New Hampshire, and already Federalists knew of the plan to impeach Justice SAMUEL CHASE. Jefferson's desire to replace John Marshall with SPENCER ROANE was also public knowledge. Right before Marshall delivered the Court's opinion in *Marbury*, the Washington correspondent of a Republican paper wrote: "The attempt of the Supreme Court . . . by a mandamus, to control the Executive functions, is a new experiment. It seems to be no less than a commencement of war. . . . The Court must be defeated and retreat from the attack; or march on, till they incur an impeachment and removal from office."

Marshall and his Court appeared to confront unattractive alternatives. To have issued the writ, which was the expected judgment, would have been like the papal bull against the moon; Madison would have defied it, exposing the Court's impotence, and the Republicans might have a pretext for retaliation based on the Court's breach of the principle of SEPARATION OF POWERS. To have withheld the writ would have violated the Federalist principle that the Republican administration was accountable under the law. ALEXANDER HAMILTON's newspaper reported the Court's opinion in a story headed "Constitution Violated by President," informing its readers that the new President by his first act had trampled on the charter of the peoples' liberties by unprincipled, even criminal, conduct against personal rights. Yet the Court did not issue the writ; the victorious party was Madison. But Marshall exhibited him and the President to the nation as if they were arbitrary Stuart tyrants, and then, affecting judicial humility, Marshall in obedience to the Constitution found that the Court could not obey an act of Congress that sought to aggrandize judicial powers in cases of original jurisdiction, contrary to Article III of the Constitution.

The Court was treading warily. The statute in question was not a Republican measure, not, for example, the repealer of the Judiciary Act of 1801. Indeed, shortly after *Marbury*, the Court sustained the repealer in STUART V. LAIRD (1803) against arguments that it was unconstitutional. In that case the Court ruled that the practice of the Justices in sitting as circuit judges derived from the Judiciary Act of 1789, and therefore derived "from a contemporary interpretation of the most forcible nature," as well as from customary acquiescence. Ironically, another provision of the same statute, section 13, was at issue in *Marbury*, not that the bench and bar realized it until Marshall delivered his opinion. The offending section, passed by a Federalist Congress after being drafted by OLIVER ELLSWORTH, one of the Constitution's Framers and Marshall's predecessor, had been the subject of previous litigation before the Court without anyone having thought it was unconstitutional. Section 13 simply authorized the Court to issue writs of *mandamus* "in cases warranted by the principles and usages of law," and that clause appeared in the context of a reference to the Court's APPELLATE JURISDICTION.

Marshall's entire argument hinged on the point that section 13 unconstitutionally extended the Court's original jurisdiction beyond the two categories of cases, specified in Article III, in which the Court was to have such jurisdiction. But for those two categories of cases, involving foreign diplomats or a state as a litigant, the Court has appellate jurisdiction. In quoting Article III, Marshall omitted the clause that directly follows as part of the same sentence: the Court has appellate jurisdiction "with such exceptions, and under such regulations as the Congress shall make." That might mean that Congress can detract from the Court's appellate jurisdiction or add to its original jurisdiction. The specification of two categories of cases in which the Court has original jurisdiction was surely intended as an irreducible minimum, but Marshall read it, by the narrowest construction, to mean a negation of congressional powers.

In any event, section 13 did not add to the Court's original jurisdiction. In effect it authorized the Court to issue writs of *mandamus* in the two categories of cases of original jurisdiction and in all appellate cases. The authority to issue such writs did not extend or add to the Court's jurisdiction; the writ of *mandamus* is merely a remedial device by which courts implement their existing jurisdiction. Marshall misinterpreted the statute and Article III, as well as the nature of the writ, in order to find that the statute conflicted with Article III. Had the Court employed the reasoning of *Stuart v. Laird* or the rule that the Court should hold a statute void only in a clear case, giving every presumption of validity in doubtful cases, Marshall could not have reached his conclusion that section 13 was unconstitutional. That conclusion allowed him to decide that the Court was powerless to issue the writ because Marbury had sued for it in a case of original jurisdiction.

Marshall could have said, simply, this is a case of original jurisdiction but it does not fall within either of the two categories of original jurisdiction specified in Article III; therefore we cannot decide: writ denied, case dismissed. Section 13 need never have entered the opinion, although, alternatively, Marshall could have declared: section 13 authorizes this Court to issue such writs only in cases warranted by the principles and usages of law; we have no jurisdiction here because we are not hearing the case in our appellate capacity and it is not one of the two categories in which we possess original jurisdiction: writ denied, case dismissed. Even if Marshall had to find that the statute augmented the Court's original jurisdiction, the ambiguity of the clause in Article III, which he neglected to quote, justified sustaining the statute.

Holding section 13 unconstitutional enabled Marshall to refuse an extension of the Court's powers and award the judgment to Madison, thus denying the administration a pretext for vengeance. Marshall also used the case to answer Republican arguments that the Court did not and should not have the power to declare an act of Congress unconstitutional, though he carefully chose an inoffensive section of a Federalist statute that pertained merely to writs of mandamus. That he gave his doctrine of judicial review the support of only abstract logic, without reference to history or precedents, was characteristic, as was the fact that his doctrine swept way beyond the statute that provoked it.

If Marshall had merely wanted a safe platform from which to espouse and exercise judicial review, he would have begun his opinion with the problems that section 13 posed for the Court; but he reached the question of con-

stitutionality and of judicial review at the tail-end of his opinion. Although he concluded that the Court had to discharge the show-cause order, because it lacked jurisdiction, he first and most irregularly passed judgment on the merits of the case. Everything said on the merits was OB-ITER DICTA and should not have been said at all, given the judgment. Most of the opinion dealt with Marbury's unquestionable right to his commission and the correctness of the remedy he had sought by way of a writ of mandamus. In his elaborate discourse on those matters, Marshall assailed the President and his cabinet officer for their lawlessness. Before telling Marbury that he had initiated his case in the wrong court, Marshall engaged in what EDWARD S. CORWIN called "a deliberate partisan *coup*." Then Marshall followed with a "judicial *coup d'etat*," in the words of ALBERT J. BEVERIDGE, on the constitutional issue that neither party had argued.

The partisan *coup* by which Marshall denounced the executive branch, not the grand declaration of the doctrine of judicial review for which the case is remembered, was the focus of contemporary excitement. Only the passages on judicial review survive. Cases on the REMOVAL POWER of the President, especially concerning inferior appointees, cast doubt on the validity of the dicta by which Marshall lectured the executive branch on its responsibilities under the law. Moreover, by statute and by judicial practice the Supreme Court exercises the authority to issue writs of mandamus in all appellate cases and in the two categories of cases of original jurisdiction. Over the passage of time *Marbury* came to stand for the monumental principle, so distinctive and dominant a feature of our constitutional system, that the Court may bind the coordinate branches of the national government to its rulings on what is the supreme LAW OF THE LAND. That principle stands out from *Marbury* like the grin on the Cheshire cat; all else, which preoccupied national attention in 1803, disappeared in our constitutional law. So too might have disappeared national judicial review if the impeachment of Chase had succeeded.

Marshall himself was prepared to submit to review of Supreme Court opinions by Congress. He was so shaken by the impeachment of Chase and by the thought that he himself might be the next victim in the event of Chase's conviction, that he wrote to Chase on January 23, 1804: "I think the modern doctrine of impeachment should yield to an appellate jurisdiction in the legislature. A reversal of those legal opinions deemed unsound by the legislature would certainly better comport with the mildness of our character than a removal of the judge who has rendered them unknowing of his fault." The acquittal of Chase meant that the Court could remain independent, that Marshall had no need to announce publicly his desperate plan for congressional review of the Court, and that *Mar-*

bury remained as a precedent. Considering that the Court did not again hold unconstitutional an act of Congress until 1857, when it decided DRED SCOTT V. SANDFORD, sixty-eight years would have passed since 1789 without such a holding, and but for *Marbury*, after so long a period of congressional omnipotence, national judicial review might never have been established.

LEONARD W. LEVY
(1986)

Bibliography

BEVERIDGE, ALBERT J. 1916–1919 *The Life of John Marshall*, 4 vols. Vol. III:50–178. Boston: Houghton Mifflin.

CORWIN, EDWARD S. 1914 *The Doctrine of Judicial Review.* Pages 1–78. Princeton, N.J.: Princeton University Press.

HAINES, CHARLES GROVE 1944 *The Role of the Supreme Court in American Government and Politics, 1789–1835.* Pages 223–258. Berkeley: University of California Press.

VAN ALSTYNE, WILLIAM W. 1969 A Critical Guide to Marbury v. Madison. *Duke Law Journal* 1969:1–47.

WARREN, CHARLES 1923 *The Supreme Court in United States History*, 3 vols. Vol. I:200–268. Boston: Little, Brown.

MARCHETTI v. UNITED STATES
390 U.S. 39 (1968)

GROSSO v. UNITED STATES
390 U.S. 62 (1968)

HAYNES v. UNITED STATES
390 U.S. 85 (1968)

UNITED STATES v. UNITED STATES COIN & CURRENCY
401 U.S. 715 (1971)

In *Marchetti* and *Grosso* the Supreme Court, in opinions by Justice JOHN MARSHALL HARLAN from which only Chief Justice EARL WARREN dissented, held that the RIGHT AGAINST SELF-INCRIMINATION constituted an ironclad defense against a criminal prosecution for failure to register as a gambler pursuant to federal gambling statutes or to pay federal occupational and EXCISE TAXES on gambling. The Court overruled *United States v. Kahriger* (1953) and *Lewis v. United States* (1955), which had held that the Fifth Amendment right could not be asserted by professional gamblers because the federal gambling laws did not compel self-incrimination. In those earlier cases the Court reasoned that the right was inapplicable to prospective acts: a gambler had the initial choice of deciding whether to continue gambling at the price of surrendering his right against self-incrimination, or cease gambling and thereby

avoid the need to register and pay the taxes. In 1968 the Court found its earlier reasoning "no longer persuasive."

Justice Harlan explained how the statutes worked. A gambler had an obligation to register annually with the Internal Revenue Service as one engaged in the business of accepting wagers. He paid a $50 occupational tax plus an excise tax of ten percent on the gross amount of all bets. He had to keep daily records of all bets and reveal those records to IRS inspectors. The issue posed by such congressional requirements was not whether the United States may tax gambling, for the unlawfulness of an activity did not preclude its taxation. The issue, rather, was whether the registration, record-keeping, and tax provisions whipsawed gamblers into confessing criminal activities. Federal and state laws made gambling illegal, and the IRS made available to law enforcement agencies the identities of those who complied with the gambling statutes. Gamblers therefore confronted substantial hazards of self-incrimination. On pain of punishment for not complying, they had to provide prosecutors with evidence of their guilt.

Marchetti was convicted of failing to register and pay the occupational tax, Grosso for failing to pay that tax and the excises. Reversing their convictions, the Court distinguished their cases from those in which a criminal had failed to file income tax returns for fear of self-incrimination and another in which the government had required record keeping from persons not engaged in an inherently suspect activity. The mere filing of a tax return, required of all, or the failure to keep routine business records did not identify anyone as a suspect of a crime. In *Haynes*, the Court ruled that a person possessing a sawed-off shotgun is suspect and therefore cannot be compelled to register his weapon, under the National Firearms Act, because of the hazard of self-incrimination. In *United States Coin & Currency* a 5–4 Court applied the *Marchetti* reasoning to a forfeiture proceeding involving property used to violate federal gambling laws.

LEONARD W. LEVY
(1986)

MARKETPLACE OF IDEAS

The "marketplace of ideas" argument in FIRST AMENDMENT jurisprudence was first enunciated in Justice OLIVER WENDELL HOLMES's dissenting opinion in ABRAMS V. UNITED STATES (1919):

> But when men have realized that time has upset many fighting faiths, they may come to believe even more than they believe the very foundations of their own conduct that the ultimate good desired is better reached by free trade in ideas—that the best test of truth is the power of

thought to get itself accepted in the competition of the market, and that truth is the only ground upon which their wishes safely can be carried out. That at any rate is the theory of our Constitution. It is an experiment, as all life is an experiment. . . . While that experiment is part of our system I think that we should be eternally vigilant against attempts to check the expression of opinions that we loathe and believe to be fraught with death, unless they so imminently threaten immediate interference with the lawful and pressing purpose of the law that an immediate check is required to save the country.

Holmes's stirring words recall similar but distinct passages from JOHN MILTON and JOHN STUART MILL. Extravagant as Holmes's passage is, it is in significant respects more careful than the implications of Milton's rhetorical question: "[W]ho ever knew truth put to the worse, in a free and open encounter?" Holmes did not claim that truth always or even usually emerges in the marketplace of ideas. Holmes's claim was more confined—that the best test of truth is the competition of the marketplace.

On the other hand, Milton spoke of a free and open encounter; Holmes spoke of the competition of the marketplace. A recurrent problem in First Amendment cases is that these two notions are not the same. Those who seek access to the broadcast media, as in RED LION BROADCASTING V. FCC (1969), or to powerful newspapers, as in MIAMI HERALD PUBLISHING CO. V. TORNILLO (1974), argue that the competition of the marketplace is not free and open. They urge that truth cannot emerge in the market if the gatekeepers do not let it in. A more general criticism of the Holmes position is that the claim that the marketplace is the best test of truth cannot itself be tested without an independent test of truth, yet the argument by its terms denies any superior test of truth that is independent of the marketplace.

These criticisms aside, the question arises whether the marketplace argument overvalues truth. Holmes's view that the expression of opinion should be free until an immediate check is needed to "save the country" has never been adopted by the Supreme Court. Advocacy of illegal action, for example, may be restricted when it is directed to and likely to incite or produce imminent lawless action, whether or not the country itself is endangered. Indeed, if the marketplace argument extends to facts as well as opinions, it is clear that showings far more pedestrian than Holmes's proposed requirements are sufficient to justify repression. The expression of factual beliefs can be restricted in order to protect reputation or privacy, and, in the commercial sphere, to further any substantial government interest.

Nonetheless, the marketplace argument has been a powerful theme in First Amendment law. For example, some defamatory facts and all defamatory opinion are pro-

tected in order to guarantee the breathing space we need for robust, uninhibited, and wide-open debate. Ironically, however, the marketplace argument serves to restrict speech as well as to protect it. "Under our Constitution," said the Court in GERTZ V. ROBERT WELCH, INC. (1974), "there is no such thing as a false idea," yet obscenity is divorced from speech protection because it is thought to be unnecessary for the expression of any idea. At bottom, First Amendment methodology is grounded in a paradox. Government must be restrained from imposing its views of truth. But government itself determines when this principle has been abandoned.

STEVEN SHIFFRIN
(1986)

Bibliography
SCHAUER, FREDERICK 1978 Language, Truth and the First Amendment: An Essay in Memory of Harry Canter. *Virginia Law Review* 64:263, 268–272.

MARRIAGE AND THE CONSTITUTION

Although the constitutional "right to marry" was not securely confirmed by the Supreme Court until its decision in ZABLOCKI V. REDHAIL (1978), the Court had spoken of the freedom to marry as a FOURTEENTH AMENDMENT "liberty" as early as MEYER V. NEBRASKA (1923). Two WARREN COURT decisions had also laid the foundations for SUBSTANTIVE DUE PROCESS protections of marriage. GRISWOLD V. CONNECTICUT (1965) had recognized a RIGHT OF PRIVACY for the marital relationship, and LOVING V. VIRGINIA (1967) had struck down a MISCEGENATION law not only as an unconstitutional RACIAL DISCRIMINATION but also as a due process violation. The *Loving* opinion was explicit enough in speaking of the "freedom to marry," but doubt lingered that the Court meant to carry the principle beyond the racial context of the decision.

Zablocki ended the doubt. The Court held invalid, on equal protection grounds, a law forbidding a resident to marry without a judge's approval when he or she had court-ordered child support obligations. The judge could not approve the marriage unless support payments were kept current and the children were unlikely to become public charges. Some concurring Justices thought the law defective on due process grounds. *Zablocki*'s importance turns not on this doctrinal distinction but on its explicit recognition of marriage as a FUNDAMENTAL INTEREST, requiring STRICT SCRUTINY by the courts of direct and substantial governmental interference.

Just two months earlier, however, in *Califano v. Jobst* (1977), the Court had upheld a portion of the SOCIAL SE-

CURITY ACT terminating disability benefits for a disabled dependent child of a wage earner when the child married a person not entitled to benefits under the act, even though that person was also disabled. Much of the discussion in *Zablocki*'s several opinions was devoted to *Jobst*. The majority distinguished *Jobst* as lacking the "directness and substantiality of the interference with the freedom to marry" present in *Zablocki*. The message was clear: interferences with marriage would demand justification in proportion to their degrees of severity. In *Zablocki* as in *Jobst* a money cost was attached to marriage; in *Zablocki* that cost would be prohibitive in most cases covered by the law.

This version of judicial interest-balancing seems likely to uphold such state restrictions on marriage as blood tests, reasonable age requirements, and insistence on a mentally retarded person's ability to understand the nature of the marriage relationship, even when those restrictions are strictly scrutinized. On principle, the state's power to prohibit POLYGAMY or to deny homosexual couples marriage or some comparable status seems more vulnerable to attack. It would be unrealistic, however, to expect an extension of the constitutional right to marry to homosexuals in the near future. (See SEXUAL PREFERENCE AND THE CONSTITUTION.) And recognition of a constitutional right to multiple marriage is a poor bet even for the distant future.

The extension of constitutional protection to other intimate relationships more closely resembling traditional marriage is already at hand. *Griswold*'s "privacy" protections have been effectively extended to the unmarried in EISENSTADT V. BAIRD (1972) and CAREY V. POPULATION SERVICES INTERNATIONAL (1977). Some states continue to recognize common law marriage, and others have concluded that support obligations may attach to the partners to some informal unions, once the unions end. As the number of unmarried couples living together increases, and as the incidents of unwed union come to resemble those of traditional marriage, formal marriage itself is more clearly seen in its expressive aspects, as a statement of commitment. In these circumstances it makes good sense to think of the right to marry as, in part, a FIRST AMENDMENT right.

KENNETH L. KARST
(1986)

(SEE ALSO: *Freedom of Intimate Association; Same-Sex Marriage.*)

Bibliography

KARST, KENNETH L. 1980 The Freedom of Intimate Association. *Yale Law Journal* 89:624–692.
NOTE 1980 Developments in the Law: The Constitution and the Family. *Harvard Law Review* 93:1156–1383, 1248–1296.

MARSH v. ALABAMA
326 U.S. 501 (1946)

When a person sought to distribute religious literature on the streets of a company town, the Supreme Court, 5–3, upheld her FIRST AMENDMENT claim against the owner's private property claims. Stressing the traditional role of free speech in town shopping districts open to the general public, Justice HUGO L. BLACK for the Court noted that, aside from private ownership, this town functioned exactly as did other towns which were constitutionally forbidden to ban leafleting. *Marsh* served as the basis for the later attempt, aborted in HUDGENS V. NLRB (1976), to extend First Amendment rights to users of privately owned SHOPPING CENTERS.

MARTIN SHAPIRO
(1986)

MARSH v. CHAMBERS
463 U.S. 783 (1983)

A 6–3 Supreme Court sustained the constitutionality of legislative chaplaincies as not violating the SEPARATION OF CHURCH AND STATE mandated by the FIRST AMENDMENT. Chief Justice WARREN E. BURGER for the Court abandoned the three-part test of LEMON V. KURTZMAN (1971) previously used in cases involving the establishment clause and grounded his opinion wholly upon historical custom. Prayers by tax-supported legislative chaplains, traceable to the FIRST CONTINENTAL CONGRESS and the very Congress that framed the BILL OF RIGHTS, had become "part of the fabric of our society." Justice JOHN PAUL STEVENS, dissenting, asserted that Nebraska's practice of having the same Presbyterian minister as the official chaplain for sixteen years preferred one denomination over others. Justices WILLIAM J. BRENNAN and THURGOOD MARSHALL, dissenting, attacked legislative chaplains generally as a form of religious worship sponsored by government to promote and advance religion and entangling the government with religion, contrary to the values implicit in the establishment clause—privacy in religious matters, government neutrality, freedom of conscience, autonomy of religious life, and withdrawal of religion from the political arena.

LEONARD W. LEVY
(1986)

MARSHALL, JOHN
(1755–1835)

John Marshall, the third CHIEF JUSTICE of the Supreme Court (1801–1835), is still popularly known as the "Great

Chief Justice" and the "Expounder of the Constitution." He was raised in the simple circumstances of backwoods Virginia, but his mother was pious and well educated and his father was a leader of his county and a friend of GEORGE WASHINGTON. Even though Marshall had little formal education, his extraordinary powers of mind, coupled with equity and good humor, made him a natural leader as a young soldier of the Revolution, as a member of the Richmond bar (then outstanding in the country), and as a general of the Virginia militia. He became nationally prominent as a diplomat, having outwitted the wily Charles Talleyrand while negotiating with France's Directory (1797–1798), and as a legislator, having supported Washington's FEDERALISM first in the Virginia Assembly (1782–1791, 1795–1797) and then in the HOUSE OF REPRESENTATIVES (1799–1800). In June 1800 President JOHN ADAMS named Marshall to replace the Hamiltonian John Pickering as secretary of state, and in January 1801, after the strife-ridden Federalists' epochal defeat, appointed him Chief Justice when JOHN JAY, the first Chief Justice, declined to preside again over "a system so defective."

From its inception Marshall had defended the Constitution. His experience in Washington's ragtag army had made him a national patriot while rousing his disgust with the palsied Confederation. At the crucial Virginia ratifying convention (June 1788) he replied in three important speeches to the fears of PATRICK HENRY and other Anti-Federalists. The proposed Constitution, he argued, was not undemocratic, but a plan for a "well-regulated democracy." It set forth in particular the great powers of taxing and warring needed by any sound government. The state governments would retain all powers not given up expressly or implicitly; they were independently derived from the people. A mix of dependence upon the people and independence and virtue in the judges would prevent federal overreaching. If a law were not "warranted by any of the powers enumerated," Marshall remarked prophetically, the judges would declare it "void" as infringing "the Constitution they are to guard." Two other nonjudicial interpretations of the Constitution are notable. In 1799 Marshall wrote a report of the Virginia Federalists defending the constitutionality of the ill-famed Sedition Act of 1798 (a law he nevertheless had opposed as divisive in the explosive political atmosphere surrounding the French Revolution). If the NECESSARY AND PROPER CLAUSE authorizes punishment of actual resistance to law, he argued, it also authorizes punishment of "calumnious" speech, which is criminal under the COMMON LAW and prepares resistance. A speech to Congress in 1800, once famous in collections of American rhetoric, defended the President's power required by JAY'S TREATY to extradite a British subject charged with murder on a British ship. Because the criminal and the location were foreign, Marshall argued, the question was not a case in law or equity for United States courts; although a treaty is a law, it is a "political law," the execution of which lies with the President, not the courts. The judiciary has no political power whatever; the President is "the sole organ of the nation in its external relations."

As Chief Justice, Marshall raised the office and the Supreme Court to stature and power previously lacking. After having two Chief Justices in eleven years, the Court had Marshall for thirty-four, the longest tenure of any Chief Justice before or since. Individual opinions SERIATIM largely ceased, and dissents were discouraged. The Court came to speak with one voice. Usually the voice was Marshall's. He delivered the OPINION OF THE COURT in every case in which he participated during the decisive first five years, three-quarters of the opinions during the next seven years, and almost all the great constitutional opinions throughout his tenure. Marshall's captivating and equable temper helped unite a diverse group of justices, many appointed by Republican Presidents bent on reversing the Court's declarations of federal power and restrictions of state power. In the face of triumphant Jeffersonian Republicans, suspicious of an unelected judiciary stocked with Federalists, Marshall was wary and astute. His Court never erred as the JAY COURT did in CHISHOLM V. GEORGIA (1793), which had provoked the ELEVENTH AMENDMENT as a corrective. Nor did he cast antidemocratic contentions in the teeth of the Jeffersonians or their Jacksonian successors, thus to provoke (as had Justice Samuel Chase) impeachment proceedings. Marshall's judicial opinions encouraged grave respect for law, treated the Constitution as sacred and its Founding Fathers as sainted men, and fashioned a protective and compelling shield of purpose, principle, and reasoning.

His crucial judicial accomplishment was MARBURY V. MADISON (1803), which laid down the essentials of the American RULE OF LAW. Judges are to oversee executive and legislature alike, keeping the political departments faithful to applicable statutes, to the written Constitution, and to "general principles" of law protecting individual rights and delimiting the functions of each department. A series of important decisions secured individual rights, especially the right to acquire property by contract, against state and general governments. United States v. Burr (1807) expounded a narrow constitutional definition of TREASON and made prosecution difficult. STURGES V. CROWNINSHIELD (1819) set strict standards for voiding debts by bankruptcy. FLETCHER V. PECK (1810) and DARTMOUTH COLLEGE V. WOODWARD (1819) enforced as judicially protected contracts a state's sale of land and a state's grant of a corporate charter. Finally, several of Marshall's most famous opinions elaborated great powers for the national government and protected them from state encroachment.

MCCULLOCH V. MARYLAND (1819) sustained Congress's authority to charter a bank and in general to employ broad discretion as to necessary and proper means for carrying out national functions. GIBBONS V. OGDEN (1824), the steamboat case, interpreted congressional power under the COMMERCE CLAUSE to protect a national market, a right of exchange free from state-supported monopoly. COHENS V. VIRGINIA (1821) eloquently defended Supreme Court review of state court decisions involving FEDERAL QUESTIONS.

The presupposition of Marshall's CONSTITUTIONALISM was that the Constitution is FUNDAMENTAL LAW, not merely a fundamental plan, written to impose limits, not just to raise powers, and designed to be permanent, not to evolve or to be fundamentally revised. Interpretation is to follow the words and purposes of the various provisions; amendment is for subordinate changes that will allow "immortality" to the Framers' primary work. Marshall called a written constitution America's "greatest improvement on political institutions." It renders permanent the institutions raised by popular consent, which is the only basis of rightful government. Besides, the American nation was fortunate in its founding: it benefited from a remarkable plan, from a fortunate ratification in the face of jealousy and suspicion in states and people, and from the extraordinary firmness of the first President. Washington had settled the new federal institutions and conciliated public opinion, despite the "infinite difficulty" of ratification and a crescendo of attacks upon his administration as monarchic, aristocratic, and anglophile. So Marshall argued in the penetrating (if somewhat wooden) *Life of George Washington*, a biography he condensed into a schoolbook to impress on his countrymen the character and political principles of "the greatest man in the world."

Marshall understood the Constitution to establish a government, not a league such as that created by the ARTICLES OF CONFEDERATION. The new government possessed sovereign powers of two sorts, legal (the judicial power) and political (legislative and executive). The special function of judges is to apply the law to individuals. It is a power extensive although not, Marshall consistently said, political or policy-oriented. Judicial JURISDICTION extends as far as does the law: common law, statute law, Constitution, treaties, and the law of nations (which Marshall influenced by several luminous opinions). In applying the law to individuals, courts are to care for individual rights, the very object of government in general. By "nature" or by "definition," courts are "those tribunals which are established for the security of property and to decide on human rights." Such rights are contained either in explicit constitutional provisions and amendments, or in "unwritten or common law," which the Constitution presupposes as the substratum of our law (and which Marshall thought was spelled out in traditional law books, such as Sir WIL-LIAM BLACKSTONE's *Commentaries on the Laws of England*). In short, courts are to construe all law in the light of the rights of person and property that are the object of law—as well as in the light of the constitutional authority of the other branches.

Marshall was fond of contrasting the Americans' "rational liberty," which afforded "solid safety and real security," with revolutionary France's "visionary" civic liberty, which had led to a despotism "borrowing the garb and usurping the name of freedom." While trying AARON BURR, Marshall repeatedly noted the "tenderness" of American law for the rights of the accused. His *Life of Washington* mixes praise of FREEDOM OF SPEECH and of conscience with attacks on religious persecution. Yet Marshall also said that morals and free institutions need to be "cherished" by public opinion; he would not suppose that a free MARKETPLACE OF IDEAS insures progress in public enlightenment. He did suppose that a rather free economic marketplace would lead to progress in national wealth. Marshall defended property rights in the sense of rights of contract or vested rights, rights that vest under contract and originate in a right to the fruits of one's labor and enterprise. By protecting industrious acquisitions the judiciary fosters the dynamic economy of free enterprise. Rational liberty is prudent liberty, which breeds power as well as wealth: the "legitimate greatness" of a "widespreading, rising empire," extending from "the Ste. Croix to the Gulph of Mexico, from the Atlantic to the Pacific." By directly securing the rights of property, courts indirectly secure the "vast republic."

While courts are "the mere instruments of the law, and can will nothing," or at most possess a legal discretion governed by unwritten principles of individual rights, the executive and legislature enjoy broad political discretion for the safety and interrelation of all. President and Congress are indeed subordinate to the Constitution of ENUMERATED POWERS and explicit restrictions. Marshall did not follow ALEXANDER HAMILTON, and would not have followed some later Supreme Courts, in inferring a plenary legislative power. His arguments, however, take aim at enemies on the other flank, at Jeffersonian strict constructionists who allowed only powers explicit in the Constitution or necessarily deduced from explicit powers. A constitution of government is not a "legal code," Marshall replied, and its enumerated powers are vested fully and encompass the full panoply of appropriate means. In *McCulloch*, Marshall set forth the core of the American doctrine of SOVEREIGNTY: the need for great governmental powers to confront inevitable crises. Maryland had placed a prohibitive tax on a branch of the national bank, and its counsel denied federal authority to charter a bank (a power not explicit in the Constitution). Ours is a constitution, Marshall replied, "intended to endure for ages to come, and, consequently, to be adapted to the various *crises* of human affairs." Armies must be marched and taxes raised throughout the land. "Is that construction of the Constitution to be preferred which would render these operations difficult, hazardous, and expensive?" In a similar spirit Marshall defended an executive vigorous in war and FOREIGN AFFAIRS and able to overawe faction and rebellion at home. He struck down, as violating Congress's power to regulate commerce among the states, state acts imposing import taxes or reserving monopolistic privileges. The arguments are typical. Great powers are granted for great objects. A narrow interpretation would defeat the object: the words must be otherwise construed. Thus a nation is raised. Individual enterprise, a national flow of trade, and the bonds of mutual interest breach barriers of state, section, and custom. The machinery of government is geared for great efforts of direction and coercion. The national sovereign, limited in its tasks, supreme in all means needed for their accomplishment, rises over the once independent state sovereignties. Marshall acknowledged the states' independent powers as well as the complexities of federalism: America was "for many purposes an entire nation, and for others several distinct and independent sovereignties." He tried above all to protect the federal government's superior powers from what the Framers had most feared, the encroachments of the states, more strongly entrenched in the people's affections.

Like virtually all of the Framers, Marshall was devoted to popular government. Yet SHAYS' REBELLION of western Massachusetts farmers (1786–1787) had made him wonder whether "man is incapable of governing himself." He thought the new Constitution a republican remedy for the flaws of republican government, and for some time he thought constitutional restraints might suffice to rein the people to sound government. Marshall's republicanism encompassed both representative government and balanced government. The people are to grant their sovereignty to institutions for exercise by their representatives. A more substantial, virtuous, and enlightened Senate and President would balance the more popular House of Representatives, the dangerous house in a popular republic. Marshall came to be troubled by a decline in the quality of American leaders, from the great statesmen of the Revolution and founding, notably Washington, to the "superficial showy acquirements" of "party politicians." He came to be deeply disheartened by the tumultuous growth of democratic control, inspired by THOMAS JEFFERSON and consummated by ANDREW JACKSON. A "torrent of public opinion," inflamed by the French Revolution, aroused the old debtor and STATES' RIGHTS party during Washington's administration. It led to democratic societies, set up to watch the government, and then to a legislature that conveyed popular demands without much filtering. Marshall

had anticipated that Jefferson would ally himself with the House of Representatives, and become leader of the party dominating the whole legislature, thus increasing his own power while weakening the office of President and the fundamentals of balanced government. During Jackson's terms (1828–1836), with the presidency transformed from a check on the majority to the tribune of the majority, Marshall favored reduction of its power, a tenure limited to one term, and even selection of the President by lot from among the senators. He called his early republicanism "wild and enthusiastic democracy," and came to doubt that the constitutional Union could endure in the face of resurgent sectionalism and populism.

The eventual dissolution of political balances made crucial Marshall's decisive accomplishment as he and Jefferson began their terms of office: the confirmation of the judiciary as interpreter and enforcer of the fundamental law. Although Marshall's opinion in *Marbury* denied that courts can exercise political power, it gave courts power to circumscribe the forbidden sphere, to determine the powers of legislatures and executives. Marshall's argument for this unprecedented judicial authority recalled "certain principles . . . long and well established." In deciding cases judges must declare what the law is. The Constitution is the supreme law. Judges must apply the Constitution in preference to statute when the two conflict—else the Constitution is not permanent but "alterable when the legislature shall please to alter it." The argument established the Supreme Court as enforcer of the constitutional government central to America's constitutional democracy. Marshall pointed to the horrors of "legislative omnipotence," only inconspicuously bestowing on courts a ruling potency as the voice of the Constitution. Marshall's opinion, the object of intense scrutiny ever since, was faithful to the CONSTITUTIONAL CONVENTION's supposition that there will be some JUDICIAL REVIEW of statutes and to its suspicion of democratic legislatures. It did not confront certain difficulties, notably those of a Supreme Court (like the TANEY COURT in DRED SCOTT V. SANDFORD, 1857) whose decisions violate the principles of the Constitution. Marshall's judicial reasonings were his attempt to keep judges, and his country, from violating the Constitution that preserves those principles.

ROBERT K. FAULKNER
(1986)

Bibliography

BEVERIDGE, ALBERT J. 1916–1919 *The Life of John Marshall.* 4 Vols. Boston: Houghton Mifflin.

CORWIN, EDWARD S. 1919 *John Marshall and the Constitution.* New Haven, Conn.: Yale University Press.

FAULKNER, ROBERT K. 1968 *The Jurisprudence of John Marshall.* Princeton, N.J.: Princeton University Press.

HOLMES, OLIVER WENDELL 1952 John Marshall. Pages 266–271 in *Collected Legal Papers*. New York: Peter Smith.

WHITE, G. EDWARD 1976 *The American Judicial Tradition*. Pages 7–34. New York: Oxford University Press.

ZIEGLER, BENJAMIN MUNN 1939 *The International Law of John Marshall*. Chapel Hill: University of North Carolina Press.

MARSHALL, THURGOOD
(1908–)

Thurgood Marshall, the first black Justice of the Supreme Court, was born in Baltimore in 1908. After graduation from Lincoln University in Pennsylvania, Marshall attended Howard University Law School. Graduating first in his class in 1933, Marshall became one of CHARLES H. HOUSTON's protégés. He began practice in Baltimore, where he helped revitalize the local branch of the National Association for the Advancement of Colored People (NAACP). Houston, who had become special counsel to the NAACP in New York, was developing a program of litigation designed to attack segregated education in the South; Marshall joined the NAACP staff as Houston's assistant in 1936.

Of all the Justices who have served on the Supreme Court, Marshall has the strongest claim to having contributed as much to the development of the Constitution as a lawyer as he has done as a judge. At the start of his career, race relations law centered on the SEPARATE BUT EQUAL DOCTRINE. In his initial years at the NAACP, Marshall brought a number of lawsuits challenging unequal salaries paid to black and white teachers in the South. After Marshall succeeded Houston as special counsel in 1938, he became both a litigator and a coordinator of litigation, most of it challenging segregated education. He also successfully argued a number of cases involving RACIAL DISCRIMINATION in the administration of criminal justice before the Supreme Court. When social and political changes during WORLD WAR II led to increased black militancy and support for the NAACP, Marshall was able to expand the NAACP's legal staff by hiring an extremely talented group of young, mostly black lawyers. Although he continued to conduct some litigation, Marshall gradually assumed the roles of appellate advocate and overall strategist. Relying on his staff to generate helpful legal theories, he selected the theory most likely to accomplish the NAACP's goals. This process culminated in the five lawsuits decided by the Supreme Court as BROWN V. BOARD OF EDUCATION (1954). Marshall had used his staff to develop these cases and the legal theory that segregation was unconstitutional no matter how equal were the physical facilities. After the Supreme Court held that segregation was unconstitutional and that it should be eliminated "with ALL DELIBERATE SPEED," Marshall and the NAACP staff devoted much of their attention to overcoming the impediments that southern states began to place in the way of DESEGREGATION. These impediments included school closures and investigations and harassment of the NAACP and its lawyers.

Marshall left the NAACP in 1961, having been nominated by President JOHN F. KENNEDY to a position on the UNITED STATES COURT OF APPEALS for the Second Circuit. His confirmation to that position was delayed by southern opposition for over eleven months. During Marshall's four years on the Second Circuit, he wrote an important opinion holding that the DOUBLE JEOPARDY clause applied to the states, anticipating by four years the position that the Supreme Court would adopt in BENTON V. MARYLAND (1969), a decision written by Justice Marshall. He also urged in dissent an expansive interpretation of statutes allowing persons charged with crimes in state courts to remove those cases to federal court. (See CIVIL RIGHTS REMOVAL.) Marshall was nominated as solicitor general by President LYNDON B. JOHNSON in 1965. He served as solicitor general for two years, during which he supervised the disposition of criminal cases imperiled by illegal WIRETAPPING. Johnson appointed him in 1967 to succeed Justice TOM C. CLARK on the Supreme Court.

Justice Marshall's contributions to constitutional development have been shaped by the fact that for most of his tenure his views were among the most liberal on a centrist or conservative Court. As he had at the NAACP, and as have most recent Justices, Marshall relied heavily on his staff to present his views forcefully and systematically in his opinions.

For a few years after Marshall's appointment to the Court, he was part of the liberal bloc of the WARREN COURT. Despite the tradition that newly appointed Justices are not assigned important majority opinions, Justice Marshall wrote several important free speech opinions during his first two years on the Court. In STANLEY V. GEORGIA (1969), he held that a state could not punish a person merely for possessing obscene materials in his home; the only justification for such punishment, guaranteeing a citizenry that did not think impure thoughts, was barred by the First Amendment. *Amalgamated Food Employees Union v. Logan Valley Plaza* (1968) recognized the contemporary importance of privately owned SHOPPING CENTERS as places of public resort, holding that centers must be made available, over their owners' objections, to those who wish to picket or pass out leaflets on subjects of public interest. *Pickering v. Board of Education* (1968) established the right of public employees to complain about the way in which their superiors were discharging their responsibilities to the public.

With the appointment of four Justices by President

RICHARD M. NIXON, Justice Marshall rapidly found himself in dissent on major civil liberties issues. *Stanley* was limited by *United States v. Reidel* (1971) to private possession and not extended to what might have seemed its logical corollary, acquisition of obscene material for private use. *Logan Valley Plaza* was overruled in HUDGENS V. NATIONAL LABOR RELATIONS BOARD (1976), and *Pickering* was limited by a relatively narrow definition of complaints relating to public duties in *Connick v. Myers* (1983). Marshall became part of a small liberal bloc that could prevail only by attracting more conservative members, who could be kept in the coalition by allowing them to write the majority opinions. In the series of death penalty cases, for example, Justice Marshall stated his conclusion that capital punishment was unconstitutional in all circumstances, but when a majority for a narrower position could be found to overturn the imposition of the death penalty in a particular case, he joined that majority.

Thus, after 1970, Marshall rarely wrote important opinions for the Court regarding FREEDOM OF SPEECH, CRIMINAL PROCEDURE, or EQUAL PROTECTION. Two of his opinions in cases about the PREEMPTION of state law by federal regulations, *Jones v. Rath Packing Co.* (1977) and *Douglas v. Seacoast Products* (1977), seem likely to endure as statements of general principle. More often he was assigned to write opinions in which a nearly unanimous Court adopted a "conservative" position. For example, in *Gillette v. United States* (1971), Justice Marshall's opinion for the Court rejected statutory and constitutional claims to exemption from the military draft by men whose religious beliefs led them to oppose participation in some but not all wars. Undoubtedly because of his race and because of his desire to see a majority support positions helpful to blacks, Marshall rarely wrote important opinions in cases directly implicating matters of race, although he did write two significant dissents, one defending AFFIRMATIVE ACTION in REGENTS OF THE UNIVERSITY OF CALIFORNIA V. BAKKE (1978), and another emphasizing blacks' lack of access to political power in MOBILE V. BOLDEN (1980). But Justice Marshall's major contributions have come in areas where the experience of race has historically shaped the context in which apparently nonracial issues arise.

Marshall occasionally received the assignment in important civil liberties cases. His opinion in POLICE DEPARTMENT OF CHICAGO V. MOSLEY (1972) crystallized the equality theme in the law of freedom of speech. There he emphasized the importance for free expression of the rule that governments may not regulate one type of speech because of its content, in a setting where speech with a different content would not be regulated: "[G]overnment may not grant the use of a forum to people whose views it finds acceptable, but deny use to those wishing to express less favored or more controversial views . . . Selective exclusions . . . may not be based on content alone, and may not be justified by reference to content alone." Unless it were prohibited, discrimination based on content would allow governments, which ought to be controlled by the electorate, to determine what the electorate would hear. Although the *Mosley* principle is probably stated too broadly, because differential regulation of categories of speech such as OBSCENITY or COMMERCIAL SPEECH is allowed, still it serves as a central starting point for analysis, from which departures must be justified.

His opinion in *Memorial Hospital v. Maricopa County* (1974) synthesized a line of cases regarding the circumstances in which a state might deny benefits such as nonemergency medical care for INDIGENTS to those who had recently come to the state. If the benefit was so important that its denial could be characterized as a penalty for exercising the RIGHT TO TRAVEL, it was unconstitutional.

Because of the relatively rapid shift in the Court's composition, most of Justice Marshall's major contributions to the constitutional development have come through dissents. Several major dissenting opinions by Justice Marshall have helped shape the law of equal protection. The opinions criticize a rigid approach in which classifications based on race and a few other categories are to be given STRICT SCRUTINY while all other classifications must be "merely rational." Marshall, in dissents in DANDRIDGE V. WILLIAMS (1970) and SAN ANTONIO INDEPENDENT SCHOOL DISTRICT V. RODRIGUEZ (1973), offered a more flexible approach. He argued that the courts should examine legislation that affects different groups differently by taking into account the nature of the group—the degree to which it has been discriminated against in the past, the actual access to political power it has today—and the importance of the interests affected. Under this "sliding scale" approach, a statute differentially affecting access to WELFARE BENEFITS might be unconstitutional while one with the same effects on access to public recreational facilities might be permitted. A majority of the Court has not explicitly adopted the "sliding scale" approach, but Justice Marshall's sustained criticisms of the rigid alternative have produced a substantial, though not entirely acknowledged, acceptance of a more nuanced approach to equal protection problems.

As *Logan Valley Plaza* showed, Justice Marshall has urged, usually in dissent, an expansive definition of those actors whose decisions are subject to constitutional control. In JACKSON V. METROPOLITAN EDISON CO. (1974) the majority found that the decision of a heavily regulated utility to terminate service for nonpayment was not "state action" under any of the several strands of that DOCTRINE. Justice Marshall's dissent argued that state involvement was significant when looked at as a whole and, more important, pointed out that on the majority's analysis the utility could, without constitutional problems, terminate service to blacks. On the assumption, confirmed in later cases, that the result is incorrect, Justice Marshall's argument effectively demonstrated that the "state action" doctrine is actually a doctrine about the merits of the challenged decision: if it is a decision that the Justices believe should not be controlled by the Constitution, there is no "state action," whereas if it is a decision that the Justices believe should be controlled by the Constitution, there is state action.

Finally, after joining the seminal opinion in GOLDBERG V. KELLY (1968), which held that the Constitution defined the procedures under which public benefits, the "new property" of the welfare state, could be taken away, Justice Marshall dissented in later cases where the Court substantially narrowed the scope of *Goldberg*. His position, in cases such as BOARD OF REGENTS V. ROTH (1972), has been that everyone must be presumed to be entitled to those benefits, and that the presumption can be overcome only after constitutionality-defined procedures have been followed.

In most of the areas of law to which Justice Marshall's opinions have made significant contributions the linked strands of race and poverty appear. Discrimination by nominally private actors and suppression of speech on racial issues have played an important part in the black experience. Similarly, wealth and poverty as grounds for allocating public resources are classifications closely linked to race. Justice Marshall's desire to adopt a more flexible approach to equal protection law stems from his awareness that only such an approach would allow the courts to address difficulties that the ordinary routines of society cause for the poor. For example, his dissent in *United States v. Kras* (1973) objected to the imposition of a fifty dollar filing fee on those who sought discharges of their debts in bankruptcy. But it would be misleading to conclude that Thurgood Marshall's most important role in constitutional development was what he did as a Justice of the Supreme Court. Rather it was what he did as a lawyer for the NAACP before and after the decision in *Brown v. Board of Education.*

MARK TUSHNET
(1986)

Bibliography
KLUGER, RICHARD 1976 *Simple Justice.* New York: Knopf.

MARSHALL, THURGOOD
(1908–1993)
(Update)

Thurgood Marshall has earned a unique place in American history on the basis of a long, varied, and influential career as a private attorney, governement lawyer, and appellate jurist. Two achievements in particular stand out. First, as counsel for the National Association for the Advancement of Colored People (NAACP), he has shaped the litigation that destroyed the constitutional legitimacy of state-enforced racial SEGREGATION. Second, as an Associate justice of the Supreme Court—the nation's first black Justice—he boldly articulated a liberal jurisprudence on a Court dominated by conservatives. No person in the history of the Supreme Court better illustrates the limits and possibilities of the jurist as dissenter.

Marshall was born July 2, 1908, in Baltimore, Maryland, attended that city's racially segregated public schools, and was graduated from Lincoln University. Excluded from the University of Maryland Law School by that state's racial policies, he received his law degree from Howard Law School. He excelled at Howard and came to the attention of the school's dean, CHARLES H. HOUSTON, a pioneer in the use of litigation as a vehicle of social reform. Although Marshall embarked on a conventional commercial practice upon graduation, he also participated, under Houston's guidance, in important, albeit unremunerative, CIVIL RIGHTS cases. Appropriately enough, his first consisted of a successful suit against the same state university system that had earlier excluded him. In *Murray v. Maryland* (1937) Marshall convinced the Court of Appeals of Maryland that the Constitution required the state to do more for black residents seeking legal education than merely offer them scholarships to attend out-of-state law schools.

In 1939 Marshall succeeded Houston as special counsel of the NAACP. Over the next two decades he traveled ceaselessly, addressing problems of racial inequality in a wide array of settings: from obscure local courts in which he sought to extract from hostile juries and judges a measure of justice for black defendants, to Korea where he investigated the treatment of black soldiers by United States military authorities, to black churches and lodges where he encouraged people in aggrieved communities to seek to vindicate their rights. He also argued thirty-two cases before the Supreme Court, prevailing in twenty-nine of them. His brilliant advocacy helped to convince the Supreme Court to invalidate practices that excluded blacks from primary elections (SMITH V. ALLWRIGHT), to prohibit segregation in interstate transportation (MORGAN V. VIRGINIA), to overturn convictions obtained from juries from which blacks had been illicitly barred (PATTON V. MISSISSIPPI), and to prohibit state courts from enforcing racially restrictive real estate covenants (SHELLEY V. KRAEMER). Marshall's greatest triumph arose from the skillfully orchestrated litigation that culminated in BROWN V. BOARD OF EDUCATION (1954), which invalidated state-enforced racial segregation in public schooling. By the close of the 1950s, Marshall had attained widespread recognition as a leading public figure and was known affectionately in much of black America as "Mr. Civil Rights."

The next stage in Marshall's career was marked by a series of high-level appointments. In 1961, President JOHN F. KENNEDY appointed him to the United States Court of Appeals for the Second Circuit over the strong objections of segregationist senators who delayed his confirmation for nearly a year. In 1965, President LYNDON B. JOHNSON appointed Marshall SOLICITOR GENERAL of the United States. The first black American to hold this post, Marshall argued several important cases before the Court, including MIRANDA V. ARIZONA (1966), in which he successfully urged the Court to impose greater limitations on the power of police to interrogate criminal suspects; HARPER V. VIRGINIA STATE BOARD OF ELECTIONS (1966), in which he successfully argued that state POLL TAXES violated the federal Constitution; and UNITED STATES V. GUEST (1966), in which he successfully defended the federal prosecution of white supremacists in Georgia who committed a racially motivated murder during the era of the CIVIL RIGHTS MOVEMENT.

In 1967, President Johnson set the stage for Marshall to cross the color line in another area of governmental service when he named him to a seat on the Supreme Court. Marshall's elevation vividly symbolized the ascendancy of values and interests he had long sought to advance. At the outset of Marshall's career on the Court, it was presided over by Chief Justice EARL WARREN and animated by a decidedly reformist ethos. Ironically, however, the liberal wing whose ranks Marshall fortified began to disintegrate soon after he took his seat. By the mid-1970s, the appointments of Chief Justice WARREN E. BURGER and associate Justices LEWIS F. POWELL and WILLIAM H. REHNQUIST had brought to the fore a conservative ethos that has long confined Justice Marshall to the periphery of judicial power.

During his years on the Court, Justice Marshall has seldom held sway in the middle as a "swing" vote. Rather, he has made his mark as a judicial maverick—always independent, consistently bold, frequently dissenting. Keenly attentive to allegations of INVIDIOUS DISCRIMINATION, Justice Marshall has been strongly favorable to the claims of members of historically oppressed groups. However, he has repeatedly found himself at odds with the Court. MEMPHIS V. GREENE (1981) involved a city's decision to close a street, mainly used by blacks, which traversed a predominantly white neighborhood. The Court upheld the legality of the city's action. Justice Marshall perceived a violation of the THIRTEENTH AMENDMENT, concluding that the city's action constituted a racially prejudiced "badge or incident of slavery." PERSONNEL ADMINISTRATOR OF MASSACHUSETTS V. FEENEY (1979) called into question a state law that provided an absolute preference for veterans of the ARMED FORCES in civil service positions, a system of selection that tended overwhelmingly to disadvantage women in relation to men. The Court upheld the statute. Justice Marshall condemned it as a violation of the EQUAL PROTECTION clause of the FOURTEENTH AMENDMENT. MOBILE V. BOLDEN (1980) concerned an at-large voting scheme under which, for almost seventy years, no black had ever been elected to a seat on the ruling city commission in Mobile, Alabama, even though blacks constituted nearly a third of the city's population. The Court held that this electoral arrangement could be invalidated only if it were used as a vehicle of purposeful discrimination. Justice Marshall concluded that the system's racially disparate impact violated the FIFTEENTH AMENDMENT. ROSTKER V. GOLDBERG (1981) brought into question the constitutionality of a federal statute that requires men but not women to register for the military draft. Differing with the majority of his colleagues, Justice Marshall declared that the Court erred in placing its "imprimatur on one of the most potent remaining public expressions of "ancient canards about the proper role of women."

Critical of the Court for showing too little solicitude for those who have been historically victimized on the basis of race and gender, Justice Marshall has also rebuked the Court for displaying undue aggressiveness in defending the asserted rights of those who challenge affirmative action policies that provide preferences to women and racial minorities. Sharply distinguishing between benign and invidious discrimination, he has voted to uphold every AFFIRMATIVE ACTION plan the Court has reviewed. Here, too, he has been forced into dissent, objecting bitterly to decisions that have increasingly limited the permissible scope of affirmative action measures. In REGENTS OF UNIVERSITY OF CALIFORNIA V. BAKKE (1978), the first affirmative action case that the Court resolved, Justice Marshall declared that "It must be remembered that during most of the past 200 years, the Constitution as interpreted by the [Supreme] Court did not prohibit the most ingenious and pervasive forms of discrimination against the Negro. Now, when a State acts to remedy the effects of that legacy of discrimination, I cannot believe that this same Constitution stands as a barrier."

A decade later, Justice Marshall continued to rail against an interpretation of the Fourteenth Amendment that he considers perverse. In RICHMOND V. J. A. CROSON CO. (1989), for instance, he dissented against a ruling that invalidated Richmond, Virginia's policy of reserving that for enterprises owned by racial minorities a designated percentage of business generated by the city. Observing that "It is a welcome symbol of racial progress when the former capital of the Confederacy acts forthrightly to confront the effects of RACIAL DISCRIMINATION in its midst," he angrily chided his colleagues for taking "a deliberate and giant step backward." The Court's decision, he predicted, "will inevitably discourage or prevent governmental entities, particularly States and localities, from acting to rectify the scourge of past discrimination. This is the harsh reality of the majority's decision, but it is not the Constitution's command."

Other areas in which Justice Marshall's strongly held views have frequently been at odds with the Court's conclusions involve CAPITAL PUNISHMENT, ABORTION and the legal status of the poor—areas in which Marshall's jurisprudential commitments frequently overlap. Insisting that death penalties under all circumstances violate the Eighth Amendment's prohibition against CRUEL AND UNUSUAL PUNISHMENT, Justice Marshall has filed dissents against all executions that the Court has sanctioned. In AKE V. OKLAHOMA (1985), his advocacy on behalf of those charged with capital crimes succeeded in wringing from his colleagues a rare broadening of rights to which criminal defendants are entitled. Writing for the Court, Justice Marshall held that, at least in cases possibly involving the death penalty, DUE PROCESS requires states to afford indigent defendants the means to obtain needed psychiatric experts.

With respect to abortion, Justice Marshall has been among the most stalwart defenders of ROE V. WADE (1973), dissenting in every case in which the Court has upheld legislative inroads on what he views as a woman's broad right to decide whether or not to terminate a pregnancy. An example of his allegiance to *Roe v. Wade* (1973) is his dissenting opinion in MAHER V. ROE (1977), where he maintained that a state violated the Constitution by denying poor women funding for abortions while making funds available to them for expenses of childbirth. "Since efforts to overturn [*Roe v. Wade*] have been unsuccessful," he charged, "the opponents of abortion have attempted every imaginable means to circumvent the commands of the Constitution and impose their moral choices upon the rest of society." Articulating his anger with characteristic sharpness, Justice Marshall asserted that this case involved "the most vicious attacks yet devised" in that they fell on poor women—"those among us least able to help or defend themselves."

Throughout Justice Marshall's career on the Court he has vigorously attempted to improve the legal status of the poor. He has argued, for instance, that the federal courts should subject to heightened scrutiny state laws that explicitly discriminate on the basis of poverty. For the most part, however, his efforts have been stymied. One particularly memorable expression of Justice Marshall's empathy for the indigent is his dissent in *United States v. Kras* (1973), a case in which the Court held that federal law did not violate the Constitution by requiring a $50 fee of persons seeking the protections of bankruptcy. Objecting to the Court's assumption that the petitioner could readily accumulate this amount, Justice Marshall wrote that he could not agree with the majority

> that it is so easy for the desperately poor to save $1.92 *each week* over the course of six months. . . . The 1970 Census found that over 800,000 families in the Nation had annual incomes of less than $1,000 or $19.23 a week. . . . I see no reason to require that families in such straits sacrifice over 5% of their annual income as a prerequisite to getting a discharge in bankruptcy. . . . It may be easy for some people to think that weekly savings of less than $2 are no burden. But no one who has had close contact with poor people can fail to understand how close to the margin of survival many of them are. . . . It is perfectly proper for judges to disagree about what the Constitution requires. But it is disgraceful for an interpretation of the Constitution to be premised upon unfounded assumptions about how people live.

On occasion Justice Marshall's dissents have succeeded in changing the mind of the Court. An example is the Court's response to claims of racially invidious discrimination in peremptory challenges. In SWAIN V. ALABAMA (1965) the Court had ruled that prosecutors could properly use race as a basis for peremptorily excluding potential jurors so long as they did so as a matter of strategy relating to a particular trial and not for the purpose of barring blacks routinely from participation in the administration of justice. By repeatedly dissenting from orders in which the Court refused to reconsider *Swain* and by showing in detail this decision's dismal practical consequences, Marshall finally convinced the Court to reverse itself—though even when it did in BATSON V. KENTUCKY (1986), Marshall still maintained that his colleagues had neglected to go far enough in ridding the criminal justice system of invidious practices.

For much of Justice Marshall's career on the bench, he seems to have deliberately avoided any extrajudicial controversies. Beginning in the 1980s, however, he appears to have altered his habits. He publicly criticized RONALD REAGAN, declaring that his civil rights record as President of the United States was among the worst in the twentieth century. He also chided President GEORGE BUSH for selecting DAVID H. SOUTER to occupy the seat on the Court vacated by Justice Marshall's long-time ally, Justice WILLIAM J. BRENNAN. In an unprecedented action, Justice Marshall declared on a televised broadcast that, in his view, the President's choice was inappropriate.

Although Justice Marshall recieved considerable criticism for his comments on Presidents Regan and Bush, extrajudicial remarks that generated an even greater amount of contraversy stemmed from a speech that he gave in 1987 in the midst of the bicentenial celebration of the United States Constitution. Bodly challenging the iconography of American CONSTITUTIONALISM, he asserted that he did not find "the wisdom, foresight, and sense of justice exhibited by the framers [to be] particularly profound. To the contrary," he declared, "the government they devised was defective from the start," omitting, for example, blacks and women as protected members of the polity. Eschewing "flag waving fervor," Justice Marshall noted his intention to commemerate the bicentennial by recalling "the suffering, struggle, and sacrifice that has triumphed over much of what was wrong with the original document" and by also acknowleging the Constitution's unfulfilled promise.

Some detractors fault Justice Marshall on the grounds that his penchant for dissent has robbed him of influence that he might otherwise have wielded. Judging influence, however, is a dangerous endeavor. Justices JOHN MARSHALL HARLAN, OLIVER WENDELL HOLMES, JR., and LOUIS D. BRANDEIS are as well respected on the basis of their dissenting opinions as they are respected for any other aspect of their illustrious careers. History may well bequeath the same fate to Justice Thurgood Marshall. Justice Marshall resigned from the Court in 1991.

RANDALL KENNEDY
(1992)

(SEE ALSO: *Badges of Servitude; NAACP Legal Defense Fund; Race and Criminal Justice; Race-Consciousness*.)

MARSHALL v. BARLOW'S, INC.
436 U.S. 307 (1978)

In *Marshall* the Supreme Court held unconstitutional a congressional enactment authorizing Occupational Safety and Health Administration inspectors to conduct WARRANTLESS SEARCHES of employment facilities to monitor compliance with regulations. PROBABLE CAUSE for a warrant can, however, be satisfied on a lesser showing than that required in a search for criminal EVIDENCE.

JACOB W. LANDYNSKI
(1986)

MARSHALL COURT
(1801–1835)

In 1801 the Supreme Court existed on the fringe of American awareness. Its prestige was slight, and it was more ignored than respected. On January 20, 1801, the day President JOHN ADAMS nominated JOHN MARSHALL for the chief justiceship, the commissioners of the DISTRICT OF COLUMBIA informed Congress that the Court had no place to hold its February term. The Senate consented to the use of one of its committee rooms, and Marshall took his

seat on February 4 in a small basement chamber. At the close of 1809, Benjamin Latrobe, the architect, reported that the basement had been redesigned to enlarge the courtroom and provide an office for the clerk and a library room for the Justices. In 1811, however, Latrobe reported that the Court "had been obliged to hold their sittings in a tavern," because Congress had appropriated no money for "fitting up and furnishing the Court-room. . . ." After the British burned the Capitol in 1814 Congress again neglected to provide for the Court. It held its 1815 term in a private home, and for several years after met in temporary Capitol quarters that were "little better than a dungeon." The Court moved into permanent quarters in 1819. In 1824 a New York correspondent described the Court's Capitol chamber: "In the first place, it is like going down cellar to reach it. The room is on the basement story in an obscure part of the north wing. . . . A stranger might traverse the dark avenues of the Capitol for a week, without finding the remote corner in which Justice is administered to the American Republic." He added that the courtroom was hardly large enough for a police court.

The Supreme Court, however, no longer lacked dignity or respect. It had become a force that commanded recognition. In 1819 a widely read weekly described it as so awesome that some regarded it with reverence. That year THOMAS JEFFERSON complained that the Court had made the Constitution a "thing of wax," which it shaped as it pleased, and in 1824 he declared that the danger he most feared was the Court's "consolidation of our government." Throughout the 1820s Congress debated bills to curb the Court, which, said a senator, the people blindly adored— a "self-destroying idolatry." ALEXIS DE TOCQUEVILLE, writing in 1831, said: "The peace, the prosperity, and the very existence of the Union are vested in the hands of the seven Federal judges. Without them, the Constitution would be a dead letter. . . ." Hardly a political question arose, he wrote, that did not become a judicial question.

Chief Justice Marshall was not solely responsible for the radical change in the Court's status and influence, but he made the difference. He bequeathed to the people of the United States what it was not in the political power of the Framers of the Constitution to give. Had the Framers been free agents, they would have proposed a national government that was unquestionably dominant over the states and possessed a formidable array of powers breathtaking in flexibility and scope. Marshall in more than a figurative sense was the supreme Framer, emancipated from a local constituency, boldly using his judicial position as an exalted platform from which to educate the nation to the true meaning, his meaning, of the Constitution. He wrote as if words of grandeur and power and union could make dreams come true. By the force of his convictions he tried to will a nation into being.

He reshaped the still malleable Constitution, giving clarification to its ambiguities and content to its omissions that would allow it to endure for "ages to come" and would make the government of the Union supreme in the federal system. Marshall is the only judge in our history whose distinction as a great nationalist statesman derives wholly from his judicial career. Justice OLIVER WENDELL HOLMES once remarked, "If American law were to be represented by a single figure, sceptic and worshipper alike would agree without dispute that the figure could be one alone, and that one, John Marshall." That the Court had remained so weak after a decade of men of such high caliber as JOHN JAY, OLIVER ELLSWORTH, JAMES WILSON, JAMES IREDELL, WILLIAM PATERSON, and SAMUEL CHASE demonstrates not their weakness but Marshall's achievement in making the Court an equal branch of the national government.

Until 1807 he cast but one of six votes, and after 1807, when Congress added another Justice, but one of seven. One Justice, one vote has always been the rule of the Court, and the powers of anyone who is Chief Justice depend more on the person than the office. From 1812, BUSHROD WASHINGTON and Marshall were the only surviving Federalists, surrounded by five Justices appointed by Presidents Thomas Jefferson and JAMES MADISON; yet Marshall dominated the Court in a way that no one has ever since. During Marshall's thirty-five-year tenure, the Court delivered 1,106 opinions in all fields of law, and he wrote 519; he dissented only eight times. He wrote forty of the Court's sixty-four opinions in the field of constitutional law, dissenting only once in a constitutional case. Of the twenty-four constitutional opinions for the Court that he did not write, only two were important: MARTIN V. HUNTER'S LESSEE (1816), a case in which he did not sit, and OGDEN V. SAUNDERS (1827), the case in which he dissented. He virtually monopolized the constitutional cases for himself and won the support of his associates, even though they were members of the opposing political party.

Marshall's long tenure coincided with the formative period of our constitutional law. He was in the right place at the right time, filling, as Holmes said, "a strategic place in the campaign of history." But it took the right man to make the most of the opportunity. Marshall had the character, intellect, and passion for his job that his predecessors lacked. He had a profound sense of mission comparable to a religious "calling." Convinced that he knew what the Constitution should mean and what it was meant to achieve, he determined to give its purposes enduring expression and make them prevail. The Court was, for him, a judicial pulpit and political platform from which to address the nation, to compete, if possible, with the executive and legislative in shaping public opinion.

Marshall met few of the abstract criteria for a "great" judge. A great judge should possess intellectual rectitude and brilliance. Marshall was a fierce and crafty partisan who manipulated facts and law. A great judge should have a self-conscious awareness of his biases and a determination to be as detached as human fallibility will allow. In Marshall the judicial temperament flickered weakly; unable to muzzle his deepest convictions, he sought to impose them on the nation, sure that he was right. He intoxicated himself with the belief that truth, history, and the Constitution dictated his opinions, which merely declared the law rather than made the law. A great judge should have confidence in majority rule, tempered by his commitment to personal freedom and fairness. Marshall did not think men capable of self-government and inclined to favor financial and industrial capitalism over most other interests. A great judge should have a superior technical proficiency, modified by a sense of justice and ethical behavior beyond suspicion. Marshall's judicial ethics were not unquestionable. He should have disqualified himself in MARBURY V. MADISON (1803) because of his negligent complicity. He overlooked colossal corruption in FLETCHER V. PECK (1810) to decide a land title case by a doctrine that promoted his personal interests. He wrote the opinion in MCCULLOCH V. MARYLAND (1819) before hearing the case. Marshall's "juridical learning," as Justice JOSEPH STORY, his reverent admirer and closest colleague, conceded, "was not equal to that of the great masters in the profession. . . ." He was, said Story, first, last, and always, "a Federalist of the good old school," and in the maintenance of its principles "he was ready at all times to stand forth a determined advocate and supporter." He was, in short, a Federalist activist who used the Constitution to legitimate predetermined results. A great judge should have a vision of national and moral greatness, combined with respect for the federal system. Marshall had that—and an instinct for statecraft and superb literary skills. These qualities, as well as his activism, his partisanship, and his sense of mission, contributed to his inordinate influence.

So too did his qualities of leadership and his personal traits. He was generous, gentle, warm, charming, considerate, congenial, and open. At a time when members of the Court lived together in a common boarding house during their short terms in Washington, his charismatic personality enabled him to preside over a judicial family, inspire loyalty, and convert his brethren to his views. He had a cast-iron will, an astounding capacity for hard work (witness the number of opinions he wrote for the Court), and formidable powers of persuasion. He thought audaciously in terms of broad and basic principles that he expressed axiomatically as absolutes. His arguments were masterful intellectual performances, assuming that his premises were valid. Inexorably and with developing momentum he moved from an unquestioned premise to a foregone conclusion. Jefferson once said that he never admitted anything when conversing with Marshall. "So sure as you admit any position to be good, no matter how remote from the conclusion he seeks to establish, you are gone." Marshall's sophistry, according to Jefferson, was so great, "you must never give him an affirmative answer or you will be forced to grant his conclusion. Why, if he were to ask me if it were daylight or not, I'd reply, "Sir, I don't know. I can't tell." Marshall could also be imperious. He sometimes gave as the OPINION OF THE COURT a position that had not mustered a majority. According to one anecdote, Marshall is supposed to have said to Story, the greatest legal scholar in our history, "That, Story, is the law. You find the precedents."

The lengthy tenure of the members of the Marshall Court also accounts for its achievements. On the pre-Marshall Court, the Justices served briefly; five quit in a decade. The Marshall Court lasted—BROCKHOLST LIVINGSTON seventeen years, THOMAS TODD nineteen, GABRIEL DUVALL twenty-four, WILLIAM JOHNSON thirty, Bushrod Washington thirty-one, and Marshall outlasted them all. Story served twenty-four years with Marshall and ten more after his death; SMITH THOMPSON served fifteen years with Marshall and eight years after. This continuity in personnel contributed to a consistent point of view in constitutional doctrine—a view that was, substantially, Marshall's. From 1812, when the average age of the Court's members was only forty-three, through 1823—twelve successive terms—the Court had the same membership, the longest period in its history without a change, and during that period the Marshall Court decided its most important cases except for *Marbury.*

Marshall also sought to strengthen the Court by inaugurating the practice of one Justice's giving the opinion of the Court. Previously the Justices had delivered their opinions SERIATIM, each writing an opinion in each case in the style of the English courts. That practice forced each Justice to take the trouble of understanding each case, of forming his opinion on it, and showing publicly the reasons that led to his judgment. Such were Jefferson's arguments for seriatim opinions; and Marshall understood that one official opinion augmented the Court's strength by giving the appearance of unity and harmony. Marshall realized that even if each Justice reached similar conclusions, the lines of argument and explanation of doctrine might vary with style and thought of every individual, creating uncertainty and impairing confidence in the Court as an institution. He doubtless also understood that by massing his Court behind one authoritative opinion and by assigning so many opinions to himself, his own influence as well as the Court's would be enhanced. Jefferson's first appointee, Justice Johnson, sought to buck the practice for a while. He had been surprised, he later informed Jefferson, to discover the Chief Justice "delivering all the

opinions in cases in which he sat, even in some instances when contrary to his own judgment and vote." When Johnson remonstrated in vain, Marshall lectured him on the "indecency" of judges' "cutting at each other," and Johnson soon learned to acquiesce "or become such a cypher in our consultations as to effect no good at all." Story, too, learned to swallow his convictions to enhance the "authority of the Court." His "usual practice," said Story, was "to submit in silence" to opinions with which he disagreed. Even Marshall himself observed in an 1827 case, by which time he was losing control of his Court, that his usual policy when differing from majority was "to acquiesce silently in its opinion."

Like other trailblazing activist judges, Marshall squeezed a case for all it was worth, intensifying its influence. For Marshall a constitutional case was a medium for explaining his philosophy of the supreme and FUNDAMENTAL LAW, an occasion for sharing his vision of national greatness, a link between capitalism and CONSTITUTIONALISM, and an opportunity for a basic treatise. Justice Johnson protested in 1818, "We are constituted to decide causes, and not to discuss themes, or digest systems." He preferred, he said, to decide no more in any case "than what the case itself necessarily requires." Ordinary Justices decide only the immediate question on narrow grounds; but Marshall, confronted by some trivial question—whether a justice of the peace had a right to his commission or whether peddlers of lottery tickets could be fined—would knife to the roots of the controversy, discover that it involved some great constitutional principle, and explain it in the broadest possible way, making the case seem as if the life of the Union or the supremacy of the Constitution were at stake. His audacity in generalizing was impressive; his strategy was to take the highest ground and make unnerving use of OBITER DICTA; and then, as a matter of tactics, almost unnoticeably decide on narrow grounds. *Marbury* is remembered for Marshall's exposition of JUDICIAL REVIEW, not for his judicial humility in declining JURISDICTION and refusing to issue the WRIT OF MANDAMUS. COHENS V. VIRGINIA (1821) is remembered for Marshall's soaring explication of the supremacy of the JUDICIAL POWER OF THE UNITED STATES, not for the decision in favor of Virginia's power to fine unlicensed lottery ticket peddlers. GIBBONS V. OGDEN (1824) is remembered for its sweeping discourse on the COMMERCE CLAUSE of the Constitution, not for the decision that the state act conflicted with an obscure act of Congress.

Marshall's first major opinion, in *Marbury*, displayed his political cunning, suppleness in interpretation, doctrinal boldness, instinct for judicial survival, and ability to maneuver a case beyond the questions on its face. Having issued the show cause order to Madison, the Court seemingly was in an impossible position once Jefferson's supporters called that order a judicial interference with the executive branch. To decide for Marbury would provoke a crisis that the Court could not survive: Madison would ignore the Court, which had no way to enforce its decision, and the Court's enemies would have a pretext for IMPEACH-MENT. To decide against Marbury would appear to endorse the illegal acts of the executive branch and concede that the Court was helpless. Either course of action promised judicial humiliation and loss of independence. Marshall therefore found a way to make a tactical retreat while winning a great strategic victory for judicial power. After upbraiding the executive branch for violating Marbury's rights, Marshall concluded that the Court had no JURIS-DICTION in the case, because a provision of an act of Congress conflicted with Article III. He held that provision unconstitutional by, first, giving it a sweeping construction its text did not bear and, second, by comparing it to his very narrow construction of Article III. Thus he reached and decided the great question, not argued by counsel, whether the Court had the power to declare unconstitutional an act of Congress. By so doing he answered from the bench his critics in Congress who, now that they were in power, had renounced judicial review during the debate on the repeal of the JUDICIARY ACT OF 1801. Characteristically Marshall relied on no precedents, not even on the authority of THE FEDERALIST #78. Significantly, he chose a safe act of Congress to void—section 13 of the JUDICIARY ACT OF 1789, which concerned not the province of the Congress or the President but of the Supreme Court, its authority to issue writs of mandamus in cases of ORIGINAL JURISDICTION. But Marshall's exposition of judicial review was, characteristically, broader than the holding on section 13. Jefferson, having been given no stick with which to beat Marshall, privately fumed: "Nothing in the Constitution has given them a right to decide for the Executive, more than to the Executive to decide for them," he wrote in a letter. "The opinion which gives to the judges the right to decide what laws are constitutional, and what not, not only for themselves in their own sphere of action, but also for the Legislature and Executive also, in their spheres, would make the judiciary a despotic branch."

The Court did not dare to declare unconstitutional any other act of Congress which remained hostile to it throughout Marshall's tenure. STUART V. LAIRD (1803), decided shortly after Marbury, upheld the repeal of the Judiciary Act of 1801. (See JUDICIARY ACTS OF 1802.) A contrary decision would have been institutionally suicidal for the Court. Marshall's opinion in Marbury was daring enough; in effect he courageously announced the Court's independence of the other branches of the government. But he was risking retaliation. Shortly before the arguments in Marbury, Jefferson instructed his political allies in the House to start IMPEACHMENT proceedings against

JOHN PICKERING, a federal district judge; the exquisite timing was a warning to the Supreme Court. Even earlier, Jeffersonian leaders in both houses of Congress openly spoke of impeaching the Justices. The threats were not idle. Two months after Marbury was decided, Justice Chase on circuit attacked the administration in a charge to a GRAND JURY, and the House prepared to impeach him. Senator WILLIAM GILES of Virginia, the majority leader, told Senator JOHN QUINCY ADAMS that not only Chase "but all the other Judges of the Supreme Court," except William Johnson, "must be impeached and removed." Giles thought that holding an act of Congress unconstitutional was ground for impeachment. "Impeachment was not a criminal prosecution," according to Giles, who was Jefferson's spokesman in the Senate. "And a removal by impeachment was nothing more than a declaration by Congress to this effect: you hold dangerous opinions, and if you are suffered to carry them into effect, you will work the destruction of the Union. We want your offices for the purposes of giving them to men who will fill them better."

Intimidated by Chase's impending impeachment, Marshall, believing himself to be next in line, wrote to Chase that "impeachment should yield to an APPELLATE JURISDIC-TION in the legislature. A reversal of those legal opinions deemed unsound by the legislature would certainly better comport with the mildness of our character than a removal of the Judge who has rendered them unknowing of his fault." Less than a year after his Marbury opinion the fear of impeachment led an anguished Marshall to repudiate his reasoning and favor Congress as the final interpreter of the Constitution. Fortunately the greatest crisis in the Court's history eased when the Senate on March 1, 1805, failed to convict Chase on any of the eight articles of impeachment. Marshall and his Court were safe from an effort, never again repeated, to politicize the Court by making it subservient to Congress through impeachment.

The Court demonstrated its independence even when impeachment hung over it. In *Little v. Barreme* (1804) Marshall for the Court held that President Adams had not been authorized by Congress to order an American naval commander to seize a ship sailing from a French port. Justice Johnson on circuit vividly showed his independence of the President who had appointed him. To enforce the EMBARGO ACTS, Jefferson had authorized port officers to refuse clearance of ships with "suspicious" cargoes. In 1808 Johnson, on circuit in Charleston, ordered the clearance of a ship and denounced the President for having exceeded the power delegated by the Embargo Acts. Jefferson could not dismiss as partisan politics Johnson's rebuke that he had acted as if he were above the law. Justice Brockholst Livingston, another Jefferson appointee, also had occasion in 1808 to show his independence of the President. Jefferson supported a federal prosecution for

TREASON against individuals who had opposed the embargo with violence. Livingston, who presided at the trial, expressed "astonishment" that the government would resort to a theory of "constructive treason" in place of the Constitution's definition of treason as levying war against the United States and he warned against a "precedent so dangerous." The jury speedily acquitted. After the tongue-lashing from his own appointees, Jefferson won an unexpected victory in the federal courts in the case of the brig *William* (1808). Federal district judge John Davis in Massachusetts sustained the constitutionality of the Embargo Acts on commerce clause grounds. Davis, a lifelong Federalist, showed how simplistic was Jefferson's raving about judicial politics.

The evidence for the Court's nonpartisanship seems plentiful. For example, Justice Story, Madison's appointee, spoke for an independent Court in *Gelston v. Hoyt* (1818), a suit for damages against government officials whose defense was that they had acted under President Madison's orders. Story, finding no congressional authority for these orders, "refused an extension of prerogative" power and added, "It is certainly against the general theory of our institutions to create discretionary powers by implication. . . ."

On the other hand, the Court supported the theory of IMPLIED POWERS in *McCulloch v. Maryland* (1819), which was the occasion of Marshall's most eloquent nationalist opinion. *McCulloch* had its antecedent in *United States v. Fisher* (1804), when the Court initially used BROAD CONSTRUCTION to sustain an act of Congress that gave to the government first claim against certain insolvent debtors. Enunciating the DOCTRINE of implied powers drawn from the NECESSARY AND PROPER CLAUSE, Marshall declared that Congress could employ any useful means to carry out its ENUMERATED POWER to pay national debts. That the prior claim of the government interfered with state claims was an inevitable result, Marshall observed, of the supremacy of national laws. Although a precursor of *McCulloch*, *Fisher* attracted no opposition because it did not thwart any major state interests.

When the Court did confront such interests for the first time, in UNITED STATES V. JUDGE PETERS (1809), Marshall's stirring nationalist passage, aimed at states that annulled judgments of the federal courts, triggered Pennsylvania's glorification of state sovereignty and denunciation of the "unconstitutional exercise of powers in the United States Courts." The state called out its militia to prevent execution of federal judgments and recommended a constitutional amendment to establish an "impartial tribunal" to resolve conflicts between "the general and state governments." State resistance collapsed only after President Madison backed the Supreme Court. Significantly, eleven state legislatures, including Virginia's, censured Pennsylvania's doctrines and endorsed the Supreme Court as the constitutionally established tribunal to decide state disputes with the federal courts.

The *Judge Peters* episode revealed that without executive support the Court could not enforce its mandate against a hostile state, which would deny that the Court was the final arbiter under the Constitution if the state's interests were thwarted. The episode also revealed that if other states had no immediate stake in the outcome of a case, they would neither advance doctrines of state sovereignty nor repudiate the Court's supreme appellate powers. When Virginia's high court ruled that the appellate jurisdiction of the Supreme Court did not extend to court judgments and that section 25 of the Judiciary Act of 1789 was unconstitutional, the Marshall Court, dominated by Republicans, countered by sustaining the crucial statute in *Martin v. Hunter's Lessee* (1816). Pennsylvania and other states did not unite behind Virginia when it proposed the constitutional amendment initiated earlier by Pennsylvania, because *Martin* involved land titles of no interest to other states. The fact that the states were not consistently doctrinaire and became aggressive only when Court decisions adversely affected them enabled the Court to prevail in the long run. A state with a grievance typically stood alone. But for the incapacity or unwillingness of the Court's state enemies to act together in their proposals to cripple it, the great nationalist decisions of the Marshall Court would have been as impotent as the one in *Worcester v. Georgia* (1832). *Worcester* majestically upheld the supreme law against the state's despoliation of the Cherokees, but President ANDREW JACKSON supported Georgia, which flouted the Court. Even Georgia, however, condemned the SOUTH CAROLINA ORDINANCE OF NULLIFICATION, and several state legislatures resolved that the Supreme Court was the constitutional tribunal to settle controversies between the United States and the states.

The Court made many unpopular decisions that held state acts unconstitutional. *Fletcher v. Peck*, which involved the infamous Yazoo land frauds, was the first case in which the Justices voided a state act for conflict with the Constitution itself. *Martin v. Hunter's Lessee*, which involved the title to the choice Fairfax estates in Virginia, was only the first of a line of decisions that unloosed shrill attacks on the Court's jurisdiction to decide cases on a WRIT OF ERROR to state courts. In *McCulloch* the Court supported the "monster monopoly," the Bank of the United States chartered by Congress, and held unconstitutional a state tax on its Baltimore branch. In *Cohens* the Court again championed its supreme appellate powers under section 25 of the Judiciary Act of 1789 and circumvented the ELEVENTH AMENDMENT. In STURGES V. CROWNINSHIELD (1819) the Court nullified a state bankruptcy statute that aided victims of an economic panic. In

GREEN V. BIDDLE (1821) the Court used the CONTRACT CLAUSE when voiding Kentucky acts that supported valuable land claims. In OSBORN V. BANK OF THE UNITED STATES (1824) it voided an Ohio act that defied *McCulloch* and raised the question whether the Constitution had provided for a tribunal capable of protecting those who executed the laws of the Union from hostile state action.

When national supremacy had not yet been established and claims of state sovereignty bottomed state statutes and state judicial decisions that the Court overthrew, state assaults on the Court were inevitable, imperiling it and the Union it defended. Virginia, the most prestigious state, led the assault which Jefferson encouraged and SPENCER ROANE directed. Kentucky's legislature at one point considered military force to prevent execution of the *Green* decision. State attacks were vitriolic and intense, but they were also sporadic and not united. Ten state legislatures adopted resolutions against the Marshall Court, seven of them denouncing section 25 of the 1789 Act, which was the jurisdictional foundation for the Court's power of judicial review over the states. In 1821, 1822, 1824, and 1831 bills were introduced in Congress to repeal section 25. The assault on the Court was sharpest in the Senate, whose members were chosen by the state legislatures. Some bills to curb the Court proposed a constitutional amendment to limit the tenure of the Justices. One bill would have required seriatim opinions. Others proposed that no case involving a state or a constitutional question could be decided except unanimously; others accepted a 5–2 vote. One bill proposed that the Senate should have appellate powers over the Court's decisions.

Throughout the 1820s the attempts to curb the Court created a continuing constitutional crisis that climaxed in 1831, when Marshall despondently predicted the repeal of section 25 and the dissolution of the Union. In 1831, however, the House, after a great debate, defeated a repeal bill by a vote of 138–51; Southerners cast forty-five of the votes against the Court. What saved the Court was the inability of its opponents to mass behind a single course of action; many who opposed section 25 favored a less drastic measure. The Court had stalwart defenders, of course, including Senators DANIEL WEBSTER and JAMES BUCHANAN. Most important, it had won popular approbation. Although the Court had enemies in local centers of power, Americans thrilled to Marshall's paeans to the Constitution and the Union and he taught them to identify the Court with the Constitution and the Union.

A perceptible shift in the decisions toward greater tolerance for state action also helped dampen the fires under the Court in Marshall's later years. The coalition that Marshall had forged began to dissolve with the appointments of Justices Smith Thompson, JOHN MCLEAN, and Henry Baldwin. *Brown v. Maryland* (1827), MARTIN V. MOTT (1827), AMERICAN INSURANCE COMPANY V. CANTER (1828), WESTON V. CHARLESTON (1829), CRAIG V. MISSOURI (1830), and the CHEROKEE INDIAN CASES (1832) continued the lines of doctrine laid down by the earlier Marshall Court. But the impact of new appointments was felt in the decisions of *Ogden v. Saunders* (1827), WILLSON V. BLACKBIRD CREEK MARSH COMPANY (1829) and PROVIDENCE BANK V. BILLINGS (1830). In Marshall's last decade on the Court, six decisions supported nationalist claims against seventeen for state claims. During the same decade there were ten decisions against claims based on VESTED RIGHTS and only one sustaining such a claim. The shift in constitutional direction may also be inferred from the inability of the Marshall Court, because of dissension and illness, to resolve CHARLES RIVER BRIDGE V. WARREN BRIDGE, MAYOR OF NEW YORK V. MILN, and BRISCOE V. BANK OF KENTUCKY, all finally decided in 1837 under Marshall's successor against the late Chief Justice's wishes. Before his last decade the only important influence on the Court resulting from the fact that Republicans had a voting majority was the repudiation of a FEDERAL COMMON LAW OF CRIMES.

What was the legacy of the Marshall Court? It established the Court as a strong institution, an equal and coordinate branch of the national government, independent of the political branches. It established itself as the authoritative interpreter of the supreme law of the land. It declared its rightful authority to hold even acts of Congress and the President unconstitutional. It maintained continuing judicial review over the states to support the supremacy of national law. In so doing, the Court sustained the constitutionality of the act of Congress chartering the Bank of the United States, laying down the definitive exposition of the doctrine of implied powers. The Court also expounded the commerce clause in *Gibbons v. Ogden* (1824), with a breadth and vigor that provided the basis for national regulation of the economy generations later. Finally, the Court made the contract clause of the Constitution into a bulwark protecting both vested rights and risk capital. *Fletcher* supported the sanctity of public land grants to private parties, encouraging capital investment and speculation in land values. NEW JERSEY V. WILSON (1812) laid down the doctrine that a state grant of tax immunity constituted a contract within the protection of the Constitution, preventing subsequent state taxation for the life of the grant. DARTMOUTH COLLEGE V. WOODWARD (1819) protected private colleges and spurred the development of state universities; it also provided the constitutional props for the expansion of the private corporation by holding that a charter of incorporation is entitled to protection of the contract clause. The Marshall Court often relied on nationalist doctrines to prevent state measures that sought to regulate or thwart corporate development. Just as national supremacy, judicial review, and the Court's appellate jurisdiction were often interlocked, so too the interests of capitalism, nationalism, and judicial review were allied. Time has hardly withered the influence and achievements of the Marshall Court.

LEONARD W. LEVY
(1986)

Bibliography

BAKER, LEONARD 1974 *John Marshall*. New York: Macmillan.

BEVERIDGE, ALBERT J. 1919 *The Life of John Marshall*. Vols. 3 and 4. Boston: Houghton Mifflin.

CORWIN, EDWARD S. 1919 *John Marshall and the Constitution: A Chronicle of the Supreme Court*. New Haven: Yale University Press.

HAINES, CHARLES G. 1944 *The Role of the Supreme Court in American Government and Politics, 1789–1835*. Berkeley: University of California Press.

HASKINS, GEORGE LEE and JOHNSON, HERBERT Q. 1981 *Foundations of Power: John Marshall, 1801–1815*. Volume 2 of the *Oliver Wendell Holmes Devise History of the Supreme Court of the United States*. New York: Macmillan.

KONEFSKY, SAMUEL J. 1964 *John Marshall and Alexander Hamilton*. New York: Macmillan.

MORGAN, DONALD G. 1954 *Justice William Johnson: The First Great Dissenter*. Columbia: University of South Carolina Press.

WARREN, CHARLES 1923 *The Supreme Court in United States History*, 3 vols. Boston: Little, Brown.

MARSHALL PLAN

At the Harvard University commencement exercises on June 5, 1947, Secretary of State George C. Marshall proposed that the United States undertake a vast program of postwar economic aid to assist the countries of Europe to rebuild from WORLD WAR II. Neither Secretary Marshall nor President HARRY S. TRUMAN offered any constitutional authority for such a program, although some members of Congress, led by Senator ROBERT A. TAFT of Ohio, contended that the expenditure could not be justified under either the FOREIGN AFFAIRS power or the TAXING AND SPENDING POWER. Acting on the initiative of the United States, sixteen European nations formed the Organization of European Economic Cooperation (OEEC) which in turn issued a report setting forth Europe's collective needs and resources. The Soviet Union and other East European countries were invited to participate, but declined. Thereafter, on April 3, 1948, following the Soviet-sponsored coup in Czechoslovakia, which turned the tide of congressional opinion and caused the Marshall Plan expenditures to be justified as a national defense measure, the United States Congress passed the Economic Cooperation Act, to be administered by the Economic Cooperation Ad-

ministration. Within four years and after the expenditure of \$12–\$13 billion in American loans and grants-in-aid, Europe made tremendous strides toward economic recovery. Coupled with increased military security (evidenced primarily in the signing of the NORTH ATLANTIC TREATY in 1949 and formation of the North Atlantic Alliance), this extensive economic recovery helped quell fears of Soviet expansion into Western Europe. The Marshall Plan and the OEEC resulting from it also created a precedent for further economic integration among the participating states of Western Europe.

BURNS H. WESTON
(1986)

Bibliography

PRICE, HARRY BAYARD 1955 *The Marshall Plan and Its Meaning*. Ithaca, N.Y.: Cornell University Press.

MARTIAL LAW

See: Civil-Military Relations

MARTIN, LUTHER
(1748–1826)

Luther Martin represented Maryland in the CONTINENTAL CONGRESS and signed the DECLARATION OF INDEPENDENCE. He was attorney general of Maryland from 1778 to 1805 and one of the early leaders of the American bar. Martin also represented Maryland at the CONSTITUTIONAL CONVENTION OF 1787, where he was a leader of the small-state faction. Although he favored the Convention's purpose, he consistently advocated positions that would have prevented the establishment of a strong central government. Fearing tyranny, he endorsed a one-term presidency and opposed JAMES MADISON's plan to allow a congressional veto of state or local laws.

The question of congressional REPRESENTATION seemed to him one of the most vexing problems. He favored a unicameral legislature and spoke fervently against proportionate representation at the HOUSE OF REPRESENTATIVES, both in the Convention and afterward. His opposition in Philadelphia helped produce the deadlock that nearly wrecked the convention, but he served on the committee that framed the GREAT COMPROMISE and supported its recommendation. Martin favored JUDICIAL REVIEW but opposed authorizing Congress to create federal courts on the ground that state courts would suffice; they were bound by federal law and their decisions could be appealed to the Supreme Court. Martin also thought that the clause prohibiting interference with the OBLIGATION OF

CONTRACTS was unwise; he warned of the inevitability of "great public calamities and distress" when such intervention would become essential—an argument vindicated in HOME BUILDING & LOAN V. BLAISDELL (1934). As the summer progressed, Martin grew increasingly restive. He opposed allowing suspension of the writ of HABEAS CORPUS and he strongly favored granting Congress power to tax or completely prohibit the slave trade. An opponent of SLAVERY, he labeled its recognition in the Constitution "absurd and disgraceful to the last degree." Martin also concluded that later changes rendered the SUPREMACY CLAUSE, which he originally had proposed, "worse than useless." For these reasons, and because the Constitution contained no BILL OF RIGHTS, he opposed its ratification. In his influential tract of 1788 against RATIFICATION OF THE CONSTITUTION, a major anti-Federalist statement, Martin presented the fullest argument of the time in favor of equal representation of the states in Congress. Despite his opposition to the Constitution, Martin later switched his party allegiance and became known as the "Federalist bulldog."

A brilliant lawyer despite his later alcoholism, Martin appeared frequently in the Supreme Court and in state trials; he defended his old friend Justice SAMUEL CHASE at the latter's IMPEACHMENT trial in 1804 and represented AARON BURR against a TREASON charge three years later, winning both cases. (See EX PARTE BOLLMAN AND SWARTWOUT.) Among dozens of Court appearances, his most famous cases were FLETCHER V. PECK (1810) and MCCULLOCH V. MARYLAND (1819). In *McCulloch*, he eloquently defended Maryland's right to tax the federally chartered Bank of the United States, arguing for the application of the Tenth Amendment. Shortly after losing *McCulloch*, Martin suffered a severe stroke. After living as a penniless derelict for some time, he was eventually taken in by Burr. He died in 1826.

DAVID GORDON
(1986)

Bibliography

CLARKSON, PAUL S. and JETT, R. SAMUEL 1970 *Luther Martin of Maryland.* Baltimore: Johns Hopkins University Press.

MARTIN v. HUNTER'S LESSEE
1 Wheaton 304 (1816)

Appomattox ultimately settled the issue that bottomed this case: were the states or was the nation supreme? As a matter of law, the opinion of the Supreme Court supplied the definitive answer, but law cannot settle a conflict between competing governments unless they agree to abide by the decision of a tribunal they recognize as having JURISDICTION to decide. Whether such a tribunal existed was the very issue in this case; more precisely the question was whether the Supreme Court's APPELLATE JURISDICTION extended to the state courts. In 1810 Virginia had supported the Court against state sovereignty advocates. Pennsylvania's legislature had resolved that "no provision is made in the Constitution for determining disputes between the general and state governments by an impartial tribunal." To that Virginia replied that the Constitution provides such a tribunal, "the Supreme Court, more eminently qualified . . . to decide the disputes aforesaid in an enlightened and impartial manner, than any other tribunal which could be erected." (See UNITED STATES V. JUDGE PETERS.) The events connected with the *Martin* case persuaded Virginia to reverse its position. The highest court of the state, the Virginia Court of Appeals, defied the Supreme Court, subverted the JUDICIAL POWER OF THE UNITED STATES as defined by Article III of the Constitution, circumvented the SUPREMACY CLAUSE (Article VI), and held unconstitutional a major act of Congress—all for the purpose of repudiating JUDICIAL REVIEW, or the Supreme Court's appellate jurisdiction over state courts and power to declare state acts void.

The *Martin* case arose out of a complicated and protracted legal struggle over land titles. Lord Fairfax died in 1781, bequeathing valuable tracts of his property in Virginia's Northern Neck to his nephew, Denny Martin, a British subject residing in England. During the Revolution Virginia had confiscated Loyalist estates and by an act of 1779, which prohibited alien enemies from holding land, declared the escheat, or reversion to the state, of estates then owned by British subjects. That act of 1779 did not apply to the estates of Lord Fairfax, who had been a Virginia citizen. The Treaty of Peace with Great Britain in 1783, calling for the restitution of all confiscated estates and prohibiting further confiscations, strengthened Martin's claim under the will of his uncle. In 1785, however, Virginia had extended its escheat law of 1779 to the Northern Neck, and four years later had granted some of those lands to one David Hunter. JAY'S TREATY of 1794, which protected the American property of British subjects, also buttressed Martin's claims. By then a Virginia district court, which included Judge ST. GEORGE TUCKER, decided in Martin's favor; Hunter appealed to the state's high court. JOHN MARSHALL, who had represented Martin, and James Marshall, his brother, joined a syndicate that arranged to purchase the Northern Neck lands. In 1796 the state legislature offered a compromise, which the Marshall syndicate accepted: the Fairfax devisees relinquished claim to the undeveloped lands of the Northern Neck in return for the state's recognition of their claim to Fairfax's manor lands. The Marshall syndicate accepted the compromise, thereby seeming to secure Hunter's claim, yet thereafter completed their purchase. In 1806, Martin's heir conveyed the lands to the syndicate, and in 1808 he appealed to the Court of Appeals, which decided in favor of Hunter two years later.

The Martin-Marshall interests, relying on the Treaty of 1783 and Jay's Treaty, took the case to the Supreme Court on a WRIT OF ERROR under section 25 of the JUDICIARY ACT OF 1789. That section provided in part that the nation's highest tribunal on writ of error might reexamine and reverse or affirm the final judgment of a state court if the state court sustained a state statute against a claim that the statute was repugnant to the Constitution, treaties, or laws of the United States, or if the state court decided against any title or right claimed under the treaties or federal authority. Chief Justice Marshall took no part in the case, and two other Justices were absent. Justice JOSEPH STORY, for a three-member majority and against the dissenting vote of Justice WILLIAM JOHNSON, reversed the judgment of the Virginia Court of Appeals, holding that federal treaties confirmed Martin's title. In the course of his opinion Story sapped the Virginia statutes escheating the lands of alien enemies and ignored the "compromise" of 1796. The mandate of the Supreme Court to the state Court of Appeals concluded: "You therefore are hereby commanded that such proceedings be had in said cause, as according to right and justice, and the laws of the United States, and agreeable to said judgment and instructions of said Supreme Court . . ." (*Fairfax's Devisee v. Hunter's Lessee*, 1813).

The state court that received this mandate consisted of eminent and proud men who regarded the Supreme Court as a rival; the man who dominated the state court was SPENCER ROANE, whose opinion Story had reversed. Roane, the son-in-law of PATRICK HENRY, was not just a judge; he was a state political boss, an implacable enemy of John Marshall, and the man whom THOMAS JEFFERSON would have appointed Chief Justice, given the chance. To Roane and his brethren, Story's opinion was more than an insulting encroachment on their judicial prerogatives. It raised the specter of national consolidation, provoking the need to rally around the STATES' RIGHTS principles of the VIRGINIA AND KENTUCKY RESOLUTIONS. Roane consulted with Jefferson and JAMES MONROE, and he called before his court the leading members of the state bar, who spoke for six days. Munford, the Virginia court reporter, observed: "The question whether this mandate should be obeyed excited all that attention from the Bench and Bar which its great importance truly merited." The reporter added that the court had its opinions ready for delivery shortly after the arguments. That was in April 1814, when the Republican political organization of Virginia dared not say anything that would encourage or countenance the states' rights doctrines of Federalist New England, which opposed the War of 1812 and thwarted national policies. Not until De-

cember 1815, when the crisis had passed and secessionism in the North had dissipated, did the Virginia Court of Appeals release its opinions.

Each of four state judges wrote opinions, agreeing that the Constitution had established a federal system in which SOVEREIGNTY was divided between the national and state governments, neither of which could control the other or any of its organs. To allow the United States or any of its departments to operate directly on the states or any of their departments would subvert the independence of the states, allow the creature to judge its creators, and destroy the idea of a national government of limited powers. Although conflicts between the states and the United States were inevitable, the Constitution "has provided no umpire" and did not authorize Congress to bestow on the Supreme Court a power to pass final judgment on the extent of the powers of the United States or of its own appellate jurisdiction. Nothing in the Constitution denied the power of a state court to pass finally upon the validity of state legislation. The states could hold the United States to the terms of the compact only if the state courts had the power to determine finally the constitutionality of acts of Congress. Section 25 of the Judiciary Act was unconstitutional because it vested appellate powers in the Supreme Court in a case where the highest court of a state has authoritatively construed state acts. In sum, the position of the Court of Appeals was that the Supreme Court cannot reverse a state court on a matter of state or even federal law, but a state court can hold unconstitutional an act of the United States. Thus, Roane, with Jefferson's approval, located in the state courts the ultimate authority to judge the extent of the powers of the national government; in 1798 Jefferson had centered that ultimate authority in the state legislatures. At the conclusion of their opinions, the Virginia judges entered their judgment:

> The court is unanimously of opinion, that the appellate power of the Supreme Court of the United States does not extend to this court, under a sound construction of the constitution of the United States; that so much of the 25th section of the act of Congress to establish the judicial courts of the United States, as extends the appellate jurisdiction of the Supreme Court to this court, is not in pursuance of the constitution of the United States; that the writ of error, in this cause, was improvidently allowed, under the authority of that act; that the proceedings thereon in the Supreme Court were *Coram non judice* [before a court without jurisdiction], in relation to this court, and that obedience to its mandate be declined by the court.

When the case returned a second time to the Supreme Court on writ of error, Marshall again absented himself and Story again wrote the opinion. The *Martin* Court, consisting of five Republicans and one Federalist, was unanimous, though Johnson concurred separately. Story's forty-page opinion on behalf of federal judicial review is a masterpiece, far superior to Marshall's performance in MARBURY V. MADISON (1803) on behalf of national judicial review. In its cadenced prose, magisterial tone, nationalist doctrine, incisive logic, and driving repetitiveness, Story's opinion foreshadowed Marshall's later and magnificent efforts in MCCULLOCH V. MARYLAND (1819), COHENS V. VIRGINIA (1821), and GIBBONS V. OGDEN (1824), suggesting that they owe as much to Story as he to Marshall's undoubted influence on him. Because the Constitution, as Roane pointed out, had neither expressly empowered Congress to extend the Court's appellate jurisdiction to the state courts nor expressly vested the Court itself with such jurisdiction, Story had to justify BROAD CONSTRUCTION. The Constitution, he observed, was ordained not by the sovereign states but by the people of the United States, who could subordinate state powers to those of the nation. Not all national powers were expressly given. The Constitution "unavoidably deals in general language," Story explained, because it was intended "to endure through a long lapse of ages, the events of which were locked up in the inscrutable purpose of Providence." The framers of the Constitution, unable to foresee "what new changes and modifications of power might be indispensable" to achieve its purposes, expressed its powers in "general terms, leaving to the legislature, from time to time, to adopt its own means to effectuate legitimate objects. . . ." From such sweeping premises on the flexibility and expansiveness of national powers, Story could sustain section 25. He found authority for its enactment in Articles III and VI.

Article III, which defined the judicial power of the United States, contemplates that the Supreme Court shall be primarily an appellate court, whose appellate jurisdiction "shall" extend to specified CASES AND CONTROVERSIES. "Shall" is mandatory or imperative: the Court *must* exercise its appellate jurisdiction in *all* cases, in law and EQUITY, "arising under the Constitution, the Laws of the United States, and Treaties made. . . ." It is, therefore, the case, not the court from which it comes, that gives the Supreme Court its appellate jurisdiction, and because cases involving the Constitution, federal laws, and treaties may arise in state courts, the Supreme Court must exercise appellate jurisdiction in those cases. Contrary to Roane, that appellate jurisdiction did not exist only when the case came from a lower federal court. The Constitution required the establishment of a Supreme Court but merely authorized Congress to exercise a discretionary power in establishing lower federal courts. If Congress chose not to establish them, the Court's mandatory appellate jurisdiction could be exercised over only the state courts. The establishment of the lower federal courts meant that the appellate jurisdiction of the Supreme Court extended concurrently to both state and federal courts.

Article VI, the supremacy clause, made the Constitution itself, laws in pursuance to it, and federal treaties the supreme law of the land, binding on state courts. The decision of a state court on a matter involving the supreme law cannot be final, because the judicial power of the United States extends specifically to all such cases. To enforce the supremacy clause, the Supreme Court must have appellate jurisdiction over state court decisions involving the supreme law. That a case involving the supreme law might arise in the state courts is obvious. Story gave the example of a contract case in which a party relied on the provision in Article I, section 10, barring state impairments of the OBLIGATIONS OF A CONTRACT, and also the example of a criminal prosecution in which the defendant relied on the provision against EX POST FACTO laws. The Constitution, he pointed out, was in fact designed to operate on the states "in their corporate capacities." It is "crowded" with provisions that "restrain or annul the sovereignty of the States," making the Court's exercise of appellate power over state acts unconstitutional no more in derogation of state sovereignty than those provisions or the principle of national supremacy. Not only would the federal system survive the exercise of federal judicial review; it could not function without such review. The law must be uniform "upon all subjects within the purview of the Constitution. Judges . . . in different States, might differently interpret a statute, or a treaty of the United States, or even the Constitution itself: If there were no revising authority to control these jarring and discordant judgments, and harmonize them into uniformity, the laws, the treaties and the Constitution of the United States would be different in different states," and might never have the same interpretation and efficacy in any two states.

Story's opinion is the linchpin of the federal system and of judicial nationalism. It remains the greatest argument for federal judicial review, though it by no means concluded the controversy. Virginia's hostility was so intense that a case was contrived in 1821 to allow the Supreme Court to restate the principles of *Martin*. (See COHENS V. VIRGINIA, 1821.) As a matter of fact, though, federal judicial review and the constitutionality of section 25 remained bitterly contested topics to the eve of the CIVIL WAR.

LEONARD W. LEVY
(1986)

Bibliography

BEVERIDGE, ALBERT J. 1916–1919 *The Life of John Marshall*, 4 vols. Vol. IV:145–167. Boston: Houghton Mifflin.

CROSSKEY, WILLIAM WINSLOW 1953 *Politics and the Constitution*, 2 vols. Pages 785–817. Chicago: University of Chicago Press.

HAINES, CHARLES GROVE 1944 *The Role of the Supreme Court*

in *American Government and Politics, 1789–1835.* Pages 340–351. Berkeley: University of California Press.

MARTIN v. MOTT
12 Wheaton 19 (1827)

Mott, having avoided militia duty during the War of 1812, was fined by a court-martial. The Constitution authorized Congress to call forth the militia, and President JAMES MADISON, under congressional authority, had called upon the state militias for military service. Several states, which opposed the war, obstructed compliance, arguing that the national government had no authority to determine when the state militias could be called or to subject them to federal governance. Mott relied on such arguments. The Court unanimously held, in an opinion by Justice JOSEPH STORY, that the President, with congressional authorization, had exclusive power to decide when and under what exigencies the militia might be called to duty, and that his decision not only binds the states but places their militias under the control of officers appointed by the President.

LEONARD W. LEVY
(1986)

MARYLAND v. CRAIG
497 U.S. 836 (1990)

This is another Sixth Amendment case in which the Supreme Court declined to follow the express words of the text. Although the Court engaged in what is usually described as JUDICIAL ACTIVISM, it acted in a good cause and had PRECEDENT for its exception to the CONFRONTATION clause of the amendment. In every case in which HEARSAY evidence of any sort is admitted, the right of the accused to confront the witnesses against him or her becomes empty. In this case the Court held, 5–4, that the victim of child abuse may testify on closed circuit television to avoid the trauma of face-to-face confrontation with the accused.

Justice SANDRA DAY O'CONNOR, for the Court, reasoned that the state had a legitimate interest in protecting the child witness from psychological trauma. Face-to-face confrontation, assured by the text of the Sixth Amendment, turned out not to be an indispensable element of the confrontation guarantee.

Justice ANTONIN SCALIA, an unlikely spokesman for the liberal Justices who joined him, rested his dissent on the clear language of the text. He accused the majority of a line of reasoning that "eliminates the right." But his view on the admission of hearsay ("not expressly excluded by the Confrontation Clause") would also justify admission of television testimony in the presence of defense counsel—

because the amendment does not expressly exclude such a procedure. Scalia further questioned whether the evidence of a frightened child was reliable. But the state, not the Court, should decide whether the child required protection. Scalia's final proposition, that the Court is not at liberty to ignore the confrontation clause, was at war with his several illustrations to the contrary.

LEONARD W. LEVY
(1992)

MARYLAND TOLERATION ACT
(April 2, 1649)

This landmark in the protection of liberty of conscience was the most liberal in colonial America at the time of its passage by the Maryland Assembly under the title, "An Act Concerning Religion," and it was far more liberal than Parliament's TOLERATION ACT of forty years later. Until 1776 only the Rhode Island Charter of 1663 and Pennsylvania's "Great Law" of 1682 guaranteed fuller RELIGIOUS LIBERTY.

Maryland's statute, framed by its Roman Catholic proprietor, Lord Baltimore (Cecil Calvert), was the first public act to use the phrase "the free exercise" of religion, later embodied in the FIRST AMENDMENT. More noteworthy still, the act symbolized the extraordinary fact that for most of the seventeenth century in Maryland, Roman Catholics and various Protestant sects openly worshiped as they chose and lived in peace, though not in amity. The act applied to all those who professed belief in Jesus Christ, except antitrinitarians, and guaranteed them immunity from being troubled in any way because of their religion and "the free exercise thereof." In other provisions more characteristic of the time, the act fixed the death penalty for blasphemers against God, Christ, or the Trinity, and it imposed lesser penalties for profaning the sabbath or for reproaching the Virgin Mary or the apostles. Another clause anticipated GROUP LIBEL laws by penalizing the reproachful use of any name or term such as heretic, puritan, popish priest, anabaptist, separatist, or antinomian.

At a time when intolerance was the law in Europe and most of America, Maryland established no church and tolerated all Trinitarian Christians, until Protestants, who had managed to suspend the toleration act between 1654 and 1658, gained political control of the colony in 1689.

LEONARD W. LEVY
(1986)

Bibliography
HANLEY, THOMAS O'BRIEN 1959 *Their Rights and Liberties: The Beginnings of Religious and Political Freedom in Maryland.* Westminister, Md.: Newman Press.

MASON, GEORGE
(1725–1792)

An influential Virginia leader of the Revolutionary period, George Mason served only a single term (1759–1760) in the colony's House of Burgesses. Family responsibilities and a dislike for routine legislative work kept him at his estate in Fairfax County, where he was active in local public affairs. He was a member and treasurer of the Ohio Company (1752–1773), the Virginia enterprise to explore and settle the Northwest Territory. Mason opposed parliamentary taxation of the colonies and, as justice of the peace, connived at evasion of the Stamp Act. His Fairfax Resolves of 1774 were introduced by his friend and neighbor GEORGE WASHINGTON in the House of Burgesses and prefigured the Declaration and Resolves of the FIRST CONTINENTAL CONGRESS. In 1775 Mason succeeded Washington as a member of Virginia's provisional legislature and was elected to the Committee of Safety, the de facto executive. At the Virginia convention of 1776, Mason wrote the VIRGINIA DECLARATION OF RIGHTS and a major part of the constitution. At the same convention he was appointed, along with GEORGE WYTHE, EDMUND PENDLETON, and THOMAS JEFFERSON, to a committee to revise the state's laws; and, although he resigned from the committee, many of his drafts were included in the final product. Throughout the Revolution he remained active in military and western affairs, and he was the author of an early plan for ceding the Northwest Territory to Congress and organizing its government.

Mason was at the meeting at Mount Vernon in 1785 that set in train the movement toward a constitutional convention; and he was elected to, but did not attend, the Annapolis Convention. He was a delegate to the CONSTITUTIONAL CONVENTION OF 1787 where he was one of the five most frequent speakers. He made his mark at the convention as a spokesman for republican nationalism. He favored a president elected directly by the people for a single seven-year term and assisted by a council. He opposed any mention of slavery in the Constitution as degrading to the document. He was a member of the committee that proposed the GREAT COMPROMISE but bitterly opposed the later compromise which gave twenty years' protection to the slave trade. Most decisively he desired to see a BILL OF RIGHTS included in the new constitution: "The laws of the United States are to be paramount to state bills of rights," he warned, and a constitutional guarantee of rights "would give great quiet to the people." The motion to draft a bill of rights was defeated, and Mason, who had been active in framing the new Constitution, accordingly refused to sign it. He sent his proposed bill of rights to RICHARD HENRY LEE who tried, but failed, to have Congress add it before transmitting the Constitution to the states.

Mason opposed RATIFICATION OF THE CONSTITUTION in the Virginia convention of 1788 because of its supposed antirepublican tendencies, its compromise with SLAVERY, and its want of a bill of rights. When the convention voted to ratify the Constitution it appended a declaration of rights that closely followed Mason's declaration of 1776.

Mason thereafter retired from public life. He declined appointment as a United States senator in 1790. Shortly before his death he told Thomas Jefferson that the machinations of ALEXANDER HAMILTON in favor of urban monied interests were bearing out Mason's predictions about the Constitution.

Throughout his public career Mason adhered to principle even in apparent contradiction to his self-interest. Although he held some 300 slaves he abominated slavery as an institution and favored a plan of gradual compensated emancipation preceded by education. Although he was an active Anglican layman, he favored measures to end the ESTABLISHMENT OF RELIGION in Virginia.

DENNIS J. MAHONEY
(1986)

Bibliography

ROWLAND, KATE MASON 1892 *The Life of George Mason, Including His Speeches, Public Papers, and Correspondence.* New York: Putnam's.

RUTLAND, ROBERT ALLEN 1961 *George Mason, Reluctant Statesman.* Williamsburg, Va.: Colonial Williamsburg, distributed by Holt, Rinehart & Winston, New York.

MASSACHUSETTS v. LAIRD
400 U.S. 886 (1970)

In 1969, the legislature of Massachusetts attempted to nullify the VIETNAM WAR. It passed an act declaring the war unconstitutional, exempting Massachusetts citizens from service in the war, and directing the state attorney general to seek a Supreme Court ruling on the constitutionality of the war. Accordingly, the attorney general filed suit in the state's name against the secretary of defense, Melvin Laird, requesting an order prohibiting the secretary from sending any Massachusetts citizen to Vietnam. As the suit was between a state and a citizen of another state, it would have come within the ORIGINAL JURISDICTION of the Supreme Court. The Court, however, voted 6–3 to deny leave to file the complaint. Justice WILLIAM O. DOUGLAS, who passionately desired an opportunity to rule on the constitutionality of the war, filed an unusual fourteen-page dissent from the denial memorandum.

DENNIS J. MAHONEY
(1986)

MASSACHUSETTS v. MELLON

See: *Frothingham v. Mellon*

MASSACHUSETTS BAY, COLONIAL CHARTERS OF
(1629, 1691)

In 1629 King Charles I granted a royal charter to Puritan leaders of the New England Company, incorporating them as the Massachusetts Bay Colony. In the same year Puritan leaders received authorization to migrate to New England and take the charter with them. As a result the Puritans controlled Massachusetts and sought to create a godly commonwealth. The charter authorized the freemen of the company to meet in a General Court or legislature, and to choose a governor, a deputy governor, and assistants, seven of whom could function as the General Court. The charter vested power in these men to govern Massachusetts Bay in every respect and guaranteed that all inhabitants "shall have and enjoy all liberties and immunities of free and natural subjects . . . as if they . . . were born within the realm of England." The Puritans, who governed themselves, enjoyed the rights of Englishmen, and put an ocean between themselves and England, became obstinately independent.

Massachusetts admitted only church members to freemanship, but the little oligarchy in control refused to allow the freemen a right to participate in governing, a violation of the charter. In 1634 the freemen, on seeing the charter for themselves, demanded full participation in government. From then on, the freemen in the towns chose two deputies from each town as members of the General Court, making it a representative body. Conflict between the freemen and the assistants led to an agreement that without a majority vote of each no law should be passed; that soon led to BICAMERALISM. In the 1640s the battle of the freemen for their charter rights led to the MASSACHUSETTS BODY OF LIBERTIES and to the MASSACHUSETTS GENERAL LAWS AND LIBERTIES, which, with the charter, became the basis of FUNDAMENTAL LAW in the colony, the functional equivalent of a written CONSTITUTION.

In the succeeding decades Massachusetts proved to be aloof from English concerns and refractory in many ways, even claiming that its charter made it independent of Parliament. Relations deteriorated after the Restoration and finally, in 1684, England vacated the charter of 1629. In 1686 James II appointed his own governor of the new Dominion of New England, which combined the New England colonies, New York, and New Jersey. The king's governor ruled without a representative legislature and sought to insinuate the Church of England into Puritan New England. News of the overthrow of James II led to a parallel Glorious Revolution in New England—and elsewhere in America. Each of the colonies that had been absorbed within the dominion resumed its prior governmental practices.

In 1691 King William III, advised by people who had experienced the independence of Massachusetts, officially restored self-government to Massachusetts on royal terms. The charter of 1691 turned Massachusetts from comparative autonomy to a royal colony. The king appointed its governor and his deputy, and the governor could veto legislation—a model for a strong executive in later American history. The General Court consisted of two houses, the lower one elected by the people of the towns who sent two deputies each to the General Court; these elected representatives chose the governor's council, which also served as the upper house. The freemanship of church members disappeared under the new charter, which replaced the religious test with a property qualification on the right to vote. The General Court was empowered to legislate, to create a judicial system, and to elect the upper house—subject to the governor's veto. The government established by the second charter recognized a clear SEPARATION OF POWERS between the three branches. The charter also embodied the principle of liberty of conscience for "all Christians (Except Papists)" and, like the first charter, also guaranteed the rights of Englishmen.

LEONARD W. LEVY
(1986)

Bibliography

OSGOOD, HERBERT L. (1904) 1957 *The American Colonies in the Seventeenth Century.* 3 Vols. Gloucester, Mass.: Peter Smith.

MASSACHUSETTS BOARD OF RETIREMENT v. MURGIA
427 U.S. 307 (1976)

In *Murgia* the Supreme Court, asked to subject AGE DISCRIMINATION to heightened judicial scrutiny, declined the invitation, 7–1. In a per curiam opinion the Court upheld a state law limiting membership in the uniformed state police to persons under the age of fifty, irrespective of an older person's ability to pass physical or other tests of qualification. There was not a murmur in the Court's opinion about IRREBUTTABLE PRESUMPTIONS, nor was age a SUSPECT CLASSIFICATION; although the aged were not free from discrimination, they had not experienced "purposeful unequal treatment" or disabilities imposed "on the basis of stereotyped characteristics not truly indicative of their abilities." With that breathtaking inaccuracy behind it, the Court applied the most permissive form of RATIONAL BASIS review, noted that physical ability generally declines with age, and concluded that because the mandatory retirement rule was not "wholly unrelated" to the objective of maintaining a physically fit police force, the law was valid. Justice THURGOOD MARSHALL, in lone dissent, repeated his long-standing argument that the Court should abandon its "two-tier" system of STANDARDS OF REVIEW in favor of a system that matched the level of judicial scrutiny in EQUAL PROTECTION cases to the interests at stake in each case.

KENNETH L. KARST

(1986)

MASSACHUSETTS BODY OF LIBERTIES

(1641)

The Massachusetts Body of Liberties, which resulted from popular demand that the fundamental law of the colony be written, was primarily a set of constitutional safeguards protecting personal freedom and the procedures of DUE PROCESS. By 1634 the colonists were demanding publication of the colony's laws as a curb on the magistrates' discretionary powers. The magistrates opposed publication as a restraint of their lawful powers; they believed that law should develop in Massachusetts Bay as had the COMMON LAW in England, over time and by custom. More to the point, publication would invite direct comparison with English law and one provision of the charter forbade establishment of any laws repugnant to those of England.

For the remainder of the decade a number of attempts were made to formulate a document that would satisfy these demands. One plan, drawn up by the Reverend John Cotton, may have been rejected because of its biblical severity or its failure to be sufficiently comprehensive. In 1638, the Reverend Nathaniel Ward, a barrister active at Lincoln's Inn before his emigration, submitted a proposal that was eventually sent to the towns for their consideration and revision early in 1641. Despite years of inaction and obstruction by the magistrates the General Court finally adopted this draft that autumn.

The first "liberty," paraphrasing the thirty-ninth article of MAGNA CARTA, specified conformity to the traditional rights of Englishmen, as exemplified in Magna Carta and the common law, and to "the word of God." The Body of Liberties was undeniably a product of the Puritan colony: a large portion outlined ecclesiastical rights and responsibilities. One section, drawn from Cotton's code, listed twelve capital crimes and cross-referenced each one to the appropriate biblical verse.

Over forty liberties were devoted to "Juditiall Proceedings" and their adjunct rights. In addition to defining a few lesser offenses, the Body of Liberties provided extensive guarantees for each step in legal proceedings. The use of summonses was regulated and a right to BAIL was assured. Written pleadings were permitted in court and, unlike English practice, cases would not be abated for minor technical errors. Parties were granted the right to TRIAL BY JURY and to challenge any of the jurors. Other liberties protected rights now taken for granted. Among these were provisions for a SPEEDY TRIAL, a limited privilege against self-incrimination, as well as prohibitions of DOUBLE JEOPARDY and "inhumane barbarous and cruel" punishments. (See CRUEL AND UNUSUAL PUNISHMENT.) The Body of Liberties also guaranteed FREEDOM OF SPEECH in courts and public assemblies and freedom of movement. Other sections covered the "Liberties of Women," children's rights, and those of servants.

Despite these and other innovations the deputies were dissatisfied with the document. They found it overly broad and poorly defined and insisted upon specified penalties— the Body of Liberties provided them only for capital crimes—and precise limits to magisterial power. Eventually, widespread discontent resulted in the passage in 1648 of the extensively detailed MASSACHUSETTS GENERAL LAWS AND LIBERTIES.

DAVID GORDON

(1986)

Bibliography

HASKINS, GEORGE L. 1960 *Law and Authority in Early Massachusetts*. New York: Macmillan.

MASSACHUSETTS CIRCULAR LETTER

(February 11, 1768)

This document reveals the American conception of a CONSTITUTION as a supreme FUNDAMENTAL LAW limiting government by definite restraints upon power. SAMUEL ADAMS drafted the document, which the Massachusetts House of Representatives adopted and sent to the assemblies of other colonies to secure their assent to the contention that the TOWNSHEND ACTS of 1767 and all other taxes levied by Parliament on America were unconstitutional. The right to private property, Adams wrote, is an unalterable natural and constitutional right "engrafted into the British Constitution, as a fundamental law. . . ." Parliament had violated that right by TAXATION WITHOUT REPRESENTATION. Although Parliament was the supreme legislature in the empire, it could act lawfully only within the sphere of its legitimate powers. Echoing the Swiss jurist EMERICH DE VATTEL, who distinguished a constitution from ordinary statutory law, Adams declared that in all free states the constitution is fixed, and "as the supreme Legislative derives its Power and Authority from the Constitution, it cannot overleap the bounds of it, without destroying its own foundation. . . ." The constitution, Adams stated, "ascertains and limits" both SOVEREIGNTY and allegiance.

London censured the "Seditious Paper" of Massachusetts and declared that Massachusetts had subverted "the true principles of the constitution." To the British, as Sir WILLIAM BLACKSTONE contended in his *Commentaries*, Parliament could not act unconstitutionally; it knew no practical limits. To the Americans, an unconstitutional act was one that exceeded governmental authority. "Unconstitutional" did not mean impolitic or inexpedient, as it meant in Britain; it meant a lawless government act that need not be obeyed. The Massachusetts Circular Letter thus fortified the emergence of a new conception of constitutional law.

LEONARD W. LEVY
(1986)

Bibliography
MILLER, JOHN C. 1943 *Origins of the American Revolution.* Pages 257–264. Boston: Little, Brown.

MASSACHUSETTS CONSTITUTION
(October 25, 1780)

The "Constitution or Form of Government for the Commonwealth of Massachusetts" is the classic American state CONSTITUTION and the oldest surviving written constitution in the United States (or the world), distinguished in addition by the fact that it was framed by the world's first CONSTITUTIONAL CONVENTION. But for two states which merely modified their COLONIAL CHARTERS, all the original thirteen states except Massachusetts had adopted their first constitutions by 1778 and in every case the body that enacted ordinary legislation framed the constitution and promulgated it. The Massachusetts legislature also framed a constitution but resorted to the novel step of submitting it to the voters for approval, and they rejected it. Then, in accordance with a proposal first advanced in the CONCORD TOWN RESOLUTIONS of 1776, a special constitutional convention elected for the sole purpose of drawing up a document of FUNDAMENTAL LAW performed the task and sent it out for ratification, article by article. Universal manhood suffrage prevailed in the vote for delegates to the convention and for popular ratification. Massachusetts, following democratic procedures for institutionalizing the SOCIAL COMPACT THEORY of government to devise a frame of government and a supreme law, provided the model that subsequently became common throughout the United States. The Massachusetts constitution of 1780, with amendments, still continues as the constitution of that commonwealth.

JOHN ADAMS, the principal framer of the constitution, once proudly wrote, "I made a Constitution for Massachusetts, which finally made the Constitution of the United States." His exaggeration was pardonable, because no other state constitution so much influenced the framing of the national Constitution. Some earlier state constitutions had referred to the principle of SEPARATION OF POWERS but had made their legislatures dominant, even domineering. Massachusetts not only provided the fullest statement of the principle but also put it into practice. Its judges, appointed by the governor, were to hold office "during GOOD BEHAVIOR" with undiminishable salaries. Its governor was the model for the presidency of the United States. He was to be elected by the voters, rather than by the legislature as in other states, and be a strong executive. He appointed the members of his own council or cabinet and, indeed, appointed all judicial officers down to local magistrates and registers of probate as well as sheriffs, coroners, and the state attorney general. He was "commander-in-chief of the army and navy"; he had the PARDONING POWER; and he alone among the first governors of the thirteen states had a sole VETO POWER over legislation, which could be overridden only by a two-thirds vote of both houses. The state senate and house of representatives were also precursors of the national bicameral system. No original state constitution had a better system of CHECKS AND BALANCES than Massachusetts's.

Its constitution was divided into three parts: a preamble, a declaration of rights, and a frame of government. The preamble, on the general purposes of the state, explicitly embodied the social compact theory of the origin of the body politic. The declaration of rights, although containing little not found in constitutions previously framed by other states, was the most comprehensive compendium of its kind, and it phrased the rights which it guaranteed in language most influential in framing the BILL OF RIGHTS of the Constitution of the United States. The injunction against " UNREASONABLE SEARCHES and seizures" in the FOURTH AMENDMENT derives from the Massachusetts Declaration of Rights, and the injunction "shall not" instead of the pallid "ought not" ("liberty of the press ought not be restrained") was also a Massachusetts innovation. The one grave deficiency of the Massachusetts document was its creation of a multiple ESTABLISHMENT OF RELIGION that was inconsistent with its guarantee of RELIGIOUS LIBERTY.

LEONARD W. LEVY
(1986)

Bibliography
ADAMS, WILLI PAUL 1980 *The First American Constitutions.* Chapel Hill: University of North Carolina Press.

PETERS, RONALD M., JR. 1978 *The Massachusetts Constitution of 1780: A Social Compact.* Amherst: University of Massachusetts Press.

MASSACHUSETTS GENERAL LAWS AND LIBERTIES

In 1646, the General Court of Massachusetts Bay appointed a committee to "correct and compose in good order all the liberties, lawes, and orders extant with us." The committee's work, publication of which was delayed until 1648, was far more comprehensive than the earlier MASSACHUSETTS BODY OF LIBERTIES. The framing of the General Laws and Liberties capped a movement for codification that had grown because the Body of Liberties had failed to curb the magistrates' discretion. Frequent legislation compounded popular confusion over the state of the law, but even so, the General Laws did not include all the laws in force.

The new code incorporated eighty-six of the one hundred items in the Body of Liberties and covered subjects from business regulations to property laws. It generally followed English practice. Plaintiffs could easily attach land, the law guaranteed a SPEEDY TRIAL, and juries could return "special" verdicts—practices foreign to English proceedings. Also unlike English practice, forms of action were relatively unimportant; substance took precedence in Massachusetts. Like contemporary English statutory abridgments and practice manuals, the General Laws were listed alphabetically to encourage reference and use. They were revised in 1660 and 1672 and served as the prototype for other colonies' legal codes.

DAVID GORDON
(1986)

MASSACHUSETTS RESOLUTIONS

See: Embargo Acts

MASSES PUBLISHING COMPANY v. PATTEN
244 Fed. 535 (1917)

Judge LEARNED HAND's *Masses* opinion was one of the first federal opinions dealing with free speech. It remains influential even though Hand was reversed by the court of appeals and many years later himself abandoned his initial position. A postmaster had refused to accept the revolutionary monthly *The Masses* for mailing, citing the ESPIONAGE ACT. Hand, sitting in a federal district court, interpreted the act not to apply to the magazine. He noted

that any broad criticism of a government or its policies might hinder the war effort. Nevertheless, to suppress such criticism "would contradict the normal assumption of democratic government." Hand advanced a criminal incitement test. He conceded that words can be "the triggers of action" and, if they counseled violation of law, were not constitutionally protected. If, however, the words did not criminally incite and if the words stopped short "of urging upon others that it is their duty or their interest to resist the law . . . one should not be held to have attempted to cause its violation."

Hand's concentration on the advocacy content of the speech itself is thought by some to be more speech-protective than the CLEAR AND PRESENT DANGER rule's emphasis on the surrounding circumstances.

MARTIN SHAPIRO
(1986)

MASSIAH v. UNITED STATES
377 U.S. 201 (1964)

After a defendant had been indicted and released on BAIL, a bugged co-defendant who had turned police informer, engaged him in an incriminating conversation. The Supreme Court held that the Sixth Amendment prohibits deliberate elicitation of information from an indicted person in the absence of his counsel and ruled that defendant's incriminating statements were inadmissible at trial.

BARBARA ALLEN BABCOCK
(1986)

MASSON v. NEW YORKER MAGAZINE, INC.
501 U.S. 496 (1991)

A case more interesting for its facts than important for its holding, *Masson v. New Yorker Magazine, Inc.* required the Supreme Court to consider the circumstances in which the press is subject to LIBEL claims for deliberately fabricating quotations.

The case arose from an article written by Janet Malcolm for *The New Yorker* concerning Jeffrey Masson's tenure as Projects Director of the Sigmund Freud Archives—a tenure abruptly terminated when Masson accused Freud of fraud and declared the "sterility of psychoanalysis throughout the world." Malcolm's article included lengthy quotations attributed to Masson that made him appear less than attractive. As one review of the article quoted by the Court said: "Masson, the promising psychoanalytic scholar, emerges gradually as a grandiose egoist—mean-spirited, self-serving, full of braggadocio, impossibly arrogant and, in the end, a self-destructive fool. But it is not Janet Malcolm who calls him such: His own words reveal this psychological profile." Masson claimed, however, that he had not in fact said many of the words that Malcolm put in his mouth. He brought a libel suit, which focused on six statements that Malcolm had attributed to him in the article but that nowhere appeared in the more than forty hours of tape recordings she had made of their conversations.

As the case was presented to the Court, Malcolm conceded for purposes of her summary judgment motion that she had deliberately fabricated the quotations. Masson for his part conceded that he was a PUBLIC FIGURE under the Court's libel jurisprudence and therefore would have to show at trial that Malcolm published a defamatory statement with "actual malice"—that is, knowledge of the statement's falsity or reckless disregard as to its truth. The question on the summary judgment motion was whether a reasonable jury could find, on the basis of the fabricated quotations, that Masson met this constitutional requirement.

The Court held that the appropriate standard in a case of this kind was whether the deliberate alteration of the speaker's words effected a "material change" in their meaning. If the fabrication did so, and if the changed meaning then caused harm to reputation, even a public figure could recover in a libel action; if, however, the fabrication carried with it no such change in meaning, then dismissal of the suit was appropriate. The Court saw this standard as but one variant of the usual COMMON LAW principle, now treated as an integral part of the actual malice standard, that "substantial" even if not complete or literal truth will defeat a libel action. Applying its standard, the Court held that five of the six fabricated quotes at issue materially changed the meaning of what Masson had said and therefore could go to a jury.

Although the *Masson* case received considerable press attention, perhaps because of the striking contrast between the professional reputation of the journalistic defendants and the seriousness of the charges leveled against them, the Court's decision probably will matter little either to the press or to defamed individuals. The press should have little difficulty living with a rule that subjects them to liability for fabricated quotes only when these materially depart from, rather than essentially paraphrase, the substance of what their subjects say; even within the journalistic profession, almost no one believes that this rule imposes a substantial or an unreasonable burden. And the victims of deliberate falsification should have little difficulty recovering under this rule if and to the extent that they have suffered real injury; the Court's standard cuts off suit only when the alteration of the subject's words cannot be thought to have harmed reputation. However

sensational, the problem of fabricated quotes lies at the margin of journalistic behavior (indeed, this is precisely what makes the problem sensational), and the *Masson* decision occupies a similar place in the Court's by now expansive libel doctrine.

ELENA KAGAN
(2000)

Bibliography
BOLLINGER, LEE 1991 The End of *New York Times v. Sullivan:* Reflections on *Masson v. New Yorker Magazine. Supreme Court Review* 1991:1–46.

MASTER, SPECIAL

See: Special Master

MATHEWS v. ELDRIDGE
424 U.S. 319 (1976)

GOLDBERG V. KELLY (1970) established a PROCEDURAL DUE PROCESS right to an evidentiary hearing prior to the termination of state WELFARE BENEFITS. Eldridge, whose Social Security disability benefits had been terminated without a prior hearing, could be pardoned for thinking that *Goldberg* controlled his case. In the event, a 6–2 Supreme Court explained how that view was mistaken, and established its basic test for determining whether a particular procedure satisfied the demands of DUE PROCESS.

The government conceded that the disability benefit was the sort of statutory "ENTITLEMENT" that constituted a "PROPERTY" interest protected by the due process guarantee. The government nonetheless argued that a *prior* hearing was not required; rather, due process was satisfied by a posttermination hearing at which the beneficiary might review the evidence, submit evidence of his own, and make arguments for reconsideration. Under the existing procedures, a beneficiary who prevailed in such a posttermination hearing was entitled to full retroactive relief. A majority of the Court agreed with the government's argument.

In a passage often quoted in later opinions, the Court set out the factors relevant to determining "the specific dictates of due process," once a "liberty" or "property" interest is impaired: "First, the private interest that will be affected by the official action; second, the risk of an erroneous deprivation of such interest through the procedures used, and the probable value, if any, of additional or substitute procedural safeguards; and finally, the Government's interest, including the function involved and the fiscal and administrative burdens that the additional or substitute procedural requirement would entail." Here, eligibility for disability benefits was not based on need, the standard for welfare eligibility in *Goldberg*. The Court assumed that a delayed payment would harm the typical disability beneficiary less than the typical welfare recipient. The medical question of disability, in contrast with the "need" question in a welfare case, was more focused and less susceptible to erroneous decision. The costs of pretermination hearings would be great. In short, the Court balanced its factors on the government's side.

The *Eldridge* due process calculus implies a strong presumption of constitutionality of whatever procedures a legislative body or government agency may choose to provide persons deprived of liberty or property. This presumption grows naturally out of the Court's limited choice of factors to be balanced, emphasizing material costs and benefits and ignoring the role of procedural fairness in maintaining each individual's sense of being a respected, participating citizen.

KENNETH L. KARST
(1986)

MATTHEWS, STANLEY
(1824–1889)

Stanley Matthews's political connections and his legal work for railroads led to his Supreme Court nomination in 1881; these same activities also nearly prevented him from taking a place on the bench. Like his predecessor, NOAH SWAYNE, Matthews had been an Ohio antislavery Democrat and a Democratic appointee as a United States attorney. By 1860, however, he had switched to the Republican party. After CIVIL WAR military service, he became an important leader of the Cincinnati bar. Before the Ohio Supreme Court, Matthews represented the Cincinnati Board of Education and supported its authority to abolish religious instruction in the public schools. His eloquent argument defended SEPARATION OF CHURCH AND STATE as the best way to insure RELIGIOUS LIBERTY.

Matthews served as one of RUTHERFORD B. HAYES's lawyers during the contested electoral battle in 1877. Near the end of his administration, Hayes nominated Matthews to succeed Swayne, but because of internal Republican patronage feuds, as well as questions about Matthews's railroad connections, the SENATE took no action. President JAMES A. GARFIELD, under pressure from Hayes's allies and prominent business interests, resubmitted the nomination. After a long, bitter fight, the Senate confirmed Matthews by a one-vote majority.

Matthews clearly served railroad interests when he joined the Court's decision in WABASH, ST. LOUIS & PACIFIC RAILROAD CO. V. ILLINOIS (1886), substantially weakening the state regulatory doctrine of *Munn v. Illinois* (1877).

Similarly, he concurred in the nearly unanimous decision in the CIVIL RIGHTS CASES (1883), which capped a legal and political counterassault against racial equality.

The *Wabash* case, while limiting state regulation, decisively stimulated federal ECONOMIC REGULATION under the COMMERCE CLAUSE. Matthews relied on an expansive conception of national power in BOWMAN V. CHICAGO AND NORTHWESTERN RAILWAY CO. (1888), ruling invalid a state's prohibition of liquor shipments from other states. However desirable the state's regulation, Matthews said, it infringed on Congress's EXCLUSIVE POWER. In *Poindexter v. Greenhow* (1885) Matthews relied on the CONTRACT CLAUSE when he held that states could not lawfully repudiate their debts.

Matthews's most important cases involved the interpretation of the FOURTEENTH AMENDMENT. In HURTADO V. CALIFORNIA (1884) he held for the Court that even in a capital case an accusation by INFORMATION rather than INDICTMENT by a GRAND JURY did not deny DUE PROCESS OF LAW contrary to the FOURTEENTH AMENDMENT. The *Hurtado* ruling stood for nearly a half century as a barrier to any tendency toward nationalizing CIVIL RIGHTS and CIVIL LIBERTIES. Yet in YICK WO V. HOPKINS (1886) Matthews spoke for the Court on one of those rare occasions when it advanced civil rights. Holding unconstitutional the discriminatory application of a San Francisco ordinance requiring licensing of wooden laundries, used to destroy Chinese businesses, Matthews described the Fourteenth Amendment in libertarian terms that usually were reserved for corporate cases. Indeed, he cast the plight of the Chinese in language that any good entrepreneur could understand: "For, the very idea that one man may be compelled to hold his life, or the means of living, or any material right essential to the enjoyment of life, at the mere will of another, seems to be intolerable in any country where freedom prevails, as being the essence of slavery itself."

Matthews spoke for the Court in one of the Mormon anti-polygamy cases, sustaining congressional action and invoking the prevailing norms of the family and marriage. He also voted to strike down the Ku Klux Klan laws in UNITED STATES V. HARRIS (1883); he agreed with the majority that AMERICAN INDIANS were not citizens in *Elk v. Wilkins* (1884); and he concurred that state MISCEGENATION laws were constitutional in PACE V. ALABAMA (1883).

Matthews epitomized the nation's retreat from the reforming zeal of RECONSTRUCTION. The controversy surrounding Matthews's appointment eventually subsided, and he carried out his duties until his death in early 1889.

STANLEY I. KUTLER
(1986)

Bibliography

FILLER, LOUIS 1969 Stanley Matthews. In Leon Friedman and Fred L. Israel, eds., *The Justices of the Supreme Court*, Vol. 2:1351–1378. New York: Chelsea House.

MAGRATH, C. PETER 1963 *Morrison R. Waite: The Triumph of Character.* New York: Macmillan.

MAXIMUM HOURS AND MINIMUM WAGES LEGISLATION

Regulation of the employment relationship was an important aspect of the movement toward state intervention in economic affairs, which began in the late 1800s. The transition from small individual to large corporate employers and the development of a factory system with a numerous wage-earning class resulted in pervasive exploitation of employees. The principal method of alleviating the economic injustice was statutory regulation of employment conditions. The spectrum of protective legislation was wide, including factory safety, child labor, workers' compensation, and the hours and wages of employment. In these early days the laws were state laws.

The protracted constitutional contest over hours and wage legislation was one aspect of the larger theme of SUBSTANTIVE DUE PROCESS, a concept developed by the Supreme Court at the turn of the century. Liberty included FREEDOM OF CONTRACT, which included the employment contract, of which hours and wages were the main components. The Court held that laws regulating hours and wages violated the guarantee of DUE PROCESS OF LAW if the purpose of the law was invalid or if the means were not reasonably related to a valid purpose.

Hours legislation began in the 1870s. Reformers perceived the duration of the workday as related to the employees' health and safety, protection of which was a valid legislative purpose. In its first opinion on the subject, HOLDEN V. HARDY (1898), the Court sustained a law limiting the hours of men working in mines to eight a day. The hazardous nature of the work justified the limitation as a valid health and safety measure. In MULLER V. OREGON (1908) an hours limitation for women was sustained on the theory that the "weaker sex" required special protection.

Beyond these two exceptional situations the Court at first prohibited hours regulation. The prototype case was LOCHNER V. NEW YORK (1905). A 5–4 Court invalidated a law restricting the work of bakery employees to ten hours a day and sixty hours a week. Despite massive documentation, the Court refused to recognize that the baking industry posed any special health danger to which hours of work were reasonably related. More broadly, the Court concluded that the law was not truly a health law, but a "purely labor law" to regulate hours, an impermissible objective.

This strict view yielded to persistent pressures. In BUNTING V. OREGON (1917) hours regulation of adult males in factories was sustained as a valid health measure, a result clearly inconsistent with *Lochner,* which was not even mentioned in the opinion. Thereafter the validity of hours regulation was not seriously questioned.

Massachusetts passed the first minimum wage statute in 1912 and within ten years there were fifteen such state laws. Proponents urged that health was impaired by wages below a subsistence level. The Court was at first unpersuaded, and, in ADKINS V. CHILDREN'S HOSPITAL (1923), it invalidated a District of Columbia minimum wage law for women. Wages were the "heart of the contract" and, unlike hours, had no relation to health. Contrary to hours regulation, women were entitled to no special wage protection. The minimum wage was invalid also because it bore no relation to the value of the service rendered. But a law curing this deficiency was invalidated in MOREHEAD V. NEW YORK EX REL. TIPALDO (1936).

One principal justification for protective legislation was that the inequality of economic power between employers and employees made true freedom of contract illusory. This argument was expressly rejected by the Court, which candidly declared in COPPAGE V. KANSAS (1915) that it was "impossible to uphold freedom of contract and the right of private property without at the same time recognizing as legitimate those inequalities of fortune that are the necessary result of the exercise of those rights." Social Darwinism was thus enshrined in the Constitution.

In 1937, that year of constitutional revolution, minimum wage legislation became constitutional by a 5–4 vote. WEST COAST HOTEL CO. V. PARRISH upheld a minimum wage for women. *Adkins* was overruled. The Court purported surprise at the employer's reliance on liberty of contract. Not only was the health/subsistence rationale accepted but, more broadly, it was now accepted as a valid legislative purpose to prevent "exploitation of a class of workers who are in unequal position with respect to bargaining power."

Federal regulation of hours and wages was first exercised in limited contexts. An eight-hour day for railroad workers was upheld under the COMMERCE CLAUSE in WILSON V. NEW (1917). Congress has long regulated both wages and hours of work performed by employees of contractors with the federal government. Examples are the Davis-Bacon Act, which regulates wages for work on public buildings and other public works, and the Walsh-Healey Public Contracts Act, which regulates both wages and hours for work on supply contracts. The constitutionality of both statutes is unquestioned under the TAXING AND SPENDING POWER.

Finally, in the FAIR LABOR STANDARDS ACT of 1938, Congress legislated for private employment generally, superseding most state laws. The act required the payment of a minimum wage and overtime for all hours over forty a week to all employees engaged in commerce or the production of goods for commerce. The main purpose was not health but to bolster the economy. The FLSA was sustained under the commerce power in UNITED STATES V. DARBY (1941). A substantive due process argument was rejected without analysis. It was "no longer open to question" that neither Fifth nor FOURTEENTH AMENDMENT due process limited the fixing of minimum wages or maximum hours, and it made no difference that the regulations applied to both men and women.

That has been the view of the matter ever since. In other contexts the Court repudiated the *Lochner* substantive due process approach to protective legislation. What was once a burning issue now appears to be a closed chapter in constitutional law. The scope of the STATE POLICE POWER was underscored in striking fashion by the upholding in *Day-Brite Lighting, Inc. v. Missouri* (1952) of a law that required employers to give employees four hours off from work in order to vote—with full pay.

WILLIAM P. MURPHY
(1986)

Bibliography

DE VYVER, FRANK T. 1939 Regulation of Wages and Hours Prior to 1938. *Law and Contemporary Problems* 6:323–332.

DODD, E. MERRICK 1943 From Maximum Wages to Minimum Wages: Six Centuries of Regulation of Employment Contracts. *Columbia Law Review* 43:643–687.

MAXWELL v. DOW
176 U.S. 581 (1900)

This case was decided at a time when the Court was subjecting the FOURTEENTH AMENDMENT to an accordionlike motion, expanding SUBSTANTIVE DUE PROCESS to protect the rights of property and contracting PROCEDURAL DUE PROCESS for persons accused of crime. After HURTADO V. CALIFORNIA (1884), when the Court held that the concept of due process did not guarantee INDICTMENT by GRAND JURY, persons accused of crime resorted to the INCORPORATION DOCTRINE, claiming that the Fourteenth Amendment, through either its due process clause or its PRIVILEGES AND IMMUNITIES clause, incorporated provisions of the BILL OF RIGHTS, thus extending to the states the same trial standards. Utah accused Maxwell by an INFORMATION, rather than an indictment, and tried him by a jury of eight rather than twelve. The Fifth and SIXTH AMENDMENTS would have made such procedures unconstitutional in federal courts. Maxwell argued that the Fourteenth Amendment guaranteed the federal standards in state proceedings. Justice JOHN MARSHALL HARLAN, dissenting, adopted Maxwell's arguments. Justice RUFUS PECKHAM, for the remainder of the Court, held that neither the due process nor the privileges and immunities clause of the Fourteenth Amendment embodied Fifth or Sixth Amendment rights. Peckham also

ruled that TRIAL BY JURY "has never been affirmed to be a necessary requisite of due process of law" and that an eight-member jury was constitutional. In 1968 DUNCAN V. LOUISIANA, overruling *Maxwell*, held trial by jury to be a fundamental right of due process of law for persons accused of crime, but under today's constitutional law, the JURY SIZE need not be twelve members in a state proceeding.

LEONARD W. LEVY
(1986)

MAYFLOWER COMPACT

See: Social Compact Theory

MAYOR OF NEW YORK v. MILN
11 Peters 102 (1837)

This was the first case decided by the TANEY COURT involving a COMMERCE CLAUSE issue, and the Supreme Court finessed that issue. Justice JOSEPH STORY, dissenting alone, said that he took consolation in knowing that the late Chief Justice (JOHN MARSHALL) concurred in his view that the city of New York had unconstitutionally regulated FOREIGN COMMERCE, a subject exclusively belonging to Congress. The city required incoming ship captains to supply vital statistics on every immigrant they brought to harbor. The city argued that passengers were not commerce, but if they were, the voyage having ceased, no foreign commerce was involved; the requirement of the information on passengers was an exercise of the POLICE POWER, a precautionary measure against paupers, vagabonds, convicts, and pestilence.

By a vote of 6–1, in an opinion by Justice PHILIP BARBOUR, the Court sustained the regulation as a valid exercise of the police power. Barbour disavowed giving any opinion on the question whether the states shared CONCURRENT POWERS over foreign commerce. Justice SMITH THOMPSON, concurring separately, agreed with Story that the facts showed a regulation of foreign commerce, but he believed that in the absence of congressional legislation, the states retained a CONCURRENT POWER. The early and simplistic victory for the police power in this case solved little, because the Court did not face the question of the scope of the police powers when they affected SUBJECTS OF COMMERCE.

LEONARD W. LEVY
(1986)

MAYSVILLE ROAD BILL
(1830)

President ANDREW JACKSON's veto of the Maysville Road Bill challenged the INTERNAL IMPROVEMENTS component of

HENRY CLAY'S AMERICAN SYSTEM on constitutional and policy grounds and enhanced the role of the President in the legislative process.

In 1816, President JAMES MADISON vetoed the "Bonus Bill," which would have provided federal support for internal improvements such as the Cumberland Road, on the ground that the Constitution did not authorize expenditure of federal funds for anything except the powers explicitly enumerated in it. The Maysville Road Bill would have funded completion of a twenty-mile spur of the National Road entirely within the state of Kentucky. Jackson defended his veto on the ground that the Maysville Road was wholly intrastate and therefore outside the power of the federal government. Jackson also vetoed the bill in order to promote economy in the national government. He thus asserted a presidential prerogative in legislative policy, as well as a quasi-constitutional position, associated with the Democratic Party for the next thirty years, of hostility to expenditure of federal funds for internal improvements.

WILLIAM M. WIECEK
(1986)

(SEE ALSO: *Veto Power.*)

MCCARDLE, EX PARTE
7 Wallace (74 U.S.) 506 (1869)

In *Ex Parte McCardle*, Chief Justice SALMON P. CHASE, for the Supreme Court, validated congressional withdrawal of the Court's jurisdiction over appeals in HABEAS CORPUS proceedings under an 1867 statute but reasserted the Court's appellate authority in all other habeas cases.

A federal circuit court remanded William McCardle, a Mississippi editor hostile to Republican Reconstruction policies, to military custody. When he appealed to the Supreme Court, Democrats predicted that the Justices would use his case as a vehicle to hold unconstitutional the trial of civilians by military commissions in southern states undergoing RECONSTRUCTION. Democrats inferred from the earlier decision of EX PARTE MILLIGAN (1866) that a majority of the Court believed that military commissions could not constitutionally try civilians accused of crimes where courts were functioning in peacetime. Alarmed congressional Republicans, seeing this essential machinery of Reconstruction threatened, enacted a narrow statute in 1868 that revoked Supreme Court appellate authority in habeas cases under the HABEAS CORPUS ACT OF 1867.

In the *McCardle* opinion, Chief Justice Chase acknowledged the validity of this repeal under the "exceptions clause" of Article III, section 2, but pointedly reminded

the bar that the 1868 repealer "does not affect the JURISDICTION which was previously exercised." In *Ex Parte Yerger* (1869), the Court promptly affirmed this OBITER DICTUM, accepting a *habeas* appeal under section 14 of the JUDICIARY ACT OF 1789 and rebuking Congress for the 1868 repealer. *McCardle* is therefore historically significant as evidence not of judicial submission to political threats during Reconstruction but rather of the Court's uninterrupted determination to preserve its role in questions of CIVIL LIBERTIES.

McCardle remains important in the modern debate on congressional power to curtail the Supreme Court's APPELLATE JURISDICTION over cases raising controversial issues such as SCHOOL BUSING, school prayer, and abortion. Some constitutional scholars have argued that Congress cannot erode the substance of the JUDICIAL POWER of the United States vested in the Supreme Court by Article III, section 1, through jurisdictional nibbling at the Court's appellate authority, but the extent to which Congress can affect substantive rights by jurisdictional excisions remains controverted.

WILLIAM M. WIECEK
(1986)

(SEE ALSO: *Judicial System, Federal.*)

MCCARRAN ACT

See: Internal Security Act

MCCARRAN-WALTER ACT

See: Immigration and Alienage

MCCARTHY, JOSEPH R.

See: McCarthyism

MCCARTHYISM

On February 9, 1950, Senator Joseph R. McCarthy of Wisconsin claimed that 205 communists were presently "working and shaping the policy of the State Department." Although McCarthy produced no documentation for this preposterous charge, he quickly emerged as the nation's dominant Cold War politician—the yardstick by which citizens measured patriotic or scurrilous behavior. McCarthy's popularity was not difficult to explain. Americans were frightened by Soviet aggression in Europe. The years since WORLD WAR II had brought a series of shocks—

the Hiss trial, the fall of China, the KOREAN WAR—which fueled the Red Scare and kept it alive.

President HARRY S. TRUMAN played a role as well. In trying to defuse the "Communist issue," he established a federal LOYALTY-SECURITY PROGRAM with few procedural safeguards. The program relied on nameless informants; it penalized personal beliefs and associations, not just OVERT ACTS; and it accelerated the Red hunt by conceding the possibility that a serious security problem existed inside the government and elsewhere. Before long, state and local officials were competing to see who could crack down hardest on domestic subversion. Indiana forced professional wrestlers to sign a LOYALTY OATH. Tennessee ordered the death penalty for those seeking to overthrow the *state* government. Congress, not to be outdone, passed the INTERNAL SECURITY ACT of 1950 over Truman's veto, requiring registration of "Communist action groups," whose members could then be placed in internment camps during "national emergencies."

Despite his personal commitment to CIVIL LIBERTIES, President Truman appointed four Supreme Court Justices who opposed the libertarian philosophy of WILLIAM O. DOUGLAS and HUGO L. BLACK. As a result, JUDICIAL REVIEW was all but abandoned in cases involving the rights of alleged subversives. The Court upheld loyalty oaths as a condition of public employment, limited the use of the Fifth Amendment by witnesses before congressional committees, and affirmed the dismissal of a government worker on the unsworn testimony of unnamed informants. As ROBERT G. MCCLOSKEY noted, the Court "became so tolerant of governmental restriction on freedom of expression as to suggest it [had] abdicated the field."

By the mid-1950s, the Red Scare had begun to subside. The death of Joseph Stalin, the Korean armistice, and the Senate's censure of Senator McCarthy all contributed to the easing of Cold War fears. There were many signs of this, though none was more dramatic than the Supreme Court's return to libertarian values under Chief Justice EARL WARREN. In *Slochower v. Board of Higher Education* (1956) the Court overturned the discharge of a college teacher who had invoked the Fifth Amendment before a congressional committee. In *Sweezy v. New Hampshire* (1956) it reversed the conviction of a Marxist professor who had refused, on FIRST AMENDMENT grounds, to answer questions about his political associations. In WATKINS V. UNITED STATES (1957) it held that Congress had "no general authority to expose the private affairs of individuals without justification. . . ." "No inquiry is an end in itself," wrote Warren. "It must be related to and in furtherance of a legitimate [legislative] task of Congress."

The reaction in Congress was predictable. A South Carolina representative called the WARREN COURT "a greater threat to this union than the entire confines of Soviet Russia." Bills were introduced to limit the Court's JURISDICTION in national security cases, and legislators both state and federal demanded Warren's IMPEACHMENT. Although this uproar probably caused some judicial retreat in the late 1950s, the Supreme Court played an important role in blunting the worst excesses of the McCarthy era.

DAVID M. OSHINSKY
(1986)

Bibliography

OSHINSKY, DAVID M. 1983 *A Conspiracy So Immense: The World of Joe McCarthy.* New York: Free Press.

MCCLESKEY v. KEMP
481 U.S. 279 (1987)

McCleskey, a black Georgian, on being sentenced to death for the murder of a white person, sought a writ of HABEAS CORPUS on the claim that Georgia's capital-sentencing procedures violated the EQUAL PROTECTION clause of the FOURTEENTH AMENDMENT and the CRUEL AND UNUSUAL PUNISHMENT clause of the Eighth Amendment. He based his claim on "the Baldus study," a statistical examination of Georgia's more than 2,000 murder cases during the 1970s. The study showed a significant correlation between race and prosecutors' decisions to seek the death penalty and jurors' recommendations of the death penalty. For example, death was the sentence in twenty-two percent of the cases involving black defendants and white victims, in eight percent of the cases involving white defendants and white victims, and in three percent of the cases involving white defendants and black victims. The Supreme Court, held 5–4, that McCleskey did not show that Georgia had acted unconstitutionally in sentencing him to CAPITAL PUNISHMENT.

The infirmity of McCleskey's argument, according to Justice LEWIS F. POWELL, for the Court, consisted in his failure to prove that he personally had been the target of RACIAL DISCRIMINATION or that the race of his victim had anything to do with his sentence. Anyone invoking the equal-protection clause in a capital-sentencing case has the burden of showing that deliberate discrimination had a discriminatory effect "in *his* case." McCleskey's reliance on the Baldus study proved nothing with respect to him; moreover, every jury is unique, so that statistics concerning many juries do not establish anything regarding a particular one.

McCleskey also argued that the state violated the equal protection clause by enacting the death penalty statute and retaining it despite its supposedly discriminatory application. Powell dismissed this argument because it had no support from proof that the legislature passed and kept a capital punishment act because of its racially discriminatory effect. The Court had previously held in *Gregg v. Georgia* (1976) that Georgia's capital-sentencing system could operate fairly.

The Court found McCleskey's Eighth Amendment argument no more persuasive. In *Gregg* it had ruled that the jury's discretion was controlled by clear and objective standards. The statute even required the trial court to review every sentence to determine whether it was imposed under the influence of prejudice, whether the evidence supported it, and whether the sentence was disproportionate to sentences in similar cases. Moreover, the judge had to consider the question whether race had any role in the trials. Absent proof that the Georgia system operated arbitrarily, McCleskey could not prove a violation of the Eighth Amendment by showing that other defendants had not received the death penalty.

McCleskey also argued that Georgia's system was arbitrarily applied "because racial considerations may influence capital sentencing decisions." Statistics, Powell replied, show only a "likelihood," which was insufficient to establish an "unacceptable risk" of racial prejudice.

Justice WILLIAM J. BRENNAN, for the dissenters, argued the Eighth Amendment issue. He believed that a death sentence should be voided if there was a risk that it might have been imposed arbitrarily. Brennan believed that McCleskey should not have to prove discrimination in his own case; it was enough that the risk of prejudice, which Brennan believed was established by the statistical study, "might have infected the sentencing decision." McCleskey's claim warranted the Court's support because his was the first case challenging the system, not on how it might operate but "on empirical documentation of how it does operate." Black Georgians who killed whites were sentenced to death at nearly twenty-two times the rate of blacks who killed blacks and at more than seven times the rate of whites who kill blacks. This proved the point about disproportionate sentencing for the dissenters.

Justice HARRY A. BLACKMUN, who also spoke for them, used similar evidence to maintain that Georgia's capital-sentencing procedures conflicted with the equal-protection clause. Racial factors impermissibly affected the system from indictment to sentencing: "The Baldus study demonstrates that black persons are a distinct group that are singled out for a different treatment in the Georgia capital sentencing system." The BURDEN OF PROOF, Blackmun contended, should be on the state to demonstrate that racially neutral procedures yielded the racially skewed results shown by the study.

The Court's opinion is not easy to explain, unless one accepts the belief of dissenters that the Court did not wish to open a can of worms. McCleskey's claims taken to their logical conclusion undermined principles that buttressed the entire CRIMINAL JUSTICE SYSTEM. His equal-protection and "cruel and unusual punishment" arguments, if accepted, could have applied to punishments in noncapital cases and to procedures before SENTENCING and might have resulted in abolition of the death penalty as well.

LEONARD W. LEVY
(1992)

(SEE ALSO: *Capital Punishment and Race; Capital Punishment Cases of 1972; Capital Punishment Cases of 1976; Race and Criminal Justice.*)

MCCLOSKEY, ROBERT G.
(1916–1969)

Robert G. McCloskey earned his Ph.D. at Harvard University, and he taught American government at Harvard from 1948 to 1969. He was by training a political scientist and by scholarly instinct a historian concerned with contemporary events; the modern Supreme Court created a challenge that filled the major portion of his intellectual life. The philosophy of judicial self-restraint in the light of the Court's limited competence and resources appealed to McCloskey at least in part because it struck a chord in his own character. He distrusted the flamboyant, preferring cautious interpretation. By nature judicious, he was suspicious of a Court that too precipitously proclaimed eternal verities. He wrote *American Conservatism in the Age of Enterprise* (1951), *The American Supreme Court* (1961), and *The Modern Supreme Court* (published posthumously in 1972), and he edited the papers of Justice JAMES WILSON.

MARTIN SHAPIRO
(1986)

MCCOLLUM v. BOARD OF EDUCATION
333 U.S. 203 (1948)

During the late 1940s and 1950s "RELEASED TIME programs" were popular around the country. Public school boards and administrators cooperated with churches and synagogues to provide religious education for students according to their parents' choices. Under the arrangement in Champaign-Urbana, Illinois, students whose parents had so requested were excused from their classes to attend classes given by religious educators in the school buildings. Nonparticipating pupils were not excused from their regular classes.

McCollum, whose child Terry attended the public schools, challenged the Illinois practice on the grounds that it violated the establishment clause of the FIRST AMENDMENT. The case was the first church-state controversy to reach the Court since EVERSON V. BOARD OF EDUCATION the year before, and Justice HUGO L. BLACK again delivered the opinion of the Court.

Referring to the theory of strict separation announced as OBITER DICTUM in his *Everson* opinion, Black held that the Illinois arrangement fell squarely within the First Amendment's ban. He stressed particularly the utilization of tax-supported facilities to aid religious teaching.

Justice FELIX FRANKFURTER concurred in an opinion in which Justices ROBERT JACKSON, WILEY B. RUTLEDGE, and HAROLD H. BURTON joined. These four had dissented from *Everson's* approval of state aid to the transportation of children to religious schools.

Justice Jackson also concurred separately, rejecting the sweeping separationism of the Black opinion. Pointing out that there was little real cost to the taxpayers in the Illinois program, he agreed that the Court should end "formal and explicit instruction" such as that in the Champaign schools, but cautioned against inviting ceaseless petitions to the Court to purge school curricula of materials that any group might regard as religious.

Justice STANLEY F. REED, the lone dissenter, had concurred in the result in *Everson*. Here he argued that the majority was giving "establishment" too broad a meaning; unconstitutional "aid" to religion embraced only purposeful assistance directly to a church, not cooperative relationships between government and religious institutions.

McCollum seemed to represent a deepening Supreme Court commitment to the theory of strict SEPARATION OF CHURCH AND STATE, but it was significantly limited by another released-time case, ZORACH V. CLAUSEN (1952).

RICHARD E. MORGAN
(1986)

MCCRAY v. UNITED STATES
195 U.S. 27 (1904)

Together with CHAMPION V. AMES (1903), the decision in *McCray* played a seminal role in the expansion of a NATIONAL POLICE POWER. Responding to lobby pressure, Congress in 1902 passed a clearly discriminatory EXCISE TAX on oleomargarine colored yellow to resemble butter. Relying on its power to regulate INTERSTATE COMMERCE, Congress sought to force yellow oleo off the market by taxing it at a rate forty times greater than naturally colored oleo. The act was attacked as an encroachment on STATE POLICE POWERS, a TAKING OF PROPERTY without DUE PROCESS, and a violation of the fundamental principles inherent in the Constitution.

Justice EDWARD D. WHITE, for a 6–3 Court, refused to

inquire into Congress's intent and sustained the tax. He argued that the Court could not examine the wisdom of a particular act and, reiterating an OBITER DICTUM from *Champion*, said the remedy for "unwise or unjust" acts ". . . lies not in the abuse by the judicial authority of its functions, but in the people, upon whom . . . reliance must be placed for the correction of abuses." The Court pointedly dismissed WILLIAM GUTHRIE's argument that the validity of a tax ought to be determined by its natural and reasonable effect, regardless of pretext, though it would adopt his reasoning in BAILEY V. DREXEL (1922). The act's purpose—to suppress the sale of yellow oleo rather than to raise revenue—was immaterial. White concluded a judicial abdication of power in this case (although the Court would reassert it in *Bailey*) by stating that the Court could not help but sustain a congressional act even if that body "abused its lawful authority by levying a tax which was unwise or oppressive, or the result of the enforcement of which might be to indirectly affect subjects not within the powers delegated to Congress."

Chief Justice MELVILLE W. FULLER and Justices HENRY B. BROWN and RUFUS PECKHAM dissented without opinion.

DAVID GORDON
(1986)

MCCREE, WADE HAMPTON, JR.
(1920–1987)

Wade McCree was a member of the generation of black lawyers Governor G. Mennen Williams of Michigan once described as "revolutionaries," individuals who by talent and determination succeeded in opening doors that previously had been closed to members of their race. A graduate of Fisk University and Harvard Law School, McCree spent several years in private practice, but then entered upon a career of public service that continued through four decades and earned for him a reputation as one of the most distinguished lawyers of his time.

After serving as a member of the Michigan Workmen's Compensation Commission and as an elected Wayne County circuit judge, he was appointed by President JOHN F. KENNEDY to the UNITED STATES DISTRICT COURT for the Eastern District of Michigan. Five years later, in 1966, President LYNDON B. JOHNSON elevated him to the UNITED STATES COURT OF APPEALS for the Sixth Circuit, on which he served until 1977, when President JIMMY CARTER appointed him SOLICITOR GENERAL. In 1981, he joined the faculty of the University of Michigan Law School, where he served as the Lewis M. Simes Professor until his death. McCree was the first black or among the first blacks to hold each of these positions.

Widely admired for his judicious manner and temperament, his careful craftsmanship, and the breadth and depth of his knowledge, McCree quickly gained a reputation as a judge's judge. As a judge, and more particularly as a judge on an "inferior court," he was constrained within limits set by others, but within the limits of his office he sought to advance what he regarded as the deepest purposes of law, the fair treatment of individuals and the protection of their liberty and security. McCree's career, both on the bench and off, demonstrates the contribution to those goals that can be made in a life spent in the law.

TERRANCE SANDALOW
(1992)

Bibliography

TRIBUTES 1987 Wade Hampton McCree, Jr. *Michigan Law Review* 86:217–265.

MCCULLOCH v. MARYLAND
4 Wheat. 316 (1819)

Speaking for a unanimous Supreme Court, Chief JUSTICE JOHN MARSHALL delivered an opinion upon which posterity has heaped lavish encomiums. JAMES BRADLEY THAYER thought "there is nothing so fine as the opinion in *McCulloch v. Maryland*." ALBERT BEVERIDGE placed it "among the very first of the greatest judicial utterances of all time," while William Draper Lewis described it as "perhaps the most celebrated judicial utterance in the annals of the English speaking world." Such estimates spring from the fact that Marshall's vision of nationalism in time became a reality, to some extent because of his vision. Beveridge was not quite wrong in saying that the *McCulloch* opinion "so decisively influenced the growth of the Nation that, by many, it is considered as only second in importance to the Constitution itself." On the other hand, Marshall the judicial statesman engaged in a judicial coup, as his panegyrical biographer understood. To appreciate Marshall's achievement in *McCulloch* and the intense opposition that his opinion engendered in its time, one must also bear in mind that however orthodox his assumptions and doctrines are in the twentieth century, they were in their time unorthodox. With good reason Beveridge spoke of Marshall's "sublime audacity," the "extreme radicalism" of his constitutional theories, and the fact that he "rewrote the fundamental law of the Nation," a proposition to which Beveridge added that it would be more accurate to state that he made of the written instrument "a living thing, capable of growth, capable of keeping pace with the advancement of the American people and ministering to their changing necessities."

The hysterical denunciations of the *McCulloch* opinion by the aged and crabbed THOMAS JEFFERSON, by the frenetically embittered SPENCER ROANE, and by that caustic apostle of localism, JOHN TAYLOR, may justly be discounted, but not the judgment of the cool and prudent "Father of the Constitution," JAMES MADISON. On receiving Roane's "Hampden" essays assaulting *McCulloch*, Madison ignored the threat of state nullification and the repudiation of JUDICIAL REVIEW, but he agreed with Roane that the Court's opinion tended, in Madison's words, "to convert a limited into an unlimited Government." Madison deplored Marshall's "latitude in expounding the Constitution which seems to break down the landmarks intended by a specification of the Powers of Congress, and to substitute for a definite connection between means and ends, a Legislative discretion as to the former to which no practical limit can be assigned." Few if any of the friends of the Constitution, declared Madison, anticipated "a rule of construction . . . as broad as pliant as what has occurred," and he added that the Constitution would probably not have been ratified if the powers that Marshall claimed for the national government had been known in 1788–1789. Madison's opinion suggests how far Marshall and the Court had departed from the intentions of the Framers and makes understandable the onslaught that *McCulloch* provoked. Although much of that onslaught was a genuine concern for the prostration of STATES' RIGHTS before a consolidating nationalism, Taylor hit the nail on the head for the older generation of Jeffersonians when he wrote that *McCulloch* reared "a monied interest."

The case, after all, was decided in the midst of a depression popularly thought to have been caused by the Bank of the United States, a private corporation chartered by Congress, and *McCulloch* was a decision in favor of the hated bank and against the power of a state to tax its branch operations. The constitutionality of the power of Congress to charter a bank had been ably debated in Congress and in Washington's cabinet in 1791, when ALEXANDER HAMILTON proposed the bank bill. Constitutional debate mirrored party politics, and the Federalists had the votes. The Court never passed judgment on the constitutionality of the original BANK OF THE UNITED STATES ACT, though it had a belated opportunity. In 1809 a case came before the Court that was remarkably similar to *McCulloch*: state officials, acting under a state statute taxing the branches of the bank, forcibly carried away from its vaults money to pay the state tax. In *Bank of the United States v. Deveaux* (1809), Marshall for the Court, deftly avoiding the questions that he confronted in *McCulloch*, found that the parties lacked the DIVERSITY OF CITIZENSHIP that would authorize JURISDICTION. With the bank's twenty-year charter nearing expiration, a decision in favor of the bank's constitutionality might look like pro-Federalist politics by the Court, embroiling it in a dispute with President

Madison, who was on record as opposing the bank's constitutionality, and with Congress, which supported Madison's policies.

The United States fought the War of 1812 without the bank to help manage its finances, and the results were disastrous. The war generated a new wave of nationalism and a change of opinion in Madison's party. In 1816 President Madison signed into law a bill chartering a second Bank of the United States, passed by Congress with the support of young nationalists like HENRY CLAY and JOHN C. CALHOUN and opposed by a Federalist remnant led by young DANIEL WEBSTER. The political world was turned upside down. The bank's tight credit policies contributed to a depression, provoking many states to retaliate against "the monster monopoly." Two states prohibited the bank from operating within their jurisdictions; six others taxed the operations of the bank's branches within their jurisdictions. The constitutionality of Maryland's tax was the issue in *McCulloch*, as well as the constitutionality of the act of Congress incorporating the bank.

Six of the greatest lawyers of the nation, including Webster, WILLIAM PINKNEY, and LUTHER MARTIN, argued the case over a period of nine days, and only three days later Marshall delivered his thirty-six-page opinion for a unanimous Court. He had written much of it in advance, thus prejudging the case, but in a sense his career was a preparation for the case. As Roane conceded, Marshall was "a man of profound legal attainments" writing "upon a subject which has employed his thoughts, his tongue, and his pen, as a politican, and an historian for more than thirty years." And he had behind him all five Jeffersonian-Republican members of the Court.

Arguing that Congress had no authority to incorporate a bank, counsel for Maryland claimed that the Constitution had originated with the states, which alone were truly sovereign, and that the national government's powers must be exercised in subordination to the states. Marshall grandiloquently turned these propositions around. When Beveridge said that Marshall the solider wrote *McCulloch* and that his opinion echoed "the blast of the bugle of Valley Forge" (where Marshall served), he had a point. Figuratively, Old Glory and the bald eagle rise up from the opinion—to anyone stirred by a nationalist sentiment. The Constitution, declared Marshall, had been submitted to conventions of the people, from whom it derives its authority. The government formed by the Constitution proceeded "directly from the people" and in the words of the PREAMBLE was "ordained and established" in their name, and it binds the states. Marshall drove home that theme repeatedly. "The government of the Union . . . is, emphatically, and truly, a government of the people. In form and in substance it emanates from them. Its powers are granted by them, and are to be exercised directly on them,

and for their benefit." A bit later Marshall declared that the government of the Union though limited in its powers "is supreme within its sphere of action. . . . It is the government of all; its powers are delegated by all; it represents all, and acts for all." And it necessarily restricts its subordinate members, because the Constitution and federal laws constitute the supreme law of the land. Reading this later, ABRAHAM LINCOLN transmuted it into "a government of the people, by the people, for the people."

Marshall's opinion is a state paper, like the DECLARATION OF INDEPENDENCE, the Constitution itself, or the Gettysburg Address, the sort of document that puts itself beyond analysis or criticism. But there were constitutional issues to be resolved, and Marshall had not yet touched them. Madison agreed with Roane that "the occasion did not call for the general and abstract doctrine interwoven with the decision of the particular case," but *McCulloch* has survived and moved generations of Americans precisely because Marshall saw that the "general and abstract" were embedded in the issues, and he made it seem that the life of the nation was at stake on their resolution in the grandest way.

Disposing affirmatively of the question whether Congress could charter a bank was a foregone conclusion, flowing naturally from unquestioned premises. Though the power of establishing corporations is not among the ENUMERATED POWERS, seeing the Constitution "whole," as Marshall saw it, led him to the doctrine of IMPLIED POWERS. The Constitution ought not have the "prolixity of a legal code"; rather, it marked only "great outlines," with the result that implied powers could be "deduced." Levying and collecting taxes, borrowing money, regulating commerce, supporting armies, and conducting war are among the major enumerated powers; in addition, the Constitution vests in Congress the power to pass all laws "necessary and proper" to carry into execution the powers enumerated. These powers implied the means necessary to execute them. A banking corporation was a means of effectuating designated ends. The word "necessary" did not mean indispensably necessary; it did not refer to a means without which the power granted would be nugatory, its object unattainable. "Necessary" means "useful," "needful," "conducive to," thus allowing Congress a latitude of choice in attaining its legitimate ends. The Constitution's Framers knew the difference between "necessary" and "absolutely necessary," a phrase they used in Article I, section 10, clause 2. They inserted the NECESSARY AND PROPER CLAUSE in a Constitution "intended to endure for ages to come, and, consequently, to be adapted to the various crises of human affairs." They intended Congress to have "ample means" for carrying its express powers into effect. The "narrow construction" advocated by Maryland would abridge, even "annihilate," Congress's discretion in selecting its means. Thus, the test for determining the constitutionality of an act of Congress was: "Let the end be legitimate, let it be within the scope of the Constitution, and all means which are appropriate, which are plainly adapted to that end, which are not prohibited, but consist with the letter and spirit of the Constitution, are constitutional." That formula yielded the conclusion that the act incorporating the bank was valid.

Such was the BROAD CONSTRUCTION that "deduced" implied powers, shocking even Madison. The Court, he thought, had relinquished control over Congress. He might have added, as John Taylor did, that Marshall neglected to explain how and why a private bank chartered by Congress was necessary, even in a loose sense, to execute the enumerated powers. In *Construction Construed* (1820) Taylor gave five chapters to *McCulloch*, exhibiting the consequences of Marshall's reasoning. Congress might legislate on local agriculture and manufactures, because they were necessary to war. Roads were still more necessary than banks for collecting taxes. And:

> Taverns are very necessary or convenient for the offices of the army. . . . But horses are undoubtedly more necessary for the conveyance of the mail and for war, than roads, which may be as convenient to assailants as defenders; and therefore the principle of implied power of legislation will certainly invest Congress with a legislative power over horses. In short, this mode of construction completely establishes the position, that Congress may pass any internal law whatsoever in relation to things, because there is nothing with which war, commerce and taxation may not be closely or remotely connected.

All of which supported Taylor's contention that Marshall's doctrine of implied powers would destroy the states and lead to a government of unlimited powers, because "as ends may be made to beget means, so means may be made to beget ends, until the co-habitation shall rear a progeny of unconstitutional bastards, which were not begotten by the people."

Marshall's reasoning with respect to the second question in the case incited less hostility, though not by much. Assuming Congress could charter the bank, could a state tax its branch? Marshall treated the bank as a branch or "instrument" of the United States itself, and relying on the SUPREMACY CLAUSE (Article VI), he concluded that if the states could tax one instrument to any degree, they could tax every other instrument as well—the mails, the mint, even the judicial process. The result would cripple the government, "prostrating it at the foot of the States." Again, he was deducing from general principles in order to defeat the argument that nothing in the Constitution prohibits state taxes on congressionally chartered instruments. Congress's power to create, Marshall reasoned, implied a power to preserve. A state power to tax was a power

to destroy, incompatible with the national power to create and preserve. Where such repugnancy exists, the national power, which is supreme, must control. "The question is, in truth, a question of supremacy," with the result that the Court necessarily found the state act unconstitutional.

That was Marshall's *McCulloch* opinion. Roane and Taylor publicly excoriated it, and Jefferson spurred them on, telling Roane, who rejected even federal judicial review, "I go further than you do." The Virginia legislature repudiated implied powers and recommended an amendment to the Constitution "creating a tribunal for the decision of all questions, in which the powers and authorities of the general government and those of the States, where they are in conflict, shall be decided." Marshall was so upset by the public criticism that he was driven for the first and only time to reply in a series of newspaper articles. Still, Ohio allied itself with Virginia and literally defied, even nullified, the decision in *McCulloch*. (See OSBORN V. BANK OF THE UNITED STATES; COHENS V. VIRGINIA.) Pennsylvania, Indiana, Illinois, and Tennessee also conducted a guerrilla war against the Court, and Congress seriously debated measures to curb its powers. Fortunately the common enemies of the Court shared no common policies. *McCulloch* prevailed in the long run, providing, together with GIBBONS V. OGDEN (1824), the constitutional wherewithal to meet unpredictable crises even to our time. *McCulloch* had unforeseen life-giving powers. Marshall, Beveridge's "supreme conservative," laid the constitutional foundations for the New Deal and the Welfare State.

LEONARD W. LEVY
(1986)

Bibliography

BEVERIDGE, ALBERT J. 1916–1919 *The Life of John Marshall*, 4 vols. Vol. IV: 283–339. Boston: Houghton Mifflin.

HAINES, CHARLES GROVE 1944 The Role of the Supreme Court in American Government and Politics, 1789–1835 Pages 351–368. Berkeley: University of California Press.

WARREN, CHARLES 1923 *The Supreme Court in United States History*, 3 vols. Vol. I:499–540. Boston: Little, Brown.

MCELVAINE v. BRUSH

See: *Kemmler, In Re*

MCGOWAN, CARL
(1911–1987)

Carl McGowan served on the UNITED STATES COURT OF APPEALS for the District of Columbia Circuit from 1963 until his death. Before his appointment, he had a private practice and served on the law faculty of Northwestern University. He was a judge whose intelligence and humanity made him suited to the craft. His opinions were lucid in style and expression, sound in analysis, and combined intellectual acuity, practical understanding, and good sense.

McGowan could not be pigeonholed as a "liberal" or a "conservative." He was the sort of judge a lawyer might wish for before knowing which side of the case he had to argue. McGowan won the respect and affection of his colleagues on the bench as well as of the bar of the DISTRICT OF COLUMBIA. He counseled not by preaching but by example. He was learned in the law, evenhanded in approach, honest, and wise. His ability to conciliate between opposing views allowed his court to resolve cases on common ground. McGowan's dissents barely match the number of terms he served on the court—some twenty-five dissents in a quarter century's service. From the mid-1960s to the mid-1980s, the overall dissent rate in the D.C. Circuit in cases with published opinions hovered around 13 percent; indicative of McGowan's moderating influence, in cases in which he was a panel member, that rate was five percent.

Judge McGowan's patient genius worked through many perplexing constitutional issues. In *Rothstein v. Wyman* (2d Cir. 1972), for example, his opinion delineated the critical line drawn by the ELEVENTH AMENDMENT between what federal courts can and cannot order states to do. In *Nixon v. Administrator of General Services* (D.D.C. 1976) he persuasively analyzed a panoply of constitutional objections pressed on behalf of a former president. In high tribute to Judge McGowan, the Supreme Court's majority essentially adopted his reasoning on the hard questions of SEPARATION OF POWERS, EXECUTIVE PRIVILEGE, invasion of privacy, freedom of expression, and BILL OF ATTAINDER.

RUTH BADER GINSBURG
(1992)

Bibliography

POWELL, LEWIS F., JR., et al. 1988 In Memoriam Judge Carl McGowan. *George Washington Law Review* 56:681–702.

MCGOWAN v. MARYLAND

See: Sunday Closing Laws

MCGRAIN v. DAUGHERTY
273 U.S. 135 (1927)

In KILBOURN V. THOMPSON (1881) the Supreme Court had held that because Article I of the Constitution assigned Congress no power beyond the lawmaking power, Congress might constitutionally investigate "the private affairs of individuals" only for the purpose of gathering information to write new legislation. *McGrain* restated this requirement of legislative purpose, but rejected, 8–0, a challenge to the contempt conviction of the brother of Harry M. Daugherty who had failed to appear before a Senate committee investigating the failure of former Attorney General Daugherty to prosecute the malefactors in the Teapot Dome scandal.

In reality the investigation was not aimed at developing new legislation but at exposing malfeasance in the executive branch, a task that might have been deemed constitutionally appropriate for Congress if it were not for the simplistic *Kilbourn* theory. The gap between theory and reality was bridged by the creation of a presumption that congressional investigations had a legislative purpose, a presumption that was not to be overcome simply by showing that an investigation also had a purpose of public exposure.

The *McGrain* technique of requiring a legislative purpose for a congressional investigation, and then invoking a presumption of legislative purpose even when exposure was clearly a principal motive, had important consequences in post-World War II cases where anticommunist investigating committees were seeking to punish leftist speakers by public exposure precisely because the FIRST AMENDMENT prohibited Congress from passing legislation punishing such speech. The Court invoked the presumption of legislative purpose both to blind itself to the actual "exposure for exposure's sake" being conducted and to establish a congressional interest in lawmaking that outweighed whatever incidental infringement on speech the Court was willing to see.

MARTIN SHAPIRO
(1986)

(SEE ALSO: *Legislative Investigation.*)

MCHENRY, JAMES
(1753–1816)

Irish-born physician James McHenry was a Maryland delegate to the CONSTITUTIONAL CONVENTION OF 1787 and a signer of the Constitution. Absent for most of June and July, he participated little in debate; but, when present, he took detailed notes which are a valuable record of the deliberations. He was later secretary of war (1796–1800).

DENNIS J. MAHONEY
(1986)

MCILWAIN, CHARLES H.
(1871–1968)

Charles Howard McIlwain, a lawyer and political scientist, taught at Princeton and Harvard Universities. His major fields of interest were political theory and British constitutional history. His *The American Revolution: A Constitutional Interpretation* won the Pulitzer Prize in 1923. In that book he showed that the revolution was "the outcome of a collision between two mutually incompatible interpretations of the British constitution." His *Constitutionalism: Ancient and Modern* (1940, revised 1947) argued that the essence of CONSTITUTIONALISM was the balance between governmental power and the JURISDICTION of an independent judiciary and traced the roots of American constitutionalism through English history to classical Rome.

DENNIS J. MAHONEY
(1986)

MCKEIVER v. PENNSYLVANIA
403 U.S. 528 (1971)

Although IN RE GAULT (1967) extended some basic procedural rights to juvenile offenders, young people continued to be tried in most states before judges who exercised great discretion, supposedly to protect juveniles. McKeiver, a juvenile defendant, faced possible incarceration for five years and requested TRIAL BY JURY, which the state denied. By a 6–3 vote, the Supreme Court decided that DUE PROCESS OF LAW does not guarantee trial by jury to juvenile offenders. Justice HARRY BLACKMUN for a plurality of four wrote an opinion based on the unrealistic premise that the juvenile system is fundamentally sound and enlightened, but he did not explain how it assured fundamental fairness. Justice JOHN MARSHALL HARLAN found Blackmun's opinion romantic but concurred nevertheless because he still opposed DUNCAN V. LOUISIANA (1968), which extended trial by jury to the states. Justice WILLIAM J. BRENNAN concurred because he thought, mistakenly, that publicity served as a check on juvenile court judges. Justices WILLIAM O. DOUGLAS, HUGO L. BLACK, and THURGOOD MARSHALL dissented. *McKeiver* short-circuited expectations that the Court would require essentially all the rights of the criminally accused for juveniles who commit adult crimes and face the prospect of serious punishment.

LEONARD W. LEVY
(1986)

MCKENNA, JOSEPH
(1843–1926)

Few Justices sat longer upon the Supreme Court than Joseph McKenna, the son of an Irish immigrant baker, who served for twenty-seven years from 1898 until 1925 under three Chief Justices. During McKenna's tenure, the nation's political system grappled with the problems generated by industrialization, urbanization, and rising class conflict. The same problems followed many of the issues that came before the Court, whose decisions lacked consistency and predictability.

When President WILLIAM MCKINLEY named McKenna, his old House of Representatives colleague, to the seat vacated by Justice STEPHEN J. FIELD, he recognized not distinction at the bar or on the bench but loyal service. McKenna had been a four-term representative from California, a member of the Ninth Circuit Court of Appeals, and attorney general of the United States. In these roles McKenna had earned a justified reputation for devotion to the Republican party, the protective tariff, and the interests of his chief patron, the railroad mogul Leland Stanford. Even as a member of the circuit court, McKenna had written several opinions protecting Stanford's powerful Southern Pacific company from the unfriendly behavior of local and state officials who sought to regulate the carrier's rates and terminal facilities.

As a member of the Supreme Court during the high tide of the Progressive era, however, McKenna supported the efforts of THEODORE ROOSEVELT's and WILLIAM HOWARD TAFT's administrations to bring the country's major railroads under a larger measure of administrative control through the Interstate Commerce Commission (ICC). Times had changed. By the turn of the century, even the railroads desired a degree of federal regulation that would protect them from conflicting state laws and the debilitating rate wars which drained away profits. McKenna wrote opinions for the Court that confirmed the new relationship between the carriers and the federal government by upholding the ICC's statutory powers with respect to fact-gathering and rate making.

McKenna also became a robust supporter of congressional efforts to regulate other aspects of the nation's economic and social life under authority of the COMMERCE CLAUSE. He joined Justice JOHN M. HARLAN's crucial opinion in CHAMPION V. AMES (1903), which laid the foundation for a NATIONAL POLICE POWER by giving Congress the authority to exclude from the channels of INTERSTATE COMMERCE supposedly harmful goods such as lottery tickets. McKenna later applied this principle in his own opinions, which sustained the PURE FOOD AND DRUG ACT and also the Mann Act, banning the transportation of women in interstate commerce for immoral purposes.

To his great credit, McKenna was able to accept the extension of the national power doctrine to child labor in the famous case of HAMMER V. DAGENHART (1918), even while others who had endorsed the earlier decisions turned their backs upon logic and history. Nor did he join the majority in the case of ADAIR V. UNITED STATES (1908), where six Justices overturned Congress's attempt to ban YELLOW DOG CONTRACTS on the nation's railroads. McKenna's dissent placed the authority of Congress to regulate commerce above the contractual freedom of corporate management.

A stout nationalist and a moderate Republican who remained capable of accepting many progressive reforms, McKenna nonetheless displayed a checkered record with regard to state and federal efforts to assist the working class and organized labor. He refused, for example, to permit the state of Kansas to outlaw yellow dog contracts in all private industry, although he endorsed Congress's effort to do so on the interstate railroads. He cast his vote with RUFUS PECKHAM in LOCHNER V. NEW YORK (1905) and with GEORGE H. SUTHERLAND in ADKINS V. CHILDREN'S HOSPITAL (1923), when the majority struck down MAXIMUM HOURS AND MINIMUM WAGE LEGISLATION on the grounds of FREEDOM OF CONTRACT. Yet McKenna spurned that conservative shibboleth in MULLER V. OREGON (1908), WILSON V. NEW (1917), and BUNTING V. OREGON (1917). On the other hand, not many opinions could match in reactionary tone McKenna's dissent in the *Arizona Employers' Liability Cases* (1919), where he argued that liability without fault violated the DUE PROCESS clause of the FOURTEENTH AMENDMENT.

Like most of his brethren on the WHITE COURT, McKenna gave the green light to federal and state efforts to stamp out dissent during WORLD WAR I. He voted to uphold the convictions of Charles Schenck and Eugene V. Debs as well as those of Jacob Abrams and Joseph Gilbert, although the latter two cases provoked sharp dissents from OLIVER WENDELL HOLMES and LOUIS D. BRANDEIS. If sometimes contractual freedom had to give way before the power of Congress, McKenna believed, so, too, did the liberty to protest against the government in time of war.

MICHAEL E. PARRISH
(1986)

Bibliography

MCDEVITT, BROTHER MATTHEW 1946 *Joseph McKenna: Associate Justice of the United States.* Washington, D.C.: Catholic University Press.

SEMONCHE, JOHN E. 1978 *Charting the Future: The Supreme Court Responds to a Changing Society, 1890–1920.* Westport, Conn.: Greenwood Press.

MCKINLEY, JOHN
(1780–1852)

Like several other Jacksonian Justices on the TANEY COURT, John McKinley was a product of the Southwest. Born in Virginia, he went with his family to Kentucky where he learned law and began practice. In 1818 he moved to Huntsville, Alabama, then a frontier town, where he practiced law and pursued a diversified political career—first as a supporter of HENRY CLAY and then, when Clay's fortunes waned in Alabama, of ANDREW JACKSON. This timely shift got him a Senate seat in 1826. He served there until 1830, when he lost reelection. He then returned to the Alabama legislature, and in 1832 he went to the United States House of Representatives where he served for one term. After another term in the state legislature in 1836, he was elected by that body to the Senate but chose instead to accept an appointment to the Supreme Court from MARTIN VAN BUREN in 1837.

McKinley's legislative career lacked distinction, but the policy preferences he revealed were those that would guide his work on the Court: in addition to unswerving loyalty to Jackson and Van Buren, he was a strict states' rights man, though he never argued out his case philosophically or constitutionally. In good Jacksonian fashion he was suspicious of monopolies and hated the second Bank of the United States. He also had a strong preference for land laws that favored small settlers and a firm belief that SLAVERY was a state problem and that property in slaves was entitled to legal protection.

McKinley's fifteen years on the Supreme Court (1837–1852) were unproductive and frustrating, both for him and for those who worked with him. In general, states' rights ideas guided his judicial behavior, but he never spoke for the Court in any important cases. He took his duties seriously, as Chief Justice ROGER B. TANEY pointed out in his brief eulogy, and was decent and fairminded to the best of his ability. But during his entire tenure, which was interrupted by illness and frequent absences, he wrote only about twenty opinions for the Court, all routine.

Perhaps his most notorious opinion came in BANK OF AUGUSTA V. EARLE (1839) where, both on circuit and in a lone dissent at Washington, he held that a CORPORATION chartered in one state (a bank in the *Earle* case) could not do business within the boundaries of another state without the latter's express consent. McKinley's position was consistent with a deep concern for state SOVEREIGNTY, but it was, as Justice JOSEPH STORY observed in dismay, totally unrealistic in an age when interstate corporate business was increasingly the norm. McKinley dissented twenty-three times but none of his dissents attracted support and none pioneered new law. Many were unwritten, evidence of the Justice's increasing isolation from the ongoing operations of the Court.

McKinley was also isolated on his own circuit, although Supreme Court Justices, as senior circuit judges, ordinarily dominated the district judges with whom they sat. Not so on the Fifth Circuit where district judges Philip K. Lawrence and, to a lesser extent, Theodore H. McCaleb held the upper hand. There is evidence also that leading members of the circuit bar held the Justice in disrepute. Part of the problem was the 10,000 miles of annual travel (which left McKinley little time to study cases) and the large number of cases (2,700 at each of the two terms in 1839 by his reckoning). His circuit also included Louisiana, where the civil law received from France and the COMMON LAW formed a mixture that was well-nigh incomprehensible to all save lawyers who grew up with it. The main difficulty on circuit as on the full Court, however, was McKinley himself. His talents were simply too modest for the duties of his office. Even his eulogizers found nothing about his legal ability to praise, and all evidence points to the correctness of CARL B. SWISHER's assessment: that John McKinley, of all the Justices on the Taney Court, was the least distinguished.

R. KENT NEWMYER
(1986)

Bibliography

GATELL, FRANK O. 1969 John McKinley. In Leon Friedman and Fred L. Israel (eds.), *The Justices of the United States Supreme Court 1789–1969*, Vol. 1, pages 769–792. New York: Chelsea House.

Proceedings in Relation to the Death of the Late Judge McKinley 1852 14 Howard iii–v.

MCKINLEY, WILLIAM
(1843–1901)

William McKinley, an Ohio Republican who was President of the United States from 1897 to 1901, spent most of his term in office preoccupied with foreign affairs. An imperialist, he advocated the annexation of Hawaii and, after successfully prosecuting a war against Spain, acquired the Philippines and PUERTO RICO for the United States. McKinley continued the domestic policies of his predecessor, GROVER CLEVELAND, but unlike most Chief Executives in the late nineteenth century, McKinley saw the presidency as a powerful office. He frequently relied on expert and academic commissions to offer him advice on specific problems.

McKinley's lack of interest in enforcing the SHERMAN ANTITRUST ACT paralleled BENJAMIN HARRISON's, but McKinley's failure to enforce the law vigorously is more significant because he held office during the second greatest merger movement in American history. His three attorneys general—one of whom, JOSEPH MCKENNA, would be his sole appointment to the Supreme Court—initiated only three cases under the act. The most important ANTITRUST cases decided during McKinley's tenure, UNITED STATES V. TRANS-MISSOURI FREIGHT ASSOCIATION (1897) and *Addyston Pipe & Steel Co. v. United States* (1899), had been started under prior administrations.

DAVID GORDON
(1986)

Bibliography

GOULD, LEWIS L. 1980 *The Presidency of William McKinley.* Lawrence: Regents Press of Kansas.

MCLAUGHLIN, ANDREW C.
(1861–1947)

A protégé of THOMAS COOLEY at the University of Michigan, Andrew Cunningham McLaughlin took over his course in American constitutional history and later taught that subject at the University of Chicago for thirty years. In his 1914 presidential address before the American Historical Association, McLaughlin criticized CHARLES BEARD's monolithic emphasis on economic factors. McLaughlin also rejected the tone of exaltation that imbued the work of JOHN FISKE and others on the CONSTITUTIONAL CONVENTION OF 1787. In his first major book, *Confederation and Constitution* (1905), McLaughlin emphasized the constructive aspects of the ARTICLES OF CONFEDERATION and of the Confederation period. He construed the Articles as the product of a war against centralism and as the world's first written CONSTITUTION to establish a federal system, whose origins he traced to the British Empire. His other important works, distinguished for their judicious interpretations, were *Courts, Constitutions, and Parties* (1912), *Foundations of American Constitutionalism* (1932), and *Constitutional History of the United States* (1935), which won a Pulitzer Prize.

LEONARD W. LEVY
(1986)

MCLAUGHLIN v. FLORIDA

See: Miscegenation

MCLAURIN v. OKLAHOMA STATE REGENTS

See: *Sweatt v. Painter*

MCLEAN, JOHN
(1785–1861)

John McLean's appointment to the Supreme Court on March 6, 1829, was ANDREW JACKSON's first and the first from the old Northwest and Ohio, where McLean had grown to manhood. He studied law with Arthur St. Clair, Jr., was admitted to the bar in 1807, and maintained an active full-time practice in Lebanon, Ohio, until his 1812 election to Congress, where he served two terms. As a

National Republican, he favored a protective tariff and a national bank. From 1816 to 1822 he served as judge of the Ohio Supreme Court where he gained a respect for the COMMON LAW and developed a penchant for bending it "to the diversity of our circumstances," as he put it in one case. While serving on that court, McLean assiduously cultivated political favor, first with JAMES MONROE and JOHN QUINCY ADAMS, and, when the latter began to falter, with Jackson. His efforts paid off, first in 1822 with an appointment as Commissioner of the General Land Office, then in 1823 as Postmaster General, where his brilliant administrative abilities won him a national reputation. Adams reappointed him to head the Post Office Department, and Jackson was willing to do the same but nominated him to the Supreme Court when McLean indicated an unwillingness to make political removals.

McLean served as Associate Justice from 1829 to 1861, during a period of rapid transition in American law. At the outset the new Justice inclined toward Jacksonian STATES' RIGHTS dogma, as in his dissent from CONTRACT CLAUSE orthodoxy in CRAIG V. MISSOURI (1830). More revealing yet was his practical-minded opinion for the majority in BRISCOE V. BANK OF THE COMMONWEALTH OF KENTUCKY (1837), which held that the notes of the Commonwealth Bank were not BILLS OF CREDIT prohibited by Article I, section 10, even though the state owned the bank and the notes circulated as legal tender.

Despite his result-oriented approach in such cases as *Briscoe* and MAYOR OF NEW YORK V. MILN (1837) (where he supported STATE POLICE POWER regulations against the charge that they were regulations of INTERSTATE COMMERCE), McLean was not a Jacksonian judge. Indeed, he moved steadily toward a conservative nationalism similar to that of Justice JOSEPH STORY, who became his closest friend on the Court. That McLean was solidly conservative on property rights and CORPORATION questions is clear from his majority opinion in behalf of contractual sanctity in PIQUA BRANCH BANK V. KNOOP (1854). His nationalism was apparent in the CHEROKEE INDIAN CASES (*Worcester v. Georgia*) in 1832 (where he joined JOHN MARSHALL against Georgia and Jackson), and in *Holmes v. Jennison* in 1840 (where he concurred in ROGER B. TANEY's dissent which asserted the supremacy of the federal government in the area of foreign policy). His "high-toned FEDERALISM" in COMMERCE CLAUSE cases can be seen in the LICENSE CASES (1847) and PASSENGER CASES (1849) and in his majority opinion in *Pennsylvania v. Wheeling and Belmont Bridge Company* (1852) which struck down a Virginia law authorizing a bridge that obstructed commerce over a navigable river. His dissent in COOLEY V. BOARD OF WARDENS OF PHILADELPHIA (1851) reaffirmed the theory of his friend Story that the power to regulate foreign and interstate commerce belonged exclusively to Congress.

McLean disliked SLAVERY and his opinions often revealed his free-soil sentiments; but he regularly conceded the legality of the institution. Thus his separate opinion in PRIGG V. PENNSYLVANIA (1842) upheld the right of northern states to protect free Negroes from unlawful rendition, but it also affirmed the power of Congress to require the states to return fugitives. Equivocation was unavoidable, too, in GROVES V. SLAUGHTER (1841) where in a separate opinion McLean argued that slavery was a local institution under state control and that the power of Congress to regulate interstate commerce did not prevent a state from regulating the importation of slaves. Free states presumably could prohibit slaves from being brought into their jurisdiction and liberate slaves once they arrived, but slave states could also regulate imports and exports of slaves for sale. On circuit McLean also ruled against freedom when he thought the law obliged him to do so.

McLean's proslavery decisions, which were condemned in the free-soil press, increasingly ran counter to his presidential plans which, to the distress of some of his colleagues, he relentlessly pursued from the bench. In DRED SCOTT V. SANDFORD (1857) his political ambition, now focused on the Republican party, influenced his judicial behavior. In a separate dissent, he argued that Congress had the power to prohibit slavery in the TERRITORIES, that Negroes could be citizens, and that Dred Scott was free by virtue of his residence in a free state and a free territory. McLean has been unfairly blamed for the Court's wide-ranging, politically explosive decision—a burden we now know should fall most heavily on Taney and JAMES M. WAYNE. But there is no doubt that McLean's determination to dissent gave Taney and Wayne a good excuse to confront the whole problem of SLAVERY IN THE TERRITORIES.

McLean was not a legal scholar, he pioneered no new DOCTRINE, and he did not greatly refine the process of constitutional adjustment to new circumstances that was the hallmark of the TANEY COURT. Greatness, however, is not only rare but relative, and on a Court burdened with mediocrity McLean looked good. His opinions were generally solid and persuasive (as in the great copyright case of *Wheaton v. Peters* in 1834) and he assuredly carried more than his share of the Court's heavy work load (with nearly 250 majority opinions and numerous dissents). He was one of the few Justices of the period who went to the considerable trouble of publishing his circuit opinions (in six volumes) and whose circuit opinions were worth publishing. It is true that his political ambition contributed to the politicization of the judicial process. Still, he cherished the Court as an institution and worked diligently through it to preserve the Union under the Constitution.

R. KENT NEWMYER
(1986)

Bibliography

GATELL, FRANK O. 1969 John McLean. In Leon Friedman and Fred L. Israel (eds.), *The Justices of the United States Supreme Court, 1789–1969*, Vol. 1, pages 535–567. New York: Chelsea House.

WEISENBURGER, FRANCIS P. 1937 *The Life of John McLean: A Politician on the United States Supreme Court*. Columbus: Ohio State University Press.

MCNABB-MALLORY RULE

Partly in response to the problem posed by the VOLUNTARINESS test, the Supreme Court made an unexpected departure from that test in *McNabb v. United States* (1943) and *Mallory v. United States* (1957). Under the "McNabb-Mallory Rule," a confession obtained by law enforcement officers during a period of unnecessary delay in bringing an arrested person before a magistrate for arraignment was inadmissible in federal prosecutions. The rule was based not on constitutional grounds but on the Court's supervisory authority over the administration of criminal justice in the federal courts. The rule created more problems than it attempted to solve, and in 1968, Congress abolished it.

In *McNabb*, five brothers were arrested for murder and held in barren detention cells for forty-eight hours. Isolated from friends and family, and without the assistance of counsel, they were repeatedly interrogated until confessions were obtained. (See POLICE INTERROGATIONS AND CONFESSIONS.) Only after they confessed were they taken before a magistrate for arraignment. The confessions were admitted into EVIDENCE at trial and the McNabbs were convicted.

The Court, with only Justice STANLEY F. REED dissenting, reversed the convictions on the ground that they were unlawfully obtained during a period of prolonged custodial delay. Federal laws in effect at the time of the Court's decision required officers to take an arrested person "immediately" before a magistrate for arraignment. At arraignment, the magistrate advises the defendant of the charges against him, of his constitutional rights, and sets a preliminary hearing date at which the government must show legal cause for the detention.

Justice FELIX FRANKFURTER devoted much of his opinion for the Court to an analysis of the policies behind the immediate arraignment laws. He concluded that they were intended to protect the rights of arrested persons and to deter the police from secret third-degree interrogation of persons not yet arraigned.

Finding that the officers who arrested the McNabbs had acted in willful disobedience of the laws requiring immediate arraignment, the Court suppressed the confessions. Suppression, Frankfurter explained, would promote the policies behind the laws and ensure the fair and effective administration of the federal criminal justice system by disallowing convictions based on unfair police procedures.

Two years after *McNabb*, Congress adopted Rule 5(a) of the FEDERAL RULES OF CRIMINAL PROCEDURE. The rule required that an arrested person be taken, "without unnecessary delay," before the nearest available commissioner or any other nearby officer empowered to commit persons charged with offenses against the laws of the United States. The rule, by failing to include remedies for its violation, left intact the *McNabb* mandate that confessions obtained during a period of unlawful detention be suppressed. Any questions regarding the continuing viability of the *McNabb* rule were put to rest by the Court's opinion in *Mallory*.

Mallory was arrested with two other suspects on rape charges. Although the police had sufficient evidence to consider Mallory the prime suspect, he was not arraigned until ten hours after his arrest, during which time he was continually interrogated and finally signed a written confession. At trial, the signed confession was introduced into evidence; Mallory was convicted and received the death sentence.

Frankfurter delivered the opinion of a unanimous Court, which held the confession inadmissible because Mallory had not been arraigned without unnecessary delay as required by Rule 5(a). The Court's interpretation of Rule 5(a) was based on the principles announced earlier in the *McNabb* decision. Delays in arraignment must be prevented in order to prevent abusive and unlawful law enforcement practices aimed at obtaining confessions of guilt from suspects in custody who have not been informed by a judicial officer of the charges against them or of their constitutional rights.

After *Mallory* the law prevailing in the federal courts, commonly referred to as the "McNabb-Mallory Rule," was that any confession made by a suspect under arrest, in violation of Rule 5(a), was inadmissible in evidence. The problem with the McNabb-Mallory Rule was that it operated arbitrarily to exclude from evidence otherwise free and voluntary confessions merely because of delay in arraignment. In other words, the United States Supreme Court had failed to consider the obvious: a delayed arraignment does not imply the involuntariness of a confession.

Criticized as illogical and unrealistic, the McNabb-Mallory Rule was abolished in 1968 when Congress enacted Title II of the OMNIBUS CRIME CONTROL AND SAFE STREETS ACT. The act provides in part that confessions shall not be inadmissible solely because of delay in arraignment, if they are voluntary and made within six hours of arrest or during a delay in arraignment that is reasonable, considering the transportation problems in getting a defendant before a magistrate. Thus, the voluntary nature of the confession is the test of its admissibility, and delay in arraignment is only one factor for the judge to consider.

WENDY E. LEVY
(1986)

Bibliography

STEPHENS, OTIS H., JR. 1973 *The Supreme Court and Confessions of Guilt.* Pages 63–89. Knoxville: University of Tennessee Press.

MCREYNOLDS, JAMES C.
(1862–1946)

James Clark McReynolds, a Tennessee Democrat, first came to national attention as an antitrust prosecutor during the THEODORE ROOSEVELT and WILLIAM HOWARD TAFT administrations. He was a Tennessee Gold Democrat, friendly with Colonel Edward House, WOODROW WILSON's key adviser. His antitrust reputation led to his appointment as Wilson's attorney general in 1913. Within a year, however, McReynolds found himself at odds with the administration and powerful congressmen. Wilson "kicked McReynolds upstairs" to the Supreme Court in 1914. From then until his retirement in 1941, McReynolds distinguished himself as a consistent and implacable foe of Progressive and NEW DEAL regulatory programs.

McReynold's hostility to trusts largely derived from his ideas of individualism and freedom from arbitrary restraints. Throughout his judicial career he resolutely supported the business community and was instinctively suspicious of governmental regulation. "If real competition is to continue, the right of the individual to exercise reasonable discretion in respect of his own business methods must be preserved," McReynolds wrote in FEDERAL TRADE COMMISSION V. GRATZ (1920). In that case, the Court limited the authority of the FTC, the creation of which had been one of the Wilson administration's primary achievements; McReynolds wrote that the courts, not the commission, would decide the meaning of "unfair method of competition." In *St. Louis and O'Fallon Railroad v. United States* (1929) the Court resolved a long-standing dispute between the Interstate Commerce Commission (ICC) and railroads as to whether original or replacement costs should be considered for valuation and rate purposes. Speaking for a narrow majority, McReynolds overturned ICC policy by ruling that the commission had to base its determination of rates on replacement costs, which were higher.

McReynolds resisted the claims of organized labor. For example, he joined his colleagues in rejecting federal child labor laws and a District of Columbia minimum wage statute. When the Court in 1919 sustained an Arizona law holding employers responsible for on-the-job accidents whether or not they were negligent, McReynolds dissented, caustically arguing that such laws served "to stifle enterprise, produce discontent, strife, idleness and pauperism."

Without exception, McReynolds supported the conviction of political radicals during the "Red Scare" period following WORLD WAR I a decade later, when the Court turned against restrictive state measures on speech and press, McReynolds parted company with the majority, dissenting in STROMBERG V. CALIFORNIA (1931) and NEAR V. MINNESOTA (1931). Similarly, McReynolds's ill-concealed contempt for blacks led to dissent from decisions striking down an all-white primary law and ordering a new trial for the Scottsboro defendants. Finally, when the Court, in MISSOURI EX REL. GAINES V. CANADA (1938), began its long process of overturning segregation, McReynolds bitterly assailed the majority opinion.

Some of McReynolds's opinions defending individual rights remain relevant. In MEYER V. NEBRASKA (1923) he spoke for the Court in striking down a state statute prohibiting German language instruction in the public schools; in PIERCE V. SOCIETY OF SISTERS (1925) he ruled against an Oregon statute that had the effect of proscribing parochial school education; and in CARROLL V. UNITED STATES (1925) he vehemently protested against violations of the FOURTH AMENDMENT in enforcing PROHIBITION. In MYERS V. UNITED STATES (1926) he dissented from what he considered to be an almost unlimited approval of presidential power to remove federal officials, a view vindicated nine years later when the Court unanimously rejected President FRANKLIN D. ROOSEVELT's attempt to remove a federal trade commissioner.

The New Deal years provide the sharpest focus for McReynolds's views of constitutional law, both when he joined in majority opinions and later in the bitter dissents that represent his most familiar legacy. McReynolds combined his ideological reaction to the New Deal with a passionate, almost pathological, hatred for Franklin D. Roosevelt. The Justice was scathing in his private remarks and, at times, indiscreet in public. In his courtroom dissent in the GOLD CLAUSE CASES (1935) McReynolds emotionally proclaimed: "This is Nero at his worst. The Constitution is gone!" When the New Deal gained a few early Court victories, McReynolds dissented, as in the gold clause cases, in NEBBIA V. NEW YORK (1934), and in ASHWANDER V. TENNESSEE VALLEY AUTHORITY (1936). As one of the "Four Horsemen," he participated in striking down thirteen New Deal measures between 1934 and 1936. When the Court made its famous shift, beginning in 1937 with WEST COAST HOTEL COMPANY V. PARRISH and the WAGNER ACT

CASES, McReynolds joined his fellow conservatives in outraged dissent. As their spokesman in *National Labor Relations Board v. Friedman-Marks Clothing* (1937), he argued that the WAGNER ACT regulated production, not commerce, and thus exceeded the boundaries of congressional power as set in long-standing precedents. Similarly, he considered the SOCIAL SECURITY ACT unconstitutional; he registered a lone dissent against the approval of the securities registration provisions of the PUBLIC UTILITIES HOLDING COMPANY ACT; and, finally, he provided the sole dissent to the Court's recognition in 1940 that labor PICKETING was entitled to protection as an exercise of FREEDOM OF SPEECH.

Few Supreme Court Justices have been more outspoken or more doctrinaire than McReynolds; and few have been so incompatible with colleagues. McReynolds refused to speak to fellow Wilson appointee John H. Clarke, who was too liberal, and to LOUIS D. BRANDEIS and BENJAMIN N. CARDOZO, who were both liberal and Jewish. Even Chief Justice Taft found him "selfish and prejudiced" and difficult to like. He was committed to laissez-faire individualism and racial segregation, and he was unyielding and hostile to any political beliefs he regarded as deviant.

STANLEY I. KUTLER
(1986)

Bibliography

MASON, ALPHEUS THOMAS 1956 *Harlan Fiske Stone: Pillar of the Law.* New York: Viking.

PASCHAL, JOEL F. 1951 *Mr. Justice Sutherland: A Man Against the State.* Princeton, N.J.: Princeton University Press.

MECHANICAL JURISPRUDENCE

This pejorative epithet was introduced in 1908 by the American jurist ROSCOE POUND. It and similar rubrics— "the jurisprudence of conceptions," "slot machine, phonograph, T-square theories of law"—were widely used to caricature patterns of juristic thought and judicial action that deduced conclusions from unexamined, predetermined conceptions by purely mechanical logical processes, disregarded socioeconomic realities and practical consequences, and understated the degree of judicial lawmaking by attributing a machinelike automatism to the judicial process.

The "sociological jurisprudence" and "legal realism" of Justices OLIVER WENDELL HOLMES, HARLAN FISKE STONE, and BENJAMIN N. CARDOZO were often hailed as correctives for mechanical jurisprudence because they viewed law and logic instrumentally as means to social ends, and they acknowledged judicial lawmaking.

A perennial juristic allurement, mechanical jurispru-

dence was exemplified by many Supreme Court "economic DUE PROCESS" and COMMERCE CLAUSE decisions between 1895 and 1937. In due process cases such as LOCHNER V. NEW YORK (1905) and ADKINS V. CHILDREN'S HOSPITAL (1923), the Court invoked the laissez-faire doctrine, FREEDOM OF CONTRACT, which regarded workers and employers as bargaining equals, in holding state and federal legislation unconstitutional. In commerce clause cases such as UNITED STATES V. E. C. KNIGHT CO. (1895) and CARTER V. CARTER COAL CO. (1936), the Court used economically unrealistic distinctions between "commerce" and PRODUCTION, and "direct" and "indirect" EFFECTS ON COMMERCE in invalidating federal legislation. A classic expression of mechanical jurisprudence is the passage of Justice Owen Roberts's opinion in UNITED STATES V. BUTLER (1936) where he said the Court had only to compare the statute with the appropriate constitutional clause to see if they squared.

Such decisions led finally to President FRANKLIN D. ROOSEVELT's 1937 "Court reform" bill, designed, he said, "to save the Constitution from the Court and the Court from itself." But the Court swiftly reversed and reformed itself, abandoning these mechanical constitutional interpretations. Later, in WICKARD V. FILBURN (1942), it reemphasized that its recognition of economic realities had made "the mechanical application of legal formulas no longer feasible."

HOWARD E. DEAN
(1986)

Bibliography

POUND, ROSCOE 1908 Mechanical Jurisprudence. *Columbia Law Review* 8:605 623.

STERN, ROBERT L. 1951 The Problems of Yesteryear—Commerce and Due Process. *Vanderbilt Law Review* 4:446–468.

MEDIA AND THE CONSTITUTION

See: Broadcasting; Freedom of the Press; Free Press/Fair Trial; Journalistic Practices, Tort Liability, and the Freedom of the Press

MEESE COMMISSION

The Attorney General's Commission on Pornography, better known as "The Meese Commission" after Attorney General Edwin Meese, was charged to "determine the nature, extent, and impact on society of pornography in the United States, and to make specific recommendations to the Attorney General concerning more effective ways in which the spread of pornography could be contained, consistent with constitutional guarantees." The committee included three attorneys, two psychologists, a city council member, a federal judge, a social worker, a magazine editor, and a priest. It had a balanced religious and political composition as well.

After a year of extensive hearings, field trips, and study, the commission produced a 1,960-page report. If the size of the report were not daunting enough, the findings of the commission were relatively inconclusive. Although the commission did take a stand on the issue of PORNOGRA-PHY—something a similar presidential commission established during the Nixon administration failed to do—it did not wholly condemn pornography as the right, especially the religious right, and feminists had hoped. Instead, it unanimously condemned sexually explicit material that is violent in nature; sexually explicit materials that show situations where women are humiliated, demeaned, and subjugated; and CHILD PORNOGRAPHY in any form.

A major problem the commission faced was its inability to define key terms. The commission found it difficult to define "pornography," "obscenity," and "hardcore." In the end, it could do no better than Justice POTTER J. STEWART had in JACOBELLIS V. OHIO (1964). Stewart, although not defining pornography, qualified it by stating, "I know it when I see it." Hampered by the inability to define key terms, the commission called for further research.

JEFFREY D. SCHULTZ
(1992)

Bibliography

ATTORNEY GENERAL'S COMMISSION ON PORNOGRAPHY 1986 *Final Report.* Washington, D.C.: U.S. Government Printing Office.

KEATING, CHARLES H., JR., 1970 *Report of Charles H. Keating, Jr., Commissioner: Commission of Obscenity and Pornography.* Cincinnati, Ohio: Charles H. Keating, Jr.

STANMEYER, WILLIAM 1986 The Pornography Commission Report: A Plea for Decency. *Benchmark* II:227–236.

MEIKLEJOHN, ALEXANDER
(1872–1964)

Alexander Meiklejohn was a philosopher, president of Amherst College, and director of an experimental college at the University of Wisconsin. After his long academic career he became a CIVIL LIBERTIES publicist. His *Free Speech and Its Relation to Self-Government* (1948) presented the FIRST AMENDMENT as the foundation of political democracy. He advocated that citizens should have the same unlimited FREEDOM OF SPEECH as their representatives. Regarding the CLEAR AND PRESENT DANGER TEST and BALANCING TESTS as annulments of the First Amendment, he criticized OLIVER WENDELL HOLMES and ZECHARIAH CHAFEE as proponents of a stunted interpretation of free

speech. In the McCarthy period he defended the right of communists to teach. His essay, "The First Amendment Is An Absolute," written when he was almost ninety, summarized his position, which was not really absolutist. Distinguishing "the freedom of speech" from "speech," he believed that private defamation, OBSCENITY, perjury, false advertising, and solicitation of crime were not constitutionally protected. His ABSOLUTISM seems to have extended to speech concerning all matters of public policy, education, philosophy, arts, literature, and science, but he believed that even protected speech was subject to reasonable regulations of time and place. Meiklejohn was closer to Holmes and Chafee than he admitted.

LEONARD W. LEVY
(1986)

MEMOIRS v. MASSACHUSETTS
383 U.S. 413 (1966)

Nine years after ROTH V. UNITED STATES, still unable to agree upon a constitutional definition of OBSCENITY, the Supreme Court reversed a state court determination that John Cleland's *Memoirs of a Woman of Pleasure*, commonly known as *Fanny Hill*, was obscene. The three-Justice PLURALITY OPINION, written by Justice WILLIAM J. BRENNAN, held that the constitutional test for obscenity was: "(a) the dominant theme of the material taken as a whole appeals to a prurient interest in sex; (b) the material is patently offensive because it affronts contemporary community standards relating to the description or representation of sexual matters; and (c) the material is utterly without redeeming social value."

Despite an OBITER DICTUM in JACOBELLIS V. OHIO (1964), it was believed—and the Massachusetts courts had held—that *Roth* did not require unqualified worthlessness before a book might be deemed obscene. Justice Brennan twisted the *Roth* reasoning (that obscenity was unprotected because it was utterly worthless) into a constitutional test that was virtually impossible to meet under criminal standards of proof. Thus a finding of obscenity would become rare, even where the requisite prurient interest appeal and offensiveness could be demonstrated.

The Massachusetts courts had tried the book in the abstract; a host of literary experts testified to its social value. The circumstances of the book's production, sale, and publicity were not admitted. Justice Brennan noted that evidence that distributors commercially exploited *Fanny Hill* solely for its prurient appeal could have justified a finding, based on the purveyor's own evaluation, that *Fanny Hill* was utterly without redeeming social importance.

Justices HUGO L. BLACK, WILLIAM O. DOUGLAS, and POTTER J. STEWART concurred in the result, Black and Douglas adhering to their view that obscenity is protected expression. Stewart reiterated his view that the First Amendment protected all but "hard-core pornography."

Justice TOM C. CLARK, dissenting, rejected the importation of the "utterly without redeeming social value" standard into the obscenity test, which he believed would give the "smut artist free rein." Reacting against the continuous flow of pornographic materials to the Supreme Court, he reasserted that the Court should apply a "sufficient evidence" standard of review of lower courts' obscenity decisions.

Justice JOHN MARSHALL HARLAN, dissenting, argued that although the federal government could constitutionally proscribe only hard-core pornography, the states could prohibit material under any criteria rationally related to accepted notions of obscenity.

Justice BYRON R. WHITE, also dissenting, argued that *Roth* counseled examination of the predominant theme of the material, not resort to minor themes of passages of literary worth to redeem obscene works from condemnation.

KIM MCLANE WARDLAW
(1986)

MEMORANDUM ORDER

Most orders of any court are not accompanied by opinions, but are simply stated in memorandum form. The Supreme Court issues thousands of such memorandum orders each year, granting or denying such requests as applications for review, applications for permission to appear IN FORMA PAUPERIS, applications for permission to file briefs AMICI CURIAE, or PETITIONS FOR REHEARING.

Some memorandum orders effectively decide cases; the denial of a petition for CERTIORARI is one example, and another is the dismissal of an APPEAL "for want of a substantial federal question." Occasionally the Court summarily affirms the decision of a lower court, issuing no opinion but only a memorandum order. The denial of certiorari generally has little force as a PRECEDENT; however, both lower courts and commentators do draw conclusions concerning the Court's view when they see a consistent pattern of refusal to review lower court decisions reaching the same conclusion. The summary affirmance of a decision in a memorandum order does establish a precedent, but the precedent is limited to the points necessarily decided by the lower court, and does not extend to the reasoning in that court's opinion. The practice of deciding major issues through memorandum orders is often criticized on the ground that decisions will not be understood as principled if they are not explained.

KENNETH L. KARST
(1986)

Bibliography

BROWN, ERNEST J. 1958 The Supreme Court, 1957 Term—Foreword: Process of Law. *Harvard Law Review* 72:77–95.

MEMPHIS v. GREENE
451 U.S. 100 (1981)

Because the City of Memphis blocked a street at the point where a white neighborhood bordered a black neighborhood, residents of the black neighborhood had to drive around the white neighborhood in order to get to and from the city center. Black residents brought a CLASS ACTION against the city, seeking an INJUNCTION to keep the street open. They failed in the federal district court, but the court of appeals held that the closing violated their right to hold and enjoy property, guaranteed by the CIVIL RIGHTS ACT OF 1866.

The Supreme Court, with Justice JOHN PAUL STEVENS writing for a 6–3 majority, rejected the statutory claim, saying the street closing had caused only minor inconvenience, and had not damaged the plaintiff's property values. The question remained whether the THIRTEENTH AMENDMENT, of its own force, forbade anything but slavery itself. The Court did not reach this broad question, saying only that the street closing here was not a BADGE OF SERVITUDE. Justice THURGOOD MARSHALL, for the dissenters, scored the majority for ignoring "the plain and powerful symbolic message of the 'inconvenience' ": to fence out "undesirables."

KENNETH L. KARST
(1986)

MENTAL ILLNESS AND THE CONSTITUTION

Mental illness has played two apparently different roles in American law generally: as a limitation on state authority to impose ordinary legal standards on individuals and as a basis for increasing state authority over individuals. The paradigmatic limiting use of mental illness is the defense of insanity for conduct that would otherwise be subject to criminal liability. Its paradigmatic use to increase state authority is in civil commitment of people who, apart from their mental illness, would not be subject to state confinement or control. In both guises, however, the same underlying justification is advanced—that a mentally ill person deserves specially beneficial treatment from the state, either to excuse him from ordinary standards of criminal liability or to protect and treat him under civil commitment laws.

Until the 1960s, constitutional doctrine paid scant attention to any of the legal usages for mental illness. Beginning in that decade, lower federal courts began to scrutinize these uses and to invoke constitutional norms in the service of that scrutiny. The central problem was that the promise of special beneficence for mental illness proved false on close examination. Although insanity was denoted a defense to criminal liability, in practice defendants thus found "not guilty" were automatically confined to state maximum security institutions indistinguishable from prisons (and often with harsher custodial conditions), were provided with virtually no psychiatric treatment, and were typically held for longer terms than if they had been convicted of the offenses charged. Similarly, individuals who were civilly committed, ostensibly for protection and treatment, in fact were regularly confined in brutal state institutions, provided no semblance of psychiatric treatment, subjected to degrading impositions such as numbing, physically harmful drug dosages, strait-jacketed isolation, and confined for long terms.

Confronted with these facts, federal courts found various violations of constitutional rights, all derived essentially from the proposition that DUE PROCESS required the state to justify any deprivation of liberty and, where that justification was based on a promise of beneficent treatment, to fulfill that promise. Thus the District of Columbia Circuit Court held in *Rouse v. Cameron* (1966) that those found not guilty by reason of insanity had a "right to treatment" and not simply custodial confinement, and in *Bolton v. Harris* (1968) that these defendants could not be automatically confined after an insanity acquittal but only if found "mentally ill" and "in need of treatment" according to civil commitment standards. For civilly committed people generally, that court found in *Lake v. Cameron* (1966) a liberty-based presumption against automatic commitment to a secure institution and a consequent right to treatment in the "least restrictive alternative" setting. Other federal courts concluded that civilly committed people generally had a constitutional right to treatment and that civil commitment must rest on proof of "danger to self or others," not simply mental illness as such, and proof moreover that would satisfy the criminal law "beyond REASONABLE DOUBT."

For more than a decade after these rulings, the Supreme Court held back from any definitive holding either to endorse or to reject these doctrinal innovations. During the 1960s, the Court did demonstrate concern for the problem of unfulfilled and even hypocritical state promises of therapeutic benefits as a justification for increased social controls. The most significant context for this Supreme Court concern was not mental illness but rather the juvenile court system, where states sought to justify the absence of criminal law procedural protections by invoking the promise of therapy. In IN RE GAULT (1967) the Court found these promises insufficiently convincing and required extensive recasting of juvenile court procedures.

In 1972 the Supreme Court first addressed the systemic implications of this same problem for state authority generally premised on mental illness. In *Jackson v. Indiana* the Court overturned common state practice regarding criminal defendants found mentally incompetent to stand trial. Traditional doctrine purported to excuse such disabled defendants from standing trial, ostensibly to benefit them; but the practical consequence was that these defendants were treated in the same way and as badly as those found not guilty by insanity. The defendants were given long-term, even lifetime, confinement in harsh facilities without semblance of psychiatric care, even if the offense charged were a petty MISDEMEANOR. The Court ruled in *Jackson* that this disposition violated due process; the conditions of this confinement must provide treatment with reasonable prospect that the defendant will be made competent to stand trial. The practical result of this ruling has been substantially to increase the treatment resources provided to defendants found incompetent for trial. To justify the confinement of defendants who, after a substantial period of confinement, remain disabled for trial purposes, a state must invoke its civil commitment laws.

With this one exception, however, the Supreme Court was hesitant during the 1970s to address the constitutional law issues raised by state invocations of mental illness. The dominant motif of the Court's work during this time can be seen in its resolution in 1979 of the question of the requisite BURDEN OF PROOF in civil commitment proceedings. The Court acknowledged that substantial due process liberty interests were at stake, but nonetheless concluded that the state's beneficent purpose toward the allegedly mentally ill person justified a less stringent burden than the criminal standard of proof; hence in *Addington v. Texas* (1979) the Court required an intermediate standard of "clear and convincing evidence."

This impulse to find some seeming middle ground between fundamentally opposed premises is also apparent in the Court's equivocal approach to the question of a constitutional right to treatment for persons confined to state mental institutions. In O'CONNOR V. DONALDSON (1975) the Court ruled that a state could not commit a person on grounds of mental illness alone but only with an added finding of danger to self or others. The Court refused, however, to decide whether a state was obliged to provide treatment to such a person rather than impose merely custodial confinement. The same issue returned to the Court in *Youngberg v. Romeo* (1982), this time regarding an institutionalized person who was retarded rather than mentally ill. Again the Court avoided a definitive resolution, ruling that the plaintiff was constitutionally entitled to "minimal treatment" that reasonably promised to reduce his aggressive outbursts—as opposed to the harsh behavior controls, such as prolonged shackling, that the state had used. The Court did not, however, reach the broader issue whether the state was obliged to provide treatment with any promise of greater benefits such as ultimate freedom from confinement.

In 1983 the Court departed from its previous pattern of equivocation in these matters. In a 5–4 decision the Court held in *Jones v. United States* that a criminal defendant found not guilty by insanity could be confined to a mental institution without regard to the maximum term for which he might have been sentenced for the offense charged. The Court ruled, moreover, that the insanity acquittal itself justified the defendant's confinement without any necessary invocation of civil commitment standards, thus effectively disapproving the 1968 court of appeals decision in *Bolton*. The Court in effect treated the "criminally insane" as different from either "criminals" or the "insane." This differential treatment can work a marked disadvantage, as the defendant in the *Jones* case found. But, the Court appeared to conclude, the defendant chooses to plead criminal insanity and thus knowingly embraces the risk of his ultimate disadvantage. Indeed, in AKE V. OKLAHOMA (1985) the Court made it easier to invoke the insanity defense by ruling that an indigent defendant is entitled to a court-appointed psychiatrist. The specific context of that case was a capital offense, where the risk of indefinite confinement following an insanity acquittal might seem invariably worthwhile; but the Court did not limit its holding to capital cases.

It is not clear whether the Court's definitive rulings in the context of criminal insanity will be followed by similar resolutions in other aspects of state authority regarding mentally ill people. The Court may have felt a special need to address criminal insanity as such because of the extraordinary public attention resulting from John Hinckley's acquittal for insanity in 1982 on the charge of attempting to assassinate President RONALD REAGAN. Whatever the future directions of judicial rulings, however, the underlying questions regarding the justifications for and scope of state authority in these matters remain difficult.

The dominant theme of the constitutional principle set out by lower courts in the 1960s and 1970s has been that mental illness is relevant to the exercise of state power only where the state promises therapeutic benefit, and that the Constitution requires that this promise be kept. Keeping the promise, however, is easier said than done. Both diagnosis and treatment of mental illness is uncertain. Furthermore, adequate therapy, either in state institutions or in community treatment facilities, will require supervision of complex bureaucracies and large expenditures of funds. Supervision of this process will severely strain both the courts' enforcement capacities and traditional conceptions of judicial authority. Some observers thus conclude that the lower courts were correct in seeing the failure and even hypocrisy of states regarding their therapeutic promises, but these courts merely compounded this error by invoking the Constitution to add new promises that similarly cannot be fulfilled.

If courts cannot and should not attempt to enforce the promise of therapy, what response is proper in the face of egregious state abuses? Some have argued that states should simply be barred from giving mental illness special legal relevance in any circumstances, as a justification either for increasing or withholding state power over individuals. In this view, states could confine people for "dangerousness" only by applying ordinary criminal law standards, and those standards should make no special dispensation for the mentally ill. A few states have essentially abolished the insanity defense and sharply limited the availability of civil commitment. Similarly, some judicial decisions such as *Rogers v. Okin* (1980) have found a constitutional right to *refuse* treatment, notwithstanding that a person has been civilly committed as mentally ill and dangerous. The premise of these decisions is not that the state might fail to keep its therapeutic promise; it is rather that the promise may be kept with excessive rigor, and that the state may thereby transgress valued boundaries of individual integrity and dignity. Though these lower court decisions do not directly embrace the view that would abolish all state mental illness powers, they share the underlying suspicion of therapeutically justified state impositions, and they apparently prefer modes of social control that do not directly purport to invade mental processes, such as imprisonment for criminal convictions.

This underlying premise is a temptingly plausible response to the sorry history of state abuse of the mentally ill. But the premise fails both as social policy and as constitutional doctrine. The consequences were disastrous for large numbers of people who were removed from state institutions in the 1960s and 1970s, in part as a response to court decisions, and were "dumped" into communities with no facilities to receive them or willingness to respond to their special needs. As constitutional doctrine, the abolitionist doctrine relies on a conception of due process "liberty" that takes insufficient account of the psychological conditions of individual autonomy that lie beneath this prized constitutional right. This conception ignores the ways in which mental illness can distort an individual's capacity to acknowledge his need for help, including state-administered assistance. It may be that state power can never be trusted to provide this help, that this is the lesson of the history of state abuse of mentally ill people in the criminal and civil law context. But this lesson has not yet been clearly written into constitutional doctrine.

ROBERT A. BURT
(1986)

(SEE ALSO: *Disabilities, Rights of Persons With; Disability Discrimination.*)

Bibliography

BROOKS, ALEXANDER D. 1974 *Law, Psychiatry and the Mental Health System,* and 1980 *Supplement.* Boston: Little, Brown.

BURT, ROBERT A. 1979 *Taking Care of Strangers: The Rule of Law in Doctor-Patient Relations.* New York: Free Press.

SCULL, ANDREW 1977 *Decarceration: Community Treatment and the Deviant: A Radical View.* Englewood Cliffs, N.J.: Prentice-Hall.

MENTAL ILLNESS AND THE CONSTITUTION
(Update)

Beginning in the 1960s, lower federal courts scrutinized with increasing intensity state claims that special statutory treatment of mental illness, either as a basis for civil commitment to psychiatric institutions or for apparent exemptions from ordinary criminal liability, were in fact beneficial to the affected individual. For almost two decades the Supreme Court was cautiously supportive of this effort, though only equivocally addressing the lower courts' most expansive findings of constitutional protections. In 1983, however, the Court definitively rejected one protective path that some lower courts had pursued; in *Jones v. United States,* the Court ruled that a criminal defendant found not guilty by reason of insanity could be confined to a mental institution without regard to the maximum term for which he might have been sentenced for the offense charged and, moreover, that the defendant could be confined without regard to the standards for mental illness civil commitment.

Two significant decisions since 1983 suggest that the Court more generally has resolved to abandon its prior tolerance, if not wholehearted support, for judicial scrutiny of state authority regarding mental illness. In *Allen v. Illinois* (1986), the Court ruled that the Fifth Amendment RIGHT AGAINST SELF-INCRIMINATION does not apply to commitment proceedings based on mental illness, thus upholding the use of derogatory evidence obtained from a court-ordered psychiatric interview. The Court accepted at face value both the state's characterization of the proceedings as "civil" (even though the statute under review

applied only to mentally ill people who were "sexually dangerous" and had already been charged with a criminal offense) and the state's claim that the purpose of the commitment was "treatment, not punishment" (even though the person would be confined for an indeterminate term in a maximum-security facility adjoining, though administratively distinct from, a state prison). Similarly, in WASHINGTON V. HARPER (1990) the Court ruled that a criminally convicted prisoner could be compelled to take psychotropic medication without any recourse to judicial proceedings to examine either the prisoner's mental competency or need for the medication. The Court thus effectively disapproved the extensive prior efforts of lower federal courts to establish constitutional protections against forced medication for civilly committed people, as in *Rennie v. Klein* (1983) and *Rogers v. Okin* (1984).

The Supreme Court's disavowal of this kind of judicial scrutiny comes at a time of popular arousal about homeless people in urban areas, many of whom appear to be mentally ill. Their visibly disturbing presence has been widely blamed on past judicial inquiries into conditions in mental institutions and the "deinstitutionalization" movement given impetus by these court decisions. Many states have responded to this popular concern by enacting more liberal standards for civil commitment, not only to avert "dangerous" conduct but also to forestall "substantial mental deterioration." Though some lower courts have constitutionally invalidated such liberalized criteria, it is unlikely that the Supreme Court today would agree.

In one limited context the Supreme Court has recently enlarged the state's obligation to give special advantage to mentally ill people; in FORD V. WAINWRIGHT (1986) the Court ruled that states are constitutionally prohibited from executing a mentally incompetent person. But this apparent beneficence has a twist that ironically corresponds to the overall direction of the Court's recent jurisprudence regarding mental illness: the state will now provide psychiatric treatment to incompetent people so that, when cured, they can be killed.

ROBERT A. BURT
(1992)

Bibliography

KIESLER, CHARLES A. and SIBULKIN, AMY E. 1987 *Mental Hospitalization: Myths and Facts About a National Crisis.* Newbury Park, Calif.: Sage.

MENTAL RETARDATION AND THE CONSTITUTION

The Supreme Court first addressed the constitutional status of mentally retarded people in BUCK V. BELL (1927).

In an opinion by Justice OLIVER WENDELL HOLMES, the Court upheld a state statute authorizing compulsory STERILIZATION of "mental defectives." In dismissing the claim that this imposition wrongly discriminated against retarded people and thereby denied them EQUAL PROTECTION under the FOURTEENTH AMENDMENT, Holmes appeared to invoke "minimal scrutiny" (as it was later termed), holding that the legislature might reasonably find retardation both inheritable and socially harmful. It was not until the 1970s that courts took a different, more protective stance toward retarded people. In so doing, they challenged the social attitudes of fear and aversion that lay beneath not only sterilization laws but also the general state policy, dating from the late nineteenth century, of excluding retarded people from community facilities (such as public schools) and consigning them to large, geographically isolated residential institutions.

The modern decisions involved two constitutional approaches. The first approach was to recognize a constitutional "right to treatment" for residents of state institutions. This right was initially formulated in 1971 when a federal district court held that brutal custodial conditions in an Alabama institution must be remedied by intensive educational and treatment programs conducted by new cadres of professionally qualified staff. In *Youngberg v. Romeo* (1982) the Supreme Court effectively endorsed this constitutional holding, deriving as a proposition of SUBSTANTIVE DUE PROCESS that, although the state was not required to offer any services to retarded people, if the state chose to provide residential facilities, then those facilities must meet certain minimal standards.

The second constitutional approach was initially formulated in 1972, when a federal district court overturned a state statute excluding retarded children from public schools on the ground that they were "ineducable." The court appeared to conclude that all retarded people were educable to some degree. This holding was quickly adopted by other federal courts to overturn similar state statutes and, moreover, was endorsed by Congress in the EDUCATION OF ALL HANDICAPPED CHILDREN ACT (1975) requiring education of all children, no matter how severely impaired, as a condition on federal funding of public schools.

These two constitutional approaches of substantive due process and equal protection analysis were blended by a 1977 district court ruling that a state institution for the retarded must be wholly closed and its residents moved to small-scale community homes on the grounds that the "right to treatment" could not be effectively protected in any large, isolated institutional setting and that, like racial SEGREGATION, separation of retarded people from contact with mentally normal people was INVIDIOUS DISCRIMINA-

TION. A congressional act of 1975 also indicated preference for community over institutional retardation facilities; but the Supreme Court, in PENNHURST STATE SCHOOL V. HALDERMAN (1981) without addressing the initial constitutional ruling, held that Congress had spoken only with "hortatory" rather than mandatory intention.

In 1985 the Supreme Court finally did address the question whether mentally retarded people warranted specially protected constitutional status, but its answer was ambiguous. The specific issue in CLEBURNE V. CLEBURNE LIVING CENTER (1985) was the validity of a local ZONING ordinance that specifically excluded group residences for "feeble-minded" people, even though fraternity and sorority houses, dormitories, and nursing homes for "convalescents or aged" people were explicitly permitted. The Fifth Circuit overturned the ordinance, citing the immutability of retardation, its stigmatized social history (as evidenced by sterilization laws based on spurious scientific findings and by brutalizing, isolated institutional residences), and the political vulnerability of retarded people. Because retardation could be relevant to some state classifications such as school programming or employment eligibility, however, the court found that it was more like gender than like race, a "quasi-suspect" rather than a SUSPECT CLASSIFICATION. Applying intermediate scrutiny, the court found insufficient justification for the zoning exclusion.

The Supreme Court declined to follow this analysis. It concluded that retardation classifications warranted no special judicial scrutiny for several reasons: the legitimate relevance of retardation for some classificatory purposes, the nonjudicial expertise seemingly required to evaluate such purposes, and the political strength of retardation advocates as evidenced by the 1975 congressional acts (notwithstanding that Congress had also acted against race and gender discrimination in recent decades). The Court nonetheless invalidated the zoning ordinance on the ground that it was based merely on "vague, undifferentiated fears" about retarded people. This rationale does not readily fit the conventional conception of "minimal scrutiny" equal protection analysis, given that fears regarding the irrationality and uncontrollability of retarded people have some plausible claim to factuality, even though this claim is unreliably documented and inapplicable to most retarded people.

The Court's invalidation of the zoning ordinance in *Cleburne* must thus rest on an unacknowledged premise, either that minimal scrutiny equal protection analysis (as applied to all state classifications) now requires more clearly demonstrated reasonableness than has heretofore been demanded or that retarded people do warrant some degree of special judicial protection to ensure that differential classifications of them have factual bases beyond "vague, undifferentiated fears."

ROBERT A. BURT
(1986)

(SEE ALSO: *Disabilities, Rights of Persons With; Disability Discrimination.*)

Bibliography

BURT, ROBERT A. 1985 Pennhurst: A Parable. Pages 265–364 in Robert Mnookin, ed., *In the Interest of Children.* New York: W. H. Freeman.

MERCY KILLING

See: Euthanasia; Right to Die

MERE EVIDENCE RULE

A SEARCH WARRANT must identify the place to be searched and the items to be seized. Such items may include fruits or instrumentalities of crime (such as stolen money or burglar's tools) or contraband (such as illegal drugs). In *Gouled v. United States* (1921) the Supreme Court held that search warrants could not issue to seize mere EVIDENCE of crime.

In WARDEN V. HAYDEN (1967), however, the Court held that warrants could issue for mere evidence so long as there was a "nexus" between the evidence and the criminal behavior. ZURCHER V. STANFORD DAILY (1978) illustrates the effect of the rule's abandonment. The Stanford University student newspaper published photographs of a campus disturbance between the police and demonstrators. Because the police observed only two of their assailants, a warrant was obtained for a search of the newspaper's offices. The warrant affidavit did not allege any involvement in the unlawful acts by newspaper staff members. During the search, police examined the paper's photographic labs, files, desks, and waste paper baskets. Since no new evidence was discovered, no items were taken.

One commentator has summarized the "mere evidence rule" after *Zurcher* as follows: *Zurcher* represents a case in which none of the items searched for by the police was a fruit or instrumentality of a crime, or contraband. Under the pre-*Hayden* rule, the warrant used in *Zurcher* could not have been issued. Yet the present broad rule is so well established that the Supreme Court's majority opinion did not even discuss the issue.

CHARLES H. WHITEBREAD
(1986)

Bibliography

WHITEBREAD, CHARLES H. 1980 *Criminal Procedure.* Mineola, N.Y.: Foundation Press.

MERITOR SAVINGS BANK, FSB v. VINSON
477 U.S. 57 (1986)

In *Meritor* the Supreme Court unanimously held that sexual harassment that created a "hostile environment" in the workplace constituted EMPLOYMENT DISCRIMINATION in violation of Title VII of the CIVIL RIGHTS ACT OF 1964. The Court thus gave its blessing to an interpretation that was already well established in the guidelines of the Equal Employment Opportunity Commission (EEOC) and in the lower federal courts.

A woman who had been employed by a bank for four years sued her branch manager and the bank for injunctive relief and for both compensatory and punitive damages, alleging that the manager had demanded and obtained sexual favors from her, including some incidents of forcible rape. She stated that she had not reported these facts to the manager's superiors because she was afraid of her manager. The manager disputed these allegations, and the bank contended that it neither knew nor approved of any sexual harassment by the manager. The bank further argued that the prohibitions of Title VII were limited to discrimination causing economic or tangible loss, not psychological harm.

Justice WILLIAM H. REHNQUIST, writing for the Court, rejected the latter argument. Title VII was intended to strike at all disparate treatment of men and women. The EEOC guidelines were also persuasive authority that Title VII is concerned with noneconomic injury. The guidelines had explicitly recognized sexual harassment that creates "an intimidating, hostile, or offensive working environment" to be a form of SEX DISCRIMINATION that violates the act, and lower courts had arrived at a similar interpretation in cases involving both racial harassment and sexual harassment.

Even if the plaintiff's sexual relationship with the manager were "voluntary," the Court said, that is not a defense to a Title VII action; rather, the question is whether the manager's sexual advances were "unwelcome," a determination to be made on the totality of the circumstances shown in the record. The Court declined to rule in the abstract on the question of the bank's liability for the actions of its manager. It followed the EEOC's brief, agreeing that an employer is absolutely liable when a supervisory employee offers economic benefits for sexual favors, but refusing to extend the rule of absolute liability to a "hostile environment" case. The Court also rejected the bank's argument that the mere existence of a grievance procedure insulated it from liability. The issue of the employer's liability, the Court suggested, should first be addressed by the lower courts in the context of specific findings of fact.

Justice THURGOOD MARSHALL, writing for four Justices, concurred separately to address the question of employer liability. He would follow the EEOC guidelines on this point. These guidelines went beyond the EEOC's own brief to the Court, making an employer generally responsible for supervisory employees' sexual harassment whether or not that conduct was authorized or forbidden and whether or not the employer knew or should have known of the conduct.

KENNETH L. KARST
(1992)

Bibliography

ABRAMS, KATHRYN   1989   Gender Discrimination and the Transformation of Workplace Norms. *Vanderbilt Law Review* 42: 1183–1248.

MacKINNON, CATHARINE A.   1979   *Sexual Harassment of Working Women.* New Haven, Conn.: Yale University Press.

METRO BROADCASTING, INC. v. FCC
497 U.S. 547 (1990)

In this decision the Supreme Court, 5–4, upheld two aspects of an AFFIRMATIVE ACTION program approved by Congress in the area of BROADCASTING. In 1986 members of racial and ethnic minorities, who constitute about one-fifth of the nation's population, owned just over two percent of the radio and television broadcasting stations licensed by the Federal Communications Commission (FCC). Two FCC policies aim to bring a greater racial and ethnic diversity to broadcast ownership. First, the FCC considers minority ownership as one factor among many in making comparative judgments among applicants for new licenses. Second, the FCC seeks to increase minority ownership through a "distress sale" policy. Normally, a licensee cannot transfer its license during the time when the FCC is considering whether the license should be revoked. As an exception to this policy, such a broadcaster may sell its license before the revocation hearing to a minority-controlled broadcaster that meets the FCC's qualifications, provided that the price does not exceed seventy-five percent of the station's value. Congress, in appropriating money for the FCC, ordered that these programs be continued.

In *Metro Broadcasting* both of these policies were challenged as denials of the guarantee of EQUAL PROTECTION

that the Court has recognized in the Fifth Amendment's DUE PROCESS clause. Writing for the majority, Justice WILLIAM J. BRENNAN strongly emphasized Congress's adoption of the two minority ownership policies. The proper STANDARD OF REVIEW for congressional affirmative action was not STRICT SCRUTINY but the intermediate standard that the Court has previously used, for example, in cases of SEX DISCRIMINATION. This standard requires that Congress have an "important" purpose for its legislation and that the racial classification be "substantially related" to achieving that purpose.

For the majority of the Court, the FCC's policies easily satisfied this test. The interest in diversifying broadcast programming accorded with the long-recognized policy of the Federal Communications Act to ensure the presentation of a wide variety of views. The Supreme Court had recognized this need in the context of the scarcity of electronic frequencies in RED LION BROADCASTING CO. V. FCC (1969), sustaining the FCC's "fairness doctrine." The FCC had quite reasonably determined that racial and ethnic diversity in broadcast ownership would promote diversity in programming, and Congress had repeatedly endorsed this view by rejecting proposals that would arguably reduce opportunities for minority ownership, such as a proposal to deregulate broadcasting. The Court, said Justice Brennan, must give great weight to the joint administrative-congressional determination of a connection between minority ownership and programming diversity. The minority ownership policies did not rest on impermissible stereotyping, but on the need to diversify programming. The FCC had considered other means of achieving this diversification and had reasonably concluded that these means were relatively ineffective. The burden imposed by these two policies on nonminority applicants for broadcast licenses was not impermissibly great.

Justice SANDRA DAY O'CONNOR wrote for the four dissenters. Arguing that any race-conscious program must pass the test of strict scrutiny, she rejected the claim that broadcasting diversity was a COMPELLING STATE INTEREST or even an important one. Furthermore, the policies were not narrowly tailored; they assumed a connection between minority ownership and program content, and they ignored other race-neutral means of assuring programming to serve a diversity of audiences, such as direct regulation of programming.

The importance of *Metro Broadcasting* as a precedent remains to be seen. Justice Brennan's retirement from the Court may lead to a resurgence of the rhetoric of strict scrutiny, even for congressional programs of affirmative action. However, as Justice O'Connor noted in her concurrence in WYGANT V. JACKSON BOARD OF EDUCATION (1986), the practical difference between compelling and important purposes, or between necessary and substantially related means, may be less than a surface reading of opinions suggests.

KENNETH L. KARST
(1992)

Bibliography

EULE, JULIAN N. 1990 Promoting Speaker Diversity: *Austin* and *Metro Broadcasting. Supreme Court Review* 1990:105–132.

METROPOLITAN LIFE INSURANCE CO. v. WARD
470 U.S. 869 (1985)

This decision departed from a long series of Supreme Court decisions upholding the constitutionality of state taxes against attack under the EQUAL PROTECTION clause. Alabama taxed the gross premiums of insurance companies by imposing a one percent tax on companies organized in Alabama, and a tax of three percent or four percent on companies organized in other states. In an opinion by Justice LEWIS F. POWELL, the Supreme Court held, 5–4, that this discrimination failed even the RATIONAL BASIS test, because its only articulated purpose—to create a tax advantage for domestic economic interests over out-of-state interests—was illegitimate. Congress, in its 1945 act permitting the states to discriminate in favor of local insurance companies, had insulated such laws from attack under the COMMERCE CLAUSE, but had not purported to speak to any issue of equal protection.

In an unusual division of the Court, Justice SANDRA DAY O'CONNOR dissented, joined by Justices WILLIAM J. BRENNAN, THURGOOD MARSHALL, and WILLIAM H. REHNQUIST. Justice O'Connor pointed to previous decisions recognizing the legitimacy of state efforts to promote domestic industry, and made the unanswerable point that Alabama's tax scheme was rationally related to such a purpose. Furthermore, she said, Congress in 1945 understood that it was authorizing laws of this very kind. She also accused the majority of reviving active judicial scrutiny of state ECONOMIC REGULATION. Although the latter prediction seems unlikely to come true, the fear that it expresses is not dispelled by the majority's opinion.

KENNETH L. KARST
(1986)

Bibliography

COHEN, WILLIAM 1985 Federalism in Equality Clothing: A Comment on *Metropolitan Life Insurance Company v. Ward. Stanford Law Review* 38:1–27.

MEYER v. NEBRASKA
262 U.S. 390 (1923)

Meyer represented an early use of SUBSTANTIVE DUE PROCESS doctrine to defend personal liberties, as distinguished from economic ones. Nebraska, along with other states, had prohibited the teaching of modern foreign languages to grade school children. Meyer, who taught German in a Lutheran school, was convicted under this law. The Supreme Court, 7–2, held the law unconstitutional. Justice JAMES C. MCREYNOLDS wrote for the Court in *Meyer* and in four companion cases from Iowa, Ohio, and Nebraska. Justice OLIVER WENDELL HOLMES, joined by Justice GEORGE SUTHERLAND, dissented in all but the Ohio cases.

McReynolds began with a broad reading of the "liberty" protected by the FOURTEENTH AMENDMENT: "it denotes not merely freedom from bodily restraint, but also the right of the individual to contract, to engage in any of the common occupations of life, to acquire useful knowledge, to marry, establish a home and bring up children, to worship God according to the dictates of his own conscience, and, generally, to enjoy those privileges long recognized at common law as essential to the orderly pursuit of happiness by free men." State regulation of this liberty must be reasonably related to a proper state objective; the legislature's view of reasonableness was "subject to supervision by the courts." The legislative purpose to promote assimilation and "civic development" was readily appreciated, given the hostility toward our adversaries in World War I. However, "no adequate reason" justified interfering with Meyer's liberty to teach or the liberty of parents to employ him during a "time of peace and domestic tranquillity."

Holmes concurred in the Ohio cases, because Ohio had singled out the German language for suppression. But he could not say it was unreasonable for a state to forbid teaching foreign languages to young children as a means of assuring that all citizens might "speak a common tongue." Because "men might reasonably differ" on the question, the laws were not unconstitutional.

Meyer was thus a child of LOCHNER V. NEW YORK (1905), taking *Lochner*'s broad view of the judicial role in protecting liberty. Yet, although substantive due process has lost its former vitality in the field of ECONOMIC REGULATION, *Meyer*'s precedent remains vigorous in the defense of personal liberty. *Meyer* was reaffirmed in GRISWOLD V. CONNECTICUT (1965), LOVING V. VIRGINIA (1967), and ZABLICKI V. REDHAIL (1978), three modern decisions protecting the FREEDOM OF INTIMATE ASSOCIATION.

KENNETH L. KARST
(1986)

MIAMI HERALD PUBLISHING COMPANY v. TORNILLO
418 U.S. 241 (1974)

It may be argued that FREEDOM OF SPEECH is meaningless unless it includes access to the mass media so that the speech will be heard. Here the Supreme Court unanimously struck down a Florida statute requiring a newspaper to provide a political candidate free space to reply to its attacks on his personal character. Noting that the statute infringed upon "editorial control and judgment," the Court held that "any [governmental] compulsion to publish that which 'reason' tells . . . [the editors] . . . should not be published is unconstitutional."

Tornillo was a major blow to proponents of a right of access. When compared to RED LION BROADCASTING COMPANY V. FEDERAL COMMUNICATIONS COMMISSION (1969), it raises the question whether the FIRST AMENDMENT provides greater protection for the press than for the electronic media. In light of the large number of one-newspaper towns, the scarcity rationale for allowing government to compel access to broadcast channels would seem to apply even more strongly to the print media. Ultimately the distinction may be between the public ownership of the channels and the private ownership of the print media. If so, the Court has not explained or defended this linking of speech rights to property rights.

MARTIN SHAPIRO
(1986)

MICHAEL M. v. SUPERIOR COURT
450 U.S. 464 (1981)

A boy of 17 was convicted of rape under a California statute making it a crime for a male to have intercourse with a female under 18; the girl's age was 16. A fragmented Supreme Court voted 5–4 to uphold the conviction against the contention that the statute's SEX DISCRIMINATION—the same act was criminal for a male but not for a female—denied the EQUAL PROTECTION OF THE LAWS.

There was no opinion for the Court. The majority Justices, however, agreed in accepting the California Supreme Court's justification for the law: prevention of illegitimate teen-age pregnancies. The risk of pregnancy itself, said Justice WILLIAM H. REHNQUIST, served to deter young females from sexual encounters; criminal sanctions on young males only would roughly "equalize" deterrents.

The dissenters argued that California had not demonstrated its law to be a deterrent; thirty-seven states had adopted gender-neutral statutory rape laws, no doubt on the theory that such laws would provide even more deter-

rent, by doubling the number of persons subject to arrest. When both parties to an act are equally guilty, argued Justice JOHN PAUL STEVENS, to make the male guilty of a FELONY while allowing the female to go free is supported by little more than "traditional attitudes toward male-female relations."

KENNETH L. KARST
(1986)

MICHELIN TIRE COMPANY v. ADMINISTRATOR OF WAGES
423 U.S. 276 (1976)

Opening the way for increased local revenue, a unanimous Court overruled *Low v. Austin* (1872) and sustained a state property tax on imported goods even though they retained their character as imports. The Court held that the IMPORT-EXPORT CLAUSE did not prohibit such a tax if it were imposed without discrimination on all goods in the state.

DAVID GORDON
(1986)

(SEE ALSO: *Original Package Doctrine.*)

MICHIGAN v. LONG

See: Adequate State Grounds; Stop and Frisk

MICHIGAN v. SUMMERS
452 U.S. 692 (1981)

A 6 3 Supreme Court held that if the police had a valid warrant to search a home for illegal drugs, they had authority to detain the occupants of the premises during the search. They could therefore lawfully require a suspect to remain in the house, arrest him after finding the contraband, and search his person incident to the arrest. The dissenters argued that the FOURTH AMENDMENT prevented the police from seizing a person without PROBABLE CAUSE in order to make him available for arrest should probable cause be revealed by the search.

LEONARD W. LEVY
(1986)

MICHIGAN DEPARTMENT OF STATE POLICE v. SITZ
496 U.S. 444 (1990)

Recent FOURTH AMENDMENT cases reflect a pattern of rejection by the Supreme Court of claims based on the right against unreasonable SEARCH AND SEIZURE. This case fits that pattern, yet the decision of the Court seems right.

Because of the slaughter on public highways caused by drunk drivers, the Michigan State Police instituted a program of sobriety checkpoints. All drivers passing through a checkpoint, usually after midnight, were stopped and examined briefly for signs of intoxication. Suspected drunk drivers were directed out of the flow of traffic for further investigation; all others were permitted to continue. The average stop took twenty-five seconds.

A 6–3 Supreme Court held that although the stop was a seizure in the sense of the Fourth Amendment, it was a reasonable one because the intrusion was slight and served a substantial public interest. The dissenters, led by Justice JOHN PAUL STEVENS, believed that the intrusion violated the Fourth Amendment. Much of Steven's opinion challenged the wisdom of the legislative policy authorizing the sobriety-checkpoint program. His challenge to its constitutionality was founded on the absurd proposition that "unannounced investigatory seizures are, particularly when they take place at night, the hallmarks of regimes far different from ours," and he referred to Nazi Germany. Moreover, Stevens weakened his argument based on the Fourth Amendment by offering the opinion that a permanent, nondiscretionary checkpoint program would not violate the amendment. He supposed that a state could condition the use of its roads on the uniform administration of a breathalizer test to all drivers, thereby keeping drunks off the roads.

The intrusiveness of the means upheld by the Court's majority, led by Chief Justice WILLIAM H. REHNQUIST, was considerably less than that of the means favored by Stevens. In addition, the majority did not debate the wisdom of the policy before it. Its deference to the legislature seemed submissive, however, and its constitutional analysis stopped when it took notice of the twenty-five-second intrusion.

LEONARD W. LEVY
(1992)

MIDDENDORF v. HENRY
425 U.S. 25 (1976)

A 5–3 Supreme Court ruled that servicemen have no RIGHT TO COUNSEL in summary courts-martial. Justice WILLIAM H. REHNQUIST's majority opinion concluded that such proceedings did not constitute criminal prosecutions within the Sixth Amendment's guarantee, and he also disposed of a Fifth Amendment DUE PROCESS claim as without merit.

DAVID GORDON
(1986)

MIFFLIN, THOMAS
(1744–1800)

General Thomas Mifflin, a wealthy Philadelphia Quaker, was a member of the Pennsylvania Assembly and of the First and Second Continental Congresses before serving as quartermaster general of the Army (1775–1778). He was elected to Congress in 1782, and in 1783 became President of the United States in Congress Assembled. Mifflin was speaker of the Pennsylvania Assembly in 1787, when he was chosen as chairman of his state's delegation to the CONSTITUTIONAL CONVENTION OF 1787. The records of the convention do not indicate that Mifflin ever spoke in the debates, although he did sign the Constitution. In 1790 he presided over the state CONSTITUTIONAL CONVENTION. He served as governor of Pennsylvania from 1790 to 1799, a period that included the WHISKEY REBELLION.

DENNIS J. MAHONEY
(1986)

Bibliography

ROSSITER, CLINTON 1966 *1787: The Grand Convention.* New York: Macmillan.

MILITARY AND THE CONSTITUTION

See: Armed Forces; Military Justice; Sexual Orientation and the Armed Forces

MILITARY JUSTICE

The Constitution, in language taken from the ARTICLES OF CONFEDERATION, empowers Congress to "make Rules for the Government and Regulation of the land and naval Forces." Congress has enacted Articles of War and Articles for the Government of the Navy since 1775, but in 1950 the two systems were fused in the Uniform Code of Military Justice (UCMJ).

Criminal justice under the UCMJ resembles that in civilian courts more than it differs. As in most states, the type of trial court depends on the gravity of the offense. Petty offenses are dealt with by nonjudicial punishment or summary court-martial; more serious offenses may be tried before a special or general court-martial. The types of court-martial differ in number of members and in the maximum punishment they may impose. The rules of EVIDENCE are about the same as in the federal courts; and a defendant tried by a special or general court-martial enjoys the RIGHT TO COUNSEL at government expense. The Supreme Court held in *Middendorf v. Henry* (1976) that the right to free counsel does not apply in summary courts-martial, which more closely resemble administrative hearings than criminal trials.

The major difference between military and civilian criminal justice is the absence of a jury. The members of the court are appointed by the convening authority, who can, theoretically, "pack the court." However, the accused can avoid the possibility of command influence by electing trial by a military judge sitting alone, who is responsible only to the Judge Advocate General of his service. When the military judge sits with members of a court-martial his role is like that of a civilian judge, except that the members determine the sentence if the accused is convicted. There is an elaborate system of review but, except in a limited class of cases, APPEAL to the Court of Military Appeals (three civilian judges appointed by the President) is not by right.

The UCMJ does not provide for review by any civilian court: findings and sentences of courts-martial, as affirmed under the code, are "final and conclusive" and "binding upon all . . . courts . . . of the United States." The Supreme Court has always held that, absent provision by Congress, there can be no direct appeal from the decisions of military tribunals. The federal courts have, however, developed several techniques of collateral review—notably HABEAS CORPUS, MANDAMUS, and suits for back pay in the COURT OF CLAIMS—which effectively ensure that military courts are subject to constitutional supervision.

The federal courts had long collaterally reviewed court-martial convictions to ensure that there was JURISDICTION over person, offense, and sentence. The Supreme Court after World War II imposed new limits on court-martial jurisdiction over person and offense. In the UCMJ, courts-martial were granted jurisdiction over many categories of civilians, including honorably discharged servicemen and civilians accompanying the armed forces outside the United States. In a series of decisions, including UNITED STATES EX REL. TOTH V. QUARLES (1955) and REID V. COVERT (1956), the Supreme Court held that a court-martial could not constitutionally try any civilian in peacetime. There are still some gray areas, such as jurisdiction over retired regulars and certain reservists.

Thereafter the Court held that a court-martial could not constitutionally try a member of the armed forces for an offense that had no "service connection"; the leading case, O'Callahan v. Parker (1969), involved the attempted rape of a civilian by a soldier off-post, on leave, and out of uniform. Despite a subsequent decision in which the Court suggested a dozen factors to be considered in determining whether a crime was "service-connected," there are still many doubtful cases, particularly those involving off-post use or possession of drugs. The Court of Military Appeals and the inferior federal courts have made two

exceptions to the requirement of service connection. Considering that O'Callahan was based on the loss of TRIAL BY JURY, they have permitted courts-martial to try offenses regardless of service connection committed outside the jurisdiction of American civilian courts or punishable by not more than six months' confinement, so that the accused would not in any case be constitutionally entitled to a jury.

Until after World War II the BILL OF RIGHTS had no application to courts-martial: if jurisdiction existed over person, offense, and sentence, federal courts would not consider allegations of even the grossest unfairness. Chief Justice SALMON P. CHASE, concurring in EX PARTE MILLIGAN (1866), declared that "the power of Congress, in the government of the land and naval forces, is not affected by the fifth or any other amendment." Historical evidence concerning the framers of the Bill of Rights justifies Chase's dictum: President JAMES MADISON, for example, approved the conviction of General William Hull in 1814, although the court-martial had denied Hull's request for the assistance of counsel.

The Supreme Court has never set aside a court-martial conviction for denial of constitutional DUE PROCESS, but it would almost certainly do so if confronted with a clear case of such denial. No such case has yet reached the Court because the protections of the Bill of Rights (except trial by jury and the right to BAIL) are embodied in the UCMJ. A coerced confession, for example, would violate not only the Fifth Amendment but also the UCMJ and thus constitute a denial of "military due process." In addition the Court of Military Appeals has consistently construed the UCMJ in such a way as to avoid conflict with the Supreme Court's construction of the Constitution. Military exigency may, however, justify some relaxation of civilian standards. Military rulings on constitutional issues must conform to Supreme Court standards, absent a showing that special military conditions require a different rule. Thus PARKER V. LEVY (1974) held that the "general articles" which prohibit "conduct unbecoming an officer and a gentleman" and "disorders and neglects to the prejudice of good order and discipline" are not unconstitutionally vague or overbroad.

JOSEPH W. BISHOP, JR.
(1986)

(SEE ALSO: *Armed Forces*.)

Bibliography

BISHOP, JOSEPH W., JR. 1974 *Justice under Fire: A Study of Military Law*. Chaps. 2, 3, 4. New York: Charterhouse.
WIENER, FREDERICK BERNAYS 1958 Courts-Martial and the Bill of Rights: The Original Practice. *Harvard Law Review* 72:1–49, 266–304.

MILITARY RECONSTRUCTION ACTS
15 Stat. 2 (1867)
15 Stat. 14 (1867)

The first Military Reconstruction Act established procedures for the resumption of self-government and normalized constitutional status for ten states of the former Confederacy. Though it preserved extant governments intact for the time being, it authorized military peacekeeping and required adoption of new state constitutions. It also mandated black suffrage.

By February 1867, congressional Republicans realized that the FOURTEENTH AMENDMENT, even if ratified, constituted an insufficient program of RECONSTRUCTION. They were unwilling to accept the forfeited-rights theory of southern state status propounded by Rep. THADDEUS STEVENS, or to sanction indefinite military governance. However, the intransigence of President ANDREW JOHNSON and the Machiavellian politics of congressional Democrats, who both demanded immediate and unconditional restoration of white rule in the South, convinced the Republicans that federal supervision of the process of recreating state governments was essential if the freedmen and Republican war objectives were not to be abandoned.

The first Military Reconstruction Act divided the ex-Confederate states (Tennessee excepted) into five military districts each under the command of a regular brigadier general, who was charged with peacekeeping responsibilities. He was empowered to use either ordinary civilian officials or military commissions to accomplish this objective. Though the commissions were authorized to overrule civilian authorities if necessary, the act did not replace the state governments previously created under presidential authority. Rather, under the first and subsequent Military Reconstruction Acts (1867–1868), the commanding general was required to call for the election of delegates to CONSTITUTIONAL CONVENTIONS. In these elections, blacks were entitled to vote, and whites disfranchised by the Fourteenth Amendment were excluded. The new state constitution had to enfranchise blacks. When it was ratified by a majority of eligible voters, elections were to be held under it for new state governmental officials. Only then would the existing governments cede authority. The new legislature had to ratify the Fourteenth Amendment and present its state constitution to Congress. Congress would then complete the process by admitting the state's congressional delegation to their seats.

President Johnson vetoed the first measure, asserting several grounds for its unconstitutionality. First, it imposed an "absolute domination of military rulers" whose "mere will is to take the place of all law," subjecting the southern people to "abject slavery." Second, Congress lacked power to impose governments on the southern states, particularly because those states remained part of the Union. Third, the act would deny individual liberties, including the requirements of TRIAL BY JURY, warrants, DUE PROCESS, and HABEAS CORPUS. Johnson also opposed the measure because the requirements of black suffrage would "Africanize the southern part of our territory," and, finally, because the anomalous status of the ten states which had been denied representation in Congress since 1865 cast a cloud over legislation affecting them. Congress immediately overrode the veto.

Under the procedure specified by the Military Reconstruction Acts, all southern states were reorganized and readmitted between 1868 and 1870. The military presence remained for nearly another decade, however, because of turbulence caused by antiblack and anti-Unionist terrorism. The Republican governments established under congressional Reconstruction were overthrown by "Conservative" or "Redeemer" white-supremacist Democratic regimes by 1877, when the process of Reconstruction was effectively terminated.

WILLIAM M. WIECEK
(1986)

(SEE ALSO: *Constitutional History, 1865–1877.*)

MILITIAS, MODERN

The mid-1990s have included the presence in American political life of paramilitary "militia movements" organized, by their lights, to serve as the first line of defense against the loss of basic constitutional freedoms. Their opponents altogether plausibly describe them as ultrachauvinistic, often racist, radical movements based largely in rural America and threatened by the modern bureaucratic state, general social developments within American society, and the implications of an increasingly globalized political economy. From this perspective, they are far more likely to be threats to, rather than defenders of, constitutional liberty.

What entitles these modern militias to a place in a book on the U.S. Constitution is their claim to be the entities protected by the very words of the SECOND AMENDMENT: "A well regulated Militia, being necessary to the security of a free State, the right of the people to keep and bear Arms, shall not be infringed." That is, members of organized militias describe themselves as precisely those persons explicitly protected against federal (and, through the FOURTEENTH AMENDMENT, state) regulation of the private possession of firearms.

Their opponents instead argue that the amendment's

reference to "a well regulated Militia" limits any constitutional protection to an official militia organized and regulated by states themselves. The modern militia movement, on the other hand, has no ties with any formal government and therefore has no special constitutional protection.

An 1886 decision by the Supreme Court, *Presser v. Illinois,* offers some support for this view, inasmuch as it upheld an Illinois law prohibiting "any body of men whatever, other than the regular organized volunteer militia of the State, and the troops of the United States . . . to drill or parade with arms in any city, or town, of this State, without the license of the Governor thereof." The Court, however, also rejected the applicability of the Second Amendment to the states at all—this was well before the Court began "incorporating" the BILL OF RIGHTS against the states—so it is not dispositive as to the meaning of the amendment, though it would occasion great surprise if the modern Court were in fact to deviate from the *Presser* DOCTRINE. (A number of western states have adopted similar prohibitions of military training.)

Still, defenders of the legal rights of the modern militia movement would undoubtedly note that "militia," as an eighteenth-century term of art, referred to a group considerably broader than a discrete body of citizens organized into a state-regulated body. No less a worthy than George Mason, one of the primary advocates of a Bill of Rights—indeed, he refused to sign the Constitution because it lacked one—wrote "Who are the Militia? They consist now of the whole people." He was not alone in this view, and many discussants at the time distinguished the "general militia" from a "select militia." Given that one of the reasons to protect the right to bear arms was a profound fear of a corrupt state, they would scarcely have been happy with a definition of militia that protected only those deemed worthy by the state itself.

These arguments are scarcely frivolous, as an intellectual matter, but it is impossible, as a practical matter, to believe that mainstream legal analysts able to gain nomination and confirmation to the federal courts will be receptive to them. Instead, one can fairly confidently predict that the judiciary will be no more willing to interpret the Second Amendment in ways that would protect members of the militia movement than were judges to interpret the considerably clearer words of the FIRST AMENDMENT in the 1950s to protect members of the Communist Party. Those viewed by the mass public as genuine security threats will rarely be protected by the judiciary, regardless of constitutional language.

SANFORD LEVINSON
(2000)

(SEE ALSO: *Incorporation Doctrine; Radical Constitutional Interpretation; Right of Revolution.*)

Bibliography

KONIAK, SUSAN   1996   When Law Risks Madness. *Cardozo Studies in Law & Literature* 8:65–107.

MALCOLM, JOYCE   1994   *To Keep and Bear Arms: The Origins of an Anglo American Right.* Cambridge, Mass.: Harvard University Press.

WILLIAMS, DAVID C.   1996   The Militia Movement and the Second Amendment Revolution: Conjuring with the People. *Cornell Law Review* 81:879–952.

MILKOVICH v. LORAIN JOURNAL CO.
497 U.S. 1 (1990)

This is a major free press case that has been widely misunderstood, especially by the news media. The *Los Angeles Times,* for example, called it a "huge setback" for freedom of the press. Under the heading, "Supreme Court Strips Away "Opinion' as Libel Defense," the *Times* announced that the Court had unanimously demolished "a widely used media defense against libel suits, ruling that a writer or speaker may be sued for statements that express opinion." The *Times* censured the Court for having acted "with astonishing recklessness . . . when it overturned nearly two decades of precedent and ruled that the First Amendment does not automatically protect expressions of opinion from being found libelous." A dramatic increase in LIBEL litigation was foreseen as a result of the Court's chilling just the sort of "serious speech the First Amendment was intended to protect." Every critic, editorialist, cartoonist, and commentator faced trial, the *Times* predicted.

In fact, the Court did not diminish the First Amendment's protection of opinion and overruled no precedents, let alone two decades of them. It did hold, however, that opinion requires no new constitutional protection because the conventional safeguards of freedom of expression adequately protect opinion in libel cases. It held, too, that if an expression of opinion implied an assertion of objective fact on a matter of public concern, no liability for defamation would exist unless the party bringing suit proved that the publication was false and published with malice in the case of a public official or a PUBLIC FIGURE, or false and published with "some level of fault" in the case of a private individual involved in a matter of public concern.

In this case, the publication accused a private individual of perjuring himself in a judicial proceeding on a matter of public concern, but the accusation was couched in terms of opinion, for example, "anyone who attended the [wrestling] meet . . . knows in his heart that [Coach] Milkovich . . . lied at the hearing." Chief Justice WILLIAM H. REHNQUIST, for the Court, observed that the writer should not escape liability merely because he used words such as "I think," because he might do as much damage to an individual's reputation as he would by saying flatly that he had lied.

The publishing company sought a special rule distinguishing "fact" from "opinion" and exempting opinion from the law of libel. This is what the Court refused to do because some opinions connoted facts for which their authors ought to be responsible. The Court made clear, however, that "a statement of opinion relating to a matter of public concern which does not contain a provably false factual connotation will receive full constitutional protection."

Justices WILLIAM J. BRENNAN and THURGOOD MARSHALL dissented, but only on the question as to whether the publisher in this case should be held accountable for libel. Significantly, Brennan, who was the Court's foremost exponent of FREEDOM OF THE PRESS in libel cases, declared that Rehnquist addressed the issue of First Amendment protection of opinion "cogently and almost entirely correctly. I agree with the Court that . . . only defamatory statements that are capable of being proved false are subject to liability under state libel law." Thus, the Court did not diminish constitutional protections of opinion and held, properly, that existing First Amendment doctrines adequately served to insulate from libel prosecutions the expression of sheer opinion in matters of public interest.

LEONARD W. LEVY
(1992)

MILL AND FREEDOM OF EXPRESSION

Chapter Two of John Stuart Mill's *On Liberty*, first published in 1859, remains to this day the classic exposition of the liberal argument for FREEDOM OF SPEECH. Mill wrote the essay with the active collaboration of his wife Harriet Taylor, who died during the interval between its original composition and publication. Although the argument purports to rest on a utilitarian claim regarding the net consequences of unregulated expression, his treatment of the subject can be read instead as grounded in the character ideal of the inquisitive, open-minded person, an ideal that might justify a policy of toleration independent of any empirical calculation of collective consequences.

Mill wrote *On Liberty* at what he perceived to be the dawn of the age of mass society, in the wake of the Industrial Revolution and the most significant broadening of the franchise in English history. In the essay he identifies the greatest threat to liberty to be not the transgressions of tyrants or corrupt factions but rather laws and informal social sanctions supported by large popular majorities. He considered the spirit of his age to be inhospitable to in-

dependent thought and unconventional experiments in living. He lamented that mid-Victorian England had become a nation of timid, complacent, constricted persons, conformist in outlook and suspicious of innovators. He urged a robust principle of free expression, together with a more general principle of liberty, as an antidote.

Mill's treatment of the liberty of thought and discussion considers the reasons for tolerating speech under three different assumptions regarding its truth. First, an unconventional idea, at risk of suppression by means of legal or social sanctions, might be true. Second, it might be wholly false. Third, it might be partly true and partly false.

If an idea is true, there is an obvious case for letting it circulate. However, why should would-be regulators be guided by this possibility in the case of heretical ideas they know with great confidence to be false? Mill responds that such confidence is frequently misplaced. To act on it is to assume one's infallibility. Mill's point is more empirical than logical. Proponents of speech regulation usually concede the logical possibility that ideas they hold to be true could be false, and vice versa. But they seldom, in particular instances, give credence to that possibility for the purpose of guiding their actions. Mill finds this troubling because he is impressed by how regularly the conventional wisdom of one time and place is seen by later ages and different peoples to be the sheerest folly. In *On Liberty* he catalogues many such dramatic alterations of understanding, including the modern assessment in retrospect of the executions of Socrates and Christ, and of the persecution of the early Christians by the Emperor Marcus Aurelius, one of the wisest, most learned men of his day.

In the course of urging a greater appreciation of the possibility that heretical ideas might actually be true, Mill addresses the argument that truth has inherent power to prevail over falsehood. If so, the costs of suppressing nascent true ideas would be only temporary, and the fact that a widely held belief has gained adherents over time would be strong evidence of its validity. Mill denies that truth has any such inherent power to prevail: "the dictum that truth always triumphs over persecution is one of those pleasant falsehoods which men repeat after one another till they pass into commonplaces, but which all experience refutes." The only advantage truth possesses, he asserts, is that a suppressed true idea may be rediscovered at a later time when conditions for its reception are more favorable.

A final argument for suppressing heretical ideas even if they might be true is that the received wisdom may be socially useful independent of its truth value. Mill is scornful of this notion. He asserts that an idea's social utility depends to a large extent, even if not exclusively, on its truth. We cannot assess the usefulness of an idea if we cannot consider reasons why it may not be true.

Mill does not deny that the received wisdom could in

fact be true. Indeed, among the strongest arguments in *On Liberty* are those that proceed from the assumption that the ideas society wishes to suppress are wholly false. Mill concedes that a society's confidence in its most cherished tenets could strengthen the capacity to act on those beliefs. He maintains, however, that such confidence flows not from the suppression of false ideas but from the willingness to consider all points of view, and from the consequent perception that the best that could be said in opposition to the received wisdom has been articulated and found wanting.

Not only confidence but lively understanding ensues from the experience of fending off the challenges of dissenters, Mill claims. He decries "the deep slumber of a decided opinion" and asserts that in the absence of controversy "teachers and learners go to sleep at their post." He notes that Cicero claimed to study the arguments of his opponents with much greater care and imagination than he devoted to learning his own side of a case. Mill recommends that practice for those engaged in truth seeking as well as forensics. He goes so far as to say that we ought to thank someone who has produced a skillful challenge to our beliefs, for such a person has done for us that which we otherwise should feel the need to do on our own.

Most ideas at risk of legal or social suppression, Mill observes, are neither wholly true nor wholly false but rather contain a mixture of truth and falsity. It is important that such ideas be allowed to circulate because they contribute to the process of adaptation. Wisdom is not so much a matter of demonstrative proof or refutation but of finding the right balance between "the standing antagonisms of practical life"—between, for example, stability and reform, cooperation and competition, luxury and abstinence, or liberty and discipline. Progress ordinarily entails the replacement of one partial truth with another that is somewhat better adapted to its time.

Although his critics sometimes accuse him of intellectual elitism, Mill himself considered his principle of liberty to be for the masses. It is not, he says, "to form great thinkers that freedom of thinking is required. On the contrary, it is as much, and even more indispensable, to enable average human beings to attain the mental stature which they are capable of." Progress is most often achieved, he maintains, when "the dread of heterodox speculation is for a time suspended" and "the yoke of authority" is broken. Only then, will "the mind of a people" be stirred up from its foundations so as to raise "even persons of the most ordinary intellect to something of the dignity of thinking beings."

Mill did not advocate an unqualified freedom of expression. "[E]ven opinions lose their immunity," he says, "when the circumstances in which they are expressed are such as to constitute their expression a positive instigation to some mischievous act." He offered an example to illustrate the limits of his principle: "An opinion that corn-dealers are starvers of the poor, or that private property is robbery, ought to be unmolested when simply circulated through the press, but may justly incur punishment when delivered orally to an excited mob assembled before the house of a corn-dealer, or when handed about among the same mob in the form of a placard."

Mill's discussion of the liberty of thought and expression constitutes just one part of his comprehensive treatment of the subject of liberty. The full essay *On Liberty*, he states in the introduction, is designed to assert "one very simple principle." He describes that principle as follows: "The only purpose for which power can rightfully be exercised over any member of a civilized community, against his will, is to prevent harm to others." Given the centrality of this harm principle to Mill's overall project, it is perhaps surprising that his discussion of free speech does not explore the various ways that expression and communication might cause harm. This omission has led some observers to conclude that his argument for free speech has more to do with a claim about the irreducible attributes of personhood or the essential conditions for human flourishing than with any sort of balanced calculation of consequences. Although Mill disclaims any reliance on the notion of NATURAL RIGHT, his emphasis on individual character and on "the liberty of conscience, in the most comprehensive sense" suggests that he wished to protect free speech not because he thought it does no or little harm but because he considered it fundamental to life itself.

VINCENT BLASI
(2000)

Bibliography

BERLIN, ISAIAH 1969 John Stuart Mill and the Ends of Life. In *Four Essays on Liberty*. London: Oxford University Press.
McCLOSKEY, H. J. 1970 Liberty of Expression: Its Grounds and Limits. *Inquiry* 13:219–237.
STEPHEN, JAMES FITZJAMES 1873 *Liberty, Equality, Fraternity*. New York: Holt & Williams.
WALDRON, JEREMY 1992 Mill and the Value of Moral Distress. In *Liberal Rights*. Cambridge, Eng.: Cambridge University Press.

MILLER, SAMUEL F.
(1816–1890)

Samuel Freeman Miller was a towing figure on the Supreme Court from his appointment by ABRAHAM LINCOLN in 1862 until his death in 1890. He sat with four Chief Justices, participated in more than 5,000 decisions of the Court, and was its spokesman in ninety-five cases involving construction of the Constitution. No previous member of the Court had written as many constitutional opinions.

Miller's contemporaries regarded him as one of the half-dozen great Justices in American history, a remarkable achievement for a self-educated lawyer who had never held public office, either in his native Kentucky or in adopted Iowa, prior to his appointment to the Court. Justice HORACE GRAY claimed that if his legal training had been less "unsystematic and deficient," Miller would have been "second only to [JOHN] MARSHALL."

Miller looked and acted the part of a great magistrate. He was tall and massive; he had a warm, unaffected disposition and was said to be "as ready to talk to a hod-carrier as to a cardinal." His instinct for what he often called "the main points, the controlling questions," his impatience with antique learning and philosophical abstraction, and his unrivaled reputation for industry, integrity, and independence all enhanced his stature. Candor and intellectual self-reliance pervaded his opinions, and he often stated quite bluntly his assumption that law and practical good sense were of one piece: "This is the honest and fair view of the subject, and we think it conflicts with no rule of law" (*Pettigrew v. United States*, 1878); "if this is not DUE PROCESS OF LAW it ought to be" (*Davidson v. New Orleans*, 1878); "this is just and sound policy" (*Iron Silver Mining Co. v. Campbell*, 1890).

Statecraft rather than formal jurisprudence was Miller's forte, and he emerged as the Court's balance-wheel soon after coming to the bench. His career ultimately spanned three tumultuous decades in which the Justices constantly quarreled, often rancorously, about the scope of federal and state powers and the Court's role in protecting private rights against the alleged usurpations of both. Scores of cases involved highly charged political issues. Yet Miller always remained detached. He never permitted differences of opinion to affect personal relations with his brethren; he met counsels of heat and passion with chilly distaste. Miller's capacity for detachment was, in part, a matter of personality. But it was also a function of his modest view of the Court's role in the American system of government. He resisted doctrinal formulations that curtailed the discretion of other lawmakers, spoke self-consciously about "my conservative habit of deciding no more than is necessary in any case," and often succeeded in accommodating warring factions of more doctrinaire colleagues by narrowing the issue before the Court. As early as 1870, Chief Justice SALMON P. CHASE said he was "beyond question, the dominant personality upon the bench."

The first principles of Miller's constitutional understanding were derived from HENRY CLAY and the Whig party. Although he abandoned the Whigs for the Republican party in 1854, Miller never ceased to regard Clay as the quintessential American statesman or to reaffirm the Kentucky sage's belief in a BROAD CONSTRUCTION of national powers, the primacy of the legislative department in shaping public policy, and the duty of government at all levels to encourage material growth. Miller's adherence to the first two principles was especially apparent in his work on the CHASE COURT. In EX PARTE MILLIGAN (1866), he joined the minority of four, concurring, who suggested that Congress might constitutionally have established martial rule in Indiana. And in *Tyler v. Defrees* (1870), a confiscation case, Miller flatly rejected the doctrine "long inculcated, that the Federal Government, however strong in a conflict with a foreign foe, lies manacled by the Constitution and helpless at the feet of a domestic enemy." Early in 1868, when the movement to impeach President ANDREW JOHNSON gathered momentum and the Court initially established jurisdiction in EX PARTE MCCARDLE, Miller conceded privately that "in the threatened collision between the Legislative branch of the government and the Executive and judicial branches I see consequences from which the cause of free government may never recover in my day." He added, however, that "the worst feature I now see is the passion which governs the hour in all parties and persons who have a controlling influence." In contrast, Miller not only counseled caution and delay while Congress proceeded to divest the Court of jurisdiction over *McCardle* but also dissented in TEXAS V. WHITE (1869). He regarded the status of states still undergoing military reconstruction as a POLITICAL QUESTION which only Congress could decide. *Hepburn v. Griswold* (1870), the first of the LEGAL TENDER CASES, evoked his most celebrated defense of congressional authority. There Miller sharply criticized the majority's reliance on the "spirit" of the Constitution, which, he insisted, "substitutes . . . an undefined code of ethics for the Constitution, and a court of justice for the National Legislature. . . . Where there is a choice of means, the selection is for Congress, not the Court."

Miller was not always such a positivist in rejecting considerations arising from the spirit of the Constitution. In the SLAUGHTERHOUSE CASES (1873), which came up during fierce public debate over the Enforcement and Klu Klux Klan Acts, Miller intervened decisively to preserve "the main features" of the federal system. Although the powers of Congress were not directly at issue, his opinion for the Court undercut every FOURTEENTH AMENDMENT theory that had been advanced in other cases to justify federal jurisdiction over perpetrators of racially motivated private violence. The Fourteenth Amendment's PRIVILEGES AND IMMUNITIES clause, Miller explained for a majority of five, protected only the handful of rights that necessarily grew out of "the relationship between the citizen and the national government." The really fundamental privileges and immunities of CITIZENSHIP, including the rights to protection by the government, to own property, and to contract, still remained what they had been since 1789—rights of state citizenship. To bring all CIVIL RIGHTS under the umbrella of national citizenship, Miller concluded, would be "so great a departure from the structure and spirit of our institutions" and would so "fetter and degrade the State governments by subjecting them to the control of Congress" that it should not be permitted "in the absence of language which expresses such purpose too clearly to admit of doubt."

Over the succeeding seventeen years, Miller's voting record in civil rights cases remained consistent with the views he expounded in 1873. He joined the majority in UNITED STATES V. CRUIKSHANK (1876) and the CIVIL RIGHTS CASES (1883), both of which severely reduced the range of "appropriate legislation" Congress was authorized to enact; he voted to invalidate the Ku Klux Klan Act altogether in UNITED STATES V. HARRIS (1883). In EX PARTE YARBROUGH (1884), an important Enforcement Act case, Miller consolidated his formal approach to protecting civil rights in a federal system. Speaking for a unanimous Court, he sustained federal jurisdiction over persons who violently interfered with the exercise of VOTING RIGHTS in a federal election. Congress's authority to reach private action in *Yarbrough*, he explained, flowed not from the FIFTEENTH AMENDMENT but from both its power to regulate the time, place, and manner of federal elections and its duty "to provide, in an election held under its authority, for security of life and limbs to the voter." By emphasizing the national ramifications of private action in *Yarbrough*, Miller managed to distinguish *Cruikshank* in much the same way that he had distinguished between rights of national citizenship and rights of state citizenship in the *Slaughterhouse Cases*. Both formulations were designed to set principled limits to the exercise of Congress's affirmative powers to protect civil rights.

The impulse to preserve "the main features" of the federal system also shaped Miller's work in cases involving governmental interventions in economic life. He was certainly not immune to the laissez-faire ethos of the late nineteenth century, and his opinion for the Court in LOAN ASSOCIATION V. TOPEKA (1875) has long been regarded as one of the most significant expressions of natural law constitutionalism in American history and as an important building block in the growth of SUBSTANTIVE DUE PROCESS. There he held that a contract for $100,000 in municipal bonds, issued to lure a manufacturing firm to Topeka, was unenforceable. The people's tax dollars, he proclaimed, could not "be used for purposes of private interest instead of public use." Yet Miller resisted the urge, spearheaded by Justice STEPHEN J. FIELD, to link the "public use" principle with the Fourteenth Amendment and the concept of "general jurisprudence" in order to limit the exercise of all the states' inherent powers—police, taxation, and eminent domain.

The sweeping doctrines advanced by Field and other doctrinaire advocates of laissez-faire conflicted with three working principles of Miller's constitutional understanding, each of which militated against dramatic enlargement of federal judicial power at the expense of the states. The first was his Whiggish predisposition to allow state governments ample room to channel economic activity and develop resources for the general good. A broad construction of the Fourteenth Amendment, he asserted in the *Slaughterhouse Cases*, "would constitute this Court a perpetual censor upon all legislation of the States" and generate state inaction, even in the face of clear public interests, for fear of endless litigation. Miller also believed that it was not the function of federal courts to sit in judgment on state courts expounding state law. He repeatedly invoked this second working principle in the long line of cases that began with GELPCKE V. DUBUQUE (1864). There the Court insisted that municipal bonds issued to subsidize railroad construction were unquestionably for a "public use" despite recent state court decisions to the contrary. The *Gelpcke* majority defended federal judicial intervention on the ground that municipal bonds were a species of commercial paper and therefore the question of bondholder rights "belong[ed] to the domain of general jurisprudence." Miller dissented. In his view, extension of the principle of SWIFT V. TYSON (1842) to the construction of state statute law was an unconscionable act of federal usurpation, and he accurately predicted that it would spawn a generation of conflict between federal courts and recalcitrant state and local officials.

The apparent inconsistency between Miller's opinion in *Loan Association v. Topeka* and his stance in the *Slaughterhouse Cases* and in the *Gelpcke* line of municipal-bond cases is readily explained. All of them did raise similar conceptual issues; each hinged, in part, on the application of the "public use" principle to governmental aid of private enterprise in the form of either monopoly grants or cash subsidies. But for Miller, if not for his colleagues, the controlling factor in *Loan Association v. Topeka* was that it had been tried under the DIVERSITY JURISDICTION of a federal court, and pertinent state law had not yet been framed on the subject. As a result, Miller later explained in *Davidson v. New Orleans* (1878), the Court had been free to invoke "principles of general constitutional law" which the Kansas court was equally free to adopt or reject in subsequent cases involving similar circumstances. The concepts of substantive due process and "general jurisprudence," on the other hand, failed to maintain the ample autonomy for state governments which Miller regarded as an indispensable component of the American polity.

Miller ultimately failed to stave off the luxuriation of substantive due process, just as he had failed to curb the majority's impulse to invoke *Swift* in the municipal-bond cases. "It is in vain to contend with judges who have been at the bar the advocates for forty years of rail road companies, and all the forms of associated capital," he told his brother-in-law late in 1875. "I am losing interest in these matters. I will do my duty but will fight no more." Yet Miller's views did make a difference, particularly in the conference room. What remained influential was Miller's third working principle of constitutional interpretation. He recommended resistance to Field's syllogistic reasoning and quest for immutable principles; he suggested, instead, that once the Court had determined to protect private rights against state interference, it was best to decide cases on the narrowest possible grounds, to employ open-ended doctrinal formulas amenable to subsequent alteration, and to elaborate the meaning of due process through what he called a "gradual process of inclusion and exclusion." Thus Miller described local aid of manufactures as "robbery" in *Loan Association v. Topeka,* but he added that "it may not be easy to draw the line in all cases so as to decide what is a public use in this sense and what is not." He also endorsed the notoriously vague doctrine of "business AFFECTED WITH A PUBLIC INTEREST" in *Munn v. Illinois* (1877). And in CHICAGO, MILWAUKEE & ST. PAUL RY. V. MINNESOTA, (1890), when the Court finally invalidated a state law on due process grounds, Miller concurred "with some hesitation" but filed an opinion cautioning his colleagues against the adoption of a rigid formula, such as "fair value," to determine whether rate-making authorities had acted "arbitrarily and without regard to justice and right."

Miller's immediate successors disregarded the advice, but during the 1930s interest revived in his conception of the judicial function, particularly among FELIX FRANKFURTER's circle at the Harvard Law School. Frankfurter, who called Miller "the most powerful member of his Court," insisted in 1938 that judging was not at all like architecture. Rather than framing doctrinal structures with clean lines and the appearance of permanence, Frankfurter explained, "the Justices are cartographers who give temporary location but do not ultimately define the evershifting boundaries between state and national power, between freedom and authority." Miller could not have described his own views with greater clarity or force.

CHARLES W. McCURDY
(1986)

Bibliography

FAIRMAN, CHARLES 1938 *Mr. Justice Miller and the Supreme Court, 1862–1890.* Cambridge, Mass.: Harvard University Press.

FRANKFURTER, FELIX (1938) 1961 *Mr. Justice Holmes and the Supreme Court.* Cambridge, Mass.: Harvard University Press.

GILLETTE, WILLIAM 1969 Samuel Miller. Pages 1011–1024 in Leon Friedman and Fred Israel, eds., *The Justices of the Supreme Court, 1789–1965.* New York: Chelsea House.

MILLER v. CALIFORNIA
413 U.S. 15 (1973)

PARIS ADULT THEATRE I v. SLATON
413 U.S. 49 (1973)

For the first time since ROTH V. UNITED STATES (1957), a Supreme Court majority agreed on a definition of OBSCENITY. The Court had adopted the practice of summarily reversing obscenity convictions when at least five Justices, even if not agreeing on the appropriate test, found the material protected. The states were without real guidelines; and the requirements of JACOBELLIS V. OHIO (1964) that each Justice review the material at issue had transformed the Court into an ultimate board of censorship review.

To escape from this "intractable" problem, the *Miller* Court reexamined obscenity standards. Chief Justice WARREN E. BURGER's majority opinion, reaffirming *Roth,* articulated specific safeguards to ensure that state obscenity regulations did not encroach upon protected speech. The Court announced that a work could constitutionally be held to be obscene when an affirmative answer was appropriate for each of three questions:

(a) whether "the average person applying contemporary community standards" would find that the work, taken as a whole, appeals to the prurient interes. . . . ;
(b) whether the work depicts or describes, in a patently offensive way, sexual conduct specifically defined by the applicable state law; and
(c) whether the work, taken as a whole, lacks serious literary, artistic, political or scientific value.

Three aspects of the *Miller* formula are noteworthy. First, the work need not be measured against a single national standard, but may be judged by state community standards. Second, state obscenity regulations must be confined to works that depict or describe sexual conduct. Moreover, the states must specifically define the nature of that sexual conduct to provide due NOTICE to potential offenders. Third, the Court rejected the "utterly without redeeming social value" standard of MEMOIRS V. MASSACHUSETTS (1966). To merit FIRST AMENDMENT protection, the work, viewed as a whole, must have serious social value. A token political or social comment will not redeem an otherwise obscene work; nor will a brief erotic passage condemn a serious work.

In a COMPANION CASE, *Paris Adult Theater I,* the Court held that regulations concerning the public exhibition of obscenity, even in "adult" theaters excluding minors, were permissible if the *Miller* standards were met. The prohibition on privacy grounds against prosecuting possession of obscene material in one's home, recognized in STANLEY

v. GEORGIA (1969), does not limit the state's power to regulate commerce in obscenity, even among consenting adults.

Justice WILLIAM J. BRENNAN, joined by Justices POTTER J. STEWART and THURGOOD MARSHALL, dissented in both cases. Abandoning the views he expressed in *Roth* and *Memoirs*, Brennan concluded that the impossibility of definition rendered the outright suppression of obscenity irreconcilable with the First Amendment and the FOURTEENTH AMENDMENT. The Court's inability to distinguish protected speech from unprotected speech created intolerable fair notice problems and chilled protected speech. Furthermore, "institutional stress" had resulted from the necessary case-by-case Supreme Court review. Instead of attempting to define obscenity, Brennan would balance the state regulatory interest against the law's potential danger to free expression. He recognized the protection of juveniles or unconsenting adults as a state interest justifying the suppression of obscenity. Justice WILLIAM O. DOUGLAS, separately dissenting, also denounced the vague guidelines that sent persons to jail for violating standards they could not understand, construe, or apply.

The Court's attempt to articulate specific obscenity standards was successful to the extent it reduced the number of cases on the Supreme Court docket. Nevertheless, as Justice Brennan noted, and the history of obscenity decisions confirms, any obscenity definition is inherently vague. The Court thus remains the ultimate board of censorship review.

KIM MCLANE WARDLAW
(1986)

Bibliography

LOCKHARD, WILLIAM B. 1975 Escape from the Chill of Uncertainty. *Georgia Law Review* 9:533–587.

MILLER v. JOHNSON
515 U.S. 900 (1995)

In *Miller v. Johnson*, the Supreme Court overturned Georgia's Eleventh Congressional District, which was nowhere near as ill-compact as North Carolina's Twelfth Congressional District challenged in SHAW V. RENO (1993) but whose creation could be laid almost entirely to insistence by the U.S. Department of Justice that Georgia create two additional black-majority congressional districts. Writing for the majority, Justice ANTHONY M. KENNEDY asserted that the Department of Justice had made improper use of its preclearance authority under section 5 of the VOTING RIGHTS ACT OF 1965 (as amended) in pursuit of a policy of maximizing the number of black-majority districts, and

that racial considerations were predominant in the creation of the Eleventh District. *Miller* demonstrated that even districts that were not especially ill-compact or in blatant violation of traditional districting criteria could be struck down under the *Shaw* standard if the Court majority were convinced that existing irregularities could only be explained in racial terms.

Miller also showed the importance of the views of Justice SANDRA DAY O'CONNOR as a pivotal vote. O'Connor, in addition to joining the MAJORITY OPINION, wrote a two-paragraph CONCURRING OPINION in which she sought to reassure critics of *Shaw* that the Court was not going throw out all use of race as a districting criterion. In particular, she asserted that the *Shaw* test was "a demanding one," and that to invoke STRICT SCRUTINY, "a plaintiff must show that the State has relied on race in substantial disregard of customary and traditional districting practices." However, what this latter phrase means in practice seems very much in the eyes of the beholder. The DISSENTING OPINION, written by Justice RUTH BADER GINSBURG (and joined in whole or part by three other Justices), in effect denied that the district violated this test.

BERNARD GROFMAN
(2000)

(SEE ALSO: *Electoral Districting; Voting Rights.*)

Bibliography

GROFMAN, BERNARD, ed. 1998 *Race and Redistricting in the 1990s.* New York: Agathon Press.

MILLETT v. PEOPLE OF ILLINOIS
117 Illinois 294 (1886)

This was the first case in which a court held a regulatory statute unconstitutional on the ground that it violated the doctrine of FREEDOM OF CONTRACT. Illinois required coal-mine owners to install scales for the weighing of coal in order to determine the wages of miners. Millett, an owner, contracted with his miners, in violation of the statute, to pay by the boxload rather than by weight. The state supreme court, overturning his conviction, unanimously declared that the statute deprived him of DUE PROCESS substantively construed. Miners, the court said, could contract as they pleased in regard to the value of their labor, and owners had the same freedom of contract. The court summarily dismissed the contention that the regulation was a valid exercise of the POLICE POWER on the ground that the legislature had not protected the miners' safety or the property of others. A few months later the Pennsylvania high court, in *Godcharles v. Wigeman* (1886), held unconstitutional a state act that prohibited owners of mines or factories from paying workers in kind rather than in money wages. Such cases were forerunners of LOCHNER V. NEW YORK (1905) and its progeny.

LEONARD W. LEVY
(1986)

MILLIGAN, EX PARTE
4 Wallace 2 (1866)

In 1861, Chief Justice ROGER B. TANEY contrived a possibility of executive-judicial, civil-military clashes (*Ex parte Merryman*); in 1863 the Supreme Court averted similar confrontations (EX PARTE VALLANDIGHAM; PRIZE CASES). But in 1866–1867, the CHASE COURT, in the TEST OATH and *Ex parte Milligan* decisions, overcame its restraint.

In 1864, an Army court sentenced Lambden (spelling various) Milligan, a militantly antiwar, Negrophobe Indianan, to death for overtly disloyal activities. President ANDREW JOHNSON commuted the sentence to life imprisonment. Milligan's lawyer, employing the 1863 HABEAS CORPUS ACT, in 1865 appealed to the federal circuit court in Indiana for release. The judges, including Justice DAVID DAVIS, divided on whether a civil court had JURISDICTION over a military tribunal and on the legitimacy of military trials of civilians. This division let the petition go to the Supreme Court. There, in 1866, Attorney General HENRY STANBERY denied that any civil court had jurisdiction; special counsel BENJAMIN F. BUTLER insisted on the nation's right to use military justice in critical areas.

Milligan's lawyers included JAMES A. GARFIELD, JEREMIAH BLACK, and DAVID DUDLEY FIELD. Milligan, they argued, if indictable, was triable in civil courts for TREASON. Alternatively, they insisted that the Army court had failed to obey the 1863 Habeas Corpus Act's requirement to report on civilian prisoners. Further, they asserted that the Constitution's barriers against the use of military power in a state not in rebellion were fixed and unmodifiable, though Congress, they admitted, had authority to use military justice in the South.

All the Justices concurred about the military court's dereliction in not reporting Milligan's arrest. For the Court's bare majority, Justice Davis held that neither President nor Congress could establish military courts to try civilians in noninvaded areas, and, implicitly, that the final decision as to what areas were critical was the Court's. Martial law must never exist where civil courts operated, he stressed, although both had co-existed since the war started. SALMON P. CHASE, speaking also for Justices Samuel Miller, Noah Swayne, and JAMES WAYNE, disagreed. Congress could extend military authority in Indiana under the WAR POWERS without lessening BILL OF RIGHTS protections,

Chase asserted. The option was Congress's, not the Court's.

The majority view in *Milligan* was at once seized upon by supporters of President Johnson, the white South, and the Democratic party, though even Justice Davis stressed that he referred not at all to the South. Until military reconstruction clarified matters, the duties of the Army, acting under President Johnson's orders and the FREEDMEN'S BUREAU statute, were complicated greatly by misuses of the *Milligan* decision in the southern state courts, complications increased by the Test Oath decisions. Taken together, the *Milligan* and the Test Oath decisions greatly limited the capacity of both the nation and the states to provide more decent, color-blind justice in either civil or military courts (including those of the Freedmen's Bureau), and to exclude from leadership in politics and the professions persons who had sparked SECESSION and war.

In subsequent decades, legal writers THOMAS COOLEY and ZECHARIAH CHAFEE reconstructed *Milligan* into a basic defense of individual liberty and of civilian primacy over the military. Both men were flaying dragons perceived by Victorian Social Darwinists and by critics of WORLD WAR I witch-hunts. Milligan was never a merely theoretical threat. Neither the civil police and courts of Indiana nor the federal government, except for the Army, evidenced capacity to deal with him. In light of existing alternatives, the Army's decision to try Milligan (not its failure to report its decision and verdict) is defensible.

Republican criticism of the *Milligan* decision never threatened the Court. Instead, from 1863 through 1875, the Congress increased the Court's habeas corpus jurisdiction as well as that in admiralty, bankruptcy, and claims. The *Milligan* decision, paradoxically, became a major step in the Court's successful effort to regain the prestige that it had squandered in DRED SCOTT V. SANDFORD (1857), and that Taney had risked dissipating altogether in *Merryman*.

HAROLD M. HYMAN
(1986)

Bibliography

GAMBIONE, JOSEPH G. 1970 *Ex Parte Milligan:* The Restoration of Judicial Prestige? *Civil War History* 16:246–259.
KUTLER, STANLEY I. 1968 *Judicial Power and Reconstruction Politics.* Chaps. 6–8. Chicago: University of Chicago Press.

MILLIKEN v. BRADLEY
418 U.S. 717 (1974)
433 U.S. 267 (1977)

The DESEGREGATION of public schools in many large cities poses a problem: the cities are running out of white pupils, as white families move to the suburbs. In the early 1970s, some federal district judges began to insist on desegregation plans embracing not only city districts but also surrounding suburban districts. In the first such case to reach the Supreme Court, the Justices divided 4–4, thus affirming without opinion the DECISION of the court of appeals, which had reversed the district court's order for metropolitan relief. The case had come from Richmond, Virginia; Justice LEWIS F. POWELL, the former president of the Richmond school board, had disqualified himself.

Milliken, the Detroit school desegregation case, came to the Court the next year. Justice Powell participated, and a 5–4 Court held that interdistrict remedies were inappropriate absent some showing of a constitutional violation by the suburban district as well as the city district. Chief Justice WARREN E. BURGER wrote for the majority, joined by the other three appointees of President RICHARD M. NIXON and by Justice POTTER STEWART. Justices THURGOOD MARSHALL, BYRON R. WHITE, and WILLIAM O. DOUGLAS all wrote dissenting opinions, and Justice WILLIAM J. BRENNAN also dissented.

This decision was the first major setback for school desegregation plaintiffs, but it did not entirely foreclose metropolitan relief. Justice Stewart, who joined the majority opinion, concurred separately as well, saying he would be prepared to accept metropolitan relief not only where a suburban district had committed a constitutional violation, but also where state officials had engaged in racially discriminatory conduct such as racial gerrymandering of district lines or discriminatory application of housing or ZONING laws.

When the Detroit case returned to the Court three years later, it added a weapon to the arsenal of desegregation remedies. As part of a desegregation decree, the district court ordered the establishment of remedial education programs; the Supreme Court unanimously affirmed, with the Chief Justice again writing for the Court. The remedy must not exceed the constitutional violation, he wrote, but here, unlike the situation in *Milliken I,* the remedy was "tailored to cure the condition that offend[ed] the Constitution."

KENNETH L. KARST
(1986)

MILTON AND
FREEDOM OF EXPRESSION

The renowned poet John Milton's *Areopagitica,* written in 1644, is the earliest extended essay on the FREEDOM OF THE PRESS that continues to be read today. The essay was prompted by a decision of Parliament to reinstate the practice of licensing all books and pamphlets. This occurred a few short years after the institutions of crown censorship, including the infamous Star Chamber, had been abolished as part of a general challenge by the legislature to royal authority. In the interim after the abolition of crown licensing, as a civil war was raging, the leaders of Parliament became distressed both by the efflorescence of radical religious ideas circulating in the streets and by the effectiveness of propaganda then being disseminated by forces loyal to the King. Milton, along with many of his Puritan brethren, was disillusioned by this return to centralized control over thought. He implored the Parliament to have more faith in the English people by trusting them with unlicensed books and pamphlets.

Milton's argument is divided into four parts. First, he asserts that licensing writings is a relatively recent practice, developed by the Roman Catholic Church to thwart the Protestant Reformation and reaching its logical culmination in the Spanish Inquisition. Enlightened regimes tracing back to ancient Greece and Rome eschewed the policy of licensing, Milton claims. In identifying the regulation of speech with the Catholic Church, Milton appealed to the sympathies of his overwhelmingly Protestant audience, and to their widely held fears that the Stuart monarchs planned to return England to the Catholic fold.

Second, Milton argues that exposure to evil is necessary to knowledge of the good. He notes how the wisest thinkers throughout history have made it a point to study the systems of thought they were ultimately to reject and refute. "I cannot praise," says Milton, "a fugitive and cloistered virtue, unexercised and unbreathed, that never sallies out and sees her adversary. . . ." The theological notion of temptation figures prominently in this part of the argument. "[T]hat which purifies us is trial," Milton asserts, "and trial is by what is contrary."

The third section of the essay develops the claim that as a practical matter the licensing of books and pamphlets will not achieve its intended objectives. It is not easy, Milton observes, to determine which writings are truly evil and dangerous. What is to be done, for example, with "books which are partly useful and excellent, partly culpable and pernicious. . . ." If all such works were denied publication, the "commonwealth of learning" would be badly damaged. To evaluate writings in a discerning manner, a licenser "had need to be a man above the common measure, both studious, learned, and judicious. . . ." But this sort of work will not attract such a person, for "there cannot be a more tedious and unpleasing journey-work, a greater loss of time levied upon his head, than to be made the perpetual reader of unchosen books and pamphlets, oft times huge volumes." Given the drudgery of the job, "we may easily foresee what kind of licensers we are to expect hereafter, either ignorant, imperious, and remiss, or basely pecuniary."

Moreover, even if censors were discerning, evil writings

would circulate underground. And evil ideas can be spread by means other than books and pamphlets. Milton likens the futile project of licensing to "the exploit of that gallant man who thought to pound up the crows by shutting his park gate."

The fourth part of the argument of *Areopagitica* is the longest and the most impassioned. Here Milton waxes poetic regarding the harm that censorship does to the spirit of inquiry, both religious and political. It is an assault on the dignity of a writer, he says, to distrust him as though he were a truant schoolboy, to make him "trudge to his leave-giver" to obtain permission to publish. This demeaning distrust extends also to the general population of readers. If we "dare not trust them with an English pamphlet," says Milton, "what do we but censure them for a giddy, vicious, and ungrounded people, in such a sick and weak state of faith and discretion, as to be able to take nothing down but through pipe of a licenser."

One crucial consequence of the distrust implicit in licensing is its devastating effect on the general level of spiritual and political energy. Images of sloth and torpor abound in the essay. "[O]ur faith and knowledge thrives by exercise," Milton contends. Truth can be compared to "a streaming fountain; if her waters flow not in perpetual progression, they sicken into a muddy pool of conformity and tradition." The aim of censorship is a debilitating stasis, "a dull ease and cessation of our knowledge," an "obedient unanimity," the "forced and outward union of cold and neutral and inwardly divided minds."

Milton's regard for dynamism and ferment caused him to express a much higher opinion of the religious radicals of his day than was common, even among other proponents of toleration. Parliament's return to the practice of licensing had been prompted in part by the outpouring of bizarre, extravagant versions of Protestant theology that had greeted the lifting of crown censorship. This caught the mainstream Protestants who controlled Parliament by surprise and alarmed them greatly because they took seriously the notion of blasphemy and considered the stakes to be nothing less than divine favor at a pivotal moment in the history of both the Reformation and the English nation. Milton, in contrast, viewed the radical sectarians as a source of energy and potential revelation, despite his own rather more conventional theological views. "Where there is much desire to learn, there of necessity will be much arguing, much writing, many opinions; for opinion in good men is but knowledge in the making." Parliament's fear of heresy, he says, is exactly the wrong theological response: "Under these fantastic terrors of sect and schism, we wrong the earnest and zealous thirst after knowledge and understanding which God hath stirred up in this city. What some lament of, we rather should rejoice at, should rather praise this pious forwardness among

men, to reassume the ill-deputed care of their religion into their own hands again."

Milton's disdain for censorship derived in part from his belief that each person must take responsibility for his religious convictions and must form those convictions by an active process of inquiry. Also central to his position was his belief that the capacity of mortals to know the truth is very limited such that human laws designed to protect the known truth from heretical opinions are more likely to preserve error than to serve their intended purposes. Milton considered the search for truth to be never-ending until the Second Coming, and a matter of slow, fitful, halting progress. "[H]e who thinks we are to pitch our tent here, and have attained the utmost prospect of reformation that the mortal glass wherein we contemplate can show us, till we come to beatific vision, that man by this very opinion declares that he is yet far short of truth." The problem of false appearances figures prominently in Milton's argument. Truth, he asserts, "may have more shapes than one." Its "first appearance to our eyes, bleared and dimmed with prejudice and custom, is more unsightly and unplausible than many errors, even as the person is of many a great man slight and contemptible to see to."

Milton's understanding of the relationship between the FREEDOM OF SPEECH and the search for truth was informed not only by his notions of personal responsibility and human incapacity but also by his belief in divine providence. The circulation of heretical ideas is not as threatening as the proponents of censorship suppose because just when "false teachers" are "busiest in seducing" the populace, "God then raises to his own work men of rare abilities, and more than common industry" to revise previous errors and "go on some new enlightened steps in the discovery of truth." "For who knows not that truth is strong, next to the Almighty?" Because of divine providence, "though all the winds of doctrine were let loose to play upon the earth, so Truth be in the field, we do injuriously by licensing and prohibiting, to misdoubt her strength. Let her and falsehood grapple; who ever knew Truth put to the worse in a free and open encounter?"

As much as he insisted upon personal responsibility and struggle in matters of faith, and as impressed as he was with the limitations of human knowledge, Milton nevertheless explicitly excepted Roman Catholics from his argument for toleration. "I mean not tolerated popery," he says, "and open superstition, which, as it extirpates all religions and civil supremacies, so itself should be extirpate. . . ." Defenders of Milton have observed that almost all his fellow proponents of toleration made this exception and that the fear of Catholic military designs dominated the politics of Stuart England, not least the political struggle during the civil war between the Parliament and the Crown for the allegiance of the general populace. Had

Milton urged the toleration of Catholics he would have lost credibility with his intended Parliamentary audience. Milton's critics point out that an argument that emphasizes the need to confront supposed falsehood would seem to require the toleration of the most feared and powerful "supposed falsehood" of the day.

The *Areopagitica* is noteworthy as a rich repository of images and characterizations pertaining to censorship and free inquiry, and as an imaginative development of the point that there is positive value in grappling with ideas that may turn out to be false and evil. Interpretative debates persist regarding whether Milton's argument is limited solely to controversies over the regulation of *religious* speech, whether it constitutes only a case against the prior licensing of speech with no implications for disputes over other forms of control such as criminal penalties, and whether the author's refusal to tolerate Catholics renders his plea for free expression incoherent and/or hypocritical. The extent to which Milton's analysis was informed by his deep faith in divine providence and by the particular view of truth he derived therefrom raises questions regarding how much the *Areopagitica* has to offer the modern age. However these matters are resolved, Milton's observations about the importance of maintaining energy and his penetrating satirical comments about the dynamics and pretensions of censorship preserve the continuing value of the essay.

VINCENT BLASI
(2000)

Bibliography

BARKER, ARTHUR 1942 *Milton and the Puritan Dilemma.* Toronto: University of Toronto Press.
HALLER, WILLIAM 1955 *Liberty and Reformation in the Puritan Revolution.* New York: Columbia University Press.
KOLBRENER, WILLIAM 1997 *Milton's Warring Angels.* Cambridge, Eng.: Cambridge University Press.
LOEWENSTEIN, DAVID 1992 *Milton and the Drama of History.* Cambridge, Eng.: Cambridge University Press.
SMITH, NIGEL 1990 Areopagitica: Voicing Contexts 1643–45. In David Loewenstein and James Turner, eds., *Politics, Poetics, and Hermeneutics in Milton's Prose.* Cambridge, Eng.: Cambridge University Press.

MINERSVILLE SCHOOL DISTRICT v. GOBITIS

See: Flag Salute Cases

MINIMUM WAGES

See: Maximum Hours and Minimum Wages Legislation

MINISTERIAL ACT

A ministerial act is one an official performs as a matter of legal duty, without any personal discretion and without judging the merits. For example, in MARBURY V. MADISON (1803), Chief Justice JOHN MARSHALL described delivery of an appointee's commission as a ministerial act of the secretary of state.

DENNIS J. MAHONEY
(1986)

MINNESOTA v. BARBER
136 U.S. 313 (1890)

The Supreme Court unanimously held unconstitutional as a violation of the COMMERCE CLAUSE a Minnesota statute that prohibited the sale for human consumption of meat slaughtered in another state and not inspected in Minnesota. The statute, the Court declared, forced citizens to buy only Minnesota meat, denying them the benefits of competition in INTERSTATE COMMERCE.

LEONARD W. LEVY
(1986)

MINNESOTA RATE CASES
230 U.S. 352 (1913)

In these cases a unanimous Supreme Court reaffirmed state power to regulate INTRASTATE COMMERCE even if it should indirectly affect INTERSTATE COMMERCE. Justice CHARLES EVANS HUGHES stressed the supremacy of federal authority but, reaching back to COOLEY V. BOARD OF WARDENS OF PHILADELPHIA (1852), held that states could regulate interstate commerce when Congress had not yet chosen to act.

The cases before the Court represented extensive litigation throughout the country. The Railroad & Warehouse Commission of Minnesota and the state legislature had issued orders fixing maximum rail rates within the state. Although the rates they set were purely intrastate, both sides agreed that interstate rates would be affected. The cases arose as STOCKHOLDERS' SUITS to prevent the application of the prescribed rates to interstate operators. (See EX PARTE YOUNG.) On the principal question whether the orders fixed rates that interfered with interstate commerce, Hughes agreed that if the rates imposed a direct burden on commerce, they must fall. He then began a lengthy exposition of the nature of commercial regulation in the federal system, concluding that "it is competent for a state to govern its internal commerce . . . although interstate commerce may incidentally or indirectly be involved." Unless and until Congress acted, state action might well be legal even if touching interstate commerce. Only Congress could judge the necessity for action and, having decided to, it could intervene "at its discretion for the complete and effective government" of even local conduct affecting interstate commerce. The Minnesota actions were, therefore, within the state's power but would be superseded if Congress acted. The Court thus broadly upheld state ratemaking authority; it also implicitly affirmed federal power over intrastate railroad activity affecting interstate commerce, a significant step it would take explicitly the following year in HOUSTON, EAST & WEST TEXAS RAILWAY COMPANY V. UNITED STATES, (1914).

DAVID GORDON
(1986)

MINOR v. HAPPERSETT
21 Wallace 162 (1875)

MORRISON R. WAITE delivered the unanimous opinion of the Supreme Court holding that a woman, though a citizen of the United States and of the state in which she resides, had no right to vote as a privilege of national CITIZENSHIP protected by the PRIVILEGES AND IMMUNITIES clause of the FOURTEENTH AMENDMENT. The laws of her state allowed only men to vote, and the amendment did not change that by making any new voters.

LEONARD W. LEVY
(1986)

MINTON, SHERMAN
(1890–1965)

Born in Indiana in 1890, Sherman Minton attended Indiana University and Yale Law School. After military service during WORLD WAR I, several years in private practice, and brief service as attorney for an Indiana state agency, Minton was elected to the United States Senate in 1934. A fervent advocate of President FRANKLIN D. ROOSEVELT's "NEW DEAL," Minton supported measures expanding the federal government's role in ECONOMIC REGULATION powers despite his concern that the Supreme Court might declare such measures unconstitutional. As the Court repeatedly struck down New Deal legislation, Minton proposed that the votes of at least seven Justices be necessary to invalidate an act of Congress; in 1937, Minton worked vigorously for the enactment of Roosevelt's Court reorganization plan. After Minton was defeated for reelection in 1940, he served briefly as one of Roosevelt's special assistants. In the spring of 1941 Roosevelt appointed Minton to the Seventh Circuit Court of Appeals. In 1949 President HARRY S. TRUMAN appointed Minton to the Supreme

Court to fill the vacancy created by the death of Justice WILEY B. RUTLEDGE; this appointment was as much a product of Truman's close friendship with Minton as of Truman's desire to appoint Justices with prior judicial experience. Ill health forced Minton's retirement in 1956.

Minton believed that the Supreme Court could not impose libertarian standards upon a government and a people that did not favor them. Minton's commitment to judicial restraint and his resistance to what he perceived as JUDICIAL POLICYMAKING followed directly from his frustration as a senator with the Court's opposition to New Deal legislation and his participation in efforts to curb the Court's powers.

Minton disappointed liberals who had hoped that he would work as vigorously for judicial protection of individual liberties as for the legitimation of governmental economic regulation. He consistently voted to uphold statutes and other governmental programs intended to protect the national security, rejecting challenges asserting violation of individual liberties. In CRIMINAL PROCEDURE cases, Minton tended to uphold convictions. For example, in UNITED STATES V. RABINOWITZ (1950) Minton held for the Court that the FOURTH AMENDMENT permits WARRANTLESS SEARCHES and seizures, so long as they are reasonable. Where litigants sought review of state criminal decisions, Minton was reluctant to disturb state procedures or court decisions absent a showing of significant unfairness affecting the verdict. Minton was ready to invalidate STATE ACTION discriminating against minorities, but he was disinclined to find state action. He emphasized the literal meaning of congressional statutes, rarely resorting to external aids or evidence of legislative intent; in the absence of express statutory language, federal regulation did not preempt concurrent state regulation.

Minton stressed the importance of the Court's collegial atmosphere. He disliked personal disputes among the Justices and did his best to reduce their intensity or to dissipate them altogether. Minton viewed the task of writing opinions for the Court as the preparation of functional instruments of collective policy. He rarely wrote concurrences or dissents, for he believed that separate opinions tended to vitiate the authority of majority opinions and to sow discord among the Justices. After his retirement in 1956, Minton minimized the significance of his tenure on the Court; he believed that his most important judicial act was his vote in BROWN V. BOARD OF EDUCATION (1954) to strike down SEGREGATION of public schools.

RICHARD B. BERNSTEIN
(1986)

Bibliography

WALLACE, HARRY L.   1959–1960   Mr. Justice Minton: Hoosier Justice on the Supreme Court. *Indiana Law Journal* 34:145–205, 383–424.

MIRANDA v. ARIZONA
384 U.S. 436 (1966)

Miranda is the best known as well as the most controversial and maligned self-incrimination decision in the history of the Supreme Court. Some of the harshest criticism came from the dissenters in that case. Justice BYRON R. WHITE, for example, declared that the rule of the case, which required elaborate warnings and offer of counsel before the RIGHT AGAINST SELF-INCRIMINATION could be effectively waived, would return killers, rapists, and other criminals to the streets and have a corrosive effect on the prevention of crime. The facts of *Miranda*, one of four cases decided together, explain the alarm of the four dissenters and of the many critics of the WARREN COURT. The majority of five, led by Chief Justice EARL WARREN, reversed the kidnap-and-rape conviction of Ernesto Miranda, who had been picked out of a LINEUP by his victim, had been interrogated without mistreatment for a couple of hours, and had signed a confession that purported to have been voluntarily made with full knowledge of his rights, although no one had advised him that he did not need to answer incriminating questions or that he could have counsel present. The Court reversed because his confession had been procured in violation of his rights, yet had been admitted in EVIDENCE. Warren conceded that the Court could not know what had happened in the interrogation room and "might not find the . . . statements to have been involuntary in traditional terms." Justice JOHN MARSHALL HARLAN, dissenting, professed to be "astonished" at the decision. Yet the Court did little more than require that the states follow what was already substantially FEDERAL BUREAU OF INVESTIGATION (**FBI**) procedure with respect to the rights of a suspect during a custodial interrogation.

The doctrinal significance of the case is that the Fifth Amendment's self-incrimination clause became the basis for evaluating the admissibility of confessions. The Court thus abandoned the traditional DUE PROCESS analysis that it had used in state cases since BROWN V. MISSISSIPPI (1936) to determine whether a confession was voluntary under all the circumstances. (See POLICE INTERROGATIONS AND CONFESSIONS.) Moreover, the Court shifted to the Fifth Amendment from the Sixth Amendment analysis of ESCOBEDO V. ILLINOIS (1964), when discussing the RIGHT TO COUNSEL as a means of protecting against involuntary confessions. *Miranda* stands for the proposition that the Fifth Amendment vests a right in the individual to remain silent unless he chooses to speak in the "unfettered exercise of his own will." The opinion of the Court lays down a code of procedures that must be respected by law enforcement officers to secure that right to silence whenever they take a person into custody or deprive him of his freedom in any significant way.

In each of the four *Miranda* cases, the suspect was not effectively notified of his constitutional rights and was questioned incommunicado in a "police-dominated" atmosphere; each suspect confessed, and his confession was introduced in evidence against him at his trial. The Court majority demonstrated a deep distrust for police procedures employed in station-house interrogation, aimed at producing confessions. The *Miranda* cases showed, according to Warren, a secret "interrogation environment," created to subject the suspect to the will of his examiners. Intimidation, even if only psychological, could undermine the will and dignity of the suspect, compelling him to incriminate himself. Therefore, the inherently compulsive character of in-custody interrogation had to be offset by procedural safeguards to insure obedience to the right of silence. Until legislatures produced other procedures at least as effective, the Court would require that at the outset of interrogation a person be clearly informed that he has the right to remain silent, that any statement he makes may be used as evidence against him, that he has the right to the presence of an attorney, and that if he cannot afford an attorney, one will be appointed to represent him.

These rules respecting mandatory warnings, Warren declared, are "an absolute prerequisite to interrogation." The presence of a lawyer, he reasoned, would reduce coercion, effactually preserve the right of silence for one unwilling to incriminate himself, and produce an accurate statement if the suspect chooses to speak. Should he indicate at any time before or during interrogation that he wishes to remain silent or have an attorney present, the interrogation must cease. Government assumes a heavy burden, Warren added, to demonstrate in court that a defendant knowingly and intelligently waived his right to silence or to a lawyer. "The warnings required and the waiver necessary in accordance with our opinion today are prerequisites," he emphasized, "to the admissibility of any statement made by a defendant."

Warren insisted that the new rules would not deter effective law enforcement. The experience of the FBI attested to that, and its practices, which accorded with the Court's rules, could be "readily emulated by state and local law enforcement agencies." The Constitution, Warren admitted, "does not require any specific code of procedures" for safeguarding the Fifth Amendment right; the Court would accept any equivalent set of safeguards.

Justice TOM C. CLARK, dissenting, observed that the FBI had not been warning suspects that counsel may be present during custodial interrogation, though FBI practice immediately altered to conform to Warren's opinion. Clark, like Harlan, whose dissent was joined by Justices POTTER STEWART and Byron White, would have preferred "the more pliable dictates" of the conventional due process analysis that took all the circumstances of a case into account. Harlan also believed that the right against self-incrimination should not be extended to the police station and should not be the basis for determining whether a confession is involuntary. White wrote a separate dissent, which Harlan and Stewart joined, flaying the majority for an opinion that had no historical, precedential, or textual basis. White also heatedly condemned the majority for weakening law enforcement and for prescribing rules that were rigid, but still left many questions unanswered. (See MIRANDA RULES.)

LEONARD W. LEVY
(1986)

Bibliography

KAMISAR, YALE 1980 *Police Interrogations and Confessions.* Pages 41–76. Ann Arbor: University of Michigan Press.

WHITEBREAD, CHARLES H. 1980 *Criminal Procedure.* Pages 292–310. Mineola, N.Y.: Foundation Press.

MIRANDA RULES

In MIRANDA V. ARIZONA (1966) the Supreme Court held that a person subject to custodial POLICE INTERROGATION must be warned that any statement he makes can be used against him, that he has a right to remain silent, and that he has a right to the presence of an attorney and that one will be appointed for him if he is indigent. A defendant may waive these rights. A WAIVER must be voluntary and intelligent. In the absence of a fully effective alternative, these warnings must be given and a valid waiver taken as the constitutional prerequisite to the admissibility of any product of custodial police interrogation.

The *Miranda* opinion left unresolved numerous issues. For example: When is a person in custody? What constitutes interrogation? What are the standards for measuring the validity of a purported waiver of the *Miranda* rights? May voluntary statements that are inadmissible for failure to comply with *Miranda* be introduced to impeach the credibility of a defendant's trial testimony? How is the burden of proving VOLUNTARINESS and compliance with the *Miranda* requirements allocated?

Post-*Miranda* cases have lessened considerably the constraints the decision had imposed upon law enforcement officials. For example, the police are required to give a suspect the *Miranda* warnings only if the suspect is in custody at the time of interrogation. In OROZCO V. TEXAS (1969) the Court held that a person is in custody any time that he is not free to leave whether in his own home, a hospital, a police car, or the stationhouse. ESTELLE V. SMITH (1981) held that when an indicted defendant, who has not put his mental state in issue, is compelled to undergo a court-ordered psychiatric examination, he is in custody and is entitled to the *Miranda* warnings prior to the evaluation by a mental health professional. However, most courts have held that a suspect is not in custody when in an open, natural environment. Examples include STOP AND FRISK situations, traffic arrests, accident investigations, or searches at international borders.

The second prerequisite to requiring the *Miranda* warnings is that the suspect be the subject of interrogation. The *Miranda* opinion defined interrogation as "questioning initiated by law enforcement officers." In RHODE ISLAND V. INNES (1980), the Court elaborated, stating that "interrogation" meant "express questioning or its functional equivalent" including "any words or actions on the part of the police . . . reasonably likely to elicit an incriminating response from the subject." By contrast, a statement freely and voluntarily made without any interrogation is admissible as a "threshold confession" or "spontaneous statement." If, for example, a person walks into a police station and states that he has killed someone, the police are not required to stop the person wishing to speak and give that person the warnings.

If both custody and interrogation are present, the police must give the warnings or take a valid waiver before proceeding. The police may not presume that a suspect knows of the *Miranda* rights. The form of the warnings may vary, however, so long as the words used give a clear, understandable warning of all the rights, taking into account the circumstances and the characteristics of the suspect.

In OREGON V. ELSTAD (1985) the Supreme Court held that an invalid confession obtained without the suspect being informed of his *Miranda* rights would not invalidate a later confession made after the suspect was informed of his rights, so long as the confession was obtained without coercion. However, in NEW YORK V. QUARLES (1984) the Court established a "public safety" exception, stating that if reasonable concern for public safety is present, a police officer need not recite the *Miranda* warnings before questioning a suspect in custody.

The accused, after receiving the warnings, may voluntarily waive any of his *Miranda* rights. The government must demonstrate voluntariness under all the circumstances. A signed waiver form is strong, but not conclusive, evidence of voluntariness. An effective waiver need not be written, however, and it may be implied from the accused's conduct.

Once the suspect terminates the interrogation or requests counsel, he may not be reinterviewed without being provided access to the requested attorney even if the suspect is given a second set of *Miranda* warnings. In EDWARDS V. ARIZONA (1981) the Court held that once an accused requests counsel, questioning must cease until counsel is present or until the accused "initiates further communication, exchanges or conversation with the police." In *Smith v. Illinois* (1984), the Court followed this precedent by holding that, once the accused has requested an attorney, no further questions or responses may be used to cast doubt on the request.

By contrast, in *Fare v. Michael C.* (1979) the Court held that a juvenile's request for a probation officer during questioning does not have the same constitutional effect as a request for a lawyer. The Court based its distinction on the fact that a lawyer's principal responsibility is to defend his client, while a probation officer has a duty to report and prosecute misconduct by a juvenile. In addition, probation officers are not necessarily qualified to provide legal assistance. Consequently, a juvenile's request for his probation officer is not a per se invocation of the *Miranda* RIGHT TO COUNSEL.

The issue of voluntariness arises in nonwaiver contexts as well. The Court has held that voluntary confessions obtained in violation of the *Miranda* rules, though not admissible in the State's case-in-chief as evidence of guilt, may be admitted to impeach a testifying defendant's credibility. In the leading case, HARRIS V. NEW YORK (1971), the defendant denied in court that he had sold heroin to an undercover agent. During cross-examination, Harris was asked whether he had made certain statements following his arrest that were inconsistent with his in-court testimony. Even though the prosecution conceded that the statements were obtained in violation of *Miranda*, the Supreme Court upheld the trial judge's ruling that the statements could be considered by the jury in evaluating the defendant's credibility.

When the defendant's statements are truly involuntary, they may not be admitted into evidence for any purpose. *Mincey v. Arizona* (1978) is illustrative, holding that the defendant's statements were inadmissible because they were obtained while the defendant was hospitalized and barely able to speak.

Whether the issue arises in the waiver or in the impeachment context, the burden of proving voluntariness under all the circumstances rests on the government. *Miranda* described it as a "heavy burden," a term which a number of courts have interpreted as requiring proof beyond a REASONABLE DOUBT. The Supreme Court, however, stopped this trend by holding, in *Lego v. Twomey* (1972), that proof by a preponderance of the evidence will suffice in federal court, though the states may impose a higher burden in state proceedings.

CHARLES H. WHITEBREAD
(1986)

Bibliography

WHITEBREAD, CHARLES H. 1980 *Criminal Procedure*. Mineola, N.Y.: Foundation Press.

MIRANDA RULES
(Update)

MIRANDA V. ARIZONA (1966) held that a statement obtained from a criminal defendant through custodial interrogation is inadmissible against that defendant unless the police obtained a waiver of the RIGHT AGAINST SELF-INCRIMINATION after warning the suspect of both the right to remain silent and the RIGHT TO COUNSEL. Recently, the Supreme Court has issued decisions favorable to the government concerning several *Miranda* issues: the definition of custodial interrogation, in *Arizona v. Mauro* (1989); the adequacy of warnings provided to persons in custody, in *Duckworth v. Eagan* (1989); and the standard that governs the validity of waiver, in *Colorado v. Spring* (1987) and *Colorado v. Connelly* (1986). Although in *Arizona v. Robertson* (1988) the Court reaffirmed the proscription of questioning until counsel appears, once the suspect requests counsel, the police need not advise the suspect of a lawyer's efforts to consult with him or her, as the Court held in *Moran v. Burbine* (1986).

The most significant of these developments is the holding in *Connelly* and *Spring* that a *Miranda* waiver is valid so long as the police did not obtain the waiver through conduct that would render a confession "involuntary" as a matter of PROCEDURAL DUE PROCESS. The *Miranda* opinion stated that "a heavy burden rests on the Government to demonstrate that the defendant knowingly and intelligently waived his privilege against self-incrimination and his right to . . . counsel." Connelly, a lunatic, confessed at the behest of "the voice of God." Spring waived *Miranda* rights after government agents led him to believe that the questioning would concern an illegal firearms transaction, but the interrogation eventually included questions about a homicide. Spring's waiver was not knowing, and Connelly's was not intelligent. The Court nonetheless approved admission of both CONFESSIONS, stating in *Connelly* that "there is obviously no reason to require more in the way of a "voluntariness' inquiry in the *Miranda* waiver context than in the FOURTEENTH AMENDMENT confession context."

The Justices would not likely approve waiver of the right to counsel *at trial* by a person in Connelly's condition or by a person like Spring, who misunderstood the seriousness of the charge. Yet in *Patterson v. Illinois* (1988), the Court held that in the interrogation context the claimed waiver of the Sixth Amendment right to counsel, a right initiated by a formal charge with the prospect of a trial, is tested under the *Connelly* standard. Ironically, the standard governing the waiver of rights is strictest in the courtroom, where coercion and deception are least likely, and most lenient in the stationhouse or the police cruiser, where these dangers are greatest.

Not many police departments are likely to depart from the verbal formulation of the warnings given by the *Miranda* opinion, and in few cases does a lawyer attempt to advise an arrested person who did not invoke the *Miranda* right to counsel. Commonly, however, the government claims that the accused waived his or her *Miranda* rights. The ability of police interrogators to induce suspects to waive their rights explains the consistent empirical finding that the *Miranda* doctrine has had a negligible effect on police effectiveness. Because *Miranda* was inspired by dissatisfaction with the vacuous and unpredictable due process approach, stating the test for waiver in the same terms as the voluntariness test comes close to full circle from the law that preceded *Miranda*.

But the Court's retrenchment of the *Miranda* doctrine is not the whole story. In one sense, the most important development in confessions law is *Miranda*'s continued survival, emphasized by cases such as *Roberson*, in which the Court approved the exclusion of valuable evidence obtained without police brutality. At least since HARRIS V. NEW YORK (1971), a majority of the Justices have believed that *Miranda* was wrongly decided. A majority continues to describe the *Miranda* rules as prophylactic safeguards rather than constitutional entitlements, a distinction that is not compatible with *Miranda*'s presumption that statements obtained without a valid waiver are compelled within the meaning of the Fifth Amendment. Despite the erosion of their Fifth Amendment foundation, the Court refuses to abandon the *Miranda* rules.

The failure of recent efforts to have *Miranda* overruled confirms that STARE DECISIS, even without more, will sustain the decision. During the presidency of RONALD REAGAN, the Justice Department's Office of Legal Policy issued a lengthy report calling for *Miranda*'s demise. The report effectively pointed out the inconsistency of *Harris* and its progeny with *Miranda* itself; but on several points, including the key issue of law enforcement effectiveness, the report made an embarassingly weak case for obliterating a landmark. Not only did the Court as a whole reject the department's effort; the report was not approved by a single Justice in any concurring or dissenting opinion.

So *Miranda* lives, a symbol of commitment to civil liberty that conveniently does little to obstruct the suppression of crime. But at the borders of the *Miranda* rules, a skeptical Supreme Court majority has taken frequent opportunities to limit their scope. The most likely future development along these lines is approval of the suggestion advanced by two Justices, concurring in *Duckworth v. Eagan*, to the effect that claims by state prisoners that their convictions violated *Miranda* should not be cognizable in federal HABEAS CORPUS proceedings.

DONALD A. DRIPPS
(1992)

(SEE ALSO: *Police Interrogation and Confessions; Procedural Due Process of Law, Criminal.*)

Bibliography

KAMISAR, YALE et al. 1989 *Modern Criminal Procedure*, 6th ed. St. Paul, Minn.: West Publishing Co.

UNITED STATES DEPARTMENT OF JUSTICE, OFFICE OF LEGAL POLICY 1986 *Report to the Attorney General on the Law of Pre-trial Interrogation.* Washington, D.C.: U.S. Government Printing Office.

MISCEGENATION

The fear of racial mixture migrated to the New World with the earliest colonists. In 1609, planters headed for Virginia were reminded by a preacher of the injunction that "Abrams posteritie keepe to themselves." Of course, they did no such thing. From the beginning, there was a shortage of women; white men freely interbred with both Indian and black women, even before the great waves of slave importation. During the era of SLAVERY, interracial sex cut across all strata of the white male population, from the poorest indentured servants to the wealthiest planters. THOMAS JEFFERSON was merely the most celebrated of the latter. Mulattoes were, in fact, deliberately bred for the slave market. Miscegenation laws, forbidding an interracial couple to marry or live together, were not designed to prevent interracial sex but to prevent the transmission of wealth and status from white fathers to their interracial offspring. Laws governing ILLEGITIMACY served a similar purpose, particularly in southern states. To this day, a majority of "blacks" in the United States are of interracial descent.

The adoption of the FOURTEENTH AMENDMENT offered an obvious opportunity for the Supreme Court to hold miscegenation laws unconstitutional on EQUAL PROTECTION grounds. When the occasion arose in PACE V. ALABAMA (1883), however, the Court unanimously upheld such a law, saying that it applied equally to punish both white and black partners to an intimate relationship. The constitutional validity of miscegenation laws went largely unquestioned until the great mid-twentieth-century rediscovery of racial equality as the Fourteenth Amendment's central meaning. Following BROWN V. BOARD OF EDUCATION (1954), it was only a matter of time before the miscegenation issue would reach the Supreme Court. As it happened, the period of time was short. In *Naim v. Naim* (1955–1956) the Court fudged, dismissing an appeal in a jurisdictional evasion that Herbert Wechsler properly scored as "wholly without basis in the law." Unquestionably, the Court adopted this avoidance technique because of the political storm that had greeted the *Brown* decision. Playing on the white South's fear of race mixture was a standard scare tactic of politicians favoring SEGREGATION. Recognizing this fear, the NAACP, in planning its assault on segregated higher education, had deliberately chosen as its plaintiff in MCLAURIN V. OKLAHOMA STATE REGENTS (1950) a sixty-eight-year-old graduate student. The *Brown* opinion itself had been carefully limited to the context of education, and the *Naim* evasion was cut from the same political cloth.

For a decade, the Court was spared the inevitable confrontation. In *Mclaughlin v. Florida* (1964), it invalidated a law forbidding unmarried cohabitation by an interracial couple. Assuming for argument the validity of the state's law forbidding interracial marriage, the Court nonetheless held that the cohabitation law denied equal protection. The reasoning of *Pace v. Alabama*, the Court said, had not withstood analysis in more recent decisions. Finally, in LOVING V. VIRGINIA (1967), the Court put an end to the whole ugly pretense about "racial purity," holding invalid a law forbidding interracial marriage. Equal protection and SUBSTANTIVE DUE PROCESS grounds served as alternative basis for the decision. *Loving* thus stands not only for a principle of racial equality but also for a broad "freedom to marry." (See FREEDOM OF INTIMATE ASSOCIATION.) The principle of equality is often liberty's cutting edge.

KENNETH L. KARST
(1986)

Bibliography

FRAZIER, E. FRANKLIN   1939   *The Negro Family in the United States.* Chap. IV. (rev. ed. 1966). Chicago: University of Chicago Press.

MYRDAL, GUNNAR   1944   *An American Dilemma: The Negro Problem and Modern Democracy.* Chap. 5. New York: Harper & Brothers.

MISDEMEANOR

A misdemeanor is one of a class of offenses considered less heinous, and punished less severely, than FELONIES. Generally, misdemeanors are punishable by fine or by incarceration in facilities other than penitentiaries for terms of up to one year. Federal law and most state statutes classify all crimes other than felonies as misdemeanors. Two standards have traditionally been used to distinguish felonies from misdemeanors: the place of imprisonment (a penitentiary as opposed to a jail); and the length of imprisonment (more than one year for felonies, a lesser term for misdemeanors).

The Supreme Court has held that criminal defendants charged with misdemeanors are entitled to certain guarantees of the BILL OF RIGHTS. In ARGERSINGER V. HAMLIN (1972), an indigent defendant was convicted of carrying a concealed weapon, a misdemeanor offense, and sentenced to ninety days in jail. An attorney was not appointed to represent the defendant even though he did not waive this right. The Supreme Court ruled that the RIGHT TO COUNSEL was applicable to misdemeanors where the defendant received a jail term. In *Scott v. Illinois* (1979), however, the Supreme Court declined to find a right to counsel at trial where loss of liberty is merely a possibility and does not, in fact, occur.

The Supreme Court also held, in BALDWIN V. NEW YORK (1970), that the Sixth Amendment requires that defendants accused of serious crimes be afforded the right to TRIAL BY JURY. This right applies to misdemeanors where imprisonment for more than six months is authorized. (See INFORMATION.)

CHARLES H. WHITEBREAD
(1986)

Bibliography

LAFAVE, W. and SCOTT, A.   1972   *Criminal Law.* St. Paul, Minn.: West Publishing Co.

MISHKIN v. NEW YORK

See: *Memoirs v. Massachusetts*

MISSISSIPPI v. JOHNSON
4 Wallace (71 U.S.) 475 (1867)

GEORGIA v. STANTON
6 Wallace (73 U.S.) 50 (1868)

In these cases, the Supreme Court refused to enjoin President ANDREW JOHNSON and Secretary of War EDWIN M. STANTON from enforcing the MILITARY RECONSTRUCTION ACTS. The Justices unanimously refused to act in the Mississippi case, holding that legislatively mandated executive duties were not enjoinable. Georgia subsequently argued that the military laws threatened its corporate sovereignty, but Justice SAMUEL NELSON found this a POLITICAL QUESTION unfit for judicial scrutiny. Nelson hinted, however, that the Court might favorably consider an action based on property rights. Shortly afterward, in an unreported case (*Mississippi v. Stanton*, 1868), the Justices evenly divided on that question. Consequently, the judiciary never ruled on the constitutionality of military reconstruction; yet these decisions involved an important recognition of SEPARATION OF POWERS and the limits of JUDICIAL POWER.

STANLEY I. KUTLER
(1986)

MISSISSIPPI UNIVERSITY FOR WOMEN v. HOGAN
458 U.S. 718 (1982)

Joe Hogan, a male registered nurse, was rejected by a state university's all-female school of nursing. A 5–4 Supreme Court held that Hogan's exclusion violated his right to EQUAL PROTECTION OF THE LAWS. For the majority, Justice SANDRA DAY O'CONNOR rejected the argument that, by excluding males, the university was compensating for discrimination against women. Rather, the all-female policy "tends to perpetuate the stereotyped view of nursing as an exclusively woman's job." The university thus failed the test set by CRAIG V. BOREN (1976) for SEX DISCRIMINATION cases. The dissenters, making a case for diversity of types of higher education, emphasized that Hogan could attend a coeducational state nursing school elsewhere in Mississippi.

KENNETH L. KARST
(1986)

MISSOURI v. HOLLAND
252 U.S. 416 (1920)

Missouri v. Holland confirmed the status of treaties as supreme law. Although becoming "perhaps the most famous and most discussed case in the constitutional law of foreign relations" it arose from a narrower Progressive era desire to prevent indiscriminate killing of migratory birds, which key states had proved unable or unwilling to end by themselves. Congress first legislated hunting restrictions in March 1913, but lower federal courts invalidated them on TENTH AMENDMENT grounds as exceeding the federal government's commerce power, intruding on STATE POLICE POWERS, and usurping the states' well-established position in American law as trustees for their citizens of wild animals. The federal government feared the outcome of a final test of the 1913 act sufficiently to delay Supreme Court action. Instead, responding to suggestions from Elihu Root and others, the Wilson administration concluded the Migratory Bird Treaty of 1916 with Great Britain (acting on behalf of Canada). This committed both nations to restrict hunting of the birds, and in the United States President WOODROW WILSON signed implementing legislation in July 1918.

Several lower courts, including one that had ruled against the 1913 legislation, quickly upheld the 1918 act. In one of these cases the state of Missouri had sought to enjoin federal game warden Ray P. Holland from enforcing the new law. Appealing to the Supreme Court, Missouri argued that because, in the absence of a treaty, the legislation would be clearly invalid on Tenth Amendment grounds, it must fall even with a treaty base, for otherwise constitutional limitations would become a nullity. The Supreme Court upheld the 1918 legislation in a 7–2 vote (but with no written dissent filed).

Echoing the government's defense of the challenged act, the core of Justice OLIVER WENDELL HOLMES's opinion for the Court was a standard federal supremacy argument. Whether or not the 1913 legislation had been invalid, the 1918 act implemented a treaty; because the Constitution explicitly delegated the TREATY POWER to the federal government and gave status as supreme law to treaties made "under the authority of the United States," Tenth Amendment objections had no force.

Less restrained, even cryptic, was Holmes's language, which provided a basis for years of controversy. After questioning whether the requirement that treaties be made under the authority of the United States meant more than observance of the Constitution's prescribed forms for treaty-making, Holmes defended an organic, expansive conception of the Constitution. Its words had "called into life a being the development of which could not have been foreseen completely by the most gifted of its begetters." The Migratory Bird Case needed consideration "in light of our whole experience." The question finally became whether the treaty was "forbidden by some invisible radiation from the general terms of the 10th Amendment." Holmes thereby camouflaged his admissions that treaties must involve matters of national interest and must not contravene specific constitutional prohibitions.

In the 1920s and early 1930s, when the Court often adhered to the doctrine of DUAL FEDERALISM, *Missouri v. Holland* arguably offered constitutional grounds for otherwise suspect federal legislation if appropriate treaties were concluded. (Proponents of child labor regulation toyed with the approach.) Fears about its potential in this respect lingered into the 1950s, when the case was a frequent target for backers of the BRICKER AMENDMENT. Yet after 1937 the Supreme Court routinely accepted broader interpretations of TAXING AND SPENDING POWERS, the COMMERCE CLAUSE, and the FOURTEENTH AMENDMENT, so in practice the case's importance diminished.

CHARLES A. LOFGREN
(1986)

Bibliography

HENKIN, LOUIS 1972 *Foreign Affairs and the Constitution.* Mineola, N.Y.: Foundation Press.

LOFGREN, CHARLES A. 1975 *Missouri v. Holland* in Historical Perspective. *Supreme Court Review* 1975:77–122.

MISSOURI v. JENKINS
495 U.S. 33 (1990)

Jenkins produced a unanimous result but with two sharply differing opinions on an important question concerning the power of federal courts to remedy school DESEGREGATION. A federal district court, after ordering the desegregation of the Kansas City school district, ordered the state of Missouri and the district to share the costs of the remedy, which included substantial capital improvements to make the integrated schools more attractive and thus to reduce "white flight." The district had exhausted its capacity to tax as defined by state law, and so the court ordered the district's property-tax levy increased through the next several fiscal years. The court of appeals affirmed the tax increase order, but the Supreme Court unanimously reversed. The majority, in an opinion by Justice BYRON R. WHITE, held that the district court had abused its discretion in imposing the tax itself when an alternative to such an intrusive order was available. That alternative, said Justice White, would be for the district court to order the school district to levy property taxes at a rate adequate to fund the desegregation remedy.

Justice ANTHONY M. KENNEDY, joined by three other Justices, concurred in the result but disagreed strongly with the majority's conclusion that the district court had power to order the district to levy such a tax. That order, he said, would exceed the JUDICIAL POWER OF THE UNITED STATES established in Article III of the Constitution. Taxation would be a legislative function, and the hiring and supervision of a staff to administer the funds so levied would be a political function. Justice Kennedy distinguished GRIFFIN V. COUNTY SCHOOL BOARD OF PRINCE EDWARD COUNTY (1964), in which the Court had upheld the power of a district court to order a school district to levy taxes to reopen schools that had been closed in evasion of a desegregation order. Griffin, he said, involved an order to exercise an existing power to tax; in Jenkins, the school district would have to exceed its powers under state law. He suggested that the district court might have accomplished the desegregation of Kansas City's schools—although not with the particular remedies chosen—by means that did not require funding beyond the district's current means. Desegregating schools was an important objective, he said, but the limits on judicial power must be strictly observed.

KENNETH L. KARST
(1992)

(SEE ALSO: *Judicial Power and Legislative Remedies*.)

MISSOURI v. JENKINS
515 U.S. 70 (1995)

In *Missouri v. Jenkins,* the Supreme Court considered once again the limits on the type of relief that a federal district court judge can order in a SCHOOL DESEGREGATION case. At issue was an ambitious DESEGREGATION order requiring salary increases for teachers and staff in the Kansas City school district and the continued funding of an extensive remedial education program.

The Court, in a 5–4 decision, struck down this desegregation order, holding that it went beyond the scope of the constitutional violation it sought to redress. The Court, with Chief Justice WILLIAM H. REHNQUIST writing for the majority, argued that the dominant purpose of the desegregation order was to attract nonminority students from outside the predominantly minority Kansas City school district and thereby to increase racial mixing in the Kansas City schools. The Court concluded that because the district court had found unlawful segregation only within the Kansas City school district, it did not have authority, in accordance with MILLIKEN V. BRADLEY (1974), to fashion a remedy for the purpose of increasing interdistrict desegregation.

In a DISSENTING OPINION, Justice DAVID H. SOUTER argued that district judges in school desegregation cases must have broad latitude to remedy the vestiges of segregation and to utilize remedies that may affect other school districts.

The decision reflects the Court's ongoing desire to end the era of judicial supervision of school districts and to return the control of schools to local officials.

DAVISON M. DOUGLAS
(2000)

Bibliography

JOONDEPH, BRADLEY W. 1996 *Missouri v. Jenkins* and the De Facto Abandonment of Court-Enforced Desegregation. *Washington Law Review* 71:597–681.

MISSOURI COMPROMISE
(1820)

The Missouri Compromise provided a simple constitutional and geographical expedient for resolving a crisis of the Union growing out of SLAVERY's expansion into the western TERRITORIES. Because the compromise formed the basis of a balance of the free and slave states in the Union for a generation, its abrogation in the 1850s destabilized the constitutional system and intensified the disruption of the Union.

In 1819, Representative James Tallmadge of New York offered an amendment to the Missouri statehood enabling bill that would prohibit the further introduction of slavery into Missouri and would free all children born to slaves after the state's admission, but hold them in servitude until age 25. Free-state congressmen supported congressional power thus to restrict the admission of Missouri by arguments derived from four constitutional sources: the new states clause of Article IV, section 3, giving Congress discretionary authority to admit new states into the Union; the territories clause of the same article and section, empowering Congress to make "Regulations respecting the Territory" of the nation; the slave trade clause of Article I, section 9, permitting congress to control the "Migration" of persons; and the GUARANTEE CLAUSE of Article IV, section 4, which required all states to have a REPUBLICAN FORM OF GOVERNMENT. Supporters of the Tallmadge amendment, citing the DECLARATION OF INDEPENDENCE, argued that slavery was incompatible with republican government.

Opponents of the Tallmadge amendment rejected all these arguments, insisting particularly that the logical implications of the republicanism argument would subvert slavery in the states where it already existed. The first Missouri crisis was resolved by a package of statutes that admitted Missouri without the Tallmadge restriction, admitted Maine as a free state, and prohibited the introduction of slavery into the remainder of the Louisiana Purchase territory north of Missouri's southern boundary. This compromise was subsequently supplemented by an informal process of admitting paired free and slave states, thus preserving a balance between the sections in the SENATE.

On the eve of its statehood Missouri precipitated the second crisis by adopting provisions in its new constitution that would have prohibited the abolition of slavery without the consent of slaveholders and that required the state legislature to prohibit the ingress of free blacks. Constitutional arguments over the second controversy turned on the PRIVILEGES AND IMMUNITIES clause of Article IV, section 2, which introduced the question of the constitutional status of free black people. This issue went unresolved because the compromise that settled the second crisis simply provided that nothing Missouri might do in legislative compliance with the constitutional mandate should be construed to deny any citizen a privilege or immunity to which he was entitled, a toothless provision that Missouri flouted in 1847 by excluding free blacks.

THOMAS JEFFERSON warned at the time that "a geographical line, coinciding with a marked principle, moral and political, once conceived and held up to the angry passions of men, will never be obliterated." His somber prediction was fulfilled in the 1850s. The WILMOT PROVISO of 1846, which would have prohibited the introduction of slavery into territories acquired as a result of the Mexican War, inaugurated a period of controversy that terminated in the destruction of the Union in 1860. Democrats and southern political leaders in 1848 began to insist that the first Missouri restriction was unconstitutional and to demand its repeal. Repeal was accomplished by the KANSAS-NEBRASKA ACT of 1854; and Chief Justice ROGER B. TANEY gratuitously held that the Missouri Compromise had been unconstitutional all along in his opinion in DRED SCOTT V. SANDFORD (1857). Yet during Secession Winter, Senator JOHN J. CRITTENDEN resurrected the Missouri Compromise as the centerpiece of his compromise proposals, which recommended extrapolating the Missouri line all the way to the Pacific. But by 1860 sectional developments had made the constitutional settlement of 1820 obsolete.

WILLIAM M. WIECEK
(1986)

Bibliography

MOORE, GLOVER 1953 *The Missouri Controversy, 1819–1821.* Lexington: University of Kentucky Press.

MISSOURI EX REL. GAINES v. CANADA
305 U.S. 337 (1938)

This was the first decision establishing minimum content for equality within the SEPARATE BUT EQUAL DOCTRINE. Missouri law excluded blacks from the state university; Gaines, a black applicant, was thus rejected by the university's law school. Missouri's separate university for blacks had no law school, and so the state offered to pay his tuition at a law school in a neighboring state. Represented by NAACP lawyers, Gaines sought a WRIT OF MANDAMUS to compel his admission to the state university law school. The state courts denied relief, and the Supreme Court reversed, 6–2.

Chief Justice CHARLES EVANS HUGHES, for the majority, said, "The admissibility of laws separating the races in the enjoyment of privileges afforded by the State rests wholly upon the equality of the privileges which the laws give to the separated groups within the State." The case was thus a doctrinal milestone on the road to BROWN V. BOARD OF EDUCATION (1954). Henceforth the Court would demand real equality in a segregated system of education. Because the education of blacks in the southern and border states had emphasized separateness and deemphasized equality—even equality of physical facilities and school spending—it would have been enormously expensive for the states to satisfy the test of *Gaines* by providing parallel educational systems. *Brown*'s question—whether segregation itself imposed an unconstitutional inequality—was a natural extension of the inquiry launched in *Gaines*.

KENNETH L. KARST
(1986)

MISSOURI PACIFIC RAILROAD v. HUMES
115 U.S. 512 (1885)

A CORPORATION, invoking the FOURTEENTH AMENDMENT, employed SUBSTANTIVE DUE PROCESS against a state statute, but the Supreme Court, led by Justice STEPHEN J. FIELD, unanimously construed due process in an exclusively procedural sense. A statute might seriously depreciate the value of property, Field declared, but "if no rule of justice is violated in the provisions for the enforcement of such a statute," it could not be said to deprive a person of property without due process. The case was a replay of *Davidson v. New Orleans* (1878), which Field quoted. In 1886, the Court began to abandon the *Davidson-Humes* view of due process. (See STONE V. FARMERS' LOAN & TRUST CO.)

LEONARD W. LEVY
(1986)

MISTRETTA v. UNITED STATES
488 U.S. 361 (1989)

In *Mistretta* the Supreme Court, 8–1, upheld the Sentencing Reform Act of 1984 against the constitutional challenges that it was an unconstitutional DELEGATION OF POWER and that it violated the principle of SEPARATION OF POWERS by intruding the federal judiciary into functions that are legislative.

Congress has the power to fix the sentence for a federal crime. Historically Congress has, in practical effect, delegated a considerable part of this power to the judicial branch through the mechanism of setting a range of possible sentences for the same offense—for example, one to five years of imprisonment. This scheme gives the judge authority to select the sentence appropriate in a particular case—typically including the possibility of probation—in light of the circumstances of the offense, the defendant's history and sense of responsibility, and the like. The possibility of a presidential pardon remained. In recent years, too, Congress allowed the judge to sentence the defendant to an indeterminate term, leaving the actual release date to the U.S. Parole Commission, an agency located in the executive branch. The system not only divided power among the three branches of the federal government, but also produced wide-ranging variation in the severity of sentences.

These disparities persisted despite the best efforts of sentencing institutes, judicial councils, and the Parole Commission. Concern for sentencing inequities, combined with a desire to express a tough attitude toward crime, led Congress to adopt the 1984 act. This act authorized the creation of the United States Sentencing Commission, "an independent commission in the judicial branch" composed of seven members appointed by the President with the ADVICE AND CONSENT of the Senate. Three of the members must be federal judges chosen by the President from a list of six submitted by the JUDICIAL CONFERENCE OF THE UNITED STATES. The commission was authorized to prepare guidelines for essentially determinate SENTENCING, specifying sentences for various types of crimes and categories of defendants. A judge must adhere to the guidelines except when a case presents aggravating or mitigating circumstances of a kind not specified in the guidelines. The commission is to review and revise the guidelines periodically.

John Mistretta, sentenced on the basis of the guidelines by a federal district court for the sale of cocaine, appealed to the UNITED STATES COURT OF APPEALS and petitioned the Supreme Court for CERTIORARI before judgment in the court of appeals. The Supreme Court granted the petition and affirmed the sentence. Justice HARRY A. BLACKMUN, writing for the Court, quickly rejected *Mistretta's* delegation of power challenge. Congress can constitutionally delegate its legislative power to an agency if it specifies clear standards for the agency to follow in carrying out its rule-making power. Congress gave the Sentencing Commission a clear set of specific goals, including lists of the factors to be considered in establishing grades of offense and categories of defendants. These lists leave considerable discretion to the commission, but the statute's standards are sufficiently clear to allow a reviewing court to determine whether the commission had followed the will of Congress.

Justice Blackmun wrote at greater length in rejecting the broader separation of powers challenge that the Sentencing Commission was a judicial body exercising legislative powers. The commission's work undoubtedly involved political judgment, but the practical consequences of locating the commission within the judicial branch did not threaten to undermine either the integrity of the judiciary or the power of Congress. On the question of locating the commission within the judicial branch, Justice Blackmun emphasized that the commission is not a court and does not exercise judicial power; that Congress can override the commission's determinations at any time; and that the questions assigned to the commission had long been exercised by the judiciary in the aggregate, deciding case by case.

Justice Blackmun found "somewhat troublesome" the

participation in the commision of judges appointed under Article III of the Constitution. Nonetheless, he concluded that the constitution does not prohibit Article III judges from taking on extrajudicial functions in their individual capacities, that Congress and the President had historically aquiesced in federal judges' assumption of such duties, and that the Court's own precedents supported the constitutionality of the practice. Some kinds of extrajudicial service might have adverse effects on the public's sense of the judiciary's independence, but the commision's work was "essentially neutral" in the political sense and designed primarily to govern tasks done entirely within the judicial branch. Although the President could remove the commision members for neglect of duty or malfeasance, this power did not extend to the dismissal of federal judges as judges. Justice Blackmun made clear that there were limits to such extrajudicial services by judges of the CONSTITUTIONAL COURTS, but he could find no constitutionally significant practical effect on the work of the judicial branch from these judge's service on this commision. The emphasis on "practical" and "functional" considerations is the central theme throughout Justice Blackmun's opinion.

Justice ANTONIN SCALIA dissented, arguing that Congress could not constitutionally delegate its legislative power to an agency whose sole power was to make laws, even laws going under the name of "guidelines." This opinion represents the strongest effort in the modern era to revive the delegation doctrine as a serious limit on congressional authority to enlist other agencies in lawmaking. Justice Scalia lamented the Court's tendency to tolerate blurring of the lines separating the powers of the three branches of the federal government. Scolding the majority in a manner now familiar, he offered a restatement of today's operative rule: "the functions of the Branches should not be commingled too much—how much is too much to be determined, case-by-case, by this Court." If we disregard the tone, this restatement seems exactly on the mark. Even so, it is not clear how the national government can be run on a formalistic model of separation of powers that already seemed too confining in 1794 when JOHN JAY, while he was Chief Justice of the United States, went to London to negotiate the agreement we now call JAY'S TREATY.

KENNETH L. KARST
(1992)

MITCHUM v. FOSTER
407 U.S. 225 (1972)

The federal anti-INJUNCTION statute prohibits a federal court from granting an injunction to stay state court proceedings "except as expressly authorized by Act of Congress, or where necessary in aid of its JURISDICTION, or to protect or effectuate its judgments." In *Mitchum*, relying on the "basic alteration" in our federal system wrought by the RECONSTRUCTION-era legislation, the Supreme Court decided that SECTION 1983, TITLE 42, UNITED STATES CODE (originally part of the Civil Rights Act of 1871), constituted an exception to the prohibition despite the absence of an express reference in section 1983 to the anti-injunction statute. Recent scholarship, which implicitly supports *Mitchum*, suggests that the original 1793 version of the anti-injunction statute sought merely to prohibit individual Supreme Court Justices from enjoining state proceedings and was not intended to be a comprehensive ban on federal injunctions against state proceedings. The Court's prior decision in YOUNGER V. HARRIS (1971) limits *Mitchum*'s practical importance. *Younger*, which relied on nonstatutory grounds, severely restricted federal courts' discretion to enjoin pending state proceedings.

THEODORE EISENBERG
(1986)

M. L. B. v. S. L. J.
519 U.S. 102 (1996)

A Mississippi trial court terminated M. L. B.'s parental rights to two minor children. When she sought to appeal, the state insisted on advance payment of some $2,300 in fees for preparation of the trial record; because she lacked the money to pay the fees, her appeal was dismissed. The Supreme Court held, 6–3, that conditioning appeal from a trial court termination of parental rights on a parent's ability to pay violated the DUE PROCESS and EQUAL PROTECTION clauses of the FOURTEENTH AMENDMENT.

Writing for the Court, Justice RUTH BADER GINSBURG recognized that previous decisions had not extended the rule of GRIFFIN V. ILLINOIS (1957) to guarantee ACCESS TO THE COURTS in all civil cases. She noted, however, that in cases "involving controls or intrusions on family relationships" the Court had been more receptive to both due process and equal protection claims. Mississippi's policy was not an ordinary refusal to subsidize the exercise of a constitutional right. Here, by analogy to a criminal case, M. L. B. sought "to be spared from the State's devastatingly adverse action." Justice ANTHONY M. KENNEDY, concurring, would have placed the decision solely on due process grounds.

Dissenting, Justice CLARENCE THOMAS relied on the argument of the second Justice JOHN MARSHALL HARLAN in his dissent in *Griffin:* that due process did not require an appeal, and that equal protection was not violated by a state's failure to make up for an indigent's ability to pay for a service necessary to secure an appeal. Chief Justice WILLIAM H. REHNQUIST and Justice ANTONIN SCALIA joined in this part of the dissent. Thomas, joined only by Scalia, also said he would be inclined to OVERRULE *Griffin*.

KENNETH L. KARST
(2000)

MOBILE v. BOLDEN
446 U.S. 55 (1980)

A fragmented Supreme Court majority upheld, 6–3, Mobile's at-large system for electing city commissioners, although the system diluted the voting strength of black voters by submerging them in a white majority. The plurality found that purposeful RACIAL DISCRIMINATION had not been demonstrated. (See WASHINGTON V. DAVIS; ROGERS V. LODGE.) In 1982 Congress amended the VOTING RIGHTS ACT OF 1965 to permit reliance on racially discriminatory "results" to show a violation of the act's prohibitions.

KENNETH L. KARST
(1986)

MONELL v. DEPARTMENT OF SOCIAL SERVICES
436 U.S. 658 (1978)

In 1961, MONROE V. PAPE had held municipalities effectively immune from suit under SECTION 1983, TITLE 42, UNITED STATES CODE. *Monell* reinterpreted the legislative history relied upon in *Monroe* to conclude that municipalities may be sued under section 1983 but are liable only for acts constituting official policy. Not every violation of federal rights by municipal employees gives rise to an action against the municipality.

THEODORE EISENBERG
(1986)

MONETARY POWER

The monetary power of Congress flows from one express constitutional grant and a melange of others, cemented by the NECESSARY AND PROPER CLAUSE. The enumerated power deals with coin and has never been significant in American constitutional law. Congress's more important powers over the money supply—to charter banks and endow them with the right to issue circulating notes, to emit BILLS OF CREDIT, and to make government paper a legal tender— are only implied. From the administration of GEORGE WASHINGTON to the age of FRANKLIN D. ROOSEVELT, few questions were debated with more intensity than the nature and scope of Congress's IMPLIED POWERS over the currency. At no point, however, did the Supreme Court offer sustained resistance to the extension of Congress's authority. In MCCULLOCH V. MARYLAND (1819), the lodestar case on the monetary power, the MARSHALL COURT upheld incorporation of a bank as an appropriate means for executing "the great powers, to lay and collect taxes; to borrow money; to regulate commerce; to declare and conduct a war; and to raise and support armies and navies." The HUGHES COURT invoked the same undifferentiated list of enumerated powers, reinforced by the necessary and proper clause, in the GOLD CLAUSE CASES (1935), where the last potential limitation on Congress's monetary power was swept away.

Two factors account for the Court's acquiescence. The ambiguous legacy of the CONSTITUTIONAL CONVENTION OF 1787 was especially important. Monetary questions loomed large in the political history of the Confederation era, and some of the Founders, perhaps a majority, wanted to constitutionalize a settlement. They acted decisively to curtail state power. Article I, section 10, provides that "no state shall . . . coin money; emit bills of credit; [or] make anything but gold and silver coin a tender in payment of debts." But the Founders were more circumspect when dealing with the scope of national power. JAMES MADISON's motion to vest Congress with a general power "to grant charters of incorporation" was not adopted because, as RUFUS KING explained, the bank question might divide the states "into parties" and impede ratification. JAMES WILSON suggested that the power to incorporate a bank was implied anyway; but GEORGE MASON, the only other delegate to speak on the matter, disagreed.

Conflicting conceptions of implied powers also materialized without being resolved in the much longer debate on Congress's authority to augment the money supply with government paper. The original draft of the Constitution, as reported to the convention by the Committee of Detail, empowered Congress "to borrow money and emit bills on the credit of the United States." When this section was reached in debate, GOUVERNEUR MORRIS moved to strike out the emission clause; the motion was ultimately carried by a vote of nine states to two. Yet there was no meeting of minds on the implications of Morris's motion before the roll call. Wilson, Mason, and virtually everyone else who spoke assumed that striking out the emission power was equivalent to prohibiting congressional exercise of such a power. Morris said that "the monied interest will oppose the plan of government if paper emissions be not prohibited." But NATHANIEL GORHAM remarked that he was for "striking out, without inserting any prohibition." And that was precisely what happened. Gorham neither mentioned the concept of implied powers nor flatly stated that eliminating the power to emit was by no means equivalent to prohibiting it. His remarks nonetheless suggest that at least some of the Founders assumed, despite Morris's protestations to the contrary, that to vote for his motion was to leave the paper money question to be settled as problems arose.

The sequence of federal legislation on banking and the currency was the second factor that shaped the growth of Congress's monetary power in constitutional law. Once the Constitution had been ratified, Congress was required to assert implied powers either to incorporate a bank or to issue paper money. Sanctioned exercise of one power could be expected to provide at least a modicum of constitutional authority for assertion of the other. Yet the Founders' distrust of government paper was so intense that it was possible for a skillful statesman to obscure the close constitutional relationship between the powers to incorporate banks and emit paper money by treating the former as a conservative policy alternative to the latter. ALEXANDER HAMILTON was such a statesman.

In his Report on the National Bank (1790) Hamilton stressed the "material differences between a paper currency, issued by the mere authority of Government, and one issued by a Bank, Payable in coin." The proposed national bank, he said, would serve as a financial arm of the government and a ready lender to the Treasury; its capital stock, consisting primarily of public securities, would be monetized in the form of bank notes redeemable in specie, thereby multiplying the nation's active capital and stimulating trade. Paper money, in contrast, was just too "seducing and dangerous an expedient," for "there is almost a moral certainty of its becoming mischievous." Much of the constitutional theory he mustered later to justify Congress's power to incorporate a bank was equally applicable to its power to issue paper money. But it is unlikely that the congressmen who approved the BANK OF THE UNITED STATES ACT or President Washington, who signed the bill despite forceful constitutional arguments against it by THOMAS JEFFERSON and others, would have sanctioned Hamilton's BROAD CONSTRUCTION of the government's implied powers in order to facilitate emissions of paper money. In view of JOHN MARSHALL's language regarding the sanctity of contracts in OGDEN V. SAUNDERS (1827), it is equally significant the McCulloch involved national bank notes rather than depreciated government paper.

Between 1812 and 1815 there occurred another series of events with implications almost as great as McCulloch for the development of Congress's monetary power. The First Bank's charter expired in 1811; its successor was not created until 1816. When the War of 1812 began, then, the government had to finance its operations without the aid of a national banking system. On four separate occasions Congress followed President Madison's recommendation and authorized the emission of Treasury notes, fundable into government bonds and receivable for all duties and taxes owed to the government. Every piece of

paper issued in 1812, 1813, and 1814 had a large denomination, carried a fixed term, and bore interest. But the 1815 issue was of bearer notes without interest, in denominations from three, five, and ten dollars upward, receivable in payments to the United States without time limit. Debate in Congress suggests that the notes were fully expected to circulate as currency. Nobody objected to them on constitutional grounds and all were retired soon after the war. Nevertheless, the 1815 Treasury notes provided what John Jay Knox later called "a fatal precedent."

Knox's was a shrewd observation. The Madison administration's Treasury notes were indistinguishable from the bills of credit which Gouverneur Morris and others thought they had prohibited at the Constitutional Convention. In defense of his motion to strike the emission clause, Morris had emphasized that "a responsible minister" could meet emergencies without resort to bills of credit. The remaining power "to borrow money," he had explained, would enable the Treasury to issue "notes"—a term which he understood to mean interest-bearing, fixed-term paper in contradistinction to "bills" which he defined as interest-free paper issued by the government in payment of its obligations. The Treasury notes emitted by the Madison administration were clearly of the latter variety. Moreover, the receivability of those notes for all public debts undermined Madison's own constitutional understanding of 1787. He had suggested that the Convention ought to retain the emission power while expressly prohibiting the power to make government paper a legal tender.

As he noted in his journal, however, Madison had "acquiesce[d]" in the Convention's decision once he "became satisfied that striking out the words would not disable the Government from the use of public notes as far as they could be safe and proper; and would only cut off the pretext for a paper currency and particularly for making the bills a tender either for public or private debts." At Philadelphia, moreover, only Madison had emphasized the legal tender question. And as the bullionists on the Court learned during the post-Civil War LEGAL TENDER CASES, it was extremely difficult to deny Congress the legal tender power once its power to emit bills of credit had been conceded and McCulloch had established its discretion in the choice of appropriate means.

Yet the distrust of money-supply decisions made by legislation retained such great vitality during the nineteenth century that an attempt was made to proscribe irredeemable government paper on constitutional grounds. It came in Hepburn v. Griswold (1870). Speaking for a 4–3 majority, Chief Justice SALMON P. CHASE declared that the legal tender legislation he had recommended during his tenure as ABRAHAM LINCOLN's secretary of the treasury was invalid insofar as it impaired the value of preexisting private debts. Chase began by reiterating Marshall's McCulloch commentary on implied powers and "the painful duty of this tribunal" with regard to laws inconsistent with the "letter and spirit" of the Constitution. He admitted that Congress had an "undisputed power" to emit bills of credit; in VEAZIE BANK V. FENNO (1869) he had said that Congress might even levy prohibitive taxes on the notes of state-chartered banks in order "to provide a currency for the whole country." But the legal tender power was distinguishable. It was not necessary, though perhaps convenient, for Congress to impart legal tender qualities to its paper in order to guarantee circulation. And legislation that impaired contracts was not only contrary to the "spirit" of the Constitution as Marshall and others had understood it but also deprived creditors of property without DUE PROCESS or JUST COMPENSATION.

The narrow construction of Congress's authority expounded in *Hepburn* did not endure. SAMUEL MILLER, dissenting along with NOAH SWAYNE and DAVID DAVIS, had claimed that the majority's reliance on the "spirit" of the Constitution substituted "an undefined code of ethics for the Constitution." In their view, *McCulloch* had established that "where there is a choice of means, the selection is for Congress, not the Court." WILLIAM STRONG and JOSEPH BRADLEY, whom ULYSSES S. GRANT nominated to the Court on the very day *Hepburn* was decided, agreed with the *Hepburn* dissenters and voted to overrule Chase's previous majority in *Knox v. Lee* (1871). Bradley stated in a concurring opinion that once the power to emit bills of credit had been conceded, "the incidental power of giving such bills the quality of legal tender follows almost as a matter of course." Strong's opinion for the Court responded forcefully to the "TAKING" claims advanced in *Hepburn*. An 1834 act passed pursuant to Congress's power "to coin money and regulate the value thereof," he pointed out, had established a new regulation of the weight and value of gold coins. Creditors had sustained consequential injuries as a result, for antecedent debts had become "solvable with six per cent less gold than was required to pay them before." But it had never been imagined that Congress had taken property without due process of law. Congress's implied monetary powers, Strong concluded, were as plenary as its enumerated monetary power: "Contracts must be understood as made in reference to the possible exercise of the rightful authority of the government, and no obligation of contract can extend to the defeat of legitimate governmental authority."

Two other Chase Court decisions, *Bronson v. Rodes* (1869) and *Trebilock v. Wilson* (1872), reflected the law's continuing favor for freedom in private contract despite Strong's sweeping language regarding the plenary nature of Congress's monetary power. There the Court held that agreements specifically requiring payment in gold and silver coin could not be satisfied by tenders of irredeemable government paper. Coin was still a legal tender under federal law, the Court explained; because the Legal Tender Acts did not expressly prohibit parties from drafting contracts requiring payment in specie, it remained "the appropriate function of courts . . . to enforce contracts according to the lawful intent and understanding of the parties." Creditors found *Bronson* and *Trebilock* particularly reassuring in the Populist era. Although the Civil War greenbacks became redeemable at par in 1879, apprehensions of currency devaluation by "free coinage" of silver prompted virtually all draftsmen of long-term debt obligations to specify repayment in gold coin of a given weight and fineness. But the monetary crisis of 1933 led not only to another, apparently final abandonment of the gold standard and a substantial depreciation of the currency but also to a joint resolution of Congress that proclaimed gold clauses in private contracts to be "against public policy" and void. Eight years later, EDWARD S. CORWIN remarked that "no such drastic legislation from the point of view of property rights had ever before been enacted by the Congress."

The Court nonetheless sustained the resolution by a 5–4 margin in the GOLD CLAUSE CASES (1935). In *Bronson* and *Trebilock*, Chief Justice CHARLES EVANS HUGHES explained for the majority, the Court had mandated the enforcement of contracts containing gold clauses at a time when Congress had not prohibited such agreements. Now Congress had acted; "parties cannot remove theirs transactions from the reach of dominant constitutional power by making contracts about them." JAMES MCREYNOLDS filed a discursive dissent in which he claimed, among other things, that the Constitution "is gone." In one respect his argument had some merit. Many of the Founders, perhaps a majority, had assumed that adoption of Gouverneur Morris's motion to strike the power to emit bills of credit precluded all government paper designed to circulate as money. Yet contracts were enforceable in government paper and only government paper after 1933. From another perspective, however, McReynolds's claim was simply perverse. The constitutional text does not forbid Congress to issue paper money, and American constitutional law not only sets limitations on what government does but also legitimizes government's authority to act affirmatively in the face of changing public interests. It was no accident that when Marshall emphasized the importance of remembering that "it is a *constitution* we are expounding," he did so in the leading case involving Congress's monetary power.

CHARLES W. MCCURDY
(1986)

Bibliography

CORWIN, EDWARD S. 1941 *Constitutional Revolution, Ltd.* Claremont, Calif.: Claremont Colleges.

DAM, KENNETH W. 1982 The Legal Tender Cases. *Supreme Court Review* 1981:367–412.

HURST, JAMES WILLARD   1973   *A Legal History of Money in the United States, 1774–1970.* Lincoln: University of Nebraska Press.

KNOX, JOHN JAY   1882   *United States Notes: A History of the Various Uses of Paper Money by the Government of the United States.* New York: Scribner's.

MONROE, JAMES
(1758–1831)

James Monroe was the last veteran of the AMERICAN REVOLUTION to serve as President of the United States. He had abandoned his studies at the College of William and Mary to join the army, and he rose to the rank of lieutenant colonel. He later read law under THOMAS JEFFERSON and, in 1782, was elected to the legislature of his native Virginia. From 1783 to 1786 he represented Virginia in Congress, where one of his chief concerns was the unsuccessful attempt to amend the ARTICLES OF CONFEDERATION to provide for a stronger central government. A committee chaired by Monroe drafted an amendment that would have given Congress the power to regulate commerce, but no action was taken on the amendment.

Notwithstanding his views on the Confederation, Monroe opposed RATIFICATION OF THE CONSTITUTION, primarily because it created too strong a central government and vested too much power in the President. He publicly professed to see in the proposed system a tendency toward monarchy and aristocracy, and he privately complained that the South would be outvoted on sectional issues.

From 1790 to 1794, Monroe represented Virginia in the United States Senate. There he was a leader of the Republican party and an opponent of the programs of ALEXANDER HAMILTON and especially of the BANK OF THE UNITED STATES ACT. He left the Senate in 1794 to become ambassador to France. He served as governor of Virginia (1799–1802), then held diplomatic posts abroad for the Jefferson administration, including an assignment as one of the negotiators of the LOUISIANA PURCHASE TREATY. He was again elected governor in 1811 but resigned to become secretary of state under President JAMES MADISON. During the War of 1812 he also acted as secretary of war.

Monroe's presidency (1817–1825) was notable for the rhetoric of constitutional literalism and STRICT CONSTRUCTION. He opposed congressional schemes for federally funded INTERNAL IMPROVEMENTS (such as highways and canals) on the grounds that there was no constitutional authority for them; but he suggested a constitutional amendment to confer such authority. In 1820, despite reservations about the constitutionality of its conditions on admission of a state, Monroe approved the MISSOURI COMPROMISE limiting expansion of SLAVERY IN THE TERRITORIES.

And in 1823, on the advice of Secretary of State JOHN QUINCY ADAMS, he asserted presidential control over FOREIGN AFFAIRS by proclaiming the MONROE DOCTRINE. During his administration, the opportunity for peaceful westward development was assured by the negotiation of treaties fixing the borders of the United States with Canada and with the Spanish and Russian possessions in North America.

The most pressing constitutional question of his time was the place of slavery in the American republic. Himself a slaveholder, Monroe favored gradual, compensated emancipation followed by settlement of ex-slaves in Africa. To that end he was a founding member of the American Colonization Society; and the capital of Liberia, the African state settled through the society's efforts, was named in his honor.

Monroe's last active role in public affairs was as president of the Virginia CONSTITUTIONAL CONVENTION of 1829.

DENNIS J. MAHONEY
(1986)

Bibliography

AMMON, HARRY   1971   *James Monroe: The Quest for National Identity.* New York: McGraw-Hill.

MONROE v. PAPE
365 U.S. 167 (1961)

This case, a fountainhead of modern CIVIL RIGHTS doctrine, arose out of an unconstitutional search conducted by Chicago police officers. The victim sought damages in an action brought under SECTION 1983, TITLE 42, UNITED STATES CODE, which authorizes suits for deprivations, under COLOR OF LAW, of rights, privileges, or immunities secured by the Constitution and laws of the United States. *Monroe* settled that section 1983 protects all FOURTEENTH AMENDMENT rights and not merely those narrowly defined rights that the SLAUGHTERHOUSE CASES (1873) found to be protected by the Fourteenth Amendment's PRIVILEGES AND IMMUNITIES clause. Early litigation under section 1983 had suggested possible links between the scope of the privileges and immunities clause and the rights protected by section 1983. *Monroe* also confirmed earlier holdings in federal civil rights cases that the phrase "under color of" law in section 1983 includes official acts not authorized by state law. *Monroe's* third holding, that cities could not be made defendants in section 1983 cases, was overruled in MONELL V. DEPARTMENT OF SOCIAL SERVICES (1978).

THEODORE EISENBERG
(1986)

MONROE DOCTRINE
2 Richardson, *Messages and Papers of the Presidents* 207 (1823)

The United States, the first true revolutionary nation, became, in 1823, the guardian of the emerging revolutionary states of the New World. The American constitutional ideal of republican, LIMITED GOVERNMENT, founded on NATURAL RIGHTS and SOCIAL COMPACT, stood in opposition to the constitutional system of Europe, based on hereditary privilege. The countries of the Western Hemisphere, becoming independent in the early nineteenth century, would, in rejecting the European system, seem naturally to embrace the American ideal.

JOHN QUINCY ADAMS, secretary of state to President JAMES MONROE, perceived the threat to the Americas from the reactionary Concert of Europe and the Holy Alliance. Adams formulated, and Monroe announced, a policy of resistance to any attempt to restore European hegemony in the Americas. Although Adams counseled use of diplomatic channels, Monroe, on the advice of Secretary of War JOHN C. CALHOUN, announced the doctrine in his 1823 State of the Union Message.

The proclamation of the Monroe Doctrine was a significant assertion of executive power in FOREIGN AFFAIRS. Although Monroe's address repeatedly stressed America's neutrality in European wars and in the colonial revolutions against Spain, his declaration that "we should consider any attempt on their part to extend their system to any portion of this hemisphere as dangerous to our peace and safety" was a clear warning that American interests would be vindicated by force, if necessary. The President, therefore, committed the country to potential military action outside its borders and announced the fact to Congress rather than asking for congressional authorization.

The Constitution, of course, makes no provision for so sweeping an assertion of executive authority over foreign affairs or so general a commitment of American power abroad. Yet the Monroe Doctrine swiftly became part of the UNWRITTEN CONSTITUTION, the accretion of customs and precedents that fill the constitutional lacunae.

DENNIS J. MAHONEY
(1986)

Bibliography

PERKINS, DEXTER 1955 *A History of the Monroe Doctrine.* Boston: Little, Brown.

MONTESQUIEU
(1689–1755)

The political philosophy of Charles de Secondat, Baron de la Brede et de Montesquieu, was an important influence on American constitutional thought. The leading republican theorist of the generation immediately preceding the American Revolution, he was referred to more frequently by the delegates to the CONSTITUTIONAL CONVENTION OF 1787 than any other theoretical writer. JAMES MADISON (in THE FEDERALIST #43) called him "the oracle . . . who is always consulted and cited." In the debates on the RATIFICATION OF THE CONSTITUTION the authority of Montesquieu was invoked by partisans ranging from Luther Martin to ALEXANDER HAMILTON.

Montesquieu's most important work was *The Spirit of the Laws* (1748). The book seems obscure and difficult to most readers, at least partly because the author tried to combine a philosophic inquiry, intended for a few readers only, with practical political advice meant for a much wider audience. In Montesquieu's practical teaching, based on observation, philosophic reflection, and first-hand experience, the American founders found the apparent resolution of two key problems of American politics: how to reconcile popular government with a vast extent of territory and how to reconcile energetic government with the security of liberty.

Montesquieu was the first political philosopher to treat FEDERALISM at any length. He believed, with the classical theorists, that republican government was possible only in small societies, for there alone could be found the virtue and public-spiritedness necessary if people are to govern themselves. But small republics are in constant danger from larger, despotic neighbors. The solution was the federal republic: "a convention by which several bodies politic consent to become citizens of a larger state . . . a society of societies who form a new one, which can enlarge itself through new associates who join."

But a large republic, even a federal republic, is liable to destruction through internal strife. Sectional and religious differences divide the people and make republican virtue impossible. For this, too, Montesquieu had an answer: "Commerce cures destructive prejudices; and it is almost a general rule that wherever there is commerce there are gentle ways of life." Commerce tends to make people peaceful and tolerant, and it makes them aware of their interdependence for security and comfort.

Montesquieu's greatest influence on American CONSTITUTIONALISM is seen in the twin doctrines of SEPARATION OF POWERS and CHECKS AND BALANCES. Montesquieu adopted the idea of separation of powers from JOHN LOCKE, but he fundamentally modified it by defining the three branches of government as legislative, executive, and judicial. Although Montesquieu introduced separation of powers in a famous chapter "On the Constitution of England," that chapter actually comprises not a description of the English government but rather a presentation of the conditions necessary for liberty and safety. Checks and balances, according to Montesquieu, are modifications of separation of powers necessary to keep any one branch of government from becoming despotic and to promote harmony of action.

DENNIS J. MAHONEY
(1986)

Bibliography

ALLEN, WILLIAM BARCLAY 1972 Montesquieu: The Federalist-Anti-Federalist Debate. Unpublished Ph.D. dissertation, Claremont Graduate School.

PANGLE, THOMAS L. 1973 *Montesquieu's Philosophy of Liberalism.* Chicago: University of Chicago Press.

MOODY, WILLIAM H.
(1853–1917)

After studying law in the offices of novelist-lawyer Richard Henry Dana, William Henry Moody of Massachusetts first came to national attention as a special prosecutor in the Fall River ax-murder case of Lizzie Borden (1892). In 1895 he went to Congress where he served as a Republican until President THEODORE ROOSEVELT appointed him secretary of the navy in 1902. When PHILANDER C. KNOX left the administration for the Senate in 1904, Moody replaced him as attorney general. Philosophically comfortable with the President, Moody spent much of his tenure directing the prosecution of the Beef Trust. Although Knox had begun the case, Moody successfully argued SWIFT & COMPANY V. UNITED STATES (1905) before the Supreme Court, helping to lay the basis for the STREAM OF COMMERCE doctrine. As attorney general, Moody directed active participation by the Department of Justice in many facets of national ECONOMIC REGULATION, from antitrust proceedings to railroad regulation under the ELKINS ACT.

Roosevelt rewarded Moody's service and his commitment to a strong national government by appointing him to succeed Justice HENRY B. BROWN on the Supreme Court in 1906. Although Moody's service on the Court formally lasted until 1910, he was rarely present the last two years. Moody took part in relatively few cases during his tenure, but his opinions fulfilled Roosevelt's expectations and reflected Moody's moderate PROGRESSIVISM. As a Justice, Moody continued his support of regulatory legislation, often voting with the Court to extend or strengthen federal authority. Moody joined the majority in LOEWE V. LAWLOR (1908), holding that the SHERMAN ANTITRUST ACT covered labor boycotts, and he wrote for the dissenters in the first EMPLOYERS' LIABILITY CASES (1908), asserting that Congress had power to regulate employer-employee relations in INTERSTATE COMMERCE issues. Although that dissent typified Moody's willingness to expand the reach of federal powers,

he also supported exercises of STATE POLICE POWER when they worked no interference with federal powers. An adherent of judicial self-restraint, Moody opposed judicial legislation and he silently concurred in MULLER V. OREGON (1908), in which the BRANDEIS BRIEF offered convincing EVIDENCE to the Court of the benefits of maximum hours legislation. In TWINING V. NEW JERSEY (1908), perhaps his best-known opinion, Moody, for the Court, declared that the RIGHT AGAINST SELF-INCRIMINATION was not an "essential element" of DUE PROCESS OF LAW incorporated in the FOURTEENTH AMENDMENT and applicable to the states. If the people of the state were dissatisfied with the law, he declared, recourse "is in their own hands."

Stricken with acute rheumatism, Moody retired in 1910 and died, a semi-invalid, seven years later.

DAVID GORDON
(1986)

MOORE, ALFRED
(1755–1810)

A staunch FEDERALIST in an ANTI-FEDERALIST state, Alfred Moore served as North Carolina's attorney general from 1782 to 1791 and was prominent in securing RATIFICATION OF THE CONSTITUTION there. He defended the state Confiscation Act in BAYARD V. SINGLETON (1787), opposing JUDICIAL REVIEW. President JOHN ADAMS appointed him to the Supreme Court in 1799 but he resigned in 1804 because of ill health. During his tenure Moore wrote only one opinion, in *Bas v. Tingy* (1800), a prize case. Moore's unexceptional opinion, together with those of the other Justices, lent support to congressional legislation dealing with the quasi-war with France.

DAVID GORDON
(1986)

MOORE v. CITY OF EAST CLEVELAND
431 U.S. 494 (1977)

Although it produced no OPINION OF THE COURT, *Moore* is a major modern Supreme Court precedent confirming the Constitution's protection of the family. A 5–4 Court held invalid a city ordinance limiting occupancy of certain residences to single families and defining "family" in a way that excluded a family composed of Inez Moore, her son, and two grandsons who were not brothers but cousins. Justice LEWIS F. POWELL, for a plurality of four Justices, concluded that "such an intrusive regulation of the family" required careful scrutiny of the regulation's justification. The city's asserted justifications—avoiding overcrowding, traffic and parking problems, and burdens on its schools—were served only marginally by the ordinance. The plurality thus concluded that the ordinance denied Mrs. Moore liberty without DUE PROCESS OF LAW.

Justice JOHN PAUL STEVENS, concurring, characterized the ordinance as a TAKING OF PROPERTY without due process or compensation. Chief Justice WARREN E. BURGER, dissenting, would have required Moore to exhaust her state administrative remedies before suing in federal court. Three other Justices dissented on the merits, rejecting both due process and EQUAL PROTECTION attacks on the ordinance and more generally opposing heightened judicial scrutiny of legislation merely on the basis of its effect on a family like the Moores.

The PLURALITY OPINION has become a standard citation for the reemergence of SUBSTANTIVE DUE PROCESS, and more specifically for a constitutional right of an extended—but traditional—family to choose its own living arrangements. In a wider perspective the decision can be seen as part of the growth of a FREEDOM OF INTIMATE ASSOCIATION. The decision was not, however, a blow against covert RACIAL DISCRIMINATION. East Cleveland was a predominantly black city, with a black commission and city manager. The ordinance, like ordinances in many white communities, was designed to maintain middle-class nuclear family arrangements. In this perspective, the PLURALITY OPINION is seen to collide with *Village of Belle Terre v. Boraas* (1974), which had upheld an ordinance excluding "unrelated" groups from single-family residences. Justice Powell's distinction of *Belle Terre* amounted to this: families are different. But he offered no definition of "family" apart from a generalized bow to "a larger conception of the family," including an extended family of blood relatives, for which he found support in "the accumulated wisdom of civilization." Of such stuff is substantive due process made.

KENNETH L. KARST
(1986)

Bibliography

BURT, ROBERT A. 1979 The Constitution of the Family. *Supreme Court Review* 1979:329, 388–391.

MOORE v. DEMPSEY
261 U.S. 86 (1923)

Moore was a landmark for two of the twentieth century's most important constitutional developments: the emergence of the DUE PROCESS clause of the FOURTEENTH AMENDMENT as a limitation on state CRIMINAL PROCEDURE, and the assumption by the federal judiciary of a major responsibility for supervising the fairness of state criminal processes, through HABEAS CORPUS proceedings.

For all its importance, the case began as a squalid episode of racist ferocity. Returning from WORLD WAR I, a black Army veteran sought to organize black tenant farmers of Phillips County, Arkansas, into a farmers' union. In October 1919—a year disfigured by racial violence in both North and South—these farmers held a meeting in a rural church to plan efforts to obtain fair accountings from their white landlords. At this remove in time it requires effort to understand that such a meeting, in such a place, for such a purpose, was seen as revolutionary. A sheriff's deputy fired at the church; blacks who were armed fired back, killing the deputy and wounding his companion. Hundreds of new deputies were sworn; they and hundreds of troops arrested most of the county's black farmers, killing resisters. Responsible estimates of the black dead ranged from twenty-five to 200.

About 120 blacks were indicted for various crimes, including the murder of the deputy. The trial juries, like the grand jury that had issued the INDICTMENTS, were all white. Twelve men were convicted of murder and sentenced to death; dozens of others were sentenced to long prison terms. The twelve sentenced to death filed APPEALS in two groups of six each. One group, after multiple appeals, was released in 1923 by order of the Arkansas Supreme Court, for excessive delay in their retrial. The convictions of the remaining six, however, were affirmed by the state supreme court, and the U.S. Supreme Court denied certiorari. They unsuccessfully sought habeas corpus in the state courts, and again the Supreme Court declined to review the case.

By now the NAACP had mounted a national fund-raising drive to support the six petitioners. Their execution, set for September 1921, was postponed by the filing of a habeas corpus petition in the federal district court. That court dismissed the writ. On direct appeal, the Supreme Court reversed, 7–2, with an opinion by Justice OLIVER WENDELL HOLMES. (The opinion refers, apparently erroneously, only to the five petitioners who were tried together; the petition of the sixth was consolidated for hearing and decision.)

On REMAND to the district court, counsel for the six petitioners struck a deal; the habeas corpus petition would be dismissed and the sentence commuted to twelve years' imprisonment, making the men eligible for immediate parole. In 1925 the governor of Arkansas granted an "indefinite furlough," releasing them along with the others convicted following the Phillips County "insurrection."

The federal habeas corpus petition in *Moore* alleged that counsel appointed to represent the five defendants tried together did not consult with his clients before the trial; requested neither delay nor change of VENUE nor separate trials; challenged not a single juryman; and called no defense witnesses. The trial took forty-five minutes, and the jury "deliberated" less than five minutes. A lynch mob had been dissuaded from carrying out its purpose by a local committee, appointed by the governor to combat the "insurrection," who assured the mob that justice would be done swiftly. Two black witnesses swore they had been whipped and tortured into testifying as the prosecution wished. Holmes summarized the petition: "no juryman could have voted for an acquittal and continued to live in Phillips county, and if any prisoner, by any chance, had been acquitted by a jury, he could not have escaped the mob."

The Supreme Court held that these facts, if proved, justified two conclusions: the state had violated PROCEDURAL DUE PROCESS, and the federal district court should grant the writ of habeas corpus. Today both conclusions seem obvious. In 1923, however, the Supreme Court had not yet begun to impose significant federal constitutional limitations on the fairness of state criminal proceedings. *Moore* lighted the path that would lead, in less than half a century, to an expansion of the liberty protected by the due process clause, applying virtually the entire BILL OF RIGHTS to the states. (See INCORPORATION DOCTRINE.)

Moore's other conclusion, concerning the reach of federal habeas corpus, also broke new ground. In FRANK V. MANGUM (1915), a case involving strikingly similar facts, the Court had rejected a claim to federal habeas corpus relief on the ground that the state courts had provided a full "corrective process" for litigating the accused's federal constitutional claims. Only in the absence of such a corrective process, the Court had held, could a federal habeas corpus court intervene. *Moore* did not explicitly overrule *Frank*, but it did look in a different direction. Justice Holmes, in his characteristically laconic way, said only that if "the whole proceeding is a mask," with all participants in the state trial swept to their conclusion by a mob, and if the state courts fail to correct the wrong, "perfection in the [state's] machinery for correction" could not prevent the federal court from securing the accused's constitutional rights. The right claimed in *Moore*, of course, goes to the essence of due process of law; when the basic fairness of a state criminal trial is challenged, the fact that the state courts have already had a chance to look into the matter seems a weak justification for barring federal habeas corpus.

From *Moore* through FAY V. NOIA (1963), the Supreme Court steadily widened access to federal habeas corpus for persons challenging constitutionality of state convictions. STONE V. POWELL (1976) and WAINWRIGHT V. SYKES (1977) marked the BURGER COURT's reversal of the direction of doctrinal change. Indeed, *Stone* revived the doctrine of *Frank v. Mangum* in cases involving claims based on the

FOURTH AMENDMENT's guarantee against UNREASONABLE SEARCHES and seizures. Yet, despite these limitations, *Moore's* legacy, even in the field of federal habeas corpus, remains vital to a system of national constitutional standards of fairness for persons accused of crime.

KENNETH L. KARST
(1986)

Bibliography

BATOR, PAUL M. 1963 Finality in Criminal Law and Federal Habeas Corpus for State Prisoners. *Harvard Law Review* 76: 441, 483–493.

WATERMAN, J. S. and OVERTON, E. E. 1933 The Aftermath of Moore v. Dempsey. *St. Louis Law Review* (now *Washington University Law Review*) 18:117–126.

MOOSE LODGE #107 v. IRVIS
407 U.S. 163 (1972)

Irvis, a black, was refused service at a Harrisburg, Pennsylvania, branch of the Moose Lodge, a fraternal organization whose fraternity knew bounds. Irvis sued under federal CIVIL RIGHTS laws for an INJUNCTION requiring the Pennsylvania liquor board to revoke the lodge's license so long as it continued to discriminate on the basis of race. The Supreme Court held, 6–3, in an opinion by Justice WILLIAM H. REHNQUIST, that Irvis was not entitled to the relief he sought. The state's licensing was not, of itself, sufficient to satisfy the STATE ACTION limitation of the FOURTEENTH AMENDMENT, and the Constitution offered no protection against RACIAL DISCRIMINATION by a private club.

In the majority's view, nothing in the case approached the "symbiotic relationship" between the state and private racial discrimination shown in BURTON V. WILMINGTON PARKING AUTHORITY (1961). Although Pennsylvania liquor licensees were subjected to a number of state regulations, that supervision did not "encourage" racial discrimination. Furthermore, because many liquor licenses had been issued in the area, the lodge's license fell short of creating a state-supported monopoly. Thus the state had not implicated itself in the lodge's discriminatory policies.

Justices WILLIAM O. DOUGLAS and WILLIAM J. BRENNAN wrote separate DISSENTING OPINIONS, each joined by Justice THURGOOD MARSHALL. The dissenters emphasized the degree of monopoly power of clubs licensed to sell liquor and the state's detailed regulation of licensees.

KENNETH L. KARST
(1986)

MOOTNESS

Article III's CASE OR CONTROVERSY restriction precludes federal courts from declaring law except in the context of litigation by parties with a personal stake in a live dispute that judicial decision can affect. They may not resolve moot questions—questions whose resolution can no longer affect the litigants' dispute because events after the commencement of litigation have obviated the need for judicial intervention. However live the issues once were, however much the parties (and the public) may desire a declaration of law, and however far the litigation may have progressed when the mooting events occur, Article III requires dismissal of the lawsuit. Common examples include a criminal defendant's death during appeal of a jail sentence, enactment of a new statute superseding one whose enforcement the plaintiff seeks to enjoin, or full satisfaction of a party's litigation demands.

Other cases exhibit less certainty that the substantive issues raised no longer need judicial action to forestall anticipated harm. In these cases, mootness questions are more troublesome. They inevitably introduce discretion to exercise or withhold judgment, discretion potentially influenced by the substantive issues' public importance. Thus, in DEFUNIS V. ODEGAARD (1974) a divided Supreme Court refused to decide the constitutionality of a race-conscious AFFIRMATIVE ACTION program for law school admissions when it appeared fairly certain that the challenger, who had only become a student through lower court victories, would be graduated irrespective of the lawsuit's outcome.

Several DOCTRINES reveal mootness to be a matter of degree. First, when changed circumstances moot the main dispute, but adjudication could produce collateral consequences, the issue is not moot, as when a prisoner's sentence expires before his appeal is decided, but the conviction might subject him to other civil or criminal penalties. Second, cases where defendants voluntarily agree to refrain from challenged behavior are not moot absent proof that they are unlikely to resume the behavior. This rule protects plaintiffs by preventing defendants from manipulating the mootness doctrine to avoid adverse decisions. Third, issues are not moot, despite passage of the immediate problem, when they are "capable of repetition, yet evading review," that is, when they arise sporadically, do not persist long enough to be reviewed before ceasing each time, and are reasonably likely to threaten the challengers again. Suits challenging ELECTION rules, where the immediate election passes before judicial resolution but the rules probably would affect the challengers in subsequent elections, or litigation challenging an abortion restriction that necessarily can apply to a woman only during the term of pregnancy are important instances where an unbending application of the mootness doctrine might deny judicial protection to persons periodically subject to harm. Finally, the Court generously allows a CLASS ACTION to continue, despite developments eliminating any

need to protect the party bringing the lawsuit on behalf of the class, if the case is not moot as to other members of the class.

These refinements give federal courts some flexibility either to reach issues of their choice without pressing necessity to protect the parties or to decline to rule by insisting on a higher degree of probability that the threat of harm continues. Like other JUSTICIABILITY doctrines, mootness is not only a constitutional doctrine itself but a somewhat pliable tool of constitutional governance.

JONATHAN D. VARAT
(1986)

Bibliography

NOTE 1974 The Mootness Doctrine in the Supreme Court. *Harvard Law Review* 88:373.

MOOTNESS
(Update)

Constitutional litigation often takes place on two distinct planes. First, the parties disagree about whether government has wrongfully injured the plaintiff's liberty or PROPERTY interests. Second, the subject matter of the litigation sets the stage for a larger legal and ideological debate. If some event ends the parties' disagreement about the plaintiff's injury, so that a judicial decision would have no consequences for the parties, the case is said to be moot. The question is whether the case may continue to serve as a vehicle for settling the larger debate.

In general, the Supreme Court has answered this question negatively. A relatively straightforward case of mootness was presented in *Arizonans for Official English v. Arizona* (1997). The voters of Arizona had narrowly approved a ballot INITIATIVE establishing English as the state's official language. The plaintiff, Maria-Kelly Yñíguez, was a state insurance claims manager who in her daily work spoke Spanish to clients who understood only Spanish. Worried that the new law would prohibit her from speaking any Spanish on the job, she sued state officials, claiming that the initiative violated the EQUAL PROTECTION clause.

After the trial court ruled in her favor, Yñíguez resigned from state employment to take another job, thus mooting the case. Yet both Yñíguez and backers of the initiative urged the courts to settle the constitutionality of the "OFFICIAL ENGLISH" LAW. The Supreme Court not only refused to allow the suit to go forward, but vacated all the proceedings in the courts below. Lacking a personal stake in the constitutionality of the initiative, Yñíguez no longer had a JUSTICIABLE dispute against the state.

The Court sometimes uses the mootness rules to adjust

the timing of controversial decisions. In DEFUNIS V. ODE-GAARD (1974), the Court refused to decide a challenge to AFFIRMATIVE ACTION in law school admissions, even though the "capable of repetition, yet evading review" exception used the previous term in ROE V. WADE (1973) appeared to apply. After the issue had percolated for four years, the Court decided REGENTS OF UNIVERSITY OF CALIFORNIA V. BAKKE (1978), brushing aside a weighty argument that the case was moot. In another dubious opinion, *Boston Firefighters Union, Local 718 v. Boston Chapter, NAACP* (1983), the Court found a challenge to affirmative action in public hiring moot, only to decide the same issue the next year in a case that seemed no less moot, FIREFIGHTERS LOCAL UNION NO. 1784 V. STOTTS (1984).

In using the mootness DOCTRINE to refine the timing of its controversial decisions, the Court has consciously or unconsciously followed a practice once urged by Professor ALEXANDER M. BICKEL. He argued that the Court should use the mootness, STANDING, RIPENESS, and POLITICAL QUESTION doctrines in a frankly unprincipled manner so that proper timing would allow the Court to decide the merits of cases in a principled manner. Rather than hand down a decision when it would be especially divisive, the Court should wait until public opinion has matured to some degree.

History has yet to pronounce on the wisdom of this practice. Making unprincipled rulings on mootness grounds creates a tension with the Court's tradition of giving reasoned explanations for its decisions. Lawyers and lower court judges puzzle over technical-looking opinions that add up to little more than, "Better wait." Worse yet, unprincipled decisionmaking threatens the very public credibility that the Court seeks to protect.

EVAN TSEN LEE
(2000)

Bibliography

BICKEL, ALEXANDER M.   1986   *The Least Dangerous Branch: The Supreme Court at the Bar of Politics*, 2nd ed. New Haven, Conn.: Yale University Press.
FALLON, RICHARD H., JR.   1984   Of Justiciability, Remedies, and Public Law Litigation: Notes on the Jurisprudence of *Lyons*. *New York University Law Review* 59:1–75.
LEE, EVAN TSEN   1992   Deconstitutionalizing Justiciability: The Example of Mootness. *Harvard Law Review* 105:603–669.

MOREHEAD v.
NEW YORK EX REL. TIPALDO
298 U.S. 587 (1936)

In June 1936 the Supreme Court ended its term with an opinion so startling that even the Republican party repudiated it at the party's national convention. The Republi-can plank read: "We support the adoption of State laws to abolish sweatshops and child labor and to protect women and children with respect to MAXIMUM HOURS, MINIMUM WAGES and working conditions. We believe that this can be done within the Constitution as it now stands." "This" was precisely what the Court had ruled could not be done. It had defended STATES' RIGHTS as it struck down national legislation, and in NEBBIA V. NEW YORK (1934) it had declared, "So far as the requirement of DUE PROCESS of law is concerned, a state is free to adopt whatever economic policy may reasonably be deemed to promote public welfare. . . ." Just two weeks before the *Tipaldo* decision, the Court had announced, in CARTER V. CARTER COAL COMPANY (1936), as it had in the SCHECHTER POULTRY CORP. V. UNITED STATES (1935), that the regulation of labor was a local matter reserved by the TENTH AMENDMENT to the states, and specifically the Court had referred to the fixing of wages as a state function. Thus the resolution of *Tipaldo* came as a surprise. The Court used the FREEDOM OF CONTRACT doctrine, derived from SUBSTANTIVE DUE PROCESS, to hold that the states lack power to enact minimum wage laws. The precedent that controlled the case, the Court ruled, was ADKINS V. CHILDREN'S HOSPITAL (1923).

Although *Adkins* had seemed to block minimum wage legislation, the Court grounded that decision on the statute's failure to stipulate that prescribed wages should not exceed the value of labor services. New York had carefully framed a minimum wage law for women and children that embodied the Court's *Adkins* standard: the state labor commission was empowered to fix wages "fairly and reasonably commensurate with the value of the service or class of service rendered." By a 5–4 vote the Court held the state act unconstitutional. Justice PIERCE BUTLER, speaking for the majority, declared, "Forcing the payment of wages at a reasonable value does not make applicable the principle and ruling of the Adkins Case." The right to make contracts for wages in return for work "is part of the liberty protected by the due process clause," Butler said, and the state was powerless to interfere with such contracts. Women were entitled to no special consideration. Any measure that deprived employers and women employees the freedom to agree on wages, "leaving employers and men employees free to do so, is necessarily arbitrary."

Chief Justice CHARLES EVANS HUGHES dissented on ground that the statute was a reasonable exercise of the POLICE POWER, and he distinguished this case from *Adkins* because the *Tipaldo* statute laid down an appropriate standard for fixing wages. Justices HARLAN FISKE STONE, LOUIS D. BRANDEIS, and BENJAMIN N. CARDOZO concurred in Hughes's opinion but in a separate dissent by Stone they went much further. Stone accused the majority of having decided on the basis of their "personal economic predilections." He repudiated the freedom of contract DOC-TRINE, adding: "There is grim irony in speaking of the freedom of contract of those who, because of their economic necessities, give their services for less than is needful to keep body and soul together." Following the reasoning of Justice OLIVER WENDELL HOLMES, dissenting in *Adkins,* Stone declared that it made no difference what wage standard the statute fixed, because employers were not compelled to hire anyone and could fire employees who did not earn their wages. Stone would have followed the principle of *Nebbia,* which the majority ignored, and he would have overruled *Adkins.* A year later, after President FRANKLIN D. ROOSEVELT proposed packing the Court, it overruled *Adkins* and *Tipaldo* in WEST COAST HOTEL V. PARRISH (1937).

LEONARD W. LEVY
(1986)

Bibliography

LEONARD, CHARLES A. 1971 *A Search for a Judicial Philosophy: Mr. Justice Roberts and the Constitutional Revolution of 1937.* Pages 88–93. Port Washington, N.Y.: Kennikat Press.

MORGAN v. VIRGINIA
328 U.S. 373 (1946)

This was the first transportation SEGREGATION case brought to the Supreme Court by the NAACP; counsel for the appellant were THURGOOD MARSHALL and WILLIAM H. HASTIE. A Virginia law required racial segregation of passengers on buses. A black woman, riding from Virginia to Maryland, refused to move to a rear seat; she was convicted of a MISDEMEANOR and fined $10. Eighteen states forbade such segregation of passengers, and ten states required it. In 1878 the Supreme Court had invalidated a state law forbidding racial segregation on an interstate carrier as an undue burden on INTERSTATE COMMERCE in HALL V. DECUIR. The NAACP lawyers rested on the *Hall* precedent, and did not argue that the Virginia law violated the FOUR-TEENTH AMENDMENT.

In an opinion by Justice STANLEY F. REED, the Supreme Court held, 7–1, that the law unduly burdened interstate commerce. Although the usual analysis of a STATE REGU-LATION OF COMMERCE involves a balance of burdens on commerce against competing state interests such as health or safety, the Court avoided any discussion of a state interest in segregation, saying only that a uniform national rule of passenger seating was required for interstate carriers, if any rule was to be adopted. Justice HAROLD BURTON dissented.

KENNETH L. KARST
(1986)

MORMON CHURCH v. UNITED STATES

See: *Church of Jesus Christ of Latter Day Saints v. United States*

MORRILL ACT
12 Stat. 503 (1862)

The Morrill Land Grant College Act provided a basis for state support of public universities and thereby profoundly influenced the course of American higher EDU-CATION.

Under the Land Ordinance of 1785, section 16 of every township was sold and the proceeds used to create a "school fund." In the late 1850s, Vermont Republican Justin Morrill promoted the "Illinois Idea," which would have authorized further land grants to create an "industrial college" in each state. But southern Democrats objected on constitutional grounds, seeing in Morrill's bill a threat to STATES' RIGHTS. In 1862, with these opponents withdrawn from Congress, the Land Grant College Act was passed. It provided that 30,000 acres of public lands be assigned to each state for each of its senators and representatives (or land scrip in an equivalent amount issued to states lacking available public lands). The proceeds of the land sales were to be invested to support a college "to teach such branches of learning as are related to agriculture and the mechanic arts," as well as "military tactics," "in order to promote the liberal and practical education of the industrial classes." The American land-grant colleges are the result of this policy.

WILLIAM M. WIECEK
(1986)

MORRIS, GOUVERNEUR
(1752–1816)

A lawyer and businessman descended from a wealthy, landed family, Gouverneur Morris was elected to New York's first provincial congress in 1775. The next year, he was a member of the committee that drafted the state's first CONSTITUTION and wrote the message to New York's delegates to the Continental Congress instructing them to vote for the DECLARATION OF INDEPENDENCE. He was himself sent to the Continental Congress in 1778 and was a signer of the ARTICLES OF CONFEDERATION. In 1780 he moved to Philadelphia and served as assistant superintendent of finance under ROBERT MORRIS. In this last capacity, he drafted a report to Congress that contained the first official proposal for a national currency: a decimal coinage based on the Spanish dollar.

Gouverneur Morris was elected to Pennsylvania's delegation to the CONSTITUTIONAL CONVENTION OF 1787. In the debates of the Convention he spoke more frequently than any other delegate. He was an advocate of strong national government, but also of aristocratic privilege. His view of humankind was extraordinarily cynical, and, distrusting any higher motives, he desired to institutionalize private interests as a guarantee of liberty. Although, like Robert Morris, he proposed a senate chosen for life from men of great wealth, the proposal arose partly out of fear that otherwise the rich would corrupt the democratic elements of the regime. He favored a provision to allow Congress to veto state laws and wanted to unite the executive and judiciary in a council of revision to veto national legislation. He favored direct election of the President and congressional representation proportional to taxation; he opposed any constitutional protection of slavery or the slave trade. He was against giving Congress the power to admit new states on terms of equality, and throughout his life he advocated governing the western territories as provinces while retaining power in the East.

Morris was elected to the Committee on Style, along with WILLIAM SAMUEL JOHNSON (its chairman), JAMES MADISON, JAMES WILSON, and RUFUS KING. The committee entrusted Morris with the duty of preparing its report, and so Morris became the principal author of the actual words of the Constitution. He also devised the formula for signing the document—the signatures bearing witness to the unanimous consent of the states—and drafted the letter by which the Convention transmitted its work to Congress.

ALEXANDER HAMILTON asked Morris to collaborate in writing THE FEDERALIST, but Morris declined. He served as a senator from New York from 1800 to 1803, supporting the JUDICIARY ACT OF 1801 and advocating the annexation—by force if necessary—of Louisiana. His public career also included a brief term as minister to France and the founding chairmanship of the Erie Canal Commission.

Morris opposed the War of 1812 as sectional and ill-conceived. The former champion of strong national government became an advocate of STATES' RIGHTS; he even counseled SECESSION of New York and New England from the Union. Morris was disappointed when the HARTFORD CONVENTION resolutions failed to embody that step.

DENNIS J. MAHONEY
(1986)

Bibliography

MINTZ, MAX M. 1970 *Gouverneur Morris and the American Revolution.* Norman: University of Oklahoma Press.

ROOSEVELT, THEODORE 1888 *Gouverneur Morris.* (American Statesman Series.) Boston: Houghton Mifflin.

MORRIS, ROBERT
(1734–1806)

The English-born merchant and patriot Robert Morris was an early supporter of colonial rights, opposing the Stamp Act and signing the Non-Importation Agreement in 1765. As a member of the Second Continental Congress (1776–1788), Morris voted against the DECLARATION OF INDEPENDENCE because it was premature; but he later signed the Declaration as well as the ARTICLES OF CONFEDERATION. He earned the nickname "Financier of the Revolution" because of his role in raising money to support the Army. In 1781, Congress chose him to be superintendent of finance. While serving in that capacity he organized the Bank of North America, chartered by Congress as a device for borrowing money to pay the costs of the new government. In 1783, he resigned the "insupportable situation" of superintendent of finance, giving as his reason that "to increase our debts while the prospect of paying them diminishes does not consist with my ideas of integrity."

He was a member of the Pennsylvania delegation to the CONSTITUTIONAL CONVENTION OF 1787. There he nominated GEORGE WASHINGTON to be presiding officer, but otherwise, despite his reputation in Pennsylvania politics as a speaker who "bears down all before him," he remained silent throughout the debates. He was a strong nationalist, and desired a Senate comprising men of great and established property appointed for life. Morris signed the Constitution, and, in a letter, recommended it as "the subject of infinite investigation, disputation, and declamation," but still the work not of angels or devils but of "plain, honest men."

Morris and his friends supported the Constitution not least because it promised economic stability, security of contracts, and relief from the harassment of the Bank of North America by the state governments. But Morris's support for ratification seems only to have increased the fervor of some anti-Federalists.

Morris would have been a leading candidate to become the first secretary of the treasury, but he did not want the post. Instead, in 1789, he was elected to the United States SENATE, where he became a leader of the FEDERALIST faction and a key ally of ALEXANDER HAMILTON in the matter of the assumption of state debts.

Morris retired from public life in 1795, and devoted his time to the management of his financial affairs, including his speculation in western lands. That speculation brought him, in 1797, to financial ruin and to three and one-half years in debtors' prison.

DENNIS J. MAHONEY
(1986)

MORRISON v. OLSON

See: Constitutional History, 1980–1989; Independent Counsel; Special Prosecutor

MORROW, WILLIAM W.
(1843–1929)

William W. Morrow served nearly thirty-two years on the federal bench. President BENJAMIN HARRISON in 1892 appointed him to the Northern District of California; President WILLIAM MCKINLEY in 1897 elevated him to the Ninth Circuit Court of Appeals, where he served until retirement in 1923.

His most influential opinion came in *In Re Wong Kim Ark* (1897). Morrow relied on history and precedent in the Ninth Circuit to define a COMMON LAW basis for CITIZENSHIP. He held that under the first section of the FOURTEENTH AMENDMENT a child whose parents were subjects of the emperor of China but domiciled in the United States at the time of the child's birth derived his citizenship from the place of birth rather than the father's citizenship. Morrow's opinion, which the Supreme Court affirmed in UNITED STATES V. WONG KIM ARK (1898), confirmed the claims of thousands of Chinese to American citizenship.

Morrow's opinion in *United States v. Wheeler et al* (1912) revealed his profound suspicion of federal authority. Arizona officials had refused to prosecute the perpetrators of the Bisbee deportations, in which private citizens had forcibly removed over 200 members of the Industrial Workers of the World from Arizona to New Mexico. The United States sought to prosecute the leaders of the deportation under the conspiracy section of the FORCE ACT OF 1870. Morrow, however, rejected federal intervention. He held that the Fourteenth Amendment applied only to those rights explicitly provided for by Congress and which had not been historically entrusted to the states. Morrow reasoned that the acts of private individuals did not constitute STATE ACTION under the amendment, that the 1870 act applied only to the rights of freedmen, and that Congress had not passed any statute making kidnapping a federal crime. Morrow refused to allow the federal government to intervene, no matter how just the cause, in an area traditionally left to the STATE POLICE POWER.

Morrow's conservative jurisprudence paralleled his Republican politics. Through three decades of service on the Ninth Circuit he provided leadership to a court committed, like himself, to precedent and DUAL FEDERALISM.

KERMIT L. HALL
(1986)

Bibliography

JURY, JOHN G. 1921 William W. Morrow. *California Law Review* 10:1–7.

MUELLER v. ALLEN
463 U.S. 388 (1983)

In this major case on the SEPARATION OF CHURCH AND STATE, the Supreme Court altered constitutional law on the issue of state aid to parents of parochial school children. The precedents had established that a state may not aid parochial schools by direct grants or indirectly by financial aids to the parents of the children; whether those aids took the form of tax credits or reimbursements of tuition expenses did not matter. In this case the state act allowed taxpayers to deduct expenses for tuition, books, and transportation of their children to school, no matter what school, public or private, secular or sectarian.

Justice WILLIAM H. REHNQUIST for a 5–4 Court ruled that the plan satisfied all three parts of the purpose, effect, and no-entanglement test of LEMON V. KURTZMAN (1971). That all taxpaying parents benefited from the act made the difference between this case and the precedents, even though parents of public school children could not take advantage of the major tax deduction. Rehnquist declared that the state had not aided religion generally or any particular denomination and had not excessively entangled the state with religion even though government officials had to disallow tax deductions for instructional materials and books that were used to teach religion. According to the dissenters, however, the statute had not restricted the parochial schools to books approved for public school use, with the result that the state necessarily became enmeshed in religious matters when administering the tax deductions. The dissenters also rejected the majority point that the availability of the tax deduction to all parents distinguished this case from the precedents. The parents of public school children simply were unable to claim the large deduction for tuition. Consequently the program had the effect of advancing the religious mission of the private sectarian schools.

LEONARD W. LEVY
(1986)

MUGLER v. KANSAS
123 U.S. 623 (1887)

In *Mugler* the Supreme Court took a significant step toward the acceptance of SUBSTANTIVE DUE PROCESS, announcing it would henceforth examine the reasonableness involved in an exercise of STATE POLICE POWER. A Kansas statute prohibited the manufacture or sale of intoxicating liquor; the state arrested Mugler for making and selling malt liquor and also closed a brewery for being a public nuisance.

Justice JOHN MARSHALL HARLAN addressed the issue: did the Kansas statute violate the FOURTEENTH AMENDMENT guarantee of DUE PROCESS OF LAW? He declared that such a prohibition "does not necessarily infringe" any of those rights. Although an individual might have an abstract right to make liquor for his own purposes, as Mugler contended, that right could be conditioned on its effect on others' rights. The question became who would determine the effects of personal use on the community? Harlan found that power lodged squarely in the legislature which, to protect the public health and morals, might exercise its police power. But, bowing to JOSEPH CHOATE's argument, he admitted that such power was limited. Harlan asserted that the courts would not be bound "by mere forms [or] . . . pretenses." They had a "solemn duty—to look at the substance of things"; absent a "real or substantial relation" of the act to its objects, the legislation must fall as a "palpable invasion of rights secured by the FUNDAMENTAL LAW." The Kansas statute easily passed this test, however, and Harlan denied any interference or impairment of property rights. Harlan likewise dismissed the contention that the closing of a brewery amounted to a TAKING OF PROPERTY without JUST COMPENSATION, thereby depriving its owners of due process. Justice STEPHEN J. FIELD dissented in part, urging the Court to adopt substantive due process.

DAVID GORDON
(1986)

(SEE ALSO: *Allgeyer v. Louisiana.*)

MULLER v. OREGON
208 U.S. 412 (1908)

Despite the Supreme Court's previous rejection of a maximum hour law for bakers in LOCHNER V. NEW YORK (1905), here the Justices unanimously sustained an Oregon statute limiting women to ten hours' labor in "any mechanical establishment, or factory, or laundry." The sole issue was the law's constitutionality as it affected female labor in a laundry. Lawyers for Muller contended that the law violated FREEDOM OF CONTRACT, that it was class legislation, and that it had no reasonable connection with the public health, safety, or welfare. The state countered with LOUIS D. BRANDEIS's famous brief elaborately detailing similar state and foreign laws, as well as foreign and domestic experts' reports on the harmful physical, economic, and social effects of long working hours for women.

Justice DAVID BREWER, speaking for the Court, based his opinion on the proposition that physical and social differences between the sexes justified a different rule respecting labor contracts, thereby allowing him to distinguish *Lochner*. Although the Constitution imposed unchanging limitations on legislative action, Brewer acknowledged that the FOURTEENTH AMENDMENT's liberty of contract doctrine was not absolute. He invoked HOLDEN V. HARDY (1898), sustaining an eight-hour day for Utah miners, and portions of *Lochner* that similarly approved some exceptional regulations. Brewer declared that although the legislation and opinions cited in the BRANDEIS BRIEF were not "authorities," the Court would "take judicial cognizance of all matters of general knowledge."

The accepted wisdom that women were unequal and inferior to men animated Brewer's opinion. Women's physical structure and their maternal functions, he said, put them at a disadvantage. Long hours of labor, furthermore, threatened women's potential for producing "vigorous" children; as such their physical well-being was a proper object of interest "in order to preserve the strength and vigor of the race." Beyond Brewer's concerns for the "future well-being of the race," he contended that the long historical record of women's dependence upon men demonstrated a persistent reality that women lacked "the self-reliance which enables one to assert full rights." Legislation such as the Oregon maximum hour law, Brewer concluded, was necessary to protect women from the "greed" and "passion" of men and therefore validly and properly could "compensate for some of the burdens" imposed upon women.

Taken out of context, Brewer's remarks obviously reflected paternalistic and sexist notions. Yet they also reflected prevailing sentiments, which he invoked to justify an exception to his normally restrictive views of legislative power. The same arguments were advanced by those who sought an opening wedge for ameliorating some of the excesses of modern industrialism.

Although the *Muller* decision did not overrule *Lochner*, it reinforced a growing line of precedents to counter *Lochner*. *Muller* eventually led to BUNTING V. OREGON (1917), approving maximum hour laws for both sexes, a decision that Chief Justice WILLIAM HOWARD TAFT believed in 1923 had tacitly overruled *Lochner*—mistakenly, as it turned out, for the Court invoked *Lochner* to strike down a minimum wage law in ADKINS V. CHILDREN'S HOSPITAL (1923).

STANLEY I. KUTLER
(1986)

(SEE ALSO: *Sex Discrimination.*)

Bibliography

MASON, ALPHEUS T. 1946 *Brandeis: A Free Man's Life.* New York: Viking Press.

MULTIMEMBER DISTRICT

A multimember district (MMD) is a political district with more than one representative. European countries with proportional REPRESENTATION divide multiple representatives proportionally by party vote, normally producing many small, doctrinaire parties and volatile, schismatic governments. In United States MMDs, at-large, winner-take-all elections have been the rule, notably with ELECTORAL COLLEGE delegations. Winner-take-all puts more than proportional value on shiftable votes. Scholars believe that it has helped produce the American pattern of stable, center-seeking, two-party coalitions attentive to minorities who can form part of a winning coalition.

A ten-member, winner-take-all MMD offers less demographic variety—and less direct claim on any particular representative—than ten single-member districts; so MMDs have often been attacked for depersonalizing representation and submerging minorities. On the other hand, voters in MMDs have a mathematical advantage over voters in single-member districts (SMDs) because a 110 vote for ten representatives has more chance of affecting the overall election outcome than a full vote for one representative. Moreover, MMD representatives, who answer to one large constituency rather than to ten small ones, are thought more likely to vote as a bloc than SMD representatives. Hence, an MMD voter may have less access to his representative than does an SMD voter, but he also may have more power over electoral and legislative outcomes.

MMDs share with GERRYMANDERS the "standards problem": the incommensurability of the various ways in which dilution or concentration of a group can enhance or diminish the group's power for different purposes. Short of ordering proportional representation, there is no way to equalize a group's (or a group member's) effective power. Accordingly, the Supreme Court has been cautious in intervening against MMDs, as it has against gerrymanders. In *Delaware v. New York* (1966) it was unmoved by Delaware's argument that New York voters, with sixty-four delegates to the Electoral College, has 2.3 times as much chance to affect the election outcome as Delaware voters, with only three delegates.

Likewise, with the exceptions of judicially created MMDs and legislatively created ones drawn with the proven intent of submerging minorities, the Court has been tolerant of MMDs, even where their effect has been to submerge minorities. In *Whitcomb v. Chavis* (1971) and MOBILE V. BOLDEN (1980) the Court held that submerging a minority is not per se a violation of the FOURTEENTH or FIFTEENTH AMENDMENT. Purposeful discrimination must also be shown, as in *White v. Regester* (1973) and ROGERS V. LODGE (1982), where the plaintiffs demonstrated intentional discrimination against minority groups. Congressional critics (of the *Mobile* case) in 1982 succeeded in amending the VOTING RIGHTS ACT OF 1965 to make racially disproportionate election results one "circumstance" relevant to the determination of a violation of the act. The amendment added a proviso that racially proportional representation is not required, but it left to the courts the task of giving meaning to its calculatedly uncertain operative language.

WARD E. Y. ELLIOT
(1986)

Bibliography

BANZHAF, JOHN E. 1966 Multi-Member Electoral Districts—Do They Violate the "One Man, One Vote" Principle? *Yale Law Journal* 75:1309–1338.

ELLIOT, WARD E. Y. 1975 *The Rise of Guardian Democracy: The Supreme Court's Role in Voting Rights Disputes, 1845–1969.* Cambridge, Mass.: Harvard University Press.

MULTINATIONAL CORPORATIONS, GLOBAL MARKETS, AND THE CONSTITUTION

Multinational corporations (MNCs) are regulated by domestic and INTERNATIONAL LAW. In the United States, CORPORATIONS are normally established pursuant to state law, and their activities are regulated by state and federal law as limited by the Constitution. The authority of the United States to regulate activities of MNCs abroad is subject to limits established by international law.

Typically a "parent" MNC will conduct its operations in countries abroad through "subsidiary" corporations that the parent owns or controls. Under international law a corporation takes the nationality of the country in which it is incorporated, and that country thereby acquires the authority to regulate the conduct of its corporate nationals anywhere in the world. Thus, the United States has international law authority to tax and otherwise to regulate the worldwide conduct of its parent MNCs. In cases such as *Blackmer v. United States* (1932), the Supreme Court has confirmed the constitutional authority of Congress to adopt such LEGISLATION. Politically, however, Congress has generally been reluctant to impose U.S. economic regulation on American MNCs abroad for fear of putting them at a competitive disadvantage as against European and Asian competitors. The principal exceptions have been where regulation had high foreign policy significance, as in economic sanctions, or was important domestically, as in ANTITRUST and anticorruption legislation.

Most controversially the United States has claimed authority to regulate the conduct of foreign subsidiaries of U.S. parent MNCs in the case of economic sanctions legislation, even though those subsidiaries are also nationals of the foreign country where they are incorporated. The result has often been a conflict between the respective countries' trade and economic policies (involving countries such as China, the former Soviet Union, Iran, Libya, and Cuba), with the result that major trading partners of the United States have challenged its authority under international law to impose such regulation extraterritorially. In the face of intense opposition the United States has negotiated compromises, provided administrative and judicial relief to otherwise applicable penalties, and otherwise moderated its claims in particular cases, but it continues to defend the legitimacy under international law of its extraterritorial application of nationality-based economic sanctions law. The Supreme Court has never denied Congress's constitutional authority to adopt such legislation. Indeed, the Supreme Court has repeatedly held that, for purposes of determining the law to be applied in American courts, a subsequent statute supersedes an earlier inconsistent international rule—that is to say, Congress may violate international law. The International Court of Justice has not ruled on the U.S. position regarding the legality of its extraterritorial economic sanctions legislation under international law, although European courts have rejected it.

Under international law a country also has authority to regulate the conduct of MNCs within its territory, and Congress has similar power in the United States under the COMMERCE CLAUSE. Here too the United States has asserted the power to apply its law extraterritorially, for example, over the foreign conduct of foreign MNCs having a direct and substantial effect in the United States. These assertions have also been controversial politically and have been challenged as violative of international law. The Supreme Court has nevertheless upheld Congress's authority to pass such legislation. American courts normally construe ambiguous statutes to be consistent with international law, and Justice ANTONIN SCALIA has recently opined that international law requires a narrow construction of the antitrust laws in an extraterritorial context. The majority of the Supreme Court, however, declined to so hold. Thus, even the foreign activities of foreign MNCs are constitutionally subject to U.S. regulation if they cause a direct and substantial effect here. Again, an act of Congress supersedes international law as far as American courts are concerned.

Despite the potentially bewildering maze of nationality- and territorial-based regulation, and the potentially significant conflict that could result, MNCs' exploitation of global markets has been facilitated by international law. To the extent that legitimate economic regulation is strictly limited to a nation's territory or to its own corporate nationals, MNCs can better plan their operations. In addition, the free-trade regime centered on the World Trade Organization (WTO) provides stable rules on tariffs, quotas, taxation, subsidies, and unfair pricing of traded goods. The objective of the regime is to promote free trade, and the WTO now supervises related subjects including trade in services, intellectual property protection, and protection of investment and capital flows. All these international law guarantees significantly benefit MNCs in their development of global markets. Moreover, the WTO has introduced a legal dispute–settlement system, which promises to be more effective than previous international law institutions. Some of the U.S. assertions of extraterritorial application of law described above can even be challenged in the new WTO courts, so that Congress may be further inhibited from exercising its full constitutional power to regulate MNCs abroad.

To date, the focus of international law has been to support MNCs, with less attention to the ancillary social and environmental consequences of their access to global markets. Efforts in the United Nations to draft a Code of Conduct to regulate the behavior of MNCs have never been completed. Other codes, like those produced by the Organization for Economic Cooperation and Development (OECD), the International Labor Organization (ILO), and MNCs themselves, are either voluntary or are not legally binding. Consequently, the only effective regulation of MNCs is national legislation and even this alternative is limited by international law.

PHILLIP R. TRIMBLE
(2000)

Bibliography

BORN, GARY B. and WESTIN, DAVID 1992 *International Civil Litigation in United States Courts,* 2nd ed. Boston: Kluwer Law and Taxation Publishers.

MUNDT-NIXON BILL
(1948–1949)

Karl Mundt of South Dakota and RICHARD M. NIXON of California, members of the HOUSE COMMITTEE ON UN-AMERICAN ACTIVITIES, sponsored the first anticommunist bill of the

Cold War era. They contended that a house-cleaning of the executive department and a full exposure of past derelictions regarding communists would come only from a body in no way corrupted by ties to the administration. The measure (HR 5852) contained antisedition provisions but also reflected the view that the constitutional way to fight communists was by forcing them out into the open. The bill thus would have required the Communist party and "front" organizations to register with the Department of Justice and supply names of officers and members. It would also require that publications of these organizations, when sent through the mails, be labeled "published in compliance with the laws of the United States, governing the activities of agents of foreign principals."

The measure passed the HOUSE by a large margin but failed in the SENATE after becoming a controversial factor in the presidential campaign of 1948. The bill was denounced by the Republican candidate, Thomas E. Dewey, and numerous respected national publications as a form of unwarranted thought control.

PAUL L. MURPHY
(1986)

(SEE ALSO: *Subversive Activity*.)

Bibliography

COHEN, MURRAY and FUCHS, ROBERT F. 1948 Communism's Challenge and the Constitution. *Cornell Law Quarterly* 34: 182–219, 352–375.

MUNICIPAL BANKRUPTCY ACT
48 Stat. 798 (1934)

This legislation, amending the Bankruptcy Act of 1898, declared "a national emergency caused by increasing financial difficulties of many local governmental units." Hearings on the bill disclosed that over 2,000 municipalities in all forty-eight states were in default—including such cities as Detroit and Miami—to an estimated total of nearly three billion dollars. The act conferred ORIGINAL JURISDICTION on federal bankruptcy courts in proceedings for the relief of "any municipality or other political subdivision of any State." Such taxing districts were thus enabled to file petitions asserting their inability to meet their debts. The act required submission of a "plan of readjustment" to accommodate a municipality's debts. The courts could enforce a plan that was "fair [and] equitable" and was approved by either two-thirds or three-quarters of the creditors, depending on the nature of the district. Section 80(k) stated that "nothing contained in this chapter shall be construed to limit or impair the power of any State to

control . . . any political subdivision" and required state approval of these bankruptcy petitions.

A 5–4 Supreme Court invalidated this act in ASHTON V. CAMERON COUNTY WATER DISTRICT (1936), but the Court sustained a substantially similar act in *United States v. Bekins* (1938).

DAVID GORDON
(1986)

Bibliography

JACKSON, ROBERT H. 1941 *The Struggle for Judicial Supremacy.* New York: Knopf.

MUNICIPAL IMMUNITY

Although precise practice varied among the states, two distinctions shaped municipalities' COMMON LAW liability. First, cities were immune from harms resulting from the exercise of governmental functions, such as fire protection, but they were not immune for harms attending proprietary functions, such as running a business. This sovereignlike immunity drew upon cities' legal connection to sovereign states, but it was independent of the ELEVENTH AMENDMENT immunity which states enjoy from suit in federal court. Since *Lincoln County v. Luning* (1890), cities and counties have not been viewed as part of the state for Eleventh Amendment purposes. Second, courts distinguished between discretionary functions, for which cities were immune, and ministerial activities, for which cities were not immune. As long as municipal liability was largely a branch of common law liability, courts articulated no significant distinctions between the treatment of federal claims against cities and claims brought under state law.

MONROE V. PAPE (1961), which reinvigorated SECTION 1983, TITLE 42, UNITED STATES CODE, and transformed the liability of state and local officials for violations of federal law into a question of federal statutory interpretation, laid the groundwork for greater municipal liability for violations of federal rights. But *Monroe* also retarded this development by interpreting section 1983 not to authorize suits against municipalities for violations of federal law. Indeed, the Court suggested that Congress doubted its constitutional authority to do so.

Between 1961 and 1978 litigants employed, with mixed success, various techniques to exploit *Monroe*'s federalization of official liability law, while at the same time avoiding *Monroe*'s holding that section 1983 did not authorize suits against cities. While these techniques were still developing, MONELL V. DEPARTMENT OF SOCIAL SERVICES (1978) drastically changed the law of municipal liability. *Monell* reinterpreted the legislative history relied on in *Monroe*, concluded that Congress had meant to subject cities to suit for violations of federal law, and overruled *Monroe's* limitation on suits against cities. But *Monell* also held that Congress had not intended cities to be liable merely because they had employed an individual wrongdoer. Under *Monell*, cities are liable for violation of federal law only if the violation is "by its lawmakers or by those whose edicts or acts may fairly be said to represent official policy."

The question whether an alleged violation of federal law may be characterized as official policy became even more critical when, in OWEN V. CITY OF INDEPENDENCE (1980), the Court held that cities may not rely on the good faith defense available to individual officials as part of the law of EXECUTIVE IMMUNITY. *Owen* also severed the final links between municipalities' common law immunities and their modern amenability to suit under federal law. The Court rejected reliance by cities on sovereign-based immunities; a higher sovereign, the United States, had in section 1983 commanded municipal liability. The immunity for discretionary acts fell because "a municipality has no 'discretion' to violate the Federal Constitution." Cities achieved a modest victory when, in *City of Newport v. Fact Concerts, Inc.* (1981), the Court reaffirmed their traditional immunity from punitive damages claims.

THEODORE EISENBERG
(1986)

Bibliography

SCHNAPPER, ERIC 1979 Civil Rights Litigation After *Monell*. *Columbia Law Review* 79:213–266.

MUNN v. ILLINOIS

See: Granger Cases

MURDOCK v. PENNSYLVANIA
319 U.S. 105 (1943)

A city ordinance required anyone offering goods for sale or engaged in solicitation (as opposed to sale from fixed premises) to obtain a license and pay a fee. Jehovah's Witnesses charged with violating the ordinance challenged it as a violation of the free exercise clause of the FIRST AMENDMENT.

Justice WILLIAM O. DOUGLAS, delivering the OPINION OF THE COURT, held that although the Witnesses offered literature for sale, their activity was "as evangelical as the revival meeting," occupying the same high estate under the First Amendment as worship in churches and preaching from pulpits. On the same day the Court vacated the judgment in *Jones v. Opelika* (1942), where the Court had previously upheld such an ordinance against a similar challenge.

Justice STANLEY F. REED dissented, arguing that *Jones v. Opelika* had been correctly decided. Justices OWEN ROBERTS, FELIX FRANKFURTER, and ROBERT H. JACKSON joined Reed's dissent. Justice Frankfurter also dissented separately, arguing that persons are not constitutionally "exempt from taxation merely because they may be engaged in religious activities or because such activities may constitute the exercise of a constitutional right."

Murdock represented a step away from the traditional doctrine of REYNOLDS V. UNITED STATES (1879) which had held that otherwise valid secular regulations could be enforced against nonconforming behavior even if that behavior were religiously motivated. (See RELIGIOUS LIBERTY.)

RICHARD E. MORGAN
(1986)

MURPHY, FRANK
(1890–1949)

President FRANKLIN D. ROOSEVELT appointed Frank Murphy to the Supreme Court in 1940. Murphy, who had been mayor of Detroit and governor of Michigan, was ATTORNEY GENERAL at the time of his appointment as a Justice. As attorney general he created the Civil Rights Section (now division) of the Department of Justice and supported a vigorous antitrust program. As spokesman for the Supreme Court in constitutional matters, Murphy made modest but significant contributions. But as author of CONCURRING and DISSENTING OPINIONS in constitutional areas of individual freedom, Murphy voiced some of the more eloquent and impassioned defenses of human liberty in the Court's history.

Murphy's tenure on the Court spanned the decade of the 1940s. That period witnessed the consolidation of the federal and state power to deal with pressing economic and social problems. Murphy eagerly joined in this judicial retreat from the philosophy of LOCHNER V. NEW YORK (1905). Murphy's contribution to the de-Lochnerization of constitutional law was highlighted by his opinions for the Court in *North American Co. v. Securities & Exchange Commission* (1946) and *American Power & Light Co. v. Securities & Exchange Commission* (1946). Those decisions validated the "death sentence" clauses of the PUBLIC UTILITY HOLDING COMPANY ACT of 1935, the last major piece of NEW DEAL legislation to be challenged. In language reminiscent of JOHN MARSHALL's language in GIBBONS V. OGDEN (1824), Murphy declared that the COMMERCE CLAUSE is "an affirmative power commensurate with the national needs." It gives Congress authority "to undertake to solve national problems directly and realistically, giving due recognition to the scope of state power," as well as to other constitutional provisions.

His first assignment to write a Court opinion produced a historic chapter in the development of FREEDOM OF SPEECH. In THORNHILL V. ALABAMA (1940) the Court held an Alabama antipicketing statute unconstitutional on its face. Murphy wrote that information concerning labor disputes is "within the area of free discussion . . . guaranteed by the Constitution." Such speech can be abridged only if there is a CLEAR AND PRESENT DANGER that substantive evils may arise before the merits of the discussion can be tested in the market of public opinion. The Court, though later permitting certain "time, place, and manner" restrictions on picketing, has never repudiated the *Thornhill* doctrine.

Another landmark free speech opinion written by Murphy was CHAPLINSKY V. NEW HAMPSHIRE (1942). Although controversial, the decision proved to be an influential forerunner of the Court's doctrinal notion that certain kinds of speech are of such slight social value as not to deserve full FIRST AMENDMENT protection. Such speech, said Murphy, includes "the lewd and obscene, the profane, the libelous, and the insulting or 'FIGHTING' WORDS—those which by their very utterance inflict injury or tend to incite an immediate BREACH OF THE PEACE."

Murphy also made a provocative contribution to the once raging judicial battle over whether the FOURTEENTH AMENDMENT totally or only selectively incorporates the BILL OF RIGHTS. While agreeing with Justice HUGO L. BLACK's total INCORPORATION DOCTRINE, Murphy in a dissent in *Adamson v. California* (1947) proposed an "incorporation plus" approach. A state proceeding, he wrote, may be so wanting in DUE PROCESS as to warrant constitutional condemnation "despite the absence of a specific provision in the Bill of Rights." Murphy's suggestion has proved functionally similar to the Court's final choice of the "selective incorporation approach."

Murphy was seldom assigned to write majority opinions in other constitutional areas. Among the few that he did write were the short-lived Fourth Amendment opinion in TRUPIANO V. UNITED STATES (1948) and the influential FULL FAITH AND CREDIT opinion in *Industrial Commission v. McCartin* (1947). Thus most of his deeply held views on the constitutional rights of individuals had to find expression in concurring and dissenting opinions. Through these he developed his judicial philosophy and expressed his ardent opposition to restricting the constitutional rights of racial and religious minorities, the economically disadvantaged, and those accused of crime.

The most durable and the most highly praised of all these individualized opinions is his dissent from what

Murphy called "this legalization of racism" in KOREMATSU V. UNITED STATES (1944). The Court there upheld the wartime relocation of all persons of Japanese ancestry residing on the West Coast. Murphy dissected the military report upon which the relocation was based, and found the report filled with discredited and questionable racial and sociological factors beyond the realm of expert military judgment. To Murphy, the relocation was nothing more than racial discrimination that was "utterly revolting among a free people who have embraced the principles set forth in the Constitution of the United States." This dissent has been described by commentators as a classic in Supreme Court literature, and as one that "should be engraved in stone."

In *Falbo v. United States* (1944), Justice Murphy wrote that the law "knows no finer hour than when it cuts through formal concepts and transitory emotions to protect unpopular citizens against discrimination and persecution." His instinctive empathy for the constitutional rights of the oppressed and the unpopular constitutes Murphy's lasting contribution to the development of constitutional law.

EUGENE GRESSMAN
(1986)

Bibliography

FINE, SIDNEY   1984   *Frank Murphy: The Washington Years.* Ann Arbor: University of Michigan Press.
HOWARD, J. WOODFORD   1968   *Mr. Justice Murphy.* Princeton, N.J.: Princeton University Press.

MURPHY, PAUL L.
(1923–1997)

Born in Caldwell, Idaho in 1923, Paul L. Murphy earned his B.A. at the College of Idaho in 1947 and his M.A. and Ph.D. at the University of California at Berkeley in 1948 and 1953, respectively. At the time of his death in 1997, he was Regents' Professor of History and American Studies and Adjunct Professor of Political Science at the University of Minnesota, Twin Cities, and Distinguished Adjunct Professor at Hamline University School of Law. He was also serving as President of the American Society for Legal History. Murphy expressed his deep personal commitment to individual autonomy, individual dignity, and individual self-determination in his teaching and scholarship and his active involvement in the AMERICAN CIVIL LIBERTIES UNION. He was an inspirational teacher, a superb scholar, and a loving friend.

In 1963 Murphy reminded scholars, lawyers, and judges of the importance of history in CONSTITUTIONAL INTERPRETATION. He challenged historians to reclaim constitutional history and accord the field its proper place within American history generally and to provide "the most accurate, thoroughly documented, and impeccable history we are capable of producing" to help lawyers and judges build "a new order seeking a new level of equal rights and social justice through law." Murphy set the example with his own scholarship. His books include *The Constitution in Crisis Times, 1918–1969* (1972); *The Meaning of Freedom of Speech: First Amendment Freedoms from Wilson to FDR* (1972), which won the ABA's Silver Gavel Award; and *World War I and the Origin of Civil Liberties in the United States* (1979). With James Morton Smith, he edited a document collection, *Liberty and Justice,* long regarded as a standard text in United States constitutional history. Murphy also published numerous articles, essays, and reviews in professional journals, law reviews, and book chapters on such diverse subjects as POLITICAL PARTIES, Native American rights, the Passaic Textile Strike of 1926, various BILL OF RIGHTS guarantees, and judges.

Murphy's scholarship, like his teaching, was interdisciplinary. His approach emphasized the importance of social, economic, political, and cultural contexts in which constitutional cases arise and judicial decisions are made. Through prodigious research in remarkably wide-ranging materials, which he synthesized into crisp narrative, Murphy explained changing legal DOCTRINE within the evolving social, economic, and political structures of twentieth-century America. Political activists, minorities, social and political elites, public interest groups, economic and social organizations, business institutions, professional associations, and academics play important roles in shaping public attitudes toward CIVIL LIBERTIES and individual rights, which, in turn, affect judicial outcomes. As a scholar and an academic, Murphy embodied the best of the American liberal tradition. A student and custodian of the FIRST AMENDMENT, a sacred article of his personal constitution, Murphy championed the role of law in securing individual freedom, justice, and equality.

ROBERT J. KACZOROWSKI
(2000)

Bibliography
MURPHY, PAUL L. 1963 Time To Reclaim: The Current Challenge of American Constitutional History. *American Historical Review* 69:64–79.
———— 1972 *The Constitution in Crisis Times, 1918–1969.* New York: Harper & Row.
———— 1972 *The Meaning of Freedom of Speech: First Amendment Freedoms From Wilson to FDR.* Westport, Conn.: Greenwood Press (Winner of the American Bar Association Gavel Award).
———— 1979 *World War I and The Origin of Civil Liberties in the United States.* New York: W.W. Norton.

MURPHY v. FLORIDA
421 U.S. 794 (1975)

Jack "Murph the Surf" Murphy appealed a Florida robbery conviction. He claimed that he was denied a FAIR TRIAL because the jurors learned about his previous robbery and murder convictions, and about the circumstances of the instant case, from newspaper reports. The Supreme Court, 8–1, sustained his conviction.

Speaking through Justice THURGOOD MARSHALL, the Court held that juror exposure to information concerning the accused does not presumptively deny DUE PROCESS OF LAW. Since the VOIR DIRE did not discover juror hostility and there was no inflamed community sentiment, the totality of circumstances did not show inherent or actual prejudice.

DENNIS J. MAHONEY
(1986)

(SEE ALSO: *Free Press/Fair Trial.*)

MURPHY v. FORD
390 F. Supp. 1372 (1975)

On September 8, 1974, President GERALD R. FORD granted to his predecessor, RICHARD M. NIXON, a "full, free and absolute pardon . . . for all offenses" that he might have committed while President. A Michigan lawyer brought suit in federal District Court for a DECLARATORY JUDGMENT invalidating the pardon. The District Court judge dismissed the suit, holding that the PARDONING POWER is unlimited, except in cases of IMPEACHMENT, and may as properly be exercised before criminal proceedings begin as after conviction. Citing THE FEDERALIST, the judge argued that the intention of the Framers in establishing the pardoning power was to provide for just such instances.

DENNIS J. MAHONEY
(1986)

(SEE ALSO: *Articles of Impeachment of Richard M. Nixon; Watergate and the Constitution.*)

MURPHY v. WATERFRONT COMMISSION OF N.Y. HARBOR

See: Two Sovereignties Rule

MURRAY, WILLIAM
(Lord Mansfield)
(1705–1793)

The leading Tory constitutionalist of the eighteenth century, William Murray was appointed a judge after a career as a barrister and parliamentarian and service as attorney general. As Baron (later Earl) Mansfield, he was Lord Chief Justice of the Court of King's Bench from 1756 until 1788. He was active in the debates of the House of Lords and served for fifteen years in the cabinet. He opposed repeal of the Stamp Act in 1766, arguing that since the colonists were virtually represented in Parliament their complaints of TAXATION WITHOUT REPRESENTATION were without merit. Mansfield was a firm advocate of coercion in dealing with America, and he was the author of the Quebec Act of 1775.

In the WILKES CASES of 1763–1770 he held GENERAL WARRANTS illegal. He was tolerant of religious deviance and disapproved of prosecution of either Roman Catholic recusants or Protestant dissenters. In SOMERSET'S CASE (1772) he freed an escaped slave who had been recaptured in England, ruling that slavery was too odious to be supported by COMMON LAW. In SEDITIOUS LIBEL cases he allowed the jury to decide only the fact of publication, reserving the question of law—whether the published words were libelous—to be decided by the judge.

DENNIS J. MAHONEY
(1986)

MURRAY'S LESSEE v. HOBOKEN LAND & IMPROVEMENT COMPANY
18 Howard 272 (1856)

This case raised the question whether an act of Congress provided DUE PROCESS OF LAW in the proceedings it laid down for exacting payments due to the treasury by collectors of the customs. For the first time the Supreme Court expounded the meaning of due process of law, which limited all branches of government. The Court interpreted due process exclusively in terms of PROCEDURAL DUE PROCESS. The settled usages and modes of proceedings in English law, "before the emigration of our ancestors," that were not unsuited to the civil and political conditions of America constituted due process.

LEONARD W. LEVY
(1986)

MUSKRAT v. UNITED STATES
219 U.S. 346 (1911)

In one of a series of TEST CASES, the Court here refused to hear the suits involved because the parties failed to meet the constitutional requirement of CASES OR CONTROVERSIES (Article III, section 2). Congress had authorized certain Indians to sue the United States in the COURT OF CLAIMS and directed the ATTORNEY GENERAL to defend. The object

was to determine the validity of certain congressional acts regarding Indian lands. The Court dismissed the suits, denying that Congress had the authority to create a case and designate parties to it.

DAVID GORDON
(1986)

(SEE ALSO: *Ashwander v. Tennessee Valley Authority; Collusive Suit.*)

"MUST CARRY" LAW

The development of the cable television industry has revolutionized the way most Americans watch television. Until the 1960s, television signals were broadcast through the air into people's homes and picked up by receivers in the television sets. Such signals used the electromagnetic spectrum, which has limited frequencies, and could only travel relatively short distances. Because of these technological limitations, Congress, through the Federal Communications Commission, claimed the power to regulate BROADCASTING in order to license and control the use of the limited number of frequencies or "channels" and to impose certain content restrictions and public interest obligations on the broadcasters given those licenses.

Because of the short range of broadcast signals, viewers could only receive programs transmitted by local broadcasting "stations," and people in remote areas got very poor signal reception. Cable television fundamentally changed the picture. First, cable transmits video signals through fiberoptic cables, not electromagnetic frequencies, and thus has the capacity to carry dozens, if not hundreds, of different channels at one time. Second, by transmitting their signals through cable wires, rather than through the air, cable operators can easily send their programs to distant places.

Initially, cable was used primarily to improve reception of broadcast stations in crowded urban or remote rural areas. But because of the large number of channels a cable station could transmit, the cable industry developed a large number of new sources of programming, and hundreds of new cable networks, such as Nickelodeon, The Discovery Channel, and Cable News Network (CNN), were created. Because of better reception and wider programming, cable soon became the source of transmission of programming to approximately 60 percent of the households in America.

Broadcasters felt threatened by this new source of programming and, more importantly, by the control that cable operators had over the broadcasters' ability to reach their audience. The broadcasters were dependent on cable operators to carry their programs over cable wires into homes that had switched to cable. Yet, the broadcasters were in competition with the cable industry over channels and programming. What was to keep the local cable company from refusing to carry the local broadcasting stations in order to enhance the market for the new cable networks and programs? And, if broadcasters were forced out of business, they argued, that would reduce the diversity of programming, and also harm the 40 percent of the American families that did not subscribe to cable. Cable operators had a "chokehold" over broadcasters and television programming.

At the urging of the broadcast industry and others, Congress passed the Cable Television Consumer Protection and Competition Act of 1992. That law mandated that all cable operators had to carry a reasonable number or percentage of "local commercial television stations" and local "noncommercial educational television stations" among the channels on their cable systems. The larger the number of channels, the more broadcast stations the system had to carry. Overall, the result was that approximately one-third of the channels on any cable system had to be made available for use by local commercial or noncommercial broadcast stations.

These "must carry" rules were challenged as violating the FIRST AMENDMENT rights of cable operators and programmers. But in a 1994 ruling, TURNER BROADCASTING SYSTEM V. FCC, the Supreme Court held that those rules were constitutional.

JOEL M. GORA
(2000)

Bibliography

MASETH, MICHAEL W. 1995 Comment: The Erosion of First Amendment Protections of Speech and Press: The "Must Carry" Provisions of the 1992 Cable Act. *Capital University Law Review* 24:423–456.

MEYERSON, MICHAEL I. 1995 Authors, Editors, and Uncommon Carriers: Identifying the "Speaker" Within the New Media. *Notre Dame Law Review* 71:79–125.

SYMPOSIUM 1997 Telecommunications Law: Unscrambling the Signals, Unbundling the Laws. *Columbia Law Review* 97:819–1201.

MYERS v. UNITED STATES
272 U.S. 52 (1926)

An 1876 statute authorized presidential appointment and removal of postmasters with the ADVICE AND CONSENT of the SENATE. (See APPOINTING AND REMOVAL POWER.) President WOODROW WILSON appointed Myers with Senate consent but later removed him without consulting that body. Myers filed suit in the COURT OF CLAIMS and appealed that court's adverse decision to the Supreme Court.

Chief Justice, and former President, WILLIAM HOWARD TAFT, in a broad construction of Article II, found the statute unconstitutional. For a 6–3 majority he insisted upon the necessity for the nation's chief executive officer to be able to remove subordinates freely: "To hold otherwise would make it impossible for the President . . . to take care that the laws be faithfully executed."

Justices OLIVER WENDELL HOLMES, JAMES C. MCREYNOLDS, and LOUIS D. BRANDEIS dissented. Brandeis declared that implying an unrestricted power of removal from the power of appointment "involved an unnecessary and indefensible limitation upon the constitutional power of Congress." History and present state practice demonstrated "a decided tendency to limit" the executive's removal power, and he also cited the DOCTRINES of CHECKS AND BALANCES and the SEPARATION OF POWERS.

The Court limited the doctrinal reach of *Myers* in HUMPHREY'S EXECUTOR V. UNITED STATES (1935).

DAVID GORDON
(1986)

NAACP v. ALABAMA
357 U.S. 449 (1958)

In this decision the Supreme Court first recognized a FREEDOM OF ASSOCIATION guaranteed by the FIRST AMENDMENT. Alabama, charging that the NAACP had failed to qualify as an out-of-state CORPORATION, had sought an INJUNCTION preventing the association from doing business in the state. In that proceeding, the state obtained an order that the NAACP produce a large number of its records. The association substantially complied, but refused to produce its membership lists. The trial court ruled the NAACP in contempt and fined it $100,000. The state supreme court denied review, and the U.S. Supreme Court unanimously reversed.

Justice JOHN MARSHALL HARLAN wrote for the Court. First, the NAACP had STANDING to assert its members' claims; to rule otherwise would be to require an individual member to forfeit his or her political privacy in the act of claiming it. On the constitutional merits, Harlan wrote: "Effective advocacy . . . is undeniably enhanced by group association"; thus "state action which may have the effect of curtailing the freedom to associate is subject to the closest scrutiny." The privacy of association may be a necessary protection for the freedom to associate "where a group espouses dissident beliefs." Here, disclosure of NAACP membership in Alabama during a time of vigorous civil rights activity had been shown to result in members' being fired from their jobs, physically threatened, and otherwise harassed. Only a COMPELLING STATE INTEREST could justify this invasion of political privacy. That compelling interest was not shown here. The names of the NAACP's rank-and-file members had no substantial bearing on the state's interest in assuring compliance with its corporation law.

This same technique—solemnly accepting the state's account of its purposes, ignoring possible improper motives, and concluding that those state interests were not "compelling"—was employed in other cases involving efforts by southern states to force disclosures of NAACP membership such as *Bates v. Little Rock* (1960) and *Shelton v. Tucker* (1960).

KENNETH L. KARST
(1986)

(SEE ALSO: *Gibson v. Florida Legislative Investigation Commission.*)

NAACP v. BUTTON
371 U.S. 415 (1962)

The Supreme Court held that Virginia statutes forbidding one person to advise another that his legal rights had been violated and to refer him to a particular attorney were unconstitutional as applied to activities of the NAACP and its legal defense fund. The furtherance of litigation designed to challenge the constitutionality of RACIAL DISCRIMINATION was a mode of expression and association protected by the FIRST and FOURTEENTH AMENDMENTS. The Court acknowledged that INTEREST GROUP LITIGATION, aimed at changing constitutional law through TEST CASES, was not only professional legal activity subject to state regulation but also constitutionally protected political activity.

MARTIN SHAPIRO
(1986)

NAACP v. CLAIBORNE HARDWARE COMPANY

See: Labor and the Constitution

NAACP LEGAL DEFENSE & EDUCATIONAL FUND

The NAACP Legal Defense & Educational Fund, Inc., was founded in 1939 by board members of the National Association for the Advancement of Colored People to conduct the legal program of the association through a corporation qualified to receive tax deductible contributions. The association was not tax exempt, because it lobbied. Board members of the association served on the board of the Fund; the Fund's director and some of its lawyers also were employees of the association.

In 1957 the Internal Revenue Service (IRS) objected to the interlocking staff and board because it enabled an organization not tax exempt to influence one entitled to tax exemption. The IRS required termination of the interlocking arrangement. Thereafter the Fund and the association were no longer formally linked, and the Fund functioned entirely independently with its own board, staff, budget, and policies. The Fund has since represented individuals and organizations with no relationship to the association at all as well as members and branches of the association.

In 1984 the Fund's staff consisted of twenty-four lawyers, with offices in New York and Washington, D.C., and several hundred cooperating lawyers across the United States. Its budget was $6.7 million. It has served as a model for the public interest law movement generally, including other legal defense funds, such as those dealing with discrimination against Hispanics, Asians, women, the handicapped, homosexuals, and the aged, as well as public interest firms representing environmental, consumer, migrant worker, and other groups.

The Fund's director-counsel was THURGOOD MARSHALL, who served until 1961 and was succeeded by Jack Greenberg, who directed the organization until 1984, when he was succeeded by Julius L. Chambers. The Fund has been involved in most of the leading cases dealing with racial discrimination in the United States, including BROWN V. BOARD OF EDUCATION (1954), which held unconstitutional racial SEGREGATION in public education, the principle of which was ultimately extended to all other governmental activities. *Brown* was the culmination of a planned litigation effort which built upon earlier Fund cases involving RACIAL DISCRIMINATION in graduate and professional schools. In the 1960s, the Fund provided representation in most of the cases generated by the CIVIL RIGHTS movement, including representation of MARTIN LUTHER KING, JR., Thereafter, following passage of the Civil Rights Acts of the mid-1960s, the Fund brought most of the leading cases enforcing those laws. The Fund has represented civil rights claimants in more than 2,000 cases dealing with education, employment, VOTING RIGHTS, housing, CAPITAL PUNISHMENT, health care, and other areas of the law.

JACK GREENBERG
(1986)

Bibliography

RABIN, ROBERT L. 1976 Lawyers for Social Change: Perspectives on Public Interest Law. *Stanford Law Journal* 28:207–261.

NAFTA

See: North American Free Trade Agreement

NARCOTICS REGULATION

See: Drug Regulation

NARDONE v. UNITED STATES
302 U.S. 379 (1937)

After the Supreme Court largely exempted ELECTRONIC EAVESDROPPING from constitutional control in OLMSTEAD V. UNITED STATES (1928), protection against WIRETAPPING was sought legislatively. In 1934, Congress passed the COMMUNICATIONS ACT, section 605 of which provided that "no person" could intercept and divulge radio and wire communications. In *Nardone v. United States* the Supreme Court ruled that section 605 extended to federal agents; later the Court applied it also to state officers in *Benanti v. United States* (1957). The Justice Department construed section 605 very narrowly, however, and it was rarely invoked. It has been largely superseded by Title III of the OMNIBUS CRIME CONTROL AND SAFE STREETS ACT (1968).

HERMAN SCHWARTZ
(1986)

NASHVILLE CONVENTION RESOLUTIONS
(1850)

Fearing that Congress might enact the WILMOT PROVISO, abolish the slave trade in the DISTRICT OF COLUMBIA, or adopt other antislavery measures, southern separatists called for a convention of slave states to meet at Nashville in June 1850. The convention adopted resolutions asserting that: the TERRITORIES were the joint property of the people of all the states; Congress could not discriminate among owners of different kinds of property in the territories, and hence could not exclude slaves; and the federal government must protect all forms of property, including slaves, in the territories. However, the moderates who dominated the convention added that if the free states refused to recognize these principles, the slave states would accept a division of the territories by extending the MISSOURI COMPROMISE line to the Pacific, an extraordinary concession on the central constitutional issue that disgusted the radicals. A poorly attended adjourned session of the convention, dominated by radicals, met in November 1850, denounced the COMPROMISE OF 1850, advocated SECESSION, but proposed no immediate program. The resolutions of the Nashville Convention are thus significant principally as an indication of the slave states' inability to unite on a secessionist platform.

WILLIAM M. WIECEK
(1986)

(SEE ALSO: *Slavery and the Constitution*.)

Bibliography

POTTER, DAVID M. 1976 *The Impending Crisis, 1848–1861*. New York: Harper & Row.

NATIONAL ASSOCIATION FOR THE ADVANCEMENT OF COLORED PEOPLE

See: NAACP Legal Defense & Educational Fund

NATIONAL EMERGENCIES ACT

See: Emergency Powers

NATIONAL ENDOWMENT FOR THE ARTS v. FINLEY

See: First Amendment; Freedom of Speech; Public Forum

NATIONAL ENVIRONMENTAL POLICY ACT

See: Environmental Regulation and the Constitution

NATIONAL INDUSTRIAL RECOVERY ACT
48 Stat. 195 (1933)

The National Industrial Recovery Act (NIRA) was the best-known and, perhaps, in President FRANKLIN D. ROOSEVELT's words, "the most important and far-reaching legislation ever enacted" by the NEW DEAL Congress. The act was designed to curb unemployment, stimulate business recovery, and end the competitive wars of the Great Depression. By May 1935, over 750 codes covering some twenty-three million people had been created under the NIRA's authority. Even before Roosevelt's inauguration, his "brain trust" had begun to plan a recovery bill. Introduced May 17, 1933, the bill raised questions of constitutionality. Congress passed it, however, and Roosevelt signed it into law on June 16.

The act declared a national emergency and justified congressional action under the COMMERCE CLAUSE and the GENERAL WELFARE CLAUSE. Section 2 established the National Recovery Administration (NRA) to supervise the NIRA, limiting its operation to two years. The heart of the act, section 3, provided for the framing of "codes of fair competition" by private businessmen and trade associations. After meeting certain requirements and obtaining presidential approval, these codes became "standards of fair competition" with the full force of federal law, regulating industrywide prices, wages, and practices. Such an extraordinary DELEGATION OF POWER was unprecedented: it allowed private citizens to draft codes to rule industry and provided, at best, minimal policy guidelines and standards. Violations of the codes "in any transaction in or affecting INTERSTATE or FOREIGN COMMERCE [were] deemed an unfair method of competition in commerce within the meaning of the FEDERAL TRADE COMMISSION ACT." Upon complaint or failure of an industry to formulate a code, the President could establish a compulsory code. Section 7 prescribed three mandatory provisions for every code: availability of COLLECTIVE BARGAINING, employee freedom from coercion to join or refrain from joining a union, and compliance with regulated MAXIMUM HOURS AND MINIMUM WAGES. The various clauses of this section constituted the broadest regulation of wages and hours in American history to that date. The NRA also incorporated in its "blanket code" a provision outlawing child labor in industries without specific codes. Although the NIRA prohibited monopolies and monopolistic practices, it exempted code-covered industries from the antitrust laws. Title II of the NIRA established a Public Works Administration to stimulate construction and, by spending its $3.3 billion budget, to increase purchasing power.

Serious questions of the act's constitutionality eventually reached the Supreme Court, however, and in SCHECH-TER POULTRY CORP. V. UNITED STATES (1935) a unanimous Court voided the NIRA for unconstitutionally delegating power to the President and exceeding the limits of the commerce power. Despite this decision and PANAMA REFIN-ING COMPANY V. RYAN (1935), invalidating other provisions, Congress gradually replaced the act with new and more effective legislation. Although historians debate whether the NRA impeded or encouraged recovery and reform, the lessons of this experiment in economic planning provided valuable experience for drafting later legislation such as the WAGNER (NATIONAL LABOR RELATIONS) and FAIR LABOR STANDARDS ACTS.

DAVID GORDON
(1986)

Bibliography

LYON, LEVERETT S. et al. 1935 *The National Recovery Admin-istration: An Analysis and Appraisal.* Washington, D.C.: Brookings Institution.

ROOS, CHARLES F. 1937 *NRA Economic Planning.* Blooming-ton: Indiana University Press.

NATIONAL LABOR RELATIONS ACTS

See: Taft-Hartley Labor Relations Act; Wagner Act

NATIONAL LEAGUE OF CITIES v. USERY
426 U.S. 833 (1976)

This case proved that obituaries for DUAL FEDERALISM were premature. It arose after Congress amended the FAIR LA-BOR STANDARDS ACT (FLSA), in 1974, to extend wages-and-hours coverage to nearly all public employees. Several states, cities, and intergovernmental organizations sought to enjoin enforcement of the new provisions. Admitting that the employees in question would come within the federal commerce power if they worked in the private sec-tor, the plaintiffs argued that congressional regulation of employment conditions for state and municipal workers violated "the established constitutional DOCTRINE of IN-TERGOVERNMENTAL IMMUNITY." A three-judge district court disagreed, ruling that under *Maryland v. Wirtz* (1968), which had upheld the application of wages and hours reg-ulations to public schools and hospitals, an employee's public status was irrelevant to the scope of congressional authority. On APPEAL, the Supreme Court reversed the lower court, 5–4, holding that the FLSA amendments

could not constitutionally be applied to public employees performing "traditional governmental functions."

Writing for the Court, Justice WILLIAM H. REHNQUIST initially confronted the sweep of the COMMERCE CLAUSE recognized in GIBBONS V. OGDEN (1824). The grant of congressional power was plenary, he conceded, but did not override "affirmative limitations" on Congress. The TENTH AMENDMENT provided the most explicit source for such a limitation, for in *Fry v. United States* (1975) the Court had offered the dictum that the amendment "expressly de-clared the constitutional policy that Congress may not ex-ercise power in a fashion that impairs the States' integrity or their ability to function effectively in a federal system." Yet Rehnquist emphasized a less explicit limitation—the overall federal structure. Within it, states perform essen-tial governmental functions, and state decisions about these functions, which include fire protection and law en-forcement, must be free from federal interference. Wages and hours legislation constituted a forbidden infringe-ment, because it "operate[s] directly to displace the States' freedom to structure integral operations in areas of tra-ditional governmental functions. . . ." Indeed, he expressly held the Court had wrongly decided *Wirtz.*

But the meaning of *National League of Cities* as pre-cedent is not clear. Justice HARRY A. BLACKMUN qualified his crucial fifth vote with a concurrence that interpreted the Court as "adopt[ing] a balancing approach." For him, the decision did not preclude regulation of states in areas, such as environmental protection, where the federal in-terest was demonstrably greater. And the Court itself ex-pressly left open the power of Congress to regulate even traditional state functions by employing the TAXING AND SPENDING POWER or by enforcing the FOURTEENTH AMEND-MENT. (See FITZPATRICK V. BITZER.)

In dissent, Justice WILLIAM J. BRENNAN charged that the decision contained "an ominous portent of destruction of our constitutional structure" and delivered a "catastrophic body blow" to the commerce power. In his view, Rehn-quist had misread earlier case law and had abandoned the plain meanings of the commerce and SUPREMACY CLAUSES. Moreover, Rehnquist's "essential function test" was "con-ceptually unworkable," for it failed to clarify the distinc-tion between essential and other state activities.

The Court's opinion did lack a reasoned test for deter-mining the essential functions of states "*qua* states." It also ran counter to forty years of judicial acceptance of broad congressional power under the commerce clause. Accord-ingly, *National League of Cities* led to further litigation over state immunity from federal regulation and injected the Supreme Court into issues long dormant. In GARCIA V. SAN ANTONIO METROPOLITAN TRANSIT AUTHORITY (1985) a dif-ferent 5–4 majority flatly overruled *National League of*

Cities, but the dissenters promised that disinterment of the 1976 decision awaited only one more vote.

CHARLES A. LOFGREN
(1986)

Bibliography

BARBER, SOTIRIOS A. 1976 *National League of Cities v. Usery:* New Meaning for the Tenth Amendment? *Supreme Court Review* 1976:161–182.

LOFGREN, CHARLES A. 1980 The Origins of the Tenth Amendment: History, Sovereignty, and the Problem of Constitutional Intention. Pages 331–357 in Ronald K. L. Collins (ed.), *Constitutional Government in America.* Durham, N.C.: Carolina Academic Press.

NAGEL, ROBERT F. 1981 Federalism as a Fundamental Value: *National League of Cities* in Perspective. *Supreme Court Review* 1981:81–109.

NATIONAL POLICE POWER

The "national police power" is not, strictly speaking, a constitutional power of Congress. Rather, it is a phrase describing the power of Congress, acting under the enumerated powers, to enact "police legislation." The term "police legislation" includes criminal law as well as health, morals, safety, antidiscrimination, and environmental statutes.

Under our federal system, national police power regulation has always been controversial. Police matters are historically state or local concerns, and yet some problems seem to call for a national solution. The recurring issues, therefore, are whether Congress should address a problem that has historically been attacked at the state or local level and whether the courts can articulate any principled limits on congressional power to do so.

The Constitution provides a number of sources of power for national police legislation. The most important are the congressional powers to regulate commerce, to tax, and to spend. However, several other powers should not be overlooked. The postal power makes possible laws to protect consumers from fraudulent or obscene materials transmitted through the mails, subject to significant First Amendment limitations. The enabling clauses of the THIRTEENTH and FOURTEENTH AMENDMENTS open the way for a variety of antidiscrimination laws. (See JONES V. ALFRED H. MAYER CO. (1968), racial discrimination in housing; UNITED STATES V. GUEST (1966), violence against minorities in the use of public facilities.)

Because such local activities as manufacturing or gambling are not themselves interstate commerce, they are not, without more, subject to federal commerce clause regulation. However, constitutional developments during the twentieth century have marked out two techniques which, alone or in combination, permit virtually unlimited regulation of local activity under the aegis of the COMMERCE CLAUSE: prohibition of INTERSTATE COMMERCE and linking a local activity to an "effect" on interstate commerce.

A few early statutes prohibited particular forms of interstate commerce (such as transportation of diseased cattle or use of unsafe locomotives) because they physically endangered the stream of commerce. In 1895, however, Congress took a further critical step by prohibiting the interstate transportation of lottery tickets. Transportation of the tickets harmed nobody; Congress was obviously concerned that the use of the tickets in the receiving state was harmful to public morals. Thus the prohibition on transportation really was a technique to assist the states in stamping out national (or international) lotteries. Under traditional assumptions, of course, the regulation of gambling or of consumer fraud was a state responsibility, but individual state regulation of lotteries had proved ineffectual.

In CHAMPION V. AMES (1903), often referred to as "The Lottery Case," the Supreme Court upheld the federal statute by a 5–4 vote. The majority believed that the shipment of articles in interstate commerce that were harmful to the public safety or morals was a "misuse" of commerce, the prohibition of which lay well within the commerce power. This rationale paved the way for many later statutes which treated various goods or persons as "outlaws" of commerce and thus prohibited their shipment. For example, the courts upheld regulation or prohibition of interstate transportation of adulterated food, prostitutes, obscene literature, and stolen cars upon the authority of *Champion.* In addition, the Court upheld statutes banning the interstate shipment of items (such as liquor or goods produced by convict labor) that violated the laws of the receiving state.

In addition to permitting regulation of interstate transportation of goods, *Champion* provided authority for regulation of the use of the goods after they arrived. Finally, although most of the commerce-prohibition cases involved regulation of purely commercial activity, the Court in *Caminetti v. United States* (1917) found no constitutional objection to punishing a man for transporting a woman to whom he was not married across the state lines for immoral, but wholly noncommercial, purposes. (See HOKE V. UNITED STATES.)

The usefulness of the commerce-prohibiting technique suffered a temporary but sharp reverse after Congress decided to use it for the purpose of abolishing child labor. In HAMMER V. DAGENHART (1918) the Supreme Court held that Congress could not prohibit the transportation in interstate commerce of goods made by children, because the goods were lawfully produced in the state of origin and harmless both to interstate commerce and to users in the receiving state. The government tried to show that the law was necessary to achieve fair interstate competition, because states allowing child labor had an unfair advantage over those prohibiting it. The Court said that Congress had no power to equalize comparative advantages or disadvantages among the states.

Justices OLIVER WENDELL HOLMES's dissent in *Hammer* seemingly demolished the majority opinion and ultimately became the law when UNITED STATES V. DARBY overruled *Hammer* in 1941. *Darby* made clear that Congress could prohibit the interstate shipment of harmless goods manufactured by workers whose wages or working hours violated the FAIR LABOR STANDARDS ACT. The Court in *Darby* accepted the theory, rejected by the *Hammer* majority, that Congress could use the commerce-prohibiting technique to improve labor conditions in the state of origin and to achieve fair competition among states. After *Darby*, therefore, there was no longer any obstacle to the achievement of police goals by the prohibition of interstate commerce in people or goods, absent the violation of some other constitutional norm.

In the landmark commerce clause case of GIBBONS V. OGDEN (1824) Chief Justice JOHN MARSHALL seemingly established that a local activity could be regulated by Congress under the commerce clause if the activity "affected" other states. Nevertheless there arose a confusing body of case law on the extent to which local affairs could be regulated because of their effect on interstate commerce. On the one hand, for example, the Shreveport case, HOUSTON, EAST AND WEST TEXAS RAILWAY V. UNITED STATES (1914), allowed the Interstate Commerce Commission to regulate intrastate railroad rates because low rates for intrastate hauls and high rates for interstate hauls unfairly discriminated against interstate commerce. On the other hand, early antitrust cases, including UNITED STATES V. E. C. KNIGHT CO. (1895), cast doubt on Congress's power to regulate monopolies in manufacturing because manufacturing was considered local; the Court evidently assumed that granting regulatory power to the national government would prevent the states from regulating the activity.

In several cases during the 1930s, narrow majorities of the Supreme Court invalidated New Deal legislation that sought to regulate local activity affecting interstate commerce (such as labor relations in coal mining in CARTER V. CARTER COAL CO., 1936). By the late 1930s, however, these cases had been disapproved. By the time of WICKARD V. FILBURN (1942) there was no longer any dobt that Congress had power to regulate purely local and individually trivial activities which (when cumulated) substatially affected in-

terstate commerce. In that case the Court ruled that Congress could regulate home consumption of wheat because of its aggregate effect on an inerstate market.

Thus the "affecting commerce" rationale was available when Congress turned to national police legislation. The Fair Labor Standards Act not only prohibited interstate transportation of goods manufactured by persons whose wages or hours violated the act; it also directly prohibited the production of such goods for interstate commerce. *United States v. Darby* upheld the manufacturing prohibition on two distinct theories. The Court held that manufacturing could be prohibited (even if transportation had not been prohibited) because production of goods under substandard labor conditions was a form of unfair competition that substantially affected interstate commerce. In addition, the Court upheld the manufacturing ban as a necessary and proper incident of Congress's power to prohibit interstate transportation of the goods. This latter theory opened the way for Congress to ban virtually any local activity if it also bans interstate transportation of the persons who conduct the activity or the goods produced by it.

Congress has frequently resorted to the "affecting commerce" rationale when it pursues fundamentally noneconomic objectives. The Court has generously upheld federal statutes upon determining that Congress has "rationally" concluded that a local activity substantially affected commerce. For example, the Court upheld in KATZENBACH V. MCCLUNG (1964) a federal prohibition on racial discrimination, as applied to a restaurant that had purchased food from a local seller who had purchased it in interstate commerce. The Court's tenuous theory was that Congress could rationally conclude that discrimination in such restaurants decreased interstate sales of food. (See HEART OF ATLANTA V. UNITED STATES.)

The "affecting commerce" rationale has opened the way for a vast expansion of federal criminal law. In PEREZ V. UNITED STATES (1971) the Court upheld a conviction under the federal loan-sharking statute, even though the defendant had no apparent contact with interstate commerce. In previous cases, such as *Katzenbach v. McClung*, the characteristic used to identify the regulated party had a connection to interstate commerce, but in *Perez*, the characteristic ("loan-sharking") had no such connection. However, the Court deferred to congressional findings that loan-sharking is used by multistate organized crime rings to raise or launder money to take over legitimate businesses. It then held that because loansharks as a "class" substantially affect interstate commerce, any member of the class can be reached by a federal criminal statute, regardless of the individual's actual interstate connections. Of course, this approach is drastically overinclusive, but it is justifiable because it is difficult to ascertain in a given case whether a particular loanshark has connections to organized crime and thus to interstate commerce. The *Perez* theory that Congress can criminalize an entire class, when some members of that class substantially affect interstate commerce, undergirds several other federal racketeering, gambling, and drug abuse statutes. (See LAW ENFORCEMENT AND FEDERAL-STATE RELATIONS.)

The "prohibiting commerce" and the "affecting commerce" techniques, used separately or together, thus provide the authority for virtually limitless expansion of national police power. Given only slight ingenuity in statute-drafting, a local activity which Congress wishes to regulate or prohibit can be linked somehow to interstate commerce.

Nevertheless, the Court has employed a number of low-visibility judicial techniques to slow the federalization of police power. It has frequently construed narrowly statutes that make unexpected intrusions into local domains, reasoning that Congress should clearly state its intention to expand national police power. Moreover, in construing federal criminal statutes, the Court takes into account its view of an appropriate balance between state and federal law enforcement. These constructional techniques require Congress at least to face and consider the implications of a drastic extension of federal power. Similarly, the Court may hold that an ambiguous criminal statute fails to give fair warning to those affected by it if a broad construction would punish essentially local activity.

In considering congressional police power under the commerce clause, the most important open question is whether a majority of the Supreme Court will hold that a "trivial" effect on interstate commerce is an insufficient foundation. A number of Justices have written that questions of degree are important to them and that the cumulative effect on commerce of the class of regulated activities must be "substantial." In several cases involving federal stripmining legislation, for example, including HODEL V. VIRGINIA SURFACE MINING AND RECLAMATION ASSOCIATION and *Hodel v. Indiana* (1981), the court unanimously upheld statutes which regulated stripmining on steep slopes and on farmland against claims that land use control is a uniquely local function. The Court found that Congress had acted rationally in identifying the environmental effects of stripmining as substantial burdens on interstate commerce and that the means chosen by Congress were rational. Two Justices wrote separately to emphasize that their concurrence was based on the substantiality of the effect. In the past, other Justices have expressed similar reservations. If a majority of the Supreme Court were actually to assess the substantiality of the effect on commerce of the class of regulated activities before upholding a statute, it would be much less clear than it seems today that the Constitution imposes no effective limit on the national police power under the commerce clause.

By using its power to tax an activity, Congress can discourage, regulate, or prohibit the activity. Consequently, a power intended to furnish Congress with the means for raising revenue can be effectively employed for police purposes. Occasional taxpayers have contended that a so-called tax is really regulatory in purpose and effect, and consequently not a tax at all. In early cases, such as UNITED STATES V. DOREMUS (1919), the Court upheld tax statutes with patently obvious regulatory goals, taking the tax label at face value. The court turned a blind eye to the fact that the tax would destroy the taxed business, that it produced little or no revenue, or that its administrative provisions were inappropriate for tax collection.

However, when Congress sought to prohibit child labor by taxing income from the sale of products made by children, the Court rebelled. In BAILEY V. DREXEL FURNITURE CO. (1922) it concluded that the tax was actually a regulatory measure, for it provided for a tax of ten percent on annual net income if the taxpayer knowingly used child labor on even a single occasion. Thus, said the Court, Congress had used the taxing power as a pretext for an attempt to regulate manufacturing—something it had previously held beyond Congress's power.

Ultimately, the court abandoned any effort to distinguish taxation from regulation. In upholding the federal gambling tax, which obviously was intended to stamp out illegal gambling rather than to raise revenue, the Court noted that a federal tax is valid even though it may destroy the taxed activity, raises little revenue, and contains enforcement provisions more appropriate to a criminal statute than a tax provision. In *United States v. Kahriger* (1953), decided over a strong dissent by Justice FELIX FRANKFURTER, the Court held that unless the tax law contains penalty or administrative provisions "extraneous to any tax need," it is valid.

The Court later limited its *Kahriger* precedent. MARCHETTI V. UNITED STATES (1968) held that the registration requirement for gamblers entailed coerced self-incrimination, in violation of the Fifth Amendment. Nevertheless, unless a tax runs afoul of a specific provision of the Bill of Rights, it seems unlikely that the Court will ever again seek to patrol the troubled border between taxation and regulation. There is little need for the distinction, now that virtually any activity it seeks to regulate through taxation could be easily reached through the commerce power.

Through its power to spend for the general welfare,

Congress can enlist state or private cooperation in achieving an endless list of regulatory goals. All it needs to do is place conditions on offers of federal money. If the offer is sufficiently generous, the recipients are virtually certain to accept the conditions.

In the 1930s the Supreme Court made a doomed attempt to limit the traditional practice of regulation through conditional grants. It held that a federal program of payments to farmers, upon condition that they contractually agree to limit their acreage, was an invalid attempt to regulate agriculture and thus an incursion into a matter left to the states. In UNITED STATES V. BUTLER (1936) it declared that Congress could not purchase submission to a regulation that it could not impose directly.

The *Butler* prohibition on conditional spending lasted only a year. The SOCIAL SECURITY ACT contained a joint federal-state taxing and spending program to pay unemployment compensation. To induce the states to participate, Congress imposed a payroll tax on employers. However, a taxpayer received a credit of ninety percent of the federal tax if its state levied a payroll tax and adopted a system for distributing benefits that complied with the federal statute. As a practical matter, this credit, which had the effect of a federal expenditure, required states to participate in the program. Nevertheless, the court upheld that statute in STEWARD MACHINE COMPANY V. DAVIS (1937), approving the concept of "cooperative federalism" and declaring that no state was coerced into adopting an unemployment compensation system. However, the Court indicated that it might have some doubts if the federal law imposed conditions that were unreasonable or unrelated in subject matter to legitimate national objectives or entailed surrender by states of quasi-sovereign powers.

Since *Steward Machine*, the Court has consistently upheld conditional spending programs in the few cases that have raised the issue. For example, in *Oklahoma v. Civil Service Commission* (1947) it sustained a system of conditional highway construction grants to states. A recipient state had to consent to a provision in the HATCH ACT precluding administration by any person involved in political campaigns. Because the state was free to reject federal funding, no coercion was involved.

Conditional federal grants have been used to achieve a wide variety of federal police objectives, particularly in the areas of environmental protection, affirmative action, education, and health services. However, in PENNHURST STATE SCHOOL V. HALDERMAN (1981) the Court sounded a warning. If a state is to be bound by a condition on its receipt of federal funds, the condition must be unambiguously stated in the statute. Otherwise, a state's acceptance might not have been knowing and voluntary. Like the requirement that Congress make a clear statement that it intends a criminal statute to reach an essentially local activity, the clear statement rule of *Pennhurst* requires Congress to focus on the issue of federalism when it adopts a conditional spending program.

Congress has ample power to achieve national police power objectives. The commerce clause, the postal, taxing, and spending power, and the enabling clauses of the Thirteenth and Fourteenth Amendments furnish authority for almost any conceivable expansion of national regulatory jurisdiction. However, the Court has suggested (sometimes in OBITER DICTUM) potential limitations on these powers which might someday be invoked to constrain an extension of federal authority.

Much more important than any judicially imposed limits are the political constraints on the national police power. Various structural elements of the national government assure sympathetic treatment for arguments based on federalism; for example, states opposing federal intrusion are protected by the fact that each state has two senators (regardless of population). Among other factors, state legislative control over House districting and the state-oriented organization of national political parties also assure respectful treatment for state or local contentions that extension offederal regulation is unnecessary. Similarly, the selection of the President by the Electoral College emphasizes the importance of states. The powerful representation of states at the national level, the tradition that police regulation is performed at the state level, and the inertia of Congress all work together to assure that intrusions by the national government into matters of state concern are likely to occur only when a broad national consensus emerges that centralization is necessary.

MICHAEL ASIMOW
(1986)

Bibliography

CUSHMAN, ROBERT E. 1919 National Police Power under the Commerce Clause of the Constitution. *Minnesota Law Review* 3:289–319, 381–412, 452–483.

——— 1920 National Police Power under the Postal Power of the Constitution. *Minnesota Law Review* 4:402–440.

KADEN, LEWIS B. 1979 Politics, Money and State Sovereignty: The Judicial Role. *Columbia Law Review* 79:847–897.

STERN, ROBERT L. 1973 The Commerce Clause Revisited: Federalization of Intrastate Crime. *Arizona Law Review* 15:271–285.

WECHSLER, HERBERT 1954 The Political Safeguards of Federalism: The Role of the States in the Composition and Selection of the National Government. *Columbia Law Review* 54:543–560.

NATIONAL PROHIBITION CASES

See: Amending Process; Eighteenth Amendment

NATIONAL SECURITY ACT
69 Stat. 495 (1947)

This act embodies the most comprehensive reorganization ever undertaken of the means by which the WAR POWERS are to be exercised. The act unified the command of the armed forces, officially organized the Joint Chiefs of Staff, created the Air Force department, and established the office of secretary of defense. The separate army and navy establishments recognized in the Constitution, together with the air force, became a single, permanent "National Military Establishment."

Furthermore, the act erected, within the executive branch, the National Security Council. The original intention of Congress seems to have been to constrict the President's freedom of action in defense and FOREIGN AFFAIRS by prescribing the persons to be consulted and the manner of consultation in national security decision making. In fact, however, strong and politically skillful Presidents have used the council to strengthen their own positions, as, for example, President JOHN F. KENNEDY did during the Cuban missile crisis of 1962.

Under the National Security Council the act created the Central Intelligence Agency (CIA), with a broad charter to conduct foreign intelligence-gathering activities, as well as to process and disseminate intelligence gathered by other agencies. The act specifically prohibited domestic intelligence activities on the part of the CIA.

DENNIS J. MAHONEY
(1986)

NATIONAL SECURITY AND THE FOURTH AMENDMENT

The right to individual privacy and the preservation of national security have jarred against each other for centuries. "National security cases . . . often reflect a convergence of First and FOURTH AMENDMENT values not present in cases of 'ordinary' crime," wrote Justice LEWIS F. POWELL for a unanimous Supreme Court in UNITED STATES V. UNITED STATES DISTRICT COURT (1972). The early English cases, such as the WILKES CASES (1763–1770), establishing the right to keep the government out of a home unless it has PROBABLE CAUSE and a judicially approved warrant to enter, arose from successful challenges by political dissidents to searches by royal officers hunting for seditious writings. Preventing such infringements on both personal security and free expression was the main purpose of the Fourth Amendment. Today, Presidents claim inherent executive power to break into homes, to make physical SEARCHES AND SEIZURES, to open mail, and to video-tape, WIRETAP, and bug—again in order to protect national security.

Where the surveillance is directed against national security threats by *domestic* groups or individuals, the Supreme Court has held that the President has no inherent executive power, and a warrant must first be obtained. The government's needs will not be presumed to outweigh the threats such a power poses for the rights of free speech and personal security; rather, a search against domestic threats must be approved in advance by a neutral magistrate. The Court did suggest that Congress could authorize less stringent procedures for domestic intelligence gathering than for crime detection, but so far Congress has not done so.

Foreign national security issues have been treated very differently. Courts have generally accepted the claim of inherent presidential power to use electronic surveillance, video-tapes, and physical entries against both foreigners and Americans in order to obtain foreign intelligence, without obtaining prior judicial approval. The power is justified on several grounds: the need for stealth, speed, and secrecy to counter foreign threats; the executive's superior experience and knowledge of FOREIGN AFFAIRS and the judiciary's relative lack of competence in such matters; and the executive's primacy in foreign affairs in the constitutional scheme. This power is limited to intelligence gathering, so that when the investigation becomes a criminal investigation and the warrantless interception is made for the purpose of gathering evidence for a prosecution, the requirements of Title III of the OMNIBUS CRIME CONTROL AND SAFE STREETS ACT must be satisfied. This inherent intelligence gathering power, moreover, can be exercised only by the President or the attorney general; a lower-level official cannot authorize intelligence-gathering break-ins or wiretaps on his own, without judicial approval.

In 1976, a Senate committee issued a massive documentation of the many abuses of Fourth Amendment rights perpetrated by executive officers and the intelligence agencies from the 1930s through the 1970s. The Central Intelligence Agency, for example, admitted wiretapping people it considered "left-wingers" both in this country and abroad in a project it called "Operation Chaos," even though the agency had no authority to operate domestically. It was trying to find links between antiwar groups and foreign powers, which were never found. The military eavesdropped on radio messages in the late 1960s and early 1970s in connection with civil disorders, with full knowledge that such eavesdropping was illegal. In 1969, President RICHARD M. NIXON authorized taps on four journalists and thirteen government employees, allegedly to discover who was leaking foreign affairs information; these taps were kept in operation for over two years even though it quickly became clear that nothing pertinent to the leaks was being learned.

In reaction to these revelations and to the Watergate

abuses, Congress in 1978 banned electronic surveillance for foreign national security purposes within the United States, without prior judicial approval. Under the Foreign Intelligence Surveillance Act (FISA) the executive branch no longer has inherent power to tap and bug for foreign intelligence-gathering purposes. With the approval of the attorney general, a federal official may apply to a specially selected court (composed of regular federal judges) which sits in secret. The court must issue a warrant if it finds probable cause to believe, first, that the target is a foreign power or agent, and, second, that certain procedures to minimize the interception have been set up; an American who, on behalf of a foreign power, engages in clandestine intelligence gathering that may involve criminal activity, may be considered a foreign agent, though not for activities protected by the FIRST AMENDMENT. Other control procedures are also established, though they are less stringent than those for electronic surveillance for crime detection under Title III. The FISA applies to foreign intelligence gathering by any type of electronic, mechanical, or other surveillance device, but not to physical break-ins, mail openings, and the like—these remain subject to the more traditional claims of inherent presidential power.

Although the FISA was held constitutional by a federal district court, there is still no definitive Supreme Court ruling on the existence of inherent executive power to break into homes for foreign national security purposes or to eavesdrop on Americans without a warrant.

HERMAN SCHWARTZ
(1986)

Bibliography

CARR, JAMES G.   1977 (1981 supp.)   *The Law of Electronic Surveillance.* New York: Clark Boardman.

SCHWARTZ, HERMAN   1977   *Taps, Bugs, and Fooling the People.* New York: Field Foundation.

UNITED STATES, CONGRESS, SENATE SELECT COMMITTEE TO STUDY GOVERNMENTAL OPERATIONS WITH RESPECT TO INTELLIGENCE ACTIVITIES   1976   *III Final Report.* 94th Congress, 2d session.

NATIONAL TREASURY EMPLOYEES UNION, UNITED STATES v.
513 U.S. 454 (1995)

The U.S. Congress in 1989 prohibited federal employees from receiving any compensation for any outside speeches or articles. In challenging the statute's constitutionality, the National Treasury Employees Union condemned the law's broad sweep, noting that postal workers were banned from accepting fees for lectures on religion and federal scientists could not supplement their income by writing

dance reviews. The Supreme Court, by a 6–3 vote, agreed that the statute violated the FREEDOM OF SPEECH rights of federal employees below the level of GS-16, but left questions concerning upper-level federal employees unanswered.

The MAJORITY OPINION, authored by Justice JOHN PAUL STEVENS, emphasized the public interest in permitting federal employees to speak on matters of public concern, and the ways in which bans on compensation might chill such speech. Nathaniel Hawthorne and Herman Melville wrote major works while on the public payroll, and the Justices seemed concerned that the statute under attack might deter future literary geniuses in the civil service. The majority opinion further recognized that banning low-level PUBLIC EMPLOYEES from being compensated for their outside speeches and articles would not improve the efficiency of the workplace by improving morale or preventing corruption, though few employers encourage their employees to moonlight.

United States v. National Treasury Employees Union offers less to public employees than meets the eye. A Court committed to judging the free-speech rights of public employees on a case-by-case basis merely seemed offended by the crudeness of the restriction under constitutional attack. In the last half of the 1990s, federal employees retain the right to criticize the local production of *Swan Lake*, but place themselves at risk if they publicly challenge decisions made by their agencies.

MARK A. GRABER
(2000)

(SEE ALSO: *First Amendment; Patronage; Public Employees and Free Speech; Waters v. Churchill.*)

NATIONAL TREASURY EMPLOYEES UNION v. VON RAAB
489 U.S. 656

In this companion case to SKINNER V. RAILWAY LABOR EXECUTIVES ASSOCIATION, the Supreme Court upheld 5–4, the constitutionality of federal regulations requiring urine testing of all Customs employees involved in drug interdiction, carrying weapons, or handling classified materials. Justices ANTONIN SCALIA and JOHN PAUL STEVENS, who had supported the majority in *Skinner*, joined the *Skinner* dissenters in this case.

Scalia believed that considerations of public safety and the relation between drugs and accidents had justified the departure from individualized suspicion in *Skinner*. These considerations did not prevail in this case. No EVIDENCE existed to show that Customs employees used drugs, let alone that such use jeopardized the public. Accordingly, the public safety could not be furthered by the urinalysis required of these employees. The search itself, Scalia believed, was "particularly destructive of privacy and offensive to personal dignity." The Court majority, however, remained convinced that the government had a compelling interest in ensuring the physical fitness of the employees required to submit to urine testing.

LEONARD W. LEVY
(1992)

NATIONAL UNITY, GROUP CONFLICT, AND THE CONSTITUTION

Writing on behalf of the Supreme Court in SHAW V. RENO (1993), Justice SANDRA DAY O'CONNOR complained that race-sensitive REAPPORTIONMENT schemes reinforce "the perception that members of the same racial group . . . think alike, share the same political interests, and will prefer the same candidates at the polls." In her view, "Racial GERRYMANDERS, even for remedial purposes, may balkanize us into competing racial factions." She accordingly concluded that the Constitution prohibits states from drawing bizarrely shaped legislative districts on the basis of racial criteria.

O'Connor's argument highlights some basic principles of American democracy. Democracy cannot be reduced to majoritarianism. In a purely majoritarian system, 40 percent of the people can lose 100 percent of the time. That would be unfair; true democracy requires that government speak on behalf of the whole people, rather than a mere part of the people—even if the part is a majority.

Nevertheless, American democracy relies heavily on majoritarian elections. These elections are likely to be a satisfactory means for implementing democracy only if one of two conditions holds. The first possibility is that interests might vary greatly from person to person, so that everybody is in the majority on some issues. If so, everybody would occasionally benefit from majoritarian procedures.

The second possibility is that citizens might take an interest in one another. They might, in other words, place an affirmative value upon the happiness of their fellow citizens, including citizens in the minority. If so, members of the minority would enjoy virtual REPRESENTATION through the concerns of the majority.

Both conditions are put in jeopardy by enduring, cohesive political factions. When such factions exist, interests vary from group to group, rather than from person to person. As a result, members of minority groups may find that they are consistent losers in a polarized political process. Moreover, people in one faction are likely to be hostile to those in competing factions.

Shaw thus relied on sound premises. National unity is a structural principle of American democracy, much like FEDERALISM or the SEPARATION OF POWERS. The constitutional aspiration to establish democratic government requires that the state presume Americans can best flourish if they live and work together. Laws that "balkanize [Americans] into competing factions" may thus be unconstitutional even if they meet with the approval of minority groups. Indeed, when rival factions dislike or distrust one another, they may find separation more appealing than cooperation.

As the *Shaw* Court recognized, racial divisions—and especially the divisions between black and white Americans—have always been the most potent source of political factionalism in the United States. Nevertheless, although *Shaw* relied on sound principles, its application of them was dubious. The Court treated racial gerrymanders as though they segregated citizens on the basis of race. In fact, though, the districts reviewed in *Shaw* were among the most integrated in America.

Shaw's antisegregation rhetoric would have been more appropriate in BOARD OF EDUCATION OF KIRYAS JOEL VILLAGE SCHOOL DISTRICT V. GRUMET (1994). *Kiryas Joel* involved a school district gerrymandered so that a village inhabited solely by Hasidic Jews could run its own school system. The Hasidim had previously sent their children to the neighboring Monroe-Woodbury school district, but the Hasidic children had been teased and mistreated. Since neither community liked the other, both were happy with the segregated district.

The constitutional commitment to national unity, however, forbids the state from endorsing this kind of separatist impulse. The Court rightly held the Kiryas Joel school district unconstitutional under the ESTABLISHMENT CLAUSE. In a CONCURRING OPINION, Justice JOHN PAUL STEVENS called attention to the fact that New York had "affirmatively support[ed] a religious sect's interest in segregating itself." Stevens rightly said that it would have been better for New York to "further the strong public interest in promoting diversity and understanding in the public schools."

CHRISTOPHER L. EISGRUBER
(2000)

(SEE ALSO: *Electoral Districting; Religious Liberty.*)

Bibliography

EISGRUBER, CHRISTOPHER L. 1994 Political Unity and the Powers of Government. *UCLA Law Review* 41:1297–1336.
——— 1997 Democracy, Majoritarianism, and Racial Equal-

ity: A Response to Professor Karlan. *Vanderbilt Law Review* 50:347–360.

KARST, KENNETH L. 1989 *Belonging to America: Equal Citizenship and the Constitution.* New Haven, Conn.: Yale University Press.

SYMPOSIUM 1997 Group Conflict and the Constitution: Race, Sexuality and Religion. *Yale Law Journal* 106:2313–2561.

NATIVE AMERICANS

See: American Indians and the Constitution; Cherokee Indian Cases; Tribal Economic Development and the Constitution

NATIVE HAWAIIAN SOVEREIGNTY MOVEMENTS

The Kingdom of Hawai'i was an independent country with formal treaty relationships with the United States and other countries until it was overthrown in 1893 by a rebellious group of westerners, many of whom were U.S. citizens, with the active support of U.S. diplomats and military troops. President GROVER CLEVELAND condemned the overthrow and rejected the request of the rebels that Hawai'i be annexed to the United States. But congressional leaders refused to support his desire to restore the monarchy and for five years Hawai'i was governed by those that had led the revolution. In 1898, after WILLIAM MCKINLEY had become President and gave his support to annexation, this option was formally presented to Congress. The two-thirds vote necessary for the U.S. SENATE to ratify a TREATY could not be obtained, but a simple majority in both the U.S. HOUSE OF REPRESENTATIVES and the Senate adopted a JOINT RESOLUTION supporting annexation, and Hawai'i became a TERRITORY OF THE UNITED STATES. Pursuant to this annexation, 1,800,000 acres of land that had been previously governed by the monarchs and government of the Kingdom of Hawai'i were "ceded" to the United States.

In 1921, Congress transferred 200,000 of these acres to the Hawaiian Home Lands Commission to be made available to persons with at least 50 percent Native Hawaiian ancestry. In 1959, the residents of Hawai'i voted overwhelmingly to became the fiftieth state. Congress then accepted Hawai'i into the Union and transferred about 1,200,000 acres of the ceded lands to the state, to be used for specific public purposes, including "the betterment of the conditions of the Native Hawaiian people." In 1978, the people of Hawai'i amended the state constitution to create the Office of Hawaiian Affairs (OHA), which thereafter received 20 percent of the revenues produced by the ceded lands held by the state government to promote Native Hawaiian culture and economic interests.

The U.S. Congress passed another joint resolution in 1993, which President WILLIAM J. CLINTON signed, apologizing for the participation of U.S. agents in the overthrow, characterizing the overthrow as "illegal" and in violation of INTERNATIONAL LAW, acknowledging that the subsequent "cession" of 1,800,000 acres of lands to the United States was "without the consent of or compensation to the Native Hawaiian people of Hawai'i or their sovereign government," and calling for steps to be taken to achieve a "reconciliation" between the Native Hawaiian people and the U.S. government. Hawai'i's state legislature has enacted statutes expressing similar views, and has taken steps to facilitate the establishment of a sovereign Native Hawaiian nation.

Since 1972, Congress has included Native Hawaiians in many federal programs designed to benefit AMERICAN INDIANS and Alaskan Natives. In *Morton v. Mancari* (1947), the Court ruled that preferential and separate programs for natives are based on a "political" relationship rather than a "racial" classification, and are constitutional if they are rationally linked to the protection or promotion of self-government, self-sufficiency, or native culture. Congress has stated explicitly in many enactments that a special political relationship exists between the United States and the Native Hawaiian people, similar to the status of other Native Americans. However, the legitimacy of this conclusion is occasionally challenged by those who argue that preferences for Native Hawaiians constitute RACIAL DISCRIMINATION. This issue is being reviewed by the Supreme Court in *Rice v. Cayetano* during the 1999–2000 session.

Many Native Hawaiians have acted individually or through organizations to promote the establishment of a sovereign Native Hawaiian government. Some Native Hawaiians favor complete independence from the United States, arguing that the 1993 Apology Resolution recognizes the illegitimacy of U.S. annexation of Hawai'i and that the 1959 vote for statehood was tainted because Native Hawaiians were not properly educated, because the option of independence was not given to the voters, and because the United States violated international law by allowing nonnatives to immigrate to the islands and surpass the Native Hawaiians numerically.

Other Native Hawaiians favor a nation-within-a-nation model similar to the relationship between federally recognized Indian tribes and the United States. Under this approach, the Native Hawaiian nation would determine its own membership, control land and resources, tax and zone, charter CORPORATIONS, establish schools, administer justice, and so on. It would have a direct relationship with the U.S. government and would be immune from most state regulations. A final approach sometimes mentioned is the state-within-a-state model; that is, to become a political subdivision of the state. Under this model, Native Hawaiians would have the same rights as a county or municipality, with some autonomy and control of land and resources, but subject to overall regulation by the state.

In 1996, the Hawaiian Sovereignty Elections Council, a twenty-member group established by the state legislature, organized the Native Hawaiian Vote, a mail ballot asking whether Native Hawaiians supported moving toward self-determination. About 73 percent of those who responded voted yes, but this process was criticized by some Native Hawaiians because fewer than half of those who received the mail ballots returned them. In 1997, the Hawai'i Legislature enacted a statute calling for a "lasting reconciliation" and "a comprehensive, just, and lasting resolution," and established a joint committee to determine which lands should be transferred to the Native Hawaiians.

As of this writing, most of the Native Hawaiian groups interested in sovereignty are meeting together to develop a process to create a Native Hawaiian nation. Although difficult issues remain to be resolved, the momentum to achieve this goal now seems irreversible.

JON M. VAN DYKE
(2000)

NATURAL GAS REGULATION

See: Economic Regulation

NATURALIZATION

Naturalization was defined by the Supreme Court in *Boyd v. Nebraska ex rel. Thayer* (1892) as "the act of adopting a foreigner, and clothing him with the privileges of a native citizen." Congress, under Article I, section 8, of the Constitution, has complete discretion to determine what classes of ALIENS are eligible for naturalization; an individual may claim naturalization as a right only upon compliance with the terms that Congress imposes. Exercising this discretion in the Immigration and Nationality Act of 1952, Congress denied eligibility to those persons who advocate the violent overthrow of the government and limited it to those who have resided in the United States for at least five years, are of "good moral character," and take an oath in open court to support and defend the Constitution, to bear true faith and allegiance to the same, and to bear arms or perform noncombative service in behalf of the United States.

Any naturalized citizen who is proved to have taken the oath of CITIZENSHIP with mental reservations or to have concealed acts or affiliations that, under the law, would disqualify him for naturalization, is subject, upon these facts being conclusively shown in a proper proceeding, to cancellation of his certificate of naturalization. While this action remedies a fraud on the naturalization court that the United States would otherwise be powerless to correct, it subjects a naturalized citizen to possible loss of CITIZENSHIP from which native-born citizens are spared and thus arguably calls into question Justice WILLIAM O. DOUGLAS's announcement in *Schneider v. Rusk* (1964) that "the rights of citizenship of the native-born and of the naturalized person are of the same dignity and are coextensive."

Although naturalization normally is accomplished through individual application and official response on the basis of general congressional rules, naturalization can also be extended to members of a group, without consideration of their individual fitness. Such collective naturalization can be authorized by Congress, as in cases of naturalization of all residents of an annexed TERRITORY or of a territory made a state, or by a treaty.

RALPH A. ROSSUM
(1986)

Bibliography

GORDON, CHARLES and ROSENFIELD, HARRY N. 1984 *Immigration Law and Procedure*, Vol. 3, chaps. 14–18. New York: Matthew Bender.
HERTZ, MICHAEL T. 1976 Limits to the Naturalization Power. *Georgetown Law Journal* 64:1007–1045.

NATURAL LAW

See: Higher Law; Natural Rights and the Constitution

NATURAL RIGHTS AND THE CONSTITUTION

The Constitution as it came from the Philadelphia convention contained no bill of rights. Indeed, the word right (or rights) appears only once in it, and there only in the context of Congress's power to promote the progress of science and useful arts "by securing for limited Times to Authors and Inventors the exclusive Right to their respective Writings and Discoveries" (Article 1, section 8). In the view of the Anti-Federalists, the Constitution should have begun with a statement of general principles, or of "admirable maxims," as PATRICK HENRY said in the Virginia ratifying debates, such as the statement in the VIRGINIA DECLARATION OF RIGHTS OF 1976: "That all men are by nature equally free and independent, and have certain inherent rights, of which, when they enter a state of society, they cannot by any compact deprive or divest their posterity; namely, the enjoyment of life and liberty, with the means of acquiring and possessing property, and pursuing and obtaining happiness and safety." In short, a bill of rights ought to be affixed to the Constitution containing a statement of natural rights.

The Federalists disagreed. They conceded that the Constitution might properly contain a statement of *civil* rights, and they were instrumental in the adoption of the first ten amendments which we know as the BILL OF RIGHTS, but they were opposed to a general statement of first principles in the text of the Constitution. However true, such a statement, by reminding citizens of the right to abolish government, might serve to undermine government, even a government established on those principles. And, as Publius insisted, the Constitution was based on those principles: "the Constitution is itself, in every rational sense, and to every useful purpose, A BILL OF RIGHTS" (THE FEDERALIST #84). It is a bill of natural rights, not because it contains a compendium of those rights but because it is an expression of the natural right of everyone to govern himself and to specify the terms according to which he agrees to give up his natural freedom by submitting to the rules of civil government. The Constitution emanates from us, "THE PEOPLE of the United States," and here in its first sentence, said Publius, "is a better recognition of popular rights than volumes of those aphorisms which make the principal figure in several of our State bills of rights and which would sound much better in a treatise of ethics than in a constitution of government." Natural rights point or lead to government, a government with the power to secure rights, and only secondarily to limitations on governmental power.

This is not to deny the revolutionary character of natural rights, or perhaps more precisely, of the natural rights teaching. The United States began in a revolution accompanied by an appeal to the natural and unalienable rights of life, liberty, and the pursuit of happiness. But these words of the DECLARATION OF INDEPENDENCE are followed immediately by the statement that "to secure these rights, Governments are instituted among Men." Natural rights point or lead to government in the same way that the Declaration of Independence points or leads to the Constitution: the rights, which are possessed by all men equally by nature (or in the state of nature), require a well-governed civil society for their security.

The link between the state of nature and civil society, or between natural rights and government, is supplied by the laws of nature. The laws of nature in this (modern) sense must be distinguished from the natural law as understood in the Christian tradition, for example. According to Christian teaching, the natural law consists of commands and prohibitions derived from the inclinations (or the natural ordering of the passions and desires), and

is enforced, ultimately, by the sanction of divine punishment. According to Hobbes and Locke, however—the principal authors in the school of natural rights—the laws of nature are merely deductions from the rights of nature and ultimately from the right of self-preservation. Because everyone has a natural right to do whatever is necessary to preserve his own life, the state of nature comes to be indistinguishable from the state of war where, in Hobbes's familiar phrase, life is solitary, poor, nasty, brutish, and short; even in Locke's more benign version, and for the same reason, the state of nature is characterized by many unendurable "inconveniences." In short, in the natural condition of man the enjoyment of natural rights is uncertain and human life itself becomes insufferable. What is required for self-preservation is peace, and, as rational beings, men can come to understand "the fundamental law of nature" which is, as Hobbes formulates it, "to seek peace, and follow it." From this is derived the second law of nature, that men enter in a contract with one another according to which they surrender their natural rights to an absolute sovereign who is instituted by the contract and who, from that time forward, represents their rights. More briefly stated, each person must consent to be governed, which he does by laying down his natural right to govern himself. In Locke's version, political society is formed when everyone "has quitted his natural power"—a power he holds as of natural right—and "resigned it up into the hands of the community." In the same way, Americans of 1776 were guided by "the Laws of Nature and of Nature's God" when they declared their independence and constituted themselves as a new political community. Commanding nothing—for these are not laws in the proper sense of commands that must be obeyed—the laws of nature point to government as the way to secure rights, a government that derives its "just powers from the consent of the governed." (See SOCIAL COMPACT THEORY.)

It is important to understand that in the natural rights teaching neither civil society nor government exists by nature. By nature everyone is sovereign with respect to himself. Civil society is an artificial person to which this real person, acting in concert with others, surrenders his natural and sovereign powers, and upon this agreement civil society becomes the sovereign with respect to those who consented to the surrender. It is civil society, in the exercise of this sovereign power, that institutes and empowers government. So it was that "we [became] the People of the United States" in 1776 and, in 1787–1788, that we ordained and established "this Constitution for the United States of America." The Constitution is the product of the "will" of the sovereign people of the United States (*The Federalist* #78).

The power exercised by this people is almost unlimited. Acting through its majority, the people is free to determine the form of government (for, as the Declaration of Independence indicates, any one of several forms of government—democratic, republican, or even monarchical—may serve to secure rights) as well as the organization of that government and the powers given and withheld from it. It will make these decisions in the light of its purpose, which is to secure the rights of the persons authorizing it. This is why the doctrine of natural rights, if only secondarily, leads or points to limitations on government; and this is why the people of the United States decided to withhold some powers and, guided by the new "science of politics" (*The Federalist* #9), sought to limit power by means of a number of institutional arrangements.

Among the powers withheld was the power to coerce religious opinion. Government can have authority over natural rights, said THOMAS JEFFERSON, "only as we have submitted [that authority] to them, [and] the rights of conscience we never submitted, we could not submit."

Among the institutional arrangements was the SEPARATION OF POWERS, and the scheme of representation made possible by extending "the sphere of society so as to take in a greater variety of parties and interests thus making it less probable that a majority of the whole will have a common motive to invade the rights of other citizens" (*The Federalist* #10). First among these rights, according to Locke, is the property right, for, differing somewhat from Hobbes in this respect, Locke understood the natural right of self-preservation primarily as the right to acquire property. Publius had this in mind when he said that "the first object of government . . . [is] the protection of different and unequal faculties of acquiring property" (*The Federalist* #10). The large (commercial) republic is a means of securing this natural right as well as the natural right of conscience, for, within its spacious boundaries, there will be room for a "multiplicity of [religious] sects" as well as a "multiplicity of [economic] interests" (*The Federalist* #51).

Just as a "respect to the opinions of mankind" required Americans to announce the formation of a people that was assuming its "separate and equal station . . . among the powers of the earth," so a jealous concern for their natural rights required this people to *write* a Constitution in which they not only empowered government but, in various complex ways, limited it.

WALTER BERNS
(1986)

Bibliography

JAFFA, HARRY V. 1975 *The Conditions of Freedom: Essays in Political Philosophy.* Pages 149–160. Baltimore: Johns Hopkins University Press.
STORING, HERBERT J. 1978 The Constitution and the Bill of Rights. Pages 32–48 in M. Judd Harmon, ed., *Essays on the Constitution of the United States.* Port Washington, N.Y.: Kennikat.
STRAUSS, LEO 1953 *Natural Right and History.* Introduction and chap. 5. Chicago: University of Chicago Press.

NAVIGABLE WATERS

See: Subjects of Commerce

NAZIS

See: Extremist Speech

NEAGLE, IN RE

See: Sawyer, Lorenzo

NEAL v. DELAWARE
103 U.S. 370 (1881)

Justice JOHN MARSHALL HARLAN, for a majority of 7–2, laid down an important principle in JURY DISCRIMINATION cases: the fact that no black person had ever been summoned as a juror in the courts of a state presents "a *prima facie* case of denial, by the officers charged with the selection of grand and petit jurors, of that equality of protection" secured by the FOURTEENTH AMENDMENT. *Neal* differed from VIRGINIA V. RIVES (1880), here reaffirmed, because the prisoner in *Rives* had merely alleged the exclusion of blacks, which the state denied, while here the state conceded the exclusion. The state chief justice explained that "the great body of black men residing in this State are utterly unqualified by want of intelligence, experience or moral integrity, to sit on juries." Harlan called that a "violent presumption." *Neal* did nothing to prevent the elimination of blacks from juries in the South, because in the absence of a state confession of constitutional error, blacks had the burden of proving deliberate and systematic exclusion of their race. (See NORRIS V. ALABAMA.)

LEONARD W. LEVY
(1986)

NEAR v. MINNESOTA
283 U.S. 697 (1931)

Although GITLOW V. NEW YORK (1925) had accepted for the sake of argument that the FIRST AMENDMENT'S FREEDOM OF SPEECH guarantees were applicable to the states through the DUE PROCESS clause of the FOURTEENTH AMENDMENT,

Near was the first decision firmly adopting the INCORPORATION DOCTRINE and striking down a state law in its totality on free speech grounds. Together with STROMBERG V. CALIFORNIA (1931), decided in the same year and also with a 5–4 majority opinion by Chief Justice CHARLES EVANS HUGHES, *Near* announced a new level of Supreme Court concern for freedom of speech.,

A Minnesota statute authorizing injunctions against a "malicious, scandalous and defamatory newspaper, magazine or other periodical" had been applied against a paper that had accused public officials of neglect of duty, illicit relations with gangsters, and graft. Arguing that hostility to PRIOR RESTRAINT AND CENSORSHIP are the very core of the First Amendment, the Court struck down the statute. Yet *Near*, the classic precedent against prior restraints, is also the doctrinal starting point for most defenses of prior restraint. The Court commented in OBITER DICTUM that "the protection even as to previous restraint is not absolutely unlimited," and listed as exceptions wartime obstruction of recruitment and publication of military secrets, OBSCENITY, INCITEMENTS, to riot or forcible overthrow of the government, and words that "may have all the effect of force."

In emphasizing the special First Amendment solicitude for criticisms of public officials, whether true or false, *Near* was an important way station between *Gitlow*'s implicit acceptance of the constitutional survival in the United States of the English COMMON LAW concept of SEDITIOUS LIBEL and the rejection of that concept in NEW YORK TIMES V. SULLIVAN (1964).

MARTIN SHAPIRO
(1986)

NEBBIA v. NEW YORK
291 U.S. 502 (1934)

Both the desperate economic conditions in the American dairy industry and the legal responses to the dairy crisis, during the depression years 1929–1933, exemplified the dilemmas that the Great Depression posed for American law. Vast, unmarketable surpluses of fluid milk and other dairy products, widespread mortgage foreclosures in dairy centers of rural America, and wild swings in dairy prices and consumption, all spelled extreme distress for the industry and its marketing institutions.

Among the states that responded with new legislation was New York, whose dairy industry constituted about half the value of its farm income and served the great urban concentration of population in the city of New York and its metropolitan area. In framing a program to deal with the crisis, New York's lawmakers knew they were forced to walk through a constitutional minefield. Despite provisions of the 1933 federal AGRICULTURAL ADJUSTMENT ACT intended to give the states some latitude in control of dairy commerce involving interstate milksheds, federal district courts around the country had struck down state laws seeking to control interstate movements of fluid milk or the terms on which it could be marketed. In addition, even laws seeking to regulate only in-state production and distribution were challenged as invalid under the AFFECTED WITH A PUBLIC INTEREST rule; indeed, in numerous previous decisions the Supreme Court had in obiter dicta listed dairies among the enterprises that clearly were "ordinary" or "purely private" businesses, not affected with a public interest and therefore not subject to price regulation. In NEW STATE ICE CO. V. LIEBMANN (1932), for example, the Court had denied the legislature of Oklahoma authority to regulate ice manufacturing and selling on the ground that it was "a business as essentially private in its nature as the business of the grocer, the dairyman, the butcher, the baker, the shoemaker, or the tailor."

Mindful of this background, the New York legislature conducted a lengthy investigation of the fluid milk industry and its travails. In addition to making a record, thereby, as to the condition of the farmers and distribution system, the price collapse and its consequences, and the extensive effects of the crisis on the state's economy, when the legislature drafted a new Milk Control Law in March 1933, it explicitly denominated it as emergency legislation and provided for its termination one year following. By this maneuver, the legislators hoped to slip the knot of "affected with a public interest" and give the Milk Control Law safe harbor in the EMERGENCY POWERS and POLICE POWER area in the event that courts proved unimpressed with the statute's assertion that the milk industry was "a business affecting the public health and interest."

Like similar legislation enacted in New Jersey, Illinois, and other dairy states, the New York law included power to fix prices in the virtually plenary grant of authority to the milk control agency that was established. The board was also empowered to license producers, establish maximum retail prices and the spread between prices paid producers and charged consumers, and regulate interstate fluid milk entrants to the New York market.

The price-fixing provision came before the bench in an appeal from the conviction of a storekeeper for selling milk at retail below the price established by the new milk control agency. When the New York Court of Appeals affirmed the conviction, the case was carried to the Supreme Court. Counsel contended that price control violated the "affected with a public interest" standard, subjecting Nebbia to improper regulation in violation of his FOURTEENTH AMENDMENT right to DUE PROCESS.

By a 5–4 vote, the Court upheld the New York law.

Justice OWEN J. ROBERTS's opinion did not rest on the narrow grounds that the milk control program was of an emergency nature; instead, it addressed in broadest possible terms the nature of the police power and the constitutional limitations upon which states might exercise it. The long history of the "affected with a public interest" doctrine came to an end with *Nebbia*, the majority opinion going back to Chief Justice MORRISON R. WAITE's language in *Munn v. Illinois* (1877). (See GRANGER CASES.) Waite had used the phrase "affected with a public interest" as the equivalent of "subject to the exercise of the police power," the Court now declared: "It is clear that there is no closed class or category of businesses affected with a public interest, and the function of courts in the application of the Fifth and Fourteenth Amendments is to determine in each case whether circumstances vindicate the challenged regulation as a reasonable exertion of governmental authority or condemn it as arbitrary or discriminatory." By repudiating the doctrine of affection with a public interest, which was based on SUBSTANTIVE DUE PROCESS OF LAW, the Court weakened the due process clause as a bastion of property rights. The due process clause, Roberts observed, made no mention of sales, prices, business, contracts, or other incidents of property. Nothing, he added, was sacred about the prices one might charge. The state, Roberts declared, "may regulate a business in any of its aspects, including the prices to be charged for the products or commodities it sells." The crux of this opinion, which prefigured a transformation in constitutional law, was this statement: "So far as the requirement of due process is concerned ... a state is free to adopt whatever economic policy may reasonably be deemed to promote public welfare, and to enforce that policy by legislation adapted to its purpose. The courts are without authority either to declare such policy, or, when it is declared by the legislature, to override it."

Handed down not long after HOME BUILDING LOAN ASSOCIATION V. BLAISDELL (1934), a decision that did extensive damage to once sacrosanct CONTRACT CLAUSE doctrine, the *Nebbia* decision was anathema to property-minded conservatives who saw the juridical scaffolding for VESTED RIGHTS as collapsing in the early New Deal years, even before the Court fight and the wholesale reversal of doctrine that came after 1935. Indeed, *Nebbia* may be read as present-day constitutional law.

HARRY N. SCHNEIBER
(1986)

Bibliography

GOLDSMITH, IRVING B. and WINKS, GORDON W. 1938 Price Fixing: From *Nebbia* to *Guffey*. Pages 531–553 in Douglas B.

Maggs, ed., *Selected Essays on Constitutional Law*. Chicago: Association of American Law Schools.

NEBRASKA PRESS ASSOCIATION v. STUART
427 U.S. 539 (1976)

In *Nebraska Press Association v. Stuart* the Court addressed for the first time the constitutionality of a prior restraint on pretrial publicity about a criminal case. Noting the historic conflict between the FIRST and SIXTH AMENDMENTS, the Court refused to give either priority, recognizing that the accused's right to an unbiased jury must be balanced with the interests in a free press. At issue was a narrowly tailored GAG ORDER in a sensational murder case restraining the press from publishing or broadcasting accounts of the accused's confessions or admissions or "strongly implicative" facts until the jury was impaneled.

Applying the standard of DENNIS V. UNITED STATES (1951) and inquiring whether "the gravity of the 'evil,' discounted by its improbability justified such invasion of free speech as is necessary to avoid the danger," the Court struck down the gag order. To determine whether the record supported the extraordinary measure of a prior restraint on publication, the Court considered the nature and extent of pretrial news coverage, the likelihood that other measures would mitigate the effects of unrestrained pretrial publicity, and the effectiveness of a restraining order to prevent the threatened danger, and, further, analyzed the order's terms and the problems of managing and enforcing it. The gag order was critically flawed because it prohibited publication of information gained from other clearly protected sources.

Justice WILLIAM J. BRENNAN, joined by Justices POTTER J. STEWART and THURGOOD MARSHALL, concurring, argued that a prior restraint on the press is an unconstitutionally impermissible method for enforcing the Sixth Amendment. Refusing to view the First and Sixth Amendments as in irreconcilable conflict, he noted that there were numerous less restrictive means by which a fair trial could be ensured. Justice BYRON R. WHITE doubted whether prior restraints were ever justifiable, but did not believe it wise so to announce in the first case raising that question. Justice LEWIS F. POWELL emphasized the heavy burden resting on a party seeking to justify a prior restraint.

KIM McLANE WARDLAW
(1986)

(SEE ALSO: *Free Press/Fair Trial; Prior Restraint and Censorship*.)

NECESSARY AND PROPER CLAUSE

The enumeration of powers in Article I, section 8, gives Congress the power to do such specific things as "regulate commerce . . . among the several States" and "raise and support Armies." At the end of the list is the power "to make all Laws which shall be necessary and proper for carrying into execution the foregoing Powers, and all other Powers vested by this Constitution in the Government of the United States, or in any Department or Officer thereof." The ANTI-FEDERALISTS called this the "elastic clause" or the "sweeping power." They predicted it would centralize all governmental power in the national government. JAMES MADISON denied this charge in THE FEDERALIST #23. He observed that the clause spoke of power to execute only those powers that were specified elsewhere in the document, and that the power vested by the clause would have been implicit in the grant of other powers even without the clause. (See IMPLIED POWERS.) The clause, therefore, did not conflict with the principle of enumerated national powers, Madison argued. Events have vindicated Anti-Federalist fears.

THOMAS JEFFERSON and ALEXANDER HAMILTON took opposing positions on the meaning of the word "necessary" in the clause during their debate in 1791 on the constitutionality of the first BANK OF THE UNITED STATES ACT. Hamilton argued that the nation needed a BROAD CONSTRUCTION of congressional powers so that the government could employ a wide variety of means useful to the discharge of its responsibilities. Jefferson countered that a broad construction would enable Congress to encroach upon the reserved powers of the states whenever its measures might serve as means to ends within its enumerated powers. To safeguard STATES' RIGHTS, such encroachments should be permitted only when "absolutely necessary," said Jefferson—only, that is, when failure to encroach would nullify the grant of federal power. Hamilton's view prevailed first with President GEORGE WASHINGTON in 1791 and later in the Supreme Court, when JOHN MARSHALL's opinion in MCCULLOCH V. MARYLAND upheld the second national bank in 1819.

Marshall construed national powers in terms of a few authorized national ends. Most important, he understood the COMMERCE POWER and related powers as authorizing the pursuit of national prosperity and the various military and diplomatic powers as authorizing the pursuit of national security. This ends-oriented conception of national powers was the view of *The Federalist* #41, which also gave greatest emphasis to the goals of national prosperity and security. When Marshall held in *McCulloch* that Congress could pursue its authorized ends without regard for the reserved powers of the states, he was saying, in effect, that Congress could do what it wanted relative to state pow-

ers so long as it gave the right reasons. Marshall suggested a hierarchy of constitutional values, with state powers subordinated to Congress's version of national prosperity and security. The opinion thus brought virtually all state powers within Congress's potential control, because, with changing conditions, Congress might consider any social practice (education, for example) as an instrument of the nation's prosperity and security.

But to suggest that Congress can act for the right reasons is not to say that Congress can disregard states' rights at will. Marshall's theory of the necessary and proper clause was still consistent with the idea of enumerated powers because it presupposed a limited number of nationally authorized ends. Marshall thus stated that the judiciary would be prepared to invalidate pretextual uses of national power to reach ends reserved to the states. In the twentieth century, the Supreme Court refused to give effect to Marshall's commitment to invalidate pretextual uses of congressional power, thus fulfilling the Anti-Federalist prediction of what the clause eventually would be.

The Court first upheld pretextual uses of power as means to eliminating state bank notes in VEAZIE BANK V. FENNO (1869) and margarine colored to resemble butter in *McRay v. United States* (1904). These acts were aimed at what Congress considered the nation's economic health. They were therefore valid under Marshall's theory of the commerce power. But, in the meanwhile, the Court had moved away from Marshall's conception to a limited view of the nation's commerce as those things that crossed state lines. Pretexts were necessary unless the Court chose to abandon this artificial view; instead of correcting the mistake which necessitated pretexts, the Court established precedents for them. Later the Court upheld enactments that obviously were not aimed at the national goals implicit in Congress's enumerated powers. The Court thus upheld the TAXING POWER as a weapon against drug abuse in UNITED STATES V. DOREMUS (1919) and the commerce power as a means of combating gambling, illicit sex, and other practices usually said to be reserved to the STATE POLICE POWER, as in HOKE V. UNITED STATES (1913). These decisions turned Marshall's theory of the necessary and proper clause on its head. Where Marshall had upheld incursions into state powers as means to nationally authorized ends, the Court was now upholding national powers as means to state ends. As a result the NATIONAL POLICE POWER can today be used to reach an indefinite variety of purposes, and the necessary and proper clause authorizes almost anything that might be useful for addressing what Congress views as a national problem.

Limits on national power do remain in the BILL OF RIGHTS, in other sources of individual rights such as the CIVIL WAR amendments, and in principles derived from the Constitution's institutional arrangements. Because the states do constitute a part of those arrangements, the Court still says it will protect various state rights to participate in federal government action, such as the right to equal representation in the Senate. But such states' rights limitations on national power are of little contemporary significance. For the most part, the necessary and proper clause has been construed in a way that has destroyed the notion that the enumeration of powers limits the national government.

SOTIRIOS A. BARBER
(1986)

Bibliography

BERNS, WALTER 1961 The Meaning of the Tenth Amendment. Pages 126–148 in Robert A. Goldwin, ed., *A Nation of States*. Chicago: Rand McNally.

GUNTHER, GERALD, eds. 1969 *John Marshall's Defense of McCulloch v. Maryland*. Stanford, Calif.: Stanford University Press.

NELSON, SAMUEL
(1792–1873)

On March 5, 1845, Samuel Nelson became a Justice of the Supreme Court and judge of the Second Circuit. President JOHN TYLER nominated the New York Democrat in the belief that his record of moderation compiled over twenty-one years in the New York courts, including thirteen as associate and then chief justice of the state supreme court, would resolve eighteen months of wrangling between the chief executive and the SENATE over the high court vacancy. Unanimous Senate confirmation made Nelson the Court's thirty-first justice.

Nelson's most significant contribution to constitutional development involved the admiralty clause in Article III, section 2, of the Constitution. That clause specified that the federal courts should exclusively exercise the ADMIRALTY AND MARITIME JURISDICTION. He interpreted the clause to extend federal JURISDICTION while retaining for the states an area of constitutional responsibility. Nelson first suggested the position, later adopted by the full Court in PROPELLER GENESEE CHIEF V. FITZHUGH (1851), that where INTERSTATE COMMERCE was involved the admiralty clause extended federal jurisdiction to inland rivers and lakes (*New Jersey Steam Navigation Co. v. Merchant's Bank*, 1848). He carefully rooted this expansion in an 1845 act that established admiralty jurisdiction in "certain cases, upon the lakes and navigable waters connecting with" the oceans. Nelson left to state courts responsibility for vessels that operated on lakes and rivers exclusively within the same state. This interpretation rested on two constitutional themes that pervaded his other opinions: congres-

sional domination of matters of law as opposed to constitutional principles, and belief in a scheme of dual SOVEREIGNTY.

Even in this single instance of doctrinal leadership Nelson lost the initiative. New members of the Court and the quickening tempo of commercial life in the western United States rendered his emphasis on dual sovereignty obsolete. Almost always eager for accommodation, he acquiesced. In 1869 he spoke for the Court in holding that from the time of *Genesee Chief* federal admiralty jurisdiction on the lakes and rivers stemmed from the JUDICIARY ACT OF 1789 rather than from the act of 1845 (*The Eagle v. Frazer*, 1869). Through this about-face, Nelson acknowledged that litigants could use federal district courts in admiralty cases arising in INTRASTATE COMMERCE.

The concept of dual sovereignty also informed his attitude toward the COMMERCE CLAUSE. In the LICENSE CASES (1847) and PASSENGER CASES (1849) he concurred with Chief Justice ROGER B. TANEY's opinions sustaining STATE POLICE POWER, and in the 1849 cases he was the only Justice not to write a separate opinion. When Congress acted under the commerce clause, Nelson supported national power. Speaking for the Court in *Pennsylvania v. Wheeling and Belmont Bridge Co.* (1856), his most important commerce clause opinion, he confirmed Congress's power to deal with navigation and interstate commerce on inland rivers.

Nelson's constitutional jurisprudence also stressed JUDICIAL SELF-RESTRAINT and SEPARATION OF POWERS. He voted only once with a majority to strike down a federal law in *Hepburn v. Griswold* (1870). He deferred to presidential management of FOREIGN AFFAIRS, but dissented in the PRIZE CASES (1863) because he thought President ABRAHAM LINCOLN had infringed on Congress's war-making powers.

Nelson believed that federal JUDICIAL POWER should protect slaveholders, but that the Court should exercise it benignly. Acting on this belief, he persuaded the Court in 1856 to rehear DRED SCOTT V. SANDFORD (1857). In his draft opinion for the Court, he argued that the laws of Missouri made Scott a slave and that the Court could ignore the questions of the legal status of slaves and the constitutionality of the MISSOURI COMPROMISE. This position raised the hackles of Justices JOHN MCLEAN and BENJAMIN R. CURTIS, and Chief Justice Taney took from Nelson responsibility for preparing the Court's opinion. Nelson, believing that the Chief Justice's decision to reach major issues was unwise, submitted his draft opinion for the Court as his own, even retaining the pronoun "we" in the printed version.

Nelson continued in the post-CIVIL WAR era as a hard-working jurist and able legal technician. He agreed in February 1871 to serve on the *Alabama* Claims Commission. His appointment by a Republican president underscored as much his reputation as an impartial jurist as it did his knowledge of admiralty, maritime, and prize law.

Nelson resigned from the Court on November 28, 1872. Often described as a doughface (a Northerner who took a southern view on slavery), Nelson is better understood as a political moderate concerned about the fate of the Union, disposed to antislavery rather than proslavery views, and committed to the position that the judicial role should emphasize discretion, restraint, and deference to legislative leadership. In view of his twenty-six years on the Court, he contributed surprisingly little to constitutional jurisprudence.

KERMIT L. HALL
(1986)

Bibliography

GATELL, FRANK OTTO   1969   Samuel Nelson. Pages 817–839 in Leon Friedman and Fred L. Israel, eds., *The Justices of the United States Supreme Court 1789–1969: Their Lives and Major Opinions.* New York: Chelsea House.

NEUTRAL PRINCIPLES

"Neutral principles" refers to a debate that took place throughout the late 1950s and the 1960s (and still resonates today) regarding the role of the judiciary in American democracy. Participants in the debate were, for the most part, law professors and judges, but their debate spilled into the broader society in the form of widely publicized speeches and articles published in the popular press. In essence, the debate was about whether there is a way to distinguish the judicial function from ordinary politics, and about the power of judges to strike down laws as unconstitutional.

The neutral principles debate arose in the context of controversial decisions rendered by the Supreme Court under the leadership of Chief Justice EARL WARREN. In 1954, the Court decided BROWN V. BOARD OF EDUCATION, which ordered the DESEGREGATION of public schools. The Court was criticized, especially in the South, but academic commentary for a time was largely positive. Then, in 1957 and 1958, the Court decided a number of cases favoring the rights of Communists and communist-sympathizers, and there was a strong backlash against the Court in some quarters. It was against this backdrop that, in February 1958, Judge LEARNED HAND delivered his famous Holmes Lecture at the Harvard Law School. Hand was regarded as one of the preeminent judges in the country. His address surprised many people, for in it he was very critical of the Court. Hand attacked the idea of an activist judiciary, and even took the Court to task for its decision in *Brown.*

The following year, Professor Herbert Wechsler delivered his Holmes Lecture, entitled *Toward Neutral Principles of Constitutional Law,* in which he responded to Hand. Wechsler supported the idea of JUDICIAL REVIEW, but insisted that when courts decide constitutional cases, the most important factor is that they reach their decision by applying "neutral principles" that "transcend the case at hand." Although he said he personally favored the decision in *Brown,* Wechsler was unable to identify a neutral principle equally applicable to "a Negro or a segregationist" that made it clear that the Constitution's requirement of EQUAL PROTECTION OF THE LAWS required the desegregation of schools. According to Wechsler, *Brown* was about the FREEDOM OF ASSOCIATION, and he could not find a way to choose between "denying the association to those individuals who wish it or imposing it on those who would avoid it."

Wechsler's address set off a furious debate over the idea of neutral principles. Some, such as Professor Louis Pollak, supported the idea of neutrality, but felt it was possible to identify a neutral principle to justify *Brown:* No majority race should subjugate a minority race. Many other constitutional scholars felt that the very idea of neutrality as advanced by Wechsler was naïve or bankrupt. Although their views differed, these scholars, among them ALEXANDER M. BICKEL, Arthur Selwyn Miller, Eugene Rostow, Charles Black, Martin Shapiro, and Jan Deutsch generally believed that what mattered ultimately was whether any given decision of the Court was morally correct and could garner acceptance among the body politic.

The neutral principles position taken by Wechsler must be understood in its broader social and jurisprudential context. In the first half of the twentieth century, a group of scholars commonly referred to as the LEGAL REALISTS argued that legal outcomes inevitably were influenced by the views of the judges applying the law, and by the social milieu in which decisions were rendered. This Realist insight troubled many, for it seemed to deny law its neutrality and to equate law with politics. A later group of scholars developed a school of thought known as the "Legal Process" school, which sought to preserve a unique role for law apart from politics. In the view of the Legal Process school, the secret to sound constitutional decisions was "reasoned elaboration." By relying on reason, courts could differentiate their work from that of the more political branches of government. Wechsler was a Legal Process scholar, and it was in this context that he challenged the Court to rely on neutral principles to avoid being seen as a "naked power organ." Other Legal Process scholars who advocated reliance on reasoned elaboration were HENRY M. HART, JR., and PHILLIP B. KURLAND. Opponents of the Legal Process scholars doubted whether reason alone either achieved the sort of neutrality that

Wechsler advocated, or was a sufficient basis for deciding cases.

Neutral principles played an important role in the more enduring debate over the role of the Court and JUDICIAL REVIEW. Many of the WARREN COURT'S progressive decisions, such as those involving FREEDOM OF SPEECH, RACIAL DISCRIMINATION, and REAPPORTIONMENT won broad popular support, but that support declined by the late 1960s. The Court expanded the rights of criminal suspects at a time when crime rates were rising, and RICHARD M. NIXON was elected President vowing to appoint Justices to the Supreme Court who would follow closely the original meaning of the Constitution. The Court became a special target of controversy after it decided ROE V. WADE (1973), which guaranteed a woman the right to ABORTION. Many critics of *Roe* complained that the right to abortion could not be found in the Constitution. In the face of skepticism about neutral principles and the power of reasoned elaboration, these critics now began to insist that Supreme Court Justices adhere closely to the text of the Constitution and the intentions of those who drafted and ratified it, in order to avoid imposing judicial preferences on the body politic. Thus, the neutral principles debate served as a bridge between the insights of the Legal Realists, and the modern-day debate over the proper method of constitutional interpretation.

BARRY FRIEDMAN
(2000)

(SEE ALSO: *Constitutional Interpretation; Constitutional Theory; Original Intent; Originalism.*)

Bibliography

DUXBURY, NEIL 1995 *Patterns of American Jurisprudence.* New York: Oxford University Press.

FRIEDMAN, BARRY 1997 Neutral Principles: A Retrospective. *Vanderbilt Law Review* 50:503–536.

HAND, LEARNED 1958 *The Bill of Rights.* Cambridge, Mass: Harvard University Press.

HOROWITZ, MORTON J. 1992 *The Transformation of American Law 1870–1960: The Crisis of Legal Orthodoxy.* New York: Oxford University Press.

MILLER, ARTHUR SELWYN and HOWELL, RONALD F. 1960 The Myth of Neutrality in Constitutional Adjudication. *University of Chicago Law Review* 27:661–695.

PELLER, GARY 1988 Neutral Principles in the 1950's. *University of Michigan Journal of Law Reform* 21:561–622.

POLLAK, LOUIS H. 1959 Racial Discrimination and Judicial Integrity: A Reply to Professor Wechsler. *University of Pennsylvania Law Review* 108:1–34.

SEBOK, ANTHONY J. 1996 Reading the Legal Process. *Michigan Law Review* 94:1571–1595.

SHAPIRO, MARTIN 1963 The Supreme Court and Constitutional Adjudication: Of Politics and Neutral Principles. *George Washington Law Review* 31:587–606.

WECHSLER, HERBERT 1959 Toward Neutral Principles of Constitutional Law. *Harvard Law Review* 73:1–35.

NEW CHRISTIAN RIGHT

See: Religious Fundamentalism

NEW DEAL

During the New Deal years, from 1933 to the end of WORLD WAR II, the nation experienced an era of protracted economic crisis and social dislocation, a dramatic change in national political alignments, and then mobilization for total war. A society contending with changes and emergencies of this order, especially with an enormously popular reformist President in office, cannot easily avoid profound challenges to its constitutional order; and so it was for America in this era. Every major aspect of political controversy in this period found expression of varying kinds in constitutional discourse and conflict, and these constitutional battles both reflected and actively intensified the bitter ideological polarization that bedeviled the nation's politics.

When the New Deal era came to a close just after the war, the constitutional as well as political landscape of the country had been transformed. With respect both to governmental institutions and policies and to formal constitutional doctrine, things as they had stood in 1933 had been largely swept away. The transformations of governance and politics in the New Deal era brought far-reaching reform of constitutional law, accomplished without benefit of formal constitutional amendment on any question except the repeal of PROHIBITION. The new constitutional order that emerged, moreover, would stand firmly for half a century as the basic framework of the modern welfare, regulatory, and national-security state. In most particulars, the new order proved durable enough to survive determined efforts by neoconservatives in the 1980s to overturn some of the most important New Deal doctrines and reforms.

President FRANKLIN D. ROOSEVELT at the outset of his presidency characteristically struck a pose that seemed to dismiss offhandedly the need for worries about constitutional difficulties. "Our Constitution is so simple and practical," he declared in his first inaugural address in 1933, "that it is possible always to meet extraordinary needs by changes in emphasis and arrangement without loss of essential form." But what changes in "emphasis" and "arrangement" he had in mind! Even the legislative programs and executive actions of the "First Hundred Days" posed a broad challenge to prevailing doctrines in constitutional law, especially regarding the protection of vested economic rights against government's hand and the proper limits of the national government's authority in the federal system. Nor did the challenge recede or soften significantly in the years immediately following, as Roosevelt and his party generated a prolix legislative and administrative record that would repeatedly inspire bitter constitutional controversies.

Virtually every element of the New Deal administration's policies, especially their idealistic nuances and implications, bore the imprint of Roosevelt's own thinking. The direction and extraordinary scope of the New Deal's challenge to the traditional role and perogatives of the states, for example, were signaled early by Rooselvelt when he was governor of New York: "In our business life and in our social contracts," he declared in 1929, "we are little controlled by the methods and practices employed by our forefathers." Why, then, he asked, be "content . . . to accept and continue to use the local machinery of government which was first devised generations or even centuries ago?" This kind of iconoclasm and willingness to experiment with governmental structures structures was soon to be directed against the states. Impatience with antiquated institutional legacies was linked with Roosevelt's robust "Old Progressive" faith in bringing enterprise to bear on social and economic problems. Hence, the President readily endorsed the regional approach (exemplified by the TENNESEE VALLEY AUTHORITY ACT OF 1933) to problems that trascended state lines. Similarly, he was sypathetic to a national planning approach (as was espoused by his National Resource Planning Board and the agricultural price-support and production-controll efforts); and he also fostered the system of direct federal grant-in-aid support to city governments for public housing, airports, and other projects in ways that dramaically enhanced municipal autonomy within the states.

Perhaps of greatest long-run importance to governmental practice was Roosevelt's own proclivity to devolve on appointive agencies and their expert staffs the responsibility for defining the "public interest" in the course of setting regulatory policies—a preference shared by the New Deal majorities in Congress as they crafted the design of new regulatory agencies. Roosevelt regularly pressed on Congress and the public the urgency of the social and economic programs he was proposing—both the programs of the "Hundred Days," designed to break the terrible spiral of despair, and those of the ensuing years, designed to effect enduring reforms, including a systematic (and, to many, a radical) redistribution of income and wealth. The argument for urgent action, for room to experiment, and for administration with maximal flexibility and discretion was cast from the start in terms of the necessities associated with a "national emergency." As New Deal programs expanded, however, this view was

translated into the more general argument for wide-ranging agency discretion and a reliance on experts for policy making. In the context of the war emergency after 1938, this tendency became even more pervasive.

The question remained: what constitutional principles, if any, restrained such claims by the chief executive? The New Deal answer in light of the Depression crisis tended increasingly to be couched as a majoritarian rationale: "Does anybody believe," asked Senator Lewis Schwellenbach of Washington, one of Roosevelt's closest allies in Congress, "that the founding fathers intended to set up a form of government which would prevent that government from solving the current problems of the people?" Roosevelt phrased the issue similarly in his first radio speech of his second term, the address in which he fired the first shot in the COURT-PACKING battle. It was the entire "modern movement for social and economic progress through legislation" that was at stake, the President declared, referring dramatically to "one-third of a nation ill-nourished, ill-clad, ill-housed." He rejected as outrageous the notion that the judiciary might deny Congress the authority "to protect us against catastrophe by meeting squarely our modern social and economic conditions."

In private correspondence with Schwellenbach, the President referred to their common view of the constitutional issues as the cause of "liberal democracy." New Deal victories by "overwhelming" popular majorities in 1932 and 1936, the President repeatedly contended in his public messages on the constitutional question, had provided an "overwhelming mandate" for immediate action to put the programs of "liberal democracy" in place.

Roosevelt and the constitutional imperatives embodied in his programs for this "liberal democracy" successfully prevailed beginning in 1937, as a new majority in support of the New Deal emerged virtually overnight on the HUGHES COURT and later became a dependable reliance for Roosevelt as he made new appointments. Similarly, the President would prevail in virtually all particulars when he assumed vastly expanded executive emergency authority in the military and foreign-policy realms during the pre-war neutrality period and the years of combat in a global arena that followed the Pearl Harbor disaster.

The President thus placed his personal stamp on the most dramatic political initiatives of the era; however, there were also more enduring legacies of the New Deal in the nation's constitutional development. An inventory of this heritage from the 1930s and World War II must embrace not only the dramatic changes that were ardently debated in their own day, but also the various effects of conflict and innovation only dimly discerned by either friends or critics of Roosevelt's social and economic programs and the wartime initiatives.

Prominent in the inventory of change was the movement of national authority and active intervention into many vital areas of social and economic life that before 1933 had been left by Congress largely to the states and had been only marginally affected by national law. A vast array of legislation from 1933 to 1937 bespoke this dramatic occupation by Congress of policy areas that traditionally had been extremely decentralized in practice; some of them, moreover, had been specifically designated by the Supreme Court's conservative majority as being within the exclusive purview of the states as a matter of TENTH AMENDMENT guarantees, or as a matter of judicially defined categories that differentiated "national" from "local" activities under terms of the COMMERCE CLAUSE or in light of the doctrine of a limited number of enumerated powers.

Thus, by 1941 the working constitutional system had become a system in which formal constitutional issues of FEDERALISM had been recast completely in light of new realities generated by New Deal innovations. A definitive redistribution of both policy responsibilities and power had occurred. There was comprehensive restructuring of agriculture as a managed sector, a formal preemption of labor law through the Wagner Act and its guarantees of the right to organize, adoption of minimal federal standards for wages and hours, and the establishment of a vast regional energy and economic development program through the Tennessee Valley Authority. Federal regulatory authority was extended over the securities markets, and there was a dramatic expansion of national regulation in the transportation, antitrust, and banking fields. The New Deal also instituted the first massive ENTITLEMENT programs with the passage of the SOCIAL SECURITY ACT in 1935; this measure became the foundation stone of the modern national WELFARE STATE.

One concomitant of this powerful move toward centralization of governmental responsibilities was a transformation in the distribution of funds and expenditures. In 1929, with expenditures of $2.6 billion, the budget of the national government was only one-third the amount of state and local expenditures; but a decade later, federal expenditures were $9 billion, exceeding the combined amounts spent by state and local government. Linked with this aspect of new "giant government"—emergence of the national government as a modern Leviathan—was the New Deal's explicit adoption in 1938 of Keynesian principles for fiscal policy. Although growth of the national government establishment was not in itself a development that implicated constitutional questions directly, as a reality of governance and power, "big government" transformed the entire context of the debate over constitutional principles.

More explicitly cast in constitutional terms was the matter of federal grants in aid to state and local government,

which rose from $193 million in 1933 to a floodtide level of $2.9 billion in 1939. Although welfare and relief comprised some eighty percent of these sums in each year, the vast aggregate amount in 1939 embraced a range of new programs for natural-resources management, public housing, and health services as well as the more traditional highway aid and agricultural research funds. In this arena of initiative, the Supreme Court posed no serious obstacles; in the 1923 case of FROTHINGHAM V. MELLON, it already had upheld the practice of attaching conditions to federal grants. Decisions in the late 1930s reaffirmed this view. Taken as a whole, the grant-in-aid programs became an important element of what has been termed the modern system of COOPERATIVE FEDERALISM, displacing the older principles and practices of DUAL FEDERALISM.

In its devastating response to the early New Deal measures for industrial reorganization and agricultural market controls, the Supreme Court in SCHECHTER POULTRY CORPORATION V. UNITED STATES (1935) did strike down key legislation in part because of what it found to be a promiscuous violation of the principles of SEPARATION OF POWERS. After the new liberal majority had established the credo of Roosevelt's "liberal democracy" in a dominant position in the Court's decisions after 1936, however, the delegation of rule-making authority to the new administrative and regulatory agencies won virtually routine approval with the Justices. Indeed, judicial deference to agency discretion became one of the most durable—and also most problematic—features of the longer-term New Deal legacy in American law.

For the most part, it was regulation of economic interests that was at stake when challenges were raised against administrative prerogatives; and as the Court abandoned its commitment to defend economic or entrepreneurial liberty on the same basis as it would the political elements of liberty (see PREFERRED FREEDOMS), such challenges lost their doctrinal authoritativeness. Not until the 1960s did political leaders and legal scholars entirely sympathetic with the goals of New Deal-style benefit programs and regulatory regimes begin to worry much about excessive paternalism and discretion. They became concerned particularly with the degree to which the New Deal legacy had produced a system of social benefits, franchises, subsidies, and services that were dispensed by elaborate bureaucracies. In this system, some groups and individuals were favored, while others might be held virtually in thrall because of Byzantine or Kafkaesque procedural standards or simply because of high-handedness and capriciousness. Only then, thirty years after the system had begun to emerge from New Deal legislation and twenty years after the Administrative Procedure Act became law, were the Constitution's procedural guarantees reappraised with a view toward real equality of treatment and fairness in the agencies' administration of social programs and regulations.

When war broke out in Asia and Europe, the Roosevelt administration's policies carried the "emergency" doctrine and delegation of powers to an entirely new level. In September 1939, the President declared a "limited emergency" by EXECUTIVE ORDER, thereby assuming the authority to expand the military forces and to take other measures under war statutes. After the Pearl Harbor attack, the two WAR POWERS ACTS (December 1941 and March 1942) gave the President unprecedented delegated powers under which he erected a massive bureaucracy with coercive powers to direct mobilization. The March 1941 Lend-Lease Act also delegated the spending power, providing the legal basis for over $50 billion in grants of supplies and credits to the Allies.

In one of the most extraordinary documents in the entire history of American constitutional law, Roosevelt in September 1942 threatened that if Congress failed to meet his wishes with respect to repealing a section of the price-control laws in light of the war emergency, he would assume the power to nullify the law on his own authority. Congressional deference averted a constitutional confrontation on the issue.

The war period was of special importance with respect to civil liberties. In one of the most grievous violations of any groups' rights in the modern era, the Roosevelt administration authorized by EXECUTIVE ORDER 9066 (later validated by Congress) the removal in 1942 of the entire Japanese-ancestry population from the West Coast and their prolonged internment in concentration camps until nearly the end of the war. Meanwhile, the army took advantage of a declaration of martial law in Hawaii by the territorial governor in the hours after Pearl Harbor, maintaining a comprehensive military regime with suspension of civilian justice in criminal matters until late 1944, long after any credible threat of invasion of the Hawaiian Islands had passed. In the notorious JAPANESE AMERICAN CASES (1943–1944), the Supreme Court upheld the removal and internment decisions; but when the Hawaiian policy was finally challenged (DUNCAN V. KAHANAMOKU), the Court ruled that the army had acted illegally in suspending civilian government and justice beyond the time justified by military necessity.

Although the wartime record on CIVIL LIBERTIES was thus marred by excesses of the military authorities—and although the army in each instance had full support of the White House—the more enduring heritage of the New Deal in race relations and constitutional equal protection has a different face. Although failing to support federal antilynching bills or any positive CIVIL RIGHTS legislation that would have attacked SEGREGATION, Roosevelt and the agency administrators generally pressed hard to see that blacks received an equitable share of the benefits of federal welfare and relief programs. The President supported the Justice Department's creation in 1939 of what became the Civil Rights Division; and within a few years, this unit's lawyers had undertaken a variety of prosecutions—the most significant being the case of UNITED STATES V. CLASSIC (1941)—challenging RACIAL DISCRIMINATION in the electoral process in the southern states. The Justice Department's new concern for equal rights and civil liberties also served to enhance the significance of Supreme Court decisions (including especially HAGUE V. CIO in 1939) (that were then strengthening FIRST AMENDMENT guarantees and laying the essential doctrinal groundwork for the much farther-reaching civil liberties and civil rights jurisprudence of the WARREN COURT era. In sum, racial equality and civil liberties had been brought within the ambit of the New Deal agenda—the essential counterweight to unrestrained majoritarianism that many feared was embodied in Roosevelt's attack on the Court in 1936 and even, albeit in a more reflective mode, in the constitutional theories calling for "judicial self-restraint" championed in the wake of the Court fight (see JUDICIAL REVIEW AND DEMOCRACY).

The American constitutional order in 1945, at President Roosevelt's death, had thus witnessed far-reaching changes in the allocation of state versus federal powers, in the extent and style of intervention by government in social and economic affairs, and in the role of the national authorities in regard to individual rights and liberties. In the realm of doctrine, the Supreme Court had reinterpreted the commerce clause so completely that the Justices would soon declare it to be simply "as broad as the economic needs of the nation" (*American Power & Light v. SEC*). After the decision of WICKARD V. FILBURN (1942), the economic regulatory powers of the Congress seemed to be plenary, with no economic activity protected from congressional determination of what was of national significance. As early as 1934, in NEBBIA V. NEW YORK, the Court had discarded traditional economic due process and AFFECTED WITH A PUBLIC INTEREST doctrine—two of the main props of traditional VESTED RIGHTS analysis that had been used to restrain severely the state's regulatory powers. In UNITED STATES V. DARBY LUMBER COMPANY (1941) the Court cast into the dustbin of history, it seemed, the old view of the Tenth Amendment, declaring now that the amendment "states but a truism" and was merely "declaratory." Meanwhile, the New Deal administration posed a new challenge to state sovereignty over valuable natural resources by asserting a federal property claim based on "paramount rights" over the offshore oil and any other resources of the continental shelf, long considered to be under state ownership out to a distance of three miles. With the emergence of the new civil rights and civil liberties jurisprudence exemplified by *Classic*, the university-segregation decision of MISSOURI EX REL. GAINES V. CANADA (1938), and other decisions, the potentialities of the emerging changes in law became clear. Whether one interprets these changes, as friends of the Roosevelt Administration sought to do, as a "return to the Constitution" (a reversal of conservative doctrines that had become dominant in violation of correct principles), or instead, as a positive advancement of law to meet the urgent requirements of a modern industrial society in crisis, the New Deal era did indeed bequeath to postwar America a constitutional order dramatically transformed.

HARRY N. SCHEIBER
(1992)

Bibliography

BIXBY, DAVID M. 1981 The Roosevelt Court, Democratic Ideology, and Minority Rights: Another Look at United States v. Classic. *Yale Law Journal* 90:741–814.

HURST, JAMES WILLARD 1977 *Law and the Social Order in the United States.* Ithaca, N.Y.: Cornell University Press.

MURPHY, PAUL L. 1972 *The Constitution in Crisis Times, 1918–1969.* New York: Harper & Row.

PARRISH, MICHAEL E. The Great Depression, the New Deal, and the American Legal Order. *Washington Law Review* 59:723–750.

SCHEIBER, HARRY N. 1989 Economic Liberty and the Constitution. In *Essays in the History of Liberty.* San Marino, Calif.: The Huntington Library.

——— and SCHEIBER, JANE L. 1990 Constitutional Liberty in World War II: Army Rule and Martial Law in Hawaii. *Western Legal History* 3:341–378.

NEW DEAL
(Constitutional Significance)

The NEW DEAL era was a time of extraordinary constitutional ferment, witnessing significant constitutional change in a strikingly wide variety of areas. Just as the Supreme Court was evincing increasing solicitude for CIVIL RIGHTS and CIVIL LIBERTIES, particularly in the realms of FREEDOM OF SPEECH and CRIMINAL PROCEDURE, the Justices substantially eroded the DOCTRINE of INTERGOVERNMENTAL IMMUNITY from taxation, dramatically relaxed the restraints imposed upon state governments by the CONTRACT CLAUSE, and sanctioned a major reorientation of monetary policy. At the same time, the executive branch emerged with significantly enhanced authority in both domestic and FOREIGN AFFAIRS. Yet the expansions of the powers of Congress to regulate INTERSTATE COMMERCE and to spend for the GENERAL WELFARE, along with the demise of economic SUBSTANTIVE DUE PROCESS OF LAW, are generally regarded as the period's signal contributions to the modern American constitutional landscape.

Of these three, developments in the TAXING AND SPENDING POWER jurisprudence were arguably the least significant. To be sure, the Court's embrace of the Hamiltonian interpretation of the spending power, announced in UNITED STATES V. BUTLER (1936) and confirmed in the *Social Security Cases*, freed future Congresses from concern that the power to spend was limited to ends identified in the other ENUMERATED POWERS of Article I, section 8. Yet federal grants-in-aid to states and municipalities, widely employed in such New Deal programs as the Public Works Administration, were already a well-established feature of American "cooperative" FEDERALISM. Moreover, exercises of the spending power could easily be insulated from JUDICIAL REVIEW under the taxpayer STANDING doctrine announced in FROTHINGHAM V. MELLON (1923). So long as Congress appropriated the funds to be spent from general revenue rather than from an account funded by a particular tax, no taxpayers had standing to challenge the propriety of the expenditure. While the New Deal ushered in the modern welfare state with its dramatic increases both in the volume of federal expenditures and in the purposes to which Washington's largesse was directed, such congressional capacity was already latent in the structure of contemporary constitutional doctrine.

Indeed, the American constitutional order on the eve of the Great Depression was hardly an unregulated regime of *laissez-faire*. By 1930 the Court had already upheld a vast array of state POLICE POWER statutes, including regulations of working hours and child labor, worker's compensation statutes, wage and payment regulations, utility and price regulations, and state ANTITRUST laws. Far more notorious, however, were cases in which the Court had invalidated a workplace or price prescription on the ground that it interfered with the FREEDOM OF CONTRACT or applied to a business that was not "affected with a public interest." The HUGHES COURT excised these closely related substantive due process doctrines from the constitutional lexicon, upholding extensive legislative control of wages, prices, and collective bargaining. Henceforth "regulatory legislation affecting ordinary commercial transactions" would enjoy a virtually irrebuttable presumption that it provided DUE PROCESS OF LAW. In tandem with contemporaneous developments in COMMERCE CLAUSE jurisprudence, these decisions cleared the remaining impediments to the emergence of the modern regulatory state.

Federal regulation of the economy was of course not a New Deal innovation. By 1930 the Court had already sanctioned extensive regulation of business practices in interstate commerce, upholding initiatives ranging from the FEDERAL TRADE COMMISSION ACT and federal antitrust laws to the PURE FOOD AND DRUG ACT. The Court had similarly approved extensive federal supervision of the railroad industry, stamping its imprimatur on not only the INTERSTATE COMMERCE ACT, but the Federal Employers Liability Act, the Safety Appliance Act, and the Railway Labor Act as well. Under the SHREVEPORT DOCTRINE, federal regulatory power over the railroads extended even to intrastate activities when they bore a "close and substantial" relation to interstate commerce. Such "local" activities as mining, manufacturing, and agricultural production were typically held to affect interstate commerce only "indirectly," and were thus frequently beyond congressional control. However, even local activities such as transactions in stockyards and on grain exchanges could be reached by Congress if they were situated in a "current" or "stream" of interstate commerce. Under both the Shreveport doctrine and the current of commerce doctrine, however, federal regulation of local enterprise was limited by the due process requirement that the business regulated be, like railroads, stockyards, and grain exchanges, "affected with a public interest."

Two events of the New Deal period dramatically expanded the scope of federal power. First, by lifting the "affected with a public interest" limitation in due process jurisprudence, the Court allowed more general application of commerce clause PRECEDENTS previously restricted to a handful of enterprises. This development opened new opportunities for federal regulation of such domains as industrial labor relations and the agriculture and energy sectors. Second, by 1942 the Court had explicitly retired the old local/national and direct/indirect dichotomies that had framed commerce clause jurisprudence for more than half a century. The consequences of this abandonment were twofold. First, a plenary commerce power underwrote unprecedented expansion of both the national administrative state and the role of federal law in daily life. Much of the nation's economic activity would become subject to the JURISDICTION of REGULATORY AGENCIES, and the commerce power eventually became the vehicle of choice for federal oversight of everything from civil rights to street crime. Second, because these old distinctions had also been central to DORMANT COMMERCE CLAUSE jurisprudence, their exile from the affirmative commerce clause context prompted the Court to reformulate the clause's negative implications. In years to come such cases would focus not on whether the activity regulated was "local" or the regulation affected commerce "directly," but rather on whether the state or local government was discriminating against or unduly burdening interstate commerce. Decoupling affirmative and dormant commerce clause doctrine served to prevent omnicompetent federal power from implicitly obliterating state and local regulatory prerogatives.

Recent years have seen a revival of academic interest in the New Deal. Central to the lively scholarly discussion has been the question of how best to characterize the period's constitutional development. Some scholars see an abrupt constitutional "revolution" in 1937; others claim a more gradual "transformation" began earlier in the decade (if not earlier in the century) and concluded in the early 1940s. Some see in this development a "rediscovery" of the Constitution after a period of activist corruption, whereas others view it as a mistaken departure from established and appropriate constitutional norms. Where some detect a "translation" or adaptation of the Constitution to changed circumstances, still others observe a shift in interpretive practice that transformed the very meaning of constitutional adaptivity. One prominent scholar contends that the Constitution was actually "amended" outside the procedure specified by Article V when the Court forged new constitutional law in response to the will of the people expressed in the "critical election" of 1936. The debate has taken on greater urgency in an era of political and judicial retrenchment, as some commentators seek not only to describe the change, but also to legitimate and draw prescriptive force from it. Yet beneath these differences in characterization rests a consensus that the New Deal era was the principal constitutional watershed of the twentieth century.

BARRY CUSHMAN
(2000)

(SEE ALSO: *Amendment Process (Outside of Article V); Constitutional History, 1933–1945; Roosevelt, Franklin D.*)

Bibliography

ACKERMAN, BRUCE 1998 *We the People: Transformations.* Cambridge, Mass.: Harvard University Press.
CUSHMAN, BARRY 1998 *Rethinking the New Deal Court: The Structure of a Constitutional Revolution.* New York: Oxford University Press.
FRIEDMAN, RICHARD D. 1994 Switching Time and Other Thought Experiments: The Hughes Court and Constitutional Transformation. *University of Pennsylvania Law Review* 142: 1891–1984.
LESSIG, LAWRENCE 1995 Understanding Changed Readings: Fidelity and Theory. *Stanford Law Review* 47:395–472.
LEUCHTENBURG, WILLIAM E. 1995 *The Supreme Court Reborn: The Constitutional Revolution in the Age of Roosevelt.* New York: Oxford University Press.
WHITE, G. EDWARD 1997 The "Constitutional Revolution" as a Crisis in Adaptivity. *Hastings Law Journal* 48:867–912.

NEW HAMPSHIRE SUPREME COURT v. PIPER
470 U.S. 274 (1985)

In *Piper* the Supreme Court followed *United Building and Construction Trades Council v. Camden* (1984) and applied a two-step analysis for applying the PRIVILEGES AND IMMUNITIES clause of Article IV. The Court held, 8–1, that

New Hampshire's rule limiting the practice of law to New Hampshire citizens violated the clause. First, the clause was properly invoked; doing business in the state is a privilege that is "fundamental" to the preservation of interstate harmony. Second, the state had not sufficiently justified its exclusion of Piper, who lived in Vermont, 400 yards from the New Hampshire border, and intended to maintain a law office in New Hampshire.

KENNETH L. KARST
(1986)

NEW JERSEY v. T. L. O.
469 U.S. 325 (1985)

In *New Jersey v. T. L. O.* a unanimous Supreme Court held that the FOURTH AMENDMENT's prohibition against unreasonable SEARCHES AND SEIZURES applies to searches of students conducted by public school officials. A majority of the Court (6–3) also held that school officials need not obtain a SEARCH WARRANT before searching a student under their authority and that their searches can be justified by a lower standard than probable cause to believe that the subject of the search has violated or is violating the law. Instead, the legality of the search depends on the reasonableness of the search under all the circumstances.

According to Justice BYRON R. WHITE's majority opinion, determining reasonableness requires a twofold inquiry: first, whether the search was justified at its inception, and, second, whether the search as actually conducted was reasonably related in its scope to the circumstances that initially justified it. Ordinarily, the search is justified at its inception if there are reasonable grounds for suspecting that the search will produce EVIDENCE that the student has violated or is violating either the law or the school rules. The search is permissible in scope if the measures adopted are reasonably related to the objectives of the search and are not excessively intrusive in light of the age and sex of the student and the nature of the infraction.

PATRICK DUTTON
(1986)

Bibliography

DUTTON, PATRICK 1985 School Searches: Recent Applications of the United States and California Constitutions. *Journal of Juvenile Law* 9:106–128.

NEW JERSEY v. WILSON
7 Cranch 164 (1812)

This case was the vehicle by which the Supreme Court made a breathtaking expansion of the CONTRACT CLAUSE. In the colonial period New Jersey had granted certain lands to an Indian tribe in exchange for a waiver by the Indians of their claim to any other lands. The grant provided that the new lands would be exempt from taxation in perpetuity. In 1801, over forty years later, the Indians left the state after selling their lands with state permission. The legislation repealed the tax exemption statute and assessed the new owners, who challenged the constitutionality of the repeal act.

A unanimous Supreme Court, overruling the state court, held that the grant of a tax immunity was a contract protected by the contract clause. By some species of metaphysics the Court reasoned that the tax immunity attached to the land, not to the Indians, and therefore the new holders of the land were tax exempt. Chief Justice JOHN MARSHALL's opinion, voiding the state tax, gave a retroactive operation to the contract clause; the grant of tax immunity predated the clause by many years. More important, Marshall ignored the implications of his DOCTRINE that such a grant was a contract. According to this decision, a state, by an act of its legislature, may contract away its sovereign power of taxation and prevent a successive legislature from asserting that power. The doctrine of VESTED RIGHTS, here converted into a doctrine of tax immunity, handicapped the revenue capabilities of the states, raising grave questions about the policy of the opinion. As a matter of political or constitutional theory, the Court's assumption that an attribute of SOVEREIGNTY can be surrendered by a legislative grant to private parties or to their property was, at the least, dubious. Although Marshall restricted the states, he allowed them to cede tax powers by contract rather than thwart the exercise of those powers on rights vested by contract.

The growth of CORPORATIONS revealed the significance of the new doctrine of tax immunity. States and municipalities, eager to promote the establishment of banks, factories, turnpikes, railroads, and utilities, often granted corporations tax immunity or other tax advantages as an inducement to engage in such enterprises, and the corporations often secured their special privileges by corrupt methods. This case permitted the granting of tax preferences and constitutionally sanctioned political corruption and the reckless development of economic resources. But permission is not compulsion; the legislatures, not the judiciary, granted the contracts. The Court simply extended the contract clause beyond the intentions of its framers to protect vested rights and promote business needs.

LEONARD W. LEVY
(1986)

NEW JERSEY COLONIAL CHARTERS

New Jersey received its first charter from its proprietors, John Berkeley and George Carteret, in 1664. The charter established representative institutions of government, contained a clause on RELIGIOUS LIBERTY similar to that in the RHODE ISLAND CHARTER of 1663, and guaranteed that only the general assembly could impose taxes. In 1676 Berkeley sold his share of New Jersey to Quakers, leaving Carteret proprietor of East New Jersey. In 1677 the Quaker proprietors issued a "Charter or Fundamental Laws, of West New Jersey," the work, probably, of WILLIAM PENN. The charter included clauses on liberty of conscience, TRIAL BY JURY, and several protections for the criminally accused; the charter is memorable, however, because it functioned as a written CONSTITUTION of FUNDAMENTAL LAW. It began with the provision that the " COMMON LAW or fundamental rights" of the colony should be "the foundation of the government, which is not to be altered by the Legislative authority . . . constituted according to these fundamentals. . . ." The legislature was enjoined to maintain the fundamentals and to make no laws contradicting or varying from them.

In 1682 a Quaker group headed by Penn gained control of East New Jersey and in the following year issued "The Fundamental Constitutions" for that province. The charter of 1683, which was modeled on the Pennsylvania Frame of Government of 1682 (see PENNSYLVANIA COLONIAL CHARTERS), recognized CONSCIENTIOUS OBJECTION, banned any ESTABLISHMENT OF RELIGION, paraphrased chapter 39 of MAGNA CARTA, and included a variety of provisions that resembled a bill of rights, far more numerous than in the English BILL OF RIGHTS of 1689. Although New Jersey became a royal colony in 1702, the seventeenth-century Quaker charters are significant evidence of the grip which CONSTITUTIONALISM had upon influential colonial thinkers.

LEONARD W. LEVY
(1986)

Bibliography

ANDREWS, CHARLES MCLEAN 1936 *The Colonial Period of American History.* Vol. 3:138–180. New Haven, Conn.: Yale University Press.

NEW JERSEY PLAN

The adoption of the VIRGINIA PLAN by the CONSTITUTIONAL CONVENTION OF 1787 frightened state sovereignty supporters and nationalists from small states. A BICAMERAL Congress apportioned on the basis of population would have enabled the great states to dominate the new government. On June 15, 1787, WILLIAM PATERSON of New Jersey introduced a substitute plan that retained the "purely federal" (confederated) character of the ARTICLES OF CONFEDERATION. Under the Article a unicameral Congress in which

each state had one vote preserved the principle of state equality.

As CHARLES PINCKNEY observed, if New Jersey had an equal vote, she would "dismiss her scruples, and concur in the national system." The New Jersey plan, though merely amending the Articles, was a small states' nationalist plan, not a state sovereignty plan. It recommended a Congress with powers to regulate commerce and to raise revenue from import and stamp duties, and it would have authorized requisitions from the states enforceable by a national executive empowered to use the military against states defying national laws and treaties. The plan recommended a national judiciary with broad JURISDICTION, extending to cases arising out of the regulation of commerce and the collection of the revenue. The nucleus of the SUPREMACY CLAUSE, making national law the supreme law of the states, was also part of the plan. It was a warning to large-state nationalists that they would have to compromise on the issue of REPRESENTATION. The Committee of the Whole defeated the plan 7–3, with one state divided. The Convention was thereafter stymied until the GREAT COMPROMISE was adopted. (See CONSTITUTIONAL HISTORY, 1776–1789.)

LEONARD W. LEVY
(1986)

Bibliography

BRANT, IRVING 1950 *James Madison: Father of the Constitution, 1787–1800.* Pages 46–54. Indianapolis: Bobbs-Merrill.

NEW ORLEANS v. DUKES
427 U.S. 297 (1976)

Only once since 1937 has the Supreme Court struck down a state ECONOMIC REGULATION as a denial of the EQUAL PROTECTION OF THE LAWS. That case was *Morey v. Doud* (1957). In *Dukes*, the Court unanimously overruled *Morey*; a per curiam opinion reaffirmed the appropriateness of the RATIONAL BASIS standard of review in testing economic regulations against the demands of both equal protection and SUBSTANTIVE DUE PROCESS.

Dukes involved a New Orleans ordinance prohibiting the sale of food from pushcarts in the French Quarter, but exempting vendors who had been selling from pushcarts for eight years. This GRANDFATHER CLAUSE, said the Court, was rationally related to the city's legitimate interest in preserving the area's distinctive character while accommodating substantial reliance interests of long-term businesses.

KENNETH L. KARST
(1986)

NEW RIGHT

As a political phenomenon New Right jurisprudence is a reaction against the broad protection of individual rights advanced by the WARREN COURT. Intellectually the New Right proposes a style of CONSTITUTIONAL INTERPRETATION that emphasizes fidelity to received historical materials and legal forms in order to foreclose judicial reliance on moral philosophy. Among the most prominent proponents of New Right jurisprudence are former Attorney General Edwin Meese, Chief Justice WILLIAM H. REHNQUIST, and scholar-jurist Robert H. Bork.

The great aim in fashioning an approach to constitutional interpretation must, for the New Right, be to find public, politically neutral standards that curb judicial willfulness. "The framers' intentions with respect to freedoms," as Bork put it, "are the sole legitimate premise from which constitutional analysis may proceed." The great temptation for judges armed with the power to review legislative acts (and for losers in the political process who retain the capacity to influence judges) is to strike down laws that they do not like on the grounds furnished by some broad, vague, and easily manipulated constitutional phrase. The only antidote for judicial tyranny is history—the authority of the original, public sense of what a particular phrase or clause was meant to accomplish.

This reliance on ORIGINAL INTENT, however, cannot be a mechanical process. Principles must be discerned and applied to particular circumstances and problems (such as WIRETAPPING) that the Framers could not have foreseen. Most originalists seek to discern and apply the primary purpose of a clause rather than the Framers' specific intentions. And so even a practice specifically accepted by the Framers of the EQUAL PROTECTION clause of the FOURTEENTH AMENDMENT, such as segregated schooling, might be unconstitutional.

The second element in New Right jurisprudence is an emphasis on democracy or majority rule as the touchstone of constitutional authority. Against the background of POPULAR SOVEREIGNTY, the power of unelected judges to strike down laws made by the people's representatives appears anomalous and in need of close containment. The emphasis on popular rule also supports the resort to historical intentions: When judges rely on the Framers' intentions, they can claim simply to be upholding a superior expression of popular will (the Constitution as originally understood) to an inferior one (the will of this legislature).

The New Right's third basic commitment is its foursquare opposition to the role of moral theory in constitutional interpretation. Whatever one might think of natural law or moral objectivity, in political practice moral arguments must always be regarded as nothing more than expressions of personal preferences and desires. Thus, according to Bork, "every clash between a minority claiming freedom from regulation and a majority asserting its freedom to regulate requires a choice between the gratifications (or moral positions) of the two groups." The New Right believes that to allow moral judgment any substantial role in constitutional interpretation licenses judges to overturn duly made laws on personal, ideological grounds.

The fourth and final plank in the New Right program is the identification of the extension of individual rights with an assault on community in the name of moral relativism. Both Bork and Meese approvingly quote the conservative British jurist Lord Patrick Devlin: "What makes a society is a community of ideas, not political ideas alone but also ideas about the way its members should behave and govern lives." More judicially mandated individual freedom, it seems, equals more relativism and less community.

Each of the components of New Right jurisprudence has been subjected to criticism. Original intentions, it has been said, are often extremely difficult to discern. What is to count as evidence? How do we distinguish intentions from hopes and aspirations? Did the Framers intend us to be guided by their intentions? Perhaps most tellingly, what do we make of the broad moralistic language that was often chosen and written into the Constitution? Bork wants to regard the NINTH AMENDMENT and the Fourteenth Amendment's PRIVILEGES AND IMMUNITIES clause as unintelligible "ink blots" on the document because to treat them as the broad delegations that they appear to be would give too much power to judges. The New Right's sense of how much JUDICIAL POWER is too much seems, in spite of professions of political neutrality, rooted less in a careful reading of history than in a reaction against the JUDICIAL ACTIVISM spawned by the Warren Court.

The New Right's emphasis on the Constitution's basically democratic character misses, some have charged, the equally basic role of individual liberty in the founding design. A basic commitment to broad individual rights helps legitimate the powers of a Court remote from popular passions and prejudices. The practical moral skepticism of the New Right is also subjected to debate: Do we not have widely shared working standards of morality? Does not the New Right itself implicitly invoke and depend upon a democratic political morality and an ethic of judicial self-restraint?

The New Right's claim that individual rights will replace community morality with relativism seems highly dubious, not to mention odd, in light of the New Right's own professed skepticism. In becoming more tolerant, open, and respectful of individual freedom a community would seem to be changing, perhaps even improving, its morality rather than dropping it. With its capacity to insist that majorities treat minorities reasonably, the Supreme

Court appears well situated to improve community morality.

New Right jurisprudence appeals to political skeptics who identify judicial activism, new and old, with elite tyranny. The sharpest opponents of the New Right are those who believe that the Constitution itself raises moral questions for interpreters and that an active, morally reflective Court advances the causes of individual liberty and reasonable self-government.

STEPHEN MACEDO
(1992)

(SEE ALSO: *Bork Nomination; Conservatism; Constitution and Civic Ideals; Critical Legal Studies; Deconstructionism; Liberalism; Originalism; Political Philosophy of the Constitution; Segregation.*)

Bibliography

BERGER, RAOUL 1977 *Government by Judiciary.* Cambridge, Mass.: Harvard University Press.

BORK, ROBERT H. 1990 *The Tempting of America: The Political Seduction of the Law.* New York: Free Press.

MACEDO, STEPHEN 1987 *The New Right v. the Constitution.* Washington, D.C.: Cato Institute.

REHNQUIST, WILLIAM H. 1976 The Notion of a Living Constitution. *Texas Law Review* 54:693–704.

NEWSMAN'S PRIVILEGE

See: Reporter's Privilege

NEW STATE ICE COMPANY v. LIEBMANN
285 U.S. 262 (1932)

An Oklahoma law required ice dealers to obtain a license before entering the market because their business was AF-FECTED WITH A PUBLIC INTEREST. A 6–2 majority could find no exceptional circumstances such as monopoly or emergency—that is, no public interest in regulation—justifying the restriction and so struck down the law as a violation of DUE PROCESS. Echoing Justice OLIVER WENDELL HOLMES's dissent in TYSON BROTHER V. BANTON (1927), Justice LOUIS D. BRANDEIS, with Justice HARLAN FISKE STONE concurring, insisted that the assessment of local conditions and requirements was a legislative concern. Seeking to justify a state's right to experiment with social and economic legislation, Brandeis wrote: ". . . we must be ever on our guard, lest we erect our prejudices into legal principles."

DAVID GORDON
(1986)

(SEE ALSO: *Nebbia v. New York; Ribnik v. McBride.*)

NEW YORK v. BELTON

See: Automobile Search

NEW YORK v. FERBER
458 U.S. 747 (1982)

This decision demonstrated the BURGER COURT's willingness to add to the list of categories of speech excluded from the FIRST AMENDMENT's protection. New York, like the federal government and most of the states, prohibits the distribution of material depicting sexual performances by children under age 16, whether or not the material constitutes OBSCENITY. After a New York City bookseller sold two such films to an undercover police officer, he was convicted under this law. The Supreme Court unanimously affirmed his conviction.

Justice BYRON R. WHITE, for the Court, denied that state power in this regulatory area was confined to the suppression of obscene material. The state's interest in protecting children against abuse was compelling; to prevent the production of such materials, it was necessary to forbid their distribution. CHILD PORNOGRAPHY—the visual depiction of sexual conduct by children below a specified age—was "a category of material outside the protection of the First Amendment."

The Court also rejected the argument that the law was overbroad, thus abandoning a distinction announced in BROADRICK V. OKLAHOMA (1973) to govern OVERBREADTH challenges. Henceforth the overbreadth doctrine would apply only in cases of "substantial overbreadth," whether or not the state sought to regulate the content of speech.

KENNETH L. KARST
(1986)

NEW YORK v. MILN

See: *Mayor of New York v. Miln*

NEW YORK v. QUARLES
467 U.S. 649 (1984)

Justice WILLIAM REHNQUIST, for a 5–4 Supreme Court, announced a public safety exception to the MIRANDA RULES. In a situation where concern for the public safety must supersede adherence to MIRANDA V. ARIZONA (1966), the prosecution may use in EVIDENCE incriminating statements made during a custodial interrogation before the suspect receives notice of his constitutional rights. Here, the Court reinstated a conviction based on the evidence of a gun and information concerning its whereabouts. Dissenters disagreed on whether the case showed a threat to the public safety, but produced no principled argument against the exception to *Miranda*.

LEONARD W. LEVY
(1986)

NEW YORK v. UNITED STATES
505 U.S. 144 (1992)

In GARCIA V. SAN ANTONIO METROPOLITAN TRANSIT AUTHORITY (1985), the Supreme Court seemed to reject a strong JUDICIAL ROLE in protecting states from congressional regulatory authority. But in *New York v. United States* and *Printz v. United States* (1997), the Court renewed its earlier commitment to protecting state autonomy. Together, *New York* and *Printz* hold that Congress may not commandeer state or local legislative or executive officials to formulate or administer a federal regulatory program that otherwise falls within the Article I authority of Congress. These decisions leave Congress with ample authority to encourage states to implement federal policies, but limited authority to coerce them to do so.

In *New York*, the Court invalidated the "take title" provision of the Low-Level Radioactive Waste Policy Amendments Act of 1985. This provision required each state by 1996 either to regulate, in congressionally acceptable ways, the disposal of publicly or privately generated radioactive WASTE, or to take title to the waste and hence assume liability for it. The Court offered two main arguments for its conclusion. The first concerned ORIGINAL INTENT: In replacing the ARTICLES OF CONFEDERATION with the Constitution, claimed the Court, the Framers intended to replace an ineffectual regime in which Congress could regulate only the states and not individual citizens, with the conceptually opposite regime in which Congress could regulate only individual citizens but not states. The Court also professed a concern for maintaining clear lines of political accountability, and claimed that commandeering might lead citizens within a state erroneously to ascribe responsibility for unpopular policy decisions to "puppet" state officials rather than the actual federal decisionmakers behind the scenes.

Printz involved a challenge to provisions of the federal Brady Handgun Violence Prevention Act that required state law enforcement officers to expend a "reasonable effort" to conduct background checks as part of a federal handgun control policy. Defending the statute, the United States argued that *New York* was distinguishable because the Brady Act coerced only the administration of federally defined law, rather than state legislative lawmaking in pursuance of general federal objectives. By compelling only relatively ministerial activities, asserted the United States, the act neither interfered with the state's sovereign lawmaking capacity and autonomy, nor did it realistically threaten to muddle political accountability. But the Court rejected these efforts to distinguish *New York*, making clear that Congress cannot commandeer state executive officials any more than legislative ones, by imposing ministerial burdens any more than regulatory ones. The Court replied that the principle of state autonomy inherent in the notion of "dual sovereignty" is undermined whenever Congress targets states for the imposition of affirmative regulatory or executory duties.

The doctrinal rule emerging from *New York* and *Printz*—Congress may not conscript state officials to do its bidding—may seem intuitively appropriate as an interpretation of dual sovereignty, and has the further merit of establishing a bright line capable of easy judicial enforcement. The Court's reasoning in these decisions has been criticized, however, for its overly formalist quality. While the Court invoked commonplace clichés about how state autonomy may frustrate federal tyranny, the Court failed to consider carefully how an anticommandeering rule serves the values underlying our federalist regime. Moreover, the Court's formalist structural and historical arguments purporting to deduce an anticommandeering rule from abstract notions of dual sovereignty seem somewhat forced, belying any suggestion that the REHNQUIST COURT is less "activist" as defined by aggressive review of democratically enacted statutes than either the WARREN COURT or BURGER COURT.

Both *New York*'s and *Printz*'s practical impact on federal–state relations may be quite limited. First, the cases leave open the possibility that Congress may still commandeer state administrative resources pursuant to a few specific grants of power, including the power of Congress under the FOURTEENTH AMENDMENT, SECTION 5 to enforce that amendment's rights against the states. Second, the cases affirmed the authority of Congress to encourage states to enact and enforce regulations designed to achieve federal goals through either of two noncoercive means. Congress may condition federal subsidies on the willingness of states to administer federally desired programs, and Congress may threaten to PREEMPT state programs unless they conform to federal standards. As Congress has employed these noncoercive tools far more frequently than coercive ones, *New York* and *Printz* may have greater symbolic than practical import for our regime of FEDERALISM.

EVAN H. CAMINKER
(2000)

(SEE ALSO: *Dual Federalism; López, United States v.; Sovereignty; State Immunity from Federal Law*.)

Bibliography

CAMINKER, EVAN H. 1995 State Sovereignty and Subordinacy: May Congress Commandeer State Officers to Implement Federal Law? *Columbia Law Review* 95:1001–1089.

——— 1997   Printz, State Sovereignty, and the Limits of Formalism. *The Supreme Court Review* 1997:199–248.

PRAKASH, SAIKRISHNA B.   1993   Field Office Federalism. *Virginia Law Review* 79:1957–2037.

POWELL, H. JEFFERSON   1993   The Oldest Question of Constitutional Law. *Virginia Law Review* 79:633–689.

NEW YORK CENTRAL RAILROAD COMPANY v. WHITE
243 U.S. 188 (1917)

The New York Workmen's Compensation Act of 1914 made employers liable to compensate injured workers in certain cases without regard to fault. The statute thereby departed from time-honored COMMON LAW rules of liability, particularly the fellow-servant doctrine and contributory negligence. The act established a graduated scale of compensation based on the loss of earning power, prior wages, and the character and duration of the disability suffered. Death benefits would be paid according to the survivors' needs.

Here, a night watchman was injured while guarding tools and materials used in the construction of a new station and tracks designed for INTERSTATE COMMERCE. A 9–0 Supreme Court held that the watchman was not in interstate commerce within the meaning of the first EMPLOYERS' LIABILITY ACT. Justice MAHLON PITNEY, for the Court, declared that his work "bore no direct relation to interstate transportation." Pitney rejected claims that the New York act violated the FOURTEENTH AMENDMENT's prohibition against a TAKING OF PROPERTY without DUE PROCESS OF LAW and deprived both parties of the FREEDOM OF CONTRACT. "It needs no argument to show that such a rule [fellow-servant] is subject to modification or abrogation by a state upon proper occasion." Because "the public has a direct interest in this as affecting the common welfare," the Court sustained the act as a reasonable exercise of the STATE POLICE POWER. Pitney also rejected the argument that the exclusion of certain workers from the statute's coverage was an arbitrary classification in violation of the EQUAL PROTECTION clause of the Fourteenth Amendment. He concluded that the classification was reasonable in view of the "inherent risks" associated with the various occupations.

DAVID GORDON
(1986)

NEW YORK CHARTER OF LIBERTIES AND PRIVILEGES
(October 30, 1683)

The first enactment of the first general assembly in New York was a statute but had the characteristics of a charter or CONSTITUTION of FUNDAMENTAL LAW. Its purpose was to establish a government "that Justice and Right may be Equally done to all persons . . . ," an early forerunner of the principle of EQUAL PROTECTION OF THE LAWS. After describing the organs of government and empowering every freeholder to vote for representatives, the statute paraphrased chapter 39 of MAGNA CARTA and provided that no taxes should be imposed but by the general assembly. Then followed protections of the rights of the criminally accused, including a right to INDICTMENT by GRAND JURY in criminal cases. Another provision of the document, after protecting RELIGIOUS LIBERTY, created a multiple ESTABLISHMENT OF RELIGION. It allowed the towns on Long Island to elect Christian ministers of their choice, to be supported by town rates, and declared that "all" the other Christian churches in the province were "priviledged Churches . . . Established" by law. Elsewhere in Christendom, an established church meant a church of a single denomination preferred over all others.

The Privy Council disallowed the statute in 1686. In 1691, after James II was overthrown, the general assembly substantially reenacted it but again it was disallowed, probably because it curbed the royal prerogative. Although the statute never became law, it is early evidence of the high regard that colonists had for Magna Carta, written guarantees of their liberties, and the principle that there should be no TAXATION WITHOUT REPRESENTATION.

LEONARD W. LEVY
(1986)

Bibliography

ANDREW, CHARLES McLEAN   1936   *The Colonial Period of American History.* Vol. 3:114–121. New Haven, Conn.: Yale University Press.

NEW YORK STATE CLUB ASSOCIATION v. NEW YORK CITY

See: Freedom of Association

NEW YORK TIMES CO. v. SULLIVAN
376 U.S. 254 (1964)

MARTIN LUTHER KING, JR., was arrested in Alabama in 1960 on a perjury charge. In New York a group of entertainers and civil rights activists formed a committee to help finance King's defense. They placed a full-page advertisement in the *New York Times* appealing for contributions. The ad charged that King's arrest was part of a campaign to destroy King's leadership of the movement to integrate public facilities and encourage blacks in the South to vote.

It asserted that "Southern violators" in Montgomery had expelled King's student followers from college, ringed the campus with armed police, padlocked the dining hall to starve them into submission, bombed King's home, assaulted his person, and arrested him seven times for speeding, loitering, and other dubious offenses.

L. B. Sullivan, a city commissioner of Montgomery, filed a libel action in state court against the *Times* and four black Alabama ministers whose names had appeared as endorsers of the ad. He claimed that because his duties included supervision of the Montgomery police, the allegations against the police defamed him personally.

Under the common law as it existed in Alabama and most other states, the *Times* had little chance of winning. Whether the statements referred to Sullivan was a fact issue; if the jury found that readers would identify him, it was immaterial that the ad did not name him. Because the statements reflected adversely on Sullivan's professional reputation they were "libelous per se"; that meant he need not prove that he actually had been harmed. The defense of truth was not available because the ad contained factual errors (for example, police had not "ringed the campus," though they had been deployed nearby; King had been arrested four times, not seven). A few states recognized a privilege for good faith errors in criticism of public officials, but Alabama was among the majority that did not.

The jury awarded Sullivan $500,000. In the Alabama Supreme Court, the *Times* argued such a judgment was inconsistent with FREEDOM OF THE PRESS, but that court merely repeated what the United States Supreme Court had often said: "The First Amendment of the United States Constitution does not protect libelous publications."

When the case reached the Supreme Court in 1964, it was one of eleven libel claims, totaling $5,600,000, pending against the *Times* in Alabama. It was obvious that libel suits were being used to discourage the press from supporting the CIVIL RIGHTS movement in the South. The *Times* urged the Court to equate these uses of libel law with the discredited doctrine of SEDITIOUS LIBEL and to hold that criticism of public officials could never be actionable.

Only three Justices were willing to go that far. The majority adopted a more limited rule, holding that public officials could recover for defamatory falsehoods about their official conduct or fitness for office only if they could prove that the defendant had published with "actual malice." This was defined as "knowledge that [the statement] was false or with reckless disregard of whether it was false or not." The Court further held that this element had to be established by "clear and convincing proof," and that, unlike most factual issues, it was subject to independent review by appellate courts. The Court then reviewed Sullivan's evidence and determined that it did not meet the new standard.

The decision was an important breakthrough, not only for the press and the civil rights movement but also in FIRST AMENDMENT theory. Until then, vast areas of expression, including libel and commercial speech, had been categorically excluded from First Amendment protection. Also, the decision finally repudiated the darkest blot on freedom of expression in the history of the United States, the Sedition Act of 1798.

Over the next few years, the Court went out of its way to make the new rule effective. It defined "reckless disregard" narrowly (*St. Amant v. Thompson*, 1967). It extended the *Sullivan* rule to lesser public officials (*Rosenblatt v. Baer*, 1966), to candidates for public office (*Monitor Patriot Co. v. Roy*, 1971), to PUBLIC FIGURES (*Associated Press v. Walker*, 1967), and to criminal libel (*Garrison v. Louisiana*, 1964). After 1971 the Court retreated somewhat, declining to extend the *Sullivan* rule to private plaintiffs and permitting a de facto narrowing of the public figure category.

From its birth the rule has been criticized, by public officials and celebrities who believe it makes recovery too difficult, and by the news media, which argue that the rule still exposes them to long and expensive litigation, even though ultimately they usually win. The Court, however, has shown no inclination to revise the rule. In *Bose Corp. v. Consumers Union* (1984), the Court was invited to dilute it by abandoning independent appellate review of findings of "actual malice." The Court refused, holding such review essential "to preserve the precious liberties established and ordained by the Constitution."

DAVID A. ANDERSON
(1986)

Bibliography

KALVE, HARRY, JR. 1964 The New York Times Case: A Note on "The Central Meaning of the First Amendment." *Supreme Court Review* 1964:191–221.

PIERCE, SAMUEL R., JR. 1965 The Anatomy of an Historic Decision: *New York Times Co. v. Sullivan. North Carolina Law Review* 43:315–363.

NEW YORK TIMES CO. v. UNITED STATES
403 U.S. 713 (1971)

New York Times Co. v. United States, more commonly known as the Pentagon Papers case, is one of the landmarks of contemporary prior restraint doctrine. Only NEAR V. MINNESOTA (1931) rivals it as a case of central importance in establishing the FIRST AMENDMENT's particular and extreme aversion to any form of official restriction applied prior to the act of speaking or the act of publication.

The dramatic facts of the case served to keep it before the public eye even as it was being litigated and decided. On June 12, 1971, the *New York Times* commenced publication of selected portions of a 1968 forty-seven-volume classified Defense Department study entitled "History of United States Decision Making Process on Vietnam Policy" and a 1965 classified Defense Department study entitled "The Command and Control Study of the Tonkin Gulf Incident Done by the Defense Department's Weapons Systems Evaluation Group in 1965." Collectively these documents came to be known as the Pentagon Papers. Within a few days other major newspapers, including the *Washington Post,* the *Los Angeles Times,* the *Detroit Free Press,* the *Philadelphia Inquirer,* and the *Miami Herald* also commenced publication of the Pentagon Papers. The papers had been provided to the *New York Times* by Daniel Ellsberg, a former Defense Department official and former government consultant. Ellsberg had no official authority to take the Pentagon Papers; his turning over the papers to the *New York Times* was similarly unauthorized.

When the newspapers commenced publication, the United States was still engaged in fighting the VIETNAM WAR. Claiming that the publication of the Pentagon Papers jeopardized national security, the government sought an INJUNCTION against any further publication of the papers, including publication of scheduled installments yet to appear. In the United States District Court for the Southern District of New York, Judge Murray Gurfein issued a temporary restraining order against the *New York Times,* but then denied the government's request for a preliminary injunction against publication, finding that, in light of the extremely high hurdle necessary to justify a prior restraint against a newspaper, "the publication of these historical documents would [not] seriously breach the national security." (See PRIOR RESTRAINT AND CENSORSHIP.) The United States immediately appealed, and the Court of Appeals for the Second Circuit, on June 23, 1971, remanded the case for further consideration in light of documents filed by the United States indicating that publication might pose "grave and immediate danger to the security of the United States." The Second Circuit continued to enforce the stay it had previously issued, in effect keeping the *Times* under the restraint of the temporary restraining order. On the same day, however, the United States Court of Appeals for the District of Columbia Circuit, in a case involving the *Washington Post's* publication of the Pentagon Papers, affirmed a decision of the district court refusing to enjoin further publication. On June 24, the *New York Times* filed a petition for a WRIT OF CERTIORARI and

motion for expedited consideration in the Supreme Court, and on the same day the United States asked that Court for a stay of the District of Columbia circuit's ruling in the *Washington Post* case. The two cases were consolidated and accelerated, with briefs filed on June 26, oral argument the same day, and a decision of the Supreme Court on June 30, only seventeen days after the first publication of the papers in the *New York Times.*

In a brief PER CURIAM opinion, the Supreme Court affirmed the District of Columbia Circuit, reversed the Second Circuit, and vacated the restraints. Noting the "heavy presumption" against prior restraints, and the consequent "heavy burden of . . . justification" necessary to support a prior restraint, the Court found that the United States had not met that especially heavy burden.

The Court's per curiam opinion was accompanied by a number of important separate opinions by individual Justices. Justices HUGO L. BLACK and WILLIAM O. DOUGLAS made it clear that in their view prior restraints were never permissible. Justice WILLIAM J. BRENNAN would not go this far, but found it noteworthy that "never before has the United States sought to enjoin a newspaper from publishing information in its possession." For him "only governmental allegation and proof that publication must inevitably, directly, and immediately cause the occurrence of an evil kindred to imperiling the safety of a transport already at sea [citing *Near v. Minnesota*] can support even the issuance of an interim restraining order." In agreeing that the restraint was improper, Justice THURGOOD MARSHALL emphasized the absence of statutory authorization for governmental action to enjoin a newspaper. And Justice JOHN MARSHALL HARLAN, joined by Chief Justice WARREN E. BURGER and Justice HARRY A. BLACKMUN, dissented. The dissenters were disturbed by the alacrity of the proceedings, and in addition thought that the executive's "constitutional primacy in the field of FOREIGN AFFAIRS" justified a restraint at least long enough to allow the executive to present its complete case for the necessity of restriction. The most doctrinally illuminating opinions, however, were those of Justices POTTER J. STEWART and BYRON R. WHITE. For them only the specific nature of the restriction rendered it constitutionally impermissible. Had the case involved criminal or civil sanctions imposed after publication—subsequent punishment rather than prior restraint—they indicated that the First Amendment would not have stood in the way.

As highlighted by the opinions of Justices Stewart and White, therefore, the *Pentagon Papers* case presents the problem of prior restraint in purest form. The judges had the disputed materials in front of them, and thus there was no question of a restraint on materials not before a court, or not yet published. And the evaluation of the likely effect of the materials was made by the judiciary, rather than by a censorship board, other administrative agency, or police officer. Under these circumstances, why might a prior restraint be unconstitutional when a subsequent punishment for publishing the same materials would be upheld? What justifies a constitutional standard higher for injunctions than for criminal sanctions? It cannot be that prior restraints in fact "prevent" more things from being published, for the deterrent effect of a criminal sanction is likely to inhibit publication at least as much as an injunction. Someone who is willing knowingly to violate the criminal law, in order to publish out of conscience, may also be willing to violate an injunction. Is the special aversion against prior restraint, visible in the Pentagon Papers case, based on principle, or is it little more than an anachronism inherited from JOHN MILTON and WILLIAM BLACKSTONE, and transferred from a milieu in which prior restraint was synonymous with unreviewable determinations of an administrative censorship board?

The result in the Pentagon Papers case was not inconsistent with prior cases. The case did, however, present more clearly the puzzling nature of the virtually absolute prohibition against prior restraints under circumstances in which subsequent punishment of the very same material would have been permissible. Yet the case is also significant for reasons that transcend the doctrine of prior restraint. When confronted with a constitutional objection to a governmental policy, a court typically must evaluate the justification for the policy, and assess the likelihood of some consequences that the policy is designed to prevent. When that consequence and the governmental attempt to forestall it relates to war, national security, or national defense, judicial deference to governmental assertions of likely consequences has traditionally been greatest, even if the putative restriction implicates activities otherwise protected by the Constitution. When national security has been invoked, constitutional protection has often been more illusory than real. At every level in the Pentagon Papers case the courts conducted their own independent assessments of the likely dangers to national security and to troops overseas. The Supreme Court's decision was at least partly a function of the Justices' unwillingness to accept governmental incantation of the phrase "national security" as dispositive. Certainly executive determinations concerning the effect of publications on national security still receive greater deference than do other executive predictions about the effect of publications. But the Pentagon Papers case stands for the proposition that even when national security is claimed the courts will scrutinize for themselves the necessity of restriction. The decision, therefore, speaks not only to prior restraint but also, and more pervasively, to the courts' willingness to protect con-

stitutional rights even against wartime governmental restrictions imposed in the name of national security.

FREDERICK SCHAUER
(1986)

Bibliography

HENKIN, LOUIS 1971 The Right to Know and the Duty to Withhold: The Case of the Pentagon Papers. *University of Pennsylvania Law Review* 120:271–280.

JUNGER, PETER 1971 Down Memory Lane: The Case of the Pentagon Papers. *Case Western Reserve Law Review* 23:3–75.

KALVEN, HARRY, JR. 1971 Foreword: Even When a Nation Is at War. *Harvard Law Review* 85:3–36.

NIEMOTKO v. MARYLAND
340 U.S. 268 (1951)

The VINSON COURT here unanimously reversed the convictions of two Jehovah's Witnesses who had been charged with disorderly conduct for attempting to hold religious services in a city park without a permit. Local officials had refused to issue the permit, citing ordinances or administrative standards that governed the procedure, but such permits had been routinely approved for other religious and patriotic groups. The city's refusal to issue a permit to the Jehovah's Witnesses under these circumstances, the Court held, was both an unconstitutional prior restraint on speech and a denial of EQUAL PROTECTION.

MICHAEL E. PARRISH
(1986)

NIMMER, MELVILLE B.
(1923–1985)

After his graduation from Harvard Law School Melville Nimmer practiced law in Los Angeles for more than a decade. During that time he wrote the foundational article elaborating the "right of publicity," a right to control the commercial use of one's own identity. He also produced *Nimmer on Copyright* (1st ed., 1963), a four-volume treatise rightly called "magisterial," which soon became the nation's leading authority on copyright law. In 1962 he joined the law faculty of the University of California, Los Angeles, where he was a much-loved teacher of copyright law (later expanded into entertainment law), contracts, and constitutional law.

Although Nimmer's constitutional law scholarship ranged over such diverse topics as American CIVIL RIGHTS legislation and judicial review in Israel, the main focus of his attention was the FIRST AMENDMENT. He practiced what he preached, serving the AMERICAN CIVIL LIBERTIES UNION as counsel in a number of cases, including COHEN V. CALIFORNIA (1971). In *Cohen* the Supreme Court adopted Nimmer's argument severely restricting the assumption, casually made in CHAPLINSKY V. NEW HAMPSHIRE (1942), that profanity lay outside the First Amendment's protection. The case produced one of Justice JOHN MARSHALL HARLAN's most noteworthy opinions, and today it is widely taught in law school courses dealing with the FREEDOM OF SPEECH.

Nimmer's First Amendment articles dealt with movie censorship, LIBEL and invasion of privacy (see PRIVACY AND THE FIRST AMENDMENT), SYMBOLIC SPEECH, national security secrets, the special role of the press clause, and—inevitably—the relation of COPYRIGHT to the First Amendment. (He wrote on three of these topics for this *Encyclopedia*.) In these writings he developed a theory of "definitional balancing" that became one of the theoretical centerpieces of his last major work on constitutional law, *Nimmer on Freedom of Speech: A Treatise on the Theory of the First Amendment* (1984). Nimmer planned to supplement this treatise regularly, and specifically to apply his theories to "national security, breach of the peace, commercial speech and obscenity." When he died the next year, his colleagues and the larger community lost much more than those products of a gifted legal mind.

KENNETH L. KARST

(1992)

Bibliography

MELVILLE B. NIMMER SYMPOSIUM 1987 *UCLA Law Review* 34: 1331–1903 (includes a complete list of Nimmer's published works).

NINETEENTH AMENDMENT

Ratification of the women's suffrage amendment in 1920 marked the culmination of a struggle spanning three quarters of a century. Under the leadership of organizations including the National Woman's Suffrage Association and the National Women's Party, over 2 million women participated in some 900 campaigns before state and federal legislators, party officials, and referendum voters. By the time the amendment was adopted, a majority of the states had already given some recognition to women's VOTING RIGHTS.

Political agitation for enfranchisement began in 1848, at the first women's rights convention in SENECA FALLS, New York. In its Declaration of Sentiments, the convention included suffrage as one of the "inalienable rights" to which women were entitled. As the century progressed, the vote assumed increasing importance, both as a symbolic affirmation of women's equality and as a means to address a vast array of sex-based discrimination in employment, education, domestic law, and related areas. Once the Supreme Court ruled in MINOR V. HAPPERSETT (1875) that suffrage was not one of the PRIVILEGES AND IMMUNITIES guaranteed by the FOURTEENTH AMENDMENT to women as citizens, the necessity for a state or federal constitutional amendment became apparent.

The struggle for women's rights was a response to various forces. Urbanization, industrialization, declining birth rates, and expanding educational and employment opportunities tended to diminish women's role in the private domestic sphere while encouraging their participation in the public sphere. So too, women's involvement, first with abolitionism and later with other progressive causes, generated political commitments and experiences that fueled demands for equal rights.

Those demands provoked opposition from various quarters. The liquor industry feared that enfranchisement would pave the way for PROHIBITION, while conservative political and religious leaders, as well as women homemakers, painted suffrage as an invitation to socialism, anarchism, free love, and domestic discord. Partly in response to those claims, many leading suffragists became increasingly conservative in their arguments and increasingly unwilling to address other causes and consequences of women's inequality. That strategy met with partial success. As they narrowed their social agenda, women's rights organizations expanded their political appeal. The growing strength of the suffrage movement, together with women's efforts in WORLD WAR I, finally helped prompt the United States to join the slowly increasing number of Western nations that had granted enfranchisement.

Yet to many leading women's rights activists, the American victory proved scarcely less demoralizing than defeat. The focus on enfranchisement had to some extent deflected attention from other issues of critical importance for women, such as poverty, working conditions, birth control, health care, and domestic relations. Without a unifying social agenda beyond the ballot, the postsuffrage feminist movement foundered, splintered, and for the next half century, largely dissolved. During that period, women did not vote as a block on women's issues, support women candidates, or, with few exceptions, agitate for women's rights. Despite their numerical strength and access to the ballot, women remained subject to a vast range of discrimination in employment, education, WELFARE BENEFITS, credit standards, family law, and related areas. Although the Nineteenth Amendment itself was urged as a ground for qualifying women to serve on juries, most courts rejected this argument except where jury service was tied to voter status.

Yet however limited its immediate affects, the Nineteenth Amendment marked a significant advance toward equal rights. Enfranchisement was a necessary if not sufficient condition for women to exercise significant political leverage. Moreover, the skills, experience, and self-esteem that women gained during the suffrage campaign helped lay the foundation for a more egalitarian social order.

DEBORAH L. RHODE
(1986)

(SEE ALSO: *Anthony, Susan Brownell; Stanton, Elizabeth Cady; Woman Suffrage; Woman Suffrage Movement.*)

Bibliography

CATT, CARRIE CHAPMAN and SHULER, NETTIE ROGERS 1970 *Woman Suffrage and Politics.* New York: Americana Library Edition.

STANTON, ELIZABETH CADY et al., eds. 1881–1922 *History of Woman Suffrage.* New York: Fowler Wells.

NINTH AMENDMENT

Largely ignored throughout most of our history, the Ninth Amendment has emerged in the past twenty years as a possible source for the protection of individual rights not specifically enumerated in the Constitution's text. Although no Supreme Court decision has yet been based squarely on an interpretation of the Ninth Amendment, it has been mentioned in several leading cases in which the Court enlarged the scope of individual rights. Lawyers, scholars, and judges are understandably intrigued by a provision that, on the basis of language, seems ideally suited to provide a constitutional home for newly found rights: "The enumeration of certain rights in the Constitution shall not be construed to deny or disparage others retained by the people."

The historical origins of the Ninth Amendment lay in JAMES MADISON's concern that the inclusion of specified rights in the BILL OF RIGHTS might leave other rights unprotected. He recognized, moreover, that the inherent limitations of language could thwart the intent of the authors of the Bill of Rights to provide a permanent charter of personal freedom. These concerns, which led Madison originally to question the wisdom of a Bill of Rights, caused him to propose, in the First Congress, a resolution incorporating the present language of the Ninth Amendment. It was adopted with little debate.

It is not surprising that the Ninth Amendment lay dormant throughout most of our history. The holding in BARRON V. BALTIMORE (1833) that the Fifth Amendment was not applicable to the states limited the scope of the Ninth Amendment also: all provisions of the Bill of Rights restricted the United States only. Moreover, the federal government, being one of limited powers, did not move into those areas of activity that would trigger claims of infringement of rights not specified in the Constitution. Challenges to federal actions were more likely to take the form that the President or Congress lacked power under the Constitution rather than that the actions abridged an individual right. Even the specific guarantees of the Bill of Rights spawned only a trickle of litigation until well into the twentieth century.

The states, of course, had broad POLICE POWERS to legislate in the areas of welfare, health, education, morality, and business. Until the latter part of the nineteenth century, however, the Supreme Court's review of state legislation served primarily to assure that states did not unduly burden or tax interstate businesses. Court decisions in these areas were not based on individual rights but rather on a judicially created doctrine that Congress's power to regulate INTERSTATE COMMERCE carried with it a prohibition against state laws that were viewed by the Court as unreasonably burdensome or discriminatory as applied to interstate businesses. The post-Civil War Amendments provided the textual basis for challenges to state law as violating individual rights.

The Supreme Court, however, moved quickly to limit the scope of the THIRTEENTH AMENDMENT and FOURTEENTH AMENDMENT. In the famous SLAUGHTERHOUSE CASES (1873) the Court virtually eliminated the PRIVILEGES AND IMMUNITIES clause of the Fourteenth Amendment as a protection for individual rights by limiting the clause to such rights as interstate travel, petitioning the federal government for redress of grievances, protection while abroad, or the privilege of HABEAS CORPUS. The EQUAL PROTECTION and DUE PROCESS clauses were also narrowly interpreted so as to preclude broad challenges to state regulatory statutes, as was the Thirteenth Amendment in *Slaughterhouse* and the CIVIL RIGHTS CASES (1883).

Despite the *Slaughterhouse Cases*, those seeking constitutional support for the protection of property rights against ECONOMIC REGULATION looked elsewhere in the Fourteenth Amendment, and ultimately found a home in the due process clause. Toward the end of the nineteenth century the Court expanded the meaning of "liberty" and "property" to include the right to enter into business relationships. Hundreds of state laws were invalidated under this expanded concept of SUBSTANTIVE DUE PROCESS. This view of the Fourteenth Amendment, together with narrow interpretations of Congress's power under the COMMERCE CLAUSE and the TAXING AND SPENDING POWER, led to the NEW DEAL constitutional crisis of the 1930s. In the spring of 1937 a narrow Court majority shifted ground, broadening Congress's enumerated powers and limiting the due process clause to its present scope, namely, that state regulatory laws should bear a reasonable relationship to a valid legislative purpose. Throughout this long constitutional journey the Ninth Amendment was an unused instrument, because those who challenged state laws relied primarily on the Fourteenth Amendment's due process clause whose scope had been so broadened that there was no need to develop a theory of unenumerated rights.

As the Court in the 1930s and 1940s finally rejected the claim that the Constitution contained rights that protected business against government regulation, the enumerated rights in the Bill of Rights were gradually being incorporated into the meaning of the words "liberty" and "property" of the Fourteenth Amendment's due process clause. By the end of the 1960s, substantive rights guaranteed by the FIRST AMENDMENT, and most of the procedural rights of the Fourth, Fifth, Sixth, and Eighth Amendments were made binding on the states. In this legal development the Ninth Amendment was inconsequential, because the Court employed the judicial technique of incorporating into the due process clause rights enumerated in the Bill of Rights. There was little need to develop the concept of "unenumerated" rights, so long as the due process clause of the Fourteenth Amendment provided the vehicle for making the Bill of Rights binding on the states.

Thus, during the early 1960s, as the process of incorporating the Bill of Rights into the Fourteenth Amendment was moving forward, the Supreme Court maintained a consensus developed as early as UNITED STATES V. CAROLENE PRODUCTS CO. (1938). On matters of economic and social legislation (the type of law that gave rise to the substantive due process controversies of the pre-New Deal era) the Supreme Court would have a limited role to play. Legislation (either state or federal) would be assumed to be valid unless arbitrary or unreasonable, or unless shown to violate a specific provision of the Constitution. Laws reflecting prejudice against certain minorities, or laws infringing personal liberties of the kind enumerated in the Bill of Rights, or other specific provisions of the Constitution, would be subject to a more demanding form of judicial scrutiny.

The Court remained divided on the meaning of specific constitutional guarantees, but these divisions resulted from differences over the meaning of enumerated rights, rather than from differences over whether newly identified, unenumerated, rights should be read into the Constitution. In this constitutional world, an amendment that spoke of unenumerated rights had little to offer as a defense of personal rights. However, a Connecticut law that prohibited the use of contraceptives jolted this consensus and led to the emergence of the Ninth Amendment as a possible vehicle for the protection of rights not specifically guaranteed in other provisions of the Constitution. After two decades of not enforcing its statute, and after thwarting attempts to overturn it in the Supreme Court, Connecticut prosecuted a doctor who was giving contraceptive advice to a married couple in a BIRTH CONTROL clinic. He was charged with "aiding and abetting" a violation of the law prohibiting the use of contraceptives.

The case, GRISWOLD V. CONNECTICUT (1965), presented a difficult problem for a Court majority wedded to the notion that only arbitrary, or capricious, or invidiously discriminatory laws, or those that violated a specific constitutional right, could be invalidated. All of the Justices agreed that the Connecticut statute was foolish, but the Court was obviously troubled as to why it was unconstitutional for a state to decide that it wished to discourage extramarital sexual relations and that the ready availability of contraceptives, including contraceptives for married persons, increased the likelihood of extramarital sex by eliminating the fear of pregnancy. Connecticut claimed that in order to achieve the objective of deterring sex outside of marriage the state could prohibit the use of all contraceptives, thus making them less available. If no specific constitutional right had been violated, why could not Connecticut make its own mistakes, leaving it to the people, through their elected representatives, to correct them?

The Supreme Court's answer, in an opinion by Justice WILLIAM O. DOUGLAS, was to create a right of marital privacy which was found in "penumbras, formed by emanations" from other guarantees found in enumerated rights, specifically those in the First, Third, Fourth, and Fifth Amendments. The Ninth Amendment was also mentioned, but the constitutional approach of the majority was to expand existing rights in order to create a new right of marital privacy which the Connecticut law was held to contravene.

Three Justices (Chief Justice EARL WARREN and Justices ARTHUR GOLDBERG and WILLIAM J. BRENNAN), in an opinion by Goldberg, relied specifically on the Ninth Amendment as an additional basis for striking down the law. Justice Goldberg's standard for defining rights "retained by the people" seemed to strike a widely criticized note of open-ended substantive due process. He referred to FUNDAMENTAL RIGHTS and to the "traditions" and "conscience of our people" in order to determine whether a right was to be regarded as "fundamental." It is not surprising that this language prompted a vigorous dissent from Justice HUGO L. BLACK, who regarded the majority and concurring Justices as having engaged in the same unprincipled personal jurisprudence as the conservative Justices who had written the concept of FREEDOM OF CONTRACT into the Constitution in the early part of the twentieth century.

Viewed in isolation, the *Griswold* case might have been regarded merely as involving a slight broadening of enumerated rights to encompass the basic right to decide whether or not to conceive a child. Whether the Court reached this result by finding the new right lurking in "penumbras" formed by "emanations" from existing rights, or by discovering new "unenumerated" rights, was probably of no great concern, because the Connecticut statute was so unreasonable, even in the context of the state's asserted objective of promoting moral behavior, that the law should have been declared invalid under a REASONABLENESS standard. But strong movements were developing in the country during the 1960s and 1970s. Women were moving rapidly toward equality of opportunity to participate in American life. Attitudes about private sexual behavior, marriage, cohabitation, and family relationships were all changing toward an increased respect for individual choice.

In the 1970s the Court responded by recognizing some of these new attitudes and enshrining them in constitutionally protected rights. In EISENSTADT V. BAIRD (1972), for example, the principles of *Griswold* were extended to include the right of an unmarried person to the acquisition and use of contraceptives. The culmination of this trend was ROE V. WADE (1973), where the Court recognized constitutional protection of a woman's right to procure an abortion, particularly during the first twenty-six weeks of pregnancy. *Roe v. Wade*, in turn, generated renewed debate among constitutional scholars over the proper role of the Court in intervening to overturn the legislative decisions of democratically elected legislatures. In this debate the Ninth Amendment started to assume new significance because it provided a possible textual basis for an expanded jurisprudence of individual liberty.

The Ninth Amendment was mentioned in *Roe v. Wade*, but only as one of a number of constitutional provisions to support the Court's conclusion that "liberty" encompassed a woman's child-bearing decision. Justice Douglas who had written the majority opinion in *Griswold*, based his concurrence in *Roe v. Wade* primarily on the Ninth Amendment and suggested a broad range of personal autonomy rights such as "control over development and expression of one's intellect, interest, tastes, and personality," "freedom of choice in the basic decisions of one's life respecting marriage, divorce, procreation, contraception, and the education and upbringing of children," "freedom to care for one's health and person, freedom from bodily restraint or compulsion, freedom to walk, stroll, or loaf."

After *Roe v. Wade* (perhaps relying on Justice Douglas's expansive concurrence) some litigants sought to use the Ninth Amendment as a basis for expanding personal autonomy rights beyond the scope of sexual privacy. Many lower courts appeared receptive to such claims as the right, under the Ninth Amendment, to control one's personal grooming and appearance and the right to be protected from disclosing personal information. However, in *Kelley v. Johnson* (1976) the Supreme Court upheld a

regulation limiting the length of a police officer's hair. Personal autonomy issues continue to be litigated, but the Ninth Amendment is rarely involved as a basis for decision.

Because interest in the Ninth Amendment started with cases involving sexual privacy, it is not surprising that the amendment continues to be used to attack state antisodomy laws. Apart from a summary affirmance in 1976 of a district court opinion, the Court has not specifically addressed the issue of the rights of homosexuals. In 1985 the Court of Appeals for the Fourth Circuit upheld a Ninth Amendment claim that right of private consensual sexual behavior was beyond the reach of state regulation. But even if the Supreme Court should sustain the decision of the Circuit Court the Supreme Court's preferred rationale is likely to be substantive due process, that is, enlarging the definition of "sexual privacy" as part of the "liberty" protected by the Fourteenth Amendment.

One could well conclude that the Ninth Amendment should be allowed to return to the oblivion it experienced prior to the *Griswold* case. Persistent references to the Ninth Amendment by lower court judges, however, and even by Supreme Court Justices (for example, Chief Justice WARREN E. BURGER in RICHMOND NEWSPAPERS, INC. V. VIRGINIA, 1980) suggest that the amendment could serve as an analytical tool for the appraisal of new claims of constitutional rights. If it is to serve as something more than a superfluous additional citation, the Ninth Amendment must offer the promise of the development of a more coherent body of law than has thus far emerged as the Court has recognized new claims of unenumerated constitutional rights.

At present the Court deals with such rights primarily through the technique employed in *Griswold* and its progeny. The Court usually tries to base its decisions on one or more specific constitutional provisions, and then expands those provisions to include new rights. Typical was the *Richmond Newspaper* case, where the Court held that the public had a right of access to criminal trials. Chief Justice Burger's PLURALITY OPINION was based on principles said to derive from the First Amendment, even though the amendment itself specifically guarantees, for these purposes, only the rights of speech, press, and assembly. The Chief Justice made specific reference to rights that were not "enumerated" in the Constitution and pointed out that James Madison's concern with the danger of protecting only enumerated rights led to the adoption of the Ninth Amendment.

Despite his reference to the Ninth Amendment, the Chief Justice's approach in *Richmond Newspapers* would appear to be similar to earlier cases, including *Griswold*, where new rights were recognized because they were analogous to existing rights. Freedom of association is a judicially recognized derivation of the First Amendment protection for freedom of expression, and the requirement of proof beyond a REASONABLE DOUBT is derived from the enumerated guarantee of due process. Recognizing the right of marital privacy or the right to terminate a pregnancy may involve a greater leap from the enumerated rights in the First, Fourth, and Fifth Amendments, but the technique of deriving the rights from enumerated rights did not start with *Griswold* or *Roe v. Wade*. Once the leap is made, the further development of the right becomes merely a matter of interpretation of the newly perceived rights.

An alternate approach to the development of unenumerated rights would look instead to the open-ended clauses of the Constitution such as the PRIVILEGES AND IMMUNITIES clauses in Article IV and the Fourteenth Amendment, or the due process clause—or even no clause at all. Some Justices have viewed the developments since *Griswold* as a revival of open-ended substantive due process. This view has characterized the approach of Justices FELIX FRANKFURTER and JOHN MARSHALL HARLAN to the incorporation of procedural rights into the Fourteenth Amendment. They would have relied on the meaning of "liberty" rather than on the lifting of a "right" from the Bill of Rights and transferring the right to the Fourteenth Amendment (the approach of Justice Brennan and ultimately a majority of the Court).

If the Ninth Amendment is to serve as a meaningful vehicle for the protection of UNENUMERATED RIGHTS, it should, at the least, have something more to offer than the expansion of enumerated rights exemplified by *Roe v. Wade* and *Richmond Newspapers* or the open-ended substantive due process approach of Justices Frankfurter, Harlan, and Stewart. The Ninth Amendment offers two potential contributions: historical justification and constitutional standard. The historical justification, articulated by Justice Goldberg in *Griswold* and by Chief Justice Burger in *Richmond Newspapers*, provides a powerful support for the argument that "unenumerated rights" have a place in the Constitution.

The same history also suggests a constitutional standard: a range of rights protected by the entire text of the Constitution. To leave the Ninth Amendment open-ended, with no obligation on the part of judges to link unenumerated rights to enumerated rights, would render the amendment indistinguishable from the nontextually based substantive due process. Moreover, confining "retained" rights to those analogous to enumerated rights would be consistent with Madison's conception of the Ninth Amendment. He was not seeking to create new rights. He was concerned that the enumeration of the rights in the Bill of Rights could not possibly take into account similar but undefined rights that could not be fully delineated in a constitutional text. The Ninth Amendment was the original "safety net" to compensate for the imperfection of language and the inability to provide for changing circumstances. Such an approach leaves room for a gradual expansion of rights, but requires some grounding for each newly recognized right in the constitutional text. A text-based standard is one that requires far less justification, in terms of democratic political theory, than a frankly noninterpretivist standard.

Does the Ninth Amendment, as so limited, add an additional dimension to the technique employed in *Griswold* or *Richmond Newspapers*? If rights "retained" under the Ninth Amendment are those analogous to rights found elsewhere in the Constitution, how does this approach differ from the approach of Justice Douglas in *Griswold*, which found rights in the "penumbras" formed by "emanations" from existing rights?

One obvious response is that the Ninth Amendment is itself a textual, historically valid justification for this approach to the enforcement of enumerated rights. It thus has a "leg-up" in the quest for legitimacy of judicial intervention. Moreover, Ninth Amendment analysis should derive from the entire text of the Constitution and not merely from other rights. Thus, as Justice Brennan noted in *Zobel v. Williams* (1982), the RIGHT TO TRAVEL can be discerned as a necessary consequence of nationhood as embodied in several constitutional provisions. Similarly, protection of VOTING RIGHTS can be derived from constitutional provisions that contemplate broad voter participation. The Ninth Amendment has never defined absolute rights. Rather, jurisprudence based on the Ninth Amendment will require placing on the balancing scales those individual unenumerated rights that might otherwise be ignored but that are sufficiently analogous to enumerated rights, or to our governmental structure, as to require constitutional protection.

NORMAN REDLICH
(1986)

Bibliography

BLACK, CHARLES 1981 *Decision According to Law.* New York: Norton.

DUNBAR, L. 1956 James Madison and the Ninth Amendment. *Virginia Law Review* 42:627–643.

ELY, J. H. 1980 *Democracy and Distrust: A Theory of Judicial Review.* Cambridge, Mass.: Harvard University Press.

LAYCOCK, DOUGLAS 1981 Taking Constitutions Seriously: A Theory of Judicial Review by John Hart Ely. *Texas Law Review* 59:343–394.

PATTERSON, B. 1955 *The Forgotten Ninth Amendment* 27; *The Constitution of the United States of America: Analysis and Interpretations*, S. Doc. No. 92–82, 92d Cong.

REDLICH, N. 1961 Are There Certain Rights . . . Retained by the People? *NYU Law Review* 37:787, 802–808.

RHOADES, LYMAN and PATULA, RODNEY R. 1973 The Ninth Amendment: A Survey of Theory and Practice in the Federal Courts Since *Griswold v. Connecticut. Denver Law Journal* 50:153–176.

VAN ALSTYNE, WILLIAM 1981 Slouching Toward Bethlehem with the Ninth Amendment. *Yale Law Journal* 91:207–216.

NINTH AMENDMENT
(Update)

The Supreme Court's reliance on the Ninth Amendment to justify a constitutional RIGHT OF PRIVACY in the landmark cases of GRISWOLD V. CONNECTICUT (1965) and ROE V. WADE (1973) ignited great interest in the long-ignored amendment. Scholars wrote a flurry of articles about it, and lower federal courts began accepting Ninth Amendment challenges to a variety of statutes. After *Roe*, however, the Supreme Court consistently abstained from any further use of the Ninth Amendment. Its most notable rejection came in BOWERS V. HARDWICK (1986). In *Bowers*, the federal court of appeals had held a statute criminalizing sodomy unconstitutional because it violated the right of privacy protected by, among other provisions, the Ninth Amendment. The Court, in a 5–4 decision, reversed. Though the Court noted that "[r]espondent does not defend the judgment below based on the Ninth Amendment, the Equal Protection Clause, or the Eighth Amendment," its refusal to extend the right of privacy grounded in the DUE PROCESS clause to this type of statute, together with its earlier refusals to rely on the Ninth Amendment, signaled that future legal challenges based on the Ninth Amendment would not likely be successful.

This is where the situation might have remained had President RONALD REAGAN not nominated appellate court judge Robert H. Bork to the Court in 1987. During his famously televised confirmation hearing, Bork was questioned by SENATE JUDICIARY COMMITTEE Chairman Joseph Biden, as well as by Senators Strom Thurmond, Ted Kennedy, and Dennis DeConcini, about whether the right of privacy was supported by the Ninth Amendment. Bork initially suggested that the rights "retained by the people" referred solely to rights mentioned in state constitutions. Later he added: "I would be delighted" to use the Ninth Amendment "if anybody showed me historical evidence" as to what the Framers meant. Then Bork offered a provocative analogy that received wide attention: "I do not think you can use the ninth amendment unless you know something of what it means. For example, if you had an amendment that says 'Congress shall make no' and then there is an ink blot and you cannot read the rest of it and that is the only copy you have, I do not think the court can make up what might be under the ink blot if you can-

not read it." Bork said he knew of no evidence that the Framers of the Ninth Amendment intended it to protect a "dynamic category of rights, that is, under the ninth amendment the court was free to make up more Bill of Rights."

Analogizing any part of the Constitution's text to an "ink blot"—while invoking the absence of historical inquiry—was sure to elicit an academic response. Bork's very public dialogue, followed by the SENATE's denial of his confirmation, sparked a renewed interest in the Ninth Amendment among constitutional scholars and an explosion of new articles and books on the subject ensued. Most, but not all, academic writers were friendlier to the use of the amendment than was either Bork or the Court. New historical research undercut the state constitutional rights thesis posited by Bork and others and supported the view that the rights "retained by the people" was a reference to inherent or NATURAL RIGHTS. What still divides scholars is whether the Ninth Amendment authorizes the judicial protection of the natural rights to which it refers.

Paralleling the academic response to Bork's treatment of the Ninth Amendment was the reaction of subsequent Court nominees when each was asked about the amendment. Justice DAVID H. SOUTER, for example, testified that "the starting point for anyone who reads the Constitution seriously is that there is a concept of limited governmental power which is not simply to be identified with the enumeration of those specific rights or specifically defined rights that were later embodied in the bill. If there were any further evidence needed for this, of course, we can start with the ninth amendment." Souter's denial that he had anything novel to contribute to the jurisprudence of the Ninth Amendment provoked Biden to respond: "It is novel that you acknowledge it, based on our past hearings in this committee. One of the last nominees said it was nothing but a waterblot on the Constitution, which I found fascinating." Souter went on to testify that he had no reason to doubt that the Ninth Amendment "was an acknowledgment that the enumeration was not intended to be in some sense exhaustive and in derogation of other rights retained." In response to the question of whether a majority acting through government can violate inherent rights that precede the state, Souter testified that the job of the Court is "to define and protect this point beyond which government simply cannot go or cannot go without the most strong justification."

Souter's testimony was to prove prophetic. In PLANNED PARENTHOOD V. CASEY (1992), the Court overturned portions of a Pennsylvania ABORTION law. Speaking for a plurality in a rare jointly authored opinion, Justices ANTHONY M. KENNEDY, SANDRA DAY O'CONNOR, and Souter relied explicitly on the Ninth Amendment: "Neither the Bill of Rights nor the specific practices of States at the time of the adoption of the Fourteenth Amendment marks the outer limits of the substantive sphere of liberty which the Fourteenth Amendment protects. See U.S. Const., Amdt. 9." It then quoted with approval the statement of the second Justice JOHN MARSHALL HARLAN that "the full scope of the liberty guaranteed by the Due Process Clause cannot be found in or limited by the precise terms of the specific guarantees elsewhere provided in the Constitution. This 'liberty' is not a series of isolated points pricked out in terms of the taking of property; the freedom of speech, press, and religion; the right to keep and bear arms; the freedom from unreasonable searches and seizures; and so on. It is a rational continuum which, broadly speaking, includes a freedom from all substantial arbitrary impositions and purposeless restraints, . . . and which also recognizes, what a reasonable and sensitive judgment must, that certain interests require particularly careful scrutiny of the state needs asserted to justify their abridgment."

Casey represents the high-water mark, to date, of judicial willingness to use the Ninth Amendment. Following *Casey,* and throughout the 1990s, the Court did not employ the Ninth Amendment or even refer to it and, unlike the rush of enthusiasm that followed *Griswold* and *Roe,* neither did lower courts increase their receptivity to Ninth Amendment arguments. Off the bench, Justice ANTONIN SCALIA has expressed skepticism about the Ninth Amendment, and its future will undoubtedly depend on the judicial philosophies of future nominees to the Court. It will also depend on whether judges or academics can develop ways to put the Ninth Amendment into effect without seeming to authorize unbridled judicial discretion to strike down statutes. As Biden observed during Justice Kennedy's confirmation hearing, Justices "are reluctant to use it because once you start down that road on the ninth amendment, then it becomes very difficult to figure where to stop; what are those unenumerated rights."

One possibility involves modifying the prevailing "presumption of constitutionality." Under this judicially created DOCTRINE, as explained in the famous Footnote 4 of UNITED STATES V. CAROLENE PRODUCTS CO. (1938), courts will presume a statute to be constitutional unless "it appears on its face to be within a specific prohibition of the Constitution, such as those of the first ten amendments. . . ." But if the courts shift the presumption only when a statute violates "a specific prohibition," do they not disparage or deny" the "other" rights "retained by the people" in violation of the Ninth Amendment? If courts do not evenhandedly employ heightened scrutiny whenever a statute infringes on *any* rightful exercise of a citizen's liberty, have they not disparaged those liberties that were unenumerated?

Although distinguishing "rightful exercises of liberty" from mere "license" appears to pose the same problem of indeterminacy that attaches to identifying unenumerated rights directly, the problem may be less serious than first appears. State tort, property, and contract law doctrines routinely distinguish rightful from wrongful exercises of liberty, and federal judges regularly defer to state law in deciding cases between private parties in which there is DIVERSITY JURISDICTION. Moreover, federal courts frequently identify "liberty interests" that they then balance against governmental interests. Such liberty interests are, however, indistinguishable from rightful exercises of liberty (as opposed to license). In addition, the people, acting through state INITIATIVES or REFERENDUMS, could directly declare certain liberties to be fundamental.

Perhaps, then, federal courts could protect unenumerated rights by increasing the scrutiny of federal statutes restricting the exercise of individual liberties that constitute legitimate "liberty interests" insofar as they are neither tortious nor violative of the contract or property rights of another person. It would then fall to the federal government to show why such interferences with liberty are truly "necessary and proper," the legal standard supplied by the NECESSARY AND PROPER CLAUSE.

Adopting such a "presumption of liberty" would protect the unenumerated rights retained by the people in a manner very similar, if not identical, to the way the enumerated liberties of FREEDOM OF SPEECH and FREEDOM OF THE PRESS are protected under the FIRST AMENDMENT. Such a presumption would effectively negate the inference that JAMES MADISON sought to avoid when he drafted the Ninth Amendment: "that those rights which were not singled out, were intended to be assigned into the hands of the general government." As for protecting unenumerated liberties from infringements by states, the current weight of scholarly opinion is that, contrary to the SLAUGHTER-HOUSE CASES (1873), this protection is best accomplished by reference to the PRIVILEGES OR IMMUNITIES clause of the FOURTEENTH AMENDMENT—though the existence of the Ninth Amendment argues against rigidly limiting these privileges and immunities solely to "the enumeration in the constitution of certain rights."

RANDY E. BARNETT
(2000)

(SEE ALSO: *Bork Nomination.*)

Bibliography

BARNETT, RANDY E., ed. 1989, 1993 *The Rights Retained by the People: The History and Meaning of the Ninth Amendment,* Vols. 1 & 2. Fairfax, Va.: George Mason University Press.
BARNETT, RANDY E. 1997 Necessary and Proper. *UCLA Law Review* 44:745–793.
MASSEY, CALVIN R. 1995 *Silent Rights: The Ninth Amendment and the Constitution's Unenumerated Rights.* Philadelphia: Temple University Press.

SYMPOSIUM 1988 Interpreting the Ninth Amendment. *Chicago-Kent Law Review* 64:37–268.

YOO, JOHN CHOON 1993 Our Declaratory Ninth Amendment. *Emory Law Journal* 42:967–1043.

NIX v. WILLIAMS
467 U.S. 431 (1984)

A 7–2 Supreme Court held that although an accused's incriminating statements could not be admitted as EVIDENCE because police had interrogated him in violation of his RIGHT TO COUNSEL, physical evidence discovered on the basis of his incriminating statements could be introduced against him if the prosecution, by a preponderance of proof, could show that such evidence would inevitably have been discovered even in the absence of accused's statements. The case produced an "inevitable discovery" exception to the EXCLUSIONARY RULE: any FRUIT OF THE POISONOUS TREE may be used as evidence if it would have been inevitably or ultimately discovered, just as if it had been discovered on the basis of independent or uncontaminated leads. (See BREWER V. WILLIAMS.)

LEONARD W. LEVY
(1986)

NIXON, RICHARD M.
(1913–1994)

Richard Milhous Nixon, the thirty-seventh President of the United States, was born in Yorba Linda, California. An alumnus of Whittier College and Duke University Law School, he practiced law in Whittier, California, from 1937 to 1942. After a brief stint in the enforcement of wartime price controls, he entered the Navy and served with it in the South Pacific. Upon his release from duty he was elected to the HOUSE OF REPRESENTATIVES from the Twelfth District of California. Shortly he gained national prominence as a member of the HOUSE COMMITTEE ON UN-AMERICAN ACTIVITIES, and he played a decisive role in generating the perjury case against Alger Hiss. Nixon was elected to the SENATE from his home state in 1950, gaining new notoriety in denouncing the Democrats for having "lost" China to communism. In 1952 he was elected vice-president as the running mate of DWIGHT D. EISENHOWER. Nixon had riveted national attention—once again—with an impassioned defense on radio and television of his acceptance of money from a political "slush" fund. As vice-president he drew international notice through his "kitchen debate" with Soviet Premier Nikita Khrushchev. Nixon was nominated for President by his party in 1960, but lost to the Democrats' JOHN F. KENNEDY in a close elec-tion. Two years later Nixon ran for governor of California and lost. He reentered the private practice of law, this time in New York City. Maintaining and broadening his political contacts, he was again nominated for the presidency by the Republicans in 1968. His campaign theme was a pledge to heal the divisions in the nation that the Vietnam War had created and to bring the hostilities to an honorable conclusion. He won a plurality of the popular vote over the Democrats' HUBERT H. HUMPHREY and George C. Wallace, candidate of the American Independence Party.

As President, Nixon took advantage of the dramatic expansion of the office that had been taking place since the time of FRANKLIN D. ROOSEVELT, recognizing that the public had grown accustomed to regarding the Chief Executive as the undisputed architect of national policies. But Nixon stretched his authority with less restraint than his predecessors, undertaking steps violative of the law and of the Constitution itself. A full explanation for his actions may never be forthcoming. Possibly he felt keenly that his party's inability to capture or control Congress would continue to frustrate his desire to dismantle many New Deal and Great Society programs. He may also have been guided by inner compulsions of ambition and feelings of inadequacy he never articulated. Nixon, at any rate, interpreted by his own lights the constitutional prerogatives of his office, including an assumed right to ignore or modify the letter and intent of laws.

Nixon, for example, did not consider himself obligated to respect the law of 1972 requiring that EXECUTIVE AGREEMENTS arrived at with foreign governments be reported to Congress within sixty days, cavalierly submitting them late. Moreover, he sometimes negotiated them at a lower diplomatic level and labeled them "arrangements." Under Nixon's stewardship, executive agreements were entered into on major matters and formal treaties almost invariably on minor matters—a reversal of the traditional relationship between the two forms of diplomatic undertakings.

Although a few Presidents had sometimes impounded funds appropriated by Congress, the step was generally taken in conformity with congressional intent or under the President's authority as COMMANDER-IN-CHIEF. Nixon broke fresh ground in his assertion of a constitutional power to decline to spend appropriated funds. For him IMPOUNDMENT was a legitimate tool of the President to alter policy set by Congress—and he employed it on a scale hitherto unknown. While some of the funds he refused to release came out of military, space, and public works appropriations, vast amounts also came out of social and environmental programs. By 1973 Nixon's impoundments totaled about $18 billion, between seventeen and twenty percent of the funds he could claim to control. Nixon and his aides maintained that he was following patterns established by previous Presidents. The evidence is, however, that his predecessors did not aim to contravene the will of Congress, but merely postpone immediate expenditure. Nixon, on the other hand, used impoundment to terminate or curtail programs. He defended his actions on the ground that the executive power of the President included a constitutional right to be the people's defender against Congress's inability to hold down nondefense spending.

Nixon's boldness had the effect of giving the executive an item veto of appropriation bills—a remedy long sought by Presidents, and provided for in the CONFEDERATE CONSTITUTION, but consistently withheld from Presidents since first requested by President ULYSSES S. GRANT in 1873. Whatever the merit of the device, Nixon's insistence on exercising it in defiance of Congress was a usurpation of power.

Although WIRETAPPING without formal authorization had long been employed occasionally by Presidents, Nixon was the first Chief Executive who systematically resorted to its use. His practice of it grew out of a determination to keep under wraps the "secret" B-52 raids over Cambodia in 1969. Nixon was apparently fashioning a new conception of his office, metamorphosing it into a "plebiscitary presidency"—one in which the Chief Executive would assume widened power under the Constitution, relying on a reshaped Supreme Court to validate his actions. Nixon's expressed concern was that leaks of information about the "secret war" were putting national security in jeopardy. He ordered the tapping of telephones of members of the National Security Council staff and of several newspaper reporters. The taps were conducted without court order and in patent violation of Title III of the OMNIBUS CRIME CONTROL AND SAFE STREETS ACT of 1968. By countenancing not only illegal wiretapping but, shortly, burglary (in the case of Daniel Ellsberg, who revealed the so-called Pentagon Papers), the hiring of *agents provacateurs* (to conduct "dirty tricks" in election campaigns), and the subverting of the Internal Revenue Service (to punish "enemies"), Nixon was substituting his personal sanction for established law.

In assuming this prerogative, Nixon believed he was exercising what he regarded as INHERENT POWER to maintain national and domestic security. This claim of "inherent power," sometimes also set forth by previous Presidents, has never been recognized as valid by the courts. In *United States v. United States District Court* (1972) the Supreme Court by an 8–0 vote ruled unconstitutional the Nixon administration's practice of engaging in domestic electronic surveillance without a judicial warrant.

Nixon's assertion of an EXECUTIVE PRIVILEGE to reject a SUBPOENA became the issue in the case of UNITED STATES V. NIXON (1974). The suit revolved around Nixon's refusal to surrender tapes containing information relevant to the prosecution of some of his close aides for offenses that included obstruction of justice by "covering up" the administration's involvement in the WATERGATE break-in. In its unanimous decision requiring the President to turn over the tapes, the Supreme Court recognized that a President is entitled to confidentiality of communication— needful for "protection of the public interest in candid, objective, and even blunt or harsh opinion in presidential decisionmaking." But, the Court concluded, "when the ground for asserting privilege as to subpoenaed material sought for use in a criminal trial is based only on the generalized interest in confidentiality, it cannot prevail over the fundamental demands of DUE PROCESS OF LAW in the fair administration of criminal justice. The generalized assertion of privilege must yield to the demonstrated, specific need for EVIDENCE in a pending criminal trial."

Nixon toyed with the idea of disobeying the decision, but decided to comply, surrendering the tapes covered in the decision. Indeed, he published their contents, thus providing the House Judiciary Committee with the "smoking gun"—the now famous words in which the President counseled inducing the Central Intelligence Agency to limit the FBI's investigation of the Watergate burglary.

Nixon's use of the POCKET VETO was also remarkable. As intended by the Framers of the Constitution it may be used at the end of a session of Congress when a President who does not sign a bill cannot return it to Congress because it stands adjourned. Nixon unhesitatingly used pocket vetoes when Congress was merely in brief recess. In *Kennedy v. Simpson* (1973) a district court overturned as misused Nixon's pocket veto of the Family Practice of Medicine Bill, which had been opposed by only three members of Congress.

Nixon's transgressions of the law and the Constitution contributed to the passage of two major pieces of legislation. One was the CONGRESSIONAL BUDGET AND IMPOUNDMENT CONTROL ACT of 1974, which detailed the arrangements under which Congress may monitor the deferral by a President of appropriated funds. The second law, responding to the deployment of troops in Asia, first by President LYNDON B. JOHNSON and then by Nixon, was the War Powers Resolution of 1973, severely restricting the ability of a President to use military force outside the United States without congressional authorization. Nixon and all succeeding Presidents have denounced this law as an unconstitutional abridgment of the power of the President to direct the armed forces.

Nixon made two nominations to the Supreme Court that failed of confirmation. In 1969 he submitted the name of Judge Clement F. Haynsworth of South Carolina, a designation that met implacable opposition from CIVIL RIGHTS groups and labor unions. Early the following year Nixon sent forward the name of Judge G. Harrold Carswell of the Fifth Circuit Court of Appeals in Florida. Denounced as a racist in many quarters, although he had renounced his older views on race, Carswell was also opposed as lacking the superior qualifications required for a seat on the highest court.

In addition to placing HARRY A. BLACKMUN of Minnesota, LEWIS F. POWELL, JR., of Virginia, and WILLIAM H. REHNQUIST of Arizona on the Supreme Court, Nixon also appointed the fourteenth Chief Justice, Judge WARREN E. BURGER of the District of Columbia Court of Appeals, whose conservative speeches and advocacy of judicial restraint appealed to the President. Nixon had been especially impressed by an address that Burger delivered in 1967 on the subject of "law and order," from which Nixon had borrowed during the 1968 campaign for the Presidency. He was mindful, too, of the support Burger had given him during his critical time in the 1952 campaign.

Nixon was the first Chief Executive to resign the Presidency—a consequence of the Watergate affair that convulsed the nation from 1972 to 1974. The reasons for the burglary—carried out by Nixon's political aides at the headquarters of the Democratic party—have never been adduced. From the start of the investigation the administration tried to cover up its connection to the crime. In the long drawnout effort to get at the truth, the focus of the quest became the President himself: what did he know and when did he know it? The evidence lay in the recordings of conversations in his office that Nixon was revealed to have been making for years. The President turned over the critical tapes just as the House of Representatives seemed on the verge of voting to impeach him. He surrendered his office on August 9, 1974. The following month, his successor, GERALD R. FORD, issued the former President a "full, free, and absolute" pardon for any crimes he may have committed.

HENRY F. GRAFF
(1986)

(SEE ALSO: *Articles of Impeachment of Richard M. Nixon; Impeachment.*)

Bibliography

KURLAND, PHILLIP B. 1978 *Watergate and the Constitution.* Chicago: University of Chicago Press.

NATHAN, RICHARD P. 1973 *The Plot That Failed: Nixon and the Administrative Presidency.* New York: Wiley.

NIXON, RICHARD M. 1978 *R.N.: The Memoirs of Richard Nixon.* New York: Grosset Dunlap.

SCHLESINGER, ARTHUR M., JR. 1973 *The Imperial Presidency.* Boston: Little, Brown.

WHITE, THEODORE H. 1975 *Breach of Faith: The Fall of Richard Nixon.* New York: Atheneum.

NIXON, UNITED STATES v.
418 U.S. 683 (1974)

This litigation unfolded contemporaneously with congressional investigation of the Watergate affair and with proceedings in the HOUSE OF REPRESENTATIVES for the IMPEACHMENT of President RICHARD M. NIXON. (See WATERGATE AND THE CONSTITUTION.) A federal GRAND JURY had indicted seven defendants, including Nixon's former attorney general and closest White House aides, charging several offenses, including conspiracy to obstruct justice by "covering up" the circumstances of a burglary of Democratic party offices in Washington. The grand jury named Nixon as an unindicted co-conspirator. A special prosecutor had been appointed to handle this prosecution. To obtain evidence, the special prosecutor asked Judge John Sirica to issue a SUBPOENA ordering Nixon to produce electronic tapes and papers relating to sixty-four White House conversations among persons named as conspirators, including Nixon himself.

Judge Sirica issued the subpoena in mid-April 1974; on May 1, Nixon's counsel moved to quash the subpoena and to expunge the grand jury's naming of the President as a co-conspirator. Sirica denied both motions and ordered Nixon to produce the subpoenaed items. When Nixon appealed, the special prosecutor asked the Supreme Court to hear the case, bypassing the court of appeals. The Court granted that motion and advanced argument to July 8. On July 24 the Court upheld the subpoena, 8–0, including the votes of three Nixon appointees. Justice WILLIAM H. REHNQUIST, formerly a Justice Department official under the indicted ex-attorney general, had disqualified himself. A week following the decision, before Nixon had complied with it, the House Judiciary Committee recommended his impeachment. When Nixon turned over the tapes on August 5, they included a conversation that even his strongest supporters called a "smoking gun." On August 9 the President resigned.

A year earlier a White House press officer had said Nixon would obey a "definitive" decision of the Supreme Court about the tapes. At ORAL ARGUMENT in the Supreme Court, however, Nixon's counsel, pressed to say that the President had "submitted himself" to the Court's decision, evaded any forthright promise of compliance. Even after the Court's decision, the press reported, Nixon and his aides debated for some hours whether he should comply with the subpoena. Some have reported that the Court's unanimity was an important factor influencing that decision.

The Court itself seems to have been impressed with the need for unanimity; its bland opinion, formally attributed to Chief Justice WARREN E. BURGER, bore the external marks of a document hurriedly negotiated—as investigative reporters have said it was. The Court brushed aside objections to its JURISDICTION, such as the FINAL JUDGMENT RULE. Nixon also argued that the courts had no jurisdiction over an "intra-branch" dispute between the President and his subordinate, the special prosecutor. Responding, the Court emphasized the "uniqueness" of the conflict, but apart from that comment its argument bordered on incoherence. After gratuitously remarking that the executive branch had exclusive discretionary control over federal criminal prosecutions, the Court reversed field, discovering a guarantee of independence for the special prosecutor in the regulation that appointed him and promised not to remove him absent a consensus among certain congressional leaders. Both the Court's propositions were dubious. (See APPOINTING AND REMOVAL POWER.) Yet the Court marched on to some heroic constitutional issues concerning relations between the executive and judicial branches.

Both sides had appealed to the abstraction of SEPARATION OF POWERS. Nixon argued first that the judiciary lacked power "to compel the President in the exercise of his discretion," and second that the President enjoyed an EXECUTIVE PRIVILEGE to keep confidential his conversations with his advisers. The first argument blurred two separate issues: the President's immunity from judicial process and the POLITICAL QUESTION issue of his discretion to control disclosure of his conversations. This latter claim of absolute executive privilege overlapped his second main argument. That argument began with an absolute privilege claim, but if that claim failed the President sought to persuade the Court to recognize a wide scope for a qualified privilege.

The special prosecutor, opposing both PRESIDENTIAL IMMUNITY and the claim of absolute privilege, assumed the existence of a qualified privilege. That privilege was lost, he argued, when there was substantial reason to believe that the participants in a presidential conversation had been planning a crime.

The Court's opinion, like Nixon's argument, blurred the boundaries of separate issues in the case. The decision to uphold the subpoena, however, implicitly rejected the claim of presidential immunity, and the Court expressly rejected the claim of absolute privilege. A qualified privilege did exist, the Court said—by way of assumption, not demonstration—but the privilege was defeated when the specific confidential information sought was shown to be relevant, admissible evidence for a pending federal prosecution. The Court thus disposed of the case without mentioning Nixon's own possible complicity in crime; it dismissed the question whether the President could constitutionally be named as a co-conspirator.

Today some form of a qualified executive privilege is assumed to exist, but the scope of the privilege remains largely undefined. *Nixon's* most important contribution to our constitutional law, however, lay elsewhere: in its reaffirmation that even the highest officer of government is not beyond the reach of the law and the courts. Nixon's brief had included this remark, designed to reassure: "it must be stressed we do not suggest the President has the attributes of a king. *Inter alia,* a king rules by inheritance and for life." The *Nixon* decision reminded us that there are also other differences.

KENNETH L. KARST
(1986)

Bibliography

SYMPOSIUM   1974   United States v. Nixon. *UCLA Law Review* 22:1–140.

WOODWARD, BOB and ARMSTRONG, SCOTT   1979   *The Brethren: Inside the Supreme Court.* Pages 285–347. New York: Simon and Schuster.

NIXON v. ADMINISTRATOR OF GENERAL SERVICES
433 U.S. 425 (1977)

Ex-president RICHARD M. NIXON sued to prevent implementation of the Presidential Recordings and Materials Preservation Act. In upholding the constitutionality of the act, the Supreme Court rejected Nixon's contentions that it violated SEPARATION OF POWERS and EXECUTIVE PRIVILEGE, abridged Nixon's RIGHT OF PRIVACY and FREEDOM OF ASSOCIATION, and constituted a BILL OF ATTAINDER.

DENNIS J. MAHONEY
(1986)

NIXON v. CONDON
286 U.S. 73 (1932)

After the decision in NIXON V. HERNDON (1927), Texas amended its statute, giving a political party's state executive committee the power to set voting qualifications for the party's PRIMARY ELECTIONS. The Democratic party's committee limited primary voting to whites. Nixon, a black, again was denied a primary ballot and again sued election officials for DAMAGES. The Supreme Court reversed a dismissal of the action, holding, 5–4, that the committee's conduct was STATE ACTION in violation of the FOURTEENTH AMENDMENT. The line of "Texas primary cases" continued with GROVEY V. TOWNSEND (1935).

KENNETH L. KARST
(1986)

NIXON v. FITZGERALD
457 U.S. 731 (1982)

HARLOW v. FITZGERALD
457 U.S. 800 (1982)

In these cases the Supreme Court significantly expanded the scope of EXECUTIVE IMMUNITY in actions for DAMAGES brought by persons injured by official action. Fitzgerald sued former President RICHARD M. NIXON and two of his aides, alleging that he had been dismissed from an Air Force job in retaliation for revealing to a congressional committee a two billion dollar cost overrun for a transport aircraft.

In *Nixon* the Court held, 5–4, that the President is absolutely immune from civil damages—not merely for the performance of particular functions but for all acts within the "outer perimeter" of his official duties. Justice LEWIS F. POWELL, for the majority, rested his decision not on the text of the Constitution but on "the constitutional tradition of the SEPARATION OF POWERS." Unlike other executive officers, who have only a qualified immunity from damages actions, the President occupies a unique place in the government. He must be able to act without fear of intrusive inquiries into his motives. The dissenters agreed that some of the President's functions should be clothed in absolute immunity, but argued that a qualified immunity from suit was sufficient in most cases to protect presidential independence.

In *Harlow* the Court, 8–1, rejected the aides' claim of absolute immunity, but broadened the scope of qualified executive immunity. Under previous decisions, this immunity was lost when the official negligently violated "clearly established" rights or acted with malicious intention to deprive constitutional rights or to cause harm. The Court here eliminated the "malicious intention" test for losing the immunity. A great many actions for damages against executive officials are based on claims of right that are not "clearly established." *Harlow* forbids damages in such a case even though the official acts with malice.

KENNETH L. KARST
(1986)

NIXON v. HERNDON
273 U.S. 536 (1927)

This decision was the first in a series of "Texas primary cases." Texas law disqualified blacks from voting in Democratic party PRIMARY ELECTIONS. Nixon, refused a ballot under this law, sued election officers for damages under the federal CIVIL RIGHTS laws, asserting a denial of EQUAL PROTECTION OF THE LAWS under the FOURTEENTH AMEND-MENT and a denial of the right to vote on account of race, in violation of the FIFTEENTH AMENDMENT. (See VOTING RIGHTS.) The Supreme Court reversed a dismissal of the action, holding for Nixon on his equal protection claim and not discussing the Fifteenth Amendment. The next case in the series was NIXON V. CONDON (1932).

KENNETH L. KARST
(1986)

NIXON v. UNITED STATES
506 U.S. 224 (1993)

In *Nixon v. United States*, the Supreme Court held that a challenge to the U.S. SENATE's practice of permitting a committee to hear evidence against an impeached judge presented a nonjusticiable POLITICAL QUESTION. The petitioner Walter Nixon, a federal judge, had made false statements to a federal GRAND JURY that was investigating him for bribery. He argued that having a body smaller than the Senate receive evidence deprived him of a "trial" by the Senate, which, under Article I, section 3 has "the sole Power to try all Impeachments." A six-member majority of Justices found that "the use of the word 'try' in the first sentence of the Impeachment Trial Clause lacks sufficient precision to afford any judicially manageable standard of review of the Senate's actions." It further held that JUDICIAL REVIEW was precluded by the vesting in the Senate of the "sole" power of trial and conviction: "If the courts may review the actions of the Senate . . . , it is difficult to see how the Senate would be 'functioning . . . independently . . .'"

Had the majority reached the merits, Nixon probably still would have lost, as Justice BYRON R. WHITE argued in a CONCURRING OPINION. Many federal adjudications entail initial evidence-gathering by an official or entity other than the ultimate trier of fact. In contrast, the majority's nonmerits reasoning is peculiar. Given the constitutional inferences that the Court has confidently drawn in other adjudicative contexts, it seems incredible that the federal judiciary would be incompetent to determine what constitutes a legally sufficient impeachment trial. Nor would circumscribed judicial review seem to deprive the Senate of its "sole" power to conduct such trials.

Because impeachment is Congress's only constitutionally authorized check on miscreant judges, it is easy, however, to understand the Court's desire to exhibit self-restraint in policing the process. The Court may also have wanted to signal to the executive branch that it would not interfere with Congress's exclusive mechanism for forcing the removal of corrupt public officials.

PETER M. SHANE
(2000)

(SEE ALSO: *Judicial Impeachment.*)

Bibliography

GERHARDT, MICHAEL J. 1993 The Senate's Process for Removing Federal Judges. Pages 139–242 in National Commission on Judicial Discipline and Removal, *Research Papers of the National Commission on Judicial Discipline and Removal, Vol. I.* Washington, D.C.: U.S. Government Printing Office.

—— 1994 Rediscovering Nonjusticiability: Judicial Review of Impeachments after *Nixon. Duke Law Journal* 44:231–276.

NLRB v. FRIEDMAN-HARRY MARKS CLOTHING CO.

See: Wagner Act Cases

NLRB v. FRUEHAUF TRAILER CO.

See: Wagner Act Cases

NLRB v. JONES & LAUGHLIN STEEL CORP.

See: Wagner Act Cases

NO-KNOCK ENTRY

Police are not allowed to enter a house to search or make an ARREST unless they have procured a warrant based on PROBABLE CAUSE, according to PAYTON V. NEW YORK (1980) and *Vale v. Louisiana* (1970). If police cannot get a warrant because of EXIGENT CIRCUMSTANCES, they may act on probable cause alone. In either case, the Supreme Court has not articulated specific rules for no-knock entries. At COMMON LAW, police could not make a forcible entry unless admittance was refused after they announced their authority and purpose, and the FEDERAL CODE OF CRIMINAL PROCEDURE prescribes the same requirements. But the Court has not made this rule into a formal FOURTH AMENDMENT requirement. Rather, the Court emphasizes that entries must always be reasonable, and forcible entries must be based on exigent circumstances. A few states authorize by statute the issuance of no-knock warrants, but any blanket sanctioning of such entries probably would be held to violate the Fourth Amendment.

CATHERINE HANCOCK
(1986)

Bibliography

LAFAVE, WAYNE R. 1978 *Search and Seizure: A Treatise on the Fourth Amendment.* Vol. 2:122–140. St. Paul, Minn.: West Publishing Co.

NOLO CONTENDERE

(Latin: "I do not choose to contest [it].") This statement, variously defined as plea and not a plea, indicates that the defendant will not fight a charge against him. Of the same immediate effect as a guilty plea, it admits the facts charged but cannot be used as a confession of guilt in any other proceeding. Acceptance by a court is discretionary.

DAVID GORDON
(1986)

NONINTERPRETIVISM

This ungainly name was invented as a counterpart of INTERPRETIVISM, the view that courts, in deciding on the meaning of the Constitution, should find their authoritative sources only in the constitutional text and the clearly established intentions of those who adopted the text. A noninterpretivitst, then, was one who believed that courts might properly go beyond these sources, enforcing constitutional norms not readily discernible in the text or the Framers' intentions, narrowly conceived. These terms lost their vogue fairly quickly because few commentators (and no judges) wanted to admit that their views were anything other than interpretations of the Constitution.

Today's commentary uses other terms that are more descriptive of their referents. "Textualism," for example, refers to a view that focuses closely on the Constitution's words. Almost no commentators now profess to be strict textualists. Justice HUGO L. BLACK is the modern Supreme Court's strongest claimant to being a textualist, and even he had his moments of backsliding. ORIGINALISM, which limits the authoritative sources to the text and the ORIGINAL INTENT of the Framers, has a number of adherents among today's commentators and a smaller number among the federal judiciary, but none among the Justices. By the end of the 1980s, however, sightings of noninterpretivists had become rarer than sightings of Bigfoot.

KENNETH L. KARST
(1992)

Bibliography

BREST, PAUL 1980 The Misconceived Quest for the Original Understanding. *Boston University Law Review* 60:204–238.

ELY, JOHN HART 1980 *Democracy and Distrust: A Theory of Judicial Review,* chaps. 1 and 2. Cambridge, Mass.: Harvard University Press.

LEVY, LEONARD W. 1988 *Original Intent and the Framers' Constitution.* New York: Macmillan.

PERRY, MICHAEL J. 1982 *The Constitution, the Courts, and Human Rights.* New Haven, Conn.: Yale University Press.

TUSHNET, MARK V. 1983 Following the Rules Laid Down: A Critique of Interpretivism and Neutral Principles. *Harvard Law Review* 96:781–827.

NONJUDICIAL INTERPRETATION OF THE CONSTITUTION

The requirement in Article VI, section 3, that public officers "support the Constitution" applies to all three branches of government, not merely the judiciary. In compliance with this constitutional mandate, legislators and executive officials have made major contributions over the years in interpreting and shaping the Constitution. Because jucidial doctrines often exclude the courts from deciding certain questions, the meaning of the Constitution may depend exclusively on determinations reached by the legislative and executive branches.

In the early decades of the American republic, before the Supreme Court began to establish PRECEDENTS for constitutional law, the Constitution had to be interpreted solely by members of Congress and executive officials. Such critical issues as FEDERALISM, INTERSTATE COMMERCE, the President's APPOINTING AND REMOVAL POWER, the investigative power of Congress, the TREATY POWER and FOREIGN AFFAIRS, SLAVERY, and INTERNAL IMPROVEMENTS were debated and resolved by the political branches without any assistance from the judiciary. Many of these constitutional judgments were later accepted by the federal courts as binding interpretations.

The idea of JUDICIAL SUPREMACY begins with Chief Justice JOHN MARSHALL's declaration in MARBURY V. MADISON (1803) that it is "emphatically the province and duty of the judicial department to say what the law is." Bold words, but the political situation required Marshall to finesse the legal issue to avoid a confrontation with President THOMAS JEFFERSON he knew he could not win. Significantly, Marshall never again, throughout his long tenure on the bench, invalidated another act of Congress.

It is doubtful whether Marshall actually believed that the Supreme Court possessed the exclusive authority to decide the meaning of the Constitution. After Congress impeached and removed Judge JOHN PICKERING in 1804 and began proceedings to impeach Supreme Court Justice SAMUEL J. CHASE (with Marshall probably next in line), Marshall wrote to Chase on January 23, 1804, suggesting that members of Congress did not have to impeach judges because they objected to their legal opinions. Congress could simply reverse the decisions. Marshall advised Chase, "I think the modern doctrine of impeachment should yield

to an appellate jurisdiction in the legislature. A reversal of those legal opinions deemed unsound by the legislatures would certainly better comport with the mildness of our character that [would] a removal of the Judge who has rendered them unknowing of his fault."

Marshall's letter to Chase is somewhat ambiguous. Could Congress reverse only statutory interpretations or constitutional decisions as well? Did reversal require a constitutional amendment or merely a statute? The context of Marshall's statement implies that he was quite willing to share with the other two branches the task of CONSTITUTIONAL INTERPRETATION.

Obviously, neither Congress nor the Presidents accepted the Court as the final arbiter of constitutional law. Jefferson believed that constitutional decisions by one branch, including the judiciary, were to be given "no control to another branch." Each branch "has an equal right to decide for itself what is the meaning of the Constitution in the cases submitted to its action; and especially, where it is to act ultimately and without APPEAL." An example is the President's PARDONING POWER. Although the ALIEN AND SEDITION ACTS of 1798 had never been declared unconstitutional in the federal courts, Jefferson considered it a nullity when he became President and, accordingly, pardoned those who had been convicted under it. Congress later appropriated funds to reimburse individuals who had been fined under the Sedition Act, declaring in committee reports that the statute was "unconstitutional, null, and void." The Court later admitted in NEW YORK TIMES V. SULLIVAN (1964) that the Sedition Act had been repudiated not by a court of law, but by the "court of history."

President ANDREW JACKSON also believed that each branch of government had an independent duty to interpret the Constitution. The Court upheld the constitutionality of the BANK OF THE UNITED STATES in MCCULLOCH V. MARYLAND (1819), and Congress passed legislation to recharter it, but Jackson nevertheless vetoed the bill on the ground that Congress, the President, and the Court "must each for itself be guided by its own opinion of the Constitution. Each public officer who takes an oath to support the Constitution swears that he will support it as he understands it, and not as it is understood by others." This broad concept of the VETO POWER has been adopted by all subsequent Presidents.

In a series of speeches in 1858, ABRAHAM LINCOLN denied that the Court's decision in DRED SCOTT V. SANDFORD (1857) represented the "last word" on the slavery issue, particularly with regard to the power of Congress to prohibit SLAVERY IN THE TERRITORIES and the rights of blacks. Lincoln considered the Court a coequal, not a superior, branch of government. In his inaugural address in 1861, he warned that if government policy on "vital questions affecting the whole people is to be irrevocably fixed" by the Court, "the people will have ceased to be their own rulers."

The Supreme Court may be the ultimate interpreter of the Constitution in a particular case, but once it releases an opinion, it is helpless to control the political forces and pressures that shape constitutional meaning. In 1918 and again in 1922, the Court struck down congressional efforts to regulate child labor. The first statute, according to the Court, exceeded Congress's power under the COMMERCE CLAUSE because manufacturing was not "interstate commerce." The second statute, the Court held, exceeded the taxing power because the tax was really a "regulation." Despite these precedents, the New Deal Congress passed legislation in 1938 to regulate wages and hours in manufacturing, relying again on the commerce clause, and a unanimous Court overrode the 1918 child labor decision and upheld the statute in UNITED STATES V. DARBY LUMBER COMPANY (1941).

For a period of several decades in the twentieth century, the Supreme Court invoked its power of JUDICIAL REVIEW to restrict the power of Congress to regulate the national economy. These decisions did little more than delay the momentum for national control. In time, the constitutional meaning of interstate commerce and federalism fell almost exclusively to Congress and the President. In PRUDENTIAL INSURANCE COMPANY V. BENJAMIN (1946) the Court conceded: "the history of judicial limitation of congressional power over commerce, when exercised affirmatively, has been more largely one of retreat than of ultimate victory." In GARCIA V. SAN ANTONIO METROPOLITAN TRANSIT AUTHORITY (1985) the Court essentially delegated to Congress the responsibility for defining federalism.

Relying on the commerce clause and its powers to enforce the Civil War amendments, Congress has taken the initiative to establish the constitutional rights of black citizens in such areas as education, housing, VOTING RIGHTS, employment, and equal access to PUBLIC ACCOMMODATIONS. Virtually all these legislative actions in recent decades have been sustained by the courts.

Dissenting in GERTZ V. ROBERT WELCH, INC. (1974), Justice WILLIAM J. BRENNAN claimed that the courts are "the ultimate arbiters of all disputes concerning clashes of constitutional values." Two hundred years of history present quite a different picture. Clashes of constitutional values are fought out in every arena—national and state—and within all of the branches of government. No single branch can claim ultimate control. Constitutional judgments of the courts are frequently overturned by the political branches.

In ZURCHER V. STANFORD DAILY (1978) the Court balanced the right of a free press against the needs of law enforcement officials and sided with the latter. In 1980,

Congress passed legislation giving much greater protection to FIRST AMENDMENT interests. In *United States v. Miller* (1976) the Court supported the right of law enforcement agents to subpoena banks for information in a depositor's account. Two years later, Congress passed legislation that placed limits on warrantless searches of bank and credit records.

Another example of a Court-Congress dialogue, with Congress again defending constitutional rights left unprotected by the judiciary, is GOLDMAN V. WEINBERGER (1986). The Court upheld an Air Force regulation that prohibited an Orthodox Jew from wearing his yarmulke indoors while on duty. The Court reasoned that the Air Force's values of obedience, discipline, and unity outweighed any interference with the religious beliefs of Captain Goldman. Congress disagreed, passing legislation the next year that told the Air Force to change its regulation to permit officers and airmen to wear religious apparel while in uniform.

On special occasion, an authoritative and binding decision by the Supreme Court may be helpful in resolving a political impasse. The unanimous decision in COOPER V. AARON (1958) defused the smoldering Little Rock crisis, but the CIVIL RIGHTS stalemate persisted until the two political branches confronted the issue squarely and passed the CIVIL RIGHTS ACT OF 1964. This statute provided more of a "last word" on the constitutional rights of black citizens than any court decision, including such landmark rulings as BROWN V. BOARD OF EDUCATION (1954). Similarly, the unanimous decision in UNITED STATES V. NIXON (1974) signaled a dramatic turn in the WATERGATE affair, leading to the resignation of President RICHARD M. NIXON, but the decision added little clarity to the constitutional meaning of EXECUTIVE PRIVILEGE and even introduced new areas of confusion and uncertainty.

Sometimes an effort by the Court to announce the last word on a divisive constitutional issue simply backfires, attempting to do through the judiciary what must be accomplished through the political process. A notable example is the inaugural address by one President who explained that a difficult constitutional issue was before the Supreme Court, where it belonged, and that it would be "speedily and finally settled." The address was by JAMES BUCHANAN, two days before the Court announced the *Dred Scott* case.

The belief that the judiciary is the ultimate arbiter of constitutional issues finds no support in our history. The Court itself often shows a keen awareness that CONSTITUTIONAL INTERPRETATION is an exceedingly delicate and complex task that must be shared with Congress, the President, the states, and society at large.

LOUIS FISHER
(1992)

Bibliography

ANDREWS, WILLIAM G., ed. 1969 *Coordinate Magistrates: Constitutional Law by Congress and the President.* New York: Van Nostrand Reinhold.

FISHER, LOUIS 1988 *Constitutional Dialogues: Interpretation as Political Process.* Princeton, N.J.: Princeton University Press.

MURPHY, WALTER F. 1986 Who Shall Interpret? The Quest for Ultimate Constitutional Interpreter. *Review of Politics* 48: 401–423.

NONJUDICIAL INTERPRETATION OF THE CONSTITUTION
(Update)

The Constitution of the United States demands interpretation. Its textual language is often less than clear, as is its surrounding history. As a result, ordinary citizens as well as constitutional scholars frequently debate the meaning of the Constitution's terms. Moreover, so too do government officials, legislative and executive, high and petty, in the numerous contexts in which the Constitution potentially constrains the performance of their duties. And of course judges, state and federal, and at all levels of the judicial hierarchy, must routinely engage in CONSTITUTIONAL INTERPRETATION in applying the law to the cases before them. In all of these settings, it is uncontroversial that the Constitution is the supreme law of the land, and that all other laws must be compatible with it, but it is often controversial just what it is that the Constitution means.

In situations in which there are no Supreme Court interpretations of the Constitution, government officials, including those sitting as judges of state courts and lower federal courts, must interpret the Constitution for themselves. In these circumstances, no question arises regarding the propriety of such officials doing the best they can to interpret the Constitution that both informs and constrains their work.

When the Supreme Court has offered an interpretation of some constitutional provision, however, a new question arises, because it is controversial whether lower court judges and nonjudicial officials must obey what they believe to be erroneous interpretations of the Constitution just because those interpretations come from the Supreme Court. May such lower court judges and nonjudicial officials follow their own interpretations of the Constitution regardless of what the Supreme Court has said?

The responses to this question, both in judicial opinions and in the scholarly literature, fall into three broad categories. One response denies to Supreme Court interpretations any binding force except in the specific case in which the interpretation was offered. In support of this position, some commentators argue that Article III of the Constitution, which describes and creates the JUDICIAL POWER OF THE UNITED STATES and thus the power of the Supreme Court, restricts the power of the federal courts to the decision of CASES AND CONTROVERSIES. Thus, although the Supreme Court may bind the parties and the lower courts to its interpretation in the particular case before it—a power that follows from the very idea of a supreme court—the Supreme Court has no power to bind officials or courts in other cases to its interpretation. Indeed, according to this position, the Court has no power even to bind itself, through the DOCTRINE OF STARE DECISIS, to any constitutional interpretation that it subsequently deems to be erroneous.

This position, which denies to the Supreme Court the power to bind anyone other than the litigants and lower courts in particular cases, strikes many observers as anarchical, inevitably productive to an unworkable cacophony of conflicting constitutional interpretations. A second and less-extreme position, therefore, holds that Supreme Court interpretations of the Constitution should be accorded considerable but not absolute weight by courts other than the Supreme Court, and should be accorded moderate weight by the Supreme Court itself. Under this position, the fact of an existing Supreme Court interpretation is relevant (but not necessarily dispositive) in an authoritative and not merely persuasive way in cases other than the case in which the interpretation first arose. Especially with respect to interpretations by legislative and executive officials, the details of this position are often less than clear, since there is a great deal of room to maneuver around the question of what it is for a decision to have "considerable" but not "absolute" authoritative force. Thus, commentators who hold this second position have diverse views about when officials should act contrary to Supreme Court interpretations that those officials believe to be erroneous. All agree that some "dialogue" between the Court and other branches of government is a good thing and conducive to better constitutional interpretation, but there is disagreement about what is to happen when disagreement persists even after the most robust dialogue.

The third position, which is the one the authors endorse, accords Supreme Court interpretations of the Constitution the status of supreme law of the land, and thus the status that the Constitution declares itself to have. According to this position, a Supreme Court interpretation of the Constitution becomes part of the Constitution for all practical purposes, and to lower court judges and nonjudicial officials there should be no difference between what the Constitution says and what the Supreme Court says the Constitution says. (The most extreme version of this position would make Supreme Court interpretations authoritative for the Supreme Court itself in later cases; and at a minimum this position entails that such interpretations may not be overturned by the Court merely because the Court thinks them wrong.) Undergirding this position is a respect for the values of consistency and uniformity that support the reason for having a constitution in the first place. The virtue of a constitution is not in the fact that it takes a position on controversial issues of political morality, but that it settles controversial issues of political morality. Insofar as the meaning of the Constitution itself remains unsettled, this central function and virtue of constitutionalism remains unsatisfied. A Supreme Court interpretation of the Constitution, if given the authoritative status of the Constitution itself, can provide the settlement that the Constitution is meant to provide but often does not.

The Supreme Court itself has endorsed this third position in COOPER V. AARON (1958), and again more recently in *City of Boerne v. Flores* (1997). That the Supreme Court itself has endorsed the position, however, is neither surprising nor dispositive, for the question of what weight others should give to Supreme Court interpretations cannot be settled by the Supreme Court itself. Thus, the question is not what the Supreme Court has said about the authoritativeness of its own interpretations, but whether this position—JUDICIAL SUPREMACY (but not exclusivity) with respect to matters of constitutional interpretation—best serves the goals of a constitutional system. And although such a view might on occasion produce excess deference to erroneous Supreme Court interpretations, the opposing view might, on even more frequent occasions, produce an unwillingness in the executive and legislative branches to take seriously the idea that the Constitution constrains and thus invalidates even some outcomes that might be desirable, in the short run, on both policy and political grounds. The question is therefore not whether the Supreme Court is in some way a "better" interpreter than the other branches. Rather, it is whether, in light of the relevant systemic incentives and goals, a system of authoritative Supreme Court interpretation of the Constitution will produce better results, in the aggregate and in the long term, than a system in which each judge, each legislator, and each executive official may decide for himself or herself what the Constitution means.

LARRY ALEXANDER
FREDERICK SCHAUER
(2000)

(SEE ALSO: *Religious Freedom Restoration Act.*)

Bibliography

ALEXANDER, LARRY and SCHAUER, FREDERICK 1997 On Extrajudicial Constitutional Interpretation. *Harvard Law Review* 110:1359–1387.

DEVINS, NEAL and FISHER, LOUIS 1998 Judicial Exclusivity and Political Instability. *Virginia Law Review* 84:83–106.

NAGEL, ROBERT F. 1998 Judicial Supremacy and the Settlement Function. *William and Mary Law Review* 39:849–864.

PAULSEN, MICHAEL STOKES 1994 The Most Dangerous Branch: Executive Power to Say What the Law Is. *Georgetown Law Journal* 83:217–345.

SYMPOSIUM 1987 Perspectives on the Authoritativeness of Supreme Court Opinions. *Tulane Law Review* 61:977–1095.

NONMARITAL CHILDREN

Beginning with *Mills v. Hableutzel* (1982), the Supreme Court invalidated a series of laws that sharply limited the time during which a paternity suit might be brought to secure child support from the father of a child born outside marriage. In *Mills*, a Texas law imposed a limitation of one year from the birth of the child; the state imposed no limit on the time in which such a suit could be brought against the father of a child born within marriage. The Court was unanimous in striking down the law, and five Justices added their view that even a longer limitations period might be invalid. In *Pickett v. Brown* (1983) the Court was again unanimous; a two-year limitation imposed by Tennessee was held invalid. These two opinions did little to clear up the confusion in the Court's earlier discussions of the appropriate STANDARD OF REVIEW in cases involving nonmarital children.

In *Clark v. Jeter* (1988), however, the Court—again unanimously—held invalid Pennsylvania's six-year limitation period for such a lawsuit. Now Justice SANDRA DAY O'CONNOR wrote for the Court, explicitly holding that discrimination based on "ILLEGITIMACY" must survive the intermediate scrutiny that the Court had been using in cases of SEX DISCRIMINATION. Perhaps the most remarkable feature of this series of decisions is that Justice WILLIAM H. REHNQUIST (by 1988, Chief Justice) joined in the move to heighten judicial scrutiny, a step he had refused to take in earlier times. Some commentators have detected a move to the center of the Court on the part of the Chief Justice in these cases. His concurrence in the result of the sex discrimination case of UNITED STATES V. VIRGINIA (1996) similarly embraces the intermediate scrutiny standard he had resisted during its formative years.

KENNETH L. KARST
(2000)

NONTESTIMONIAL COMPULSION

See: Testimonial and Nontestimonial Compulsion

NORMAN v. BALTIMORE & OHIO RAILROAD COMPANY

See: Gold Clause Cases

NORRIS, GEORGE W.
(1861–1944)

George William Norris, a progressive Republican from Nebraska, served in the HOUSE OF REPRESENTATIVES from 1903 to 1913. He led the revolt against Speaker Joseph Cannon that, in 1910, broke the power of the speaker to control virtually all legislation in the house. As a United States senator (1913–1943) Norris was the author of the TWENTIETH AMENDMENT, which ended the "lame duck" sessions of Congress, and co-author of the NORRIS-LAGUARDIA ACT (1932), which outlawed YELLOW DOG CONTRACTS and restricted use of federal court INJUNCTIONS against labor strikes, and of the TENNESSEE VALLEY AUTHORITY ACT (1933). Norris supported most of President FRANKLIN D. ROOSEVELT's "NEW DEAL" and criticized Supreme Court decisions that held such legislation unconstitutional. Although he favored a constitutional amendment to restrict national JUDICIAL REVIEW, he opposed Roosevelt's plan to pack the Court with pro-administration justices.

DENNIS J. MAHONEY
(1986)

Bibliography

LOWITT, RICHARD 1963–1978 *George W. Norris.* 3 Vols. Syracuse, N.Y.: Syracuse University Press; Urbana, Ill.: University of Illinois Press.

NORRIS v. ALABAMA
294 U.S. 587 (1935)

Clarence Norris, one of the Scottsboro boys (see POWELL V. ALABAMA), on retrial moved to quash the INDICTMENT and trial venire (pool of potential jurors) on the ground that qualified black citizens were systematically excluded from jury service solely on the basis of race. On denial of his motion by the trial judge, Norris was retried and again found guilty. The state supreme court affirmed the JUDGMENT of the trial court that no JURY DISCRIMINATION existed. The Supreme Court, voting 8–0, reversed the judgment after reviewing the evidence for itself for the first time in such a case. The evidence showed that for a generation or more no black person had been called for jury service in the county and that a substantial number of black persons qualified under state law. In an opinion by Chief Justice CHARLES EVANS HUGHES, the Court ruled that the evidence of black exclusion made a *prima facie* case of denial of the EQUAL PROTECTION guaranteed by the FOURTEENTH AMENDMENT. *Norris* began a line of cases that led to the virtual extinction of RACIAL DISCRIMINATION in the composition of juries.

LEONARD W. LEVY
(1986)

NORRIS-LAGUARDIA ACT
47 Stat. 70 (1932)

Reeling from a string of adverse court decisions, labor saw the Norris-LaGuardia Act of 1932 as Congress's long overdue remedy for Supreme Court antipathy. A panel of experts, including Professor FELIX FRANKFURTER, helped to draft a bill to end the abuse of labor INJUNCTIONS, and, as eventually passed by large majorities in Congress, the act greatly diminished the use of federal injunctions in labor disputes. The act recognized the need for COLLECTIVE BARGAINING and encouraged union formation, ending years of misinterpretation of the spirit, if not the letter, of the CLAYTON ACT. One of the key provisions of the new act (section 4) outlawed the issuance of federal injunctions against those who "whether acting singly or in concert" might strike, aid, or publicize strikes, join unions, or assemble peacefully. YELLOW DOG CONTRACTS, sustained in HITCHMAN COAL COKE COMPANY V. MITCHELL (1917), were also rendered unenforceable (section 3). In DUPLEX PRINTING PRESS COMPANY V. DEERING (1921) the Court had unjustifiably declared that the Clayton Act provision covering labor disputes applied only to related parties, employer and employee, not to those engaged in a secondary boycott. Section 13 rewrote that practice by redefining "labor dispute" so that the parties need no longer be in "proximate relation" to each other. Although the act divested federal courts of injunctive power, it provided exceptions where illegal acts or injury were likely. Moreover, the employers had to make "every reasonable effort" to negotiate a settlement before seeking an injunction (section 8).

The act's explicitly stated purpose was to foster labor's right to organize and act without federal judicial interference. The act created no new substantive rights but enlarged the area in which labor could operate. The act's procedures would be upheld in *Lauf v. E. G. Shinner*

Company (1938) and its substance upheld in *New Negro Alliance v. Sanitary Grocery Company* (1938).

DAVID GORDON
(1986)

NORTH AMERICAN FREE TRADE AGREEMENT
32 I.L.M. 296 (Parts One Through Three)
32 I.L.M. 612 (Parts Four Through Eight)
(1993)

The North American Free Trade Agreement between the Government of the United States of America, the Government of Canada, and the Government of the United Mexican States (NAFTA) was signed on December 17, 1992 by Canadian Prime Minister Brian Mulroney, Mexican President Carlos Salinas de Gortari, and U.S. President GEORGE H. W. BUSH. The U.S. government concluded NAFTA as a congressional–executive agreement, pursuant to a delegation of "fast track" negotiating authority set forth in section 1103 of the Omnibus Trade and Competitiveness Act of 1988 and section 151 of the Trade Act of 1974. The North American Free Trade Agreement Implementation Act—the vehicle for congressional approval and implementation of the Agreement—passed the U.S. HOUSE OF REPRESENTATIVES on November 17, 1993 by a 234–200 margin, and then passed the U.S. SENATE on November 20 by a 61–38 vote. President WILLIAM J. CLINTON signed the bill on December 8, enabling NAFTA to enter into force on January 1, 1994.

NAFTA consists of eight parts organized into twenty-two chapters (plus scores of annexes and schedules), which together liberalize North American trade in goods and services. Whether a good qualifies for the application of NAFTA's trade-liberalizing rules is determined by the Rules of Origin (chapter four). The principle of national treatment must be applied to all qualifying goods and services. Tariffs, quotas, and other trade restrictions on qualifying goods are eliminated over a ten-year period. By eliminating these barriers to "substantially all trade" between the constituent territories, NAFTA is a free trade agreement within the meaning of Article XXIV of the General Agreement on Tariffs and Trade. In addition, NAFTA liberalizes investment rules, requires protection of intellectual property, provides for temporary entry of business persons, and disciplines the parties' customs procedures, government procurement practices, administration of antidumping and countervailing duty laws, use of technical barriers to trade, and application of sanitary and phytosanitary measures. Several academic and government studies suggest that these NAFTA rules are causing a shift of some labor-intensive production to Mexico and some production requiring high-skilled labor to the United States and Canada.

While party governments may employ NAFTA's general dispute settlement procedures (chapter twenty), natural or legal PERSONS other than the party governments generally lack STANDING to participate in NAFTA dispute settlement. However, nationals of the parties may appeal party antidumping or countervailing duty determinations directly to a NAFTA dispute settlement panel (chapter nineteen), and certain disputes between a party and an investor of another party may be settled by binding arbitration (chapter eleven).

The Free Trade Commission, comprising cabinet-level representatives of the parties or their designees, carries out the agreement's implementation, elaboration, and supervision. Commission decisions must be taken by consensus. The commission is serviced by a secretariat that is often referred to as a "virtual secretariat," because each country houses in its capital its own "national Section" of the trinational secretariat.

Environmental and labor concerns associated with North American trade liberalization led to the conclusion of three supplementary international agreements: the North American Agreement on Environmental Cooperation, the Agreement Concerning the Establishment of a Border Environment Cooperation Commission and a North American Development Bank, and the North American Agreement on Labor Cooperation.

Of several challenges to NAFTA's constitutionality, three have generated significant debate. First, since congressional debate began on approval and implementation of NAFTA, Laurence Tribe and others have asserted that NAFTA should not have been concluded as a congressional–executive agreement, a device that is nowhere contemplated in the Constitution and that Tribe argues is unconstitutional. Instead, they assert that NAFTA should have been concluded as a TREATY pursuant to Article II, subject to approval by two-thirds of the Senate present—a proportion of Senate support that NAFTA did not garner. Despite this challenge, the prevailing view set forth in the Restatement (Third) of Foreign Relations Law of the United States is that the congressional–executive agreement can be used as an alternative to the treaty method in every instance. Legal scholars Louis Henkin, Myres McDougal, and Detlev Vagts have advanced this latter view at various times in the last fifty years. And in the context of this NAFTA debate, Bruce Ackerman and David Golove offered a political–historical explanation for the development and legitimacy of congressional–executive agreements as interchangeable with treaties.

Second, some have argued that NAFTA's chapter nineteen provision for appeal of a party's antidumping or countervailing duty decision to NAFTA dispute settlement contravenes Article III, which vests "[t]he judicial Power of the United States . . . in one supreme Court, and in such inferior Courts as the Congress may establish." However, the prevailing view appears to be that chapter nineteen dispute settlement panels are legitimate "courts" because the governmental interest in establishing and maintaining NAFTA outweighs individual traders' interests in review by constitutional courts. Therefore, chapter nineteen would survive the BALANCING TEST set forth in *Commodity Futures Trading Commission v. Schor* (1986).

Finally, some have argued that chapter nineteen of NAFTA contravenes the APPOINTMENTS CLAUSE because chapter nineteen dispute settlement panelists are required to interpret and apply U.S. antidumping and countervailing duty law. Hence, the panelists appear to be "exercising significant authority pursuant to the laws of the United States," which would place them within the definition of "Officers of the United States" set forth in BUCKLEY V. VALEO (1976) and so require compliance with the appointments clause procedure. However, the prevailing view among commentators who advised Congress during the NAFTA debate is that the panels will in actuality be international bodies exercising their authority pursuant to an international agreement, thus rendering the clause inapplicable. Despite the view that chapter nineteen would survive constitutional scrutiny, the NAFTA implementing LEGISLATION did establish special procedures for constitutional challenges to the panel system.

RICHARD H. STEINBERG
(2000)

(SEE ALSO: *Executive Agreement.*)

Bibliography

ACKERMAN, BRUCE and GOLOVE, DAVID   1995   Is NAFTA Constitutional? *Harvard Law Review* 108:799–929.

BELLO, JUDITH H.; HOLMER, ALAN F.; and NORTON, JOSEPH J., eds. 1994   *The North American Free Trade Agreement: A New Frontier in International Trade and Investment in the Americas.* Washington, D.C.: American Bar Association.

BOYER, ETHAN   1996   Article III, the Foreign Relations Power, and the Binational Panel System of NAFTA. *International Tax and Business Lawyer* 13:101–142.

DAVEY, WILLIAM J.   1992   The Appointments Clause and International Dispute Settlement Mechanisms: A False Conflict. *Washington and Lee Law Review* 49:1315–1328.

TRIBE, LAURENCE H.   1995   Taking Text and Structure Seriously: Reflections on Free-Form Method In Constitutional Interpretation. *Harvard Law Review* 108:1221–1303.

NORTH ATLANTIC TREATY
63 Stat. 2241 (1949)

Following WORLD WAR II, the Soviet Union rapidly expanded its influence in Eastern and Central Europe. Fearing a further "Communist offensive," the West, led initially by Belgium, Canada, France, Luxembourg, the Netherlands, the United Kingdom, and the United States, negotiated the North Atlantic Treaty which, it was hoped, would deter Soviet expansionism. The treaty was signed by twelve countries on April 4, 1949, and presently lists a total of sixteen countries among its signatories. The primary objectives of the treaty are as stated in its preamble: "to promote stability and well-being in the North Atlantic area" and "to unite . . . for collective defense and for the preservation of peace and security." The treaty stipulates that "an armed attack against one or more of the [State] Parties in Europe or North America shall be considered an attack against them all" and that, in the event of such an attack, each State Party shall take "such action as it deems necessary, including the use of armed force, to restore and maintain the security of the North Atlantic area." Some commentators have suggested that this language may effect an unconstitutional delegation of United States authority to declare war. The argument is of minimal concern, however, inasmuch as Article 11 of the treaty provides that all of the treaty's provisions shall be "carried out by the Parties in accordance with their respective constitutional processes." The discretionary language of Article 5 ("such action as it deems necessary") reinforces this conclusion.

BURNS H. WESTON
(1986)

(SEE ALSO: *Status of Forces Agreement; Treaty Power.*)

Bibliography

FOX, WILLIAM T. and SCHILLING, WARNER R., eds.   1973   *European Security and the Atlantic System.* New York: Columbia University Press.

SAULLE, MARIA RITA   1979   *NATO and Its Activities.* Dobbs Ferry, N.Y.: Oceana Publications.

NORTHERN PIPELINE CONSTRUCTION COMPANY v. MARATHON PIPE LINE COMPANY
458 U.S. 50 (1982)

If Congress were to make a wholesale transfer of JURISDICTION over matters within the JUDICIAL POWER of the United States to ADMINISTRATIVE AGENCIES or LEGISLATIVE

COURTS, the result would be a serious risk of undermining the independence of the judiciary. Then, under what circumstances can Congress make any such transfer? The question blurs constitutional doctrine with practical statecraft. In *Marathon* the Supreme Court had an opportunity to illuminate this subject, which has long seemed impervious to light.

In the BANKRUPTCY ACT (1978) Congress created a category of bankruptcy judges, who would hold office not during good behavior (as do judges of CONSTITUTIONAL COURTS) but for fourteen-year terms. The act authorized the bankruptcy judges to decide not only matters peculiar to bankruptcy, such as the marshaling and distribution of assets and the discharge of bankrupts from certain liabilities, but also "related" matters, including actions on behalf of bankrupts against other persons, based on state law. The Supreme Court, 6–3, held that the grant of jurisdiction over the "related" matters exceeded the limits of Article III.

Four Justices concluded that federal jurisdiction over matters not involving "public rights"—dealings between the national government and others, or subject to that government's regulation—must be vested in constitutional courts, with certain limited exceptions. Three Justices espoused balancing Article III's concerns for judicial independence against other practical needs of administering the governmental system. Neither view commanded a majority of the Court, and the doctrinal murk deepened.

KENNETH L. KARST
(1986)

(SEE ALSO: *Thomas v. Union Carbide Agricultural Products Co.*)

NORTHERN SECURITIES CO. v. UNITED STATES
193 U.S. 197 (1904)

A bare majority of the Supreme Court, in a broad construction of congressional power under the COMMERCE CLAUSE, upheld the constitutionality of the SHERMAN ANTITRUST ACT as applied to holding companies. The Court thus extended the scope of the Sherman Act to companies not directly engaged in such commerce which nevertheless controlled INTERSTATE COMMERCE.

The formation in 1901 of the Northern Securities Company, a holding company comprising both the Hill-Morgan and the Harriman interests, united parallel competing lines. In March 1902, the government filed an EQUITY suit to dissolve the company. The question was clear: was a holding company, whose subsidiaries' operations were its only connection with interstate commerce, exempt from the Sherman Act? The Court split 5–4 but without a majority opinion.

Justice JOHN MARSHALL HARLAN, for the plurality, followed UNITED STATES V. TRANS-MISSOURI FREIGHT ASSOCIATION (1897) and other cases, arguing that the Sherman Act established competition as a test for interstate commerce. Harlan declared that a combination need not be directly in commerce to restrain it: intent to restrain or potential for restraint was all that was needed, and here potential restraint could be found in the reduction of competition resulting from the holding company's formation. Harlan refused to interpret the statute using the RULE OF REASON. He also broadly construed the commerce clause, curtly dismissing defense allegations that the INJUNCTION violated state sovereignty and the TENTH AMENDMENT. Justice DAVID J. BREWER concurred only in Harlan's result. Abandoning his earlier opinions, Brewer now embraced the rule of reason but concluded that even under that rule the Northern Securities Company clearly constituted an unlawful restraint of trade.

Justices EDWARD D. WHITE and OLIVER WENDELL HOLMES each wrote dissents. The former followed the definition of interstate commerce in UNITED STATES V. E. C. KNIGHT COMPANY (1895), stressing that stock ownership did not place the defendants within the scope of the Sherman Act. Holmes's first written dissent on the Supreme Court emphasized a COMMON LAW reading of the statute. He believed that the holding company device was neither a combination nor a contract in restraint of trade. Holmes asserted that this case so nearly resembled *Knight* as to require no deviation from that opinion.

Counted by THEODORE ROOSEVELT "one of the greatest achievements of my administration because it emphasized the fact that the most powerful men in this country were held to accountability before the law," this decision's importance lay both in Harlan's insistence on the supremacy of federal law and in the reinvigoration of a law that business had hoped the Court rendered ineffectual in *Knight*.

DAVID GORDON
(1986)

Bibliography

APPEL, R. W., JR. 1975 The Case of the Monopolistic Railroadman. In John A. Garraty, ed., *Quarrels That Have Shaped the Constitution*. New York: Harper & Row.

NORTHWESTERN FERTILIZER CO. v. HYDE PARK
97 U.S. 659 (1878)

In 1867 the Illinois legislature chartered the company for a term of fifty years to manufacture fertilizer, from dead animals, outside the city limits of Chicago. The nearby village of Hyde Park regarded the company's factory as an unendurable nuisance, injurious to the public health. Immediately before the legislature chartered the company it empowered the village to abate public nuisances excepting the company. The village passed an ordinance prohibiting the existence of any company engaged in any offensive or unwholesome business within a distance of one mile. The ordinance put the fertilizer company out of business. It invoked its chartered rights against the ordinance, which it claimed violated the CONTRACT CLAUSE.

On the basis of past decisions the Court should have accepted the company's argument, holding that the village had no authority to abate its factory. By a vote of 7–1, however, the Supreme Court ruled that the village had validly exercised its police power to protect the public health. Justice NOAH SWAYNE for the Court declared that the company's charter must be construed narrowly and held that it provided no exemption from liability or nuisances. Swayne quoted from the decision earlier that term in BOSTON BEER CO. V. MASSACHUSETTS in which the Court announced the DOCTRINE of INALIENABLE POLICE POWER. Both cases had the result of weakening the contract clause's traditional protection of chartered rights.

LEONARD W. LEVY
(1986)

NORTHWEST ORDINANCE
(1787)

This congressional enactment, which applied to the territory northwest of the Ohio River, was the most significant accomplishment of the United States under the ARTICLES OF CONFEDERATION. In effect the ordinance provided for self-government under constitutional law in the TERRITORIES, thus "solving" a colonial problem by avoiding it. The pattern for government, which subsequently was extended to other western territories, allowed for growth from a system of congressional government to statehood and admission to the Union "on an equal footing with the original States, in all respects whatever. . . ." As soon as a district reached a population of 5,000 males of voting age, each one possessing a fifty-acre freehold was entitled to vote for representatives to a general assembly. The assembly had authority to elect a delegate to Congress with the right to debate but not to vote. When the population reached 60,000, the territory could apply for admission as a state, on condition that it had a REPUBLICAN FORM OF GOVERNMENT and a state constitution. Ohio, Illinois, Indiana, Michigan, and Wisconsin were formed out of the Northwest Territory; this ordinance established a model for territorial governance and the admission of other states in the American West.

The ordinance was the first federal document to contain a bill of rights. To extend "the fundamental principles of civil and RELIGIOUS LIBERTY," Congress provided articles that were to have constitutional status, remaining "forever . . . unalterable" except by common consent. These articles guaranteed that the inhabitants of a territory should always be entitled to the writ of HABEAS CORPUS, TRIAL BY JURY, representative government, and judicial proceedings "according to the course of the COMMON LAW" (in effect, a provision for DUE PROCESS OF LAW.) As an extra safeguard the articles encapsulated a provision from MAGNA CARTA by insuring that no person should be deprived of liberty or property "but by the judgment of his peers, or the LAW OF THE LAND." In addition, the articles protected the right to BAIL except in capital cases, enjoined that all fines should be "moderate," and prohibited CRUEL OR UNUSUAL PUNISHMENT. Another article that provided a federal precedent for a similar provision in the BILL OF RIGHTS of the Constitution of the United States dealt with EMINENT DOMAIN: no person's property could be taken except in a public exigency, when he must be fully compensated for its value. The CONTRACT CLAUSE of the Constitution also originated in this ordinance: one article declared that no law should ever be made or have force that in any manner interfered with or affected existing private contracts made in good faith and without fraud. Other articles encouraged "schools and the means of education" and protected Indian lands and liberties. One provision of the ordinance had the effect of reducing sex discrimination in land ownership and preventing the introduction of the law of primogeniture; it ordained that the property of anyone dying intestate (without a will) should be distributed in equal parts to all children or next of kin. The ordinance also protected the religious sentiments and modes of worship of all orderly persons, without exception, and in a precedent-making clause declared, "There shall be neither slavery nor involuntary servitude" in the Northwest Territory or states formed from it. The ordinance, which was probably drafted in the main by RUFUS KING and NATHAN DANE, remains one of the most constructive and influential legislative acts in American history.

LEONARD W. LEVY
(1986)

Bibliography

PHILBRICK, FRANCIS S. 1965 *The Rise of the New West, 1754–1830.* Pages 120–133. New York: Harper & Row.

NORTZ v. UNITED STATES

See: Gold Clause Cases

NOTICE

When unsure what is right, American society often falls back on a process in which people on all sides of a disputed question have their say before a decision is rendered. Moreover, even if one cannot participate in a governmental decision, our notions of the state require that one know in advance the standards by which officials will judge us. To have one's say or to conform one's behavior to a standard one must know of the proceeding or the standard. Because such knowledge is so essential to this scheme of things, the Constitution at numerous points requires that those affected by governmental actions receive notice.

Clauses as diverse and specific as the requirement that Congress publish a journal and the prohibitions against EX POST FACTO laws and BILLS OF ATTAINDER, as well as the more general requirements of the DUE PROCESS clauses require notice in various circumstances. Because of its generality the due process clause has generated most of the litigation about constitutionally required notice. In PROCEDURAL DUE PROCESS cases courts have struggled to distinguish two situations: those in which persons need have only the *opportunity* of finding out about contemplated government actions, and situations in which they must receive more individualized attention. The maxim that ignorance of the law is no excuse expresses the proposition that the legislature need not tell each of us that it has passed some law. We rely instead on the hope that our legislators represent us and on the opportunity we have to adjust our behavior after the law takes effect. The Supreme Court has, however, required that laws defining criminal acts be sufficiently specific to enable persons who *do* look at them to tell what acts are prohibited.

As the focus of government attention narrows from all citizens (the subject of statutes) to more specific contexts, the Constitution requires more elaborate and specific forms of notice, notice that is often linked with a subsequent hearing. Thus the Court has not required the Colorado legislature to notify all the citizens of Denver before altering their property assessments, but it has required notice (and a hearing) for individual property owners on a block to be assessed on the basis of frontage feet. Similarly with administrative or judicial adjudication: persons whose property or liberty stands in jeopardy must receive notice of the threatened governmental action.

Even in such individual adjudication, however, due process requires only that parties who will be bound by official decisions receive the best notice practicable given the circumstances. For example, in a suit to approve the trustee's stewardship of a common trust fund with more than a hundred beneficiaries, the Court required individual notice only to those beneficiaries who could easily be located;

members of the group thus notified shared an interest with the unnotified and would represent them, the Court said in *Mullane v. Central Hanover Bank Trust* (1950).

Once it has notified them with appropriate specificity, government requires much of its citizens; until such notice, however, it can require little.

STEPHEN C. YEAZELL
(1986)

Bibliography

TRIBE, LAURENCE H.   1978   *American Constitutional Law.* Chap. 10. Mineola, N.Y.: Foundation Press.

NOXIOUS PRODUCTS DOCTRINE

The first step in development of a NATIONAL POLICE POWER was the "noxious products doctrine," which Justice JOHN MARSHALL HARLAN propounded in CHAMPION V. AMES (1903). According to this doctrine, Congress has the power to prohibit INTERSTATE COMMERCE in any item that is so injurious to the public—in this case, lottery tickets—as to pollute the commerce of which it is a part. In HAMMER V. DAGENHART (1918), the doctrine became a limitation on the commerce power: because the products of child labor were not inherently more harmful than those of adult labor, Congress lacked power to forbid their interstate transportation. The doctrine was abandoned after UNITED STATES V. DARBY LUMBER (1941).

DENNIS J. MAHONEY
(1986)

NUDE DANCING

Is a sexually titillating dance performed in a bar or in a booth at an "adult" bookstore by a totally nude woman speech protected by the FIRST AMENDMENT? Or is it conduct that can be banned by state or local regulation? For decades the Supreme Court avoided deciding this question. For instance, in SCHAD V. VILLAGE OF MT. EPHRAIM (1981) the Court invoked the OVERBREADTH DOCTRINE to invalidate a citywide ban on all live entertainment, including nude dancing in a booth in an adult bookstore. Earlier and more dubiously, the Court in *California v. La Rue* (1972) invoked the state's power under the TWENTY-FIRST AMENDMENT to regulate alcohol as a basis for upholding a ban on nude dancing in places where liquor was served—a rationale subsequently disavowed in *44 Liquormart v. Rhode Island* (1996). It was not until 1991, in *Barnes v. Glen Theatre, Inc.*, that the Court finally reached the merits of the FREEDOM OF SPEECH issues raised by the prohibition of nude dancing. The Court held that although totally nude dancing was expressive conduct entitled to some First Amendment protection, it could nonetheless be banned. The Court in *Barnes* was sharply divided, both as to result and rationale. Five justices (Chief Justice WILLIAM H. REHNQUIST, and Justices SANDRA DAY O'CONNOR, ANTHONY M. KENNEDY, ANTONIN SALIA, and DAVID H. SOUTER) held that Indiana could constitutionally apply its general ban on public nudity to forbid totally nude dancing in bars and adult bookstores. Four Justices (BYRON R. WHITE, THURGOOD MARSHALL, HARRY A. BLACKMUN, and JOHN PAUL STEVENS) found that applying the ban on public nudity to nude dancing violated the First Amendment.

Although four opinions were issued in *Barnes*, no opinion spoke for a majority. Writing for a plurality consisting of himself, Kennedy, and O'Connor, Rehnquist grudgingly acknowledged that nude dancing was expressive conduct "within the outer perimeters of the First Amendment [although] only marginally so." As such it was entitled to the protection provided by the four-part test of UNITED STATES V. O'BRIEN (1968). Under *O'Brien*, regulation of expressive conduct will be upheld if "it is within the constitutional power of government; if it furthers an important or substantial governmental interest; if the governmental interest is unrelated to the suppression of free expression; and if the incidental restriction on alleged First Amendment freedoms is no greater than is essential to the furtherance of that interest." Applying *O'Brien*, the PLURALITY OPINION found Indiana's ban on public nudity constitutional "despite its incidental limitations on some expressive activity." The prohibition reflected "moral disapproval of people appearing nude among strangers in public places." The plurality found that the ban on public nudity was thus "clearly within the constitutional power of the state" and that it "furthers a substantial government interest in protecting order and morality." The plurality also concluded that this interest was "unrelated to the suppression of free expression." Rehnquist's opinion rejected the argument that the reason Indiana applied its ban on public nudity to nude dancing was to prevent its erotic message, emphasizing that the state equally prevents public nudity with little, if any, erotic message, such as nude sunbathing on public beaches. "Public nudity is the evil the State seeks to prevent," explained the Chief Justice, "whether or not it is combined with expressive activity." Finally, the plurality concluded that "the incidental restriction on First Amendment freedom [was] no greater than is essential to the furtherance of the governmental interest." The prohibition on public nudity, the plurality explained, "is not a means to some greater end, but an end in itself." Additionally, the restriction was in the plurality's view "narrowly tailored," since Indiana required only that the dancers wear "pasties and G-strings," the "bare minimum" (so to speak) "necessary to achieve the State's purpose."

The most controversial part of the plurality's analysis is the holding that the state's interest in promoting morality qualifies as a "substantial or important" justification for banning expressive activity protected by the First Amendment. In support of this holding the plurality relies on two cases, *Paris Adult Theater I v. Slaton* (1973) and BOWERS V. HARDWICK (1986). In both cases the Court held that the state may legitimately enact morals legislation. However, these cases found only that the state's interest in morality supplied a "legitimate" or a RATIONAL BASIS for legislation; neither suggested that this interest was sufficiently weighty to justify the prohibition of a constitutionally protected activity. Thus in *Bowers* it was only after finding that the DUE PROCESS clause of the FOURTEENTH AMENDMENT did not confer a FUNDAMENTAL RIGHT to engage in homosexual sodomy that the Court held that the state's interest in morality provided a rational basis for banning such conduct. Similarly, *Slaton* held only that the state had a "legitimate" interest in promoting morality, and therefore might invoke this interest to ban OBSCENITY, material long held to be without First Amendment protection.

Concurring in the JUDGMENT in *Barnes*, Scalia took a very different approach. Because Indiana's ban on public nudity was a general law regulating conduct and not specifically directed at expression, Scalia would have found the regulation "not subject to First Amendment scrutiny at all." In his view, where there is no constitutional protection of the activity at issue, the state's interest in promoting morality provides a constitutionally sufficient justification for banning the activity. Scalia thus would abandon the "intermediate" level of First Amendment protection extended to expressive conduct by the four-part *O'Brien* test. Such a development would not, he insisted, mean that expressive conduct would be bereft of all First Amendment protection. "Where the government prohibits conduct precisely because of its communicative attributes," Scalia explained, the regulation is unconstitutional. If, on the other hand, the government can adduce some speech-neutral justification for the regulation, such as promoting morality in the case of nude dancing, "that is the end of the matter so far as First Amendment guarantees are concerned." In essence, Scalia would adopt the third part of the *O'Brien* test as the sole criterion for measuring the First Amendment validity of state regulation of expressive conduct. Such limited scrutiny of laws of general applicability despite their impact on fundamental rights would mirror the Court's controversial approach to the First Amendment right of RELIGIOUS LIBERTY under the free exercise clause developed in Scalia's opinion for the Court in EMPLOYMENT DIVISION, DEPARTMENT OF HUMAN RESOURCES OF OREGON V. SMITH (1990).

Souter also concurred in the judgment upholding Indiana's ban on public nudity as applied to nude dancing in bars and adult bookstores. He agreed with the plurality that nude dancing is entitled to "a degree of First Amendment protection" and that the appropriate level of protection is provided by the four-part *O'Brien* analysis. Unlike the plurality and Scalia, however, Souter did not invoke the state's interest in morality. Rather, he relied exclusively on the state's interest in combating the pernicious "secondary effects" said to be caused by this type of nude dancing, including prostitution and sexual assaults. In REN-TON (CITY OF) v. PLAYTIME THEATRES, INC. (1986), the Court found that a city's interest in avoiding similar "secondary effects" provided a legitimate, speech-neutral justification for imposing onerous ZONING requirements on movie theaters showing sexually oriented films. In concluding that this "secondary effects" rationale supported a total ban on activity protected by the First Amendment, however, Souter significantly increased the speech restrictive impact of this rationale.

The four dissenting Justices, in an opinion by White, agreed with the plurality and Souter that the nude dancing at issue was expressive conduct protected by the First Amendment. The DISSENTING OPINION, however, took issue with the plurality's basic premise, shared by Scalia, that Indiana's regulation was a general prohibition of conduct. White pointed out that the ban on nudity did not apply in the home. This observation seems wide of the mark. As Scalia notes, the rationale for the ban was not that nudity was immoral but that *public* nudity was immoral. The dissent offered a stronger argument that the nudity ban was not truly general, claiming that the ban did not apply to nudity in theatrical productions such as "Hair" or to nudity in ballets or operas such as "Salome." The dissent also disagreed with the conclusion that the purpose of the ban was unrelated to the expressive aspect of nude dancing. In the dissent's view it was the "emotions and feelings of eroticism and sensuality" generated by nude dancing that the state sought to regulate, "apparently on the assumption that creating or emphasizing such thoughts and ideas in the minds of spectators may lead to increased prostitution and degradation of women." Consequently, the dissent found Indiana's ban on nude dancing to be an unconstitutional content-based regulation of protected expression.

To the extent that *Barnes* allows the state to ban totally nude dancing in bars and adult book stores, it represents a relatively constrained view of the scope of free speech protection. There are, nonetheless, several speech-protective aspects to this decision. Eight members of the Court found that nude dancing was "expressive conduct" entitled to some degree of First Amendment protection. A clear majority of the Court appeared to reject the plurality's view that the state's interest in promoting morality was sufficient justification for even incidental bans on constitutionally protected expression. Finally, *Barnes* strongly

suggests that the state may not constitutionally ban nudity in theatrical productions. Souter, whose vote was necessary to uphold the ban, noted that it would be difficult to see how nudity in productions such as "Hair" and "Equus" could possibly cause harmful "secondary effects." On the other hand, this result can also be read as unjustifiably discriminating between "high brow" entertainment that appeals to the Justices and the "low brow" entertainment of the masses.

JAMES WEINSTEIN
(2000)

Bibliography

BLASI, VINCENT   1992   Six Conservatives in Search of the First Amendment: The Revealing Case of Nude Dancing. *William and Mary Law Review* 33:611–663.

NULLIFICATION

THOMAS JEFFERSON first suggested the doctrine of nullification in the second Kentucky Resolutions (1799), where he asserted that the sovereign states are the only proper judges of whether the federal government has violated the Constitution and "that a nullification . . . [by] those sovereignties, of all unauthorized acts . . . is the rightful remedy." (See VIRGINIA AND KENTUCKY RESOLUTIONS.) In the 1820s, South Carolinians Robert J. Turnbull and Whitemarsh Seabrook laid the doctrinal foundations of an expanded nullification argument by denouncing the expansion of federal authority. In *Consolidation* (1824), THOMAS COOPER argued that the states remained independent sovereigns, having given only limited and express powers to Congress.

JOHN C. CALHOUN systematized and refined the Carolinians' constitutional arguments. He maintained that the people of the separate states never relinquished their SOVEREIGNTY, and that sovereignty was indivisible. In ratifying the Constitution, the states created a government of limited, specified, and delegated authority. Calhoun used the legal doctrine of agency to explain the federal relationship: "The States . . . formed the compact, acting as sovereign and independent communities. The General Government is but [their] creature . . . a government emanating from a compact between sovereigns . . . of the character of a joint commission . . . having, beyond its proper sphere, no more power than if it did not exist." ("Address on the Relation of the States and the Federal Government," 1831.) When the federal government (the agent) exceeded its authority, the states (the principals), in the exercise of their sovereign power, could "interpose" their authority by nullifying the federal statute or action, which would be void in the nullifying states. If three-fourths of the other states adopted a constitutional amendment empowering the federal government to perform the nullified act, the state then had the choice of acquiescing or of withdrawing from the compact (the federal Constitution) by SECESSION. But Calhoun emphasized that nullification was a peaceable alternative, not a preliminary step, to secession.

Calhoun's theory found application in a dispute, ostensibly over protective tariffs, that produced the Nullification Crisis of 1832. For a decade, Carolinians had declared that their objections to specific federal programs such as INTERNAL IMPROVEMENTS or the national bank were merely specific parts of a larger objection to federal intrusion into the states' internal autonomy. The antitariff struggle was, in James Henry Hammond's metaphor, a "battle at the outposts" to prevent an assault on the real "citadel," slavery. When the Tariff of 1832 failed to meet Carolinian demands for an abrogation of the 1828 Tariff of Abominations, a South Carolina convention adopted an ordinance nullifying it and prohibiting its enforcement in the state.

President ANDREW JACKSON reacted forcefully. In his "Proclamation to the People of South Carolina" (1832), he denounced the theory of secession, insisting that the federal government was a true government to which the states had surrendered a part of their sovereignty. (See JACKSON'S PROCLAMATION.) "Disunion by armed force is treason," he warned. Congress enacted the FORCE ACT (1833), which provided for alternative means of collecting the tariff in South Carolina and enhanced the president's power to use militia and regular forces to suppress resistance to federal authority. Congress also began a downward revision of the tariff. With the crisis over the tariff assuaged, the South Carolina legislature denounced Jackson's "Proclamation" and a subsequent convention made the empty gesture of nullifying the Force Act.

In 1837, Calhoun offered six congressional resolutions that would have opened all federal TERRITORIES to slavery. Congress adopted four of these, including one declaring that the federal government was only a "common agent" of the states and possessed only "delegated" powers. But antislavery agitation in the North increased, and many Northerners endorsed the WILMOT PROVISO (1846), which would have excluded slavery from the territories acquired as a result of the Mexican War. To meet this threat, other southern radicals, including Robert Barnwell Rhett, Edmund Ruffin, and William Lowndes Yancey, turned to secession, which subsumed nullification.

Though the Union victory in the CIVIL WAR left the doctrines of state sovereignty, INTERPOSITION, nullification, and secession all defunct, southern political leaders briefly and ineffectually exhumed interposition theories during efforts in the late 1950s to thwart desegregation in southern universities and schools.

WILLIAM M. WIECEK
(1986)

Bibliography

CURRNET, RICHARD W. N. 1963 *John C. Calhoun.* New York: Washington Square Press.

FREEHLING, WILLIAM W. 1965 *Prelude to Civil War: The Nullification Controversy in South Carolina, 1816–1836.* New York: Harper & Row.

NULLIFICATION CONTROVERSY

See: Constitutional History, 1829–1848

OBITER DICTUM

(Latin: "Said in passing.") In an opinion, a judge may make observations or incidental remarks. Because these comments are unnecessary to the DECISION, they are not a part of the HOLDING and thus do not bind the court in later cases. Such statements are often referred to by the plural, dicta.

DAVID GORDON
(1986)

OBLIGATION OF CONTRACTS

The CONSTITUTIONAL CONVENTION OF 1787, engaged as it was in producing a frame of national government, provided in the Constitution for only a very few restrictions on the LEGISLATIVE POWER of the STATES. Among these was the proscription of any state law impairing the obligation of contracts; that the delegates omitted to include a similar prohibition as to Congress is attributable entirely to the fact that they did not contemplate the existence of national contract law. The phrase "obligation of contracts" did not exist as a term of art, but originated in the Constitution; its meaning is not as obvious as it may seem.

The moral obligation of contracts derives from the voluntary agreement of parties who promise to perform certain duties in exchange for some valuable consideration. In the NATURAL RIGHTS political philosophy of the Framers of the Constitution, the obligation to obey the law itself derives from a SOCIAL COMPACT, in which the individual obliges himself to obey in exchange for the state's guarantee of security for his life, liberty, and property. The moral obligation of contracts, of course, cannot be impaired by state law.

But contracts are also legally binding under the COMMON LAW (as modified from time to time by statute). One of the things that induces men to enter into contracts is the knowledge that the state, by its courts and officers, stands ready to enforce the contractual duties undertaken by the parties. This knowledge is especially important when, as in contracts for lending money, one party will have already performed his side of the bargain while the promise of the other party remains "executory," that is, to be performed in the future. The CONTRACT CLAUSE of the Constitution was intended to prevent state law from undermining the enforceability at law of obligations voluntarily entered into.

The Framers of the Constitution well knew the temptation to repudiate obligations improvidently undertaken. SHAYS' REBELLION, which had just been suppressed in Massachusetts, had been directed against judicial enforcement of farm mortgage loans. The CONTINENTAL CONGRESS, sitting at the same time as the Convention, recognized the same danger and wrote into the NORTHWEST ORDINANCE a provision that "no law ought ever to be made or have force in the said territory, that shall, in any manner whatever, interfere with or affect private contracts, or engagements, *bona fide*, and without fraud previously formed."

The history of the constitutional guarantee against impairment of contracts has been the story of slow, but steady, erosion. Much of the erosion has been effected by limiting the extent of the legal obligation or by discovering remedies that purport to leave the obligation intact while depriving the obligee of the benefit of his bargain. In STURGES V. CROWNINSHIELD (1819) Chief Justice JOHN MARSHALL defined the obligation of a contract as "the law which binds the parties to perform their agreement." Subsequently, in OG-DEN V. SAUNDERS (1827), over Marshall's vigorous dissent, the majority held that the "law" in Marshall's definition was the municipal law of contracts in force where and when the contract was entered into, which local law became part of the contract regardless of any contrary intent of the parties to it. The legislature (or courts) may alter the law of contracts so long as the alteration is prospective in effect. Even after *Ogden v. Saunders,* however, the Supreme Court continued to read the contract clause as proscribing retroactive state legislation affecting contracts.

In times of economic distress, when the number of debtors exceeds the number of creditors, the majority tends to use the political process to shield itself from the consequences of improvident engagements. When the economic hardship is prolonged, even constitutional barriers may be unable to withstand the pressure for relief. Under such pressure, courts have held debtors' relief legislation constitutional by distinguishing the obligation of the contract from the remedies available when the contract is breached. Thus, for example, in HOME BUILDING AND LOAN COMPANY V. BLAISDELL (1933) the HUGHES COURT held that a state law extending the contractual time for repayment of mortgage loans and precluding creditors from exercising their contractual right to sell the mortgaged property to satisfy the debt did not impair the obligation of the loan contract (because the debtor still owed the money) but merely altered the remedy. This sophistical holding permitted the form of the constitutional guarantee to endure even as its substance drained away.

In recent years the Court has partially repudiated the rationale of *Blaisdell* and has revived the contract clause as a check on state ECONOMIC REGULATION. In UNITED STATES TRUST CO. V. NEW JERSEY (1977) as regards public contracts, and in ALLIED STRUCTURAL STEEL CO. V. SPANNAUS (1978) as regards private contracts, the Court subjected statutes that apparently impaired the obligation of contracts to a higher STANDARD OF REVIEW than is commonly applied to economic legislation.

DENNIS J. MAHONEY
(1986)

Bibliography

FRIED, CHARLES 1981 *Contract as Promise: A Theory of Contractual Obligation.* Cambridge, Mass.: Harvard University Press.

O'BRIEN, UNITED STATES v.
391 U.S. 367 (1968)

The *O'Brien* opinion is today widely cited in briefs and judicial opinions defending governmental action against claims of violation of the FREEDOM OF SPEECH. In 1965 Congress amended the SELECTIVE SERVICE ACT to make it a crime to destroy or mutilate a draft registration card. The amendment's legislative history made clear that it was aimed at antiwar protest, but the Supreme Court nonetheless upheld, 8–1, the conviction of a protester for DRAFT CARD BURNING, rejecting his FIRST AMENDMENT claims.

Writing for the Court, Chief Justice EARL WARREN assumed that SYMBOLIC SPEECH of this kind was entitled to First Amendment protection. However, he announced a doctrinal formula now dear to the hearts of government attorneys, a formula that seemed to apply generally to all First Amendment cases: "[W]e think it clear that a government regulation is sufficiently justified if it is within the constitutional power of the Government; if it furthers an important or substantial governmental interest; if the governmental interest is unrelated to the suppression of free expression; and if the incidental restriction on alleged First Amendment freedoms is no greater than is essential to the furtherance of that interest."

This very case seemed appropriate for application of the formula to overturn the protesters' conviction, but it was not to be. Here, Warren said, the power of the federal government to "conscript manpower" was clear; further, he placed great importance on the government's interests in keeping draft cards intact. As for the purpose to suppress expression, the Chief Justice took away what he had just given to First Amendment challengers: the Court should not inquire, he said, into possible improper congressional motivations for an otherwise valid law. (See LEGISLATION.) Finally, he said, the government's interests could not be served by any less restrictive means.

It is hard to avoid the conclusion that the Justices, embattled on political fronts ranging from SEGREGATION to school prayers, thought it prudent not to add to the Court's difficulties a confrontation with Congress and the President over the VIETNAM WAR. Justice WILLIAM O. DOUGLAS, however, dissented alone on the ground that the Court should consider the constitutionality of military CONSCRIPTION in the absence of a DECLARATION OF WAR by Congress.

KENNETH L. KARST
(1986)

Bibliography

ELY, JOHN HART 1975 Flag Desecration: A Case Study in the Roles of Categorization and Balancing in First Amendment Analysis. *Harvard Law Review* 88:1482–1508.
NIMMER, MELVILLE B. 1973 The Meaning of Symbolic Speech under the First Amendment. *UCLA Law Review* 21: 29–62.

O'BRIEN v. BROWN
409 U.S. 1 (1972)

This decision involved challenges to the unseating of delegates to the Democratic National Convention. The Supreme Court refused to decide the case and stayed the lower court's decision, since the full convention had not met on the question and little time was available to decide delicate, "essentially political" issues. Three Justices dissented.

WARD E. Y. ELLIOTT
(1986)

O'BRIEN FORMULA

The Supreme Court has occasionally stated that the test set out in UNITED STATES V. O'BRIEN (1968) should be employed in cases involving the content-neutral regulation of speech. Under that test such a regulation is "sufficiently justified if it furthers an important or substantial government interest . . . and if the incidental restriction on alleged FIRST AMENDMENT freedoms is no greater than is essential to the furtherance of that interest."

Current doctrine is more complicated than such statements imply. First, the O'Brien test often is not employed in important cases involving content-neutral regulations. For example, when speakers seek access to government property, the Court turns to a body of tests and rules that fall under the heading of PUBLIC FORUM doctrine. The O'Brien test has been largely absent from the opinions in those cases.

Second, even when the O'Brien test is applied, the Court often deviates from the test's original language in ways that seem to make the test more speech-protective. For example, the O'Brien test implies that the furtherance of a substantial state interest by the appropriate means always outweighs the interest in FREEDOM OF SPEECH. But the Court will sometimes ask whether the government interest is sufficiently substantial to justify the effect of the ordinance on expression. In addition, the Court may consider factors not mentioned in the test—principally, the adequacy of alternative channels of communication.

Nonetheless, the Court's application of the test has been less rigorous than its wording might connote. Indeed, some commentators have been led to suggest that the O'Brien test really means that the government always wins. This is a plausible reading of the test's treatment in the Supreme Court, but not of its treatment in the lower courts. In fact, the O'Brien test is simply a mangled attempt to state that courts should consider competing interests and arrive at appropriate decisions.

STEVEN SHIFFRIN
(1992)

Bibliography

SHIFFRIN, STEVEN H. 1990 *The First Amendment, Democracy, and Romance.* Cambridge, Mass.: Harvard University Press.

OBSCENITY

Obscenity laws embarrass ALEXIS DE TOCQUEVILLE's claim that there is "hardly a political question in the United States which does not sooner or later turn into a judicial one." It is not merely that the obscenity question became a serious judicial issue rather much later than sooner. It is that the richness of the questions involved have been lost in their translation to the judicial forum.

Obscenity laws implicate great questions of political theory including the characteristics of human nature, the relationship between law and morals, and the appropriate role of the state in a democratic society. But these questions were barely addressed when the Court first seriously considered a constitutional challenge to obscenity laws in the 1957 cases of ROTH V. UNITED STATES and *Alberts v. California.*

The briefs presented the Court with profoundly different visions of FIRST AMENDMENT law. Roth argued that no speech including obscenity could be prohibited without meeting the CLEAR AND PRESENT DANGER test, that a danger of lustful thoughts was not the type of evil with which a legislature could be legitimately concerned, and that no danger of antisocial conduct had been shown. On the other hand, the government urged the Court to adopt a balancing test that prominently featured a consideration of the value of the speech involved. The government tendered an illustrative hierarchy of nineteen speech categories with political, religious, economic, and scientific speech at the top; entertainment, music, and humor in the middle; and libel, obscenity, profanity, and commercial PORNOGRAPHY at the bottom. The government's position was that the strength of public interest needed to justify speech regulation diminished as one moved down the hierarchy and increased as one moved up.

In response to these opposing contentions, the Court took a middle course. Relying on cases like BEAUHARNAIS V. ILLINOIS (1952), the Court seemed to embrace what HARRY KALVEN, JR., later called the TWO-LEVEL THEORY of the First Amendment. Under this theory, some speech is beneath the protection of the First Amendment; only that speech within the amendment's protection is measured by the clear and present danger test. Thus some speech is at the bottom of a two-level hierarchy, and the *Roth* Court sought to explain why obscenity deserved basement-level nonprotection.

History, tradition, and consensus were the staple of the Court's argument. Justice WILLIAM J. BRENNAN explained that all "ideas having even the slightest redeeming social importance" deserve full First Amendment protection. But, he said, "implicit in the history of the First Amendment is the rejection of obscenity as utterly without redeeming social importance." Then he pointed to the consensus of fifty nations, forty-eight states, and twenty obscenity laws passed by the Congress from 1842 to 1956. Finally, relying on an OBITER DICTUM from CHAPLINSKY V. NEW HAMPSHIRE (1942), the Court explained that obscene utterances "are of such slight social value as a step to truth that any benefit that may be derived from them is clearly outweighed by the social interest in order and morality."

From the perspective of liberal, conservative, or feminist values, the Court's reliance on the *Chaplinsky* quotation amounts to a cryptic resolution of fundamental political questions. Liberals would advance several objections. Some would suggest that the Court underestimates the contribution to truth made by sexually oriented material. David Richards, for example, has suggested that

> pornography can be seen as the unique medium of a vision of sexuality . . . a view of sensual delight in the erotic celebration of the body, a concept of easy freedom without consequences, a fantasy of timelessly repetitive indulgence. In opposition to the Victorian view that narrowly defines proper sexual function in a rigid way that is analogous to ideas of excremental regularity and moderation, pornography builds a model of plastic variety and joyful excess in sexuality. In opposition to the sorrowing Catholic dismissal of sexuality as an unfortunate and spiritually superficial concomitant of propagation, pornography affords the alternative idea of the independent status of sexuality as a profound and shattering ecstasy [1974, p. 81].

Even some liberals might find these characterizations overwrought as applied to Samuel Roth's publications, such as *Wild Passion* and *Wanton by Night*. Nonetheless, many of them would argue that even if such publications have no merit in the MARKETPLACE OF IDEAS, individuals should be able to decide for themselves what they want to read. Many would argue along with JOHN STUART MILL that "[T]he only purpose for which power can be rightfully exercised over any member of a civilized community, against his will, is to prevent harm to others." Such a principle is thought to advance the moral nature of humanity, for what distinguishes human beings from animals is the capacity to make autonomous moral judgments. From this perspective, the *Roth* opinion misunderstands the necessity for individual moral judgments and diminishes liberty in the name of order without a proper showing of harm.

Conservatives typically agree that humans are distinguished from animals by their capacity to make rational moral judgments. They believe, however, that liberals overestimate human rational capacity and underestimate the importance of the state in promoting a virtuous citizenry. Moreover, they insist that liberals do not sufficiently appreciate the morally corrosive effects of obscenity. From their perspective, obscenity emphasizes the base animality of our nature, reduces the spirituality of humanity to mere bodily functions, and debases civilization by transforming the private into the public. As Irving Kristol put it, "When sex is a public spectacle, a human relationship has been debased into a mere animal connection."

Feminists typically make no objection to erotic material and make no sharp separation between reason and passion. Their principal objection is to the kind of sexually oriented material that encourages male sexual excitement in the domination of women. From their perspective, a multibillion dollar industry promotes antifemale propaganda encouraging males to get, as Susan Brownmiller put it, a "sense of power from viewing females as anonymous, panting playthings, adult toys, dehumanized objects to be used, abused, broken and discarded." From the feminist perspective, the *Roth* opinion's reference to the interests in order and morality obscures the interest in equality for women. From the conservative perspective, the opinion is underdeveloped. From the liberal perspective, it is wrongheaded.

Liberals gained some post-*Roth* hope from the Court's treatment of the obscenity question in STANLEY V. GEORGIA (1969). In *Stanley* the Court held that the possession of obscenity in the home could not be made a criminal offense without violating the First Amendment. More interesting than the holding, which has since been confined to its facts, was the Court's rationale. The Court insisted that "our whole constitutional heritage rebels at the thought of giving government the power to control men's minds." It denied the state any power "to control the moral content of a person's thoughts." It suggested that the only interests justifying obscenity laws were that obscene material might fall into the hands of children or that it might "intrude upon the sensibilities or privacy of the general public."

Many commentators thought that *Stanley* would be extended to protect obscene material where precautions had been taken to avoid exposure to children or nonconsenting adults. Indeed such precautions were taken by many theaters, but the Supreme Court (the composition of which had changed significantly since *Stanley*) reaffirmed *Roth* and expanded on its rationale in *Paris Adult Theatre I v. Slaton* (1973).

The Court professed to "hold that there are legislative interests at stake in stemming the tide of commercialized obscenity, even assuming it is feasible to enforce effective safeguards against exposure to the juvenile and the passerby. These include the interest of the public in the quality of life and the total community environment, the tone of commerce in the great city centers, and, possibly, the public safety itself." The Court did not suggest that the link between obscenity and sex crimes was anything other than arguable. It did insist that the "States have the power to make a morally neutral judgment that public exhibition of obscene material, or commerce in such material, has a tendency to injure the community as a whole . . . or to jeopardize, in Chief Justice Earl Warren's words, the State's "right . . . to maintain a decent society."

Several puzzles remain after the Court's explanation is dissected. First, "arguable" connections to crime do not ordinarily suffice to justify restrictions of First Amendment liberties. A merely arguable connection to crime supports restriction only if the speech involved is for some other reason outside FirstAmendment protection. Second, as the Court was later to recognize in YOUNG V. AMERICAN MINI THEATRES, INC. (1976), the reference to quality of life, the tone of commerce in the central cities, and the environment have force with respect to all sexually oriented bookstores and theaters whether or not they display obscene films or sell obscene books. The Court in MILLER V. CALIFORNIA (1973) limited the definition of obscenity to that material which the "average person, applying contemporary community standards" would find that "taken as a whole appeals to the prurient interest" and "depicts and describes, in a patently offensive way, sexual conduct specifically defined by the applicable state law"; and which, "taken as a whole, lacks serious literary, artistic, political, or scientific value." No one has suggested that these restrictions on the definition bear any relationship to the tone of commerce in the cities.

Moreover, if the intrusive character of public display were the issue, mail order sales of obscene material should pass muster under the First Amendment; yet there is no indication that the Court is prepared to protect such traffic. As interpreted in the *Paris Adult Theatre* opinion, *Stanley v. Georgia* appears to protect only those obscene books and films created and enjoyed in the home; the right to use in the home amounts to no more than that. There is no right to receive obscene material—even in plain brown wrappers.

Perhaps least convincing is the Court's attempt to harmonize its *Paris Adult Theatre* holding with liberal thought. It claims to have no quarrel with the court's insistence in *Stanley* that the state is without power "to control the moral content of a person's thoughts." Because obscene material by the Court's definition lacks any serious literary, artistic, political, or scientific value, control of it is said to be "distinct from a control of reason and the intellect." But this is doubletalk. The power to decide what has serious artistic value is the power to make moral

decisions. To decide that material addressing "reason" or the "intellect" is all that is important to human beings is ultimately to make a moral decision about human beings. Implicit in the latter idea, of course, is the belief that the enjoyment of erotic material for its own sake is unworthy of protection. But the view is much more general. The Court supposes that human beings have a rational side and an emotional side, that the emotional side needs to be subordinated and controlled, and that such suppression or control is vital to the moral life. That is why the Court believes that the contribution of obscenity to truth is outweighed by the state's interest in morality. The Court's insistence on the right to maintain a decent society is in fact an insistence on the state's interest in the control of the "moral content of a person's thoughts."

Finally, it is simply dazzling for the Court to suggest that the states are engaged in a "morally neutral" judgment when they decide that obscene material jeopardizes the right to maintain a decent society. When states decide that "a sensitive key relationship of human existence, central to family life, community welfare, and the development of human personality can be debased and distorted by commercial exploitation of sex," they operate as moral guardians, not as moral neutrals. Nonetheless, the Courts' bows to liberal theory in *Paris Adult Theatre* are revealing, and so are the guarded compromises of the obscenity test adopted in *Miller v. California*. The bows and compromises reflect, as do the opinions of the four dissenting Justices in *Paris Adult Theatre*, that America is profoundly divided on the relationship of law to morality and on the meaning of free speech. Since *Paris Adult Theatre* and *Miller*, and despite those decisions, the quantity of erotic material has continued to grow. At the same time, feminist opposition to pornography has ripened into a powerful political movement. The Supreme Court's decisions have neither stemmed the tide of commercial pornography nor resolved the divisions of American society on the issue. These political questions will continue to be judicial questions.

STEVEN SHIFFRIN
(1986)

Bibliography

CLOR, HARRY M. 1969 *Obscenity and Public Morality*. Chicago: University of Chicago Press.

KALVEN, HARRY, JR. 1960 The Metaphysics of the Law of Obscenity. *Supreme Court Review* 1960:1–45.

LEDERER, LAURA, ed. 1980 *Take Back the Night: Women on Pornography*. New York: Bantam Books.

RICHARDS, DAVID A. J. 1974 Free Speech and Obscenity Law: Toward a Moral Theory of the First Amendment. *University of Pennsylvania Law Review* 123:45–99.

OCEAN LAW
AND THE CONSTITUTION

Constitutional adjudication in the field of admiralty law has always taken account of rules and principles accepted as "customary law" in the jurisprudence of INTERNATIONAL LAW. Outside the admiralty field, however, the Supreme Court has seldom been inclined to engage in any systematic engrafting of substantive doctrines from international law into the fabric of American law. Hence, it is remarkable to find that in cases requiring the Court to rule on the physical boundaries of individual states of the Union—that is to say, in performing one of its most basic functions, as "umpire" of the federal system—the Court has relied on evolving international law as the basis for such important decisions.

The cases in question include *United States v. California* (1965), the Texas and Louisiana Boundary Cases of 1969 (*United States v. Louisiana et al.*), and *United States v. Alaska* (1997). In each of them, the Court decided disputes between the federal government and state governments concerning the outermost seaward boundaries of those states' jurisdiction. At issue was the ownership of submerged land, beyond the physical limits of the coastline; the economic stakes were high, because of the value of offshore oil deposits in the beds of the offshore waters. In each instance, the state sought to validate a claim as proprietor of the submerged lands, hoping to gain the advantage of substantial potential oil revenues that would otherwise go to the federal government.

Specifically at issue in all four cases was interpretation of two 1953 statutes, the Submerged Lands Act and the Outer Continental Shelf Lands Act, by which Congress had ceded to the coastal states title to submerged lands (together with their oil deposits and other resources) out to a limit of three miles beyond the coastline. Congress's intent, in these statutes, was to "correct" the decision of the Court in *United States v. California* (1947), in which the Court had ruled that the national government had "paramount rights" in all offshore waters and their resources, out to whatever limit the President and Congress declared to be the outer seaward boundary of the nation's jurisdiction. What remained at issue, once Congress had thus granted to the states title to submerged land out to three miles, was the question of exactly how to define "coastline" for purposes of measuring to the mandated offshore boundary.

In each of the four cases, the Court relied on an international agreement, the 1958 Convention on the Territorial Sea and the Contiguous Zone, which had been ratified by the United States in 1964, as providing "the best and most workable definitions available." Over Justice HUGO L.

BLACK's objections in dissent that Congress had intended to leave this delicate and (in his view) purely domestic question in the hands of a federal executive agency, the Court's majority in the 1969 cases declared that Congress had deliberately left to the judiciary final authority in the matter of defining offshore boundaries.

With regard to eroded shorelines, dredged channels into the sea, and elevations that emerged only during low tide, among other questions regarding physical features of the coast and offshore waters, the Court relied for its definitions not only on language in the 1958 convention itself but also—most extraordinarily—upon the "legislative history" behind that agreement; specifically, the 1958 report of the International Law Commission. This commission had been charged by the United Nations to develop a draft for the convention, together with scholarly commentary on customary law and general principles applicable to the definition of coastlines. Thus, the Court relied on technical discussion in the commission's report and its draft convention text as determinative evidence of the meaning of otherwise ambiguous or perplexing language in the convention as to the coastline boundary definition. Deciding in favor of the federal government in all four cases, the Court also relied on the convention and general principles of international ocean law to reassert the authority of the national government, as ultimate sovereign responsible for foreign policy, to exercise discretion in selecting from among the options available to it under the terms of the convention.

In 1994, the codification of ocean law as a distinctive branch of international law advanced dramatically with the entering into force of the United Nations Convention on the Law of the Sea (UNCLOS), first opened for signature in 1982. This convention specifies duties and responsibilities of signatory states across the entire spectrum of ocean uses (fisheries, navigation, naval power, scientific research, environmental protection), and also establishes the legitimacy of a 200-mile "exclusive economic zone" offshore of coastal and island states.

President RONALD REAGAN refused to sign the UNCLOS agreement, objecting to the convention's establishment of collective international management and revenue rights in high-seas ocean bed resources beyond the 200-mile limit; but he declared that the other terms of UNCLOS were already established as customary law and would be honored as such by the United States. Although President WILLIAM J. CLINTON did sign UNCLOS in 1994, the Republican majority in the U.S. SENATE declined to debate it, or even to hold committee hearings, because of the intransigent opposition of some key senators to the convention's terms as a potential threat to American SOVEREIGNTY in ocean affairs. Especially controversial was UNCLOS's establishment of a United Nations International Tribunal for the

Law of the Sea, with power to interpret the convention's terms and with jurisdiction in cases arising under the agreement. Hence, even after the convention was essentially amended by a new agreement in 1994, eliminating the collectivist terms that Reagan had found objectionable as to seabed resource exploitation, the United States remained in 1999 formally a nonparticipant standing outside the processes and framework of one of the most important and far-reaching innovations in international law in modern history.

HARRY N. SCHEIBER
(2000)

Bibliography

BRISCOE, JOHN   1995   The Division of America's Offshore Zones as Between Nation and States. In *Implications of Entry into Force of the Law of the Sea Convention for U.S. Ocean Governance.* Newark, Del.: Ocean Governance Study Group and the University of Delaware.

SCHEIBER, HARRY N. and CARR, CHRIS   1992   Constitutionalism and the Territorial Sea: An Historical Study. *Territorial Sea Journal* 2:67–90.

O'CONNOR, SANDRA DAY
(1930–   )

Sandra Day O'Connor, the first woman Justice to serve on the Supreme Court, was appointed by President RONALD REAGAN in 1981. She had served previously as the nation's first woman senate majority leader in her home state of Arizona and as a member of the Arizona Court of Appeals. In announcing her nomination the President extolled her as someone who would be a rigid adherent of constitutional principles, taking an exacting view of the SEPARATION OF POWERS as a limitation on JUDICIAL ACTIVISM, and respecting the role of FEDERALISM in the constitutional scheme. Although there is little doubt that one motivation in appointing O'Connor was to deprive the Democrats of the opportunity of appointing the first woman Justice, the President's expectations have, by and large, not been disappointed.

For O'Connor constitutional jurisprudence means, above all, an adherence to enduring constitutional principles, recognizing that, while the application of these principles may change, the principles themselves are rooted in the constitutional text and in the precepts that animate the Constitution. In her dissent in *Akron v. Akron Center for Reproductive Health* (1983), O'Connor complained that the majority's decision rested "neither [on] sound constitutional theory nor [on] our need to decide cases based on the application of neutral principles." It is not entirely clear yet whether the Justice mistakenly iden-

tifies constitutional principles with "neutral principles." Her opinions generally indicate an awareness that the Constitution is not neutral with respect to its ends and purposes. She has refused to accept the prevailing view that the Constitution is merely a procedural instrument that is informed by no purposes or principles beyond the procedures themselves.

In CRIMINAL PROCEDURE cases O'Connor has adhered to the principle she enunciated in KOLENDER V. LAWSON (1983): "Our Constitution is designed to maximize individual freedoms within a framework of ORDERED LIBERTY. Statutory limitations on those freedoms are examined for substantive authority and content as well as for definiteness or certainty of expression." The Justice has used this rationale to resist unwarranted attempts to expand criminal DUE PROCESS rights beyond those clearly prescribed or fairly implied by the Constitution. For example, in OREGON V. ELSTAD (1985) O'Connor refused to extend the FRUIT OF THE POISONOUS TREE doctrine either to uncoerced inculpatory statements made after police violation of the MIRANDA RULES, or as in NEW YORK V. QUARLES (1984), to nontestimentary EVIDENCE produced as a result of a *Miranda* violation. In the latter case O'Connor concluded that Justice WILLIAM H. REHNQUIST's majority opinion had created "a finespun new DOCTRINE on public safety exigencies incident to custodial interrogation, complete with the hair-splitting distinctions that currently plague our FOURTH AMENDMENT jurisprudence." Moreover, dissenting in *Taylor v. Alabama* (1982), O'Connor would not have allowed an illegal ARREST to taint a confession that followed appropriate *Miranda* warnings; nor in *South Dakota v. Neville* (1983) would she allow the claim that the refusal to take a blood-alcohol test is protected by the RIGHT AGAINST SELF-INCRIMINATION.

O'Connor has been no less resolute in her efforts to protect the constitutional role of the states in the federal system. In her dissent in GARCIA V. SAN ANTONIO METROPOLITAN TRANSIT AUTHORITY (1985) she remarked that the principle of "state autonomy . . . requires the Court to enforce affirmative limits on federal regulation of the states." The majority opinion, she continued, created the "real risk that Congress will gradually erase the diffusion of power between state and nation on which the Framers based their faith in the efficiency and vitality of our Republic." O'Connor has also staunchly supported the "exhaustion" doctrine of federal HABEAS CORPUS review as a means "to protect the state courts' role in the enforcement of federal law and prevent disruption of state judicial proceedings." The rule that all federal claims must first be exhausted in state court proceedings is, as she wrote in *Engle v. Isaac* (1982), a recognition that "the State possesses primary authority for defining and enforcing the criminal law." She continued that "[f]ederal intrusions into State criminal trials frustrate both the States' sovereign power to punish offenders and their good-faith attempts to honor constitutional rights." And in HAWAII HOUSING AUTHORITY V. MIDKIFF (1984) O'Connor made clear that the Court would accord the utmost deference to state legislatures in matters of "social legislation."

O'Connor was less deferential, however, in the instance where a state maintained a women-only nursing school. Writing for the majority in MISSISSIPPI UNIVERSITY FOR WOMEN V. HOGAN (1982), O'Connor stated that in "limited circumstances a gender-based classification favoring one sex can be justified if it intentionally and directly assists members of the sex that is disproportionately burdened." Here, the SEX DISCRIMINATION actually harmed the intended beneficiaries by perpetuating "stereotyped" and "archaic" notions about the role of women in society.

O'Connor has urged the Court to reexamine some important issues connected with the ESTABLISHMENT OF RELIGION clause of the FIRST AMENDMENT. Concurring in WALLACE V. JAFFREE (1985), O'Connor agreed that an Alabama law providing for a moment of silence was unconstitutional because it sought to sanction and promote prayer in public schools. She dissented, however, from the Court's decision in AGUILAR V. FELTON (1985) striking down the use of federal funds to provide remedial education by public school teachers for parochial school students. While agreeing in LYNCH V. DONNELLY (1983) that every governmental policy touching upon religion must have a secular purpose, O'Connor suggested that the entanglement test propounded in LEMON V. KURTZMAN (1971) should be reexamined.

In the area of EQUAL PROTECTION rights, O'Connor has taken the firm stance that rights belong to individuals. In *Ford Motor Company v. Equal Employment Opportunity Commission* (1982), and in her concurring opinion in FIREFIGHTERS LOCAL #1784 V. STOTTS (1984), O'Connor argued that remedies must be limited to those who can demonstrate actual injury and must be fashioned in a way that protects the settled expectations of innocent parties. She thus adheres to the original intention of the framers of the FOURTEENTH AMENDMENT and of the CIVIL RIGHTS ACT OF 1964, reaffirming the principle that lies at the heart of constitutional jurisprudence—that rights belong to individuals and not to the racial or gender group of which they are members. Employing narrowly construed and analytical opinions, O'Connor has begun to build a solid base for the Court's return to a jurisprudence that looks to the articulation of the Constitution's enduring principles.

EDWARD J. ERLER
(1986)

Bibliography

CORDRAY, RICHARD A. and VRADLIS, JAMES T. 1985 The Emerging Jurisprudence of Justice O'Connor. *University of Chicago Law Review* 52:389–459.

O'CONNOR, SANDRA DAY 1981 Trends in the Relationships between the Federal and State Courts from the Perspective of a State Court Judge. *William and Mary Law Review* 22:801–815.

O'CONNOR, SANDRA DAY
(1930–)
(Update 1)

Sandra Day O'Connor was born in Arizona in 1930. After leaving high school at the age of sixteen, she completed both her undergraduate and law degrees at Stanford University in five years. She spent the next decade as a county attorney and in private practice in Arizona and elsewhere, and she became an Arizona assistant attorney general in 1965. She served in the Arizona state senate from 1969 until 1974, when she moved into the state judiciary—first as a trial judge and later on the state's intermediate court of appeals. President RONALD REAGAN nominated her as the first female Justice of the Supreme Court of the United States in 1981.

O'Connor took the oath of office on September 25, 1981, as the first Supreme Court appointee of the most conservative President since CALVIN COOLIDGE. Not surprisingly, she immediately became part of the conservative wing of the Court, voting with Justice WILLIAM H. REHNQUIST more than ninety percent of the time by 1984. She has continued to be a reliable conservative vote in CRIMINAL PROCEDURE and FEDERALISM cases. After 1984, however, she began striking out on her own in several areas. She became considerably less predictable in cases involving SUBSTANTIVE DUE PROCESS, discrimination, and complex jurisdictional or procedural questions.

By 1989 O'Connor had become a pivotal center vote on the Court. Although this change resulted in part from the appointment of two more conservative Justices, it was also the result of the changes in O'Connor's own views: by 1987 she was voting with Rehnquist only seventy-eight percent of the time. Moreover, during this period O'Connor often wrote separate concurrences and dissents, approaching cases from independent points of view; and by the end of the 1988 term, her originally solo viewpoints commanded majorities in several doctrinal areas. Three topics illustrate both her influence and her central position on the Court: the ESTABLISHMENT CLAUSE of the FIRST AMENDMENT, AFFIRMATIVE ACTION, and CAPITAL PUNISHMENT.

At the time O'Connor joined the Court, establishment clause challenges were virtually always governed by the test of LEMON V. KURTZMAN (1971): a statute violates the establishment clause if it has a primary purpose or a primary effect of advancing or inhibiting religion, or if it causes excessive government entanglement with religion. Beginning with LYNCH V. DONNELLY (1984), O'Connor proposed a "refinement" of the LEMON TEST emphasizing the questions "whether the government's purpose is to endorse religion and whether the statute actually conveys a message of endorsement." Unlike the standard view of the *Lemon* test, which centers on the practical effect of governmental action, O'Connor's test focuses on the communicative or symbolic aspects of that action. Thus, O'Connor would find a constitutional violation when "[e]ndorsement sends a message to non-adherents that they are outsiders, not full members of the political community, and an accompanying message to adherents that they are insiders, favored members of the political community."

Between 1984 and 1989, O'Connor's application of this principle made her the swing vote in many establishment-clause cases. She provided the fifth vote to uphold a public Christmas display including a crèche in *Lynch v. Donnelly* and to uphold federal funding of religious family-planning organizations in BOWEN V. KENDRICK (1988). She also provided the fifth vote to invalidate a state-mandated moment of silence for meditation or prayer at the beginning of the public school day in WALLACE V. JAFFREE (1985) and to invalidate a public Christmas display of a crèche alone in COUNTY OF ALLEGHENY V. ACLU (1989). In *County of Allegheny*, moreover, she appeared to have converted a majority of the Court to her test, at least where the display of religious symbols is at issue.

O'Connor also fashioned what has become the majority test for constitutional challenges to affirmative action programs. For over a decade, the Court was unable to produce a majority opinion in any constitutional case involving affirmative action. Badly fragmented, the Court could not agree on either the level of scrutiny to be applied to such challenges or the factual prerequisites that might make an affirmative action program valid. Beginning with WYGANT V. JACKSON BOARD OF EDUCATION (1986), O'Connor wrote several separate opinions answering both questions with great specificity: affirmative action programs should be tested by STRICT SCRUTINY, and such scrutiny typically requires that there be a remedial need for the program, shown by some evidence—not necessarily contemporaneous—of prior government discrimination (remedying past societal discrimination is an insufficient governmental interest). In 1989, in RICHMOND (CITY OF) V. J. A. CROSON CO. (1989), O'Connor obtained majority support for her position.

O'Connor has also had a significant influence in cases dealing with the death penalty for juveniles. Although she has not generally been the swing vote in ordinary capital cases, her vote has been crucial in deciding whether the state may execute persons who committed crimes when they were under the age of majority. In THOMPSON V. OKLAHOMA (1988), she voted with the four liberal Justices to overturn a death sentence imposed on a girl who had com-

mitted murder at the age of fifteen. O'Connor did not join Justice JOHN PAUL STEVENS's plurality opinion, however, because it categorically denied the constitutionality of executing anyone who was under sixteen when the crime was committed. Instead, O'Connor concluded that the legislature, in failing to set any minimum age limit, did not give proper consideration to a question on which no national consensus existed and, thus, that the penalty was CRUEL AND UNUSUAL PUNISHMENT.

This distinctive approach allowed her to vote the very next year in STANFORD V. KENTUCKY (1989) to uphold death sentences imposed on two juveniles who had committed crimes at the ages of sixteen and seventeen. Again she was the fifth vote, this time combining with the conservative wing of the Court, and again she wrote a separate concurrence basing her decision on a "sufficiently clear . . . national consensus." In a case decided the same day as *Stanford*, PENRY V. LYNAUGH (1989), O'Connor provided the pivotal vote (and wrote the majority opinion) for two separate majorities: one concluding that the Eighth Amendment generally permits the execution of mentally retarded adults and the other reversing the death sentence of the particularly mentally retarded defendant on the ground that the jury instructions deprived the jury of any meaningful opportunity to take the defendant's handicap into account as a mitigating factor.

Finally, O'Connor may prove to be the crucial vote on ABORTION. From 1981 to 1989, O'Connor consistently voted to uphold all antiabortion laws; and in *Akron v. Akron Center for Reproductive Health* (1983), she even wrote that ROE V. WADE (1973) was "on a collision course with itself." In WEBSTER V. REPRODUCTIVE HEALTH SERVICES (1989), however, O'Connor declined to join with the four other Justices wishing to modify *Roe*. Instead, she wrote a separate concurrence upholding the challenged statute under *Roe* itself and explicitly refusing to reach the question of *Roe's* continued validity. Indeed, her earlier opinions had suggested that the Court abandon the trimester approach to abortion and instead ask whether a challenged statute "unduly burdens" a woman's right to an abortion. In *Webster*, Rehnquist's plurality opinion adopted this approach almost verbatim, but O'Connor nevertheless declined to join his opinion.

Two additional trends are evident in O'Connor's opinions. First, she frequently writes separately in order to "clarify" the majority's opinion. Her clarifying concurrences are often attempts to point out the limits of the Court's decision or to minimize the distance between the majority and dissent. In *Wygant*, for example, her concurrence stressed that there was little difference in application between a "compelling" governmental interest and an "important" one and that both majority and dissenting opinions agreed that remedying past discrimination constitutes such an interest. In other cases she has made a great effort to specify what issues the Court has not decided.

The second common thread during O'Connor's tenure on the Court to date is her tendency to demand fact-specific decision making in a wide variety of contexts. For example, in *Lanier v. South Carolina* (1985), she wrote a separate concurrence to a per curiam opinion on the voluntariness of a confession, stressing that on remand the Court should look at the particular circumstances of the confession. In two cases involving the appropriate state statute of limitations to be borrowed in SECTION 1983 actions, she dissented from nearly unanimous Court decisions imposing a single standard, preferring instead to examine the circumstances of each section 1983 suit (*Wilson v. Garcia* and *Goodman v. Lukens Steel Co.*). In a series of HABEAS CORPUS cases, she wrote majority opinions fashioning a test whereby defendants who could produce evidence of "actual innocence" might avoid the newly strengthened strictures of the "cause and prejudice" test (*Smith v. Murray* and *Murray v. Carrier*). In COY V. IOWA (1988), she concurred in a decision invalidating on CONFRONTATION clause grounds a state statute permitting courts to place a screen between the accused and the accuser in child sexual abuse cases, but refused to join the majortity's conclusion that such screens *always* violate the right to confrontation. In ALLEN V. WRIGHT (1984), she demanded greater specificity by parents seeking STANDING to challenge Internal Revenue Service regulations that they alleged were inadequate to prevent discriminatory private schools from obtaining and keeping charitable exemption status. Finally, her position on affirmative action, noted above, makes clear the need for some factual predicate for the adoption of any affirmative-action plan.

When O'Connor joined the Court in 1981, it was expected that her votes would reflect three influences: her CONSERVATISM would align her with the right wing of the Court, her state legislative background would give her a strong STATES' RIGHTS tilt, and her gender would make her more receptive to claims of SEX DISCRIMINATION. Only the last of these expectations has proved both accurate and significant. Although as already indicated, she has voted conservatively on some issues, in other cases she has followed an independent path. Her deference to state legislatures is reasonably consistent, but she has virtually always been outvoted, as in GARCIA V. SAN ANTONIO METROPOLITAN TRANSIT AUTHORITHY (1985) and *South Dakota v. Dole* (1987).

O'Connor has, however, been a consistent supporter of gender equality. During her tenure on the Court, she has joined the majority—and sometimes provided a crucial vote—in making partnership decisions subject to Title VII (*Hishon v. King Spalding*), declaring sexual harassment as actionable under the same statute (MERITOR SAVINGS BANK V. VINSON), rejecting a PREEMPTION challenge to a state law requiring employers to give pregnancy leave to employees who want one (*California Federal Savings Loan v. Guerra*), upholding discrimination claims based on sexual stereotyping (*Price Waterhouse v. Hopkins*), invalidating an all-female state nursing school (MISSISSIPPI UNIVERSITY FOR WOMEN V. HOGAN), and upholding an affirmative action program for women (JOHNSON V. TRANSPORTATION AGENCY). Only in the area of abortion has her support of women's rights been less consistent.

Thus, after eight years on the Court, O'Connor has proved herself an independent and sometimes unpredictable thinker. It is clear, however, that the first female Supreme Court Justice has already left her mark on the Court and will continue to do so.

SUZANNE SHERRY
(1992)

Bibliography

CORDRAY, RICHARD M. and VRADELIS, JAMES I. 1985 The Emerging Jurisprudence of Justice O'Connor. *University of Chicago Law Review* 52:389–459.

O'CONNOR, SANDRA DAY 1981 Trends in the Relationship Between the Federal and State Courts from the Perspective of a State Court Judge. *William and Mary Law Review* 22:801–815.

SHEA, BARBARA C. S. 1986 Sandra Day O'Connor—Woman, Lawyer, Justice: Her First Four Terms on the Supreme Court. *University of Missouri, Kansas City Law Review* 55:1–32.

SHERRY, SUZANNA 1986 Civic Virtue and the Feminine Voice in Constitutional Adjudication. *Virginia Law Review* 72:543–616.

O'CONNOR, SANDRA DAY
(1930–)
(Update 2)

Sandra Day O'Connor was appointed to the Supreme Court by President RONALD REAGAN in 1981. The first woman appointed to the Court, O'Connor brought to the Court a background in state law and politics. She had served on the Arizona state legislature, eventually ascending to senate majority leader, and had been a member of the Arizona Court of Appeals.

When O'Connor joined the Court in 1981, she and then-Justice WILLIAM H. REHNQUIST were its most conservative members. As the Court's composition has shifted over the intervening years and liberal Justices such as WILLIAM J. BRENNAN, JR., and THURGOOD MARSHALL have been replaced by those with other views, her jurisprudence increasingly has provided a middle ground around which other views can rally.

O'Connor is a strong and highly intelligent individual

with a judicial inclination toward PRAGMATISM. She is committed to applying the Constitution's complex requirements faithfully. She eschews the notion that there is a "Grand Unified Theory" that will cover all cases falling under a particular constitutional clause. On her reading, the Constitution is a practical weapon against tyranny, not the locus of a grand metaphysics. It is also a bulwark against the sacrifice of higher ideals to contemporary pressures. In her words, the Constitution "protects us from our own best intentions. It divides power among sovereigns and among branches of government precisely so that we may resist the temptation to concentrate power in one location as an expedient solution to the crisis of the day."

In key constitutional areas—FEDERALISM, ABORTION regulation, AFFIRMATIVE ACTION, and SEPARATION OF CHURCH AND STATE—the Court's DOCTRINE has evolved toward O'Connor's views.

The Court's federalism jurisprudence has developed in fits and starts over the last twenty years. Influenced in no small part by her experiences as a state legislator and judge, O'Connor is a strong advocate of STATES' RIGHTS and the Constitution's limits on federal powers. The Court's trend toward placing more meaningful limits on Congress's power to regulate the states reflects O'Connor's allegiance to state autonomy in the Constitution's scheme of DUAL FEDERALISM. In NATIONAL LEAGUE OF CITIES V. USERY (1976), the Court, per Rehnquist, struck down the 1974 law that extended the Fair Labor Standards Act to cover employees of state and local governments, on the ground that it impaired the states' sovereign integrity. That decision was OVERRULED less than a decade later in GARCÍA V. SAN ANTONIO METROPOLITAN TRANSIT AUTHORITY (1985), in which O'Connor joined the dissenters who predicted that such an assault on states' rights would not continue to command a majority of the Court. By 1992, O'Connor wrote the majority opinion in NEW YORK V. UNITED STATES (1992), which held that Congress does not have the power to compel states to provide for the disposal of radioactive WASTE within their borders. Her subsequent votes in the Court's leading federalism holdings—UNITED STATES V. LÓPEZ (1995), *Printz v. United States* (1997), *Seminole Tribe v. Florida* (1996), *Florida v. College Savings Bank* (1999), and *College Savings Bank v. Florida* (1999)—and her joinder in the reasoning of the majority in *Boerne (City of) v. Flores* (1997) confirm her allegiance to state autonomy.

From her earliest writings in the abortion cases, O'Connor has characterized the BALANCING TEST established in ROE V. WADE (1973), which weighed the states' legitimate interest in the life of a fetus against a pregnant woman's interest in autonomy, as a requirement that the state may regulate abortion but may not place "undue burdens" upon a woman's desire to obtain an abortion. Although various members of the Court have disagreed over

whether *Roe* required STRICT SCRUTINY and whether *Roe* was legitimate, O'Connor has been persistent in her devotion to the undue burden standard as the proper constitutional guide for states attempting to regulate abortion. Consistent with her views on states' rights, the standard creates a great deal of latitude for states to regulate abortion, but does not give states *carte blanche*. She voted to invalidate a state law forcing minors to notify both parents before obtaining an abortion in HODGSON V. MINNESOTA (1990) and to invalidate a state law forcing married women to notify their husbands before obtaining an abortion in PLANNED PARENTHOOD V. CASEY (1992). When the discord at the Court over the validity of *Roe* reached its peak, O'Connor's undue burden test garnered the support of Justices ANTHONY M. KENNEDY and DAVID H. SOUTER. O'Connor, Kennedy, and Souter formed a plurality that voted to reaffirm the "core meaning" of *Roe* (along with liberal Justices Marshall, Brennan, and HARRY A. BLACKMUN). The plurality adopted O'Connor's "undue burden" approach, asserting that the test adhered to *Roe* by retaining its "essential holding."

In an area previously fraught with discord, O'Connor has led the Court to a more consistent position on the constitutionality of race-based affirmative action programs. In RICHMOND (CITY OF) V. J. A. CROSON CO. (1989), she wrote the majority opinion holding that affirmative action plans must be subjected to the strictest of scrutiny and that a city could not constitutionally create preferences for minorities in government contracting in the absence of evidence of a history of RACIAL DISCRIMINATION and proof that the plan was narrowly tailored to remedy the particular history of discrimination. The same reasoning was extended to the federal government in ADARAND CONSTRUCTORS, INC. V. PEÑA (1995) and now governs all affirmative action programs in government employment and in government contracting. The Court's establishment of a more certain test in this arena has prompted a serious reexamination of such programs by the federal and state governments.

Since joining the Court, O'Connor has been the crucial swing vote in the Court's cases addressing the separation of church and state. Three years after joining the Court, she began to advocate a modification of the previously applied LEMON TEST. In LEMON V. KURTZMAN (1971), the Court surveyed ESTABLISHMENT CLAUSE precedent and concluded that a statute violates that clause if it has a primary purpose or effect of advancing or inhibiting religion, or if it causes excessive entanglement between church and state. O'Connor suggested reading this test with an emphasis on "whether the government's purpose is to endorse religion and whether the statute actually conveys a message of endorsement." Endorsement is a constitutional evil, as she explained in LYNCH V. DONNELLY (1984), because it "sends a message to non-adherents that they are outsiders, not full members of the political community, and an accompanying message to adherents that they are insiders, favored members of the political community."

The endorsement test has led O'Connor to draw fine distinctions in the Court's ESTABLISHMENT OF RELIGION cases. She voted to uphold a city's Christmas display that included a crèche in *Lynch* but to invalidate a public Christmas display of a crèche alone in COUNTY OF ALLEGHENY V. AMERICAN CIVIL LIBERTIES UNION (1989). The Court moved toward her endorsement test in LEE V. WEISMAN (1992), which held that a public school graduation prayer was unconstitutional, and followed her reasoning on state aid to church organizations in AGOSTINI V. FELTON (1997), which permitted public school teachers to teach secular subjects on parochial school grounds.

O'Connor also has had considerable influence in cases involving SEX DISCRIMINATION, ELECTORAL REDISTRICTING, HABEAS CORPUS, and CAPITAL PUNISHMENT.

O'Connor's contributions to the United States are not limited to her role as Associate Justice. She is also an ardent advocate of democratization in Eastern Europe. She has spent a great deal of time visiting and advising many of the world's emerging democracies, with special emphasis on the importance of the RULE OF LAW. O'Connor will have made her mark not simply by being the first woman Justice but rather by dint of her strength, intelligence, and contributions to jurisprudence around the world.

MARCI A. HAMILTON
(2000)

(SEE ALSO: *Constitutional History, 1980–1989; Constitutional History, 1989–1999; Rehnquist Court; Religious Liberty; Sovereign Immunity; Voting Rights.*)

Bibliography

COLLECTION　1996　Tribute to Justice Sandra Day O'Connor. *Annual Survey of American Law* 1996:i–1vii.

O'CONNOR, SANDRA DAY　1981　Trends in the Relationship Between the Federal and State Courts from the Perspective of a State Court Judge. *William and Mary Law Review* 55:1–32.

SYMPOSIUM　1991　The Jurisprudence of Justice Sandra Day O'Connor. *Women's Rights Law Reporter* 13:53–170.

O'CONNOR v. DONALDSON
422 U.S. 563 (1975)

Donaldson was initially billed as the case that would decide whether a mental patient held in custody had a constitutional "right to treatment." Ultimately the Court did not decide that issue, but it did make some important pronouncements on the relation between MENTAL ILLNESS AND THE CONSTITUTION.

Kenneth Donaldson was committed to a state hospital at the request of his father; the committing judge found that he suffered from "paranoid schizophrenia." Although the commitment order specified "care, maintenance, and treatment," for almost fifteen years Donaldson received nothing but "milieu therapy"—the hospital superintendent's imaginative name for involuntary confinement. Donaldson finally sued the superintendent and others for damages under SECTION 1983, TITLE 42, UNITED STATES CODE, claiming they had intentionally denied his constitutional rights. The federal district judge instructed the jury that Donaldson's rights had been denied if the defendants had confined him against his will, knowing that he was neither dangerous nor receiving treatment. The jury awarded damages, and the court of appeals affirmed, specifically endorsing the district court's theory of a mental patient's constitutional right to treatment.

The Supreme Court unanimously held that Donaldson had stated a valid claim, but remanded the case for reconsideration of the hospital superintendent's assertion of EXECUTIVE IMMUNITY. Justice POTTER STEWART, for the Court, said that a finding of mental illness alone could not justify a state's confining a person indefinitely "in simple custodial confinement." The Court did not reach the larger question of a "right to treatment"; it disclaimed any need to decide whether persons dangerous to themselves or others had a right to be treated during their involuntary confinement by the state, or whether a nondangerous person could be confined for purposes of treatment. But when the state lacked any of the usual grounds for confinement of the mentally ill—the safety of the person confined or others, or treatment for illness—involuntary confinement was a denial of liberty without DUE PROCESS OF LAW. Confinement was not justified, for example, in order to provide the mentally ill with superior living standards, or to shield the public from unpleasantness. To support the latter point, the Court cited FIRST AMENDMENT decisions including COHEN V. CALIFORNIA (1971). Chief Justice WARREN E. BURGER concurred in the Court's opinion, but wrote separately to express his opposition to any constitutional "right to treatment."

KENNETH L. KARST
(1986)

OFFICE OF MANAGEMENT AND BUDGET

The rapid growth of the federal government in the twentieth century has created the need for an institution to coordinate both fiscal and substantive policy. In 1921, Congress empowered the President to prepare and submit a BUDGET for the government. Previously, the government had had no central budgeting function: the various agencies had made funding requests directly to the appropriations committees in Congress. The President exercises the budgeting function through the Office of Management and Budget (OMB). Although OMB controls the requests that Congress receives, Congress is free to appropriate any amount that it considers appropriate.

The budgeting function accords the President an important opportunity to set the agenda for congressional deliberations over appropriations. Notwithstanding the modern presence of a budget process within Congress itself, Congress finds itself responding initially to the President's views of the best resource allocation for the government. And, of course, Congress is aware that its departure from the President's recommended budget may result in the presidential veto of an appropriations bill. In consequence, through OMB the President exercises great influence on actual appropriations. Moreover, appropriations usually confer discretion concerning the amounts to be spent and the precise uses to be made of the funds. The President supervises the agencies' actual spending through OMB.

OMB also exercises limited control over the substantive policies that the agencies follow. The Supreme Court, in MYERS V. UNITED STATES (1926), recognized presidential power to "supervise and guide" the executive agencies in their exercise of power that Congress has delegated to them. This does not extend to the independent regulatory commissions because, in HUMPHREY'S EXECUTOR V. UNITED STATES (1935), the Supreme Court declared those commissions to be independent of the President except for the constitutional power to appoint their members, and except for powers over them that Congress explicitly grants the President, such as budget review.

Policy supervision therefore concentrates on the executive agencies. In part because of doubts about the extent of the President's power to dictate policy even when it is formed in the executive agencies, OMB has usually limited its supervision to requiring agencies to comply with procedural directives imposed by Presidential EXECUTIVE ORDERS. These directives are thought to be less intrusive than outright commands setting substantive policy. Several Presidents have directed the agencies to prepare analyses of the costs and benefits of their regulations, and to submit them to OMB for review and comment. In view of the size of the executive establishment and the complexity of the issues it considers, this kind of procedural supervision and occasional ad hoc consultation on major policy decisions is the most that the relatively small bureaucracy that serves the President in OMB can hope to accomplish.

HAROLD H. BRUFF
(1986)

"OFFICIAL ENGLISH" LAWS

Many Americans assume that English is already the official language of the United States. In fact, though, the Framers explicitly refrained from giving English any preferred constitutional status. In their view, the natural advantages of English would make it preeminent, while efforts to make it official would crystallize resistance among non-English-speakers and delay English acquisition. Despite the Framers' view, state and local officials have periodically decided to give English some kind of official endorsement. During the WORLD WAR I era, for example, some states tried to limit the use of languages other than English in private as well as public schools. Relying on the DUE PROCESS clause, the U.S. Supreme Court struck down these statutes as an unwarranted interference with both the right of parents to bring up children as they see fit and the right of foreign-language instructors to pursue their livelihood.

Since the 1980s, the status of English as an official language has garnered new attention. With rising levels of immigration, the proportion of non-English-speakers in the United States has grown steadily. In response, by 1996, a total of eighteen states had laws making English their official language, most of them passed in the last fifteen years. These laws vary widely. Some state legislatures have adopted purely symbolic measures, declaring English to be the state language in the same way that the robin might be declared the state bird or the bluebell the state flower. Other provisions have real teeth, allowing private citizens to sue for enforcement of English's official status. Stringent laws like these are often state constitutional amendments, many of which are enacted by popular INITIATIVE

Despite a proliferation of state and local provisions, official English advocates have yet to enjoy much success in declaring English the official language at the federal level. As a result, federal protections for linguistic minorities have limited the impact of state and local measures. For example, federal law now requires schools to provide some special assistance to children with limited English skills, and federal statutes also mandate that some political jurisdictions offer bilingual ballots and election materials upon request. Under the Sixth Amendment and FOURTEENTH AMENDMENT, non-English-speaking defendants in criminal cases are entitled to interpreters at their trials so that they can confront witnesses and consult with counsel.

In the area of social services, however, relatively few federal protections apply. To the extent that official English provisions threaten bilingual assistance provided by these agencies, constitutional challenges have resulted. In Arizona, voters used the popular initiative to amend the state constitution to make English the official language. The amendment provided that "the State and all political subdivisions of [the] State shall act in English and in no other language." A bilingual government worker, who assisted Spanish-speaking clients with medical malpractice claims against the state, sued to block enforcement of the provision. She contended that the policy violated her FIRST AMENDMENT right to FREEDOM OF SPEECH. Because she feared that she would be fired for speaking Spanish on the job, the official English provision had a CHILLING EFFECT on her ability to communicate. The Ninth Circuit Court of Appeals agreed, but the U.S. Supreme Court vacated the judgment on the ground of MOOTNESS in ARIZONANS FOR OFFICIAL ENGLISH V. ARIZONA (1997). Because the employee had already left her position, there was no live controversy for the federal courts to consider.

Subsequently, however, the Arizona courts passed on the constitutionality of the amendment. The state litigation involved claims by four elected officials, five state employees, and one public school teacher, all of whom were bilingual and who asserted that the official English provision denied them freedom of speech and EQUAL PROTECTION OF THE LAWS while they performed government business. The Arizona superior court rejected the First Amendment free speech claim because the official English requirement was content-neutral; that is, it did not attempt to regulate what public officials and employees talked about but only the manner in which they communicated. The superior court found no equal protection violation under the Fourteenth Amendment, either, because there was no proof that Arizona voters acted with discriminatory intent or animus when they approved the official English requirement. The Arizona court of appeals, relying on judicial comity, adopted the views of the Ninth Circuit Court of Appeals, even though that court's opinion had been vacated by the U.S. Supreme Court.

On appeal, the Arizona Supreme Court ultimately concluded that the official English measure "violates the First Amendment by depriving elected officials and public employees of the ability to communicate with their constituents and with the public." In the court's view, the provision went "too far" by "effectively cut[ting] off governmental communication with thousands of limited-English-proficient and non-English-speaking persons in Arizona, even when the officials and employees have the ability and desire to communicate in a language understandable to them." In addition, the Arizona court found that the official English requirement infringed on the fundamental RIGHT TO PETITION the government for redress of grievances and correspondingly, to participate on an equal basis in the political process. As a result, the plaintiffs did not need to prove discriminatory intent; instead, discrimination was presumed, and the state's action therefore was subject to STRICT SCRUTINY under equal protection law. Assuming arguendo that the state had a compelling need to promote a uniform language, the Arizona court held that

the official English requirement swept too broadly in prohibiting all non-English usage. Because such severe intrusions were not necessary to achieve Arizona's objective, the provision denied plaintiffs equal protection. The U.S. Supreme Court has yet to address the merits of the Arizona Supreme Court's conclusions.

Tensions surrounding the use of languages other than English are likely to persist. Formal measures to declare English the official language are not likely to solve the problem, so long as newcomers bring linguistic diversity with them. Recent immigrants will struggle to learn English to improve their social and economic opportunities, while English-speakers chafe at the sounds of foreign languages during the transition. The linguistic clashes associated with today's demographic changes are as unlikely to be legislated away as were the conflicts among colonial languages during the Framers' times. The role of English as the language of opportunity, rather than as the official language, will be decisive in resolving these differences.

RACHEL F. MORAN
(2000)

Bibliography

CRAWFORD, JAMES 1992 *Hold Your Tongue: Bilingualism and the Politics of "English Only."* Reading, Calif.: Addison-Wesley.

CRAWFORD, JAMES, ed. 1992 *Language Loyalties: A Source Book on the Official English Controversy.* Chicago: University of Chicago Press.

HEATH, SHIRLEY BRICE 1981 English in Our Language Heritage. Pages 6–20 in Charles A. Ferguson and Shirley Brice Heath, eds., *Language in the USA.* Cambridge, Eng.: Cambridge University Press.

PEREA, JUAN F. 1992 Demography and Distrust: An Essay on American Languages, Cultural Pluralism and Official English. *Minnesota Law Review* 77:269–373.

OFFICIAL IMMUNITY

See: Executive Immunity; Immunity of Public Officials; Judicial Immunity; Legislative Immunity; Municipal Immunity; Presidential Immunity; Sovereign Immunity

OGDEN v. SAUNDERS
12 Wheaton 213 (1827)

Ogden established the doctrine that a state bankruptcy act operating on contracts made after the passage of the act does not violate the OBLIGATION OF A CONTRACT. The majority reasoned that the obligation of a contract, deriving from positive law, is the creature of state laws applicable to contracts. A contract made after the enactment of a bankruptcy statute is, therefore, subject to its provisions; in effect the statute enters into and becomes part of all contracts subsequently made, limiting their obligation but not impairing it.

For a minority of three, Chief Justice JOHN MARSHALL dissented, losing control of his Court in a constitutional case for the first and only time during his long tenure. He would have voided all state bankruptcy acts that affected the obligation of contracts even prospectively. Grounding his position in the immutable HIGHER LAW principles of morality and natural justice, he maintained that the right of contract is an inalienable right not subject to positive law. The parties to a contract, not society or government, create its obligation. Marshall believed that the majority's interpretation of the CONTRACT CLAUSE would render its constitutional prohibition on the states "inanimate, inoperative, and unmeaning." Had his opinion prevailed, contractual rights of property vested by contract would have been placed beyond government regulation, making the contract clause the instrument of protecting property that the Court later fashioned out of the DUE PROCESS clause substantively construed. Until then, despite Marshall's fears, the contract clause remained the principal bastion for the DOCTRINE of VESTED RIGHTS. This case, however, ended the Court's doctrinal expansion of that clause. *Ogden* prevented constitutional law from confronting the nation with a choice between unregulated capitalism and socialism.

LEONARD W. LEVY
(1986)

OHIO v. AKRON CENTER FOR REPRODUCTIVE HEALTH

See: *Hodgson v. Minnesota*

OHIO LIFE INSURANCE AND TRUST CO. v. DE BOLT

See: *Piqua Branch of the State Bank of Ohio v. Knoop*

OKANOGAN INDIANS v. UNITED STATES

See: Pocket Veto Case

OLIVER, IN RE
333 U.S. 257 (1948)

Since 1917 Michigan had maintained a unique GRAND JURY system, allowing a single judge to be a grand jury with all its inquisitorial powers as well as retain his judicial power to punish for contempt any witness whose testimony he believed to be false or evasive. In the course of a secret grand jury proceeding, a judge summarily sentenced Oliver for contempt. The Supreme Court held the Michigan procedure a violation of SIXTH AMENDMENT rights—denial of PUBLIC TRIAL and of an opportunity to defend himself—without DUE PROCESS OF LAW, contrary to the FOURTEENTH AMENDMENT. Justice HUGO L. BLACK spoke for a 7–2 majority.

LEONARD W. LEVY
(1986)

OLIVER v. UNITED STATES
466 U.S. 170 (1984)

A 6–3 Supreme Court, speaking through Justice LEWIS F. POWELL, reinvigorated the sixty-year-old "OPEN FIELDS" DOCTRINE, according to which the FOURTH AMENDMENT, whose language protects "persons, houses, papers, and effects," does not extend to open fields. No one doubts that the police, or public, may view land from a plane. The question in *Oliver* was whether the police could ignore "No Trespassing" signs and make a warrantless investigation of fenced-in backlands used to grow marijuana, seize EVIDENCE, and introduce it in court despite a TRESPASS on private property. Powell declared that no one could reasonably have a constitutionally protected expectation of privacy in an open field, well away from the curtilage or land immediately surrounding a house (and therefore part of the area to which the Fourth Amendment's protection extends). The dissenters objected that the language of the amendment does not expressly include many areas which the Court has ruled to be within its protection, such as telephone booths, offices, curtilages, and other places which one may reasonably expect to be secure against warrantless police intrusion.

LEONARD W. LEVY
(1986)

OLMSTEAD v. UNITED STATES
277 U.S. 438 (1928)

Federal agents installed WIRETAPS in the basement of a building where Roy Olmstead, a suspected bootlegger, had his office and in streets near his home. None of Olmstead's property was trespassed upon. A sharply divided Supreme Court admitted the wiretap EVIDENCE in an opinion that virtually exempted ELECTRONIC EAVESDROPPING from constitutional controls for forty years. The dissents by Justices OLIVER WENDELL HOLMES and LOUIS D. BRANDEIS are classic statements of the government's obligation to obey the law.

Olmstead argued that because the prosecution's evidence came entirely from the wiretaps, it could not be used against him; wiretapping, he claimed, was a SEARCH AND SEIZURE under the FOURTH AMENDMENT, and because the amendment's warrant and other requirements had not been met, the wiretap evidence was illegally obtained. He also claimed that use of the wiretap evidence violated his RIGHT AGAINST SELF-INCRIMINATION under the Fifth Amendment; further, that because the agents had violated a state statute prohibiting wiretapping, the evidence was inadmissible, apart from the Fourth and Fifth Amendments.

Chief Justice WILLIAM HOWARD TAFT, writing for a five-Justice majority, rejected all Olmstead's contentions. The self-incrimination claim was dismissed first: the defendants had not been compelled to talk over the telephone but had done so voluntarily. This aspect of *Olmstead* has survived to be applied in cases such as HOFFA V. UNITED STATES (1966). As to the Fourth Amendment claims: first, the Court ruled that the amendment was violated only if officials trespassed onto the property of the person overheard, and no such trespass had taken place—the agents had tapped Olmstead's telephones without going onto his property. Second, the Court limited Fourth Amendment protection to "material things," not intangibles like conversations. Third, the Court seemed to deny any protection for the voice if projected outside the house. As to the claim that the agents' violation of the state statute required excluding the evidence, the Chief Justice found no authority for such exclusion.

Justice Holmes wrote a short dissent, condemning the agents' conduct as "dirty business." Justice Brandeis wrote the main dissent in which he disagreed with the majority's reading of the precedents, its very narrow view of the Fourth Amendment, and its willingness to countenance criminal activity by the government. For him, the Fourth Amendment was designed to protect individual privacy, and he warned that the "progress of science in furnishing the Government with means of espionage" called for a flexible reading of the amendment to "protect the right of personal security." He stressed that because a tap reaches all who use the telephone, including all those who either call the target or are called, "WRITS OF ASSISTANCE or GENERAL WARRANTS are but puny instruments of tyranny and oppression when compared with wiretapping." Responding to the argument that law enforcement justified both a narrow reading of the amendment and indifference to the agents' violation of state law, he wrote: "Experience should teach us to be most on our guard to protect liberty when the Government's purposes are beneficent.... The greatest dangers to liberty lurk in insidious encroachment by men of zeal, well-meaning but without understanding...."

Our Government is the potent, the omnipresent teacher. For good or for ill, it teaches the whole people by its example."

Although the decision was harshly criticized, it endured. In *Goldman v. United States* (1942), *Olmstead* was read to allow police to place a microphone against the outside of a wall, because no trespass onto the property was involved. Wiretapping itself remained outside constitutional controls, though section 605 of the COMMUNICATIONS ACT of 1934 was construed by the Supreme Court in NARDONE V. UNITED STATES (1937) to bar unauthorized interception and divulgence of telephone messages.

In 1954, however, *Olmstead* began to be undermined. In IRVINE V. CALIFORNIA (1954), the Court indicated that intangible conversations were protected by the Fourth Amendment. The Court found a trespass when the physical penetration was only a few inches into a party wall as in SILVERMAN V. UNITED STATES (1961) or by a thumbtack as in *Clinton v. Virginia* (1964). Finally, in KATZ V. UNITED STATES (1967), the Supreme Court overruled *Olmstead*, holding that a trespass was unnecessary for a violation of the Fourth Amendment and that the amendment protects intangibles, including conversations.

HERMAN SCHWARTZ
(1986)

Bibliography

MURPHY, WALTER F. 1966 *Wiretapping on Trial: A Case Study in the Judicial Process.* New York: Random House.

OLNEY, RICHARD
(1835–1917)

In 1893 President GROVER CLEVELAND offered the post of ATTORNEY GENERAL to Richard Olney. A Massachusetts Democrat and highly successful railroad lawyer, Olney sought the advice of his major clients. All agreed he should accept the office and one even continued him on the payroll after he took the post, a conflict of interest that reflected the biases Olney allowed to influence his actions in office.

Olney was one of a few lawyers in the country who had litigated the recently passed SHERMAN ANTITRUST ACT; he had successfully defended the Whiskey Trust, and he believed that section 2 of the act was "void because of vagueness, indefiniteness, and ambiguity." While Olney served as attorney general, the Department of Justice initiated no new antitrust suits against business combinations.

Olney is most often remembered for his weak presentation of the government case in UNITED STATES V. E. C. KNIGHT COMPANY (1895). Although the prosecution had been begun under President BENJAMIN HARRISON, Olney was responsible for choosing *Knight* to test the Sherman Act's constitutionality. Even as attorney general he specifically rejected the belief that "the aim and effect of this statute are to prohibit and prevent" trusts, and he contended that "literal interpretation" of the act was "out of the question" because of the act's overbroad terms. His ineffective prosecution contributed to a government loss, crippling enforcement of the Sherman Act for nearly a decade. Olney saw *Knight* as a vindication of his personal views and as an excuse to ignore the law; although he ought to have chosen a stronger case, the federal judges who so narrowly construed the act must share responsibility for the outcome.

Olney's antipathy to the Sherman Act ran deep. He was determined to break the Pullman strike in 1894, and although he had to rely on the Sherman Act to secure lower court INJUNCTIONS, he abandoned that successful tack in the Supreme Court. He convinced a unanimous Court in IN RE DEBS (1895) to rely instead upon the inherent power of the executive branch to protect the national interest in the flow of INTERSTATE COMMERCE.

Olney also argued POLLOCK V. FARMERS' LOAN TRUST COMPANY (1895) before the Supreme Court, although his actions resulted in insufficient time for government preparation and may have cost the government its case. The Court struck down the tax, a decision Olney considered "a great blow to the power of the Federal government . . . a national misfortune."

DAVID GORDON
(1986)

Bibliography

EGGERT, GERALD 1074 *Richard Olney: Evolution of a Statesman.* University Park: Pennsylvania State University Press.

O'LONE v. ESTATE OF SHABAZZ
482 U.S. 342 (1987)

Regulations at a New Jersey prison forbade minimum-security inmates who worked outside the main prison building from reentering the building during the day, thus preventing certain Muslim PRISONERS from attending their weekly worship service held on Fridays. Required by the Koran to attend the service, the prisoners filed suit, claiming violation of their rights under the free exercise clause. Adopting what was essentially a COMPELLING STATE INTEREST test, the court of appeals held that the prison had to prove "that no reasonable method exists by which [the prisoners'] religious rights can be accommodated without creating bona fide security problems." In a 5–4 decision the Supreme Court reversed, ruling that the court of appeals paid insufficient deference to prison officials, who

have authority to enact any prison regulations "reasonably related to legitimate penological interests."

Justice WILLIAM J. BRENNAN, writing for the dissenters, accused the majority of uncritically accepting the assertions of prison administrators. Brennan did not claim that the courts should never defer to the judgment of prison authorities; but when the prison completely deprives prisoners of a right and where the activity in question is not presumptively dangerous, Brennan maintained that prison officials should be required to show that the denial of the right is no greater than necessary to achieve the government's objective.

Shabazz foreshadowed the Court's eventual abolition of the compelling-state-interest test for all free-exercise cases in EMPLOYMENT DIVISION, DEPARTMENT OF HUMAN RESOURCES OF OREGON V. SMITH (1990).

JOHN G. WEST, JR.
(1992)

OLSEN v. NEBRASKA EX REL. REFERENCE & BOND ASSOCIATION
313 U.S. 236 (1941)

Sustaining a Nebraska statute regulating fees charged by private employment agencies, the Supreme Court specifically reversed RIBNIK V. MCBRIDE (1928). Justice WILLIAM O. DOUGLAS reiterated earlier dissents of Justices OLIVER WENDELL HOLMES (see TYSON BROTHER V. BANTON, 1927) and LOUIS D. BRANDEIS (see NEW STATE ICE COMPANY V. LIEBMANN, 1932), declaring that the need and appropriateness of legislation concerning the public interest ought to be left to state legislatures.

DAVID GORDON
(1986)

OMNIBUS ACT
15 Stat. 73 (1868)

The Omnibus Act readmitted six of the Confederate states to full congressional representation and terminated military governance in them.

After the process of restoration mandated by the MILITARY RECONSTRUCTION ACTS was largely completed, Congress readmitted Arkansas in June 1868 and, three days later, by the Omnibus Act readmitted Alabama, Florida, Georgia, Louisiana, North Carolina, and South Carolina. The Omnibus Act declared that each of the six states had complied with the conditions specified in the Military Reconstruction Acts, required each to ratify the FOURTEENTH AMENDMENT, and imposed the "fundamental condition" that the state constitutional provisions for black suffrage be inviolate. All the congressmen and senators of these states were seated by late July 1868.

Georgia's full readmission was delayed for two years, however, because the state legislature excluded all black members and admitted several whites disfranchised by the Fourteenth Amendment or the Military Reconstruction Acts. Congress by special legislation forced a rescission of these actions, and Georgia once again underwent military supervision until its readmission. Virginia, Mississippi, and Texas were also readmitted in 1870, thus bringing the formal process of RECONSTRUCTION to a close.

WILLIAN M. WIECEK
(1986)

OMNIBUS CRIME CONTROL AND SAFE STREETS ACT
92 Stat. 3795 (1968)

The most extensive anticrime legislation in the nation's history, this measure reflected the public's fear of rising crime and its demand for federal protection. Congress enacted a massive and restrictive piece of legislation, called by its critics an invasion of basic CIVIL LIBERTIES. Particularly distasteful to President LYNDON B. JOHNSON, who signed it with reluctance, were titles permitting broad use of WIRETAPPING in federal and state cases, and a section seeking to overturn controversial Supreme Court rulings on the rights of defendants.

The act authorized law enforcement grants to aid local police departments in planning, training, and research and a block grant procedure whereby funds were given to the states to be allocated to their communities under a statewide plan. It channeled funds to improve techniques for combating organized crime and for preventing and controlling riots. The most controversial provision of the act purported to overturn Supreme Court decisions in *Mallory v. United States* (1957), MIRANDA V. ARIZONA (1966), and UNITED STATES V. WADE (1967), authorizing greater freedom in POLICE INTERROGATION of suspects accused of crimes against the United States, and in the use of LINEUPS to identify criminals.

The measure specified permissive new conditions under which confessions could be introduced in federal courts. The trial judge was to determine the issue of voluntariness, out of the hearing of the jury, basing that determination on such criteria as time lapse between arrest and arraignment, whether the defendant knew the nature of the charged offense, when the defendant was advised of or knew of the right to remain silent and the RIGHT TO COUNSEL, and whether the defendant was without assistance of counsel when questioned and giving the confession.

The act's provisions on ELECTRONIC EAVESDROPPING permitted warrant-approved wiretapping and bugging in investigations of a wide variety of specified crimes, and authorized police to intercept communications for forty-eight hours without a warrant in an "emergency" where organized crime or NATIONAL SECURITY was involved. Further, it authorized any law officer or any other person obtaining information in conformity with such a process to disclose or use it as appropriate. The law forbade the interstate shipment to individuals of pistols and revolvers, and over-the-counter purchase of handguns by individuals who did not live in the dealer's state. But it specifically exempted rifles and shotguns from these controls.

Passed overwhelmingly a few hours after the assassination of ROBERT F. KENNEDY, the act still drew the opposition of liberals troubled by its criminal law sections and concerned that its permissive wiretap section did not contain proper constitutional safeguards. Constitutional issues aside, the act failed to achieve its objectives.

PAUL L. MURPHY
(1986)

Bibliography

NATIONAL COMMISSION ON THE CAUSES AND PREVENTION OF VIO-
LENCE 1970 *Law and Order Reconsidered.* Washington,
D.C.: Government Printing Office.

O'NEIL v. VERMONT

See: *Kemmler, In Re*

ONE PERSON, ONE VOTE

The National Municipal League popularized the slogan "one man, one vote" from the 1920s to the 1960s to promote REAPPORTIONMENT to equalize political districts. Reapportionment had lagged far behind urban growth, leaving the largest urban districts by 1960 with only half the legislative representatives per capita of the smallest rural ones.

Urban spokesmen claimed that "malapportionment" produced stagnant "barnyard governments" indifferent to urban concerns and needs. They demanded one person, one vote to stop urban blight and revitalize state governments. These conjectural claims did not win reapportionment from legislators reluctant to tamper with their own districts, nor from voters, who repeatedly defeated reapportionment INITIATIVES. But they did persuade political and legal writers and study commissions, who called for courts or commissions to order reapportionment where legislators and voters would not.

The Supreme Court declined this invitation in COLE-

GROVE V. GREEN (1946) but accepted one person, one vote in REYNOLDS V. SIMS (1964) as the "fundamental principle" of the Constitution. Political scientists, black rights groups, the *New York Times*, and the DWIGHT D. EISENHOWER and JOHN F. KENNEDY administrations had endorsed that principle.

Some critics thought that the Court had confused individual suffrage with group REPRESENTATION, misconstrued the FOURTEENTH AMENDMENT, and ignored the "standards problem" of equalizing group representation, because gerrymandering could still deny equal weight to votes. Others saw little evidence of revitalization or greater equality in substance to match the greater equality in form, and they believed that by overriding legislative and popular majorities, the Court seemed to have devalued the very representative institutions to which it granted equal access in form.

The WARREN COURT's adoption of one person, one vote was a remarkable political success, affecting more people than school DESEGREGATION or criminal justice cases, with less help from Congress and less damaging backlash. But its practical contributions to equal representation and vital government remain a matter of dispute.

WARD E. Y. ELLIOTT
(1986)

Bibliography

ELLIOTT, WARD E. Y. 1975 *The Rise of Guardian Democracy: The Supreme Court's Role in Voting Rights Disputes, 1845–1969.* Cambridge, Mass.: Harvard University Press.

ON LEE v. UNITED STATES
343 U.S. 737 (1952)

The Supreme Court held, 5–4, that government informers who deceptively interrogated criminal suspects and simultaneously transmitted the conversations to other government agents via electrical transmitters had not violated the FOURTH AMENDMENT or the antiwiretap provisions of section 605 of the COMMUNICATIONS ACT; the agents who listened might testify to the overheard conversations. Because entry had been consented to—although the consent was obtained deceptively—it was not a TRESPASS, and under OLMSTEAD V. UNITED STATES (1927) the intrusion did not violate the Fourth Amendment. It was also not WIRETAPPING, nor did it become illegal because it might be immoral. The Court reaffirmed *On Lee* in UNITED STATES V. WHITE (1971).

HERMAN SCHWARTZ
(1986)

OPEN FIELDS DOCTRINE

The FOURTH AMENDMENT protects "persons, houses, papers, and effects against unreasonable searches and seizures." The amendment, held to embody a RIGHT OF PRIVACY, shelters certain enclaves from arbitrary government examination and interference. Within these enclaves, roughly defined as places where persons have a subjective expectation of privacy that society recognizes as reasonable—the paradigmatic case is the home—governmental SEARCHES AND SEIZURES are unreasonable unless authorized by a SEARCH WARRANT issued on PROBABLE CAUSE. There are some exceptions to this rule against WARRANTLESS SEARCHES, however, and the open fields doctrine presents one of them.

In applying the Fourth Amendment to detached dwellings the Supreme Court has held that persons have a REASONABLE EXPECTATION OF PRIVACY in the home and its "curtilage." Curtilage is the area immediately surrounding the home that harbors the intimate activities associated with domestic life and home privacies. Proximity to the home, containment within an enclosure surrounding the home, use for domestic and private purposes, and steps taken to protect the area from observation all help to define its ambit.

The open fields doctrine permits warrantless searches of private land outside the curtilage. The right of privacy that the Fourth Amendment protects is therefore not congruent with the right of property ownership, and exercise of the COMMON LAW right to exclude persons from land cannot make governmental searches of it unlawful. Further, under the doctrine open fields need be neither open nor fields, but only areas of land outside the curtilage. Fenced dense woods could therefore qualify as open fields. Consequently, neither the natural seclusion of property, which might be thought to make it private, nor efforts to keep trespassers out, such as posting with signs or surrounding with fences, secures it from governmental search.

GARY GOODPASTER
(1992)

(SEE ALSO: *Plain View Doctrine.*)

Bibliography

LaFAVE, WAYNE 1987 *Search and Seizure: A Treatise on the Fourth Amendment.* St. Paul, Minn.: West Publishing Co.

OPEN HOUSING LAWS

Many believe housing, the last major area covered by Congress's 1960s CIVIL RIGHTS program, to be the key to at least short-term progress in INTEGRATION. Despite numerous ANTIDISCRIMINATION LAWS, segregated housing patterns threaten much of the civil rights agenda, including integrated public education. Yet until the 1960s the federal government promoted segregated housing. Federal housing agencies, such as the Federal Housing Administration, required racially RESTRICTIVE COVENANTS in federally assisted projects. In Executive Order 11063 (1962), President JOHN F. KENNEDY prohibited housing discrimination in federal public housing and in housing covered by mortgages directly guaranteed by the federal government. Title VI of the CIVIL RIGHTS ACT OF 1964, which outlawed discrimination in programs receiving federal financial assistance, extended the ban to nearly all federally assisted housing.

Title VIII of the CIVIL RIGHTS ACT OF 1968 was the first comprehensive federal open housing law. Title VIII bans discrimination on the basis of race, color, religion, or national origin in the sale, lease, and financing of housing, and in the furnishing of real estate brokerage services. A 1974 amendment extends the ban to discrimination on the basis of sex. Title VIII exempts single-family houses sold or rented by owners and small, owner-occupied boarding houses. Congress's consideration of Title VIII was affected by the assassination of MARTIN LUTHER KING, JR. House opponents of the measure had tried to delay its consideration in the hope that intervening national events would sway Congress against it. But during the delay, Dr. King was assassinated and passage of the act followed swiftly.

Courts have construed Title VIII to cover activities other than the direct purchase, sale, or lease of a dwelling. For example, Title VIII prohibits discriminatory refusals to rezone for low-income housing. Most courts find that practices with greater adverse impact on minorities, even if undertaken without discriminatory purposes, impose some burden of justification. This view links Title VIII litigation to a similar line of EMPLOYMENT DISCRIMINATION cases decided under Title VII of the Civil Rights Act of 1964.

To enforce its provisions, Title VIII authorizes the secretary of housing and urban development to seek to conciliate disputes, but the Department of Housing and Urban Development (HUD) initially must defer to state or local housing agencies where state law provides relief substantially equivalent to Title VIII. In *Gladstone, Realtors v. Village of Bellwood* (1979) the Supreme Court held that Title VIII also authorized direct civil actions in federal court without prior resort to HUD or to state authorities. An ATTORNEY GENERAL finding a pattern or practice of housing discrimination is authorized to seek relief in federal court.

Two months after Title VIII's enactment the Supreme Court found Section 1982, Title 42, United States Code,

a remnant of section 1 of the CIVIL RIGHTS ACT OF 1866, to be another federal open housing law. Section 1982 grants all citizens the same right "as is enjoyed by white citizens" to purchase and lease real property. In JONES V. ALFRED H. MAYER CO. (1968) the Court construed section 1982 to prohibit a racially motivated refusal to sell a home to a prospective black purchaser. In *Sullivan v. Little Hunting Park, Inc.* (1969) the Court found that violations of section 1982 may be remedied by damages awards or by injunctive relief. There are, therefore, two federal open housing laws, which, in the area of RACIAL DISCRIMINATION, overlap. But section 1982 contains none of Title VIII's exemptions, provides for none of its administrative machinery, and contains no express list of remedies.

THEODORE EISNENBERG
(1986)

Bibliography

BELL, DERRICK A., JR. 1980 *Race, Racism and American Law,* 2nd ed. Boston: Little, Brown.

DORSEN, NORMAN et al. 1976–1979 *Political and Civil Rights in the United States,* 4th ed. II:1063–1149. Boston: Little, Brown.

OPERATION RESCUE

See: Anti-Abortion Movement

OPINION OF THE COURT

An appellate court would give little guidance to inferior courts, the legal community, or the general public concerning the law if it merely rendered a DECISION and did not explain the RATIO DECIDENDI, or the grounds for its decision. It is the court's reading of the law and the application of legal principles to the facts that gives a reported case value as PRECEDENT and permits the judicial system to follow the doctrine of STARE DECISIS. By ancient custom, Anglo-American judges, at least at the appellate level, publish opinions along with their decisions.

The general practice of English courts at the time of the American Revolution, and the general practice today in most of the British Commonwealth, is for the members of multijudge courts to deliver their opinions SERIATIM, that is, severally and in sequence. This practice was followed by the United States SUPREME COURT during its early years. However, when JOHN MARSHALL became CHIEF JUSTICE in 1801 he instituted the practice of delivering a single "opinion of the court." The effect of this change was to put the weight of the whole Court behind a particular line of reasoning (usually Marshall's), and so to make that line of reasoning more authoritative. At the time, Marshall's innovation was criticized by many, including President THOMAS JEFFERSON, either because it permitted lazy Justices to evade the responsibility of thinking through the cases on their own or because it fortified the Federalist majority in its conflicts with Republican legislators and state governments.

The opinion of the court is not necessarily unanimous. A majority of the Justices customarily endorses a single opinion, however, and that majority opinion is issued as the opinion of the court, with the Chief Justice—or the senior Justice, if the Chief Justice is not in the majority—assigning responsibility for writing the opinion. A Justice who disagrees with the decision of the case may file a DISSENTING OPINION; a Justice who agrees with the result, but disagrees with the rationale, or desires to supplement the majority opinion, may file a CONCURRING OPINION. When there is no majority opinion, the opinion signed by the largest number of Justices in support of the decisions is called the PLURALITY OPINION, and no opinion of the court is issued. In some important cases in the past, and increasingly during the BURGER COURT years, the number of separate opinions has presented an appearance resembling a return to seriatim opinions.

DENNIS J. MAHONEY
(1986)

ORAL ARGUMENT

Lawyers argue points of law orally before courts at all levels. The Supreme Court regulates oral argument by court rule. Some cases are decided summarily, without full briefing and argument, on the papers filed by the parties seeking and opposing Supreme Court review. About 150 cases per TERM are decided with briefs and oral argument. The arguments begin in October, early in the term, and (absent extraordinary circumstances) end in the following April, so that all opinions can be finished by the end of the term.

In the Court's early years oral argument was a leisurely affair; argument in MCCULLOCH V. MARYLAND (1819) lasted nine days. Today, given the increase in the Court's business and increasing doubt that illumination is proportional to talk, argument is normally limited to one-half hour for each side. More time may be allocated to a case that is unusually complicated or important. Permission to argue is only rarely granted to an AMICUS CURIAE, except for the SOLICITOR GENERAL, who is often allowed to argue orally for the United States as amicus curiae.

The Justices have already read the briefs when they hear counsel. Accordingly, oral argument is no longer a place for oratory. Justices interrupt with their questions and even conduct debates with each other through rhetorical questions to counsel. Time limits on argument are strictly enforced; the red light flashes on the lectern, and counsel stops.

Normally within a few days after oral argument the Justices meet in CONFERENCE to discuss groups of cases and vote tentatively on their disposition. The Justices regularly say that oral argument, fresh in their minds, influences their thinking in "close" cases. Whether a case is close, however, is a characterization very likely formed before a Justice hears what counsel have to say.

KENNETH L. KARST
(1986)

Bibliography
STERN, ROBERT L. and GRESSMAN, EUGENE 1978 *Supreme Court Practice*, 5th ed. Chap. 14. Washington, D.C.: Bureau of National Affairs.

ORDERED LIBERTY

A loosely used term, diversely applied in scholarly literature and judicial opinions, "ordered liberty" suggests that fundamental constitutional rights are not absolute but are determined by a balancing of the public (societal) welfare against individual (personal) rights. In this dialectical perspective, the thesis is "order," its antithesis "liberty"; the synthesis, "ordered liberty," describes a polity that has reconciled the conflicting demands of public order and personal freedom.

Justice BENJAMIN N. CARDOZO's majority opinion for the Court in PALKO V. CONNECTICUT (1937) provided what was probably the first judicial recognition of "ordered liberty." Acknowledging the difficulty of achieving "proper order and coherence," Cardozo identified some constitutionally enumerated rights that were *not* of the essence of a scheme of "ordered liberty," and thus not incorporated in the FOURTEENTH AMENDMENT and applied to the states: "to abolish [these rights] is not to violate a principle of justice so rooted in the traditions and conscience of our people as to be ranked fundamental." On the other hand, rights such as "freedom of thought and speech" were "of the very essence of a scheme of ordered liberty" because they constituted "the matrix, the indispensable condition, of nearly every other form of freedom."

HENRY J. ABRAHAM
(1986)

Bibliography
ABRAHAM, HENRY J. 1987 *Freedom and the Court: Civil Rights and Liberties in the United States*, 5th ed. New York: Oxford University Press.

ORDINANCE OF 1784

One of the most important constitutional questions of the founding era was that of the status of the western TERRITORIES. In 1783, as a concession to secure ratification of the ARTICLES OF CONFEDERATION, states with claims to western lands ceded them to Congress. In April 1784 Congress adopted an ordinance of government for the ceded territory drafted by THOMAS JEFFERSON. That ordinance, although it never went into effect, embodied the principle that the territories were not to be mere colonies but would become states within the Union. The principle was fulfilled under the NORTHWEST ORDINANCE and the Constitution.

The Ordinance of 1784 created eight "states" in the West and prescribed for them three stages of evolution culminating in full equality with the original thirteen states. But, unlike the Northwest Ordinance, which provided for gradual advance toward self-government by the settlers, the Ordinance of 1784 conferred self-government immediately. Jefferson's proposal to ban SLAVERY from the territories was defeated in Congress by a vote of seven states to six.

Rather than allow squatters to benefit, Congress made the Ordinance effective only when the western lands were officially offered for sale, and that did not happen until after the Ordinance was superseded.

DENNIS J. MAHONEY
(1986)

OREGON v. BRADSHAW

See: *Edwards v. Arizona*

OREGON v. ELSTAD
470 U.S. 298 (1985)

The Supreme Court reaffirmed MIRANDA V. ARIZONA (1966) yet made another exception to it. For a 6–3 majority, Justice SANDRA DAY O'CONNOR held that initial failure to comply with the MIRANDA RULES does not taint a second confession made after a suspect has received the required warnings and has waived his rights. In this case the suspect had not blurted out an incriminating statement before police questioned him. They arrested him, with a warrant, at his home and began an interrogation without advising him of his rights. He confessed. They took him to the station and gave him the warnings, but they did not inform him that his prior confession could not be used against him as proof of his guilt. O'Connor, commenting that a contrary decision might "disable the police," ruled that the second confession need not be suppressed because of the illegality of the first. She treated the illegal confession as if it had been voluntarily made. Her focus on the voluntariness of that initial confession suggested that if coercion had then been present, it would have tainted a second confession made after the *Miranda* warnings. The Court, therefore, reaffirmed *Miranda*. Nevertheless, the case taught that the police may ignore *Miranda*, secure a confession, and then give the warnings in the hope of getting an admissible confession once the suspect thinks "the cat is out of the bag." Justice WILLIAM J. BRENNAN savaged the Court's opinion in a dissent that O'Connor claimed had an "apocalyptic tone" and distorted much of what she had said. She denied Brennan's accusation that the majority's opinion had a "crippling" effect on *Miranda*.

LEONARD W. LEVY
(1986)

OREGON v. HASS

See: Police Interrogation and Confessions

OREGON v. MITCHELL
400 U.S. 112 (1970)

This decision suggested some short-lived constitutional limits on Congress's power to regulate voting. The 1970 amendments to the VOTING RIGHTS ACT OF 1965 lowered from twenty-one to eighteen the minimum voting age for federal, state, and local elections, suspended LITERACY TESTS throughout the nation, prohibited states from imposing RESIDENCE REQUIREMENTS in presidential elections, and provided for uniform national rules for absentee registration and voting in presidential elections. (See VOTING RIGHTS AMENDMENTS.) The Supreme Court unanimously upheld the suspension of literacy tests and over Justice JOHN MARSHALL HARLAN'S dissent, found the residency and absentee voting provisions valid. Four Justices found the age limit reduction constitutional for all elections and four Justices found it unconstitutional for all elections. Because Justice HUGO T. BLACK found the age limit reduction constitutional only for federal elections, the case's formal HOLDING, though reflecting only Justice Black's view, was to sustain the age reduction only in federal elections. The many separate opinions in *Mitchell* also reviewed the question, first addressed in KATZENBACH V. MORGAN (1966), of Congress's power to interpret and alter the scope of the FOURTEENTH AMENDMENT. In 1971, in reponse to *Mitchell*, the TWENTY-SIXTH AMENDMENT lowered the voting age to eighteen in all elections.

THEODORE EISENBERG
(1986)

ORGANIZED CRIME CONTROL ACT
84 Stat. 922 (1970)

Heralded as the most comprehensive federal law ever enacted to combat organized crime, this act was not limited to that use alone. Its provisions applied to a wide range of offenses, on the theory that the involvement of organized crime in a particular criminal act is not always clear. The detection of such involvement was one purpose of the law.

The LEGISLATION contained thirteen titles, a number of which aroused sharp criticism on constitutional grounds. One controversial title reinforced and expanded the investigatory power of GRAND JURIES by authorizing special grand juries to return INDICTMENTS and to report to UNITED STATES DISTRICT COURTS concerning criminal misconduct by appointive public officials involving organized criminal activity or concerning organized crime conditions in their areas. An individual named in such a report was entitled to a grand jury hearing, with the right to call witnesses and to file a rebuttal to the report. Another title replaced all previous laws governing witness IMMUNITY GRANTS; the title authorized federal legislative, administrative, and judicial bodies to grant witnesses immunity from prosecution using their testimony. The new section thus substituted "use immunity" for the "transaction immunity" that had previously protected such witnesses from prosecution for any events mentioned in or related to their testimony regardless of independent evidence against them.

Other provisions authorized detention of recalcitrant witnesses for CONTEMPT until they complied with court orders to testify, but for no longer than eighteen months, authorized convictions for perjury based on obviously contradictory statements made under oath (no longer requiring proof of the crime by any particular number of witnesses or by any particular type of EVIDENCE), and the use of depositions in criminal cases subject to constitutional guarantees and certification by the ATTORNEY GENERAL that the case involved organized crime. Still other sections limited to five years the period in which government action to obtain evidence could be challenged as illegal and limited the disclosure of government records previously required by ALDERMAN V. UNITED STATES (1969). Finally, the act authorized increased sentences up to twenty-five years for persons convicted of felonies, provided they were found to be dangerous and to be "habitual" offenders, "professional" criminals, or "organized crime figures."

Although the whole measure was denounced by the New York City Bar Association as containing "the seeds of official repression," only the narrowed witness immunity provisions were challenged. In KASTIGAR V. UNITED STATES (1972) the Supreme Court ruled that they did not violate the Fifth Amendment RIGHT AGAINST SELF-INCRIMINATION.

PAUL L. MURPHY
(1986)

Bibliography

CONGRESSIONAL QUARTERLY 1973 *Congress and the Nation*, vol. 3. Washington, D.C.: Congressional Quarterly.

ORIGINAL INTENT

"Original intent" is a shorthand term for both a familiar topic of CONSTITUTIONAL HISTORY and a problematic theory of CONSTITUTIONAL INTERPRETATION. As a historical problem, the quest for original intent seeks to discover what particular provisions of the Constitution meant at the moment of their adoption, whether to the Framers in the CONSTITUTIONAL CONVENTION OF 1787 (or Congress, in the case of subsequent amendments), the ratifiers in the state conventions and legislatures, or the citizenry in general. As a mode of constitutional interpretation, however, original intent suggests that the true meaning of these provisions was in some sense fixed at the point of their adoption and that later interpreters of the Constitution should adhere to that original meaning.

The earliest version of original intent can be traced as far back as the 1790s, when JAMES MADISON sought to develop a mode of interpretation that could counter the loose canon of Hamiltonian construction. More recently, the call for a return to a "jurisprudence of original intent" held a central place in the campaign by the administration of RONALD REAGAN to challenge controversial decisions taken by the Supreme Court under Chief Justices EARL WARREN and WARREN E. BURGER. In many areas of constitutional law, conservatives argued, the Court had freely ignored the original meaning of particular provisions of the Constitution in order to impose its own values on society. In so doing, conservatives further alleged, the Court had also usurped powers the Constitution vested in the political branches of government, thereby violating its original meaning in a second and more fundamental sense.

Yet the appeal of the theory of original intent has never been confined to conservatives alone. On many issues, liberals can invoke the authority of the Framers and ratifiers of the Constitution just as easily. In recent controversies over the conduct of FOREIGN AFFAIRS, for example, liberals have effectively argued that the Framers and ratifiers of the Constitution did not expect the executive to have unilateral initiative in making foreign policy or the power to commit American forces to combat without the active approval of Congress. Judged pragmatically, the theory of original intent is neither inherently conservative nor inherently liberal. It is, instead, a style of constitutional argument that particular parties can invoke whenever the available historical evidence promises to support their immediate cause.

Modern proponents of a jurisprudence of original intent rest their case on democratic norms. The Constitution is the supreme law of the land not merely because Article VI says so but because its authority can be traced to extraordinary acts of POPULAR SOVEREIGNTY, whether in the state ratification conventions of 1787–1790 or through the congressional and state legislative supermajorities required to secure amendments. By contrast, the Supreme Court Justices who ultimately interpret the Constitution are the least politically accountable officers in the entire system of governance. When judges abuse the power of JUDICIAL REVIEW to impose values not securely rooted in the constitutional text, originalists argue, they effectively nullify the sovereign will of the people as that will is expressed in the great acts of constitution-making or in the ordinary legislative decisions the Court chooses to overturn. If fundamental constitutional change is called for, originalists suggest, it should be achieved through the amendment procedures of Article V, not by judicial fiat.

Critics of this modern version of ORIGINALISM challenge this position on several grounds. They argue, first, that the unwieldy requirements of Article V render the Constitution so difficult to amend that it is far better to rely on constitutional evolution through judicial interpretation and political innovation than to insist that its original meaning be preserved inviolate until the necessary supermajoritarian consensus can be mobilized. Nor is it clear why decisions made by judges who are appointed by politically accountable Presidents and senators should be regarded as more arbitrary or less democratic than those earlier decisions imposed by generations dead and gone. Finally, the criticism that judges act undemocratically by extending the definition and protection of constitutional rights misses the obvious point that it has always been the duty of the judiciary to protect individual and minority rights against majority abuse.

These objections are, in a sense, normative: they ask whether a jurisprudence of original intent is desirable, not whether it is practicable. But other reservations about the merits of this theory of interpretation rest on narrower grounds of practicality. Some of these reservations concern the adequacy of the historical evidence on which all appeals to the original meaning rest; others reflect doubts about the capacity of judges or other officials to use this evidence intelligently and objectively. The idea that adherence to original intent would always work to constrain judges is itself questionable. A historical record that is ambiguous or murky may actually broaden the interpretive latitude within which a willful judge might choose to roam.

Perhaps the single most telling problem of evidence involves the difficult task of recovering what the ratifiers of the Constitution understood they were adopting when they expressed the sovereign will of the people. Under the strict theory of original intent, the understandings of the ratifiers command the greatest weight in interpretive efforts, because it was their actions—as opposed to the proceedings in the Federal Convention or Congress—that alone gave legal force to the constitutional text. Unfortunately, the records of the debates in the state ratification conventions of 1787–1788 (or in the state legislatures for the BILL OF RIGHTS and later amendments) seem less than adequate. Whole days of debate—and in some states, entire conventions—went unreported; numerous provisions of the Constitution went unexamined; and in the end, the delegates who passed judgment on the Constitution voted only on whether or not they wanted to accept the document as a whole. Thus, although the ratification records are rich enough to allow scholars to survey the general grounds on which the Constitution was supported or opposed, they cannot conclusively illuminate what its various provisions meant to the obscure state politicians who ratified it, much less the anonymous—though sovereign—people they represented.

James Madison was aware of this problem when, in the mid-1790s, he first argued that the understanding of the ratifiers could legitimately constrain the reach of interpretation. Although Madison never explained exactly how one could determine what the Constitution meant in a positive sense, he did believe that it was possible to challenge interpretations that either had not been offered at the time of adoption or would have been rejected out of hand if they had been candidly stated.

Regardless of the legal arguments that favor the authority of the ratifiers, in practice few interpreters of the Constitution are inclined to ignore evidence about the intentions of its actual Framers. Much of the debate about the original allocation of the WAR POWERS, for example, centers on the Federal Convention's decision to substitute the verb "declare" for "make" in the clause giving Congress the authority to declare war. Scholars have similarly canvassed the congressional debates about the FOURTEENTH AMENDMENT for clues about the original meaning of its frequently controverted clauses.

The great advantage that inquiries into the Framers' intentions enjoy over ratifiers' understandings is that the former may better help to explain how and why a particular provision acquired its precise textual form. Yet even then, there is no ready way to demonstrate how well any one comment or set of comments represented the range of intentions and expectations that typically inform any collective political decision. Many studies of legislative voting suggest that all exercises in collective decision making are inherently ambiguous.

Given all these difficulties, it is not surprising that most judicial forays into originalist interpretation receive low marks from knowledgeable scholars. Judges and their law clerks are not trained historians, and they repeatedly err in their treatment of the historical evidence on which they necessarily rely. On this basis alone it can be strongly argued that originalism can never offer much more than a rhetorical strategy to justify decisions taken on more complex grounds.

That argument does not imply, however, that originalism has no role to play in modern CONSTITUTIONALISM. Even if it is impossible to ascertain fixed original meanings for the Constitution's most disputed and "open-textured" clauses, a sound historical approach can still reconstruct the general contours of the debates from which they emerged. Moreover, the fact that Americans repeatedly invoke the authority of Framers and ratifiers—especially "the founders" of 1787–1788—in their constitutional disputes may reveal something important about American political culture. Originalism can never be a dispositive theory of interpretation, but neither can it be entirely deposed from the place it has repeatedly claimed in American constitutional discourse.

JACK N. RAKOVE
(1992)

(SEE ALSO: *Conservatism; Deconstructionism; Incorporation Doctrine and Original Intent; Interpretivism; Liberalism; Noninterpretivism; Political Philosophy of the Constitution; Strict Construction.*)

Bibliography

LEVY, LEONARD W. 1988 *Original Intent and the Framers' Constitution.* New York: Macmillan.
LOFGREN, CHARLES 1986 *"Government from Reflection and Choice": Constitutional Essays on War, Foreign Relations, and Federalism.* New York: Oxford University Press.
RAKOVE, JACK N., ed. 1990 *Interpreting the Constitution: The Debate over Original Intent.* Boston: Northeastern University Press.

ORIGINALISM

"Originalism" is a term used to describe the view that judicial decisions regarding the Constitution must be based on the ORIGINAL INTENT of those who participated in the framing and enactment of the original Constitution and later amendments. For example, originalists regard the issue of the constitutional validity of the death penalty as easily resolved by the explicit references in the Fifth and Fourteenth Amendments to the deliberate taking of life by government, indicating that the Constitution expressly contemplates the imposition of the death penalty. The Fifth Amendment states that "[n]o person shall be held to answer for a capital, or otherwise infamous crime, . . . put in jeopardy of life or limb; . . . be deprived of life, liberty, or property . . ." and the FOURTEENTH AMENDMENT, likewise guarantees that "[n]o state shall . . . deprive any person of life, liberty, or property. . . ."

Originalists justify their view on the grounds that focusing on original intent both limits the intrusion of the subjective political values of judges in constitutional decisions and gives due respect to democratic processes. Originalists argue that the intent of the Framers will sometimes accord with the personal views of judges and sometimes not. Application of this intent, therefore, will limit the ability of judges to impose their personal views on various issues upon the nation. Originalists also point out that the Constitution contains democratic amendment procedures and that the use of criteria other than original intent would enable judges to subvert both the democratic processes that led to the enactment of particular constitutional provisions and the democratic processes that provide for amendments. Finally, originalists argue that originalism is the only theory that can legitimate the institution of judicial review, which is a method of ensuring that the Constitution, as a superior law adopted by the people, constrains all organs of government, including the courts. MARBURY V. MADISON, 5 U.S. (1 Cranch) 137, 179–180 (1803).

Critics of originalism generally rely on two lines of attack. The first line is that the intent of the Framers is difficult and often impossible to determine. As Justice WILLIAM J. BRENNAN said: "It is arrogant to pretend that from our vantage we can gauge accurately the intent of the Framers on application of principle to specific, contemporary questions." Doubt as to our present ability to learn the intent of the Framers fuels the suspicion among observers more cynical than Justice Brennan that lip service to supposed evidence of original intent is actually a façade behind which judges weave their subjective political values into the fabric of constitutional law. Second, critics argue that our concepts of civilized rule constantly evolve and that originalism affords too niggardly a protection for profoundly important rights. Again, Justice Brennan put the matter succinctly in describing his position on the constitutionality of the death penalty: "Because we are the last word on the meaning of the Constitution, our views must be subject to revision over time, or the Constitution falls captive, again, to the anachronistic views of long-gone generations." He thus felt free to argue that the Eighth Amendment's prohibition on CRUEL AND UNUSUAL PUNISHMENT (applicable to the states through the Fourteenth Amendment) prohibits the death penalty notwithstanding the specific references to the death penalty in the Fifth Amendment, which was part of the BILL OF RIGHTS package that included the Eighth, and the more general reference to the death penalty in the Fourteenth Amendment itself.

In response to the first criticism—that the intent of the

Framers regarding contemporary constitutional litigation is not ascertainable—originalists divide into what might be called an "intentionalist" school of thought and an "interpretivist" school of thought.

Members of the intentionalist school search for the actual state of mind of the Framers at the pertinent time, based on the language of the constitutional text, preconstitutional precedents, sometimes involving British law, or explicit legislative history. In their view, a judicial decision that is not based on explicit constitutional language or direct evidence of an actual intent held by the Framers is an illegitimate decision. The intentionalist school is best illustrated by the work of Raoul Berger. Berger has thus concluded that BROWN V. BOARD OF EDUCATION OF TOPEKA (1954) was an illegitimate decision because of the lack of an explicit reference to DESEGREGATION in the Fourteenth Amendment and because of evidence that some of the Framers stated during the framing and ratification period that public, segregated, educational institutions would pass constitutional muster under the Fourteenth Amendment. He has also denied the existence of an EXECUTIVE PRIVILEGE because of the failure of the Constitution to mention such a privilege and the lack of precedent in colonial or preexisting law.

INTERPRETIVISM, on the other hand, insists only that constitutional decisions be, in Dean John Hart Ely's (not himself an originalist) words, "in accord with an inference whose starting point, whose underlying premise, is fairly discoverable in the Constitution. That the complete reference will not be found there—because the situation is not likely to have been foreseen—is generally common ground." For interpretivists, the name originalism is thus a bit of a misnomer, at least to the extent that it suggests that express language of the Constitution or evidence of the actual state of mind of the Framers are the sole legitimate criteria for constitutional adjudication.

Interpretivists take the view that CONSTITUTIONAL INTERPRETATION must apply the conventional legal criteria used by lawyers in interpreting other legal texts. As Judge Robert H. Bork, certainly the most noted originalist, has stated, the search for original intent is "the everyday procedure of lawyers and judges when they must apply a statute, a contract, a will, or the opinion of a court." These criteria, of course, are designed to determine the purposes of the text. Democratic processes demand that statutory interpretation be governed by LEGISLATIVE INTENT. Contract law stresses the purposes of the parties, estate law stresses the intent of the testator, and the doctrine of STARE DECISIS stresses the meaning of prior decisions. Drawing on an analogy between these fields of law and constitutional law, interpretivists believe that constitutional law must stress the meaning of the document, which for them, as Professor Henry Monaghan has stated, is not so much

the state of mind of the Framers as the "*public* understanding" of what particular constitutional provisions were intended to achieve.

Constitutional adjudication is thus for interpretivists much more than a search for express language, colonial or English precedent, or direct evidence of intent (or lack thereof) that produces a mechanical result in each case. Language or other direct evidence of intent is of course important in their view and dispositive when, as in the case of the death penalty, explicit consideration was given to the particular issue. Certainly, they would argue, the fact that the Fifth and Fourteenth Amendments prohibit imposition of the death penalty without DUE PROCESS OF LAW is inconsistent with a judicial decision holding that the death penalty violates the Constitution in any and all circumstances.

Beyond such cases in which direct evidence of intent, such as language in the Constitution or legislative history, is dispositive, the interpretive view of originalism provides considerable scope for the exercise of judgment and for disagreement. This is not surprising because the conventional legal criteria applied by lawyers in interpreting statutes, contracts, or other legal documents extend well beyond language or express intent. Legal documents frequently provide evidence of only a very general purposebb that courts must adapt to the circumstances of each case. Courts legitimately, therefore, read into statutes commands or exceptions to commands that have no basis in the express statutory language, but are believed necessary to effectuate the overall legislative purpose. For example, in *Reves v. Ernst Young* (1990), the Supreme Court held that the phrase "any note" in the definitional section of the Securities Exchange Act of 1934 does not literally mean "any note," but must be understood in terms of what Congress sought to accomplish by enacting the statute; and in *Haggar Co. v. Helvering* (1940), the Court held in light of the statutory purpose that "[a] timely amended return is as much a "first return' . . . as is a single return filed by the taxpayer. . . ." Courts must do this because of the inability of drafters to anticipate the myriad circumstances in which the meaning of the statute must be divined, obvious drafting errors, or changes in the relevant industrial practice or technology. Similarly, courts may adapt contractual language to changed circumstances or impose duties, such as the duty to act in good faith where the contract accords considerable discretion to one party, notwithstanding the lack of express contractual language. Application of this mode of analysis to constitutional interpretation is essential because constitutional language is more general than most statutes and private contracts, and the interstices thus tend to be considerably wider.

Interpretivists believe that the Framers could not foresee all of the circumstances to which particular constitutional provisions might be applied and that judges must attempt to adapt what evidence of purpose there is to changed circumstances. Many interpretivists thus believe that contrary to Raoul Berger's conclusion *Brown* was fully legitimate. The interpretivists argue that the specific expectations of those Framers who stated that segregated education would survive the enactment of the Fourteenth Amendment were not faced with direct evidence that segregated educational systems were palpably inconsistent with the amendment's core purpose of relieving blacks of obstacles imposed by law. The interpretivist school thus takes into account the very limited experience these Framers had with both segregated schools and public education itself and feels free to override their particularized expectations in order to satisfy the basic philosophy of the EQUAL PROTECTION clause.

Similarly, the interpretivist school is willing to adapt constitutional provisions to other changed circumstances. For example, in *Ollman v. Evans* (D.C. Circuit, 1984), Judge Bork wrote with regard to the interplay of the First Amendment and the law of LIBEL:

> We know very little of the precise intentions of the framers and ratifiers of the speech and press clauses of the first amendment. But we do know they gave into the judges' keeping the value of preserving free expression and, in particular, the preservation of political expression, which is commonly conceded to be the value at the core of these clauses. Perhaps the framers did not envision libel actions as a major threat to that freedom. . . . But if, over time, the libel action evolves so that it becomes a threat to the central meaning of the first amendment, why should not judges adapt their doctrines? . . . It is no different to refine and evolve doctrine here, so long as one is faithful to the basic meaning of the amendment, than it is to adapt the fourth amendment to take account of electronic means of surveillance, the commerce clause to adjust to interstate motor carriage, or the first amendment to encompass the electronic media. . . .

Moreover, interpretivists feel free to draw what Professor Charles L. Black has called inferences "from the structures and relationships created by the Constitution." Again, this interpretive method is commonly used by lawyers and judges to interpret legal texts. The Supreme Court's opinions regarding private actions under the securities laws brim with inferences as to the scope and content of one remedial provision drawn from the scope and content of other remedial provisions. Interpretation of contracts also often requires courts to infer obligations from the structure of the parties' relationship.

Because the Constitution established a nation to be governed by a designated governmental structure, this interpretive method is particularly suited to constitutional law. Black has thus argued that an inference from structure reconciles the Supreme Court's scrutiny of state regulation claimed to discriminate against INTERSTATE COMMERCE with the absence in the constitutional texts of any explicit prohibition of such state conduct; the freedom of commerce from local discrimination is implicit in the economic structure of nationhood and the fact that "we are one people, commercially as otherwise. . . ." One can similarly infer some form of executive, legislative, or judicial privilege from the Constitution's SEPARATION OF POWERS. Were one branch routinely to compel disclosure of the internal decisional consultations of another branch, the latter branch might find its decision making skewed and the exercise of its legitimate powers subject to substantial encroachment by the other branch. This result would be contrary to the Constitution's purpose of establishing separate and independent branches of government.

Drawing inferences from structure and relationships is thus a legitimate method of determining the intent of the Framers. This intent, of course, is not the Framers' conscious thoughts or expectations, but the adaptation of the general principle they sought to establish to particular factual situations. Indeed, unless a judge is willing to draw such inferences, the intent of the Framers may go unfulfilled. For example, as Black has argued, even if the First Amendment had not been adopted, a judge might legitimately conclude that the various provisions for free elections for federal office could not fulfill their purpose if either federal or state governments were free to prohibit speeches by candidates for federal office or their supporters. To effectuate the purposes of the electoral provisions—to effectuate original intent—some form of protection for political speech similar to First Amendment doctrine would have to be fashioned by courts.

Having concluded that neither the constitutional text, legislative history, nor inferences from structures and relationships address a claim of a right, originalists believe that courts should not recognize that right. Originalists thus typically argue that ROE V. WADE (1973) was incorrectly decided because there is no evidence that either the generalized RIGHT TO PRIVACY relied on in the decision's brief doctrinal discussion or the specific issue of ABORTION has even been addressed by any constitutional provision. This view is fortified in the minds of originalists by the seeming disarray among *Wade*'s defenders as to the doctrinal basis for the decision, which ranges from an implied right of privacy protecting individual autonomy in sexual or procreative matters to the First Amendment's religion clause, to the equal protection clause, and to the THIRTEENTH AMENDMENT's prohibition on involuntary servitude.

In some cases, evidence of purpose or inferences drawn from structures or relationships may yield no guidance for interpretation of a particular constitutional provision. In such a case, originalists believe that judges should accord no judicially enforceable meaning to that provision because the only available criteria for establishing that meaning are the judiciary's subjective views of what is good constitutional policy. Originalists thus typically view the NINTH AMENDMENT ("The powers not delegated to the United States by the Constitution, nor prohibited by it to the States, are reserved to the states respectively, or to the people") or the PRIVILEGES AND IMMUNITIES clause of the Fourteenth Amendment ("No state shall make or enforce any law which shall abridge the privileges or immunities of citizens of the United States") as such clauses. The language of these provisions does not make any cogent choice between alternative legal rules, and their history appears to lack any evidence of judicially enforceable purpose. This being the case, originalist theory holds that judges should not undertake to attribute meaning to these provisions. To the argument that the Framers may have intended that courts undertake the task of giving meaning to such clauses, originalists generally answer that there is nothing in the constitutional record to suggest that such substantial power was to be accorded to the judiciary.

On one issue—adherence to PRECEDENT—originalist theory is unclear. As the preceding discussion has indicated, the interpretive school of originalism calls simply for the application of conventional legal criteria to constitutional interpretation. In nonconstitutional areas, such criteria certainly include judicial precedent. Thus, one does not infrequently encounter statutes whose interpretation over time seems to have departed rather far from their language or legislative purpose. The doctrine of stare decisis, however, generally precludes courts from undoing settled interpretations. Similarly, contractual clauses are used by lawyers to achieve particular purposes, even though the purposes and the particular language seem at best distantly related. Lawyers continue to use them, however, because courts have previously attributed to these clauses the purposes in question.

One would therefore expect interpretivists at least to put a heavy weight on precedent and to overrule precedent only infrequently. However, this expectation clashes with the argument that a reluctance to overrule precedent gives an advantage to those who would base constitutional decisions on criteria deemed by originalists to be invalid. Unless originalists are willing to overrule precedent, it can be argued, the Constitution will, over time, spawn a body of law considerably at odds with original intent. Indeed, Professor Monaghan has pointed out that much of present constitutional law "is at variance with what we know of the original understanding."

With regard to the criticism that originalism affords inadequate protection for profoundly important rights, originalists rarely answer with a denial. Originalism does not claim to offer a comprehensive formula for civilized rule or an optimal set of individual rights. Rather, it purports to offer the correct role for the judiciary in a democratic society. It posits that lodging the ultimate decision-making power of the state in a nonelected branch of government must ultimately subordinate the elected branches and subvert democratic rule itself. It denies the existence of a natural law that can be discovered and applied by judges in a manner consistent with democratic principles. Originalists see in the various attempts by scholars to fashion nonoriginalist criteria for constitutional decision making faintly disguised political movements seeking to achieve in court what they have been unable to secure in elections.

At bottom, then, originalism is based on the view that judges must confine their role to the application and enforcement of principles that have become constitutional law through the adoption of the Constitution or the amendment of the Constitution itself. Originalism is neutral with regard to particular rights in the sense that a persuasive argument that a right is necessary to civilized rule will not carry the day in court without an anchoring of that argument in the Constitution; nevertheless, originalism is not a nihilistic philosophy. Rather, it prizes democratic rule and demands that restrictions on this rule be the result of the adoption and amendment procedures set out in the Constitution. Originalists thus view the orderly democratic procedures of the Constitution as superior to claims of substantive rights that have not been adopted through such procedures. For originalists, rule by judiciary is not the road to civilized rule or optimal individual rights.

The future of originalism is unclear. The Senate's failure to confirm Judge Bork was based in part on the criticisms of originalism previously described. Many originalists are puzzled at the recent controversy over their view because many of their critics seem not to quarrel with the application of conventional legal criteria to other legal texts such as statutes or contracts. Moreover, originalists view their methodology as politically neutral. Nevertheless, the Bork controversy illustrated the difficulty of defending originalism in a political context. Because originalists do not believe that the Constitution enshrines every right necessary to avoid every wrong—including serious wrongs—originalists can be mistakenly perceived as favoring those wrongs. Judge Bork was thus depicted by some as favoring POLL TAXES because he had written that such taxes did not violate the equal protection clause.

Originalists fear that the difficulty of defending their position politically will fundamentally alter the American system of government. In their view, judicial nominations and Senate confirmation proceedings may, in the worst-case scenario, become highly politicized in the sense that nominees may be required to make commitments about future decisions equivalent to political promises. These promises will be made to appease groups that seek to constitutionalize their claims and have sufficient political power to extract such promises. If so, originalists fear, constitutional law will become an incoherent body of rules having no connection with the document and resulting from random constellations of political forces and the idiosyncratic views of particular Supreme Court Justices.

RALPH K. WINTER
(1992)

Bibliography

BLACK, CHARLES L. 1969 *Structure and Relationship in Constitutional Law.* Baton Rouge, La.: Louisiana State University Press.

BORK, ROBERT H. 1990 *The Tempting of America: The Political Seduction of the Law.* New York: Free Press.

FEDERALIST SOCIETY 1986 *Interpreting Our Written Constitution* (Occasional Paper No. 2). Washington, D.C.: The Federalist Society.

McDOWELL, GARY 1985 *The Constitution and Contemporary Constitutional Theory.* Cumberland, Va.: Center for Judicial Studies.

MONAGHAN, HENRY 1981 Our Perfect Constitution. *New York University Law Review* 56:353–376.

ORIGINAL JURISDICTION

The original jurisdiction of a court (as distinguished from APPELLATE JURISDICTION) is its power to hear and decide a case from the beginning. In the federal court system, the district courts originally hear the overwhelming majority of cases. Most discussion and litigation concerning the JURISDICTION OF FEDERAL COURTS centers on the district courts' original JURISDICTION. Yet the term "original jurisdiction" is heard most frequently in discussion and litigation concerning the jurisdiction of the Supreme Court.

The Constitution itself establishes the Supreme Court's original jurisdiction. After setting out the types of cases subject to the JUDICIAL POWER OF THE UNITED STATES, Article III distributes the Supreme Court's jurisdiction over them: "In all cases affecting ambassadors, other public ministers and consuls, and those in which a state shall be a party, the Supreme Court shall have original jurisdiction. In all other cases mentioned, the Supreme Court shall have appellate jurisdiction. . . ."

From the beginning, Congress has given the district courts CONCURRENT JURISDICTION over some of the cases within the Supreme Court's original jurisdiction, offering plaintiffs the option of commencing suit in either court. The Supreme Court has given this practice its stamp of constitutional approval. Furthermore, because the Court is hard-pressed by a crowded docket, it has sought ways of shunting cases to other courts. Thus, even when a case does fall within the Court's original jurisdiction, the court has conferred on itself the discretion to deny the plaintiff leave to file an original action. Typically the Court decides only three or four original jurisdiction cases each year, conserving its institutional energies for its main task: guiding the development of federal law by exercising its appellate jurisdiction.

Congress, however, cannot constitutionally diminish the Court's original jurisdiction. Nor can Congress expand that jurisdiction; the dubious reading of Article III in MARBURY V. MADISON (1803) remains firmly entrenched. However, the Supreme Court does entertain some actions that have an "original" look to them, even though Article III does not list them as original jurisdiction cases: HABEAS CORPUS is an example; so are the common law WRITS OF MANDAMUS and PROHIBITION. The Court hears such cases only when they can be characterized as "appellate," calling for Supreme Court supervision of actions by lower courts.

Of the two types of original jurisdiction cases specified in Article III, the state-as-party case has produced all but a tiny handful of the cases originally decided by the Supreme Court. Officers of foreign governments enjoy a broad diplomatic immunity from suit in our courts, and, for motives no doubt similarly diplomatic, they have not brought suits in the Supreme Court. (The "ambassadors" and others mentioned in Article III, of course, are those of foreign governments, not our own.)

The state-as-party cases present obvious problems of SOVEREIGN IMMUNITY. The ELEVENTH AMENDMENT applies to original actions in the Supreme Court; indeed, the amendment was adopted in response to just such a case, CHISHOLM V. GEORGIA (1793). Thus a state can no more be sued by the citizen of another state in the Supreme Court than in a district court. However, when one state sues another, or when the United States or a foreign government sues a state, there is no bar to the Court's jurisdiction.

The spectacle of nine Justices of the Supreme Court jointly presiding over a trial has a certain Hollywood allure, but the Court consistently avoids such proceedings. The SEVENTH AMENDMENT commands TRIAL BY JURY in any common law action, and at first the Supreme Court did hold a few jury trials. The last one, however, took place in the 1790s. Since that time the Court has always managed to identify some feature of an original case that makes it a suit in EQUITY; thus jury trial is inappropriate, and findings of fact can be turned over to a SPECIAL MASTER, whose report is reviewed by the Court only as to questions of law.

The source of the substantive law applied in original actions between states is FEDERAL COMMON LAW, an amalgam of the Anglo-American common law, policies derived from congressional statutes, and international law principles. Thus far no state has defied the Supreme Court sufficiently to test the Court's means of enforcing its decrees, but some states have dragged out their compliance for enough years to test the patience of the most saintly Justice.

KENNETH L. KARST
(1986)

Bibliography

NOTE   1959   The Original Jurisdiction of the United States Supreme Court. *Stanford Law Review* 11:665–719.

ORIGINAL PACKAGE DOCTRINE

In BROWN V. MARYLAND (1827) the Supreme Court had before it a challenge to a state statute requiring all importers of goods from foreign countries to take out a $50 license. Instead of simply holding that such a license tax imposed only on importers from foreign countries violated the constitutional clause prohibiting states from laying "any IMPOSTS or duties on imports or exports," Chief Justice JOHN MARSHALL used the occasion to decide just when goods imported from abroad ceased being imports exempted from taxation by the states. He concluded that no tax could be imposed on the goods or their importer so long as the goods had not been sold and were held in the original packages in which they were imported. He also said the principles laid down "apply equally to importations from a sister state."

The original package DOCTRINE had a long career as applied to goods imported from abroad. In *Low v. Austin* (1872) the Court held that a state could not collect its uniform property tax on cases of wine which the importer held in their original package on tax day. Much later, in *Hooven Allison Co. v. Evatt* (1945), the Court applied the doctrine to immunize bales of hemp from state property taxation, so long as the importer held them in their original package—the bales. Along the way, not surprisingly, the Court struggled in many cases with such problems as what constitutes the original package, and when it is broken.

Finally, in MICHELIN TIRE CORP. V. WAGES (1976) the Court upheld the imposition of a nondiscriminatory property tax upon tires imported from abroad and held in their original packages. It discussed at length the decision in *Low v. Austin*, overruled it, and appeared to be saying that only taxes discriminating against FOREIGN COMMERCE will be held invalid. Hence, it appears that the rules governing taxation of imports will now be similar to those applied to taxing such goods from other states, with the original package doctrine playing no part in the decisions.

Marshall's suggestion in *Brown v. Maryland* that the original package doctrine applied to state *taxation* of goods imported from other states was early rejected. In WOODRUFF V. PARHAM (1869) the Court upheld a state sales tax applied to an auctioneer who brought goods from other states and sold them in the taxing state in the original and unbroken packages. The IMPORT-EXPORT CLAUSE was determined to apply only to traffic with foreign nations, not to interstate traffic. The Court indicated its feeling that it would be grossly unfair if a resident of a state could escape from state taxes on all merchandise that he was able to import from another state and keep in its original package.

In 1890, however, the Court held that the original package doctrine applied to invalidate state *regulations* of goods imported from other states until the goods were sold or the package broken. The decision, LEISY V. HARDIN (1890), invalidated a state prohibition law as applied to sales within the state by the importer of kegs and cases of beer. Federal statutes were then enacted permitting states to exclude alcohol even in original packages. But the original package doctrine persisted with reference to other state regulations for nearly half a century. The Court found reasons in many cases to avoid applying the doctrine but did not effectively repudiate it until 1935. In *Baldwin v. G. A. F. Seelig* (1935) the Court, after reviewing the cases applying the original package doctrine said:

> "In brief, the test of the original package is not an ultimate principle. . . . It makes a convenient boundary and one sufficiently precise save in exceptional conditions. What is ultimate is the principle that one state in its dealing with another may not place itself in a position of economic isolation. Formulas and catchwords are subordinate to this overmastering requirement."

Today the original package doctrine is of interest only to historians.

EDWARD L. BARRETT, JR.
(1986)

(SEE ALSO: *State Regulation of Commerce; State Taxation of Commerce.*)

Bibliography

NOWAK, JOHN E.; ROTUNDA, RONALD D.; and YOUNG, NELSON J. 1979   *Handbook on Constitutional Law.* Pages 285–290. St. Paul, Minn.: West Publishing Co.

POWELL, THOMAS R.   1945   State Taxation of Imports: When Does an Import Cease to Be an Import? *Harvard Law Review* 58:858–876.

RIBBLE, F. D. G.   1937   *State and National Power over Commerce.* New York: Columbia University Press.

OROZCO v. TEXAS
394 U.S. 324 (1969)

In an opinion by Justice HUGO L. BLACK, the Supreme Court held that a conviction based on incriminating admissions obtained by police in the absence of notification of the MIRANDA RULES, even though the prisoner was at home, away from the coercive surroundings of a stationhouse, violated the RIGHT AGAINST SELF-INCRIMINATION.

LEONARD W. LEVY
(1986)

OSBORN v. BANK OF THE UNITED STATES
9 Wheaton 738 (1824)

On its constitutional merits, *Osborn* was a replay of MCCULLOCH V. MARYLAND (1819). Ohio had sought to drive out the congressionally chartered bank by taxing its branches $50,000 each and by seizing money from its vaults. The bank sued the state auditor in a federal court for recovery of the money. The state argued that the ELEVENTH AMENDMENT barred the court from taking JURISDICTION, but, on APPEAL to the Supreme Court, Chief Justice JOHN MARSHALL concluded that the amendment applied only when the state was named as a party defendant—a position abandoned by the Court in later decisions. (See EX PARTE YOUNG.) On the principles of *McCulloch*, the auditor was liable for his TRESPASS.

Osborn's lasting doctrinal contribution was its sweeping definition of congressional power under Article III to confer FEDERAL QUESTION JURISDICTION on the federal courts. Marshall's view, which remains good law, was that cases "arising under" the Constitution, or federal laws, or treaties included—for purposes of defining congressional power to confer jurisdiction—any case in which federal law might *potentially* be dispositive. It made no difference that federal law was not implicated in the bank's complaint for trespass; the arguable invalidity of the bank's charter might possibly be raised as a defense to such an action. Although similar words ("arises under") are used in the statutes defining federal question jurisdiction, they have been interpreted more narrowly. *Osborn* thus defines congressional power, not its exercise.

The *Osborn* decision heightened the vehemence of state denunciations of the Court's judicial nationalism and even of its appellate jurisdiction. President ANDREW JACKSON's veto of the bank bill of 1832 probably reflected the prevailing belief—despite *McCulloch* and *Osborn*—that Congress had no constitutional authority to charter a corporation.

LEONARD W. LEVY
KENNETH L. KARST
(1986)

OSBORNE v. OHIO

See: Child Pornography

O'SHEA v. LITTLETON
414 U.S. 488 (1974)

Protesters against RACIAL DISCRIMINATION in Cairo, Illinois, obtained a federal court INJUNCTION against a state judge and magistrate, forbidding continuation of various discriminatory BAIL, sentencing, and jury-fee practices in criminal cases. The Supreme Court reversed, 6–3, on RIPENESS grounds. Although some plaintiffs had previously suffered such discrimination, none were now threatened with prosecution. Thus there was no live CASE OR CONTROVERSY.

Once a prosecution was commenced, YOUNGER V. HARRIS (1971) would forbid a federal injunction. (See ABSTENTION DOCTRINE.) Thus potential plaintiffs in such cases must file their complaints within a narrow time period.

KENNETH L. KARST
(1986)

OTIS, JAMES, JR.
(1725–1783)

Massachusetts lawyer, Harvard graduate (1743), and ideologue of the AMERICAN REVOLUTION, James Otis, Jr., became constitutionally significant with PAXTON'S CASE (1761), which concerned the issuance of WRITS OF ASSISTANCE by the Superior Court of Massachusetts. Confronted with the reality that the writs, which empowered customs officers to search all suspected houses, typified many kinds of general SEARCH WARRANTS within British law, Otis resorted to the HIGHER LAW. Using sources from MAGNA CARTA to BONHAM'S CASE (1610), Otis argued not only that incompatibility with natural and COMMON LAW rendered general searches void but also that the court should proclaim that invalidity. Although he did not advocate outright JUDICIAL REVIEW of an act of Parliament by a colonial court, the interpretation of the writs that Otis urged on the court would have had that result.

Although Otis's present fame derives heavily from *Paxton's Case*, he gained little contemporary notice from his performance in it, for his brief was not published until 1773. Rather, the principal constitutional services of the case were that it resulted in Otis's election to the Massachusetts General Court (legislative), thereby giving him a forum for his views and enabling him to assemble and rehearse the constitutional arguments that he later applied to those issues that directly generated the American Revolution.

Limiting the power of Parliament was central to Otis's thought: "To say the Parliament is absolute and arbitrary is a contradiction. The parliament cannot make 2 and 2, 5; Omnipotency cannot do it; the supreme power in a state is JUS DICERE [to announce the law] only;—JUS DARE [to construct the law] strictly speaking belongs only to God. . . . Should an act of Parliament be against any of his natural laws, which are immutably true, their declaration would be contrary to eternal truth, equity and justice, and consequently void." Otis's constitutional significance, however, does not emanate from this belief, which most contemporaries shared, but from the corollaries he extracted from it. Otis first transformed the British constitution into a fixed rather than a flexible barrier to Parliament, which he redefined as a subordinate creature of the constitution rather than one of its components. Of even greater import, Otis characterized the courts as umpires of Parliament's power. "The judges of England," he wrote, "have declared in favor of these sentiments when they expressly declare; that acts of Parliament against natural equity are void. That acts against the fundamental principles of the British Constitution are void." To assert that all earthly power, even that of Parliament, had limits was a ubiquitous platitude; to imply that agencies outside Parliament could calibrate and enforce these limits challenged the axiom of parliamentary supremacy that, for most Englishmen, lay at the foundation of their constitution.

A disembodied and didactic use of sources, ranging from Magna Carta to Hugo Grotius, provided Otis's intellectual ammunition. In *Bonham's Case*, for example, the *Reports* of Sir EDWARD COKE mentioned courts' controlling acts of Parliament and adjudging them void. Coke's meaning, however, was constructive rather than constitutional and involved no judicial effort to subjugate Parliament. The case pitted not the legislature against the courts but two clashing private parties and raised questions of which conflicting laws applied. Coke reasoned that the common law courts, acting with, rather than against, another court in the form of Parliament, should give the laws a reasonable construction that was jointly desired. Otis bloated the case, however, into precedent for constitutional regulation of Parliament under judicial aegis.

Otis repeatedly denied the revolutionary implications of his ideology, stressing that Parliament was the British Empire's supreme but not absolute legislature and could alone rescind its statutes. Despite these denials, however, Otis's assumptions intrinsically approached the threshold of the right to revolution against unconstitutional parliamentary acts.

Having asserted limits to Parliament's authority, Otis enumerated the colonial rights that lay beyond them. As a delegate to the STAMP ACT CONGRESS (1765) and in his *Rights of the British Colonies* (1764), written against the Sugar Act, Otis condemned taxation of the colonists by a Parliament to which they had directly elected no representatives. (See TAXATION WITHOUT REPRESENTATION.) As

moderator of the Boston town meetings, he also opposed juryless trials under the TOWNSHEND ACTS of 1767.

Widely regarded as the premier theorist of the radical cause in the 1760s, Otis had great influence on the constitutional ideology of the developing revolution. He edited many of the *Farmer's Letters* (1767) by JOHN DICKINSON, while JOHN ADAMS adapted much of Otis's reasoning in *Paxton's Case* against juryless ADMIRALTY trials in *Sewall v. Hancock* (1768–1769).

WILLIAM J. CUDDIHY
(1986)

Bibliography

WATERS, JOHN 1968 *The Otis Family.* Chapel Hill: University of North Carolina Press.

OVERBREADTH

Judges frequently encounter the claim that a law, as drafted or interpreted, should be invalidated as overbroad because its regulatory scope addresses not only behavior that constitutionally may be punished but also constitutionally protected behavior. The normal judicial response is confined to ruling on the law's constitutionality as applied to the litigant's behavior, leaving the validity of its application to other people and situations to subsequent adjudication. Since THORNHILL V. ALABAMA (1940), however, the Supreme Court has made an exception, most frequently in FIRST AMENDMENT cases but applicable to other precious freedoms, when it is convinced that the very existence of an overbroad law may cause knowledgeable people to refrain from freely exercising constitutional liberties because they fear punishment and are unwilling to litigate their rights. In such cases, the aggregate inhibition of guaranteed freedom in the regulated community is thought to justify both holding the overbroad law INVALID ON ITS FACE and allowing one to whom a narrower law could be applied constitutionally to assert the overbreadth claim. Unlike the alternative of narrowing the unconstitutional portions of an overbroad statute case by case, facial invalidation prevents delay in curing the improper deterrence. Moreover, courts most effectively can address the inhibition of those who neither act nor sue by allowing those who do to raise the overbreadth challenge.

Like a VAGUENESS challenge, an overbreadth challenge implicates judicial governance in two controversial ways. First, if successful, the challenge completely prohibits the law's enforcement, even its constitutional applications, until it is narrowed through reenactment or authoritative interpretation. Second, the challenge requires a court to gauge the law's applications to unidentified people in circumstances that must be imagined, often ignoring the facts of the situation before them—a practice of hypothesizing that is at odds with the court's usual application of law to the facts of concrete CASES OR CONTROVERSIES.

Overbreadth differs from vagueness in that the constitutional defect is a law's excessive reach, not its lack of clarity; yet the defects are related. A law that punished "all speech that is not constitutionally protected" would, by definition, not be overbroad, but it would be unduly vague because people would have to speculate about what it outlawed. A law that prohibited "all speaking" would be unconstitutionally overbroad, but it also might be vague. Although clear enough if taken literally, it might be understood that the legislature did not intend the full reach of its broadly drafted law, and the public would have to speculate about what the contours of the intended lesser reach might be. A law that banned "all harmful speech" would be both overbroad and vague on its face. The key connection, however, is the improper inhibiting effect of the broad or vague law.

As with vagueness, the federal courts approach overbreadth challenges to state and federal laws differently. A federal court must interpret a federal law before judging its constitutionality. In doing so, the court may reduce the law's scope, if it can do so consistently with Congress's intent, a course that may minimize constitutional problems of overbreadth. Only state courts may authoritatively determine the reach of state laws, however. Consequently, when the Supreme Court reviews an overbreadth challenge to a state law on appeal from a state court—which review usually occurs because the challenger raised the claim in defense of state court proceedings against him—the Court must accept the state court's determination of the law's scope and apply its own constitutional judgment to the law as so construed. By contrast, if parties threatened with enforcement of a state statute sue in federal court to have the law declared unconstitutionally overbroad before they are prosecuted or sued in state court, the federal court faces the additional complication of determining the overbreadth question without the guidance of any state court interpretation of the law in this case. If past interpretations of the law's terms make its breadth clear, there is no more difficulty than in Supreme Court review of a state court case. But if there is some question whether a state court might have narrowed the state law, especially in light of constitutional doubts about it, the federal court faces the possibility of making its own incorrect interpretation and basing an overbreadth judgment on that unstable premise.

With other constitutional claims involving uncertain state laws, a federal court normally will abstain from deciding the constitutional question until clarification is sought in state court. However, because the prolongation of CHILLING EFFECTS on constitutionally protected conduct

is the basis of the vagueness of overbreadth doctrines, the Supreme Court indicated in DOMBROWSKI V. PFISTER (1965) and *Baggett v. Bullitt* (1964) that abstention is generally inappropriate if the problem would take multiple instances of adjudication to cure. *Babbitt v. United Farm Workers* (1979) followed the implicit corollary, requiring abstention where a single state proceeding might have obviated the need to reach difficult constitutional issues. But BROCKETT V. SPOKANE ARCADES, INC. (1985) shunned abstention in a case where state court clarification was feasible in an expeditious single proceeding, but where the litigants objecting to overbreadth were not people to whom the law could be validly applied but people who desired to engage in constitutionally protected speech. In that circumstance, at least where the unconstitutional portion of the statute was readily identifiable and severable from the remainder, the Court chose to strike that portion rather than abstain to see if the state court would remove it by interpretation.

Brockett also expressed a preference for partial over facial invalidation whenever challengers assert that application of a statute to them would be unconstitutional. The Court's ultimate objective is to invalidate only a statute's overbroad features, not the parts that legitimately penalize undesirable behavior. It permits those who are properly subject to regulation to mount facial overbreadth attacks only to provide an opportunity for courts to eliminate the illegitimate deterrent impact on others. Partial invalidation would do such people no good, and those who are illegitimately deterred from speaking may never sue. In order to throw out the tainted bathwater, the baby temporarily must go too, until the statute is reenacted or reinterpreted with its flaws omitted. Where, as in *Brockett*, one asserts his own right to pursue protected activity, however, no special incentive to litigate is needed. The Court can limit a statute's improper reach through partial invalidation and still benefit the challenger. *Brockett*'s assumption that the tainted part of the statute does not spoil the whole also undercuts Henry Monaghan's important argument that allowing the unprotected to argue overbreadth does not depart from normal STANDING rules because they always assert their own right not to be judged under an invalid statute. The part applied to them is valid, and they are granted standing to attack the whole only to protect others from the invalid part. Finally, the claim that a law is invalid in all applications because based on an illegitimate premise has elements of both partial and facial invalidation. As the invalid premise affects the challenger as well as everyone else, there is no need to provide a special incentive to litigate, but because the whole law is defective, total invalidation is appropriate.

The seriousness of striking the whole of a partially invalid law at the urging of one to whom it validly applies, together with doubts about standing and the reliability of constitutional adjudication in the context of imagined applications, renders overbreadth an exceptional and controversial DOCTRINE. The determination of what circumstances are sufficiently compelling to warrant the doctrine's use has varied from time to time and among judges. The WARREN COURT focused mainly on the scope of the laws' coverage, the chilling effect on protected expression, and the ability of the legislature to draw legitimate regulatory boundaries more narrowly. The Court seemed convinced that overbroad laws inhibited freedom substantially, and thus made that inhibition the basis of invalidation, especially when the laws were aimed at dissidents and the risk of deliberate deterrence was high, as in APTHEKER V. SECRETARY OF STATE (1964), *United States v. Robel* (1967), and *Dombrowski v. Pfister* (1965). The BURGER COURT has continued to employ the overbreadth doctrine when deterrence of valued expression seems likely, as in *Lewis v. New Orleans* (1974), which struck down a law penalizing abusive language directed at police, and in SCHAD V. MT. EPHRAIM (1981), which struck down an extremely broad law banning live entertainment.

Justice BYRON R. WHITE has led that Court, however, in curtailing overbreadth adjudication. As all laws occasionally may be applied unconstitutionally, there is always a quantitative dimension of overbreadth. White's majority opinion in BROADRICK V. OKLAHOMA (1973) held that the overbroad portion of a law must be "real and substantial" before it will be invalidated. That standard highlights the magnitude of deterrent impact, which depends as much on the motivations of those regulated as on the reach of the law. *Broadrick* also emphasized the need to compare and offset the ranges of a statute's valid and invalid applications, rather than simply assess the dimensions of the invalid range. This substituted a judgment balancing a statute's legitimate regulation against its illegitimate deterrence of protected conduct for a judgment focused predominantly on the improper inhibition.

Broadrick initially limited the "substantial overbreadth" approach to laws seemingly addressed to conduct, leaving laws explicitly regulating expression, especially those directed at particular viewpoints, to the more generous approach. In *Ferber v. New York* (1982) and *Brockett*, however, substantial overbreadth was extended to pure speech cases as well. That these cases involved laws regulating OBSCENITY might suggest that some Justices find the overbreadth doctrine an improper means to counter deterrence of marginally valued expression. More likely, however, the Court generally is abandoning its focus on the subject of a law's facial coverage in favor of a comparative judgment of the qualitative and quantitative dimensions of a law's legitimate and illegitimate scope, whatever speech or conduct be regulated.

Still, the reality of deterrence and the value of the liberty deterred probably remain major factors in overbreadth judgments, even if more must be considered. For example, the Court's pronouncement in *Bates v. State Bar of Arizona* (1977) that overbreadth analysis generally is inappropriate for profit-motivated advertising rested explicitly on a judgment that advertising is not easily inhibited and implicitly on the historic perception of COMMERCIAL SPEECH as less worthy of protection.

Overbreadth controversies nearly always reflect different sensitivities to the worth of lost expression and of lost regulation of unprotected behavior, or different perceptions of the legitimacy and reliability of judicial nullification of laws that are only partially unconstitutional, or different assessments of how much inhibition is really likely, how easy it would be to redraft a law to avoid overbreadth, and how important broad regulation is to the effective control of harmful behavior. Despite controversy and variations in zeal for application of the overbreadth doctrine, however, its utility in checking repression that too sweepingly inhibits guaranteed liberty should assure its preservation in some form.

JOHNATHAN D. VARAT
(1986)

Bibliography
ALEXANDER, LAWRENCE A. 1985 Is There an Overbreadth Doctrine? *San Diego Law Review* 22:541–554.
MONAGHAN, HENRY P. 1981 Overbreadth. *Supreme Court Review* 1981:1–39.
NOTE 1970 The First Amendment Overbreadth Doctrine. *Harvard Law Review* 83:844–927.

OVERRULING

The authority of the Supreme Court to reconsider and overrule its previous DECISIONS is a necessary and accepted part of the Court's power to decide cases. By one estimate, the Supreme Court overruled itself on constitutional issues 159 times through 1976 and in each case departed from the DOCTRINE of STARE DECISIS.

The basic tenet of *stare decisis*, as set forth by WILLIAM BLACKSTONE, is that PRECEDENTS must generally be followed unless they are "flatly absurd" or "unjust." The doctrine promotes certainty in the law, judicial efficiency (by obviating the constant reexamination of previously settled questions), and uniformity in the treatment of litigants. The roots of the doctrine, which is fundamental in Anglo-American jurisprudence, have been traced to Roman civil law and the Code of Justinian.

Justices and commentators have disagreed about the proper application of *stare decisis* to constitutional decision making. Justice (later Chief Justice) EDWARD D. WHITE, in his dissenting opinion in POLLOCK V. FARMERS LOAN TRUST CO. (1895), observed:

> The fundamental conception of a judicial body is that of one hedged about by precedents which are binding on the court without regard to the personality of its members. Break down this belief in judicial continuity, and let it be felt that on great constitutional questions this court is to depart from the settled conclusions of its precedessors, and to determine them all according to the mere opinion of those who temporarily fill its bench, and our Constitution will, in my judgment, be bereft of value and become a most dangerous instrument to the rights and liberties of people.

Under this view, *stare decisis* should be applied with full force to constitutional issues.

The more commonly accepted view is that *stare decisis* has a more limited application in CONSTITUTIONAL INTERPRETATION than it does in the interpretation of statutes or in ordinary common law decision making. Although Congress, by a simple majority, can override the Supreme Court's erroneous interpretation of a congressional statute, errors in the interpretation of the Constitution are not easily corrected. The AMENDING PROCESS is by design difficult. In many instances only the Court can correct an erroneous constitutional decision.

Moreover, the Court will on occasion make decisions that later appear to be erroneous. As Chief Justice JOHN MARSHALL remarked in MCCULLOCH V. MARYLAND (1819), the Constitution requires deductions from its "great outlines" when a court decides specific cases. Because the modern Supreme Court generally accepts for review only cases in which principles of broad national importance are in competition, its decisions necessarily involve difficult questions of judgment. In view of the difficulties inherent in amending the Constitution, any errors made by the Court in the interpretation of constitutional principles must be subject to correction by the Court in later decisions.

The classic statement of this view was expressed by Justice LOUIS D. BRANDEIS in his dissenting opinion in *Burnet v. Coronado Oil Gas Co.* (1932): "[I]n cases involving the Federal Constitution, where correction through legislative action is practically impossible, this Court has often overruled its earlier decisions. The Court bows to the lessons of experience and the force of better reasoning, recognizing that the process of trial and error, so fruitful in the physical sciences, is appropriate also in the judicial function." The Court has relied on Brandeis's reasoning in later decisions, such as EDELMAN V. JORDAN (1974), overruling previous constitutional precedents.

An additional reason for applying *stare decisis* less rigidly to constitutional decisions is that the judge's primary obligation is to the Constitution itself. In the words of Justice FELIX FRANKFURTER, concurring in *Graves v. New York* (1939), "the ultimate touchstone of constitutionality is the Constitution itself and not what we have said about it."

Some critics of *stare decisis* suggest that it has no place whatsoever in constitutional cases. For example, Chief Justice ROGER B. TANEY reasoned in the PASSENGER CASES (1849) that a constitutional question "is always open to discussion" because the judicial authority of the Court should "depend altogether on the force of the reasoning by which it is supported." The more generally accepted view, however, was stated by the Court in *Arizona v. Rumsey* (1984): "Although adherence to precedent is not rigidly required in constitutional cases, any departure from the doctrine of *stare decisis* requires special justification." Consistent with this view, the Supreme Court generally seeks to provide objective justification for the overruling of past precedents, apart from the fact that the Court's personnel may have changed.

One of the most commonly expressed reasons for overruling a previous decision is that it cannot be reconciled with other rulings. This rationale is in a sense consistent with *stare decisis* in that the justification for the overruling decision rests on competing but previously established judicial principles. In GIDEON V. WAINWRIGHT (1963), for example, which overruled BETTS V. BRADY (1942), the Court asserted not only that the rationale of *Betts* was erroneous but also that *Betts* had abruptly departed from well-established prior decisions. *Betts* had held that the DUE PROCESS clause of the FOURTEENTH AMENDMENT does not impose on the states, as the Sixth Amendment imposes on the federal government, the obligation to provide counsel in state criminal proceedings. *Gideon* expressly rejected this holding, thereby ruling that indigent defendants have the right to appointed counsel in such cases. Similarly, in WEST COAST HOTEL CO. V. PARRISH (1937) the Court concluded that it had no choice but to overrule its earlier decision in ADKINS V. CHILDREN'S HOSPITAL (1923), which had held a minimum wage statute for women unconstitutional under the due process clause. The Court reasoned that *Adkins* was irreconcilable with other decisions permitting the regulation of maximum hours and other working conditions for women.

The Court frequently argues, too, that the lessons of experience require the overruling of a previous decision. In ERIE RAILROAD CO. V. TOMPKINS (1938), for example, the Court reasoned that in nearly one hundred years the doctrine of SWIFT V. TYSON (1842) "had revealed its defects, political and social." And in MAPP V. OHIO (1961) the Court held the EXCLUSIONARY RULE applicable to the states, saying that the experience of various states had made clear that remedies other than the exclusionary rule could not effectively deter unreasonable searches and seizures. The

Court therefore overruled WOLF V. COLORADO (1949), which only two decades earlier had ruled that states were free to devise their own remedies for enforcing SEARCH AND SEIZURE requirements applicable to the states through the due process clause of the Fourteenth Amendment.

The Court also justifies overruling decisions on the basis of changed or unforeseen circumstances. In BROWN V. BOARD OF EDUCATION (1954), for example, the Court referred to the change in status of the public schools in rejecting the application of the SEPARATE BUT EQUAL DOCTRINE of PLESSY V. FERGUSON (1896). And in PROPELLER GENESEE CHIEF V. FITZHUGH (1851), one of the earliest overruling decisions, the Court stressed that when it had erroneously held in *The Thomas Jefferson* (1825) that the ADMIRALTY AND MARITIME JURISDICTION of the federal government was limited "to the ebb and flow of the tide," commerce on the rivers of the West and on the Great Lakes had been in its infancy and "the great national importance of the question . . . could not be foreseen."

Other considerations may also suggest a decision's susceptibility to being overruled. Thus a decision on an issue not fully briefed and argued may be entitled to less precedential weight than one in which the issue received full and deliberate consideration. Or, the fact that an issue was decided by a closely divided Court may suggest a higher probability of error and make later reconsideration more likely. By contrast, as the Court recognized in *Akron v. Akron Center for Reproductive Health* (1983), a carefully considered decision, repeatedly and consistently followed, may be entitled to more respect than other constitutional holdings under principles of *stare decisis*.

As the Court develops constitutional doctrine, it may limit or distinguish a previous decision, gradually eroding its authority without expressly overruling it. Such a doctrinal evolution may both portend an overruling decision and establish the groundwork for it.

The Court's willingness to reconsider its prior constitutional decisions and in some instances to overrule itself is implicit in the general understanding of the Constitution as a document of broad outlines intended to endure the ages. Yet it has been suggested that the Court risks a loss of confidence as a disinterested interpreter of the Constitution whenever it overrules itself. Because of its antimajoritarian character, the Court must be sensitive to the need for restraint in exercising its power of JUDICIAL REVIEW. If it overrules itself too frequently and without adequate justification, its reputation may suffer. The Constitution's general language, however, leaves wide room for honest differences as to its interpretation and application. An objective and detached overruling opinion, which faithfully seeks to apply constitutional principles on the basis of the constitutional text and history, is on occasion to be expected and need not jeopardize public confidence in the Court.

JAMES R. ASPERGER
(1986)

Bibliography

BERNHARDT, CHARLOTTE C. 1948 Supreme Court Reversals on Constitutional Issues. *Cornell Law Quarterly* 34:55–70.

BLAUSTEIN, ALBERT P. and FIELD, ANDREW H. 1958 "Overruling" Opinions in the Supreme Court. *Michigan Law Review* 57:151–194.

ISRAEL, JEROLD H. 1963 Gideon v. Wainwright: The "Art" of Overruling. *Supreme Court Review* 1963:211–272.

NOLAND, JON D. 1969 Stare Decisis and the Overruling of Constitutional Decisions in the Warren Years. *Valparaiso University Law Review* 4:101–135.

REED, STANLEY 1938 Stare Decisis and Constitutional Law. *Pennsylvania Bar Association Quarterly* 1938:131–150.

OVERT ACTS TEST

The overt acts test originated in the seventeenth century in suggestive remarks by ROGER WILLIAMS, William Walwyn, and Baruch Spinoza, primarily to promote the cause of RELIGIOUS LIBERTY. To the same end, PHILLIP FURNEAUX, in the next century, developed the test and THOMAS JEFFERSON adopted it. Such libertarians advocated the test as an alternative to the prevailing BAD TENDENCY TEST, according to which the expression of an opinion was punishable if it tended to stir animosity to the established religion of a state or to the government or its officers or measures. Thus, the preamble to Jefferson's VIRGINIA STATUTE OF RELIGIOUS FREEDOM declared that allowing the civil magistrate to restrain the profession of opinions "on the supposition of their ill tendency . . . at once destroys all religious liberty." The government's rightful purposes, Jefferson continued, were served if its officers did not interfere until "principles break out into overt acts against peace and good order." The overt acts test, therefore, sharply distinguished words from deeds, and, in Furneaux's words, was based on the proposition that the "penal laws should be directed against overt acts only."

When the Sedition Act of 1798 incorporated the principles of ZENGER'S CASE (1735), libertarians who had advocated those principles finally abandoned them as inadequate protections of the FREEDOM OF THE PRESS and embraced the overt acts test. Only a radical minority ever advocated the test in cases of political expression, yet it survived down to the twentieth century. Justices HUGO L. BLACK and WILLIAM O. DOUGLAS found the test admirably suited to their ABSOLUTISM. Dissenting in YATES V. UNITED STATES (1957), Black said, "I believe that the FIRST AMEND-

MENT forbids Congress to punish people for talking about public affairs, whether or not such discussion incites to action, legal or illegal."

The overt acts test would provide the utmost protection for words and make the principle of FREEDOM OF SPEECH immunize every kind of verbal crime. The test ignores the fact that in some instances words themselves can be crimes (contempt of court, perjury, OBSCENITY, the verbal agreement in a CRIMINAL CONSPIRACY) or can violate laws validly governing the time and place of assemblies, parades, PICKETING, and SOUNDTRUCKS AND AMPLIFIERS. Words can also cause severe injury, constitute INCITEMENT TO UNLAWFUL CONDUCT, or otherwise solicit crime. The overt acts test draws a bright but fake constitutional line between speech and action; an indistinct zone would be more appropriate. Nevertheless, the Supreme Court in BRANDENBURG V. OHIO (1969), a leading free speech case, almost flirted with the overt acts test when it held that a state may not constitutionally "forbid or proscribe advocacy of the use of force or of law violation except where such advocacy is directed to inciting or producing imminent lawless action and is likely to incite or produce such action."

The Constitution contains a different overt acts test in the TREASON clause (Article 3, section 3), which specifies that unless a person accused of treason confesses in open court, two witnesses to the same overt act must prove his guilt. The clause also defines the required overt act as making war against the United States or "adhering to their Enemies, giving them aid and comfort." The treason clause, therefore, prevents the punishment of "constructive" treason, which consists of any words or acts construed by the government or a court to be tantamount to treason. Thus, the overt acts provision of the treason clause helps guarantee CIVIL LIBERTY by preventing the crime of treason from being used expansively to silence opponents of the government.

LEONARD W. LEVY
(1986)

Bibliography

GREENAWALT, KENT 1980 Speech and Crime. *American Bar Foundation Research Journal* 1980:647–785.

OWEN v. CITY OF INDEPENDENCE
445 U.S. 622 (1980)

In MONELL V. DEPARTMENT OF SOCIAL SERVICES (1978) the Supreme Court held that municipalities may be liable under SECTION 1983, TITLE 42, UNITED STATES CODE, for deprivations of constitutional rights if the deprivation results from official policy. In *Owen*, the Court held that municipalities may not avail themselves of the good-faith defense or qualified immunity enjoyed by individual defendants in section 1983 cases. Thus, a municipality may be liable for unconstitutional acts even if its officials reasonably believe in good faith that their acts are constitutional.

THEODORE EISENBERG
(1986)

OYAMA v. CALIFORNIA
332 U.S. 633 (1948)

In *Terrace v. Thompson* (1923) the Supreme Court had upheld the power of a state to limit land ownership to U.S. citizens. *Oyama*, together with TAKAHASHI V. FISH AND GAME COMMISSION (1948), both undermined *Terrace* and signaled a changing judicial attitude toward RACIAL DISCRIMINATION.

California's Alien Land Law forbade land ownership by ALIENS ineligible for CITIZENSHIP; under existing federal law, that category was largely limited to persons of Asian ancestry. Invoking its law, California sought to take over title to land held in the name of a young U.S. citizen, on the ground that it was really owned by his father, an alien ineligible for citizenship. The father had paid for the land, and so under the law was presumed its owner. A similar presumption would not apply to ownership of land by citizens of other races. Without purporting to rule on the general validity of the Alien Land Law, the Supreme Court held, 7–2, that the presumption denied the EQUAL PROTECTION OF THE LAWS.

KENNETH L. KARST
(1986)

P

PACE v. ALABAMA
106 U.S. 583 (1883)

To white supremacists, the MISCEGENATION issue was crucially important. The often unexpressed fear of interracial sex involving white women underlay all sorts of RACIAL DISCRIMINATION. The states punished adultery and fornication much more severely when the parties were of different races than when both were of the same race. *Pace* challenged the constitutionality of Alabama's statute, but the Supreme Court unanimously held that the unequal punishment did not violate the EQUAL PROTECTION clause of the FOURTEENTH AMENDMENT because both the interracial fornicators were subject to the same punishment.

LEONARD W. LEVY
(1986)

(SEE ALSO: *Loving v. Virginia*.)

PACIFISTS

See: Conscientious Objection

PACKERS & STOCKYARDS ACT
42 Stat. 159 (1921)

After a Federal Trade Commission investigation damaging to the meat-packing industry in 1919–1920, popular sentiment demanded decisive action. Congress responded with this statute regulating both the packers and the stockyards. As one of its sponsors declared, the statute merely reenacted old principles in order to restore and maintain competition. Indeed, the clause banning "unfair" competition restated section 5 of the FEDERAL TRADE COMMISSION ACT. Other provisions forbade giving "undue or unreasonable advantage" (repeating section 3 of the INTERSTATE COMMERCE ACT) or apportioning items by geographic area (ICA, section 5; SHERMAN ANTITRUST ACT, section 1). Violators might be brought before the secretary of agriculture, who could issue CEASE-AND-DESIST ORDERS; APPEALS lay to federal CIRCUIT COURTS. Stockyards subject to the act were required to register and provide "reasonable" services and charges. The secretary could determine new rates and order compliance, although the act provided no standards for his guidance. Perhaps because of a CONSENT DECREE negotiated with the industry in 1920, the Department of Justice was reluctant to prosecute the packers. Their disinclination, and the packers' efforts to avoid the consent decree, materially contributed to the act's passage. In enacting this statute, Congress emphasized public concern over and commitment to strict accountability to the nation's antitrust laws. (See STAFFORD V. WALLACE.)

DAVID GORDON
(1986)

Bibliography

GORDON, DAVID 1983 The Beef Trust: Antitrust Law and the Meat Packing Industry, 1902–1922. Ph.D. diss., Claremont Graduate School.

PAINE, THOMAS
(1737–1809)

Thomas Paine, the son of an English Quaker tradesman, became the great propagandist of the American and French revolutions. Before sailing to Philadelphia in 1774, with a letter of recommendation from BENJAMIN FRANKLIN, Paine had been a corsetmaker, a privateer, a tax assessor, a songwriter, and a tobacconist. In Philadelphia, he became editor of the *Pennsylvania Magazine*, crusading for abolition of slavery, proscription of dueling, greater rights for women, and easier availability of divorce.

Paine became the spokesman for the AMERICAN REVOLUTION when, in January 1776, he published a pamphlet called *Common Sense*. The pamphlet sharply attacked "the constitutional errors of the English form of government," including monarchy and CHECKS AND BALANCES. Paine declared that "the constitution of England is so complex, that the nation may suffer for years together without being able to discover in which part the fault lies." He argued for minimal government: "Society is in every state a blessing, but government even in its best state is but a necessary evil." Paine concluded *Common Sense* with a proposal for a "Continental Charter" of government based on large and equal REPRESENTATION and featuring a presidency rotated among the provincial delegations.

Between 1776 and 1783, Paine published a series of thirteen essays called *The Crisis*, chronicling "the times that try men's souls." Although in *Common Sense* he had denounced the English constitution, by the time he wrote *The Crisis* #7 in 1778, Paine had come to wonder "whether there is any such thing as the English constitution?" *The Crisis* #13, published in 1783, presented an argument for a strong and permanent national union, because "we have no other national SOVEREIGNTY than as the United States."

As the CONSTITUTIONAL CONVENTION OF 1787 met, however, Paine was en route to Europe to promote a scheme for building iron bridges. The outbreak of the French Revolution in 1789 found him in Paris. He became a French citizen and a member of the revolutionary Convention; he was the principal author of the Declaration of the Rights of Man and Citizen. When Edmund Burke denounced the French Revolution, Paine responded with *The Rights of Man*, the nearest thing he ever wrote to a systematic treatise on politics. Not an originator of ideas but a popularizer, Paine grounded his case for the revolution in the concepts of NATURAL RIGHTS and SOCIAL COMPACT. "Every civil right," he wrote, "has for its foundation some natural right pre-existing in the individual, but to the enjoyment of which his individual power is not, in all cases, sufficiently competent."

In 1792 the French revolutionary government fell into the hands of a radical faction; Paine was imprisoned and only narrowly escaped the guillotine. During his year in prison he wrote *The Age of Reason*, an apology for deism and religious rationalism with an anti-Christian tenor.

Paine's release from prison was arranged by the American ambassador, JAMES MONROE. For nearly a decade Paine remained in France as a journalist and political commentator. In 1802 he returned to America where he wrote polemical articles for the newspapers in support of THOMAS JEFFERSON's Republican party until his death in 1809.

DENNIS J. MAHONEY
(1986)

Bibliography

CANAVAN, FRANCIS 1972 Thomas Paine. Pages 652–658 in Leo Strauss and Joseph Cropsey, eds., *History of Political Philosophy*. Chicago: Rand McNally.

HAWKE, DAVID FREEMAN 1974 *Paine*. New York: Harper & Row.

PALKO v. CONNECTICUT
302 U.S. 319 (1937)

Palko, decided in the sesquicentennial year of the Constitution, highlights the difference between the constitutional law of criminal justice then and now. The *Palko* Court, which was unanimous, included five of the greatest judges in our history—CHARLES EVANS HUGHES, LOUIS D. BRANDEIS, HARLAN FISKE STONE, HUGO L. BLACK, and the Court's spokesman, BENJAMIN N. CARDOZO. In one respect Cardozo's opinion is a historical relic, like HURTADO V. CALIFORNIA (1884), MAXWELL V. DOW (1900), and TWINING V. NEW JERSEY (1908), which he cited as governing precedents. In another respect, *Palko* rationalized the Court's INCORPORATION DOCTRINE of the FOURTEENTH AMENDMENT by which it selected FUNDAMENTAL RIGHTS to be safeguarded against state violation.

Palko was sentenced to life imprisonment after a jury found him guilty of murder in the second degree. The state sought and won a new trial on the ground that its case had been prejudiced by errors of the trial court. Palko objected that a new trial on the same INDICTMENT exposed him to DOUBLE JEOPARDY, but he was overruled. At the second trial the jury's verdict of murder in the first degree resulted in a sentence of death. Had the case been tried in a federal court, the double jeopardy claim would have been good. The question raised by Palko's case was whether a double standard prevailed—one for state courts and the other for federal—or whether the Fifth Amendment's guarantee against double jeopardy applied to the state through the DUE PROCESS clause of the Fourteenth Amendment.

Cardozo declared that Palko's contention was even broader: "Whatever would be a violation of the original BILL OF RIGHTS (Amendments 1 to 8) if done by the federal government is now equally unlawful by force of the Fourteenth Amendment if done by a state." The Court answered, "There is no such general rule," thus rejecting the theory of total incorporation. Nevertheless, said Cardozo, by a "process of absorption"—now referred to as selective incorporation—the Court had extended the due process clause of the Fourteenth Amendment to include FIRST AMENDMENT freedoms and the RIGHT TO COUNSEL in certain cases, yet it had rejected the rights of the criminally accused, excepting representation by counsel for ignorant INDIGENTS in capital prosecutions. The rationalizing principle that gave coherence to the absorption process, Cardozo alleged, depended on a distinction among the various rights. Some were "fundamental" or "of the very essence of a scheme of ORDERED LIBERTY," like FREEDOM OF SPEECH or religion. By contrast, TRIAL BY JURY, indictment by GRAND JURY, and the RIGHT AGAINST SELF-INCRIMINATION were not: justice might be done without them. The right against double jeopardy, the Court ruled summarily, did not rank as fundamental and therefore received no protection against the states from the due process clause of the Fourteenth Amendment. BENTON V. MARYLAND (1969) overruled *Palko*, showing that even "fundamental" value judgments change with time. All that remains of *Palko* is the abstract principle of selective incorporation.

LEONARD W. LEVY
(1986)

Bibliography
ABRAHAM, HENRY J. 1977 *Freedom and the Court*, 3rd ed. Pages 64–70. New York: Oxford University Press.

PALMER, ALEXANDER M.
(1872–1936)

Appointed attorney general in 1919, Alexander Mitchell Palmer soon faced violence stirred up by the extreme left. After a series of bombings, Palmer campaigned against CIVIL LIBERTIES and unsuccessfully urged adoption of a new SEDITION law. His overreaction to alleged domestic radicals, particularly his "Red Raids" into private homes, mass arrests, and deportations of aliens, earned him widespread censure. Palmer also used the emergency WAR POWERS to attempt an end to the coal strike in 1919, exciting further criticism. These circumstances all contributed to his losing the 1920 Democratic presidential nomination for which he had been a leading contender. He nevertheless remained a party regular and helped write the 1932 party platform.

DAVID GORDON
(1986)

Bibliography
COBEN, STANLEY (1963) 1972 *A. Mitchell Palmer: Politician*. New York: Da Capo Press.

PALMER v. THOMPSON
402 U.S. 217 (1971)

Under a federal court order to integrate its public recreational facilities, Jackson, Mississippi, closed four of its five public swimming pools and surrendered the city's lease on the fifth pool. In a 5–4 decision, the Supreme Court sustained the closings, stating that a legislative act does not "violate EQUAL PROTECTION solely because of the motivations of the men who voted for it." *Palmer's* statement that legislative motive is irrelevant was undermined in WASHINGTON V. DAVIS (1976) and ARLINGTON HEIGHTS V. METROPOLITAN HOUSING DEVELOPMENT CORPORATION (1977).

THEODORE EISENBERG
(1986)

PALMER RAIDS
(1919–1920)

In the aftermath of WORLD WAR I and the Russian Revolution, waves of European IMMIGRATION aggravated domestic inflation and unemployment. LABOR strikes, often violent, were rampant, and the Communist party was organized.

Under pressure from the press and the public, WOODROW WILSON's attorney general, A. MITCHELL PALMER, conducted a series of raids between autumn 1919 and spring 1920 against the homes and offices of suspected ALIENS and radical leaders. The raids were conducted without ARREST WARRANTS or SEARCH WARRANTS, and those detained were denied the right to HABEAS CORPUS. Several thousand persons were detained, and over 500 alien radicals were deported.

DENNIS J. MAHONEY
(1986)

PALMORE v. SIDOTI
466 U.S. 429 (1984)

When Linda Palmore was divorced from Anthony Sidoti, a Florida court awarded custody of their daughter to Palmore. Later, Sidoti sought custody on the ground that Palmore, a white woman, had been cohabiting with a black man, whom she shortly married. The state court changed the custody on the sole ground that the mother had "chosen for herself and her child, a life-style unacceptable to her father and to society." The child would, if she remained with her mother, be "more vulnerable to peer pressures" and would suffer from "social stigmatization." The Supreme Court unanimously reversed.

For the Court, Chief Justice WARREN E. BURGER reaffirmed the need for STRICT SCRUTINY of governmental action based on race. Racial prejudice indeed existed, but the potential injury from such private biases was not a constitutionally acceptable basis for the custody change. The decision has symbolic importance, but seems unlikely to make much difference in actual awards of child custody, which can be rested on a variety of grounds in the name of the "best interests of the child" without any explicit consideration of race.

KENNETH L. KARST
(1986)

PANAMA CANAL TREATIES
33 Stat. 2234 (1903)
TIAS 10030 (1977)

At the turn of the twentieth century the United States emerged as a major power in world politics. Central to that major-power status were America's merchant shipping and the navy that protected it. The disadvantage of being a continental power with shores on two oceans became obvious during the Spanish American War when redeployment of warships from the Pacific to the Atlantic Ocean, by way of Cape Horn, took two months to complete. The United States government determined to construct a canal across Central America through the Isthmus of Panama. The United States negotiated a treaty with Colombia, in which the isthmus was located, but that treaty was rejected by the Colombian Senate in August 1903.

In November 1903, with American encouragement, Panama declared its independence from Colombia; two weeks later Panama signed a treaty (sometimes called the Hay-Bunau Treaty) permitting the United States to build the Panama Canal. The United States Senate gave its ADVICE AND CONSENT to ratification of the treaty the following February.

In the treaty the United States undertook to defend both the canal and the Republic of Panama and to make nominal annual payments to Panama from the revenue of the canal. The treaty gave the United States permanent control "as if it were sovereign" over the Panama Canal Zone, a strip of land ten miles wide dividing the republic—which retained nominal sovereignty over the zone—in two. For nearly three-quarters of a century the Canal Zone was governed as an American TERRITORY. When President LYNDON B. JOHNSON made (mostly symbolic) concessions to Panama following civil unrest there in the 1960s, members of Congress accused him of usurping Congress's exclusive power over the territories.

Negotiations between four successive administrations and the Panamanian government, conducted over more than thirteen years, resulted in two pacts signed in 1977, the Panama Canal Treaty and the Panama Canal Neutrality Treaty. Together, these agreements abolished the Canal Zone, returned the zone and the canal to Panamanian SOVEREIGNTY, and provided for the future operation of the waterway under joint, and ultimately under Panamanian, control. The campaign to win the advice and consent of the Senate to the treaties proved to be a major test of the constitutional roles of the executive and the Senate in the exercise of the TREATY POWER. The original Panama Canal Treaty had been approved after an unprecedentedly short debate; the length of the debate over the new treaties was exceeded in the twentieth century only by that over the Treaty of Versailles.

Ratification of the treaties in 1978, with numerous amendments and "conditions," proved to be only the beginning of a new struggle. The treaties were not self-executing but required implementing legislation; that gave members of the HOUSE OF REPRESENTATIVES, some of whom objected to the President and the SENATE giving away "American territory" without their participation, a chance to affect the terms of the transfer. Over the objections of both President JIMMY CARTER and the Panamanian government, Congress wrote into the implementing legislation provisions authorizing the President to intervene militarily to protect American interests in the former Canal Zone. The episode serves to illustrate the extent of congressional power, under the Constitution, to influence the conduct of FOREIGN AFFAIRS, over which the President is often assumed to have exclusive control.

DENNIS J. MAHONEY
(1986)

Bibliography

CRABB, CECIL V. and HOLT, PAT M.   1980   The Panama Canal Treaties. *Invitation to Struggle: Congress, the President and Foreign Policy.* Chap. 3. Washington, D.C.: Congressional Quarterly.

PANAMA REFINING CO. v. RYAN
293 U.S. 388 (1935)

In 1933 the price of wholesale gasoline had fallen to two and a half cents a gallon, that of crude oil to ten cents a barrel. The states, unable to cut production and push up prices, clamored for national controls. Congress responded with section 9(c) of the NATIONAL INDUSTRIAL RECOVERY ACT, authorizing the President to prohibit the shipment in INTERSTATE COMMERCE of petroleum produced in excess of quotas set by the states. By a vote of 8–1 the Supreme Court, in an opinion by Chief Justice CHARLES EVANS HUGHES, for the first time in history held an act of Congress unconstitutional because it improperly delegated legislative powers to the President without specifying adequate standards to guide his discretion. Moreover, the act did not require him to explain his orders. Vesting the President with "an uncontrolled legislative power," Hughes said, exceeded the limits of delegation; he did not explain how much delegation is valid and by what standards.

Justice BENJAMIN N. CARDOZO disagreed. He found adequate standards in section 1 of the statute: the elimination of unfair competitive practices and conservation of natural resources. These objectives guided the President's discretion, Cardozo explained. The principle of SEPARATION OF POWERS, which the majority used to underpin its opinion, should not be applied with doctrinaire rigor. Moreover, the statute, Cardozo observed, "was framed in the shadow of a national disaster" which raised unforeseen contingencies that only the President could face from day to day. The standards for his discretion had to be broad, and he need never give reasons for EXECUTIVE ORDERS. Cardozo's opinion notwithstanding, the Court in effect removed the oil industry from effective controls, to its detriment and that of the national economy. This case marked the NEW DEAL's debut before the Court.

LEONARD W. LEVY
(1986)

(SEE ALSO: *Delegation of Power.*)

PAPACHRISTOU v. JACKSONVILLE

See: Vagrancy Laws

PARADISE, UNITED STATES v.
480 U.S. 149 (1987)

For several decades, the Alabama Department of Public Safety excluded blacks from employment as state troopers. Only after a federal district court imposed a hiring quota in the early 1970s did the department finally change its ways. Even then, however, the department failed to promote the black officers it hired. Thereafter, the district court again intervened, this time requiring the department to institute promotion procedures without an adverse impact on black officers. When the department failed to institute such procedures within a timely period, the court imposed a promotion quota until the department developed acceptable promotion procedures of its own. Under the court's scheme, one black officer had to be promoted for every white officer promoted. The United States challenged the court's order, claiming that it violated the EQUAL PROTECTION clause of the FOURTEENTH AMENDMENT. The Supreme Court disagreed and upheld the order 5–4.

Writing for a plurality, Justice WILLIAM J. BRENNAN noted that members of the Court disagreed about what level of scrutiny to apply to discrimination remedy cases, but argued that this did not matter because the race-conscious remedy under review survived even the Court's highest standard of STRICT SCRUTINY because it was "narrowly tailored" to serve a COMPELLING STATE INTEREST.

Rejecting the strict scrutiny approach in discrimination-remedy cases, Justice JOHN PAUL STEVENS concurred in the judgment, but stressed that the federal judiciary has "broad and flexible authority" to fashion even race-conscious remedies once a violation of the Fourteenth Amendment has occurred.

Justice SANDRA DAY O'CONNOR vigorously disagreed. Writing for three of the dissenters, O'Connor not only insisted that all remedies be subjected to strict scrutiny but she also took the plurality to task for adopting "a standardless view" of strict scrutiny's requirement that a remedy be narrowly tailored to accomplish its purpose. Maintaining that "there is simply no justification for the use of racial preferences if the purpose of the order could be achieved without their use," O'Connor argued there was no evidence that the district court considered any alternatives to the RACIAL QUOTA, even though several alternatives in fact existed, including an invocation of the court's CONTEMPT POWER.

JOHN G. WEST, JR.
(1992)

PARDEE, DON ALBERT
(1837–1919)

President JAMES A. GARFIELD on May 3, 1881, appointed Don Albert Pardee judge of the Fifth Circuit Court. From 1891 to his death Pardee presided as senior judge of the Fifth Circuit Court of Appeals.

Pardee's most significant constitutional opinions involved the STATE POLICE POWER and VESTED RIGHTS. In *New Orleans Water-Works Co. v. St. Tammany Water-Works Co.* (1882) the judge held that the Louisiana legislature had exceeded its powers by incorporating a new company to compete with an enterprise that had enjoyed a monopoly over the distribution of the water supply to the city of

New Orleans. "Arguments in cases like the one under consideration," Pardee observed, "are generally based on the assumption that the sovereign . . . is absolutely unfettered with regard to . . . all the rights of property. I am not prepared to take this advanced ground." He enjoined the new company from further construction and held that the legislature could not invoke its police power "without compensation of the vested rights of the New Orleans Water-Works Company."

Pardee did accept broader legislative discretion under the police power when moral objectives were involved. In *United States ex rel. Hoover v. Ronan, Sheriff* (1887) he rejected an argument that a Georgia statute violated the DUE PROCESS and EQUAL PROTECTION provisions of the FOURTEENTH AMENDMENT by requiring would-be saloonkeepers in unincorporated towns and cities to obtain signatures from residents in order to secure a retail license. In *Ex Parte Kinnerbrew* (1888), he found on moral benefit grounds that the Georgia local option liquor law was compatible with the federal COMMERCE CLAUSE.

Pardee insisted on the power of the federal judiciary to frame a constitutional jurisprudence that separated the state police power into public and private sector concerns. As a result, reverence for vested property rights and public morality gilded his judicial conservatism.

KERMIT L. HALL
(1986)

Bibliography

BRYAN, PAUL E. 1964 Don Albert Pardee. *Dictionary of American Biography*, Vol. 14:201–202. New York: Scribner's.

plenary. There is the constitutional limitation that pardon may not be used to relieve from impeachment or its sanctions. Otherwise, a pardon can be granted before conviction, indeed before indictment, and it can be conferred absolutely or conditionally, provided that the conditions themselves are not unconstitutional. However, whether a pardon can be conferred over the objection of the grantee is not clear, for acceptance of a pardon is generally thought to be an acknowledgment of commission of a crime.

On the whole, the pardon power has not been used for political ends as was anticipated. The partisan strife of the Old World did not, with rare exceptions, see its counterpart on the American scene. The political nature of the power can be seen in the pardons to the WHISKEY REBELS, to those convicted under the ALIEN AND SEDITION ACTS, and in the AMNESTY—granted by Congress—to the rebels of the CIVIL WAR. President GERALD R. FORD's pardon of ex-President RICHARD M. NIXON after the WATERGATE affair was, perhaps, the most blatant partisan use of the power.

The Supreme Court, in SCHICK V. REED (1974), has legitimated the almost unlimited power of executive pardon. Although the history of the origins as recounted in *Schick* is somewhat suspect, *Schick* remains the definitive statement, unless and until the Court revises it through later opinions.

PHILLIP B. KURLAND
(1986)

Bibliography

CORWIN, EDWARD S. 1957 *The President: Office and Powers 1787–1957*, 4th ed. New York: New York University Press.

PARDONING POWER

The power of pardon—the power to relieve a person of the legal sanctions imposed for illegal conduct—was reluctantly put in the hands of the President by the CONSTITUTIONAL CONVENTION OF 1787. The reluctance derived from the fact that it was too much akin to the royal prerogative to afford dispensation to favorites from obedience to the law, a prerogative supposedly eliminated by the English BILL OF RIGHTS in 1689. The Framers were concerned lest the power should be used to shelter the treasonous activities of a President and his henchmen. The most persuasive argument on behalf of a presidential pardoning power was its potential use to reconcile warring factions. Because it would, for this purpose, be an effective tool only if it were readily available to strike a deal at any time, and because Congress was not expected to be in session all, or even most, of the time, it properly devolved on the executive.

The power of pardoning for criminal activities is all but

PARHAM v. HUGHES

See: Illegitimacy

PARHAM v. J. R.
442 U.S. 584 (1979)

The notion of "voluntary" civil commitment of mental patients takes on a special meaning when the patients are children: under a typical state's law they can be committed by the joint decision of their parents and mental hospital authorities. This case, a CLASS ACTION on behalf of all children detained in Georgia mental hospitals, was brought in order to establish a child's PROCEDURAL DUE PROCESS right to an adversary hearing before being so committed. Although the lower federal court agreed with the plaintiff's theory, the Supreme Court reversed in an opinion by Chief Justice WARREN E. BURGER.

The Court was unanimous in rejecting the broadest due

process claim in behalf of the children. There were constitutionally protected "liberty" interests at stake in a commitment, both the freedom from bodily restraint and the freedom from being falsely labeled as mentally ill. However, applying the interest-balancing calculus suggested in MATHEWS V. ELDRIDGE (1976), the Court concluded that a child's due process rights did not extend to an adversary precommitment hearing. The majority concluded that due process required no more than informal "medical" inquiries, once near the time of commitment and periodically thereafter, by a "neutral fact-finder" who would determine whether the standards for commitment were satisfied. There need be no adversary proceeding, but this neutral decision maker should interview the child.

The Court's opinion emphasized the importance of maintaining parents' traditional role in decision making for their children. (See CHILDREN'S RIGHTS.) Although some parents might abuse their authority, the law had historically "recognized that natural bonds of affection lead parents to act in the best interests of their children." On the surface, *J. R.* is a "family autonomy" decision. Yet, as Robert Burt has shown, the Court's solicitude for parental authority was expressed in the context of parental decisions validated by state officials. Other decisions suggest that the Court's primary deference runs not to parents but to "state-employed behavioral professionals."

Justice WILLIAM J. BRENNAN, for three partially dissenting Justices, agreed that pre-confinement hearings were not constitutionally required in all cases where parents sought to have their children committed, but he argued that due process did require at least one postadmission hearing. The informal inquiries approved by the Court did not moot this standard.

KENNETH L. KARST
(1986)

(SEE ALSO: *Mental Illness and the Constitution.*)

Bibliography

BURT, ROBERT A. 1979 The Constitution of the Family. *Supreme Court Review* 1979:329–395.

PARIS ADULT THEATRE I v. SLATON

See: *Miller v. California*

PARKER v. BROWN
317 U.S. 341 (1943)

A California statute compelled raisin growers to comply with the orders of a state-sponsored marketing monopoly.

Farmers could sell thirty percent of their crop on the open market; the remainder went to the state commission, which controlled the interstate supply and price. This law survived challenge when a unanimous bench followed reasoning laid out earlier by Justice HARLAN FISKE STONE in DISANTO V. PENNSYLVANIA (1927). Here Stone dismissed statutory objections: the SHERMAN ANTITRUST ACT applied only to individual, not state, action; neither did the COMMERCE CLAUSE forbid this state regulation. Most important, Congress, in the AGRICULTURAL MARKETING AGREEMENT ACT, did not preempt this state legislation but reflected a congressional policy to encourage it.

DAVID GORDON
(1986)

(SEE ALSO: *State Regulation of Commerce.*)

PARKER v. DAVIS

See: Legal Tender Cases

PARKER v. LEVY
417 U.S. 733 (1974)

In a celebrated trial of the VIETNAM WAR era, Captain Howard Levy, an Army physician, was convicted by COURT MARTIAL for violating provisions of the UNIFORM CODE OF MILITARY JUSTICE that penalized willful disobedience of the lawful command of a superior officer, "conduct unbecoming an officer and a gentleman," and conduct "to the prejudice of good order and discipline in the armed forces." The Third Circuit Court of Appeals had held that these provisions were unconstitutionally vague in violation of the DUE PROCESS clause of the Fifth Amendment and overbroad in violation of the FIRST AMENDMENT.

Justice WILLIAM H. REHNQUIST, for the Supreme Court, reversed and upheld Levy's conviction. Rehnquist's opinion rejected the contention that the provisions of the Uniform Code of Military Justice were too vague and overbroad. "The fundamental necessity for obedience, and the consequent necessity for imposition of discipline, may render permissible within the military that which would be constitutionally impermissible outside it," he wrote. Justices WILLIAM O. DOUGLAS, WILLIAM J. BRENNAN, THURGOOD MARSHALL, and POTTER STEWART dissented. The last wrote, "I cannot believe that such meaningless statutes as these can be used to send men to prison under a Constitution that guarantees due process of law."

MICHAEL E. PARRISH
(1986)

PARLIAMENTARY PRIVILEGE

Parliamentary privilege, a term originating in England, refers to a bundle of rights that Parliament and every American legislature claimed and exercised. Article I of the Constitution safeguards several of these rights, including the right of the HOUSE OF REPRESENTATIVES to choose its speaker, the right of each house to judge the elections and qualifications of members, the right of the houses to determine their own rules of procedure, and the rights of members to be free from arrest while performing their duties and to enjoy FREEDOM OF SPEECH in carrying out their duties. (See SPEECH OR DEBATE CLAUSE.) In addition, parliamentary privilege included the right, which derived from the judicial authority of Parliament, to punish for contempt.

The power to punish for contempt in both England and America proved to be incompatible with freedom of speech for critics of government, especially of the legislature. In colonial America the most suppressive body was the popularly elected assembly, which in effect enforced the law of SEDITIOUS LIBEL by punishing contempts or breaches of parliamentary privilege. An assembly, needing no GRAND JURY to indict and no PETIT JURY to convict, could summon, interrogate, and fix criminal penalties against anyone who had written, spoken, or printed words tending to impeach the assembly's conduct, question its authority, derogate from its honor, affront its dignity, or defame its members.

The practice of punishing seditious scandals or contempts against the government began in America with the first assembly that met in Virginia and continued well after the adoption of the Constitution. In 1796, for example, the New York Assembly jailed a lawyer for his offensive publications, and in 1800 the United States SENATE found a Jeffersonian editor guilty of a "high breach of privileges" because of his seditious libels. As late as 1874 the Texas legislature, having expelled a hostile journalist, ordered his imprisonment for violating its order. The Supreme Court has held that the House of Representatives has the implied power to punish for contempt. Theoretically Congress still retains that power; in practice Congress refers its charges to a federal prosecutor who seeks a grand jury INDICTMENT. (See LEGISLATIVE CONTEMPT POWER.)

LEONARD W. LEVY
(1986)

Bibliography

CLARKE, MARY PATTERSON (1943) 1971 *Parliamentary Privilege in the American Colonies*. New York: Da Capo Press.
WITTKE, CARL (1921) 1970 *The History of English Parliamentary Privilege*. New York: Da Capo Press.

PAROCHIAL SCHOOLS

See: Government Aid to Religious Institutions

PARTIES, POLITICAL

See: Political Parties; Political Parties, Elections, and Constitutional Law; Political Parties in Constitutional Law

PASSENGER CASES
7 Howard 283 (1849)

Two states imposed a tax on the masters of vessels for each ALIEN passenger they landed in the country. By a 5–4 vote, the Supreme Court held the state acts unconstitutional. Each of the Justices in the majority wrote an opinion, and none spoke for the Court. Three of the four dissenters wrote opinions. The report of the cases takes 290 pages and reflects chaos in judicial interpretation. The Justices squabbled about CONCURRENT POWERS, and the COMMERCE CLAUSE in relation to the POLICE POWER, but they settled nothing doctrinally.

LEONARD W. LEVY
(1986)

PATENT

Article I grants to Congress the power to "promote the Progress of Science and useful Arts, by securing for limited times to Authors and Inventors the exclusive Right to their respective Writings and Discoveries." This clause confers on the federal government authority to provide for both patents and COPYRIGHTS.

United States patent law derives from the English experience. During Tudor times, English monarchs granted various monopolies (such as ones over salt) to royal favorites. The populace arose against the high prices charged by such monopolies. In 1623, Parliament enacted the germinal Statute of Monopolies. The statute declared monopolies void but as an exception allowed letters patent for fourteen years to the "true and first inventors" of "new manufactures."

In America, some states prior to adoption of the Constitution granted patents to inventors. But in listing the limited and specific powers of the federal legislature, the drafters of the Constitution agreed that patents and copyrights should be among those powers. As JAMES MADISON argued in THE FEDERALIST #43, "the States cannot separately make effectual provision for either." The drafters perceived that the interests of both a unified national economy and a strong system of incentives for invention required that a patent power lie in the federal government.

The constitutional power specifies both the *end* of the patent system (progress of the useful arts) and the *means* for achieving it (secure for a limited time to inventors the exclusive right to their discoveries). The power is only an enablement and does not of its own force create any patent rights. Nevertheless, the first Congress in 1790 enacted a patent statute. An 1836 statute revised the patent laws and created the Patent Office. A 1952 statute restated the patent laws in their current form. An inventor of a new and useful product or process may obtain from the Patent Office a patent granting for a number of years (currently seventeen) the right to exclude others from making, selling, or using the invention defined by the claims in the patent.

Although most questions concerning patentability are defined by statute, the Constitution limits Congress's power to authorize patent monopolies. In *Graham v. John Deere Co. of Kansas City* (1966), the Supreme Court stressed that Congress may not authorize patents that "remove existent knowledge from the public domain." Rejecting a NATURAL RIGHTS theory of patents for inventions, the Court emphasized the utilitarian function of patents: they stimulate innovation and the disclosure of new knowledge. Patents may issue only for inventions that advance the state of technology. This constitutional standard of innovation finds expression in the patent law DOCTRINE of "nonobviousness," which bars a patent for any discovery that would have been obvious at the time of invention to a person with ordinary skill in the pertinent art who had knowledge of all the prior art.

A patent may issue for virtually any type of useful product or process. In *Diamond v. Chakrabarty* (1980), the Supreme Court upheld the potential patentability of a live, genetically altered strain of microorganism.

DONALD S. CHISUM
(1986)

Bibliography

CHISUM, DONALD S. 1978 *Patents: A Treatise on the Law of Patentability, Validity and Infringement.* New York: Matthew Bender.

MACHLUP, FRITZ 1958 An Economic Review of the Patent System. Study No. 15, Subcommittee on Patents, Trademarks & Copyrights, Judiciary Committee, 85th Congress, 2d Session.

PATENT
(Update)

A patent is a grant issued by the federal government that gives an inventor the right to exclude others from making, using, or selling his invention for a specific period of time. The historical purpose of granting these exclusive rights has not changed to this day: it is to encourage public disclosure of new scientific and technological developments that would have a favorable impact upon society and the ECONOMY.

The American patent system was largely based on early European concepts. As far back as 1440, English "letters patent" were issued for a method of processing salt. Often, however, such royal grants of monopolies were offered not to encourage invention or business development but to reward court favorites. They generated a great deal of controversy and ultimately led to passage of the Statute of Monopolies (1623), which, by making a patent an exceptional case in which exclusive rights could be granted, restricted the crown's power to confer a monopoly.

The Framers of the Constitution, realizing the importance of stimulating science and technology, authorized Congress to establish and control a patent system. In September 1787 the CONSTITUTIONAL CONVENTION adopted Article I, section 8: "The Congress shall have Power . . . To promote the Progress of Science and useful Arts, by securing for limited Times to Authors and Inventors the exclusive Right to their respective Writings and Discoveries."

Congress exercised this power by passing the Patent Act of 1790. The statute placed the burden of granting patents upon a committee made up of the secretary of state, the secretary of war, and the ATTORNEY GENERAL. Secretary of State THOMAS JEFFERSON, an early champion of the idea that "ingenuity should receive liberal encouragement," became the first patent examiner.

For several decades there was no requirement that an inventor demonstrate his invention's patentability (its novelty and usefulness) in order to obtain exclusive rights. As a result, a patent was issued almost immediately upon receipt of an application. The process was modified in 1836, when the commissioner of patents was charged with examining every proposal to determine that an invention was both new and useful in concept (though not necessarily that it worked well in practice). These criteria are still applied, together with a requirement that the invention must be "unobvious to one skilled in the art."

Patents are to be distinguished from trademarks and COPYRIGHTS; generally, the claiming of one does not preclude the claiming of any other, even though they may all apply to a single product. A copyright protects an author's original writing (the tangible expression of an idea). A trademark covers any words used to distinguish one product from another. For example, a computer's interior mechanism and software may be protected by a patent, its instruction manual by a copyright, and its market identification by a trademark. All three legal protections are now considered part of a larger jurisprudential framework called "intellectual property."

A patent may be obtained by anyone who invents or discovers a new, useful, and "unobvious" device or process. If a patent is granted, the inventor gains exclusive rights for a period of seventeen years (fourteen years for the developer of a new design). Any unauthorized manufacture, use, or sale of a patented device or design (or their equivalents) constitutes an infringement.

Patent cases begin at the district court level, may be appealed to the UNITED STATES COURT OF APPEALS FOR THE FEDERAL CIRCUIT, and can be reviewed by the Supreme Court. In *Graham v. John Deere Co. of Kansas City* (1968) the Court defined the three statutory conditions of patentability: novelty, usefulness, and nonobviousness. The classic modern doctrine of "equivalents" was described in *Graver Tank & Manufacturing Co. v. Linde Air Products Co.* (1950). One of the largest recent infringement cases was *Polaroid Corp. v. Eastman Kodak Co.* (1989).

KENNETH LASSON
(1992)

Bibliography

CHISUM, DONALD S. 1978 *Patents: A Treatise on the Law of Patentability, Validity and Infringement.* New York: Matthew Bender.

DELLER, ANTHONY W. 1964 *Walker on Patents.* New York: Lawyers Co-operative.

LASSON, KENNETH 1986 *Mousetraps and Muffling Cups: One Hundred Brilliant and Bizarre United States Patents.* New York: Arbor House.

PATERSON, WILLIAM
(1745–1806)

William Paterson played a major role in the framing of the United States Constitution. His stubborn advocacy of state equality influenced the kind of government that was formed. He also was an active member of the United States Supreme Court who served as an important link between the Framers of the Constitution and the Supreme Court of JOHN MARSHALL.

Born in Ireland, Paterson moved to New Jersey at an early age, graduated from the College of New Jersey (Princeton), studied law, and was admitted to the bar in 1768. Supporting the movement for independence, he soon became a prominent member of New Jersey's revolutionary generation and served in its provincial legislature. Paterson drafted the state's first constitution and became its first attorney general. During the 1780s he built up his legal practice by defending the interests of wealthy landowners and creditors. In the political battles of that decade he advocated the supremacy of the peace treaty of 1783 over state laws, opposed the emission of paper money, and supported the movement to create a strong central government.

In 1787 New Jersey selected Paterson as one of its delegates to the CONSTITUTIONAL CONVENTION. Although he favored increasing the power of the national government, Paterson vigorously opposed the proposal of the VIRGINIA PLAN, as drafted by JAMES MADISON and presented by EDMUND RANDOLPH, that REPRESENTATION in both houses of the national legislature be apportioned according to population. Paterson feared this provision would give too much power to the larger states and place smaller states like New Jersey, Connecticut, and Delaware at a disadvantage. As an alternative he proposed the NEW JERSEY PLAN of government. Its principal feature was the continuance of the unicameral legislature of the ARTICLES OF CONFEDERATION in which each state had only one vote. The plan also would have: provided the federal government with the power to levy imposts and regulate trade and collect funds from states that did not comply with federal requisitions; created a Supreme Court with broad powers; and made the laws and treaties of the United States the supreme law of the land, with the state judiciaries bound to obey them despite any contrary state laws. Should a state or individuals within a state refuse to obey the laws of Congress or its treaties, the federal government would have had the right to use force to compel obedience. In other words, the central issue separating the proponents of the New Jersey Plan from those who favored the Virginia Plan was representation, not nationalism. Although the convention rejected Paterson's proposal, the delegates from the small states remained strongly opposed to proportional representation in Congress. In fact, the convention almost foundered on this issue, but it finally resolved the matter by adopting the so-called GREAT COMPROMISE that provided for representation by population in the lower house of a bicameral Congress and equal representation of each state in the upper house. With this matter settled, Paterson threw his complete support behind the new Constitution.

In 1789 the New Jersey legislature elected Paterson to the first United States Senate where, along with OLIVER ELLSWORTH, he helped to write the JUDICIARY ACT OF 1789. This law created a system of lower federal courts, broadly defined their JURISDICTION, created the office of attorney general, and gave the Supreme Court APPELLATE JURISDICTION over the final decisions of state courts in all matters relating to the Constitution and federal laws and treaties. As a senator, Paterson also enthusiastically supported ALEXANDER HAMILTON's proposals to fund the national debt at face value with full interest, and for the federal government to assume all state debts. In November 1790 Paterson resigned his seat in the Senate to become governor of New Jersey. In this capacity he undertook the task of codifying the state's laws, which were published in 1800. He also worked closely with Hamilton in 1791 to form the generally unsuccessful "Society for Establishing Useful Manufactures"; the society created a small industrial city on the banks of the Passaic River, which became known as Paterson.

Early in 1793 President GEORGE WASHINGTON appointed Paterson to the United States Supreme Court. For the next decade he had an active career on the bench participating in almost all the important decisions rendered by the high court. These decisions reveal Paterson to have been, above all else, a firm advocate of the supremacy of the federal over the state governments. In *Penhallow v. Doane's Administrators* (1795) he expounded an extremely nationalist interpretation of the origins and nature of the Union, arguing that even during the 1780s the Continental Congress represented the "supreme will" of the American people. In the important and controversial case of WARE V. HYLTON (1796) Paterson held that the treaty of peace with Great Britain (1783), which guaranteed that no legal obstacles would be placed in the way of the recovery of debts owed by Americans to British creditors, was part of the "supreme law of the land," rendering invalid a Virginia statute (1777) that allowed the sequestration of debts owed to British subjects before the Revolution.

Paterson also believed in a strong and independent judiciary. In 1795 while on circuit in Pennsylvania he delivered an opinion in VAN HORNE'S LESSEE V. DORRANCE that espoused the doctrine of VESTED RIGHTS and the right of the courts to void a statute repugnant to the Constitution. Although the case involved a state law that contradicted a state constitution, Paterson's argument had broader theoretical implications, and his remarks on the subject of JUDICIAL REVIEW are the fullest and most important statements by a Justice of the United States Supreme Court before John Marshall's opinion in MARBURY V. MADISON (1803). In HYLTON V. UNITED STATES (1796) Paterson agreed with the other Justices in upholding the constitutionality of a federal tax on carriages enacted in 1794. Because the key issue was whether the carriage tax was a DIRECT TAX or an excise tax, Paterson's opinion contained a long discussion of the intention of the Framers of the Constitution as to what kinds of taxes required apportionment among the states according to population. Paterson also expounded on the intention of the Framers in *Calder v. Bull* (1798) when he concurred with the rest of the Court in interpreting the provision of Article I, section 10, prohibiting state legislatures from enacting EX POST FACTO laws as extending only to criminal, not civil laws.

Like so many Federalists, Paterson refused to recognize the legitimacy of the Republican opposition during the 1790s. When Congress passed the ALIEN AND SEDITION ACTS, in 1798, he vigorously enforced them. While riding circuit in Vermont he urged a federal grand jury to indict Democratic-Republican Congressman Matthew Lyon for bringing the President and the federal government into disrepute with his various criticisms. "No government," Paterson observed, "can long subsist when offenders of this kind are suffered to spread their poison with impunity." In the trial that followed Paterson continued to pursue Lyon, emphasizing that the tendency of the Congressman's words be made the test of his intent. Paterson also made clear his belief that the Supreme Court alone had the final authority to determine the constitutionality of laws of Congress, a position the Republican defense had denied. After the jury convicted Lyon, Paterson imposed a harsh sentence of four months in jail and a $1,000 fine. In 1800 Paterson also presided over the trial of Anthony Haswell, a Bennington, Vermont, newspaperman who had rallied to Lyon's defense, and following Haswell's conviction sentenced him to two months in prison and fined him $200. Paterson's actions during the crisis of 1798, along with those of SAMUEL CHASE, are among the clearest examples of the partisan nature of the Federalist judiciary during the late 1790s. Many Jeffersonians were incensed by the proceedings, and had the attempt to remove Chase from the Supreme Court proven successful in 1805, they probably would have gone after Paterson next.

When Oliver Ellsworth resigned as Chief Justice in 1800, most Federalists in the Senate felt the post should go to Paterson. But by then President JOHN ADAMS had openly broken with the Hamiltonian wing of the party, and he appointed John Marshall instead. Paterson accepted this development graciously; in fact, he described the new Chief Justice as "a man of genius" whose "talents have at once the lustre and solidity of gold." When the Jeffersonians took political power in 1801, Paterson backed away from his earlier extremism and supported Marshall's strategy of avoiding direct political confrontations with the Republican majority in Congress. When the JUDICIARY ACT OF 1801 was repealed, some of the more belligerent Federalists, including Justice Chase, wanted the Supreme Court to declare the repeal act unconstitutional. Riding circuit in Virginia, Marshall opposed this strategy, and declared the law constitutional in STUART V. LAIRD. The decision was immediately appealed to the Supreme Court where Marshall would not be allowed to participate in the case because he had already ruled on it in the lower court. In early 1803 Paterson delivered the Supreme Court's decision on the question. Not only did he side with Marshall, he delivered a warning to the more combative Federalists that "the question is at rest and ought not now to be disturbed." Among other things, the decision clearly indicated that the Federalist-dominated Supreme Court was willing to acquiesce in the "Revolution of 1800." It also went a long way toward reducing concerns, at least among moderates in THOMAS JEFFERSON's administration, about the high court's tendency to engage in partisan politics.

In the fall of 1803, Paterson was injured in a carriage accident. He missed the February 1804 term of the Supreme Court; and although he rode circuit the following year, he never fully recovered. He died in 1806.

RICHARD E. ELLIS
(1986)

Bibliography

GOEBEL, JULIUS, JR. 1971 *History of the Supreme Court of the United States, Vol. I: Antecedents and Beginnings to 1801.* New York: Macmillan.

O'CONNOR, JOHN E. 1979 *William Paterson: Lawyer and Statesman, 1745–1806.* New Brunswick, N.J.: Rutgers University Press.

PATERSON PLAN

See: New Jersey Plan

PATIENTS' RIGHTS

The constitutional status of patients' rights can be distilled into three general doctrinal propositions: First, there are constitutional constraints on state authority to force medical treatment on an unwilling person; second, when a person is in state custody (for whatever reason), the state is constitutionally obliged to provide at least minimally adequate health care; and third, the state is not otherwise constitutionally required to provide even a minimal level of health care to anyone. The Supreme Court has not been so solicitous, however, toward implementing the first and second propositions as it has been toward the third.

The Court long ago held, in JACOBSON V. MASSACHUSETTS (1905) regarding smallpox vaccination, that an individual may be constitutionally subjected to involuntary medical treatment to protect community health. Beginning in the 1970s, in cases involving MENTAL ILLNESS, the Court found that forced treatment implicated FOURTEENTH AMENDMENT "liberty" interests and, accordingly, required the state to demonstrate, by "clear and convincing evidence," both the existence of mental illness and some measure of harm either to the affected individual or others that would follow without treatment. The principal decisions in this area were O'CONNOR V. DONALDSON (1975) and *Addington v. Texas* (1979). The Court, however, has not been expansive in applying the "liberty" principle to require state respect for individuals' autonomous choice to refuse treatment even where the possibility of harm appears limited to themselves alone.

Two 1990 decisions exemplify this restrictive construction. In *Washington v. Harper* (1990) the Court ruled that a prisoner could be forced to take psychotropic medication without any judicial determination of his or her need for the medication or mental competency to refuse it. While the Court acknowledged the existence of a "significant liberty interest" and said that the state's purposes in forcibly administering the medication must be "therapeutic" rather than "punitive," the Court found that internal administrative determinations made by prison psychiatric professionals would be adequate to protect the PRISONER'S RIGHTS.

Cruzan v. Missouri Department of Health (1990) considered the rights of patients to refuse medical treatment in an apparently different context; and yet, the result, in the Court's restricted construction of the liberty interest at stake, seems strikingly similar. In *Cruzan*, the patient was in a state hospital, having been without cognitive function (in a "persistent vegetative state") since an automobile accident seven years earlier. Hospital staff refused to discontinue medical treatment without judicial authorization, notwithstanding the request of the patient's parents, and the state court found that there was no "clear and convincing evidence" that patient herself would have wanted termination of treatment. The Supreme Court ruled that a competent adult had a Fourteenth Amendment liberty interest against unconsented medical care, but that the state was free to erect stringent evidentiary standards in evaluating claims on behalf of incompetent patients.

There were special factors in these two cases that might have limited the Court's inclination to apply the liberty interest that it abstractly had endorsed. In *Harper*, the Court cited "legitimate needs of institutional confinement," including state "interests in prison safety and security," as a basis for withholding application of the prisoner's claimed right to refuse medication; there was, however, no specific factual finding that the prisoner's condition endangered prison safety or security. In *Cruzan*, the autonomy claim was advanced on behalf of an obviously incompetent patient; there was, however, evidence (which the state court refused to credit) that before her incapacitating accident, the patient had explicitly opposed such medical treatment. In accepting the restrictive evidentiary standard, the Supreme Court was apparently unconcerned with the practical likelihood that most people will not make clear prior indications of their wishes regarding medical treatment (notwithstanding the statutory recognition in many states of so-called "living wills"). The Court, moreover, referred favorably to the state's interest in prohibiting suicide, a reference that suggests that the state is free to impose stringent mental competency tests on individuals who, unlike Cruzan, have current capacity to articulate their resistance to treatment—tests so stringent as to undermine in practice the liberty interest to refuse medical treatment that the Court abstractly endorsed.

The Court may, however, be more hospitable to the practical implementation of patients' right to refuse treatment in future cases than it was in *Harper* or *Cruzan*. Indeed, there were strong dissents in both cases (three in *Harper* and four in *Cruzan*) urging respect for the refusal rights and although Justice SANDRA DAY O'CONNOR concurred in the Court's opinion in *Cruzan*, she wrote separately to suggest that states may be constitutionally required to respect not only prior formal statements made by an individual, as in a "living will," but also the wishes of a surrogate decision maker who had been formally designated by the individual before incapacitating illness.

As in the current constitutional doctrine regarding a patient's right to refuse treatment, there is a disjunction in the Supreme Court's case law between the abstract formulation that the state must provide medical treatment to persons in its custody and the specific standards adopted to assure practical implementation of that right. The disjunction was visible on the face of the first opinion in which the Court announced that prisoners have a right to medical treatment: In *Estelle v. Gamble* (1976) the Court held that failure to provide necessary treatment could constitute CRUEL AND UNUSUAL PUNISHMENT in violation of the Eighth Amendment, but only if such failure amounted to a "deliberate indifference to serious medical needs." Similarly, in *Youngberg v. Romeo* (1982), the Court found that a resident of a state mental retardation institution had a constitutional right to receive "minimally adequate or reasonable training" programs; at the same time, however, the Court held that in determining the minimal standards for adequacy of reasonableness, judges must defer to medical and behavioral professionals. (Indeed, in Chief Justice WILLIAM H. REHNQUIST's opinion for the Court in *Cruzan*, the force even of this minimally bestowed treatment right was subtly undermined with the observation that "the liberty interest" in *Youngberg* addressed only "safety and freedom from bodily restraint [and] did not deal with decisions to administer or withhold medical treatment.")

Whatever the uncertainties of its acknowledgment of the right to refuse medical treatment or the right to receive treatment while in state custody, the Court has been quite clear in rejecting the existence of any generally applicable constitutional right for the provision of medical services. The Court explicitly stated in *Youngberg* that there was no such right to "substantive services." In MAHER V. ROE (1977) and HARRIS V. MCRAE (1980), moreover, the Court had held that neither state nor federal governments are constitutionally required to provide ABORTIONS for women who are INDIGENT; although these cases were col-

ored by the surrounding public controversy about whether abortion should be considered an ordinary medical procedure, the decisions are nonetheless consistent with the Court's long-standing resistance to finding any constitutional ENTITLEMENTS not only for medical care but for WELFARE BENEFITS generally.

In *Cruzan* none of the other Court members joined with Justice ANTONIN SCALIA in his separate statement that "the Constitution has nothing to say" about the right to refuse medical treatment. Notwithstanding the pervasive role of state and federal governments in the provision and regulation of health care, however, the Constitution—as currently construed by the Supreme Court—says very little about patients' rights generally.

ROBERT A. BURT
(1992)

Bibliography

ANNAS, GEORGE J.; LAW, SYLVIA; ROSENBLATTE, RAND; and WING, KENNETH 1990 *American Health Law.* Chapter VI, pages 561–666. Boston: Little, Brown.

KATZ, JAY 1984 *The Silent World of Doctor and Patient.* New York: Free Press.

PATRONAGE

Political patronage has had a long tradition in parts of the United States, particularly in cities dominated by so-called "machine politics." Patronage entails government officials' exchanging government jobs or other discretionary government benefits for political support. In the first Mayor Daley's Chicago, for example, city employees were expected to work for the election of Democratic Party candidates as well as to contribute 2 percent of their salary to the party if they wanted to keep their jobs.

Beginning with a PLURALITY OPINION in the 1976 case of *Elrod v. Burns,* the Supreme Court has made it increasingly difficult for government officials to take party affiliation into account in making employment or contracting decisions. In *Elrod,* the newly elected Democratic sheriff of Cook County, Illinois sought to fire Republican employees in the Sheriff's office. Justice WILLIAM J. BRENNAN, JR., in a three-Justice plurality opinion, held that firing a government employee based solely on the employee's party affiliation violated the employee's FIRST AMENDMENT right of FREEDOM OF ASSOCIATION. Two additional Justices concurred in the result that the sheriff's conduct violated the First Amendment.

The sheriff had argued that patronage practices could be justified on three grounds: (1) insuring effective government and the efficiency of public employees; (2) insuring employees' political loyalty so that employees would not block implementation of a new administration's policies; and (3) preserving the democratic process through a strong party system. Applying STRICT SCRUTINY, the *Elrod* plurality rejected the first and third of these interests outright. It stated that the sheriff's interest in effective and efficient government could be protected through the less restrictive means of discharging employees for cause. It also disbelieved that the elimination of patronage practices would bring about the demise of party politics.

The plurality agreed that the sheriff's second asserted ground of insuring employees' political loyalty was valid insofar as it applied to employees in "policymaking positions," but it did not serve to "validate patronage wholesale." In the 1980 case of *Branti v. Finkel,* a majority further explained that a government official could take party affiliation into account in firing employees only when such affiliation is "an appropriate requirement for the effective performance of the public office involved." The *Branti* Court held that party affiliation was not an appropriate requirement for an assistant public defender.

Justice LEWIS F. POWELL, JR., dissented in both *Elrod* and *Branti,* arguing in both cases that political patronage strengthened POLITICAL PARTIES, and that strong political parties are required for effective democratic government. He also argued in *Branti* that the policymaking test articulated by the majority was uncertain and ill-advised.

In *Rutan v. Republican Party of Illinois* (1990), a 5–4 majority extended the *Elrod* rule to other employment decisions, including hiring, promotions, transfers, and recalls of employees after layoffs. Justice ANTONIN SCALIA wrote a scathing dissent, raising and elaborating on many of the points Powell had made in his earlier dissents. Besides arguing that the *Elrod* line should be overturned, Scalia contended that strict scrutiny should not be applied to cases in which the government acted as an employer.

Four of the five Justices in the *Rutan* majority left the Court before it decided its most recent pair of patronage cases in 1996, *O'Hare Truck Service v. City of Northlake* and *Umbehr v. Heiser,* leading commentators to predict that the Court would use these decisions to reverse the *Elrod* line. In the event, Chief Justice WILLIAM H. REHNQUIST, and Justices ANTHONY M. KENNEDY and SANDRA DAY O'CONNOR switched sides from their dissenting position in *Rutan.* Kennedy, writing for a 7–2 majority in *O'Hare,* held that the *Elrod* rule applied to independent contractors.

In an important development, the Court in *Umbehr* and *O'Hare* distinguished the *Elrod* line of cases, in which government based its employment decisions solely on the employee's party affiliation, from the *Pickering v. Board of Education* (1968) line of cases, in which government based its employment decisions on its employee's speech, such as employee speech criticizing the government. *Elrod* places the burden on the hiring authority to show that a political affiliation requirement is appropriate for the effective performance of the employee's office. In contrast, *Pickering* requires a balancing of the employee's rights with the government's legitimate interest as an employer in the latter.

After holding in *O'Hare* and *Umbehr* that independent contractors of the government must receive the same constitutional protection as government employees, the *O'Hare* Court explained that the initial question in future patronage cases must be whether the government's decision was based purely on the employee's or contractor's party affiliation or whether it also (or solely) involved the employee's or contractor's speech. Cases in the first category are governed by *Elrod,* but mixed cases of affiliation and speech (as well as pure speech cases) are governed by *Pickering.* Scalia in dissent believed this standard is unworkable, asking for example whether the statement "I am a Republican" moves a case from *Elrod* strict scrutiny to *Pickering* balancing. Most probably, the *Elrod* line henceforth will be reserved primarily for cases involving wholesale, nonindividualized decisions by the government to condition employment or contracting on the party affiliation of the employees or contractors.

Though the debate over the constitutionality of patronage turns in part on the Justices' varied beliefs about how coercive or unfair a party affiliation requirement is to government employees or contractors, the most contentious issue appears to be whether patronage practices support a strong democratic government. The majority in the *Elrod* line of cases characterizes patronage as inefficient and corrupt, and especially prone to entrenchment of one-party rule. The dissenters have a more benign view of patronage, noting its abuses but contending that states should have the right to find an optimal mix of patronage and merit that can strengthen the major political parties. Though a majority of the Court now appears to believe that the state has a strong interest in promoting the two-party system, TIMMONS V. TWIN CITIES AREA NEW PARTY (1997), no current majority believes that patronage practices promote the two-party system.

In part, the debate over the virtues of patronage comes too late. The replacement of party-centered, labor-intensive political campaigns with candidate-centered, capital-intensive ones has lessened politicians' demand for patronage employment. Politicians want money for media campaigns, not precinct workers. This increased demand for campaign contributions puts pressure on politicians to exchange government favors, including contracts, for such contributions. *O'Hare,* however, limits these exchanges, making it the patronage case most likely to have a strong effect on our political system.

RICHARD L. HASEN
(2000)

(SEE ALSO: *Employee Speech Rights (Public); Freedom of Speech.*)

Bibliography

BOWMAN, CYNTHIA GRANT 1991 "We Don't Want Anybody Anybody Sent": The Death of Patronage Hiring in Chicago. *Northwestern University Law Review* 86:57–95.

—— 1996 The Law of Patronage at a Crossroads. *Journal of Law and Politics* 12:341–363.

HASEN, RICHARD L. 1993 An Enriched Economic Model of Political Patronage and Campaign Contributions: Reformulating Supreme Court Jurisprudence. *Cardozo Law Review* 14:1311–1341.

JOHNSON, RONALD N. and LIBECAP, GARY D. 1994 *The Federal Civil Service System and the Problem of Bureaucracy: The Economics and Politics of Institutional Change.* Chicago: University of Chicago Press.

PATTERSON v. MCLEAN CREDIT UNION
491 U.S. 164 (1989)

This decision's constitutional significance lies in what the Supreme Court did not do. The CIVIL RIGHTS ACT OF 1866 guarantees "all persons . . . the same right . . . to make and enforce contracts . . . as is enjoyed by white persons." In RUNYON V. MCCRARY (1976) the Court had held that this provision not only required a state to give blacks and whites the same legal rights in contracting but also forbade private racial discrimination in the making of contracts. Later decisions had applied the same section to employment contracts. *Patterson* raised the issue of whether this section gave a black employee a right to damages against her employer for acts of racial harassment. In 1988, after oral argument on this issue and without any prompting from the parties, a 5–4 majority of the Court set the case down for reargument and asked the parties to consider whether *Runyon v. McCrary* should be overruled.

Four Justices bitterly dissented from this order, and outside the Court a clamor of protest rose. The majority that supported the order consisted of the two *Runyon* dissenters and the three Justices appointed by President RONALD REAGAN, and the order appeared to be the opening salvo in an assault on some of the major gains of the CIVIL RIGHTS MOVEMENT. If *Runyon* were overruled, why should the Court not overrule JONES V. ALFRED H. MAYER CO. (1968)? *Jones* was the landmark decision that (1) interpreted a parallel provision of the 1866 Act to forbid private racial discrimination in the disposition of property, and (2) upheld the law, as so interpreted, on the basis of Congress's power to enforce the THIRTEENTH AMENDMENT. The latter possibility seems, in retrospect, to have been unlikely, but the depth of concern is understandable. Sixty-six United States senators and 118 representatives

filed a brief urging the Court not to overrule *Runyon*, and so did the attorneys general of forty-seven states.

In the event, the Court unanimously reaffirmed the *Runyon* PRECEDENT. The majority opinion (the same majority that had agreed on the reargument order) simply applied the doctrine of STARE DECISIS. The Court went on to read the 1866 act extremely narrowly, rejecting the conclusion of most lower federal courts that the law allowed damages for a private employer's racial harassment of an employee.

Patterson's narrow interpretation of the 1866 act is vulnerable to criticism, as the opinion of the four dissenters and Congress's recent effort to overturn it both attest. But the Court's reaffirmation of *Runyon* stants as the doctrinal consolidation of a broad political consensus on CIVIL RIGHTS that had seemed threatened in the 1980s.

KENNETH L. KARST
(1992)

Bibliography

KARST, KENNETH L. 1989 Private Discrimination and Public Responsibility: Patterson in Context. *Supreme Court Review* 1989:1–51.

PATTON v. UNITED STATES
281 U.S. 276 (1930)

In this case a unanimous Supreme Court, speaking through Justice GEORGE SUTHERLAND, held that the constitutional right to a jury in a federal court included exactly twelve members who were to render a unanimous verdict. (See JURY SIZE; JURY UNANIMITY.) Sutherland also declared that a defendant might waive his right to a jury or consent to a jury of less than twelve. Forty years later, in WILLIAMS V. FLORIDA (1970), a case involving a state court, the Court held that fixing the number of required jurors at twelve was a "historical accident" and "cannot be regarded as an indispensable component of the Sixth Amendment."

DAVID GORDON
(1986)

(SEE ALSO: *Waiver of Constitutional Rights.*)

PAUL v. DAVIS
424 U.S. 693 (1976)

Even before GOLDBERG V. KELLY (1970) the Supreme Court assumed that the guarantee of PROCEDURAL DUE PROCESS attached to state impairments of "liberty" or "property" interests—concepts that bore their own constitutional meanings as well as their traditional COMMON LAW meanings. *Goldberg* and its successors added to those meanings a new category of protected "entitlements" established by statute or other state action. BISHOP V. WOOD (1976) and *Paul v. Davis* turned this development upside down, using the idea of "entitlements" under state law to *confine* the reach of due process.

In *Paul*, police officers circulated a flyer containing the names and photographs of persons described as "active shoplifters." Davis, one of those listed, had been arrested and charged with shoplifting, but the case had not been prosecuted and the charge had been dismissed. He sued a police officer in a federal district court, claiming damages for a violation of his federal constitutional rights. The Supreme Court held, 5–3, that the alleged harm to Davis's reputation did not, of itself, amount to impairment of a "liberty" interest protected by the due process guarantee. For the majority, Justice WILLIAM H. REHNQUIST manhandled precedents that had established reputation as a "core" constitutionally protected interest, asserting that the Court had previously offered protection to reputation only when it was harmed along with some other interest established by state law, such as a right to employment. Justice WILLIAM J. BRENNAN, for the dissenters, showed how disingenuous was this characterization of the precedents.

Probably the majority's main concern was to keep the federal CIVIL RIGHTS laws from becoming a generalized law of torts committed by state officers, with the federal courts as the primary forum. Yet the majority opinion cannot be taken at face value. Unquestionably the notion of "liberty" interests protected by due process still includes a great many interests not defined by state law, such as FIRST AMENDMENT liberties.

KENNETH L. KARST
(1986)

PAUL v. VIRGINIA
8 Wallace 168 (1869)

In 1866, Virginia prohibited out-of-state insurance companies from doing business without a substantial deposit; domestic companies were not so required. Convicted of violating the 1866 act, Paul filed a WRIT OF ERROR and BENJAMIN R. CURTIS argued his case. Justice STEPHEN J. FIELD, for a unanimous Supreme Court, rejected Paul's Article IV PRIVILEGES AND IMMUNITIES argument, declaring that CITIZENSHIP could apply only to natural persons. Field further asserted that insurance contracts were not articles of commerce and that the issuance of a policy was not a transaction in INTERSTATE COMMERCE. *Paul* was often cited as a limitation on congressional power on the incorrect assumption that congressional and state regulatory power were mutually exclusive. *Paul* remained law until virtually

overturned in UNITED STATES V. SOUTH-EASTERN UNDERWRITERS ASSOCIATION (1944), involving congressional power, after which Congress authorized state regulation.

DAVID GORDON
(1986)

PAXTON'S CASE
Gray, *Mass. Repts.*, 51 469 (1761)

In *Paxton's Case*, the Massachusetts Superior Court considered whether to continue issuing WRITS OF ASSISTANCE, which, by a British statute of 1662, empowered customs officers to search all houses for contraband. Massachusetts opposed these writs; its legislation had repudiated the general SEARCH WARRANTS they resembled in favor of uniformly specific warrants. Other stimulants to the case were frequent searches under the writs, tense relations with local British customs officers, the belief that customs regulations had been enforced against local merchants with discriminatory rigor, and the thwarted ambitions of the powerful Otis family for appointment to the Superior Court.

The death of King George II terminated existing writs after six months, and local merchants asked the court not to replace them. In the initial hearing Josiah Gridley argued the positions of the customs establishment that the act of 1662 defined writs of assistance as general search warrants and that a local statute had empowered the court to issue them by giving it the same jurisdiction as the one that issued them in England. Oxenbridge Thacher and JAMES OTIS, JR., representing the merchants, inaccurately replied that the local court had not recently exercised the powers of the English tribunal, the Court of Exchequer.

Otis, son of the candidate for a seat on the Superior Court, cited a magazine article to prove that the writs did not currently operate as GENERAL WARRANTS in Britain and had not been so intended by the statute of 1662. Legions of British laws authorized general searches, however, and Otis relied primarily on the HIGHER LAW. Since general searches allegedly violated natural and COMMON LAW, Otis reasoned that writs of assistance were intrinsically void if worded as the statute prescribed and should be judicially construed as specific search warrants.

Otis's use of sources was heavily didactic. He cited Sir EDWARD COKE, whose *Institutes* exaggerated MAGNA CARTA into a prohibition of general search warrants, and he wrongly read into Coke a further requirement that all search warrants be specific. Otis also stretched BONHAM'S CASE (1610) to hold that common law courts could "control" unreasonable Parliamentary legislation and render it void. Only private interests had actually clashed in *Bon-*

ham's Case, not levels of law or government as Otis implied. Although Otis had not advised the court explicitly to disallow a Parliamentary statute, he misused *Bonham's Case* to advocate a judicial construction of the act that would have had the effect of disallowance.

Persuaded by Otis's eloquence, the court delayed its decision, found that the writs used in England were general, and approved their local issuance over Otis's continued objections. The Massachusetts legislature responded by reducing the salaries of the judges and passing a bill, vetoed by the governor, to define the writs as specific warrants. THOMAS HUTCHINSON, whose appointment as Chief Justice had blocked the judicial aspirations of the Otises, later traced his political demise to his courtroom support of writs of assistance. *Paxton's Case* is one of the leading precedents for the FOURTH AMENDMENT and probably inspired the rejection by later Massachusetts courts (1763–1766) of customary search warrants against felons in *Bassett v. Mayhew* and other cases.

WILLIAM J. CUDDIHY
(1986)

Bibliography

SMITH, M. H. 1978 *The Writs of Assistance Case.* Berkeley: University of California Press.

PAYNE v. TENNESSEE
501 U.S. 808 (1991)

Writing for a 6–3 majority, Chief Justice WILLIAM H. REHNQUIST held that victim impact evidence in CAPITAL PUNISHMENT cases is not barred by the Eighth Amendment's CRUEL AND UNUSUAL PUNISHMENT clause. *Payne* OVERRULED a contrary decision, BOOTH V. MARYLAND (1987), handed down only four years earlier by a Court divided 5–4.

The drug-crazed and sexually driven Payne stabbed to death a young mother and her two-year-old daughter, and attacked and seriously injured her three-year-old son. At Payne's trial, the grandmother was allowed to testify that the boy cried for his lost relatives. The prosecutor, in closing argument, poignantly portrayed a child in mourning, who would never be kissed good-night by his mother or be able to play with his little sister.

In upholding the admission of testimony relating to the effect of the murders on the boy, the majority rejected *Booth's* holding that victim impact evidence subverts the reasoned decisionmaking process required for the imposition of the death penalty. Rehnquist denied that victim impact evidence introduced factors irrelevant to proper sentencing goals (such as retribution and deterrence) or encouraged jurors to base sentences on the perceived moral or social worth of victims or their families (thereby creating an impermissible risk that the penalty would be determined arbitrarily). Rather, he opined, victim impact evidence is designed to show each victim's uniqueness as a human being and provides a needed counterweight to the virtually unlimited proof that the defendant is permitted to adduce concerning his circumstances, character, and record.

In dissent, Justice JOHN PAUL STEVENS echoed the arguments accepted in *Booth*, while Justice THURGOOD MARSHALL accused the majority of abandoning PRECEDENT solely because of a change in the personnel of the Court.

VIVIAN BERGER
(2000)

Bibliography

BERGER, VIVIAN 1992 *Payne* and Suffering—A Personal Reflection and a Victim-Centered Critique. *Florida State Law Review* 20:21–65.

COYNE, RANDALL 1992 Inflicting *Payne* on Oklahoma: The Use of Victim Impact Evidence During the Sentencing Phase of Capital Cases. *Oklahoma Law Review* 45:589–628.

PAYTON v. NEW YORK
445 U.S. 573 (1980)

The FOURTH AMENDMENT, which the FOURTEENTH makes applicable to the states, says that the "right of people to be secure in their . . . houses . . . shall not be violated." *Payton* was the first case in which the Supreme Court confronted the issue whether police may enter a private home, without an ARREST WARRANT or consent, to make a FELONY arrest. New York, sustained by its courts, authorized warrantless ARRESTS, by forcible entry if necessary, in any premises, if the police had PROBABLE CAUSE to believe a person had committed a felony. In Payton's case the police seized EVIDENCE in PLAIN VIEW at the time of arrest and used it to convict him.

A 6–3 Supreme Court, in an opinion by Justice JOHN PAUL STEVENS, reversed and held the state statute unconstitutional. Absent EXIGENT CIRCUMSTANCES, "a man's house is his castle" and unlike a public place may not be invaded without a warrant. Stevens found slight guidance in history for his position on the special privacy of the home in the case of a felony arrest, but he insisted that the Fourth Amendment required a magistrate's warrant. Justice BYRON R. WHITE for the dissenters declared that the decision distorted history and severely hampered law enforcement; the amendment required only that a warrantless felony arrest be made on probable cause in daytime. (See STEAGALD V. UNITED STATES.)

LEONARD W. LEVY
(1986)

PECKHAM, RUFUS W.
(1838–1909)

Rufus Wheeler Peckham, the last of President GROVER CLEVELAND's four appointees to the Supreme Court, was commissioned in 1896 following eight years of service on the New York Court of Appeals. His name is linked most often with one of the half dozen most fulsomely denounced Supreme Court decisions in American history. Speaking for a majority of five in LOCHNER V. NEW YORK (1905), Peckham invoked the SUBSTANTIVE DUE PROCESS doctrine of "liberty of contract," which he had established in an incipient form in ALLGEYER V. LOUISIANA (1897), and invalidated a statute regulating the hours worked by bakeshop employees. (See FREEDOM OF CONTRACT.) Peckham's opinion infuriated progressive reformers, evoked one of Justice OLIVER WENDELL HOLMES's most famous dissents, and ultimately contributed a new term to the lexicon of constitutional discourse in America. More than four generations later, "Lochnerism" is habitually used by commentators to describe the horrible consequences of interventionist JUDICIAL REVIEW in defense of doctrinally abstract constitutional rights.

Holmes once remarked that the "major premise" of Peckham's jurisprudence was "God damn it." It was an apt observation. Peckham was outraged by the increasing propensity of state legislatures and the Congress to transcend "the proper functions of government," and he not only conceptualized the judicial function in essentially negative terms but also regarded the Court as an appropriate forum for battling the ominous evils of centralization and socialism. For Peckham, the Court's role in constitutional adjudication was to police the boundaries separating the rights of the individual, the powers of the states, and the authority of the general government in such a way as to keep each within its proper sphere. Otherwise, he warned while still on the New York bench, "in addition to the ordinary competition that exists throughout all industries, a new competition will be introduced, that of competition for the possession of the government."

Peckham had boundless confidence in his capacity to draw objective lines between these mutually limiting spheres. He dissented in CHAMPION V. AMES (1903) on the ground that a federal statute prohibiting interstate distribution of lottery tickets was not a regulation of commerce at all but rather an attempt by Congress to usurp the reserved power of the states to regulate public morals. And in *Lochner* Peckham conceded that state governments might prevent individuals from making certain kinds of contracts, only to conclude that there was no "direct relation" between the hours worked by bakeshop employees and either the public health or the health, safety, and mor-

als of the workers. Peckham, in short, knew a police regulation or an exercise of the commerce power when he saw one. Holmes may have been astonished when Peckham claimed that legitimate governmental interventions were readily distinguishable from those with only a "pretense" of legitimacy. But most Americans were accustomed to the claim. The spate of veto messages issued by President Cleveland were strikingly similar to Peckham's judicial opinions in both substance and style.

Peckham's voting record in cases involving race relations reflected another principal goal of the Cleveland Democracy—"home rule" for the South. The great spokesman for liberty of contract joined the majority in HODGES V. UNITED STATES (1906), which denied federal JURISDICTION over conspiracies to prevent blacks from making or carrying out labor contracts. He also concurred in BEREA COLLEGE V. KENTUCKY (1908), where the Court upheld a statute prohibiting even voluntary interracial education. If Peckham perceived a principled difference between the right of employers and employees to contract in *Lochner* and the right of individuals freely to associate in *Berea College,* he never described it. Yet it appears that Peckham rarely worried about such overarching conceptual problems. He not only managed to keep race relations and employment contract issues in separate analytical compartments but also voted to impose more stringent PUBLIC USE requirements on state governments when they regulated prices under the POLICE POWER than when they exercised the EMINENT DOMAIN power. Peckham stridently criticized the DOCTRINE of *Munn v. Illinois* (1877) throughout his career, arguing that storage rates charged by grain elevator firms were not subject to regulation because the owners had not devoted their property "to any public use, within the meaning of the law." (See GRANGER CASES.) In *Clark v. Nash* (1905), however, he sustained a law that permitted individuals to condemn rights-of-way across their neighbors' land for irrigation and mining purposes. "What is a public use," Peckham declared, "may frequently and largely depend upon the facts surrounding the subject, and . . . the people of a State . . . must in the nature of things be more familiar with such facts" than the federal judiciary.

Peckham wrote 448 opinions during his fourteen years on the Court, more than thirty percent of which were dissents. Very few of his majority opinions have stood the test of time. Modern commentators almost unanimously regard most of the results he reached to be insupportable and his mode of reasoning unfathomable. But it was Peckham himself who best summed up both the implications of his work for American public life and the internal contradictions that hastened its demise. "At times there seems to be a legal result which takes no account of the obviously practical result," he wrote in *Sauer v. City of New York*

(1907). "At times there seems to come an antithesis between legal science and common sense."

CHARLES W. MCCURDY
(1986)

Bibliography

SKOLNIK, RICHARD 1969 Rufus Peckham. Pages 1685–1703 in Leon Friedman and Fred L. Israel, eds., *The Justices of the United States Supreme Court, 1789–1967.* New York: Chelsea House.

PEIK v. CHICAGO & NORTHWESTERN RAILWAY CO.

See: Granger Cases

PELL v. PROCUNIER
417 U.S. 817 (1974)

In a case that helped delineate the boundaries between the traditional FIRST AMENDMENT freedoms and the expanding area of PRISONERS' RIGHTS, several prisoners and professional journalists challenged the constitutionality of a California prison regulation that forbade press interviews with particular inmates. The argument for the prisoners' rights was that this regulation abridged their FREEDOM OF SPEECH; the journalists claimed the rule inhibited their newsgathering capabilities, thus violating the FREEDOM OF PRESS. The Justices voted 6–3 against the inmates and 5–4 against the journalists. Because the prisoners had alternative means of communication (friends or family, for example) the California regulation did not violate their rights. The majority based its rejection of the journalists' position on the purpose of the regulation— to prevent particular individuals from gaining excessive influence through special attention—and the reporters' otherwise free access to prisoners. Furthermore, the regulation did not prohibit the press from publishing what it chose.

DAVID GORDON
(1986)

PENDENT JURISDICTION

When a federal court has JURISDICTION over a case presenting a FEDERAL QUESTION, the court may also take jurisdiction over closely related claims based on state law. According to *Gibbs v. United Mine Workers of America* (1966), pendent jurisdiction over a state law claim is appropriate when the state and federal claims share "a common nucleus of operative fact." If the federal claim is itself insubstantial, or is dismissed before the case is tried, it will not serve as a basis for getting a state claim heard by the federal court; such a case should be dismissed. The federal court has discretion to decline pendent jurisdiction over a state claim when the state issues are apt to predominate in the case (making it more appropriate for hearing in a state court), or when the combination of federal and state claims is apt to produce jury confusion. (See ANCILLARY JURISDICTION.)

In PENNHURST STATE SCHOOL & HOSPITAL V. HALDERMAN (1984) the Supreme Court drastically curtailed use of pendent jurisdiction in CIVIL RIGHTS cases. The Court held that the ELEVENTH AMENDMENT bars a federal court from entertaining an action—whether for DAMAGES or for INJUNCTION—against a state officer, when the action is based on an alleged violation of state law.

KENNETH L. KARST
(1986)

Bibliography

WRIGHT, CHARLES ALAN 1983 *The Law of Federal Courts,* 4th ed. Pages 103–109. St. Paul, Minn.: West Publishing Co.

PENDLETON, EDMUND
(1721–1803)

Admitted to the bar in 1745, Edmund Pendleton became a justice of the peace in 1751 and a member of the Virginia House of Burgesses in 1752. He was a leader of the conservative patriot faction in Virginia and opposed PATRICK HENRY on many issues, including colonial reaction to the Stamp Act of 1765. Pendleton opposed the act and, as a justice of the peace, declared it unconstitutional, but he did not approve of Henry's famous resolutions against it. He became a member of the committee of correspondence in 1773 and a delegate to the FIRST CONTINENTAL CONGRESS in 1774. Between 1774 and 1776 he was president of both the Virginia convention (the provisional legislature) and the Committee of Safety (the de facto executive). He presided over the Virginia convention of 1776 which passed the resolution Pendleton had drafted instructing Virginia's delegates to the CONTINENTAL CONGRESS to seek a DECLARATION OF INDEPENDENCE, adopted the VIRGINIA DECLARATION OF RIGHTS AND CONSTITUTION, and appointed a committee, including Pendleton, GEORGE WYTHE, and THOMAS JEFFERSON, to revise the state's laws. He was elected speaker of the first House of Delegates under the new constitution (1776–1777) and then appointed first presiding judge of the court of chancery (1777–1779). In 1779 he became presiding judge of the court of appeals, the state's highest court, a position he held until his death. In COMMONWEALTH V. CATON (1782), he stated that laws repugnant to the state constitution were void, but he reserved the question of whether his court could so declare them.

Pendleton was unanimously chosen president of the Virginia convention of 1788 at which he argued and voted for the RATIFICATION OF THE CONSTITUTION. He declined President GEORGE WASHINGTON's offer of a federal district judgeship in order to remain on the state court. As an indication of his virtues as a judge, it is said that only one of his judicial decisions was ever reversed, and in that case he reversed himself.

DENNIS J. MAHONEY
(1986)

PENDLETON ACT
22 Stat. 403 (1883)

A fundamental change in the operation of American government began with the adoption of the Civil Service Act of 1883—known as the Pendleton Act, for its sponsor, Senator George H. Pendleton (Democrat of Ohio). The act created a merit system for selection of non-policymaking employees of the United States government to replace the "spoils" system which rewarded political supporters. Although the immediate stimulus for adoption of the act was the assassination of President JAMES GARFIELD by a disappointed office seeker, a politically independent civil service had been a major goal of reformers for many years.

The act based eligibility for affected federal employment on performance in competitive examinations, and it created a Civil Service Commission to supervise the examinations and handle personnel administration. Initially extending to less than ten percent of federal employees, the competitive civil service now includes over ninety percent. Much of this growth was a result of the Ramspeck Act (Civil Service Act of 1940) which authorized the President to place virtually all federal employment under the system by EXECUTIVE ORDER. The Civil Service Reform Act (1978) abolished the Civil Service Commission but retained the principle of political neutrality established by the Pendleton Act.

DENNIS J. MAHONEY
(1986)

Bibliography

ROSENBLOOM, DAVID H. 1971 *Federal Service and the Constitution*. Ithaca, N.Y.: Cornell University Press.

PENN, WILLIAM
(1644–1718)

The scion of a wealthy English family, William Penn attended Oxford University, studied law, and managed the family's estates before becoming a Quaker in the mid-1660s. Throughout the rest of his life Penn engaged in Quaker preaching and propaganda. He was imprisoned on at least three occasions for publishing pamphlets about his religious beliefs. His acquittal in 1670 on a charge of unlawful preaching led to BUSHELL'S CASE, which ended the punishment of jurors who decided contrary to a judge's instructions. In the political campaigns of the late 1670s, Penn agitated for RELIGIOUS LIBERTY and frequent parliamentary elections.

Penn's involvement with America began in 1682, when he became a trustee of the colony of West Jersey, which he and eleven others had purchased for settlement by Quakers, and helped to frame its charter. King Charles II granted the proprietary colony of Pennsylvania to Penn in 1681 as settlement of a large debt that the king owed Penn's father; the following year Penn leased the area now known as Delaware and added it to the colony. Penn described his intentions for the colony as a "holy experiment" in religious and political liberty. In 1682, during a two-year sojourn in America, he wrote a Frame of Government (constitution) for the colony, granting the settlers freedom of religion, procedural guarantees in criminal cases, and limited self-government.

In 1697 Penn drafted, and submitted to the Board of Trade, the first proposal for a federal union of the English colonies in North America. His plan would have created a "congress," comprising two representatives from each colony, competent to legislate on any matter related to "the public tranquility and safety."

During a visit to Pennsylvania in 1701 Penn granted the residents a new charter, the Charter of Privileges, creating a unicameral legislature, greatly expanding the scope of colonial self-government, and providing for Delaware's establishment as a separate entity. Shortly thereafter, he returned to England, where he died.

DENNIS J. MAHONEY
(1986)

(SEE ALSO: *Pennsylvania Colonial Charters*.)

Bibliography

WILDES, HARRY E. 1974 *William Penn*. New York: Macmillan.

PENN CENTRAL TRANSPORTATION CO. v. NEW YORK CITY
438 U.S. 104 (1978)

Some governmental regulations of the use of property are severe enough to be called TAKINGS OF PROPERTY, for which JUST COMPENSATION must be made under the explicit terms of the Fifth Amendment (governing federal government action) or interpretations of the FOURTEENTH AMENDMENT's

DUE PROCESS clause (governing state action). This decision illustrates how difficult it is to persuade the Supreme Court that a regulation constitutes a "taking."

A New York City ordinance required city approval before a designated landmark's exterior could be altered. The owner of Grand Central Terminal sought to build a tall office building on top of the terminal, and was refused permission on aesthetic grounds. The Supreme Court held, 6–3, that this regulation did not constitute a "taking."

Justice WILLIAM J. BRENNAN, for the majority, conceded that the takingregulation distinction had defied clear formulation, producing a series of "ad hoc factual inquiries." This regulation, however, was analogous to ZONING under a comprehensive plan; over 400 landmarks had been designated. Further, the owner's loss was reduced by transferring its air-space development rights to other property in the city.

For the dissenters, Justice WILLIAM H. REHNQUIST argued that the law's severely destructive impact on property values was not justified by either of the usual "exceptions": the banning of "noxious uses," or the imposition of widely shared burdens to secure "an average reciprocity of advantage" (as in the case of zoning). Penn Central had suffered a huge loss of value, not offset by benefits under the landmark law.

KENNETH L. KARST
(1986)

PENNHURST STATE SCHOOL & HOSPITAL v. HALDERMAN
451 U.S. 1 (1981)
457 U.S. 1131 (1984)

Pennhurst worked major changes in the interpretation of the ELEVENTH AMENDMENT and in the PENDENT JURISDICTION of federal courts over claims based on state law. These changes remove one important weapon from the arsenal of CIVIL RIGHTS plaintiffs.

Terri Lee Halderman, a resident of Pennhurst, a state institution for the mentally retarded, commenced a CLASS ACTION in federal district court against Pennhurst and a number of state and local officials. She alleged that squalor, abuse of residents, and other conditions at Pennhurst violated the federal DEVELOPMENTALLY DISABLED ASSISTANCE AND BILL OF RIGHTS ACT of 1975, the DUE PROCESS clause of the FOURTEENTH AMENDMENT, and Pennsylvania's statute governing mental retardation. After a long trial, the district court agreed with her on all counts, and held that mentally retarded people in the state's care had a due process right to live in "the least restrictive setting" that would serve their needs. The court's INJUNCTION ordered the defendants to close Pennhurst and place its residents

in "suitable living arrangements." The court of appeals affirmed, but rested decision only on the federal statute. The Supreme Court reversed, instructing the lower courts to consider whether the district court's order was justified on the basis of the Constitution or state law. On REMAND, the court of appeals avoided the constitutional issue, holding that state law required reaffirmance of the "least restrictive setting" ruling. When the case returned to the Supreme Court, the Court held, 5–4, that the Eleventh Amendment barred the district court's injunction. (The case was then settled, with the state agreeing to close Pennhurst and to move its residents to their home communities, or to other institutions if they were aged or ill.)

Justice LEWIS F. POWELL'S OPINION OF THE COURT announced that the doctrine of SOVEREIGN IMMUNITY is a constitutional principle, based on the Eleventh Amendment, which gives a state immunity from suit in a federal court by an individual plaintiff. In Powell's novel reading, EX PARTE YOUNG (1908) stands for a narrow exception to this immunity, allowing a suit in federal court for an injunction against a state officer only when the plaintiff's claim is based on a violation of the federal Constitution. (Perhaps violations of federal statutes will fit within this category, because of the operation of the SUPREMACY CLAUSE.) Suits in federal court against state officers—even suits for injunctive relief—are thus barred by the Eleventh Amendment when they are based on claimed violations of state law.

Prior to *Pennhurst* an action in federal court founded on FEDERAL QUESTION JURISDICTION could include a claim for relief on state law grounds, when both the federal and state claims arose out of the same facts. However, Powell said, this doctrine of pendent jurisdiction rests only on concerns for efficiency and convenience, concerns that must give way to the force of the Eleventh Amendment.

For the dissenters, Justice JOHN PAUL STEVENS decried the Court's overruling of some two dozen precedents, and defended the long-established understanding of *Ex parte Young*: that when a state officer's conduct is illegal (under either federal or state law), the officer is "stripped" of the cloak of the sovereign's immunity. Here it was perverse to clothe Pennsylvania's officers with the state's Eleventh Amendment immunity when they were acting in violation of their sovereign's commands as embodied in state law. Justice WILLIAM J. BRENNAN, dissenting separately, argued that the amendment does not bar a suit by a citizen against the citizen's own state.

The *Pennhurst* majority opinion is vulnerable to criticism for its historical analysis of the Eleventh Amendment, for its casual dismissal of the importance of the federal courts' pendent jurisdiction, and for its choice to confer immunity on wrongdoing officials in the name of the sovereignty of the very state that had made the officials' conduct illegal. These criticisms seem minor, however, in the light of another one that is far more grave. The majority, in denying private citizens a vital judicial remedy against official lawlessness, weakened the rule of law.

KENNETH L. KARST
(1986)

Bibliography

SHAPIRO, DAVID L. 1984 Wrong Turns: The Eleventh Amendment and the Pennhurst Case. *Harvard Law Review* 98:61–85.

PENNSYLVANIA v. NELSON
350 U.S. 497 (1956)

The Supreme Court banned outright state prosecutions for SEDITION against the United States by ruling, in *Pennsylvania v. Nelson,* that Congress had already preempted that field of SOVEREIGNTY. The decision had the effect of limiting the states to punishing sedition against state or local, but not federal, government.

Steve Nelson, an avowed communist, had been convicted for violating Pennsylvania's stringent sedition law by his words and actions concerning the federal government; he was sentenced to serve twenty years in prison and pay large fines. The state supreme court reversed, holding the state law had been superseded by the Smith Act. The Supreme Court upheld and extended this ruling. Chief Justice EARL WARREN used three criteria or a three-part criterion in ruling that there was no longer room for state action in this field. The scheme of federal regulation, he maintained, which included the Smith Act, the INTERNAL SECURITY ACT of 1950, and the COMMUNIST CONTROL ACT of 1954, was "so pervasive" as to leave no room for state regulation. Further, these federal statutes demonstrated a federal interest "so dominant" as to preclude state action on the same subject; and for the state to enforce its federal law presented a "serious danger of conflict" with the administration of the federal program. Three Justices dissented, arguing that Congress had not intended to preempt the internal security field.

Following the decision all pending proceedings under the state sedition laws were dismissed or abandoned. Congress considered a measure to set aside the decision but failed to enact it.

PAUL L. MURPHY
(1986)

PENNSYLVANIA
COLONIAL CHARTERS
(April 25, 1682; October 28, 1701)

WILLIAM PENN, the proprietor of Pennsylvania, was a Quaker, a humanitarian, a champion of RELIGIOUS LIBERTY, and a stalwart advocate of CIVIL LIBERTIES. His two charters for his colony gave it representative institutions of government and bills of rights far in advance of the times. The 1682 Frame of Government called itself a "charter of liberties" that had the character of FUNDAMENTAL LAW. Any act of government that "infringed" on the designated liberties, said the Frame, "shall be held of no force or effect." Inhabitants possessing one hundred acres of land "at one penny an acre" were declared "freemen" capable of electing or being elected representatives, including members of the upper house—an innovation. The Frame separated church and state and guaranteed religious liberty by its provision that all persons professing God should be free to worship as they pleased and not be compelled to frequent or maintain any worship or ministry. FAIR TRIAL, which Penn and the Quakers had been denied in England, was here protected. At a time when defendants could not testify on their own behalf, the Frame allowed all persons to plead their own cases. Trial by a twelve-member jury of the VICINAGE, whose judgment was to be "final" (see BUSHELL'S CASE, 1670) and INDICTMENT by GRAND JURY in capital cases were guaranteed. The RIGHT TO BAIL was recognized and excessive fines were banned.

The 1701 Charter of Privileges, which replaced the Frame and remained the basis of government in Pennsylvania until 1776, also had the character of a CONSTITUTION to which ordinary legislation must conform or be of no effect. Its provisions for the "Enjoyment of Civil Liberties" and for religious liberty, and its ban against an ESTABLISHMENT OF RELIGION extended to all inhabitants "for ever." Among their innovations was a guarantee that "all criminals shall have the same Privileges of Witnesses and Council [sic] as their Prosecutors," the source of the comparable clauses in the SIXTH AMENDMENT. England did not allow counsel to all defendants until 1836. Pennsylvania's colonial charters had a marked influence on the development of the concept of a bill of rights in America.

LEONARD W. LEVY
(1986)

Bibliography

PERRY, RICHARD L., ed. 1959 *Sources of Our Liberties.* Pages 204–221, 251–260. New York: American Bar Foundation.

PENNSYLVANIA CONSTITUTION
OF 1776
(August 16, 1776)

Pennsylvania's short-lived first CONSTITUTION, superseded in 1790, is notable because it was the most unorthodox and democratic of the constitutions of the original states. Although the extralegal "convention" that framed the document exercised full powers of government and remained in session as the legislature, the constitution was FUNDA-MENTAL LAW. Its preamble, stressing NATURAL RIGHTS theory, declared that it was "for ever" unalterable; its declaration of rights was made part of the constitution and inviolable; and its frame of government created a legislature without the power "to add to, alter, abolish, or infringe" any part of the constitution.

The declaration of rights was superior to the more famous VIRGINIA DECLARATION OF RIGHTS, Pennsylvania's model. Pennsylvania omitted the right to BAIL and the ban against excessive fines and CRUEL AND UNUSUAL PUNISH-MENTS but added FREEDOM OF SPEECH, assembly, and petition; separated church and state; recognized the right of CONSCIENTIOUS OBJECTION; protected the RIGHT TO COUNSEL in all criminal cases; and provided for the right to bear arms and the RIGHT TO TRAVEL or emigrate—all constitutional "firsts" in the United States. To create a political democracy controlled by the people, the frame of government established a powerful unicameral legislature, with no upper house to check the lower and no governor to veto its legislation. The legislature's proceedings had to be made public and its doors were to be open to the public. In effect all males of voting age could vote, because the constitution enfranchised all taxpayers (all men had to pay a POLL TAX) and their sons, and anyone who could vote was eligible to hold office. Proportional representation, based on the number of taxable inhabitants, governed the apportionment of the legislature.

In place of a governor the constitution established a council, elected by the people, representing each county, with a president or chairman. The council had weak executive powers but for the power to make appointments, including all judges. The constitution instituted few checks and did recognize SEPARATION OF POWERS. Its strangest institution was the council of censors, a popularly elected body that met for one year in every seven and was charged with the responsibility of seeing that the constitution was preserved inviolate; it could review the performance of all public officers, order IMPEACHMENTS, recommend repeal of legislation, and call a convention to revise the constitution. That council met only once and was so politically divided that it did nothing. But the VER-MONT CONSTITUTION OF 1777, based on Pennsylvania's, copied the council of censors and kept it until 1869. The Pennsylvania Constitution of 1790 followed the MASSACHU-SETTS CONSTITUTION OF 1780.

LEONARD W. LEVY
(1986)

Bibliography

SELSON, J. PAUL (1936) 1971 *The Pennsylvania Constitution of 1776.* New York: Da Capo Press.

PENRY v. LYNAUGH
492 U.S. 302 (1989)

In this case on the prohition against CRUEL AND UNUSUAL PUNISHMENT imposed by the Eighth Amendment and the FOURTEENTH AMENDMENT, the Court ruled that to inflict CAPITAL PUNISHMENT on a mentally retarded prisoner was not necessarily unconstitutional. The Court, speaking through Justice SANDRA DAY O'CONNOR, also held that the ban on cruel and unusual punishments would be violated in a capital case if the sentencing jury were not instructed to consider all circumstances mitigating against the imposition of the death penalty. In this case, the jury had not properly considered whether Penry's MENTAL RETAR-DATION and history of childhood abuse diminished his moral culpability and made capital punishment a disproportionate sentence. Because the Eighth Amendment mandates an individualized assessment of the appropriateness of the death penalty, no mitigating factor may be withheld from the jury. Punishment must be directly related to the personal culpability of the criminal. Accordingly, the Court vacated the death sentence and remanded the case for resentencing under proper jury instruction.

Nonetheless, Justice O'Connor, for the Court, rejected Penry's second claim, ruling that the Eighth Amendment does not categorically prohibit the execution of a criminal who is mentally retarded. One who is profoundly or severely retarded and wholly lacking in the capacity to understand the wrongfulness of his or her actions cannot, in the face of the amendment, be executed. But the degree of mental retardation must be considered. In Penry's case, that of an adult with the reasoning capacity of a child not more than seven years of age, there was some proof that his diminished abilities disabled him from controlling his impulses and learning from his mistakes; yet a jury could properly conclude that his disabilities did not substantially reduce his level of blameworthiness for a capital offense. The Court refused to accept mental age as a line-drawing principle in such cases.

Four dissenters argued that the execution of mentally retarded prisoners invariably violates the "cruel and unusual punishment" clause because such people lack the culpability that is prerequisite to the proportionate imposition of the death penalty.

The *Penry* decision also made law on the subject of HABEAS CORPUS relief in federal courts, extending the non-retroactivity principle of *Teague v. Lane* (1989) to capital cases.

LEONARD W. LEVY
(1992)

PENSACOLA TELEGRAPH CO. v. WESTERN UNION TELEGRAPH CO.
96 U.S. 1 (1878)

This case is significant because the Supreme Court, following GIBBONS V. OGDEN (1824), declared that the congressional power to regulate INTERSTATE COMMERCE extends to newly invented instrumentalities of commerce, here the telegraph. In 1866 Congress had prohibited the states from granting telegraph monopolies. Florida, seeking to control telegraphic transmission within its JURISDICTION, conferred exclusive rights on the Pensacola company. A 7–2 Court, speaking through Chief Justice MORRISON R. WAITE, held the state act unconstitutional for conflict with the act of Congress. Accordingly, the company had no valid chartered right to exclude competitors.

LEONARD W. LEVY
(1986)

PENUMBRA THEORY

Writing for the Supreme Court in GRISWOLD V. CONNECTICUT (1965), Justice WILLIAM O. DOUGLAS commented that "specific guarantees in the BILL OF RIGHTS have penumbras, formed by emanations from those guarantees that help give them life and substance." The occasion for this shadowy suggestion was the Court's decision holding unconstitutional the application to a BIRTH CONTROL clinic of a state law forbidding the use of contraceptive devices, even by the married couples whom the clinic had aided. Although nothing in the Constitution specifically forbade such a law, Justice Douglas rested decision on a RIGHT OF PRIVACY founded in this "penumbra" theory. A number of constitutional guarantees created "zones of privacy." One such zone included the "right of association contained in the FIRST AMENDMENT." Other protections of privacy were afforded by the THIRD AMENDMENT's limitations on the quartering of troops, the FOURTH AMENDMENT's protections against unreasonable SEARCHES AND SEIZURES, and the Fifth Amendment's RIGHT AGAINST SELF-INCRIMINATION. "The present case, then, concerns a relationship lying within the zone of privacy created by several fundamental constitutional guarantees."

This "penumbra" theory, which has had no generative power of its own, is best understood as a last-ditch effort by Justice Douglas to avoid a confrontation with Justice HUGO L. BLACK over a doctrinal issue dear to Black's heart. In his famous dissent in *Adamson v. California* (1947), Black had derided "the natural-law-due-process formula" that allowed judges, with no warrant in the constitutional text, "to trespass, all too freely, on the legislative domain of the States as well as the Federal Government." Douglas

had joined Black's *Adamson* dissent, and perhaps hoped that his *Griswold* opinion, by maintaining a formal tie to the specifics of the Bill of Rights, might persuade Black to come along. Black, of course, would have none of it: "I get nowhere in this case by talk about a constitutional 'right of privacy' as an emanation from one or more constitutional provisions. I like my privacy as well as the next one, but I am nevertheless compelled to admit that government has a right to invade it unless prohibited by some specific constitutional provision."

The Court subsequently relocated its new right of privacy in the liberty protected by the DUE PROCESS clause of the FOURTEENTH AMENDMENT, and no further "penumbras" have been seen in the land. Nonetheless, the *Griswold* decision has been an unusually influential precedent, not only for the Supreme Court's abortion decisions but also for the development of a generalized FREEDOM OF INTIMATE ASSOCIATION. Not every penumbra darkens the road ahead.

KENNETH L. KARST
(1986)

Bibliography

KAUPER, PAUL G. 1965 Penumbras, Peripheries, Emanations, Things Fundamental and Things Forgotten: The Griswold Case. *Michigan Law Review* 64:235–282.

PEONAGE

Peonage is a system of debt bondage, in which a laborer is bound to personal service in order to work off an obligation to pay money. The system originated in the newly independent countries of Spanish America early in the nineteenth century, and in Hawaii and the Philippines later, as a substitute for various institutions used in the colonial era to marshal a labor force. In some of these countries the system continues to exist. In its classic form, peonage involves a trivial advance of money to a worker, in exchange for a contractual obligation to work for a term, or until the debt is repaid. From then on, the laborer is bound by law to serve the employer, and efforts to quit are met with the force of the state: arrest, imprisonment, return to the employer's service.

Peonage was also part of a larger system of involuntary servitude that emerged in the American South after the CIVIL WAR. As such, though whites have sometimes been its victims, peonage has served as a substitute for black SLAVERY. After the slave states were forced by emancipation to shift from a labor regime based on status and force to one of free labor based on contract and choice, peonage emerged as a system that hid the wolf of involuntary servitude in the sheep's clothing of contract.

Peonage as a customary system for coerced black labor had its origin in the contract-enforcement sections of the BLACK CODES (1865–1875) and other labor-related statutes of the era. These provided both civil and criminal penalties for breach of labor contracts, punished VAGRANCY, prohibited enticement of laborers from their jobs, and hampered or penalized agents inducing the emigration of laborers. Southern states also permitted the leasing of convict labor and adopted a criminal-surety system, whereby a person convicted of a MISDEMEANOR would have his fine and costs paid by a prospective employer and then be obliged to work for the surety. Though the Black Codes were soon repealed, the FREEDMEN'S BUREAU at the same time emphasized labor contracts as the nexus of the employer-employee relationship for former slaves, and this later encouraged the use of contracts as a device for forcing black labor.

In 1867, when Congress enacted the Peonage Act to abolish peonage in New Mexico Territory, it also made it applicable to "any other Territory or State of the United States." The act made it a FELONY to hold a person in a condition of peonage, or to arrest a person for that purpose. It voided statutes and "usages" enforcing the "voluntary or involuntary service or labor of any persons as peons in liquidation of a debt or obligation, or otherwise."

United States District Judge Thomas G. Jones began the legal struggle against peonage in a vigorous GRAND JURY charge, reported as *The Peonage Cases* (1903), defining peonage broadly as "the exercise of dominion over their persons and liberties by the master, or employer, or creditors, to compel the discharge of the obligation, by service or labor, against the will of the person performing the service." In *Clyatt v. United States* (1905), the Supreme Court upheld the use of the Peonage Act for the prosecution of a peon-master. Brushing aside both STATE ACTION and DUAL SOVEREIGNTY arguments, Justice DAVID J. BREWER found authorization for direct federal power over peonage in the enforcement clause (section 2) of the THIRTEENTH AMENDMENT. But he also held that debt was the "basal fact" of peonage, thus limiting federal action to cases where an actual debt could be shown.

After publication of the "Report on Peonage" (1908) by the United States Department of Justice, prompted by discovery of occasional instances of white peonage (usually of immigrants), the Supreme Court, in BAILEY V. ALABAMA (1911), used the Peonage Act to strike down Alabama contract-enforcement statutes that permitted quitting to be *prima facie* evidence of an intent to defraud the employer. The Court held that the Peonage Act voids "all legislation which seeks to compel the service or labor by making it a crime to refuse or fail to perform it." In *United States v. Reynolds* (1914), the Court invalidated Alabama criminal-surety statutes, describing the plight of a black peon caught in them as being "chained to an everturning wheel of servitude." But peonage has proved to be a remarkably tenacious form of servitude for blacks in the rural South, highlighted by the 1921 massacre of eleven black peons by their Georgia master, and by the establishment of peonage under federal and state auspices in refugee camps after the 1927 Mississippi River flood.

While physical force or threat of prosecution plainly constitute peonage, other forms of compulsion present interpretive problems. Thus subterfuges as well as outright violations of the Peonage Act persist into the present, despite the invalidation or repeal of the state labor-contract statutes that provided the original basis of peonage. The threat of deportation has proved an effective means of keeping alien migrant workers in a condition of involuntary or underpaid labor, and lower federal courts have divided as to whether this constitutes peonage.

WILLIAM M. WIECEK
(1986)

Bibliography

COHEN, WILLIAM 1976 Negro Involuntary Servitude in the South, 1865–1940: A Preliminary Analysis. *Journal of Southern History* 42:31–60.

DANIEL, PETE 1972 *The Shadow of Slavery: Peonage in the South, 1901–1969.* Urbana: University of Illinois Press.

NOVAK, DANIEL A. 1978 *The Wheel of Servitude: Black Forced Labor After Slavery.* Lexington: University Press of Kentucky.

PEOPLE v. CROSWELL
3 Johnson's Cases (N.Y.) 336 (1804)

The state of New York, run by Jeffersonians, indicted Harry Croswell, a Federalist editor, for the crime of SEDITIOUS LIBEL, because he wrote that President THOMAS JEFFERSON had paid a scurrilous journalist to defame GEORGE WASHINGTON. Croswell was convicted at a trial presided over by the Jeffersonian chief justice of the state, Morgan Lewis, who embraced the position of the prosecution in ZENGER'S CASE (1735). Lewis ruled that truth was not a defense against a charge of seditious libel and that the jury's sole task was to decide whether the defendant had published the statements charged, leaving the court to decide their criminality as a matter of law.

ALEXANDER HAMILTON, representing Croswell on his appeal to the state's highest court, advocated the protections of the Sedition Act of 1798: truth as a defense and determination by the jury of the criminality of the publication. FREEDOM OF THE PRESS, declared Hamilton, was "the right to publish, with impunity, truth, with good motives for justifiable ends, though reflecting on government, the magistracy, or individuals." Spenser Ambrose, the Jeffersonian prosecutor, defended the remote BAD TENDENCY TEST. By the time the court decided the case, Ambrose had become a member of it. Had he been eligible to vote, the court would have supported the suppressive views of Lewis and Ambrose. As it was, the court split 2–2. Judge BROCKHOLST LIVINGSTON joined Lewis, while Judge SMITH THOMPSON joined the opinion of JAMES KENT, a Federalist who adopted Hamilton's argument.

In 1805 the state legislature enacted a bill allowing the jury to decide the criminality of a publication and permitted truth as a defense if published "with good motives for justifiable ends." On the whole that was the standard that prevailed in the United States until NEW YORK TIMES V. SULLIVAN (1964).

LEONARD W. LEVY
(1986)

PER CURIAM

(Latin: "By the court.") A *per curiam* opinion represents the views of the court and summarily disposes of the issue before the court by applying settled law. (See RES JUDICATA). Generally the opinion is short and it is always unsigned, although dissents will occasionally be filed.

DAVID GORDON
(1986)

PEREMPTORY CHALLENGES

Peremptory challenges are challenges given to both parties to a litigation allowing them to dismiss prospective jurors during jury selection without having to give a reason. In recent years, the Supreme Court has recognized constitutional limits on peremptories; as a result, there are some circumstances in which a reason must be given for challenging a juror.

In both federal and states courts, prospective jurors are summoned from the community for JURY SERVICE. They are assigned to panels, known as venires, and from the venire a jury is selected. Before a prospective juror is seated on a jury, however, there is a process during which the judge and/or attorneys question the prospective juror; this questioning is known as VOIR DIRE. One purpose of voir dire, whether it is conducted by the judge or by the attorneys, is to ensure that the jurors selected to serve on the jury can be impartial; those who cannot be impartial will be removed.

There are two ways to remove a prospective juror from a jury. One way is for an attorney to raise a challenge "for cause." The attorney must give a reason for such a challenge. Among accepted reasons are that the prospective juror is related to one of the participants in the trial, or

that the prospective juror has admitted that he or she cannot be impartial in the case. The decision whether to grant a for-cause challenge is up to the trial judge. Trial judges do not grant for-cause challenges readily, perhaps because there is another way for attorneys to remove a prospective juror from the jury.

The second way to remove a prospective juror is through the use of a peremptory challenge. In every trial, whether in state or federal court or whether the trial is for a civil or criminal matter, the parties are allotted a certain number of peremptory challenges. The number varies, depending on the type of case and whether it is in federal or state court. The number of peremptories is provided by statute and/or by court rules. For example, according to federal statute, in federal court in a civil trial each side is entitled to three peremptory challenges. According to a federal rule, in federal court in a criminal trial, the number of peremptories varies depending on the type of offense charged. For example, if the offense charged is punishable by imprisonment for more than one year, the prosecutor is entitled to six peremptories, whereas the defendant is entitled to ten.

The exercise of a peremptory challenge, unlike the exercise of a for-cause challenge, is ordinarily left to the attorney's discretion. Attorneys can use their allotted peremptories to remove prospective jurors with whom they feel uncomfortable or whom they believe might not be impartial. Usually the attorney does not have to give a reason to explain why he or she is using a peremptory challenge to dismiss a particular juror.

A recent line of Supreme Court cases, however, has identified a few circumstances in which attorneys must give reasons for their peremptories. In SWAIN V. ALABAMA (1965), the Court held that if an African American defendant could show that in case after case a prosecutor was exercising peremptory challenges to exclude prospective jurors who were of the defendant's race, then the defendant would have established that the prosecutor was violating the defendant's right to EQUAL PROTECTION OF THE LAWS under the FOURTEENTH AMENDMENT to the Constitution. In *Swain*, the Court set an evidentiary burden for the defendant so high that only the rare defendant could meet it. As a result, individual prosecutors who were of a mind to discriminate could continue to use peremptories to exclude jurors based on race.

Twenty years later, the Court revisited the issue in BATSON V. KENTUCKY (1986). The Court in *Batson* OVERRULED the evidentiary burden established in *Swain*, and held that a defendant could establish that the prosecutor violated his right to equal protection based on the prosecutor's use of peremptories in his case alone. In *Batson*, the Court tried to strike a balance between preserving the peremptory and preventing it from perpetuating RACIAL DISCRIM-

INATION. *Batson* requires a defendant to establish a prima facie case that the prosecutor used peremptories based on race. To establish this, the defendant must show that he or she is a member of a cognizable racial group; that the prosecutor had exercised peremptories to remove from the venire prospective jurors of the defendant's race; and that these and other circumstances raise an inference of discrimination. After defendant's prima facie showing, the burden shifts to the prosecution to offer a race-neutral reason for its challenges. The trial judge determines whether the prosecution's reason is race neutral; if it is, then the peremptory is permitted; if it is not, then the peremptory is prohibited.

This modification of the peremptory was clearly a compromise, and left critics on both sides dissatisfied. Justice THURGOOD MARSHALL, writing a concurrence in *Batson*, urged that peremptories be eliminated so that they could no longer be used in a discriminatory manner, whereas Chief Justice WARREN E. BURGER, writing in dissent, claimed that no reason should ever have to be given for the exercise of a peremptory and to the extent that *Batson* required a reason, it signaled the demise of the peremptory challenge.

In recent cases, the Court has extended the reach of *Batson*. In *Powers v. Ohio* (1991), the Court held that a defendant did not have to be of the same race as the excluded juror to raise a *Batson* challenge. In *Edmonson v. Leesville Concrete Co.* (1991), the Court extended *Batson* to civil cases, and in *Georgia v. McCollum* (1992), the Court held that the defense, just like the prosecution, could not exercise peremptories based on race. Most recently, in *J. E. B. v. Alabama* (1994), the Court held that peremptories could not be exercised based on gender.

NANCY S. MARDER
(2000)

Bibliography

ABRAMSON, JEFFREY 1995 *We, the Jury.* New York: Basic Books.
ALSCHULER, ALBERT W. 1989 The Supreme Court and the Jury: Voir Dire, Peremptory Challenges, and the Review of Jury Verdicts. *University of Chicago Law Review* 56:153–233.
HOFFMAN, MORRIS B. 1997 Peremptory Challenges Should Be Abolished: A Trial Judge's Perspective. *University of Chicago Law Review* 64:809–871.
MARDER, NANCY S. 1995 Beyond Gender: Peremptory Challenges and the Roles of the Jury. *Texas Law Review* 73:1041–1138.
MONTOYA, JEAN 1996 The Future of the Post-*Batson* Peremptory Challenge: Voir Dire by Questionnaire and the "Blind" Peremptory. *University of Michigan Journal of Law Reform* 29:981–1030.

PEREZ v. BROWNELL

See: *Trop v. Dulles*

PEREZ v. UNITED STATES
402 U.S. 146 (1971)

In sustaining a conviction for the federal crime of "loansharking," the Supreme Court upheld Title II of the Consumer Credit Protection Act as valid under the COMMERCE CLAUSE. For an 8–1 Court, Justice WILLIAM O. DOUGLAS rehearsed a congressional committee's finding that extortionate credit practices were linked to organized, interstate crime and vitally affected INTERSTATE COMMERCE. He rejected petitioner's contention that the crime of loansharking was necessarily local in nature. Justice POTTER STEWART, in dissent, argued that there had been no showing of interstate movement or effect in Perez's case, and worried that Congress might preempt the whole field of criminal law.

DENNIS J. MAHONEY
(1986)

PERRY v. UNITED STATES

See: Gold Clause Cases

PERRY EDUCATION ASSOCIATION v. PERRY LOCAL EDUCATORS' ASSOCIATION
460 U.S. 37 (1983)

Perry provided the leading modern opinion setting guidelines governing FIRST AMENDMENT claims of access to the PUBLIC FORUM. A school district's collective bargaining agreement with a union (PEA) provided that PEA, but no other union, would have access to the interschool mails and to teacher mailboxes. A rival union (PLEA) sued in federal district court, challenging the constitutionality of its exclusion from the school mails. The district court denied relief, but the court of appeals held that the exclusion violated the EQUAL PROTECTION clause and the First Amendment. The Supreme Court reversed, 5–4, rejecting both claims.

Justice BYRON R. WHITE wrote for the Court, setting out a three-category analysis that set the pattern for later "public forum" cases such as CORNELIUS V. NAACP LEGAL DEFENSE AND EDUCATIONAL FUND, INC. (1985). First, the streets and parks are "traditional" public forums, in which government cannot constitutionally forbid all communicative activity. Any exclusion of a speaker from such a traditional public forum based on the content of the speaker's message must be necessary to serve a COMPELLING STATE INTEREST. Content-neutral regulations of the "time, place, and manner" of expression in such places may be enforced when they are narrowly tailored to serve significant state interests and they leave open "ample alternative channels" of communication.

Second, the state may open up other kinds of public property for use by the public for expressive activity. The state may close such a "designated" public forum, but so long as it remains open it must be made available to all speakers, under the same constitutional guidelines that govern traditional public forums.

Third, communicative uses of public property that is neither a traditional nor a designated public forum may be restricted to those forms of communication that serve the governmental operation to which the property is devoted. The only constitutional limits on such restrictions on speech are that they be reasonable, and that they not be imposed in order to suppress a particular point of view. The *Perry* case, said Justice White, fit this third category: the school mail system was neither a traditional public forum nor designated for public communicative use; rather it could be limited to school-related communications, including those from PEA, the teachers' elected bargaining agent. Such a limitation did not exclude PLEA because of its point of view.

Justice WILLIAM J. BRENNAN, for the four dissenters, argued that the exclusion of PLEA was "viewpoint discrimination," and thus that the case did not turn on the characterization of the school mails as a public forum.

The *Perry* formula capped a process of doctrinal development focused on what HARRY KALVEN, JR., named "the concept of the public forum." In its origin, the concept expanded the First Amendment's protections of speech. *Perry* marks the success of a campaign, highlighted by Justice WILLIAM H. REHNQUIST's opinion in *United States Postal Service v. Greenburgh Civic Association* (1981), to convert the public forum concept into a preliminary hurdle for would-be speakers to clear before they can establish their claims to the FREEDOM OF SPEECH on government property or in government-managed systems of communication.

KENNETH L. KARST
(1986)

PERSON

The Constitution contains dozens of references to "persons" but nowhere defines the term. When the Framers of the original document identified persons who might hold federal office or be counted in determining a state's representation in Congress or the ELECTORAL COLLEGE, they used "persons" in its everyday sense—even when they provided that slaves should be counted as "three fifths of all other Persons." Focusing on the allocation of

governmental powers, they had little occasion to ponder the philosopher's question: what does it mean to be a person? It was the addition to the Constitution of a body of constitutional rights against the government—first in the BILL OF RIGHTS and later in the FOURTEENTH AMENDMENT—that gave the philosopher's question constitutional significance.

In court, that question is never raised in wholesale terms but always in the context of particular issues. The Fourteenth Amendment's DUE PROCESS and EQUAL PROTECTION clauses, for example, offer their protections to "any person." Should those protections extend to a corporation? To a fetus? A philosopher, asked to say whether a corporation or a fetus more closely resembles some ideal model of a person, might be forgiven for failing to predict the Supreme Court's conclusions in *Santa Clara County v. Southern Pacific Railroad* (1886) and ROE V. WADE (1973) that corporations were included but fetuses were not. The Court, like many another human institution, defines its terms with substantive purposes in mind.

The notion that a corporation might be a "person" for some constitutional purposes had been suggested early in the nineteenth century. The point was not explicitly argued to the Supreme Court, however, until *San Mateo County v. Southern Pacific Railroad* (1882). In that case former Senator ROSCOE CONKLING, representing the railroad, made use of the journal of the joint congressional committee that had drafted the Fourteenth Amendment, a committee on which he had served. Conkling strongly intimated that the committee had used the word "person" for the specific purpose of including corporations. The case was dismissed for MOOTNESS, but in the *Santa Clara* case Chief Justice MORRISON R. WAITE interrupted ORAL ARGUMENT to say that the Court had concluded that the equal protection clause, in referring to a "person," extended its benefit to a corporation—a ruling that has since been followed consistently in both equal protection and due process decisions. Much of the later development of SUBSTANTIVE DUE PROCESS as a guarantee of FREEDOM OF CONTRACT and a protection against ECONOMIC REGULATION thus rested on a proposition of law whose basis was never articulated in an opinion of the Supreme Court.

To be a person, for constitutional purposes, is to be capable of holding constitutional rights. Our system of rights is premised on the idea that a right either "belongs" to someone—some person—or does not exist. The DOCTRINES of STANDING and mootness, as they govern our federal courts, reflect this assumption. We are accustomed to speak of "individual rights." Yet any claim to any right is an appeal to principle—and a principle is an abstraction that governs a great many "cases" not in court. Every claim of "individual" right, in other words, is a claim on behalf of a group composed of all those who fit the claim's underlying principle. Only a person can claim a constitutional right, but every such claim is made by a person as an occupant of a role: a homeowner whose house has been searched by the police, a would-be soapbox orator, a natural father disqualified from having custody of his child.

Although corporations—or even whole states—are capable of asserting constitutional claims, and although every "individual" constitutional right is capable of being generalized to extend to a group, nonetheless there remains an important sense in which we hold constitutional rights as persons. Today's constitutional law recognizes a body of substantive rights founded on the essentials of being a person. Here the philosopher's question must be asked; some model of what it means to be a person is implicit in such developments as the emergence of a RIGHT OF PRIVACY or a FREEDOM OF INTIMATE ASSOCIATION.

These rights of "personhood" (to use the Supreme Court's expression in *Roe v. Wade*) attach to natural persons. They rest on the assumption, usually not articulated, that although each human being is unique, we all share certain elements of our common humanity. The assumption is that each of us is conscious of a continuing identity; has some conception of his or her own good; is capable of forming and changing purposes; has a sense of justice— is, in short a "moral person" and not just a biological organism. Of course, the biological person has received its own constitutional protections: the FOURTH AMENDMENT's guarantee against unreasonable searches and seizures runs in part to our "persons"; a woman's right to have an abortion is based on her right to control the use of her body. It is the moral person, however, who is the focus of the newer rights of "personhood."

The principal doctrinal foundation for these rights has been a renascent SUBSTANTIVE DUE PROCESS. Yet similar values form the substantive core of the Fourteenth Amendment's guarantee of the equal protection of the laws. That guarantee originated as part of the nation's response to slavery and to efforts in the postabolition South to create a system of serfdom to substitute for slavery. In law, of course, a slave was not a person; an item of property could claim no rights. Yet the original Constitution's two provisions recognizing slavery referred not to "slaves" but to "persons"—as if the draftsmen, resigned to the necessity of their unholy bargain with the southern states, nonetheless could not bring themselves to deny their common humanity with the men and women held as slaves. Seventy years later, in DRED SCOTT V. SANDFORD (1857), Chief Justice ROGER B. TANEY expressed quite another view of the Framers' understanding. At the nation's founding, Taney said, blacks had been considered "an inferior class of beings," incapable of CITIZENSHIP. The modern revival of the Fourteenth Amendment's principle of equal citizenship serves, above all, to protect the claim of each of us to be treated by the society as a person—one who has rights as a respected, responsible, participating member of our community.

KENNETH L. KARST
(1986)

Bibliography

GRAHAM, HOWARD JAY 1938 The "Conspiracy Theory" of the Fourteenth Amendment. *Yale Law Journal* 47:371–403; 48: 171–194.

HORWITZ, MORTON J. 1985–1986 *Santa Clara* Revisited: The Development of Corporate Theory. *West Virginia Law Review* 88:173–224.

NOONAN, JOHN T., JR. 1976 *Persons and Masks of the Law: Cardozo, Holmes, Jefferson, and Wythe as Makers of the Masks*. New York: Farrar, Straus & Giroux.

TRIBE, LAURENCE H. 1978 *American Constitutional Law*. Chap. 15. Mineola, N.Y.: Foundation Press.

VINING, JOSEPH 1978 *Legal Identity: The Coming of Age of Public Law*. New Haven, Conn.: Yale University Press.

PERSONAL LIBERTY LAWS

Between 1826 and 1858, all the free states east of Illinois enacted "personal liberty laws" providing one or more procedural remedies to persons seized as fugitive slaves. These included the writs of HABEAS CORPUS and personal replevin. Some personal liberty laws also provided jury trial to alleged fugitives; prohibited kidnaping or enticement of black persons out of state; imposed more stringent state procedures for recaptions; or provided the services of state's attorneys to alleged fugitives. The Vermont Freedom Act of 1858 declared every slave who came into the state free.

In PRIGG V. PENNSYLVANIA (1842), Justice JOSEPH STORY held that state statutes interfering with recaptures under the 1793 Fugitive Slave Act were unconstitutional. But in an OBITER DICTUM unique to him, Story stated that state officials need not participate in a recapture under federal authority. This spurred enactment of statutes prohibiting state officials such as judges and sheriffs from participating in fugitive recaptures and prohibiting the use of state facilities such as jails to slave-catchers trying to hold runaways. Proslavery spokesmen tirelessly denounced the personal liberty laws. In his last annual message, President JAMES BUCHANAN blamed the crisis of 1860 on them. South Carolina cited the laws as justification for its SECESSION.

WILLIAM M. WIECEK
(1986)

(SEE ALSO: *Fugitive Slavery*.)

Bibliography

MORRIS, THOMAS D. 1974 *Free Men All: The Personal Liberty Laws of the North, 1780–1861.* Baltimore: Johns Hopkins University Press.

PERSONNEL ADMINISTRATOR OF MASSACHUSETTS v. FEENEY
442 U.S. 256 (1979)

In selecting applicants for state civil service positions, Massachusetts preferred all qualifying veterans of the armed forces over any qualifying nonveterans. Because fewer than two percent of Massachusetts veterans were women, the preference severely restricted women's public employment opportunities. A nonveteran woman applicant challenged the preference as a denial of the EQUAL PROTECTION OF THE LAWS; the Supreme Court, 7–2, upheld the preference's constitutionality.

The Court, speaking through Justice POTTER STEWART, followed WASHINGTON V. DAVIS (1976) and held that SEX DISCRIMINATION, like RACIAL DISCRIMINATION, is to be found only in purposeful official conduct. A discriminatory impact, of itself, is thus insufficient to establish the sex discrimination that demands the judicial scrutiny set out in CRAIG V. BOREN (1976). Here the veterans preference disadvantaged nonveteran men as well as women; there was no basis for assuming that the preference was "a pretext for preferring men over women." Rather it was aimed at rewarding the sacrifices of military service and easing the transition from military to civilian life.

Justice THURGOOD MARSHALL dissented, joined by Justice WILLIAM J. BRENNAN: legislators act for a variety of reasons; the question is whether an improper purpose was one motivating factor in the governmental action. Here the discriminatory impact of the law was not merely foreseeable but inevitable. The result was to relegate female civil servants to jobs traditionally filled by women. Other less discriminatory means were available for rewarding veterans (bonuses, for example); the state's choice of this preference strongly suggested intentional gender discrimination. A similar "foreseeability" argument was persuasive to a majority of the Court four weeks later, in the context of school segregation. (See COLUMBUS BOARD OF EDUCATION V. PENICK.)

KENNETH L. KARST
(1986)

PETERS, RICHARD
(1744–1828)

President GEORGE WASHINGTON on April 11, 1792, commissioned Richard Peters judge of the United States District Court for Pennsylvania, a position he filled until his death. His duties included presiding with a Supreme Court Justice over the federal CIRCUIT COURT in the state.

Peters contributed significantly to the development of a distinctly American ADMIRALTY AND MARITIME LAW, including features borrowed from civil and COMMON LAW precedents. In cases like *Warder v. LaBelle Creole* (1792), he was among the first American judges to advance a risk-reward calculus intended to facilitate the expansion of commerce.

His constitutional opinions touched the civil and criminal JURISDICTIONS of the lower federal courts and the law of TREASON. Peters in 1792 joined his fellow circuit court judges in HAYBURN'S CASE in refusing to determine the qualifications of Revolutionary War pensioners under a congressional act. This task, the judges concluded, fell outside the JUDICIAL POWER OF THE UNITED STATES. Peters, however, had a broad view of federal judicial power. In *United States v. Worrall* (1798) he urged recognition of a FEDERAL COMMON LAW OF CRIMES, a position subsequently rejected by the Supreme Court.

Peters's nationalism also shaped his views of treason and the supremacy of the federal courts. In *United States v. John Fries* (1800) he charged the jury that "levying war against the United States" included armed opposition to the collection of taxes. (See FRIES' REBELLION.) During the famous *Olmstead* controversy in Pennsylvania, Peters ordered the governor and the General Assembly to pay a judgment outstanding against the state in the federal court. Peters withheld issuing compulsory process for fear of an armed clash, but Chief Justice JOHN MARSHALL in UNITED STATES V. JUDGE PETERS (1809) vindicated the judge's nationalism.

Peters's Federalist political principles flowed into his jurisprudence. He was a "Republican Schoolmaster," who exploited the lower federal bench to promote commercial development, federal judicial independence, and national authority.

KERMIT L. HALL
(1986)

Bibliography

PRESSER, STEPHEN B. 1978 A Tale of Two Judges: Richard Peters, Samuel Chase, and the Broken Promise of Federalist Jurisprudence. *Northwestern University Law Review* 73:26–111.

PETITION FOR REDRESS OF GRIEVANCES

See: Freedom of Petition

PETITION OF RIGHT
(June 7, 1628)

This statute is among the foremost documents in Anglo-American constitutional history. The Petition of Right protected the liberty of the subject and contributed to the development of the RULE OF LAW and the concept of FUNDAMENTAL LAW. The Framers of the Constitution regarded the act of 1628 as part of their COMMON LAW inheritance establishing rights against government. In its time, however, the statute limited only the royal prerogative or executive authority.

In 1626 Charles I, exercising his prerogative, had exacted a "forced loan" from his subjects. The poor paid it by having to quarter soldiers in their homes and having to serve in the army or face trial by a military tribunal. Five knights refused to make a contribution of money to the crown on the grounds that it was an unconstitutional tax; they were imprisoned by order of the king's council. When they sought a writ of HABEAS CORPUS, the Court of King's Bench, in *Darnel's Case* (1627), ruled that because the return to the writ showed the prisoners to be held on executive authority, no specific cause of imprisonment had to be stated.

The forced loan and the resolution of *Darnel's Case* caused a furor. After the House of Commons adopted resolutions against arbitrary taxation and arbitrary imprisonment, Sir EDWARD COKE introduced a bill to bind the king. The House of Lords sought to "save" the SOVEREIGNTY of the king by allowing a denial of habeas corpus for reasons of state. Coke, opposing such an amendment to the bill, argued that it would weaken MAGNA CARTA, and he warned: "Take heed what we yield unto: Magna Charta [sic] is such a fellow that he will have no "sovereign." The Lords finally agreed and the king assented.

The Petition of Right reconfirmed Magna Carta's provision that no freeman could be imprisoned but by lawful judgment of his peers or "by the LAW OF THE LAND." The Petition also reconfirmed a 1354 reenactment of the great charter which first used the phrase "by DUE PROCESS OF LAW" instead of "by the law of the land." By condemning the military trial of civilians, the Petition invigorated due process and limited martial law. One section of the Petition provided that no one should be compelled to make any loan to the crown or pay any tax "without common consent by act of parliament." Americans later relied on this provision in their argument against TAXATION WITHOUT REPRESENTATION. Other sections of the act of 1628 provided that no one should be imprisoned or be forced to incriminate himself by having to answer for refusing an exaction not authorized by Parliament. Condemnation of imprisonment without cause or merely on executive authority strengthened the writ of habeas corpus. (See HABEAS CORPUS ACT OF 1679; BILL OF RIGHTS (ENGLISH).) The THIRD AMENDMENT of the Constitution derives in part from the Petition of Right.

LEONARD W. LEVY
(1986)

Bibliography

RELF, FRANCIS H. 1917 *The Petition of Right.* Minneapolis: University of Minnesota Press.

PETIT JURY

The petit jury is the trial jury, as distinguished from the GRAND JURY. The petit jury decides questions of fact in cases at law, and renders the verdict, formally declaring its findings. Traditionally, in Anglo-American law, the jury decided by unanimous vote of twelve members, but this is not constitutionally required.

DENNIS J. MAHONEY
(1986)

(SEE ALSO: *Jury Discrimination; Jury Size; Jury Unanimity; Trial by Jury.*)

PEYOTE, RELIGIOUS USE OF

See: *Employment Division, Department of Human Resources of Oregon v. Smith*

PHELPS, EDWARD J.
(1822–1900)

Edward John Phelps was a Vermont Democrat who, in frequent appearances before the Supreme Court, championed the rights of private property. An outstanding orator—he was frequently likened to DANIEL WEBSTER or WILLIAM EVARTS—Phelps served as president of the American Bar Association (1880–1881) and as Kent Professor of Law at Yale (1881–1900). He declared that America's problems stemmed from "a vicious and altogether unnecessary enlargement of the electorate"; this attitude explained his belief that the Constitution was too hallowed to be "hawked about the country, debated in the newspapers . . . [and] elucidated by pot-house politicians, and dung-hill editors."

DAVID GORDON
(1986)

PHILADELPHIA v. NEW JERSEY
437 U.S. 617 (1978)

In a 7–2 decision, the Supreme Court invalidated a New Jersey environmental protection law that prohibited the importation of solid waste originating or collected out of state. Justice POTTER STEWART, writing for the majority, concluded that the law unduly burdened INTERSTATE COMMERCE. The worthlessness of the regulated commodity did not exclude it from the operation of the COMMERCE CLAUSE; nor was the law permissible because its goals were environmental rather than economic. New Jersey could not require other states to bear the whole burden of conservation of its landfill sites. (See ENVIRONMENTAL REGULATION AND THE CONSTITUTION.)

DENNIS J. MAHONEY
(1986)

PHILADELPHIA & READING RAILROAD CO. v. PENNSYLVANIA
(State Freight Tax Case)
Wallace 232 (1873)

Pennsylvania imposed a tonnage tax on all freight transported within the state, including freight shipped out of and into the state. The transportation of freight for exchange or sale, said Justice WILLIAM STRONG for a 7–2 Supreme Court, is commerce, and a clear tax on such commerce among states is an unconstitutional burden on INTERSTATE COMMERCE that might injure commercial intercourse in the country. Strong added that the transportation of persons or merchandise through a state or from one to another is a subject of national importance requiring, under the rule of COOLEY V. BOARD OF WARDENS (1852), uniform and exclusive regulation by Congress. This still is an important case on STATE TAXATION OF COMMERCE.

LEONARD W. LEVY
(1986)

PHILOSOPHY AND THE CONSTITUTION

The Constitution is one of the great achievements of political philosophy; and it may be the only political achievement of philosophy in our society. The Framers of the Constitution and the leading participants in the debates on RATIFICATION shared a culture more thoroughly than did any later American political elite. They shared a knowledge (often distorted, but shared nevertheless) of ancient philosophy and history, of English COMMON LAW, of recent English political theory, and of the European Enlightenment. They were the American branch of the Enlightenment, and salient among their membership credentials was their belief that reasoned thought about politics could guide them to ideal political institutions for a free people. They argued passionately about the nature of SOVEREIGNTY, of political REPRESENTATION, of republicanism, of CONSTITUTIONALISM; and major decisions in the ferment of institution-building that culminated in 1787 were influenced, if never wholly determined, by such arguments. The final form of the new federal Constitution embodied radically new views about the location of sovereignty—now located "in the people" in a stronger sense than any philosopher except Jean-Jacques Rousseau would have recognized—and about the function of the SEPARATION OF POWERS and BICAMERALISM.

Philosophy has never again played the role it played at the founding of the Republic, except perhaps in inspiring some ABOLITIONIST CONSTITUTIONAL THEORY. To be sure, "philosophy" in a loose sense has always influenced politicians and judges, who are part of society. The Supreme Court in the late nineteenth and early twentieth centuries expressed in its decisions a laissez-faire "philosophy" compounded of Darwinism, a version of NATURAL RIGHTS theory, and conservative economic beliefs. When the Court abandoned that "philosophy," they adopted another, more progressivist and pragmatic, and more attuned to, though at most only loosely connected with, the renascent empiricism among academic philosophers. Occasionally, the Court has adverted to specific philosophical doctrines, from JOHN MARSHALL in FLETCHER V. PECK (1810) to GEORGE H. SUTHERLAND in UNITED STATES V. CURTISS-WRIGHT EXPORT CORP. (1936) (on the necessary existence of sovereign power). Individual Justices like OLIVER WENDELL HOLMES may have been influenced by philosophical reading and by contact with professional philosophers. But, on the whole, while "philosophy" has had an influence, philosophy has had little—except to the extent that the "philosophy" of the present is always shaped in part by the philosophy of the past. (The decreased influence of philosophy has not lessened the relevance of philosophical issues.)

There are a number of reasons for the decreased influence of philosophy. In the open society the Framers helped to create, their style of argument, dependent on a relatively homogeneous and classically educated elite, could not maintain its political importance. Also, political philosophy itself became less unified. Widely divergent views were united under the umbrella of the Enlightenment by common opposition to entrenched privilege and hieratic religion. Once common enemies were vanquished, philosophical comrades parted company.

Another reason for the decreased influence of philosophy is that philosophy admits of no binding authorities, while law does, and does essentially. The Framers were creating a new political system. No one since then, except to some extent the RECONSTRUCTION Congresses, has had that luxury. Later contributors to our constitutional development have always had to interpret, and to attempt to maintain at least the appearance of continuity with, what has gone before.

Curiously, while recent philosophical thinking has had little discernible influence on constitutional law, the reverse is not true. The decisions of the WARREN COURT and the public discussion they generated certainly contributed, probably significantly, to the revival of interest among American philosophers in social and political questions, a revival that became apparent in the CIVIL RIGHTS era of the 1950s and 1960s and that is still in full flower.

Whatever the influence or lack of it of philosophy on constitutional law, philosophical discussion among academic constitutional lawyers may have reached greater intensity in the 1980s than at any time since the 1780s. Constitutional law, like law in general, raises deep and perplexing philosophical questions. The questions that arise most immediately are questions of political philosophy, and of these the one that has generated most discussion is what is known as the "antimajoritarian difficulty": how can it be appropriate for the enormously consequential power of JUDICIAL REVIEW to be vested ultimately in nine individuals who are not chosen by the people and who are not politically accountable to anyone at all? The problem is especially vexing when the Court, in the space of three decades, has outlawed SEGREGATION, forbidden religious activity in the public schools, required REAPPORTIONMENT of the state legislatures and local government, created a constitutional code of CRIMINAL PROCEDURE, established a right to abortion, and found in the EQUAL PROTECTION clause a command that government shall not engage in SEX DISCRIMINATION.

There are three principal types of answer to the question how a democratic society can countenance such judicial power. The first answer, and the natural answer for any lawyer, is the claim that the Supreme Court has this power because the Constitution says it does. But the Constitution does not say that, at least not explicitly. The power of judicial review is nowhere explicitly granted. Now, in a sense, the lawyer's answer is still right. The Constitution as it has been interpreted from 1803 to the present does create the power of judicial review. The propriety of some form of judicial review is disputed by no one. Even so, it is noteworthy that at the very foundation of American constitutional law we encounter the problem of CONSTITUTIONAL INTERPRETATION.

Given a document, and given agreement that its commands are to be put into practice by legal institutions, how

do we decide what it commands? How do we decide what it means? Neither the words alone nor anything we know about the writers' intentions is likely to answer straightforwardly all the questions time will bring forth. For that matter, is it the document we are primarily concerned to interpret, or the political and doctrinal tradition proceeding from the document that we are concerned to interpret and to continue? And how are interpretation and continuation related?

It is important to distinguish between the document and the tradition and to ask how our commitments to each are interrelated. For example, we are firmly committed, by our allegiance to the tradition, to certain DOCTRINES, such as the effective application of the BILL OF RIGHTS to the states and of the equal protection clause to the federal government, which can be deduced from the document only by extremely generous canons of interpretation. Some argue that if we are committed to these doctrines, then we must accept and continue to apply those generous canons. But that conclusion does not follow at all. Law, like any tradition, can sanctify mistakes.

The problem of interpretation does not arise only at the stage of justifying judicial review. It arises also at every application of judicial review. What is the Court to do with this power? The lawyerly answer, and again clearly the right answer in some sense, is that the Court should enforce the Constitution. But once more, how do we decide what the Constitution means?

The lawyerly exponent of judicial review also invites, by appealing to the Constitution, the most fundamental question: why do we care about the document or the tradition at all? It may be that to ask this question is to go beyond the domain of the lawyer as lawyer; but lawyers and judges are people, and every person who bears allegiance to the document or the tradition must face this question. Note, however: even though all lawyers and judges must face this question of political philosophy in deciding whether to carry out their roles, it does not follow that they must also appeal to substantive political philosophy in the course of carrying out their roles. Whether they must do that, and whether they could avoid doing that if they tried, are further issues.

The difficulties with the lawyerly justification and exposition of judicial review have prompted two other main theories of judicial review. In one theory, judicial review is justified by the need to protect individual rights against infringement by majoritarian government. Exponents of this theory have drawn heavily on a neo-Kantian strain of contemporary American political philosophy in attempting to elucidate individual rights and the limits of the majority's legitimate power. In the other theory, judicial review does not purport to limit but merely to purify the democratic process. Judicial intervention is necessary to protect political speech and participation and to prevent distortion of the process by majority prejudice, but all in the name of more perfect majoritarianism.

Opposed as they are on the significance of individual rights, these two theories share an ambivalent relationship to the Constitution and the interpretive tradition. Whence comes the notion that individual autonomy should be protected, or that majoritarian democracy should be purified but not otherwise limited? Is it just that the Constitution says so? The Constitution says neither of these things explicitly; and it says both too much and too little to make either of these views a completely satisfactory reading of the document as a whole.

On the other hand, if someone claims to read the Constitution as protecting individuality (or purified majoritarianism) because of the independent moral weight of those values, why does the historical document come into it at all? Is not every appeal to the Constitution by a proponent of independently grounded values of autonomy or purified majoritarianism in some sense mere manipulation of other people's allegiance to the Constitution for itself?

We see that the questions raised by the lawyerly approach to judicial review are not so easily avoided. Still, the competing approaches we have noted alert us to dimensions of the problem not previously apparent. First, if the justification for judicial review is to promote general values such as autonomy or purified majoritarianism, that may help us decide how specific bits of the Constitution should be interpreted. Second, the tradition may refer to certain goals—justice, autonomy, democracy—which the tradition itself views as having a value and grounding outside and independent of the tradition. If the tradition commands allegiance both to its own specific content and to external values, it contains within itself the seeds of possible contradiction. What does faithfulness to the tradition then require?

As of the 1980s, the newest philosophical interest of academic constitutional lawyers is in hermeneutics. Whether there are answers here, and whether any such answers will influence the course of constitutional law, remains to be seen. Hermeneutics may bring new insight into the various meanings of the idea of operating in a tradition. Barring some remarkable feat of philosophical bootstrapping, hermeneutics will not answer the most fundamental philosophical question about constitutional law: why care about the tradition at all? And there is a final irony. Because the political community is made up of individuals who must confront this fundamental question, the community must confront it also, even though from another perspective it is by shared allegiance to the tradition that the community is defined.

DONALD H. REGAN
(1986)

Bibliography

DWORKIN, RONALD   (1977) 1978   *Taking Rights Seriously.* Cambridge, Mass.: Harvard University Press.
ELY, JOHN H.   1980   *Democracy and Distrust: A Theory of Judicial Review.* Cambridge, Mass.: Harvard University Press.
LAYCOCK, DOUGLAS   1981   Taking Constitutions Seriously: A Theory of Judicial Review. *Texas Law Review* 59:343–394.
TRIBE, LAURENCE H.   1978   *American Constitutional Law.* Mineola, N.Y.: Foundation Press.
WOOD, GORDON S.   1969   *The Creation of the American Republic, 1776–1787.* Chapel Hill: University of North Carolina Press for the Institute of Early American History and Culture at Williamsburg, Va.

PHYSICIAN-ASSISTED SUICIDE

See: Right to Die

PICKERING, JOHN
(1738?-1805)

In March 1803 the HOUSE OF REPRESENTATIVES impeached John Pickering, federal district judge for New Hampshire, of habitual drunkenness, uttering blasphemy and profanity from the bench, and making decisions contrary to law. During his SENATE trial Pickering introduced a defense of insanity; but the Senate, in a partisan vote, found him "guilty as charged" and removed him from office. The vote was a warning to other Federalist judges that Congress did not need to convict them of a specific crime in order to remove them. (See JUDICIAL IMPEACHMENT.)

DENNIS J. MAHONEY
(1986)

PICKETING

Picketing typically consists of one or more persons patrolling or stationed at a particular site, carrying or wearing large signs with a clearly visible message addressed to individuals or groups approaching the site. Some form of confrontation between the pickets and their intended addressees appears an essential ingredient of picketing. Congress and the National Labor Relations Board have distinguished between picketing and handbilling, however, and merely passing out leaflets without carrying a placard does not usually constitute picketing. What stamps picketing as different from more conventional forms of communication, for constitutional and other legal purposes, ordinarily seems to be the combination of a sign big enough to be seen easily and a confrontation between picketer and viewer.

Constitutional determinations concerning picketing

have usually involved LABOR unions that are advertising a dispute with employers and appealing to the public or fellow employees for support. The assistance sought might be a refusal by customers to patronize the picketed business or a refusal by workers to perform services or make deliveries there. In addition, picketing has often been a weapon of CIVIL RIGHTS demonstrators, political and religious activists, environmentalists, and other interest groups.

The leading Supreme Court decision upholding picketing as an exercise of FREEDOM OF SPEECH protected by the FIRST AMENDMENT is THORNHILL V. ALABAMA (1940). In striking down a state antipicketing statute, Justice FRANK MURPHY declared that an abridgment of the right to publicize through picketing or similar activity "can be justified only where the clear danger of substantive evils arises under circumstances affording no opportunity to test the merits of ideas by competition for acceptance in the market of public opinion." Despite this sweeping language, the actual holding in *Thornhill* was narrow. The Alabama courts were prepared to apply a criminal statute to prohibit a single individual from patrolling peacefully in front of an employer's establishment carrying a sign stating truthfully that the employer did not employ union labor.

Following *Thornhill* two principal themes have dominated the Supreme Court's analysis of the constitutional status of picketing. One is the "unlawful objectives" test and the other is the concept of picketing as "speech plus." Under the first approach, as illustrated by GIBONEY V. EMPIRE STORAGE & ICE CO. (1949), even peaceful picketing may be proscribed if its "sole, unlawful immediate objective" is the violation of a valid public policy or statutory mandate. Picketing is treated like any other type of communication, oral or written, which may also be forbidden if it produces a CLEAR AND PRESENT DANGER of, or a direct INCITEMENT to, substantive evils that government is entitled to prevent. A message delivered by pickets, however, might constitute a clearer and more present danger than the same message in a newspaper advertisement, for picketing physically confronts the addressee at the very moment of decision.

A conceptual weakness of the "unlawful objectives" test is that it can sustain almost any restriction on picketing by too loose a characterization of the pickets' purpose as illegal. In *Teamsters Local 695 v. Vogt, Inc.* (1957), a 5–3 Supreme Court upheld a state court INJUNCTION against peaceful organizational picketing on the ground that its purpose was to coerce the employer to force its employees to join the union. Even so, in *Amalgamated Food Employees Union v. Logan Valley Plaza* (1968) Justice THURGOOD MARSHALL could sum up the prior DOCTRINE by declaring that the cases in which picketing bans had been approved "involved picketing that was found either to have been directed at an illegal end . . . or to have been

directed to coercing a decision by an employer which, although in itself legal, could validly be required by the State to be left to the employer's free choice."

Picketing as "speech plus" refers to two elements that arguably distinguish it from pure speech. First, it involves physical activity, usually the patrolling of a particular location. It is therefore subject to TRESPASS laws, and to other laws governing the time, place, and manner of expression, such as laws limiting sound levels, regulating parades, or forbidding the obstruction of public ways. Furthermore, picketing enmeshed with violence or threats of violence may be enjoined or prosecuted as assault and battery. Second, picketing may serve as a "signal" for action, especially by organized groups like labor unions, without regard to the ideas being disseminated. Some scholars have challenged the "pure speech/speech plus" dichotomy, contending that all speech, oral or written, has certain physical attributes, and can evoke stock responses from a preconditioned audience.

A further strand of Supreme Court free speech analysis is the notion that government may not engage in "content control." Thus, in POLICE DEPARTMENT OF CHICAGO V. MOSLEY (1972) the Court invalidated a city ordinance that forbade all picketing next to any school while it was in session, but exempted "peaceful picketing of any school involved in a labor dispute." That constituted "an impermissible distinction between labor and other peaceful picketing." The "no content control" doctrine obviously must be qualified by the "unlawful objectives" test.

In 1980 the Supreme Court extended the "unlawful objectives" test so far as to strip it of any practical limitations. A 6–3 majority held in *NLRB v. Retail Employees Local 1001 (Safeco)* that picketing asking customers not to buy a nonunion product being distributed by a second party was an unlawful BOYCOTT of the distributor. Six Justices considered the prohibition justified constitutionally by Congress's purpose of blocking the "coercing" or "embroiling" of neutrals in another party's labor dispute. In *Safeco*, for the first time ever, the Supreme Court clearly sustained a ban on peaceful and orderly picketing addressed to, and calling for seemingly lawful responses by, individual consumers acting on their own.

Safeco might be explained on the basis that labor picketing is only "economic speech," like commercial advertising, and thus subject to lesser constitutional safeguards than political or ideological speech. Although such a distinction would contradict both established precedent and the traditional recognition of picketing as the working person's standard means of communication, at least it would preserve full-fledged free speech protections for picketing to promote political and ideological causes.

THEODORE J. ST. ANTOINE
(1986)

Bibliography

COX, ARCHIBALD   1951   Strikes, Picketing and the Constitution. *Vanderbilt Law Review* 4:574–602.

GREGORY, CHARLES O. and KATZ, HAROLD A.   (1946) 1979   *Labor and the Law.* New York: Norton.

JONES, EDGAR A., JR.   1956   Free Speech: Pickets on the Grass, Alas!—Amidst Confusion, a Consistent Principle. *Southern California Law Review* 29:137–181.

PIERCE, FRANKLIN
(1804–1869)

A New Hampshire attorney and politician, Pierce was nominated as a compromise presidential candidate by the Democrats in 1852. Pierce was a supporter of the COMPROMISE OF 1850 and a long-time opponent of abolitionists and antislavery Democrats. In 1854 he supported the KANSAS-NEBRASKA ACT, which led to a mini-civil war in "bleeding Kansas." Pierce's role in the passage of this act and his generally pro-southern positions undermined most of his other legislative proposals and his popularity in the North. During the CIVIL WAR Pierce's shrill attacks on ABRAHAM LINCOLN's administration made Pierce appear to be a full-fledged Copperhead.

PAUL FINKELMAN
(1986)

Bibliography

NICHOLS, ROY F.   1931   *Franklin Pierce: Young Hickory of the Granite State.* Philadelphia: University of Pennsylvania Press.

PIERCE, WILLIAM
(1740?–1789)

William Pierce, a veteran of the Revolutionary War and a member of Congress, was a delegate from Georgia to the CONSTITUTIONAL CONVENTION OF 1787. He spoke only infrequently, and he left the Convention on July 1, under pressure of private business difficulties. Pierce did not sign the Constitution but wrote to ST. GEORGE TUCKER: "I approve of its principles and would have signed it with all my heart, had I been present."

Pierce kept fairly detailed notes of the debates while he was present. The notes were published in 1828 and include brief character sketches of each of the delegates.

DENNIS J. MAHONEY
(1986)

PIERCE v. SOCIETY OF SISTERS
268 U.S. 510 (1925)

Pierce provided a doctrinal link between the SUBSTANTIVE DUE PROCESS of the era of LOCHNER V. NEW YORK (1905) and that of our own time. The Supreme Court unanimously invalidated an Oregon law requiring children to attend public schools. A church school and a military school, threatened with closure, sued to enjoin the law's enforcement. Although the law threatened injury to the schools, their challenge to it was based not on their own constitutional rights but on the rights of their pupils and the children's parents. By allowing the schools to make this challenge, the Court made a major exception to the usual rule denying a litigant's STANDING to assert the constitutional rights of others. Here there was a close relationship between the schools and their patrons, and failure to allow the schools to assert the patrons' rights might cause injury to the schools that no one would contest in court. Parents, fearing prosecution and unwilling to bear the expense of suit, might simply send their children to public schools.

In an opinion by Justice JAMES C. MCREYNOLDS, the Court held that the law unconstitutionally invaded the parents' liberty, guaranteed by the FOURTEENTH AMENDMENT's due process clause, to direct their children's education and upbringing. The decision rested squarely on the notion that important personal liberties could be seriously restricted by the state only upon a showing of great public need. Although *Pierce* thus traced its lineage to earlier decisions protecting economic liberty, it provided support for a later generation of decisions protecting marriage and family relationships against state intrusion. (See FREEDOM OF INTIMATE ASSOCIATION.)

Pierce is also cited regularly as a RELIGIOUS LIBERTY precedent, defending the right of parents to choose religious education for their children. (See WISCONSIN V. YODER.)

KENNETH L. KARST
(1986)

PIERSON v. RAY
386 U.S. 547 (1967)

Pierson is an important case involving individual immunities from suits under SECTION 1983, TITLE 42, UNITED STATES CODE. Clergymen who violated an unlawful "whites only" waiting room policy in a Jackson, Mississippi, bus terminal were arrested and convicted. They brought an action under section 1983 against the arresting police officers and a state judge for depriving the clergymen of their constitutional rights. The Supreme Court both reaffirmed what it asserted to be the absolute immunity of judges from suit at COMMON LAW and refused to interpret section 1983 to abolish that traditional immunity. Although the police officer defendants were not granted absolute immunity, the Court did grant them a defense if the otherwise unconstitutional arrests were made in good faith and with PROBABLE CAUSE.

THEODORE EISENBERG
(1986)

PINCKNEY, CHARLES
(1757–1824)

Charles Pinckney, a wealthy and ambitious young lawyer from South Carolina, was one of the most active members of the CONSTITUTIONAL CONVENTION OF 1787. A supporter of strong national government, Pinckney had already proposed in Congress several amendments to strengthen the government under the ARTICLES OF CONFEDERATION. He had unsuccessfully urged Congress to call a convention to amend the Articles.

Selected as a delegate to the Federal Convention, Pinckney drafted a comprehensive plan for revising the articles which he introduced immediately after EDMUND RANDOLPH proposed the VIRGINIA PLAN. The PINCKNEY PLAN was never debated in the Convention or the Committee of the Whole, although the Committee of Detail may have drawn some ideas or phrases from it.

Pinckney was one of the most frequent speakers in the debates, but the Constitution, as written, reflected his influence only in minor points and details. In a speech before signing, Pinckney announced that he would support the Constitution despite "the contemptible weakness and dependence of the Executive."

In his later career, Pinckney was a delegate to the South Carolina ratifying convention and to the state CONSTITUTIONAL CONVENTION of 1790, three times governor, a member of the legislature and of both houses of Congress, and minister of the United States to Spain.

DENNIS J. MAHONEY
(1986)

PINCKNEY, CHARLES COTESWORTH
(1746–1825)

A British-educated, slaveholding lawyer, General Charles Cotesworth Pinckney represented South Carolina at the CONSTITUTIONAL CONVENTION OF 1787 and signed the Constitution. In the convention he worked for a strong national government and for protection of the slaveholding interests. As a leading spokesman for RATIFICATION in South Carolina, he defended the compromises on SLAVERY and argued that a BILL OF RIGHTS was unnecessary.

In 1791, Pinckney declined President GEORGE WASHINGTON's offer of a seat on the Supreme Court. The chief leader of the southern FEDERALISTS, Pinckney was nominated for Vice-President in 1800, and for President in both 1804 and 1808.

DENNIS J. MAHONEY
(1986)

Bibliography

ZAHNISER, MARVIN R. 1967 *Charles Cotesworth Pinckney, Founding Father.* Chapel Hill: University of North Carolina Press.

PINCKNEY PLAN
(1787)

The brash young South Carolinian CHARLES PINCKNEY arrived at the CONSTITUTIONAL CONVENTION OF 1787 bearing his own comprehensive draft of a new CONSTITUTION based on proposals he had made to amend the ARTICLES OF CONFEDERATION during his three years in Congress. He presented it to the convention immediately after EDMUND RANDOLPH presented the VIRGINIA PLAN. The Pinckney Plan was never debated, but it was referred to the Committee on Detail which may have drawn some ideas or phrases from it.

There was no copy of the Pinckney Plan among the papers of the convention. Pinckney himself later published what he claimed was his plan, but this was actually a fabrication closely resembling the finished Constitution. On the basis of this (fraudulent) published version and Pinckney's own extravagant claims about his influence, many historians and popular writers have attributed more significance to the Pinckney Plan and its author than either actually had.

In the twentieth century, historians J. Franklin Jameson and ANDREW C. MCLAUGHLIN reconstructed the details of the original Pinckney Plan. The proposal was certainly quite nationalistic, with no state role in the election of either house of Congress, an unconditional congressional veto over state laws, and a very powerful national executive.

DENNIS J. MAHONEY
(1986)

Bibliography

MCLAUGHLIN, ANDREW C. 1904 The Pinckney Plan. *American Historical Review* 9:135–147.

PINK, UNITED STATES v.
315 U.S. 203 (1942)

In *Pink*, the Supreme Court reaffirmed a DOCTRINE articulated five years earlier in UNITED STATES V. BELMONT

(1937): that the President has exclusive constitutional authority to recognize foreign governments and to take all steps necessary to effect such recognition. In *Belmont*, the Court recognized the federal government's STANDING to sue to enforce an EXECUTIVE AGREEMENT known as the "Litvinov Agreement." As part of the process of recognition of the Soviet Union by the United States in 1933, this agreement assigned to the United States nationalized Russian assets located within the United States.

In *Pink*, the Court was again confronted with the controversial Litvinov Assignment. In this case, while recognizing the federal government's rights under the Litvinov Assignment as required by *Belmont*, the New York courts rejected the government's claims of ownership of the assets in question, contending that to enforce the assignment would violate New York public policy against the confiscation of private property. The Supreme Court reversed, 5–2, emphasizing that an executive agreement, like a TREATY, is part of the "supreme law of the land" that no state may frustrate without interfering unconstitutionally with the federal government's exclusive competence in respect of FOREIGN AFFAIRS. In so doing, the Court reasserted the supremacy of an executive agreement over all inconsistent state law or policy.

BURNS H. WESTON
(1986)

Bibliography

CARDOZO, MICHAEL H. 1962 The Authority in Internal Law of International Treaties: The Pink Case. *Syracuse Law Review* 13:544–553.

FORKOSCH, MORRIS D. 1975 The Constitution and International Relations. *California Western International Law Journal* 5.210, 240–249.

HENKIN, LOUIS 1972 *Foreign Affairs and the Constitution.* Mineola, N.Y.: Foundation Press.

LEARY, M. A. 1979 International Executive Agreements: A Guide to the Legal Issues and Research Sources. *Law Library Journal* 72:1–11.

PINKNEY, WILLIAM
(1764–1822)

William Pinkney studied law under SAMUEL CHASE and subsequently practiced in Baltimore. Although he opposed the RATIFICATION OF THE CONSTITUTION in the Maryland convention of 1788, he later became one of the nation's foremost constitutional lawyers. He held public office continuously from 1788 until his death, serving in the state legislature, in both houses of Congress, as a diplomat in important foreign capitals, and as ATTORNEY GENERAL of the United States under President JAMES MADISON. Although as a young man he favored gradual compensated emancipation in Maryland, Pinkney was a vigorous spokesman for the slave states in the Senate debates over the MISSOURI COMPROMISE (1820).

Between political and diplomatic assignments Pinkney conducted what was probably the most lucrative legal practice in the United States, arguing seventy-two cases before the Supreme Court. He was counsel for the New Hampshire state appointed board of trustees in DARTMOUTH COLLEGE V. WOODWARD (1819), unsuccessfully arguing that the college was a public CORPORATION whose charter could be altered by the state. In MCCULLOCH V. MARYLAND (1819), however, he won the day, contending for the constitutionality of a congressionally chartered bank and against the power of the state to tax it. And in COHENS V. VIRGINIA (1821) he successfully argued for the Supreme Court APPELLATE JURISDICTION over state criminal cases.

As an advocate, Pinkney won the praise of both judges and opposing counsel. Chief Justice JOHN MARSHALL called him "the greatest man I ever saw in a court of justice" and Marshall's successor, ROGER B. TANEY, said that in thirty years, "I have seen none to equal Pinkney." His enduring significance in American constitutional history derives from his incisive and original arguments in cases of first impression.

PAUL FINKELMAN
(1986)

Bibliography

PINKNEY, REV. WILLIIAM 1853 *The Life of William Pinkney.* New York: D. Appleton & Co.

PIQUA BRANCH OF THE STATE BANK OF OHIO v. KNOOP
16 Howard 369 (1854)

In NEW JERSEY V. WILSON (1812) the Supreme Court had held that a state grant of a tax immunity was a contract within the protection of the CONTRACT CLAUSE. In this case Ohio chartered a bank with the proviso that six percent of its net profits would be taxed in lieu of other taxation. The states competed with each other to entice private business to settle within their borders on the supposition that the more banks, railroads, and factories a state had, the greater would be its prosperity. Special privileges to CORPORATIONS were common, and they often wrote their own charters. Ohio, gripped by an anticorporate movement, reneged by passing an act to tax banks at the same rate as other properties. The bank refused to pay the new tax on the ground that its charter was a contract the obligation of which had been impaired by the tax. (See OBLIGATION OF CONTRACTS.) By a vote of 6–3 the Supreme Court invalidated the tax. To the contention that the power to tax was an inalienable attribute of SOVEREIGNTY, which could not be contracted away, the Court replied that the making of a public contract is an exercise of sovereignty. To the argument that one legislature, by granting a charter of tax immunity, could not bind its successors, the Court replied that the contract clause made the charter binding. In effect the Court cautioned the states to govern wisely, because the Court would not shield them from their imprudence if it took the form of contracts. Corporations throughout the country profited enormously.

LEONARD W. LEVY
(1986)

PITNEY, MAHLON
(1858–1924)

Mahlon Pitney was the last of President WILLIAM HOWARD TAFT's appointments to the Supreme Court. Organized labor and some progressives vigorously protested the nomination because of Pitney's antilabor opinions as a New Jersey state judge, but his views paralleled Taft's. During Pitney's decade on the bench (1912–1922), he made prophets of his critics, as his opinions reflected a consistent hostility to the claims of organized labor. Nevertheless, Taft, as Chief Justice, derided Pitney as a "weak" member of his Court.

In COPPAGE V. KANSAS (1915) Pitney concluded that a Kansas statute prohibiting YELLOW DOG CONTRACTS violated FREEDOM OF CONTRACT. The opinion largely followed doctrine laid down in LOCHNER V. NEW YORK (1905), and reinforced in ADAIR V. UNITED STATES (1908), when the Court nullified an 1898 congressional law prohibiting railroads from imposing yellow dog contracts. In *Coppage*, Pitney attacked the state law as a restraint on a worker's right to contract, a right he saw as essential to the laborer as to the capitalist, "for the vast majority of persons who have no other honest way to begin to acquire property, save by working for money." Rejecting the statute's avowed intent of enabling workers to organize and bargain collectively, Pitney held that its primary effect was to interfere with "the normal and essentially innocent exercise of personal liberty or of property rights."

Two years later, Pitney wrote the Supreme Court's opinion favoring labor INJUNCTION and again sustained the validity of yellow dog contracts. In HITCHMAN COAL AND COKE CO. V. MITCHELL (1917) he upheld an injunction forbidding the United Mine Workers from seeking to organize workers who had previously agreed not to join a union. Every miner who had affiliated with the union "was guilty of a breach of contract," he said; furthermore, Pitney found that the union knowingly had violated the employer's "legal and constitutional right to run its mine 'non-union.'"

Pitney's implacable defense of yellow dog contracts and injunctions galvanized labor's growing antagonism to the federal judiciary and its demands for congressional relief. Eventually, in 1932, the NORRIS-LAGUARDIA ACT forbade federal courts to enforce yellow dog contracts or issue labor injunctions, thus severely limiting the effects of Pitney's COPPAGE and HITCHMAN opinions.

In DUPLEX PRINTING CO. V. DEERING (1921) Pitney reinfoced the judicial ban on secondary BOYCOTTS, thus frustrating organized labor's understanding that the CLAYTON ACT (1914) had legalized such practices. Pitney followed an earlier decision against secondary boycotts (LOEWE V. LAWLOR, 1908) and argued that a sympathetic strike supporting a secondary boycott could not be deemed "peaceful and lawful persuasion as allowed in the Clayton Act." Although Pitney regularly invoked judicial doctrines that inhibited labor's right to organize, he occasionally defied prediction. In *Mountain Timber Co. v. Washington* (1917) Pitney led a 5–4 majority that sustained a state WORKERS' COMPENSATION law requiring all employers to contribute to a general state fund, regardless of wheter their employees had been injured. He found that the statute did not deprive employers of their property without DUE PROCESS OF LAW, and furthermore, it had a reasonable relationship to the GENERAL WELFARE. Four years later, in TRUAX V. CORRIGAN (1921), he joined OLIVER WENDELL HOLMES, LOUIS D. BRANDEIS, and JOHN H. CLARKE in dissent against Chief Justice Taft's opinion invalidating an Arizona law modeled on the labor provisions of the Clayton Act. In another rare deviation from his norm, Pitney joined the dissenters who favored the dissolution of the United States Steel Corporation.

Typically, judges such as Pitney would presume that regulatory laws such as Kansas's prohibition of yellow dog contracts and the labor provisions of the Clayton Act violated liberty of contract or property rights. Yet Pitney made no such assumption when an individual confronted the criminal process. In the notorious case of FRANK V. MANGUM (1915), for example, Pitney maintained that the state of Georgia had "fairly and justly" done its duty. Pitney also vigorously supported the national government's prosecution of dissenters and radicals following WORLD WAR I. In *Pierce v. United States* (1920) he sustained the conviction of socialists who "knowingly" and "recklessly" distributed "highly colored and sensational" and "grossly false" statements about the government's conduct of the war. The *Pierce* decision solidified the Court's shift from Holmes's CLEAR AND PRESENT DANGER interpretation of the FIRST AMENDMENT to the less speech-protective BAD TENDENCY TEST.

Pitney approved the Court's invalidation of the child labor laws; he dissented from the majority's approval of widening the authority of the Interstate Commerce Commission; and he dissented from Justice CHARLES EVANS HUGHES's expansive reading of the COMMERCE CLAUSE in the "Shreveport Case," *Houston, East and West Texas Railway Company v. United States* (1914). In short, Pitney's judicial career faithfully reflected the conservative reaction to much of the political and legal thrust of the Progressive movement.

STANLEY I. KUTLER
(1986)

Bibliography

LEVITAN, DAVID M. 1954 Mahlon Pitney—Labor Judge. *Virginia Law Review* 40:733–770.

PITT, WILLIAM
(Lord Chatham)
(1708–1778)

William Pitt the elder was one of Britain's greatest statesmen and one of freedom's staunchest friends. He led Britain from near defeat in the Seven Years War to victory and worldwide empire.

In the WILKES CASES debates (1763–1770) Pitt denounced GENERAL WARRANTS as illegal and subversive of liberty and opposed any surrender of PARLIAMENTARY PRIVILEGE. During the 1766 debate over repeal of the Stamp Act, Pitt insisted that "the distinction between legislation and taxation is essentially necessary to liberty," and that while Britain was "sovereign and supreme, in every circumstance of government and legislation whatsoever," Parliament had no right to tax those not represented therein. "There is," he declared, "a plain distinction between taxes levied for purposes of raising a revenue, and duties imposed for the regulation of trade." Later that year, as earl of Chatham, Pitt was again called to head the government. During his administration (but while he was incapacitated by illness) his chancellor of the exchequer procured passage of the TOWNSHEND ACTS.

In the 1770s Chatham urged conciliation with the American colonies, but he opposed any measure tending toward dissolution of the empire. His final speech, delivered in 1778, was against a motion to withdraw British troops and recognize American independence.

DENNIS J. MAHONEY
(1986)

PLAIN FEEL DOCTRINE

The FOURTH AMENDMENT prohibits the government from conducting unreasonable seizures of effects. This protection, however, does not require the government to obtain a warrant in every instance. In *Minnesota v. Dickerson* (1993), the Supreme Court established the plain feel or plain touch DOCTRINE, based on the premise that tactile information can justify a warrantless seizure. The plain feel doctrine extends the principle of the PLAIN VIEW DOCTRINE, which rests on the sense of sight, to the sense of touch. The doctrine permits a law enforcement officer to seize an object if its nature is immediately apparent during a touching permitted by the Fourth Amendment. Thus *Dickerson* held that an officer authorized to touch clothing or a container may acquire PROBABLE CAUSE to believe the felt object is contraband or evidence and thereby justify a further Fourth Amendment intrusion.

The plain feel doctrine does not provide authority to touch. It merely permits the officer to act on tactile information concerning a felt object. Authority to feel the object in the first instance must be found elsewhere. In many cases, the officer derives authority from the STOP-AND-FRISK principles of TERRY V. OHIO (1968) which allow a pat down for weapons. In others, the officer has consent for the touching. Authority to touch may also rest on the need to move an object or on other permitted conduct involving contact with the object.

In every case, however, the officer's authority to engage in tactile exploration is limited. When the prosecution relies on the plain feel doctrine, the court should determine not only whether the object could be recognized by touch as contraband or evidence, but also whether its tactile characteristics are so pronounced that it could be recognized within the scope of the permitted search. An officer may not extend the scope of a search in an attempt to obtain probable cause. The *Dickerson* Court recognized authority to seize items felt during a pat down but emphasized that a *Terry* frisk for weapons is strictly circumscribed and does not permit an officer to probe an object that does not feel like a weapon. The officer's continued manipulation in *Dickerson* went beyond the authorized intrusion and also belied any claim that it was immediately apparent that the lump was crack cocaine.

The prosecution needs to rely on the plain feel doctrine only when an officer without probable cause to arrest a defendant seizes a nonweapon-like item recognizable by feel. Because few seizable items other than weapons can be identified by feel, one might expect plain feel to be a tool of limited utility. On the contrary, prosecutors often rely on plain feel to justify seizures. Plain feel cases fall into a predictable pattern. The prosecution most often invokes the doctrine to uphold a seizure of drugs, drug paraphernalia, or evidence of drug trafficking from the defendant's person. The touching typically occurs during a *Terry* frisk or a consensual pat down following an authorized stop.

Determining whether the nature of the seized item was

immediately apparent to the officer is critical to justify a seizure based on plain feel. Although *Dickerson* used "immediately apparent" to describe the standard for seizure, it is clear from *Arizona v. Hicks* (1987) that plain feel, like plain view, requires probable cause.

The "immediately apparent" requirement for seizing items that do not feel weapon-like should be distinguished from the *Terry* basis for seizing items that feel like weapons. *Terry* allows the officer to frisk to detect and remove weapons. The *Terry* frisk is biased to protect the safety of the officer and public. Generally, any object of sufficient hardness and size can be explored, even though its shape does not advertise it as a gun or knife. If clothing obscures the contents from tactile detection, courts often approve investigation of the object.

By contrast, the plain feel doctrine is not biased to permit exploration of suspicious objects. The *Dickerson* Court emphasized that the tactile information obtained during the authorized touching must immediately raise probable cause to believe the object is seizable. Mere reasonable suspicion that an object is contraband does not support further intrusion.

ANNE BOWEN POULIN
(2000)

(SEE ALSO: *Search and Seizure; Unreasonable Search.*)

PLAIN VIEW DOCTRINE

The FOURTH AMENDMENT protects persons and their effects against unreasonable SEARCHES AND SEIZURES. However, articles exposed to the plain view of others are subject to a warrantless seizure on PROBABLE CAUSE, for no search is involved and hence no invasion of privacy results. (Plain view differs from abandonment. Exposure of an article to plain view may result from carelessness; abandonment signifies a deliberate relinquishment of the right of ownership. In either case, there is no constitutionally protected interest in the privacy of the article.)

Three conditions must be met for a plain view seizure to be constitutional, according to the decision in COOLIDGE V. NEW HAMPSHIRE (1971). First, the officer who sees the article must have a legal right to be where he is. Second, discovery of the article by the police must be "inadvertent," not a result of prior information that would have enabled the police to obtain a warrant beforehand. (This requirement is relaxed in a SEARCH INCIDENT TO ARREST, where a seizure made within the limited scope of the authorized search is lawful even if the finding of the evidence was anticipated.) Finally, the incriminating nature of the evidence must be "immediately apparent," so that no additional intrusion on privacy is necessary in order to es-

tablish that fact. (The term "immediately apparent" was modified in *Brown v. Texas* (1983) to mean probable cause; certainty is not required.)

An emergency "hot pursuit" of a suspect into private premises, as in WARDEN V. HAYDEN (1967), provides the widest latitude for a plain view seizure; the search for the suspect and his weapons is permitted to extend throughout the entire place until he is apprehended. Barring emergencies, however, a plain view of the interior of a house, obtained through a window or open door, does not permit a warrantless entry of premises any more than does testimony of the senses (say, the odor of marijuana) that criminal activity is afoot. In searches of buildings, therefore, the plain view serves to authorize a seizure only when a lawful search is already in progress when the view is obtained. A different standard applies to automobiles: a plain view of evidence in an automobile on the road not only permits seizure of the evidence but also may provide probable cause for a WARRANTLESS SEARCH of the entire vehicle. Since *Brown*, even a closed container may be seized under the plain view doctrine if the contents can be reliably inferred from its outside appearance—for example, a tied balloon of a type commonly used to carry narcotics.

JACOB W. LANDYNSKI
(1986)

Bibliography

LAFAVE, WAYNE R. 1978 *Search and Seizure: A Treatise on the Fourth Amendment.* Vol. 2:589–595, 601–605. St. Paul, Minn.: West Publishing Co.

PLAIN VIEW DOCTRINE
(Update)

Under the plain view doctrine of COOLIDGE V. NEW HAMPSHIRE (1971), certain items found in a lawful search may be seized without a SEARCH WARRANT though they were not among the items that were legitimate objectives of the search. Though this issue also arises in other contexts, it most frequently comes into play when police, executing a search warrant naming certain things to be seized, find and immediately seize other items unnamed in the warrant.

The Supreme Court in *Coolidge* declined to hold that in such circumstances the police must always seek another warrant, reasoning that such a procedure "would often be a needless inconvenience, and sometimes dangerous—to the evidence or to the police themselves." At the same time, the Court was not prepared to uphold warrantless seizures made either without PROBABLE CAUSE or as a consequence of an earlier circumvention of the warrant requirement, as where the police intended from the very beginning to seize the unnamed objects. Consequently, the *Coolidge* plurality concluded that a warrantless seizure was permissible only if three requirements were met: (1) there must have been a prior valid intrusion into the place where the seized evidence was found; (2) the discovery of the seized items must have been "inadvertent"; and (3) it must have been "immediately apparent" that the seized items were evidence of crime.

The *Coolidge* plurality did not explain what it meant by "inadvertent." It did not state explicitly what degree of expectation would make the subsequent discovery of an item other than inadvertent. Most lower courts took the inadvertent-discovery limitation to mean that a discovery is inadvertent, without regard to the hopes or expectations of the police, if there were not sufficient grounds to get a search warrant for that item. Moreover, for probable cause to nullify an inadvertent claim those grounds must have been in the hands of the police at a time when it would have been feasible to obtain a warrant, for otherwise the police cannot be faulted for failing to obtain a warrant also naming the seized item.

Even so interpreted, the inadvertent-discovery limitation is unsound. It is a limitation on seizure, not search, and thus protects possessory interests only, not privacy interests. Yet, one consequence of the inadvertence requirement is that lawfully discovered items seized on probable cause may be excluded merely because the officer, out of an abundance of caution, failed to seek a magistrate's approval for a more intrusive search through the premises for those items. If, as the Court declared in HOFFA V. UNITED STATES (1966), "the police are not required to guess at their peril the precise moment at which they have probable cause," this result is not a desirable one. Such a result will no longer obtain, for in *Horton v. California* (1990) the Court rejected the inadvertent-discovery limitation on the plain view doctrine.

The "immediately apparent" limitation does not require the police to be certain of the incriminating character of the seized object; probable cause will suffice. But when must this probable cause become apparent? Assume a case in which police executing a search warrant for stolen stereo equipment see in the searched premises a television set. They turn the television set around to expose its serial number, and then determine that the number matches that of a set recently reported stolen. Many courts interpreted *Coolidge* to mean that such movement of the television set, though not authorized by the warrant, was nonetheless a lawful search if undertaken upon reasonable suspicion that the set was stolen. The appealing rationale of these cases was that the slight movement of the object to examine its exterior was such a minimal intrusion upon

FOURTH AMENDMENT interests as to not require full probable cause.

Though these decisions arguably found support in the Supreme Court's decision in *United States v. Place* (1983), holding that personal effects in transit such as luggage could be briefly detained for investigation upon mere reasonable suspicion, the Court in *Arizona v. Hicks* (1987) held that *Coolidge*'s "immediately apparent" requirement means full probable cause must exist before the television set is even moved. The Court in *Hicks* reasoned that such movement was part of "a dwelling-place search," for which full probable cause had always been required, and distinguished such cases as *Place* on the ground that the "special operational necessities" existing there were not present. *Hicks* made the plain view doctrine of the *Coolidge* plurality a doctrine endorsed by a majority of the Justices, and *Hicks* held that the doctrine may not be invoked when the police have less than probable cause to believe that an item should be seized as evidence of crime.

WAYNE R. LAFAVE
(1992)

(SEE ALSO: *Search and Seizure; Unreasonable Search; Warrantless Searches.*)

Bibliography

LAFAVE, WAYNE R. 1987 *Search and Seizure: A Treatise on the Fourth Amendment*, 2nd ed. St. Paul, Minn.: West Publishing Co.

MOYLAN, CHARLES E. 1975 The Plain View Doctrine: Unexpected Child of the Great Search Incident Geography Battle. *Mercer Law Review* 26:1047–1101.

PLANNED PARENTHOOD v. ASHCROFT

See: Reproductive Autonomy

PLANNED PARENTHOOD v. CASEY
505 U.S. 833 (1992)

In *Planned Parenthood v Casey*, a slim majority of the Supreme Court, to the surprise of many, dramatically rejected the vigorous and caustic calls of four dissenting Justices to overrule ROE V. WADE (1973), decided nineteen years earlier. The majority instead reaffirmed *Roe*'s "core" as it struck down a spousal notice provision in a Pennsylvania ABORTION statute. A different majority, however, OVERRULED portions of two of *Roe*'s successor decisions, by upholding the statute's informed consent provisions for adult women, including a twenty-four–hour waiting period and a prescribed set of oral and written disclosures by the physician of "objective, non-judgmental . . . accurate scientific information" about fetal development, social services, and adoption. This latter majority also upheld a parental consent provision (with a judicial bypass) for minors seeking abortion and a clinic data collection and reporting requirement.

Among the notable features of this case was the gravitas of the PLURALITY OPINION by the three Justices in the conservative middle of the Court. Justices ANTHONY M. KENNEDY, SANDRA DAY O'CONNOR, and DAVID H. SOUTER jointly authored and signed the opinion, an exceptional step reminiscent of the COOPER V. AARON (1958) opinion signed by each of the nine WARREN COURT Justices to emphasize their commitment to BROWN V. BOARD OF EDUCATION (1955). Drawing back from their expressions of hostility to *Roe* in prior opinions, Kennedy and O'Connor joined with Souter to reaffirm *Roe*'s "core" holdings that a woman has a FUNDAMENTAL RIGHT to terminate her pregnancy prior to fetal viability; after viability a state can ban abortion except where the woman's life or health are endangered; and from the start of a pregnancy the state has a legitimate interest in protecting the health of the woman and a growing interest in protecting the life of the fetus.

In contrast to Justices JOHN PAUL STEVENS and HARRY A. BLACKMUN, who in separate opinions adhered more fully to the Court's opinion in *Roe*, the joint plurality opinion rejected *Roe*'s "trimester structure" for evaluating state regulation of abortion in favor of an "undue burden" standard. By this, the plurality meant that a state cannot constitutionally impose a rule that leaves a woman with merely a formal right or that "has the purpose or effect of placing a substantial obstacle" to the effective exercise of the abortion right. Moreover, a burden that affects only a small fraction of women can nonetheless constitute an undue burden as to them. Thus, while the spousal notice provision may interfere with the choice of only some women, it was struck down as a substantial burden. By contrast, the plurality did not deem the impediments that a twenty-four–hour waiting period clearly impose to be a substantial obstacle, on the evidence offered in this facial challenge. It remains to be seen how courts will implement the "undue burden" standard in evaluating regulations that make abortion more difficult and more costly. Although the dissenters disparaged this standard as a newly minted DOCTRINE without content, some scholars have suggested that the undue burden standard accurately describes the Court's traditional approach, across a broad range of constitutional issues, to determining whether a right has been infringed.

In applying the undue burden standard, the Court notably did not apply the dicta in UNITED STATES V. SALERNO (1987) that, outside of FIRST AMENDMENT cases, a facial challenge can succeed only if there is "no set of circumstances" under which the statute is valid.

The joint opinion tied its application of the undue burden standard to the important question of the affirmative role of the state in creating a decisional framework for individuals to help secure to them conditions supporting the exercise of their autonomy; and this concern, in turn, implicitly implicates the related questions of GOVERNMENT SPEECH and the speech of professionals. The opinion indicated that the state may seek to further its interest in "potential life" prior to fetal viability only by means "calculated to inform the woman's free choice, not hinder it," and may require physicians to provide patients with certain information "to ensure that this choice is thoughtful and informed" and specifically informed of the philosophic and social arguments that favor a state's "preference" for childbirth.

In describing the woman's interest in reproductive autonomy, the joint opinion spoke more of liberty than the RIGHT OF PRIVACY; linked aspects of this liberty to the right of bodily integrity the Court has identified in, among other cases, *Cruzan v. Director, Missouri Department of Health* (1990); and sympathetically emphasized that reproduction and abortion are unique in that they touch upon the very core of personhood and conscience (as individuals seek to apprehend "the mystery of human life") and involve for women a unique intimacy, burden, and pain. Moreover, the opinion recognized the essential role of reproductive autonomy in affording women opportunities "to participate equally in the economic and social life of the Nation. . . ." Despite the views of some commentators, it would appear that the opinion necessarily, although implicitly, treated the woman's interest as fundamental. In so doing, the joint opinion forthrightly reaffirmed that the "liberty" the DUE PROCESS clause protects includes fundamental rights that are identified by a judicial exercise of "reasoned judgment" and not only by a search for the Framers' ORIGINAL INTENT or for America's specific historical traditions. Among those identified liberties endorsed by the joint opinion is the fundamental right to use contraceptives, including postconception contraceptives.

Despite its sympathetic elaboration of the woman's interests, the joint opinion intimated that some of its authors might not have joined *Roe* when originally decided, and that for them STARE DECISIS was determinative of their judgment. Because *Roe* was workable, had induced serious reliance by a generation of women, and was not an anachronism undermined by subsequent changes in either doctrine or facts, the plurality found no warrant to overturn *Roe* under traditional principles of stare decisis in constitutional matters. The plurality nonetheless acknowledged that these factors would not preclude reexamination of even so repeatedly reaffirmed a case as *Roe*, given the depth of the constitutional and political controversy surrounding it. However, after reviewing more than a century of CONSTITUTIONAL HISTORY, the opinion concluded that *Roe* was one of those rare cases in which the Court "calls the contending sides of a national controversy to end their national division by accepting a common mandate rooted in" the Court's interpretation of the Constitution. Unless the circumstances facing the nation have fundamentally altered, the opinion asserts, later Justices must adhere to the judgment in such a case in order to maintain the Court's constitutional legitimacy and avoid appearing to "surrender to political pressure."

Perhaps the authors of the joint opinion understood that, had they joined in overruling *Roe*, they would have appeared to be doing exactly what the Republican Presidents RONALD REAGAN and GEORGE H. W. BUSH who nominated them wanted. For these Presidents had engaged in an unprecedented attempt to reshape the federal judiciary by ideologically screening judicial nominations, especially with respect to abortion, and by occasionally disregarding other traditional criteria of nomination, including professional and senatorial judgments. In declining to vote the party line, however, these Justices may have aided the REPUBLICAN PARTY electorally by continuing to place the abortion right beyond Republican political reach—at least until additional retirements from the Court lead some to try once again to place the issue of *Roe* before the electorate and the Court.

ROBERT D. GOLDSTEIN
(2000)

Bibliography

BROWNSTEIN, ALAN 1994 How Rights Are Infringed: The Role of Undue Burden Analysis in Constitutional Doctrine. *Hastings Law Journal* 45:867–959.

GOLDSTEIN, ROBERT D. 1988 *Mother-Love and Abortion: A Legal Interpretation.* Berkeley, Calif.: University of California Press.

——— 1996 Reading *Casey:* Structuring the Woman's Decisionmaking Process. *William & Mary Bill of Rights Journal* 4:787–880.

PLANNED PARENTHOOD OF CENTRAL MISSOURI v. DANFORTH
428 U.S. 52 (1976)

Following ROE V. WADE (1973), Missouri adopted a comprehensive law regulating ABORTION. Planned Parenthood, which operated an abortion clinic, and two eminent physicians sued in federal district court challenging the constitutionality of most of the law's provisions. On appeal, the Supreme Court unanimously upheld three of the state's requirements and by divided vote invalidated four others. Justice HARRY A. BLACKMUN wrote for the Court.

The Court sustained the law's definition of "viability" of a fetus: "when the life of the unborn child may be continued indefinitely outside the womb by natural or artificial life-supportive systems." The state's failure to set a specific time period survived a challenge for VAGUENESS; the Court assumed that the physician retained the power to determine viability. The Court also upheld a requirement of written certification by a woman of her "informed" consent to an abortion, and certain record-keeping requirements.

The Court invalidated, 6–3, a requirement of consent to an abortion by the husband of the pregnant woman, and invalidated, 5–4, a parental consent requirement for unmarried women under age eighteen. Recognizing the husband's strong interest in the abortion decision, the Court concluded that when spouses disagreed, only one of them could prevail; that one must be the woman. As for parental consent, the opinion offered no broad charter of CHILDREN'S RIGHTS but concluded that a "mature" minor's right to have an abortion must prevail over a parent's contrary decision (*H. L. v. Matheson*, 1981). The state had little hope of restoring a family structure already "fractured" by such a conflict.

The Court invalidated, 6–3, a prohibition on saline amniocentesis as an abortion technique. The procedure was used in more than two-thirds of all abortions following the first trimester of pregnancy; its prohibition would undermine *Roe*. Finally, the state had required a physician performing an abortion to use professional skill and care to preserve the life and health of a fetus. The requirement was held invalid, 6–3, because it was not limited to the time following the stage of fetal viability.

The question of the doctor's role in determining viability and preserving fetal life returned to the Court in *Colautti v. Franklin* (1979). There the Court invalidated, 6–3, on vagueness grounds, a Pennsylvania law requiring a doctor to exercise care to protect a fetus when there was "sufficient reason to believe that the fetus may be viable." As in *Roe* and *Danforth*, the Court paid considerable deference to physicians, leaving undefined their control over their patients' constitutional rights.

KENNETH L. KARST
(1986)

(SEE ALSO: *Reproductive Autonomy.*)

Bibliography

COHEN, LESLIE ANN 1980 Fetal Viability and Individual Autonomy: Resolving Medical and Legal Standards for Abortion. *UCLA Law Review* 27:1340–1364.

PLEA BARGAINING

The overwhelming majority of convictions in American criminal courts occur when the accused pleads guilty to a charge; few defendants receive a full judicial trial. "Plea bargaining" describes a variety of incentives and pressures that produce this result and that are commonly encountered in American criminal courts. Some plea bargaining is explicit: defendants are led by the prosecutor or the judge to plead guilty in return for the promise of some concession or in fear of harsh treatment meted out to those who insist on a trial. The reward for defendants may be release on bail before trial, the dropping or reduction of charges, or the lightening of punishment imposed after conviction. Some defendants may plead guilty out of a sense of contrition, but more probably acquiesce in conviction because they expect more lenient treatment if they do not insist on their right to trial.

Overt negotiation to induce a defendant to plead guilty is often not necessary. The incentive structure is built into the culture of the courthouse and into the substantive criminal code itself. Those accused of crime learn the culture from cellmates, friends, and lawyers. Under most modern American penal codes, the same criminal conduct typically permits the defendant to be charged with one or more of several distinct offenses, each carrying different levels of potential punishment. Some of the potential sentences are severe: not just CAPITAL PUNISHMENT but punishment for common offenses by prison terms that may exceed the length of a person's vigorous adulthood. It would be practically impossible and morally unthinkable to apply such severe sanctions in a substantial portion of the cases.

The system is thus dominated at every level by official discretion; police, prosecutors, judges, and correctional officials are expected to extend leniency to most offenders lest the system become brutal and the courthouses overloaded. The guilty plea thus provides incentives for the state as well as the defendant. The courts are prepared to try only about ten percent of the cases potentially before them, and prosecutors value convictions obtained without the effort and expense of trial.

The relationship of this system of official discretion, including plea bargaining, with constitutional norms is strained, to say the least. Enforcement of criminal laws in America is predominantly the responsibility of over 3,000 distinct and varying local systems for the administration of criminal justice. The system generally gives a central role to professional police and prosecutorial organizations rather than to the active supervising magistracy that the Fourth, Fifth, and Sixth Amendments apparently contemplated for federal prosecutions.

The dominance of plea bargaining and the discretionary power to bring and dismiss charges tend to reduce the likelihood of direct confrontation between constitutional doctrine and everyday law enforcement practice. Officials are motivated to settle cases in which the lawfulness of their behavior appears likely to be challenged. Moreover, the dominance of discretion permits some rationalization of enforcement policies, better managerial control of scarce resources, and reduction of the uncertainties of trial for both officials and defendants. The system also permits the public at large to avoid facing the contradictions inherent in the penal policies embodied in the criminal codes of most states.

The guilty plea system potentially conflicts with constitutional norms in three principal ways. First, the system is in some tension with DUE PROCESS standards. In America the guilty plea wholly substitutes for a judicial trial. In Europe, the judge typically must conduct an independent investigation of guilt, whether or not the accused confesses. Even before the modern constitutional revolution in criminal justice, the Supreme Court recognized the dangers inherent in convictions based solely upon guilty pleas, insisting in such cases that convictions be based on knowing and voluntary WAIVER OF RIGHTS. In a series of decisions between 1960 and 1970 the Court spelled out this requirement in specific terms: an admission of guilt in open court by an accused who is adequately counseled and informed by a neutral judge of his rights and of the possible consequences of waiving them by pleading guilty. This formula requires only a rather formalistic colloquy between defendant and judge in open court to ascertain the accused's knowledge and VOLUNTARINESS of the plea. It also precludes active participation by the judge in the negotiations that induce the plea, through promises of leniency or threats of severity. It is also understood that bargains, once struck, must be observed by the government. Beyond these requirements due process is satisfied so long as the bargaining is fair according to the standards of commercial bargaining. Thus a defendant may be held to his plea despite his insistence that he is innocent. Troubling issues arise when an accused pleads guilty, despite his belief in his own innocence, because he recognizes the long odds against acquittal and the high risk of a more severe penalty after conviction at trial. Although the Court has held such pleas to be voluntary and to satisfy due process standards, doubts continue regarding the voluntariness of many such pleas.

A second cluster of constitutional concerns about the guilty plea system centers on the question of equal treatment for all similarly situated defendants. The guarantees of due process and EQUAL PROTECTION somewhat limit the arbitrary and disparate imposition of punishment. Yet the plea bargaining system grants to some defendants concessions that are unlikely to be extended to all. Indeed, if the concessions were equally available, they would lose much of their force in persuading defendants to plead guilty. Moreover, the process of negotiation operates outside the formal protections of the criminal process, within an area of official discretion that is seldom subjected to independent scrutiny. Opportunities abound for arbitrary discrimination.

The third and most pressing set of constitutional concerns about plea bargaining has received the least satisfactory treatment by the Supreme Court. When a defendant pleads guilty, he waives a host of constitutionally protected rights, including TRIAL BY JURY or by a judge, the RIGHT AGAINST SELF-INCRIMINATION, the right to CONFRONTATION and cross-examination of witnesses, and the right to challenge evidence against him. Government officials encourage the waiver of these rights by promising reduced punishment, and by threatening greater punishment for those who insist on their constitutionally guaranteed rights. This process appears to be an UNCONSTITUTIONAL CONDITION on the exercise of rights.

Despite these constitutional concerns, and despite widespread public dissatisfaction, plea bargaining seems to be a permanent feature of the American system of criminal justice. If the Supreme Court has thus far acquiesced in the system's constitutionality, perhaps the Court is not yet persuaded that a satisfactory alternative has been demonstrated.

ARTHUR ROSSETT
(1986)

Bibliography

ROSSETT, ARTHUR I. and CRESSY, DONALD 1976 *Justice by Consent: Plea Bargains in the American Courthouse.* Philadelphia: Lippincott.
SCHULHOFER, STEPHEN J. 1984 Is Plea Bargaining Inevitable? *Harvard Law Review* 97:1037–1107.

PLESSY v. FERGUSON
163 U.S. 537 (1896)

Until BROWN V. BOARD OF EDUCATION (1954), *Plessy* was the constitutional linchpin for the entire structure of Jim Crow in America. Borrowed from LEMUEL SHAW in ROBERTS V. BOSTON (1851), the *Plessy* Court established the SEPARATE BUT EQUAL DOCTRINE: black persons were not denied the EQUAL PROTECTION OF THE LAWS safeguarded by the FOURTEENTH AMENDMENT when they were provided with facilities substantially equal to those available to white persons.

Florida enacted the first Jim Crow transportation law in 1887, and by the end of the century the other states of the old Confederacy had followed suit. Louisiana's act, which was challenged in *Plessy*, required railroad companies carrying passengers in the state to have "equal but separate accommodations" for white and colored persons by designating coaches racially or partitioning them. Black citizens, who denounced the innovation of Jim Crow in Louisiana as "unconstitutional, unamerican, unjust, dangerous and against sound public policy," complained that prejudiced whites would have a "license" to maltreat and humiliate inoffensive blacks. Plessy was a TEST CASE. Homer A. Plessy, an octoroon (one-eighth black), boarded the East Louisiana Railroad in New Orleans bound for Covington in the same state and sat in the white car; he was arrested when he refused to move to the black car. Convicted by the state he appealed on constitutional grounds, invoking the THIRTEENTH and FOURTEENTH AMENDMENTS. The Court had already decided in Louisville, New Orleans & *Texas Pacific Ry. v. Mississippi*, (1890) that Jim Crow cars in INTRASTATE COMMERCE did not violate the COMMERCE CLAUSE.

Justice JOHN MARSHALL HARLAN was the only dissenter from the opinion by Justice HENRY B. BROWN. That the state act did not infringe the Thirteenth Amendment, declared Brown, "is too clear for argument." The act implied "merely a legal distinction" between the two races and therefore had "no tendency to destroy the legal equality of the two races, or reestablish a state of involuntary servitude." Harlan, believing that STATE ACTION could have no regard to the race of citizens when their CIVIL RIGHTS were involved, would have ruled that compulsory racial SEGREGATION violated the Thirteenth Amendment by imposing a BADGE OF SERVITUDE.

The chief issue was whether the state act abridged the Fourteenth Amendment's equal protection clause. One reads Brown's opinion with an enormous sense of the feebleness of words as conveyors of thought, because he conceded that the object of the amendment "was undoubtedly to enforce the absolute equality of the two races before the law," yet he continued the same sentence by adding, "but in the nature of things it could not have been intended to abolish distinctions based on color. . . ." As a matter of historical fact the intention of the amendment was, generally, to abolish legal distinctions based on color. The Court pretended to rest on history without looking at the historical record; it did not claim the necessity of adapting the Constitution to changed conditions, making untenable the defense often heard in more recent years, that the decision fit the times. *Plessy* makes sense only if one understands that the Court believed that segregation was not discriminatory, indeed that it would violate the equal protection clause if it were discriminatory. Brown conceded that a statute implying a legal inferiority in civil society, lessening "the security of the right of the colored race," would be discriminatory, but he insisted that state-imposed segregation did not "necessarily imply the inferiority of either race to the other. . . ." There was abundant evidence to the contrary, none of it understandable to a Court that found fallacious the contention that "the enforced separation of the two races stamps the colored race with a badge of inferiority. If this be so, it is not by reason of anything found in the act, but solely because the colored race chooses to put that construction on it." That segregation stamped blacks with a badge of inferiority was not fallacious. The fallacy was that only they imputed inferiority to segregation. Jim Crow laws were central to white supremacist thought. That blacks were inherently inferior was a conviction being stridently trumpeted by white supremacists from the press, the pulpit, and the platform, as well as from the legislative halls, of the South. The label, "For Colored Only," was a public expression of disparagement amounting to officially sanctioned civil inequality. By the Court's own reasoning, state acts compelling racial segregation were unconstitutional if inferiority was implied or discrimination intended.

The separate but equal doctrine was fatally vulnerable for still other reasons given, ironically, by the Court in *Plessy.* It sustained the act as a valid exercise of the POLICE POWER yet stated that every exercise of that power "must be reasonable, and extend only to such laws as are enacted in good faith for the promotion of the public good, and not for the annoyance or oppression of a particular class." Jim Crow laws were not only annoying and oppressive to blacks; they were not reasonable or for the public good. The Court asserted that the question of reasonableness must be determined with reference "to the established usages, customs and traditions" of the people of the state. The proper standard of reasonableness ought to have been the equal protection clause of the Constitution, not new customs of the white supremacists of an ex-slave state. Even if the custom of segregation had been old, and it was not, the Court was making strange doctrine when implying that discrimination becomes vested with constitutionality if carried on long enough to become customary. Classifying people by race for the purpose of transportation was unreasonable because the classification was irrelevant to any legitimate purpose.

The only conceivable justification for the reasonableness of the racial classification was that it promoted the public good, which Brown alleged. The effects of segregation were inimical to the public good, because, as Harlan pointed out, it "permits the seeds of race hate to be planted under the sanction of law." It created and perpetuated interracial tensions. Oddly the Court made the public-good argument in the belief that the commingling of the races would threaten the public peace by triggering disorders. In line with that assumption Brown declared that legislation is powerless to eradicate prejudice based on hostile "racial instincts" and that equal rights cannot be gained by "enforced commingling." These contentions seem cynical when announced in an opinion sanctioning inequality by sustaining a statute compelling racial segregation. The argument that prejudice cannot be legislated away overlooked the extent to which prejudice had been legislated into existence and continued by Jim Crow statutes.

Harlan's imperishable dissent repeated the important Thirteenth Amendment argument that he had made in the CIVIL RIGHTS CASES (1883) on badges of servitude. That amendment, he declared, "decreed universal civil freedom in the country." Harlan reminded the Court that in STRAUDER V. WEST VIRGINIA (1880), it had construed the Fourteenth Amendment to mean that "the law in the States shall be the same for the black as for the white" and that the amendment contained "a necessary implication of a positive immunity, or right . . . the right to exemption from unfriendly legislation against them distinctively as colored—exemption from legal discriminations, implying inferiority in civil society, lessening the security of their enjoyment of rights which others enjoy. . . ." To Harlan, segregation was discriminatory per se. The state act was unreasonable because segregation was not germane to a legitimate legislative end. He meant that the Fourteenth Amendment rendered the state powerless to make legal distinctions based on color in respect to public transportation. A railroad, he reminded the Court, was a public highway exercising public functions available on the same basis to all citizens. "Our Constitution," said Harlan, "is color-blind, and neither knows nor tolerates classes among citizens." He thought the majority's decision would prove in time to be as pernicious as DRED SCOTT V. SANDFORD (1857). As for the separate but equal doctrine, he remarked that the "thin disguise" of equality would mislead no one "nor atone for the wrong this day done."

Plessy cleared the constitutional way for legislation that forced the separation of the races in all places of public accommodation. Most of that legislation came after *Plessy.* In the CIVIL RIGHTS CASES, the Court had prevented Congress from abolishing segregation, and in *Plessy* the Court supported the states in compelling it. Not history and not the Fourteenth Amendment dictated the decision; it reflected its time, and its time was racist. As Justice Brown pointed out, even Congress in governing the DISTRICT OF COLUMBIA had required separate schools for the two races. The Court did not invent Jim Crow but adapted the Constitution to it.

LEONARD W. LEVY
(1986)

Bibliography

KLUGER, RICHARD 1973 *Simple Justice: The History of Brown v. Board of Education and Black America's Struggle for Equality.* Pages 71–83. New York: Knopf.
OBERST, PAUL 1973 The Strange Career of *Plessy v. Ferguson. Arizona Law Review* 15:389–418.

OLSON, OTTO, ed. 1967 *The Thin Disguise: Turning Point in Negro History: Plessy v. Ferguson.* New York: Humanities Press.

WOODWARD, C. VANN 1971 The National Decision Against Equality. Pages 212–233 in Woodward, *American Counterpoint: Slavery and Racism in the North-South Dialogue.* Boston: Little, Brown.

PLURALITY OPINION

In some cases the majority of Justices of the Supreme Court, although agreeing on the DECISION, do not agree on the reasoning behind the decision. In such cases, there is no OPINION OF THE COURT; instead there are two or more opinions purporting to explain the decision. If one opinion is signed by more Justices than any other, it is called the "plurality opinion." A plurality opinion may be cited as precedent in later cases, but, unlike a majority opinion, it is not an authoritative statement of the Court's position on the legal or constitutional issues involved.

DENNIS J. MAHONEY
(1986)

PLYLER v. DOE
457 U.S. 202 (1982)

Experimenting with ignorance, the Texas legislature authorized local school boards to exclude the children of undocumented ALIENS from the public schools, and cut off state funds to subsidize those children's schooling. The Supreme Court, 5–4, held that this scheme denied the alien children the EQUAL PROTECTION OF THE LAWS. The OPINION OF THE COURT, by Justice WILLIAM J. BRENNAN, contains the potential for important future influence on equal protection DOCTRINE.

The Court was unanimous on one point: the Fourteenth Amendment's guarantee of equal protection for all PERSONS extends not only to aliens lawfully admitted for residence but also to undocumented aliens. The question that divided the Court was what that guarantee demanded—an issue that the Court's recent opinions had typically discussed in language about the appropriate STANDARD OF REVIEW. In SAN ANTONIO INDEPENDENT SCHOOL DISTRICT V. RODRIGUEZ (1973) the Court had rejected the claim that EDUCATION was a FUNDAMENTAL INTEREST, and had subjected a state system for financing schools to a deferential RATIONAL BASIS standard. A significant OBITER DICTUM, however, had suggested that a total denial of education to a certain group of children would have to pass the test of STRICT SCRUTINY. (See GRIFFIN V. COUNTY SCHOOL BOARD OF PRINCE EDWARD COUNTY.) Furthermore, although alienage was, for some purposes, a SUSPECT CLASSIFICATION, the Court had not extended that characterization to laws discriminating against aliens who were not lawfully admitted to the country.

Justice Brennan's analysis blurred the already indistinct lines dividing levels of judicial scrutiny in equal protection cases. He suggested that some form of "intermediate scrutiny" was appropriate, and even hinted at a preference for strict scrutiny. Eventually, though, he came to rest on rhetorical ground that could hold together a five-Justice majority. Because the Texas law imposed a severe penalty on children for their parents' misconduct, it was irrational unless the state could show that it furthered "some substantial goal of the State," and no such showing had been made. In a concurring opinion, Justice LEWIS F. POWELL remarked that heightened scrutiny was proper, on analogy to the Court's decisions about classifications based on ILLEGITIMACY. Justice THURGOOD MARSHALL, also concurring, repeated his argument for recognition of a "sliding scale" of standards of review, and accurately noted that this very decision illustrated that the Court was already employing such a system. No one should be surprised when the Court holds invalid a supremely stupid law that imposes great hardship on a group of innocent people.

Chief Justice WARREN E. BURGER, writing for the four dissenters, agreed that the Texas policy was "senseless." He argued nonetheless that the Court, by undertaking a "policymaking role," was "trespass[ing] on the assigned function of the political branches." In allocating scarce state resources, Texas could rationally choose to prefer citizens and lawfully admitted aliens over aliens who had entered the country without permission; for the dissenters, that was enough to validate the law.

The *Plyler* opinion was narrow, leaving open the question whether a similar burden of substantial justification would be imposed on a discrimination against undocumented aliens who were adults, or even against innocent children when the discrimination was something less than a total denial of education. Justice Brennan did suggest that judicial scrutiny might properly be heightened in cases of discrimination against aliens—even undocumented aliens—who had established "a permanent attachment to the nation." Although it is unlikely that this view could command a majority of the Court today, the remark may bear fruit in the future.

KENNETH L. KARST
(1986)

(SEE ALSO: *Immigration and Alienage.*)

POCKET VETO

If Congress adjourns within ten days after passing a bill, the President can prevent the bill's enactment by merely withholding his signature (Article I, section 7, clause 3, of the Constitution). By means of this extension of the VETO POWER, the President can kill legislation without giving any reason and without the possibility of being overridden.

DENNIS J. MAHONEY
(1986)

POCKET VETO CASE
Okanogan Indians v. United States
279 U.S. 655 (1929)

A unanimous Supreme Court, speaking through Justice EDWARD SANFORD, held that a bill passed by Congress, but not signed by the President, had died when the 69th Congress adjourned between its first and second sessions. The POCKET VETO may therefore be used during the adjournment between sessions, and not merely at the final adjournment, of a particular Congress.

In *Wright v. United States* (1938) and *Kennedy v. Sampson* (1965) federal courts established that the pocket veto could not be used during intrasession adjournments.

DENNIS J. MAHONEY
(1986)

POELKER v. DOE

See: *Maher v. Roe*

POINTER v. TEXAS
380 U.S. 400 (1965)

A state court had allowed the introduction in EVIDENCE of the transcript of an absent witness's testimony given at a preliminary hearing when the defendant, unrepresented by counsel, could not effectively cross-examine. The Supreme Court, disallowing an exception to the HEARSAY RULE, held that "the SIXTH AMENDMENT's right of an accused to confront the witnesses against him is a fundamental right and is made obligatory on the State by the FOURTEENTH AMENDMENT." The Court also held that the RIGHT OF CONFRONTATION is governed by the same standards in state and federal courts.

LEONARD W. LEVY
(1986)

POLICE ACTION

The phrase "police action" is not a term of art, or one having any precise legal significance, but simply an expression or euphemism occasionally employed to describe the use of the armed forces of the United States and other nations to resist what is perceived as a violation of international law, a notable example being American use of the armed forces against the North Korean invasion of South Korea in 1950. (See KOREAN WAR.) President HARRY S. TRUMAN based his decision to use American forces to defend South Korea on the fact that the North Korean aggression constituted a violation of the UNITED NATIONS CHARTER, as declared in a resolution of the Security Council. (The Soviet Union, which of course treated the North Korean invasion as "self-defense," chose to absent itself from that meeting of the Council and thereby lost the opportunity to veto the resolution.) Subsequently, in 1957, Senator John Bricker and other conservative congressmen who were opposed to American intervention in Korea (not because they had any sympathy for communist imperialism but because they were isolationists) attempted to remove such justifications of presidential use of troops by unsuccessfully proposing that the Constitution be amended to require affirmative action by Congress before a treaty obligation could be implemented. (See STATE OF WAR; BRICKER AMENDMENT.)

The phrase has occasionally been employed, although not officially, in other situations in which the United States has used its armed forces without a DECLARATION OF WAR or other explicit sanction by Congress, such as President JOHN F. KENNEDY's 1962 blockade of Cuba. A pejorative variation of it was sometimes employed by opponents of American intervention in VIETNAM, who contended that the United States should not act as an "international policeman" or "international gendarme." Although it would have been appropriate, it seems to have been used by no one to describe President JIMMY CARTER's unsuccessful attempt, in April 1980, to mount a military raid to free American hostages in Iran.

The characterization has never been officially or generally applied to a declared war.

JOSEPH W. BISHOP, JR.
(1986)

Bibliography
SEARS, KENNETH C. 1956 Bricker-Dirksen Amendment. *Hastings Law Journal* 8:1–17.

POLICE DEPARTMENT OF CHICAGO v. MOSLEY
408 U.S. 92 (1972)

Mosley is the leading modern decision linking EQUAL PROTECTION doctrine with the FIRST AMENDMENT. Chicago adopted an ordinance prohibiting PICKETING within 150 feet of a school during school hours, but excepting peaceful labor picketing. Earl Mosley had been picketing on the public sidewalk adjoining a high school, carrying a sign protesting "black discrimination," and after the ordinance was adopted he sought declaratory and injunctive relief, arguing that the ordinance was unconstitutional. The Supreme Court unanimously agreed with him.

Justice THURGOOD MARSHALL, for the Court, concluded that the exemption of labor picketing violated the equal protection clause of the FOURTEENTH AMENDMENT. This conclusion followed the lead of Justice HUGO L. BLACK, concurring in COX V. LOUISIANA (1965). Yet Justice Marshall's opinion speaks chiefly to First Amendment values and primarily cites First Amendment decisions. "[A]bove all else, the First Amendment means that government has no power to restrict expression because of its message, its ideas, its subject matter, or its content." As Chief Justice WARREN E. BURGER noted in a brief concurrence, so broad a statement is not literally true; the Court has upheld regulations of speech content in areas ranging from DEFAMATION to OBSCENITY. Yet *Mosley* properly stakes out a presumption in favor of "equality of status in the field of ideas"—a phrase borrowed from ALEXANDER MEIKLEJOHN.

The *Mosley* opinion makes two main points. First, regulations of message content are presumptively unconstitutional, requiring justification by reference to state interests of compelling importance. Second, "time, place, and manner" regulations that selectively exclude speakers from a PUBLIC FORUM must survive careful judicial scrutiny to ensure that the exclusion is the minimum necessary to further a significant government interest. Together, these statements declare a principle of major importance: the principle of equal liberty of expression.

KENNETH L. KARST
(1986)

Bibliography

KARST, KENNETH L.   1976   Equality as a Central Principle of the First Amendment. *University of Chicago Law Review* 43:20–68.

POLICE INTERROGATION AND CONFESSIONS

In the police interrogation room, where, until the second third of the century, police practices were unscrutinized and virtually unregulated, constitutional ideals collide with the grim realities of law enforcement. It is not easy to talk about the defendant's right to silence and his RIGHT TO COUNSEL when the defendant has confessed to a heinous crime—for example, the rape and murder of a small child as in BREWER V. WILLIAMS (1977) or the kidnapping,

robbery, and murder of a cab driver, by a shotgun blast to the back of the head, as in RHODE ISLAND V. INNIS (1980)— and the confession seems quite credible. Thus, for many years few matters have split the Supreme Court, troubled the legal profession, and agitated the public as much as the confession cases.

Not surprisingly, the most famous confession case of all, MIRANDA V. ARIZONA (1966), is regarded as the high-water mark of the WARREN COURT's "DUE PROCESS revolution." Nor is it surprising that the decision became the prime target of those who attributed an increase of crime to the softness of judges. *Miranda*, which finally applied the RIGHT AGAINST SELF-INCRIMINATION to the informal proceedings in the interrogation room, emerged only after a long struggle, and increasing dissatisfaction, with the test for admitting confessions that preceded it—the "voluntariness" test based on the "totality of circumstances." *Miranda* can be understood only in light of the Court's prior efforts to deal with the intractable confession problem.

Until well into the eighteenth century, doctrines concerning confessions did not affect the admissibility of extrajudicial narrative statements of guilt offered as EVIDENCE, but dealt only with the conditions under which immediate conviction followed a confession as a plea of guilty. It was not until *The King v. Warickshall* (1783) that an English court clearly expressed the notion that confessions might be unworthy of credit because of the circumstances under which they were obtained. In that case the judges declared: "A free and voluntary confession is deserving of the highest credit, because it is presumed to flow from the strongest sense of guilt, and therefore it is admitted as proof of the crime to which it refers; but a confession forced from the mind by the flattery of hope, or by the torture of fear, comes in so questionable a shape when it is to be considered as the evidence of guilt, that no credit ought to be given to it; and therefore it is rejected."

Because a separate rule against coerced confessions emerged in eighteenth-century English cases nearly a century after the right against self-incrimination had become established, JOHN H. WIGMORE, the great master of the law of evidence, concluded that the two rules had no connection. But Leonard W. Levy, the leading student of the origins of the right against self-incrimination, strongly disagrees. He maintains that "[t]he relationship between torture, *compulsory* self-incrimination, and *coerced* confessions was an historical fact as well as a physical and psychological one" and that "in the 16th and 17th centuries, the argument against the three, resulting in the rules that Wigmore said had no connection, overlapped" (Levy 1968, pp. 265, 288–289 n.102).

Levy points out that Baron Geoffrey Gilbert, in his *Law*

of Evidence, "written before 1726 though not published until thirty years later, stated that though the best evidence of guilt was a confession, 'this confession must be voluntary and without compulsion; for our Law in this differs from the Civil Law, that it will not force any Man to accuse himself; and in this we do certainly follow the Law of Nature, which commands every Man to endeavor his own Preservation . . .'" (Levy 1968, p. 327). Baron Gilbert's phrasing, "our Law . . . will not force any Man to accuse himself," Levy says, "expressed the traditional English formulation of the right against self-incrimination, or rather against compulsory self-incrimination. The element of compulsion or involuntariness was always an essential ingredient of the right and, before the right existed, of protests against incriminating interrogations" (ibid., pp. 327–328).

Although Levy insists that this was a historical blunder, both in the United States and in England the confession rules and the right against self-incrimination were divorced and, with the one notable exception of *Bram v. United States* (1897), went their separate ways—until the two rules were intertwined in MALLOY V. HOGAN (1964) and fused in the famous *Miranda* case (1966). Moreover, for most of its life the voluntariness test was essentially an alternative statement of the rule that a confession was entitled to credit so long as it was free of influence that made it untrustworthy or "probably untrue." Wigmore reflected the law prevailing at the time when in 1940 he pointed out that a confession was not inadmissible because of "any *breach of confidence*" or "any *illegality* in the method of obtaining it," or "because of any connection with the *privilege against self-incrimination.*"

In *Bram v. United States* (1897) the Supreme Court did rely explicitly on the self-incrimination clause of the Fifth Amendment in holding a confession inadmissible. But the Court soon abandoned the *Bram* approach, perhaps stung by the criticism of Wigmore and others that it had misread history, and until the mid-1960s *Bram* amounted only to an early excursion from the prevailing due process-voluntariness test.

The right against self-incrimination was not deemed applicable to the states until 1964, and by that time the Supreme Court had decided more than thirty state confession cases. Moreover, even if the Fifth Amendment right against self-incrimination had been deemed applicable to the states much earlier, the law pertaining to "coerced" or "involuntary" confessions still would have developed without it. For until *Miranda* (1966), the prevailing view was that the suspect in the police interrogation room was not being compelled to be a witness against himself within the meaning of the privilege; he was threatened neither with perjury for testifying falsely nor con-

tempt for refusing to testify at all. Because the police have no legal authority to compel statements, there is no legal obligation to answer, ran the argument, to which a privilege can apply.

So long as police interrogators were not required to advise suspects of their rights nor to permit them to consult with lawyers who would do so, there could be little doubt that many a suspect would assume that the police had a legal right to an answer. Still worse, there could be little doubt that many a suspect would assume, or be led to believe, that there were *extralegal* sanctions for refusing to cooperate. Small wonder that commentators decried the legal reasoning that excluded the privilege against self-incrimination from the stationhouse for so many years as "casuistic," "a quibble," and a triumph of logic over life.

Wigmore long condemned the statement of the confession rule in terms of voluntariness for the reason that "the fundamental question for confessions is whether there is any danger that they may be untrue . . . and that there is nothing in the mere circumstance of compulsion to speak in general . . . which creates any risk of untruth." But only two years after the Supreme Court handed down its first FOURTEENTH AMENDMENT due process cases, BROWN V. MISSISSIPPI (1936), Charles McCormick defended the voluntariness terminology on the ground that it might reflect a recognition that the confession rule not only protects against the danger of untrustworthiness but also protects an interest closely akin to that protected by the right against compulsory self-incrimination. Three decades later, the *Miranda* Court would agree. McCormick also suggested that the entire course of decisions in the confessions field could best be understood as "an application to confessions both of a privilege against evidence illegally obtained . . . and of an overlapping rule of incompetency which excludes the confessions when untrustworthy" (1954, p. 157). In the advanced stages of the voluntariness test, the Court would again make plain its agreement with McCormick.

Thus, in *Spano v. New York* (1959) the Court, speaking through Chief Justice EARL WARREN, pointed out that the ban against involuntary confessions turns not only on their unreliability but also on the notion that "the police must obey the law while enforcing the law; that in the end life and liberty can be as much endangered from illegal methods used to convict those thought to be criminals as from the actual criminals themselves." And the following year, in *Blackburn v. Alabama* (1960), the Court, again speaking through Chief Justice Warren, recognized that "a complex of values underlies the stricture against use by the state of confessions which, by way of convenient shorthand, this Court terms involuntary."

The "untrustworthiness" rationale, the view that the

rules governing the admissibility of confessions were merely a system of safeguards against false confessions, could explain the exclusion of the confession in *Brown v. Mississippi* (1936), where the deputy sheriff who had presided over the beatings of the defendants conceded that one had been whipped, "but not too much for a Negro." And the untrustworthiness rationale was also adequate to explain the exclusion of confessions in the cases that immediately followed the *Brown* case such as CHAMBERS V. FLORIDA (1940), *Canty v. Alabama* (1940), *White v. Texas* (1940), and *Ward v. Texas* (1942), for they, too, involved actual or threatened physical violence.

As the crude practices of the early cases became outmoded and cases involving more subtle pressures began to appear, however, it became more difficult to assume that the resulting confessions were untrustworthy. In *Ashcraft v. Tennessee* (1944), for example, although the confession was obtained after some thirty-six hours of almost continuous interrogation, there was good reason to think that the defendant had indeed been involved in the murder. The man whom the defendant named as his wife's killer readily admitted his involvement and accused the defendant of hiring him to do the job. Moreover, after the interrogation had ceased and the defendant had been examined by his family physician, he made what the doctor described as an "entirely voluntary" confession, in the course of which he explained why he wanted his wife killed. Nevertheless, calling the extended questioning "inherently coercive," a 6–3 majority, speaking through Justice HUGO L. BLACK, held that Ashcraft's confession should not have been allowed into evidence. Under the circumstances, the *Ashcraft* case seemed to reflect less concern with the reliability of the confession than disapproval of police methods which appeared to the Court to be dangerous and subject to serious abuse.

Although he dissented in *Ashcraft*, Justice FELIX FRANKFURTER soon became the leading exponent of the "police misconduct" or "police methods" rationale for barring the use of confessions. According to this rationale, in order to condemn and deter abusive, offensive, or otherwise objectionable police interrogation methods, it was necessary to exclude confessions produced by such methods regardless of how relevant and credible they might be, a point underscored in ROGERS V. RICHMOND (1961). After more conventional methods had failed to produce any incriminating statements, a police chief pretended to order petitioner's ailing wife brought down to headquarters for questioning. Petitioner promptly confessed to the murder for which he was later convicted. The trial judge found that the police chief's pretense had "no tendency to produce a confession that was not in accord with the truth" and in his charge to the jury he indicated that the admissibility of the confession should turn on its probable reliability. But the Court, speaking through Justice Frankfurter, held that convictions based on involuntary confessions must fall

not because such confessions are unlikely to be true but because the methods used to extract them offend an underlying principle in the enforcement of our criminal law; that ours is an accusatorial and not an inquisitorial system. . . . Indeed, in many of the cases in which the command of the Due Process Clause has compelled us to reverse state convictions involving the use of confessions obtained by impermissible methods, independent corroborating evidence left little doubt of the truth of what the defendant had confessed. Despite such verification, confessions were found to be the product of constitutionally impermissible methods in their inducement. . . . The attention of the trial judge should have been focused, for purpose of the Federal Constitution, on the question whether the [police behavior] was such as to overbear petitioner's will to resist and bring about confessions not freely self-determined—a question to be answered with complete disregard of whether or not petitioner in fact spoke the truth.

The "voluntariness" test seemed to be at once too wide and too narrow. In the sense of wanting to confess, or doing so in a completely spontaneous manner, as one might confess to rid one's soul of guilt, no confession reviewed by the Court under the "voluntariness" test had been voluntary. On the other hand, in the sense that the situation always presented a choice between two alternatives, all confessions examined by the Court had been voluntary.

As the voluntariness test evolved, it became increasingly clear that terms such as "voluntariness" and "coercion" were not being used as tools of analysis, but as mere conclusions. When a court concluded that the police had resorted to unacceptable interrogation techniques, it called the resulting confession "involuntary" and talked of "overbearing the will." When, on the other hand, a court concluded that the methods the police had employed were permissible, it called the resulting confession "voluntary" and talked of "self-determination." Moreover, such terms as "voluntariness," "coercion," and "overbearing the will" focused directly on neither of the two underlying reasons that led the courts to bar the use of confessions—the offensiveness of police interrogation methods or the risk that these methods had produced an untrue confession.

Another problem with the due process "totality of the circumstances"—voluntariness test was that it was amorphous, elusive, and largely unmanageable. Almost everything was relevant—for example, whether the suspect was advised of his rights; whether he was held incommunicado; the suspect's age, intelligence, education, and prior criminal record; the conditions and duration of his detention—but almost nothing was decisive. Except for direct physical coercion no single factor or combination of them guaranteed exclusion of a confession as involuntary. Because there were so many variables in the voluntariness equation that one determination seldom served as a useful precedent for another, the test offered police interrogators and trial courts little guidance. Trial courts were encouraged to indulge their subjective preferences, and appellate courts were discouraged from active review.

In the thirty years between *Brown* (1936) and *Miranda* (1966) the Court had reviewed about one state confession case per year and two-thirds of these had been death penalty cases. Indeed, the Court's workload had been so great that it had even denied a hearing in most death penalty cases. Not surprisingly, Justice Black remarked in the course of the oral argument in *Miranda:* "If you are going to determine [the admissibility of the confession] each time on the circumstances, [if] this Court will take them one by one, [it] is more than we are capable of doing."

The Supreme Court's dissatisfaction with the elusive "voluntariness" test and its quest for a more concrete and manageable standard led to the decisions in MASSIAH V. UNITED STATES (1964) and ESCOBEDO V. ILLINOIS (1964) and culminated in the 1966 *Miranda* decision.

Massiah grew out of the following facts: After he had been indicted for various federal narcotics violations and retained a lawyer, and while he was out on bail, Massiah was invited by his codefendant, Colson, to discuss the pending case in Colson's car. Massiah assumed that he was talking to a partner in crime, but Colson had become a secret government agent. A radio transmitter had been concealed in Colson's car to enable a nearby federal agent to overhear the Massiah-Colson conversation. As expected, Massiah made incriminating statements.

Despite the fact that Massiah was neither in "custody" nor subjected to "police interrogation," as that term is normally used, the Supreme Court held that his damaging admissions should have been excluded from evidence. The decisive feature of the case was that after adversary criminal proceedings had been initiated against him—and Massiah's RIGHT TO COUNSEL had "attached"—government agents had deliberately elicited statements from him in the absence of counsel.

Massiah was soon overshadowed by *Escobedo*, decided a short five weeks later. When Danny Escobedo had been arrested for murder he had repeatedly but unsuccessfully asked to speak to his lawyer. Instead, the police induced Escobedo to implicate himself in the murder. Although Escobedo had incriminated himself before he had been indicted or adversary criminal proceedings had otherwise commenced against him, a 5–4 majority held that under the circumstances "it would exalt form over substance to make the right to counsel . . . depend on whether at the

time of the interrogation, the authorities had secured a formal indictment." At the time the police had questioned him, Escobedo "had become the accused and the purpose of the investigation was to "get him' to confess his guilt despite his constitutional right not to do so."

Until *Miranda* moved the case off center-stage two years later, the meaning and scope of *Escobedo* was a matter of widespread disagreement. In large part this was due to the accordion-like quality of Justice ARTHUR J. GOLDBERG's majority opinion. At some places the opinion suggested that a suspect's right to counsel was triggered once the investigation ceased to be a general inquiry into an unsolved crime and began to "focus" on him, regardless of whether he was in "custody" or asked for a lawyer. Elsewhere, however, the opinion seemed to limit the holding to its special facts (Escobedo had specifically requested and been denied an opportunity to seek his lawyer's advice, the police had failed to warn him of his right to remain silent, and he was in police custody).

The *Escobedo* dissenters read the majority opinion broadly: "The right to counsel now not only entitles the accused the counsel's advice and aid in preparing for trial but stands as an impenetrable barrier to any interrogation once the accused has become suspect. From that very moment apparently his right to counsel attaches." The dissenters expressed a preference for a self-incrimination approach, rather than a right to counsel approach. The right against self-incrimination, after all, proscribed only compelled statements. "It is incongruous to assume," they argued, "that the provision for counsel in the Sixth Amendment was meant to amend or supersede the self-incrimination provision of the Fifth Amendment, which is now applicable to the States." Two years later, in *Miranda*, the Court would focus on the Fifth Amendment, but it would define "compulsion" within the meaning of the privilege in a way that displeased the four *Escobedo* dissenters (all of whom also dissented in *Miranda*).

Dissenting in *Ashcraft* in 1944, Justice ROBERT H. JACKSON agreed that custody and questioning of a suspect for thirty-six hours is "inherently coercive," but quickly added: "And so is custody and examination for one hour. Arrest itself is inherently coercive and so is detention. . . . But does the Constitution prohibit use of all confessions made after arrest because questioning, while one is deprived of freedom, is "inherently coercive'?" Both Jackson and Justice Black, who wrote the majority opinion in *Ashcraft*, knew that in 1944 the Court was not ready for an affirmative answer to Jackson's question. But by 1966 the Court had grown ready.

Ernesto Miranda had been arrested for rape and kidnapping, taken to a police station, and placed in an "interrogation room," where he was questioned about the crimes. Two hours later the police emerged from the room with a signed confession. In the 1940s or 1950s Miranda's confession unquestionably would have been admissible under the voluntariness test; his questioning had been mild compared to the objectionable police methods that had rendered a resulting confession involuntary in past cases.

The Supreme Court, however, had become increasingly dissatisfied with the voluntariness test. Miranda's interrogators admitted that neither before nor during the questioning had they advised him of his right to remain silent or his right to consult with an attorney before answering questions or his right to have an attorney present during the interrogation. These failures were to prove fatal for the prosecution.

In *Miranda* a 5–4 majority, speaking through Chief Justice Warren, concluded at last that "all the principles embodied in the privilege [against self-incrimination] apply to informal compulsion exerted by law-enforcement officers during in-custody questioning." Observed the Court:

> An individual swept from familiar surroundings into police custody, surrounded by antagonistic forces, and subjected to the persuasions [described in various interrogation manuals, from which the Court quoted at length] cannot be otherwise than under compulsion to speak. As a practical matter, the compulsion to speak in the isolated setting of the police station may well be greater than in courts or other official investigations, where there are often impartial observers to guard against intimidation or trickery. . . . Unless adequate protective devices are employed to dispel the compulsion inherent in custodial surroundings, no statement obtained from the defendant can truly be the product of his free choice.

The adequate protective devices necessary to neutralize the compulsion inherent in the interrogation environment are the now familiar "*Miranda* warnings." Although *Miranda* is grounded primarily in the right against self-incrimination, it also has a right to counsel component designed to protect and to reinforce the right to remain silent. Thus, prior to any questioning a person taken into custody or otherwise deprived of his freedom of action in any significant way must not only be warned that he has a right to remain silent and that "anything said can and will be used against [him]," but must also be told of his right to counsel, either retained or appointed. "[T]he need for counsel to protect the Fifth Amendment privilege," stated the Court, "comprehends not merely a right to consult with counsel prior to any questioning but also to have counsel present during any questioning if the defendant so desires."

A suspect, of course, may waive his rights, provided he does so voluntarily, knowingly, and intelligently. But no valid WAIVER OF CONSTITUTIONAL RIGHTS can be recognized unless specifically made after the warnings have been given. Moreover, "[t]he mere fact that [a person] may have answered some questions or volunteered some statements . . . does not deprive him of the right to refrain from answering any further inquiries until he had consulted with an attorney and thereafter consents to be questioned."

Although a great hue and cry greeted the case, *Miranda* may fairly be viewed as a compromise between the old voluntariness test (a standard so elusive and unmanageable that its safeguards were largely illusory) and extreme proposals (based on an expansive reading of *Escobedo*) that threatened to "kill" confessions.

Miranda allows the police to conduct general on-the-scene questioning even though the person arrested is both uninformed and unaware of his rights. It allows the police to question a person in his home or office, provided they do not restrict the person's freedom to terminate the meeting. (Indeed, the opinion seems to recommend that the police question a suspect in his home or place of business.) Moreover, "custody" alone does not call for the *Miranda* warnings. The Court might have held that the inherent pressures and anxieties produced by arrest and detention are substantial enough to require neutralizing warnings. But it did not. Thus, so long as the police do not question one who has been brought to the station house, *Miranda* leaves them free to hear and act upon volunteered statements, even though the volunteer neither knows nor is advised of his rights. (This point was recognized by dissenting Justice BYRON R. WHITE in *Miranda*.)

Surprisingly, *Miranda* does not strip police interrogation of its characteristic secrecy. To the extent that any lawyer worth his salt will tell a suspect to remain silent it is no less clear that any officer worth his salt will be sorely tempted to get the suspect to do just the opposite. But no stenographic transcript (let alone an electronic recording) of the waiver transaction, or the questioning that follows a waiver, need be made; no disinterested observer (let alone a judicial officer) need be present. There is language in *Miranda* suggesting that the police must make an objective record of the waiver transaction but this language has been largely overlooked or disregarded by the lower courts. And nowhere in the *Miranda* opinion does the court explicitly require the police to make either tape or verbatim stenographic recordings of the crucial events.

On the eve of *Miranda*, there were doubts that law enforcement could survive if the Court were to project defense counsel into the police station. But the *Miranda* Court did so only in a quite limited way. It never took the final step (and, as a practical matter, the most significant one) of requiring that the suspect first consult with a lawyer, or actually have a lawyer present, in order for his waiver of constitutional rights to be considered valid.

Whether suspects are continuing to confess because

they do not fully grasp the meaning of the *Miranda* warnings or because the police are mumbling, hedging, or undermining the warnings, or whether the promptings of conscience and the desire "to get it over with" are indeed overriding the impact of the warnings, or whether admissions of guilt are quid pro quos for reduced charges or lighter sentences, it is plain that in-custody suspects are continuing to confess with great frequency. This result would hardly have ensued if *Miranda* had fully projected counsel into the interrogation process, requiring the advice or presence of counsel before a suspect could waive his rights.

Because *Miranda* was the centerpiece of the Warren Court's revolution in CRIMINAL PROCEDURE, and one of the leading issues of the 1968 presidential campaign, almost everyone expected the BURGER COURT to treat *Miranda* unkindly. And it did, but only for a decade.

The first blow was struck in HARRIS V. NEW YORK (1971), which held that statements preceded by defective *Miranda* warnings, and thus inadmissible to establish the prosecution's initial case, could nevertheless be used to impeach the defendant's credibility if he took the stand. The Court noted, but seemed untroubled, that some comments in the landmark opinion seemed to bar the use of statements obtained in violation of *Miranda* for any purpose.

A second impeachment case, *Oregon v. Hass* (1975), seemed to inflict a deeper wound. In *Hass*, the police advised the suspect of his rights and he asserted them. Nevertheless, the police refused to honor the suspect's request for a lawyer and continued to question him. That such a flagrant violation of *Miranda* should produce evidence that may be used for impeachment purposes is especially troublesome; under these circumstances, unlike those in *Harris*, it is fair to assume that no hope of obtaining evidence usable for the government's case-in-chief operates to induce the police to comply with *Miranda. Hass,* then, was a more harmful blow to *Miranda* that was *Harris*.

Even more disturbing than the impeachment cases is their recent extension to permit the use of a defendant's prior silence to impeach his credibility if he chooses to testify at his trial. In JENKINS V. ANDERSON (1980) the Court held that a murder defendant's testimony that he had acted in self-defense could be impeached by showing that he did not go to the authorities and report his involvement in the stabbing. In *Fletcher v. Weir* (1982) the Court held that even a defendant's post-arrest silence—so long as he was not given and need not have been given the *Miranda* warnings—could be used to impeach him if he decided to testify at trial.

Still other blows were struck by *Michigan v. Mosley* (1975) and *Oregon v. Mathiason* (1977). Although language in *Miranda* can be read as establishing a per se rule against any further questioning of one who had asserted his right to silence, *Mosley* held that under certain circumstances, which the case left unclear, if the police cease questioning on the spot, they may try again and succeed at a later interrogation session. *Mathiason*, a formalistic, crabbed reading of *Miranda*, demonstrates that even police station interrogation is not necessarily "custodial." (The suspect had agreed to meet a police officer in the state patrol office and had come to the office alone.)

For supporters of *Miranda*, the most ominous note of all was struck by Justice WILLIAM H. REHNQUIST, speaking for the Court in *Michigan v. Tucker* (1974). The *Tucker* Court viewed the *Miranda* warnings as "not themselves rights protected by the Constitution" but only "prophylactic standards" designed to "safeguard" or to "provide practical reinforcement" for the right against self-incrimination. And it seemed to equate "compulsion" within the meaning of that right with "coercion" or "involuntariness" under the pre-*Miranda* due process test. It seemed to miss the point that much greater pressures were necessary to render a confession "involuntary" under the old test than are needed to make a statement "compelled" under the new. That was one of the principal reasons the old test was abandoned in favor of *Miranda*.

A lumping together of self-incrimination "compulsion" and pre-*Miranda* "involuntariness," which appears to be what the Court did in *Tucker*, seemed to approach a rejection of the central premises of *Miranda*. Moreover, the Supreme Court has no supervisory power over state criminal justice. By stripping *Miranda* of its most apparent constitutional basis without explaining what other bases for it there might be, the Court in the *Tucker* opinion seemed to be preparing the way for the eventual overruling of *Miranda*.

A decade later, in NEW YORK V. QUARLES (1984) and in OREGON V. ELSTAD (1985), a majority of the Court, relying heavily on language in the *Tucker* opinion, again drew a distinction between statements that are actually "coerced" or "compelled" and those that are obtained merely in violation of *Miranda*'s "procedural safeguards" or "prophylactic rules." *Quarles* admitted a statement a handcuffed rape suspect had made when questioned by police about the whereabouts of a gun he had earlier been reported to be carrying. The Court, speaking through Justice Rehnquist, "conclude[d] that the need for answers to questions in a situation posing a threat to the public safety outweighs the need for the prophylactic rule protecting [the] privilege against self-incrimination." *Elstad* held that the failure to give *Miranda* warnings to a suspect who made an incriminating statement when subjected to custodial interrogation in his own home did not bar the use of a subsequent station house confession by the suspect when the second confession was immediately preceded by *Miranda* warnings. The court, speaking through Justice SANDRA DAY O'CONNOR, rejected the argument that a *Miranda* violation "necessarily breeds the same consequences as police infringement of a constitutional right, so that evidence uncovered following an unwarned statement must be suppressed as "fruit of the poisonous tree." Although *Quarles* and *Elstad* can be read very narrowly, and *Tucker*, too, can be limited to its special facts, the Court's language in these cases—language that "deconstitutionalizes" *Miranda*—may prove to be far more significant than the cases' specific holdings.

In light of the *Tucker* majority's undermining of the basis for *Miranda* and against the background of such cases as *Harris*, *Hass*, and *Mathiason*, a 1980 confession case, *Rhode Island v. Innis*, posed grave dangers for *Miranda*. The defendant had been convicted of heinous crimes: kidnapping, robbery, and murder. He had made incriminating statements while being driven to a nearby police station, only a few minutes after being placed in the police vehicle. Any interrogation that might have occurred in the vehicle was brief and mild—much more so than the direct, persistent police station interrogation in *Miranda* and its companion cases. Two police officers conversing with one another in the front of the car, but in Innis's presence, had expressed concern that because the murder occurred in the vicinity of a school for handicapped children, one of the children might find the missing shotgun and injure himself. At this point, Innis had interrupted the officers and offered to lead them where the shotgun was hidden.

The Court might have taken an approach suggested by earlier dissents and limited *Miranda* to custodial station house interrogation or its equivalent (for example, a five-hour trip in a police vehicle). It did not do so. The Court might have taken a mechanical approach to interrogation and limited it, as some lower courts had, to situations where the police directly address a suspect. Again, it did not do so. It might have limited interrogation to situations where the record establishes (as it did not in *Innis*) that the police intended to elicit an incriminating response, an obviously difficult test to administer. It did not do this either.

Instead, the Court, speaking through Justice POTTER STEWART (one of the *Miranda* dissenters), held that "*Miranda* safeguards come into play whenever a person in custody is subjected to either express questioning or its functional equivalent." The term "interrogation" includes "any words or actions on the part of the police (other than those normally attendant to arrest and custody) that the police should know are reasonably likely to elicit as incriminating response from the suspect." Although the *Innis* case involved police "speech," the Court's definition embraces police tactics that do not. Thus, the Court seems to have repudiated the position taken by a number of lower courts that confronting a suspect with physical evidence or with an accomplice who has already confessed is not interrogation because it does entail verbal conduct on the part of the police.

One may quarrel, as the three dissenters did, with the Court's application of its definition of "interrogation" to the *Innis* facts (the Court concluded that the defendant had not been interrogated). But *Innis* ia a harder case than most because there was "a basis for concluding that the officer's remarks were for some purpose *other* than that of obtaining evidence from the suspect. An objective listener could plausibly conclude that the policeman's remarks . . . were made solely to express their genuine concern about the danger posed by the hidden shotgun" and thus not view their conversation "as a demand for information" (White 1980, pp. 1234–1235).

In any event, considering the various ways in which the *Innis* Court might have given *Miranda* a grudging interpretation, its generous definition of "interrogation" seems much more significant than its questionable application of the definition to the particular facts of the case. In *Innis* the process of qualifying, limiting, and shrinking *Miranda* came to a halt. Indeed, it seems fair to say that in *Miranda*'s hour of peril the *Innis* Court rose to its defense.

If *Innis* encouraged *Miranda*'s defenders, EDWARDS V. ARIZONA (1981) gladdened them even more. For *Edwards* was the first clear-cut victory for *Miranda* in the Burger Court. Sharply distinguishing the *Mosley* case, which had dealt with a suspect's assertion of his right to remain silent, the *Edwards* Court, speaking through Justice White (another of the *Miranda* dissenters), held that when a suspect invokes his right to counsel the police cannot try again. Under these circumstances, a valid waiver of the right to counsel cannot be established by showing "only that [the suspect] responded further to police-initiated custodial interrogation," even though he was again advised of his rights at a second interrogation session. He cannot be questioned anew "until counsel has been made available to him, unless [he] himself initiates further communication, exchanges or conversation with the police." Thus, *Edwards* reinvigorates *Miranda* in an important respect. (But a more recent case, *Oregon v. Bradshaw* (1983), interprets "initiation of further communication" so broadly that it seems to sap *Edwards* of much of its vitality.)

Although *Miranda* maintained the momentum generated by *Escobedo*, it represented a significantly different approach to the confession problem. Although the *Miranda* Court understandably tried to preserve some continuity with the loose, groping *Escobedo* opinion, it has become increasingly clear that, by shifting from a right to counsel base to a self-incrimination base, *Miranda* actually marked a fresh start in describing the circumstances under which Fifth and Sixth Amendment protections attach. *Escobedo* assigned primary significance to the amount of guilt available to the police at the time of questioning; the opinion therefore contains much talk about "focal point" and the "accusatory stage." But *Miranda* attaches primary significance to the conditions surrounding or inherent in the interrogation setting; thus the opinion contains much discussion of the "interrogation environment" or the "police-dominated" atmosphere that "carries its own badge of intimidation."

If the requisite inherent pressures exist, *Miranda* applies whether or not the individual being questioned is a "prime suspect" or has become "the accused." On the other hand, if these pressures are not operating, an individual is not entitled to the *Miranda* warnings—no matter how sharply the police have focused on him or how much they consider him the "prime suspect" or "the accused." In short, *Miranda* did not enlarge *Escobedo* so much as displace it.

The same, however, cannot be said for *Massiah*. Although *Miranda* has dominated the confessions scene ever since it was handed down, *Massiah* has emerged as the other major Warren Court confession doctrine. As strengthened by two Burger Court decisions, *Brewer v. William* (1977) (often called "the Christian burial speech" case) and *United States v. Henry* (1980), the *Massiah* doctrine holds that once "adversary" or "judicial" proceedings have commenced against an individual (by way of INFORMATION, or initial appearance before a magistrate), deliberate government efforts to elicit incriminating statements from him, whether done openly by uniformed police officers (as in *Williams*) or surreptitiously by secret government agents (as in *Massiah* and *Henry*) violate the individual's right to counsel.

Williams revivified *Massiah*. Indeed, one might even say that *Williams* disinterred it. For until the decision in *Williams* there was good reason to think that *Massiah* had only been a steppingstone to *Escobedo* and that both cases had been largely displaced by *Miranda*.

But *Massiah* is alive and well. And the policies underlying the *Massiah* doctrine are quite distinct from those underlying *Miranda*. The *Massiah* doctrine represents a pure right to counsel approach. It comes into play regardless of whether a person is in custody or is being subjected to interrogation in the *Miranda* sense. There need not be any compelling influences at work, inherent, informal, or otherwise.

The most recent *Massiah* case, *United States v. Henry* (1980), applied *Massiah* to a situation where the Federal Bureau of Investigation (FBI) had instructed its secret agent, ostensibly a fellow prisoner, not to question the defendant about the crime and there was no showing that he had. Nevertheless, the defendant's incriminating statements were held inadmissible. It sufficed that the government had "intentionally create[d] a situation likely to induce [the defendant] to make incriminating statements without the assistance of counsel." The FBI created such a situation when it instructed its secret agent to be alert to any statements made by the defendant, who was housed in the same cellblock. Even if the agent's claim were accepted that he did not intend to take affirmative steps to obtain incriminating statements, the agent "must have known that such propinquity likely would lead to that result." *Henry* not only reaffirmed the *Massiah* doctrine but significantly expanded it. Thus, the *Massiah* doctrine has emerged as a much more potent force than it ever had been during the Warren Court era.

The Burger Court's generous reading of *Miranda* in *Innis* and *Edwards* and its even more generous reading of *Massiah* in the *Henry* case have reaffirmed the Court's commitment to control police efforts to obtain confessions by constitutional rules that transcend "untrustworthiness' and "voluntariness."

Regardless of its shortcomings and the hopes it never fulfilled (or the fears about the case that proved unfounded), *Miranda* was an understandable and long-overdue effort—and the Court's most ambitious effort ever—to solve the police interrogation-confession problem. At the very least it formally recognized an interrogated suspect's self-incrimination privilege, and a right to counsel for rich and poor alike designed to protect and effectuate that privilege; generated a much greater general awareness of procedural rights; and emphatically reminded the police that they neither create the rules of interrogation nor act free of JUDICIAL REVIEW.

Miranda was an attempt to do in the confessions area what the Warren Court had done elsewhere—take the nation's ideals down from the walls, where they had been kept framed to be pointed at with pride on ceremonial occasions, and live up to them. The degree to which *Miranda* actually succeeded is debatable, but the symbolic quality of the decision extends far beyond its actual impact upon police interrogation methods.

YALE KAMISAR
(1986)

Bibliography

BAKER, LIVA 1983 *Miranda: Crime, Law and Politics.* New York: Atheneum.
BERGER, MARK 1980 *Taking the Fifth: The Supreme Court and the Privilege against Self-Incrimination.* Lexington, Mass.: Lexington Books.
GRAHAM, FRED 1970 *The Self-Inflicted Wound.* New York: Macmillan.
KAMISAR, YALE 1980 *Police Interrogation and Confessions: Essays in Law and Policy.* Ann Arbor: University of Michigan Press.
LEVY, LEONARD W. 1968 *Origins of the Fifth Amendment.* New York: Oxford University Press.

McCormick, Charles T.   1954   *Evidence*. St. Paul, Minn. West Publishing Co.

Stephens, Otis   1973   *The Supreme Court and Confessions of Guilt*. Knoxville: University of Tennessee Press.

White, Welsh S.   1981   Interrogation without Questions. *Michigan Law Review* 78:1209–1251.

Wigmore, John Henry   1940   *Evidence*, 3rd ed. Boston: Little, Brown.

POLICE INTERROGATION AND CONFESSIONS
(Update 1)

The government must comply with three constitutional requirements to use a confession against a defendant in a criminal case: a voluntariness requirement, a RIGHT TO COUNSEL requirement, and a warning requirement.

A court will refuse to admit into evidence a confession that was not voluntarily made by the defendant for two reasons. First, an involuntary confession may not be reliable. Second, the DUE PROCESS clauses of the Fifth Amendment and FOURTEENTH AMENDMENT and the Fifth Amendment's RIGHT AGAINST SELF-INCRIMINATION prevent the government from using unconscionable methods to induce a person to confess to criminal activity.

A confession is not "involuntary" unless the police obtained the confession through means that were unfair and coercive. Thus, if the police use physical force, or the threat of physical force, against the defendant or against the defendant's family or friends in order to make a defendant confess to a crime, the defendant's confession is involuntary. The police may use a confession that they gained by lying to, or tricking, the defendant so long as the lies or tricks were not both unfair and coercive. A judicial finding of coercive police activity is a prerequisite to finding that a confession should be excluded from evidence under the voluntariness test. In *Colorado v. Connelly* (1986) the Supreme Court ruled that the government could use a confession from a man who, according to psychiatric testimony offered at trial, suffered from a psychosis that reduced his ability to invoke his right to remain silent when he was asked a question by police officers. The Supreme Court held that the defendant's statements were voluntary because the police had not used any unfair and coercive tactics to obtain his statement.

The Sixth Amendment guarantees each defendant a right to counsel. It does not restrict government questioning of a suspect prior to the time that criminal proceedings have been initiated against that suspect. However, the right to counsel is violated when the government actively elicits information from a defendant outside the presence of his attorney after the beginning of criminal proceedings.

The Sixth Amendment does not protect a defendant who voluntarily gives information to a government employee who did not actively elicit that information but only listened to the defendant's statement. Thus, after a defendant has been charged with a crime and placed in a jail cell, the police may place a government informant disguised as a prisoner in the cell with the defendant. If the informant asks the defendant questions, the defendant's answers cannot be used against the defendant at trial. If the informant does not actively elicit information from the defendant, and the defendant makes incriminating statements to the informant, the defendant's incriminating statements may be used against him at his trial.

In *Patterson v. Illinois* (1988) the Supreme Court ruled that a defendant who agreed to waive his Sixth Amendment right to counsel after he was given the *Miranda* warnings had made a knowing and intelligent waiver of his right to counsel and that his subsequent confession could be used against him. All questions whether a defendant waived his constitutional rights prior to confessing to a crime are to be determined by reference to the MIRANDA RULES, which comprise the third limitation on confessions.

In MIRANDA V. ARIZONA (1966) the Supreme Court held that the police may not interrogate a person who is in police custody (or who has otherwise been deprived of his freedom by the police) unless the police clearly inform the person (1) that he has a right to remain silent; (2) that anything he says may be used against him in court; (3) that he has the right to an attorney and to have an attorney present during any questioning; and (4) that an attorney will be appointed for him if he is INDIGENT.

What happens after the suspect is given the *Miranda* warnings? If, following the *Miranda* warnings, the defendant "knowingly" and "intelligently" waives his right to remain silent and his right to an attorney, the police may interrogate him, and his subsequent confession may be used against him. If the person in custody indicates (either before or during the interrogation) that he does not want to talk to the police, the police must stop questioning the person. However, if the defendant has not requested an attorney, the police may at a later time give the defendant the *Miranda* warnings again and ask whether the defendant will waive his rights and talk with them. If the defendant says either before or during questioning that he wants to meet with an attorney, the police may not question the defendant at any later time, or ask the defendant at a later time to waive his rights, until the defendant has met with an attorney.

In the 1980s the Supreme Court ruled that a defendant's WAIVER OF CONSTITUTIONAL RIGHTS after the *Miranda* warnings would be effective unless the police had used unfair coercive methods to secure his waiver. In *Colorado v. Spring* (1987) the Court held that a defendant who had waived his rights after receiving the Miranda warnings did not have a right to be informed as to the nature of the charges that might be brought against him or the nature of the crime that was being investigated. In *Moran v. Burbine* (1986) the Court held that a defendant made a "knowing and intelligent" waiver of his rights following *Miranda* warnings, so that his statements could be used against him at trial, even though the police who gave him the warnings failed to tell him that an attorney had attempted to contact him.

The police are not required to use any specific set of words to inform the defendant of his rights so long as the statements made by the police to the defendant encompass the substance of the *Miranda* warnings. For example, in *Duckworth v. Eagan* (1989) the police gave the defendant the *Miranda* warnings and then added, "We have no way of giving a lawyer, but one will be appointed for you, if you wish, if and when you go to court." The Supreme Court found that the statement did not undercut the substance of the *Miranda* warnings because it did not induce the defendant to waive his rights to forgo the presence of counsel at questioning. Therefore, the defendant's subsequent waiver of his rights was a valid waiver; his confession could be used against him.

In the 1980s confession cases, the Supreme Court was lenient in admitting into evidence incriminating statements made by defendants so long as the police did not engage in any coercive activity. However, the Court continues to protect the integrity of the adversary process by requiring police to honor a defendant's request for an attorney and to avoid any attempt at gaining information from a defendant outside of the presence of his counsel after judicial proceedings have been instituted against the defendant.

JOHN E. NOWAK
(1992)

Bibliography

KAMIZAR, YALE; LaFAVE, WAYNE R.; and ISRAEL, JEROLD H. 1990 *Modern Criminal Procedure: Cases, Comments, and Questions,* 7th ed. St. Paul, Minn.: West Publishing Co.

LaFAVE, WAYNE R. and ISRAEL, JEROLD H. 1985 *Criminal Procedure.* St. Paul, Minn.: West Publishing Co.

POLICE INTERROGATION AND CONFESSIONS
(Update 2)

Three constitutional law DOCTRINES may make a confession of a crime inadmissible in court. First, it may violate DUE PROCESS OF LAW for the prosecution to use a defendant's involuntary confession against him. In determining whether a confession is involuntary, a court ordinarily considers the totality of the circumstances, including the environment and techniques of police interrogation and the interrogee's special characteristics of strength or weakness. A court may also consider the need for interrogation in the particular case. If the suspect refuses to speak or demands to see a lawyer, the police need not stop the interrogation. Police persistence will be a relevant point against admissibility, but not necessarily a determinative one. The inherent vagueness of the involuntariness doctrine has made it hard for courts to be consistent. The vagueness of the involuntariness rule has also made it possible for courts to hold confessions admissible even though obtained by significant police pressure.

Second, admission of an incriminating statement into evidence may also violate the Sixth Amendment RIGHT TO COUNSEL if the prosecution uses a statement that the police or their agents have deliberately elicited from a suspect, after the onset of adversary judicial proceedings, without first obtaining a valid waiver of the right to counsel. This doctrine affords suspects no protection in the vast majority of cases since police interrogation ordinarily occurs before any judicial proceeding has taken place.

The third relevant doctrine is found in the MIRANDA RULES, which were developed to protect the Fifth Amendment RIGHT AGAINST SELF-INCRIMINATION. These rules make inadmissible any incriminating statements obtained by police interrogation of a person in custody unless the police have first given a proper *Miranda* warning and obtained a valid waiver of both the right against self-incrimination and the right to counsel. If the suspect asserts the right against self-incrimination, the police must disengage from the interrogation. However, the police may later reengage the suspect for the purpose of soliciting a waiver. If the suspect asserts the right to counsel, the police must also disengage. However, the police may not later solicit a waiver unless the suspect has first initiated some case-related communication with the police. *Miranda* is thus more protective of the suspect than the involuntariness rule, which does not require the police to disengage or take no for an answer.

Must the police disengage if the suspect makes an ambiguous reference to counsel (e.g., "Maybe I should talk to a lawyer.")? In *Davis v. United States* (1994), the Supreme Court unanimously held that disengagement was not required. Five justices additionally held that the police were under no obligation to clarify the ambiguity and could immediately proceed with the interrogation. This holding continues the long-standing denigration of *Miranda*, weakens its protectiveness, and thus throws more cases into the uncertain coverage of the involuntariness rule.

LAWRENCE HERMAN
(2000)

Bibliography

HERMAN, LAWRENCE 1987 The Supreme Court, The Attorney General, and the Good Old Days of Police Interrogation. *Ohio State Law Journal* 48:733–755.

——— 1992 The Unexplored Relationship Between the Privilege Against Compulsory Self-Incrimination and the Involuntary Confession Rule (Parts I and II). *Ohio State Law Journal* 53:101–209, 497–553.

LEO, RICHARD A. and THOMAS, GEORGE C., III 1998 *The Miranda Debate: Law, Justice, and Policing.* Boston: Northeastern University Press.

POLICE POWER

The police power is the general power of a government to legislate for the comfort, safety, health, morals, or welfare of the citizenry or the prosperity and good order of the community.

                                    DENNIS J. MAHONEY
                                    (1986)

(SEE ALSO: *Inalienable Police Power; National Police Power; Reserved Police Power; State Police Power.*)

POLICE PURSUITS AND CONSTITUTIONAL RIGHTS

In *County of Sacramento v. Lewis* (1998), the Supreme Court sent an unfortunate message to innocent citizens trapped in the midst of vehicular police pursuits: they lack the constitutional protections afforded those injured by the unrestricted use of firearms by the police.

Although no single government agency maintains an exhaustive accounting of all pursuits in a given year, from 1980 to 1996, the National Highway Traffic Safety Administration reported 5,306 vehicular-pursuit deaths in the United States. Despite the staggering frequency of pursuits ending in tragedies, the Supreme Court declined to consider the police vehicle as a deadly weapon for which officers should train with the same attention as that afforded the use of firearms.

In *Tennessee v. Garner* (1985), the Supreme Court curtailed the unrestricted use of firearms against suspected criminals by stating: "The use of deadly force to prevent the escape of all felony suspects, whatever the circumstances, is constitutionally unreasonable. It is not better that all felony suspects die than that they escape."

The U.S. Court of Appeals for the Ninth Circuit relied upon *Tennessee v. Garner* and reversed a lower court's grant of summary judgment in favor of a police officer who engaged in a vehicular pursuit of two unarmed youths on a motorcycle who posed no threat of imminent harm to human life. The pursuit ended in the death of the minor passenger, Philip Lewis. In a lawsuit filed against the county and the pursuing officer, James Everet Smith, Lewis's parents asserted that the chase violated their son's FOURTEENTH AMENDMENT SUBSTANTIVE DUE PROCESS rights.

In reversing the Ninth Circuit, the Supreme Court ruled that rather than deliberate indifference to their son's constitutional rights, the Lewis's were required to establish that the pursuing officer's conduct was so egregious and outrageous that it "shocks the conscience." What is shocking is the Supreme Court's failure to recognize an officer's fundamental duty to weigh the risks of a vehicular pursuit against the need for immediate apprehension. If that analysis is constitutionally required when an officer reaches into his or her holster, then it must also extend when that officer decides to launch a two-ton vehicle through a community.

                                    LYNNE A. DUNN
                                    (2000)

Bibliography

ALPERT, GEOFFREY P. 1997 The Constitutional Implications of High Speed Police Pursuit Under A Substantive Due Process Analysis: Homeward Through The Haze. *University of Memphis Law Review* 27:599–662.

ALPERT, GEOFFREY P. and FRIDELL, LORIE A. 1992 *Police Vehicles and Firearms: Instruments of Deadly Force.* Prospect Heights, Ill.: Waverly Press.

FALCONE, DAVID 1992 *Police Pursuit in Pursuit of Policy: The Pursuit Issue, Legal and Literature Review and An Empirical Study.* Normal, Ill.: Illinois State University Press.

POLITICAL ACTION COMMITTEES

For political action committees (PACs) and for all other contributors to campaigns for public office, the modern constitutional era began in 1976 with the Supreme Court's decision in BUCKLEY V. VALEO. In sorting out the constitutionality of the many parts of the FEDERAL ELECTION CAMPAIGN ACT (FECA) of 1971 and 1974, the Court reaffirmed the protections of the FIRST AMENDMENT'S FREEDOM OF ASSEMBLY AND ASSOCIATION for PACs, citing a long line of precedents that included NAACP V. ALABAMA (1958). The Court further held all campaign contributions and expenditures to be the expression of political views and thus protected by the First Amendment.

The protections of the First Amendment notwithstanding, the Court permitted much of the congressional regulation of PACs in the FECA to stand as a legitimate exercise of Congress's right to prevent "corruption or the appearance of corruption." All PAC contributions are limited to $5,000 per candidate per election. Moreover, in *California Medical Association v. FEC* (1981), Congress was within its constitutional powers in forbidding them to accept more than $5,000 per year from any group or individual. But because the Court in *Buckley* extended greater protections to campaign spending than to campaign contributions, PACs are free to pursue unregulated independent spending in campaigns—spending done, that is, without the cooperation or knowledge of the candidate being aided.

For a subset of PACs, those with sponsoring parent organizations, the burden of regulation is heavier. If a parent organization is a corporation or labor union, it is (and has long been) prohibited under federal law (and the laws of some states) from making direct political expenditures. The PAC, then, must be a "separate, segregated fund" that raises its own money for its political spending. The parent organization, however, is free under federal law to pay the overhead costs of the PAC and to direct its decisions. PACs with parent organizations are further restricted by law in their fund-raising: PACSs of membership organizations may solicit only their members; with a few rarely used exceptions, union PACs may solicit only their members; and corporate PACs may solicit only stockholders and nonunion employees. These limits were upheld in *FEC v. National Right to Work Committee* (1982).

Even though the major constitutional precedents in this area have arisen largely in cases under the FECA, they apply to state legislation as well—with one exception. In *Citizens Against Rent Control v. Berkeley* (1981) the Court ruled that those states with initiative and referendum elections are less free to limit PAC contributions in those elections. Because no potential officeholders receive campaign funds during such elections, there is no possibility of the campaign contributions eventually corrupting public officials.

By 1988 there were 4,268 PACs registered under federal law as against 608 in 1974; their contributions to congressional candidates had jumped from $12.5 million in 1974 to $148.1 million in 1988. That growth has given rise to proposals for new restrictions, proposals that have raised new constitutional questions. President GEORGE BUSH in 1989 proposed that PACs with parent organizations be banned. No details were forthcoming, but certainly an outright ban would raise serious constitutional issues, more than, say, a change in the law to prohibit parent organizations from paying PAC overhead costs. Other common proposals would cut the limit on PAC contributions to candidates from $5,000 to $3,500 or even lower. One must determine, however, at what point restrictions on contributions become an invasion of First Amendment rights. Still other proposals would limit the total receipts

a candidate might accept from PACs. As limits on receipts appear to stand logically between limits on contributions and limits on spending, these, too, would appear to be in a zone of constitutional uncertainty.

Clearly, the Supreme Court has not moved very far into the balancing of the legitimate regulatory interests of Congress and the First Amendment rights of PACs. It has in fact dealt only with one extended piece of legislation at one point in time; Congress has passed no major regulation of PACs since 1976, and the states began to do so only in the late 1980s. New issues will reach the courts (e.g., state limits on candidates' receipts from PACs), forcing new constitutional interpretations. Moreover, the changing status quo in campaign finance, and especially the growth of PACs, put old rules and precedents in a new legislative context.

FRANK J. SORAUF
(1992)

(SEE ALSO: *Campaign Finance.*)

Bibliography

GOTTLIEB, STEPHEN E. 1985 Fleshing Out the Right of Association: The Problem of the Contribution Limits of the Federal Election Campaign Act. *Albany Law Review* 49:825–854.

SORAUF, FRANK J. 1986 Caught in a Political Thicket: The Supreme Court and Campaign Finance. *Constitutional Commentary* 3:97–121.

POLITICAL PARTIES

The United States Constitution is virtually silent on politics. It touches upon elections, but even here the subject is treated in a most gingerly fashion by delegating the power to set the "Times, Places and Manner of holding Elections for Senators and Representatives" to the legislature of each state. Even the qualification for voting in national elections was left to the states, by the provision that whoever was qualified to vote for members of the "most numerous branch of the State Legislature" could also vote for members of the HOUSE OF REPRESENTATIVES.

The Founders saw peril in politics. The Constitution was an effort to provide a solution to politics. To JAMES MADISON in THE FEDERALIST #10, one of the greatest virtues of the Constitution was that it provided an antidote to the "mischiefs of faction." Because attempting to prevent the emergence of faction would be a cure worse than the disease, the only alternative was to provide a system of FEDERALISM on a continental scale so that no faction or conspiracy among factions could reach majority size, thereby becoming a party. Representative government centered in a legislature became the superior form of government because the "temporary or partial considerations" of factions would be regulated by "passing them through the medium of a chosen body of citizens, whose wisdom . . . will be more consonant to the public good than if pronounced by the people themselves. . . ." GEORGE WASHINGTON in his Farewell Address (the drafting of which was shared by Madison and ALEXANDER HAMILTON) warned of "the danger of parties in the State [founded on] geographical discriminations [and] against the baneful effects of the spirit of party generally."

The Constitution was designed also to solve the political problems inherent in the presidency. In effect, Article II provided for a two-tiered presidential selection: *nomination* by the electors and *election* by the House of Representatives. Under the original Article II the process began with selection of electors in a manner provided by each state legislature. In the first election under the Constitution, in 1788–1789, the electors were chosen by legislature in seven states and by voters in six. Next, electors were to meet in their state capitals, never nationally. There is no ELECTORAL COLLEGE; that term is nowhere to be found in the Constitution or in *The Federalist*. At the prescribed meeting at the state capital each elector had the right and obligation to cast ballots for *two persons*—not two votes, but separate votes for two different people, one not from the same state as the elector. If a candidate received an absolute majority of all electoral votes, he was declared the President; the candidate with the second largest vote became vice-president. If no candidate received an absolute majority, the House of Representatives would choose from the top five names, with each state having one vote, regardless of the population of the state. If two candidates received an absolute majority in a tie vote (as happened between THOMAS JEFFERSON and AARON BURR in 1800), the House would choose between the top two.

This system was virtually designed to produce a *parliamentary* government—a strong executive elected by the lower house of the legislature. During the first two decades of the Republic, the primary functions of the national government were to implement the scheme of government contemplated by the Constitution, and that required one-time-only policies, such as the establishment of the major departments, the establishment of the judiciary, and the exercise of SOVEREIGNTY as a nation-state among nation-states, manifest in various kinds of treaties. Policies had to be adopted to assume all the debts previously incurred by the CONTINENTAL CONGRESS and the national government under the ARTICLES OF CONFEDERATION; laws were also adopted to assume all the debts incurred during the war by the thirteen states. All these policies and many others emanated from the executive branch. Congress looked to President Washington for leadership

and accepted Secretary of the Treasury Alexander Hamilton as Washington's representative. Although consensus around Washington was replaced with polarization, even before JOHN ADAMS became President, the Federalists carried the necessary majorities through legislative meetings (caucuses) led mainly by Hamilton. But at the same time, all the power to enact the policies—all the power "expressly delegated" to the national government by Article I, section 8—was lodged in Congress. Inevitably, politics came out as a modified parliamentarism, with a strong executive elected by the lower house.

These arrangements seem to have been intentional on the part of the Framers of the Constitution. Without a national meeting, and with each elector having to cast ballots for two separate persons, it was to be expected that several candidates for President would be identified. The concept of the "favorite son" actually goes back to George Washington himself, and the expectation that there would be a large number of favorite sons is strongly implied by the provision that in the event of no absolute majority the top five names would be submitted to the House. Surely this means that more than five meaningful candidates would normally be produced and that final election in the House would be the norm also. With this modified parliamentary system, the Constitution and politics became synonymous. The politics of the two to three decades of the founding period followed the lines prescribed by the Constitution—or, to put it another way, flowed fairly strictly within channels established by the Constitution.

This original system was transformed within a generation following the founding. At some point during the Jefferson administration, the regime of the founding was replaced by a regime of ordinary government. One-time-only policies were replaced by routine and repeatable policies, such as INTERNAL IMPROVEMENTS, land grants, personal claims, tariffs, PATENTS, surveys, and other services. This type of national government is precisely what was intended by Article I, section 8. The TENTH AMENDMENT (1791) merely made more explicit what was already unmistakably clear in Article I, that the important powers of governing were to be reserved to the states. What was not intended, however, was that the political solution prevailing during the first generation would come unstuck. Political parties had already emerged despite Washington's warnings, and the discipline of their members virtually destroyed the so-called Electoral College by requiring that each elector be pledged to a presidential candidate "nominated" prior to their selection as electors. Political parties captured the *nominating* phase of presidential selection. For twenty years thereafter the method of nomination was by legislative caucus—derisively called King Caucus. As the two major parties spread their influence to districts where they had voters but no members of Congress, the party leaders had to work out a method of nomination more representative than King Caucus. That solution, the presidential nominating convention, was adopted in 1832 and remained the institution of party government until 1952.

The national party system was by this time no longer working within prescribed constitutional channels but had created some new channels for itself. *More significantly, the party system in the 1820s and 1830s created a realm of politics independent of the Constitution.*

In another sense, however, the Constitution was having the last word. First, Congress had become the central power of the national government. There was no longer any development toward parliamentary government but clearly toward congressional government, as WOODROW WILSON put it in his important text later in the nineteenth century. Second, the nominating convention, in providing the President with a popular base independent of Congress, produced the SEPARATION OF POWERS that many feel the Constitution had intended—a system of coequal branches each with its own separate constituency.

Third, and most important, the functions of the national government had come more into proportion with the intent of Article I, section 8. That is to say, a politics independent of the Constitution came only at the expense of the kinds of functions the national government had been required to perform during the founding decades. In fact, the relationship ought to be put the other way around. The change of functions from the one-time-only policies of the founding to the ordinary policies of the rest of the nineteenth century had been responsible for the political changes, thus confirming a fundamental and well-nigh universal pattern. *every regime tends to create a politics consonant with itself.* Thus, when the regime (the Constitution and its government) of the founding shifted to a regime of policies arising literally under the provisions of Article I, section 8, politics changed accordingly. For more than a century after 1832 the national government was congressional government; the national politics during that epoch was a function of party government; and together, government and politics were consistent with, and reinforced, a strictly *federal* Constitution in which the national government had a highly limited and specialized role in the life of the country.

A third regime emerged out of the NEW DEAL, not from the increased size of the national government but from the addition to that government of significant new functions. The significant departure from tradition arose out of the enactment of a large number of policies that can be understood only as regulatory and redistributive policies. In effect, the national government acquired its own POLICE POWERS and added its own regulatory and redistributive policies to those of the states. These additions—which

were validated by the Supreme Court—brought on a third regime.

Congress did more than enact the new policies that gave the national government its new functions and its directly coercive relationship to citizens. Congress also literally created a new form of government by delegating powers to the executive branch. Each of the new regulatory policies adopted by Congress identified broadly the contours of a problem and then delegated to the executive virtually all the discretion necessary to formulate the actual rules to be imposed on citizens. Technically, this is called the DELEGATION OF POWER, and the rationalization was that Congress had indeed passed the law and left to administrative agencies the power only to "fill in the details." But in fact the executive branch filled in more than details. Just as Woodrow Wilson called the national government of the nineteenth century congressional government, we can with no greater distortion entitle the regime following the New Deal as presidential government.

National politics began to change accordingly. Signs of the weakening of party democracy were already fairly clear during the New Deal. President FRANKLIN D. ROOSEVELT had tried to rebuild the Democratic party into a programmatic kind of presidential party. The most dramatic moment in that effort was the "purge of 1938," an unprecedented effort by a President to defeat or demote the opposition within his own party in order to make it into a modern instrument of program development and enactment. History records that Roosevelt failed, but the meaning of that failure was not lost on the Democrats or Republicans: the President can no longer depend on locally organized opportunistic parties and must develop his own, independent base of popular support. If this support could no longer be found through political parties, the President would have to do it directly, through the media of mass communication. The President's constituency became the public *en masse.*

The presidential conventions of 1952 were the last of the traditional conventions, where parties still controlled the nominations through the control that state party leaders had over the delegates. And if ANDREW JACKSON can be considered the revolutionary who gave birth to the national conventions, DWIGHT D. EISENHOWER was a revolutionary who turned them into vestigial organs. As the 1952 Republican Convention approached, the Eisenhower forces had to confront the fact that ROBERT A. TAFT was ahead. Their only available strategy was to question the credentials of several state delegations whose members, pledged to Taft, had been selected by the traditional method of virtual appointment by state leaders and were pledged to vote slavishly for the candidate designated by the state leadership. Failing to convince the credentials committee, the Eisenhower leaders took their objections to the convention floor in the form of a "fair play" motion. The debate took place over national television—despite Taft's objections—and the Eisenhower motion swayed enough neutral delegations to gain the majority vote and the momentum sufficient to win the nomination. More important than the immediate victory was the long-range result, which was to weaken the foundations of the traditional party system itself. Progressively from that time, delegates came to be treated as factors in their own right, as individuals to be courted rather than as pawns within a state delegation controlled by state party leaders.

Once the delegates became meaningful individuals, the process of selection had to be democratized. Just as the nominating convention once was a means of democratizing the legislative caucus, the primaries became the means of democratizing conventions. But the primaries are as much a reflection as a cause of the decline of party government, including the decline of party control of the presidential selection process. Party government was already seriously undermined before the spread of selection of pledged delegates by primary elections. The transformed convention was, then, a reflection of the broader process of the decline of state and national political parties. The presidential nomination was becoming an open process by which presidential candidates amassed individual delegates, who had little in common with each other or with the candidate to whom they were pledged. The popular base of the presidency became a mass base. It was no longer the outcome of a process by which state party leaders and their delegations formed coalitions around the candidate most likely to win the nomination and election for President.

Serious students of American political parties have been arguing for more than a decade over the political reforms of the 1960s and 1970s associated with the loosening of the national parties and the virtual displacement of the national conventions. Some argue that the decline of political parties and of the convention as the institution of party government was unintentionally caused by the reforms. Others argue that parties had already declined and that the decline of conventions as the real decision-making body was already happening; therefore, the reforms were more a reflection of the decline than a cause of it. Most significant, however, is the emergence of the new regime: a new form of politics consonant with the regime of regulation and redistribution, with its presidential government.

Many of the current disagreements continue because we are still in the midst of the transformation and the ultimate form has not yet fully emerged. Two distinct scenarios or models can be drawn from the prevailing political analyses. One is "dealignment," tending toward mass democracy—that is, a direct relationship between the President and the masses of people unmediated by any representative institution at all, whether party or legislature. The second scenario is an alignment or realignment model anticipating the restoration of the two major parties. Such a development could require the abolition of some reforms instituted in the 1960s and 1970s that radically unhinged certain features of the traditional party system, and adoption of new measures aimed at restoring the power of party bosses in the presidential nominating process.

The resolution is likely to be a fusion of the two models. The entire functioning of the national government has come to rest upon the President; the expectations of all Americans focus there, and the relationship between the President and the people will continue to be direct. This is the essence of mass politics. At the same time, however, there is strong evidence of a resurgence in the headquarters of the national political parties. Yet there is no place for these parties in the direct line of communication between the President and his mass base. Thus, if these parties are to survive and prosper at the national level they will have to find functions other than the traditional ones of intervening between the masses and the President by controlling the nominating process and political campaigns. The creation of such new functions would require the national leadership to organize from the bottom up, district by district, but in fact the national headquarters are organizing from the top down. They are developing their base in the electorate by collecting data for the computerized analysis of categories of voters. These techniques permit efficient mass mailings to solicit voters and, more important, sponsors who will make millions of donations in units of less than $50 apiece. These are not electoral parties in the traditional sense. Nor are they European-style "mass parties" or social democratic parties. They are what, for lack of an established word, can be called "taxation parties," whose main function is to defray the tremendous cost of the capital necessary to maintain the computers, collect the data, analyze the data, write the letters and stuff the envelopes, and design and communicate the spot announcements and other commercial messages on extremely expensive network television.

American national politics has been in a state of transition for a long time. Professional students of elections, polling, and political parties have all been expecting some kind of "realignment" at least since 1964. Major reforms of the parties and of elections have followed each presidential election since that time; their main result has been to prevent forever the outcome of the previous convention and election. Although the Democrats have been the major reformers, mainly because they have been the major losers in national elections, the Republicans have followed them in these reforms almost immediately. The national political process has not yet adjusted effectively to the regime of regulation and redistribution. In other words, although politics ultimately takes some form consonant with the regime, there is no guaranteeing that the adjustments will be successful and stable.

This fact points to the most important contrast between the present regime and the two previous ones: National politics is flowing through channels increasingly independent of the Constitution; that is, efforts to restore party government have been oblivious to the historic relationship between the Constitution and politics.

This is not to suggest that politics is operating unconstitutionally or outside the spirit of Supreme Court decisions. It means only that efforts to restore the parties, and to reform nominations and elections accordingly, have concentrated on the flow itself rather than on the constitutional structure that ultimately determines the flow. Having recognized the many problems with American politics since the New Deal, reformers have attempted to change the politics. They have persisted in this approach even while recognizing two grievous perils in it. First, because some interests inevitably gain or lose from any political reform, there is always a suspicion that these gains were known and sought in advance. The legitimacy of the system can be badly hurt by the more generalized suspicion that the established electoral process is being manipulated. Second, some reform efforts have come close to violating the FIRST AMENDMENT, and in fact the Supreme Court declared such a violation in BUCKLEY V. VALEO (1976), striking down a law attempting to set limits on the amounts individuals could spend in campaigns. That case is definitely not the end of litigation involving First Amendment rights involved in political reforms (See PO-LITICAL PARTIES AND THE SUPREME COURT.)

Politics can be understood as the never-ending process of adjusting to a given structure of government, or regime, by seeking sufficient power and consensus to change the structure or influence its direction. If a change in the conduct of politics is sought, the appropriate route is the exercise of the historic right to change the Constitution and the structure of government. The forms of politics would change accordingly. We have constitutional rights to change our government. As Madison argued in *The Federalist* #10, the attempt to regulate politics is a cure worse than the disease. If there are problems with American national politics—and there appears to be wide agreement on this proposition throughout the political spectrum— then the time may have come to reexamine the structure of government, including the Constitution itself. An extensive revision of the Constitution is neither necessary nor appropriate. The last major constitutional change was triggered by the New Deal, without a single constitutional amendment. Once we recognize that politics is most stable

and most respected when it is consonant with constitutional forms, reformers might be convinced to focus at least some of their energies away from political reform and toward constitutional reform.

THEODORE J. LOWI
(1986)

Bibliography

AGAR, HERBERT 1966 *The Price of Union.* Boston: Houghton Mifflin.

BINCKLEY, WILFRED 1947 *President and Congress.* New York: Knopf.

BURNHAM, WALTER DEAN 1970 *Critical Elections and the Mainsprings of American Politics.* New York: Norton.

CHARLES, JOSEPH 1961 *The Origins of the American Party System.* New York: Harper & Row.

GINSBER, BENJAMIN 1982 *The Consequences of Consent.* Reading, Mass.: Addison-Wesley.

LOWI, THEODORE J. (1967) 1975 Party, Policy and Constitution in America. In William N. Chambers and Walter Dean Burnham, eds., *The American Party System—Stages of Political Development.* New York: Oxford University Press.

POLSBY, NELSON 1983 *Consequences of Party Reform.* New York: Oxford University Press.

SHEFTER, MARTIN 1978 Party Bureaucracy and Political Change. In Louis Maisel and Joseph Cooper, eds., *Political Parties: Development and Decay.* Beverly Hills, Calif.: Sage Publications.

POLITICAL PARTIES
(Update)

The judiciary has struggled to build a coherent jurisprudential approach to the constitutional handling of political parties. The difficulty of this task is due in large part to the absence of parties from the text of the Constitution itself. The Framers were indifferent, if not outright hostile, to political parties and made no provision for them in the constitutional scheme.

Indeed, the very structure of the Constitution makes it difficult for parties to flourish. The dispersal of power among branches and levels of government, the system of CHECKS AND BALANCES, the delegation of a large measure of the definition of party authority to state law, all combine to create a constitutional environment inhospitable to parties. Parties and the party system are always in some tension with the Constitution.

Yet FIRST AMENDMENT protections of FREEDOM OF SPEECH and the FREEDOM OF ASSOCIATION have been extended to include political parties. The Supreme Court has considered the constitutional status of parties in a variety of contexts, from the propriety of party PATRONAGE practices to the parties' role in BALLOT ACCESS. In the process, the

Court has been influential in determining how parties function. Yet, the parties' extraconstitutional nature has prevented the Court from treating them in a consistent or theoretically sound manner. The Court appears to lack a clear normative understanding of parties; it has often been indifferent to them as tools of representative democracy.

Constitutional disputes implicating political parties continue to find their way to the court. In *Colorado Republican Federal Campaign Committee v. FEC* (1996), the REHNQUIST COURT rendered a relatively party-friendly decision in the realm of CAMPAIGN FINANCE. Building on the leading decision of BUCKLEY V. VALEO (1976), the Court determined that party spending independent of a specific candidate's campaign was constitutionally protected and not subject to statutory limits. The consequences of the decision demonstrate in dramatic fashion the practical impact of the Court on the electoral process. The national parties responded by spending unprecedented amounts of so-called soft money—that is, money contributed to the parties rather than to specific candidates—bolstering financial support for candidates on all levels. The decision may, in the end, yield more integrated and cohesive parties. At the same time, recent developments have intensified the demands for reform of an electoral system considered already too expensive. Interestingly, four of the nine Justices in the case were prepared to cast aside as unconstitutional any restrictions on parties' role in financing electoral campaigns. That question may well come before the Court in the not-so-distant future.

The uniquely American two-party system itself came under scrutiny in TIMMONS V. TWIN CITIES AREA NEW PARTY (1996). The two major parties perpetuate their control of state legislatures by imposing ballot access and public financing laws disadvantageous to minor parties. In *Timmons*, the Court rejected a constitutional attack on this legal entrenchment of the two-party system. The Court upheld a state ban on fusion, a practice used by minor parties to gain exposure by nominating as their candidate someone who has also been endorsed or nominated by one of the major parties. The Court found a state interest in promoting political stability through a healthy two-party system; states are thus constitutionally free to maintain the substantial barriers facing third parties in the American political arena. This judicially sanctioned party duopoly further insulates the major parties from minor party challenges; in the process, the Court may become an obstacle to party reform. By diminishing the associational rights of minor parties, the Court may be complicit in propping up a party system that fails the test of representativeness.

The Rehnquist Court's decisions, however, have not been uniformly party friendly. In *Morse v. Republican Party of Virginia* (1996), the Court impaired the autonomy and associational rights of parties to define for themselves how they conduct their PRIMARY ELECTIONS.

Despite the short-term advantages the *Timmons* and *Colorado Republican Federal Campaign Committee* cases might confer upon the major parties, their ultimate impact depends on the extent to which the parties can use them to sharpen their traditional democratic functions, and demonstrate clearly that they are worthy of constitutionally protected freedom.

DAVID K. RYDEN
(2000)

Bibliography

EPSTEIN, LEON   1986   *Political Parties in the American Mold.* Madison: University of Wisconsin Press.
ISSACHAROFF, SAMUEL; KARLAN, PAMELA S.; and PILDES, RICHARD H. 1998   *The Law of Democracy: Legal Structures of the Political Process.* New York: Foundation Press.
LOWENSTEIN, DANIEL H.   1995   *Election Law: Cases and Materials.* Durham, N.C.: Carolina Academic Press.
RYDEN, DAVID K.   1996   *Representation in Crisis: The Constitution, Interest Groups, and Political Parties.* New York: State University of New York Press.
———   1999   'The Good, The Bad, and The Ugly': The Judicial Shaping of Party Activities. Pages 50–65 in John Green and Daniel Shea, eds., *The State of the Parties*, 3rd ed. Boulder, Colo.: Roman & Littlefield.

POLITICAL PARTIES, ELECTIONS, AND CONSTITUTIONAL LAW

Since the mid-1980s the Supreme Court has decided three significant FIRST AMENDMENT cases affecting POLITICAL PARTIES and one that will hamper states' efforts to reform the INITIATIVE process.

In *Tashjian v. Republican Party of Connecticut* (1986), the REPUBLICAN PARTY sought to "open" its PRIMARY ELECTION for high-level offices by permitting independent voters to participate, but the Democratic legislature refused to modify statutes limiting participation to party registrants. The Supreme Court held that the First Amendment FREEDOM OF ASSOCIATION guarantees a party the right to control its own nomination process; it therefore ruled that state law could not prohibit the Republicans from opening their primary.

Tashjian was a mixed blessing for adherents of the party-renewal movement, who were pleased by the extension of association rights to parties but who tend to favor a closed primary as more conducive to strong political parties with relatively sharp ideological focus. The party renewalists welcomed more uniformly the Court's unanimous decision in *Eu v. San Francisco County Democratic Central Committee* (1989), which relied on the parties' right of association to rule that state legislation can neither prevent party committees from endorsing candidates in primary elections nor require a particular governing structure for party organizations.

In *Tashjian* and *Eu*, the Court ignored a point that has been made by numerous commentators, that the extension of rights of association to parties is in tension with *Smith v. Allwright* (1944) and other cases, which treated parties, at least when they are conducting primary elections, as instrumentalities of the state for purposes of the doctrine of STATE ACTION. Within the logic of the state action doctrine, it may be anomalous for the same entity to be treated as part of the state and yet to enjoy constitutional rights against the state. Nevertheless, the conclusion that parties should be protected by the First Amendment and at the same time barred from denying EQUAL PROTECTION and other constitutional rights to citizens is not likely to offend many people.

A more serious deficiency in the Court's approach is its failure to recognize that party associational claims may reflect intraparty disputes rather than the typical CIVIL LIBERTIES claim by a private person against the state. This was not the case in *Tashjian*, where, as Justice THURGOOD MARSHALL noted in his majority opinion, a united Republican party was prevented from opening its primary by Democratic legislators. But in *Eu* the statutes governing each major party reflected the wishes of that party's delegation in the state legislature.

Eu establishes that over some range of decision making affecting parties, the wishes of state party committees or other extragovernmental party structures will prevail when they conflict with the wishes of the party's elected officials as reflected in state legislation. Mere invocation of the concept of freedom of association cannot establish that this result will strengthen parties in the long run or have other desirable consequences.

In RUTAN V. REPUBLICAN PARTY OF ILLINOIS (1990), the Court significantly extended the range of its antipatronage doctrine. In *Elrod v. Burns* (1976) and BRANTI V. FINKEL (1980), the Court had held that to fire nonpolicymaking PUBLIC EMPLOYEES because of nonaffiliation with the party in power violated the employees' First Amendment rights of speech and association. In *Rutan* this principle was extended to transfers, promotions, and even hiring of public employees based on party affiliation.

Whereas *Tashjian* and *Eu* have been welcomed by many as empowering parties, *Rutan* has been criticized as weakening them. As Justice LEWIS F. POWELL argued in dissent in *Elrod*, the prospect of reward often has been a stronger inducement to party activism than ideological conviction, and at many times and in many places, the main reward for party service has been public employment.

It may be doubted whether any of the recent party decisions actually will have the pro- or antiparty effects that have been ascribed to them. The actual points at issue in *Tashjian* and *Eu*—open or closed primaries, party endorsements in primary elections, details of party governance—are not likely to have more than marginal consequences for the American party system. For example, some have hoped that the availability of party endorsements in primaries would permit party organizations to impose party discipline on public officials. But in the first primary held in California after the *Eu* decision, the Republican party opted not to make endorsements and the two statewide candidates in competitive races who were endorsed by the Democratic party were losers in the primary.

If *Tashjian* and *Eu* were extended to the point that parties could not be required by state law to use primaries at all to select their candidates, the effect on the American system could be considerable. Though Justice ANTONIN SCALIA argued in dissent that just such a result was implied by *Tashjian*, there is no reason to expect the majority to press its reasoning that far. Even if it does, perhaps few, if any, party organizations would opt for nomination processes that could be perceived as less democratic than primaries.

The patronage cases, if enforced in a different era, might have had major effects. Even by the time of *Elrod*, patronage practices had declined sharply in most parts of the United States. *Rutan* may deliver a deathblow to patronage more surely than *Elrod* did, but even so, its effects on the political system should be limited to relatively few localities.

Meyer v. Grant (1988), though not affecting political parties, will be a significant restraint in those states whose STATE CONSTITUTIONS provide for the initiative process. *Meyer* struck down a Colorado statute that prohibited the use of paid circulators to qualify initiative measures for the ballot.

Meyer came just as the "initiative industry" was exploding in California and beginning to spread to other initiative states. This industry assures a ballot position for proponents with deep pockets while rendering volunteer petition drives virtually obsolete.

As popular resistance grows to increased numbers of initiative measures proposed by well-funded but sometimes narrowly based groups, state legislatures are likely to look for ways of evading *Meyers v. Grant* or, if no such ways can be found, to increase the signature requirements as a means of cutting the number of proposals that qualify for the ballot.

DANIEL H. LOWENSTEIN
(1992)

Bibliography

EPSTEIN, LEON D.   1986   *Political Parties in the American Mold.* Madison: University of Wisconsin Press.
LOWENSTEIN, DANIEL HAYS and STERN, ROBERT M.   1989   The

First Amendment and Paid Initiative Petition Circulators: A Dissenting View and a Proposal. *Hastings Constitutional Law Quarterly* 17:175–224.

POLITICAL PARTIES IN CONSTITUTIONAL LAW

"No America without democracy, no democracy without politics, no politics without parties. . . ." So begins Clinton Rossiter's commentary on American political parties. Nonetheless, the Supreme Court has said in *Elrod v. Burns* (1976) that "partisan politics bears the imprimatur only of tradition, not the Constitution." Despite the absence of constitutional reference to political parties, the Constitution has had substantial influence in shaping the two-party system and in defining the contested boundary between governmental authority and political party autonomy.

Frank Sorauf has observed that "[t]he major American political parties are in truth three-headed political giants, tripartite systems of interactions. . . . As a political structure they include a party organization, a party in office, and a party in the electorate. . . ." All three branches of political parties are defined, limited, and authorized, at least in part, by constitutional DOCTRINE. All three are shaped in part by specific constitutional arrangements.

Two-party politics, which has persisted throughout the nation's history, began in the struggle between FEDERALISTS and ANTI-FEDERALISTS over the RATIFICATION OF THE CONSTITUTION. Provisions of the Constitution have reinforced the two-party system, especially Article II, section 1, empowering each state to select presidential electors, and the TWELFTH AMENDMENT, requiring an absolute majority of the ELECTORAL COLLEGE or, failing that, of state delegations in the House of Representatives for election of the President. The majority rule tends to compel the coalition of disparate factions into two parties, because only the establishment of broad coalitions offers any prospect of securing the majority necessary for election of the President.

Although no constitutional rule requires that members of the House of Representatives be elected by plurality vote or from single-member districts, these understandings soon took root after ratification of the Constitution. The popular election of the United States senators mandated by the SEVENTEENTH AMENDMENT has the effect of creating single-member districts for the selection of members of that house. These constitutional practices strengthen the two-party system, requiring broad coalitions to secure a majority, the only guarantee of electoral victory under these rules.

The Constitution's provision for a federal structure of government also shapes the party system. Unlike the majority rule's incentive for factions to consolidate into two parties, the federal structure encourages wide dispersion of influence within the party ranks. Because offices and powers at the state and local levels are more accessible and often more important than those in the national government, party organizations in each state and locale grow independent of one another and are largely free from sanctions imposed by any national party organization. This dispersion of party organization is heightened by the mandate of Article I, section 1, and the Twelfth Amendment for state-by-state selection of the electors who choose the President.

States began to regulate political parties in the late eighteenth century, and these regulations became commonplace during the Progressive era. The STATE POLICE POWER was regarded as a sufficient basis for the imposition of governmental authority upon the parties. The state-prescribed Australian ballot, antifusion legislation, and state-operated primaries were introduced at the same time as laws regulating the structure and activities of political parties. All of these were intended to curb political "bosses" and "machines."

By the beginning of WORLD WAR II, the constitutions of seventeen states and the statutes in virtually all states referred to political parties—conferring rights on them, regulating their activities, or both. State regulatory schemes went beyond prescribing the methods by which parties would select nominees for office and the qualifications of parties for places on the ballot. Many states also regulated the selection and composition of district, county, and state political party committees, the authority and duties of those committees, and the rules for their operation.

Whether the national government has similar authority to regulate political parties has seldom been tested, for Congress has not chosen to enact legislation recognizing party associations or regulating their structure and activities. Any such federal power could, however, be thought to derive from several constitutional sources.

Article IV, section 1, of the Constitution grants Congress a broad power to regulate the time, place, and manner of electing senators and representatives. In UNITED STATES V. CLASSIC (1941) the Supreme Court construed this provision to allow Congress to regulate individual conduct and also to modify those state regulations of federal elections that the Constitution authorizes. The Court has also cited the NECESSARY AND PROPER CLAUSE as an additional source of congressional authority over federal elections, and in EX PARTE YARBROUGH (1884) it declared that Congress has the power, as an attribute of republican government, to pass laws governing federal elections, especially to protect them against fraud, violence, and other practices that undermine their integrity. And, although no constitutional provision explicitly extends the authority of

Congress to regulate presidential elections, the Court affirmed this power in *Burroughs v. United States* (1934), OREGON V. MITCHELL (1970), and BUCKLEY V. VALEO (1976).

Congressional power to regulate elections does not necessarily imply power to regulate political parties. But the Supreme Court has taken a major step in that direction by bringing federal PRIMARY ELECTIONS, which are principally a party process for selecting candidates, within the ambit of Article I. In *United States v. Classic* the Justices held that: "Where state law has made the primary an integral part of the procedure of choice, or where in fact the primary effectively controls the choice, the right of the elector to have his ballot counted at the primary is . . . included in the right [to vote in congressional elections] protected by Article I, sec. 2." This right to vote in congressional elections may be protected by Congress under Article I, section 4. Subsequently, the Court has treated *Classic* as recognizing a general congressional power to regulate primary elections for federal offices.

A wholly distinct doctrinal technique for imposing judicial limits upon party affairs, which may extend congressional legislative authority to party activities, grew out of the White Primary Cases. In NIXON V. HERNDON (1927) the Supreme Court held that because the sponsorship of a primary election by a state was STATE ACTION subject to the FOURTEENTH AMENDMENT, the exclusion of black voters from such a primary was unconstitutional. Even when the state authorized the party executive committee to determine party membership, NIXON V. CONDON (1932) held the ensuing primary to constitute state action. State authorization of a ballot position for candidates selected in party-sponsored primaries, without any state-prescribed primary rules or state operation of the primary, was held in SMITH V. ALLWRIGHT (1944) to be state action in violation of the FIFTEENTH AMENDMENT.

Many commentators and judges regard TERRY V. ADAMS (1953)—the last of the White Primary Cases—as extending constitutional limitation to party activities beyond primary elections. In *Terry* the Supreme Court held that the Fifteenth Amendment prohibited a local group, the Jaybird Democratic Association, from excluding blacks from a preprimary straw vote, paid for and operated exclusively by the association, to endorse candidates to run in the statutorily recognized Democratic party primary. The four-member plurality of the *Terry* Court concluded that the Jaybirds were part of the Democratic party. Only three Justices said that the Jaybird straw vote was limited by the Fifteenth Amendment because it was "an integral part, indeed the only effective part, of the electoral process."

Nonetheless, most judicial decisions now treat party organizations as state-affiliated agencies. State laws often closely prescribe the structure, organization, and duties of local, district, and state party units. Hence, the lower federal court cases have held that the EQUAL PROTECTION CLAUSE governs the selection and apportionment of members of local, district, and state party committees and conventions. Several decisions of the Court of Appeals for the District of Columbia have also applied the Fourteenth Amendment to national party conventions, because those conventions are integral parts of the process of selecting the President. But in at least one case that court suggested that the developing law of "state action," as defined by the Supreme Court, had excluded party conventions from the scope of the Fourteenth Amendment.

In defining the scope of the Fourteenth and Fifteenth Amendments, and thus the scope of congressional power to enforce those amendments, several appellate courts have distinguished between parties' candidate selection activities and their management of "internal affairs." Ronald Rotunda has suggested "a functional standard" in which "all integral steps in an election for public office are public functions and therefore state action subject to some judicial scrutiny." The functional distinction, though plausible and attractive, is difficult to apply in practice. Party activists often seek to influence the selection of party candidates, presumably to assure that party nominees reflect the policies of the party organization. Working through party organizations, they endorse candidates in the primary, expend money on their behalf, and mobilize primary voters for them. These activities could easily be construed as part of the selection of candidates; yet it seems unlikely that they fall within the reach of the prohibitions of the Fourteenth and Fifteenth Amendments—and thus the reach of Congress's power to enforce those amendments.

One further source of governmental authority to regulate political parties is the power to attach restrictions to special statuses or benefits accorded to candidates and parties under federal and state laws. Generally, the Supreme Court has rejected legislation that requires the surrender of constitutional rights as a condition for attaining a governmental benefit. (See UNCONSTITUTIONAL CONDITIONS.) Although it recognized in *Buckley v. Valeo* (1976) that political expenditures constitute protected speech under the FIRST AMENDMENT, the Supreme Court nonetheless upheld the PRESIDENTIAL ELECTION CAMPAIGN FUND ACT's limits on political party expenditures for nomination conventions and on candidate spending in presidential nomination and general election campaigns subsidized by federal money. This decision has broad implications for state regulatory authority in the thirteen states that provide public grants to candidates and political parties.

In virtually all states political parties receive automatic access to the ballot if they obtain a certain percentage of votes cast in a prior election. And in every state the ballot carries the party label to identify the candidates nominated by qualified political parties. These state benefits to political parties may justify state regulation of the structure, organization, and operation of political parties. Moreover, these benefits may strengthen claims that party activities constitute state action, thus bringing them within the ambit of both judicial and congressional authority under the Civil War amendments.

Although the Constitution has been interpreted to allow government to extend special recognition to political parties, especially major parties, governmental assistance to parties is circumscribed by constitutional limits. In *Buckley v. Valeo* the Supreme Court not only held that financial subventions were within congressional authority under the GENERAL WELFARE CLAUSE; it also sustained definitions of eligibility that tended to reinforce the position of the major parties. Full public financing is available only to a party whose presidential candidate in the previous election received at least 25 percent of the popular vote. Some minor parties and candidates are eligible for lesser funding; others are not.

The party, seen as part of the electorate, is recognized by state eligibility requirements for voter participation in primary elections. Connecticut's closed party primary survived the challenge that it abridged independent voters' right to vote and freedom of association. A lower federal court held that the state law validly served "to protect party members from 'intrusion by those with adverse political principles,' and to preserve the integrity of the electoral process," and the Supreme Court affirmed in *Nader v. Schaffer* (1976). The courts have not decided whether political parties' freedom of association protects them from intrusion into the nominating process by persons who are not party members.

State authority to protect the integrity of party membership rolls is limited by the Fourteenth Amendment. A voter's freedom to associate with a party is apparently abridged if state-mandated enrollment rules unduly delay participation in a party primary. In *Kusper v. Pontikes* (1973) the Supreme Court invalidated a law requiring party enrollment twenty-three months in advance of a primary in which the voter wished to participate.

States also have power to protect the integrity of party nominating procedures by limiting independent or third-party candidacies by those who have been affiliated with another party. Hence, in *Storer v. Brown* (1974) the Supreme Court sustained a state law requiring an independent or new-party candidate to disaffiliate from his prior party at least a year in advance of his new party's primary. And in *American Party of Texas v. White* (1974) the Justices upheld a state law prohibiting persons who had voted in a party's most recent primary from signing petitions to qualify another party's candidate or an independent candidate for the ballot. The Court has also intimated

that it would sustain "sore loser" statutes which prohibit a candidate who has participated in a party's nominating contest from subsequently qualifying as an independent candidate or opposition party aspirant in the same election. But in the same case, *Anderson v. Celebrezze* (1983), the Court held that states may not protect established parties by setting early filing deadlines that bar independent candidates arising from opposition to the platforms or candidates of major parties, when those become known.

The Constitution has been interpreted to allow preferred ballot access to established parties. Hence, in *Jennes v. Fortson* (1971) the Court sustained a statute giving automatic ballot access to parties that had obtained twenty percent or more of the vote in the prior election, while requiring others to gain ballot placement by obtaining petition signatures equivalent to five percent of those eligible to vote in the prior election. Nonetheless, in *Williams v. Rhodes* (1968) the Court rejected statutory schemes so complex or burdensome as to make it virtually impossible for any but the Democratic and Republican parties to obtain ballot access.

Promotion of political parties through minimal restrictions on the First Amendment right to associate and on the right to vote are justified by a wide array of governmental interests. The Supreme Court has said that states may protect political parties in order to assure "stability of the political system," to avoid confusion or deception, to "avoid frivolous or fraudulent candidacies prompted by short-range political goals, pique, or personal quarrel." Congress, in providing public financing of parties and candidates, can seek to avoid funding hopeless candidacies with large sums of public money or fostering proliferation of splinter parties. In the aggregate these justifications represent a constitutional hospitality toward political parties, at least when legislators grant them special statuses.

Several developments in constitutional doctrine suggest that long-established governmental regulation of political parties may now stand on treacherous ground. The 1950s saw the emergence of an independent First Amendment freedom of association, principally in cases involving dissident or oppressed groups, especially the Communist party. As early as 1952, in *Ray v. Blair*, the Supreme Court sustained a Democratic party requirement that candidates for presidential elector swear to vote for the presidential and vice-presidential candidates selected by the national Democratic party. Such an oath "protects a party from intrusion by those with adverse political principles." But until the 1970s there was little other judicial recognition that the freedom of association might secure rights of major political parties against governmental regulation.

In *Cousins v. Wigoda* (1975) and *Democratic Party v. LaFollette* (1981) the Supreme Court specifically announced that the First Amendment protected national party conventions in their establishment of rules for the selection of delegates, even in the face of contrary state laws or local party practices. In both cases, the Supreme Court announced that "the National Democratic party and its adherents enjoy a constitutionally protected right of political association." Both cases also applied the traditional standard in First Amendment cases; only a COMPELLING STATE INTEREST warranted abridgment of the "rights of association" of the national Democratic party.

In *LaFollette* the Court concluded that Article II, section 1, of the Constitution, which empowers each state to "appoint" presidential electors in the manner directed by the legislature, bears such a "remote and tenuous" connection to "the means by which political party members in a State associate to elect delegates to party nominating conventions . . . as to be wholly without constitutional significance." This conclusion sets aside one possible constitutional basis for state power to regulate party activities in selecting presidential nominees. Together, *Cousins* and *LaFollette* signal judicial reluctance to sweep every stage in the candidate selection process, especially those conducted by the parties themselves, within the scope of governmental regulation.

Indeed, in *Cousins* the Supreme Court specifically declined to "decide" or to "intimate" decisions on several critical issues of governmental authority to regulate parties, thus suggesting that large areas of the law remain open despite the assumption of past practices and of lower court decisions that party affairs are subject to extensive regulation. First, the Court did not decide "whether the decisions of a National Political Party in the area of selection constitute state or governmental action" limited by the Fourteenth and Fifteenth Amendments, and thus subject to congressional regulation. Second, the Justices left open the question "whether national political parties are subject to the principles of the REAPPORTIONMENT decisions, or other constitutional restraints, in their methods of delegate selection or allocation." Third, the Court did not decide "whether or to what extent national political parties and their nominating conventions are regulable by, or only by, Congress."

Although the sweeping associational rights of political parties recognized in *Cousins* and *LaFollette* have sometimes been regarded as limited by the Supreme Court's reference to the special "national interest" in presidential nominating conventions, the Court has relied on those decisions to protect party autonomy below the national level. In *Rivera-Rodriguez v. Popular Democratic Party* (1982) the Court cited *Cousins* and *LaFollette* in holding that a territorial political party, empowered by law to select a replacement for a deceased territorial legislator originally elected on the party ticket, was "entitled to adopt its own procedures to select . . . [a] replacement" and "was not required to include nonmembers in what can be analogized to a party primary election."

These developments suggest that the emerging First Amendment rights of parties may give them broad autonomy to order their affairs. At a minimum, party organizations can make a strong claim to order the selection, structure, and operation of party committees and conventions free from state regulation, even if those committees and conventions participate actively in candidate selection primaries. The federal courts have held that a state law prohibiting party committees from endorsing candidates in primaries violated First Amendment speech and associational rights; they avoided deciding, however, whether party campaign activities such as contributing money were similarly protected in those primary contests. If party assemblies actually select candidates, they may claim autonomy under *Cousins* and *LaFollette*, which held that party rules overrode contrary state laws in prescribing the selection of delegates to national party nominating conventions.

At the farthest reaches, the First Amendment might be construed to allow parties a substantial role in prescribing party membership and qualifying candidates for participation in party primaries established by the states. A state has a legitimate interest in an orderly election process that encourages qualified persons to participate in elections free of fraud, intimidation, and corruption; but its interests do not warrant limitations on the First Amendment associational rights of political parties. Parties may therefore establish voter enrollment and candidate eligibility rules to prevent the intrusion into party primaries of candidates and voters who do not share the party's goals. These party rules would, of course, be subject to the limits that the Supreme Court has already imposed to protect the constitutional rights to vote and associate. Such a theory of party autonomy is consistent with the modern understanding of the First Amendment and with contemporary Supreme Court declarations of party associational rights. It is a theory awaiting full explication and recognition.

DAVID ADAMANY
(1986)

Bibliography

GEYH, CHARLES 1983 "It's My Party and I'll Cry If I Want To": State Intrusions upon the Associational Freedoms of Political Parties. *Wisconsin Law Review* 1983:211–240.

GOTTLIEB, STEPHEN E. 1982 Rebuilding the Right of Association: The Right to Hold a Convention as a Test Case. *Hofstra Law Review* 11:191–247.

KESTER, JOHN G. 1974 Constitutional Restrictions on Political Parties. *Virginia Law Review* 60:735–784.

NOTE 1978 Equal Representation of Party Members on Political Party Central Committees. *Yale Law Journal* 88:167–185.

ROSSITER, CLINTON L. 1960 *Parties and Politics in America.* Ithaca, N.Y.: Cornell University Press.

ROTUNDA, RONALD D. 1975 Constitutional and Statutory Restrictions on Political Parties in the Wake of *Cousins v. Wigoda. Texas Law Review* 53:935–963.

SORAUF, FRANK J. 1980 *Party Politics in America.* Boston: Little, Brown.

POLITICAL PHILOSOPHY OF THE CONSTITUTION

It is a commonplace that the Constitution provides for a LIMITED GOVERNMENT, one that depends upon a system of CHECKS AND BALANCES. And this in turn is said to reflect a realistic opinion both about the nature of man and about the purposes and risks of government. The general government is limited in that much is left to the states to do, to the extent and in the ways the states choose to act. The very existence of the states and many of the things they do are taken for granted; they do not depend upon the Constitution. Even the states formed pursuant to the Constitution automatically assumed, upon admission to the Union, virtually all of the prerogatives (or STATES' RIGHTS) of the original thirteen, including the status of being largely independent of the other states and in many respects independent of the general government.

The states play vital parts in the periodic choices of United States senators, representatives, and presidential electors. Otherwise, the Constitution, once ratified, depends upon the states for relatively few things in order to permit the general government to function within its appointed sphere. Various restrictions are placed upon the states, primarily with a view to preventing interferences by them with the proper activities of the general government. In addition, the states are obliged by the Constitution to respect various legal determinations in other states. But, by and large, the states are left fairly autonomous, however republican they are required and helped to be under the Constitution. (Although the CIVIL WAR and its RECONSTRUCTION amendments had effects upon the original constitutional dispensation, these amendments are consistent with, if not the natural culmination of, the initial dedication of the Constitution to liberty and equality.)

The general government is limited in still another critical respect by the SEPARATION OF POWERS, which makes the Constitution seem far less simple than it really is. Virtually everything that may be done by any branch of that government must take account, if it does not require the immediate cooperation, of the other two branches. Thus, Congress can enact laws alone, but it is easier to do so in collaboration with the President; how the judges will understand and how the President will execute these laws must be anticipated. The President alone commands the armed forces, but what those forces consist of and how they are equipped depends on congressional provisions, as does the very declaration of the wars in which such forces may be used. The judges interpret and apply laws, but, apart from the Supreme Court, all courts of the general government depend for their JURISDICTION and for their very existence upon the Congress, and for the execution of their decrees upon the President. Many other such interdependencies are evident.

We can even see in the references to divinity in the DECLARATION OF INDEPENDENCE an oblique anticipation of the qualified separation of powers found in the Constitution itself. There are four references of this kind in the Declaration. The first reference to God, and perhaps the second as well, regarded God as legislator; it is He that orders things, ordaining what is to be. That is, He first comes to sight as lawgiver or lawmaker. Next, God is seen as judge. Finally, He is revealed as executive, as One Who extends protection, enforcing the laws that have been laid down (with a suggestion as well of the dispensing power of the executive). Thus, the authors of the Declaration portrayed even the government of the world in the light of their political principles.

The constitutional dispersal of powers (between state and general governments, among branches of the general government, and between congressional houses with quite different constituencies) testifies to the recognition that those who wield power have to be watched, and perhaps shackled or at least hobbled. This understanding may be seen also in the ways the people discipline themselves, agreeing to proceed in accordance with constitutional forms. Such precautions make sense, however, only if there is indeed a considerable power to be exercised.

Preeminent among the powers of the general government are those that must be exercised countrywide if they are to be used effectively. These include the plenary (but not necessarily exclusive) powers of the general government with respect to commerce "among the several States," taxes, "the common defense," and international relations, all of which are reinforced by the NECESSARY AND PROPER CLAUSE. And so there has been no need for a "living" Constitution to "grow," except perhaps to grow out of the artificial limitations imposed by those periodic misinterpretations of the Constitution that have failed to appreciate the full extent of the powers intended to be vested in the general government.

Here and there the Constitution restricts the exercise of the plenary powers conferred upon the general government—but those restraints tend to be "procedural." "Substantive" restraints upon such powers would be unreasonable should they have to be employed in unpredictable but grave circumstances. The Constitution assumes the prudence of those who wield power. Thus, for example, no matter how the tax power is hedged in, Congress can still so use its discretion here as to ruin the country.

The prudence relied upon is to be directed to the advancement of the goals enumerated in the Preamble. There are elsewhere in the Constitution further indications of what is taken for granted as legitimate ends of government, such as in references to "the Progress of Science and useful Arts," to "public safety," to the control of "disorderly Behaviour," to a "Republican Form of Government," and to "the Law of Nations." And, of course, the Declaration of Independence states in an authoritative manner the enduring ends of American government rooted in the inalienable rights of men.

That the Declaration of Independence is taken for granted is evident even in the way the Constitution is dated: "in the Year of our Lord one thousand seven hundred and Eighty seven and of the Independence of the United States of America the Twelfth." It seems to be taken for granted as well that the prudence relied upon both in the Declaration and in the Constitution is generally to be promoted by free discussion of public issues, however salutary a temporary secrecy may be on occasion. Such discussion is presupposed by the relations of the various branches of government to one another and by what they say to each other. Thus, judges deliberate and set forth their conclusions in published opinions; the President, in exercising his VETO POWER, is to give "his Objections," which objections are to be considered by Congress; the members of Congress are protected in their exercise of freedom of speech as legislators. A continental FREEDOM OF SPEECH and FREEDOM OF THE PRESS were presupposed as well, even before the ratification of the FIRST AMENDMENT, by the repeated indications in the Constitution of 1787 that it is an ultimately sovereign people who establish and continually assess the government.

The SOVEREIGNTY of the people is central to the constitutional system, moderated though the people's control may be by the use of representatives and by indirect selections of various officers of government. Each of the seven articles of the original Constitution, including the judiciary article, testifies to the understanding that the people are ultimately to have their way, however carefully they have disciplined themselves in restricting the manner in which they insist upon having their way. The people are sovereign, and for good reasons: it is a government designed for their happiness; they themselves have ordained it and are to support it. Besides, no one else is obviously better qualified to decide what is in the best interests of the country.

An essential equality among people is indicated in various ways, including in the equal status of the states and in the freedom of citizens to move among the states. Majority rule is taken for granted again and again. No male-female or rich-poor distinction is recognized. The Constitution does not even recognize an intrinsic difference among the races, however much grudging accommodation there may have had to be to existing slavery institutions. And, of course, no government in the United States may grant TITLES OF NOBILITY.

To defer to the genuine sovereignty of the people is to submit, in effect, to that rule of law contemplated by MAGNA CARTA. It is only through law that a people, in their political capacity, can truly speak or be spoken to. Dependence upon the RULE OF LAW points to LEGISLATIVE SUPREMACY, which is indicated again and again in the Constitution, not least in its IMPEACHMENT provisions. It is peculiar, then, that we rely as much as we now do on JUDICIAL REVIEW—that is, on the duty of courts to assess congressional enactments for their constitutionality. Of course, this duty, too, can be put in terms of respect for the rule of law. But it is difficult to find in the text of the Constitution any provision for judicial review or even any indication that it was ever anticipated by the Framers. In fact, the care with which the President's veto (the executive counterpart to judicial review) is established argues against the opinion that judges are intended by the Constitution to examine formally sufficient acts of Congress for their constitutionality, except perhaps whenever the prerogatives of the courts themselves are immediately threatened. What does seem to be anticipated by the Constitution is an even more considerable power for judges than judicial review seems to offer, but one which the appellate courts of the general government have largely surrendered. This is their indirect but nevertheless critical power of supervising the COMMON LAW (and hence the moral sensibilities) of the country, subject to whatever regulations legislatures may choose to provide. In any event, these courts are entitled, perhaps even obliged, to interpret acts of Congress in accordance with the Constitution, proceeding in each case before them on the reasonable assumption (until Congress clearly indicates otherwise) that nothing unconstitutional or unjust is intended.

In the American constitutional system, both the rule of law and an ultimate dependence upon the sovereignty of the people mean that property is to be respected. (And this respect probably implies, considering the evident commercial presuppositions of the Constitution, that economic interests are to be advanced.) Respect for property is the private counterpart to that political deference to the public seen in genuine republican government. The protections of property in the THIRD, FOURTH, FIFTH, SEVENTH, and EIGTH AMENDMENTS draw upon a principle that is already evident in the original Constitution.

Deference to the public, and to republicanism, also takes the form of a concern for "the Blessings of Liberty." That a considerable liberty is taken for granted by the Constitution may be seen in its assurances with respect to HABEAS CORPUS, to BILLS OF ATTAINDER, to the crime of TREASON, to RELIGIOUS TESTS, and to " Indictment, Trial, Judgment and Punishment, according to Law." It may be seen as well in the spirit of liberty which pervades the governmental system, making much of a people's freely choosing what they will have done for them, by whom, and upon what terms.

But however much liberty, property, and equality are to be respected, there is no question under the Constitution but that there should be effective governance, and governance with respect to the most important matters facing the country as a whole. However "limited" the exercise of power may be, primarily because of the different parts played by the three branches of the general government and by the states, great powers do exist for the general government to exercise. In any extended contest, the Constitution assumes that a determined Congress can have its way both with the President and with the courts. The Constitution was itself fashioned by a deliberative body which resembles much more the Congress than it does either the presidency or the judiciary. In the very nature of things, lawmaking (whether entrusted to one hand or to many) is at the heart of sovereignty, providing the necessary mandates for those who either interpret or execute the laws.

Lawmaking may be seen as well in what the people at large in their sovereign capacity have done in "ordain[ing] and establish[ing] this Constitution." Thus, the preeminence of lawmaking may be seen not only in what the CONSTITUTIONAL CONVENTION did in drafting the Constitution but even more in what the people did in the RATIFICATION OF THE CONSTITUTION. The provision of a workable AMENDING PROCESS also presupposes that the people retain their ultimate authority—and that standards exist by which they may examine and modify constitutional arrangements from time to time.

The Framers of the Constitution applied those standards, set forth in the Declaration of Independence, to the needs and opportunities of their day. Such standards were understood to be rooted in nature. The American people considered themselves sanctified by Providence, or at least peculiarly fitted because of their experiences and circumstances, to discern and to follow the guidance of nature. Americans looked to political philosophers and other students of law and government for help in their recourse to nature—and they invoked with confidence writers from Plato and Aristotle to John Locke and Adam Smith. But none of these writers was authoritative; all of them could be exploited, along with the considerable historical record (sacred and profane, ancient and modern) repeatedly drawn upon in debate. The diversity of the many sources casually, if not cavalierly, put to use by the Framers suggests that the astute political thought of eighteenth-century Americans was, in certain respects, distinctive to them. They were eminently practical and yet high-minded constitutionalists who seemed willing to leave many private concerns, and vital personal virtues, to the ministrations of local government and of common-law judges (as well as to church and family), while they entrusted the government of the United States both with the GENERAL WELFARE (including the economy of the country) and with external affairs (including the common defense).

However extensive and even awesome those governmental powers may be, the powers retained by the people to revise whatever is done by government in their name remain even greater. The ultimate sovereignty of the people may be seen not only in the constitutional provision for amendments but also in that natural RIGHT OF REVOLUTION vigorously relied upon in the Declaration of Independence.

Intrinsic to the political philosophy of the Constitution is the recognition that a bad law may still be constitutional, and hence that the political must be distinguished from the legal (or judicial). This understanding means that in order for the constitutional government empowered by the people (as well as for the all-powerful people themselves) to contribute to the common good in a regular and enduring manner, there must be constant and informed recourse by Americans (citizens and public servants alike) to the instructive dictates of prudence.

GEORGE ANASTAPLO
(1986)

Bibliography

ALVAREZ, LEO PAUL DE, ed. 1976 *Abraham Lincoln, the Gettysburg Address and American Constitutionalism.* Irving, Texas: University of Dallas Press.

ANASTAPLO, GEORGE 1965 The Declaration of Independence. *St. Louis University Law Journal* 9:390–415.

—— 1971 *The Constitutionalist: Notes on the First Amendment.* Dallas, Texas: Southern Methodist University Press.

—— 1984 Mr. Crosskey, the American Constitution, and the Natures of Things. *Loyola University of Chicago Law Journal* 15:181–260.

—— 1987 *The Constitution of 1787: A Commentary.* Athens, Ohio: Swallow Press/Ohio University Press. (Reprinted from *Loyola University of Chicago Law Journal* [1986] 18:1.)

CROSSKEY, WILLIAM W. 1953 *Politics and the Constitution in the History of the United States.* Chicago: University of Chicago Press.

EIDELBERG, PAUL   1968   *The Philosophy of the American Constitution: A Reinterpretation of the Intentions of the Founding Fathers.* New York: Free Press.

SHARP, MALCOLM P.   1973   Crosskey, Anastaplo and Meiklejohn on the United States Constitution. *University of Chicago Law School Record* 20:3–18.

STORY, JOSEPH   1833   *Commentaries on the Constitution of the United States.* Boston: Hilliard, Gray & Co.

POLITICAL PHILOSOPHY OF THE CONSTITUTION
(Update)

To speak of the political philosophy of the Constitution is to invite immediate controversy. Many allege that the Constitution has no coherent political philosophy; and those who maintain otherwise often regard its political philosophy as far from commendable.

Those who contend that the Constitution is theoretically incoherent point to its various inconsistences and the many provisions that were the products of compromise. The more charitable of such analysts try to make a virtue of the Constitution's supposed lack of an overarching political theory, arguing that this demonstrates the Framers' laudable ability to ignore their own prejudices. In the words of law professor Donald Horowitz: "What we ought to revere is the spirit of compromise the Framers brought to Philadelphia—compromise that accommodated large states and small, north and south, numbers and wealth, legislative supremacists and proponents of a strong executive."

Probably the most significant obstacle to this view is presented by THE FEDERALIST, the contemporaneous exposition of the Constitution by ALEXANDER HAMILTON, JAMES MADISON, and JOHN JAY. Written during the turmoil of the battle for RATIFICATION, *The Federalist* presents a remarkably comprehensive and coherent exposition of the constitutional system, fleshing out its fundamental principles of NATURAL RIGHTS, CHECKS AND BALANCES, BICAMERALISM, SEPARATION OF POWERS, and FEDERALISM. *The Federalist*, which was utilized extensively by ratification proponents, goes a long way toward explaining the shared principles that underlay the compromises of the CONSTITUTIONAL CONVENTION OF 1787.

Perhaps a more challenging attack on the coherence of the Constitution comes from those who juxtapose its REPUBLICANISM with its sanction of SLAVERY. Article IV, section 2, effectively compelled northern states to return fugitive slaves to their southern masters; and Article I, section 9, protected the importation of slaves until 1808. Many of those who criticize the Constitution on this account accuse the Founders of having a contradictory understanding of inalienable rights, claiming that the Founders did not think such rights applied to black Americans. These critics often cite as evidence for this proposition Justice ROGER BROOKE TANEY's assertion in DRED SCOTT V. SANDFORD (1857) that the Founders regarded black Americans "as beings . . . so inferior, that they had no rights the white man was bound to respect."

Yet Taney's claim in *Dred Scott* was a palpable fiction, one that Taney himself had rejected as defense counsel for an abolitionist preacher earlier in his career. In reality, the Founders were not inconsistent in understanding the principle of inalienable rights; but they were inconsistent in applying it, as they themselves recognized. Slaveholders such as GEORGE WASHINGTON and THOMAS JEFFERSON knew that slavery abrogated the natural rights on which the Constitution was premised and therefore had to be abolished. The question was how to abolish slavery. Although it is easy to condemn the Framers for their compromise on this issue, one may legitimately wonder how much longer the horrible oppression of slavery would have lasted if the bargain had not been struck and the South had stayed out of the Union.

Incoherency, however, is not the only charge leveled against the political philosophy of the Constitution. Other critics chide the Founders for creating a constitutional system that cannot sustain itself because it is based almost entirely on self-interest. They claim that the philosophy of the Constitution is best summarized by the statement in *The Federalist* #51 that one must supply "by opposite and rival interests, the defect of better motives." According to these observers, the two pillars of the constitutional system are the extended republic, which fosters such a multiplicity of factions that it will be difficult for any one of them to dominate the rest, and the separation of powers, which similarly aims at preventing any single faction from controlling the government by dividing and arranging "the several offices in such a manner as that each may be a check on the other—that the private interest of every individual may be a sentinel over the public rights."

According to this view, the Founders thought that if the Constitution was properly structured to rely on self-interest, good character on the part of citizens would become expendable. This thesis has been maintained, more or less vigorously, by a variety of scholars from across the political spectrum, including Richard Hofstadter, Benjamin Barber, and Martin Diamond. Yet there are grave difficulties with this interpretation, not the least of which is its negative formulation of the Constitution's principles. According to these critics, devices such as bicameralism, checks and balances, and separation of powers use self-interest to prevent a tyrannical concentration of authority. But this is only part of the story. The Framers also believed that these devices would promote good government by attracting virtuous leaders to federal office and by supplying those leaders with the tools needed to perform their governmental duties properly.

Nowhere can this be seen more clearly than in the separation of powers. The Framers believed that powers should be separated not only to prevent tyranny, but also because the executive, legislative, and judicial powers require by their very natures different talents in order to be exercised well. The executive power requires the capacity for energy, secrecy, and quick and decisive action; the legislative power demands deliberation, or the free and full consideration of diverging points of view; and the judicial power calls for a cool and dispassionate application of the laws. The Framers of the Constitution subsequently structured each of the three branches of government in such a way as to encourage these characteristics. The Framers provided for a unitary executive, believing that this would facilitate quick and decisive action. They created a bicameral legislature to promote the best kind of deliberation. Finally, they provided that federal judges would hold their posts during GOOD BEHAVIOR, thus insulating them from the partisan battles of the moment and promoting the impartial and dispassionate application of the laws.

In sum, the Framers sought to supply each branch of government with the tools necessary to carry out its assigned tasks in the best manner possible. Of course, this was not the same as assuring each branch *would* carry out its duties in the best manner possible. A despot elected President, for example, might use the power to pardon to shield the criminal activities of his or her subordinates; unscrupulous senators might hold presidential appointments hostage to extract special favors from the executive branch; and corrupt judges might use their lifetime tenure as a shield for their corruption. Thus, the structure of the various offices ensures that good people, if elected, can more easily fulfill the functions of their offices; but it does not guarantee that good and virtuous people will actually fill those offices.

The Framers of the Constitution were well aware of this, however, and they carefully crafted the selection procedures for the various offices to encourage the choice of persons eminent in both ability and virtue. For example, the Framers believed that the election process for the presidency would tend to elect outstanding individuals because it required a candidate to achieve a national consensus in order to win in the ELECTORAL COLLEGE; no candidate who pandered to narrow or local interests would be likely to obtain such a national majority. Similarly, the selection of senators by their state legislatures would likely encourage the selection of distinguished statesmen because the legislatures would want to choose representatives that might bring luster and distinction to their respective states. More generally, higher age require-

ments for the offices of senator and President made it more probable that candidates for these offices would have the wisdom and stature that comes from experience.

The Constitution also fosters virtuous leadership in yet another manner: it encourages persons of eminent ability to *seek* federal office by assuring them that they will have enough time to prosecute their projects for the public good. This is why the Constitution contains no provision for the rotation of offices; the Framers thought that renewability of terms would help attract the best people to federal office. In the case of the presidency, wrote Alexander Hamilton, a great man will be more likely to consider running for President if he knows that he will have the time to complete as well as to undertake "extensive and arduous enterprises for the public benefit. . . ."

In many different ways, then, the very structure of the Constitution aspires to cultivate virtue in government. One may readily question, of course, whether the Constitution's structural mechanisms are *sufficient* to bring about good government. To point to only one example: the Founders were certainly correct that the national consensus needed for the election of the President ensures that a candidate of merely local interests will likely fail in his or her bid for office, but this does not necessarily mean that the person chosen will be someone preeminent in ability and virtue. If the citizenry were consumed by self-interest, they might instead elect the most pliable candidate—the one they think can be bullied into supporting their interests by their representatives in Congress. In other words, even the electoral college cannot produce a good President in and of itself. The presidential electors— and ultimately, those who select those electors—must still be good enough to care about justice and virtue.

In the end then, the Constitution can only do so much. It is not a cure-all. But contrary to the claims of some critics, the Founders themselves recognized this. They did not believe that the Constitution was a machine that would run itself. They knew that its perpetuation ultimately depended on the character of the nation's citizens. Hence, even in *The Federalist*, "a dependence on the people" is acknowledged as the primary safeguard for republicanism, whereas the Constitution's various checks and balances are described as "auxilliary precautions."

Some may object that if the Founders truly considered the character of the citizenry important, they would have mentioned civic virtue in the Constitution explicitly. After all, certain early STATE CONSTITUTIONS contained appeals to both God and virtue. The PREAMBLE to the U.S. Constitution, in contrast, seems but a pale reflection of these earlier documents. It does speak of establishing justice, but instead of going on and listing the requisite civic virtues, it merely stresses the importance of "the blessings of Liberty." Some have interpreted the Founders' emphasis on liberty rather than virtue as proof that they envisioned a republic where self-interest, rather than self-sacrifice, was to be the guiding light. Yet those who interpret "liberty" in this manner are interpolating their own modern conceptions back into the founding.

It is not difficult to understand the reason for the confusion. Today, liberty is equated with the absence of all restraint. Indeed, people who call themselves "libertarians" argue against all government regulation of business and object to criminalizing PORNOGRAPHY, hallucinogenic drugs, and prostitution. Yet the Founders' conception of liberty was entirely different. Echoing the Aristotelian understanding of virtue, the Founding generation saw liberty as the golden mean between two extremes: it was the contrary of *both* slavery and anarchy. Liberty was freedom, but freedom within the confines of the laws of nature and of nature's God. It was the freedom to organize one's own affairs, live where one wanted, participate in politics, and buy and sell property, as long as a person did not violate the immutable moral law. In short, early Americans thoroughly agreed with JOHN MILTON's aphorism that "none can love freedom heartily, but good men; the rest love not freedom but license."

That this was the Founder's true conception of liberty should become self-evident to even the most cynical observers when they examine the public actions of the Founding Fathers. The same George Washington who presided over the Constitutional Convention of 1787 declared in his Farewell Address: "Of all the dispositions and habits which lead to political prosperity, Religion and Morality are indispensable supports." The same Congress that recommended the Constitution to the states enacted an ordinance for the Northwest Territories that announced: "Religion, morality and knowledge being necessary to good government . . . schools and the means of education shall forever be encouraged."

But perhaps it was Supreme Court Justice JAMES WILSON, arguably the most systematic political thinker during the founding, who best expressed the necessity of schooling Americans in their civil rights and civic responsibilities. In his inaugural law lecture at the College of Philadelphia, attended by such luminaries as Washington and Jefferson, Wilson declared:

On the public mind, one great truth can never be too deeply impressed—that the weight of the government of the United States, and of each state composing the union, rests on the shoulders of the people.

I express not this sentiment now, . . . with a view to flatter: I express it now, as I have always expressed it heretofore, with a far other and higher aim—with an aim to excite the people to acquire, by vigorous and manly exercise, a degree of strength sufficient to support the weighty burthen, which is laid upon them—with an aim

to convince them, that their duties rise in strict proportion to their rights; and that few are able to trace or to estimate the great danger, in a free government, when the rights of the people are unexercised, and the still greater danger, when the rights of the people are ill exercised.

JOHN G. WEST, JR.
(1992)

(SEE ALSO: *Conservatism; Constitution and Civic Ideals; Constitutional History Before 1776; Constitutional History, 1776–1789; Liberalism.*)

Bibliography

BARLOW, J. JACKSON; LEVY, LEONARD W.; and MASUGI, KEN, eds. 1988 *The American Founding: Essays on the Formation of the Constitution.* New York: Greenwood Press.

HORWITZ, ROBERT H., ed. 1986 *The Moral Foundations of the Republic,* 3rd ed. Charlottesville: University Press of Virginia.

JAFFA, HARRY V. 1987 What Were the 'Original Intentions' of the Framers of the Constitution of the United States? *University of Puget Sound Law Review* 10:343–423.

KESLER, CHARLES R., ed. 1987 *Saving the Revolution: The Federalist Papers and the American Founding.* New York: Free Press.

POLITICAL QUESTION DOCTRINE

As early as MARBURY V. MADISON (1803) the Supreme Court recognized that decisions on some governmental questions lie entirely within the discretion of the "political" branches of the national government—the President and Congress—and thus outside the proper scope of JUDICIAL REVIEW. Today such questions are called "political questions."

Among the clauses of the federal Constitution held to involve political questions, the one most frequently cited has been Article IV, section 4, under which the federal government "shall guarantee to every State in this Union a REPUBLICAN FORM OF GOVERNMENT." Federal courts, and particularly the Supreme Court, have argued that as the definition of "republican" is at the heart of the American political system, only the "political branches," which are accountable to the sovereign people, can make that definition. The electorate can ratify or reject the definition by reelecting or defeating their representatives at the next election. The choice of definition, Justice FELIX FRANKFURTER said, dissenting in BAKER V. CARR (1962), entails choosing "among competing theories of political philosophy," which is not a proper judicial function.

Thus the Supreme Court has refused to review political decisions in cases involving two governments, each claiming to be the legitimate one of a state (LUTHER V. BORDEN, 1849); the question whether the post-CIVIL WAR RECON-

STRUCTION governments in southern states were republican (*Georgia v. Stanton* and MISSISSIPPI V. JOHNSON, 1867); the "republican" nature of the INITIATIVE and REFERENDUM (*Pacific Telephone & Telegraph Co. v. Oregon*, 1912; *Hawke v. Smith*, 1920); lack of REAPPORTIONMENT by state legislatures (COLEGROVE V. GREEN, 1946); contested elections (*Taylor & Marshall v. Beckham*, 1900); certain presidential actions (*Mississippi v. Johnson*, 1867); certain cases arising in Indian territory (CHEROKEE INDIAN CASES, 1831–1832); and FOREIGN AFFAIRS (*Foster v. Neilson*, 1829; *Charlton v. Kelly*, 1913).

The Supreme Court has never successfully differentiated those questions proper for judicial interpretation from those that are reserved to the "political" branches. A plurality of the Justices having held in *Colegrove v. Green* (1946) that a state legislature's failure to reapportion itself after the decennial federal census was a political question, for example, the Court in *Baker v. Carr* decided that such inaction raised a question under the equal protection clause of the FOURTEENTH AMENDMENT rather than the guarantee clause, and therefore raised an issue proper for judicial decision. After having handed down a line of cases holding that contested elections were matters in which the final decision could come only from the relevant legislative body, the Court overturned the refusal by the HOUSE OF REPRESENTATIVES (POWELL V. MCCORMACK, 1969) to seat a member who, in the Court's view, had been excluded unconstitutionally.

The Court has been relatively consistent in holding various foreign relations issues to constitute political questions, because of the necessity for the country to speak with one voice, the inability of courts to develop a body of principles to govern such issues, and what Justice Frankfurter described in *Perez v. Brownell* (1958) as the "constitutional allocation of governmental function" concerning foreign affairs to the President and Congress. Matters such as the existence of a state of war, the relevance of a treaty, the boundaries of the nation, and the credentials of foreign diplomats have been left to congressional and presidential diplomats. But the Court stated in REID V. COVERT (1957) that even the provisions of a treaty or EXECUTIVE AGREEMENT are reviewable if citizens assert violations of their rights. And, in the face of government claims that the travel of Americans abroad raises diplomatic issues fit only for executive discretion, the Court has enunciated the RIGHT TO TRAVEL abroad and has made substantive rulings for and against claims of that right (KENT V. DULLES, 1958; APTHEKER V. SECRETARY OF STATE, 1964; ZEMEL V. RUSK, 1965).

The Supreme Court's variable commitment to the political question doctrine may be explained by reasons that are nondoctrinal. The Court appears to resort to the doctrine when only two substantive judgments are possible, the first being unacceptable to the Court because it would likely go unenforced and the second being equally unacceptable because it would violate a major tenet of American political ideology. In *Colegrove v. Green*, for example, the plurality suggested that the Illinois legislation might ignore a HOLDING that the legislature's refusal to redesign badly malapportioned congressional districts was unconstitutional—and the House of Representatives might take no action. Yet upholding such a malapportionment, which gave some citizens a vote of far greater weight than that of others, would have run contrary to the American belief that all citizens are equal in the electoral process. Similarly, the Court in *Mississippi v. Johnson* had the choice of deciding that the Reconstruction state governments were illegitimate, a ruling that the President and Congress surely would have ignored; or that the governments, which had been imposed by the federal government on citizens denied the right to participate in the election process, were legitimate—which would have offended the basic American idea of SOVEREIGNTY of the people. In both cases the Court invoked the political question doctrine and left decision in the hands of the "political branches."

The very notion of "political branches," however, is untenable. Article III of the Constitution makes the federal judiciary indirectly accountable insofar as it may enable the people's representatives in Congress to strip the courts of JURISDICTION over matters the people believe the courts to have mishandled. Federal judges, too, are liable to IMPEACHMENT—although this resource has never been taken for purely political purposes since the earliest days of the nineteenth century.

Court decisions necessarily affect power. The decision in PLESSY V. FERGUSON (1896) legitimizing SEPARATE BUT EQUAL railroad cars for black and white passengers encouraged southern states to establish racially segregated schools; the holding of BROWN V. BOARD OF EDUCATION (1954) that "separate but equal" schools violated the equal protection clause stripped the states of that power, transferring the power to define SEGREGATION and integration to the federal courts, the Congress, and, in some cases, to the President. The Court's upholding of ECONOMIC REGULATION affecting wages, hours, unionization, social security, job safety, and competition shifted power from employers to state and federal legislatures, executives, and REGULATORY AGENCIES, as well as to unions, and enabled the United States to consolidate a system of welfare capitalism under which privately owned property is systematically regulated by governmental bodies.

The Court nonetheless insists that the judicial branch is apolitical, because its own institutional power depends on the electorate's belief that the Court is above politics.

As JAMES MADISON pointed out in THE FEDERALIST #51, the Court possesses neither the power of the purse nor that of the sword. It is entirely dependent for the enforcement of its decisions on the willingness of the population and public officials to carry them out. Were the Court's decisions to be ignored, the Court's prestige would suffer; in a circular fashion, the loss of prestige would increase the possibility that subsequent decisions would go unheeded.

The Court's decisions find ready compliance when the decisions reflect a societal consensus. The difference between the Court's 1946 *Colegrove* decision that malapportionment was a political question and its contrary 1962 *Baker* decision can be linked to the large-scale movement of population to urban areas underrepresented in the legislatures. By 1962 a majority of the nation's population could be expected to concur in a decision that enhanced its political power. Promise of additional support from the President was implicit in the appearance of Attorney General ROBERT F. KENNEDY before the Court to argue as AMICUS CURIAE for reapportionment, for Kennedy was, of course, the brother of President JOHN F. KENNEDY, who owed his office to urban votes.

The political question device derives its legitimacy from the necessity to preserve an independent judiciary in the American political system. The device is justifiable because it enables the judiciary to maintain its independence by withdrawing from no-win situations. In addition, it prevents the courts from usurping the role of the ballot box. The Supreme Court, declaring the presence of a political question, tacitly admits that it cannot find and therefore cannot ratify a social consensus that does not violate basic American beliefs. The Court has no moral right to impose rules upon a country not yet ready for them. The political question doctrine, which permits the Court to restrain itself from precipitating impossible situations that might tear the social fabric, gives the electorate and its representatives time to work out their own rules, which can ultimately be translated into constitutional doctrine through judicial decision. The doctrine of political questions is more than a self-saving mechanism for the Court; it is also an affirmation of a governmental system based on popular sovereignty.

PHILIPPA STRUM
(1986)

Bibliography

BICKEL, ALEXANDER M. 1962 *The Least Dangerous Branch*. Indianapolis: Bobbs-Merrill.

SCHARPF, FRITZ W. 1966 Judicial Review and the Political Question: A Functional Analysis. *Yale Law Journal* 75:517–546.

STRUM, PHILIPPA 1974 *The Supreme Court and "Political Questions."* University: University of Alabama Press.

POLITICAL QUESTION DOCTRINE
(Update 1)

Is the constitutionality of clandestine American involvement in Nicaragua an issue that the federal judiciary may decide? If the legislatures of two-thirds of the states apply to Congress to call a convention for proposing amendments and Congress ignores their application, should a federal court entertain an action by the states against Congress? Should the decision of the Republican National Committee not to seat a group of delegates at the party's national convention be subjected to federal court challenges?

All of these questions, in one way or another, implicate the political question DOCTRINE. This doctrine counsels the judiciary to refrain from deciding constitutional questions involving subject matters or issues appropriate for resolution only by the national political branches—Congress and the executive. In effect, the doctrine aims to divide "politics" from the "law," which is the proper sphere of judicial interpretation.

The Supreme Court has long considered the identification of political questions necessary to national SEPARATION OF POWERS. As early as MARBURY V. MADISON (1803), the Court recognized that although federal courts are obliged to enforce the mandatory requirements of the Constitution, a life-tenured, unelected, and politically unaccountable judiciary must reserve discretionary policymaking for the elected representatives of the American people.

Not until BAKER V. CARR (1962), however, did the Court articulate doctrinal standards for distinguishing a political question. Several of the *Baker* criteria call directly for judicial interpretation of the meaning and force of the Constitution's language; for example, does the text commit an issue to determination by the national political branches, and does the text lend itself to judicially manageable standards for resolving the issue? Other criteria require judges to assess realistically and pragmatically the political effects of a decision, such as asking if there is a significant potential for embarrassing or showing disrespect for Congress or the executive or whether the finality of a prior political decision is more important than its legality. Applying these standards, the *Baker* Court held that the Tennessee state legislature's failure to reapportion electoral districts after substantial migration of rural populations to urban centers raised a question of unconstitutional vote dilution and that the federal judiciary was competent to develop manageable standards for the vote dilution issue; it further held that the text of the FOURTEENTH AMENDMENT did not commit an EQUAL PROTECTION claim to the Congress or executive for decision and that the federal political branches had taken no action that required finality and respect.

Judges and scholars have launched serious attacks on the *Baker* approach to the definition of political questions. As the Constitution does not even provide expressly for the federal judiciary's review powers, it is difficult to argue that the text discriminates between those provisions enforceable by the judiciary and those consigned to Congress or the executive for construction. In addition, the individual-rights doctrines most fully developed by the judiciary are based on language in the BILL OF RIGHTS and the Fourteenth Amendment that is cryptic and open-ended, embodying no apparent and manageable judicial standards. Moreover, the Court may undermine the legitimacy of its own constitutional decisions by relying on pragmatic claims of institutional incompetence to supervise the policy decision making of administrative experts.

Nevertheless, the Supreme Court has shown no inclination to rethink the political question doctrine. In the most controversial political question ruling over the past five years, a solid majority of the Court expressly declined an invitation to modify or abandon the *Baker* standards. When several Indiana Democrats sued to invalidate a state legislative REAPPORTIONMENT plan for gerrymandering election district lines so as to disadvantage Democratic candidates, the Court applied the *Baker* criteria point by point and concluded that a political group's claim to fair representation does not present a political question. The opinion of Justice BYRON R. WHITE in *Davis v. Bandemer* (1986) declared that the Constitution does not generally dedicate vote dilution issues to the Congress or President for resolution and that the courts are institutionally competent to formulate workable rules for deciding such claims, even though they had not yet devised a precise method for identifying an unconstitutional political GERRYMANDER.

Several reasons may explain the Court's reluctance to reexamine the functionality of the political question doctrine. First, the judiciary has relied increasingly on other devices to limit its intervention in federal administrative policymaking, including the Supreme Court's rulings on STANDING, STATE ACTION, SOVEREIGN IMMUNITY, and constraints on equitable remedies. These alternatives have certain tactical and ideological advantages over the traditional political question doctrine: they apply to constitutional challenges against state and municipal, as well as federal, government violations, and without overruling the political question standards established during the WARREN COURT's expansive enforcement of CIVIL RIGHTS, the BURGER COURT and REHNQUIST COURT have exploited these relatively fluid devices to impose more severe restrictions on judicial regulation of government operations.

A second reason the Court may be unwilling to reexamine the doctrine is that scholarly criticism has challenged the integrity of a conceptual division of politics and law. Surely there can be no definitive and principled distinction between a political decision and a legal one in terms of their real-world consequences. A legal decision will have political effects, just as any political decision might. For example, deciding whether federal minimum-wage standards for state employees unduly interfere with the sovereign authority of state government or whether federal restrictions on political campaign contributions violate a contributor's FREEDOM OF SPEECH rights requires the judiciary either to approve the current balance of powers and rights struck by Congress or to disapprove it and redistribute the balance by imposing constitutional restraints on Congress. In another and less obvious sense, many constitutional decisions will turn on questions that are not essentially legal. Thus, some questions—for example, whether the state's interest in the preservation of fetal life during a woman's pregnancy is any less compelling before the point of viability than after it and whether a political party has been disadvantaged enough by a political gerrymander to claim unconstitutional vote dilution—may be legal because they are framed in intellectual ways familiar to lawyers and the federal judiciary assumes power to decide them. But the same questions are political in the sense that they cannot be answered except by reference to some theory of value which is inherently political (in the examples, a theory underlying a right of reproductive choice or a right to an undiluted vote). The stronger the system of judicial supervision of governmental policymaking, the more likely it is that a legal question will implicate political considerations and consequences.

Reasonably, the Court may be loath to recognize a collapse of the formal distinction between politics and law, for the merger of political and legal questions muddles the role of the federal judiciary in the tripartite national governmental system. If the questions underlying most constitutional claims involve obvious political considerations, what justifies the federal judiciary in second-guessing the policy decisions of the political branches? Ultimately, the analytical flaws of the political question doctrine threaten to unseat the Court as the primary interpreter of the Constitution.

DAVID M. SKOVER
(1992)

(SEE ALSO: *Campaign Finance; Constitutional Interpretation; Equity; Judicial Policymaking.*)

Bibliography

BICKEL, ALEXANDER 1962 *The Least Dangerous Branch: The Supreme Court at the Bar of Politics.* Indianapolis, Ind.: Bobbs-Merrill.

KOMESAR, NEIL 1984 Taking Institutions Seriously: Introduction to a Strategy for Constitutional Analysis. *University of Chicago Law Review* 56:366–446.

NAGEL, ROBERT 1989 Political Law, Legalistic Politics: A Recent History of the Political Question Doctrine. *University of Chicago Law Review* 56:643–669.

REDISH, MARTIN 1985 Judicial Review and the "Political Question." *Northwestern University Law Review* 79:1031–1061.

SCHARPF, FRITZ 1966 Judicial Review and the Political Question: A Functional Analysis. *Yale Law Journal* 75:517–597.

POLITICAL QUESTION DOCTRINE
(Update 2)

Since its modern-era recognition of the political question DOCTRINE in BAKER V. CARR (1962), the Supreme Court has never signaled a weakening of its nominal commitment to the principle that some issues do not lend themselves to adjudication in a court of law. In an increasingly large majority of cases in which a party has argued that the doctrine bars adjudication, however, the Court has found it to be an insufficient justification for departure from the normal presumption of JUDICIAL REVIEW.

The scope of the political question doctrine has been shaped as much by cases in which the Court found it not to apply as by cases in which the Court applied the doctrine. Indeed, the Court has repeatedly refused to dismiss even cases falling within categories that many commentators had thought were defined as "political" in nature. These include cases involving FOREIGN AFFAIRS and TREATIES; political GERRYMANDERING; legislative apportionment; structural requirements on the internal workings of the legislative branch; and specific grants of power to Congress such as the power to control IMMIGRATION; and the authority over AMERICAN INDIAN affairs. From these decisions, it is clear that the Court does not avoid adjudication merely because of the topic involved in the litigation. Indeed, some commentators believe that to do so would be an abdication of the Court's responsibility to decide CASES AND CONTROVERSIES.

The key to the Court's recognition of a nonjusticiable issue is the nature of the legal wrong. If the plaintiff can allege a concrete injury caused by the defendant's violation of a legal provision, the Court will ordinarily consider that claim on the merits, unless the provision at stake does not specify enforceable limits on the defendant's behavior. Even if the law involves politically sensitive areas or matters over which the other branches may have wide latitude for discretion, the Court has been willing to adjudicate as long as it can identify those legal limits against which the defendant's conduct can be evaluated. In the rare case in which no limits are specified, such as in the clause guaranteeing a REPUBLICAN FORM OF GOVERNMENT, the Court will dismiss.

NIXON V. UNITED STATES (1993) is the first post-*Baker* case in which a majority of the Court dismissed a claim on political question grounds. The Court found that the alleged violation—the failure of the U.S. SENATE properly to "try" the IMPEACHMENT of a federal judge—rested on an unusual provision of the Constitution that by its terms excluded the Court by granting to the Senate the "sole power to try impeachments." Because no constitutional provision other than the impeachment clauses grants "sole" power, there is little to suggest that this holding will have an impact outside the impeachment context. Thus, developments in the political question doctrine appear to confirm the view of those who have argued that the doctrine does not provide license for the Court to avoid decisions on the merits.

REBECCA L. BROWN
(2000)

Bibliography

BROWN, REBECCA L. 1993 When Political Questions Affect Individual Rights: The Other *Nixon v. United States*. *Supreme Court Review* 1993:125–155.

HENKIN, LOUIS 1976 Is There a "Political Question" Doctrine? *Yale Law Journal* 85:597–625.

MULHERN, J. PETER 1998 In Defense of The Political Question Doctrine. *University of Pennsylvania Law Review* 137:97–176.

POLITICAL SPEECH

See: Anonymous Political Speech; Campaign Finance; Electoral Process and the First Amendment; First Amendment; Freedom of Speech

POLITICAL TRIALS

Among Chief Justice JOHN MARSHALL's better-known observations is his declaration in MARBURY V. MADISON (1803) that the United States has "a government of laws and not of men." The assertion calls forth visions of a politically neutral legal system, dispensing evenhanded justice without regard to partisan concerns or to the identities of the parties. Yet, much in American legal history belies Marshall's aphorism. This country's past is replete with political trials, and they have done more than a little to shape its constitutional law.

In a sense, of course, all trials are political. Courts, judges, and the other institutions and individuals involved in the administration of justice are part of a system of government; even when they do no more than punish an ordinary crime or resolve a private dispute, they help to demonstrate the utility of that system and to maintain its authority. To most people, though, the term "political trial" connotes something more; it designates a type of legal proceeding having peculiar properties that distinguish it from ordinary civil and criminal litigation. There is much disagreement about what those defining attributes are, but a political trial is probably best defined as any civil or criminal trial or IMPEACHMENT proceeding that immediately affects, or is intended to affect, the structure, personnel, or policies of government; that is the product of political controversy; or that results when those in control of the machinery of government seek to use the courts to disadvantage their rivals or preserve their own economic or social position. Some commentators would dispute the inclusion of civil proceedings within this definition, but from the earliest days of the Republic, suits seeking damages, injunctions, and various special writs have been used to mobilize judicial machinery in support of political causes and to suppress critics of the government.

Most political trials are criminal, however. In some, the defendants are charged with offenses that are political in nature, involving direct challenges to governmental authority. TREASON is the most serious crime of this type. Others include SEDITIOUS LIBEL, subversion, sabotage, and espionage. Prosecutions for bribery, corruption, abuse of official power, and vote fraud also belong in this category.

A trial can be political even if the defendant is not charged with one of these political offenses, for sometimes political issues pervade trials for ordinary crimes. As Otto Kirchheimer has pointed out, "political coloring [can] be imported to such a garden-variety criminal trial by the motives or objectives of the prosecution or by the political background, affiliation, or standing of the defendant." The 1886 Haymarket case, in which defendants were prosecuted and convicted on charges of CONSPIRACY to commit murder and being accessories after the fact in a fatal bombing only because they were anarchists, is an example of the kind of proceeding to which he refers.

Like many political trials, the Haymarket case was a product of political persecution. Sometimes, though, the defendant imports the political coloring to a criminal case. A courtroom provides the accused with a public forum and an audience for his political message. Thus, during the 1920s, General Billy Mitchell deliberately provoked his superiors into court-martialing him for conduct prejudicial to the discipline and good order of the army so that he could gain a hearing for his views on air power and publicize what he regarded as the military's misuse of aviation.

Not all political trials involve such deliberate exploitation of judicial machinery for political purposes. Some earn this designation simply because political considerations determined their outcome. An example is the WORLD WAR I trial of Joe Hill. Hill's affiliation with a radical labor

organization, the Industrial Workers of the World (IWW), was unknown when he was arrested for a murder, but it was the reason for his ultimate unfair conviction on that charge.

A trial should also be considered political if the ordinary crime of which the defendant was accused was a product of political controversy or committed for political reasons. The WATERGATE burglary and coverup conspiracy trials exemplify this type of proceeding. The offenses with which the government charged the defendants were not inherently political, but the fact that the defendants were alleged to have committed them to advance RICHARD M. NIXON's reelection campaign and to protect the reputation of his administration gave their trials a clearly political character.

Legal proceedings can sometimes take on that coloration simply because they happen to affect substantially the politics of their time. During the VIETNAM WAR, Lieutenant William Calley was court-martialed for his role in the massacre of more than one hundred civilians at My Lai. Because it symbolized for hawks and doves alike all that they believed was wrong with the American military effort in Southeast Asia, the Calley case became one of the major political issues of the early 1970s.

Many of America's best-known political trials have arisen against the backdrop of military conflict. Both the AMERICAN REVOLUTION and the CIVIL WAR generated prosecutions for treason and other explicitly political offenses. During and just after World War I the federal government and numerous states launched legal assaults on radicals and dissenters. WORLD WAR II produced a circuslike sedition trial of some of the most vitriolic right-wing critics of President FRANKLIN D. ROOSEVELT, as well as postwar prosecutions of U.S. citizens alleged to have collaborated with the enemy and of leaders of the defeated Axis powers. Scores of American communists found themselves on trial during the KOREAN WAR. The Vietnam War also unleashed a torrent of political trials, produced by the efforts of the administrations of LYNDON B. JOHNSON and Richard Nixon to repress dissent and the determination of antiwar activists to obtain a judicial declaration of the war's illegality. International tensions falling short of shooting wars have also given rise to numerous political trials, such as those of Jeffersonian politicians and editors during the Quasi-War between the United States and France in the 1790s and, more recently, the trials of domestic communists during the early days of the Cold War.

Second only to military confrontations as a cause of political trials are conflicts between labor and capital. Indeed, during the period 1870–1930 they were more important. During that era big business exercised a growing influence over all levels and branches of government, and it could generally count on the assistance of prosecutors and judges in putting down challenges to its economic power. Prominent union leaders, such as EUGENE V. DEBS of the American Railway Union and "Big Bill" Haywood of the IWW, found themselves cast as defendants in highly politicized legal proceedings, as did numerous other labor activists. During World War I federal criminal prosecutions devastated the IWW.

After the rise of organized labor to political power during the 1930s, labor-management conflict ceased to generate a significant number of political trials. Racial problems continued to do so, as they had since antebellum days when white southerners sometimes tried rebellious slaves, and numerous northern abolitionists suffered prosecution for interfering with enforcement of the FUGITIVE SLAVE Law of 1850. The most spectacular political trial of the antebellum era was the 1859 state treason prosecution of abolitionist firebrand John Brown for his raid on Harpers Ferry, Virginia (now West Virginia). Although the Civil War destroyed SLAVERY, it did not put an end to political trials whose root cause was race. From West Point Cadet Johnson Whitaker in the 1880s to members of the Black Panther party in the late 1960s and early 1970s, African Americans who challenged white supremacy, whether violently or peacefully, found themselves defendants in political trials. The peak period for such prosecutions was the decade around 1970, which produced the highly publicized LeRoi Jones, Angela Davis, Bobby Seale, and Panther Twenty-one cases.

All of these black militants had positioned themselves well outside the political mainstream. Like the defendants in most American political trials, they were essentially scapegoats who lacked real power and posed threats to the system that were more symbolic than real. Seldom have those in authority hauled serious rivals into court. Early American history does offer some examples of legal attacks on potent challengers to incumbent regimes, such as the SEDITION ACT prosecutions of the Republican opposition in the late 1790s. But most such trials occurred before the concept of a legitimate political opposition had fully established itself, and most triggered a popular reaction against those who had initiated them. There have been few prosecutions of mainstream opposition groups since the Civil War.

Nor has the United States produced many examples of that staple of political justice elsewhere, the "successor regime trial," a criminal prosecution brought by those who have recently captured control of the government to discredit their predecessors in power. The principal reason for this is no doubt the constitutional stability that has kept America under the same system of government for over two hundred years. But even after the North forcefully displaced the state and national governments of the South during the Civil War, it tried few leaders of the defeated

Confederate regime. In the United States, political trials have usually occurred, not after wrenching transfers of power, but at times when the status quo was under challenge because of social and political ferment unleashed by war, economic conflict, or racial discord.

Although not associated with cataclysmic constitutional change, such legal proceedings have helped to shape the Constitution. In some doctrinal areas the precedents that supplement the language of the document itself are entirely the products of political trials. This is most obviously true of the procedures worked out by the House and Senate to supplement the purely political process of impeachment. The law of treason is also a product of political trials.

So are some FREEDOM OF SPEECH doctrines. Justices OLIVER WENDELL HOLMES, JR., and LOUIS D. BRANDEIS worked out their CLEAR AND PRESENT DANGER test in response to appeals by radicals prosecuted during World War I and the postwar Red Scare. That test gained the endorsement of a majority of the Supreme Court in HERNDON V. LOWRY (1937), only to be restrictively reinterpreted in DENNIS V. UNITED STATES (1951). Both cases arose out of political trials of communists. In BRANDENBURG V. OHIO (1969) the Court, in the process of overturning a conviction of a Ku Klux Klansman for the political offense of CRIMINAL SYNDICALISM, articulated a new principle even more protective of expression than the original clear and present danger test had been.

Political trials have affected other facets of constitutional law as well. For example, UNITED STATES V. NIXON (1973), which recognized but limited the doctrine of EXECUTIVE PRIVILEGE, arose out of the efforts of SPECIAL PROSECUTOR Leon Jaworski to obtain White House tapes for use in the Watergate conspiracy trial. The ringing declaration in EX PARTE MILLIGAN (1866) that the Constitution "covers with the shield of its protection all classes of men, at all times, and under all circumstances" and cannot be "suspended during any of the great exigencies of government" represents a doctrinal response to the ABRAHAM LINCOLN administration's efforts to use military commissions to punish civilian dissidents. Even *Marbury v. Madison*, the case in which the Supreme Court first applied the doctrine of JUDICIAL REVIEW, was a product of efforts to use judicial machinery to achieve political objectives.

The Court has, to be sure, exhibited some reluctance to decide issues thrust before it in this way. The POLITICAL QUESTION doctrine is evidence of that attitude, as is the Court's refusal during the Vietnam conflict to hear appeals pressed upon it by litigants hoping to get the war declared unconstitutional. Nevertheless, political trials have led to rulings that have created precedents and shaped doctrine in important areas of the law. As ALEXIS DE TOQUEVILLE wrote in *Democracy in America*, "Scarcely any political question arises in the United States that is not resolved, sooner or later, into a judicial question." Often that resolution has begun in the context of a political trial. Although often condemned, such proceedings are an integral part of the American constitutional tradition.

MICHAEL R. BELKNAP
(1992)

(SEE ALSO: *Iran-Contra Affair; Military Justice; Politics; Special Prosecutor.*)

Bibliography

BECKER, THEODORE L., ed. 1971 *Political Trials.* Indianapolis, Ind.: Bobbs-Merrill.

BELKNAP, MICHAEL R., ed. 1981 *American Political Trials.* Westport, Conn.: Greenwood Press.

HACKMAN, NATHAN 1972 Political Trials in the Legal Order: A Political Scientist's Perspective. *Journal of Public Law* 21:73–126.

KIRCHHEIMER, OTTO 1961 *Political Justice: The Use of Legal Procedure for Political Ends.* Princeton, N.J.: Princeton University Press.

POLITICS

Constitutions are fundamentally linked to the character of politics. At the most obvious level constitutions structure the political process. The United States Constitution defines who may serve in various elected offices, the terms of office (the frequency of election), the number of representatives, and the manner of their election. But, as important if not as obvious, constitutions in general and the United States Constitution in particular are also shaped by basic concerns about the character of politics and its malfunctions or evils. These concerns are reflected in the structures of politics established in the Constitution, the debates about the Constitution, and the evolution of constitutional law over the last two hundred years.

Two basic visions of political malfunction—one that stresses fear of the many (majoritarian bias) and one that stresses fear of the few (minoritarian bias)—coexist in traditional American views of government and constitutional history. Minoritarian bias supposes an inordinate power in the few at the expense of the many. Political power and influence, whether gained by graft, propaganda, or campaign support, often require organization and resources. Here a majority, each of whose members suffers only small loss from a government action, can be at a significant disadvantage to a minority with large per capita gains. The total loss to the majority may far outweigh the gains to the minority, but if the per capita loss is small enough, members of the majority may not even recognize that loss. Even if a member of the majority knows of the proposed legislation and recognizes its dangers, each individual has

small incentive to spend time or money in organizing others. These efforts are further frustrated by the likelihood that other members of the majority will be inclined to "free ride" (i.e., refuse to participate or assume that others will carry the load).

Majoritarian bias is a completely opposite response to the same skewed distribution of impacts that characterizes minoritarian bias. Here the numerical majority, with its small per capita interests, imposes disproportionate losses on an intense, concentrated minority. The difference between majoritarian and minoritarian bias lies in suppositions about the political process. If we suppose that everyone understands and votes his interests and if we assume a political process that counts votes for or against but does not consider the severity of impact or the intensity of feeling about the issue, a low-impact majority can prevail over a high-impact minority, even though the majority gains little and the minority is harmed greatly. The power of the many lies simply in numbers, and malfunctions arise because the few are disproportionately harmed.

Concerns about both majoritarian and minoritarian bias have been with Americans throughout their constitutional history, from the framing of the original Constitution to the modern era. The period of the framing and RATIFICATION OF THE CONSTITUTION shows clear concern about these forms of bias. Indeed, the two opposing constitutional positions of the time FEDERALISM and ANTI-FEDERALISM—can be defined by differences in their concern about majoritarian and minoritarian bias.

The authors of THE FEDERALIST recognized the existence of both forms of bias, expressed concern about both, but seemed to worry more about majorities. JAMES MADISON, in particular, placed great emphasis on the dangers of the majority in *Federalist #10*:

> If a faction consists of less than a majority, relief is applied by the republican principle, which enables the majority to defeat its sinister views by regular vote: It may clog the administration, it may convulse the society; but it will be unable to execute or mask its violence under the forms of the Constitution. When a majority is included in a faction, the form of popular government on the other hand enables it to sacrifice to its ruling passion or interest, both the public good and the rights of other citizens....
>
> The majority ... must be rendered, by their number and local situation, unable to concert and carry into effect schemes of oppression....
>
> A pure Democracy, by which I mean, a Society, consisting of a small number of citizens, who assemble and administer the Government in person, can admit of no cure for the mischiefs of faction.

Madison's comments reveal the major Federalist response to the perceived danger: the removal or insulation of federal government decision makers from local populations. They sought this insulation in several ways. First, the decision makers were physically distanced. The national capital was generally much farther from most citizens than was the seat of state or LOCAL GOVERNMENT; physical distance was no small factor at a time when travel was so difficult. Second, each of the decision makers was to represent a large number of constituents, thereby making organization of a majority more difficult. Third, they served for relatively long terms, ranging from two to six years, so that their constituents had infrequent access through the ballot box and a complex record to decipher and judge. Fourth, the Senate and President were indirectly elected—the Senate by state legislatures and the President by the ELECTORAL COLLEGE.

The opponents of the Federalists, the more heterogeneous Antifederalists, appeared far more concerned about minoritarian bias. The Antifederalists feared that indirectly elected senators serving long terms would devolve into an aristocracy and combine with the indirectly elected President to allow an easy conduit for "the advantage of the few over the many." In response, they sought rotation in office, shorter terms, the possibility of recall, and easier IMPEACHMENT. They also feared that the House of Representatives was insufficiently numerous to enable it "to resemble the people" and therefore would be subject to influence and corruption. They feared "the superior opportunities for organized voting which they felt to be inherent in the more thickly populated areas." They feared that a Supreme Court not subject to popular control would favor the rich. These fears were all signs of concern about minoritarian bias.

The tension between the Federalist and Antifederalist positions centered significantly on the controversy over the relative roles of large and small jurisdictions—in particular, the role of the states in relation to the national government. The Federalists, who feared the power of the majority more than that of the minority, believed in a strong national government and the indirect election of government officials. The Antifederalists believed in small jurisdictions and feared that as government grew larger and more remote, the concentrated few would subvert the process.

The Federalist and Antifederalist positions both possess inadequacies and inconsistencies. Antifederalists can be seen as heirs to the tradition of classical republicanism. They envisioned a republic small in size, with a small and homogeneous population. The great problem for the Antifederalists was the extrapolation of republican ideals to a large, dispersed, and heterogeneous population. They did not have an alternative for a national government.

For the Federalists, whose vision of government was more directly embodied in the Constitution, the problems were both more subtle and more important. Madison and

the Federalists stressed government on a relatively large scale, with political decision makers (legislators and executives) removed from the mass of the populace both by distance and by mode of selection. The analysis of political malfunction employed here suggests that to the extent that the Federalist structure achieved the insulation of officials from the general populace, it traded one bias for another.

Greater distance, more complex modes of selection, and larger, more diverse constituencies provide protection from the masses but not complete isolation. Other paths of influence—and therefore sources of bias—remain and in fact flourish. The more complex setting enhances the power of organization and the accumulation of funds and helps cover underhanded dealings. Isolation provides respite from the masses but far easier access to concentrated minorities. In other words, greater insulation of public officials may purchase protection from majoritarian bias by increasing the potential for minoritarian bias.

Madison and the Federalists were not necessarily wrong to emphasize majoritarian over minoritarian bias. The correct choice depends on a number of factors (such as size of the jurisdiction or complexity of the issues) that may make one or the other bias more likely. It is intriguing to wonder whether the correct choice might be different if one were writing a constitution on a clean slate for the larger, more complex United States of the late twentieth century than it was for the United States of Madison and the Federalists.

The tradeoffs and tensions between majoritarian and minoritarian bias have surfaced elsewhere in American constitutional history. The famous footnote four from UNITED STATES V. CAROLENE PRODUCTS CO. (1938), where the Supreme Court set out the general outlines of modern constitutional law, is a microcosm of these tradeoffs and tensions. Footnote four reads:

> There may be narrower scope for operation of the presumption of constitutionality when legislation appears on its face to be within a specific prohibition of the Constitution, such as those of the first ten amendments, which are deemed equally specific when held to be embraced within the Fourteenth.
>
> It is unnecessary to consider now whether legislation which restricts those political processes which can ordinarily be expected to bring about repeal of undesirable legislation, is to be subjected to more exacting judicial scrutiny under the general prohibitions of the FOURTEENTH AMENDMENT than are most other types of legislation. On restrictions upon the right to vote; on restraints upon the dissemination of information . . . ; on interferences with political organizations . . . ; as to prohibition of peaceable assembly. . . .
>
> Nor need we enquire whether similar considerations enter into the review of statutes directed at particular re-

ligious, or national, or racial minorities; or whether prejudice against discrete and insular minorities may be a special condition, which tends seriously to curtail the operation of those political processes ordinarily to be relied upon to protect minorities, and which may call for a correspondingly more searching judicial inquiry.

Examined from the perspective of the tension between majoritarian and minoritarian bias, the various components of *Carolene Products*—the holding of the case and the principle concerns expressed in the footnote—are very much interrelated.

In *Carolene Products* the Court applied minimal scrutiny to uphold the economic regulation before it. The legislation at issue in *Carolene Products* banned the interstate sale of "filled milk," skim milk supplemented with nonmilk fats such as coconut oil. It does not take much scrutiny to see the dairy lobby at work behind the passage and enforcement of the Filled Milk Act. Indeed, the dairy industry's efforts to employ legislation to keep "adulterated" products from grocery shelves and vending booths have a long history. It is perhaps not too uncharitable to suggest that concern for the dairies' pocketbooks rather than for the consumer's health best explains the dairy lobby's efforts: the dairy industry benefited from reduced competition and the resultant higher prices paid by consumers.

The holding of the case abandons serious judicial review of ECONOMIC REGULATION, thereby leaving dispersed majorities like consumers without direct judicial protection from the minoritarian bias that can characterize governmental decisions about economic regulation like that in *Carolene Products* itself. Seemingly in response to these concerns, paragraph two of the *Carolene Products* footnote promises indirect aid to dispersed majorities by strengthening their access to and participation in the political process. By protecting access to information, organization, and the vote, the Court focused on activities that would decrease the relative advantage of concentrated interests that trade upon their superiority in gathering information, organizing, and gaining access to power through nonvoting channels.

Yet, although these protections reduce minoritarian bias, they may do little for, and in fact aggravate, majoritarian bias. Government officials whose manipulations of programs reflect the will of a majority have little to fear from public exposure or an expanded franchise. Majoritarian bias is generated when simple democracy works too well. The majority knows its interest and votes it. Because that interest is unweighted, however, a minority suffers substantial losses for disproportionately small gains to the majority. From this vantage, judicial responses like the basic rule of American VOTING RIGHTS—ONE PERSON, ONE VOTE—are well suited to the dissipation of minoritarian

bias, but can reinforce majoritarian bias. In the extreme, if it were possible to fully perfect the process by making every citizen totally aware of his or her own interest and able immediately to translate that interest into an effective vote, minoritarian bias would disappear, but majoritarian bias would be worse.

Paragraph three of the *Carolene Products* footnote responds to the need to protect against this danger of majoritarian bias by promising special judicial examination of those actions most likely infected by majoritarian bias. Subsequent equal protection law decisions made these concerns a central feature of modern constitutional law.

These important historical episodes indicate that the character of constitutions and the character of politics are tightly interwoven. Constitutions determine, and are determined by, the character of politics.

NEIL K. KOMESAR
(1992)

(SEE ALSO: *Conservatism; Federalists; Jacksonianism; Jeffersonianism; Liberalism; Populism; Pragmatism; Progressivism; Republican Party.*)

Bibliography

KOMESAR, NEIL K. 1984 Taking Institutions Seriously. *University of Chicago Law Review* 51:366–446.
——— 1987 Back to the Future—An Institutional View of Making and Interpreting Constitutions. *Northwestern Law Review* 81:191–219.
——— 1987 Paths of Influence—Beard Revisited. *George Washington Law Review* 56:124–135.
——— 1988 A Job for the Judges: The Judiciary and the Constitution in a Massive and Complex Society. *Michigan Law Review* 86:657–721.

POLK, JAMES KNOX
(1795–1849)

The eleventh President's constitutional beliefs blended STRICT CONSTRUCTION, expediency, and continental vision. He returned to a central theme of Jacksonian constitutionalism to harmonize these divergent interests: the President was the tribune of the people, the only nationally elected federal official.

Polk stressed the SEPARATION OF POWERS in order to legitimate the popularly based presidential power he exercised. He recognized that congressional committees had legitimate claims to information held by the executive branch, but he spurned congressional requests that intruded upon areas of constitutional responsibility he believed assigned to the President, most notably FOREIGN AFFAIRS. He rebuffed, in 1848, SENATE advice to negotiate a treaty of extradition with Prussia and to secure the purchase rights of the Hudson's Bay Company on the Columbia River. Yet Polk acknowledged that Congress commanded a broad sphere of constitutional responsibility; he vetoed only three legislative acts.

Polk contributed significantly to the constitutional development of the COMMANDER-IN-CHIEF clause. Unlike ABRAHAM LINCOLN, he believed that the clause granted only military leadership to the President. Yet Polk made use of this power to implement his policy of continentalism. He ordered General ZACHARY TAYLOR into disputed territory between the United States and Mexico knowing that such actions were likely to precipitate hostilities. When the Mexicans responded with force, Congress was left to ratify a war rather than to fulfill its constitutional mandate to declare it. Throughout the ensuing conflict Polk established the precedent that a vigorous conception of the commander-in-chief clause meant control over military affairs.

Tough and efficient, Polk was a transitional figure in the constitutional evolution toward the modern presidency. Unlike his twentieth-century counterparts, Polk, with his strict constructionist beliefs, did not think that the right of self-defense or the inherent authority of the commander-in-chief bestowed on him the power to wage war against another country without congressional authorization.

KERMIT L. HALL
(1986)

Bibliography

MCCOY, CHARLES A. 1960 *Polk and the Presidency.* Austin: University of Texas Press.

POLLAK, WALTER H.
(1887–1940)

Walter H. Pollak, an active supporter of CIVIL LIBERTIES, argued a number of important cases before the Supreme Court. He represented the defendant in GITLOW V. NEW YORK (1925) and, although he lost that case, succeeded in convincing the Court that the FOURTEENTH AMENDMENT incorporates the FIRST AMENDMENT guarantees of FREEDOM OF THE PRESS and FREEDOM OF SPEECH against the states. With ZECHARIAH CHAFEE, Pollak served on the Wickersham Committee and investigated "lawlessness in law enforcement." He also took part in WHITNEY V. CALIFORNIA (1927) and successfully defended the "Scottsboro boys" in POWELL V. ALABAMA (1932) and NORRIS V. ALABAMA (1935).

DAVID GORDON
(1986)

POLLOCK v. FARMERS' LOAN & TRUST CO.
157 U.S. 429 and 158 U.S. 601 (1895)

CHARLES EVANS HUGHES called these decisions a "self-inflicted wound" comparable to the decision in DRED SCOTT V. SANDFORD (1857). Here the Supreme Court held unconstitutional an 1894 act of Congress that fixed a flat tax of two percent on all annual incomes over $4,000. Pollock filed a STOCKHOLDER'S SUIT against the trust company to prevent it from complying with the statute which, he claimed, imposed a DIRECT TAX without apportioning it among the states on the basis of population. The trust company, the party of record on the side of the tax, avoided the appearance of collusion by hiring the president of the American Bar Association, James Coolidge Carter; Richard Olney, attorney general of the United States, was on the same side as AMICUS CURIAE. Theirs was the easy task because history and all the precedents proved that the clause of Article 1, section 9, referring to direct taxes, meant only taxes on people or on land. The Court had so declared in HYLTON V. UNITED STATES (1796) and in several other cases, especially SPRINGER V. UNITED STATES (1881), a direct precedent; the Court there had unanimously sustained an earlier income tax as imposing an indirect tax and therefore not subject to the requirement of apportionment.

Counsel for Pollock, led by JOSEPH H. CHOATE, buttressed a weak case with an impassioned argument intended to provoke judicial fear and reflecting the panic felt by many conservatives. Choate warned that the Court had to choose between "the beginning of socialism and communism" and the preservation of private property, civilization, and the Constitution. He appealed to the Court to substitute its discretion for that of Congress.

Justice HOWELL E. JACKSON not having participated, an eight-member Court decided the case. All agreed that the federal tax on municipal bonds was unconstitutional, because government instrumentalities were exempt from taxation (see INTERGOVERNMENTAL IMMUNITIES). On the question of the validity of the tax on income from personal property, the Court divided evenly. But on the question of the validity of the tax on income from real estate, the Court voted 6–2 that it was a direct tax unconstitutionally assessed. Nothing favorable can be said about Chief Justice MELVILLE W. FULLER's opinion for the majority. He took for granted the very proposition he should have proved, asserting that a tax on the income from land was indistinguishable from a tax on the land itself. Clearly, however, the income that may derive from rents, timber, oil, minerals, or agriculture is distinguishable from a tax on acreage or on the assessed value of the land itself.

Fuller distinguished away the precedents: *Hylton* had decided only that a tax on carriages was not a direct tax, and *Springer* had decided only the narrow point that a tax on a lawyer's fees was not a direct one. Neither case, Fuller declared, dealt with a tax on the income from land, and he made much of the point that such a tax is unique because of the undisputed fact that a tax on the land itself is undoubtedly a direct tax. Justices EDWARD D. WHITE and JOHN MARSHALL HARLAN, dissenting, concluded that history and STARE DECISIS demanded a different ruling, and they warned that when the Court virtually annulled its previous decisions on the basis of the policy preferences of a majority that happened to dominate the bench, the Constitution was in jeopardy.

The tie vote of the Court on all other issues meant that the decision of the CIRCUIT COURT prevailed, leaving in force the taxes on corporate income, wages and salaries, and returns from investments. Accordingly, Choate moved for a rehearing, which was granted, and Justice Jackson attended. The trust company, which was supposed to defend the income tax act, did not retain Carter or replace him, thus leaving Olney to defend it. He took half the time permitted by the Court for his presentation.

The arguments the second time focused on the validity of the tax on the income from personal property, mainly interest and dividends. Fuller, speaking for a bare majority, again read the Court's opinion. Six weeks earlier he had based his position on the uniqueness of a tax on the income from land; now he took the opposite view, reasoning that if a tax on the income from land is a direct tax, so is a tax on the income from personal property. Having found the statute void in significant respects, he reasoned next that the invalidity of some sections contaminated the rest: since the sections were inseparable, all were void because some were.

When Fuller finished his opinion, Harlan began to read his dissent; it sizzled in its language and delivery. He ended a systematic refutation by pounding his desk, shaking his finger in the face of the Chief Justice, and shouting, "On my conscience I regard this decision as a disaster!" (*The Nation* magazine described Harlan as an "agitator" who expounded "the Marx gospel from the bench.") He accused the majority of an unprecedented use of judicial power on behalf of private wealth by striking down a statute whose policy they disliked and by doing it against all law and history. He also pointed out, as did the other dissenters, Justices White, Jackson, and HENRY B. BROWN, that the parts of the statute that were not unconstitutional per se, and might be reenacted if Congress chose, taxed the income of people who earned their money from wages and salaries but who derived no income from land or invested personal property. The decision, said Brown, is "nothing less than a surrender of the taxing power to the moneyed

class" making for "a sordid despotism of wealth." It "takes invested wealth," said White, and "reads it into the Constitution as a favored and protected class of property. . . ." It was, said Jackson, "the most disastrous blow ever struck at the constitutional power of congress" and made the tax burden fall "most heavily and oppressively upon those having the least ability" to pay.

Public opinion was opposed to the Court, though it had vigorous supporters especially among the Republican newspapers in the East. The *New York Sun* exclaimed in delight, "Five to Four, the Court Stands Like a Rock." The *New York Herald Tribune* hailed the Court for halting a "communist revolution." The Democratic party, however, recommended an amendment to the Constitution vesting Congress with the power denied by the Court. The SIXTEENTH AMENDMENT was not ratified, though, until 1913, by which time the nation's maldistribution of wealth had intensified. For eighteen years, as EDWARD S. CORWIN wrote, "the veto of the Court held the sun and moon at pause," while the great fortunes went untaxed. The government during that time raised almost all of its revenues from EXCISE TAXES and tariffs, whose burden fell mainly on consumers. In 1913 the average annual income in the United States was $375 per capita.

LEONARD W. LEVY
(1986)

Bibliography

CORWIN, EDWARD S. 1932 *Court over Constitution.* Pages 177–209. Princeton, N.J.: Princeton University Press.

KING, WILLARD L. 1950 *Melville Weston Fuller.* Pages 193–221. New York: Macmillan.

PAUL, ARNOLD M. 1960 *Conservative Crisis and the Rule of Law: Attitudes of Bar and Bench, 1887–1895.* Pages 159–220. Ithaca, N.Y.: Cornell University Press.

SHIRAS, GEORGE, 3RD, and SHIRAS, WINFIELD 1953 *Justice George Shiras Jr. of Pittsburgh.* Pages 160–183. Pittsburgh: University of Pittsburgh Press.

POLLOCK v. WILLIAMS
322 U.S. 4 (1944)

A Florida statute made the failure to perform services according to an agreement (for which an advance had been made) *prima facie* evidence of an intent to defraud. The Supreme Court, in an opinion by Justice ROBERT H. JACKSON, voided the statute, 7–2, as a violation of the THIRTEENTH AMENDMENT and of the Anti-Peonage Act of 1867. At issue before the Court was a HABEAS CORPUS petition for "an illiterate Negro laborer in the toils of law for the want of $5." His failure to perform agreed-upon labor for that advance resulted in a $100 fine, in default of which he was sentenced to sixty days' imprisonment. Jackson held that the Thirteenth Amendment and the Anti-Peonage Act "raised both a shield and a sword against forced labor because of debt."

DAVID GORDON
(1986)

POLL TAX

A poll tax (CAPITATION TAX, head tax) is typically levied on every adult (or adult male) within the taxing JURISDICTION. An old technique for raising revenue, the tax in its compulsory form raises no important constitutional questions. (Under Article I, section 9, Congress can levy a poll tax only by apportionment to the national census. Congress has not in fact raised revenue this way.)

Serious constitutional issues have been raised in this century by poll taxes whose payment is "voluntary," enforced only by conditioning voter registration on their payment. Early in the nation's history, payment of such taxes came to replace property ownership as a qualification for voting. By the CIVIL WAR, however, widespread acceptance of universal suffrage had virtually eliminated the poll tax as a condition on voting.

In a number of southern states, the poll tax returned in the 1890s along with SEGREGATION as a means of maintaining white supremacy. In theory and in early practice, poor whites as well as blacks were kept from voting by this means. Later, however, some registrars learned to use the device mainly for purposes of RACIAL DISCRIMINATION, requiring only black would-be voters to produce their receipts for poll tax payments—in some states for payments going back to the voter's twenty-first year. The poll tax gradually fell from favor as a means of keeping blacks from voting; "good character" requirements and LITERACY TESTS, for example, were more readily adapted to this purpose. By 1940 only seven states retained the poll tax as a voting condition.

In BREEDLOVE V. SUTTLES (1937), a case involving a white applicant for registration, the Supreme Court upheld Georgia's use of the poll tax as a condition on voting. The poll tax remained a CIVIL RIGHTS issue, kept alive in Congress by the regular introduction of bills to abolish its use. Southern committee chairmanships and senatorial filibusters succeeded in sidetracking this legislation. When the TWENTY-FOURTH AMENDMENT was finally submitted to the states in 1962, it forbade the use of poll taxes as a condition on voting only in federal, not state, elections. The Amendment was ratified in 1964.

Two years later, the Supreme Court held, in HARPER V. VIRGINIA BOARD OF ELECTIONS (1966), that conditioning voting in state elections on poll tax payments denied the

EQUAL PROTECTION OF THE LAWS. Only four states still retained the device, but its elimination eloquently symbolized the relation between VOTING RIGHTS and the equal CITIZENSHIP of all Americans.

KENNETH L. KARST
(1986)

Bibliography

MYRDAL, GUNNAR 1944 *An American Dilemma: The Negro Problem and Modern Democracy.* Chaps. 22–23. New York: Harper & Brothers.

POLLUTION

See: Environmental Regulation and the Constitution; Federalism and Environmental Law; Waste, Pollution, and the Constitution

POLYGAMY

Because polygamy was one of the early tenets of the Mormon Church, the movement to eradicate plural MARRIAGE became bound up with religious persecution. The Supreme Court has consistently held that the FIRST AMENDMENT's protections of RELIGIOUS LIBERTY do not protect the practice of plural marriage. Thus REYNOLDS V. UNITED STATES (1879) upheld a criminal conviction for polygamy in the Territory of Utah, and DAVIS V. BEASON (1880) upheld a conviction for voting in the Territory of Idaho in violation of an oath required of all registrants forswearing belief in polygamy. The corporate charter of the Mormon Church in the Territory of Utah was revoked, and its property forfeited to the government, in CHURCH OF JESUS CHRIST OF LATTER-DAY SAINTS V. UNITED STATES (1890). The church's First Amendment claim was waved away with the statement that belief in polygamy was not a religious tenet but a "pretense" that was "contrary to the spirit of Christianity."

It would be comforting if this judicial record were confined to the nineteenth century, but it was not. In *Cleveland v. United States* (1946), the Court upheld a conviction of Mormons under the MANN ACT for transporting women across state lines for the purpose of "debauchery" that took the form of living with them in polygamous marriage. The Court's opinion, citing the nineteenth-century cases and even quoting the "spirit of Christianity" language with approval, was written by none other than Justice WILLIAM O. DOUGLAS.

More recently, the Court has recognized a constitutional right to marry, and in a number of contexts has afforded protection for a FREEDOM OF INTIMATE ASSOCIATION. With or without the ingredient of religious freedom, SUB-

STANTIVE DUE PROCESS doctrine seems amply to justify an extension of these rights to plural marriage among competent consenting adults. Yet the force of conventional morality in constitutional adjudication should not be underestimated; the Supreme Court is not just the architect of principle but an institution of government. Polygamy is not on the verge of becoming a constitutional right.

KENNETH L. KARST
(1986)

Bibliography

LARSON, GUSTAVE O. 1971 The "Americanization" of Utah for Statehood. San Marino, Calif.: Huntington Library.

POMEROY, JOHN NORTON

See: Commentators on the Constitution

POPULAR SOVEREIGNTY

"Popular sovereignty" was a solution proposed by some northern Democrats to the problem of slavery's access to the TERRITORIES. As an alternative to the WILMOT PROVISO, Michigan Senator Lewis Cass proposed in 1847 that slavery be left "to the people inhabiting [the territories] to regulate their internal concerns their own way." He later concluded that congressional prohibition of SLAVERY IN THE TERRITORIES was unconstitutional. Popular sovereignty was a radical innovation: never before had residents of the territories been thought to be invested with SOVEREIGNTY, let alone a territorial sovereignty implying that the federal government lacked substantive regulatory power over the territories.

Illinois Senator STEPHEN A. DOUGLAS took up popular sovereignty in 1854, recommending that the MISSOURI COMPROMISE be jettisoned in order to get the slavery question out of Congress and leave it to the settlers of the territories. Though adopted in the KANSAS-NEBRASKA ACT, popular sovereignty soon fell into disfavor in both the North and the South. Douglas and other northern Democrats rejected the travesty made of it by President JAMES BUCHANAN in his attempt to force slavery into Kansas, while southern leaders abandoned it in favor of a constitutional program that would have forced slavery into all the territories.

WILLIAM M. WIECEK
(1986)

Bibliography

JOHANNSEN, ROBERT W. 1973 Stephen A. Douglas. New York: Oxford University Press.

POPULAR SOVEREIGNTY IN DEMOCRATIC POLITICAL THEORY

The Constitution's first words bespeak its derivation from popular authority: "We the people of the United States . . . do ordain and establish this Constitution." The DECLARATION OF INDEPENDENCE expresses the principle of this act: "to secure these rights, governments are instituted among men, deriving their just powers from the consent of the governed." The specific doctrine of popular sovereignty behind these familiar phrases still needs to be clarified and distinguished from related but distinct doctrines.

This doctrine of popular SOVEREIGNTY relates primarily not to the Constitution's operation but to its source of authority and supremacy, ratification, amendment, and possible abolition. When JAMES MADISON wrote in THE FEDERALIST #49 that "the people are the only legitimate fountain of power," he referred to what he had called in The Federalist #40 (paraphrasing the Declaration) "the transcendent and precious right of the people to "abolish or alter their governments." Legitimate power derives primarily from the people's original consent to their form of government, not from their continuing role in it. Because popular consent is the "pure, original fountain of all legitimate authority," ALEXANDER HAMILTON, in The Federalist #22, presents the RATIFICATION OF THE CONSTITUTION by conventions specially elected by the people, a mode recently pioneered by the states, as crucial to its legitimacy. The Federalist both opens and closes remarking that for a whole people so to choose their constitution by voluntary consent, far from being typical, is an unprecedented prodigy.

This American mode of popular consent to the institution of government formalized the notion in JOHN LOCKE's Second Treatise of "the Constitution of the Legislative being the original and supreme act of the Society, antecedent to all positive Laws in it, and depending wholly on the People." It provides a peaceful, certain, and solemn alternative to violent and irregular acts but remains ultimately an expression of the right to revolution; Madison almost admits in The Federalist #40 that adoption of the Constitution was authorized not under the ARTICLES OF CONFEDERATION but only by popular consent as an exercise of revolutionary right. Such popular sovereignty could always be exercised again not only by regular amendment but by revolution.

For the Founders, legitimate government not only had to derive its powers originally from the consent of the people but also had to gain the consent of their regularly elected representatives to legislate for them and tax them. The revolutionary controversy was fundamentally waged, first, over the American invocation of Locke's position that government "must *not raise Taxes* on the Property of the People, *without the Consent of the People,* given by themselves, or their Deputies," and then over its extension to no legislation without REPRESENTATION.

Such popular sovereignty still is not identical with popular government. The Founders generally regarded the British constitution, for example, with its hereditary king and lords, as a legitimate and even free government because the British (unlike the American) people were represented (albeit imperfectly) in the House of Commons. Republican government, although the form of government best exhibiting the capacity of mankind for self-government, was not the only form compatible with popular consent as the basis of legitimate power. Because Madison correctly believed that the character of the American people makes them unlikely to exercise their sovereign right to replace their republican government with one of another form, this point is relevant less to our domestic than to our foreign policy, which in principle should recognize the right of other sovereign peoples to consent to other forms of government.

Republican government itself differs for the Founders from the populism some later doctrines equate with popular sovereignty. *The Federalist* treats republican government as a species of popular government in that it is administered by officials appointed directly or indirectly by the people and holding office for limited periods or during GOOD BEHAVIOR. It differs from the other species, which they called "democracy" and by which they meant direct democracy, by its reliance on representation. *The Federalist* regards this difference not as an evil necessitated by size (as some Anti-Federalists did) but as a superiority making possible both size, with all its advantages, and government by "men who possess most wisdom to discern, and most virtue to pursue, the common good of the society." (THOMAS JEFFERSON in a letter to JOHN ADAMS called such republican officials "the natural aristocracy.") Republican representatives should refine and enlarge the public views because the reason, not the passion, the cool and deliberate sense, not the temporary errors and delusions, of the public should prevail. The Founders regarded the American republic as embodying the sovereignty of the public reason because it was so constructed as to encourage representatives, especially the Senate, President, and courts, to withstand popular error and passion until popular good sense could respond to argument and events. Their opinion that such an outcome would generally emerge in the few years allowed by the Constitution reveals confidence in both representatives and constituents as well as distrust.

The supremacy of the Constitution and JUDICIAL RE-VIEW, distinctive features of American CONSTITUTIONALISM, are paradoxical results of this doctrine of popular sovereignty. Hamilton in *The Federalist* #78, like JOHN MARSHALL in MARBURY V. MADISON (1803), based them on the Constitution's being the special act of the sovereign people: "the Constitution ought to be preferred to the statute, the intention of the people to the intention of their agents." The equation of popular sovereignty with the supremacy of the Constitution, let alone with judicial review, may become problematic once the people who ordained and established the Constitution are long dead. Jefferson suggested in a letter to an unpersuaded Madison that all constitutions naturally expire every generation. Madison in reply adduced the danger of faction and the need of even the most rational government for the prejudice that results from stability, but Jefferson continued to believe in the right of each generation to choose its own form of government. The jural argument for constitutional supremacy was stated by Hamilton in *Phocion* #2 (and echoed in *The Federalist* #78): "The constitution is the compact made between the society at large and each individual. The society therefore, cannot without breach of faith and injustice, refuse to any individual, a single advantage which he derives under that compact . . . until the compact is dissolved with the same solemnity and certainty with which it was made." Ultimately the identity of popular sovereignty with constitutional supremacy depends on an enlightened public opinion animated by the spirit of the Constitution.

That the Founders tended not to call the doctrine expounded here "popular sovereignty" reflects their being republicans and constitutionalists rather than populists. Not the people simply but their reason especially as solemnly embodied in their Constitution is sovereign. More fundamentally, since governments are instituted by consent "to secure these rights," their legitimacy depends not only on consent but on the security of individual rights. Debates such as that over "popular sovereignty" between ABRAHAM LINCOLN and STEPHEN DOUGLAS reveal the potential tension between popular consent and equal rights.

NATHAN TARCOV
(1986)

Bibliography

EPSTEIN, DAVID F. 1984 *The Political Theory of the Federalist.* Chicago: University of Chicago Press.

JAFFA, HARRY V. (1959) 1982 *Crisis of the House Divided: An Interpretation of the Issues in the Lincoln-Douglas Debates.* Chicago: University of Chicago Press.

TARCOV, NATHAN 1985 American Constitutionalism and Individual Rights. Pages 101–125 in Robert Goldwin and William

Schambra, eds., *How Does the Constitution Secure Rights?* Washington, D.C.: American Enterprise Institute.

POPULISM

The industrialization of the United States in the late nineteenth century caused enormous social, economic, and political upheavals in nearly every sector of the nation. Perhaps no group suffered greater dislocations than the farmers, whose livelihood and prosperity were now subject to forces over which they had no direct control. In a series of movements, farmers joined together seeking remedies to their ills. Agrarian protest reached its peak in the Populist movement in the early 1890s, when farmers took to politics in an effort to implement specific economic and political programs.

One will find little evidence of a direct impact of populism on American constitutional development. Rather, the Populists, as part of their larger reform agenda, did make particular proposals that eventually found fruition in the Progressive era. The clearest statement of these demands can be found in the People's party platform of 1896.

The platform is notable for several reasons. First, it summed up two decades of resentment by the farmers against a system they believed ignored their needs and exploited them mercilessly. Several of the complaints directly addressed the structure and operation of government. To begin with, the Populists denounced the recent Supreme Court decision in POLLOCK V. FARMERS' LOAN TRUST CO. (1895) that had invalidated the 1894 income tax rider to the tariff. To the Populists, this decision represented another example of the government's siding with the rich, and the platform demanded "a graduated income tax, to the end that aggregated wealth shall bear its proportion of taxation." In *Pollock*, they argued, the Supreme Court had misinterpreted the Constitution and invaded "the rightful powers of Congress" over taxation.

The Populists were not the first to denounce the *Pollock* decision, but they did add a strong voice to the chorus demanding an income tax. The proposal for a constitutional amendment gradually gained support throughout the country, culminating in ratification of the SIXTEENTH AMENDMENT in 1913.

The platform also called for the election of the President, Vice-President, and the Senate by "a direct vote of the people." Under the Constitution, an ELECTORAL COLLEGE selected the two executive officers, with each state's electors equal to the sum of its senators and representatives. Originally each state could chose its electors as it saw fit, but within a relatively short period of time all states adopted a system in which the popular vote determined which candidate received each state's electoral college ballots—typically in a winner-take-all system. This arrangement emphasized the importance of the larger states and created the possibility that a candidate with a majority of the popular vote could lose in the electoral college. The system has been criticized for decades, and constitutional amendments to abolish the electoral college are periodically introduced in Congress. So far, however, there has been no popular groundswell to carry through a change.

Initially, state legislatures also chose United States senators. In the Gilded Age, bribery and influence peddling often led to the selection of rich industrialists, so that by the 1890s the Senate had come to be known as a "millionaires' club." A few states had preferential primary elections to allow voters to indicate their choice for senator, but the Populists wanted direct election to eliminate what they saw as the corrupting influence of great wealth.

Any change in the election method would require a constitutional amendment, and the House of Representatives passed such an amendment in 1894, 1898, 1900, and 1902; in each session the Senate turned it down. By 1912, thirty states had preferential primaries, and the Senate finally bowed to the inevitable. It passed the SEVENTEENTH AMENDMENT, authorizing the direct election of senators, and the states ratified it the following year.

The 1896 Populist platform also called for other political reforms, some of which could be achieved without constitutional amendment. This list included the adoption of a secret ballot, limiting the use of the injunction in labor disputes, and public ownership of the railroad and telegraph. The Populists also proposed "a system of direct legislation through the initiative and referendum, under proper Constitutional safeguards."

The Populists saw many of their platform items enacted within a relative short period of time. They did not cause the adoption of the Sixteenth and Seventeenth Amendments, but certainly by adding their voices to the demand they helped to achieve these reforms. Except in wartime, we have never had government ownership or control of railroads and telegraph, but the regulatory powers finally given to the Interstate Commerce Commission in the first decade of the twentieth century provided an equivalent to the Populist demands—that public welfare take precedence over private interests.

The states did adopt secret ballots, and many of them also enacted initiative and referendum measures. Although the secret ballot proved effective in buttressing democratic elections, the other two proposals never proved as effective or easy to use as the Populists had anticipated. The elimination of the injunction as a judicial weapon against labor unions, however, had to wait until the New Deal era.

In sum, the Populist demand for political change itself

had relatively little effect on American constitutional development. By adding their voices to the demand for change, however, they reinforced reform currents already underway.

MELVIN I. UROFSKY
(1992)

Bibliography

POLLACK, NORMAN 1987 *The Just Polity: Populism, Law, and Human Welfare.* Urbana: University of Illinois Press.

POPULIST CONSTITUTIONAL INTERPRETATION

See: Nonjudicial Interpretation of the Constitution; Radical Populist Constitutional Interpretation

PORNOGRAPHY

The Supreme Court's OBSCENITY decisions define the forms of pornography that are protected from censorship by the FIRST AMENDMENT. As a practical matter, this protection is quite broad. Most pornography is also a unique kind of speech: about women, for men. In an era when sexual equality is a social ideal, the constitutional protection of pornography is a vexing political issue. Should pornographic imagery of male dominance and female subordination be repudiated through censorship, or will censorship inevitably destroy our commitment to free speech?

In ROTH V. UNITED STATES (1957) the Court found obscene speech to be unworthy of First Amendment protection because it forms "no essential part of any exposition of ideas." Yet precisely because of pornography's ideational content, some of it was deemed harmful and made criminal. The Court could avoid examining the specific nature of this harm, once it had located obscenity conveniently outside the constitutional pale. But it could not avoid defining obscenity, and thereby identifying the justification for its censorship.

The essential characteristic of "obscene" pornography is its appeal to one's "prurient interest," which is a genteel reference to its capacity to stimulate physical arousal and carnal desire. But such pornography must also be "offensive," and so, to be censored, sex-stimulant speech must be both arousing and disgusting. The meaning of offensiveness depends upon the subjective judgment of the observer, and is best captured by Justice POTTER STEWART's famous aphorism in JACOBELLIS V. OHIO (1964): "I know it when I see it."

Given the limitations of the criminal process, obscenity laws did not make offensive pornography unavailable in the marketplace. As HARRY KALVEN, JR., pointed out, few judges took the evils of obscenity very seriously, although constitutional rhetoric made the law appear to be "solemnly concerned with the sexual fantasies of the adult population." The Court's chief goal was the protection of admired works of art and literature, not the elimination of pornographic magazines at the corner drug store. Sporadic obscenity prosecutions may occur in jurisdictions where the "contemporary community standard" of offensiveness allows convictions under MILLER V. CALIFORNIA (1973). But the constitutional validity of a legal taboo on "hard-core" pornography became largely irrelevant to its suppliers and consumers, even as that material became sexually explicit and more violent in its imagery during the 1970s.

That same decade saw a legal revolution in equality between the sexes, embodied in judicial decisions based on the guarantees of EQUAL PROTECTION and DUE PROCESS. Women won legal rights to control and define their own sexuality, through litigation establishing rights to contraception and abortion, and through legislative reforms easing restrictions on prosecutions for sexual assault. Pornography also became a women's issue, as feminists such as Catharine MacKinnon attacked it as "a form of forced sex, a practice of sexual politics, an institution of gender inequality." Women marched and demonstrated against films and magazines portraying them as beaten, chained, or mutilated objects of sexual pleasure for men. In 1984, their protests took a legal form when MacKinnon and Andrea Dworkin drafted an ordinance adopted by the Indianapolis City Council, outlawing some types of pornography as acts of SEX DISCRIMINATION.

By using the concept of equal protection as a basis to attack pornographic speech, the council set up a dramatic assault upon First Amendment doctrine, making embarrassed enemies out of old constitutional friends. As a strategic matter, however, the council needed a COMPELLING STATE INTEREST to justify censorship of speech that did not fall into the obscenity category. The ordinance defined offensive pornography more broadly than *Miller's* standards allow, because it went beyond a ban on displays of specific human body parts or sexual acts. Instead, it prohibited the "graphic sexually explicit subordination of women" through their portrayals as, for example, "sexual objects who enjoy pain or humiliation," or "sexual objects for domination, conquest, violation, exploitation, possession or use."

As a philosophical matter, sex discrimination is a good constitutional metaphor for the harms attributed to pornography, namely, the loss of equal CITIZENSHIP status for women through the "bigotry and contempt" promoted by the imagery of subordination. But as a matter of DOCTRINE, the causal link between the social presence of pornography and the harms of discrimination is fatally remote. Free speech gospel dictates that "offensive speech" may be censored only upon proof of imminent, tangible harm to individuals, such as violent insurrection (BRANDENBURG V. OHIO, 1969), a physical assault (COHEN V. CALIFORNIA, 1971), or reckless tortious injury to reputation (NEW YORK TIMES V. SULLIVAN, 1964). The closest historical analogue to the creation of a cause of action for classwide harm from speech is the criminal GROUP LIBEL statute upheld by a 5–4 Supreme Court in BEAUHARNAIS V. ILLINOIS (1952). But this remedy has been implicitly discredited by *New York Times* and *Brandenburg*, given its CHILLING EFFECT upon uninhibited criticism of political policies and officials.

It came as no surprise when early court decisions struck down Indianapolis-type ordinances as void for vagueness, as an unlawful PRIOR RESTRAINT on speech, and as an unjustified restriction of protected speech as defined by the earlier obscenity decisions. The courts could accept neither the equal protection rationale nor the breadth of the ordinances' scope, as both would permit too great an encroachment upon the freedoms of expression and consumption of art, literature, and political messages. Ironically, it is the potentially endemic quality of the imagery of women's subordination that defeats any attempt to place a broad taboo upon it.

Eva Feder Kittay has posed the question, "How is it that within our society, men can derive a sexual charge out of seeing a woman brutalized?" Her answer to that loaded question is that our conceptions of sexuality are permeated with conceptions of domination, because we have eroticized the relations of power: men eroticize sexual conquering, and women eroticize being possessed. Pornography becomes more than a harmless outlet for erotic fantasies when it makes violence appear to be intrinsically erotic, rather than something that is eroticized. The social harm of such pornography is that it brutalizes our moral imagination, "the source of that imaginative possibility by which we can identify with others and hence form maxims having a universal validity."

The constitutional source for an analysis of brutalizing pornography lies in the richly generative symbols of First Amendment law itself. That law already contains the tolerance for insistence "on observance of the civic culture's norms of social equality," in the words of Kenneth L. Karst. Any acceptable future taboo would be likely to take the form of a ban on public display of a narrowly defined class of pictorial imagery, simply because that would be a traditional, readily enforceable compromise between free speech and equality. Any taboo would be mostly symbolic, but it would matter. Only by limiting the taboo can we avoid descending into the Orwellian hell where censorship is billed as freedom.

CATHERINE HANCOCK
(1986)

(SEE ALSO: *Child Pornography; Dial-a-Porn.*)

Bibliography

BRYDEN, DAVID 1985 Between Two Constitutions: Feminism and Pornography. *Constitutional Commentary* 2:147–189.

KALVEN, HARRY, JR. 1960 The Metaphysics of Obscenity. *Supreme Court Review* 1960:1–45.

KITTAY, EVA FEDER 1983 Pornography and the Erotics of Domination. Pages 145–174 in Carol C. Gould, ed., *Beyond Domination: New Perspectives on Women and Philosophy*. Totowa, N.J.: Rowman & Allanheld.

MACKINNON, CATHARINE A. 1984 Not a Moral Issue. *Yale Law & Policy Review* 2:321–345.

NOTE 1984 Anti-Pornography Laws and First Amendment Values. *Harvard Law Review* 98:460–481.

PORNOGRAPHY AND CHILDREN

See: Child Pornography; *New York v. Ferber*

PORNOGRAPHY AND FEMINISM

In 1984 Indianapolis passed an "antipornography civil rights ordinance." PORNOGRAPHY was defined thus:

the graphic sexually explicit subordination of women, whether in pictures or in words, that also includes one or more of the following: (1) Women who are presented as sexual objects who enjoy pain or humiliation; or (2) Women [who] are presented as sexual objects who experience sexual pleasure in being raped; or (3) Women [who] are presented as sexual objects tied up or cut up or mutilated or bruised or physically hurt, or as dismembered or truncated or fragmented or severed into body parts; or (4) Women [who] are presented as being penetrated by objects or animals; or (5) Women [who] are presented in scenarios of degradation, injury, abasement, torture, shown as filthy or inferior, bleeding, bruised, or hurt in a context that makes these conditions sexual; or (6) Women [who] are presented as sexual objects for domination, conquest, violation, exploitation, possession, or use, or through postures or positions of servility or submission or display.

The ordinance afforded civil, but not criminal, remedies for trafficking in pornography (i.e., sales, exhibitions, or distribution with exceptions for libraries), forcing pornography on a person, coercing a person into pornography, attacking a person because of pornography, or causing such attacks. To some extent, the functional definition of pornography depends on the particular offense under the ordinance. For example, isolated parts of a book would not support a trafficking claim, but they could support a claim against an individual for forcing pornography on someone. Although the ordinance was crafted to protect women against SEX DISCRIMINATION, it is provided that if men, children, or transsexuals were treated in the same manner, they, too, could be afforded protection.

Although there is substantial overlap, Indianapolis's "pornography" is not the Supreme Court's "obscenity." MILLER V. CALIFORNIA (1973) defined OBSCENITY to include material that the "average person, applying contemporary community standards," would find when "taken as a whole appeals to the prurient interest" and "depicts and describes in a patently offensive way, sexual conduct specifically defined by the applicable state law," and that "taken as a whole, lacks serious literary, artistic, political, or scientific value."

Some of the material falling under the sixth category of the Indianapolis ordinance (e.g., women presented as sexual objects through postures or display) might not be ruled offensive under contemporary community standards, though probably most graphic, sexually explicit material that subordinates women and that also falls within the six specified categories would meet the *Miller* standard for obscenity. Such material would in the general run of cases be thought to appeal to prurient interests and to be patently offensive under contemporary community standards. The only substantial question would be whether particular material had the serious value specified in the *Miller* test, and it is doubtful that much of it would.

The ordinance's proponents argue, however, that obscenity law is theoretically and functionally bankrupt. As Catharine MacKinnon writes, they doubt "whether the average person, gender neutral exists; [they have] more questions about the content and process of definition of community standards than deviations from them; [they wonder] why prurience counts but powerlessness does not; why sensibilities are better protected than are women from exploitation." They ask, "If a woman is subjected, why should it matter that the work has other value? Perhaps what redeems a work's value among men *enhances* its injury to women." They contend that the ordinance focuses on the real problem (harm to women rather than offense to the community), provides for more effective enforcement (by allowing women to bring civil actions), and is more precise in its definition of the material to be sanctioned than obscenity law has ever been.

Ironically, despite its efforts at precision, the ordinance has frequently been misread. For example, one respected commentator states that the "sweep of the Indianapolis ordinance is breathtaking. It would subject to governmental ban virtually all depictions of rape, verbal or pictorial. . . . The ban would extend from Greek mythology and Shakespeare to . . . much of the world's art, from ancient carvings to Picasso . . . and a large amount of commercial advertising."

It is not the case that virtually all depictions of rape are sexually explicit—let alone Shakespeare or commercial advertising in any large amount. Some ancient carvings and works of Picasso involve nudity, but how many of them are graphic? Do they involve the subordination of women? Where do they fall under the six categories? Do *any* of them fall under the first five categories? Could any breathtaking possibilities be cured by editing the sixth category? Is one person's breathtaking possibility another person's exercise of male domination? One suspects in any event that if an ordinance of this character were upheld, its opponents would find creative possibilities for limiting its scope and its proponents would be stressing the breadth of its reach.

Were the ordinance construed narrowly, what would be the case for its constitutionality? Many categories of speech are deemed beneath the protection of the FIRST AMENDMENT, including FIGHTING WORDS, some forms of advocacy of illegal action, some forms of defamation, and obscenity. The argument for the ordinance is not that it fits within such categories. Rather, proponents argue that a new category of nonprotection is justified. If defamation causes harm to specific individuals, the proponents argue, pornography causes even more:

> The harm of pornography includes dehumanization, sexual exploitation, forced sex, forced prostitution, physical injury, and social and sexual terrorism, and inferiority presented as entertainment. The bigotry and contempt pornography promotes, with the acts of aggression it fosters, diminish opportunity for equality of rights in employment, education, property, public accommodations and public services; create public and private harassment . . . ; promote injury and degradation such as rape, battery, child abuse, and prostitution and inhibit just enforcement of laws against these acts; contribute significantly to restricting women in particular from full exercise of citizenship and participation in public life, including in neighborhoods; damage relationships between the sexes; and undermine women's equal exercise of rights to speech.

Without questioning these harms, the UNITED STATES COURT OF APPEALS for the Seventh Circuit declared the Indianapolis ordinance unconstitutional on its face in *American Booksellers Association v. Hudnut* (1985), and the Supreme Court affirmed without opinion. *Hudnut* is now the principal case in the pornography area.

Speaking for the Seventh Circuit, Judge Frank Easterbrook accepted the premise that "pornography is central in creating and maintaining sex as a basis of discrimination." Nonetheless, he maintained, the entire ordinance was premised on an unacceptable form of content discrimination: "The ordinance discriminates on the ground of the content of the speech. Speech treating women in the approved way . . . is lawful no matter how sexually explicit. Speech treating women in the disapproved way . . . is unlawful no matter how significant the literary, artistic, or political qualities of the work taken as a whole. The state may not ordain preferred viewpoints in this way. The Constitution forbids the state to declare one perspective right and silence opponents." Proceeding from this reading of the First Amendment, the court stated, "We do not try to balance the arguments for and against an ordinance such as this." The case was over.

From the court's perspective, the amount of harm to women caused by pornography was quite beside the First Amendment point and not to be weighed in the balance. But this reading of current doctrine is idiosyncratic. The categorical exceptions to First Amendment protection already involve discrimination on the basis of point of view.

The treatment of legislation involving advocacy of the overthrow of the government by force and violence is one obvious example. Obscenity is another. For example, appeals to prurient interests are defined as appeals to a "shameful or morbid interest in sex." The Court ruled in BROCKETT V. SPOKANE ARCADES (1985) that appeals to prurient interests cannot be taken to include appeals to "normal" interests in sex, that is, appeals to an interest in "good, old fashioned, healthy" sex are constitutionally protected, even if they are patently offensive to contemporary standards and lack serious literary, artistic, political, or scientific value. Appeals to an "abnormal" interest in sex are treated differently. For them, when the other requirements are satisfied, it is permissible to bring down the full weight of the law. In short, appeal to one perspective is declared right and appeal to another is declared wrong.

The *Hudnut* court's unwillingness to balance the arguments was thus supported only by misreading the treatment of content discrimination in First Amendment law. Content discrimination in general and point-of-view discrimination are disfavored in First Amendment law, but they are not absolutely disfavored. The *Hudnut* court had no difficulty showing that pornography did not fall within any of the existing categorical exceptions to First Amendment protection. But the issue presented by pornography legislation is whether pornography's harm justifies the creation of a new categorical exception to First Amendment protection. That was the issue sidestepped by the court's decision of content discrimination.

One approach to the question is by analogy. The *Hudnut* court did consider that possibility. Obscenity, it observed, has been deemed by the Supreme Court to be LOW-VALUE SPEECH, and "pornography is not low value speech within the meaning of these cases" because pornography "is thought to influence social relations and politics on a grand scale, that it controls attitudes at home and in the legislature. This precludes a characterization of the speech as low value."

If analogy were the mode of argument, the issue would not be whether pornography falls into a category denominated as low value. The Supreme Court did not use the term "low value" in creating the obscenity exception. The Court maintained in ROTH V. UNITED STATES (1957) that obscenity made such a slight contribution to truth that its possible benefits were categorically outweighed by the interests in order and morality. The proponents of pornography prohibitions insist that the same or something even stronger can be said of pornography. In addition, nothing in *Roth* speaks to the magnitude of the scale upon which obscenity was thought to influence order and morality (let alone in the home or the legislature). Certainly nothing in *Roth* or any subsequent decision supposes that if obscenity were demonstrated to have profound effects on order or morality, it would then emerge as protected speech.

The real animus of the *Hudnut* analysis is a deep hostility to the obscenity exception, a hostility that is tempered only by the view that obscenity does not matter much anyway. Thus, when Indianapolis says "pornography matters," the *Hudnut* court says, "all the more reason to protect it." But this response begs the question. First Amendment values are important; so are those of gender equality. As MacKinnon has observed, a victory for FREEDOM OF SPEECH anywhere may be a victory for freedom of speech everywhere, but a victory for sexism anywhere may be a victory for sexism everywhere.

The case for or against pornography legislation cannot be decided in the abstract. Attention must be paid to the character and amount of the harm caused (e.g., whether pornography is cathartic, stimulates aggressive and discriminatory behavior, or both, and to what extent; the extent to which the ordinance would combat that harm (e.g., whether black markets would arise, to what extent the ordinance and its application would legitimize nonpornographic but equally harmful speech, and whether the absence of pornography would cause aggressive behavior); the possibility of less restrictive alternatives (e.g., what the impact of adding a serious-value test would be) and the impact on free speech (e.g., how serious the chilling effect on speech that ought to matter would be and whether the addition of a new category based on content discrimination and the raising of questions about the particular value of speech would require quite heavy justification).

Serious arguments can be made for and against the constitutionality of legislation like the Indianapolis antipornography ordinance. The scandal is that those arguments have yet to receive serious judicial consideration and expression.

STEVEN SHIFFRIN
(1992)

(SEE ALSO: *Child Pornography; Dial-a-Porn; Feminist Theory; Meese Commission.*)

Bibliography

EMERSON, THOMAS I. 1985 Pornography and the First Amendment: A Reply to Professor MacKinnon. *Yale Law and Policy Review* 3:130–143.

MACKINNON, CATHARINE 1987 *Feminism Unmodified*. Cambridge, Mass.: Harvard University Press.

STONE, GEOFFREY R. 1986 Anti-Pornography Legislation as Viewpoint Discrimination. *Harvard Journal of Law and Public Policy* 9:461–480.

SUSTEIN, CASS R. 1986 Pornography and the First Amendment. *Duke Law Journal* 1986:589–627.

PORNOGRAPHY AND THE MEESE COMMISSION

See: Meese Commission

PORNOGRAPHY OVER THE TELEPHONE

See: Dial-a-Porn

POSADAS DE PUERTO RICO ASSOCIATES v. TOURISM COMPANY OF PUERTO RICO
478 U.S. 328 (1986)

In *Posadas* the Supreme Court upheld, 5–4, a Puerto Rico statute that authorized casino gambling but forbade advertising of casino gambling when the advertising was aimed at Puerto Rican residents. The majority, in an opinion by Justice WILLIAM H. REHNQUIST, followed the doctrinal formula in CENTRAL HUDSON GAS AND ELECTRIC CORP. V. PUBLIC SERVICE COMMISSION (1980) for testing the constitutionality of regulations of COMMERCIAL SPEECH. The advertising concerned a lawful activity and was not misleading or fraudulent. Thus, the Court proceeded to the interest-balancing part of the formula. The governmental interest was the reduction of demand for casino gambling; Puerto Rico's concerns for its residents' health, safety, and welfare was obvious, considering that a majority of the states prohibit such gambling altogether. The restrictions on advertising, said the Court, directly advanced that interest. Furthermore, the Commonwealth of Puerto Rico was not required to resort to advertising of its own as a LEAST RESTRICTIVE MEANS for discouraging casino gambling. In support of the latter point Justice Rehnquist cited lower court decisions approving restrictions on advertising of cigarettes and alcohol. Puerto Rico could have banned casino gambling altogether; this greater power included the lesser power to regulate advertising.

Justice WILLIAM J. BRENNAN, writing for three Justices, dissented, arguing the the Commonwealth had not met its burden of substantial justification for regulating commercial speech. In particular, the Commonwealth had not shown that less restrictive means would suffice. Justice JOHN PAUL STEVENS focused his dissent on the law's discrimination based on the advertising's intended audience.

There is little doubt that Congress or a state legislature could constitutionally ban the sale or use of cigarettes. Commentators have suggested that *Posadas* implies that, even if such a prohibition law were not adopted, a ban on cigarette advertising would be constitutional.

KENNETH L. KARST
(1992)

POSSE COMITATUS ACT
20 Stat. 145 (1878)

Representative James P. Knott (Democrat of Kentucky) introduced this act as an amendment to the Army Appropriation Act of 1878. It provides that "it shall not be lawful to employ any part of the Army of the United States, as a posse comitatus, or otherwise, for the purpose of executing the laws" except as specifically authorized by Congress. The act has applied to the Air Force since 1947; it has been extended to the Navy and Marine Corps by administrative regulations. Originally enacted as a step in the dismantling of RECONSTRUCTION, this provision banned the practice implicitly authorized by the JUDICIARY ACT OF 1789, and used before the CIVIL WAR to enforce the Fugitive Slave Act, of including military forces in the federal marshal's posse. The act remains on the books (section 1835, Title 18, United States Code) as an expression of the fundamental division between the military and civilian realms: the armed forces are not a LAW ENFORCEMENT agency.

Congress has authorized the use of the armed forces to suppress insurrection, domestic violence, unlawful combination, or conspiracy that obstructs the execution of federal law or impedes the course of justice, or that deprives any class of people of constitutional rights that the state authorities cannot or will not protect. That provision of the Force Act of 1871 (now section 333, Title 10, United States Code) was invoked by President DWIGHT D. EISENHOWER in 1958 when he used Army units to disperse the mob in Little Rock, Arkansas, that resisted a federal court's school DESEGREGATION order (see COOPER V. AARON), and by President RICHARD M. NIXON, in 1970, when he ordered federal troops to assist in quelling a riot in Detroit, Michigan.

DENNIS J. MAHONEY
(1986)

POSTAL POWER

Seven words of Article I, section 8, of the Constitution grant the postal power to Congress. Under the power "To Establish Post Offices and Post Roads" liberally construed, Congress has built offices and constructed roads for handling the mails and maintained an extensive nationwide delivery service. Congress has vested in the Postal Service, now in corporate form, monopoly powers over the delivery of letters and extensive, though often untested, POLICE POWERS over the mails.

The postal system in the United States traces its roots to a 1692 crown patent to Thomas Neale by William and Mary, granting a monopoly of the colonial posts, including all profits therefrom. The Post Office was established on July 26, 1775, by the CONTINENTAL CONGRESS to assure effective communications and to eliminate what was viewed as a tax by the British Post Office. The ARTICLES OF CONFEDERATION granted exclusive postal power to Congress, and the Constitution carried forward the congressional power over the mails.

At the time of the CONSTITUTIONAL CONVENTION the activities of the Post Office were widely accepted, and there was little sentiment for change or elaboration. Indeed, the postal power was virtually undebated, and only one reference to it is to be found in THE FEDERALIST. The breadth of the congressional interpretation of the postal power, therefore, finds neither support nor contradiction in the Constitution or the debates concerning its adoption.

The postal monopoly, contained in the so-called private express statutes, generally makes it unlawful for private carriers to carry letters and packets, unless postage has been paid thereon and canceled. This provision is, in effect, a 100 percent tax on the carrying of letters outside the Postal Service. The monopoly dates from colonial days, and it was and is justified on the economic grounds that it is necessary to retain monopoly power over profitable routes and services so that the Postal Service can provide uniform and inexpensive service nationwide, even along uneconomic and remote routes. The Articles of Confederation specifically granted the monopoly, giving the Congress "sole and exclusive power." The absence of these words in Article I, section 8, leaves the constitutionality of the monopoly unclear, but the few courts that have considered the question have held in its favor. Historically, monopoly had been an integral feature of the British and colonial postal systems, as well as those of many other Western nations.

The extent of the postal power has been the subject of debate in the Congress and of occasional litigation. The earliest questions concerned post roads: did Congress have authority to construct new roads, or only to designate existing state roads as postal routes? The issue had not been discussed by the Framers or, with one exception (New York), at the state conventions. Congress determined that it had power to appropriate funds to construct post roads, but not to construct them directly. The Supreme Court had never decided the question, although Chief Justice JOHN MARSHALL in OBITER DICTUM in MCCULLOCH V. MARYLAND (1819) suggested that the power included construction. In the construction of the first of these roads, the Cumberland Road, Congress and the President adopted a working compromise by seeking the consent of the affected states prior to approval of the bill. Many other post roads were constructed following similar procedures. The Supreme Court ultimately put the question of construction authority to rest in *Kohl v. United States* (1876) by holding that the federal government may condemn land, by analogy to EMINENT DOMAIN, for a post office site.

Postal statutes and regulations grant police powers to the Postal Service, imposing rules designed to protect the public welfare and limiting mailability. Safety regulations (for example, mailability of poisons and explosives) and mechanical rules (size and packaging standard), have not been the subject of serious challenge. The statute imposing fines and imprisonment for mail fraud was held constitutional in *Public Clearing House v. Coyne* (1904) and several later cases. Other statutory determinations of nonmailability have similarly been upheld. *Ex parte Jackson* (1878) upheld a criminal conviction under a federal statute prohibiting mailing of newspapers containing advertisements for lotteries. In the late eighteenth and early nineteenth centuries, relying on *Jackson* and other holdings, Congress greatly expanded the exclusionary power to cover libelous matter, OBSCENITY, and the like, and these provisions remain a part of present law. The Supreme Court has repeatedly upheld the constitutionality of the congressional power to exclude obscene materials from the mails.

From 1872 until 1970, the Post Office was an executive department and the postmaster general had CABINET status. Prompted by heavy economic losses from Post Office operations, problems with postal deliveries, and charges of political inefficiency, Congress in 1970 created the United States Postal Service to take over the functions of the Post Office Department. Removing the operations of the Post Office (including appointment of the postmaster general) from direct political influence and granting to the Post Office a substantial degree of fiscal autonomy were among the major objects of the reorganization. The new Postal System is organized as a public CORPORATION, owned entirely by the federal government, under the management of a board of governors. The board appoints the postmaster general, who is the chief executive officer of the Postal Service, but is no longer a cabinet member. The board and the officers have wide discretion with respect to management, services, and expenditures, subject to congressional oversight. Postal rates, formerly established directly by Congress, are now determined by a presidentially appointed Postal Rate Commission on the basis of recommendations made by the board of governors.

STANLEY SIEGEL
(1986)

Bibliography

JOHNSTON, JOSEPH F., JR. 1968 The United States Postal Monopoly. *Business Lawyer* 23:379–405.
PAUL, JAMES C. and SCHWARTZ, MURRAY L. 1961 *Federal Censorship: Obscenity in the Mail.* New York: Free Press.
PROJECT: POST OFFICE 1968 *Southern California Law Review* 41:643–727.
ROGERS, LINDSAY 1916 *The Postal Power of Congress.* Baltimore: Johns Hopkins University Press.

POSTMODERNISM AND CONSTITUTIONAL INTERPRETATION

It has been said that postmodernism is a victim of its own diagnosis. Postmodern thought defies systematic accounts in part because it announces an intellectual and cultural condition in which such systematic accounts have become unbelievable. Postmodern thought announces the dissolution of the grand metanarratives of the Enlightenment. It presents a view of language and thought as incapable of stabilizing meaning. It holds the possibility of establishing first premises, origins, and foundations to be a kind of illusion. It reacquaints linear thought, conceptual hierarchies, and rationalism with their status as narratives. In such cultural and intellectual circumstances, the very identity of postmodernism becomes itself mysterious, mutable, and contestable. Anyone seeking to conceptualize postmodernism must thus confront the possibility that postmodernism itself announces the impossibility of such conceptualization. One practical effect is that the meaning of postmodernism is very much in the eye of the beholder.

The possible relations of postmodernism to CONSTITUTIONAL INTERPRETATION are themselves multiple and contestable. From the perspective of the American constitutional tradition, however, it is possible to distinguish two very different kinds of postmodernism with very different implications.

Consider that the American constitutional tradition boasts a generous variety of interpretive techniques and approaches. Jurists, academics, politicians, and citizens have offered and invoked a multitude of interpretive techniques. Some believe that constitutional interpretation must focus exclusively or primarily on the words of the text. Others argue that the ORIGINAL INTENT of the Framers

must be consulted. Still others believe that what matters is the linguistic usage at the time the Constitution or its amendments were adopted. Some have argued that the problem of constitutional interpretation must be understood in light of the conundrums of JUDICIAL REVIEW. More modestly, others have viewed the problem of interpretation in terms of the authority and competencies of the various constitutional actors—the various federal branches, the states, groups, and individuals. Then too, there are those who hold that constitutional interpretation must follow popular consensus. Another view holds that the Constitution must be interpreted in light of fundamental political values such as justice or equality. Yet another approach lies in recognizing that all or some of these approaches are appropriate.

For most of the second half of the twentieth century, this eclectic mix of interpretive approaches has been viewed in terms of a characteristically modernist anxiety: The primary question for jurists, academics, politicians, and citizens alike has been which is the correct mode of interpretation? This question has featured prominently in the courts, in scholarship, in judicial confirmation hearings before the U.S. SENATE, and in the editorial pages.

One postmodern perspective—call this "weak postmodernism"—displaces this question to affirm that constitutional interpretation encompasses all of these modes. On this view, to do constitutional interpretation is nothing more than to engage in one or more of these modes of interpretation. The question, "which is the right mode of interpretation?" becomes itself another interpretive approach—no more privileged, no less legitimate than the others. It becomes one more "move" among others.

This weak postmodernism would view the eclectic mix of interpretive approaches as a function of different perspectives. The different approaches differ because the Constitution is seen in terms of different interests, concerns, hopes, and fears. This kind of postmodern thought is congenial to the practice of constitutional interpretation. It does not threaten the authority of the Constitution nor the possibility of arriving at coherent and shared meanings. To the contrary, the American tradition of constitutional interpretation is arguably already postmodern and has been so for a long time—long before "postmodernism" became a fashionable term.

There is, however, a "strong postmodernism" much more disturbing to the enterprise of constitutional interpretation and constitutional law. This strong postmodernism puts in question the identity of what it is that is being interpreted. Just about any jurist, academic, politician, or citizen would answer that it is "the Constitution" that is being interpreted. But a strong postmodernism would ask, What is the identity of this "Constitution"? Is it a text, a political instrument, an institutional organization, a site of political contestation, an expression of cultural mythology—all or some of these things and perhaps many more?

This strong postmodernism effectively transposes the entire question of how to interpret (a question of methodology) into a question about what is being interpreted (a question of identity). This strong postmodernism leads to the view that the Constitution is not a thing that is there independently of or prior to the action of interpretation. Rather, this strong postmodernism reveals "the Constitution" as a kind of cultural–intellectual artifact that is itself a construct, a creation, of the various interpretive approaches. On this view, the Constitution is not so much interpreted, as it is continuously created and re-created by those who claim to be interpreting it.

This kind of postmodernism is much more difficult, perhaps even impossible, to reconcile with American notions of constitutionalism and the rule of law. This strong postmodernism denies that the Constitution is a source of authority and meaning that exists independently of present acts of interpretation. Instead, this strong postmodernism affirms that present acts of interpretation are effectively a kind of cultural and intellectual authorship.

In terms of this strong postmodernism, the very idea of a postmodern constitutional interpretation is an oxymoron—akin to an atheistic religion. To the extent that this is right, the attempt to integrate postmodernism and constitutional interpretations would lead to a serious deformation of one or the other, and perhaps both.

PIERRE SCHLAG
(2000)

Bibliography

BALKIN, J. M. 1992 What Is a Postmodern Constitutionalism? *Michigan Law Review* 90:1966–1990.

BOBBITT, PHILIP 1991 *Conscience and the Constitution: Constitutional Interpretation.* Cambridge, Mass.: Basil Blackwell, Inc.

KAHN, PAUL 1992 *Legitimacy and History: Self-Government in American Constitutional Theory.* New Haven, Conn.: Yale University Press.

PATTERSON, DENNIS 1996 *Law and Truth.* New York: Oxford University Press.

SCHLAG, PIERRE 1996 Hiding the Ball. *New York University Law Review* 71:1681–1718.

WINTER, STEVEN L. 1990 Indeterminacy and Incommensurability in Constitutional Law. *California Law Review* 78:1441–1541.

POUND, ROSCOE
(1870–1964)

Roscoe Pound was a prominent legal educator, a distinguished philosopher of law, and a prolific writer. His major contribution to American law was his formative role in the development of SOCIOLOGICAL JURISPRUDENCE. He elaborated this instrumentalist approach during the Progressive era, the spirit of which pervaded his writings. His thought had a conservative side to it, however, which became more influential in the latter stages of his life. He expressed this conservatism not only in his eulogies of the COMMON LAW but also in his criticism of the NEW DEAL and the "service state," his indictment of administrative tribunals, and his fulminations against LEGAL REALISM.

Although Pound did not specialize in constitutional law, he promoted better understanding of the realities of the judicial process in this field through his critique of MECHANICAL JURISPRUDENCE, his explanation of the broad scope of judicial discretion and JUDICIAL POLICYMAKING, and his contrast between the "law in the books and the law in action." He was also a trenchant critic of the extreme individualism underlying numerous decisions of the Supreme Court well into the twentieth century.

The quality of Pound's voluminous writings, which spanned almost the entire *corpus juris*, varied substantially. His best scholarship consisted, in the main, of his influential articles on legal thought and reform published from 1905 to 1916. These works included "Liberty of Contract" (1909), which was one of his few publications to focus on constitutional questions. *The Spirit of the Common Law* (1921), *The Formative Era of American Law* (1938), and *The Development of Constitutional Guarantees of Liberty* (1957) are today his most useful books for students of constitutional law and history. His *Jurisprudence* (1959) was the most comprehensive statement of his legal philosophy.

WILFRID E. RUMBLE
(1986)

Bibliography

WIGDOR, DAVID 1974 *Roscoe Pound.* Westport, Conn.: Greenwood Press.

POVERTY

See: Indigent; Wealth Discrimination

POVERTY LAW

In a nineteenth-century COMMERCE CLAUSE case, the Supreme Court characterized "paupers" and "vagabonds" as a "moral pestilence" against which the state could protect itself in the exercise of its POLICE POWERS. Although we can still hear echoes of these sentiments in laws and practices segregating the poor and the institutions that serve them, the Supreme Court has now made clear that bare hostility to, or suspicion of, the poor is not a constitutionally permissible basis for STATE ACTION.

The decisive break came in the 1941 decision in EDWARDS V. CALIFORNIA, where the Court struck down as a violation of the DORMANT COMMERCE CLAUSE a state law making it a crime knowingly to aid an indigent in coming into the state. The Court said in *Edwards* that "it will not now be seriously contended that because a person is without employment and without funds he constitutes a 'moral pestilence.' Poverty and immorality are not synonymous." In a much cited concurrence, Justice ROBERT JACKSON went further, insisting that "indigence' in itself is neither a source of rights nor a basis for denying them. The mere state of being without funds is a neutral fact—constitutionally an irrelevance, like race, creed, or color."

Since *Edwards*, indigence as such cannot be the basis for the imposition of governmental burdens. For indigence, as for race, however, the ideal of constitutional irrelevance has proved elusive. In dealing with issues of poverty since *Edwards*, the Court has found itself repeatedly confronting questions of what it might mean for the state to treat something as irrelevant that matters terribly in the society of which the state is a part. It is now settled that both state and federal legislatures can take action to alleviate poverty and its effects. The difficult problems that remain revolve around whether, and when, the Constitution may require relief for the poor from some of the burdens of indigence.

Constitutional solicitude for the poor emerged first in the context of CRIMINAL PROCEDURE, with the Supreme Court holding that indigent criminal defendants were entitled to state-appointed counsel, to trial transcripts on appeal, and, more recently, to limited forms of other important assistance in resisting prosecution. The first RIGHT TO COUNSEL holding came in 1932, and the Court gradually developed a constitutional law of procedural rights for indigent criminal defendants in federal and then in state courts. These rights for the indigent accused developed without any overt prod from external influences. Expansion of the rights of the poor beyond the criminal procedure context had to await the development of larger social movements.

By the mid-1960s, problems of poverty were commanding political attention. Congress responded to President LYNDON B. JOHNSON's call for a "war on poverty" with a variety of new programs designed to deal with the symptoms and the causes of poverty in America. One of the early poverty programs was federal subsidization of civil legal aid for the poor. Charitable legal aid programs had a long history in the United States, but the new federal subsidy helped channel the reformist zeal of large numbers of new lawyers acting on behalf of poor people. Their activities left a mark on many areas of the law, including much of constitutional law beyond the criminal procedure beginnings.

For a time it even appeared that litigation on behalf of welfare recipients might yield a constitutional right to subsistence support. In 1969 the Supreme Court held in SHAPIRO V. THOMPSON that states could not impose durational RESIDENCE REQUIREMENTS for the receipt of public assistance. The decision was based on the EQUAL PROTECTION clause; the residence requirements impinged on the RIGHT TO TRAVEL interstate, a right the Court characterized as "fundamental" and hence enjoying heightened constitutional protection. But the Court also suggested that the fact that WELFARE BENEFITS were at issue was important to its decision. In the Court's words, the case involved "the very means to subsist—food, shelter, and other necessities of life." And the next year, the Court held in GOLDBERG V. KELLY (1970) that a welfare recipient had a right to an administrative hearing before her welfare benefits could be withdrawn. Again the Court emphasized the nature of the benefits at stake—"the means to obtain essential food, clothing, housing, and medical care." This and other language helped stimulate a secondary literature advocating a constitutional right to what Frank Michelman called "minimum protection" of each individual's "just wants."

No such right ever gained much of a foothold in the courts, however, for reasons that came into focus early. In DANDRIDGE V. WILLIAMS (1970), decided just one year after *Shapiro*, the Court rejected a claim that a family maximum on the size of the welfare grant deprived members of large welfare families of equal protection. The claim was plausible enough after *Shapiro*, but the prospect of continued expansion of the eligible population by virtue of equal protection decisions gave the Court pause, for it suggested that the legislative reaction might simply be to divide the same total public assistance resources among a larger eligible population. The Court's response to this tradeoff of equity and adequacy in welfare programs was to back off, saying in *Dandridge* that "conflicting claims of morality and intelligence are raised by opponents and proponents of almost every measure, certainly including the one before us. But the intractable economic, social and even philosophical problems presented by public welfare programs are not the business of this Court. . . . The Constitution does not empower this Court to second-guess state officials charged with the difficult responsibility of allocating limited public welfare funds among the myriad of potential recipients." The Court did not abandon equal protection review of discrimination within welfare programs after *Dandridge*, but that review became much more subdued than the rhetoric of *Shapiro* had suggested.

The problem to which the Court referred in *Dandridge* is real enough in the equal protection context, where the claimant typically seeks to have a group to which he belongs made eligible for assistance according to standards of need the state has already defined. Indeed, each time the Court extends eligibility, it causes a realignment of political forces that might force legislative tradeoffs with nonwelfare programs such as defense, foreign aid, and the fight against pollution. In such a case, however, the legislature does retain the option to eliminate or scale back the amount of the welfare benefits. A claim for minimum subsistence, on the other hand, would require of the Court decisions not only about those entitled to the assistance but also about the appropriate level of assistance—what, in Michelman's terms, are "just wants" and how much is "minimum protection." The Court would be requiring the expenditure of funds absolutely rather than conditionally, thus necessitating, rather than just giving a nudge to, legislative tradeoffs between welfare programs and others competing for public support. The prospect would be daunting, and the Court never did more than flirt lightly with it.

The welfare cases did somewhat alleviate recurrent confusion in constitutional law with regard to the RIGHT/PRIVILEGE DISTINCTION. Prior to those cases, when an interest characterized as a right was jeopardized by some legislative or executive action, constitutional protections were applicable; when privileges were at issue, it was sometimes said that no constitutional protections attached. This doctrine was never well developed, but it kept reappearing and posed a serious obstacle to constitutional succor for recipients under a growing array of government benefit programs, for those programs surely would fall on the privilege side of any such line. In both *Shapiro* and *Goldberg*, however, the Court rejected the distinction as constitutionally irrelevant. In subsequent cases, the notion behind the distinction has occasionally resurfaced (without the language of rights and privileges), but only as a consideration in defining the strength of constitutional protection, and not as a reason for denying protection altogether. Thus, the Supreme Court has repeatedly held that state and local governments need not subsidize ABORTION, even though a pregnant woman has a constitutionally protected interest in seeking out an abortion if she chooses. These decisions suggest that the state retains a higher degree of discretion over the dispensation of benefits than over the imposition of burdens, but they do not resurrect the sort of absolute discretion with which the rightprivilege distinction was associated.

Lawyers for the indigent did have important constitutional triumphs, but usually by joining problems of the poor to some other theme with which the Court could feel more comfortable. Expansion of the franchise and perfection of the electoral system, for instance, have been important contemporary themes in constitutional law, and the Court has been responsive to the handicaps placed on the poor in participating in democratic institutions. In 1966 the Court struck down a state POLL TAX as a condition on voting, and in subsequent cases, the Court limited property qualifications for voting in some specialized contexts. It has also restricted the filing fees that can be charged indigent candidates for public office.

The emphasis on fair process for indigents in the criminal cases and in *Goldberg* has been extended to certain civil proceedings. The movement, however, has been cautious as the Court undoubtedly keeps a wary eye on the costs involved. Thus, the state cannot require an indigent to pay court costs or filing fees as a condition to filing a divorce action. The state must pay for blood testing in a state-initiated paternity proceeding. And in compelling circumstances the state must provide counsel in an action to terminate parental rights. On the other hand, the state is not required to waive filing fees for a bankruptcy proceeding for an indigent or for an appeal of an adverse decision in a welfare hearing.

Some of the early opinions extending procedural protection to indigents in criminal cases used the language of equal protection, but the equal protection clause is not apt as a basis for procedural protections, because there is no obvious reference group with which the indigent defendant is to be compared. The more recent opinions have thus recurred to PROCEDURAL DUE PROCESS notions of fundamental fairness as the standard against which arguments for subsidy are to be judged.

This attraction to themes that do not explicitly draw on the fact of poverty means that many of the advances in constitutional poverty law have resulted from litigation on behalf of groups whose members are mostly poor but not necessarily so. The Court has, for instance, established substantial constitutional protections for ALIENS within the jurisdiction of the United States, for illegitimate children, for the mentally retarded, and for youngsters subjected to JUVENILE PROCEEDINGS. The opinions in these cases often draw on the impecuniousness of the protected group, but seldom in a way that makes the doctrines announced depend on that fact.

One important extension of constitutional rights of the poor has been snatched by state courts and state constitutional law out of the mouth of federal defeat. Primary and secondary education in the United States has been financed in large part through local property taxes, with the result that property-rich districts have been able to sustain much higher per-pupil expenditures for education than have property-poor districts. Drawing on the FUNDAMENTAL RIGHTS branch of equal protection doctrine developed in *Shapiro* and other cases, students in property-poor districts challenged these financing schemes. The Supreme Court rejected the claim in its 1973 decision SAN ANTONIO INDEPENDENT SCHOOL DISTRICT V. RODRIGUEZ, holding that there was no fundamental right to a particular level of education and that the students in property-poor districts, who need not necessarily be poor, were entitled to no heightened constitutional protection. *Rodriguez*, like the welfare cases, suggests judicial disinclination to become involved in financing decisions for major public programs.

Faced with a reluctant federal court system, however, poverty lawyers and their clients increasingly have turned to state courts and state constitutional claims. In the case of educational financing, they could draw on equal protection provisions in state constitutions or on provisions assuming state responsibility for public education. The result has been court-ordered reform of educational financing in a substantial number of states.

Twenty-five years after the war on poverty began, there is no constitutional law of the poor in the way that there is a constitutional law of race relations or INTERSTATE COMMERCE. But constitutional law has changed over that time in ways that have been important for the legal status of many people who are poor. It has changed mostly in small ways and in many different contexts, but those small and diverse changes add up to an altered landscape in which constitutional law is one tool among many in addressing the myriad legal problems that beset the poor.

ROBERT W. BENNETT
(1992)

(SEE ALSO: *Illegitimacy; Mental Retardation and the Constitution; Rights of the Criminally Accused; State Constitutions.*)

Bibliography

BENNETT, ROBERT W. 1983 The Burger Court and the Poor. Pages 46–61 in Vincent Blasi, ed., *The Burger Court*. New Haven, Conn.: Yale University Press.
LAFRANCE, ARTHUR B. et al. 1973 *Law of the Poor*. St. Paul, Minn.: West Publishing Co.
MICHELMAN, FRANK I. 1969 Foreword: On Protecting the Poor Through the Fourteenth Amendment. *Harvard Law Review* 83:7–59.
WINTER, RALPH K. 1972 Poverty, Economic Equality, and the Equal Protection Clause. *Supreme Court Review* 1972:41–102.

POWELL, LEWIS F., JR.
(1907–)

Lewis Franklin Powell, Jr., has always eluded conventional portraiture. In broad brush, Powell appears the archetypal conservative: a successful corporate lawyer, a director of eleven major companies, a pillar of Richmond, Virginia's civic and social life. The roll call of legal honors—president of the American Bar Association, the American College of Trial Lawyers, and the American Bar Foundation—does little to dispel the impression.

The portrait, however, needs serious refinement. During Virginia's "massive resistance," when the Byrd organization chose to close public schools rather than accept racial integration, Powell, as chairman of the Richmond Public School Board, fought successfully to keep Richmond's open. As vice-president of the National Legal Aid and Defender Society, he helped persuade the organized bar to support publicly financed legal services for the poor. Jean Camper Cahn, a black leader with whom he worked in that endeavor, found Powell "so curiously shy, so deeply sensitive to the hurt or embarrassment of another, so self-effacing that it is difficult to reconcile the public and private man—the honors and the acclaim with the gentle, courteous, sensitive spirit that one senses in every conversation, no matter how casual. . . ."

The portrait of the private practitioner parallels that of the Supreme Court Justice. The broad picture is again one of orthodox adherence to the canons of restraint. Powell labored diligently to limit the powers of the federal courts. He sought to narrow the STANDING of litigants invoking federal JURISDICTION to instances of actual injury in WARTH V. SELDIN (1975). He dissented when the Court in *Cannon v. University of Chicago* (1979) inferred from federal statutes a private cause of action. He greatly restricted the power of federal judges to review claims of unlawful SEARCH AND SEIZURE raised by state defendants in STONE V. POWELL (1976). And he urged the sharp curtailment of federal equitable remedies such as student BUSING for racial balance, in cases like KEYES V. DENVER SCHOOL DISTRICT #1 (1973).

While working to limit federal judicial power, Powell championed the power of others to operate free of constitutional strictures. Thus prosecutors should enjoy discretion in initiating prosecution, police and GRAND JURIES in pursuing EVIDENCE, trial judges in questioning jurors, welfare workers in terminating assistance, and military officers in conducting training. The "hands-off" view applied especially to public education. Powell, a former member of the Virginia Board of Education, wrote the Court opinion preserving the rights of states to devise their own systems of public school finance in SAN ANTONIO SCHOOL DISTRICT V. RODRIGUEZ (1973). And the former chairman of the Richmond School Board spoke for the broad discretion of school authorities to administer student suspensions and corporal punishment, dissenting in GOSS V. LOPEZ (1975) and writing for the Court in INGRAHAM V. WRIGHT (1977).

Even so, a corner of the jurist's nature has been reserved for personal circumstances of particular poignancy. An early opinion afforded a black construction worker in Mississippi, father of nine, the opportunity to confront his accusers and establish his innocence in *Chambers v. Mississippi* (1973). Another Powell opinion, in MOORE V. EAST CLEVELAND (1977), voided a municipal housing ordinance that prevented an elderly woman from living with her adult sons and grandchildren. Another, SOLEM V. HELM (1983), held unconstitutional a life sentence without parole imposed by state courts on the perpetrator of seven nonviolent felonies. Even in the sacrosanct area of education, the Justice concurred in PLYLER V. DOE (1982) rather than leave children of illegal aliens "on the streets uneducated."

The cases of compassion are remarkable in one respect. Vindication of the individual claims meant overriding the most cherished of Powell's conservative tenets: the protection of state criminal judgments from meddlesome review on petition for federal writs of HABEAS CORPUS, and the recognition of only those rights tied closely to the constitutional text. Powell, plainly nervous about damaging these principles, narrowed the rulings almost to their actual facts. The cases thus testify both to a strength and a weakness in the jurist, the strength being that of an open mind and heart, the weakness being that of cautious case-by-case adjudication that leaves law bereft of general guidance and sure content.

The dichotomy between the cases of compassion and the towering doctrinal efforts of the school finance case (*Rodriguez*) and the search and seizure case (*Stone*) illustrates the different dimensions of the man himself. Powell, for example, privately deplored the arrogance of the national communications media and the maleficence of the criminal element. But he was, by nature, reserved, considerate, as eager to listen as to talk. Thus, even on subjects of strong feeling, the tempered judgment often triumphed. This quality marked his opinions dealing with the press. In a concurrence more libertarian than the Court opinion he joined in BRANZBURG V. HAYES (1972), Powell urged that "a proper balance" be struck on a "case-by-case basis" between the claims of newsmen to protect the confidentiality of sources and the need of grand juries for information relevant to criminal conduct. In GERTZ V. ROBERT WELSH INC. (1974), perhaps his most important opinion on the FIRST AMENDMENT, Powell balanced a plaintiff's interest in his good reputation against press freedoms, permitting private citizens to recover in libel on a standard less than "knowing or reckless falsehood" but greater than liability without fault. Balancing of individual and societal claims characterized Powell's opinions involving the rights of radical campus organizations, the unconventional use of national symbols, and even many criminal cases, where fact-specific rulings on the admissibility of suspect LINEUPS, for example, began to replace the per se EXCLUSIONARY RULES of the WARREN COURT.

Balancing does not permit confident forecasting of appellate outcomes. Case-by-case weighing of facts and circumstances can constitute a dangerous delegation of the Supreme Court's own authority on constitutional matters to trial judges, police and prosecutors, and potential litigants, all of whom capitalize on the uncertainty of law to work their own wills. But balancing suited Powell's preference for a devolution of authority and, in cases like Gertz, achieved a thoughtful accommodation of competing interests.

In his most famous opinion, UNIVERSITY OF CALIFORNIA REGENTS V. BAKKE (1978), Powell, the balancer, struck a middle course on the flammable question of benign preferences based on race. The immediate question in *Bakke* was whether the medical school of the University of California at Davis could set aside sixteen of one hundred places in its entering class for preferred minorities. Eight Justices took polar positions. Four argued that Title VI of the CIVIL RIGHTS ACT OF 1964 prohibited any preference based on race. Four others contended that both the act and the constitution permitted the Davis program. Powell, the ninth and deciding Justice, alone sought to accommodate both the American belief in the primacy of the individual and the need to heal a history of oppression based on race.

It has become common to note that the Supreme Court under WARREN E. BURGER did not, as some feared, dismantle the activist legacy of the Warren Court. Many of the influential Justices, Powell, POTTER STEWART, and BYRON R. WHITE among them, were more pragmatic than ideological. Thus the Court trimmed here, expanded there, and approached complex questions cautiously. Powell's opinions exhibit, as much as those of any Justice, this Court's composite frame of mind. Like him, the Court he served has eluded conventional description.

J. HARVIE WILKINSON III
(1986)

Bibliography

GUNTHER, GERALD 1972 In Search of Judicial Quality in a Changing Court: The Case of Justice Powell. *Stanford Law Review* 24:1001–1035.

HOWARD, A. E. DICK 1972 Mr. Justice Powell and the Emerging Nixon Majority. *Michigan Law Review* 70:445–468.

SYMPOSIUM 1977 [Justice Lewis F. Powell] *University of Richmond Law Review* 11:259–445.

—— 1982 [Justice Lewis F. Powell] *Virginia Law Review* 68:161–458.

POWELL, LEWIS F., JR.
(1907–1998)
(Update)

From his appointment in 1971 until his resignation in 1987, Lewis F. Powell, Jr. was widely known as the "swing

Justice" on a closely divided Supreme Court. As the term "swing Justice" implies, Powell's position on the Court was one of both loneliness and influence. The loneliness resulted because Powell lacked a stable set of allies on many of the most contentious issues that came before the Court. The influence stemmed largely from his capacity to make 5–4 majorities. In cases involving AFFIRMATIVE ACTION, ABORTION, CAPITAL PUNISHMENT, and the FIRST AMENDMENT, Powell's finely nuanced positions caused him to move back and forth between coalitions of Justices whose decisions depended less on the peculiar facts of individual controversies.

After a Justice has retired from the Court, his influence, if any, must depend on the power of his written opinions and his judicial philosophy to command respect. The question of Powell's long-term influence remains unsettled. With regard to the resolution of specific cases, Powell's successor, ANTHONY M. KENNEDY, has contributed to a perceptible conservative drift by the REHNQUIST COURT, including erosion of some of the doctrines to which Powell was committed. In addition, Powell's characteristic "balancing" philosophy, which emerged as perhaps the Court's predominant methodology during his tenure, has recently attracted sharp criticism.

Lewis F. Powell joined the Supreme Court at the age of sixty-four after thirty-five years of successful private practice in the state of Virginia. The son of well-to-do parents, Powell graduated from Washington and Lee College in 1929 and, just two years later, finished first in his class at Washington and Lee Law School. After a year of graduate study at Harvard Law School, Powell returned to Richmond and joined the prestigious firm of Hunton, Williams, Gay, Powell, and Gibson, where, with time out for military service during World War II, he remained until 1971.

Powell achieved unusual eminence as a private lawyer. Besides winning the trust and respect of clients and serving on the boards of directors of eleven major corporations, Powell became active in a variety of lawyers' groups, including the American Bar Association, which he served as president in 1964–1965. Powell also took a leading role in a number of civic and cultural organizations. He was chairman of the Richmond school board from 1952 to 1961.

The Lewis Powell who took his seat on the Supreme Court in 1971 very much reflected his background and his experiences. In addition to possessing an acute analytical intelligence, he had a business lawyer's disposition to resolve disputes pragmatically, preferably in a way that would accommodate the reasonable interests of all parties. He also had a conservative respect for established institutions. Yet Powell was more than the archetype of the successful conservative lawyer. As chairman of the Richmond school board, he had resisted efforts by the Virginia

political establishment to close public schools rather than accept racial DESEGREGATION. And as vice-president of the National Legal Aid and Defender Society, he had worked to support publicly financed legal services for the poor.

Not surprisingly in light of his background, a respect for institutions of local government and especially for local school administration represented a consistent theme in Powell's Supreme Court opinions. Although cautious and nonideological in some areas, he consistently and even aggressively sought to protect state sovereignty interests under both the TENTH AMENDMENT and the ELEVENTH AMENDMENT. As a matter of "equitable restraint," he held that federal courts should virtually never interfere with proceedings before state courts and administrative agencies. And he favored the recognition of protective "immunities" for government officials whose official conduct entangled them in suits for money damages. Without such immunity, Powell reasoned in *Harlow v. Fitzgerald* (1982), able men and women would hesitate to accept positions of public responsibility. Powell also wrote germinal opinions in the field of STANDING that had as their effect, if not their explicit purpose, the preclusion of lawsuits challenging the constitutionality of programs and policies—including those of LOCAL GOVERNMENTS—whose effects were widely dispersed across large numbers of citizens. "Generalized grievances," he argued in an influential CONCURRING OPINION in *Schlesinger v. Reservists* (1974) and later for a majority of the Court in *Warth v. Seldin* (1975), should generally be resolved in the legislature and at the ballot box, rather than by the nondemocratic federal courts.

The theme of deference to local political decision making sounded particularly loudly in one of the earliest of Powell's major opinions, SAN ANTONIO INDEPENDENT SCHOOL DISTRICT V. RODRIGUEZ (1973). At issue in *Rodriguez* was the constitutionality of Texas's system of school funding, which relied heavily on local property taxes to finance public EDUCATION and, as administered, created a large disparity between the per-pupil expenditures in rich and poor school districts. The plaintiffs claimed that the disparate allocations offended the EQUAL PROTECTION clause. Justice Powell, who wrote for a five-member majority, disagreed. Education was not a FUNDAMENTAL RIGHT in the constitutional sense, he ruled, nor did a law disadvantaging students in impecunious school districts constitute a SUSPECT CLASSIFICATION that would trigger close judicial scrutiny. Especially because the plaintiffs' argument called into question the educational financing system of "virtually every State," Powell found judicial restraint to be appropriate. "It would be difficult to imagine a case having a greater impact on our federal system than the one now before us," he wrote. "The ultimate solutions must come from the lawmakers and from the democratic pressures of those who elect them." Powell took a similarly deferential stand in cases challenging the infliction of various kinds of punishment in the public schools and the removal of books from a school library.

While Powell was a fairly traditional conservative on questions of federal jurisdiction and of federalism, his accommodationist impulses and penchant for balancing often asserted themselves in cases under the FIRST AMENDMENT, the EIGHTH AMENDMENT, and the FOURTEENTH AMENDMENT. It was in these areas that he acquired his reputation as a swing Justice.

Powell's most famous opinion, in REGENTS OF UNIVERSITY OF CALIFORNIA V. BAKKE (1978), epitomizes both Powell's judicial style and his role on an ideologically fractured Supreme Court. The case arose when Alan Bakke, a white male who was denied admission to the medical school of the University of California at Davis, challenged the school's practice of setting aside sixteen of one hundred places in its entering class for members of disadvantaged minorities. Four Justices of the Court would have upheld affirmative action programs under considerably looser constitutional standards than applied to INVIDIOUS DISCRIMINATION. Four other Justices found all acts of RACIAL PREFERENCE, even those that favor discrete and insular minorities, to be absolutely prohibited by an applicable federal statute. That left Justice Powell, alone in the middle, to formulate the constitutional principles that would define the law of the case.

Upholding the ideal that race is irrelevant to moral worth, Powell argued that even discrimination in favor of minority persons must be subject to STRICT SCRUTINY by the courts. But, carefully parsing the state's reasons for pursuing affirmative action, he also identified an interest in student diversity that was sufficiently "compelling" to justify attaching affirmative weight to prospective students' minority backgrounds as one of many factors relevant to admissions decisions. The end result was that RACIAL QUOTAS were forbidden, but individualized "pluses" permitted. Steps could thus be taken to make amends for the legacy of past invidious racialism, but a narrow tailoring of program to rationale was required.

Although no other Justice joined Powell's opinion in *Bakke*, Powell generally succeeded in establishing both the framework and the tone for the Supreme Court's affirmative action JURISPRUDENCE over the next ten years. The legal framework, subject to possible exception only in cases of congressional action, required compelling justifications, even for noninvidious or compensatory racial preferences. The tone reflected Powell's sense that the underlying issues were too hard, both morally and legally, to be settled other than on a case-by-case basis that would permit some accommodation, however crude, of the competing values at stake. In a series of cases involving employment and promotions, Powell's vote made the majority for the proposition that racial preferences would be allowed under the Constitution when reasonably necessary to correct for past discrimination by the institution implementing an affirmative action program or subject to a remedial judicial order. But he also insisted that racial classifications should be disfavored and, writing for a plurality of the Court in WYGANT V. JACKSON BOARD OF EDUCATION (1986), held that dispreferred whites may not be required to carry too heavy a burden in order to compensate for wrongs of which they personally are likely innocent. The resulting balance was not always neat, but it reflected Powell's sense that some sort of accommodation was needed.

Careful balancing and accommodation of competing interests also marked Powell's approach to the First Amendment. Perhaps his most important opinion on this subject came in GERTZ V. ROBERT WELCH, INC. (1974), which raised an issue about the scope of constitutional protection enjoyed by the press in suits for LIBEL. The common law generally had presumed liability for all defamatory speech, with the burden resting on the defendant to prove truth as a defense. In the landmark case of NEW YORK TIMES V. SULLIVAN (1964), however, the Supreme Court had recognized a constitutional privilege in cases involving speech about public officials in the performance of their official duties. Because of the public interest in promoting free and robust debate about governmental affairs, defamations of public officials were held to be constitutionally protected unless published "with actual malice," which the Court defined to mean with knowledge of their falsity or with reckless disregard for whether they were true or false. But the Court, following *New York Times*, had not reached a consensus on the scope of constitutional protection that should be accorded to other defamatory speech.

Carefully balancing the competing interests in FREEDOM OF SPEECH, FREEDOM OF THE PRESS, and the protection of individual reputation, Powell's *Gertz* opinion sought a middle ground. In order to avoid unwarranted "chilling" of the press as a result of threats of liability, Powell held that the states may not impose liability for libel in the absence of some showing of "fault." But neither, he concluded, did the First Amendment require that the state's interest in protecting its citizens' good names and reputations be sacrificed entirely. Where "private figures" are defamed, *Gertz* permits liability based on a showing that the press was negligent in publishing a false report. In actions brought by "public figures," whose stature or notoriety allows them greater opportunity to counter false allegations in the MARKETPLACE OF IDEAS, the balance shifts, and liability requires a demonstration of actual malice.

In addition to its balancing methodology, Powell's First Amendment jurisprudence was notable for its sensitivity to the role of a free press in making democracy work. In GANNETT CO., INC. V. DEPASQUALE (1979) Powell argued in a concurring opinion that the First Amendment required at least a presumptive right of the press to attend and report on criminal trials. His views about rights of access to judicial proceedings were substantially adopted by the Court a year later in RICHMOND NEWSPAPERS V. VIRGINIA (1980). But Powell would have gone further. In provocative dissenting opinions in *Saxbe v. Washington Post Co.* (1974) and *Houchins v. KQED* (1978), he argued that the press, as a representative of the public, should have limited right of access to report on conditions inside prisons and presumably on the management of other governmental operations. From one perspective, Powell's views in these cases seem in tension with his generally respectful and deferential stance toward local government and political authority. From another, his position reflects a powerful inner logic. Local government deserves deference only insofar as it represents the informed judgments of its citizens. When government conducts its affairs in unnecessary secrecy, Powell believed, the moral foundations of democracy erode.

The need to strike a balance between deference to democratically accountable decision makers and the protection of competing constitutional values was also a main theme in Powell's opinions involving PROCEDURAL DUE PROCESS. In this area, too, he emerged as one of the Court's intellectual leaders. Writing in MATHEWS V. ELDRIDGE. (1976), Powell developed a three part BALANCING TEST that has since become ubiquitous in the Supreme Court's procedural due process cases. To determine whether the government has provided adequate procedural safeguards against the erroneous deprivation of a citizen's liberty or PROPERTY RIGHTS, Powell held, the Court must weigh and balance the magnitude of the individual interests at stake; the government's interests, including those in cheap and efficient administration; and the reduction in the risk of error that more-extensive procedures might yield.

Powell was also an important figure in cases involving SUBSTANTIVE DUE PROCESS issues. He joined the initial 7–2 majority recognizing constitutional abortion rights in ROE V. WADE (1973) and remained committed to *Roe's* analytical framework throughout his tenure on the Court. As the Court later grew more polarized on abortion issues, Powell's centrist line-drawing often proved decisive in making 5–4 majorities. Powell also cast the swing vote in BOWERS V. HARDWICK. (1986), holding that the Constitution's protection of the right of PRIVACY and the right of procreation

does not extend to homosexual sodomy. In a characteristically accommodationist gesture, however, he suggested that a severe criminal penalty might offend the constitutional prohibition against CRUEL AND UNUSUAL PUNISHMENT.

Early in his career on the Supreme Court, Justice Powell won high praise from influential commentators for his skillful and judicious use of a balancing approach to constitutional questions. Although never defined with great precision, balancing—as practiced in *Matthew v. Eldridge*, for example—calls for the identification of all relevant and competing interests, and the striking of a balance for the case at hand; slight changes in the catalogue of affected interests, or the degree of their implication, could alter the result in the next case. Partly because of the looseness with which definitions of balancing are formulated, it is difficult to say how sharply balancing differs from other approaches to CONSTITUTIONAL INTERPRETATION. Much depends on how the specification of relevant interests fit into, or competes with, judicial reliance on such factors as the constitutional text, constitutional history, precedent, constitutional structure, and traditional or consensus values.

Nevertheless, the view seems to be gaining currency that balancing is the currently predominant approach to constitutional interpretation and that Justice Powell was a leading figure in popularizing this methodology. Some commentators have offered the further argument that balancing is a deficient or even a bankrupt method of constitutional analysis. And at least one, Professor Paul Kahn, has argued that its deficiencies are damningly exhibited in Justice Powell's opinions. Powell's balancing, according to this criticism, was ad hoc, unpredictable, and subjective. Moreover, his approach to judging misconceived the JUDICIAL FUNCTION, which is to identify and hierarchically array constitutional principles of sufficient clarity and generality to offer clear guidance both to lower courts and to political decision makers.

These criticisms are at best overstated. Powell's case-by-case balancing approach located him in a time-honored tradition of practical thinking in which principles—whether legal or moral—represent the distilled wisdom of carefully individualized judgments. Adherents of this approach, which has found its way into the traditions of common law adjudication and of constitutional interpretation as well, argue forcefully that it is a practical and intellectual mistake to rest on rules that are too broad for their correctness to be rationally vindicated in advance. And Powell, when he thought rational vindication possible, did not hesitate to paint with a broad brush. He did so, for example, in establishing First Amendment lines and categories in *Gertz v. Robert Welch, Inc.*

It is a seperate charge that Powell's mode of balancing—in the affirmative action cases, for example—represented JUDICIAL POLICYMAKING that was insufficiently rooted in traditional sources of legal authority to qualify as anything more than judicial second-guessing of a political judgment. Powell, his critics argue, located himself too much "inside" the political community and wrongly tried to bring the community's values to bear on constitutional questions; instead, a Justice should locate himself outside the community in the lofty and frequently astringent principles of the Constitution. The fallacy in this criticism is that there is ultimately no helpful interpretive position "outside" the constitutional community. A Supreme Court Justice, like anyone, must read the Constitution from inside the society to which its lofty generalities must be applied. And it would be folly to think that a constitutional interpreter should try to ignore the society's needs and values. For Powell, traditional sources of legal authority retained their force. But Powell looked at them, and appropriately so, from a point of view that sought to reach sound, practical solutions to constitutional problems.

It is a somewhat more telling argument against the characteristic jurisprudence of Justice Powell that, in the search for a pragmatic balance—in the effort to keep competitive values in a position approaching equipoise or to achieve what he thought was a sensible result in a particular case—he sometimes drew lines that were too fine or too ad hoc to withstand critical scrutiny. Certainly Powell's humanitarian instincts sometimes caused him to distinguish relevant "conservative" precedents, including those that he had authored, by force of little more than ipse dixit. His concurring opinion in PLYLER V. DOE (1982), distinguishing SAN ANTONIO INDEPENDENT SCHOOL DISTRICT V. RODRIGUEZ and holding that Texas could not withhold free public education from illegal-alien children, falls into this category. Some have argued that the *Bakke* line between forbidden racial quotas and permissible individual preferences is intellectually untenable.

Finally, Powell's sense of what was prudent or practically necessary sometimes overrode both the force of contending arguments and considerations of fairness. In MCCLESKY V. KEMP (1987), for example, the petitioner introduced statistical evidence establishing that blacks are more likely to be sentenced to death than are whites and that the killers of whites are more than four times more likely to be executed than are killers of blacks. This evidence, McClesky argued, required reversal of his death sentence under both the constitutional prohibition against cruel and unusual punishment and the equal protection clause. Justice Powell disagreed. In an opinion of unusual candor, he argued that the Court must reject the plaintiff's argument partly because of the far-reaching implications of its underlying premise. "McClesky's claim, taken to its

logical conclusion, throws into serious question the principles that underlie our entire CRIMINAL JUSTICE SYSTEM," Powell wrote. If statistical demonstrations of systemic disparities could establish individual unfairness, the Court "could soon be faced with similar claims [against] other types of penalty" from members of other disadvantaged groups. Powell plainly regarded this prospect as practically intolerable.

Although happily atypical in some respects, *McClesky* was, in fact, a characteristic Powell decision. Exemplifying the role of Justice as statesman, Powell repeatedly experienced conflicts of competing values about how a Supreme Court Justice, with his mission conceived to include a component of prudent statesmanship, ought to act. In cases in which competing values conflict, it is always easy to criticize any particular decision as striking the wrong balance. The harder and more interesting question is whether Powell, in embracing the obligations of prudent statesmanship, conceived his judicial role correctly. Although retirement encomiums are perhaps not the strongest evidence, Powell, upon stepping down from the Supreme Court, was widely hailed as a model Supreme Court Justice of the modern age.

RICHARD FALLON
(1992)

Bibliography

ALEINIKOFF, T. ALEXANDER 1987 Constitutional Law in the Age of Balancing. *Yale Law Journal* 96:943–1005.

FREEMAN, GEORGE CLEMON 1988 Justice Powell's Constitutional Opinions. *Washington and Lee Law Review* 45:411–465.

GUNTHER, GERALD 1972 In Search of Judicial Quality on a Changing Court: The Case of Justice Powell. *Stanford Law Review* 24:1001–1035.

KAHN, PAUL W. 1987 The Court, the Community and the Judicial Balance: The Jurisprudence of Justice Powell. *Yale Law Journal* 97:1–60.

MALTZ, EARL M. 1979 Portrait of a Man in the Middle—Mr. Justice Powell, Equal Protection, and the Pure Classification Problem. *Ohio State Law Journal* 40:941–964.

SYNPOSIUM 1982 In Honor of Justice Lewis F. Powell, Jr. *Virginia Law Review* 68:161–458.

TRIBUTE 1987 Tribute to Justice Lewis F. Powell, Jr. *Harvard Law Review* 101:395–420.

UROFSKY, MELVIN I. 1984 Mr. Justice Powell and Education: The Balancing of Competing Values. *Journal of Law and Education* 13:581–627.

POWELL, THOMAS REED
(1880–1955)

Constitutional lawyer and political scientist Thomas Reed Powell taught for twenty-five years at Harvard Law

School. He was a prolific writer of articles on constitutional law and especially on the issues of STATE TAXATION OF COMMERCE and INTERGOVERNMENTAL IMMUNITIES from taxation. His published analyses of constitutional DOCTRINES and Supreme Court decisions frequently influenced the future course of constitutional law, as, for example, in reducing the protection from taxation afforded by the ORIGINAL PACKAGE DOCTRINE. He was also a commentator on the activities of the Supreme Court: he was critical of its anti-NEW DEAL decisions in the 1930s, of the proliferation of separate opinions in the 1940s, and of the prevalence of rhetorical excess over rigorous logic at all times. His last public lectures were published in 1956 as *Vagaries and Varieties in Constitutional Law.*

DENNIS J. MAHONEY
(1986)

POWELL v. ALABAMA
287 U.S. 45 (1932)

Powell was the famous "Scottsboro boys" case in which "young, ignorant, illiterate blacks were convicted and sentenced to death without the effective appointment of counsel to aid them. The trials were in a hostile community, far from the defendants' homes; the accusation was rape of two white women, a crime "regarded with especial horror in the community."

In an early major use of the DUE PROCESS clause to regulate the administration of criminal justice by the states, the Supreme Court held that the trials were fundamentally unfair. The facts of the case made this portentous holding an easy one: the defendants were tried in one day, the defense was entirely pro forma, and the death sentence was immediately imposed on all seven defendants without regard to individual culpability or circumstance. *Powell* was not a Sixth Amendment RIGHT TO COUNSEL case; three decades would pass before that guarantee was imported into due process in GIDEON V. WAINWRIGHT (1963). But the language of the Court in expounding the importance of counsel to a fair trial was repeatedly quoted as the Sixth Amendment right developed: "[the layman] lacks both the skill and knowledge adequately to prepare his defense, even though he has a perfect one. He requires the guiding hand of counsel at every step in the proceedings against him. Without it, though he be not guilty, he faces the danger of conviction because he does not know how to establish his innocence."

Although *Powell* is usually cited as a case in which defendants had no counsel at all, there was actually a lawyer at their side, but he came late into the case and was unfamiliar with Alabama law. In discussing the failure of due process, the Court referred to the lack of investigation and consultation by this last-minute volunteer. Thus, *Powell* has implications for the developing doctrine of ineffective assistance of counsel.

BARBARA ALLEN BABCOCK
(1986)

POWELL v. MCCORMACK
395 U.S. 486 (1969)

Adam Clayton Powell, Jr., a flamboyant clergyman of indifferent ethics, for many years represented a New York City district in Congress. In 1967, after Powell won reelection despite a conviction for criminal contempt of court and a record of misappropriation of public funds, the HOUSE OF REPRESENTATIVES denied him a seat. In a special election, he received eighty-six percent of the votes and again appeared to take his seat. The House then passed a resolution "excluding" Powell.

Powell and thirteen of his constituents then sued Speaker John McCormack and several other officers of the House of Representatives. Powell lost in both the District Court and the Court of Appeals, and his case was not heard by the Supreme Court until after the Ninetieth Congress had adjourned. Powell had, in the meanwhile, been reelected, and was seated as a member of the Ninety-First Congress.

The Supreme Court, in an 8–1 decision, declined to hold the case moot, finding that Powell's claim for back pay was sufficient for a justiciable controversy. In an opinion by Chief Justice EARL WARREN, the Court proceeded to overturn some long-standing assumptions about the constitutional status of CONGRESSIONAL MEMBERSHIP.

The Court held that the houses of Congress, although they are the judges of the qualifications provided in the Constitution itself (Article I, section 5) may not add to the qualifications provided in the Constitution (Article I, section 2). If a person elected to the House is qualified by age, CITIZENSHIP, and residence, he may not be excluded. Of course, once a member has been seated, he may be expelled by a two-thirds vote for any offense the House believes is "inconsistent with the trust and duty of a member" (*In re Chapman*, 1897). But, in Powell's case the Court held that exclusion was not equivalent to expulsion. (See POLITICAL QUESTIONS.)

DENNIS J. MAHONEY
(1986)

POWELL v. PENNSYLVANIA

See: Waite Court

PRAGMATISM

Pragmatism, generally considered to be our only indigenous school of philosophic thought, has profoundly influenced the development of American jurisprudence in the twentieth century. This influence is evident in a variety of legal settings, including the field of constitutional law, where debates over the proper interpretive role of the courts continue to focus upon issues first raised in a systematic way by the early philosophers of pragmatism, notably John Dewey.

The school of philosophical pragmatism emerged only in the late nineteenth century, but it is more deeply rooted in the American past than that date implies. Thus, we see in ALEXIS DE TOCQUEVILLE's description of the American philosophical method a preview of what later became, in the works of Charles Peirce, William James, Dewey, and others, a schematically developed general theory: "To evade the bondage of system and habit, of family-maxims, class opinions, and, in some degree, of national prejudices; to accept tradition only as a means of information, and existing facts only as a lesson to be used in doing otherwise and doing better; to seek the reason of things for oneself, and in oneself alone; to tend to results without being bound to means, and to strike through the form to the substance—such are the principal characteristics of what I shall call the philosophical method of the Americans." In this account of philosophical temperament are the core elements of the reconstruction in philosophy that came to dominate constitutional discourse in the twentieth century: an instrumental approach to knowledge based upon a rigorous empiricism, a demystification of the past as a predicate for facilitating change, and an ethical orientation that finds in the application of a norm or concept the criterion of its value.

The emergence of the pragmatic movement in philosophy occurred at a critical juncture in American constitutional history. At a time when constitutional orthodoxy was embodied in the person of Justice STEPHEN J. FIELD, the appeal of pragmatic ideas to critics of the dominant view lay in the promise it held for achieving a congruence between law and the needs of a society undergoing rapid flux and transition. In place of a formalistic approach characterized by the derivation of absolute principles that are grounded in nature and from which constitutional conclusions can be deduced with certainty in support of social inequality, the pragmatists offered the prospect of deriving relative principles that are grounded in experience and from which constitutional conclusions of a tentative nature can be inductively assembled in support of a more egalitarian society. The application of pragmatism to constitutional reasoning supported the claim that law should not be an impediment to progress, that the Constitution was not a document embodying immutable principles but one whose meaning depended upon the circumstances of time and place.

In developing their legal theory, the pragmatists both drew on and rejected existing jurisprudential schools of thought. They were critical of the syllogistic process of legal reasoning that they found common to both the philosophical and analytical schools. In the application of ethical considerations by the NATURAL RIGHTS theorists and in the abandonment of such considerations by the analytical positivists, they also found a similar detachment from the realities of the social situation. In the first case ethics was not grounded in experience, and in the second, reality was disorted by the failure to understand the ethical imperitives implied in experience. The object of the pragmatists was thus to establish an empirical jurisprudence that included a consciousness of the moral basis of law. The attraction of pragmatic philosophy was its potential for steering a middle course between the positivistic seperation of law and morality, on the one hand, and, on the other, the natural-rights fusion law and morality according to the standards derived outside of experience. Both extremes led to judicial potection of the status quo, the first by accepting the legitimacy of any existing legal arrangments and the second by freezing the law into a mold formed by metaphysical abstractions. Justice, for the pragmatists, was not to be defined a priori; nor was it identifiable with the will of the sovereign. Rather, it was to be defined "transactionally," emerging out of social experience as an end to be juridically achieved. Acceptance of this view by jurists would make it unnecessary to appeal to noncontextual sources, such as an absolute standard of right conduct embodied in the text of the Constitution.

The principal theorists of legal pragmatism, BENJAMIN N. CARDOZO and ROSCOE POUND, wrote most often about private law, but both maintained that their prescriptions applied equally well to constitutional law. Cardozo's "method of sociology" and Pound's "theory of social interests" were intended in part to translate the precepts of Dewey and James into jurisprudential terms of potentially transformative significance for the Constitution. In the case of Dewey, who had addressed himself to legal questions, the translation was fairly straightforward. In his account of the law, legal rules and principles were viewed pragmatically as "working hypotheses" whose validity was to be ascertained by their application in concrete situations. Dewey also held the work of the Founding Fathers to be much less the object of reverence than had traditionally been the case: "The belief in political fixity, of the sanctity of some form of state consecrated by the efforts of our fathers and hallowed by tradition, is one of the stumbling-blocks in the way of orderly and directed change; it is an invitation to revolt and revolution." Just as the antifoundationalist emphasis in contemporary philosophy—the denial that knowledge must be based upon certain objective truths—owes much to the work of the early pragmatists, so too does the currently popular disparagement of the doctrine of ORIGINAL INTENT in CONSTITUTIONAL INTERPRETATION. Therefore, the contention that the Constitution embodies foundational principles of justice that reflect the original intentions of its Framers, is doubly problematic, and it carries minimal weight in the pragmatic account of constitutional interpretation.

The judge most often associated with philosophical pragmatism is OLIVER WENDELL HOLMES. JR. Although he occasionally criticized some of the formulations of pragmatists, his work as a Supreme Court Justice (as well as his extrajudicial writings) often manifested a pragmatic approach to the Constitution. More important, his opinions inspired many others whose interest in pragmatism had less to do with the philosophical skepticism that appealed to Holmes than with the social reform possibilities implicit in its method. For example, Holmes's opinion in MISSOURI V. HOLLAND (1920) suggested that the needs of the twentieth century need not be held hostage to the assumptions of the eighteenth or nineteenth centuries: "The case before us must be considered in the light of our whole experience and not merely in that of what was said a hundred years ago." His famous dissenting opinion in ABRAMS V. UNITED STATES (1919) expressed in one short sentence the essence of the pragmatic conception of the Constitution. The theory of the Constitution, Holmes said, was that truth would emerge in the marketplace of ideas; the document "is an experiment, as all life is an experiment." This view often led Holmes to advocate judicial self-restraint; but in time it came to express a sentiment that provided jurisprudential support for a more activist, socially engaged judiciary. The work of the WARREN COURT exemplified an important legacy of the pragmatists (especially Dewey): the increasing reliance by the judiciary upon social science evidence. Holmes's role in this development is suggested in an observation of his that Dewey, in the elaboration of his pragmatic philosophy, saw fit to quote: "I have had in mind an ultimate dependence of law [upon science] because it is ultimately for science to determine, as far as it can, the relative worth of our different social ends."

The pragmatic conception of the Constitution has generated considerable controversy. Criticism centers on two distinct but related problems. The first is that the importation of pragmatic ideas into the arena of constitutional interpretation inevitably leads to the abandonment of any meaningful distinction between judicial and legislative modes of decision making. This has the effect, it is claimed, of undermining the legitimacy of the Supreme Court, an unfortunate outcome rendered no less unfortunate by assertions about the enhanced quality of the Court's output. The second is that a pragmatic jurisprudence provides inadequate protection for constitutional rights. By effectively reducing self-evident and immutable truths to the level of tentative rules, pragmatic judges risk sacrificing FUNDAMENTAL RIGHTS on the altar of social expedience. If the Constitution is a document lacking fixed points of reference and thus deprived of meanings that are not simply contextual (that is, situated in the experience of changing historical moments), can it serve as guarantor of rights that are in their ultimate sense expressive of an unchanging human nature?

GARY J. JACOBSOHN
(1992)

(SEE ALSO: *Conservatism; Judicial Activism and Judicial Restraint; Liberalism; Political Philosophy of the Constitution.*)

Bibliography

GREY, THOMAS C.   1989   Holmes and Legal Pragmatism. *Stanford Law Review* 41:787–870.
JACOBSOHN, GARY J.   1977   *Pragmatism, Statesmanship, and the Supreme Court.* Ithaca, N.Y.: Cornell University Press.
SUMMERS, ROBERT SAMUEL   1982   *Instrumentalism and American Legal Theory.* Ithaca, N.Y.: Cornell University Press.

PRAGMATISM
(Update)

In recent years the school of philosophy known as pragmatism has enjoyed a renaissance in legal thought. This renewal of interest can be traced to several factors, including the CRITICAL LEGAL STUDIES movement's radical critique of the notion that legal rules are neutral and apolitical; the work of feminists and postmodernists who stress the importance of situated experience in influencing our perceptions of reality; and interdisciplinary approaches to law such as LAW AND ECONOMICS THEORY, which contest the traditional view of law as an autonomous discipline. Though they differ in many particulars, these various movements within contemporary JURISPRUDENCE lead to an important question: If law does not consist of a set of immutable principles waiting to be discovered, and if our notions of truth are (to some degree) socially constructed, then how should judges and other decisionmakers choose among various competing alternatives? In the view of some scholars, pragmatism provides a coherent response to this question, as well as a method for charting a middle course between the traditional model of law as a neutral, self-contained enterprise and the nihilistic view of law as nothing more than politics by other means.

Although contemporary legal pragmatists comprise a

diverse group of scholars, falling along all segments of the political spectrum, most share a few core beliefs. First, most pragmatists agree that human knowledge is contextual, meaning that each of us views the world in light of the constraints imposed upon us by such factors as prior experience, culture, and language. The premise that knowledge is contextual in turn suggests, as Richard Warner writes in his description of legal pragmatism, that there is no external standard for evaluating our norms, but rather that "our norms of justification neither have nor need a ground outside themselves." Pragmatists therefore reject the concept known as "foundationalism," what Thomas Grey refers to as "the age-old philosopher's dream that knowledge might be grounded in a set of fundamental and indubitable beliefs." Viewing knowledge as antifoundational suggests, as Richard Rorty notes in discussing the thought of John Dewey, that law and other human institutions are best viewed not as "attempts to embody or formulate truth or goodness or beauty, but rather as instruments for solving problems." Thoughtful pragmatists, however, are careful to avoid equating pragmatic instrumentalism with utilitarianism. As Grey observes, pragmatists in the tradition of Dewey reject a sharp distinction between ends and means, claiming instead that the means we choose to implement our goals are never completely instrumental, but rather must be judged "by their intrinsic satisfactions or frustrations as well as by their consequences."

Adherence to these principles compels most legal pragmatists to reject attempts to ground the law in comprehensive "grand theories" and to reject the formalist ideal that correct outcomes can always be logically deduced from some overarching set of principles. Many pragmatists instead advocate the use of "practical reason," which Richard Bernstein describes as a way of mediating "between general principles and a concrete particular situation" through choice and deliberation. The term "practical reason" is not easily defined but, according to various formulations, denotes methods for reaching decisions based on, inter alia, an appreciation of consequences; a commitment to dialogue among competing views; and a grudging respect for "common sense" coupled with skepticism over what Joseph William Singer refers to as "unreflective reliance on commonsense intuitions."

The specific policy recommendations of legal pragmatists vary depending on their perception of the outcomes suggested by practical reason. More conservative pragmatists tend to stress the instrumental value of adherence to such socially constructed norms as fidelity to text, history, and judicial deference to other branches of government. Others take a more radical approach, arguing that a commitment to human flourishing (itself a norm that we are free to accept or reject) counsels in favor of paying closer attention to the voices of the marginalized and oppressed, whose perspectives often go unnoticed by more traditional approaches. Some pragmatists argue in favor of a greater reliance on the insights provided by the sciences, including the SOCIAL SCIENCES, while others remain skeptical.

Critiques of legal pragmatism come from many quarters. Those who find natural law or rights-based approaches to jurisprudence compelling take issue with the pragmatists' view of rights as a contingent (albeit useful) human construct. Stanley Fish argues that once pragmatists claim that specific policies "[follow] from the pragmatist account" they betray their "own first principle (which is to have none)." Still others argue that, at a general level, pragmatism consists of nothing but platitudes; and that, at the particular level, the wide divergence of opinion among pragmatist scholars suggests that pragmatism ultimately has nothing distinctive to say about law. From the pragmatic perspective, the response to these critiques is that the proof is in the pudding. If, as William James observed, the truth of a proposition resides in its consequences, then the "truth" of the pragmatic approach to law depends on its effects. Put another way, pragmatists ask that their methodology be judged by this simple standard: Does it work?

THOMAS F. COTTER
(2000)

(SEE ALSO: *Feminist Theory; Postmodernism and Constitutional Theory.*)

Bibliography

BERNSTEIN, RICHARD   1983   *Beyond Objectivism and Relativism.* Philadelphia: University of Pennsylvania Press.

COTTER, THOMAS F.   1996   Legal Pragmatism and the Law and Economics Movement. *Georgetown Law Journal* 84:2071–2141.

FARBER, DANIEL   1988   Legal Pragmatism and the Constitution. *Minnesota Law Review* 72:1331–1378.

FISH, STANLEY   1991   Almost Pragmatism. In Michael Brint and William Weaver, eds., *Pragmatism in Law & Society.* Boulder, Colo.: Westview Press.

GREY, THOMAS C.   1989   Holmes and Legal Pragmatism. *Stanford Law Review* 41:787–870.

POSNER, RICHARD A.   1988   *The Problems of Jurisprudence.* Cambridge, Mass.: Harvard University Press.

RORTY, RICHARD   1982   *Consequences of Pragmatism.* Minneapolis, Minn.: University of Minnesota Press.

SINGER, JOSEPH WILLIAM   1990   Property and Coercion in Federal Indian Law: The Conflict Between Critical and Complacent Pragmatism. *Southern California Law Review* 63:1821–1837.

SMITH, STEVEN D.   1990   The Pursuit of Pragmatism. *Yale Law Journal* 100:409–449.

WARNER, RICHARD   1993   Why Pragmatism? The Puzzling Place of Pragmatism in Critical Theory. *University of Illinois Law Review* 1993:535–563.

PRATT, CHARLES
(Lord Camden)
(1714–1794)

The leading WHIG constitutionalist of eighteenth-century England, Charles Pratt was appointed a judge after a career as a barrister and parliamentarian and service as attorney general. Arguing SEDITIOUS LIBEL cases, he had maintained that the jury was competent to decide the questions both of law and of fact. He was Chief Justice of the Court of Common Pleas from 1762 until 1766. In the WILKES CASES he declared GENERAL WARRANTS contrary to the principles of the constitution and held their issuance by secretaries of state illegal. He also discouraged prosecution of Roman Catholic recusants. As Baron (later Earl) Camden, he made his first speech in the House of Lords in 1765 supporting the American position on the Stamp Act. In the debates on the Declaratory Act he called TAXATION WITHOUT REPRESENTATION "sheer robbery" and denounced the fiction of virtual representation. He became Lord Chancellor in 1766 but resigned in 1770 after disagreeing with the cabinet about several matters, including policy toward America. He continued to support the American position in the House of Lords and, with Lord Chatham, favored reconciliation with the colonies. He returned to the cabinet in 1782 and was Lord President of the Council from 1784 until his death.

DENNIS J. MAHONEY

(1086)

PRAYERS IN SCHOOL

See: Religion in Public Schools; School Prayers

PREAMBLE

The part of the Constitution that we read first is the part of the original Constitution that was written last. The Preamble, which sets forth the noble purposes for which the Constitution is "ordained and established," was composed by the CONSTITUTIONAL CONVENTION's Committee of Style. The committee sat between September 8 and September 11, 1787, after the Convention had debated and voted on all of the substantive provisions of the Constitution; its mandate was to arrange and harmonize the wording of the resolutions adopted by the delegates during the preceding four months. The task of actually drafting the document fell to GOUVERNEUR MORRIS of New York, and so the authorship of the Preamble must be ascribed to him.

Morris made two major changes in the Preamble as it was reported by the Committee of Detail and referred to the Committee of Style. The earlier version had begun, "We, the people of the states of . . ." and then had listed the thirteen states in order, from north to south; Morris changed this to the now familiar "We, the people of the United States. . . ." And the earlier version had merely stated that the people ordained and established the Constitution; Morris added the list of purposes for which they did so. Each of these changes has been the occasion of some controversy.

The reference to the "people of the United States" was a source of irritation to the Anti-Federalists. PATRICK HENRY, for example, in the Virginia ratifying convention, denounced the use of the phrase as a harbinger of a national despotism. The Convention, he said, should have written instead, "We, the States. . . ." In ANTI-FEDERALIST CONSTITUTIONAL THOUGHT, only the states, as the existing political units, to which the people had already delegated all the powers of government, could constitute a federal union and redelegate some of their powers to the national government. Reference to the constituent authority of "the people of the United States" seemed to imply consolidation, not confederation.

It is unlikely that Morris, the Committee of Style, or the Convention had any such implication in mind. The Convention had approved a preamble that referred to the people of all thirteen states. The committee had to "harmonize" that with the provision that the Constitution would become effective when it was ratified by any nine states. There would likely be a time, therefore, when there would be nine states in the Union and four outside of it; but no one could predict which would be the nine and which the four. So long as the Constitution would become effective with less than thirteen states in the Union, listing the thirteen states in the Preamble would be misleading and inaccurate. Whichever states did ratify the Constitution would be the "United States," and it would be the people of those "United States" that had ordained the Constitution. Moreover, the Constitution provided for the future admission of additional states, and the people of those states, too, would ordain and establish the Constitution.

But Henry's objection was ill-founded for another reason. The DECLARATION OF INDEPENDENCE had pronounced the Americans "one people" and had given to their political Union the name of the "United States of America." The states and the Union had been born together on July 4, 1776, when a new nation was brought forth upon this continent. The one people certainly possessed the right to alter or abolish their former government and to establish a new government more conducive to their future safety and happiness. "We, the people of the United States," are identical to the "one people" that in the Declaration of Independence dissolved the political bonds that formerly connected us to Great Britain.

The list of purposes for ordaining and establishing the Constitution is perhaps more perplexing. The Convention had never debated or voted on such a list; and yet each delegate must have had some such purposes in mind throughout the deliberations. How else could he have gauged or judged the propriety of the measures upon which he did debate and vote? Morris and the Committee of Style must have thought it fitting to provide this terse apologia for their summer's deliberations; and the delegates apparently agreed, for there is no record of any objection to the Preamble as it was reported by the committee.

The Preamble lists the purposes for which the Constitution was created: to form a more perfect Union, to establish justice, to insure domestic tranquillity, to provide for the common defense, to promote the general welfare, and to secure the blessings of liberty, not only for the founding generation but also for "posterity." It, in effect, declares to a candid world the causes for which the people have chosen to replace the ARTICLES OF CONFEDERATION with a new Constitution. The purposes listed in the Preamble are consistent with what the Declaration of Independence asserts to be the end of all governments instituted among men, namely to secure the equal and inalienable natural rights of all to life, liberty, and the pursuit of happiness.

The Preamble does not purport to create any offices or to confer any powers; as JOSEPH STORY later wrote, "Its true office is to expound the nature and extent and application of the powers actually conferred by the Constitution, and not substantially to create them." Although COMMENTATORS ON THE CONSTITUTION have, over the years, purported to find in the Preamble justification for the exercise of INHERENT POWERS of government, no court has ever held that the Preamble independently grants power to the government or to any of its officers or agencies. In fact, in *Jacobson v. Massachusetts* (1905), the Supreme Court specifically rejected that interpretation.

The Preamble concludes by proclaiming that the people "do ordain and establish this Constitution." EDWARD S. CORWIN correctly pointed to the active voice and present tense of this phrase. The act of constituting a government occurs at a particular moment in time; but the authority of the Constitution depends on the continuous consent of the governed. The people, as Corwin wrote, " 'do ordain and establish,' *not* did ordain and establish." Thus does the Preamble play its role in the preservation of constitutional government. An afterthought of the Constitu-

tional Convention, a rhetorical flourish by the Committee of Style, the Preamble has been memorized by schoolchildren and declaimed by orators and statesmen on public occasions for two centuries. And every time it is recited it calls to mind the purposes of our federal Union and unites the people more firmly to the cause of republican liberty.

DENNIS J. MAHONEY
(1986)

Bibliography

CORWIN, EDWARD S.   1920   *The Constitution and What It Means Today.* Princeton, N.J.: Princeton University Press.
EIDELBERG, PAUL   1968   *The Political Philosophy of the Constitution.* New York: Free Press.
ROSSITER, CLINTON   1966   *1787: The Grand Convention.* New York: Macmillan.

PRECEDENT

In MARBURY V. MADISON (1803) Chief Justice JOHN MARSHALL rested the legitimacy of JUDICIAL REVIEW of the constitutionality of legislation on the necessity for courts to "state what the law is" in particular cases. The implicit assumption is that the Constitution is law, and that the content of constitutional law is determinate—that it can be known and applied by judges. From the time of the nation's founding, lawyers and judges trained in the processes of the COMMON LAW have assumed that the law of the Constitution is to be found not only in the text of the document and the expectations of the Framers but also in judicial precedent: the opinions of judges on "what the law is," written in the course of deciding earlier cases. (See STARE DECISIS.)

Inevitably, issues that burned brightly for the Framers of the Constitution and of its various amendments have receded from politics into history. The broad language of much of the Constitution's text leaves open a wide range of choices concerning interpretation. As the body of judicial precedent has grown, it has taken on a life of its own; the very term "constitutional law," for most lawyers today, primarily calls to mind the interpretations of the Constitution contained in the Supreme Court's opinions. For a lawyer writing a brief, or a judge writing an opinion, the natural style of argumentation is the common law style, with appeals to one or another "authority" among the competing analogies offered by a large and still growing body of precedent.

The same considerations that support reliance on precedent in common law decisions apply in constitutional adjudications: the need for stability in the law and for evenhanded treatment of litigants. Yet adherence to precedent has also been called the control of the living by the dead. Earlier interpretations of the Constitution, when they seem to have little relevance to the conditions of society and government here and now, do give way. As Chief Justice EARL WARREN wrote in BROWN V. BOARD OF EDUCATION (1954), "In approaching [the problem of school SEGREGATION, we cannot turn the clock back to 1868 when the [FOURTEENTH] AMENDMENT was adopted, or even to 1896 when PLESSY [V. FERGUSON] was written. We must consider public education in the light of its full development and its present place in American life. . . ." Justice OLIVER WENDELL HOLMES put the matter more pungently: "It is revolting to have no better reason for a rule of law than that so it was laid down in the time of Henry IV."

Although the Supreme Court decides only those issues that come to it in the ordinary course of litigation, the Court has a large measure of control over its own doctrinal agenda. The selection of about 150 cases for review each year (out of more than 4,000 cases brought to the Court) is influenced most of all by the Justices' views of the importance of the issues presented. (See CERTIORARI, WRIT OF.) And when the Court does break new doctrinal ground, it invites further litigation to explore the area thus opened. For example, scores of lawsuits were filed all over the country once the Court had established the precedent, in BAKER V. CARR (1962), that the problem of legislative REAPPORTIONMENT was one that the courts could properly address. The Justices see themselves, and are seen by the Court's commentators, as being in the business of developing constitutional DOCTRINE through the system of precedent. The decision of particular litigants' cases today appears to be important mainly as an instrument to those lawmaking ends. The theory of *Marbury v. Madison*, in other words, has been turned upside down.

Lower court judges pay meticulous attention to Supreme Court opinions as their main source of guidance for decision in constitutional cases. Supreme Court Justices themselves, however, give precedent a force that is weaker in constitutional cases than in other areas of the law. In a famous expression of this view, Justice LOUIS D. BRANDEIS, dissenting in *Burnet v. Coronado Oil & Gas Co.* (1932), said, "in cases involving the Federal Constitution, where correction through legislative action is practically impossible, this court has often overruled its earlier decisions. The court bows to the lessons of experience and the force of better reasoning, recognizing that the process of trial and error, so fruitful in the physical sciences, is appropriate also in the judicial function."

Although this sentiment is widely shared, Justices often are prepared to defer to their reading of precedent even when they disagree with the conclusions that produced the earlier decisions. Justice JOHN MARSHALL HARLAN, for example, regularly accepted the authoritative force of

WARREN COURT opinions from which he had dissented vigorously. The Court as an institution occasionally takes the same course, making clear that it is following the specific dictates of an earlier decision because of the interest in stability of the law, even though that decision may be out of line with more recent doctrinal developments.

The Supreme Court is regularly criticized, both from within the Court and from the outside, for failing to follow precedent. But a thoroughgoing consistency of decision cannot be expected, given the combination of three characteristics of the Court's decisional process. First, the Court is a collegiate body, with the nine Justices exercising individual judgment on each case. Second, the body of precedent is now enormous, with the result that in most cases decided by the Court there are arguable precedents for several alternative doctrinal approaches, and even for reaching opposing results. Indeed, the system for selecting cases for review guarantees that the court will regularly face hard cases—cases that are difficult because they can plausibly be decided in more than one way. Finally, deference to precedent itself may mean that issues will be decided differently, depending on the order in which they come before the Court. The Court's decision in *In re Griffiths* (1973), that a state cannot constitutionally limit the practice of law to United States citizens, is still a good precedent; yet, if the case had come up in 1983, almost certainly it would have been decided differently. (See ALIENS.)

The result of this process is an increasingly fragmented Supreme Court, with more PLURALITY OPINIONS and more statements by individual Justices of their own separate views in CONCURRING OPINIONS and dissents—thus presenting an even greater range of materials on which Justices can draw in deciding the next case. In these circumstances, it is not surprising that some plurality opinions, such as that in MOORE V. CITY OF EAST CLEVELAND (1977), are regularly cited as if they had a precedent value equal to that of OPINIONS OF THE COURT.

The range of decisional choice offered to a Supreme Court Justice by this process is so wide as to call into the question the idea of principled decision on which the legitimacy of judicial review is commonly assumed to rest. Yet the hard cases that fill the Supreme Court's docket—the very cases that make constitutional law and thus fill the casebooks that law students study—do not typify the functioning of constitutional law. A great many controversies of constitutional dimension never get to court, because the law seems clear, on the basis of precedent; similarly, many cases that do get to court are easily decided in the lower courts. Although we celebrate the memory of our creative Justices—Justices who are remembered for setting precedent, not following it—the body of constitutional law remains remarkably stable. In a stable society it could not be otherwise. As Holmes himself said in another context, "historic continuity with the past is not a duty, it is only a necessity."

KENNETH L. KARST
(1986)

Bibliography

EASTERBROOK, FRANK H.   1982   Ways of Criticizing the Court. *Harvard Law Review* 95:802–832.

LEVI, EDWARD H.   1949   *An Introduction to Legal Reasoning.* Chicago: University of Chicago Press.

LLEWELLYN, KARL N.   1960   *The Common Law Tradition.* Boston: Little, Brown.

MONAGHAN, HENRY P.   1979   Taking Supreme Court Opinions Seriously. *Maryland Law Review* 39:1–26.

PREEMPTION

The SUPREMACY CLAUSE of the Constitution (Article VI, clause 2) requires that inconsistent state laws yield to valid federal laws. Preemption is the term applied to describe invalidation of state laws by superior federal law.

Strictly speaking, the issue of preemption is not one of constitutional law. The issue is not what Congress has the power to do, but what Congress has done. Where Congress has made an articulate decision whether particular state laws should survive a new scheme of federal regulation, the issue is settled. For example, in enacting minimum federal standards for automobile pollution control equipment in 1967, Congress prohibited states from enforcing more restrictive standards but made an exception for the State of California. There has been no need for litigation to mark the contours of preemption in that context. Insofar as there is a "doctrine" of preemption, it concerns the treatment of preemption by federal laws where Congress has ignored the issue.

Since preemption cases theoretically turn on construction of federal statutes to determine whether Congress intended to preempt state laws, there are limits to generalizations that can be drawn from the decisions. Each case construes a federal statute with a distinct regulatory structure and legislative history. It is particularly difficult to classify the simplest form of preemption cases—those where the claim is made that the terms of federal and state law are flatly inconsistent. Federal law may, for example, give express permission to engage in conduct prohibited by state law. An early famous case of this type was GIBBONS V. OGDEN (1824).

The most complex issues of preemption arise where it is concededly possible to comply with mandates of both state and federal law. The question then arises whether Congress intended to "occupy the field," or whether the challenged state law's enforcement would interfere inordinately with the policies of the federal law. State law may provide additional sanctions for conduct prohibited by federal law. (In *California v. Zook,* 1949, the Court sustained a state law that punished interstate motor transport operating without a federal permit.) State law may impose more stringent regulations than federal law. (In *Napier v. Atlantic Coast Line R.R.,* 1926, the Court held that a state law requiring railroad safety equipment was preempted by a federal law that required less equipment.) Finally, it may be argued that state law is, in some general way, inconsistent with the purposes of federal law. (In *New York Telephone Co. v. New York State Department of Labor,* 1979, the Court sustained state payment of unemployment compensation benefits to strikers as not inconsistent with the policy of free COLLECTIVE BARGAINING under federal labor law.)

The Court has announced general tests for determining whether Congress has "occupied the field." An often-quoted summary of the standards for finding congressional intent to preempt state law is contained in *Rice v. Santa Fe Elevator Corp.* (1947). "The scheme of federal regulation may be so pervasive as to make reasonable the inference that Congress left no room for the States to supplement it. . . . Or the Act of Congress may touch a field in which the federal interest is so dominant that the federal system will be assumed to preclude enforcement of state laws on the same subject. . . . Or the state policy may produce a result inconsistent with the objective of the federal statute." These standards are peculiarly devoid of content, as the Court admitted in the sentence following those just quoted: "It is often a perplexing question whether Congress has precluded state action or by the choice of selective regulatory measures has left the POLICE POWER of the States undisturbed except as the state and federal regulations collide."

The lack of any pattern to the preemption cases can be explained in that each case seeks to ascertain congressional intent in a unique context. Since, however, contentious preemption questions arise precisely because Congress has ignored the existence of related state laws, the "intent of Congress" is a fiction that fails to describe the Court's decision process. The controlling factors in judicial decision are similar to those that would have confronted the intelligent legislator who had grappled with them. The judges' social values, views as to the legislative wisdom of the federal and state laws, and general views of the federal system may be as decisive as technical consideration of how well the federal and state schemes would mesh.

In many cases, there are potential issues of constitutional validity of the challenged state law in addition to the preemption question. Some preemption decisions can be explained as a part of the Court's general practice of avoiding unnecessary constitutional questions. Often, the preemption question is decided, articulately or *sub silentio*, by the same criteria that would have governed the avoided constitutional question. The preemption doctrine may be preferred by the Court because the judicial decision striking down a state law is tentative, and congressional attention is invited to the issue. If Congress does nothing, the issue is avoided. If Congress makes an articulate choice to withdraw the preemption barrier, the inescapable constitutional question benefits from the additional data supplied by congressional decision. A final attraction of the preemption rationale, beyond the tentativeness of a preemption decision, may be that each decision can be truly ad hoc, resting on a fictional finding of congressional intent to preempt that governs only the particular federal statutory scheme before the Court.

WILLIAM COHEN
(1986)

Bibliography

COHEN, WILLIAM 1982 Congressional Power to Define State Power to Regulate Commerce: Consent and Pre-emption. Pages 523–547 in Terrance Sandalow and Eric Stein, eds., *Courts and Free Markets: Perspectives from the United States and Europe.* Oxford: Clarendon Press.

CRAMTOM, ROGER 1956 Pennsylvania v. Nelson: A Case Study in Federal Preemption. *University of Chicago Law Review* 26:85–108.

PREEMPTION
(Update)

Preemption means that, as a result of the exercise of federal authority in a given regulatory area, preexisting concurrent state authority to regulate that same area comes to an end. Although earlier in this century, the Supreme Court viewed preemption as an automatic consequence of federal entry into a regulatory field, the modern view understands preemption as a discretionary constitutional power of Congress (and, by delegation, of federal ADMINISTRATIVE AGENCIES), the exercise of which requires manifestation of an intent to preempt the states. This change is reflected in the modern presumption against preemption, a presumption that concurrent state authority survives the exercise of federal regulatory power.

Congress has the power to rebut this presumption and preempt state authority regardless of the content of any state law—even if, for example, existing state law is substantively identical to the federal scheme of regulation or there is no state law at all in the relevant area. By exercising its power of preemption, the federal authority elects to monopolize a regulatory field, in whole or in part.

The fact that conflict between the contents of state and federal law is not necessary for preemption to occur distinguishes preemption from the related but separate principle of the supremacy of federal law enshrined in the SUPREMACY CLAUSE of the Constitution. This principle means that a valid federal law trumps an otherwise valid state law if (and only if) the two conflict with each other. Unlike preemption, the operation of the supremacy clause does not end general state authority in an area, but results in the trumping of a particular state law by a particular federal law where the two conflict. So, for example, a new state law passed to avoid the conflict would not be prevented from taking full legal effect. Moreover, once Congress has exercised its power of preemption, no state authority survives in the preempted field so that there can no longer be a valid state law in conflict with the federal one to trigger operation of the supremacy clause. The latter operates only where concurrent state authority exists and has not already been preempted.

Preemption thus not only differs from the principle of supremacy but also constitutes a broader inroad on state authority than the latter. One important implication of this point is that the (greater) federal power to preempt state authority cannot derive from the (lesser) principle of supremacy contained in the supremacy clause—as is widely assumed—but must have some other source in the Constitution.

The Court's "preemption doctrine" holds that Congress can exercise its preemption power either expressly—by clearly stating in the legislative text whether, and to what extent, state authority survives its new regulatory scheme—or impliedly. Notwithstanding the absence of any explicit statement on the issue, Congress's intent to preempt may be implicitly contained in a statute's structure and purpose.

The Court has recognized two types of such implied preemption. The first, termed "field preemption," is, according to *Rice v. Santa Fe Elevator Corp.* (1947), where the scheme of federal regulation is "so pervasive as to make reasonable the inference that Congress left no room for the States to supplement it." The second, known as "conflict preemption," is, according to *Hines v. Davidowitz* (1941), where compliance with both federal and state regulation is a physical impossibility or where state law "stands as an obstacle to the accomplishment and execution of the full purposes and objectives of Congress."

There is obviously significant tension between the general notion of implied preemption and the modern presumption against preemption. Because the presumption means the states are not preempted unless that is "the clear and manifest purpose of Congress," it might well be thought that such purpose can, or at least should, only be expressly manifested. Even assuming the general legitimacy of inferring preemptive intent, however, there are specific problems with both types of implied preemption. First, the doctrine of field preemption is arguably too blunt an interpretive instrument and ignores alternative readings of congressional intent that might be reached by an unmediated interpretation of the relevant statute. The proposition that in itself the pervasiveness or comprehensiveness of a scheme of federal regulation makes reasonable an inference of preemptive intent may be both overinclusive and underinclusive with respect to any particular scheme. Overinclusive because, notwithstanding its comprehensiveness, Congress may (1) intend that the states be permitted to supplement it, (2) not have considered the issue, or (3) have considered it but not reached agreement. Underinclusive because Congress may intend to preempt state law while leaving the field relatively, or even entirely, unregulated by any level of government.

Second, the DOCTRINE of conflict preemption is either a contradiction in terms or it similarly imputes to Congress an intent that may be highly questionable in practice. On its face, the proposition that state law is preempted if it conflicts with federal law appears to express the most basic confusion between the distinct principles of preemption and supremacy. The trumping of an otherwise valid state law by supreme federal law is not an instance of preemption at all but a straightforward operation of the principle of supremacy. It neither ends concurrent state authority nor turns on congressional purpose. If, however, the claim is the more subtle one that such a conflict provides the necessary evidence for implying congressional intent to preempt, this generally appears to be an unlikely piece of STATUTORY INTERPRETATION. Where preexisting state regulation is followed by a conflicting federal statute that neither "occupies the field" nor contains an express preemption provision, it seems more reasonable to infer that Congress only intended to trump the relevant state statutes without divesting the states of their concurrent legislative authority in that field.

STEPHEN GARDBAUM
(2000)

Bibliography

ENGDAHL, DAVID 1987 Constitutional Federalism in a Nutshell, 2nd ed. St. Paul, Minn.: West.

GARDBAUM, STEPHEN 1994 The Nature of Preemption. Cornell Law Review 79:767–815.

PREFERRED FREEDOMS

Because FIRST AMENDMENT freedoms rank at the top of the hierarchy of constitutional values, any legislation that ex-plicitly limits those freedoms must be denied the usual presumption of constitutionality and be subjected to STRICT SCRUTINY by the judiciary. So went the earliest version of the preferred freedoms doctrine, sometimes called the preferred position or preferred status doctrine. It probably originated in the opinions of Justice OLIVER WENDELL HOLMES, at least implicitly. He believed that a presumption of constitutionality attached to ECONOMIC REGULATION, which needed to meet merely a RATIONAL BASIS test, as he explained dissenting in LOCHNER V. NEW YORK (1905). By contrast, in ABRAMS V. UNITED STATES (1919) he adopted the CLEAR AND PRESENT DANGER test as a constitutional yardstick for legislation such as the ESPIONAGE ACT OF 1917 or state CRIMINAL SYNDICALISM statutes, which limited FREEDOM OF SPEECH.

Justice BENJAMIN N. CARDOZO first suggested a more general hierarchy of constitutional rights in PALKO V. CONNECTICUT (1937), in a major opinion on the INCORPORATION DOCTRINE. He ranked at the top those "fundamental principles of liberty and justice which lie at the base of all our civil and political institutions." He tried to distinguish rights that might be lost without risking the essentials of liberty and justice from rights which he called "the matrix, the indispensable condition, of nearly every other form of freedom." These FUNDAMENTAL RIGHTS came to be regarded as the preferred freedoms. A year later Justice HARLAN F. STONE, in footnote four of his opinion in UNITED STATES V. CAROLENE PRODUCTS (1938), observed that "legislation which restricts the political processes" might "be subjected to more exacting judicial scrutiny" than other legislation. He suggested, too, that the judiciary might accord particularly searching examination of statutes reflecting "prejudice against DISCRETE AND INSULAR MINORITIES."

The First Amendment freedoms initially enjoyed a primacy above all others. Justice WILLIAM O. DOUGLAS for the Court in MURDOCK V. PENNSYLVANIA (1943) expressly stated: "FREEDOM OF THE PRESS, freedom of speech, FREEDOM OF RELIGION are in a preferred position." In the 1940s, despite bitter divisions on the Court over the question whether constitutional rights should be ranked, as well as the question whether the Court should ever deny the presumption of constitutionality, a majority of Justices continued to endorse the doctrine. Justice WILEY B. RUTLEDGE for the Court gave it its fullest exposition in Thomas v. Collins (1945). Justice FELIX FRANKFURTER, who led the opposition to the doctrine, called it "mischievous" in KOVACS V. COOPER (1949); he especially disliked the implication that "any law touching communication" might be "infected with presumptive invalidity." Yet even Frankfurter, in his Kovacs opinion, acknowledged that "those liberties . . . which history has established as the indispensable conditions of an open as against a closed society come to the Court with a momentum for respect lacking when appeal is made to liberties which derive merely from shifting economic arrangements."

The deaths of Murphy and Rutledge in 1949 and their replacement by TOM C. CLARK and SHERMAN MINTON shifted the balance of judicial power to the Frankfurter viewpoint. Thereafter little was heard about the doctrine. The WARREN COURT vigorously defended not only CIVIL LIBERTIES but CIVIL RIGHTS and the rights of the criminally accused. The expansion of the incorporation doctrine and of the concept of EQUAL PROTECTION OF THE LAWS in the 1960s produced a new spectrum of FUNDAMENTAL INTERESTS demanding special judicial protection. Free speech, press, and religion continued, nevertheless, to be ranked, at least implicitly, as very special in character and possessing a symbolic "firstness," to use EDMOND CAHN's apt term. Although the Court rarely speaks of a preferred freedoms doctrine today, the substance of the doctrine has been absorbed in the concepts of strict scrutiny, fundamental rights, and selective incorporation.

LEONARD W. LEVY
(1986)

Bibliography

MCKAY, ROBERT B. 1959 The Preference for Freedom. *New York University Law Review* 34:1184–1227.

PRESENTMENT

A presentment is a written accusation of criminal offense prepared, signed, and presented to the prosecutor by the members of a GRAND JURY, acting on their own initiative rather than in response to a bill of INDICTMENT brought before them by the government. By returning a presentment, the grand jury forces the prosecutor to indict. The presentment procedure permits the grand jury to circumvent prosecutorial inertia or recalcitrance to initiate criminal proceedings. The grand jury's presentment power originated long before there were government prosecutors. The presentment is a descendant of the grand jury's original function: to initiate criminal proceedings by accusing those whom the grand jurors knew to have reputedly committed offenses.

CHARLES H. WHITEBREAD
(1986)

Bibliography

TESLIK, W. RANDOLPH 1975 *Prosecutorial Discretion: The Decision to Charge.* Washington, D.C.: National Criminal Justice Reference Service.

PRESIDENT AND THE TREATY POWER

Article II of the Constitution authorizes the President to "make" treaties with the ADVICE AND CONSENT of the SENATE, provided two-thirds of the senators concur. An "Article II" treaty may be a bilateral or multilateral international agreement and is brought into force as an international obligation of the United States by the formal act of ratification or accession. This formal act (hereinafter called "ratification") is separate from the act of signing the treaty and is accomplished pursuant to an instrument executed by the President. Accordingly, the TREATY POWER is a presidential power that requires Senate participation before its exercise.

The decision to open a treaty negotiation, like the process of negotiation itself, is an exclusive EXECUTIVE PREROGATIVE. The Senate or individual senators may influence the course of a negotiation, but the Senate has no constitutionally recognized role before the submission of a treaty for advice and consent to ratification. The original understanding of the treaty power envisioned Senate participation before the negotiation and conclusion of treaties. However, this understanding was quickly reinterpreted in an informal manner. In 1789, in connection with an upcoming negotiation, President GEORGE WASHINGTON personally appeared before the Senate and asked its advice on a series of specific negotiating questions. The Senate postponed consideration of all but one such question to a second session. This procedure was unsatisfactory to both the President and the Senate and was abandoned. Even the practice initiated by Washington of seeking written advice on particular negotiating questions was abandoned by him before the end of his first administration. A congressional study reported that "[b]y 1816 the practice had become established that the Senate's formal participation in treaty-making was to approve, approve with conditions, or disapprove treaties after they had been negotiated by the President or his representative." An attempt in 1973 to affirm the "historic" role of the Senate in treaty making by constituting it as a council of advice for that purpose came to naught in the face of executive branch, constitutional objections. The Senate and individual senators may nevertheless informally influence the course of negotiations through expressions of views at hearings, participation as advisors to the U.S. delegation to a negotiation, and other informal methods.

If a negotiation produces an international agreement, the president must choose the most appropriate basis in domestic constitutional law for bringing the agreement into force. There are four distinct sources of authority for presidential conclusion of an international agreement on behalf of the United States. The President may submit the agreement as an Article II treaty to the Senate for its advice and consent to ratificaiton. Alternatively, the President may seek congressional authorization of an international agreement by JOINT RESOLUTION or act of Congress or may use existing legislation as a basis for ratification of the agreement. These agreements are called congressional-executive agreements. This alternative procedure has become accepted as constitutionally equivalent to the Article II procedure. Any international agreement so authorized is binding on the United States as a matter of international law, and both congressional-executive agreements and "self-executing" Article II treaties supercede earlier inconsistent federal statutes as a matter of domestic law. In general, a self executing treaty is one that is intended by the United States to take effect as domestic law upon ratification.

Third, an international agreement may be contemplated by an earlier Article II treaty and may derive its authority from the earlier treaty. Such an agreement has the same legal force internationally and domestically as an Article II treaty. Fourth, an international agreement may be concluded on the basis of the President's power in FOREIGN AFFAIRS. An international agreement concluded pursuant to the President's foreign-affairs power has the same effect internationally as an Article II treaty, but the President does not normally use a presidential EXECUTIVE AGREEMENT if it would be inconsistent with domestic law (for an exception see DAMES & MOORE V. REGAN, 1981). Any international agreement, including an Article II treaty, supersedes inconsistent state law.

The President's choice as to whether to submit an international agreement to the Senate as an Article II treaty is guided by the State Department's Circular 175 Procedure. This State Department regulation reqnuires that due consideration be given to such factors as the formality, importance and duration of the agreement, the preference of Congress, the need for implementing LEGISLATION by Congress, the effect on state law, and past U.S. and international practice. Under Circular 175, officials of the executive branch may consult with the Senate Foreign Relations Committee as to the choice of constitutional procedure. Although the "Circular 175" factors are rather general and may sometimes suggest alternative inconsistent choices and although the choice of constitutional procedure is in part a political choice, historical factors are often decisive. Thus, international agreements dealing with boundaries, arms control, military alliances, extradition, and investment are normally submitted to the Senate as Article II treaties. In contrast, international agreements dealing with trade, finance, energy, fisheries, and aviation are normally concluded as congressional-executive agreements. Sometimes an agreement may be concluded as an Article II treaty that is non-self-executing and is therefore subject to the enactment of implementing legislation by Congress before its ratification. This procedure may be preferable if the treaty requires regular appropriation of funds.

If the President chooses to submit an international agreement to the Senate as an Article II treaty, the Senate may consent to its ratification subject to conditions that bind the President if the President chooses to ratify the treaty. These conditions may require the President to attach a reservation to United Sates adherence to the treaty or to amend the treaty by agreement with the other treaty party or parties. Senate-imposed conditions may also require the President to make a specified declaration to the other treaty party or parties in connection with ratification, or a Senate-imposed condition may state an understanding that the Senate seeks to impose on the President or the U.S. Courts—for example, an understanding regarding a particular interpretation or the treaty's domestic effect. The President normally included Senate-imposed conditions requiring agreement by, or communication to, the other treaty party or parties in an instrument exchanged with the treaty partner or deposited specifically in connection with ratification. However, the President has claimed the constitutional power to comply with Senate-imposed conditions outside the formal ratification proces. A Senate-imposed condition must relate to the subject matter of the treaty and may not infringe on other provisions of the Constitution, such as the BILL OF RIGHTS or the President's foreign-affairs power. In MISSOURI V. HOLLAND (1920), the Supreme Court upheld the validity of a treaty-related act of Congress that, absent the treaty, arguably contravened the TENTH AMENDMENT. This decision caused considerable concern that a treaty might supersede other constitutional provisions, including the Bill of Rights. However, in REID V. COVERT (1957), a plurality of justices opined that a treaty may not contravene individual liberty specifically protected by the Bill of Rights. Of course, the content of such a right may be altered by the existence of a treaty and the foreign location of the governmental activity.

Following the Senate's advice and consent, the President makes an independent decision as to whether to ratify the treaty, thereby bringing it into force as an international obligation of the United States subject to the conditions imposed by the Senate. Until 1950, ratified treaties were published in the *Statutes at Large*. Now they are published separately by the Department of State as part of the series entitled *United States Treaties and Other International Agreements*. The President has also exercised the power to accept or reject proposed reservations by other parties to a treaty without the participation of the Senate.

Once a treaty has been ratified, the President has the power to interpret it, unilaterally or in agreement with treaty partners, pursuant to the President's foreign-affairs power. However, the President normally does not commit the interpretation of treaties to third-party dispute resolution, such as arbitration or adjudication by the International Court of Justice, without Senate or congressional acquiescence or approval. Moreover, if the President changes an earlier, commonly held interpretation, Congress may use its legislative and appropriations powers to force the President to reconsider. The reinterpretation controversy involving the 1972 U.S.-U.S.S.R. Treaty on the Limitation of Anti-Ballistic Missile Systems (hereinafter called the "ABM Treaty") is a good example of this phenomenon. When the President sent the ABM Treaty to the Senate for its advice and consent to ratification, executive branch officials told the Senate that the treaty prohibited the development and testing of space-based ABM systems based on "other physical principles" than those existing in 1972, such as lasers. Thirteen years later the administration of RONALD REAGAN "reinterpreted" the treaty to permit the development and testing of those space-based ABM systems. However, several senators, former officials who negotiated the treaty, and academic commentators vigorously disputed the administration's case. Congress used its legislative and appropriations powers to force the executive branch to limit development and testing of ABM systems to activities permitted under the original interpretation.

In addition to the controversy over the substantive question of how the ABM Treaty should be interpreted, the reinterpretation attempt of the ABM Treaty sparked a dispute over the constitutional limits on presidential interpretation power. In 1987, the Senate considered, but declined to adopt, Senate Resolution 167, a general resolution stating that the meaning of a treaty cannot be unilaterally changed by the President from "what the Senate understands the treaty to mean when it gives its advice and consent to ratification." After another round of debate of the constitutional issue, the Senate attached a similar condition in its consent to ratification of the 1987 U.S.-U.S.S.R. Treaty on the Elimination of Intermediate-range and Shorter-range Missiles (hereinafter called the "INF Treaty") applicable only to that treaty. The President questioned the constitutionality of that condition, but only after he had ratified the INF Treaty.

After all the controversy, little is settled. Most commentators probably would agree that the President may not reinterpret fundamental treaty provisions in major respects, even with the agreement of a treaty partner, without seeking Senate or congressional approval. Such a change would probably be classified as a "major amendment" to the treaty and, as such, would require that consent. It would also seem that other reinterpretations could be made by the President with Senate or congressional acquiescence. If Congress disagrees with a presidential interpretation, it may reflect its nonacquiescence through its legislative or appropriations power. Finally, conditions formally adopted, like that to the INF Treaty, should bind the President if the President chooses to ratify the treaty.

Another area of recent controversy concerns the termination of treaties. President JIMMY CARTER terminated an Article II defense treaty in accordance with its terms, despite a "sense of the Congress" expression that he should consult with Congress before any such change in policy. In GOLDWATER V. CARTER (1979) the Supreme Court dismissed a complaint filed by some members of Congress to enjoin the presidential action. The PLURALITY OPINION invoked the POLITICAL QUESTION doctrine. Since that time, the President has claimed the right to terminate Article II treaties in accordance with their terms. Congress has acquiesced. The President has also successfully asserted the right to declare a treaty partner to be in "material breach" of its terms so the United States may withdraw from the treaty. Finally, the President has successfully asserted the right to violate the terms of a treaty or other norms of international law in the course of conducting the nation's foreign relations, at least in the absence of congressional action prohibiting such a violation. Those rights are based on the President's foreign-affairs power.

Because the judiciary rarely adjudicates SEPARATION OF POWERS issues on the merits in foreign-affairs cases, the best guide to constitutional law defining presidential power in this area is recent historical practice; it constitutes a common law reflecting the pattern of accommodations reached by the President, the Senate, and the Congress in allocating responsibilities under the treaty power.

PHILLIP R. TRIMBLE
(1992)

(SEE ALSO: *Congress and Foreign Policy; Congressional War Powers; Presidential War Powers; Senate and Foreign Policy*.)

Bibliography

BESTOR, ARTHUR 1989 "Advice" from the Very Beginning, "Consent" When the End Is Achieved. *American Journal of International Law* 83:718–727.

CONGRESSIONAL RESEARCH SERVICE 1984 *Treaties and Other International Agreements: The Role of the United States Senate.* S-Print 98–205, 98th Congress, Second Session.

GLENNON, MICHAEL J. 1990 *Constitutional Diplomacy.* Princeton, N.J.: Princeton University Press.

HENKIN, LOUIS 1972 *Foreign Affairs and the Constitution.* Mineola, N.Y.: Foundation Press.

KOH, HAROLD HONGJU 1990 *The National Security Constitution.* New Haven, Conn.: Yale University Press.

SYMPOSIUM 1989 Arms Control Treaty Interpretation. *University of Pennsylvania Law Review* 137:1351–1557.

PRESIDENTIAL ELECTION CAMPAIGN FUND ACT

See: Federal Election Campaign Acts

PRESIDENTIAL IMMUNITY

The Constitution has no provision regarding presidential immunity akin to the SPEECH OR DEBATE CLAUSE that protects members of Congress in performing their official duties. Nevertheless, most Presidents have claimed the constitutional structure implicitly protects their ability to execute their constitutional obligations.

The Supreme Court first recognized presidential immunity formally in UNITED STATES V. NIXON (1973). The Court concluded the privilege was not absolute but presumptive and ordered President RICHARD M. NIXON to comply with a SUBPOENA requesting some tapes of his conversations with his aides. The Court determined that Nixon's "generalized" need for "confidential communications" with staff was outweighed by the need for the materials sought in a pending criminal prosecution against members of his staff.

In NIXON V. FITZGERALD (1982), the Court held 5–4 the President—but not his staff—was absolutely immune from civil actions based on his official actions. The Court explained the "President occupies a unique position in the constitutional scheme. [Because] of the singular importance of the President's duties, diversion of his energies by concern with private lawsuits would raise unique risks to the effective functioning of government."

In CLINTON V. JONES (1997), a unanimous Court acknowledged the President's "unique" constitutional status but held he was not immune from civil actions based on his unofficial conduct. The Court left unaddressed whether a President may be criminally prosecuted or imprisoned before IMPEACHMENT and removal from office, though it suggested for official actions a President "may be disciplined principally by impeachment, not by private lawsuits for damages." Although Justice JOSEPH STORY maintained a President was immune from criminal prosecution and imprisonment while discharging his duties, it is arguable that *Clinton v. Jones* sanctions any lawsuits, even criminal ones, based on a President's unofficial conduct. Moreover, no other federal officials, not even Vice Presidents, are immune while in office from criminal prosecution or imprisonment.

MICHAEL J. GERHARDT
(2000)

PRESIDENTIAL ORDINANCE-MAKING POWER

As a means of carrying out constitutional and statutory duties, Presidents issue regulations, proclamations, and EXECUTIVE ORDERS. Although this exercise of legislative power by the President appears to contradict the doctrine of SEPARATION OF POWERS, the scope of administrative legislation has remained broad. Rules and regulations, as the Supreme Court noted in *United States v. Eliason* (1842), "must be received as the acts of the executive, and as such, be binding upon all within the sphere of his legal and constitutional authority."

It is established DOCTRINE that "the authority to prescribe rules and regulations is not the power to make laws, for no such power can be delegated by the Congress," as a federal court of appeals declared in *Lincoln Electric Co. v. Commissioner of Internal Revenue* (1951). Nevertheless, vague grants of delegated authority by Congress give administrators substantial discretion to make federal policy. Over a twelve-month period from 1933 to 1934 the National Recovery Administration issued 2,998 orders. This flood of rule-making activity was not collected and published in one place, leaving even executive officials in doubt about applicable regulations.

Legislation in 1935 provided for the custody of federal documents and their publication in a "Federal Register." The Administrative Procedure Act of 1946 established uniform standards for rule-making, including notice to the parties concerned and an opportunity for public participation. Recent Presidents, especially GERALD FORD, JIMMY CARTER, and RONALD REAGAN, have attempted to monitor and control the impact of agency regulations on the private sector.

Proclamations are a second instrument of administrative legislation. Sometimes they are hortatory in character, without legislative effect, such as proclamations for Law Day. Other proclamations have substantive effects, especially when used to regulate international trade on the basis of broad grants of statutory authority. Still other proclamations have been issued solely on the President's constitutional authority, as with pardons and AMNESTIES and ABRAHAM LINCOLN's proclamations in April 1861. When a statute prescribes a specific procedure in an area reserved to Congress and the President follows a different course, proclamations are illegal and void.

From ancient times a proclamation was literally a public notice, whether by trumpet, voice, print, or posting. Yet in 1873 the Supreme Court in *Lapeyre v. United States* declared that a proclamation by the President became a valid instrument of federal law from the moment it was signed and deposited in the office of the secretary of state, even though not published. These early proclamations eventually found their way into the *Statutes at Large*, but not until the Federal Register Act of 1935 did Congress require the prompt publication of all proclamations and executive orders that have general applicability and legal effect.

Executive orders are a third source of ordinance-making power. They draw upon the constitutional power of the President or powers expressly delegated by Congress. Especially bold were the orders of President FRANKLIN D. ROOSEVELT from 1941 to 1943; without any statutory authority he seized plants, mines, and companies. Actions that exceed legal bounds have been struck down by the courts, a major example being the Steel Seizure Case (YOUNGSTOWN SHEET AND TUBE CO. V. SAWYER, 1952). Executive orders cannot supersede a statute or override contradictory congressional expressions.

Congress has used its power of the purse to circumscribe executive orders. After President RICHARD M. NIXON issued executive order 11605 in 1971, rejuvenating the SUBVERSIVE ACTIVITIES CONTROL BOARD, Congress reduced the agency's budget and expressly prohibited it from using any of the funds to implement the President's order. Congress has also prevented the President from using appropriated funds to finance agencies created solely by executive order.

LOIS FISHER
(1986)

Bibliography

FLEISHMAN, JOEL L. and AUFSES, ARTHUR H. 1976 Law and Orders: The Problem of Presidential Legislation. *Law and Contemporary Problems* 40:1–45.
HART, JAMES 1925 *The Ordinance Making Powers of the President of the United States.* Baltimore: Johns Hopkins University Press. [Reprinted in 1970 by Da Capo Press.]

PRESIDENTIAL POWERS

The powers of the American presidency are amorphous and enormous. Perhaps they can be defined only by saying that they are made adequate to the problems to which the power is addressed. Although these powers purportedly derive from the specifications of the Constitution itself, in fact their definition is to be found in the behavior of the American Presidents since 1789. During this time the executive branch, largely with the acquiescence of Congress and the encouragement of the Supreme Court, has come to resemble the monolithic authority to be found in governments that have succeeded to the authority of czars and emperors. LIMITED GOVERNMENT is now constitutionally limited only by the first eight Amendments and Article I, section 9, and even then only at the discretion of the Supreme Court.

The reason for the accumulation of power in the presidency is not hard to find. Power goes to the official who can use it. It is easy for the President to be that official because, as Justice ROBERT H. JACKSON wrote in YOUNGSTOWN SHEET & TUBE CO. V. SAWYER (1952):

Executive power has the advantage of concentration in a single head in whose choice the whole Nation has a part, making him the focus of public hopes and expectations. In drama, magnitude and finality his decisions so far overshadow any others that almost alone he fills the public eye and ear. No other personality in public life can begin to compete with him in access to the public mind through modern methods of communications. By his prestige as head of state and his influence upon public opinion he exerts a leverage upon those who are supposed to check and balance his power which often cancels their effectiveness.

The doctrine of SEPARATION OF POWERS, not to be found in terms in the Constitution, has receded to the vanishing point so far as the presidency is concerned. And the principle of CHECKS AND BALANCES, intrinsic in the Constitution as a whole, has also been diminished when it comes to putting restraints on the President.

Essentially there are two conflicting theses on the powers of American Presidents, depending in large part on whether it is believed that the opening words of the Second Article: "The Executive power shall be vested in a President of the United States," is itself a grant of power or, as was the case with Articles I and III, is simply a designation of the office with the powers of that official to be found in the provisions that followed. In sum, the question is whether everything that comes after the first sentence in Article II is a redundancy so far as presidential powers are concerned. A reading of the origins of the article would clearly deflate the concept of a presidency replete with the royal prerogatives that the nation had so roundly condemned in the DECLARATION OF INDEPENDENCE itself.

Even the view taken by THEODORE ROOSEVELT, however, is not so broad as to leave no need for separation of powers. Roosevelt asserted "that the executive power was limited only by specific restrictions and prohibitions appearing in the Constitution or imposed by Congress under its Constitutional powers." Roosevelt's immediate successor in office, WILLIAM HOWARD TAFT, had espoused a different reading: "The true view of the executive function is . . . that the President can exercise no power which cannot be fairly and reasonably traced to some specific grant of power or justly implied and included within such grant as proper and necessary." Taft's was the better reading of the origins of the constitutional provisions, although even he later turned to the Roosevelt reading when he was on the Supreme Court. But Roosevelt's was the better reading of the history of the presidency and a better prediction of what the presidency was to become.

The last important Supreme Court opinion on presidential powers, perhaps because it was one of the few outside the area of CIVIL LIBERTIES that rejected a presidential reach for power beyond his grasp, came in 1952 in the Steel Seizure Case. There the Court was thoroughly divided. The dissenters, led by Chief Justice FRED M. VINSON, read the INHERENT POWERS of the presidency as all but limitless, in keeping with the construction given by most political scientists. Justice HUGO L. BLACK went to the other extreme in his opinion for the Court. For him the chief magistrate had only those powers specifically provided by the terms of the Constitution and those powers properly conferred upon him by Congress. But of all the opinions in *Youngstown*, the one most often looked to by constitutional lawyers, including those sitting on the Court, has been that of Justice Robert H. Jackson, for whom there was no plain rule but rather a sliding scale:

1. When the President acts pursuant to an express or implied authorization of Congress, his authority is at its maximum, for it includes all that he possesses in his own right plus all that Congress can delegate. . . .

2. When the President acts in absence of either a congressional grant or denial of authority, he can only rely upon his own independent powers, but there is a zone of twilight in which he and Congress may have concurrent authority, or in which its distribution is uncertain. Therefore, congressional inertia, indifference or quiescence may sometimes, at least as a practical matter, enable, if not invite, measures of independent presidential responsibility. In this area, any test of power is likely to depend on the imperative of events and contemporary imponderables rather than on abstract theories of law.

3. When the President takes measures incompatible with the express or implied will of Congress, his power is at its lowest ebb, for then he can rely only upon its constitutional powers minus any constitutional powers of Congress over the matter. . . . Presidential claim to a power at once so conclusive and preclusive must be scrutinized with caution, for what is at stake is the equilibrium established by our constitutional system.

Jackson concluded his opinion, saying: "With all its defects, delays and inconveniences, men have discovered no technique for long preserving free government except that the Executive be under the law, and that the law be made by parliamentary deliberations. Such institutions may be destined to pass away. But it is the duty of the Court to be the last, not first, to give them up."

The concept of the RULE OF LAW continues to diminish as the nation embraces first the description in CLINTON ROSSITER's *Constitutional Dictatorship*, and then that of Arthur Schlesinger in his *Imperial Presidency*. We continue, however, to parse the sentences of the Constitution in order to justify or oppose presidential authority. But there is less reality in this exercise as each day succeeds the next.

The catalogue of presidential powers specifically stated in the Constitution is neither long nor extensive. He is given a conditional power of veto of all legislation, subject to being overridden by a two-thirds vote of each house. The remainder of his powers are specified in Article II, section 7: he is to be COMMANDER-IN-CHIEF of the armed forces, including the militia when in the service of the United States; he may require opinions from his principal cabinet officers; he may grant pardons and reprieves for offenders against the national laws; he may enter into TREATIES with foreign nations with the ADVICE AND CONSENT of two-thirds of the Senate; he is to nominate ambassadors, ministers, and consuls, members of the Supreme Court, and such other officers as are not otherwise provided for by the Constitution, plus such other officers as Congress shall provide; he may fill vacancies while the Senate is not in session; he shall address Congress on the state of the union and recommend the passage of measures he deems necessary and expedient; he may convene Congress and adjourn it when the two houses do not agree on adjournment; he shall receive ambassadors and other public ministers from foreign countries; "he shall take Care that the Laws be faithfully executed"; and he shall commission all officers of the United States. In fact, however, these bare bones of presidential authority have had much meat placed on them by presidential practices, by legislative delegation, and by judicial approval. It can hardly be gainsaid that the authors of the constitutional language would be much surprised were they to return to the scene to see what it is said that they have wrought.

The slivers of presidential power specifically authorized by the Constitution have been bundled like fasces to create huge authority in the President under the banners of FOREIGN AFFAIRS powers; WAR POWERS; fiscal powers; legislative powers and administrative powers. None of these rests exclusively on any specific authority granted by the Constitution but rather on combinations and permutations of them combined with "intrinsic" or "necessary and proper" powers, although the NECESSARY AND PROPER CLAUSE itself was a grant only to the legislative branch.

Probably the most extensive, and perhaps the most important, of the modern President's powers is to be found in his hegemony over the nation's foreign relations. As Archibald Cox has written: "The United States' assumption of a leading role in world affairs built up the presidency by focussing world attention upon the president. The constitution, combined with necessity, gives the president greater personal authority in foreign affairs than domestic matters. A succession of presidents pushed these powers to, and sometimes beyond, their limits. The personal manner in which they conducted international relations doubtless influenced their style in dealing with domestic matters." But it has been "necessity," not the Constitution, that vested this great personal power in the President. There are only two plausible grounds in the Constitution for great presidential authority in the area of foreign relations. It is he who names and receives ambassadors, which was early construed to mean that he was the sole spokesman of the nation with regard to foreign nations. It is he who is charged with the negotiation of treaties. But both in the appointment of ambassadors and in the making of treaties, the Founders required the collaboration of the Senate: a majority vote of acquiescence in the case of ambassadors and a two-thirds vote of the Senate to validate a treaty.

What the Constitution did not give the President by way of powers in this area, he has been given by Congress or he has taken for himself, and what he has taken for himself has generally been legitimated by Supreme Court decision. Much of relations with foreign nations that was committed to Congress—for example, the power over FOREIGN COMMERCE, the war-making authority—has become irrelevant to the modern Constitution. For the Supreme Court has declared that the powers over foreign affairs that are the President's do not derive from the Constitution but rather are a direct inheritance from the Crown of England. In UNITED STATES V. CURTISS-WRIGHT EXPORT CORP. (1936) the Court said: "As a result of the separation from Great Britain by the colonies acting as a unit, the powers of external SOVEREIGNTY passed from the Crown not to the colonies severally, but to the colonies in their collective and corporate capacity as the United States. . . . Sovereignty is never held in suspense. When, therefore, the external sovereignty of Great Britain in respect to the colonies ceased, it immediately passed to the Union." Not only did this power inhere in the Union; it belonged directly to the President, although where it was before there was a President is not made clear. But, said the Court, it did not come through the Constitution or the Congress. It is a "very delicate, plenary and exclusive power of the President as the sole organ of the federal government in the field of international relations—a power which does not require as a basis for its exercise an act of Congress." It is somewhat strange, if the foreign relations power never belonged to the states, that the Founders thought it necessary to take it from them in the specific words of Article I, section 10: "No state shall enter into any treaty, alliance, or confederation; grant LETTERS OF MARQUE AND REPRISAL, . . . No state shall, without the consent of Congress . . . keep troops, or ships of war in time of peace, enter into any agreement or compact with another state, or with a foreign power, or engage in war, unless actually invaded. . . ." It is strange, too, that Congress can consent to the exercise of foreign affairs powers by the states, if that power properly belongs exclusively to the President.

The coalescence of this power over foreign relations solely in the President has also had the effect of eliminating specific checks on him by the Senate. The Constitution clearly gives the power to negotiate treaties to the President, but it requires the consent of two-thirds of the Senate to validate a treaty. The requirement of Senate approval has often proved a stumbling block, as it was when the Senate refused to consent to the United States' entry into the League of Nations and when the Senate imposed qualifications on the treaty ceding the Panama Canal Zone back to Panama. But the President and the Supreme Court have found a way out of some of these restraints. An agreement with a foreign nation may be called an EXECUTIVE AGREEMENT rather than a "treaty," and an "executive agreement" does not require Senate approval, according to the decisions in UNITED STATES V. BELMONT (1937) and UNITED STATES V. PINK (1942). There is no guide, however, to say what the province of a treaty may be to distinguish it from that of an executive agreement. The justification for evading presidential responsibility to the Senate is, however, often founded on the ground that effectuation of such agreements usually requires congressional legislation, and a majority of both houses is said to be as good as or better than two-thirds of the Senate in ratifying the presidential action and easier to secure.

It has been argued, but not very cogently, that the foreign affairs powers of the President somehow derive from the Commander-in-Chief Clause of Article II. ALEXANDER HAMILTON's explanation of that provision in THE FEDERALIST #69 as to the limited authority of the commander-in-chief still seems to be the better understanding of it: "It would amount to nothing more than the supreme command and direction of the military and naval forces, as first General and Admiral of the Confederacy."

The foreign affairs powers of the President are as broad as they have become not because of constitutional delegation but because of the exigencies that have caused the Presidents to seize the power to meet the problems. Neither the public nor the Congress has shown much aversion to this presidential usurpation.

PRESIDENTIAL WAR POWERS, like presidential foreign affairs powers, rest on practice and precedent rather than on constitutional authorization. Thus, despite the provision of Article 1, section 8, giving Congress the power to declare war, wars have tended to be a consequence of executive action, sometimes confirmed by a congressional DECLARATION OF WAR and sometimes carried on without one. Five times in American history, Congress has declared war: the War of 1812, the Mexican War of 1848, the Spanish American War of 1898, WORLD WAR I (1917), and WORLD WAR II (1941). Each time American military and naval forces had been committed to action before the actual declaration took place. In most instances when military forces have been engaged against foreign powers there has been no declaration of war even when the conflict reached such vast scales as the country's commitments to the KOREAN WAR and VIETNAM WAR. It has been argued that there were de facto declarations in such instances as Korea and Vietnam by congressional silence or appropriations for the military, but that was not what the Founders had in mind. For them war was thought too serious a matter to be left to generals and Presidents.

Congress has come up with a statute attempting to resolve the problem of presidential usurpation of the war power. The WAR POWERS RESOLUTION OF 1973 provides that a President can order military action without a declaration of war by Congress, but he must inform Congress within forty-eight hours of doing so. Troops cannot be committed for more than sixty days except when Congress so authorizes, and Congress is empowered to order an immediate withdrawal of American forces by CONCURRENT RESOLUTION not subject to presidential veto. The statute is of dubious constitutional validity, giving presidential powers to Congress and congressional powers to the President. It is not likely to be the subject of a successful court test, for courts cannot act expeditiously enough nor can they effectuate a decree against the will of either of the other branches.

The essential fact is that the Constitution gives to Congress the power to declare war, to raise and support the armed forces, to make rules for the governance of the armed forces, to call up the militia, and to regulate it. It gives to the President the powers of commander-in-chief, which is only an authority to act in command of the military services so that no mere military officer shall be without civilian oversight.

The greater problem with presidential war powers is whether they enhance his authority over domestic civilian affairs. The Court has tended to sustain extraordinarily broad powers for the executive during the course of a war, as in the JAPANESE AMERICAN CASES (1943–1944), allowing relocation of native and foreign-born Japanese from the West Coast into concentration camps. When war has ended, the Court tends to look more dubiously on executive war powers, holding in DUNCAN V. KAHANOMOKU

(1946), for example, that it was an abuse of authority to declare martial law in Hawaii on the day after the Japanese bombed Pearl Harbor. So far as civilian activities are concerned, it is said that war does not give the executive any new powers but simply justifies the use of granted powers reserved for emergencies. The fact is that, in contemporary times, Congress has provided the President with more EMERGENCY POWERS than he ever has occasion to use, generally leaving to him the discretion to determine whether an emergency warrants calling such powers into play. The concept of emergency powers, itself nowhere to be found in the Constitution, has long since expanded beyond the realms of war powers to justify presidential action in the economic and social realm as well as in the areas of military combat and foreign affairs. The confiscation of Iranian assets in the United States to ransom American captives from the Iranians in 1980 affords an example of the extension of presidential authority far beyond what the Constitution provided; but in DAMES & MOORE V. REGAN (1981) the flimsiest statutory delegation was held sufficient to justify the President's actions.

The Constitution gave the President no powers over the national fisc. It was very clear at the CONSTITUTIONAL CONVENTION OF 1787 that the authority over national finance—what went into the national purse and what came out of it—belonged to Congress and Congress alone, subject, of course, to the presidential power of veto. Article 1, section 7, commands that the House of Representatives alone shall originate revenue measures. Article 1, section 8, gives to the Congress the "power to lay and collect taxes," "to pay the debts," "to borrow money," "to coin money," and to punish counterfeiting. And Article 1, section 9, clause 7, provides that "no money shall be drawn from the Treasury, but in consequence of appropriations made by law." If any principle of responsible government can be said to have been derived from the Glorious Revolution of 1688 in England and the American Revolution, it is that a popularly elected legislature is the only safe place in which to place the power of the purse.

This is not to deny that at all times in our history the executive branch has played a more or less important role in the creation and effectuation of fiscal policy, from the roles of Secretaries of the Treasury Hamilton and ALBERT GALLATIN and ANDREW JACKSON's war on the BANK OF THE UNITED STATES to contemporary times when it would appear that the executive is dominant and Congress subordinate with regard to all the fiscal powers that the Constitution gave to the Congress. But the role of the executive branch has essentially been defined by the Congress. If the executive power is now so great in fiscal matters, the reason is not that the Constitution has conferred the power on the President but that Congress has done so. Thus, one frustrating restraint on presidential fiscal policy derives from the autonomy over the money supply granted by Congress to the Federal Reserve Board, an agency independent of the President.

The nation has evolved from one in which the national government's principal role was that of the protector of the lives and property of the citizenry against encroachment by foreign governments and other citizens to one in which the government manages the economy, for better or worse, in a state where the government has assumed responsibility for the social welfare as well as the physical protection of the citizenry. And as the progression has gone on, so too has Congress relinquished more and more authority to the President. But the President can be said to have these powers only at the will of Congress and to exercise them only in order to enforce the laws faithfully. Indeed, the DELEGATION OF POWER has gone so far as for Congress to have provided by law that the President may refuse to enforce its legislation by IMPOUNDMENT of appropriated funds, provided notice is given to Congress and Congress acquiesces.

Although Congress now has its own budget-making procedures, the dominant BUDGET, derived from the President's Office of Management and Budget, is submitted to Congress more by way of command than suggestion. The concept of an executive budget derives from the 1920s when Congress first enacted a demand that the President supply one. Since then, however, the Office of Management and Budget has grown from a simple accounting agency into a fiscal ombudsman for the entire government. It is a force second only to that of the President himself within the executive branch and it has not been bashful about exercising its powers. But if the beast is a presidential pet, it is nonetheless a creature of a Congress dedicated to transferring to the President the powers that the Constitution gave to Congress.

In constitutional terms, the President's role in the legislative process was originally to be very small. Most important, of course, was the power to veto the acts passed by Congress. And even here, unlike the power of the Crown to forestall parliamentary will as expressed in legislation, the President was given only a conditional veto, subject to being overridden by two-thirds of each house of Congress. The VETO POWER is, however, fully effective only for a President who prefers a limited role for government. Obviously, his veto cannot create legislation but only prevent it. A forceful President seeking to impose his will by way of persuading Congress to action rather than inaction can, however, use the veto as a bargaining tool, a threat to cancel what Congress wants unless it gives the President what he wants. Stalemate is a frequent consequence of a profligate use of the veto power.

The President also has the power by constitutional provision to adjourn Congress, when the two houses are unable to agree on adjournment, and to convene Congress. The power to prorogue Parliament was a sore point with the colonists and they had no intention of conferring such authority on any executive of their own.

There was an imitation of the royal prerogative that was to come into existence even though it was not planned by the Founders. The Constitution provides that the President "shall from time to time give the Congress information of the state of the union, and recommend to their consideration such measures as he shall judge necessary and expedient." Like the Queen's message to the opening of Parliament, this device has been used by the executive administration to offer a legislative program to Congress. Indeed, most legislation of importance that comes to enactment in Congress tends to be that which the President has recommended to it or which the President supports by lobbying in Congress. Legislation that does not bear the imprimatur of the President seldom makes its way to enactment, although presidential recommendations are frequently amended in the process of legislative consideration and sometimes are unrecognizable by the time they emerge from both houses. But the influence of the President, utilizing the Office of Management and Budget for details, on the making of the laws is extraordinarily strong. And while there is no provision for presidential budget making in the Constitution, the fact is that the budget that he submits is the foundation on which the congressional budget-making process depends.

In fact, the President indulges in a great deal of lawmaking himself. With the demise of the ban on the delegation of legislative power, which occurred when the Supreme Court was reconstituted by FRANKLIN D. ROOSEVELT, most of the rules governing American society are made by the executive branch. Legislation has tended to take the form of generalized programs whose details are to be filled by agencies of the executive branch. Indeed, some legislation is created by the President even in the absence of authorization for it by the Congress. This takes the form of so-called EXECUTIVE ORDERS theoretically directed to the enforcement of the laws by persons in the executive branch, but usually with the same effect as rules directed to the governed rather than the governors. Very rare indeed is the instance, like the steel seizure case, when the Court has throttled an executive order. Thus, most of the rules governing the lives of Americans are to be sought not in the statutes-at-large but rather in the Federal Register where are to be found the results of the exercise of delegated legislative authority as well as executive orders that do not rest on any actual delegation.

It would seem that the originators of the departments of government thought of them as semiautonomous, with their functions defined by Congress and their secretaries responsible to either the President or the Congress, or both, as prescribed by the legislation creating those offices. The provision for a power in the President to call on the principal officers of government for their opinions would have been redundant if in fact it had been anticipated that all executive officials were directly subordinate to the President. It was probably GEORGE WASHINGTON's organization of his department chiefs into a cabinet rather than the words of the Constitution that made for the hierarchical system headed by the President that has been taken for granted since early in the nineteenth century. The cabinet is not a constitutional body and has no constitutional powers. The powers of the department heads are dependent on legislative rather than constitutional provision, except for their duties to give opinions to the President on demand. Thus by custom and by legislation, and perhaps through the charge of the Constitution to the President faithfully to execute the laws, it has come to be accepted that the executive branch, for all its multitude of offices, is an entity for which the President is responsible both to Congress through the legislature's oversight function, and to the voting public. Surely this notion of the unitary nature of the executive branch and the exceptions thereto—independent administrative agencies—underlies the judgment of the Supreme Court in MYERS V. UNITED STATES (1926) establishing the right of the President to remove officials at his will. This accepted principle is not contradicted by the obligation of the President or other executive officials to abide by their own regulations, which are created by him or them and which are subject to change by him or them. (See APPOINTMENT AND REMOVAL POWER.)

The whole of the executive branch acts subordinately to the command of the President in the administration of federal laws, so long as they act within the terms of those laws. Their offices confer no right to violate the laws, whether they take the form of constitution, statute, or treaty.

The United States does have in the presidency a "constitutional dictatorship" or a "plebiscitary President." The "benevolent monarch" of contemporary times, however, is still subject to the force of public opinion, sometimes expressed through representatives, sometimes expressed through the print and electronic media, sometimes expressed in the streets, and every four years expressed through the ballot boxes. One-term Presidents may become the rule. Despite all the centralization of authority, however, the greatest power of the presidency in this democracy is not the power of command. It is the power to lead a nation by moral suasion. It takes a great President to do that well, and that is why history records so few great Presidents.

PHILIP B. KURLAND
(1986)

Bibliography

CORWIN, EDWARD S. 1957 *The President: Office and Powers 1787–1957.* 4th rev. ed. New York: New York University Press.

COX, ARCHIBALD 1976 Watergate and the Constitution of the United States. *University of Toronto Law Journal* 26:125–139.

KOENIG, LOIS W. 1975 *The Chief Executive.* 3d ed. New York: Harcourt, Brace, Jovanovich.

KURLAND, PHILIP B. 1978 *Watergate and the Constitution.* Chicago: University of Chicago Press.

NEUSTADT, RICHARD E. 1960 *Presidential Power.* New York: John Wiley & Sons.

PIOUS, RICHARD M. 1979 *The American Presidency.* New York: Basic Books.

ROSSITER, CLINTON 1948 *Constitutional Dictatorship.* Princeton, N.J.: Princeton University Press.

SCHLESINGER, ARTHUR M., JR. 1973 *The Imperial Presidency.* Boston: Houghton Mifflin Co.

PRESIDENTIAL SPENDING POWER

The Constitution assigns to Congress the exclusive power to authorize spending. Article I, section 9, prohibits money being drawn from the Treasury "but in Consequence of Appropriations made by law." Nevertheless, the power of the purse is shared with the President because Congress has found it necessary to delegate substantial discretion over the expenditure and allocation of funds.

In his first message to Congress, President THOMAS JEFFERSON recommended that Congress appropriate "specific sums to every specific purpose susceptible of definition." He quickly recognized the impracticability of this principle, later admitting that "too minute a specification has its evil as well as a too general one." Lump-sum appropriations are routinely passed by Congress, especially during emergency periods. The magnitude of these lump sums, frequently in the billions of dollars, overstates the amount of flexibility available to administrators. Their scope of discretion is narrowed by general statutory controls, nonstatutory controls embedded in committee reports and other parts of the legislative history, and agreements and understandings entered into by Congress and the agencies.

The conflicting needs of administrative flexibility and congressional control are often reconciled by "reprogramming" agreements. An agency is given some latitude to shift funds *within* an appropriation account, moving them from one program to another. Legislative controls have gradually tightened. Initially the appropriation committees required regular reporting by the agencies, but reprogrammings over a designated dollar threshold must now be approved by appropriations subcommittees and, in some cases, by authorizing committees that have JURISDICTION over the program. Although these reprogramming procedures are largely nonstatutory and therefore fall short of legally binding requirements, they have become highly formalized and structured. They are incorporated not only in congressional documents but also in agency directives, instructions, and financial management manuals.

Another form of executive spending discretion results from transfer authority. A transfer involves the shifting of funds from one appropriation account to another (in contrast to reprogramming, where funds remain within an account). Moreover, the authority to transfer funds must be explicitly granted by statute. Transfer authority is usually accompanied by limitations, such as allowing a five percent leeway, that help preserve the general budgetary priorities of Congress. When agencies use transfer or reprogramming authority to spend funds on programs that had been previously rejected by Congress, or to enter into long-term financial commitments, Congress responds by adopting additional statutory and nonstatutory restrictions.

Agencies have access to billions of dollars that are hidden from public and congressional view. Confidential and secret funding collides with the requirement of Article I, section 9, of the Constitution: "A regular Statement and Account of the Receipts and Expenditures of all public Money shall be published from time to time." Confidential funds appeared as early as 1790, when Congress appropriated $40,000 to the President to pay for special diplomatic agents. Congress let the President decide the degree to which these expenditures would be made public. Since that time confidential (unvouchered) funds have been made available to many agencies that have domestic as well as foreign responsibilities.

Confidential funding is overt at least in the sense that the amounts are identified in appropriation or authorization bills. Secret funding is covert at every stage, from appropriation straight through to expenditure and auditing. Appropriations, ostensibly for the Defense Department or other agencies, are later siphoned off and allocated to the Central Intelligence Agency and other parts of the intelligence community. Absent congressional authorization, a federal taxpayer lacks STANDING to challenge the constitutionality of confidential or secret funding. The establishment of intelligence committees in the 1970s restored some semblance of congressional control. Legislation for the White House and the General Accounting Office has also tightened legislative control over unvouchered funds. With each increase in the scope of executive spending discretion, Congress participates ever more closely in administrative matters.

LOUIS FISHER
(1986)

(SEE ALSO: *Impoundment of Funds.*)

Bibliography
FISHER, LOUIS 1975 *Presidential Spending Power.* Princeton, N.J.: Princeton University Press.
WILMERDING, LUCIUS, JR. 1943 *The Spending Power: A History of the Efforts of Congress to Control Expenditures.* New Haven, Conn.: Yale University Press.

PRESIDENTIAL SUCCESSION

The framework for electing a President and Vice-President every four years is spelled out in the Constitution. As originally adopted, the Constitution was not clear about certain aspects of succession to the Presidency in the event something happened to the elected President. The Framers were content to establish the office of Vice-President and to add the general provisions of Article II, section 1, clause 6: "In Case of the Removal of the President from Office, or of his Death, Resignation, or Inability to discharge the Powers and Duties of the said Office, the same shall devolve on the Vice-President and the Congress may by Law provide for the Case of Removal, Death, Resignation or Inability, both of the President and Vice-President, declaring what Officer shall then act as President, and such officer shall act accordingly, until the Disability be removed, or a President shall be elected."

The Framers left unanswered questions concerning the status of a Vice-President in cases of removal, death, resignation, and inability, the meaning of the term "inability," and the means by which the beginning and ending of an inability should be determined. Because no event occurred to trigger the succession provision, these ambiguities were of no consequence during the first half century of our nation's existence. Although three Vice-Presidents died in office and another resigned, the presidency and VICE-PRESIDENCY never became vacant at the same time. If that eventuality had come to pass, the president pro tempore of the SENATE would have served as President under the provisions of a 1792 statute on presidential succession.

The ambiguities inherent in the succession provision surfaced in 1841 when President William Henry Harrison died in office. Despite protests that he had become only the "acting president," Vice-President JOHN TYLER assumed the office and title of President for the balance of Harrison's term. Tyler's claiming of the presidency, said JOHN QUINCY ADAMS, was "a construction in direct violation both of the grammar and context of the Constitution. . . ."

The precedent established by Tyler was followed twice within the next twenty-five years when Vice-Presidents MILLARD FILLMORE and ANDREW JOHNSON became President upon the deaths in office of Presidents ZACHARY TAYLOR and ABRAHAM LINCOLN. In 1881 the precedent became an obstacle to Vice-President CHESTER A. ARTHUR's acting as President during the eighty days that President JAMES A. GARFIELD hovered between life and death after being shot by an assassin. The view was strongly expressed at the time that if Arthur were to succeed to the presidency, then according to the Tyler precedent he would be President for the remainder of the presidential term regardless of whether Garfield recovered. Arthur made clear that he would not assume presidential responsibility lest he be labeled a usurper.

In the twentieth century the Tyler precedent was followed on the four occasions when Presidents died in office (WILLIAM MCKINLEY, WARREN G. HARDING, FRANKLIN D. ROOSEVELT, and JOHN F. KENNEDY.) Once again, however, it became an obstacle to a Vice-President's acting as President during the lengthy period WOODROW WILSON lay ill, unable to discharge the powers and duties of office. For the most part, presidential responsibility was assumed by the President's wife, doctor, and secretary.

Between 1955 and 1957 the lack of clarity in the succession provision was highlighted when President DWIGHT D. EISENHOWER sustained a heart attack, an attack of ileitis, and a stroke. Efforts to have Congress address the question were unsuccessful, but important groundwork for reform was established. President Kennedy's assassination in 1963 became the catalyst for implementing that reform. Congress proposed and the states ratified the TWENTY-FIFTH AMENDMENT to the Constitution to resolve the major issues surrounding the subject of presidential succession. The amendment confirmed that the Vice-President becomes President for the remainder of the term in the case of death, removal, or resignation. In the case of an inability, the amendment provided that the Vice-President serves as acting President only for the duration of the inability. The amendment provided for two methods of establishing the existence of an inability. The President was authorized to declare his own inability and, in such event, its termination. For the case where the President does not or cannot declare his own inability, it empowered the Vice-President and a majority of the Cabinet to make the decision. If the President should dispute their determination, Congress decides the issue.

The amendment also established a mechanism for filling a vice-presidential vacancy: presidential nomination and confirmation by a majority of both houses of Congress. The Twenty-Fifth Amendment is supplemented by a statute on presidential succession adopted in 1947 which provided for the Speaker of the HOUSE OF REPRESENTATIVES to serve as President in the event of a double vacancy in the offices of President and Vice-President.

The Twenty-Fifth Amendment served the nation well in the 1970s when both a President and Vice-President resigned from office during the same presidential term. Twice Vice-Presidents were nominated by the President and confirmed by Congress. The first of those Vice-Presidents, GERALD R. FORD, became President of the United States upon the resignation of RICHARD M. NIXON on August 9, 1974. Ford's succession, as did the eight preceding successions of Vice-Presidents, took place in a manner that demonstrated the stability and continuity of government in the United States.

JOHN D. FEERICK
(1986)

Bibliography

BAYH, BIRCH 1968   *One Heartbeat Away*. Indianapolis: Bobbs-Merrill.

FEERICK, JOHN D. 1965   *From Failing Hands*. New York: Fordham University Press.

——— 1976   *The Twenty-Fifth Amendment*. New York: Fordham University Press.

SILVA, RUTH 1951   *Presidential Succession*. Ann Arbor: University of Michigan Press.

PRESIDENTIAL WAR POWERS

The power of the President to initiate unilaterally military operations widened substantially under Presidents GEORGE H. W. BUSH and WILLIAM J. CLINTON. In December 1989, with Congress out of session, Bush ordered 11,000 troops into Panama to join up with 13,000 American troops already in the Canal Zone. He cited a number of justifications: protecting Americans in Panama who were in "imminent danger," bringing Panamanian General Manuel Noriega to justice in the United States, defending democracy, combating drug trafficking, and protecting the integrity of the Panama Canal treaty. Scholars of INTERNATIONAL LAW generally dismissed those arguments, but Bush on his own had used military force to invade another country without ever seeking authorization from Congress.

After Iraq, under the leadership of Saddam Hussein, invaded Kuwait on August 2, 1990, Bush began deploying U.S. forces to Saudi Arabia and elsewhere in the Middle East. At that point the operation was purely defensive—to deter further Iraqi aggression—but the doubling of U.S. forces by November gave Bush the capacity to wage offensive war. He made no effort to seek authority from Congress. Instead, he sought support from other nations and encouraged the UNITED NATIONS Security Council to authorize the use of force, which it did on November 29. Only at the eleventh hour, in January 1991, did Bush seek support (but not authority) from Congress. A legal crisis was avoided on January 12 when Congress authorized offensive action against Iraq.

In his first six years in office, Clinton repeatedly used military force without ever coming to Congress for authority. On June 26, 1993, he ordered air strikes against

Iraq as a response to the attempted assassination of former President Bush during a visit to Kuwait. Sixteen suspects, including two Iraqi nationals, had been arrested but the trial had not been completed. Clinton justified the attack as one of self-defense, but constitutional lawyers found that quite a stretch.

In September 1996, Clinton ordered the launching of cruise missiles against Iraq in response to an attack by Iraqi forces against the Kurdish-controlled city of Irbil in northern Iraq. Cruise missiles also struck air defense capabilities in southern Iraq. There was no claim here of self-defense or the need to protect the lives of Americans. Toward the end of January 1998, Clinton threatened once again to bomb Iraq, this time because Hussein had refused to give UN inspectors full access to examine Iraqi sites. The attack was postponed when UN Secretary General Kofi Annan visited Baghdad in February and negotiated a settlement with Iraq. In that same month, U.S. Secretary of State Madeleine Albright was asked how Clinton could order military action against Iraq after opposing American policy in Vietnam. Her response: "We are talking about using military force, but we are not talking about a war. That is an important distinction." How many people in the country, or in the administration, understood such distinctions? Did the President's need to obtain prior congressional authority arise only in "time of war" but not with military force? In December 1998, Clinton ordered four days of heavy bombing in Iraq and continued in 1999 with repeated air strikes.

Further military action occurred in Somalia, where an initial humanitarian effort turned bloody in June 1993 when twenty-three Pakistani peacekeepers were killed. U.S. warplanes launched a retaliatory attack. In August, four U.S. soldiers were killed when a land mine blasted apart their Humvee vehicle. As the situation deteriorated, Congress passed LEGISLATION to remove U.S. ARMED FORCES from Somalia by March 31, 1994.

On September 15, 1994, Clinton told the American public that he was prepared to invade Haiti to reinstate Jean-Bertrand Aristide as President. The UN Security Council had passed a resolution "inviting" the use of force to remove the military leaders from that island. An invasion became unnecessary when former President JIMMY CARTER negotiated an agreement in which the military leaders agreed to step down to permit Aristide's return.

Clinton ordered air strikes in Bosnia beginning in 1994. At the end of 1995 he dispatched 20,000 U.S. troops to that region for peace-keeping purposes. For authority, he cited a number of North Atlantic Treaty Organization (NATO) decisions and UN resolutions. Beginning on March 24, 1999, and operating solely through NATO, Clinton began bombing in Serbia and Kosovo. He also considered sending in U.S. armed forces as part of a mul-

tinational effort to protect refugees returning to Kosovo. At no time did Congress authorize his actions, although Clinton sent American troops into Kosovo as part of a NATO peace-keeping force upon cessation of the bombing compaign.

In August 1998, Clinton sent cruise missiles into Afghanistan to attack paramilitary camps and into Sudan to destroy a pharmaceutical factory. He justified the use of military force as a retaliation for bombings earlier in the month against U.S. embassies in Nairobi and Dar es Salaam. The administration claimed Osama bin Laden was behind the embassy attacks, that he used the training complex in Afghanistan, and that he was somehow related to the pharmaceutical plant. Questions were raised as to whether the plant was producing a precursor chemical for a nerve gas, as the administration alleged, or an agricultural pesticide. A Saudi businessman who owned the plant went to court to force the administration to release millions of dollars in assets frozen by U.S. officials on the ground that he was linked to bin Laden. The administration released $24 million of his assets but refused to clear his name.

The pattern during the Bush and Clinton years was clear: Presidents would seek authority to use military force not from Congress but from international and regional institutions. Members of Congress voted repeatedly on amendments to restrict the President's capacity to make war. With the exception of the funding restriction on Somalia, these amendments were never enacted into law.

LOUIS FISHER
(2000)

Bibliography

ADLER, DAVID GRAY and GEORGE, LARRY N. 1996 *The Constitution and the Conduct of American Foreign Policy.* Lawrence: University Press of Kansas.

ELY, JOHN HART 1993 *War and Responsibility: Constitutional Lessons of Vietnam and Its Aftermath.* Princeton, N.J.: Princeton University Press.

FISHER, LOUIS 1995 *Presidential War Power.* Lawrence: University Press of Kansas.

STERN, GARY M. and HALPERIN, MORTON H. 1994 *The U.S. Constitution and the Power to Go to War: Historical and Current Perspectives.* Westport, Conn.: Greenwood Press.

PRESUMPTION OF CONSTITUTIONALITY

See: Rational Basis; Standard of Review

PRETRIAL DISCLOSURE

The rules and practices governing pretrial disclosure to the opposing party differ dramatically in criminal and civil litigation. In civil disputes, each side has access to virtually all relevant information possessed by the other. In criminal cases, however, there has been a continuing debate which has focused on how much disclosure the prosecutor, with his superior investigative resources, should be required to make. The argument against wide-ranging disclosure is that it will result in witness intimidation and perjury. The arguments for disclosure are that a criminal trial should not be a "sporting event" in which one side tries to surprise the other, and that disclosure of the prosecution's EVIDENCE would aid the effective assistance of counsel to the accused guaranteed by the Sixth Amendment. (See RIGHT TO COUNSEL.)

Proponents of greater disclosure in criminal cases have made some gains in recent years through the expansion of DISCOVERY statutes. Rule 16 of the FEDERAL RULES OF CRIMINAL PROCEDURE is typical. The rule currently provides that, absent special circumstances, the government must disclose upon request: the defendant's own statements; his record of prior convictions; and documents, tangible evidence, or reports of examinations of the defendant or scientific tests the government intends to introduce at trial. The most striking difference between this rule and civil practice is that the criminal rule does not give the defense the power either to discover the identity of government witnesses or to compel them to testify under oath prior to trial. Several states provide for disclosure of prosecution witness lists, but Congress in 1974 rejected such a provision in the federal rules on the usual argument that disclosure of the identity of witnesses would possibly subject them to intimidation.

In addition to the slow but steady statutory expansion of pretrial disclosure by the government to the defense, there has been a reciprocal movement to entitle the prosecution to learn more about the defense case before trial. The argument that the policies underlying the Fifth Amendment RIGHT AGAINST SELF-INCRIMINATION shield the defense from any disclosure has largely been unsuccessful. Under the federal and many state rules, the defense can be requested to disclose any tangible evidence or results of physical or mental examinations it intends to introduce at trial, and to give notice of an alibi or insanity defense. The Supreme Court has upheld the constitutionality of compelling defense disclosure, provided that discovery is a two-way street; if the defendant is required to disclose alibi witnesses, for example, the government must also disclose any evidence that refutes the alibi.

Against the background of limited formal discovery rules, prosecutors frequently open files to the defense in an attempt to induce guilty pleas. Sometimes, also, judges exert informal pressure toward open discovery in order to avoid trial delays that might be caused by surprise evidence.

The Supreme Court has repeatedly held that a defendant has no general constitutional right to discovery, but it has required that the prosecution sometimes reveal "favorable" evidence. In *Brady v. Maryland* (1963) the government failed to disclose to a murder defendant that his companion had once admitted to a government agent that he had done the actual killing. The Court held that such a failure to disclose violates DUE PROCESS where the evidence is "material to guilt or punishment," irrespective of the good faith of the prosecution.

The lower courts generally gave an expansive reading to the *Brady* decision, but the Supreme Court curbed this development in *United States v. Agurs* (1976). The *Agurs* Court held that if the defense has not requested favorable evidence, or has made only a general request, a failure to disclose gives the defendant no constitutional right to a new trial unless there is a strong probability that the result of the first trial would not have been different had the favorable evidence been disclosed. Moreover, an appellate court should not grant a new trial so long as the trial judge remains reasonably convinced of the defendant's guilt. The *Agurs* Court also said that the failure to disclose evidence that reveals that the prosecution's case includes perjured testimony or the failure to disclose favorable evidence after it has been specifically requested by the defense, is "rarely excusable." In these two situations, the Constitution requires that the defendant be given a new trial if there is any reasonable possibility that the verdict would have been different had the undisclosed evidence been admitted.

Thus, *Agurs* provided some ammunition to both sides of the debate over criminal discovery: it limited the general due process right but also created a category for all but automatic reversal when the prosecution fails to respond to a defense request for specific information or when the prosecution case includes the knowing use of perjury.

BARBARA ALLEN BABCOCK
(1986)

Bibliography

BABCOCK, BARBARA 1982 Fair Play: Evidence Favorable to an Accused and Effective Assistance of Counsel. *Stanford Law Review* 34:1133–1182.

PREVENTIVE DETENTION

Preventive detention is the jailing of an accused not to prevent bail-skipping but to protect public safety pending trial. Although pretrial incarceration of criminal defendants has long been condoned when necessary to assure their appearance in court, the constitutional status of preventive detention is far less certain. The Supreme Court has never directly addressed the issue, in part because until quite recently it was rendered largely academic by a federal statutory right to BAIL in noncapital cases and by similar rights granted in most state constitutions. Since 1970, however, District of Columbia courts have been authorized to deny pretrial release in certain cases to suspects charged with "dangerous" crimes, and several states have recently amended their constitutions to allow detention under similar circumstances. Following this activity, Congress in 1984 passed a nationwide program of preventive detention, substantially curtailing the federal statutory right to bail for the first time since the right was enacted in 1789.

The constitutionality of these programs is not altogether free from doubt. To begin with, the Eighth Amendment bars the federal government from requiring "excessive bail." Commentators have waged a spirited debate over whether that prohibition implies that some bail must be set. Many constitutional scholars have argued that the Framers intended to provide an affirmative right to bail to all defendants who do not pose an unacceptable risk of flight, and that without such a right the "excessive bail" clause would be a senseless bar against the government's doing indirectly what it remained free to do directly. Others have contended that the clause is aimed at the courts, not at Congress, and that a restriction on judicial discretion in setting bail is fully consistent with legislative authority to determine the circumstances under which bail should be granted at all.

The Supreme Court's decisions and opinions on the issue have been inconclusive. In *Stack v. Boyle* (1951) the Court held that bail was "excessive" when set higher than necessary to assure the accused's presence at trial. Strictly speaking, the ruling concerned only the level at which bail may be set if it is set, but the Court also hinted that the right to bail in the first place, long accorded by federal statute, might have a constitutional dimension: "Unless this right to bail before trial is preserved, the presumption of innocence, secured only after centuries of struggle, would lose its meaning."

The rule of *Stack v. Boyle* regarding bail amounts has remained undisturbed, despite general recognition that in practice bail is frequently set with a covert eye to whether the defendant seems likely to commit crimes before trial. The Supreme Court quickly backed away, however, from its strong if cryptic endorsement of the "right to bail." In *Carlson v. Landon* (1952) the Court approved the denial of bail, for reasons of public safety, to alien communists held pending deportation hearings. The Eighth Amendment, the Court explained, does not grant "a right to bail in all cases," but only provides "that bail shall not be excessive in those cases where it is proper to grant bail." The

Court noted in particular that the amendment "has not prevented Congress from determining the classes of cases in which bail should be allowed."

Despite these seemingly categorical remarks, the effect of *Carlson* on the legacy of *Stack v. Boyle* remains unclear. The *Carlson* decision seems to have been based primarily on the differences between a criminal prosecution against a citizen and a deportation proceeding against an alien; the Court concluded only that "the Eighth Amendment does not require that bail be allowed under the circumstances of these cases."

Whether or not the Eighth Amendment provides a right to bail, preventive detention may raise questions of constitutionality under the DUE PROCESS clauses of the Fifth and FOURTEENTH AMENDMENTS. In *Bell v. Wolfish* (1979) the Supreme Court rejected a related argument, suggested in part by its own opinion in *Stack v. Boyle*, that the "presumption of innocence" limits what the government may do to a criminal defendant before conviction. The Court explained in *Wolfish* that the presumption of innocence is nothing but an evidentiary rule to be applied at trial; "it has no application to a determination of the rights of a pretrial detainee." The due process clauses, however, do apply before the commencement of trial, and *Wolfish* and later decisions have made clear that those clauses, in addition to constraining the permissible forms of detention and setting minimum procedural safeguards, also bar absolutely the "punishment" of an accused before conviction.

In testing for punishment in this context, the Supreme Court has considered, among other things, the government's reasons for imposing a given measure. The highest local court in the District of Columbia concluded in 1981 that incarceration for preventive purposes is nonpunitive and hence may be imposed before trial. The Supreme Court reasoned differently in BROWN V. UNITED STATES (1965), concluding that a preventive rationale should not stop confinement from being punishment for purposes of the BILL OF ATTAINDER clauses, but it has made no similar determination under the due process clauses.

The question whether the Constitution permits pretrial detention for purposes other than assuring a defendant's appearance in court thus remains open. A small part of the question was answered in SCHALL V. MARTIN (1984), where the Court upheld a state program of preventive detention for accused juvenile delinquents, but *Schall* relied heavily on the special prerogatives which the Constitution allows the state with respect to juveniles. Whether unconvicted adults may be jailed to keep them from committing future crimes remains a question to be decided.

The difficulty of the question reflects the strain placed on constitutional norms by the exigencies of the pretrial period. Preventive detention is difficult to reconcile with the ideal of due process, but many people are understandably made uneasy by the thought of defendants "walking the streets" while awaiting trial for serious crimes. A partial solution to the dilemma may be found in the Sixth Amendment's guarantee of a speedy trial: greater fidelity to that provision would alleviate to some extent both the risks associated with pretrial release and the inherent tension between due process and any restraint on the liberty of unconvicted defendants.

ABNER J. MIKVA
(1986)

Bibliography

VERRILLI, DONALD B., JR.   1982   The Eighth Amendment and the Right to Bail: Historical Perspectives. *Columbia Law Review* 82:328–362.

PRICE, UNITED STATES v.
383 U.S. 787 (1966)

Eighteen defendants implicated in the murder of three CIVIL RIGHTS workers in Mississippi challenged the INDICTMENTS against them under the federal CIVIL RIGHTS ACT OF 1866 and that of 1870. One act applied only to persons conspiring to violate any federally protected right, the other only to persons acting "under COLOR OF LAW" who willfully violated such rights. Previous decisions of the Supreme Court had limited the two statutes. "Under color of law" covered only officers and in effect meant STATE ACTION, thus excluding private persons from prosecution. The language of the conspiracy statute notwithstanding, the Court had previously applied it to protect only the narrow class of rights that Congress could, apart from the FOURTEENTH AMENDMENT, protect against private individuals' interference, thus excluding the bulk of civil rights. Justice ABE FORTAS for a unanimous Court ruled that when private persons act in concert with state officials they all act under color of law, because they willfully participate in the prohibited activity (deprivation of life without DUE PROCESS OF LAW) with the state or its agents. Fortas also ruled that the 1870 act meant what it said: it safeguarded *all* federally protected rights secured by the supreme law of the land. By remanding the cases for trial, the Court made possible the first conviction in a federal prosecution for a civil rights murder in the South since RECONSTRUCTION.

LEONARD W. LEVY
(1986)

PRICE-FIXING

See: Antitrust Law; Economic Regulation

PRIGG v. PENNSYLVANIA
16 Peters 539 (1842)

In 1839 Edward Prigg was convicted of kidnapping for removing an alleged fugitive slave from Pennsylvania without obtaining a warrant from a state judge as required by a Pennsylvania act of 1826. Prigg eventually appealed to the United States Supreme Court. Justice JOSEPH STORY, speaking for the Court, overturned his conviction. Story determined: (1) The federal Fugitive Slave Law of 1793 was constitutional. This was the first Supreme Court decision on that issue. (2) All state laws interfering with the rendition of fugitive slaves were unconstitutional. (3) The Fugitive Slave clause of the United States Constitution (Article IV, section 2, clause 3) was in part self-executing, and a slaveowner or his agent could capture and return a runaway slave under a right of self-help, without relying on any statute or judicial procedure, as long as the capture did not breach the peace. (4) State jurists and officials ought to help enforce the federal act of 1793, but Congress could not compel them to do so. Chief Justice ROGER B. TANEY concurred in Story's decision, but not his reasoning. Taney distorted Story's opinion by erroneously asserting that Story had declared it was illegal for state officials to aid in the rendition of fugitive slaves. In fact, Story encouraged the states to aid in the rendition process, but he believed Congress could not compel state assistance. After the decision many free states enacted PERSONAL LIBERTY LAWS which removed state support for the federal act of 1793. With few federal officials to help masters, the law went unenforced in much of the North. This situation helped lead to the passage of a new and harsher fugitive slave law in 1850.

PAUL FINKELMAN
(1986)

Bibliography

FINKELMAN, PAUL   1979   *Prigg v. Pennsylvania* and Northern State Courts: Antislavery Use of a Proslavery Decision. *Civil War History* 25:5–35.

PRIMARY ELECTION

The primary election for selecting candidates is a uniquely American innovation. First adopted in Wisconsin in 1905, it has since spread to every other state. Generally it is the required method for selecting major POLITICAL PARTIES' nominees, whose names are automatically placed on the general election ballot, and for narrowing the field in nonpartisan elections.

The Supreme Court has not heard a modern constitutional challenge to state authority to compel political parties to select their candidates at primaries or to define party membership for these purposes. In *Cousins v. Wigoda* (1975), however, the Supreme Court held that Illinois could not require the Democratic National Convention to seat delegates selected in the state's primary; and in *Democratic Party v. LaFollette* (1981) the Court held that Wisconsin's delegates could not be bound by state law to follow candidate preferences expressed by voters in the state's presidential primary. In both cases, the Justices declared that the "party and its adherents enjoy a constitutionally protected right of political association." And in *Democratic Party* the Court said that "the freedom to associate . . . necessarily presupposes the freedom to identify the people who constitute the association, and to limit association to those people only." The Justices recognized state interests in the conduct of primary elections, however, and their decisions specifically addressed attempts to regulate the conduct of national party conventions and delegates. States might be able to limit the privilege of automatic access to the ballot to those parties conforming with state primary laws.

The Supreme Court has upheld state primary laws that protect the interests of political parties. In 1976 it affirmed a lower court judgment upholding a state's closed primary against a challenge that it abridged the right to vote and violated the RIGHT OF PRIVACY in political affiliation and belief. Similarly, the Court upheld, in *Rosario v. Rockefeller* (1973), an extended waiting period for voters wishing to change party registration, thus protecting party primaries from invasion by opposition party adherents and from casual participation by independent voters. But in *Kusper v. Pontikes* (1973), the Court acknowledged a competing interest in voter participation by rejecting a waiting period so long that the voter wishing to change party affiliation was excluded entirely from at least one primary election.

The Supreme Court has concluded that Congress has authority to regulate primary elections to nominate candidates for federal office, including prohibition of fraud, bribery, and other practices that deprive voters of rights, in UNITED STATES V. CLASSIC (1941) and *Burroughs v. United States* (1934), and regulation of political finance practices, in BUCKLEY V. VALEO (1976). Additional authority to regulate primaries is encompassed within the enforcement clauses of the FOURTEENTH and FIFTEENTH AMENDMENTS.

The principal clauses of these amendments also have independent application to primary elections, apart from any regulatory legislation Congress may enact. Once a state has established the primary for nominating candidates, the ONE PERSON, ONE VOTE principle of the apportionment cases applies. RACIAL DISCRIMINATION in primaries has been held unconstitutional, whether these barriers are established by the state, as in NIXON V. HERN-

DON (1927), or by political parties pursuant to state authorization to define party membership, as in NIXON V. CONDON (1932) and SMITH V. ALLWRIGHT (1944). Racial discrimination has also been held unconstitutional in a primary operated exclusively by a political party following the state's repeal of its primary election system. The most far-reaching application of the Fifteenth Amendment, in TERRY V. ADAMS (1953), prohibited racial discrimination in a "pre-primary" straw vote conducted by an all-white political club, when such "pre-primaries" had regularly proved determinative of elections.

In *Cousins v. Wigoda* the Supreme Court held that state primary laws do not supersede the authority of national party conventions over the selection and seating of delegates, but it did not choose to make a broad decision between competing claims of FREEDOM OF ASSOCIATION of political parties and governmental authority to regulate nomination activities. On one side of this continuing constitutional controversy lie assertions of FIRST AMENDMENT rights of parties to define their own membership, to control the composition and operation of party bodies, and to nominate candidates. On the other side lie assertions of state and congressional authority to regulate elections, of congressional power specifically granted in the enforcement clauses of the Fourteenth and Fifteenth Amendments, and of the independent operation of the principal clauses of those amendments. Notwithstanding the Supreme Court's reluctance to decide this question broadly, the Court's decisions have increasingly recognized the freedom of association of political parties.

DAVID ADAMANY
(1986)

PRIMARY ELECTION
(Update)

As constitutional custodians of the electoral process, states have the power to regulate both voters' access to the polls and the conduct of the POLITICAL PARTIES. Constitutional questions pertaining to primary elections mainly stem from the tension between the state's interest in open, participatory politics and the party's interest in controlling the nominating process and voters' participation in primaries. The FIRST AMENDMENT guarantee of FREEDOM OF ASSOCIATION suggests that parties ought to be free to control participation in their primaries as they please. In contrast, the inexorable push toward broad participatory rights of individuals in all stages of the electoral process necessitates limits on the power of parties to include or exclude persons from voting in primaries. Greater individual participatory rights come at the expense of the parties' ability to select and elect candidates who embrace the party label and its programs.

The Supreme Court has repeatedly addressed the propriety of state restrictions on access to the voting booth in primary elections. These decisions have required the Court to rank the competing constitutional VOTING RIGHTS of individuals and associational rights of parties.

The Court's efforts to alleviate these tensions grew out of the discriminatory practices of the Democratic Party in the Deep South. The Court firmly established the quasi-public nature of party primary activity in the White Primary cases—notably, SMITH V. ALLWRIGHT (1944) and TERRY V. ADAMS (1953)—when it overturned the discriminatory rules of southern Democratic state parties that sought to limit participation in their primaries to white voters only. Regarding primaries, the Court viewed parties as functionally equivalent to the state, and therefore ruled that such discriminatory practices violated the EQUAL PROTECTION clause of the FOURTEENTH AMENDMENT. In *Kusper v. Pontikes* (1973), the Court again sided with individual voting rights over party associational rights, rejecting an Illinois state statute that limited primary participation based on prior party affiliation.

More recent cases have presented conflicts between party rules and state laws regulating who can participate in party primaries, conventions, or other party activities. The Court has generally deferred to party rules on these questions. Several key decisions rendered the party determinative in controlling access to the nomination process, either through open primaries or through the establishment of convention delegate selection procedures. The crux of the constitutional right of association, as the Court explained in *Tashjian v. Republican Party of Connecticut* (1986) was the party's "determination of the boundaries of its own association and the structure which best allows it to pursue its political goals." In *Eu v. San Francisco Democratic Committee* (1989), the Court unanimously invalidated a California statute that, among other things, stripped parties of the ability to endorse candidates in primary elections. These decisions gave solid constitutional protection to the parties' right of self-determination, even if the decisions watered down formal party affiliation. They ensure that parties retain control of access to primary and candidate selection processes. Some commentators have heralded these decisions as marking the reassertion of political parties over the nominating process.

This optimism received a setback in *Morse v. Republican Party of Virginia* (1996), which involved a conflict between a state party rule and a federal statute. The Court in *Morse* narrowed parties' associational right by subordinating it to the VOTING RIGHTS ACT OF 1965, striking down a party's attempt to impose a fee on those attending its state convention. By restricting participation at the convention, the fee unconstitutionally undercut individual voting rights. *Morse* suggests that federal statutes and constitutional voting rights trump the associational rights of state parties to define themselves in an exclusionary fashion. In the name of nondiscriminatory political participation, the Court subordinated the association of the party faithful to the right of peripheral "members" to take part in integral party decisionmaking. The party's freedom to identify its members yielded to the dominant impulse for more-inclusive rules and individual participation. By equating parties with the state and treating party action as STATE ACTION, *Morse* may lead to broader state intrusion into future party activity.

DAVID K. RYDEN
(2000)

Bibliography

EPSTEIN, LEON 1986 *Political Parties in the American Mold.* Madison: University of Wisconsin Press.
LOWENSTEIN, DANIEL H. 1995 *Election Law: Cases and Materials.* Durham, N.C.: Carolina Academic Press.
MAVEETY, NANCY 1991 *Representation Rights and the Burger Years.* Ann Arbor: University of Michigan Press.
RYDEN, DAVID K. 1996 *Representation in Crisis: The Constitution, Interest Groups, and Political Parties.* New York: State University of New York Press.
—— 1999 'The Good, The Bad, and The Ugly': The Judicial Shaping of Party Activities. Pages 50–65 in John Green and Daniel Shea, eds., *The State of the Parties*, 3rd ed. Boulder, Colo.: Roman & Littlefield.

PRINCE v. MASSACHUSETTS
321 U.S. 158 (1944)

Massachusetts law provided that no boy under twelve or girl under eighteen could engage in street sale of any merchandise. Prince was the guardian of a nine-year-old girl. Both were Jehovah's Witnesses and sold Witness literature. The question was whether the statute impermissibly infringed on the free exercise of religion.

Writing for the Court, Justice WILEY B. RUTLEDGE balanced the broad powers of the state to protect the health and welfare of minors against the FIRST AMENDMENT claims and held that the state's power prevailed. Justices FRANK MURPHY and ROBERT H. JACKSON dissented.

Prince follows the "secular regulation" approach to RELIGIOUS LIBERTY introduced by UNITED STATES V. REYNOLDS (1879).

RICHARD E. MORGAN
(1986)

PRINTZ v. UNITED STATES

See: Federalism; *New York v. United States*; State
Immunity from Federal Law

PRIOR RESTRAINT AND CENSORSHIP

History has rooted in our constitutional tradition of freedom of expression the strongest aversion to official censorship. We have learned from the English rejection of press licensing and from our own experiences that the psychology of censors tends to drive them to excess, that censors have a stake in finding things to suppress, and that—in systems of wholesale review before publication—doubt tends to produce suppression. American law tolerated motion picture censorship for a time, but only because movies were not thought to be "the press" in FIRST AMENDMENT terms. Censorship of the movies is now virtually dead, smothered by stringent procedural requirements imposed by unsympathetic courts, by the voluntary rating system, and, most of all, by public distaste for the absurdities of censorship in operation.

American law has tolerated requirements of prior official approval of expression in several important areas, however. No one may broadcast without a license, and the government issues licenses without charge to those it believes will serve the "public interest." Licensing is also grudgingly tolerated—because of the desirability of giving notice and of avoiding conflicts or other disruptions of the normal functions of public places—in the regulation of parades, demonstrations, leafleting, and other expressive activities in public places. But the courts have taken pains to eliminate administrative discretion that would allow officials to censor PUBLIC FORUM expression because they do not approve its message.

Notwithstanding these areas where censorship has been permitted, the clearest principle of First Amendment law is that the least tolerable form of official regulation of expression is a requirement of prior official approval for publication. It is easy to see the suffocating tendency of prior restraints where all expression—whether or not ultimately deemed protected by the First Amendment for publication—must be submitted for clearance before it may be disseminated. The harder question of First Amendment theory has been whether advance prohibitions on expression in specific cases should be discredited by our historical aversion to censorship. The question has arisen most frequently in the context of judicial INJUNCTIONS against publication. Even though injunctions do not involve many of the worst vices of wholesale licensing and censorship, the Supreme court has tarred them with the brush of "prior restraint."

The seminal case was NEAR V. MINNESOTA (1931), handed down by a closely divided Court but never questioned since. A state statute provided for injunctions against any "malicious, scandalous, and defamatory newspaper," and a state judge had enjoined a scandal sheet from publishing anything scandalous in the future. The Minnesota scheme did not require advance approval of all publications, but came into play only after a publication had been found scandalous, and then only to prevent further similar publications. Nevertheless, the majority of the Justices concluded that to enjoin future editions under such vague standards in effect put the newspaper under judicial censorship. Chief Justice CHARLES EVANS HUGHES's historic opinion made clear, however, that the First Amendment's bar against prior restraint was not absolute. Various exceptional instances would justify prior restraints, including this pregnant one: "No one would question but that a government might prevent actual obstruction to its recruiting service or the publication of the sailing dates of transports or the number and location of troops."

It was forty years before the scope of the troop ship exception was tested. The *Pentagon Papers* decision of 1971, NEW YORK TIMES CO. V. UNITED STATES, reaffirmed that judicial injunctions are considered prior restraints and are tolerated only in the most compelling circumstances. This principle barred an injunction against publication of a classified history of the government's decisions in the Vietnam war, although—unlike *Near*—the government had sought to enjoin only readily identifiable material, not unidentified similar publications in the future. Ten different opinions discussed the problem of injunctions in national security cases, and the only proposition commanding a majority was the unexplained conclusion that the government had not justified injunctive relief.

The central theme sounded in the opinions of the six majority Justices was reluctance to act in such difficult circumstances without guidance from Congress. Accepting the premise that there was no statutory authority for an injunction, several considerations support the Court's refusal to forge new rules concerning the disclosure of national secrets. First, the Court's tools are inadequate for the task; ad hoc evaluations of executive claims of risk are not easily balanced against the First Amendment's language and judicial interpretation. Second, dissemination of secret information often arises in the context of heated disagreements about the proper direction of national policy. One's assessment of the disclosure's impact on security will depend on one's reaction to the policy. Third, it would be particularly unsatisfactory to build a judge-made system of rules in an area where much litigation must be done *in camera*. Thus, general rules about specific categories of defense-related information cannot be fashioned by courts. The best hope in a nuclear age for accommodating the needs of secrecy and the public's RIGHT TO KNOW lies in the legislative process where, removed from pressures of adjudicting particular cases, general rules can be fashioned. The courts' proper role in this area is to review legislation, not try to devise rules of secrecy case by case.

Chilling this victory for freedom of the press were admonitions, loosely endorsed by four Justices, that the espionage statutes might support criminal sanctions against the *New York Times* and its reporters. No journalists were indicted, but the prosecutions of Daniel Ellsberg and Anthony Russo rested on a view of several statutes that would reach the press by punishing news-gathering activities necessarily incident to publication. Since the dismissal of these cases for reasons irrelevant to these issues, the extent of possible criminal liability for publishing national security secrets remains unclear.

The *Pentagon Papers* case underlines how little the United States has relied on law to control press coverage of national defense and foreign policy matters. For most of our history the press has rarely tested the limits of its rights to publish. Secrets were kept because people in and out of government with access to military and diplomatic secrets shared basic assumptions about national aims. The Vietnam war changed all that. The *Pentagon Papers* dispute marked the passing of an era in which journalists could be counted on to work within understood limits of discretion in handling secret information.

The third major decision striking down a judicial order not to publish involved neither national security nor scandal but the right of a criminal defendant to a fair trial. A state court enjoined publication of an accused's confession and some other incriminating material on the ground that if prospective jurors learned about it they might be incapable of impartiality. In NEBRASKA PRESS ASSOCIATION V. STUART (1976) the Supreme Court decided that the potential prejudice was speculative, and it rejected enjoining publication on speculation. The majority opinion examined the evidence to determine the nature and extent of pretrial publicity, the effectiveness of other measures in mitigating prejudice, and the effectiveness of a prior restraint in reducing the dangers. This opinion determined that the impact of pretrial publicity was necessarily speculative, that alternative measures short of prior restraint had not been considered by the lower courts, and that prior restraint would not significantly reduce the dangers presented.

On one issue of considerable importance, the Court seemed to be in full agreement. The opinions endorsed controls on parties, lawyers, witnesses, and law enforcement personnel as sources of information for journalists. These GAG ORDERS have been controversial among many journalists and publishers who think the First Amendment should guarantee the right to gather news. Although freeing the press from direct control by limiting prior restraint, the Court approved an indirect method of reaching the same result, guaranteeing that the press print no prejudicial publicity, by approving direct controls on sources of prejudicial information. The Court has subsequently held that pretrial motions may be closed to the public and the press with the consent of the prosecutor and the accused but over the objection of the press, in GANNETT CO. V. DEPASQUALE (1979). This case involved access to judicial proceedings, not prior restraints on the press, and was decided largely on Sixth Amendment grounds. The Court reached the opposite result with respect to trials in RICHMOND NEWSPAPERS V. VIRGINIA (1980), but acknowledged that the right of access to trials is not absolute.

These decisions and others have firmly established that the First Amendment tolerates virtually no prior restraints. This DOCTRINE is one of the central principles of our law of FREEDOM OF THE PRESS. On the surface, the doctrine concerns only the form of controls on expression. It bars controls prior to publication, even if imposition of criminal or civil liability following publication would be constitutional. But, as with most limitations of form, the prior restraint doctrine has important substantive consequences. Perhaps the most important of these consequences is that the doctrine is presumably an absolute bar to any wholesale system of administrative licensing or censorship of the press, which is the most repellent form of government suppression of expression. Second, the prior restraint doctrine removes most of the opportunities for official control of those types of expression for which general rules of control are difficult to formulate. The message of the prior restraint doctrine is that if you cannot control expression pursuant to general legislative standards, you cannot control it at all—or nearly at all, as the *Pentagon Papers* decision suggests, by suggesting an exception allowing an injunction in a truly compelling case of national security. A third effect of the doctrine is that by transferring questions of control over expression from the judiciary to the legislatures, it provides an enormously beneficial protection for the politically powerful mass media, if not for other elements of society with strong First Amendment interests but weaker influence in the legislative process.

Although the Supreme Court has exceeded its historical warrant in subjecting judicial injunctions to the full burden of our law's traditional aversion to prior restraints, there are sound reasons for viewing all prior controls—not only wholesale licensing and censorship—as dangerous to free expression. Generally it is administratively easier to prevent expression in advance than to punish it after the fact. The inertia of public officials in responding to a *fait accompli,* the chance to look at whether expression has actually caused harm rather than speculate about the matter, public support for the speaker, and the interposition of juries and other procedural safeguards of the usual criminal or civil process all tend to reinforce tolerance when expression can only be dealt with by subsequent punishment. Moreover, all prior restraint systems, including injunctions, tend to divert attention from the central question of whether expression is protected to the subsidiary problem of promoting the effectiveness of the prior restraint system. Once a prior restraint is issued, the authority and prestige of the restraining agent are at stake. If it is disobeyed, the legality of the expression takes a back seat to the enforcement of obedience to the prior restraint process. Moreover, the time it takes a prior restraint process to decide produces a systematic delay of expression. On the other hand, where law must wait to move against expression after it has been published, time is on the side of freedom. All in all, even such prior restraints as judicial injunctions—which are more discriminating than wholesale censorship—tend toward irresponsible administration and an exaggerated assessment of the dangers of free expression.

BENNO C. SCHMIDT, JR.
(1986)

Bibliography

BLASI, VINCENT 1981 Toward a Theory of Prior Restraint: The Central Linkage. *Minnesota Law Review* 66:11.

EMERSON, THOMAS 1955 The Doctrine of Prior Restraint *Law and Contemporary Problems* 20:648.

SCHMIDT, BENNO C., JR. 1977 Nebraska Press Association: An Expansion of Freedom and Contraction of Theory. *Stanford Law Review* 29:431.

PRIOR TESTIMONY

See: Confrontation, Right of

PRISONERS' RIGHTS

Some might think that the very term "prisoners' rights" is an oxymoron, because the essence of being imprisoned is the reduction or elimination of rights. Prisoners have traditionally been deprived of VOTING RIGHTS and, obviously, of the right to travel outside the prison confines, often of the right to communicate freely with the outside world and of the right of conjugal relationships, and, at times, of the right of ACCESS TO COURTS to complain about even those rights that they retain.

There is a tension in constitutional doctrine between the need to enforce discipline in the difficult circumstances of the prison and the necessity of recognizing that in a society of law, even prisoners ought to have remedies for violation of whatever constitutional rights they possess and also to have the right to be immune from arbitrary and capricious actions of the prison hierarchy. This tension has expressed itself in judicial opinions in two major ways: first, the enunciation of a "hands-off doctrine" that precludes JURISDICTION to review complaints of inmates; and second, the determination, either broadly or narrowly, of the nature of the rights that a prisoner might have. In times when the cluster of rights is extremely narrow, the distinction between the first mode of analysis and the second is not great.

As late as 1963 a commentator could write that there is a "conviction held with virtual unanimity by the courts that it is beyond their power to review the internal management of the prison system." Much of this changed, however, when the Supreme Court held in *Wolff v. McDonnell* (1974), as part of its expansion of PROCEDURAL DUE PROCESS to the decision making of many institutions, that "a prisoner is not wholly stripped of constitutional protections when he is imprisoned for crime. There is no iron curtain drawn between the Constitution and the prisons of this country."

Still, the definition of rights for prisoners is almost always husbanded with conditions and recognition of concerns for the difficulties the warden faces. Where the FIRST AMENDMENT is concerned, RELIGIOUS LIBERTY is guaranteed but only to the extent that the opportunities to exercise that freedom must be "reasonable." Similarly, when the right to speak and communicate is concerned, the Court limited it in PELL V. PROCUNIER (1974) to the kind of expression that is "not inconsistent with [their] status as . . . prisoner[s] or with the legitimate penological objectives of the corrections system." In *Lee v. Washington* (1968) the Court implied that even racial SEGREGATION may be tolerated when it is essential to "prison security and discipline." And the Court held in *Hudson v. Palmer* (1984), a departure from previous expansion of privacy rights, that "the FOURTH AMENDMENT had no applicability to a prison cell."

With the wonderful perversity that makes legal development fascinating, the Supreme Court, in the late 1970s, expanded prisoners' rights of access to courts, while almost simultaneously narrowing the grounds for constitutional challenge.

Litigation concerning prisoners' rights is an indicator of concern about individual rights generally. As the Court changes its views of the breadth and definition of such rights, the treatment of alleged institutional wrongs in a correctional setting is like the canary a miner takes along down the shaft. Constitutional litigation during the 1960s and 1970s created massive exposure of the internal workings of correctional institutions and pressure for change. In many instances, wholesale reforms were imposed upon these institutions as a consequence of the litigation. But the canary is weakening. (See INSTITUTIONAL LITIGATION.)

MONROE E. PRICE
(1986)

Bibliography

NOTE 1963 Beyond the Ken of the Courts: A Critique of Judicial Refusal to Review the Complaints of Convicts. *Yale Law Journal* 72:506.

PRISONERS' RIGHTS
(Update 1)

Upon conviction and imprisonment, a profound change occurs in a person's legal status. Duly convicted prisoners lose entirely many freedoms enjoyed by free persons; however, they do not relinquish all rights. As the Supreme Court noted in *Wolff v. McDonnell* (1974), "though his rights may be diminished by the needs and exigencies of the institutional environment, a prisoner is not wholly stripped of constitutional protections when he is imprisoned for crime. There is no iron curtain drawn between the Constitution and the prisons of this country."

Prisoners always retain the right to the minimal conditions necessary for human survival (i.e., the right to food, clothing, shelter, and medical care). The right of the prisoners to a non-life-threatening environment goes beyond the provision of life's necessities; it includes their right to be protected from each other and from themselves. On this last point, lower courts have been more responsive to prisoners' claim than Supreme Court and have found that prison crowding is unconstitutional. As a federal district court in Florida asserted in *Costello v. Wainwright* (1975), prison crowding "endangers the very lives of the inmates" and therefore violates the Eighth Amendment's guarantee against CRUEL AND UNUSUAL PUNISHMENT. The Supreme Court's reluctance to follow the lower courts is understandable, for emperical studies flatly contradict the assertion that crowding is life-threatening. Not only are the overall death rates, accidental death rates, and homicide and suicide rates of inmates two or three times lower than for comparable groups of parolees (controlling for age, race, and sex), but no statistically significant correlations exist between measures of crowding (density and occupancy) and inmate death rates.

Beyond agreement that inmates have the minimal right to a non-life-threatening environment, legal debate rages. Some courts and legal scholars have taken their cues from the Sixth Circuit Court of Appeals in *Coffin v. Reichard*

(1944) and have declared that prisoners retain all the rights of ordinary citizens except those expressly or by necessary implication taken by law. The Supreme Court's decision in PROCUNIER V. MARTINEZ (1974) followed this line of reasoning when it held that it would employ a STRICT SCRUTINY standard of review to evaluate claims that the rights of prisoners were being denied. It declared that it would sustain limitations of prisoners' rights only if they furthered an important or substantial governmental interest and if they were no greater than necessary to protect that interest.

Fundamentally opposed to *Coffin* and *Procunier* is the view, now dominant on the Supreme Court, that inmates are without rights except for those conferred by law or necessarily implied and that, as a consequence, courts should employ the reasonableness test to assess the legitimacy of restrictions on what prisoners assert to be their rights. In *Turner v. Safley* (1987) the Supreme Court articulated this position and rejected the use of strict scrutiny in prisoners' rights cases. Writing for a five-member majority, Justice SANDRA DAY O'CONNOR declared that "when a prison regulation impinges on inmates' constitutional rights, the regulation is valid if it is reasonably related to legitimate penological interests." O'Connor announced a four-prong test for measuring reasonableness: (1) Is there "a "valid, rational connection' between the prison regulation and the legitimate government interest put forward to justify it?" (2) "Are alternative means of exercising the right . . . open to prison inmates?" (3) What is "the impact [that] accommodation of the asserted constitutional right will have on guards and other inmates, and on the allocation of prison resources generally"? (4) Is "the absence of ready alternatives . . . evidence of reasonableness of the prison regulation"? Employing this four-prong test, Justice O'Connor rejected a FIRST AMENDMENT challenge to a Missouri ban on inmate-to-inmate correspondence because the prohibition on correspondence was "logically connected" to legitimate security concerns. In O'LONE V. ESTATE OF SHABAZZ (1987), the Court applied the same reasonableness test to sustain New Jersey prison policies that resulted in Muslim inmates' inability to attend weekly congregational services.

Security concerns generally trump the claims of prisoners' rights; the Court is hesitant to recognize inmate claims that have the potential of putting at risk the prison itself, the guards, other inmates, or the petitioner. Justice WILLIAM H. REHNQUIST, in *Jones v. North Carolina Prisoners' Union* (1977), summarized well the Court's deferential approach to these issues: "It is enough to say that they [prison officials] have not been conclusively shown to be wrong in this view. The interest in preserving order and authority in prisons is self-evident."

Applying this reasoning, the Court has denied inmates'

claims to a First Amendment right to organize as a prisoners' labor union, rejected the contention that an inmate's RIGHT OF PRIVACY protects against routine strip and body-cavity searches, and refused to recognize any inmate legal rights in the ordinary classification process or interprison transfer. As the Court said in *Moody v. Daggett* (1976), no DUE PROCESS issues are implicated by "the discretionary transfer of state prisoners to a substantially less agreeable prison, even where the transfer visit[s] a 'grievous loss' upon the inmate. The same is true of prisoner classification and eligibility for rehabilitative programs."

Beyond assuring life's necessities for inmates, the Court has consistently recognized inmates' claims in only two areas: their due process right of ACCESS TO THE COURTS and PROCEDURAL DUE PROCESS protection of their liberty interest in retaining "good time" and avoiding solitary confinement. Concerning the former, the Court has repeatedly insisted that inmates have the right to access to legal redress and that this right of access to the courts requires either an adequate law library or assistance from persons trained in law (although not necessarily lawyers). Concerning the latter, the Court held in *Wolff v. McDonnell* that inmates have a liberty interest in the good-time credit they have acquired and that they may not be stripped of these credits without a hearing before an impartial tribunal. The Court has not considered either of these rights to jeopardize prison security. Access to the courts poses no problems at all, and, as the Court made explicit in *Hewitt v. Helms* (1978) and *Superintendent v. Hill* (1985), prison disciplinary proceedings can follow (and need not precede) solitary confinement and can impose sanctions based on the lax evidentiary standard of "some evidence."

RALPH A. ROSSUM
(1992)

(SEE ALSO: *Body Search*.)

Bibliography

COHEN, FRED 1988 The Law of Prisoner's Rights: An Overview. *Criminal Law Bulletin* 24:321–349.
ROSSUM, RALPH A. 1984 The Problem of Prison Crowding: On the Limits of Prison Capacity and Judicial Capacity. *Benchmark* 1, no. 6:22–30.

PRISONERS' RIGHTS
(Update 2)

During the 1990s, the Supreme Court, with a few exceptions, continued to narrowly construe the scope of prisoners' constitutional rights. In 1974, the Court had held that a disciplinary hearing that may result in the revocation of good-time credits must be accompanied by certain procedural safeguards, such as notice of the disciplinary charge before the hearing. But in *Sandin v. Conner* (1995), the Court concluded that DUE PROCESS OF LAW affords no procedural protection to a prisoner sentenced to a disciplinary-segregation unit for thirty days for a disciplinary infraction.

In *Lewis v. Casey* (1996), the Court held that prisoners' right of access to the courts does not include the right to litigate a claim effectively. Prison officials may have to make some limited assistance available to inmates to ensure that they have a "reasonably adequate opportunity" to file nonfrivolous claims challenging their convictions, sentences, or conditions of confinement. But once their claims have been filed in court, prisoners are, as a constitutional matter, on their own.

Some of the most significant restrictions on prisoners' rights have emanated not from the Supreme Court but from Congress. Under the Prison Litigation Reform Act, for example, prisoners who have obtained injunctive relief can be required to reestablish periodically that they are entitled to the court-ordered relief. These and other restrictions to which prisoners, but not nonprisoners, are subject under the statute have provoked controversy, litigation, and debate.

LYNN S. BRANHAM
(2000)

Bibliography

BOSTON, JOHN and MANVILLE, DANIEL E. 1995 *Prisoners' Self-Help Litigation Manual*, 3rd ed. New York: Oceana Publications.
BRANHAM, LYNN S. 1998 *The Law of Sentencing, Corrections, and Prisoners' Rights in a Nutshell*. St. Paul, Minn.: West Group.

PRIVACY

See: Right of Privacy

PRIVACY ACT
88 Stat. 1896 (1974)

The Privacy Act was passed in response to public concern about "data banks" maintained by United States government agencies. Often, a person did not know what agencies held files on him or what such files contained. In addition, information provided to one government agency—often under a promise of confidentiality—was passed on to a second agency to be used for a different purpose, and that without the knowledge or consent of the individual concerned.

The act was passed by Congress and signed by President GERALD R. FORD in December 1974. According to its provisions: an individual is to have access to any files concerning him maintained by a government agency (except law-enforcement and national security files); an individual who believes that information about him in a government file is inaccurate or incomplete may seek injunctive relief to correct the file; no agency is to use information provided by an individual for other than the original purpose, or to provide the information to another agency, without the individual's consent; no agency may deny benefits to individuals who refuse to disclose their social security numbers; and no agency may maintain records describing the exercise of rights protected by the FIRST AMENDMENT.

DENNIS J. MAHONEY
(1986)

Bibliography

O'BRIEN, DAVID M. 1979 *Privacy, Law, and Public Policy.* New York: Praeger.

PRIVACY AND THE FIRST AMENDMENT

William L. Prosser has listed four categories of invasion of privacy: intrusion upon the plaintiff's seclusion or solitude, or into his private affairs; public disclosure of embarrassing private facts about the plaintiff; publicity which places the plaintiff in a false light in the public eye; and appropriation, for the defendant's advantage, of the plaintiff's name or likeness. Absent the communication of information disclosed by the intrusion, the first category of invasion raises no FIRST AMENDMENT issue.

The second category, the public disclosure of embarrassing private facts, clearly does raise a First Amendment issue. When does the FREEDOM OF THE PRESS to report "news" outbalance the individual's RIGHT TO PRIVACY, even if the disclosure is of embarrassing private facts? Thus far, the Supreme Court has only partially answered that question. In COX BROADCASTING CORPORATION V. COHN (1975) the Court held that the state could not impose liability for invasion of privacy by reason of the defendant's television news disclosure of the name of a rape victim. The Court held that the First Amendment immunized the press from such liability where the information disclosed was truthful and had already been publicly disclosed in court records. Subsequent decisions have indicated that such a First Amendment privilege applies as well to the publication of material in at least some official records designated confidential—for example, information about a criminal proceeding involving a juvenile, even though it was obtained from sources other than the public record. But what of intimate private fact disclosures that do not involve crim-

inal proceedings, or other official action? Or suppose the disclosure of private facts is embarrassing to the subject, but does not injure reputation. Which prevails, the plaintiff's right of privacy or the defendant's FREEDOM OF SPEECH? The Supreme Court thus far has been silent on these issues, and the lower courts have offered no satisfactory answers.

The third category, known as "false light" privacy, was the subject of the Supreme Court's decision in *Time, Inc. v. Hill* (1967). Defendant's report in *Life* magazine of plaintiffs' encounter with gangsters was in part false, though not reputation injuring. The Supreme Court held that the defendant was entitled to a First Amendment defense in a false-light privacy action unless the defendant knew the matter reported was false or published with reckless disregard of the truth. The Court acknowledged that this standard was borrowed from the First Amendment defense to DEFAMATION which it had fashioned in NEW YORK TIMES V. SULLIVAN (1964). Where *Sullivan* had involved statements about a public official, *Hill* seemingly extended the First Amendment privilege to statements about "a matter of public interest." The First Amendment defamation defense was later expanded in GERTZ V. ROBERT WELCH, INC. (1974) to apply to reports involving "public figures" as well as "public officials," and to require at least a negligence standard of liability as regards defamation of nonpublic figures. The Supreme Court has not had occasion to reconsider the impact of the First Amendment upon "false light" privacy cases since its decision in *Gertz*.

The fourth category is more generally referred to as the "right of publicity." It differs fundamentally from the other categories in that the injury does not consist of embarrassment and humiliation. It is based rather upon the wrongful appropriation of a person's (usually a celebrity's) name or likeness for commercial purposes. The measure of recovery is based upon the value of the use, not the injury suffered from mental distress. The only Supreme Court decision to consider the impact of the First Amendment upon the right of publicity has been *Zacchini v. Scripps-Howard Broadcasting Co.* (1977). The plaintiff performed a "human cannonball" act at a county fair. The defendant photographed his entire act and broadcast it in a local television news program. Plaintiff sued for infringement of his right of publicity. The Supreme Court held that the defendant was not entitled to a First Amendment defense. The Court regarded this as "the strongest case" for the right of publicity because it involved "the appropriation of the very activity by which the entertainer acquired his reputation in the first place." Even in the usual case, where a celebrity's name or likeness is used in order to sell a product, the lower courts have not found the First Amendment to constitute a defense, and it seems unlikely that the Supreme Court would take a contrary view. On the other hand, where the name or likeness is used as a part of an informational work, such as a biography or a biographical motion picture, in most cases the First Amendment would appear to constitute a valid defense.

MELVILLE B. NIMMER
(1986)

Bibliography

NIMMER, MELVILLE B.   1968   The Right to Speak from *Times* to *Time:* First Amendment Theory Applied to Libel and Misapplied to Privacy. *California Law Review* 56:935–967.
PROSSER, WILLIAM L.   1971   *Torts*, 4th ed. St. Paul, Minn.: West Publishing Co.

PRIVATE DISCRIMINATION

The Constitution is a document filled with restraints upon the actions of government, but for the most part it has not been interpreted to extend its reach into the private sector. The FOURTEENTH AMENDMENT to the Constitution, for example, guarantees the EQUAL PROTECTION OF THE LAWS, a command against discrimination that the Supreme Court has long read as applying only to the actions of states. The Supreme Court in BOLLING V. SHARPE (1954) applied the antidiscrimination principle to the federal government, holding that the DUE PROCESS clause of the Fifth Amendment contains within it an equal protection component. No provision of the Constitution, however, has ever been interpreted to apply rules of equal protection directly to private entities, prohibiting a private citizen or corporation from discriminating against others on the basis of race, sex, or religion.

Acts of private discrimination, nevertheless, do raise a number of significant constitutional issues. First, to what extent does the THIRTEENTH AMENDMENT's abolition of SLAVERY serve as a constitutional restraint on private acts of discrimination less severe than actual slavery? Second, when are the actions of private entities sufficiently intertwined with government to be brought within the coverage of the Fourteenth Amendment's equal protection clause under the rubric of the STATE ACTION doctrine? Third, when the United States Congress forbids private discrimination, as in CIVIL RIGHTS laws prohibiting racial bias in employment or housing, from where in the Constitution does Congress derive its affirmative authority to pass such legislation? Finally, when laws are passed at the federal, state, or local level banning discrimination by private individuals, businesses, or organizations, do such laws violate the FREEDOM OF ASSEMBLY AND ASSOCIATION embodied in the FIRST AMENDMENT?

The Thirteenth Amendment is one of the few constitutional provisions that directly implicates private conduct. That amendment, the first of the three "CIVIL WAR amendments," flatly bans slavery and involuntary servitude. It acts directly upon private entities; slaves were owned by private businesses and individuals. The Thirteenth Amendment, however, has not been interpreted to provide a significant source of constitutional proscription against acts of private discrimination. While the Amendment has been construed by the Supreme Court to protect individuals from the "badges and incidents" of slavery as well as actual slavery itself, the Supreme Court held in the CIVIL RIGHTS CASES in 1883 that the Amendment does not restrict "mere discriminations on account of race or color." The Thirteenth is thus too narrow a prohibition to be of practical use as a restraint against the types of private discrimination prevalent in modern society. In 1968, however, the Supreme Court did hold that the Thirteenth Amendment serves as an important source of congressional power to pass legislation banning private acts of discrimination.

While the equal protection clause of the Fourteenth Amendment prohibits only governmental discrimination, under the so-called state action requirement many Supreme Court decisions have recognized that ostensibly private discrimination should be treated as state action because of some connection between the private actor and the government. When the private actor is performing a "public function," for example, its activities are treated as state action, and subject to the equal protection clause. The Supreme Court has thus held that segregated primary elections conducted by political parties in Texas involved public functions and violated the Fourteenth Amendment. In MARSH V. ALABAMA (1946) the Court held that a "company town," a privately owned area encompassing both residential and business districts that looked exactly like any other town and in which the private company had assumed all the normal functions of running a city, was subject to the limitations of the First and Fourteenth Amendments. The Court has also held that apparently private activity will be treated as state action when the state and private entities have a "symbiotic relationship," as where a private restaurant leases space in a public parking garage, or when the state has commanded or encouraged acts of private discrimination.

When neither the Thirteenth Amendment nor the "state action" doctrine under the Fourteenth Amendment can be stretched to embrace a particular type of private discrimination, then the Constitution of its own force does not render the private discrimination illegal. Federal, state, and local governments may then choose to pass legislation filling this vacuum, banning discrimination through statutes and ordinances. Modern American law is pervaded with restrictions directed against private entities forbidding discrimination of all kinds, including discrimination on the basis of race, ethnic origin, sex, sexual orientation, religion, age, and physical or mental disabilities. Many of these laws are acts of Congress. When Congress attempts to outlaw private discrimination, the first constitutional question to be addressed is whether Congress has affirmative constitutional power to enact the law.

Two principal constitutional sources have been advanced to support congressional legislation banning private discrimination: the COMMERCE CLAUSE, and Congress's powers under the enforcement clauses of the Thirteenth Amendment, Fourteenth Amendment, and FIFTEENTH AMENDMENT. In the debates leading to the passage of the CIVIL RIGHTS ACT OF 1964, one of the most important modern acts of legislation dealing with private discrimination, members of Congress debated whether the act should be grounded in Congress's power to regulate INTERSTATE COMMERCE or in its power under section 5 of the Fourteenth Amendment to enforce the Amendment by "appropriate legislation." Similar enforcement clauses exist under the Thirteenth Amendment, which abolished slavery; under the Fifteenth Amendment, which granted emancipated blacks the right to vote; and under several later amendments, including the NINETEENTH AMENDMENT (WOMAN SUFFRAGE), the TWENTY-THIRD AMENDMENT (voting in the DISTRICT OF COLUMBIA), the TWENTY-FOURTH AMENDMENT (abolition of POLL TAXES), and the TWENTY-SIXTH AMENDMENT, (establishing eighteen as voting age).

The Civil Rights Act of 1964 banned most significant acts of discrimination in the private sector, including such areas as employment transportation, restaurants, and hotel accommodations. Some members of Congress argued that the act should be rooted in the enforcement clause of the Fourteenth Amendment, because it was in reality an exercise in social legislation aimed at attacking racial bias. Other members, doubtful that the Fourteenth Amendment could be used to reach private discrimination, argued for buttressing the act under the well-established powers of Congress to regulate interstate commerce. In two significant 1964 decisions shortly following passage of the act, HEART OF ATLANTA MOTEL V. UNITED STATES and *Katzenbach v. McClung*, the Supreme Court upheld the Civil Rights Act on the basis of the commerce clause, and thus did not reach the question of congressional power under the Fourteenth Amendment.

As a practical matter, virtually any enactment of Congress aimed at private discrimination would be sustained under modern commerce clause analysis. Even localized acts of discrimination may, when considered cumulatively with other such acts around the nation, have a substantial impact on interstate commerce when aggregated. Under contemporary commerce clause theory, that potential aggregate impact would be enough to uphold the legislation. Because Congress's power under the commerce clause is

so sweeping, there has been little cause for the Court to determine precisely how far congressional enforcement powers under the post-Civil War amendments may be extended to reach private-sector discrimination.

The few decisions that have dealt with congressional enforcement power under the Civil War amendments, however, indicate that Congress's power does include an ability to proscribe private activity that would not be directly prohibited by the substantive reach of the amendment itself. In an important decision involving the Thirteenth Amendment, JONES V. ALFRED H. MAYER CO. (1968), the Court upheld an application of the Civil Rights Act of 1866 to forbid private discrimination in property dealings. The Court held that Congress's power to enforce the Thirteenth Amendment included the power to identify "badges or incidents of slavery" and to pass laws NECESSARY AND PROPER to combat them.

In sum, there are ample sources of support in the Constitution for acts of Congress banning private discrimination. Congress has passed a considerable body of laws attacking such discrimination, often including in the legislation enforcement mechanisms or procedural advantages that actually make it easier to prove and obtain legal relief from acts of private discrimination than for claims based directly on the Constitution for discrimination by the government. Modern civil rights litigation frequently involves interpretation of such legislation, in which the courts are asked to determine just how far Congress has gone in a particular statute to ban discrimination in the private sector.

The final area of modern constitutional debate concerning discrimination in the private sector involves attempts by organizations engaged in discrimination to resist the application of laws banning such discrimination on the grounds that the laws infringe on the constitutional right of free association. The Civil Rights Act of 1964, and the many state and local civil rights laws passed in the 1960s and early 1970s modeled after that act, tended to reach only commercial private activity, such as employers, or stores, restaurants, and places of lodging generally "open for business to the public." A second generation of civil rights acts began to be passed by cities and states around the country, however, seeking to forbid discrimination by "private" clubs and organizations. Several of these groups claimed that these regulations violated their constitutional rights of free association.

These claims have, thus far, proved unsuccessful. In *Roberts v. United States Jaycees* (1984), the Supreme Court faced a Minnesota law that prohibited SEX DISCRIMINATION in groups such as the Jaycees. The Supreme Court established two types of FREEDOM OF ASSOCIATION: FREEDOM OF INTIMATE ASSOCIATION and "freedom of expressive association." Groups with strong claims to freedom of intimate association tend to be relatively small, exercise a high degree of selectivity, and maintain seclusion from others as critical aspects of the relationship. The Jaycees, the Court held, were basically unselective, and lacked the attributes that would qualify for recognition of intimate associational claims. The second freedom of expressive association is an incident of the FREEDOM OF SPEECH and assembly. The Court in *Roberts* held that application of state sex discrimination laws to the Jaycees would not impermissibly interfere with their freedom of expressive association, and it upheld the Minnesota law.

The Court next visited the freedom of association problem in *Board of Directors of Rotary International v. Rotary Club of Duarte* (1987). In characterizing the Rotary Club, the Court noted that although Rotary Clubs take no positions on "public questions," they do "engage in a variety of commendable service activities" protected by the First Amendment. These sorts of activities, however, posed no serious implications for infringement of the members' rights of expressive association. The lessons of these cases appear to be that attempts by private groups to resist imposition of antidiscrimination laws on free association grounds will probably fail, unless the groups possess genuinely impressive credentials as truly private organizations, with characteristics of exclusion or intimacy bordering on those of family or religious groups.

A related problem involves private religious schools that discriminate on the basis of race. The Supreme Court in *Norwood v. Harrison* (1973) held that a state could not lend textbooks to schools that practice racial SEGREGATION, even though such aid to a religious school would not be illegal under the ESTABLISHMENT CLAUSE. Notwithstanding the lack of any violation of the principle of SEPARATION OF CHURCH AND STATE, the Court held that there is no constitutional protection for state aid to RACIAL DISCRIMINATION. In BOB JONES UNIVERSITY V. UNITED STATES (1983), the Court held that the Internal Revenue Service had been authorized by Congress to deny tax-exempt status to private schools that discriminate on a racial basis, and that this denial did not prohibit the free exercise of religion.

Modern constitutional law, in conclusion, generally does not impose restraints on private discrimination through direct application of the Constitution itself. On the other hand, by refusing to recognize any significant constitutional barriers to antidiscrimination legislation, modern constitutional law facilitates efforts on the part of federal, state, and local governments to eradicate such discrimination.

RODNEY A. SMOLLA
(1992)

(SEE ALSO: *Affirmative Action; Badges of Servitude; Employment Discrimination; Fourteenth Amendment and Section 5 (Framing); Fourteenth Amendment and Section 5 (Judicial Construction); Racial Quotas; Racial Preference.*)

PRIVATIZATION AND THE CONSTITUTION

Budget pressures and concerns for efficient administration have led governments increasingly to consider privatizing functions that have traditionally been conducted by public agencies. Many correctional facilities are now operated by private CORPORATIONS, for example, and private police often supplement and sometimes replace public police. Privatization raises interesting constitutional issues, only a few of which the Supreme Court has addressed.

The government's power to privatize even the most traditional public functions is probably unlimited by the federal Constitution. (Privatization may be limited by state constitutions, but those limitations are not considered here.) One might think that public security was an essentially government function, but there is a long tradition of private policing and private provision of fire protection services, sometimes in places where there were no public police or fire services. Similarly, there seems little reason to think that the federal Constitution bars a state government from eliminating its public school system. The Court has sometimes referred to "core government functions" of the states when discussing Congress's power to regulate state governments, but those references probably have no implications for governments' decisions to eliminate even core functions.

The Constitution may not limit the government's power to privatize, but it might limit the actions of the entities conducting the activities that previously were done by the government. The STATE ACTION doctrine holds that only government action is subject to the limitations expressed in the Constitution. Privatization places pressure on the state action doctrine: If a state contracts with a private operator of correctional facilities, may the prison guards beat prisoners without violating the Eighth Amendment's prohibition of CRUEL AND UNUSUAL PUNISHMENT because the guards are employed by a private company, not the state? The Court has not yet comprehensively confronted the question of privatization.

Privatization of public functions occurs in two forms: through quasi-public corporations and through contracting-out. The government may set up a corporation to conduct some activity that previously had been done by the government itself. The United States Postal Service and Amtrak are good examples. These quasi-public corporations typically have boards of directors appointed by public authorities, but they operate without substantial direct public supervision. Their operations are financed not by appropriations in the government budget but by fees they charge the public and funds they borrow in the general market. Further, no legislative committee regularly conducts oversight hearings on their operations.

The Court initially addressed the legal status of quasi-public corporations in a series of cases involving the use of such corporations to build warships, but those cases did not raise questions about whether such corporations had to comply with the Constitution's individual rights provisions. In 1995 the Court in LEBRON V. NATIONAL RAILROAD PASSENGER CORP. held that Amtrak had to comply with constitutional requirements. The case involved a decision to exclude a political advertisement criticizing the Coors beer company for its alleged support of conservative causes. Amtrak took the position that, like any owner of private property, it could exclude the advertisement without considering any possible constitutional concerns. The Court said that Amtrak was "not a private entity but the Government itself," in large part because the President appointed a majority of Amtrak's board of directors. The decision's scope is unclear because the degree of public control over Amtrak remained unusually substantial. The result might differ if the quasi-public corporation's board of directors had only minority representation from public appointees. (The President has the power to appoint a minority of the board of directors of Comsat, the corporation that operates communications satellites.) Yet political constraints may limit extensive privatization without public control. Legislators may be unwilling to privatize unless they are assured that public appointees will have a substantial role in the quasi-public corporation's decisions. When they do have such a role, *Lebron* suggests that constitutional restraints will apply.

The Court has discussed contracting-out extensively in two cases. *Rendell-Baker v. Kohn* (1982), the more important, involved a privately owned and operated school that contracted with the state to instruct "problem" students. The school received over 90 percent of its budget from public funds, and nearly all its students were referred to it by public institutions. Rendell-Baker, a teacher, was fired by the school for disagreeing with school policies. The Court held that the school was not a "state actor," and that the FIRST AMENDMENT therefore did not restrict the school's ability to discharge its employers, as it would in the public school system. According to the Court, the school's decision to fire Rendell-Baker was not "compelled or even influenced by any state regulation."

West v. Atkins (1988) involved a private doctor who contracted to provide medical services to prisoners. The Court held that the state was subject to liability based on the doctor's failure to provide medical care that satisfied constitutional requirements. Contracting out the state's constitutional obligation to provide adequate medical care to those whose lives it controlled in its prisons did not relieve the state of responsibility. The difference from *Rendell-Baker* was apparently that the state had no federal constitutional duty to provide an education to problem students.

Rendell-Baker's approach, emphasizing whether the state directed the action in question, suggests the importance of political constraints on privatization. Those conducting activities formerly performed by the government are limited by the provisions of their contracts with the government, and by whatever other regulations the government chooses to enact. The Constitution comes into play only when the action in question is not prohibited either by the contract or by other regulations. In many circumstances, however, public officials have political reasons to include restrictive provisions in their contracts. For example, state teachers' unions may insist that schools receiving vouchers provide protections to their employees roughly equivalent to the protections public school teachers receive from the Constitution. In other circumstances, however, these political restraints may be less important. For example, legislators may face few political pressures when they contract out correctional services.

Privatization of public functions seems likely to increase, and the Court will be asked to clarify its constitutional implications. At this point, however, one can say only that privatization has constitutional implications, but not what those implications are.

MARK TUSHNET
(2000)

Bibliography

FROOMKIN, A. MICHAEL 1995 Reinventing the Government Corporation. *University of Illinois Law Review* 1995:543–634.

PRIVILEGE, EVIDENTIARY

See: Evidentiary Privileges

PRIVILEGE AGAINST SELF-INCRIMINATION

See: Right Against Self-Incrimination

PRIVILEGED COMMENT

See: Libel and the First Amendment

PRIVILEGE FROM ARREST

That legislators should be free from the threat of arrest except for notorious crimes while attending legislative sessions or en route to or from them has been recognized in English law for at least 1300 years. After the AMERICAN REVOLUTION that privilege was inserted into several state constitutions and the ARTICLES OF CONFEDERATION.

Because the privilege does not extend to "FELONY, or BREACH OF THE PEACE," it amounts in practice to immunity from arrest in civil matters, such as nonpayment of debts. The privilege is less a guarantee of legislative independence from executive abuse than a protection of public business from interference growing out of private disputes.

DENNIS J. MAHONEY
(1986)

PRIVILEGES AND IMMUNITIES

The Constitution's two privileges and immunities clauses were born of different historical circumstances and inspired by different purposes. Yet they are bound together by more than their textual similarity. Both clauses look to the formation of "a more perfect Union," both sound the theme of equality, and both have raised questions about the role of the federal judiciary in protecting NATURAL RIGHTS.

The original Constitution's Article IV set out several principles to govern relations among the states. The FULL FAITH AND CREDIT CLAUSE established one such principle, and so did the clauses providing for interstate rendition of fugitive felons and fugitive slaves. (See SLAVERY AND THE CONSTITUTION; FUGITIVE SLAVERY; FUGITIVE FROM JUSTICE.) Along with these "interstate comity" provisions was included this guarantee: "The citizens of each state shall be entitled to all privileges and immunities of citizens in the several states." Called "the basis of the Union" by ALEXANDER HAMILTON in THE FEDERALIST #80, the first privileges and immunities clause aimed at preventing a state from subjecting another state's citizens to discriminatory treatment of the kind customarily given to ALIENS. The framers saw the clause as embodying the principles of a much longer provision in the ARTICLES OF CONFEDERATION, which had begun with this statement of objective: "The better to secure and perpetuate mutual friendship and intercourse among the people of the different states in this union. . . ."

From the beginning everyone understood that Article IV's privileges and immunities clause could not mean exactly what it said. A Virginian who came to Boston surely had a right to engage in trade, but just as surely could not expect to be a candidate for governor of Massachusetts. What principle distinguished these two activities? Early in the nineteenth century, Justice BUSHROD WASHINGTON, sitting on circuit in CORFIELD V. CORYELL (1823), read the clause to guarantee equality for out-of-state citizens only as to "those privileges and immunities which are, in their nature, fundamental; which belong, of right, to the citizens of all free governments; and which have, at all times, been enjoyed by the citizens of the several states which comprise this Union. . . ." Washington went on to list "some" of those "fundamental" privileges, in language broadly inclusive of nearly every sort of right imaginable. Not only did a citizen of one state have a right "to pass through, or to reside in any other state for purposes of trade, agriculture, professional pursuits, or otherwise"; he also had the right, said Washington, to "enjoyment of life and liberty, with the right to acquire and possess property of every kind, and to pursue and obtain happiness and safety; subject nevertheless to such restraints as the government may justly prescribe for the general good of the whole." Other rights were listed, such as a right of access to a state's courts and a right to nondiscriminatory taxation. Portentously, the passage ended by mentioning "the elective franchise" as a fundamental right.

No one, not even Washington, thought a state had a constitutional duty to let out-of-staters vote in state elections. The inference arises that in offering his list of "fundamental" privileges and immunities Washington had in mind something beyond a catalogue of rights of interstate equality. That broader objective may have been to make Article IV's privileges and immunities clause into a generalized federal constitutional guarantee of liberty, available to local citizens and out-of-staters alike, with identification and enforcement of "fundamental" liberties in the hands of the federal judiciary.

This "natural rights" vision of the privileges and immunities clause of Article IV has never found favor in the Supreme Court. The Court has not interpreted the clause as a source of substantive rights, apart from the right to some measure of equality in a state's treatment of citizens of other states. The term "citizens" has been consistently limited, in this context, to natural persons who are citizens of the United States, thus excluding both corporations and aliens from the clause's protection. The substantive reach of the clause, too, was narrow in the Court's early interpretations: the right to pursue a common calling, the right to own and deal with property, the right of access to state courts.

Even in this restrictive interpretation, the interstate equality demanded by the clause overlaps with the anti-discrimination principle that restricts STATE REGULATIONS OF COMMERCE. The same law, in other words, might violate both the implied limitations of the COMMERCE CLAUSE and the privileges and immunities clause of Article IV. Yet the commerce clause has been a more significant guarantee against interstate discrimination. The commerce clause presumptively forbids a state to discriminate against INTERSTATE (or FOREIGN) COMMERCE, even when the persons engaging in that commerce are the state's own citizens. And the commerce clause, unlike the privileges and immunities clause, protects both corporations and aliens from discrimination against their activities in commerce.

A major shift in judicial attitude toward the privileges and immunities clause was signaled by TOOMER V. WITSELL (1948). South Carolina licensed shrimp boats in coastal waters, demanding license fees of $25 per boat from residents and $2,500 from nonresidents. (Since the adoption of the FOURTEENTH AMENDMENT, state residence and state citizenship have been treated as virtually equivalent.) The Supreme Court held this discrimination a violation of both the commerce clause and the privileges and immunities clause, and in its opinion reformulated the latter clause's governing doctrine. Henceforth any state discrimination against citizens of other states would be held invalid unless the state demonstrated a "substantial reason for the discrimination" apart from their out-of-state citizenship. In *Doe v. Bolton* (1973), a companion case to ROE V. WADE (1973), the Court applied the *Toomer* formula to strike down a Georgia law allowing only state residents to obtain abortions in Georgia.

Toomer seemed to have dispatched the "fundamental" privileges limitation in favor of a straightforward requirement of substantial justification for discrimination against out-of-staters. But here as elsewhere in constitutional law the idea of FUNDAMENTAL INTERESTS has had remarkable recuperative power. BALDWIN V. FISH & GAME COMMISSION (1978) revived the doctrine to uphold a Montana law that charged a state resident $9 for an elk hunting license and a nonresident $225. (The nonresident might also use the license to kill one bear and one deer, to shoot game birds, and to fish. The same package of sanguinary privileges would cost a resident $30.) Elk hunting, said the Court, was a sport, not a means to livelihood; equal access for out-of-staters to Montana elk was "not basic to the maintenance of well-being of the Union," and thus not a "fundamental" privilege protected by Article IV against interstate discrimination. Only four weeks later, in HICKLIN V. ORBECK (1978), the Court returned to the *Toomer* approach to invalidate an Alaska law giving preference to state residents in employment in jobs related to construction of the Alaska pipeline. The state had not offered substantial justification for the discrimination, the Court said, and therefore it was invalid. *Baldwin* was not cited.

The cleanest way to resolve the tension between these two decisions would have been to abandon *Baldwin* as a doctrinal sport. Instead, the Supreme Court combined both lines of decision in a new formula. In *United Building*

& Construction Trades Council v. Mayor and Council of Camden (1984) and SUPREME COURT OF NEW HAMPSHIRE V. PIPER (1985) the Court established a two-part test for determining the validity of a state law challenged under Article IV's privileges and immunities clause. The first inquiry follows *Baldwin:* the law is limited by the clause only when its discrimination against out-of-staters touches a privilege that is "fundamental" to interstate harmony. The Court made clear in *Piper* that access to a means of livelihood is such a privilege. The second inquiry follows *Toomer* and *Hicklin:* if the privilege in question is "fundamental," the discrimination is invalid unless there is a "substantial" reason for treating out-of-staters differently, and the law's discrimination bears a "substantial relationship" to that objective. The second requirement states an intermediate STANDARD OF REVIEW for judicial scrutiny of both the state's purposes and its discriminatory means.

Special problems have plagued the Supreme Court's efforts to apply the privileges and immunities clause of Article IV to cases in which the discriminating states have acted as purchasers of goods and services, or owners of property, or proprietors of enterprises. In the *Camden* case, the Court refused to recognize a general exemption of such activities from the strictures of the clause; if the activities affected a "fundamental" interest, the clause would be implicated. In the same breath, however, the Court suggested that the state's interests as a market participant might be relevant to the second part of the new two-part inquiry: the question of justification for discriminating against out-of-staters. Justification for some state preferences for local citizens may be found in the citizens' obligations to support local government. *Toomer's* teaching is that the justification must be substantial.

Thus far the privileges and immunities clause of Article IV has been applied only to state laws discriminating against out-of-staters. Concurring in *Zobel v. Williams* (1982), Justice SANDRA DAY O'CONNOR argued for a broader application of the clause that would place constitutional limits on any state law—even a law discriminating between different groups of the state's own citizens—when the law disadvantages persons who have only recently arrived in the state. Justice O'Connor would have found a violation of the clause in Alaska's law distributing the state's oil revenues to Alaska citizens in proportion to the length of their residence; she argued that the law imposed "disabilities of alienage"—a result the clause was designed to forbid. The majority, holding the law invalid on equal protection grounds, rejected this novel interpretation in favor of the conventional view: the privileges and immunities clause of Article IV is inapplicable to such a case, for the clause speaks only to discrimination against citizens of other states.

A second privileges and immunities clause was added to the Constitution in 1868 as part of the Fourteenth

Amendment: "No state shall make or enforce any law which shall abridge the privileges or immunities of citizens of the United States." Justice ROBERT H. JACKSON, concurring in EDWARDS V. CALIFORNIA (1941), said expansively that "[t]his clause was adopted to make United States citizenship the dominant and paramount allegiance among us." The fact is that the amendment's framers did not sharply differentiate the functions of the various clauses of the amendment's first section and did not speak with one voice concerning the purposes of the privileges and immunities clause. Undoubtedly, however, the clause was meant to have some effect as a limitation on the states. The amendment's opening sentence "overruled" DRED SCOTT V. SANDFORD (1857) by conferring United States citizenship and state citizenship on "all persons born or naturalized in the United States and subject to the jurisdiction thereof." The privileges and immunities clause, following immediately in the amendment's text, surely was intended to give some substantive content to the rights of citizenship, and particularly to the equal citizenship of blacks. (See EQUAL PROTECTION OF THE LAWS.) Yet the Supreme Court, in its first encounter with the clause, read it, as Justice STEPHEN J. FIELD aptly said in dissent, to be "a vain and idle enactment, which accomplished nothing." In the SLAUGHTERHOUSE CASES (1873) a 5–4 majority, distinguishing the privileges and immunities of national citizenship from those of state citizenship, confined the former to rights established elsewhere in the Constitution and federal laws and to rights that were already fairly inferable from the relation of a citizen to the national government. (Examples of the latter would be the right to United States protection in other countries, the right to enter public lands, or the right to inform federal authorities of violations of federal law.) The majority described *Corfield*'s list of "fundamental" rights as privileges of state citizenship, subject to Article IV's guarantee of interstate equality but untouched by the new privileges and immunities clause of the Fourteenth Amendment.

The Court feared that a contrary reading of the privileges and immunities clause, coupled with the power of Congress to enforce the Fourteenth Amendment, would not only "constitute this court a perpetual censor upon all legislation of the states" but also "bring within the power of Congress the entire domain of civil rights heretofore belonging exclusively to the states." Such a result, the Court accurately said, would radically restructure the federal union, centralizing power in the national government. No doubt some congressional proponents of the Fourteenth Amendment had hoped for precisely that result. The *Slaughterhouse Cases* dissenters viewed the prospect with equanimity and even sought to revive the natural rights philosophy of *Corfield* in the name of the Fourteenth Amendment. In doctrinal terms, however, they lost the battle decisively. The Court has never given the Four-

teenth Amendment's privileges and immunities clause any significant content that is distinctively its own.

Occasional flurries of activity have suggested impending revitalization of the clause. Justice HUGO L. BLACK made the clause a centerpiece in his effort to persuade the Court to recognize the total incorporation of the Bill of Rights into the Fourteenth Amendment. (See INCORPORATION DOCTRINE.) And for a season the clause came to life as a limitation on state taxing power, until MADDEN V. KENTUCKY (1940) overruled COLGATE V. HARVEY (1935). Individual Justices have promoted the clause in concurring opinions, such as that of Justice Jackson in *Edwards v. California* (1941) (right to move freely from state to state) and that of Justice OWEN ROBERTS in HAGUE V. COMMITTEE FOR INDUSTRIAL ORGANIZATION (1939) (right to assemble to discuss national legislation), but these ventures have been largely superseded by the development of other constitutional limitations on the states.

In the modern era, Justice Jackson's *Edwards* argument has borne fruit in the development of a constitutional RIGHT TO TRAVEL. The right is now well established as a limitation on state power, but the right's source in the Constitution remains unspecified. The commerce clause is one obvious candidate, and not just one but both privileges and immunities clauses have also been nominated. (Congressional interferences with the freedom of foreign travel have been tested against the Fifth Amendment's DUE PROCESS clause.) Plainly, the Supreme Court has no need to rely on either privileges and immunities clause as an independent source for the right to travel.

Although the natural rights approach to constitutional adjudication failed to make headway in the name of either of the privileges and immunities clauses, in the field of ECONOMIC REGULATION the views of the *Slaughterhouse Cases* dissenters came to prevail for almost half a century under the banner of SUBSTANTIVE DUE PROCESS. (See FREEDOM OF CONTRACT.)That experiment in JUDICIAL ACTIVISM was closed in the 1930s, but a similar philosophy has informed the revival of substantive due process as a protection of personal freedoms. Some commentators have suggested that the Fourteenth Amendment's privileges and immunities clause may be an apt vessel for these newer constitutional liberties, or even for yet-to-be-discovered affirmative constitutional obligations of government. After a century and more on the constitutional shelf, all the vessel needs is a little polishing.

KENNETH L. KARST
(1986)

Bibliography

ELY, JOHN HART 1980 *Democracy and Distrust: A Theory of Judicial Review.* Pages 22–30. Cambridge, Mass.: Harvard University Press.

FAIRMAN, CHARLES 1971 *Reconstruction and Reunion, 1864--*

88, *Part One.* Chap. 20. (Volume VI, History of the Supreme Court of the United States.) New York: Macmillan.

KURLAND, PHILIP B.   1972   The Privileges and Immunities Clause: "Its Hour Come Round at Last?" *Washington University Law Quarterly* 1972:405–420.

SIMSON, GARY J.   1979   Discrimination against Nonresidents and the Privileges and Immunities Clause of Article IV. *University of Pennsylvania Law Review* 128:379–401.

VARAT, JONATHAN D.   1981   State "Citizenship" and Interstate Equality. *University of Chicago Law Review* 48:487–572.

PRIVY COUNCIL

The Privy Council together with the monarch constitutes "the Crown," which is, in theory, the executive branch of the British government. Association of the council in the exercise of executive power was a check against the abuse of that power. The council is appointed for life and comprises members of the royal family, ministers and former ministers of state, judges, and distinguished subjects. In practice, the cabinet has become, through an evolutionary process, the executive committee of the Privy Council.

In the seventeenth and eighteenth centuries the Privy Council exercised the royal prerogative of disallowing acts of the colonial legislatures. At the same time the council was the highest court of appeal from the colonial courts (a function now exercised by the judicial committee of the Privy Council). The role of the Privy Council in the political order of the British Empire was thus suggestive of both the VETO POWER and JUDICIAL REVIEW.

Some of the early state constitutions provided for a council to share the executive power or to review acts of the legislature. At the CONSTITUTIONAL CONVENTION OF 1787 various unsuccessful proposals for a plural executive reflected the British notion of the Privy Council as a check against royal tyranny.

DENNIS J. MAHONEY
(1986)

PRIZE CASES
2 Black (67 U.S.) 635 (1863)

In the *Prize Cases*, a 5–4 majority of the Supreme Court sustained the validity of President ABRAHAM LINCOLN's blockade proclamations of April 1861, refusing to declare unconstitutional his unilateral actions in meeting the Confederacy's military initiatives.

Lincoln proclaimed a blockade of southern ports on April 19 and 27, 1861. Congress authorized him to declare a state of insurrection by the Act of July 13, 1861, thereby, at least in the view of the dissenters, giving formal legislative recognition to the existence of civil war. By the Act of August 6, 1861, Congress retroactively ratified all Lincoln's military actions. The *Prize Cases* involved seizures of vessels bound for Confederate ports prior to July 13, 1861.

For the majority, Justice ROBERT C. GRIER held that a state of CIVIL WAR existed DE FACTO after the firing on Fort Sumter (April 12, 1861) and that the Supreme Court would take judicial notice of its existence. Though neither Congress nor President can declare war against a state of the Union, Grier conceded, when states waged war against the United States government, the President was "bound to meet it in the shape it presented itself, without waiting for Congress to baptize it with a name." Whether the insurgents were to be accorded belligerent status, and hence be subject to blockade, was a POLITICAL QUESTION to be decided by the President, whose decision was conclusive on the courts. Grier reproved the dissenters by reminding them that the court should not "cripple the arm of the government and paralyze its power by subtle definitions and ingenious sophisms."

Justice SAMUEL NELSON for the dissenters (Chief Justice ROGER B. TANEY, and Justices JOHN CATRON and NATHAN CLIFFORD) argued that only Congress can declare a war and that consequently the President can neither declare nor recognize it. A civil war's "existence in a material sense . . . has no relevancy or weight when the question is what constitutes war in a legal sense." Lincoln's acts before 13 July 1861 constituted merely his "personal war against those in rebellion." Therefore seizures under the blockade proclamations were illegal.

The *Prize Cases* permitted the federal government the convenient ambiguity of treating the Confederacy as an organized insurgency and as a conventional belligerent. The opinions also had an implicit relevance to other disputed exercises of presidential authority. Defenders of a broad executive power could argue that the majority opinion's reasoning supported the constitutionality of Lincoln's call for volunteers, of his suspension of the writ of HABEAS CORPUS, and perhaps also of the EMANCIPATION PROCLAMATION.

WILLIAM M. WIECEK
(1986)

PROBABLE CAUSE

The FOURTH AMENDMENT guarantees in part that "The right of the people to be secure in their persons, houses, papers and effects, against UNREASONABLE SEARCHES and seizures shall not be violated, and no warrants shall issue but upon probable cause. . . ." The determination of probable cause necessarily turns on specific facts and often requires the courts and the police to make most difficult decisions. The need for probable cause in American CRIMINAL PROCEDURE arises in three instances: probable cause to ARREST or detain, probable cause to search, and probable cause to prosecute. The first two derive constitutional status directly from the Fourth Amendment and govern the conduct of the police. An inquiry by a judge or GRAND JURY into probable cause for prosecution is not constitutionally required in state cases; however, this check on the exercise of prosecutorial discretion is prescribed by statute or state constitutional mandate in most states and is constitutionally required by the Fifth Amendment in federal cases.

As to arrest and search, the language of the Fourth Amendment does not distinguish between SEARCHES AND SEIZURES of objects, and arrests—"seizures" of the person. While one might assume that the term would have equivalent meanings in both the search and arrest contexts, the differences between arrests of suspects and searches for evidence or contraband require the probable cause standard to be applied to different types of data for the two procedures. Probable cause for a search does not automatically support an arrest, nor does a valid ARREST WARRANT necessarily support a search.

Probable cause in the arrest context was defined by the United States Supreme Court in *Beck v. Ohio* (1964) as turning on "whether at that moment [of arrest] the facts and circumstances within [the officers'] knowledge and of which they [have] reasonably trustworthy information [are] sufficient to warrant a prudent man in believing that the [suspect] had committed or was committing an offense. There are two potential sources of information—personal knowledge and "trustworthy" secondary data. The Supreme Court has clearly established that secondary data—information not within the officer's personal knowledge—can supply sufficient grounds for an arrest. Thus, the police may rely on reports from other cities or states to support valid arrests, as in *Whitely v. Warden* (1971). Credible information supplied by an informant may also be used.

The officer's specific knowledge derived from direct contact with the arrestee is usually the primary support for a finding of probable cause. It is clear such information must be specific. Mere knowledge that, for example, a suspect has been convicted in the past coupled with an unidentified INFORMANT'S TIP alleging current criminal activity has been held to be insufficient.

Even specific EVIDENCE linking an individual to a crime will not justify an arrest if the evidence has been discovered unconstitutionally. An arrest cannot be justified by evidence seized pursuant to the arrest; as the Court said in *Sibron v. New York* (1968): "An incident search may not precede an arrest and serve as part of its justification."

Evidence discovered in an on-street investigative encounter that has not yet reached the level of an arrest may be properly used to create probable cause. For example, if as a result of a STOP-AND-FRISK encounter on the street, authorized by TERRY V. OHIO (1968), an officer feels a weapon, he has probable cause to arrest for carrying a concealed weapon. Similarly, if in the course of a temporary detention the suspect fails adequately to account for his suspicious actions or if he affirmatively discloses incriminating evidence, probable cause to arrest may be established. The same is true if the suspect runs away. While flight alone does not create probable cause to arrest, it is a significant factor to be considered in the overall assessment.

By contrast, however, as the Court held in *Brown v. Texas* (1979), the mere failure of a suspect to identify himself, without more, does not supply probable cause. Nor may a valid arrest rely on an individual's failure to protect his innocence when found with suspects for whom probable cause exists, as in *United States v. Di Re* (1948).

Di Re also stands for the proposition that mere presence of an individual in the company of others who are properly suspected of criminal activity does not constitute probable cause. Subsequent cases, however, have made clear that there are limits to this principle. The difficulties here have largely come with possessory offenses. On the one hand, the Court in *Johnson v. United States* (1947) held that a tip that opium was being smoked coupled with the smell of opium outside a hotel room did not give rise to probable cause to arrest everyone in the room. Although there was probable cause to believe a crime was being committed, there was insufficient information to determine who was committing it. Yet in KER V. CALIFORNIA (1963) the Court upheld the arrest of a married couple found in their kitchen with a brick of marijuana, even though the tip leading them there had linked only the husband to the contraband. The Court reasoned that the combination of the wife's presence in a small kitchen with obvious contraband, coupled with information that the husband had been using the apartment as a base for his drug activities, gave sufficient grounds for a reasonable belief that they were both in possession of marijuana.

This requirement of linking probable cause specifically to the arrestee was again mentioned by the Court in YBARRA V. ILLINOIS (1979). There the police procured a valid warrant to search a tavern believed to be the center of drug activity. In executing the warrant, the police searched about a dozen of the tavern's patrons, including Ybarra. While the case thus actually dealt with the legitimacy of the search rather than an arrest, the Court stated: "[W]here the standard is probable cause, a search or *seizure of a person* must be supported by probable cause particularized with respect to that person. This requirement cannot be undercut or avoided by simply pointing to the fact that coincidentally there exists probable cause to search or seize another or to search the premises where the person may happen to be." (Emphasis added.) *Ybarra* thus reinforces the requirement that probable cause be particularized to the person arrested; mere presence at a place connected with criminal activity, or in the company of suspected criminals, without more, is inadequate.

Finally, the Court held in *Gerstein v. Pugh* (1975) that whenever a suspect has been arrested without a warrant and with no prior INDICTMENT, he is entitled to a quick judicial check on the police conclusion that there is probable cause to detain him if he will undergo a "significant pretrial restraint on liberty"—more than the mere condition that he return for trial. This hearing, while constitutionally required if these conditions are met, need not be adversary and does not give rise to a RIGHT TO COUNSEL. As with the hearing to obtain an arrest warrant, this proceeding does not even require the accused's presence. The standard of proof is simply whether there is probable cause to believe the suspect has committed a crime.

The search context is the second major area in which the issue of probable cause arises. Most courts hold that probable cause for a search exists when the facts and circumstances in a given situation are sufficient to warrant a man of reasonable caution to believe that seizable objects are located at the place to be searched. (See BRINEGAR V. UNITED STATES; CARROLL V. UNITED STATES.)

The probable cause determination is generally based on the information supplied to the magistrate in the application for a search warrant. An application must be sworn to and must allege the place to be searched, the property to be seized, the person having the property if it is to be taken from his control, and the underlying crime. There is no requirement that everything must be set out in the application itself; affidavits may be attached or sworn statements taken before the magistrate. Because applications are usually submitted by police officers who do not have legal training, the language of the application is to be construed in a nontechnical way. Nevertheless, if the application is all that is submitted, and it is expressed in "conclusory" terms only, it will be insufficient to establish probable cause. Sufficient data must be contained in either the application itself or the supporting affidavits to justify the magistrate in issuing the warrant.

Although no blanket assertion can explain all cases involving probable cause for the issuance of search warrants, one useful rule of thumb is that if the affidavit and supporting documents allege facts that can explain to the magistrate the basis for the probable cause determination, a warrant based on such an affidavit is likely to be good. On the other hand, when an affidavit asserts a mere conclusion such as "we have it on good information and do believe there are drugs at the suspect's home," there is no independent basis for the magistrate's determination. A warrant based on such a showing is likely to be invalid.

The hardest issue arises when the affiant police officer is not the source of the information but is relying on an informant. Most of the Supreme Court's decisions concerning the required credibility of informants have arisen in cases involving SEARCH WARRANTS rather than arrest warrants, but the standards for use of informants in both contexts are the same.

The Supreme Court first enunciated the requirements for a valid informant-based warrant in AGUILAR V. TEXAS (1964). According to this test, the affidavit must: (a) set forth sufficient underlying circumstances to demonstrate to a neutral and detached magistrate how the informant reached hisher conclusion; *and* (b) establish the reliability or credibility of the informant. In the subsequent case, SPINELLI V. UNITED STATES (1969), the Supreme Court explained that the absence of a statement detailing the manner in which the informant's data were gathered renders it especially important that "the tip describe the accused's criminal activity in sufficient detail that the magistrate may know that he is relying on something more substantial than a casual rumor . . . or an accusation based merely on an individual's general reputation."

The *Aguilar/Spinelli* test has, however, been rejected by ILLINOIS V. GATES (1983). The Court in *Gates* introduced a totality-of-the-circumstances test, stating that it was not necessary to establish the credibility of the informant as a separate element to a valid search warrant. Instead, reliability and credibility of the informer and his basis of knowledge are considered as intertwining considerations that may illuminate the probable cause issue. In *Gates* the police received an anonymous informant's letter containing details of the defendants' involvement in drug trafficking which were corroborated by police investigations. The Court held that this provided a sufficient basis for a finding of probable cause.

Finally, according to *Henry v. United States* (1959), if the police had probable cause to arrest or search, the fact that the information on which they relied turns out to be false does not invalidate the arrest or search. Sufficient probability is the touchstone of Fourth Amendment reasonableness. (See PRELIMINARY HEARING.)

CHARLES H. WHITEBREAD
(1986)

Bibliography

LaFave, Wayne R. 1978 *Search and Seizure: A Treatise on the Fourth Amendment.* St. Paul, Minn.: West Publishing Co.

PROCEDURAL DUE PROCESS OF LAW, CIVIL

The Fifth Amendment forbids the United States to "deprive" any person of "life, liberty, or property without DUE

PROCESS OF LAW." The FOURTEENTH AMENDMENT imposes an identical prohibition on the states.

Due process is the ancient core of CONSTITUTIONALISM. It is a traditional legal expression of concern for the fate of persons in the presence of organized social power. The question of according due process arises when governments assert themselves adversely to the interests of individuals.

In modern usage "due process" connotes a certain normative ideal for decisions about the exercise of power. Very broadly, it has come to mean decisions that are not arbitrary, but are aligned with publicly accepted aims and values; are not dictatorial, but allow affected persons a suitable part in their making; and are not oppressive, but treat those affected with the respect owed political associates and fellow human beings. It is from the liberal individualist tradition that these abstract due process standards—of reason, voice, and dignity—have drawn their more concrete content. That content includes the definition of proper aims for state activity, the canons of legitimating participation and consent, and the conceptions of human personality that set the threshold of respectful treatment.

The law distinguishes between "substantive" and "procedural" due process. An arbitrary or groundless decision may violate substantive due process regardless of how it came to be made. O'CONNOR V. DONALDSON (1975), for example, held that no antecedent procedure will justify incarceration of a harmless eccentric. Conversely, a peremptory decision may violate procedural due process regardless of purposive justification. Guilt in fact will not justify sudden, final dismissal of a faithless government employee without a hearing, as the Supreme Court stated in ARNETT V. KENNEDY (1974). The due process claim is "procedural" rather than "substantive" when it questions not the state's authority to impose the harm in question by an adequate decision process, but rather the adequacy of the process actually used.

Of course, procedural demands gain much of their power from their perceived contribution to substantive accuracy and enlightenment. Justice FELIX FRANKFURTER stated in JOINT ANTI-FASCIST COMMITTEE V. MCGRATH (1951): "No better instrument has been devised for arriving at truth than to give a person in jeopardy of serious loss notice of the case against him and an opportunity to meet it. Nor has a better way been found for generating the feeling, so important to a popular government, that justice has been done."

The focal concern of procedural due process is the set of procedures, epitomized by the judicial trial, whereby governing rules and standards are brought to bear on individuals in specific cases. The doctrine also has some further extension to the formation of the governing rules and standards. Due process can support a claim for direct voice in the formation process, for example, by industry members regarding regulatory standards under consideration by an administrative agency. It can also be the ground of an objection to the nonrepresentative character of the political process in which a standard originates, for example, a restriction on professional entry adopted by a board composed of self-interested professionals. There may also be a due process failure in the way a legal standard is formulated. The standard may be too vague and ill-defined to ensure even-handed application or allow for effective submission of proofs and arguments by someone contesting its application; or, conversely, it may be so narrowly drawn as to represent an arbitrary or vindictive discrimination against a disfavored few. Lawmaking defects of these various kinds are chiefly the concern of doctrines of SEPARATION OF POWERS, unconstitutional delegation, VAGUENESS, and prohibition of BILLS OF ATTAINDER, but they cannot in practice be held entirely separate from procedural due process claims.

In *Joint Anti-Fascist Refugee Committee v. McGrath* Justice Frankfurter invoked a history in which the adversary judicial trial has dominated our law's vision of procedural due process, as the model of a procedure designed to assure reason, voice, and dignity to individuals threatened with harm by the state. Criminal due process shows the fullest development of the adversarial model, just as criminal proceedings tend to maximize the conditions bespeaking the need for adversarial safeguards: charges specifically directed against the accused individual, by highly visible officers acting in the state's name, threatening not only tangible deprivation of liberty or wealth but also public degradation. Some state-initiated proceedings against individuals, such as those brought to establish paternity or terminate parental status, while nominally civil in character, resemble criminal prosecutions in their accusatory and stigmatic implications or in the gravity of their threatened sanctions, leaving little doubt about the need to grant respondents something approaching the full set of due process safeguards. Such safeguards were required by the Court in LASSITER V. DEPARTMENT OF SOCIAL SERVICES (1981). As cases of impending state-imposed harm depart further from the criminal prosecution paradigm, however, they reveal that puzzling issues of political and legal principle are latent in the general ideal of due process. Such cases pose two distinct questions for due process doctrine. First, does the occasion demand any kind of proceeding at all? Assuming an affirmative answer, the second question is, what process is due?

Events that from certain perspectives are describable as deprivations of life, liberty, or property in which the state is implicated—for example, a creditor acting under a legal privilege to repossess consumer goods from an assertedly defaulting debtor—may occur with no provision in the law for any process at all. The most theoretically telling of recent judicial encounters with due process doctrine has been concerned with defining the occasions when some trial-type process is constitutionally required.

Due process further stands for a constitutionally mandated procedural code for the fair conduct of whatever trial-type proceedings are to occur. In this second aspect, due process doctrine is a compendium of answers to such varied questions as: May the hearing be postponed until after the onset of the deprivation (such as a summary suspension of a student from school) or must there be a pre-deprivation hearing? May the state depart from COMMON LAW rules regarding HEARSAY evidence, allow its judges to interrogate witnesses, use publication rather than personal contact as a means of notifying concerned parties of pending proceedings, or deny parties the assistance of counsel in small claims tribunals?

The answers found in due process doctrine to such questions will bind a government just insofar as it chooses, or is required by the first aspect of the doctrine, to use judicial-type forums or trial-type proceedings to carry out their pursuits. The chief problems posed by such questions are the recurrent ones of JUDICIAL REVIEW and CONSTITUTIONAL INTERPRETATION: from what sources, by what modes of reasoning, shall the answers be drawn, given the breadth and imprecision of constitutional text? Historically, the main methodological alternatives and debates have arisen in the context of criminal prosecutions and been thence carried over to the civil side.

Constitutional claims to trial-type proceedings are most obviously compelling when individuals stand to be harmed by actions of officials performing state functions or wielding state powers. Yet even in such cases the individual interests at stake may be found insufficient to call due process rights into play. On a textual level, the question plainly is whether the affected interest is identifiable as "life, liberty, or property." History, however, discloses contrasting approaches to that question. It was once commonly supposed that any serious imposition on an individual—any "grievous loss"—could qualify as a constitutionally significant deprivation. A chief feature of contemporary due process doctrine is that the potency of a harm as a due process trigger turns not on such an ordinary assessment of its weight or practical severity but rather on a technical, categorical judgment about its legal "nature." In adjudicating what categories of interests legally qualify as "life," "liberty," or "property" for due process analysis, the Court has drawn eclectically on sources both naturalistic and positivistic—on both a HIGHER LAW tradition and on currently enacted law.

This eclecticism, and indeed the entire complex practice of categorically excluding some concededly weighty interests from due process protection, has apparently evolved out of the Court's encounters with modern welfare state activism. Consider the case of a government worker unceremoniously fired, or of a disability pensioner whose monthly payments are cut off. In such cases the underlying due process values of reason, voice, and dignity may seem to call as strongly for a chance to be heard as in cases of revocation of a professional license or dispossession of land or goods. Yet neither a government job nor a disability benefit is "property" in the common speech of our own culture or that of the constitutional Framers; and although their loss might be called a loss of liberty, to speak so broadly would bring within the sweep of procedural due process many cases that evidently do not belong there, for example, denial of admission to a state university.

The Court's response, in cases like GOLDBERG V. KELLY (1970) and BISHOP V. WOOD (1976), has been to say that "property" may, indeed, include all manner of beneficial relations with the state or others, but only insofar as those relations are legal entitlements in the sense that explicit (or positive) law protects against their impairment. Thus a probationary employee lacking contractual term or statutory tenure may be peremptorily dismissed and the mere applicant peremptorily rejected; but the tenured employee has a right to be heard on the question of cause for dismissal, and the disability claimant under a statute containing definite eligibility rules may not be delisted—or even denied initial admission to benefits—without some opportunity to be heard on the issue of eligibility.

The method of equating due process protected "property" with positive legal entitlement—that is, by reference to clearly ordained, subconstitutional law—has several attractive features. It flows easily from the observation in BOARD OF REGENTS V. ROTH (1972) that a chief purpose of "the ancient institution of property" has been to "protect . . . expectations upon which people must rely in their daily lives" against being "arbitrarily undermined." Moreover, the positive-entitlement conception makes a neat fit with the idea that a fair hearing is the nub of due process. Entitlement makes directly clear what the hearing shall be about, for any law framing an entitlement must specify issues available for contest by anyone complaining of deprivation. Finally, entitlement analysis may seem to keep the judiciary clear of imposing on popularly accountable branches of government any political values or ends not accepted by those branches themselves. A judge enforcing due process rights appears to do little more than take seriously the decision of the lawmakers to create the entitlement in the first place.

The Court on some occasions has gone so far as to say that no interest qualifies as due process protected property except insofar as a legal rule safeguards its continued enjoyment. It seems clear that such statements cannot be taken literally. For example, the Court consistently refuses to approve procedures involving state officers in the repossession of goods bought on credit, without affording a prompt hearing to the buyer, no matter how clearly the applicable state law states that the buyer's entitlement to continued possession is to lapse upon the creditor's filing of notice of default (as distinguished from a judicial finding of default). Here it must be the brute reality of the buyer's established possession of the goods that comprises the constitutionally protected property, regardless of the explicit legal rules concerning its protection or duration.

The possession cases illustrate the naturalistic or higher law side of the Court's eclectic method of interest characterization. Protection of established possession against disorderly or unjustified incursion is an ancient fixture in both the rhetoric and the practice of Anglo-American common law and liberty. There are other common liberties similarly, if not all quite so anciently, esteemed: personal mobility and bodily security; liberties of conscience, intellect, and expression; domestic sanctuary, marital intimacy, and family solidarity; occupational freedom and professional autonomy. Although some of these interests find mention in the Bill of Rights, they mostly lack specific constitutional recognition.

The Court has used the "liberty" branch of the due process guarantee as a warrant for procedural protection for such interests, quite apart from their status as entitlements under positive law—and without overprecious worry about their status at ancestral common law. Regardless of whether the state's law purports, or ever did purport, to make into legal rights a schoolchild's security against corporal punishment (INGRAHAM V. WRIGHT, 1977), a parent's retention of child custody (*Santosky v. Kramer*, 1982), or a parolee's preference for remaining at liberty (*Morrissey v. Brewer*, 1972), those interests have been held protected, by the due process clause itself, against peremptory impairment by STATE ACTION. They are treated as constitutional entitlements regardless of whether they are statutory ones. It is easy to imagine why naturalist as well as positivist elements thus enter into the Court's characterizations. Welfare state activism positively invites forms of reliance and dependence which, however historically novel, evoke the essential purposes of due process; but the activist state is also prone to tread insensitively on old but still vital concerns that courts recognize as traditional freedoms.

The conclusion that an interest jeopardized by government action does qualify as someone's "life, liberty, or property" does not end the due process inquiry, for the question then remains of how much "process" is "due." It has been said that due process entails, at a minimum, "some kind of hearing" for the exposed individual. Precisely what kind depends on a judicial assessment: one which, according to the formulation in MATHEWS V. ELD-

RIDGE (1976), is supposed to take account of the gravity of the individual interest at stake, the utility of the requested procedures in avoiding factually misinformed or legally erroneous decisions, and the cost of those procedures to the pursuit of legitimate state objectives. The results of such a calculus can range from the heavy procedural armor available to criminal defendants in capital cases to the simple "opportunity to present his side of the story" that, under GOSS V. LOPEZ (1975), is due a student facing a short disciplinary suspension from school.

An important and oft-contested feature of the constitutionally guaranteed process is its timing relative to the deprivation. The Court long stood by the general proposition that (apart from "emergency" situations, such as seizure of contraband) due process meant predeprivation process. The Court continues to insist on some opportunity for in-person hearing prior to "core" deprivations such as dispossession of tangible property. In several cases, such as *Arnett v. Kennedy* and *Mathews v. Eldridge*, involving government jobs and other "benefits," the Court has accepted postponement of a live hearing until after the fall of the axe, when there has been predeprivation notice and opportunity for written protest, as long as there is adequate assurance for reparation in case the deprivation is eventually found unjustified.

Under pressure of the "mass justice" conditions imposed by modern governmental benefit programs involving very large numbers of eligibility decisions, there has been indication in recent cases and commentaries of tolerance for an alternative due process model, one less concerned than the traditional trial-type model with participation values. In this alternative managerial model, the measure of due process is not the quality of the opportunity given affected individuals for a say in the resolution of their own cases but quality control in the production of decisions. The aim is not voice for the individual but accuracy in the aggregate of the resolutions reached over a period of program administration. As advocates of this alternative model recognize, two factors are required to justify the model's use in any given setting: first, the relative dominance of individuals' interests in receiving their entitlements over their dignitary interests in participation; and, second, the value of such a systems management approach in maximizing the receipt of entitlements.

When judges find constitutional protection, under the broad cover of "liberty," for selected interests not specified as rights by constitutional text or other clearly uttered law, and when they determine just what form and quantum of process is "due" in respect of particular kinds of deprivations, they have obviously entered on the work of ranking substantive ends and values. Yet courts doing this kind of due process adjudication have not evinced great worry about usurpation of the lawmaking function. One reason may be that by merely requiring the state to provide some kind of hearing when it acts adversely to some individual's interests, a court does not consider itself ultimately to be preventing lawmakers from reaching whatever substantive results they choose.

However, the judicial act of fashioning procedural requirements, and attaching these to a select set of liberties, is not without substantive force. Procedural requirements can place serious practical obstacles in the way of legislative pursuits. They may be expensive. They may cause a formalization or distancing of some relations that lawmakers could reasonably prefer to leave more informal, close, or open, such as the relations among teachers and students in a school. They may deter valued candor—as from evaluators of candidates for jobs, promotions, university admissions, professional licenses—insofar as due process entitles the subjects of adverse reports to disclosure or CONFRONTATION. Procedural requirements may thus force lawmakers to weigh some programmatic objectives against others that would be jeopardized by pursuing the former within the procedural rules laid down by courts.

Due process protection for interests that are not entitlements established by positive law may have a subtler substantive import. If the jeopardized interest enjoys no specific protection under any law aside from the due process clause itself, there is no obvious focus for the required process. A hearing on the issue of whether the contested deprivation is "without due process" may seem pointless, lacking some legal restriction on the conditions in which the deprivation is authorized. This problem has arisen in a number of cases involving dispossession of public housing tenants, when neither the laws governing the housing programs nor the leases issued to tenants purported to restrict in any way the power of administrators to evict tenants at any time, for any reason or no reason.

Courts in this situation may supply the missing substantive entitlement on their own, by finding in the due process guarantee a protection against deprivations not rationally related to the purposes of the governmental activity in question. Thus a court may bar a public housing administrator from evicting a tenant who has been cohabiting with a nonspouse, if the court concludes that excluding the cohabitation is not rationally related to the court's understanding of the purposes of public housing. In such a case, the crossover from procedural to substantive concerns is glaringly evident.

A similar crossover is less evident, but still detectible, when a court responds to the lack of a positive law entitlement by requiring the state itself to enunciate some restrictions of purpose or circumstance on lawful impairment of the protected interest, which can provide a basis for due process hearings when official deprivations impend. For the court must then stand ready to decide whether the state's restrictions measure up to constitutional standards of protectiveness. A statute solemnly declaring that tenants may not be evicted "except as the Administrator shall decide is required for the general good" could not satisfy a court determined to afford procedural due process protection to the tenant's possessory interest viewed as an entitlement.

The alternative possibility, of requiring procedural protection even in the absence of legal restrictions on official discretion, rarely seems to have caught the Supreme Court's attention. Responsible officials, even when legally free to act at will, can always try to explain their decisions to persons adversely affected, and give the latter a chance to respond. Such an interchange will sometimes make a practical difference, by changing the officials' perceptions of the relevant facts or values. But even when it does not it may well serve any or all of the elemental purposes of due process: ensuring a voice in decisions for affected individuals, securing their recognition as persons deserving respect, and promoting consistency of official actions with goals and values that responsible officials are prepared to state and defend publicly.

Why has such a view of procedural due process, as serving process values apart from the aim of ensuring that persons receive the treatment legally due them, failed to gain judicial support? Most obviously, such an approach would cast very widely the due process net. If we see due process as broadly concerned with the quality of interaction between official and citizen, rather than more narrowly with vindication of the citizen's legal rights, then any state-inflicted "grievous loss" will seem to bring into play the constitutional standards of decisional procedure—a perhaps daunting result in light of the ubiquity of the welfare state.

The Court's limited extension of procedural protection beyond positive legal entitlements to possessory interests and a select set of liberties seems to represent its aversion to three unpalatable alternatives: first, deformation of the constitutional due process mandate by restricting its reach to entitlements specifically found in subconstitutional positive law; second, intrusive overextension of the mandate to all cases of palpably harmful state action; and third, free-form judicial choice among substantive values and policy goals. The Court apparently cannot avoid all three dangers fully and simultaneously. It has needed supplementary techniques to make good the avoidance of both trivialization and globalization of the range of the due process mandate, and these techniques have put heavy pressure on both doctrinal shapeliness and judicial self-discipline.

For example, the danger of trivialization constantly lurks in a crucial indeterminacy in the concept of legally defined entitlement as the equivalent of due process protected property. The problem is that of distributing components of a positive legal regime between the categories of substance and procedure. Suppose, as in *Bishop v. Wood*, that police officers are dismissable whenever, but only when, a designated superior has given the employee a written notice of dismissal for malfeasance in the performance of duty. Straightforwardly read, the law means to make the legal condition of dismissability not actual malfeasance but delivered written notice of dismissal. An entitlement-based due process doctrine then would logically require a hearing but only on the bootless issue of delivery of the notice. A judge can logically avoid that result by reading the law to condition dismissability on actual malfeasance, although that reading will make the law unconstitutional if the law includes no adequate provision for hearing on the malfeasance question. Whether such a reading seems unacceptably self-destructive will depend on the primacy of due process values in the reader's constitutional understanding.

Similar puzzles affect questions about whose entitlement is established by a plain statutory restriction on official discretion. A striking example is *O'Bannon v. Town Court Nursing Center* (1980), where a statute provided for financial assistance to needy elderly persons in meeting their costs of residence in officially approved nursing homes, and also set conditions of approval for the homes. Thus it was apparently unlawful for officials either to deny certification to homes meeting the conditions or to deny benefits to eligible residents of certified homes. When officials proposed to decertify a certain home, its residents claimed a due process right to be heard on the issued of the home's certifiability. The Supreme Court concluded that the residents had no constitutional right to such a hearing because their entitlement was just to benefits while residing in a certified home; the entitlement to certification belonged strictly to the nursing home operators.

Given the close practical resemblance of the residents' interests to the strongly protected interests of tenants in uninterrupted possession, a court could reasonably have concluded that they, too, were entitled to certification of their home if in fact it met the legal standards, and therefore they had due process rights to be heard on that issue. The Court's contrary conclusion was obviously influenced by concerns about overextended application of the constitutional due process mandate.

Claims to due process are not confined to situations in which the claimant's legal posture is defensive or the adversaries are government officials. They may arise also where individuals are exposed to the state's judicial power by their involvement in private legal controversies; and even where (the due process claim aside) there impends no legal proceeding at all but just some harm at a fellow citizen's hands.

The defendant in a private civil lawsuit faces possible deprivation, by officers wielding state powers, of wealth through a money judgment or of personal liberty through an injunctive decree. The occasion is obviously one to activate due process concerns, and civil defendants are held entitled to such procedural due process essentials as a fair and orderly hearing before an unbiased judge.

For reasons not quite so obvious, so are civil plaintiffs. A tempting explanation is that having allowed its courts to take charge of a private dispute, the state is obliged to have them do so in a way that satisfies the due process demand for reason, voice, and dignity. Yet this explanation seems incomplete. Some assistance is better than none. The state does not injure or oppress claimants to whom it offers procedurally flawed assistance against violators of the kinds of interests typically at stake in civil cases, unless the state is affirmatively obligated to secure those interests against violations by private as well as governmental agents. Suppose, for example (as the Supreme Court apparently did in TRUAX V. CORRIGAN, 1921) that the state is constitutionally obligated to protect landowners against disturbance by PICKETING. On such a view, a disturbed landowner can cite a refusal of protection as a deprivation of property and demand a hearing on the question of the state's justification for refusal. In other words, the landowner can demand a hearing on whether the picketing is for some special reason legally privileged. The state can meet this demand by letting the landowner sue the picketers for injunctive relief, but only if the procedural conditions of the suit satisfy due process standards of fairness from the plaintiff's point of view.

Thus denial of fair procedure to a civil plaintiff comes within the traditional due process concern about injurious treatment of individuals by the state, just insofar as we see the state's failure to protect the plaintiff's interests against the defendant's encroachments as itself a form of injury. Such is the SOCIAL COMPACT view according to which persons entering political association surrender to the state the use of force, for the safer protection of their several "lives, liberties, and estates." The state's regime of law and order then overrides the natural liberty of self-help, but only by replacing it with the state's obligation to protect.

Some such account seems necessary to complete the explanation of the conceded due process rights of civil plaintiffs. Yet other current law ostensibly rejects this account. *United States v. Kras* (1973) and *Logan v. Zimmerman Brush Co.* (1982) together indicate that the state may usually condition a would-be civil plaintiff's ACCESS TO THE COURTS on payment of filing fees, thus effectively excluding whoever cannot pay. Such a doctrine is hard to square with the idea of a state's affirmative duty to protect the litigable interests of its citizens, arising out of the latter's relinquishment of self-help by private force.

When a government sues a citizen in an otherwise ordinary civil dispute, involving property or contract rights or tort claims, the citizen sued will of course have the due process rights normally enjoyed by privately sued civil defendants. The reverse case, of a civil dispute in which the citizen is the one seeking relief for a TRESPASS, breach of contract, or other civil wrong by a governmental defendant, is complicated by the doctrine of SOVEREIGN IMMUNITY. In general, that doctrine means that the governments of the states and the Union may not be sued without the consent of their respective legislatures. If the courts find that such consent has not been given, the citizen alleging deprivation by governmental action will lack recourse in the ordinary courts, a situation presenting an obvious and a serious due process concern. In many such cases, the constitutionally guaranteed right of due process must prevail over sovereign immunity and entitle the victimized citizen to relief in constitutional litigation. That would surely be the result, for example, if government officials sought to imprison someone, or seize privately held land or goods, without ever giving the victim a fair chance to contest the legal and factual basis for such action. The citizen would be able to gain preventive relief or compensation in a CIVIL RIGHTS action based on the due process clause of the Fifth or Fourteenth Amendment.

The question of due process rights is most puzzling when seizures of possessions, or other violations of core interests generally given legal protection, are carried out by private agents with no apparent state complicity—a finance company sending its own forces to repossess an automobile securing an overdue debt, or a repair shop collecting an unpaid bill by retaining and eventually selling the repaired article. People do not usually take such "self-help" actions, or think them prudent, unless the actions are in some sense authorized, if not positively enabled, by state law. Thus lawmakers may authorize and enable a creditor's private repossession of chattel security by exempting such activity from liability for crime (theft) or civil wrong (conversion of goods). Indeed, the law usually goes farther, making it wrongful for the debtor to resist the seizure by force. The law doubtless otherwise contributes to the ability of creditors to make their seizures effective, as by securing the wealth used to pay for the requisite services. The utility of the repair shop's liquidation-by-sale depends on law allowing extinction of the debtor's legal claim to the goods in favor of the person who buys them from the repair shop. In short, self-help creditor remedies are evidently deliberate creations of state law, particular components of the state's total scheme of legally recognized and sanctioned rights and liabilities. In that sense, at least, the self-helping creditor inflicts significant deprivations under cover of the state's power, while affording no opportunity for the deprivee to be heard on the matter.

Even so, the Supreme Court concluded in FLAGG BROTHERS V. BROOKS (1978) that laws authorizing creditor self-help do not in general violate due process. In defense of this result, it might have been urged that the due process requirement is satisfied by the debtor's opportunity to sue later for restorative or compensatory relief in case the creditor's seizure was in fact unjustified. Such a rationale would accord with the holding in *Ingraham v. Wright* that paddling a student without a hearing comports with due process so long as compensatory relief for an unjustified paddling can be obtained later in a lawsuit. Yet courts have not usually explained in this way their tolerance for unilateral, peremptory creditor self-help, apparently seeing the difficulty of reconciling such an account with prevailing due process doctrine for cases of seizure by state officers, which strictly requires the state to provide some kind of judicial supervision, and a hearing for the deprivee as promptly as the case permits.

Courts instead have seen the issue presented by private self-help activities as one of state action, and, as in the *Flagg Brothers* case, have concluded that the due process guarantee has no application to such activities however much they may practically depend on the support of law. The reason for this judicial diffidence, as important as it is simple, is the difficulty of distinguishing in principle between the due process claim raised by the case of the self-helping creditor and that raised by many, if not all, other cases of intentional or foreseeable infliction, by private agents, of civilly actionable harm, that is, of torts, breaches of contract, breaches of trust, and so forth. Often, if not always, it will be possible to show compellingly how the law has contributed directly to the occasion or motive for committing the injurious act or to the injurer's practical power to inflict it, or to the practical defenselessness of the victim. But the idea of a constitutional right to a predeprivation hearing, or even an accelerated postdeprivation hearing, in all cases of ordinary private legal wrongs stretches due process too far. Every ordinary contract dispute cannot be a constitutional case.

Thus courts have been led to conclude that the deprivations of property wrought by private creditor self-help are not violations of due process for the reason that they are not attributable to the state. The position is that due process generally is not concerned with exercises of power by persons not identified with the state or perceived as acting on its behalf, in forms not conventionally understood as distinctive to the state. This position is unfortunately at odds with the premise which apparently underlies recognition of the due process rights of civil plaintiffs—the premise, that is, of an affirmative state duty to protect the persons and possessions of inhabitants against gross violation by private as well as public agents.

The difficulty is of a kind that logically must appear somewhere within any body of constitutional doctrine in which a first aim is that of securing spheres of individual liberty against social coercion, and a first institutional device is that of legal rights, themselves an obvious form of collective force. In the constitutionalist vision there is indissoluble tension between law's aim, personal liberty, and its instrument, state power. In this field of contradictory forces are situated all legal rights, including due process rights. Thus it happens that the same due process claims which from one viewpoint represent the state's liberating engagement to protect each person against incursion by others or by the social aggregate, from another perspective represent the state's oppressive oversight of affairs perhaps better and more properly left to the concerned individuals.

In no setting is the dilemma more evident than in that of the family, which in our culture has most strongly represented the value of social solidarity as opposed to that of individuals severally free to treat at arm's length in civil society. PARHAM V. J. R. (1979), a case in which due process claims were asserted on behalf of a minor child being committed by parents to a mental institution, illustrates the difficulty. The Court there assumed "that a [minor] child has a protectable interest . . . in not being . . . erroneously" committed; said that parents must be generally supposed to act in their children's best interests; said that "the risk of error inherent in the parental decision . . . [is] sufficiently great" that parental discretion cannot be "absolute and unreviewable"; and concluded, not resoundingly, that "some kind of inquiry should be made by a 'neutral fact finder' to determine whether . . . [the child] satisf[ies] the medical standards for admission."

Of the largest questions of current meaning and future role for due process in our civic culture, the Supreme Court's irresolute posture in the *Parham* case is emblematic. If due process is an epitome of libertarian law, it is also—by the same token, Max Weber would advise—an epitome of bureaucratic law. Due process as we know it is a hallmark of a formally rational law designed to liberate as it organizes and orders: to liberate energy and will by the promise of regularity, calculability, and impartiality, and by insistent strong demarcation of the private from the public sphere.

But our due process is a hallmark, too, of hierarchical formal ordering; that is, of ordering by preordained rules emanating from specialized governing authorities (representative or accountable as those authorities may be, of or to the governed). There are always spheres of life in which due process is problematic because those spheres want ordering that is more contextual and less abstract, more responsive and less prefigured, more empathic and less impersonal, more interactive and less distanced, more participatory and less authoritative, than what "due process" has traditionally signified. Conversely, "due process" invokes sensibilities resistant to a general movement toward a more thoroughly democratized polity, in which the personal and the political aspects of life would be much less sharply separated than we have tended to keep them. In any such movement due process would necessarily be transformed—transformed but not discarded, since we are unlikely to forsake the ideals of reason, voice, and dignity, or the conviction that individuals are not just parts of social wholes.

FRANK I. MICHELMAN
(1986)

Bibliography

BREST, PAUL 1982 State Action and Liberal Theory: A Casenote on *Flagg Brothers v. Brooks. University of Pennsylvania Law Review* 130:1296–1330.

FRIENDLY, HENRY J. 1975 Some Kind of Hearing. *University of Pennsylvania Law Review* 123:1267–1317.

KADISH, STANFORD 1957 Methodology and Criteria in Due Process Adjudication—A Survey and Criticism. *Yale Law Journal* 66:319–363.

MASHAW, JERRY L. 1983 *Bureaucratic Justice: Managing Social Security Disability Claims.* New Haven, Conn.: Yale University Press.

MICHELMAN, FRANK 1977 Formal and Associational Aims in Procedural Due Process. Pages 126–171 in J. Roland Pennock and John Chapman, eds., *Nomos XVIII: Due Process* New York: New York University Press.

MINOW, MARTHA 1985 Beyond State Intervention in the Family: For Baby Jane Doe. *Michigan Journal of Law Reform* 18: 933–1014.

MONOGHAN, HENRY 1977 Of "Liberty" and "Property." *Cornell Law Review* 62:405–444.

REICH, CHARLES 1964 The New Property. *Yale Law Journal* 73:733–787.

VAN ALSTYNE, WILLIAM 1977 Cracks in "The New Property": Adjudicative Due Process in the Administrative State. *Cornell Law Review* 62:445–493.

PROCEDURAL DUE PROCESS OF LAW, CIVIL
(Update 1)

A claim for procedural due process is a claim that the government cannot undertake a particular act vis-à-vis an individual or set of individuals without according them an opportunity to be heard. Depending upon the situation, a consitutionally adequate opportunity to be heard may be

private; they may use arbitrators or mediators in lieu of judges. The claims (debated in the literature and by empirical studies) are that such modes are speedier and more economic and that they produce better outcomes than does trial.

The increased reliance on procedural requirements, the "due process model," has been criticized not only by those who seek to conserve the expenditure of private and government resources but also by those who challenge government action but question the utility of the means. Some argue that procedural requirements wrongly place the risk of error on the state; others, who are proponents of state aid, argue the procedural due process model implicit in *Goldberg* wrongly equates procedural regularity and adversarial modes with good outcomes. Commentators have wondered about the utility of providing procedural opportunities to individuals with few, if any, resources to exercise them. For example, of what value is the right of cross-examination if no provision is made for a state-paid attorney? Given the resource disparities between government and individuals, procedural due process may create a façade of legitimacy for decisions that are intrinsically unfair. At a more fundamental level, this critique questions the assumptions of procedural due process opinions that a conflict between the state and the individual is inevitable. The hope is that communitarian approaches may well hold more promise for giving indigent individuals access to the riches of society. Those who endorse the *Goldberg* paradigm have been criticized for their limited vision—premised upon a classic liberal assumption of autonomous individuals confronting the state and relying on legalistic solutions.

In response, proponents of the *Goldberg* paradigm, while sympathetic to communitarian goals, note that the state "as friend" almost never materializes. Further, the formality of the *Goldberg* procedures embodies hopes of empowering actors otherwise less powerful. Although not a comprehensive solution, the requirement of formal procedure may be better than its absence. Moreover, many within the legal services community who participated in the *Goldberg* litigation did not, at the time, see its goal as procedural reform. Claims around procedural rights were used as organizing tools; the hopes were that procedural reform, along with changes in other court-based rules, such as greater use of CLASS ACTIONS, the provision of free attorneys, and easier ACCESS TO THE COURTS, would all result in diminished social inequities. Yet another possibility is that the classic due process conception of the state versus an individual can be reenvisioned as an interaction of the state, an individual, and the community in which both litigants are situated. The debate about the utility of the procedural due process model is still alive in this decade, as conferences and law-review articles address the prob-

lems of what kinds of dispute resolution governments should be offering, funding, and encouraging.

One's view of procedure, of the aspirations of *Goldberg*, of the limits imposed under the *Mathews* approach, and of the critique from both the Right and the Left depends in large measure upon one's understanding of the proper role of the state and of the relationship between government and individuals. Procedure (procedural due process included) is a vehicle for the expression of political and social values—a vision of a state in need of restraint or not, a vision of human dignity as enhanced or not enhanced by formalized interaction between decision maker and individual.

JUDITH RESNIK
(1992)

Bibliography

COVER, ROBERT M. et al. 1988 *Procedure.* New York: Foundation Press.
DELGADO, RICHARD et al. 1985 Fairness and Formality: Minimizing the Risk of Prejudice in Alternative Dispute Resolution. *Wisconsin Law Review* 1985:1359–1404.
HANDLER, JOEL 1986 *The Conditions of Discretion: Autonomy, Community, Bureaucracy.* New York: Russell Sage Foundation.
LIND, E. ALLEN et al. 1989 *The Perception of Justice: Tort Litigants' Views of the Civil Justice System.* Santa Monica, Calif.: Rand Corporation, Institute for Civil Justice.
RESNIK, JUDITH 1986 Failing Faith: Adjudicatory Procedure in Decline. *University of Chicago Law Review* 53:494–560.
SPARER, EDWARD 1984 Fundamental Human Rights, Legal Entitlements, and the Social Struggle: A Friendly Critique of the Critical Legal Studies Movement. *Stanford Law Review* 36:509–574.

PROCEDURAL DUE PROCESS OF LAW, CIVIL
(Update 2)

Procedural DUE PROCESS presupposes that the state may take a "liberty or property interest" when it has a good reason, and addresses the procedures required when it does so. The constitutionally required procedures ensure that state decisions depriving individuals of protected interests are fairly made and reasonably correct, insofar as our decisional methods allow. The determinative test balances private against governmental interests and considers the risk of error inherent in particular procedures. In general, the more important the private interest, the more fair and accurate the procedures must be. As the government's interest becomes more significant, and as procedural costs increase, the state may seek to adopt more summary procedures, less protective of private interests.

The more important the interest the government seeks to take, the more the required procedures will approximate the adversary trial paradigm. When the state seeks to take any truly important interest, and where facts are in issue, procedural due process requires notice, an oral hearing, presentation of evidence before an impartial decisionmaker, an opportunity to confront and cross-examine witnesses, counsel, and a decision on the basis of the record. Where someone will suffer serious injury pending a hearing, such as a terminated employee with no possibility of reinstatement or back pay, there should be some predeprivation hearing. Where the private interest is less important, procedural requirements are less substantial, and other exceptions turn on the taking's redressability, seriousness, and the state's need for quick and economic action. A summary predeprivation hearing, with notice, opportunity to respond, and a decision whether there are grounds to act will often serve. If necessary, a more substantial postdeprivation hearing may then follow. In emergencies, such as the need to destroy diseased animals, or where the taking harm is negligible or readily redressable, a postdeprivation hearing satisfies.

An important line of procedural due process cases deals with the question of what process the state must give when private parties seek state aid in taking another's PROPERTY, as in cases involving ex parte prejudgment attachments or garnishments. Here the balancing is between competing private interests, but as there is state involvement, procedural due process requirements apply. The Court has consistently held, as in the most recent case, *Connecticut v. Doehr* (1991), that, extraordinary circumstances aside, there must be a preattachment hearing.

The state may also act ex parte, for example when seizing property through CIVIL FORFEITURE proceedings. Where the property is movable, an extraordinary circumstance, the government may seize it ex parte without notice and hearing. Where real property is involved, as in *United States v. James Daniel Good Real Property* (1993), notice and a hearing are required, even though the seizure is justified under the FOURTH AMENDMENT. Procedural due process is an independent constitutional requirement, and forfeiture proceedings seek to take property, not merely use it as evidence.

Because procedural due process is a federal constitutional guarantee, its violation creates a federal CIVIL RIGHTS action against state officials. It may also constitute a state cause of action, such as a conversion tort when a prison guard unlawfully takes a prisoner's property. This raises a FEDERALISM concern about constitutionalizing tort litigation involving state officials. Note also that if the state provides an action for the aggrieved party, it may thereby supply all the procedural due process required, at least where a postdeprivation hearing is adequate. The Su-

preme Court, therefore, held in *Daniels v. Williams* (1986) that procedural due process protects only against deliberate, not negligent, state deprivations of protected interests. Even a deliberate state deprivation, as where a state official, "unauthorized" to do so, intentionally violates rights, may not require special procedures where there is nothing the state could have done to prevent random and unpredictable deprivations. Where, however, as in *Zinermon v. Burch* (1990), the state can institute predeprivation procedural safeguards to address a risk of deprivation—in other words, when the risk is reasonably predictable—it must do so.

GARY GOODPASTER
(2000)

Bibliography

MASHAW, JERRY L.   1985   *Due Process in the Administrative State*. New Haven, Conn.: Yale University Press.

PROCEDURAL DUE PROCESS OF LAW, CRIMINAL

The Barons at Runnymede did better than they knew. When they induced King John in 1215 to announce in MAGNA CARTA that no man should be imprisoned or dispossessed "except by the lawful judgment of his peers and by the LAW OF THE LAND," they laid the basis for a text that was to have greater significance in the development of American constitutional law than any other. In time "judgment of his peers" and "law of the land" came to be rendered alternatively as DUE PROCESS OF LAW and in that form were adopted in the Fifth Amendment to the United States Constitution as a restriction upon the federal government: "No person shall . . . be deprived of life, liberty or property, without due process of law." In 1868, substantially the same language was employed in the FOURTEENTH AMENDMENT as a restriction upon the states. Thus was embedded in the Constitution a phrase whose exegesis was to generate hundreds of decisions, libraries of commentary, and unending controversy, to this day. The Supreme Court has, over the years, used the due process clause to develop a variety of substantive restraints upon the power of government. This article, however, will deal only with the sense of due process closest to its original conception, namely, as the source of restrictions on the procedures through which governmental authority may be exercised over the individual in criminal cases.

In determining the procedures the Constitution requires of the federal government in criminal cases, the due process clause of the Fifth Amendment has been of limited significance. The BILL OF RIGHTS contains a variety of provisions explicitly directed to CRIMINAL PROCEDURE, and these rather than the due process clause have served as the principal vehicles for the development of a constitutional law of criminal procedure. So, for example, the Supreme Court has developed the constitutional law of permissible SEARCH AND SEIZURE through interpretations of the FOURTH AMENDMENT; the constitutional law with respect to DOUBLE JEOPARDY and the RIGHT AGAINST SELF-INCRIMINATION through interpretations of the Fifth Amendment; the constitutional law with respect to SPEEDY and PUBLIC TRIAL, TRIAL BY JURY, NOTICE, CONFRONTATION, of opposing witnesses, and the RIGHT TO COUNSEL through interpretations of the Sixth Amendment; and the constitutional law barring excessive BAIL, fines, and CRUEL AND UNUSUAL PUNISHMENT through interpretations of the Eighth Amendment. On the other hand, in determining the procedures the Constitution requires of state governments the due process clause of the Fourteenth Amendment has played the significant and decisive role.

What due process of law required and by what principles its meaning was to be ascertained were questions that were to preoccupy the Court for generations. They were raised early in MURRAY'S LESSEE V. HOBOKEN LAND IMPROVEMENT CO. (1856), a civil case involving the meaning of the Fifth Amendment's due process clause: "The Constitution contains no description of those procedures which it was intended to allow or forbid. It does not even declare what principles are to be applied to ascertain whether it be due process. It is manifest that it was not left to the legislative power to enact any process that might be devised. The article is a restraint on the legislative as well as on the executive and judicial powers of government, and cannot be so construed as to leave Congress free to make any process 'due process of law' by its mere will." Nor, as the Court might have added, could the article be so construed as to leave the Court free to determine what is and what is not due process by *its* mere will. The effort of the Court to come to terms with this challenge is the central feature of the constitutional history of due process.

An early effort to state a principle for interpreting due process was the test of whether a procedure was in accord with settled practices in England before the Revolution and not rejected here after settlement. A practice that met this test accorded due process; a practice that did not failed to accord due process. The test served its purpose in some cases, but it soon proved insufficient, for whatever value it had as a fixed determinant of meaning was overbalanced by its inability to reflect changing times and needs and evolving perceptions of what fairness requires. For example, the settled English practice of initiating a prosecution, customarily continued in this country, was INDICTMENT by a GRAND JURY. Did this mean that due process fastened that procedure upon the states? This was the question at issue in HURTADO V. CALIFORNIA (1884), where the Court faced a California innovation permitting a prosecutor to initiate a prosecution by filing an INFORMATION on his own, after a preliminary hearing before a magistrate on whether there was sufficient cause. The Court upheld the procedure despite its deviance from settled practice because it could find in the new procedure no significant prejudice to the rights of the accused. More decisive than the state of English practice was whether the challenged procedure comported with "those fundamental principles of liberty and justice which lie at the base of all our civil and political institutions." To regard established usage as "essential to due process of law would be to deny every quality of the law but its age, and to render it incapable of progress or improvement." Thus, the Court limited the traditional test: a practice sanctioned by immemorial usage necessarily accorded due process, but one not so sanctioned was not necessarily inconsistent with due process. In time, however, the Court rejected the remaining limb of the test as well. It had been well settled in England that a FELONY defendant had no right to be represented by counsel, and although that had been rejected in the United States Constitution and in the states, the change had not gone so far as to require appointment of counsel for INDIGENT defendants. In POWELL V. ALABAMA (1932) the Court held nevertheless that the failure to appoint counsel for uneducated and indigent defendants in a capital case in circumstances in which they had no real opportunity to present a defense denied due process of law. Of more significance to the Court was its judgment of the "fundamental nature" of the right to be represented by counsel, which in these circumstances was essential to the right to be heard at all.

The test, then, that came to prevail in judging the constitutionality of procedures in state criminal prosecutions was that of fundamental fairness in the circumstances of the particular case. Over the years a variety of formulations were used in an effort to give greater content to the test. Concerning each procedural safeguard that was being asserted, the Court would ask whether it was "of the very essence of a scheme of ORDERED LIBERTY," or whether a "fair and enlightened system of justice would be impossible without it," or whether "liberty and justice" would exist if it were sacrificed, or whether it was among those "immutable principles of justice, acknowledged . . . wherever the good life is a subject of concern." Concerning the procedure applied in the contested prosecution, the Court asked whether it violated a "principle of justice so rooted in the traditions and conscience of our people as to be ranked as fundamental," or whether its use subjected a person to "a hardship so acute and shocking that our polity would not endure it," or whether it offended "those canons of decency and fairness which express the notions of justice of English-speaking peoples even toward those charged with the most heinous offenses," for due process "embodies a system of rights based on moral principles so deeply imbedded in the traditions and feelings of our people as to be deemed fundamental to a civilized society as conceived by our whole history."

Whether any or all of these phrases succeeded in accomplishing anything more than to remit the issue to the intuitive sense of fairness of each Justice; whether, as Justice HUGO L. BLACK asked in ROCHIN V. CALIFORNIA (1952), there could possibly be "avenues of investigation . . . open to discover 'canons' of conduct so universally favored that this Court should write them into the Constitution" were issues that troubled the Justices and commentators alike. These doubts led to the development of an alternative test to determine the meaning of due process; namely, that due process should be taken to mean no more and no less than the specific guarantees of the Bill of Rights. In short, the due process clause of the Fourteenth Amendment "incorporated" as restrictions upon the states the provisions of the first eight amendments originally written as restrictions upon the federal government. The first Justice JOHN MARSHALL HARLAN was the first to advance the argument in several of his dissenting opinions, including *Hurtado* and *O'Neil v. Vermont* (1892). The issue was revived in modern times when Justice Black took up the cudgels in *Adamson v. California* (1947).

The *Adamson* case involved the constitutionality of California law allowing adverse comment to the jury on a defendant's failure to explain or deny evidence against him. In a federal prosecution this practice would have violated the Fifth Amendment's right against self-incrimination. But, of course, under the settled doctrine this was not determinative. The Court had to find that this particular aspect of the self-incrimination privilege—that which disallowed comment on its exercise—was essential to fundamental fairness to the defendant, and this the majority declined to do. The majority could find nothing in the California practice that denied the defendant a FAIR TRIAL. He was not compelled to testify. True, if he did testify he would open the record to evidence of his prior convictions, but, "When evidence is before a jury that threatens conviction, it does not seem unfair to require him to choose between leaving the adverse evidence unexplained and subjecting himself to impeachment through disclosure of former crimes." Justice Black dissented, arguing that a violation of the Fifth Amendment right against self-incrimination was necessarily a denial of due process under the Fourteenth Amendment.

Justice Black's arguments in favor of the INCORPORATION DOCTRINE, as first announced in *Adamson* and developed in later opinions, notably in his concurrence in DUNCAN V. LOUISIANA (1968), were grounded in a study of the history of the adoption of the Fourteenth Amendment, which convinced him that it was the intent of the amendment's framers that it should incorporate the Bill of Rights as a restraint upon the states. For Black, the Constitution did not endow the Court with power to expand and contract the meaning of due process to accord with the Court's assessment of what fundamental fairness required at any particular time. The fundamental fairness test was a resort to "natural law," depending "entirely on the particular judge's idea of ethics and morals instead of requiring him to depend on the boundaries fixed by the written words of the Constitution." Such a test was inconsistent with "the great design of a written Constitution." The specific language of the Bill of Rights would confine the power of the Court to read its own predilections into the Constitution.

Moreover, Black believed that the Bill of Rights, more reliably than the fundamental fairness test, would guide the Court to outcomes consistent with the values of a democratic society. In Black's view the judgment of the Framers of the Constitution would serve better than each Justice's personal judgment in determining what fairness required in criminal prosecutions. Indeed, the record of the Court's administration of its fundamental fairness test was for Black the clearest demonstration of his argument. He was speaking hyperbolically when he said in *Rochin* that the traditional test had been used "to nullify the Bill of Rights," but the fact was that in most instances the Court, as in *Adamson*, had used the fairness standard to uphold state convictions that would have been reversible had the specific provisions of the Bill of Rights been applicable.

Black's primary antagonist on this use, as on many others, was Justice FELIX FRANKFURTER, in later years joined by the second Justice JOHN MARSHALL HARLAN. They rejected Black's interpretation of the history of the Fourteenth Amendment's adoption, finding no plausible evidence that it was intended to incorporate the Bill of Rights as a restraint upon the states. But, beyond that, they advanced a very different approach to CONSTITUTIONAL INTERPRETATION. According to Frankfurter and Harlan, the provisions of the first eight amendments were not equally fundamental. Some, like the guarantees of FREEDOM OF SPEECH and religion, stated enduring values and were, therefore, binding on the states through the "independent potency" of the Fourteenth Amendment. Others, such as those protecting the right against self-incrimination and jury trials, "express the restricted views of Eighteenth-Century England regarding the best methods for the ascertainment of facts." Not every procedure that was historically protected by these provisions was necessary for fundamental fairness, though some might be of this character. Still others, such as the requirement of a grand jury indictment and the right to a jury in civil cases where the amount in controversy exceeded twenty dollars, were largely historical relics. The terms of the Bill of Rights, all of them and only them, were, therefore, an unsuitable text for carrying out the commands of fundamental justice embodied in the requirement of due process of law. Changing circumstances would create new and unforeseen problems, casting new light on the question whether a given procedural guarantee was "fundamental." Only an evolving and flexible due process could assure preservation of the procedural requirements of a free society without binding the criminal process unnecessarily to the forms of the past.

Justices Frankfurter and Harlan conceded that the Court had sustained state procedures whose use would have been forbidden under the Bill of Rights. What mattered, however, was that it had done so only after satisfying itself in each case that the defendant had not been denied fundamental fairness. For example, the Fifth Amendment might forbid a federal prosecutor to APPEAL a conviction of a lesser offense than that charged and to prosecute under the original indictment if the appeal succeeds, but, as the Court held in *Palko v. Connecticut* (1937), the requirements of civilized justice would not be compromised by permitting a state to continue a similar prosecution until it achieved a trial free of substantial error. A jury of twelve persons might be required of federal prosecutions by the Sixth Amendment, but, as the Court held in *Maxwell v. Dow* (1900), it did not follow that a person could not receive a fundamentally fair trial in a state court before a jury of fewer members. Where, on the other hand, state practices fatally infected the justice of the convictions—as in *Powell v. Alabama* (1932) where the accused was deprived of a fair opportunity to present a defense, or in BROWN V. MISSISSIPPI (1936), where torture was used to extract a confession, or in MOORE V. DEMPSEY (1923) where the trial itself was a sham and a pretense—the Court did not hesitate to employ the fundamental fairness standard of due process to strike down the convictions.

In addition, Justices Frankfurter and Harlan emphasized the importance of the Court's avoiding excessive intrusions into the autonomy of the states. The Framers had deliberately chosen to create a federal rather than a wholly centralized system, partly to assure the limitation of power through its dispersal but also to obtain the benefits of autonomy and diversity in state government. Total incorporation of the Bill of Rights into the Fourteenth Amendment would impose a constitutional straitjacket on the states, stifling experimentation by the states in the administration of justice in the name of an unneeded uniformity.

As for the peril of judges' confusing their purely personal preferences with the requirements of the Constitution, Frankfurter and Harlan argued that this risk was inherent in JUDICIAL REVIEW—no less under the incorporation doctrine than under the fundamental fairness test.

Giving meaning to particular provisions of the Bill of Rights, whose major provisions were written in open and general terms, would require judicial inquiry equally broad and open. The peril of judgment on the basis of personal preferences, they argued, must be met by judicial deference to the judgment of state governments and by a rigorous search for the fundamentals of fairness required by the nature and commitments of our society.

Though Justice Black lost the debate in *Adamson*, he continued to advance the cause of total incorporation to his final days on the Court. He never succeeded in persuading a majority, but although he lost some battles he won the war. When the dust cleared two decades after *Adamson*, the fundamental fairness standard (though significantly modified) still reigned as the accepted test of due process, but every provision of the Bill of Rights bearing on criminal procedure, with the single exception of the requirement of grand jury indictments, had been held applicable to the states.

This development occurred through the increased use of the strategy of SELECTIVE INCORPORATION, under which selected clauses of the Bill of Rights were held to be binding on the states as such in the view that they were required by fundamental fairness. Consistency with prior decisions was grounded in the view that what the Court had repeatedly rejected was the theory of total incorporation, not the view that some provisions of the Bill of Rights could be binding on the states through the due process clause. As Justice BENJAMIN N. CARDOZO, an early opponent of the total incorporation doctrine, had observed in PALKO V. CONNECTICUT (1937): "In [certain] situations immunities that are valid as against the federal government by force of the specific pledges of particular amendments have been found to be implicit in the concept of ordered liberty and thus, through the Fourteenth Amendment, become valid as against the states." Yet it is important to note that this justification for the new doctrine blurred an important distinction in the traditional view, which was that some *rights* protected by the provisions of the Bill of Rights might prove so central to ordered liberty that they were also binding on the states through the due process clause. This was not to say, however, that certain *provisions* of the Bill of Rights, in their entirety with all their interpretations, were incorporated by the due process clause.

In the decade following *Adamson* the Court was apparently not yet ready to take this leap from the traditional view to the new doctrine of selective incorporation. Instead, the Court developed a number of significant expansions in its conception of what fundamental fairness required that prepared the ground for the flowering of the selective incorporation theory a decade later. An early important instance was WOLF V. COLORADO (1949), in which the Court held, in an opinion by Justice Frankfurter, that "the security of one's privacy against arbitrary intrusion by the police—which is at the core of the Fourth Amendment—. . . is implicit in "the concept of ordered liberty" and hence enforceable against the states through the due process clause. Still, the opinion was careful not to say that the Fourth Amendment as such was applicable to the states, and the Court declined to apply the remedy it had developed for enforcing the Fourth Amendment in federal prosecutions—excluding the unlawfully seized evidence. Other cases carried the movement forward. The Court in *Rochin* found that pumping an accused's stomach to obtain incriminating evidence was so "shocking to the conscience" that due process required the conviction to be reversed. Increasingly the Court found the failure to appoint counsel for indigent defendants to violate due process under the "totality of circumstances" rule of BETTS V. BRADY (1942), which required specific prejudice to be identified in the record. The circumstances in which the Court held confessions involuntary and, therefore, barred by due process were extended in *Spano v. New York* (1959) beyond physical coercion to include situations in which the defendant's will had been overborne by more subtle means of influence, such as persistent interrogation and trickery.

In the 1960s, however, the traditional test of fundamental fairness yielded to selective incorporation as the Court's dominant approach in reviewing the constitutionality of state prosecutions. A change of mood had taken place. For a variety of reasons—change in the composition of the Court, the CIVIL RIGHTS movement, the "War against Poverty"—the consensus on the Supreme Court moved toward greater intervention on behalf of criminal defendants, the great majority of whom were poor and members of minority groups. The continued enlargement case by case of the requirements of "fundamental fairness" was one possible alternative. But if, as the Justices apparently increasingly believed, excesses in the states' administration of criminal justice required extensive judicial correction, then something more was needed than the power to intervene in occasional cases of gross injustice. As a consequence the 1960s saw one of the remarkable accomplishments of the Warren Court—the federalization of state criminal procedure through the selective incorporation of the Bill of Rights.

Mapp v. Ohio (1961) marked the beginning. Effective control of state law enforcement required a constitutional remedy for law enforcement excesses. The EXCLUSIONARY RULE, which barred admission of unconstitutionally obtained evidence, had been developed decades earlier as a remedy in federal prosecutions. In *Wolf v. Colorado* the Court had declined to apply the exclusionary rule to the states, saying that a conviction based on reliable physical evidence was not fundamentally unfair just because the police had obtained the evidence by unconstitutional means. In *Mapp* the Court overruled that holding. The Court had, after all, already held in *Wolf* that the Fourth Amendment's RIGHT OF PRIVACY was enforceable against the states. It seemed natural to take the further step of holding that the remedy used to enforce Fourth Amendment privacy rights against federal violations was no less required to enforce "due process" privacy rights against state violations. If Fourth Amendment rights were basic to liberty, so must be the only practical means for their enforcement.

The next major case, GIDEON V. WAINWRIGHT (1963), also had features that made it a relatively easy case for extending selective incorporation. The Court had earlier held in *Betts* that appointment of counsel for indigents, though required by the Sixth Amendment for federal prosecutions, was not necessarily a fundamental right protected by due process. In the special circumstances of some particular prosecution, failure to appoint counsel might constitute a lack of fundamental fairness, but absence of counsel would not necessarily create this level of prejudice in every case. However, the "special circumstances" doctrine was gradually undermined in successive cases as the Court increasingly was able to find those circumstances in cases that were typical. As Justice Harlan observed, "The Court had come to realize . . . that the mere existence of a serious criminal charge constituted in itself special circumstances requiring the services of counsel at trial." Against this background there was little resistance to overruling *Betts* and, in the process, holding that the Sixth Amendment's guarantee of counsel was one of those clauses which fundamental fairness required to be imposed upon the states by the Fourteenth Amendment.

From then on scarcely a TERM of Court in the 1960s went by without the Court's OVERRULING some prior case to hold that an additional provision of the Bill of Rights was necessary to fundamental fairness and was, therefore, incorporated in due process. In 1965, in *Griffin v. California*, the Court overruled *Adamson* and held that the Fifth Amendment right against self-incrimination was protected by due process. The Sixth Amendment right to confrontation of witnesses was held to be incorporated in *Pointer v. Texas* (1965), and the rights to a speedy and public trial and to compulsory process for obtaining witnesses were also held to be incorporated in KLOPFER V. NORTH CAROLINA and *Washington v. Texas* (1967). In DUNCAN V. LOUISIANA (1968), the Court overruled earlier decisions and held that the Sixth Amendment's right to a jury trial was incorporated in due process. In BENTON V. MARYLAND (1969), *Palko* was overruled and the double jeopardy provision was held applicable to the states. The job was done. To all intents and purposes, the contours of due process of law required of the states by the Fourteenth Amendment had come to be defined by the specific guarantees of the Bill of Rights limiting the federal government.

One may fairly ask of this constitutional tour de force how well it was defended in doctrinal analysis. The position favoring total incorporation had a forceful logic: once the initial premise was accepted, it followed that every provision of the Bill of Rights and every interpretation of those provisions developed for federal prosecutions should apply equally to state prosecutions. But how was the theory of selective incorporation to be justified? Did the Court seriously mean that all the rights the Court had previously found in selected provisions of the Bill of Rights—such as the jury trial provision of the Sixth Amendment, the Fifth Amendment's protection against self-incrimination, the Fourth Amendment restraints upon search and seizure (including the right to have even reliable evidence excluded if it were unlawfully obtained)—all were so fundamental that "a fair and enlightened system of justice would be impossible" without them? This conclusion could scarcely stand scrutiny. As the Court had noted in earlier cases holding these guarantees unprotected by due process, a large portion of the democratic world, with claims to a civilized and enlightened system of justice no less strong than ours, offers no such guarantees.

Very little effort was made to address this challenge until Justice BYRON R. WHITE (in a footnote, ironically) did so in his opinion for the Court in *Duncan v. Louisiana* (1968), holding the jury trial guarantee of the Sixth Amendment incorporated by the due process clause. He ascribed the rejection of the earlier holdings to a new interpretation of what fundamental fairness meant. The Court had previously understood it to require those guarantees that a system of justice anywhere at any time would have to accord to be called civilized. In the newer cases, however, the Court proceeded on the view that fairness required those guarantees that are necessary to an "Anglo-American regime of ordered liberty." It is not required, White noted, that a procedural guarantee be "necessarily fundamental to fairness in every criminal system that might be imagined," but that it be fundamental "in the context of the criminal processes maintained by the American states."

Whether this revision of the fundamental fairness test suffices as a basis for selecting particular provisions of the Bill of Rights for incorporation is problematic. If the new test refers to practices that have so long been accorded in American systems of justice that they have come to be regarded as among the distinguishing characteristics of American justice, then "fundamental" becomes equivalent to "traditional," all the provisions of the Bill of Rights are fundamental, and the accepted test of selective incor-

poration becomes in fact the rejected test of total incorporation. It would appear, however, that something more was meant. Criminal justice systems, like other social institutions, are complex and comprise a variety of elements that function in a delicate ecological relationship. Given the particular functioning of some procedural protection in the American system, it may be that the protection is fundamental to fairness in that system, although it would not be in a system with a different assortment of procedural elements with differing functional relationships. So, in the *Duncan* case, Justice White noted that although it was easy to imagine a fair system that used no juries, in which alternative guarantees and protections would serve the purposes the jury serves in English and American systems, no American jurisdiction had undertaken to construct such a system.

If this latter interpretation of fundamental fairness were taken seriously, the Court would be obliged to undertake in each case a factual examination of the complex functioning of the state's criminal justice system, with particular attention to how the functioning of the system as a whole colors the significance of the practice at issue. But no such inquiry was made in the *Duncan* case. The opinion drew attention to the long-standing concern about overzealous prosecutors and biased judges. But it made no effort to examine such questions as whether the routine availability of appellate review in the state courts and COLLATERAL ATTACK in the federal courts rendered a jury trial less indispensable as a protection against such abuses; or why, if the use of a jury for this purpose made it a requirement of fundamental fairness in the American system, it was not required in all civilized systems; or whether a jury of randomly chosen citizens in fact served as a check against bias rather than as a source of bias. The Court also pointed generally to the traditional acceptance in America of a jury power of nullification in the application of the law. But the Court failed to consider why this power is significant, and why, in other systems, a comparable power of nullification is not seen to be required by fundamental fairness.

The point is not that the Court could not have made a case for the conclusion that fundamental fairness required the jury in the American system of justice, but that it did not try. Nor did the Court do better in the other cases applying the doctrine of selective incorporation. In the end, therefore, there is force in the conclusion that the Court's attempt to shore up the doctrinal case for selective incorporation was an illusory post hoc rationalization.

An additional consideration, strongly pressed by Justice Harlan in his dissenting opinions, lends further support to that conclusion. Even if it be granted that a guarantee to be found in a provision of the Bill of Rights is required by fundamental fairness in an American system of justice, it does not follow that each and every interpretation of that provision developed in federal prosecutions is equally required for fundamental fairness. For example, the Fifth Amendment's privilege against self-incrimination has been held in federal prosecutions to preclude judicial or prosecutorial comment on the failure of the defendant to respond to the evidence against him. The Fifth Amendment's protection against double jeopardy has been interpreted to attach at the time the jury is first sworn. The Sixth Amendment's guarantee of a jury trial in criminal cases had once been held to require a unanimous verdict of the jury. But even if the core concept of the privilege against self-incrimination, the double jeopardy protection, and the jury trial guarantee were found to be necessary for fundamental fairness, it would scarcely follow that each and every one of these interpretations of the federal guarantees is also necessary. Yet, in sharp contrast to the requirements of the avowed theory of selective incorporation, this is what the Court had held in every instance: a conclusion that a clause of the Bill of Rights is applicable to the states necessarily entails that each and every interpretation of that clause developed in federal prosecutions, regardless of its rationale or significance, becomes fully applicable as well, as Harlan said, "jot-for-jot and case-for-case" and "freighted with [its] entire accompanying body of federal doctrine" (*Duncan v. Louisiana*, 1968; *Malloy v. Hogan*, 1964). This conclusion constitutes further evidence that the Court was not taking seriously the only theory it had advanced to support its doctrine of selective incorporation.

Putting aside the doctrinal warrant of the approach to procedural due process that has come to prevail, what has been its impact on the administration of criminal justice in the states and what is its likely bearing on the future of due process? It is clear that the values of federalism have been heavily overrun. Given the expansive, pervasive, and often highly detailed regulations the Court has imposed on the processes of criminal justice under warrant of the Bill of Rights, one has to conclude that the autonomy of state government has been drastically curtailed.

At the same time, it is almost certainly true that the procedural rights accorded the accused in state courts have been greatly expanded over what they would have been had this federalization not taken place. The expansion of constraints upon the administration of justice during the era of the Warren Court in the 1960s has been one of the notable characteristics of that Court. Few state courts and no state legislatures could have been expected on their own to have achieved anything like a comparable expansion. People will differ over whether the balance between effective law enforcement and the rights of the accused thereby achieved resulted in a preferable system of criminal justice than would have been obtained under the earlier doctrine. Most would agree, however, that the co-

alescing of the minimum constitutional rights of the accused in both state and federal prosecutions has tended to produce a constitutional jurisprudence more understandable to the citizen who does not typically distinguish between state and federal government in considering the rights of the accused.

On the other hand, the presumed advantage in using the Bill of Rights to measure what due process requires of the states—that it eliminates the uncertainty and the need for personal, subjective decision-making by judges imposed by the traditional view—has hardly been evident. In deciding what searches are "reasonable" within the Fourth Amendment, how far that Amendment protects a right of privacy against new forms of ELECTRONIC EAVESDROPPING, when noncoercive POLICE INTERROGATION becomes violative of the Fifth Amendment's right against self-incrimination, what punishment, including CAPITAL PUNISHMENT, is "cruel and unusual" within the Eighth Amendment (which the Court in TROP V. DULLES (1958) conceded had to be determined by "the dignity of man" and "evolving standards of decency"), it was readily apparent that the text of the Bill of Rights scarcely spoke for itself and in fact invited no less an assessment and choice among competing values on the basis of the Justice's sense of what justice and fairness required. Fixed meanings have not triumphed over flexible ones, and judicial subjectivity has not been contained. More seriously, insofar as the Court has proceeded on the false assumption that the need for judicial value choosing has been overcome, it has handicapped itself in the task of developing a well-considered method of decision-making that would discipline and make more rational the inevitable process of choosing among competing values.

This concern is particularly pressing because the Court has recognized that due process is still open-ended, that although due process includes the incorporated clauses of the Bill of Rights, those clauses do not exhaust the content of due process. The 1952 decision in *Rochin*, that a state denied due process by using evidence pumped from the accused's stomach against his will, was reaffirmed in SCHMERBER V. CALIFORNIA (1966) under the principle that due process precludes action against an accused that "shocks the conscience" and violates one's "sense of justice," notwithstanding the inapplicability of any other provision of the Bill of Rights. Similar evidence of the vitality of the older tests of due process where the Bill of Rights does not reach are the Court's decisions in IN RE WINSHIP (1970), holding that an essential requirement of due process in criminal cases is proof of guilt beyond a REASONABLE DOUBT, and in the CAPITAL PUNISHMENT CASES OF 1976, finding in due process a requirement of articulated criteria to guide the judge or jury in determining whether to impose capital punishment.

One may conclude that despite the victory of selective incorporation the task of developing a defensible method and set of criteria to govern the determination of those criminal procedures that are constitutionally permissible is very much before the Court. How it could best be met is uncertain. One proposed approach would entail a consideration of a number of issues. In this view the Court would begin by drawing out the implications of the basic values animating constitutional restraints on the criminal process: fairness to the accused, protection of personal dignity, and the reliability of the processes for determining guilt. Next, the Court would determine how gravely the controverted procedure impugned those values and how seriously certain restraints would prejudice the due administration of criminal justice. Finally, the Court would seek ways of rooting the inevitable final choices in ground more secure than the personal judgment of the majority of the Justices on the optimum operation of the system of criminal justice. Another approach, less oriented to consequentialist considerations, would have the Court determine the fundamental legal rights of persons, including the constitutional rights of the accused, in terms of the requirements of a general political theory that best account for the moral principles embedded in the Constitution, laws, and culture of our society. Whatever the answer, the task is a formidable one. Indeed, the effort may ultimately be futile, as those believe who view the Court as indistinguishable from any other political body in the exercise of its power. But to the extent that the Court accepts the claim that its exercise of political power is based on reason and disinterestedness—that is, on law—it can scarcely abandon the goal of writing opinions that give credence to the claim. However one may approve its results, the doctrine of selective incorporation, with its oversimplifications and misperceptions, and its dubious doctrinal underpinnings, has not served that goal well.

SANFORD H. KADISH
(1986)

Bibliography

ALLEN, FRANCIS A.   1953   Due Process and State Criminal Procedures: Another Look. *Northwestern University Law Review* 48:16–35.
DWORKIN, RONALD M.   1975   Hard Cases. *Harvard Law Review* 88:1057–1109.
FAIRMAN, CHARLES   1949   Does the Fourth Amendment Incorporate the Bill of Rights? The Original Understanding. *Stanford Law Review* 2:5–173.
FRIENDLY, HENRY   1965   The Bill of Rights as a Code of Criminal Procedure. *California Law Review* 53:929–956.
HENKIN, LOUIS   1963   "Selective Incorporation" in the Fourteenth Amendment. *Yale Law Journal* 73:74–88.
KADISH, SANFORD H.   1957   Methodology and Criteria in Due Process Adjudication—A Survey and Criticism. *Yale Law Journal* 66:319–363.
NOTE   1949   The Adamson Case: A Study in Constitutional Technique. *Yale Law Journal* 58:268–287.
NOWAK, JOHN E.   1979   Foreword: Due Process Methodology in a Post-Incorporation World. *Journal of Criminal Law and Criminology* 70:397–423.

PROCEDURAL DUE PROCESS OF LAW, CRIMINAL
(Update)

Integral to the law's aspirations is the set of variables differentiating law and politics: reason and passion, rationality and bias, free inquiry and ideology, fairness and self-interest. The law's ardent hope is that these variables permit distinctions between what will endure and what will pass, for it is the relative mix of the enduring and the ephemeral that determines whether a nation is one of disinterested laws or of self-interested individuals. Thus it is that the Supreme Court strives to justify its decisions through well-reasoned opinions. The task of the Court is to resist the allure of politics and rest judgment on principle.

But is this task possible? The difficulties are legion. Disagreements abound concerning the correct interpretative methodology, the data relevant to the various interpretive approaches, and the proper role of the judiciary in a democratic scheme. These disagreements are compounded because the Supreme Court often does not speak with one voice but instead is spoken for by each of the Justices in a setting that seriously complicates a consistent ordering of preferences in enduring legal doctrine. Super-imposed over all these difficulties is the fact that the Supreme Court is essentially a reactive institution, responding to problems generated for it by social factors beyond its control. No matter how fervently the Justices may wish to promulgate a consistent and principled JURISPRUDENCE, the diversity and unpredictability of the grist for the Court's mill make the task formidable.

The more open-ended the interpretive problem, the more formidable the task, and among the most open-ended of the Supreme Court's tasks is the interpretation of the twin DUE PROCESS OF LAW clauses in the Fifth Amendment and FOURTEENTH AMENDMENT. The language of these clauses is not confining, their historical purposes are unclear, and to the extent there is agreement concerning those purposes, their implications for contemporary issues are not obvious. The due process clause of the Fifth Amendment, for example, was adopted as part of a set of guarantees that the newly created central government would respect its proper sphere, and the similar clause of the Fourteenth Amendment was adopted to recognize and reflect the changes wrought in the country by the CIVIL WAR. Neither was adopted with the contemporary set of issues in mind to which these clauses have been asserted to be relevant by litigants and judges.

For all these reasons, the Supreme Court's interpretation of the due process clauses is consistently as much a reflection of the times as the product of timeless interpretive methodologies. The nation's first century was a time of territorial expansion and of the creation and consolidation of governmental institutions in which criminal due process adjudication played virtually no role, and there were virtually no criminal due process cases. The second century brought an increasing emphasis on the role of individual rights, which culminated in the remarkable creativity of the Supreme Court's procedural revolution in the mid-1960s. The question now is what the third century will bring.

Certain trends are already apparent. The procedural revolution is over and the resulting legal landscape is stable. Whatever its theoretical attraction, the theory of total INCORPORATION has substantially won, even though a majority of the Court has never adopted the theory. Most of the criminal provisions of the BILL OF RIGHTS have been found to be binding on the states through the due process clause of the Fourteenth Amendment. Furthermore, notwithstanding the dramatic reorientation of the Supreme Court owing to recent appointments, the Court has not overruled a single majority CRIMINAL PROCEDURE decision holding a Bill of Rights provision incorporated into the Fourteenth Amendment. The incorporationist controversy is so definitively over that the opinions of the Court addressing questions of state criminal procedure discuss directly the applicable Bill of Rights provision with at most a cursory reference to the due process clause of the Fourteenth Amendment. The casualness with which the distinction is drawn between Fourteenth Amendment due process and the specific provisions of the Bill of Rights is exemplified by the opinion for a unanimous court in *Crane v. Kentucky* (1986). In holding that due process was violated by the exclusion of testimony concerning the circumstances of a defendant's confession, the Court said that "whether rooted directly in the Due Process Clause of the Fourteenth Amendment or in the compulsory process or confrontation clauses of the Sixth Amendment, the Constitution guarantees criminal defendants "a meaningful opportunity to present a complete defense."

Justices also appear to have little interest in giving either due process clause much independent significance. In those few instances in recent years in which the Court has discussed either clause directly rather than as a surrogate for some other constitutional provision, it typically has done so to deny that due process has any meaning independent of the specific provisions of the Bill of Rights.

In *Moran v. Burbine* (1986) the Court held that there was no violation of due process when the police failed to inform a criminal suspect subjected to custodial interrogation of the efforts of an attorney to reach him. Due process also does not require appointed counsel for collateral review of a conviction (*Pennsylvania v. Finley,* 1987), not even for collateral review of capital convictions (*Murray v. Giarratano,* 1989). Similarly, in *Strickland v. Washington* (1984) the Court commented that although "the Constitution guarantees a fair trial through the Due Process Clauses, it defines the basic elements of a fair trial largely through the several provisions of the Sixth Amendment." The Court applied this approach in *Caplin & Drysdale, Chartered v. United States* (1989) to find that the Fifth Amendment due process clause adds little or nothing to the Sixth Amendment RIGHT TO COUNSEL clause and in UNITED STATES V. SALERNO (1987) to reach a similar conclusion concerning the relationship between Fifth Amendment due process and the requirement of BAIL in the Eighth Amendment.

The failure of the Court to overrule prior criminal decisions and to give independent force to the due process clauses does not mean that the creative energies of the Court are quiescent. Rather, they are finding outlets in different directions. Through the mid-1960s the Court's agenda was to tame the unruly manner in which the criminal justice process operated, particularly in the states. Employing the due process clause of the Fourteenth Amendment as its primary weapon, the Court succeeded in subjecting the state criminal justice process to the formal limits on governmental power in the Bill of Rights and in breaking down resistance to its innovations in the lower state and federal courts. One measure of this success is the increasingly common phenomenon of state supreme courts using state law to impose greater constraints on state officials than the federal constitution requires.

Because its previous messages have been largely absorbed by the lower courts and perhaps in response to increasingly conservative politics in the country, the Court has refocused the target of criminal procedural due process analysis from the specific provisions of the Bill of Rights to the question of the appropriate remedy. There are three interrelated variables driving the refocusing: first, a concern that exclusion of evidence premised upon the policy of deterring undesirable state action has a reasonable chance of advancing that goal; second, an increasingly intense belief that finality is an important value in adjudication; and third, an emphasis on accuracy in outcome.

The primary remedies that the Court has employed to effect its revisions of criminal procedure were the exclusionary rule and the threat of reversing convictions. Cases such as GIDEON V. WAINWRIGHT (1963), MAPP V. OHIO (1961), and MIRANDA V. ARIZONA (1966) fit a general pattern of announcements of new rules to be enforced by the threat of excluding EVIDENCE seized in violation of those rules or the reversals of convictions if the rules are not followed. The theory was that law enforcement officials would not jeopardize convictions by ignoring the new rules and that the threats of exclusion and reversal would thus deter unwanted behavior.

The present Court perceives two difficulties with this theory. First, as the new rules became accepted, and thus became the norm, the power of exclusion or the threat of reversal to affect law enforcement behavior diminished. It is one thing to exclude evidence or reverse a conviction because the police broke into a person's house, in the process apparently lying about whether they possessed a SEARCH WARRANT, as occurred in *Mapp*, but it is another to exclude evidence where the police made every effort to comply with the Court's pronouncements, as the Court refused to do in *United States v. Leon* (1984). Second, the nature of Supreme Court innovation is that it begins with the core problem an area poses and then expands into peripheral areas. As the cases press the logic of the original innovations further, the relationship between the cases and the policies underlying the original innovations becomes increasingly attenuated. It is one thing to sanction state officials for extensively interrogating an individual without warning him of his rights or allowing him to consult counsel, as occurred in *Miranda*, but it is another to do so because the state official gave a set of *Miranda* warnings differing somewhat from the language specifically approved in *Miranda*, as the Court refused to do in *California v. Prysock* (1981).

The Supreme Court has fashioned a number of principles to limit the EXCLUSIONARY RULE to situations in which there are reasonable prospects that deterrence will operate. Chief among these limiting principles is the GOOD FAITH EXCEPTION to the exclusionary rule fashioned in *Leon*. Exclusion of evidence is not likely to deter behavior if the law enforcement personnel had a good-faith belief in the correctness of their conduct. Similarly, the Court has refused to extend the exclusionary rule into peripheral areas where deterrence is unlikely to result, such as the GRAND JURY setting (UNITED STATES V. CALANDRA, 1974) and civil matters such as forfeiture proceedings (*United States v. Janis*, 1976) and DEPORTATION proceedings (*Immigration and Naturalization Service v. Lopez-Mendoza*, 1984).

The Court has also limited those who may litigate the legality of state action to restrict exclusion of evidence to cases where a deterrent effect is likely. Because law enforcement officials will not typically know in advance who the culprit is or who will be permitted to litigate the legality of their behavior, they will not jeopardize an investigation through illegal action so long as someone affected by their behavior may be in a position to complain. Thus, in *Rakas v. Illinois* (1987), the Court held that the passengers of a car could not contest the legality of a search of the car that included a search of the glove compartment, which had been used with the owner's apparent knowledge. In *Rawlings v. Kentucky* (1980) the Court held that the defendant could not contest the validity of the search of an acquaintance's purse where, again, the defendant had placed items with the knowledge of the purse's owner.

Intimately related to the Court's concern about the deterrent efficacy of its remedies is its growing emphasis on finality of decision. As the time increases between alleged state misbehavior and judicial intervention, the likelihood that reversals will affect behavior decreases. In addition, permitting federal relitigation of issues is an intelligent tactic if the work product of the state courts is not trusted, as was the case three decades ago; but as greater confidence in that work product is achieved, departures from finality are less desirable. A system that allows multiple attacks on the legitimacy of its work product undermines itself in various ways. Allowing repetitive relitigation of issues increases the probability of aberrational results simply because a litigant will eventually come before a court that for whatever reason—randomness, bias, or simple lack of attention—will act aberrationally. Reversals in such cases are not likely to advance deterrence of undesirable behavior or any other significant value. Allowing relitigation may also detract from the primary values of the penal system by encouraging individuals to deny responsibility for their acts. Regardless of whether confession is good for the soul, it is less likely to occur while avenues of appeal remain open.

Finality has been advanced in various ways. In particular, the scope of HABEAS CORPUS has been reduced. In STONE V. POWELL (1976) the Court held that FOURTH AMENDMENT issues could not be relitigated on habeas corpus if the defendant had been provided an adequate opportunity to litigate the issue at trial. In *Teague v. Lane* (1989) the Court held that the retroactivity of new constitutional rulings is limited to cases still pending on direct appeal at the time the new decision is handed down. In a series of cases, the Court has also developed a strict "waiver" rule to the effect that failure to raise an issue in a timely manner in state court precludes litigating it in federal habeas corpus unless failure to raise it amounted to ineffective assistance of counsel or unless a miscarriage of justice would result.

The third variable informing the Court's recent due process jurisprudence is a heightened focus on accuracy in adjudication. As the Court has become convinced that little remains of the disrespect for individual rights that it believed previously characterized the criminal justice process, it has become increasingly concerned with encouraging accurate outcomes. On the one hand, this has resulted in a further tightening of the avenues on appeal for a convicted defendant. In a series of cases beginning with *Chapman v. California* (1967), the Court has held that HARMLESS ERROR—error that does not cast doubt on the outcome of the trial—does not justify reversing a conviction. In NIX V. WILLIAMS (1984) the Court held that a conviction would not be reversed as a result of the admission of evidence illegally seized that would have been inevitably discovered by legitimate means. On the other hand, the Court has extended rights integral to the accuracy of convictions. For example, the Court has continued in its broad reading of the right to counsel, holding in EVITTS V. LUCEY (1985) that a defendant convicted of a crime is guaranteed effective assistance of counsel on a first appeal as a matter of right, even though a state is not required to provide for an appeal, and in AKE V. OKLAHOMA (1985) that a state must guarantee a criminal defendant access to a competent psychiatrist to assist in evaluation, preparation, and presentation of the defense.

The present state of due process adjudication is accurately captured by the holding in *James v. Illinois* (1990). In *James* the Court held that the principle that illegally obtained evidence can be used to impeach defendants' testimony so that exclusionary rules do not encourage perjury—first fashioned in *Walder v. United States* (1954)—did not extend to defense witnesses other than the defendant. Allowing the state to impeach witnesses other than the defendant would increase significantly the value of illegally obtained evidence, thus substantially impairing the efficacy of the exclusionary rule. Increasing the incentive of law enforcement officials to obtain evidence illegally would in turn put core constitutional values at risk. As significant as finality and accuracy are, they remain less significant than the core values of the various provisions of the Bill of Rights.

The implication of decisions like *James* is that criminal due process has evolved from a club to beat recalcitrant officials into line with the Court's innovations into a more subtle tool for adjusting the margins of the various doctrines. This use of procedural due process will surely continue for the foreseeable future. The next stage in the development of due process is presently unknowable, but its origins are predictable. The nation is in the midst of a subtle devolution of political authority from the central government to the states. Due process jurisprudence has mirrored this trend, as the Court has shown an increasing reluctance to intervene in the criminal justice process. As state officials become aware of their increasing autonomy, they will take advantage of it to rework state criminal processes. As innovations are implemented over the next decades, they will be subjected to constitutional challenges, and out of that process will come the next stage in the

continuing evolution of the meaning of the due process clauses for criminal procedure.

RONALD J. ALLEN
(1992)

(SEE ALSO: *Automobile Search; Criminal Justice System.*)

Bibliography

AMSTERDAM, ANTHONY G. 1970 The Supreme Court and the Rights of Suspects in Criminal Cases. *New York University Law Review* 45:785–815.

BLASI, VINCENT A., ed. 1983 *The Burger Court: The Counter-Revolution That Wasn't.* New Haven, Conn.: Yale University Press.

NOWAK, JOHN E. 1979 Due Process Methodology in the Postincorporation World. *Journal of Criminal Law and Criminology* 70:397–493.

WILKES, DONALD E., JR. 1985 The New Federalism in Criminal Procedure: Death of the Phoenix? Pages 166–200 in Bradley D. McGraw, ed., *Developments in State Constitutional Law.* St. Paul, Minn.: West Publishing Co.

PROCHOICE MOVEMENT

See: Abortion and the Constitution; Reproductive Autonomy

PROCLAMATION OF NEUTRALITY
(1793)

The Proclamation of Neutrality (April 22, 1793) was issued by President GEORGE WASHINGTON upon notification that France and Britain were at war. It pledged the United States to "pursue a course friendly and impartial" toward the belligerents and enjoined observance on all citizens upon pain of prosecution. Neutrality was bound to be difficult because of intense partisan feelings about the war, the privileges and obligations of the French alliance, and British rejection of American claims of neutral rights on the seas.

The importance of the proclamation for the Constitution was twofold. First, as a unilateral declaration by the President it seemed to preempt the power of Congress to decide questions of war and peace. Secretary of State THOMAS JEFFERSON, although he acquiesced in the proclamation, had made this objection in the cabinet, and it was taken up by the Republicans. In a notable series of articles under the signature Pacificus, Secretary of the Treasury ALEXANDER HAMILTON defended the proclamation. His claim of independent executive authority in FOREIGN AFFAIRS was opposed by JAMES MADISON as Helvidius, who compared it to the royal prerogative of the English constitution. (Hamilton's argument prevailed in history, though Madison's antipathy to overriding executive power has not lacked supporters.) Second, as the conduct of neutrality was executive altogether, it afforded the first instance of government by administrative lawmaking. Decisions were made in the cabinet, without statutory authority, with the guidance only of the customary law of nations. Divided and uncomfortable in this work, the cabinet officers submitted twenty-nine questions to the ruling of the Supreme Court. The court declined to rule, however, and thus established the precedent against ADVISORY OPINIONS. Meanwhile, the government's attempt to prosecute violators of the proclamation was defeated by unsympathetic juries. Not until June 1794 did Congress enact a neutrality law, which codified the rules developed in the cabinet during the preceding year.

MERRILL D. PETERSON
(1986)

Bibliography

THOMAS, CHARLES M. 1931 *American Neutrality in 1793: A Study in Cabinet Government.* New York: Columbia University Press.

PROCUNIER v. MARTINEZ
416 U.S. 396 (1974)

Speaking through Justice LEWIS F. POWELL, the Supreme Court invalidated California prison regulations censoring inmates' correspondence and prohibiting attorney-client interviews conducted by law students and legal paraprofessionals. The censorship provisions had permitted prison officials to ban correspondence in which inmates "unduly complain," "magnify grievances," or expressed "inflammatory political, racial, religious or other views or beliefs." These vague standards, the Court held, violated the FIRST AMENDMENT rights of prisoners and those with whom they corresponded. The prohibition on the use of law students and paralegals was held to be an unjustified restriction on prisoners' ACCESS TO THE COURTS.

MICHAEL E. PARRISH
(1986)

PRODUCTION

Until the transformation of the constitutional law of ECONOMIC REGULATION, beginning in 1937, "production" described economic activities that the Supreme Court regarded as local or intrastate in character and therefore beyond Congress's power to regulate under the COMMERCE CLAUSE. In 1895 the Court ruled in UNITED STATES V. E. C. KNIGHT CO. that every form of production and matters related to it were stages of economic activity that preceded the buying, selling, and transportation of goods among the states. Manufacturing, mining, agriculture, domestic fisheries, stock raising, and labor had only an "indirect" effect upon commerce, by judicial definition. Because commerce came after production the United States had no constitutional authority to extend the SHERMAN ANTITRUST ACT to monopolies in production, nor could it control the trade practices of poultry dealers, or regulate agricultural production, or fix the MAXIMUM HOURS AND MINIMUM WAGES of miners. In UNITED STATES V. DARBY (1941) the Court sustained the constitutionality of the FAIR LABOR STANDARDS ACT, which applied to workers engaged in production of goods for sale in INTERSTATE COMMERCE, in the next year the Court in WICKARD V. FILBURN (1942) ended any remaining vestiges of the doctrine that Congress could not regulate production. The Court ruled that, although certain economic activities are local or intrastate, the commerce clause extends Congress's power to them if they affect commerce, making their regulation an appropriate way of governing commerce among the states.

LEONARD W. LEVY
(1986)

PROFFITT v. FLORIDA

See: Capital Punishment Cases of 1976

PROGRESSIVE CONSTITUTIONAL THOUGHT

During the Progressive era, roughly from 1900 to 1920, the Constitution and the SUPREME COURT came in for considerable criticism on the part of historians, political theorists, statesmen, intellectuals, and journalists. The criticisms involved five issues: the origins of the Constitution's authority; claims that the Constitution, and the system of government it supported, were antiquated and needed to be modified in light of developments in modern science; protests that the Supreme Court functioned as an instrument of business interests; demands that the Constitution be reinterpreted to allow for federal regulation of industry; and similar demands that it become the agency of social reform.

Prior to the Progressive era the Constitution's authority rested on the assumption that it was a neutral document capable of rendering objective judgments based on either transcendent religious principles or secular doctrines like natural law. The first challenge to that assumption came from J. ALLEN SMITH's *The Spirit of American Government*

(1907), in which the Constitution was alleged to be a "reactionary" document designed to thwart the democratic principles of the DECLARATION OF INDEPENDENCE by means of CHECKS AND BALANCES and JUDICIAL REVIEW of legislative actions of popular majorities. But the most thorough critique of the Constitution's presumed disinterested authority fell like a blockbuster with the publication of CHARLES A. BEARD's *An Economic Interpretation of the Constitution* (1913). Here readers discovered that the movement toward RATIFICATION OF THE CONSTITUTION in 1787–1789 was led by merchants, manufacturers, creditors, and land speculators whose primary concern was to protect their own interests from what JAMES MADISON called "overbearing factions." THE FEDERALIST's authors, Beard was aware, hardly concealed the fact that they regarded protection of property as the essence of liberty. But Beard's exposure of the economic motives of the Framers did much to demystify the moral character of the Constitution by disclosing the "interests" behind it.

While the historian Beard tried to unmask the sacred image of the Constitution, political theorists tried to re-establish it on a more scientific foundation. In *The Process of Government* (1908) Arthur Bentley suggested that the scholar must penetrate beyond the formal structure of the Constitution to appreciate the forces and pressures that act upon it through interest group demands. But the dynamic of amoral interest politics was precisely what troubled WOODROW WILSON and other Progressive idealists. First in *Congressional Government* (1884), then in *Constitutional Government in the United States* (1908), and finally in a series of campaign speeches published as *The New Freedom* (1912), Wilson indicted the Constitution for weakening the executive branch of government, allowing interests and power to prevail in the legislature's standing committees, accepting as inevitable factional antagonisms detrimental to the public good, and upholding the letter of the law rather than the life of the state. Criticizing *The Federalist* for bequeathing a static, mechanist concept of government, Wilson wanted a Constitution "accountable to Darwin, not to Newton," a Constitution as "a living organism" capable of growth and adaption, one that would coordinate the branches of government so that liberty could be preserved not on the basis of diversity—Madison's premise—but of unity forged by presidential leadership.

Critical of the Constitution, Progressives also became disillusioned with a Supreme Court as an obstacle in the path of social reform. THEODORE ROOSEVELT exploded in anger when the Court invalidated state LEGISLATION involving child labor, tenement house reform, and other goals of PROGRESSIVISM. Yet, curiously, Progressives disagreed whether the Court had a right to do so. In *The Supreme Court and the Constitution* (1912), Beard argued

that the right of judicial review was the clear intent of *The Federalist*. In *Our Judicial Oligarchy* (1912) Gilbert E. Roe expounded the opposing case, arguing that the courts had usurped authority in reviewing legislative acts. While both authors scorned judges disposed to preserving property rights at the cost of social justice, they continued to differ as to whether the Supreme Court could hold unconstitutional laws void or whether it should defer to the legislative process and exercise what the followers of OLIVER WENDELL HOLMES called "judicial restraint."

Progressives were far more unified in advocating regulation. All the writers associated with the liberal *New Republic*—HERBERT CROLY, Walter Weyl, Walter Lippmann, John Dewey, and LOUIS D. BRANDEIS—wanted to see corporate enterprise subordinated to the public good by means of industrial commissions, surveillance of trusts and monopolies, banking and railroad legislation, and the like. All also agreed that standing in the way of federal regulatory policies was a debilitating Jeffersonian heritage that made private rights anterior to public responsibilities, a destructive individualism that frustrated the ideals of political authority and civic duty. "Only by violating the spirit of the Constitution," Lippmann boldly declared, "have we been able to preserve the letter of it." Many of the Progressives were Hamiltonian nationalists convinced that both the Constitution and the Republic could be preserved from the corruptions of business interests only by augmenting the authority of an efficient and enlightened state. Many were also pragmatists who believed that the Constitution should be interpreted not from within but from without, not in terms of its inherent logic or precedent but in light of its consequences as society experiences the Court's rulings.

Progressives succeeded in realizing a number of reforms through the AMENDING PROCESS, specifically the income tax, women's suffrage, and the DIRECT ELECTION of senators. As with the RECALL, and REFERENDUM in state governments, and direct PRIMARY ELECTIONS in national politics, the constitutional amendments aimed to allow people to participate more directly in the decisions affecting their lives. Whereas *The Federalist*'s authors believed that liberty could best be preserved by distancing the people from the immediate operations of government, the Progressives saw no conflict between republican liberty and participatory democracy.

JOHN PATRICK DIGGINS
(1986)

Bibliography

COMMAGER, HENRY STEELE 1950 *The American Mind: An Interpretation of American Thought and Character Since the 1890s*. New Haven, Conn.: Yale University Press.
ROSTOW, EUGENE V. 1970 The Realist Tradition in Law. Pages

203–218 in Arthur M. Schlesinger, Jr., and Morton White, eds., *Paths of American Thought*. Boston: Beacon Press.

PROGRESSIVISM

In the decades after the CIVIL WAR, American law was forced to accommodate to the increasing pace of economic change as the United States was transformed from an agrarian, rural nation of small operatives into an urban, industrial nation characterized by huge transportation, manufacturing, extractive, and financial corporations that served national rather than local or regional markets. The Standard Oil trust, formed in 1882, consisted of thirty-nine different companies that pumped oil in eight states, refined it in six, and sold it everywhere. Railroad mileage increased from 36,801 miles in 1866 to 193,346 in 1900, and the gross national product increased by a factor of twelve. By 1900, the United States was producing more steel than Great Britain and Germany combined. Nevertheless, the devastating depression of 1893–1897 underscored the pain, human suffering, and dislocation caused by industrialization—ranging from child labor to burgeoning farm tenancy, strikes, and massive unemployment (which ran as high as twenty percent during the darkest months of the depression). It also underscored the lack of rationality and order in the marketplace. The century ended with a flurry of mergers as 2,274 firms disappeared during the years 1898–1910.

Historians have questioned whether there was a "Progressive movement," disagreed about who were its leaders and followers, and argued about its dates. Around the beginning of the twentieth century, institutional reform occurred at many levels of government, but Progressives were not unified by party, class, or objectives. For example, those who favored economic efficiency, such as the conservationists, seldom showed much sympathy for those who championed social issues. Not surprisingly, the Progressives never decided how the business corporation could be made more accountable to public opinion or what role it should play in American society. Since the colonial period, American law has attempted to blend promotional and regulatory elements, though the former prevailed for most of the nineteenth century. It has proved far easier to promote economic growth—through such legal mechanisms as EMINENT DOMAIN, the power of incorporation, tax policy, and limits on liability for personal injury—than to regulate it.

For constitutional and legal scholars, it is appropriate to define the Progressive era as the years from about 1886 to 1917. Some recent historians look more charitably on the Supreme Court during this era than did scholars who wrote before the 1970s. They argue that many Justices were by training and inclination classical liberals who saw the Constitution as the embodiment of natural law. These judges wanted to preserve higher law rights and individual liberty, limit monopoly and government "paternalism," and protect the central government from expanding STATE POLICE POWER. They rejected "special privilege" in all forms. Earlier historians had charged that most members of the Court regarded the Constitution as primarily designed to protect property, that they knew little about American history and institutions, that they stubbornly clung to an organic, almost feudal view of society, and that they contributed to the growth of vast economic oligarchies. The critics insisted that state courts—particularly in their reliance on liberty of contract and in their use of injunctions to break strikes—were no less activistic, regressive, or anachronistic than the High Court.

It is not clear that the Supreme Court was out of step with public opinion or that its members held substantially more "conservative" values than did the mass of Americans. (Even in the midst of the depression, the Republicans won in a landslide in 1894 and WILLIAM MCKINLEY beat William Jennings Bryan easily in 1896.) Nevertheless, no charge was more popular during the Progressive era than that the courts had systematically violated the basic structural principle of the Constitution—the independence of the three branches of government. In 1895 the High Court rendered two decisions that struck at the heart of national LEGISLATIVE POWER. In UNITED STATES V. KNIGHT CO. the Court, which traditionally had defined the COMMERCE CLAUSE very broadly, emasculated the SHERMAN ANTITRUST ACT (1890) by ruling that the American Sugar Company, which refined more than 90 percent of the nation's supply, monopolized manufacturing but only indirectly commerce. (The Court drew the same kind of fine distinction when it refused to accept use of the commerce clause as a limit on child labor because only the products of labor, not the labor itself, was involved in INTERSTATE COMMERCE.) In the same year, the second POLLOCK V. FARMERS' LOAN AND TRUST CO. decision ignored well-settled precedent by invalidating the national income tax of 1894. And in 1896 INTERSTATE COMMERCE COMMISSION V. CINCINNATI, NEW ORLEANS, TEXAS PACIFIC RAILWAY denied that Congress had granted the Interstate Commerce Commission power to set rates.

Simultaneously, the Court, led by Justice STEPHEN J. FIELD, reinterpreted the DUE PROCESS clause of the FOURTEENTH AMENDMENT, making it a substantive protection of property against "arbitrary" and "confiscatory" state and federal regulations, not just the constitutional guarantee of a fair trial. *Munn v. Illinois* (1877) had clearly upheld the power of individual states to regulate the use of private property in the public interest; it had rejected SUBSTANTIVE DUE PROCESS as the Court had done earlier in the SLAUGH-

TERHOUSE CASES (1873). But substantive due process—which won its first great victory in STONE V. FARMERS' LOAN AND TRUST COMPANY (1886)—added new power to JUDICIAL REVIEW. A similar spirit permeated the Court's statutory interpretations, as in the RULE OF REASON articulated in STANDARD OIL COMPANY V. UNITED STATES (1911), which suggested that monopoly in and of itself was not illegal and that only the courts could define what charges, rates, or business practices were "reasonable." In LOCHNER V. NEW YORK (1905) it relied on the liberty and contract doctrine, which was based on substantive due process of law, to argue that the state could not use its police powers to regulate maximum work hours, except in dangerous jobs or jobs that immediately affected the public health; the Court held that bakers, unlike miners, did not do dangerous work. The right of workers to sell their labor at the highest price and of employers to buy it at the cheapest price took precedence. And in HAMMER V. DAGENHART (1918) the Court went against well-established precedent in declaring that the first federal child labor law went beyond Congress' commerce power, threatening the police power of the states and the balance between federal and state authority.

Many jurists and politicians fought against the conservative drift of the courts during the Progressive era, proposing reforms that included the recall of judges, the standardization of state incorporation laws, and the use of SOCIOLOGICAL JURISPRUDENCE to expand the vision and accountability of courts. But these proposals had little impact on the new industrial order. Far more important was the RULE OF LAW itself, for Progressivism was shaped by American values and faith in the American legal process. Most Americans preferred reform through law, a process of constitutional change, rather than revolution. The Progressives' faith in the rationality of man, progress, and the curative powers of law prompted such reforms as the initiative, referendum, recall, and direct elections of United States senators. They did not attack such underlying problems as poverty, racism, discrimination, and the insecurity of labor. Nor was there any major revamping of the legal system itself. Many Progressives argued that judicial review threatened the doctrine of SEPARATION OF POWERS, that it was inherently undemocratic, that it might as logically have been exercised by Congress or the President as by the Supreme Court, that most rulings of unconstitutionality had little to do with the language of the Constitution, that the frequency of 5–4 decisions violated the principle that only laws clearly unconstitutional should be invalidated, that split decisions threatened to undermine public faith in the entire justice system, and that judges had little understanding of American society. Yet Congress was unable to adopt major reforms, and most Americans remained wary of tampering with the judicial system.

Although by the 1920s the Interstate Commerce Commission, Federal Trade Commission, and the Federal Reserve Board were the only important national REGULATORY AGENCIES, by that time the commission had won out over other options (including antitrust prosecutions, which met with little enthusiasm after the Progressive era, save for a few years at the end of the 1930s). The commissions served many purposes, including fact-gathering, education, disclosure of illegal practices, encouragement of innovation, the cartelization of industries, and restrictions on monopoly and oligopoly. They combined legislative and judicial functions, or adjudication and planning, and, even more important, they maintained respect for property by following elaborate administrative hearings and procedures similar to regular courts. They built on the assumption that by removing issues from the courts and legislatures, public servants could decide the proper shape and conduct of American business. In short, the commissions fitted comfortably with American views of the legal process.

The regulation of business was one thing; basic reform of the economic system, however, was uncongenial to most Americans. The Progressives agreed that the new industrial order had to be made more predictable, accountable, and responsible; that much was obvious. They also recognized the limits of judicial regulation of business, the judges' lack of knowledge of the economic system, the inability of courts to act unless a complaint was brought to them, and the courts' inability to engage in long-range policy-making. However, while many Progressives feared bigness per se, others looked forward to a new society built on organization, cooperation, and specialization; the competition that had been so valued in the nineteenth century appeared to them as anachronistic and dangerous. The Progressives no less than those who supported the NEW DEAL could not agree on what the structure of business should be, nor could they agree on the form or forms regulation should take. Therefore, many regulatory tools—such as selective corporate taxes (as on companies that used child labor or had interlocking directorates), national incorporation, and an expansion of the NATIONAL POLICE POWER—did not receive the attention they deserved. American values were ambivalent. Most Progressives regarded laissez-faire with disdain, yet they also believed in the sanctity of private property, economic individualism, and a society driven by the harmony of self-interest rather than by the clash of classes.

DONALD J. PISANI
(1992)

(SEE ALSO: *Child Labor Amendment; Child Labor Tax Act; Conservatism; Federal Trade Commission Act; Liberalism; Progressive Constitutional Thought.*)

Bibliography

BETH, LOREN P. 1971 *The Development of the American Constitution, 1877–1917.* New York: Harper & Row.

SKLAR, MARTIN J. 1988 *The Corporate Reconstruction of American Capitalism, 1890–1916: The Market, The Law, and Politics.* Cambridge: Cambridge University Press.

SWINDLER, WILLIAM F. 1969 *Court and Constitution in the Twentieth Century: The Old Legality, 1889–1932.* Indianapolis and New York: Bobbs-Merrill Co.

PROHIBITION

A recurring theme in American constitutional history is the attempt of a majority to impose its moral standards on society by legislation. The nineteenth-century temperance movement, along with its close ally, the ABOLITIONIST movement, constituted such a moral majority. That movement sought the legal prohibition of alcoholic beverages.

State and local prohibition statutes were accepted by the Supreme Court in MUGLER V. KANSAS (1887) as valid applications of the STATE POLICE POWER. That such laws deprived citizens of their liberty and property without DUE PROCESS OF LAW had been asserted, before the CIVIL WAR, only in the state court case of WYNEHAMER V. NEW YORK (1856).

In the early twentieth century the prohibition movement acquired a new ally in the Progressive movement, and, after nineteen states adopted prohibition laws, agitation shifted to the national level. In 1917 Congress enacted prohibition as a wartime austerity measure. The same year Congress proposed the EIGHTEENTH AMENDMENT, which, when ratified in 1919, raised prohibition to constitutional status. Repeal came fourteen years later with adoption of the TWENTY-FIRST AMENDMENT.

The failure of the "noble experiment" of national prohibition is frequently cited by opponents of other types of majoritarian legislation on moral issues, such as laws against SEGREGATION, handguns, ABORTION, and drugs.

DENNIS J. MAHONEY
(1986)

PROHIBITION, WRIT OF

To lawyers as well as others, the term PROHIBITION calls to mind a law forbidding the making, distribution, or possession of intoxicating liquors. In law, however, the term has an ancient COMMON LAW meaning that retains vitality today. The writ of prohibition is an order from a higher court commanding a lower court to stop hearing a matter outside the lower court's JURISDICTION. From the beginning prohibition has been considered an extraordinary writ, one that the higher court may or may not grant, in its discretion. It is not normally to be used as a substitute for an APPEAL or a petition for a WRIT OF CERTIORARI.

A statute dating from the JUDICIARY ACT OF 1789 is interpreted to empower the UNITED STATES COURTS OF APPEALS and the Supreme Court to issue writs of prohibition to lower federal courts. Under this law, the Supreme Court can also issue writs of prohibition to state courts.

KENNETH L. KARST
(1986)

PROHIBITION OF SLAVE TRADE ACT
2 Stat. 426 (1807)

Colonial legislatures had often tried to restrict the importation of slaves for economic reasons, and THOMAS JEFFERSON's famous deleted passage in the DECLARATION OF INDEPENDENCE denounced the royal disallowance of these bills. After Independence, all the states (except Georgia until 1798) prohibited the importation of slaves from abroad. The CONSTITUTIONAL CONVENTION OF 1787 permitted Congress to legislate against the international trade but at the insistence of the South Carolina delegates prohibited it from exercising that power for twenty years (Article I, section 9). After 1790, the Pennsylvania Abolition Society and the American Convention of Abolition Societies demanded interim legislation against the trade. Their lobbying produced the Act of March 22, 1794, prohibiting Americans from fitting out in American ports for the international trade. But South Carolina shocked the nation's conscience by reopening the trade in 1803.

President Jefferson urged Congress to ban the international trade at the earliest possible moment, and Congress responded with the Act of March 2, 1807, which prohibited the importation of slaves from foreign nations and dependencies, penalized persons engaging in the trade and purchasers from them, and provided for forfeiture of slaving vessels. The Act of May 15, 1820, declared slaving to be piracy, punishable by death. But enforcement of the ban was deliberately half-hearted, and the illegal trade brought in approximately a thousand blacks a year from Africa and the Caribbean. Though some southern spokesman in the late 1850s demanded a reopening of the trade, the CONFEDERATE CONSTITUTION also prohibited it.

WILLIAM M. WIECEK
(1986)

(SEE ALSO: *Slavery and the Constitution.*)

Bibliography

WIECEK, WILLIAM M. 1977 *The Sources of Antislavery Constitutionalism in America, 1760–1848.* Ithaca, N.Y.: Cornell University Press.

PROLIFE MOVEMENT

See: Abortion and the Constitution; Anti-Abortion Movement

PROPELLER GENESEE CHIEF v. FITZHUGH
12 Howard 443 (1851)

An act of Congress extended the ADMIRALTY AND MARITIME JURISDICTION of the United States Courts in matters of contract and tort arising upon the Great Lakes and connecting navigable rivers. In the case of *The Thomas Jefferson* (1825), the Court had confined federal admiralty and maritime jurisdiction to tide waters. Here, the Supreme Court, by a vote of 8–1, sustained the constitutionality of the act of Congress by ruling that JURISDICTION should not depend on the ebb and flow of the tide as in England but on the fact that the United States has "thousands of miles" of public navigable waters in which there is no tide. The TANEY COURT thus considerably expanded federal jurisdiction.

LEONARD W. LEVY
(1986)

PROPERTY

The Constitution explicitly protects the ownership of private property, not only by the Fifth and FOURTEENTH AMENDMENTS but also through the FOURTH AMENDMENT and SEVENTH AMENDMENT as well as by the CONTRACT CLAUSE and other provisions of Article I, section 10. The Supreme Court has always regarded property as a material possession having a cash value, but the founding generation possessed a far broader view. Even JOHN LOCKE in his second treatise on government believed that the ownership of property included a right to pursue happiness; he did not restrict his understanding of property to the possession of physical assets with a cash value. A writer in the *Boston Gazette* in 1768 voiced the prevailing American opinion when he said, "Liberty and Property are not only joined in common discourse, but are in their own natures so nearly ally'd that we cannot be said to possess the one without the other." The VIRGINIA DECLARATION OF RIGHTS OF 1776, framed by GEORGE MASON, guaranteed, in part, "the enjoyment of life and liberty, with the means of acquiring and possessing property," a provision accepted by THOMAS JEFFERSON and many of the Framers, who believed that liberty and property were indissolubly linked. Many states copied this language in their constitutions.

In 1789 in the first amendment that JAMES MADISON proposed for a national BILL OF RIGHTS, he appropriated Mason's language and the Lockean meaning of property. He regarded property as a basic human right essential to one's existence, to one's independence, and to one's dignity as a person. Without property, real and personal, one could not enjoy life or liberty, or be free and independent. Only the property holder could make independent decisions and choices because he was not beholden to anyone; he had no need to be subservient. Americans cared about property not just because they were materialistic but because they cared about political freedom and personal independence. They cherished the ownership of property as a prerequisite for the pursuit of happiness, and property opened up a world of intangible values—human dignity, self-regard, and personal fulfillment.

In 1792, Madison wrote an essay entitled "Property," in which he described its "larger and juster meaning." It "embraces," he declared, "every thing to which a man may attach a value and have a right." In a narrow sense it meant one's land, merchandise, or money, but in a broader sense, "a man has property in his opinions and the free communication of them," including his religious opinions, and he has "an equal property" in the full use of his faculties or "a property in his rights" as well as a right to his property. In 1795, however, the Supreme Court endorsed the narrower meaning of property as the ownership of physical assets having financial value, and the Court added that property once vested is inviolable. "The Constitution encircles and renders it an holy thing. . . . It is sacred," said Justice WILLIAM PATERSON, who had been a member of the CONSTITUTIONAL CONVENTION. His view of the matter prevailed, and the Court showed itself as marvelously imaginative in the invention of judicial DOCTRINES of property that served to promote and protect corporate interests.

LEONARD W. LEVY
(2000)

PROPERTY RIGHTS

In the discourse of American CONSTITUTIONALISM, the idea of PROPERTY has been both primal and protean.

First, there is the text. The DUE PROCESS OF LAW clauses of both the Fifth Amendment and FOURTEENTH AMENDMENT, rank property by name with life and liberty as a chief human interest to be secured against arbitrary and excessive interference from government. The Fifth Amendment's EMINENT DOMAIN, or "taking," clause even adds a special restriction against uncompensated TAKING OF PROPERTY for public benefit. Constitutional law perceives various high aims in these general protections for property. Courts dealing with claims of taking without compensation find in property an antiredistributive principle, opposed to imposition on a select few of the costs and burdens of government operations. When the claim is one of deprivation without PROCEDURAL DUE PROCESS, modern doctrine treats property as primarily a legalistic (or bureaucratic) principle, opposed to subversion of legally warranted expectations by faithless or irregular administration of standing law. Of course, expectations build on constancy in the law itself, as well as on reliable administration. The doctrine of SUBSTANTIVE DUE PROCESS arose, in part, out of concern for protecting legally VESTED RIGHTS against retrospective disturbance by changes in law. In a more dramatic form of substantive due process, property has figured as a libertarian principle of independence from state regulation: the right of an owner, as Justice JOHN PAUL STEVENS recently wrote in MOORE V. CITY OF EAST CLEVELAND (1977), "to use her own property as she sees fit."

Second, proprietary norms and notions have inspired and organized constitutional-legal doctrine apparently far removed from the immediate scope of the property-specific clauses. Both the THIRD AMENDMENT and FOURTH AMENDMENT obviously tap special values of domestic sanctuary—refuge and privacy—from one prototypical image of property, the home or house. In GRISWOLD V. CONNECTICUT (1965) the Supreme Court marshaled these provisions with others in the BILL OF RIGHTS to construct a constitutional RIGHT OF PRIVACY in the conduct of marital intimacies at home. By the time of ROE V. WADE (1973), the Court had reconceived this as a right to choose for oneself "whether to bear or beget a child." In BUCKLEY V. VALEO (1976) the Court treated deployments of private wealth in electoral politics as exercises of the FREEDOM OF SPEECH and the FREEDOM OF ASSEMBLY AND ASSOCIATION protected by the FIRST AMENDMENT. In PERRY EDUCATION ASSOCATION V. PERRY LOCAL EDUCATORS ASSOCIATION (1983), the Court confirmed an old idea that a government acting as a proprietor (rather than as a lawmaker) is unusually free to restrict freedom of speech. In a series of cases including *Reeves, Inc. v. Stake* (1980), the Court similarly relieved states acting as owners from normal duties under the COMMERCE CLAUSE to refrain from commercial discrimination against out-of-state competitors. In contrast, courts adjudicating under the rubric of substantive due process currently treat ECONOMIC LIBERTIES (aspects of self-direction concerned with acquisition, exchanges, and deployment of property) as categorically less resistant to state regulation than more "fundamental" or "personal" aspects, such as control over family formations.

Third, on a broadly ideological level, legal depictions of property have figured strongly in imaginative conceptions of the American constitutional system. Property held a glorified place in the common lawyer's Whig history imbibed by early Americans from WILLIAM BLACKSTONE. With its naturalistic imagery of clearly demarcated "closes," property offered a paradigm of legally sanctioned authority that was supreme within its limits yet firmly delimited by law. Such an image of legal property apparently helped later generations of Americans to represent and confirm to themselves the workings of check-and-balance institutional schemes—FEDERALISM and SEPARATION OF POWERS—that depend on jurisdictional boundaries judicially patrolled. More fundamentally, the image has from the beginning helped inspire and sustain a core idea of constitutionalism: a legally LIMITED GOVERNMENT based on a secure bounding of the state's domain from those of the market and private life.

Finally, at the level of practical debate over institutions, the question of property's relation to POLITICS has always been foundational for American constitutionalism. In the strongly influential NATURAL RIGHTS philosophy traced to JOHN LOCKE, the relation is oppositional. Property—here meaning acquisition of goods by effort and exchange and retention against force and fraud—is considered a native attribute of humankind, not an artificial contingency of state power and political choice. Accordingly, the state's business is to secure natural property against breakdowns of mutual forbearance that only a supreme civil authority can prevent. For Lockeans, then, the relation of property to politics is that of an a priori external limit and a test of legitimacy.

Yet in an older tradition of civic REPUBLICANISM, to which the Founders were also heir, questions of property entitlement and distribution are inseparable from constitutional design and political ministration. By the traditional republican understanding, property, or wealth, is power in politics. Undue concentration of wealth portends either oligarchy or revolution, and warding off those contingencies is very much the business of republican government. Morevoer, in civic republican thought, "corruption" of political motives by preoccupation with private need or advantage (as opposed to public honor and common good) is a chief internal threat to the stability and success of popular governments. Elements of this traditional view, modernized and coupled with Lockean liberal ideas, plainly appear throughout THE FEDERALIST (saliently in JAMES MADISON's famous essay on "faction") and in THOMAS JEFFERSON's political writings. They appear in the Constitution, as well, and in early American constitutional practice. By such devices as indirect election and large constituencies, the Framers avowedly designed the Constitution to ensure that only men of means and repute would attain national legislative or executive office.

Moreover, it was normal in the early United States for states, which under the Constitution set electoral qualifications even for congressional and presidential elections, to restrict VOTING RIGHTS to persons of independent social status (free adult males) who also held a substantial property endowment or income of a kind not too dependent on governmental machination. In the more egalitarian democratic ethos tracing to the Jacksonian period, RECONSTRUCTION, and the CIVIL WAR amendments, WEALTH DISCRIMINATION in the field of voting rights has become constitutionally intolerable. Rather, debate has inevitably arisen over the converse claim that a democratic-republican constitution requires assurance to all, at public expense if necessary, of the material prerequisites of political independence and competence.

In summary, the American constitutional rhetoric of property and property rights is a congested manifold of cross-cutting and contested doctrinal and normative evocations. As might be expected of such an overloaded vocabulary, ambiguity and conflict affect not just normative emanations and doctrinal derivations, but the direct reference of the central terms themselves. In constitutional disputation, "property" and "property right" variously signify holdings, entitlements, and institutions. At one moment, "property" (or "property right") may refer to specific holdings of social wealth that various persons currently claim or practically enjoy; at another, to a set of legal or moral rules and principles supposed to define and condition entitlements to possession and enjoyment of parcels of social wealth; and at still another, to institutional regimes of privatization (the "free market").

This variability of reference would little surprise the generations of Anglo-American theorists—the line runs from David Hume and Jeremy Bentham to Wesley N. Hohfeld, MORRIS R. COHEN, Felix S. Cohen, Robert L. Hale, and beyond—who have attempted conceptual analysis and critiques of legal "property." Vagaries in constitutional-legal usage of "property" echo the academic discussions, which have themselves obviously been sensitive to partisan political and constitutional debates. In some respects, however, constitutional-legal usage strays from established jurisprudential positions.

It is common ground, at least, that legal "property" is a relation, not a substance. Property does not consist in parcels of wealth or "stuff." Academic sophisticates have long agreed that it also does not consist in any relation between a person and "his" stuff; neither possessory acts, proprietary intentions, nor both together constitute property. Rather, property is a matter of relations among persons: the social relations and practices that accord to bare, empirical, person-to-parcel connections a measure of public recognition, normative legitimacy, and practical reliability. But that is not all property is, either. Also indispensable to property, say the theorists, is the element of entitlement or legal sanction: there is no true "property" in a casual neighborhood practice of allowing me to farm a field and reap the fruit when we all also know that others

may stop me at any time without running afoul any law. The question then becomes whether the law that constitutes property entitlements consists strictly of the "positive" human inventions of legislatures and of courts filling gaps in the common law or, rather, is found in some method of reason or traditional understanding that composes a prelegislative "higher" or "Natural" Law. On this question, JURISPRUDENCE remains deeply divided.

It is easy to find constitutional-legal doctrine officially accepting each step of the jurisprudential consensus so far as it goes. Yet constitutional law seems also often driven to resist the abstract logic of the consensus. According to the theorists, a legal regime that secures the exclusive possession of landowners against unauthorized entry certainly constitutes a property entitlement, but so, by the same reasoning, does a legal regime that permits (and protects against interference) a particular mode of using a parcel—for example, an owner's strip mining of land. Constitutional law, by contrast, differentiates sharply between legal restrictions on use that leave possession undisturbed and laws subjecting owners to "permanent physical occupations" of land. As the Supreme Court recently confirmed in *Keystone Bituminous Coal Association v. DeBenedictis* (1987) and *Nollan v. California Coastal Commission* (1987), new use restrictions, however severe, rarely amount to constitutionally challengeable takings or deprivations of property, but state-sponsored dispossession, however trivial, almost always does. Or consider a law plainly stating that a sheriff may seize goods from a person who bought them on credit whenever the creditor tells the sheriff that the loan is in default. In the sophisticated view, such a law simply defines the extent of the installment buyer's property right and so cannot itself be a constitutionally questionable deprivation of property. Constitutional law on procedural due process officially adopted that view in BOARD OF REGENTS V. ROTH (1972), a case of peremptory unexplained dismissal from a government job expressly held at the supervisor's discretion. Yet at about the same time, in *Fuentes v. Shevin* (1972), the Court found an unconstitutional deprivation of property without procedural due process in the law authorizing unceremonious seizure of goods from an installment buyer's possession. Unlike academic jurisprudence, constitutional law has to mediate practically among demands for proprietary security, sound policy, and popular acceptance, along with the demand for consistent theory. Operating within this field of forces, courts evidently find that governmentally engineered trespasses on extant private possessions are uniquely and unacceptably insulting to property's ideological function as a paradigm of limited government, that is, as private domains secured against governmental intrusion.

A like irresolution appears in constitutional law's response to the theorists' requirement of legal entitlement as essential to property. The Court both expressly avows this requirement and rejects its full implications. Faced in *United States v. Willow River Power Co.* (1945) with a hydroelectric company's claim that the government took its property by damming a river and thereby flooding the tail end of its generating plant, Justice ROBERT H. JACKSON memorably declared that judicial delineation of property rights turns not on any intelligible essence of "property," but on discovery and construal of prior and contemporaneous law: "We cannot start the process of decision by calling [every existing economic interest or advantage] a 'property right' ... Such economic uses are property rights only when they are legally protected interests." In short, discoverable legal entitlement is required to qualify an "economic interest" as the "property" mentioned by the Fifth and Fourteenth Amendments. The Court has further perceived that those constitutional mentionings cannot themselves be read (without apparent circularity) to confer the legal status of property on any disputed "interest or advantage." Rather, according to *Regents v. Roth*, the entitlement must be grounded in "an independent source such as state law." The Court has even hitched such a "positivist" approach to the theory of federalism, declaring in PRUNEYARD SHOPPING CENTER V. ROBINS (1980) that "the United States, as opposed to the several states [is not] possessed of ... authority ... to define 'property' in the first instance."

Repeatedly, however, the Court has defied this logic and found that the Constitution's property clauses directly demand protection for interests plainly not treated as property by standing subconstitutional law. DRED SCOTT V. SANDFORD (1857) is the earliest instance. The MISSOURI COMPROMISE of 1820 established the northern portion of the Louisiana Territory as "free soil." According to the law of many jurisdictions, a slave taken by a master onto free soil was thereby emancipated. Given that as the standing legal rule, a master's legally grounded entitlement in a slave simply would not extend to retention of title after the master had taken the slave into free territory. At a time when this plainly appeared to be the applicable, governing rule, Scott's "owner" took him from Missouri to north Louisiana Territory. The Supreme Court held that to grant Scott his freedom on that basis would be to deprive Sandford of constitutionally protected property without due process of law.

Although a deservedly infamous decision, *Dred Scott* is not aberrational in its refusal to allow subconstitutional congressional and state lawmaking to dictate the limits of constitutionally protected property. In *Pennsylvania Coal Company v. Mahon* (1922) the Court granted *arguendo* the public safety justifications for a law forbidding coalmine owners to remove coal in such a way as to cause the collapse of surface structures, but still found that the law unconstitutionally took the property of mining firms on which it had confiscatory retrospective impact. Justice OLIVER WENDELL HOLMES, JR. wrote that, despite the long-established rule subordinating all property to public-safety regulation, "if regulation goes too far it will be recognized as a taking." The rule's "implied limitation" of property rights "must have its limits, or the contract and due process clauses are gone." In *Kaiser Aetna v. United States* (1979) the Court dealt similarly with the standing rule subordinating all shoreline property holdings to public rights of access to navigable waters. It refused to apply the rule strictly when doing so would have subjected the complaining owners not only to unwelcome "physical invasions," but to loss of their "distinct investment backed expectations" of privacy. Most recently, the Court's opinion in *Nollan v. California Coastal Commission* (1987) strongly implied that a state legal regime expressly subjecting all shoreline land titles to public rights of pedestrian passage would violate a baseline normative standard for property institutions contained in the Fourteenth Amendment.

The Court has thus refused to read the Constitution's property clauses as completely delegating to legislative politics the definition of legal regimes of property rights. It has refused to reduce the judiciary to the ancillary role of protecting persons against retroactive alteration and capricious administration of these subconstitutional legislative regimes. It has done so when the alternative struck it as betrayal of substantive constitutional values linked to property, notably, private sanctuary and limited government. Such cases lie along that contested boundary of JUDICIAL ACTIVISM AND JUDICIAL RESTRAINT where the demand for constitutional vindication confronts the demand for contemporary democratic accountability.

In such cases, the Court is not, however, necessarily rejecting jurisprudential insistence on legal entitlement as a prerequisite to property. It may rather be denying that property-constitutive law can be found only in the "positive" lawmaking acts of legislatures and common-law adjudicators. Not surprisingly (considering the conflicting normative pressures for both a rule of law and government of the people by the people), this choice between an exclusively "positive" and a "natural" provenance for property-constitutive law is just where the jurisprudential consensus on legal property falls apart. We can see the Court in these cases as allying the Framers with those theorists who appeal to "natural" criteria of reason or tradition for a higher-law conception of property entitlement. The Court, in effect, conceives the Framers to have been referring to such criteria when they prescribed constitutional protection for "property."

Thereby, the Court also, and to a like extent, apparently aligns itself (or the Framers) with the Lockean liberal (as opposed to civic republican) antecedents of American constitutionalism. Rather than treat the design and adjustment of property regimes as a central legitimate concern of republican government, the Court to this extent treats property rights as prior and external to state and politics. But the civic heritage may not yet be entirely expunged from American constitutional doctrine or disputation. This heritage may help explain the Court's unshakable tolerance for legislative schemes of property-use regulation that plainly and grossly exceed the bounds of any plausibly Lockean notion of POLICE POWER. More pointedly, it may help explain the settled acceptance of statutory income transfer schemes that appear to "take property from A and give it to B" in defiance of an oft-cited first principle of Lockean higher law. Commentators have argued vigorously, and vainly, that such schemes are both constitutionally obligatory and constitutionally forbidden. The modern Court's refusal of commitment to either view may be its mediation between the civic and the libertarian underpinnings of American constitutionalism.

FRANK I. MICHELMAN
(1992)

(SEE ALSO: *Economic Due Process; Economic Equal Protection; Economy; Property Rights and the Human Body.*)

Bibliography

ACKERMAN, BRUCE A. 1975 *Private Property and the Constitution.* Cambridge, Mass.: Harvard University Press.

COHEN, FELIX S. 1954 Dialogue on Private Property. *Rutgers Law Review* 9:357–387.

EPSTEIN, DAVID F. 1984 *The Political Theory of the Federalist.* Chicago: University of Chicago Press.

EPSTEIN, RICHARD 1985 *Takings: Private Property and the Law of Eminent Domain.* Cambridge, Mass.: Harvard University Press.

KENNEDY, DUNCAN 1980 Toward a Historical Understanding of Classical Legal Consciousness: The Case of Classical Legal Thought in America, 1850–1940. *Research in Law & Society* 3:3–24.

MICHELMAN, FRANK I. 1987 Possession vs. Distribution in the Constitutional Idea of Property. *Iowa Law Review* 72:1319–1350.

NEDELSKY, JENNIFER 1989 *Private Property and the Limits of American Constitutionalism: A View from the Formation.* Chicago: University of Chicago Press.

SINGER, JOSEPH WILLIAM 1982 The Legal Rights Debate in Analytical Jurisprudence from Bentham to Hohfeld. *Wisconsin Law Review* 1982:975–1059.

SYMPOSIUM 1988 The Jurisprudence of Takings. *Columbia Law Review* 88:1581–1794.

TREANOR, WILLIAM 1985 The Origins and Original Significance of the Just Compensation Clause of the Fifth Amendment. *Yale Law Journal* 94:694–716.

PROPERTY RIGHTS
(Update)

The REHNQUIST COURT has shown an interest in property rights not seen since the 1930s, and has mounted a number of rhetorical challenges to the sixty-year-long tradition of affording economic liberties less protection than "personal" rights, most notably the statement of Chief Justice WILLIAM H. REHNQUIST in DOLAN V. CITY OF TIGARD (1994) that "the Takings Clause of the Fifth Amendment is as much a part of the Bill of Rights as the First Amendment of Fourth Amendment, [and] should [not] be relegated to the status of a poor relation." Yet the Supreme Court has fallen short of renewing the constitutional protections enjoyed by PROPERTY in the heyday of ECONOMIC DUE PROCESS, and some of its recent expansions highlight unorthodox connections between property and defendants' rights.

The Court's most prominent demonstration of its renewed interest in property has been its increased willingness to hear cases concerning alleged violations of the EMINENT DOMAIN, or TAKING OF PROPERTY clause, and to hold that government action not involving direct physical appropriation triggers the obligation to pay JUST COMPENSATION under that clause. In LUCAS V. SOUTH CAROLINA COASTAL COUNCIL (1992), for example, the Court held that a land use restriction that left property without "economically beneficial use" was a per se taking, regardless of how weighty a PUBLIC PURPOSE it served. Perhaps more than any other single recent case, *Lucas* has led property owners to pursue REGULATORY TAKINGS claims, often trying to convince courts to treat separately a particular part of their property or a particular strand in their bundle of property rights to determine that the part was deprived of all economically beneficial use. In two other widely publicized cases, *Nollan v. California Coastal Commission* (1987) and *Dolan,* the Court decided that a government could condition a land use permit on donation of an interest in land to the public only if the donation mitigated some impact of the permitted use, and only if the donation were "roughly proportional" to that impact.

The DUE PROCESS OF LAW clauses of both the Fifth Amendment and the FOURTEENTH AMENDMENT have also continued to be a textual basis for Rehnquist Court decisions protective of property rights. In *BMW of North America v. Gore* (1996), the Court held that "grossly excessive" awards of PUNITIVE DAMAGES violated the doctrine of SUBSTANTIVE DUE PROCESS. In *Eastern Enterprises v. Apfel* (1998), the decisive CONCURRING OPINION of Justice ANTHONY M. KENNEDY also relied on substantive due process in striking down a statute that required companies to contribute to a health benefits fund because they had employed beneficiaries as coal miners over thirty years before the statute's passage. Some of the Court's most ardent defenders of property rights, however, did not join in these invocations of due process, no doubt in part due to antipathy toward the doctrine's use to support a right to ABORTION in ROE V. WADE (1973), and, with regard to *BMW of North America*, in part due to the view that limiting punitive damages protects "defendants rights" rather than "property rights," while curtailing the states' traditional power to punish reprehensible behavior.

The view that forfeiture cases concern "defendants' rights" rather than "property rights" may help to explain the voting lineups in a number of other closely decided recent cases that nonetheless define and protect property rights. In *United States v. James Daniel Good Real Property* (1993), for example, a bare majority of the Court held that the seizure of real property subject to CIVIL FORFEITURE without prior notice and opportunity to be heard was a violation of PROCEDURAL DUE PROCESS. In *Bennis v. Michigan* (1996), a bare majority rejected the claim that forfeiture of a woman's interest in a car in which her husband had, unbeknownst to her, engaged in illegal sexual activity with a prostitute violated the due process of law and takings clauses. And in *United States v. Bajakajian* (1998), a bare majority held for the first time that a punitive forfeiture grossly disproportional to the defendant's offense violated the excessive fines clause. The four Justices most sympathetic to takings clause claims—William H. Rehnquist, SANDRA DAY O'CONNOR, ANTONIN SCALIA, and CLARENCE THOMAS— rejected the constitutional claims in the first two of these cases, and only Thomas, in a pivotal vote that may begin to define him as the Court's most consistent libertarian, recognized the constitutional claim in *Bajakajian*.

On the issue whether the "property" protected by the federal Constitution is defined by positive subconstitutional law or by some independent method of reasoning or traditional understanding, the Court's position remains ambivalent—an ambivalence that can be found within the writings of individual Justices. Scalia, for example, seemed to draw on a nonpositivist definition when he wrote in *Nollan* that "the right to build on one's own property— even though its exercise can be subject to legitimate permitting requirements—cannot remotely be described as a 'governmental benefit.'" Yet he appealed explicitly to a positivist definition in *Lucas* where he wrote that "the Takings Clause does not require compensation when an owner is barred from putting land to a use that is proscribed by 'existing rules or understandings'" about property.

Ultimately, the Court is unlikely to strike down, on a nonpositivist theory of the substantive protection of property, a legal rule of long standing in a particular jurisdiction. That unlikeliness may be seen as a result either of an inability to construct a sufficiently strong nonpositivist theory, or of a faith that long-standing Anglo-American legal rules in fact substantially embody the correct theory. This latter resolution may be suggested by Scalia's comment in *Lucas* that state COMMON LAW principles "rarely support prohibition of the 'essential use' of land"—as presumably they should not under the correct nonpositivist theory.

When the constitutional challenge is to a recent change in law, the positivist approach reveals itself as incomplete. For if the Court is unlikely to strike down rules of long standing, it is equally unlikely to strike down all recent changes in law. Yet the positivist approach, while reframing the question of property protection in terms of legal change, does not identify which changes concern "property" in the constitutional sense, nor which of that set of property-related changes are constitutional or unconstitutional. The issue of defining which changes in law concerned "property" within the meaning of the takings and due process clauses recently split the Court in *Eastern Enterprises v. Apfel* (1998). Five members of the Court concluded that the "property" protected by the takings clause is restricted to specific, identified property interests, and does not extend to general liabilities to pay money. Those same five, however, concluded that the creation of a general liability could deprive a person of property without due process within the meaning of the due process clause (an issue pointedly avoided by the four Justices who relied on the takings clause). They then split on the issue whether the challenged law actually did violate substantive due process, reflecting continuing disagreement over the process of winnowing constitutional from unconstitutional changes in law. This disagreement surely will persist as the Court faces the next wave of constitutional property litigation over so-called deregulatory takings.

ROBERT BRAUNEIS
(2000)

Bibliography

BRAUNEIS, ROBERT 1996 "The Foundation of Our 'Regulatory Takings' Jurisprudence": The Myth and Meaning of Justice Holmes's Opinion in *Pennsylvania Coal v. Mahon. Yale Law Journal* 106:613–702.

ELY, JAMES W., JR. 1992 *The Guardian of Every Other Right: A Constitutional History of Property Rights.* Oxford, England: Oxford University Press.

FISCHEL, WILLIAM A. 1995 *Regulatory Takings: Law, Economics, and Politics.* Cambridge, Mass.: Harvard University Press.

LEVY, LEONARD W. 1996 *A License to Steal: The Forfeiture of Property.* Chapel Hill: University of North Carolina Press.

PAUL, ELLEN FRANKEL and DICKMAN, HOWARD, eds. 1990 *Liberty, Property and the Future of Constitutional Development.* Albany: State University of New York Press.

RADIN, MARGARET JANE 1993 *Reinterpreting Property.* Chicago: University of Chicago Press.

ROSE, CAROL 1994 *Property and Persuasion: Essays on the History, Theory, and Rhetoric of Ownership.* Boulder, Colo.: Westview Press.

SIDAK, J. GREGORY and SPULBER, DANIEL F. 1997 *Deregulatory Takings: The Competitive Transformation of Network Industries in the United States.* Cambridge, England: Cambridge University Press.

PROPERTY RIGHTS AND THE HUMAN BODY

PROPERTY has been described as a "bundle of rights" consisting of the right to possess, to use, to exclude, to enjoy profits, and to dispose. When it comes to property in the human body, one sees various collections of some component rights in this bundle, though never the whole bundle. Moreover, the precise contours of these component rights are often unclear, and depend on the perspective from which one approaches the body.

The perspectives available are two: from inside the body and from outside the body. That is, one can ask: what property rights do I have in my own body, or what property rights do I have in the body of another? With respect to one's own body, the COMMON LAW, which has been the primary source of property rights, has provided a set of protections that have the effect of granting certain property rights in one's own body, though the law never speaks of these rights as property. Tort law protects us from nonconsensual physical contact and physical invasions. If A punches B in the nose, A is liable for battery. A doctor who fails to get the informed consent of a patient before performing surgery commits a battery. This doctrine implies that the law gives us the right to possess our own bodies and to exclude others from using our bodies. Tort law also prohibits others from unreasonably confining us, through the tort of false imprisonment; giving us the right to direct our own bodies as we see fit. However, the common law has not articulated a clear general position on our rights to profit from our bodies or to dispose of our bodies.

With respect to the bodies of others, our property rights are considerably narrower. The common law gives to the next of kin a "quasi-property" right in the body of the decedent, which consists of the right to possess the body for purposes of burial, to recover damages for the mutilation of the body, and the right to prescribe the manner and place of burial—but not the right to sell the whole or parts of the decedent's body. This is the extent of our common law property rights in the bodies of others, at least as far as these rights have been articulated by American courts. From an early time, English courts apparently have gone further in limiting these rights; WILLIAM BLACKSTONE, in his *Commentaries on the Laws of England,* asserts that English common law gave no legal validity whatsoever to the master–slave relationship, and thus refused to recognize the claim of an absolute property right in the body of another.

Somewhere between the question of rights in one's own body and that of rights in another falls the issue of ABORTION. The early common law applied the "quickening" rule, which held the killing of an unborn infant unlawful from the moment it is able to stir in its mother's womb.

The Constitution has played a role in defining the limitations on property rights in the body. Most importantly, the THIRTEENTH AMENDMENT prohibits SLAVERY and involuntary servitude, and thus nullifies an individual's claim to have an absolute property right in the body of another or to have given such a right in his own body. The Supreme Court's ROE V. WADE (1973) decision held that state laws prohibiting abortion may violate the DUE PROCESS clause of the FOURTEENTH AMENDMENT, and articulated a rule governing the constitutionality of abortion restrictions that is analogous to the common law quickening rule in that it gives states the greatest freedom to regulate abortion in the final trimester of pregnancy. In *Washington v. Glucksberg* (1997), the Court held that the Fourteenth Amendment does not imply a protected RIGHT TO DIE with the assistance of a physician.

Today, new constitutional issues are being generated by statutes that limit the scope of property rights in the body, usually with the aim of facilitating the procurement and transplantation of human organs. Several states have enacted laws permitting coroners to remove body parts (typically corneas) from a cadaver without the consent of either the deceased or the next of kin. Pursuant to these statutes, several coroners have removed body parts without seeking consent. These removal statutes, and concomitant policies, are inconsistent with common-law quasi-property rights. Several courts have held that these policies violate the due process clause of the Fourteenth Amendment, and Erik Jaffe has suggested that the Fifth Amendment's TAKINGS clause should also apply.

Other statutes limiting property rights in the body are those prohibiting the purchase or sale of organs. The National Organ Transplant Act, a federal law, prohibits the purchase and sale of organs for transplantation. Several states have enacted similar statutes, some of them banning purchase and sale for any purpose. Although these laws were enacted on the basis of noble motives (perhaps reflecting the quality-deterioration concerns initially raised, in the context of the blood market, by Richard Titmuss), their ultimate impact is probably harmful. As transplant technology proceeds apace, and the number of suitable organ recipients increases accordingly, the shortage of human organs available for transplantation worsens every year. Allowing certain limited purchase and sale agreements, such as the postmortem transfers proposed by Lloyd Cohen, could alleviate the shortage of transplantable organs without generating the negative consequences envisioned by proponents of the sale bans.

Can or should the Constitution play a role in resolving this growing problem? If the courts were to take a broad view of our property rights in our own bodies, they might hold that statutes banning all contracts for the purchase and sale of body parts constitute takings of private property, just as a statute prohibiting individuals from selling their homes would be a taking. Or a court might find that a sweeping ban cannot survive RATIONAL BASIS review under the due process clause. The question has been unimportant until very recently, because our body parts had little value to others before the advent of transplantation. But we are approaching the day when nearly every one of our organs will have a substantial market value. As this value increases, the deprivations imposed by the sale bans may reach a level comparable to those that have been deemed unconstitutional in earlier cases.

KEITH N. HYLTON
(2000)

Bibliography

COHEN, LLOYD R. 1990 Increasing the Supply of Transplantable Organs: The Virtues of a Futures Market. *George Washington Law Review* 58:1–51.

HYLTON, KEITH N. 1990 The Law and Economics of Organ Procurement. *Law & Policy* 12:197–224.

——— 1996 The Law and Ethics of Organ Sales. *Annual Review of Law and Ethics* 4:115–136.

JAFFE, ERIK S. 1990 "She's Got Bette Davis['s] Eyes": Assessing the Nonconsensual Removal of Cadaver Organs under the Takings and Due Process Clauses. *Columbia Law Review* 90:528–574.

MUNZER, STEPHEN R. 1994 An Uneasy Case Against Property Rights in Body Parts. Pages 259–286 in Ellen Frankel Paul, Fred D. Miller Jr., and Jeffrey Paul, eds., *Property Rights*. Cambridge, England: Cambridge University Press.

SCOTT, RUSSELL 1981 *The Body as Property*. New York: Viking Press.

TITMUSS, RICHARD 1971 *The Gift Relationship: From Human Blood to Social Policy*. New York: Pantheon Books.

PROSECUTORIAL DISCRETION AND ITS CONSTITUTIONAL LIMITS

In 1992, several black men charged with federal crack-cocaine offenses alleged in defense that they were selected for prosecution because of their race. They offered affidavits stating that, of twenty-four cases closed by a federal public defender's office in 1991, all of those charged with similar crack offenses had been black; that there are an equal number of white and nonminority crack users and dealers; and that whites are more likely to be prosecuted in more lenient state courts. The Supreme Court, in *United States v. Armstrong* (1996), held that these defendants were not entitled to access to the government's records to perfect their challenge to the prosecutor's discretion because they had not made a sufficient threshold showing that the prosecution acted on the basis of race.

The Court's decision in *Armstrong* illustrates the judiciary's general deference to the prosecutor's discretion. The prosecutor may choose which crimes and which persons to prosecute. She is entitled to prosecute whenever she has PROBABLE CAUSE to believe a certain person committed a certain crime. She need not be certain that she can prove guilt beyond a reasonable doubt. In the twentieth century, there have always been many more legitimately prosecutable people than resources allow for prosecution, in addition to laws that the public has not wanted prosecutors to rigorously enforce.

In the United States, the exercise of these kinds of discretion is part of EXECUTIVE POWER, rather than LEGISLATIVE POWER or JUDICIAL POWER. Article II of the Constitution mandates the executive branch and its agents to "take Care that the Laws be faithfully executed. . . ." Prosecutorial discretion encompasses all aspects of a case; the prosecutor may decide whether to investigate, grant immunity, or allow a plea. Since the Constitution leaves these decisions in the hands of the executive, the policy of SEPARATION OF POWERS weighs against too much judicial oversight of the prosecutor's discretion.

It would be difficult for judges to correct prosecutors even if there were no doctrine of separation of powers. To know whether a prosecutor has appropriately levied a charge, a judge would have to know about the prosecutor's entire docket of similar kinds of cases. This would consume more time than most courts have. Besides, there is no good reason to believe a judge would be more competent than the prosecutor to decide whether the seriousness of the crime and the weight of the evidence justifies going forward with the case. If the judge errs, she will not be subject to the judgment of the voters. If the judiciary must pause to consider the wisdom of a prosecution, even valued prosecutions that should go forth will be delayed. Under the Anglo-American system, the judge can only control the prosecutor by dismissing a case but cannot require her to go forward. Finally, a prosecutor whose discretion will be second-guessed may refuse to exercise discretion at all by routinely filing charges on everything she sees and letting the judges go to the effort of sorting it out. For these reasons courts leave the prosecutorial decision in the hands of the prosecutors and presume that discretion has been properly exercised.

Despite this broad rule, the Constitution does not confer unfettered discretion. Under the EQUAL PROTECTION clause, courts may review a prosecutor's decision for unconstitutional motive such as race or religion. To succeed in a defense of selective prosecution, the accused must prove that prosecutorial policy had both a discriminatory effect and purpose. The Court first recognized this defense in YICK WO V. HOPKINS (1886), where a Chinese laundryman in San Francisco had been prosecuted for violating a city laundry ordinance because of his race. The Court held that "though the law be fair on its face and impartial in appearance" when "applied with an evil eye and an unequal hand" it violated the defendant's constitutional right to equal protection.

Historically, the defense of selective prosecution has rarely succeeded. To prove it is expensive. The accused must examine walls of court files to show a pattern of RACIAL DISCRIMINATION. One way to transfer some (but not all) of these costs would be to require the prosecutor to gather her own files of all the relevant cases and turn them over to the defendant for examination. In *Armstrong*, the Court held that before the defendants could look at the government's files, they must provide "clear evidence" that the government failed to prosecute other similarly situated white defendants.

Critics of *Armstrong* argue that it renders selective prosecution largely impotent as a defense; they argue that *Armstrong*'s increased hostility toward statistical evidence and the defense's increased evidentiary burden immunize prosecutors from constitutional scrutiny. Although this criticism may be true, it does not mean that *Armstrong* is improvident. The judiciary accepts as a maxim that one should not prosecute red-haired people because they are red-haired. Yet, absent a rigorous standard of proof, selective prosecution is easy for a defendant to assert and hard for a prosecutor to disprove. Even a good faith but wrongful assertion imposes costs on the government and the defendant and delays decision on the truth of the charge. Moreover, the accused says only that the prosecutor was wrong because she chose to prosecute based on an unconstitutional motive like race or creed. To claim selective prosecution is not to claim innocence: the red-haired thief hasn't claimed he didn't steal, and the Zoroastrian murderer hasn't claimed that he didn't murder.

There are two more subtle yet important reasons why *Armstrong*'s heightened burden in proving selective prosection may make sense. First, when a court rules on a selective prosecution claim it must judge the validity of the prosecutor's defense: Had the defendants in *Arm-strong* proffered clear evidence that white individuals were not similarly prosecuted, the Court would have had to evaluate whether Jamaican, Haitian, and black street gangs really did predominate crack distribution as the U.S. Attorney's office claimed. Today's judiciary is generally reluctant to involve itself in these complex and politically charged judgments and leaves it to the legislative branch to deal with them. Second, successful use of a selective prosecution defense was extremely rare even before *Armstrong* raised the bar. Most judges do not see a prosecutor's abuse of her discretion as a real problem, and little evidence supports a contrary conclusion. After all, in *Armstrong* it was Congress, not prosecutors, that imposed stiff mandatory sentencing guidelines on crack-cocaine dealers creating the disparity between powdered cocaine and crack-cocaine offenses.

JAMES B. ZAGEL
(2000)

Bibliography

HELLER, ROBERT 1998 Selective Prosecution and Federalization of Criminal Law: The Need for Meaningful Judicial Review of Prosecutorial Discretion. *University of Pennsylvania Law Review* 145:1309–1358.

JAMPOL, MELISSA L. 1997 Goodbye to the Defense of Selective Prosecution. *Journal of Criminal Law and Criminology* 87: 932–966.

LOVE, MARCI A. 1997 *United States v. Armstrong:* The Supreme Court Formulates a Discovery Standard for Selective Prosecution. *Temple Political Civil Rights Law Review* 7:191–219.

PROVIDENCE BANK v. BILLINGS
4 Peters 514 (1830)

This case anticipated the DOCTRINE of the CHARLES RIVER BRIDGE CO. V. WARREN BRIDGE CO. (1837) case and limited the doctrine of tax immunity established by NEW JERSEY V. WILSON (1812). The Court here, through Chief Justice JOHN MARSHALL, established the principle that a corporate charter should not be construed to vest more rights than are found in its express provisions. A state taxed a bank for the first time long after chartering it. The bank contended that its charter implied a tax immunity, because a state power to tax the bank could destroy it, contrary to its charter. The Court sustained the tax against the CONTRACT CLAUSE argument, reasoning that the state had made no express contract to relinquish its power to tax and that the relinquishment of that power "is never to be assumed." Chartered privileges "must be expressed . . . or they do not exist."

LEONARD W. LEVY
(1986)

PRUDENTIAL INSURANCE COMPANY v. BENJAMIN
328 U.S. 408 (1946)

The dissenters in UNITED STATES V. SOUTH-EASTERN UNDERWRITERS (1944) feared that declaring insurance to be INTERSTATE COMMERCE, subject to congressional regulation, would create chaos by rendering state regulation of that industry void. An act of Congress, however, left most such regulation standing and Justice WILEY RUTLEDGE headed a unanimous Court sustaining a state tax that discriminated against interstate commerce. Assuming that such a tax would be invalid in the absence of congressional action, here Congress had decided that uniformity of regulation and taxation was necessary and had authorized even discriminatory state regulation and taxation of the insurance business.

DAVID GORDON
(1986)

(SEE ALSO: *State Regulation of Commerce.*)

PRUNEYARD SHOPPING CENTER v. ROBBINS
447 U.S. 74 (1980)

HUDGENS V. NLRB (1976) had held that the FIRST AMENDMENT did not compel private owners of SHOPPING CENTERS to permit their property to be used for expressive activity. In *PruneYard*, California's supreme court held that the state constitution required a shopping center owner to permit the collection of signatures on a petition. The Supreme Court unanimously affirmed. Justice WILLIAM H. REHNQUIST, for the Court, concluded that the state law did not work an uncompensated TAKING OF PROPERTY. Nor did it violate the owner's First Amendment rights by compelling it to convey a message. Justice LEWIS F. POWELL, concurring, argued that under other circumstances an owner might have such a First Amendment right.

KENNETH L. KARST
(1986)

PSYCHIATRY AND CONSTITUTIONAL LAW

New impositions of legal control in the last generation have transformed traditional relationships between providers and consumers of mental health services, cabining the power physicians historically exercised over the insane. Paradoxically, the new legal limits on psychiatrists developed in a period when novel psychotropic medication—veritable wonder drugs—at last provided bases for medical paternalistic authority. Psychiatrists complained that patients would miss out on needed treatment and "rot with their rights on."

The legal developments involve processes for civilly protecting or subduing the mentally impaired, processing them through the CRIMINAL JUSTICE SYSTEM, recognizing their rights as psychiatric inpatients, and establishing for them programs of patient advocacy. Patient claims include rights to treatment; to refuse treatment; to the least intrusive alternative form of treatment; and to privacy, autonomy, liberty, information, communication, and protection while undergoing treatment. Mental health lawyers have elevated these claims to new constitutional doctrine, conveniently overlooking that many decisions recognizing them came from lower courts.

The constitutional values underlying these decisions have also found expression in other legal forms: legislative law reform, judicial interpretation of unresisting common law and statutes, and unfolding of state constitutional doctrine. Although not necessarily flying the U.S. constitutional flag, these legal developments are nevertheless based on constitutional values, such as liberty, privacy, due process, equality, and free speech. The principles invoked are not specific to mental health, but common to the modern judicial approach to protecting the vulnerable.

The Supreme Court has been slow to join these trends. In contrast to its behavior in the field of criminal justice, here the Supreme Court has followed reluctantly rather than lead. As with the rights of the criminally accused, the Court has recently retreated, leading to a development of state constitutional law.

A legislative revolution in civil commitment procedures received constitutional underpinnings in *Addington v. Texas* (1979), which mandated a standard of "clear and convincing" evidence for the fact-finding on which commitment is based. Commitment through the criminal process was limited constitutionally by the holding that incompetency to stand trial can justify incarceration only for a reasonable period during which restoration of trial capacity is foreseeable.

The Constitution seems to impose little constraint on

changes in the best-known rule in the field of psychiatry and law: the insanity defense to criminal prosecution. The state may redefine the defense and even require the defendant, rather than the prosecution, to bear the burden of proof beyond a reasonable doubt. The "least restrictive alternative" criterion for involuntary treatment, proclaimed by many lower courts, has not been adopted by the Supreme Court.

The Court has also been hesitant about a right to refuse treatment, although recognizing in theory a liberty interest in avoiding unwanted administration of antipsychotic drugs. In WASHINGTON V. HARPER (1990), it refused to hold that a prisoner had the right to refuse such treatment, taking into account that he was confined and determined to be dangerous to himself or others and that the treatment was in his medical interest. Nor was a prior judicial hearing required because the Court believed his interests would be better served by allowing medication decisions to be made by doctors rather than judges. A number of state courts have nevertheless recognized a right to refuse treatment based on common law protection of bodily integrity or state constitutional guarantees of privacy.

The right to treatment and inpatient rights have fared no better in the Supreme Court than has the right to refuse treatment. Ruling on an involuntarily committed, developmentally disabled person, *Youngberg v. Romeo* (1982) held his constitutionally protected liberty interests included minimally adequate training, as well as reasonable safety and freedom from undue bodily restraints. Presumably, the involuntarily committed mentally ill possess similar rights. But the Court eviscerated such rights by declaring that the Constitution requires only that "professional judgment" be exercised, with the courts to show deference to that judgment. "Deliberate indifference" to an inpatient's serious psychiatric needs might perhaps violate the Eighth Amendment by analogy to a holding on prisoners' medical needs.

The new legal limitations on psychiatric power seem confining only by contrast to the vast authority traditionally exercised. The mentally ill are still subject to governmental power not exercised over the healthy, on rationales of paternalism as well as protection of others. The patients' rights movement points out the hypocrisy of claims that governmental power is exercised for the patient's own good if adequate treatment is not guaranteed and if "acquittal" on the ground of insanity can result in loss of liberty for a longer period than conviction. And psychiatrists still are permitted to testify as experts, giving opinions on matters beyond their actual scientific competence, such as predicting dangerousness on the basis of clinical interviews.

The psychiatrist-patient relationship, a central focus for therapists, has been largely overlooked in constitutional case law. When the doctor is double agent for both patient and prosecutor, a *Miranda*-like warning is required before a psychiatrist examines a convicted defendant for a death penalty hearing. Psychiatric assistance itself can be a constitutional right: an indigent defendant must have access to a psychiatrist on a showing of need to prepare his or her insanity defense.

Psychiatric condition is generally not central to an individual's constitutional status. Neither psychiatric patients as a group nor MENTAL ILLNESS as a trait has yet been held to invoke specially solicitous judicial protection from elected legislatures, which is labeled heightened scrutiny under the equal protection clause. In CLEBURNE V. CLEBURNE LIVING CENTER, INC. (1985) the Supreme Court explicitly said it would not extend heightened scrutiny to the developmentally disabled. The Court nevertheless did just what it said it was not doing, on reasoning equally valid for the mentally ill. (Indeed, five Justices repudiated the whole theory of three "tiers" of equal protection scrutiny.) Psychiatric condition nevertheless has some irreducible effect on legal status: the Eighth Amendment prohibits the execution of the mentally incompetent. A finding of initial mental illness is insufficient to justify indefinite confinement; O'CONNOR V. DONALDSON (1975) requires findings of both current mental illness and dangerousness.

Constitutional law has been little affected by psychodynamic perspectives, even though twentieth-century American culture has been heavily influenced by psychoanalysis, whose models of the mind differ significantly from the law's traditions. Some cases contrast "the law's" model of the mind, involving free will and choice, with psychiatry's model, supposedly deterministic, these courts conclude that judges must disregard such psychiatric ideas. A handful of judges openly ask whether a model of the mind must be assumed for constitutional purposes. One of the law's most-cited "unreported" cases, *Kaimowitz v. Dept. of Mental Health* (1973), said that the FIRST AMENDMENT, must protect the individual's right to generate ideas if it is going to protect the right to communicate those ideas. But in *Mills v. Rogers*, although the Supreme Court cited Michael Shapiro's germinal work on the topic, it declined to rule on this point. Freedom of thought (and implicitly of emotion) was recognized in STANLEY V. GEORGIA (1969), which declared a First Amendment right to personal possession of obscene materials in the home. *Washington v. Harper* (1990) recognized that it is a substantial interference with a person's liberty interest to alter his brain's chemical balance to affect his cognitive process. And Justice LOUIS D. BRANDEIS's famous dissent in OLMSTEAD V. UNITED STATES (1928) had spoken of protecting throughts and emotions as well as beliefs.

In criminal law, the Court early had relied implicitly on a free-will model of the mind to hold a confession involuntary, based on the defendant's insanity at the time he or she confessed rather than on police coercion. This focus on the suspect's state of mind suggested that free will is a constitutional prerequisite for voluntariness. But the Court subsequently retreated from that approach.

A central lesson of psychoanalysis is that much of our mental functioning is largely inaccessible to consciousness, while nevertheless affecting our conscious thoughts, feelings, and behavior. Psychiatrists are therefore used to looking for unconscious intents and unconscious, often symbolic, meanings. The Supreme Court has recognized that actions and institutions can have not only intended but unintended psychological effects with constitutional significance, as in the famous footnote 11 of BROWN V. BOARD OF EDUCATION (1954). But the Court has not yet recognized the argument by scholars that government officials can violate the Constitution by unconscious discrimination, reflecting not overt hatred or contempt but unconscious conflict and ambivalence, aimed not only at ethnic groups and women but also at the poor and the elderly.

Lawyers' theories for interpreting the constitutional text and the motives of constitutional actors are perhaps starting to be more influenced by the experience of that other profession of interpreters, the psychotherapists. The psychoanalytic perspective assumes that multilayered contradictory intentions and symbolic meanings abound; we live lives of poetry, not prose. Speakers do not generally fully comprehend their own purposes, and the intellectual baggage we carry with us distorts our perceptions of current realities. Emotions permeate all that we do, and our rational goals are regularly compromised with dictates of conscience and defense against anxieties. Context, slips, and redundancy are important clues to meaning; useful interpretation requires an ongoing dialogue. By calling our attention to such concepts, psychiatry's chief contribution to constitutional law can be not in dealing with the abnormal but in helping us to understand one another and ourselves.

                                                    MARTIN LYON LEVINE
                                                              (1992)

Bibliography

KATZ, JAY et al. 1967 *Psychoanalysis, Psychiatry, and Law.* New York: Free Press.

LEVINE, MARTIN LYON 1988 *Age Discrimination and the Mandatory Retirement Controversy.* Baltimore: Johns Hopkins University Press.

SHAPIRO, MICHAEL H. and SPECE, ROY G., JR. 1981, 1991 *Bioethics and Law: Cases, Materials and Problems.* St. Paul, Minn.: West Publishing Co.

PUBLIC ACCOMMODATIONS

The refusal of hotels, restaurants, theaters, and other public accommodations to serve blacks was not exclusively a southern phenomenon. In the South, however, the practice was an essential part of a system of racial dominance and dependency, long after the THIRTEENTH AMENDMENT abolished slavery and the FOURTEENTH AMENDMENT recognized the CITIZENSHIP of the freed slaves. Aware of the role played by this form of RACIAL DISCRIMINATION in the system of white supremacy, Congress adopted the CIVIL RIGHTS ACT OF 1875, the last major CIVIL RIGHTS act of the Reconstruction era. The law prohibited public accommodations, including railroads along with the types already mentioned, from denying access to any person on account of race. The Supreme Court held this law unconstitutional, saying that when Congress enforced the Fourteenth Amendment it had no power to reach private action. (See CIVIL RIGHTS CASES; STATE ACTION.)

Later came the Jim Crow laws—state laws requiring racial SEGREGATION in all manner of public places, including public accommodations. This practice received the Court's blessing in PLESSY V. FERGUSON (1896), a case involving the segregation of seating in railroad cars. (See SEPARATE BUT EQUAL DOCTRINE.) By the end of the nineteenth century, the denial of access for blacks to public accommodations in the South was firmly rooted in both law and custom.

Soon after the Supreme Court decided BROWN V. BOARD OF EDUCATION (1954), the modern civil rights movement turned to the problem of access to public accommodations. The reason for direct action such as freedom rides and SIT-INS was not that seats in the front of the bus arrive at a destination before back seats do, or that black college students yearn to perch on lunch counter stools. Public accommodations became a target for civil rights demonstrators for exactly the same reason that they had been made the vehicles for racial discrimination in the first place: segregation and the refusal of service to blacks were powerful symbols of racial inferiority, highly visible denials of the entitlement of blacks to be treated as persons and citizens. Employment discrimination and housing discrimination might touch material interests of great importance, but no interest is more important than self-respect. The primary target of the civil rights movement was the stigma of caste.

Within a few years after the *Brown* decision, the Supreme Court had held unconstitutional nearly the whole range of Jim Crow laws. Racial segregation practiced by state institutions, or commanded or authorized by state laws, failed the test of the Fourteenth Amendment even before Congress reentered the public accommodations field. In most of the states of the North and West, civil rights laws commanded equal access not only to public accommodations—such laws merely reinforced the common law duties of innkeepers and common carriers—but also to other businesses. In the South, however, private discrimination continued in most hotels, restaurants, and barber shops. The Supreme Court was repeatedly invited to decide whether the Fourteenth Amendment established a right of access to such places, free of racial bias, but the Court repeatedly declined the invitation. (See BELL V. MARYLAND.)

As part of the CIVIL RIGHTS ACT OF 1964, Congress adopted a comprehensive public accommodations law, forbidding discrimination in the same types of places that had been covered by the 1875 act. (Railroads were forbidden to discriminate by modern interpretations of the Interstate Commerce Act of 1887.) Before the year was out, the Supreme Court had upheld the public accommodations portion of the 1964 act, on the basis of the power of Congress to regulate interstate commerce. (See HEART OF ATLANTA MOTEL V. UNITED STATES.)

The 1964 act is limited in its coverage, reaching an establishment only if it "affects commerce" or if its discrimination is "supported by STATE ACTION." The act exempts both private clubs and small rooming houses lived in by their proprietors. Now that the Supreme Court has interpreted the CIVIL RIGHTS ACT OF 1866 as a broad guarantee against private racial discrimination in the sale of property and other contracting, and validated the law as a congressional enforcement of the Thirteenth Amendment, at least some of the limitations of the 1964 act have been made irrelevant. For example, a barber shop is covered by the 1964 act if it is located in a covered hotel, but not if it is independent. Under recent interpretations of the 1866 act, any barber shop would violate the law by refusing service on the basis of the customer's race. (See JONES V. ALFRED H. MAYER CO.; RUNYON V. MCCRARY.)

The substantive core of the Fourteenth Amendment is a principle of equal citizenship. (See EQUAL PROTECTION OF THE LAWS.) Even in the absence of civil rights legislation, that principle demands that the organized community treat each of us, irrespective of race, as a respected, participating member. Racially based denial of access or segregation in places of public accommodations—even those privately owned—is a deliberate denial of the status of equal citizenship, as the sit-in demonstrators knew and helped the rest of us to understand.

KENNETH L. KARST
(1986)

Bibliography

LEWIS, THOMAS P. 1963 The Sit-in Cases: Great Expectations. *Supreme Court Review* 1963:101–151.
POLLITT, DANIEL H. 1960 Dime Store Demonstrations: Events and Legal Problems of the First Sixty Days. *Duke Law Journal* 1960:315–365.
WOODWARD, C. VANN 1966 *The Strange Career of Jim Crow*, 2d (rev.) ed. New York: Oxford University Press.

PUBLIC CHOICE THEORY AND CONSTITUTIONAL JURISPRUDENCE

Inasmuch as the public is often adversely affected by special interest LEGISLATION, it has a strong incentive to devise institutional mechanisms—like constitutions— that make passage of such legislation more difficult. Before one can gauge whether a constitution is designed to promote the general welfare of the public by impeding the efficacy of INTEREST GROUPS or to advance the interests of particular groups within society, it is necessary to establish guidelines by which the "public-regardingness" of a constitution can be evaluated.

The most objective means of evaluating a constitution is to examine the actual effects of the document on interest group behavior. If the constitution establishes mechanisms that facilitate rent-seeking, it is reasonable to infer that the Framers intended to encourage this result. If, on the other hand, the constitution establishes mechanisms that retard such activity by making it more costly, one can also infer that these costs were intended.

JAMES MADISON's formal, publicly articulated pronouncements indicate that controlling the ability of interest groups to achieve antimajoritarian outcomes in the legislature was a primary goal of the U.S. Constitution. As we see from examining "hidden implicit" legislation, however, it is often impossible to draw conclusions about the intentions of those who make law simply by evaluating their public pronouncements. Thus while the Framers stated publicly that reducing the political power of factions was a central feature of their constitutional design, an even more convincing indication that the Constitution was intended to promote the public interest is found by examining the results of the Framers' work.

One who observes the impressive success of interest groups in obtaining favorable legislation might conclude either that the Constitution has failed in its attempt to impede interest groups or that it was not designed to impede their activities in the first place. Such a conclusion would be erroneous.

The formation of a representative democracy establishes what economists refer to as an "agency relationship." An agency relationship calls for one person or group of people (the principal) to hire another person or group of people (the agent) to perform services and make decisions on the principal's behalf. The contract is successful

constitutional limits narrowly designed to protect public employees from invidiously selective maltreatment. This second theme protects against improper government motivation, but not against broad impact. Restrictions on the political freedom of numerous public employees are tolerated for the legitimate advantages of having a nonpartisan bureaucracy, but government may not penalize even a few for constitutionally unacceptable reasons, such as dislike of their beliefs. In UNITED STATES V. LOVETT (1946), for example, the Court struck down as a BILL OF ATTAINDER a provision of an appropriations law prohibiting payment of the salaries of three named government employees declared guilty of SUBVERSIVE ACTIVITY not by a court but by a House of Representatives subcommittee. Similarly, WIEMANN V. UPDEGRAFF (1952) took a stand against GUILT BY ASSOCIATION and held that government employment could not be denied for membership in a group advocating unlawful overthrow of the government if the member lacked knowledge of the group's unlawful aim.

With the advent of the WARREN COURT, constitutional protection for public employees expanded with the gradual adoption of a third, more complex approach that perceived several values at risk in government treatment of public employees. Increased solicitude for the employees' personal freedom, heightened awareness that jobs often carry some sense of entitlement, and growing appreciation of the part that government workers play in citizen self-government, intensified objections to blatant instances of ideologically discriminatory treatment. Reports of the death of the right-privilege distinction may have been exaggerated, but its hold weakened considerably. Various methods used to weed out allegedly subversive public employees, especially LOYALTY OATHS and compelled disclosure of an individual's associations, were invalidated on VAGUENESS and OVERBREADTH grounds, because the Court thought those methods of employment disqualification would excessively inhibit freedom of expression and association. Those developments paralleled the Warren Court's general expansion of citizen immunity from regulation affecting individual liberty and culminated in a series of decisions between 1966 and 1968, including ELFBRANDT V. RUSSELL (1966) and KEYISHIAN V. BOARD OF REGENTS (1967), that forbade public employers from requiring their employees as a condition of employment to relinquish the expanded constitutional freedoms they enjoyed as citizens. *Pickering v. Board of Education* (1968) appeared to complete the rejection of Holmes's view in *McAuliffe* by holding that a teacher could not be dismissed for speaking on issues of public concern involving her employer.

After the Warren Court era ended, the broadest implications of the demise of the right-privilege distinction were curtailed when the Court reaffirmed the constitutionality of government efforts to keep the civil service broadly—and neutrally—apolitical. The opposition to narrower but selective disadvantaging based on ideological viewpoint remained, however. The Court has disallowed the firing of public employees for belonging to the wrong political party, except where party affiliation is a legitimate qualification for the particular job. The political patronage practice may distort the political beliefs of public employees, but because it represents discrimination against ideologically disfavored viewpoints, it also elicits the narrower concern for preventing selective arbitrariness. In 1983 the Court drew an uncertain line between a worker grievance and a citizen complaint, allowing dismissal of public employees without constitutional restraint for employee speech on matters of personal interest, but retaining *Pickering's* FIRST AMENDMENT protection against dismissal for speech as a citizen on matters of public concern. It endorsed neither government's right to impose any conditions on public employment it chooses, nor the employees' personal rights of self-expression. Rather, the Court stressed the government's need for flexibility in employee discipline and the public, not personal, value of employee freedoms.

Protection against employment sanctions imposed for constitutionally unacceptable reasons also underlies the Court's public employees PROCEDURAL DUE PROCESS decisions. Significantly, these protections developed after, not before, the Court established substantive limits on the reasons the government legitimately could invoke to disadvantage its employees. The possibility of intentional government arbitrariness, rather than government indifference to valuable employment opportunities, seems to have prompted the development of procedural protections surrounding the loss of government employment benefits.

The development was part of the procedural due process revolution of the Warren Court. Government benefits that did not have to be granted at all, including employment, could not be taken away once awarded without providing certain constitutionally imposed minimum procedures. Rejecting both extremes, the Court never recognized a right to government work but also denied the government the unrestricted freedom to withhold it. Nor has the Court required that reasons and a fair process always be provided before an individual loses an employment opportunity. Instead, the Court has let the government decide whether to hold out a job as offering some job protection or security of employment. If the government bestows no entitlement by statute or practice, several rules apply. No reason is needed to discharge or refuse to hire. If defamatory reasons nonetheless are given for an adverse personnel action, the employee must have an opportunity to defend against the charge. In any event, constitutionally illegitimate reasons may not form the public basis of the adverse action. If the government does hold out a job as offering employment security of any sort, moreover, the Court disallows deprivation of the secured position until constitutionally adequate notice, reasons, and other procedures are followed. The government worker may not be deprived of employment prospects either for illegitimate reasons or for legitimate reasons that do not apply to his circumstances.

The constitutional law of public employee regulation inevitably affects the efficiency of government operations, the personal freedoms of the workers, and the public interest in checking government abuse and being apprised of how public policy is being enforced. Accommodating these interests is, and will remain, an important and complex constitutional problem.

JONATHAN D. VARAT
(1986)

Bibliography

NOTE   1984   Developments in the Law—Public Employment. *Harvard Law Review* 97:1611, 1738–1800.
VAN ALSTYNE, WILLIAM W.   1969   The Constitutional Rights of Public Employees. *UCLA Law Review* 16:751–772.

PUBLIC FIGURE

The concept of a public figure features prominently in modern FIRST AMENDMENT law involving libel suits. NEW YORK TIMES V. SULLIVAN (1964) prevented public officials (officeholders and candidates for office) from recovering damages for defamation without proof of actual malice, that is, proof that the statement was made with the knowledge that it was false or with reckless disregard whether it was or not. In *Curtis Publishing Company v. Butts* (1967) the Supreme Court extended the actual malice rule to public figures, described by the Court as private persons in positions of considerable influence or able to attract attention because they had thrust themselves into public controversies. A public figure commands public interest and therefore has sufficient access to the mass media to be able, like an officeholder, to publicize his response to falsehoods about him. He invites comment and his remarks make news. The Justices unanimously agreed that for the sake of a robust FREEDOM OF THE PRESS, the actual malice rule applies to public figures, but they disagreed in specific cases on the question whether a particular person, such as the former wife of the scion of a famous family is a public figure, the question before the court in *Time Incorporated v. Firestone* (1976). The Court

has tended to deny the press's claim that the party suing for damages is a public figure.

LEONARD W. LEVY
(1986)

PUBLIC FORUM

Laws that regulate the time, place, and manner of speech are not considered inherently problematic under the FIRST AMENDMENT, in contrast to laws that regulate the content of speech. As a general matter, would-be speakers can be denied the use of a particular public space for their expressive activities if other proper uses of that space would be unduly disturbed and if different speakers with different messages also would be denied use of the space.

The "public forum" DOCTRINE represents an important gloss on the general doctrine that accords government fairly wide authority to regulate speech in public places. For spaces that are designated public forums—streets, parks, and sidewalks, for example—the regulatory authority of government is subject to careful scrutiny under the First Amendment. Public forums, unlike other public spaces, cannot be devoted entirely to nonexpressive uses; some accommodation of the claims of would-be speakers must be made. In addition, when the content of the speech is taken into account in governing the use of a public forum, as when political criticism or commercial advertising but not expression of a labor grievance is disallowed on a public sidewalk, an especially strong presumption of invalidity stalks the regulation. Even content-neutral regulations regarding the time and manner of speech in a public forum pass muster under the First Amendment only if they are "narrowly tailored to serve a significant government interest, and leave open ample alternative channels of communication."

The historical derivation of the public forum doctrine can be traced to an oft-quoted OBITER DICTUM by Justice OWEN J. ROBERTS in HAGUE V. CIO (1939):

> Wherever the title of streets and parks may rest, they have immemorially been held in trust for the use of the public and, time out of mind, have been used for purposes of assembly, communicating thoughts between citizens, and discussing public questions. The privilege of a citizen of the United States to use the streets and parks for communication of views on national questions may be regulated in the interest of all; it is not absolute, but relative, and must be exercised in subordination to the general comfort and convenience, and in consonance with peace and good order; but it must not, in the guise of regulation, be abridged or denied.

The dictum repudiated the doctrine, endorsed by the Supreme Court forty years earlier, that government's ownership of the land on which streets and parks are situated gave officials the nearly plenary authority of a private landlord to regulate access to those spaces. The phrase "public forum" was first employed as a legal term of art by HARRY KALVEN, JR., in an influential article on the topic of speech in public places. The Supreme Court's most comprehensive discussion of the public forum doctrine is in PERRY EDUCATION ASSOCIATION V. PERRY LOCAL EDUCATORS' ASSOCIATION (1983).

Public streets, parks, state capitol grounds, and sidewalks have been held by the Court to be "quintessential" public forums. Public auditoriums and meeting rooms, state fair grounds, and public school classrooms have also been held to be public forums, although the tenor of judicial opinions suggests that officials may have somewhat more regulatory authority to preserve the special character of such places than may be exercised over open spaces such as streets and parks. The Court has denied public forum status to a jailyard, a military base portions of which were open to the public, residential mailboxes, and an internal communications system used for delivering messages and posting notices within a school district. The most important criterion for deciding whether a space constitutes a public forum is the traditional use of that type of space, not necessarily in the particular locale but rather as a general practice nationwide. Some Justices have contended that the dominant consideration should be whether the use of the space for expressive purposes is basically incompatible with other legitimate uses, but that position has not won acceptance by a majority of the Court.

The public forum doctrine has been criticized, primarily on two counts. First, it is claimed that the analytical device of categorizing public places on the basis of their general characteristics fails to give sufficient weight to considerations peculiar to each particular dispute over the use of public property for expressive purposes. Case-by-case variations in the degree to which expressive and regulatory values are implicated tend, so this criticism goes, to be overshadowed by the characterization of a place in gross as either a public forum or not. Particularly as applied to places that do not qualify as public forums, the categorization approach of the public forum doctrine permits government to regulate speech that may be highly appropriate in the particular circumstances and that may not impose serious burdens on other uses of the public space.

Second, and somewhat in tension with the first criticism, it is sometimes maintained that the public forum doctrine is misleading in that the designation of a place as a public forum or not has little resolving power in actual cases. Thus, the regulation of speech based on its content is highly disfavored, even as applied to places that are not

public forums. It is not clear what the public forum doctrine adds to the presumption against regulation based on content. In addition, because a COMPELLING STATE INTEREST can justify the regulation of speech in a public forum and because places that are not public forums typically are devoted to activities that conflict somewhat with the use of such places for expressive purposes, it is not obvious that the public forum designation alters dramatically the balancing of conflicting uses that must take place in all disputes over access to public land.

Probably the most important aspect of the public forum doctrine is the principle that public forums cannot be closed off entirely to marches, DEMONSTRATIONS, rallies, and individual acts of expression. In contrast, uniformly enforced blanket prohibitions on expressive activities in places that are not public forums are permissible as a general matter under the First Amendment. Apart from this issue of blanket prohibitions, the significance of the public forum doctrine lies mainly in the tendency of courts to weigh competing particularistic considerations more favorably to speakers when the situs in dispute is a public forum.

VINCENT BLASI
(1986)

Bibliography

KALVEN, HARRY, JR. 1965 The Concept of the Public Forum. *Supreme Court Review* 1965:1–32.

STONE, GEOFFREY 1974 Fora Americana: Speech in Public Places. *The Supreme Court Review* 1974:233–280.

PUBLIC FORUM
(Update 1)

In recent years the Supreme Court has elevated the distinction between public and nonpublic forums into "a fundamental principle of First Amendment doctrine." Apart from rules of time, place, and manner, government regulation of speech within a public forum is usually subject to the STRICT SCRUTINY ordinarily required by First Amendment jurisprudence. Government regulation of speech within a nonpublic forum, however, is accorded wide latitude and presumptive constitutionality. The Court has increasingly relied upon public forum doctrine to insulate from JUDICIAL REVIEW restrictions on speech in such settings as schools, prisons, military establishments, and state bureaucracies.

Given the dramatic constitutional difference in the government's power to regulate speech within public and nonpublic forums, the distinction between the two is a matter of some importance. The Court has offered two criteria for this distinction. The first distinguishes public from nonpublic forums on the basis of whether the government property at issue has "traditionally served as a place for free public assembly and communication of thoughts by private citizens." The second turns on whether government has deliberately opened the property at issue for indiscriminate use by the general public. The Court has never explained, however, why the exercise of ordinary First Amendment rights on government property should depend either upon tradition or upon the permission of the government. As a consequence, modern public forum doctrine has justly received nearly universal scholarly condemnation.

The explosive growth of the doctrine is nevertheless undeniable. The underlying cause of this growth appears to be that the Court is using public forum doctrine to distinguish two different kinds of government authority: management and governance. The government exercises managerial authority when it acts through institutions to achieve explicit and fixed ends. The purpose of schools is to educate the young; the goal of prisons is to punish and reform convicted criminals; the objective of the military is to safeguard the nation; and so forth. In each of these settings, the Court has used public forum doctrine to enable government to regulate speech to achieve these institutional ends. Thus, for example, the Court has classified schools as nonpublic forums to permit them to censor student speech inconsistent with the achievement of their educational mission.

Outside these narrow institutional settings, however, governmental objectives in a democracy are not fixed and given, but rather are determined by a process of public deliberation. For this reason, public speech cannot be instrumentally regulated in a managerial fashion. In public forums, therefore, the First Amendment requires that the state exercise the authority of governance, in which the regulation of speech is presumptively unconstitutional unless justified according to strict constitutional tests. These tests are designed to ensure that governmental goals and policies be perpetually subject to the evaluation of democratic deliberation.

Although the Court's doctrine has not explicitly recognized this distinction between management and governance, the pattern of its decisions has served to define the boundary between these two different forms of authority. Public forum doctrine has thus achieved important prominence in this age of the activist state, in which the rapid proliferation of government institutions has both created a legitimate need for expansive new forms of regulating speech and yet has simultaneously threatened to strangle public deliberation.

The most controversial aspect of contemporary public forum doctrine has been the Court's tendency to defer to institutional authorities on the question of whether the regulation of speech is truly necessary to achieve institutional objectives. In the 1988 decision HAZELWOOD SCHOOL DISTRICT V. KUHLMEIER, for example, the Court concluded that determinations of the educational propriety of speech should properly rest "with the school board . . . rather than with the federal courts" and that therefore judges should defer to the decisions of school officials. But such deference in effect cedes to the states enormous discretion to regulate speech and sharply raises the question of the circumstances under which courts ought to relinquish careful supervision of governmental curtailments of speech.

ROBERT C. POST
(1992)

Bibliography

FARBER, DANIEL A. and NOWAK, JOHN E. 1984 The Misleading Nature of Public Forum Analysis: Content and Context in First Amendment Adjudication. *Virginia Law Review* 70: 1219–1266.
POST, ROBERT C. 1987 Between Governance and Management: The History and Theory of the Public Forum. *Ucla Law Review* 34:1713–1835.

PUBLIC FORUM
(Update 2)

Public forum DOCTRINE initially arose out of the question whether individuals have a FIRST AMENDMENT FREEDOM OF SPEECH in such government-owned properties as streets, parks, and sidewalks. Finding that such properties have been dedicated "time out of mind" to expressive purposes, the Supreme Court has generally held that speech can be regulated, but not prohibited, in such "traditional" public forums. Thus, although government can adopt reasonable time, place, and manner regulations that channel speech in such forums, it must permit a significant opportunity for individuals to speak in public parks, march on public streets, and distribute leaflets on public sidewalks.

The question then arose, however, whether individuals have a similar right to speak in other forms of government-owned property, such as military bases, the grounds surrounding a jail, and airports. Because such properties have not been dedicated "time out of mind" to speech purposes, the Court has generally held that speech can be prohibited in such places, so long as the government acts in a content-neutral manner and there is at least a reasonable basis for the restriction. Thus, as the Court held in *Greer v. Spock* (1976), although the government must allow individuals to make speeches in public parks, it need not permit speeches on the grounds of a military base, even though the base is generally open to the public. The Court explained that "it is the business of a military installation ... to train soldiers, not to provide a public forum."

Governmental allowance of some, but not all, speech in a nonpublic forum raised more difficult issues. In LAMB'S CHAPEL V. CENTER MORICHES UNION FREE SCHOOL DISTRICT (1993), for example, a public school district permitted student groups to meet after-hours in the school's classrooms, but prohibited use of the classrooms for religious purposes. Because the classrooms were a nonpublic forum, the school district presumably could have prohibited all after-hours use of its own buildings. But once it chose to permit some student organizations to use the classrooms after-hours, could it constitutionally exclude religiously oriented organizations from using them as well?

In POLICE DEPARTMENT OF CHICAGO V. MOSLEY (1972), the Court had held that such "selective exclusions" from traditional public forums are presumptively unconstitutional and will be upheld only if they are necessary to serve a "compelling" governmental interest. The Court has applied a different approach, however, to "selective exclusions" from nonpublic forums. In this context, the Court has held that the government can constitutionally restrict access based on the "subject matter" of the speech so long as the exclusion is "reasonable and viewpoint-neutral." Applying this standard in Lamb's Chapel, the Court held that the restriction was unconstitutional because even though the classrooms were only a "limited" public forum, the denial of access to speakers who wanted to address issues from a religious perspective violated the requirement of "viewpoint-neutrality."

The most recent extension of this doctrine involves the problem of government subsidies. In ROSENBERGER V. RECTOR AND VISITORS OF UNIVERSITY OF VIRGINIA (1995), for example, the Court, following Lamb's Chapel, invalidated a University of Virginia policy authorizing payment from the Student Activities Fund for the printing costs of a variety of student publications, but prohibiting payment for any student publication that "primarily promotes or manifests a particular belief in or about a deity or an ultimate reality." In extending public forum analysis to cases like Rosenberger, which involves government PROPERTY in the form of benefits rather than a physical locale, the Court has run into particular difficulty with the concept of "viewpoint-neutrality."

In RUST V. SULLIVAN (1991), for example, the Court, in a 5–4 decision, upheld the constitutionality of federal regulations providing that federal funds appropriated to support family planning services might not be used to provide referrals for ABORTION as a method of family planning. The dissenters, in an opinion by Justice HARRY A. BLACKMUN, argued that, "until today, the Court has never upheld viewpoint-based suppression of speech simply because that suppression was a condition upon the acceptance of public funds." The Court, however, in an opinion by Chief Justice

WILLIAM H. REHNQUIST, responded that "we have here not the case of a general law singling out a disfavored group on the basis of speech content, but a case of the government refusing to fund activities, including speech, which are specifically excluded from the scope of the project funded." This line of reasoning has proved highly controversial. Critics have asked why, for example, the same argument wouldn't also hold true in cases like Lamb's Chapel and Rosenberger.

More recently, in National Endowment for the Arts v. Finley (1998), the Court upheld a federal statute that directs the NEA, in establishing procedures to judge the artistic merit of grant applications, to "tak[e] into consideration general standards of decency and respect for the diverse beliefs and values of the American public." For several reasons, the Court rejected the argument that "the provision is a paradigmatic example of viewpoint discrimination." First, the Court argued that the provision merely "adds 'considerations' to the grant-making process; it does not preclude awards to projects that might be deemed 'indecent' or 'disrespectful.'" Second, the Court observed that terms like "indecency" and "respect for diverse beliefs and values" are "susceptible to multiple interpretations" and do not necessarily "introduce considerations that, in practice, would effectively preclude or punish the expression of particular views."

The Court distinguished Rosenberger on the ground that, in "the context of arts funding, in contrast to many other subsidies, the government does not indiscriminately 'encourage a diversity of views from private speakers.' The NEA's mandate is to make aesthetic judgments, and the inherently content-based 'excellence' threshold for NEA support sets it apart from the subsidy issue in Rosenberger—which was available to all student organizations that were 'related to the educational purpose of the University.'" Finally, the Court emphasized that "we have no occasion here to address an as-applied challenge in a situation where the denial of a grant may be shown to be the product of invidious viewpoint discrimination. If the NEA were to leverage its power to award subsidies on the basis of subjective criteria into a penalty on disfavored viewpoints, then we would confront a different case." Although cases like Rust and Finley may seem a far cry from the earlier era's disputes about leafleting on public sidewalks, the common theme of access to government "property," which underlies the public forum problem, unites these decisions.

GEOFFREY R. STONE
(2000)

Bibliography

KAGAN, ELENA 1996 Private Speech, Public Purpose: The Role of Governmental Motive in First Amendment Doctrine. The University of Chicago Law Review 63:415–463.

Post, Robert 1996 Subsidized Speech. *Yale Law Journal* 106: 151–174.

Redish, Martin 1996 Government Subsidies and Free Expression. *University of Minnesota Law Review* 80:543–577.

PUBLIC INTEREST LAW

Public interest law is the work done by lawyers on behalf of poor individuals, unrepresented interests, and the general good. Public interest law services are usually provided at no cost to the beneficiaries, who are either too poor to pay or are not organized in ways that would allow them to retain lawyers. Public interest lawyers work in the courts, agencies, legislatures, and also through the media and community organizations. Although only a small number of American lawyers participate in these activities, public interest law reflects the American legal profession's commitment to values not fully served by the normal fee-for-service system of legal practice.

There is an intimate relationship between public interest law and the Constitution. First, the governmental structure created by the Constitution makes public interest law both necessary and possible. Second, without public interest law, many constitutional protections might be ineffective. Finally, the broader American tradition of CONSTITUTIONALISM depends on institutions like public interest law.

The governmental structure created by the Constitution makes legal advocacy important for the pursuit of many individual and collective interests. United States government is one by representation, not by direct participation. Although, in theory, citizens are supposed to be knowledgeable about public issues and elected representatives are supposed to take account of the interests of all constituents, in fact, most decisions are made in remote arenas and officials often are not aware of all affected interests. As a result, direct advocacy by professionals will make a difference in outcomes. If all such advocacy must be purchased in the marketplace, the system will be skewed toward the interests of the "haves." The presence of public interest advocates, at least to some degree, offsets marketplace bias.

The special role our written Constitution plays in American political life makes subsidized advocacy all the more important. Americans resolve many fundamental issues—from SLAVERY to reproductive freedom—through consitutional litigation. If free legal services are not sometimes available in these struggles, the results can be seriously skewed.

Although the constitutional structure thus makes public interest law necessary, it also helps make it possible. Of course, there is a constitutional RIGHT TO COUNSEL in criminal cases. In addition, several constitutional protections have been given to public interest lawyers. In NAACP V. BUTTON (1963) the Supreme Court ruled that litigation on behalf of a disadvantaged group was constitutionally protected speech and overturned Virginia's efforts to penalize NAACP lawyers. This ruling was extended by *In re Primus* (1978), where the Court made clear that nonprofit groups representing protected interests were exempt from normal bans on solicitation by lawyers.

The rights granted by the Constitution usually are not self-enforcing. Without legal representation, many would remain a dead letter. Protections for criminal defendants remain mere paper promises unless the accused are represented by competent lawyers. Because of the serious consequences of a deprivation of these rights, the Constitution itself guarantees counsel. But there are many other areas in which public interest law, although not constitutionally guaranteed, is equally essential. Many efforts to curb free speech, for example, would have gone unchallenged if public interest groups like the AMERICAN CIVIL LIBERTIES UNION were not available to defend this interest. The guarantee of EQUAL PROTECTION OF THE LAW might still sound completely hollow to African Americans if the subsidized services of NAACP lawyers and other public interest advocates were not available.

Public interest law spans the political spectrum. Some of the more notable liberal public interest law groups include the ACLU, the NAACP LEGAL DEFENSE AND EDUCATIONAL FUND, and the Commission on Law and Social Action of the AMERICAN JEWISH CONGRESS. Public interest law groups of a conservative persuasion include the Pacific Legal Foundation, which brings suits against governmental regulation; the Rutherford Institute, which litigates cases involving EQUAL ACCESS for religious groups and defends nonviolent protestors in the ANTIABORTION MOVEMENT; and the Washington Legal Foundation, which pursues a grab bag of causes, including JUDICIAL REVIEW of redistricting and lawsuits by crime victims.

A major aspect of American political culture is our "constitutionalism": the belief in higher values protected by the Constitution. Often, marginal and subordinated groups have looked to higher law and constitutional values as guides and inspiration for their struggle for inclusion in the American commonwealth. Women, blacks, and other groups have looked beyond existing law and institutions to a penumbra of constitutional values that, they believed, entitled them to fuller participation in economic, social, and political life. Public interest law, as idea and institution, is a reflection of this faith in the redemptive power of law and legal institutions. To be sure, law does not always fulfill the promises Americans put in it. Public interest law is often weak and ineffective; legal solutions may not lead to real gains. But public interest lawyers have won real victories and made some difference for subordinated groups. As long as America's basic political institutions remain unchanged, public interest law will be essential: it ensures that forces of the market and status quo do not overshadow democracy and constitutional values and helps preserve constitutionalism as a real force in our political life.

LOUISE G. TRUBEK
(1992)

Bibliography

ARON, NAN 1988 *Liberty and Justice for All: Public Interest Law in the 1980s and Beyond.* Boulder, Colo.: Westview Press.

CHAVKIN, DAVID F. 1987 Public Interest Advocacy. In R. Janoskik, ed., *Encyclopedia of the American Judicial System: Studies of the Principle Institutions and Processes of Law,* Vol. 2. New York: Scribners.

PUBLIC LAW LITIGATION

The WARREN COURT initiated wholesale changes in American constitutional law. Legal apartheid was dismantled. The bulk of the BILL OF RIGHTS was decreed enforceable against the states. Orchestrated public SCHOOL PRAYER was ended. Legislatures were forced to undergo REAPPORTIONMENT. Prison conditions were scrutinized. FREEDOM OF SPEECH was bolstered and made meaningful. ADMINISTRATIVE AGENCY action was rendered more easily reviewable. Access to the judicial process was expanded. And constitutionalism gained an enhanced role in the political life of the nation.

At the same time, although relatively few people noticed it, the nature of the federal litigation process began to change. Private rights were no longer the sole currency of the JUDICIAL SYSTEM. The cascade of newly recognized constitutional interests and the expanded review of administrative decisionmaking allowed by the courts opened the door to much litigation based on widely shared public values and interests. No doubt, most lawsuits continued to turn exclusively upon the competing claims of private interests. But the dramatic new acceptance of what scholars came to characterize as "public law litigation" worked to alter substantially the operation of American courts. That change will very likely remain with us, even as the Supreme Court turns in different ideological directions to reformulate substantive constitutional principles and to match its decisionmaking with the demands of the day.

Consider the contrasts. The COMMON LAW system of litigation is dominantly tied to the protection of private rights and interests. Disputes typically arise between private parties and are circumscribed by their competing claims. The litigants initiate and control its boundaries. The contested terrain concerns the rights and duties that these parties may be said to owe to each other. Courts function principally to resolve the proffered dispute, and judges act as neutral arbiters in weighing the claims. Litigation is accurately described as "bipolar"—with the parties engaged in a confrontational, winner-take-all contest. The process is, generally speaking, retrospective, designed to determine the legal significance of a fairly discrete set of past events. The remedy is intricately linked to the measurement and the determination of the legal right that provides the basis for the claim. The lawsuit is largely self-contained, its impact intended to be limited to the parties before the tribunal. Most often, judicial involvement ends with the issuance of the decree.

Public law litigation takes a decidedly different cast. The subject matter of the litigation typically concerns a dispute about the conduct of government policy—policy that likely affects not only the plaintiffs, but many others as well. The party structure is apt to be broader, and possibly more amorphous. The basis for the claim, of course, remains the assertion of deprivation of a legal right. But the focus of the attention, and of the remedy, is more likely prospective than compensatory. Litigants attempt to force the government to change its behavior, and the claims are designed to have impact well beyond the parties to the litigation. The demand for prospective, curative relief also typically entails continuing involvement or monitoring by the court. The role of the judge is altered accordingly. Public law litigation requires an active, initiating trial judge, organizing the litigation and supervising the effectiveness of the relief ordered.

Not surprisingly, perhaps, public law litigation has presented its own challenges.

First, since public claims are based on interests that are typically not the exclusive province of any one person, determining who will be allowed to bring such suits is, at the least, complex. Common law disputes typically explore whether the plaintiff is entitled to compensatory relief from a particular defendant. Lawsuits involving the validity of government policies, however, have more often involved diffuse and intangible interests: Should a legislature be apportioned more fairly? Should an environmental practice be changed to afford greater protection to natural resources? The license to bring such actions triggers an exercise of judicial authority that may well work to refashion government policy. Determining, therefore, who has STANDING to employ the judicial process has proved to be a thorny problem.

Similarly, public law litigation implicates substantial questions concerning the ability of the plaintiff appropriately to represent the interests inevitably affected by the litigation. A relatively small stake in a larger dispute may be enough to call into play an overarching use of the judicial power. As a result, traditional notions of client control and the demand that a class of litigants be tied to the fortunes of a particular member seem less relevant in a multifaceted public policy dispute in which the actual named plaintiff may have relatively little role in the proceedings. Here, to many, the courts' responses have proven unsatisfactory.

Even more starkly, public law litigation has pushed traditional notions of the federal courts' remedial powers. Declaring that the SEPARATE BUT EQUAL DOCTRINE had no place in public education proved to be only a first step in the process of DESEGREGATION. Innovative and hugely controversial remedies became necessary, however, if the asserted rights were to be meaningful protected. Reapportionment and prison cases similarly broke with traditional remedial patterns. Federal judges became managers, supervisors, magistrates, special masters, and overburdened administrators—frequently against their apparent preferences. The common law notion of the judge as passive referee seemed to become a quaint and distant memory.

Surely, the greatest question presented by the growth of public law litigation has been the most basic one—is it consistent with the limited role for the judiciary in a system marked by SEPARATION OF POWERS? To the extent that such cases are seen to vindicate the public interest rather than settle circumscribed private claims, they pose tensions not only with tradition but with perceived bases of judicial authority and legitimacy as well. Because judges are neither elected nor directly accountable to the people, extensive judicial policymaking powers present tough questions of CONSTITUTIONAL THEORY. Nor is it clear that courts are well equipped to deal with such complex and value-laden controversies. There seems little doubt, however, that judges, especially federal judges, will continue to be seen as essential partners with the other branches of government in enforcing our public values. As ALEXIS DE TOCQUEVILLE observed, "There is hardly a political question in the United States which does not sooner or later turn into a judicial one."

GENE R. NICHOL
(2000)

(SEE ALSO: *Constitutional History, 1950–1959; Constitutional History, 1960–1969; Courts and Social Change; Institutional Litigation.*)

Bibliography
CHAYES, ABRAM 1976 The Role of the Judge in Public Law Litigation. *Harvard Law Review* 89:1281–1316.
——— 1982 The Supreme Court, 1981 Term—Foreword: Public Law Litigation and the Burger Court. *Harvard Law Review* 96:4–60.
EISENBERG, THEODORE and YEAZELL, STEPHEN C. 1980 The Ordinary and the Extraordinary in Institutional Litigation. *Harvard Law Review* 93:465–517.
NICHOL, GENE R., JR. 1984 Rethinking Standing. *California Law Review* 72:68–102.
——— 1986 Injury and the Disintegration of Article III. *California Law Review* 74:1915–1950.
SCALIA, ANTONIN 1983 The Doctrine of Standing as an Essential Part of Separation of Powers. *Suffolk University Law Review* 17:881–899.
SCOTT, KENNETH E. 1975 Two Models of the Civil Process. *Stanford Law Review* 27:937–950.

PUBLIC PURPOSE DOCTRINE

The DOCTRINE of public purpose has been used, in the course of American constitutional history, as a standard by which courts have determined the legitimacy of state EMINENT DOMAIN and taxation legislation. In different periods the doctrine has been mobilized to advance divergent ideological causes and varying constitutional interpretations.

The first distinct phase in the doctrine's history ran from the early nineteenth century to the 1870s, when it was prominent as a justification for new and often far-reaching uses of eminent domain and taxation. During that period the doctrine was a bulwark of positive government. From the 1870s to the WORLD WAR I period, the doctrine became something quite different in the hands of conservatives who sought to enshrine laissez-faire policy as constitutional law. Arguments treating the public purpose doctrine as a limitation on government action were often prominent, in the new constitutional view of VESTED RIGHTS, as arguments based on FREEDOM OF CONTRACT. A third phase began in the 1930s, when state and federal courts were confronted with challenges to urban slum clearances and redevelopment projects that involved new uses of both eminent domain and taxation powers. Again the doctrine of public purpose found a prominent place in constitutional law, with legal opinion and judicial rulings seriously divided for a time as to what view of public purpose ought to prevail.

Formulation of a "public purpose" standard as a canon for testing the legitimacy of governmental action first became prominent in American decisions when states began to expand the reach of their transportation policies in the early nineteenth century. Projects such as the great Erie Canal enterprise in New York, and similar public works in other states, required powers of eminent domain for the agencies responsible for construction. When legislatures devolved the eminent domain power upon private chartered corporations that built bridges, roads, canals, and railroads, there was widespread agreement that some constitutional limitation should be formulated to prevent indiscriminate delegation of such high sovereign powers. Legal commentators and judges often invoked the Fifth

Amendment's reference to PUBLIC USE as a limitation upon eminent domain TAKINGS OF PROPERTY by state authority; many state constitutions used the same phrase in their takings clauses, and even when no express constitutional limitation referred to public use the state courts read it into their law as a fundamental principle of justice. Was a privately owned turnpike corporation engaged in a "public" activity, however? How was the distinction between "public" activities and those merely "private" to be drawn?

Gradually the phrase "public purpose" assumed nearly the same standing, as a measure of legitimacy, as "public use." One of the early decisions on turnpikes, for example, acknowledged the uniquely "public" character of such roads. They were, a New York judge declared in 1823, "the most public roads or highways that are known to exist, and in point of law, they are made entirely for public use, and the community has a deep interest in their construction and preservation." A few years later, New York's chancery court upheld the exercise of eminent domain powers by a privately owned railroad corporation. It was legitimate for the state to devolve the power to expropriate, on payment of compensation, the court declared, "not only where the safety but also where the interest or even the expediency of the state is concerned." In WEST RIVER BRIDGE V. DIX (1848), the earliest Supreme Court case during the first sixty years of the Republic's history where the eminent domain power was ruled upon directly, it was a direct taking by a state—not devolution of the power on a corporation—that was challenged; but the opinions in the case left no doubt that states enjoyed wide discretion in deciding what activities should qualify as "public" in use or purpose, hence were eligible to exercise the eminent domain power if vested in them by the legislatures.

A parallel development in legal doctrine reinforced the impact of the foregoing line of decisions. This other development was in riparian law and its relationship, which changed over time, to public law in the states. As the state legislatures enacted a growing body of law regulating interests in streams—fisheries, navigation, shoreline development, damming of waters for millpower—the courts were called upon to rule on the legitimate reach of the regulatory power. The courts derived from English COMMON LAW distinctions between streams owned by the sovereign; streams "private in ownership but public in use" and so subject to broad regulatory control; and streams strictly private in ownership and in use, whose private character immunized owners against loss from regulation or taking without compensation. Repeatedly, lawyers and judges drew the analogy between waterways in public use and the chartered railroad, canal, bridge, and road companies that were private in ownership, yet "public" in purpose and use. The analogy lent additional legitimacy to "public purpose" as a doctrine which supported state action that forced private rights to yield to communal needs. Private companies were given special privileges in promotion of drainage, wharf facilities, supply of water to urban centers, and transportation facilities, as the Ohio Supreme Court declared in 1836, "because the public has an interest in them." Hence it was consistent to force private owners to yield to takings, for purposes of such enterprises, under eminent domain.

Although the doctrine had been used initially to support a large view of eminent domain power, it was soon employed also in support of tax-financed subsidies to private business firms. As enthusiasm for railroad construction swept the country in the middle decades of the nineteenth century, voters in hundreds of local communities and many state legislatures proved willing to extend cash subsidies—money raised through taxation—to private railroads, to guarantee railroad bonds, or to purchase stock in such railroads. Again, "public purpose" proved to be the vehicle for legitimation of such use of public funds. The Michigan high court, for example, in 1852 turned back a challenge to the constitutionality of such tax-supported aid on the ground that railroad corporations were "created for public benefit" and so were distinguishable from "strictly private corporations . . . [in which] private advantage is the ultimate as well as the immediate object of their creation." The landmark state case, widely followed, was *Sharpless v. Philadelphia*, decided by the Pennsylvania court in 1853. Termed in the court's decision "beyond all comparison, the most important cause that has ever been in this Court," the case was decided in favor of the constitutionality of state subsidies. Taxation must be for a public purpose, the court emphasized, and despite private ownership the railroad companies receiving aid represented such a purpose.

The spreading practice of extending public aid to corporations alarmed many jurists, however; and by the late 1860s, opposition to such a broad reading of "public purpose" and "public use" concepts had grown strong. Emblematic of the issue was the policy of Wisconsin, where the legislature by 1874 had authorized public, tax-supported aid to telegraph, steamship, hotel, waterworks, gas, construction, bridge, canal, river improvement, and dry-dock corporations. The constitutions of the newly admitted western states commonly designated as "public purpose" enterprises firms engaged in logging, road building, irrigation and reclamation, railroads, river improvement, and drainage for mining or agriculture. Such enterprises were routinely granted eminent domain power, and many of them received subsidies. In the East and Midwest, several states allowed manufacturing corporations of all kinds to condemn and flood lands for power sites. Such laws were defended as aid to companies with an important public purpose, comparable to the grants of similar eminent domain powers to gristmills in colonial Massachusetts. In a few states—among them Georgia, New York, Alabama, and Vermont—the courts invalidated such grants of power. In most state tribunals, however, the broad view of "public purpose" continued to prevail.

Indicative of the emerging conservative jurisprudence on the issue were decisions of Judge THOMAS M. COOLEY's Michigan court in 1870 against public aid to railroads and in 1877 against a milldam flooding act. In Cooley's view, set forth more systematically in his treatise, *Constitutional Limitations* (1868), "Everything that may be done under the name of taxation is not necessarily a tax; and it may happen that an oppressive burden imposed by the government, when it comes to be carefully scrutinized, will prove, instead of a tax, to be an unlawful confiscation of property, unwarranted by any principle of constitutional government." Further distinguished authority for the same view came from the Iowa Supreme Court. Chief Justice JOHN F. DILLON—like Cooley, a treatise writer who pressed his concern for vested rights on the legal profession and the courts in the late nineteenth century—wrote an opinion for the Iowa court in 1862 that struck down railroad bond aid as a confiscation of citizens' property without compensation and a violation of DUE PROCESS.

The conservative assault led by Dillon and Cooley soon enlisted the aid of the Supreme Court. In LOAN ASSOCIATION V. TOPEKA (1874) the Court declared unconstitutional a Kansas municipal bond issue in aid of a bridge-manufacturing company. Justice SAMUEL F. MILLER's opinion for the majority denounced the use of tax funds for a "private interest instead of a public use"; and he termed it robbery to exercise the taxing power in this way. It was a sudden and surprising use of the public purpose doctrine to limit state legislative power—in contrast with its earlier use to enlarge state power and legitimate new activities.

The conservative version of public purpose did not carry the day altogether, even as the jurisprudence of vested rights was gaining ascendancy. Thus the Supreme Court repeatedly turned back assaults on state aid to railroads, with a solid majority maintaining that transportation had always been considered a "public purpose" activity and so eligible for eminent domain power and aid with tax funds. *Olcott v. The Supervisors* (1873) upheld the validity of local bonds issued to aid railroads in a Wisconsin municipality, in the face of efforts to repudiate them. In language squarely in the line of doctrine that had come down from JAMES KENT's views on turnpikes half a century earlier, the Court asserted that railroads had a "public highway character. . . . Though the ownership is private, the use is public." Use of tax funds to subsidize manufacturing companies suffered a different fate, however, in light of the *Loan Association* decision. Thus Clyde Jacobs calculated

that from 1870 to 1910 some forty public purpose cases challenging tax aid to businesses came before the federal courts and state high courts. In thirty-nine of the forty, public aid was found invalid on the ground that it was not for a public purpose. Moreover, numerous state courts interpreted the "public purpose" provisions in state constitutions to forbid subsidies or relief payments to the blind, for example, or to farmers who had suffered from weather or crop failure.

In the Supreme Court, however, a manifest softening of the commitment to public purpose as a limiting doctrine became evident in decisions on the constitutionality of grants of taxing and eminent domain power to special-purpose irrigation districts. The Court ruled in *Fallbrook Irrigation District v. Bradley* (1896) that local geographical and climatic conditions required a considerable legislative discretion as to what constituted public purpose. In other cases that tested the constitutionality of using tax revenues to finance state enterprises such as public utilities and even grain warehouses, the Court moved still further toward allowing legislatures to do so. By the early 1920s public purpose as a national constitutional doctrine was no longer a major support for vested property rights or limitation upon governmental power, even though the Court, beginning with *Fallbrook*, explicitly treated public purpose as a FOURTEENTH AMENDMENT issue.

The Supreme Court also abandoned in 1916 a residual doctrine that had enjoyed considerable judicial respect in many jurisdictions since the 1850s, the doctrine that "public use" (justifying takings by the state) should be interpreted as "use by the public" and not in broad "public purpose" terms. In *Mt. Vernon-Woodberry Company v. Alabama Power Company* (1916), Justice OLIVER WENDELL HOLMES, writing for the Court, declared flatly that "the inadequacy of the use by the general public as a universal test is established."

The deep economic crisis in the 1930s and the social dislocations it generated led to the third distinct phase of the public purpose doctrine's history. The application, throughout the nation, of federal aid to urban slum clearance and housing development produced challenges in both federal and state courts to the constitutionality of using eminent domain and taxation powers for such purposes. Especially where private real-estate and financial interests were given a key role in housing, the public purpose of takings and public expenditures for such programs was questioned. By 1940 such objections had been rejected, and the public programs upheld, in the courts of twenty-eight states. Many of these opinions concluded that where "public welfare" was served the public purpose test was met—a broad concept of legitimacy for eminent domain (and taxation) that found expression also in *United States ex rel. Tennessee Valley Authority v. Welch* (1946), a leading Supreme Court decision validating takings by a federal agency for purposes of regional development. It was for Congress to decide what was a public use, the Court declared; no "departure . . . [from] judicial restraint," with deference to the legislative branch, was warranted.

The language of the *Welch* decision was imported into state and federal courts' review of another wave of urban slum clearance programs in the 1940s and 1950s, following WORLD WAR II. In this later period, more than mere slum clearance was at issue; the urban programs often embraced comprehensive "urban redevelopment" objectives, typically employed private financial and entrepreneurial interests in the projects, and often involved sweeping condemnation programs that took land and buildings that did not fit the "slum" classification. Rejecting a public purpose challenge to comprehensive redevelopment, in which some of the property taken ended up in the hands of private developers, not government itself, a federal district court in a landmark 1953 ruling, *Schneider v. District of Columbia,* declared: "the term 'public use' has progressed as economic facts have progressed, and so projects such as railroads, public power plants, the operation of mines under some conditions, and, more recently, low-cost housing have been held to be public uses for which private property may be seized. Moreover, . . . the variation in the term from '[public] use' to '[public] purpose' indicates a progression in thought." So long as the taking is necessary to the public purpose that the legislature has determined and defined, the court concluded, eminent domain powers necessary to accomplishment of that purpose must be deemed legitimate.

The valedictory came in *Berman v. Parker* (1954), when the Supreme Court affirmed that public purpose was a concept coterminous with "public welfare," hence embraced objectives across a broad spectrum that included "public safety, public health, morality, peace and quiet, law and order," to list only "some of the more conspicuous examples." Once pursuit of public purpose in these terms was accepted, then eminent domain, taxation, or the STATE POLICE POWER might be used to accomplish the goals set forth. Judicial review under the Fifth and Fourteenth Amendments was not out of the question, at least in some jurists' views. Justice FELIX FRANKFURTER, for example, in a concurring opinion in *Welch,* wrote: "But the fact that the nature of the subject matter gives the legislative determination nearly immunity from judicial review does not mean that the power to review is wanting." In the subsequent history of taking, however, it was the eminent domain-police power distinction, and not the public purpose doctrine, on which constitutional challenges to regulation would turn. The purposes for which eminent domain or taxation could be used did seem "nearly immune," in light

of modern constitutional interpretation of the GENERAL WELFARE CLAUSE.

HARRY N. SCHEIBER
(1986)

Bibliography

JACOBS, CLYDE E.   1954   Law Writers and the Courts: The Influence of Thomas M. Cooley, Christopher G. Tiedman, and John F. Dillon upon American Constitutional Law. Berkeley and Los Angeles: University of California Press.

NICHOLS, PHILIP, JR.   1940   The Meaning of Public Use in the Law of Eminent Domain. *Boston University Law Review* 20: 615–624.

SCHEIBER, HARRY N.   1971   The Road to *Munn:* Eminent Domain and the Concept of the Public Purpose in the State Courts. *Perspectives in American History* 5:327–402.

WOODBURY, COLEMAN, ed.   1953   *Urban Redevelopment: Problems and Practices.* Chicago: University of Chicago Press.

PUBLIC TRIAL

"In all criminal prosecutions, the accused shall enjoy the right to a speedy and public trial. . . ." The language of the Sixth Amendment appears to assure that criminal courtrooms in the United States will be open—that there will be no secret trials. But the issue of openness in the process of criminal justice has only recently reached a point of consensus in the Supreme Court after nearly forty years of experimentation with successive constitutional tests.

Conflicting values underlay the debate. One was that of the open society, with the public free to observe and criticize the activities of government, including the courts. The other was fairness to someone accused of a crime: his or her right to a trial uninfluenced by public passion or prejudice. The two values do not usually conflict, but it hardly needs to be said that they may clash in a country that has known mob-dominated courtrooms and lynchings.

The constitutional conflict first surfaced in a series of cases starting with BRIDGES V. CALIFORNIA (1941). The issue was whether American, like British, judges could punish as a contempt of court any comment on a pending criminal case that had a tendency to interfere with the administration of justice. In *Bridges* two persons had been held in contempt: a labor leader for a telegram criticizing a judicial decision against his union, and a newspaper editor for an editorial admonishing a judge not to grant probation to two convicted union members. By a 5–4 vote the Supreme Court reversed both contempt convictions. The Court's opinion, by Justice HUGO L. BLACK, said the FIRST AMENDMENT barred punishment for such comments unless they presented a CLEAR AND PRESENT DANGER—the test framed by Justice OLIVER WENDELL HOLMES in the early sedition cases such as ABRAMS V. UNITED STATES (1919)—of causing "disorderly and unfair administration of justice." Later decisions made plain that it would be extremely difficult for authorities to meet that test. Justice WILLIAM O. DOUGLAS said in *Craig v. Harney* (1947): "A trial is a public event. What transpires in the courtroom is public property. . . . There is no special perquisite of the judiciary which enables it, as distinguished from other institutions of democratic government, to suppress, edit, or censor events which transpire in proceedings before it."

Nevertheless, concern remained about the possible effect of outside comment on the criminal justice process, especially on the impartiality of jurors. Justice FELIX FRANKFURTER felt so strongly about the matter that he wrote an impassioned opinion in *Maryland v. Baltimore Radio Show* (1950), when the Supreme Court refused to review a state appellate court decision reversing on First Amendment grounds the contempt conviction of a radio broadcaster who had broadcast, before a murder trial, the record of the defendant and alleged evidence of his guilt.

The Supreme Court dealt with the problem of prejudicial press comment on criminal cases another way: by reversing convictions when there was reason to think the jury might have been improperly influenced by the outside comment. The Court first found that prejudicial comment had violated a defendant's constitutional right to fair trial in IRVIN V. DOWD (1961). Justice Frankfurter, still preferring to proceed against the press itself, wrote bitterly in a concurring opinion: "The Court has not yet decided that, while convictions must be reversed and miscarriages of justice result because the minds of jurors or potential jurors were poisoned, the poisoner is constitutionally protected in plying his trade." But the device of contempt to prevent prejudicial comment never found favor with a majority. In *Sheppard v. Maxwell* (1966) the Court outlined other measures to prevent the prejudicing of juries in notorious cases: delaying or moving the trial, for example, or sequestering the jury once it had been selected.

Then a new prophylactic device was taken up by some trial courts around the country: INJUNCTIONS against press institutions and representatives forbidding reports, before trial, of evidence and other material that might prejudice potential jurors. These gag orders, as the press angrily called them, followed the approach adopted by Britain in the Criminal Justice Act of 1967. That act allowed the press to attend pretrial committal proceedings, thereby assuring scrutiny of the process, but forebade reporting on them until after the trial itself was completed—unless the defendant waived the restriction. But in 1976 the Supreme Court held that the First Amendment stood in the way of this approach, too. In NEBRASKA PRESS ASSOCIATION V. STUART the press had been enjoined from reporting, before trial, the alleged confession and other especially prej-

udicial matters about the defendant in a gruesome multiple murder case in a small Nebraska town. The Court's opinion, by Chief Justice WARREN E. BURGER, declined to adopt an absolute rule against such restraints. But the decision against them, on the extreme facts of that case, made it most unlikely that gag orders would ever be permissible; and trial courts stopped issuing them.

A last round of the constitutional debate about fair trial and free speech tested still another prophylactic device: closing the courtroom to the public and the press during sensitive phases of pretrial or trial proceedings. In GANNETT V. DEPASQUALE (1979) counsel for the defendants moved to close a pretrial hearing on motions to suppress confessions and other EVIDENCE, arguing that reports of the hearing would prejudice future jurors if the evidence were in fact suppressed. The prosecutor did not object, and the trial judge closed the courtroom. A newspaper then challenged the order. The Supreme Court decided that the "public trial" clause of the Sixth Amendment was for the benefit of the defendant alone, who could waive it, and that outsiders had no STANDING to insist on an open courtroom. The majority put aside First Amendment considerations.

A year later the Court did consider the First Amendment and decided that it limited the closing of courtrooms. In RICHMOND NEWSPAPERS V. VIRGINIA a 7–1 majority found unconstitutional the exclusion of the public (and with it the press) from a criminal trial. There was no opinion of the Court, but various Justices shared the view expressed by Chief Justice Burger that the First Amendment assures the public a "right of access" to criminal trials that can be denied only for strong and articulated reasons. Indications are that the right extends also to civil cases, and to pretrial proceedings as well as trials.

The decision was an extraordinary doctrinal conclusion to the long cycle of constitutional litigation. For the Supreme Court had for the first time said that the First Amendment was not only a shield protecting the right to speak or publish but also a sword helping the public to gain access to information about government institutions. How far that new doctrine would be taken was uncertain. But in American courtrooms, at least, a constitutional presumption favors openness.

ANTHONY LEWIS
(1986)

Bibliography

LEWIS, ANTHONY 1980 A Public Right to Know about Public Institutions: The First Amendment as Sword. *The Supreme Court Review* 1980:1–25.

SCHMIDT, BENNO C. 1977 Nebraska Press Association: An Expansion of Freedom and Contraction of Theory. *Stanford Law Review* 29:431–476.

PUBLIC UNDERSTANDING OF SUPREME COURT OPINIONS

When interpreting the Constitution, Justices of the Supreme Court—whether writing a majority, CONCURRING, or DISSENTING OPINION—should seek to reach the American people as their primary audience. They should explain with candor, in accessible and comprehensible language, what they decided, and why they decided it in that way.

That the Constitution be intelligible to the American people is essential to a government based on informed consent and open to informed dissent. The PREAMBLE to the Constitution proclaims that "We the People [not only "We Constitutional Lawyers and Teachers of Constitutional Law"], in Order to . . . establish Justice, . . . and secure the Blessings of Liberty to ourselves and our Posterity, do ordain and establish this Constitution for the United States of America."

In 1819, Chief Justice JOHN MARSHALL wrote for and to a unanimous Supreme Court in MCCULLOCH V. MARYLAND (1819) that, individually and collectively, "we must never forget that it is a *Constitution* that we are expounding"; that the Constitution derives its whole authority from the people of the nation; and that, in form and language, it is an instrument designed to be accessible and comprehensible to the public. The Constitution ought not to be converted by Court interpretations into, or be treated like, an intricate legal code detailing all of its great powers and all of the means by which they may be carried out. A Constitution, so converted, could "scarcely be embraced by the human mind" and, Marshall added, "probably would never be understood by the public."

Marshall stressed that "[s]uch is the character of human language that no word conveys to the mind, in all situations, one single definite idea." The burden of an opinion is to remove obstacles to understanding when a controversy arises between or among the governors and the governed about the Constitution's meaning. To say that is not meant to obscure the fact that the language of opinions may be no more free from ambiguity than the language of the constitutional provision being interpreted. Nevertheless, the Court's task is to clarify—to make something about the Constitution more fully understood than it was before the opinion was rendered—by explaining and giving reasons for its judgment in a concrete case.

Yet conscious ambiguity, confusion, and alteration of apparently critical facts have characterized opinions in many of the Court's most important decisions, such as those in BROWN V. BOARD OF EDUCATION (1954), COOPER V. AARON (1958), REGENTS OF UNIVERSITY OF CALIFORNIA V. BAKKE (1978), and WEBSTER V. REPRODUCTIVE HEALTH SERVICES (1989). Some Justices have been candid about the intentional muddling or misstatement of opinions.

Justice ROBERT H. JACKSON once observed that "[t]he technique of the dissenter often is to exaggerate the holding of the Court beyond the meaning of the majority and then to blast away at the excess," leaving a reader in doubt about "whether the majority opinion meant what it seemed to say or what the minority said it meant."

Chief Justice CHARLES EVANS HUGHES is reported to have admitted that "he tried to write his opinions clearly and logically, but if he needed the fifth vote of a colleague who insisted on putting in a paragraph that did not 'belong,' in it went, and let the law reviews figure out what it meant."

An opposing view, explained by Professor Burke Marshall, is that the Court has left to the legal profession and to legal scholars the task of "explain[ing] the obscure, . . . [of] construct[ing] for our students and for the people generally what it is that the Court surely meant, when the Court itself does not say what it meant." Those who hold this belief tend not to address whether this reality should be the goal of opinion writing, or whether it is simply the inevitable, albeit regrettable, product of the Court's work.

According to Professor Marshall, "Familiarity with the Court's work overwhelmingly demonstrates at a minimum that the members of the Court view their work as directed at the elite, and not to the people." But this should not lead anyone to conclude that the Justices should leave to the "experts" the task of instructing "We the People," effectively drawing a line—whether consciously or unconsciously—between the elite, those who are "in," and the rest of the people, those who are "out." Even the professional interpreters to whom the people must turn for understanding may not be able to unravel what the Court has to say, often in heavily footnoted, multiple opinions. The "experts" and even the Justices themselves, for example, may not be able to identify the constitutional principles underlying the decision in *Webster*. Its confusing, seventy-four-page set of opinions, which left unresolved the meaning of the trimester framework fashioned in ROE V. WADE (1973) for determining the constitutionality of laws permitting ABORTION, is introduced by this mind-boggling headnote:

REHNQUIST, C.J., announced the judgment of the Court and delivered the opinion for a unanimous Court with respect to Part II-C, the opinion of the Court with respect to Parts I, II-A, and II-B, in which WHITE, O'CONNOR, SCALIA and KENNEDY, J.J., joined, and an opinion with respect to Parts II-D and III, in which WHITE and KENNEDY, J.J., joined. O'CONNOR, J., . . . and SCALIA, J., . . . filed opinions concurring in part and concurring in the judgment. BLACKMUN, J., filed an opinion concurring in part and dissenting in part.

JOSEPH GOLDSTEIN
(2000)

Bibliography

GOLDSTEIN, JOSEPH 1992 *The Intelligible Constitution: The Supreme Court's Obligation to Maintain the Constitution as Something We The People Can Understand.* New York: Oxford University Press.

JACKSON, ROBERT H. 1955 *The Supreme Court in the American System of Government.* Cambridge, Mass.: Harvard University Press.

REHNQUIST, WILLIAM H. 1987 *The Supreme Court: How It Was, How It Is.* New York: Morrow.

VINING, JOSEPH 1986 *The Authoritative and the Authoritarian.* Chicago: University of Chicago Press.

WHITE, JAMES BOYD 1984 *When Words Lose Their Meaning: Constitutions and Reconstitutions of Language, Character, and Community.* Chicago: University of Chicago Press.

PUBLIC USE

The "taking" clause of the Fifth Amendment limits the power of EMINENT DOMAIN by demanding that governmental taking of private property be for a public use. The Supreme Court held in *Burlington Quincy Railroad Co. v. Chicago,* (1897) that the same requirement applies to the states through the FOURTEENTH AMENDMENT.

Although some early decisions defined the public use standard to include a right of "use by the public," that approach was repudiated by the Court. As early as 1905 in *Clark v. Nash,* the Court held that a state could authorize a private person to condemn an easement for irrigation across a neighbor's land. "What is a public use," said the Court, "may frequently and largely depend upon the facts surrounding the subject." In the arid environment of Utah, the taking of a private irrigation easement could properly be deemed a public use, because it was "absolutely necessary" to agricultural development. On similar grounds, the Court's decision in *Strickley v. Highland Boy Gold Mining Co.* (1906) sustained the statutory authority of a mining company to condemn a private easement for transporting ore to a railroad loading site. These decisions were followed by many others intimating that any use conducive to the public benefit was a public use for which eminent domain could be invoked, including reclamation of swamp lands, establishment of water and electrical power systems, development of transportation facilities, and creation of public parks.

The broad public benefit test has, in recent years, been assimilated with the RATIONAL BASIS approach invoked by the Supreme Court in reviewing regulations of economic interests under the DUE PROCESS clause. In the leading case, *Berman v. Parker* (1954), the court sustained the use of eminent domain to acquire various separate parcels of private property in blighted areas in furtherance of a community redevelopment project. The fact that the property to be condemned would be resold or leased to private persons for redevelopment purposes did not transgress the public use limitation, for "when the legislature has spoken, the public interest has been declared in terms well-nigh conclusive. In such cases the legislature, not the judiciary, is the main guardian of the public needs to be served. . . . The concept of the public welfare is broad and inclusive."

Under this expansive and deferential approach, eminent domain may be exercised as a means for achieving practically any use or objective within the power of the legislative body.

ARVO VAN ALSTYNE
(1986)

Bibliography

NICHOLS, PERRY 1983 *The Law of Eminent Domain,* Vol. 2a. New York: Matthew Bender & Co.

PUBLIC UTILITIES REGULATION

See: Economic Regulation

PUBLIC UTILITY HOLDING COMPANY ACT
49 Stat. 803 (1935)

This measure was an important part of the legislative program of President FRANKLIN D. ROOSEVELT. Two leading supporters of the bill were Senators GEORGE NORRIS and HUGO L. BLACK. The act's objective was to disperse ownership and control of the nation's gas and electric utilities, then highly concentrated in pyramids of corporations with holding companies at the top. The act required holding companies to register with the Securities and Exchange Commission and authorized the SEC to limit a company's operations to a single region. A "death sentence" provision authorized dissolution of a company that did not show, within five years, that it was serving an efficient local function.

The great holding companies sought to challenge the constitutionality of the entire act in an early TEST CASE, but government lawyers managed to persuade the Supreme Court to defer the omnibus attack and consider the act's registration requirement separately. The Court upheld that requirement in *Electric Bond & Share Co. v. SEC* (1938). The other provisions of the law came before the Court after Roosevelt had appointed seven Justices. Those provisions were sustained, with broad readings of Congress's power under the COMMERCE CLAUSE, in *North American Co. v. SEC* (1946) and *American Power & Light Co.*

v. SEC (1946). By 1952, more than 750 holding companies had been dissolved.

KENNETH L. KARST
(1986)

Bibliography

FREUND, PAUL A. 1951 *On Understanding the Supreme Court.* Pages 99–110. Boston: Little, Brown.

PUERTO RICO

Puerto Rico is the largest of the United States insular areas, both as to land area and population. It is also one of the oldest in terms of being part of the United States, having been acquired along with Guam in 1899 as a result of the Spanish American War.

The Foraker Act of 1900 established a civil government for Puerto Rico. Therefore, Puerto Rico has been an "organized" TERRITORY almost from the beginning of its affiliation with the United States. However, in *Downes v. Bidwell* (1901) the Supreme Court held that Puerto Rico had not been incorporated into the United States. Thus, Puerto Rico was deemed to be an "unincorporated" territory. Consequently, not all portions of the U.S. Constitution were applicable there. The Jones Act of 1917 granted even more autonomy to Puerto Rico and, importantly, granted all persons born there United States CITIZENSHIP. Nonetheless, in the 1922 case of *Balzac v. Porto Rico* (1922), the Court held that Puerto Rico was still an unincorporated territory. (For unknown reasons, Puerto Rico was spelled "Porto Rico" in the English language version of the Treaty of Paris of 1899, the treaty that ended the Spanish American War. "Porto Rico" remained the official spelling until 1932.)

In 1950, Congress passed Public Law 600, the effect of which was to repeal portions of the Jones Act, and to rename the remainder the "Federal Relations Act." Public Law 600 authorized the people of Puerto Rico to adopt a constitution and, significantly, contained language stating that the law was "adopted in the nature of a compact." Thereafter, Puerto Rico was deemed to be in a unique relationship with the United States, known in English as a "commonwealth."

An early case, *Mora v. Mejias* (1953), held that the compact is inalterable without the consent of the people of Puerto Rico and that the U.S. Constitution does not apply to Puerto Rico because Puerto Rico is sovereign. Subsequently, the Court held on more than one occasion— including *Harris v. Rosario* (1980) and *Califano v. Gautier Torres* (1978)—that Congress has plenary power to legislate for Puerto Rico under the territorial clause and that at least portions of the U.S. Constitution are binding on Puerto Rico.

Unlike other insular areas that have Article IV courts, Puerto Rico since 1966 has had an Article III District Court, with judges who have life tenure. Puerto Rico has only a nonvoting delegate in the U.S. Congress, and it would probably take either statehood or a constitutional amendment to give them voting REPRESENTATION. Recent REFERENDA have indicated that the people of Puerto Rico are almost evenly split over whether to seek statehood or remain a commonwealth, although an overwhelming majority favor remaining a part of the United States.

STANLEY K. LAUGHLIN, JR.
(2000)

Bibliography

LAUGHLIN, STANLEY K. 1995 *The Law of United States Territories and Affiliated Jurisdictions* (with 1997 supplement). New York: Lawyers Cooperative-West Group.

TORRUELLA, JUAN R. 1985 *The Supreme Court and Puerto Rico: The Doctrine of Separate and Unequal.* Rio Piedras, Puerto Rico: University of Puerto Rico Press.

PUERTO RICO, CONSTITUTIONAL STATUS OF

No clear definition exists of how and to what extent the Commonwealth of PUERTO RICO fits within the federal constitutional system. Undoubtedly, the *Puerto Rican Federal Relations Act*, enacted by Congress in 1950 "in the nature of a compact" between Congress and the people of Puerto Rico, and the adoption by Puerto Ricans of their own constitution in 1952 were intended to work a significant change in the previous colonial relationship between the island and the United States. The nature and scope of this change, however, have not been conclusively ascertained by federal courts ruling on the matter.

Puerto Rico, which had become a self-governing overseas province of the Kingdom of Spain under the Royal Decree of 1897, was ceded to the United States in 1898 under the Treaty of Paris which ended the Spanish American War. It became an unincorporated TERRITORY of the United States, subject to the plenary command of Congress. Under various Supreme Court decisions it is clear that, until 1952, Puerto Rico was a domestic possession of the United States, neither a foreign country nor an integral part of the nation, merely belonging to it. Congressional authority over the island and its people encompassed the entire domain of SOVEREIGNTY, both national and local, and was completely unconstrained by the federal Constitution, except as regards those basic prohibitions which go "to the very root of the power of Congress to act at all" and "which the Constitution has established in favor of human liberty and are applicable to every condition or status." (See IN-

SULAR CASES.) Wielding its plenary powers, the United States established a military government in Puerto Rico from 1898 to 1900, when a civil regime was installed under the Foraker Act, providing a meager participation of Puerto Ricans in the island's government. In 1917 Congress enacted a second Organic Act (Jones Act) providing a measure of self-government and granting United States CITIZENSHIP collectively to the people of Puerto Rico, while retaining all major elements of sovereignty.

In 1950 a bill to provide for the organization of a constitutional government by the people of Puerto Rico was introduced in Congress. Its provisions were not to be effective until accepted in a REFERENDUM by Puerto Rican voters. After a favorable vote on the new federal act by the island electorate, a CONSTITUTIONAL CONVENTION was held in Puerto Rico and the fundamental law drafted there was adopted by the majority of the islanders in 1952. In transmitting the newly adopted Puerto Rican Constitution to Congress, President HARRY S. TRUMAN recognized that with such approval "full authority and responsibility for local self-government [would] be vested in the people of Puerto Rico." In 1953 the United Nations recognized that Puerto Ricans, exercising the right of self-determination, had achieved a new constitutional status, and had "been invested with attributes of political sovereignty which clearly identify the status of self-government attained by the Puerto Rican people as that of an autonomous political entity."

It is generally accepted by federal courts that after 1952 "Puerto Rico's status changed from that of a mere territory to the unique status of COMMONWEALTH." The Supreme Court itself stated in *Examining Board v. Flores* (1976) that "the purpose of Congress in its 1950 and 1952 legislation was to accord to Puerto Rico the degree of autonomy and independence normally associated with a State of the Union." However, the precise extent of the referred "autonomy" and the constitutional basis for statelike status are very much in doubt. Thus, while the Supreme Court has now accepted that "Puerto Rico is to be deemed sovereign over matters not ruled by the federal Constitution" and that Puerto Rican legislation and court decisions deserve the same regard in federal courts as those of a state, it has also ruled in *Harris v. Rosario* (1980) that Congress under the territorial clause may still "treat Puerto Rico differently from States so long as there is a rational basis for its actions." Likewise, the Court, after acknowledging that Puerto Rico is subject to federal constitutional requirements regarding FREEDOM OF SPEECH, DUE PROCESS, EQUAL PROTECTION, and reasonable SEARCH AND SEIZURE, has indicated that such guarantees are binding either directly under the Bill of Rights or indirectly by operation of the FOURTEENTH AMENDMENT, expressly refusing to fix one or the other as the source or basis of their applicabil-

ity. The Court has yet to write on a clean slate in dealing with the new constitutional status of Puerto Rico.

JAIME B. FUSTER
(1986)

Bibliography

FUSTER, JAIME B. 1974 Origin of the Doctrine of Territorial Incorporation and Its Implications for the Power of the Commonwealth of Puerto Rico. *University of Puerto Rico Law Review* 43:259–294.

PUNISHMENT

See: Sentencing

PUNITIVE DAMAGES

The plaintiff who prevails in a tort case is entitled to compensatory DAMAGES, including damages for pain and suffering. In a limited number of cases involving aggravated wrongdoing, the plaintiff can recover punitive damages as well. Sometimes the understanding is that these damages are indeed punitive: that their intent is to punish defendants for their wrongdoing. At other times, punitive damages seem designed to provide a higher level of deterrence than would be occasioned by the mere threat of compensatory damages; at this juncture, the language of "exemplary damages" becomes apt.

Although scholars have long expressed uneasiness with punitive damages, until recently their constitutionality has been taken for granted. In recent years, however, the number of punitive-damage awards has increased, and the size of the average punitive-damage verdict has soared. These changes have encouraged the posing of new questions as to their constitutionality. In *Browning-Ferris Industries, Inc. v. Kelco Disposal, Inc.* (1989), the defendant committed a business tort against the plaintiff that resulted in $51,146 in actual damages. A jury awarded the plaintiff these damages—and six million dollars in punitive damages as well. An argument advanced by the defendant was that this award constituted an "excessive fine," forbidden by the Eighth Amendment. Amazingly, *Browning-Ferris* was the first case involving the excessive-fines clause that the Supreme Court had ever considered. The Court, divided 7–2, finally decided that punitive damages awarded in private civil actions are not "fines" and are hence unregulated by the clause. The majority opinion, authored by Justice HARRY A. BLACKMUN, left open the question as to whether the clause pertains only to proceedings that are officially criminal: rather, the rationale adopted by Blackmun was that the clause has no application to a legal proceeding in which the government is no way a party. The dissent, authored by Justice SANDRA DAY O'CONNOR, would have found the clause applicable to punitive-damage awards and, hence, would have subjected such awards to a "proportionality" analysis that O'Connor drew from the case law under the Eighth Amendment's CRUEL AND UNUSUAL PUNISHMENT clause.

Although denying the relevance of the Eighth Amendment, the *Browning-Ferris* majority acknowledged that large punitive-damage awards might raise a problem of DUE PROCESS. A concurring opinion signed by Justices WILLIAM J. BRENNAN and THURGOOD MARSHALL emphasized the likely relevance of due process. Indeed, the majority and concurring opinions together suggest two different kinds of due process issues. One is an issue of SUBSTANTIVE DUE PROCESS: that due process might be violated by punitive-damage awards that are substantively excessive. The other issue relates to PROCEDURAL DUE PROCESS; here the concern is for the lack of clarity in the standards that the jury relies on in calculating the amount of punitive damages.

If the vagueness in the standards for calculating punitive damages raise a due process problem, a related problem concerns the amorphousness in the standards relied on in determining whether or not to award punitive damages. Moreover, there are further constitutional issues that punitive-damage practices might be thought to entail. If punitive damages are regarded as sufficiently penal to render at least somewhat relevant the BILL OF RIGHTS, then the "preponderance of the evidence" standard of proof that states have traditionally relied on in punitive-damage cases might be inadequate. (Indeed, as part of the tort-reform movement of the late 1980s, several states have raised the punitive-damage standard of proof to clear and convincing evidence.) In so-called "mass-tort" situations involving such products as asbestos and the Dalkon Shield, a large number of punitive-damage verdicts can be entered against a particular defendant on account of a single (although continuing) course of harm-causing conduct. At some point, the cumulation of these awards might suggest an issue of due process or DOUBLE JEOPARDY. Indeed, in early 1989, one federal district court judge did find a constitutional violation, although a lack of adequate precedent later persuaded him to withdraw most of his holding.

The Supreme Court further considered the procedural due process issues in *Pacific Mutual Life Insurance Co. v. Haslip* (1991). This case involved an $840,000 punitive damage verdict against an insurance company for the bad faith of its agent. The majority's opinion strongly suggested that a punitive damage award resulting from "unlimited jury discretion" would offend due process. The *Haslip* jury, however, had been given at least minimal standards; and its award had then been reviewed by both the trial judge and the Alabama Supreme Court, under rather elaborate procedures. This combination of protections enabled the *Haslip* majority to conclude that the "punitive damages award in this case" did not violate due process. The majority's case-specific reasoning effectively leaves open the due process status of a large intermediate range of punitive damage practices. Although the Court affirmed Alabama's "preponderance" standard of proof, even this affirmance was tied to Alabama's special set of procedures. And since evidence of defendant's wealth is inadmissible in Alabama punitive damage actions, the Court was in a position to conclude that Alabama procedures are not biased against "a defendant with a deep pocket."

Justices Anthony Kennedy and Antonin Scalia each wrote separate opinions in *Haslip*, concurring only in the majority's result. In their view, the long-standing historical acceptance of punitive damage practices all but eliminates the due process question. Justice Sandra Day O'Connor dissented, arguing that the limited standards applied by the Alabama jury were void for vagueness and also that the Alabama trial procedures entailed a due process violation. In her view, Alabama could satisfy constitutional requirements by allowing the jury to consider the seven substantive factors that the Alabama Supreme Court itself takes into account in the course of appellate review.

GARY T. SCHWARTZ
(1992)

Bibliography

SYMPOSIUM: PUNITIVE DAMAGES 1982 *USC Law Review* 56:1–203.

——— 1989 *Alabama Law Review* 40:687–1261.

PUNITIVE DAMAGES
(Update)

After flirting with the possibility for several years, the Supreme Court has finally identified particular punitive DAMAGE awards that violate the DUE PROCESS clause of the FOURTEENTH AMENDMENT. In *Honda Motor Company v. Oberg* (1994), an alleged defect in an all-terrain vehicle injured the plaintiff. At trial, the plaintiff secured a verdict of about $920,000 in compensatory damages and $5,000,000 in punitive damages. Oregon law prohibited any review, by either the trial judge or an appellate court, of the amount of civil-action verdicts (including punitive damage verdicts), except when the record contained "no evidence" to support the verdict. The Court— emphasizing the way in which the COMMON LAW tradition has consistently recognized the need for judicial review of the level of punitive damage awards—found that the Oregon law violated due process. While the Court's opinion highlighted PROCEDURAL DUE PROCESS, the opinion also reasoned that procedure is related to substance: better procedure—such as judicial review—helps assure that punitive damage awards are not substantively excessive. The breadth of the *Oberg* holding is uncertain: It is unclear, for example, whether the Court's opinion means that the Oregon system is unconstitutional insofar as it bars judicial review of jury verdicts for compensatory damages. In any event, the *Oberg* holding may well be of limited import, for Oregon is apparently unique among American states in denying judicial review of the amount of damage awards.

Two years after *Oberg*, the Court, in *BMW of North America, Inc. v. Gore* (1996), invalidated a punitive damage judgment of $2,000,000 imposed on a car manufacturer that failed to disclose that a particular car had been damaged in transit and repainted (at a cost of $600) prior to its original sale. The purchaser of the car, eventually learning of the damage and the repainting, persuaded a jury that these events reduced the resale value of his car by $4,000. Accordingly, the jury granted him $4,000 in compensatory damages. In addition, the jury awarded $4 million in punitive damages. On appeal, the Alabama Supreme Court reduced this award to $2 million. The U.S. Supreme Court, by a 5–4 vote, then concluded that even this lower award was constitutionally excessive.

The MAJORITY OPINION focused primarily on SUBSTANTIVE DUE PROCESS. In determining whether a punitive damage award is excessive, the Court reasoned, three guidelines should be taken primarily into account: how reprehensible is the defendant's conduct, what is the ratio between compensatory damages and punitive damages, and what civil damages are provided by public law for comparable offenses. With respect to each of the three criteria, the Court concluded that the $2 million award was troublesome. As for reprehensibility, BMW's conduct posed no threat to health or safety, the relevant harm being solely economic; and while the company's nondisclosure was in a sense deliberate, its decision not to disclose its limited repainting effort was, in fact, quite legal under the regulatory schemes in effect in many other states. As for ratio, 500-to-1 raises a "suspicious judicial eyebrow." As for sanctions for comparable misconduct, in no state were they more than $10,000. Taking everything into the balance, the Court reached the conclusion that the punitive damage award was constitutionally excessive.

Given the Court's guidelines, the Court's conclusion—even if somewhat ad hoc—follows rather easily. The important question concerns the justifiability of the guidelines themselves. In explaining those guidelines, the Court reasoned that they bear on the ultimate question of whether BMW had been given "fair notice" of the likely award. This "fair notice" criterion introduces a significant element of procedural due process into the case. Moreover, it interestingly suggests that had there been prior verdicts in Alabama for comparable amounts for comparable misconduct, the award in *Gore*—however offensive in its magnitude—might well have been sustained.

A CONCURRING OPINION by Justice STEPHEN G. BREYER, speaking for three Justices, focused primarily on procedural due process. Breyer's concern was less with the excessiveness of the award and more with its possible arbitrariness. He focused on the question whether there were legal standards that adequately controlled the jury's discretion. Here Breyer noted that prior Alabama opinions had identified seven factors to take into account in considering the appropriate size of a punitive damage award. In the abstract, Breyer suggested, these standards appear sufficient. Still, insofar as they had been applied by the Alabama Supreme Court in the immediate case so as to justify an award of $2 million, that application revealed to Breyer that the standards do an inadequate job in constraining the jury's discretion.

One feature in Breyer's concurrence can be considered here—in combination with a conspicuous omission in the majority's analysis. In punitive damage cases, courts commonly say that juries can, and should, take the wealth of the defendant into account in determining the amount of a punitive damage award. Indeed, the wealth of the defendant was one of the seven factors that had been specifically endorsed in Alabama. But Breyer found this standard objectionable (at least in part) because of the way in which it "provides an open-ended basis for inflating awards when the defendant is wealthy." Furthermore, defendant wealth is conspicuously absent among the guidelines endorsed by the Court's majority. Accordingly, the constitutional status of defendant wealth as a factor that can justify large punitive damage awards is now subject to some doubt.

GARY T. SCHWARTZ
(2000)

PURE FOOD AND DRUG ACT
34 Stat. 768 (1906)

Typical of the progressive legislation passed after the turn of the century, this act extended the NATIONAL POLICE POWER to regulate the quality of food and drugs in INTERSTATE COMMERCE. A personal crusade by the chief chemist of the Department of Agriculture together with the muckrakers' stomach-churning exposés fanned public opinion. President THEODORE ROOSEVELT's backstage maneuvering also helped secure passage of this federal inspection act on June 30, 1906.

The act outlawed the manufacture of "adulterated or

misbranded" food or drugs and prohibited their introduction into interstate or FOREIGN COMMERCE. Congress gave the secretaries of agriculture, treasury, and commerce and labor authority to issue regulations enforcing the act and specifically provided PROCEDURAL DUE PROCESS for violators. The act forbade: misbranding of food; the use of imitations, substitutes, harmful additives, rotten ingredients; and concealment of "damage or inferiority." Drugs were required to meet federal standards of quality, purity, and strength or clearly label their departures from the standards.

The Supreme Court sustained this act in HIPOLITE EGG COMPANY V. UNITED STATES (1911) as a legitimate exercise of congressional power over commerce. Congress substantially tightened and extended it in the FOOD, DRUG, AND COSMETIC ACT of 1938.

DAVID GORDON
(1986)